Personal Finance 11e

E. Thomas Garman
Virginia Tech University, Professor Emeritus

Raymond E. Forgue
University of Kentucky

SOUTH-WESTERN
CENGAGE Learning

Australia • Brazil • Japan • Korea • Mexico • Singapore • Spain • United Kingdom • United States

SOUTH-WESTERN
CENGAGE Learning™

Personal Finance, Eleventh Edition

E. Thomas Garman, Raymond E. Forgue

Vice President of Editorial, Business: Jack W. Calhoun

Acquisitions Editor: Mike Reynolds

Developmental Editor: Clara Goosman

Sr. Editorial Assistant: Adele Schotz

Marketing Manager: Nathan Anderson

Sr. Content Project Manager: Holly Henjum

Sr. Media Editor: Scott Fidler

Manufacturing Planner: Kevin Kluck

Sr. Marketing Communications Manager: Jim Overly

Production Service: KnowledgeWorks Global Ltd.

Sr. Art Director: Michelle Kunkler

Cover and Internal Designer: Grannan Graphic Design

Cover Image: © Peter Dazeley/Getty Images

Permissions Acquisitions Manager/Image: Deanna Ettinger

Permissions Acquisitions Manager/Text: Audrey Pettengill

For product information and technology assistance, contact us at **Cengage Learning Customer & Sales Support, 1-800-354-9706**

For permission to use material from this text or product, submit all requests online at **www.cengage.com/permissions**
Further permissions questions can be emailed to **permissionrequest@cengage.com**

ExamView® is a registered trademark of eInstruction Corp. Windows is a registered trademark of the Microsoft Corporation used herein under license. Macintosh and Power Macintosh are registered trademarks of Apple Computer, Inc. used herein under license.

Library of Congress Control Number: 2011922187

ISBN-13: 978-1-111-53101-0

ISBN-10: 1-111-53101-3

South-Western
5191 Natorp Boulevard
Mason, OH 45040
USA

Cengage Learning products are represented in Canada by Nelson Education, Ltd.

For your course and learning solutions, visit **www.cengage.com**

Purchase any of our products at your local college store or at our preferred online store **www.cengagebrain.com**

Printed in Canada
1 2 3 4 5 6 7 15 14 13 12 11

BRIEF CONTENTS

CONTENTS

PART 2   MONEY MANAGEMENT   103

CHAPTER 4

Managing Income Taxes 104

CHAPTER 5

Managing Checking and Savings Accounts 139

CHAPTER 6

Building and Maintaining Good Credit 169

CHAPTER 9

Obtaining Affordable Housing 247

PART 3 INCOME AND ASSET PROTECTION   285

CHAPTER 10

Managing Property and Liability Risk 286

CHAPTER 11

Managing Health Expenses 319

CHAPTER 15

Investing Through Mutual Funds 456

CHAPTER 16

Real Estate and High-Risk Investments 482

PART 5 RETIREMENT AND ESTATE PLANNING 509

CHAPTER 17
Retirement Planning 510

PREFACE

A NOTE TO THE STUDENT

The 11th edition offers reassurance to readers about how to succeed in personal finance today following the Great Recession "crashes" in the world's stock, housing, and credit markets in 2007 and 2008. Despite today's sluggishly recovering economy, experts are optimistic that people can still do well financially. However, hope alone is not enough! Students need more. Thus, *Personal Finance* carefully lays out your financial "marching orders" for challenging economic times. "What to do, when to do it, and how to do it" is the mantra for this book. We give you "prescriptions" to follow that will guide you to success in your personal finances.

Personal Finance reminds students of the values of their grandparents: "work hard, study, save, invest, and live within your means." In chapter after chapter, the 11th edition demonstrates the fundamental principles of how to do well in the financial side of living life.

Personal finance is not rocket science. In fact, it is not very complicated. Making good personal financial decisions for you and your loved ones simply requires making informed choices. Learn the vocabulary of personal finance, consider our prescriptions, and then apply the principles in your everyday decision making. Ignore these suggestions at your peril, because a lack of financial literacy will guarantee your financial failure. Our goal as authors is to give you the knowledge, tools, attitudes, and skills you need to be financially sound. Along with the text, we have developed a full, rich companion website that you can use to learn as much as possible from your efforts as well as to develop your own financial plans.

TO THE INSTRUCTOR

This 11th edition of *Personal Finance* has been heavily revised, and it sets a new higher standard in the field. The text involves the student in genuinely learning the subject, particularly through newly created information presented in boxes, enhanced end-of-chapter activities, and innovative "prescriptions" from the authors. Your authors are the "Doctors of Personal Finance"—with 80 years of teaching experience, 40 years of experience writing college textbooks, and over 200 research articles written. By drawing on their years of experience, the authors have made the 11th edition more than just a compilation of what to know. This edition emphasizes what are the right things to do in personal finance and how to do them.

Why this emphasis? Because today's students need more precise guidance than those of yesteryear, particularly as a result of these extremely challenging economic times. The book's many features consistently offer normative, value-laden suggestions on getting ahead in one's personal finances.

Every chapter includes the doctors' "prescriptions" for the student. Each chapter begins with "Your Next Five Years" and later points out to the reader "Your Worst Financial Blunders." Each chapter also includes multiple "Financial Power Points" that offer practical information that can be used immediately and a concrete list of good and bad habits illustrated in "Turn Bad Habits into Good Ones." "Sean's Success Story" also appears in every chapter; Sean is a person to emulate because he does everything well in personal finance. Each chapter closes with a "Do it NOW!" feature that highlights three key personal finance actions that smart students should take immediately.

This 11th edition balances all the pieces of financial planning. In addition to updating and enhancing the quality of the content, this edition stimulates student interest in several new ways. The revised end-of-chapter activities are phenomenal. One new continuing case is that of Julia Price, whose successful financial life evolves through challenging economic times; her case ends with a question to challenge the student: "*Offer your opinions about her thinking.*" This edition now includes five or six cases in each chapter. The "Be Your Own Financial Planner" feature is also new. These activities are not busywork. They are concrete activities that require applying the knowledge provided in each chapter at a personal level. All of the "On the 'Net" activities have been designed to carefully direct students to online materials that are genuinely useful and appropriate for this time in their personal financial lives.

The 11th edition includes over 30 new headings, more than 100 new boxed inserts, dozens of new terms, and lots of new and expanded material. This edition connects all the pieces of personal finance in a comprehensive manner, shows students the relevancy of the topics, and requires students to do a reality check on their own finances. As a result, your students will succeed!

Changes in This Edition

- Chapters 5, 6, 7, 13, 14, and 15 were updated to reflect the impact of statutory and regulatory requirements of the Dodd-Frank Regulatory Reform Act of 2010.

- Chapter 4 was updated to reflect the impact of statutory and regulatory requirements of the Tax Relief, Unemployment Insurance Reauthorization, and Job Creation Act of 2010.

- Chapter 11 was updated to reflect the impact of statutory and regulatory requirements of the Patient Protectionand Affordable Health Care Act of 2010.

- Chapters 5, 6, and 7 were updated to reflect the impact of statutory and regulatory requirements of the Credit Card Accountability Responsibility and Disclosure Act of 2009 or Credit CARD (CARD) Act of 2009.

- A new boxed feature is included in every chapter—"Sean's Success Story." This feature outlines what a successful personal financial planner would do based on the topics and content of that specific chapter.

MY PERSONAL FINANCIAL PLANNER

- A new end-of-chapter exercise called "Be Your Own Personal Financial Manager." These exercises require that the student actually engage in their own personal financial management by completing the worksheets and/or mathematical calculation in that chapter. Wherever appropriate, these exercises are support by Excel spreadsheets provided on the Garman/Forgue website.

- A new end-of-chapter exercise called "Action Involvement Exercises." These exercises require that the student explore the topics in the chapter further by going out to the community to discuss the topics with friends, family members and relevant financial professionals.

- A new continuing case in each chapter in the "Financial Planning Case" end-of-chapter exercises that focuses on the financial decisions of Julia Price as she progresses financially quite well through her career. Each case describes what Julia has done in relation to her own finances on topics related to the particular chapter and then ends by asking the student to "offer your opinions on her thinking."

TOPICAL COVERAGE OF THE 11TH EDITION

We have carefully constructed the 11th edition to address instructors' concerns about getting through all the necessary material for this course. The streamlined table of contents outlines 18 chapters divided into five parts: Financial Planning, Money Management, Income and Asset Protection, Investments, and Retirement and Estate Planning. We again include a chapter entitled "Career Planning" that provides students with innovative 21st century steps they need for successful career planning, and in every chapter where relevant, we place the material in the context of today's challenging economic times.

FEATURES

We have carefully designed pedagogical features to strengthen learning opportunities for students. Each feature is designed to communicate vital information meaningfully and to maintain student interest. The following features support student understanding and retention.

You Must Be Kidding, Right?   If you typically skip the opening case, now is the time to change your ways. This feature opens every chapter with a short narrative about a financial topic and a question with four possible answers. The often surprising (and sometimes funny) answers provide an excellent opportunity to quickly engage students in a concept that is key to understanding the chapter.

What Do You Recommend?   These concise, realistic cases are pretests at the beginning of each chapter followed by leading questions asking about the most important fundamental concepts in the chapter. The case acts as a pretest because a student who has not read the chapter will be able to offer only simplistic, experience-based opinions and suggestions to respond to the questions. This will communicate to them how much they have to learn from an instructor-led classroom discussion of the chapter. A corresponding posttest, "What Do You Recommend Now?" appears as part of the end-of-chapter pedagogy. At that point, student responses should be very different: informed, practical, and action oriented. (See further discussion in the "End-of-Chapter Pedagogy" section.)

Your Next Five Years   "Your Next Five Years" boxes list the most important chapter-related actions students need to take to get off to a great start financially. These tips are sufficiently detailed to allow ready implementation. If students take these actions, they truly will become financially successful over the next five years!

Do It NOW!   "Do It NOW!" boxes in each chapter list three key personal finance actions smart students should take immediately. They focus primarily on implementing some of the most pressing "Next Five Years" tips from the chapter.

Financial Power Point   New to this edition, the "Financial Power Point" boxes provide concise, practical information on a variety of current financial issues and opportunities.

YOU MUST BE KIDDING, RIGHT?

People with no prior credit history or one that shows poor repayment patterns in the past often wonder if they will ever be able to get credit, especially in a sluggish economy when credit is difficult to obtain. Simply put, why would any lender want to trust them? Which of the following is true about the availability of credit for people in such situations?

A. No one will ever grant them credit.

B. If they wait a few years, the situation could change.

C. If they keep searching, they will find a lender that will treat them like everyone else.

D. Credit is relatively easy to obtain even today.

Answer:

The answer is B. When credit is tight, it is difficult for people with poor or no credit to obtain credit. When credit availability eases, certain lenders will accept such applicants, although they will charge high interest rates. Building and maintaining a good credit history will always get you low interest rates!

YOUR NEXT 5 YEARS

In the next five years, you can start achieving financial success by doing the following related to building and maintaining good credit:

1. Protect your credit reputation as carefully as you would safeguard your personal reputation.

2. Determine your own debt limit rather than rely on a lender before deciding to take on any debt.

3. Obtain copies of your credit bureau reports regularly, and challenge all errors or omissions you find.

4. Never cosign a loan for anyone, including relatives.

5. Always repay your debts in a timely manner.

DO IT NOW!

You know more about personal finance after reading this chapter, so get started right now by:

1. Obtaining a free copy of your credit report (www.annualcreditreport.com) from one of the three national credit bureaus.

2. Confirming the accuracy of the report and, if there are errors or omissions, challenging them with all three bureaus.

3. Repeating steps two and three every four months, staggering the bureaus to ensure that each request is free.

FINANCIAL POWER POINT

Debt Reduces Your Ability to Save and Invest

Saving and investing over long periods of time is the key to building wealth. Taking on excessive debts early in life will seriously compromise your goal of being financially successful.

RUN THE NUMBERS

Choosing Between Low-Interest-Rate Dealer Financing and a Rebate

Advertisements for new vehicles often offer low APRs for dealer-arranged loans. A cash rebate of $1000 to $3000 (or more) off the price of the car may be offered as an alternative to the low interest rate. If you intend to pay cash, then the cash rebate obviously represents the better deal. But which alternative is better when you can arrange your own financing?

To compare the two APRs accurately, you must add the opportunity cost of the forgone rebate to the finance charge of the dealer financing. The worksheet provides an example of this process. Suppose a dealer offers 2.9 percent financing for three

years with a $907 finance charge; alternatively, you can receive a $3000 rebate if you arrange your own financing. The price of the car before the rebate is $22,000. Assume you can make a $2000 down payment and that you can get a 6.5 percent loan on your own. This worksheet can be found on the *Garman/Forgue* companion website, or you can find similar worksheets at www.bankrate.com and at www.kiplinger.com.

The lower of the values obtained in steps 3 and 4 is the better deal. In this instance, the financing that you arranged on your own is more attractive. In fact, any loan you arrange that carries an APR lower than 12 percent compares favorably with the dealer-arranged financing in this case.

Step	Example	Your Figures
1. Determine the dollar amount of the rebate.	$3000	_____
2. Add the rebate amount to the finance charge for the dealer financing (dollar cost of credit).	+$ 907	_____
3. Use the n-ratio APR formula from Chapter 7 (Equation [7.2] on page 215 and replicated here as Equation [8.1]) to calculate an adjusted APR for the dealer financing.		

$$APR = \frac{Y(95P + 9)F}{12P(P + 1)(4D + F)} \quad (8.1)$$

where

APR = Annual percentage rate
Y = Number of payment periods in one **year**
F = **Finance** charge in dollars
D = **Debt** (amount borrowed)
P = Total number of scheduled **payments**

$$APR = \frac{(12)[(95 \times 36) + 9]($3000 + $907)}{12 \times 36(36 + 1)[(4 \times $20,000) + ($3000 + $907)]} = 12\%$$

4. Write in the APR that you arranged on your own.	6.5%	

ADVICE FROM A PRO

Check the Background of Your Stockbroker of Investment Advisor

You can check the background of a stockbroker or a brokerage firm via the Financial Industry Regulatory Authority (FINRA) (www.finra.org/Investors/%20ToolsCalculators/BrokerCheck/index.htm). Some investors neglect to investigate a stockbroker or firm and lose money as a result. The broker may

abscond with the investor's funds; at other times, the investor receives poor advice. Don't let it happen to you! Check out the Securities and Exchange Commission's website (www.adviserinfo.sec.gov) to review criminal complaints and regulatory problems with any of 220,000 investment advisers.

Allen Martin
California State University–Northridge

WHAT DO YOU RECOMMEND NOW?

Now that you have read this chapter on building and maintaining good credit, what would you recommend to Carrie Savarin regarding:

1. Factors she should consider regarding her ability to take on additional debt?
2. The impact of her current debt on her ability to obtain a loan to buy a vehicle?
3. Where she might obtain financing for a vehicle loan?
4. The effect of taking on a loan on her overall financial planning?

Run the Numbers These boxes guide students to their best personal finance decisions or commonly confronted choices following a step-by-step process.

Did You Know? These boxes have interesting, catchy titles that encourage students to actually read the information, and classroom research demonstrates this technique works.

Concept Checks At the end of each major segment of each chapter, we provide concept check questions tied to the major topics in that segment. These aid classroom discussion, serve as student assignments, or simply provide students with a self-check for full understanding of the material.

Advice from a Pro ... These feature boxes—written by some of the nation's best personal finance experts—offer authoritative, real-world advice on getting out of credit card debt, making purchases online, buying a used car, and paying for retirement on the layaway plan, plus many other topics.

End-of-Chapter Pedagogy The end-of-chapter pedagogy—much of which is new—carefully directs student learning of the concepts and principles that are key to success in personal finance.

What Do You Recommend Now? The same leading questions pertaining to the case at the beginning of the chapter are repeated in this section. At this point, however, instructors can anticipate higher-quality responses and a deeper level of understanding because students have read the chapter and listened to instructor-led class discussion.

Big Picture Summary of Learning Objectives Three to four sentences review the chapter content following each of the chapter learning objectives.

Let's Talk About It   Students are given an opportunity to discuss their personal experiences related to the chapter by addressing these questions. Many of these are new to this edition.

Do the Math   These questions apply the relevant quantitative mathematical calculations used in personal finance decision making. The companion website includes Excel calculators for these exercises. Many of these are new.

Financial Planning Cases   Students must apply key concepts when analyzing typical personal financial problems, dilemmas, and challenges that face individuals and couples. Because some cases are designed to be both continuous and independent of the other chapters' cases, each case can be analyzed by itself. One new continuing case is that of Julia Price, whose successful financial life evolves through challenging economic times; her case ends with a question for the student: "*Offer your opinions about her thinking.*" This edition now includes five or six cases in each chapter. The series of case questions requires data analysis and critical thinking, and this effort reinforces mastery of chapter concepts.

Be Your Own Personal Financial Planner   New to this edition, this end-of-chapter section provides concrete, personalized activities that engage students in developing aspects of their own financial plans. Where appropriate, these activities are keyed to online "My Personal Financial Planner" worksheets complete with interactive spreadsheets.

MY PERSONAL FINANCIAL PLANNER

On the 'Net   All of the "On the 'Net" exercises have been changed to carefully direct the student to online materials that are genuinely useful and appropriate for this time in their personal financial lives. Each chapter now includes several Internet-based exercises, activities, and focused questions that expand the student's learning in a guided manner, allowing the student to research and apply chapter concepts while finding the answers.

Action Involvement Activities   New to this edition, this end-of-chapter section is not busywork. Each out-of-class activity points the student toward concrete steps that require applying the knowledge provided in each chapter at a personal level, particularly aiming to have an impact on their thoughts about personal finance.

Glossary   A comprehensive end-of-text glossary includes precise definitions of all key terms and concepts.

COMPLETE INSTRUCTOR SUPPORT

- **Instructor's Manual.** Written by main text author, Ray Forgue, this ancillary includes a variety of useful components: suggested course syllabi to emphasize a general, insurance, or investments approach to personal finance; learning objectives; a summary overview for use as a lecture outline; and teaching suggestions including student application exercises and tips for bringing the Web into the classroom. This item is found on the Instructor's Resource CD and instructor website.

- **Solutions Manual.** Written by main text author, Ray Forgue, and verified by Linda Bradley, University of Kentucky. Answers and solutions to all end-of-chapter questions and problems are included. This item is found on the Instructor's Resource CD and on the instructor website.

- **PowerPoint Slides.** The PowerPoint slides contain chapter outlines, figures, and tables from the main text, which were written by main text author Ray Forgue. eLecture material is available within the PowerPoint slides.

- **Instructor's Resource CD.** This instructor support CD offers electronic versions of the **Instructor's Manual**, **Solutions Manual**, and **PowerPoint slides**. In addition, the CD includes **ExamView**, a computerized test bank that contains more than 3100 questions. Approximately 30 percent of the questions are new or revised for this

Kiplinger

edition, and all were carefully reviewed by main text author Ray Forgue. This program is very user friendly and permits editing of test questions and generation of class exams. In addition, an explanation is provided for all true-false questions for which the correct answer is "false," for all multiple-choice questions that require a mathematical computation, and for all multiple-choice questions deemed as "difficult."

- **Instructor Website.** The instructor website that accompanies *Personal Finance* provides a wealth of supplemental materials to enhance learning and aid in course management. Features of the site include PowerPoint slides, downloadable Instructor Manual and Solution Manual files, test bank content, and a DVD guide.

- **Instructor DVD.** This DVD features video discussions with numerous personal finance professionals from The Kiplinger Company. These discussions contain personal finance tips illustrating and explaining pertinent topics such as job searching, income taxes, student loans, mortgage shopping, and more.

COMPLETE STUDENT SUPPORT

- **My Personal Financial Planner** is a handbook for students to use in planning and organizing their personal finances. This booklet contains over 60 worksheets, schedules, and planners for financial planning. They are not busywork for students. Some of the worksheets mimic the calculations and planning exercises covered in the book; others are for student use in developing personal financial plans and actions. A student's use of this handbook virtually guarantees positive changes in personal financial behaviors and success in money matters.

- **Student Companion Website** is accessible without an access code. Among other assets, students can find a short interactive quiz there.

- **Finance Central Premium Student Website** contains eLecture presentations, calculators, and worksheets to complete the end-of-chapter exercises, quizzes, online glossary, games, and flashcards. This content is accessible via an optional printed access card. Standalone instant access is also available via iChapters.com.

ACKNOWLEDGMENTS

We would like to thank our reviewers and other experts, who offered helpful suggestions and criticisms to this and previous editions. This book is their book, too. We especially appreciate the assistance of the following individuals:

Tim Alzheimer, *Montana State University*

Gary Amundson, *Montana State University–Billings*

Dori Anderson, *Mendocino College*

Robert E. Arnold, Jr., *Henry Ford Community College*

Bala Arshanapalli, *Indiana University Northwest*

Hal Babson, *Columbus State Community College*

Anne Bailey, *Miami University*

Rosella Bannister, *Bannister Financial Education Services*

Richard Bartlett, *Muskingum Area Technical College*

Anne Baumgartner, *Navy Family Service Center–Norfolk*

John J. Beasley, *Georgia Southern University*

Kim Belden, *Daytona Beach Community College*

Pamela J. Bennett, *University of Central Arkansas*

Daniel A. Bequette, *Hartwell College*

Peggy S. Berger, *Colorado State University*

David Bible, *Louisiana State University–Shreveport*

George Biggs, *Southern Nazarene University*

Robert Blatchford, *Tulsa Junior College*

Susan Blizzard, *San Antonio College*

Karin B. Bonding, *University of Virginia*

Linda Bradley, *California State University–Northridge*

Dean Brassington, *Financial Educator Services*

Anne Bunton, *Cottey College*

Bruce Brunson, *Tidewater Community College*

Paul L. Camp, *Galecki Financial Management*

Chris Canellos, *Stanford University*

Andrew Cao, *American University*

Diana D. Carroll, *Carson–Newman College*

Gerri Chaplin, *Joliet Junior College*

Steve Christian, *Jackson Community College*

Ron Christner, *Loyola University*

Charlotte Churaman, *University of Maryland*

Carol N. Cissel, *Roanoke College*

Thomas S. Coe, *Xavier University of Louisiana*

Edward R. Cook, *University of Massachusetts–Boston*

Patricia Cowley, *Omni Travel*

Kathy Crall, *Des Moines Area Community College*

Sheran Cramer, *University of Nebraska–Lincoln*

Ellen Daniel, *Harding University*

Joel J. Dauten, *Arizona State University*

Carl R. Denson, *University of Delaware*

Dale R. Detlefs, *William M. Mercer, Inc.*

A. Terrence Dickens, *California State University*

Charles E. Downing, *Massasoit Community College*

Alberto Duarte, *Access Counseling*

Sidney W. Eckert, *Appalachian State University*

Marc Eiger, *Standard & Poor's*

Gregg Edwards, *Monroe Community College*

Jacolin P. Eichelberger, *Hillsborough Community College*

Gregory J. Eidleman, *Alvernia College*

Richard English, *Augustana College*

Evan Enowitz, *Grossmont College*

Don Etnier, *University of Maryland–European Division*

Judy Farris, *South Dakota State University*

Vicki Fitzsimmons, *University of Illinois*

Fred Floss, *Buffalo State College*

Paula G. Freston, *Colby Community College*

H. Swint Friday, *University of South Alabama*

Caroline Fulmer, *University of Alabama*

Wafica Ghoul, *Davenport University*

Joel Gold, *University of South Maine*

Elizabeth Goldsmith, *Florida State University*

Joseph D. Greene, *Augusta State University*

Paul Gregg, *University of Central Florida*

Jeri W. Griego, *Laramie County Community College*

Michael P. Griffin, *University of Massachusetts–Dartmouth*

Richard C. Grimm, *Grove City College*

David R. Guarino, *Standard & Poor's*

Hilda Hall, *Surry Community College*

Patty Hatfield, *Bradley University*

Andrew Hawkins, *Lake Area Technical Institute*

Janice Heckroth, *Indiana University of Pennsylvania*

Diane Henke, *University of Wisconsin–Sheboygan*

Roger P. Hill, *University of North Carolina–Wilmington*

Jeanne Hilton, *University of Nevada*

Laura Horvath, *University of Detroit Mercy*

David Houghton, *Northwest Nazarene College*

George Hruby, *University of Akron*

Samira Hussein, *Johnson County Community College*

Roger Ignatius, *University of Maine–Augusta*

James R. Isherwood, *Community College of Rhode Island*

Naheel Jeries, *Iowa State University*

Karen Jones, *SWBC Mortgage Corporation*

Marilyn S. Jones, *Friends University*

Ellen Joyner, *Liberty National Bank–Lexington*

Virginia W. Junk, *University of Idaho*

Peggy D. Keck, *Western Kentucky University*

Dennis Keefe, *Michigan State University*

Jim Keys, *Florida International University*

Haejeong Kim, *Central Michigan University*

Jinhee Kim, *University of Maryland–College Park*

Karen Eilers Lahey, *University of Akron*

Eloise J. Law, *State University of New York–Plattsburgh*

Andrew H. Lawrence, *Delgado Community College*

David W. Leapard, *Eastern Michigan State University*

Hongbok Lee, *Western Illinois University*

Charles J. Lipinski, *Marywood University*

Janet K. Lukens, *Mississippi State University*

Kenneth Marin, *Aquinas College*

Kenneth Mark, *Kansas Community College*

Julia Marlowe, *University of Georgia*

Allen Martin, *California State University–Northridge*

Lee McClain, *Western Washington University*

Billy Moore, *Delta State University*

John R. Moore, *Navy Family Services Center–Norfolk*

Diane R. Morrison, *University of Wisconsin–La Crosse*

Steven J. Muck, *El Camino College*

Randolph J. Mullis, *WEATrust*

James Nelson, *East Carolina State University*

Donald Neuhart, *Central Missouri State University*

Oris L. Odom II, *University of Texas–Tyler*

William S. Phillips, *Memphis State University*

John Piccione, *Rochester Institute of Technology*

Carl H. Pollock, Jr., *Portland State University*

Angela J. Rabatin, *Prince George's Community College*

Gwen M. Reichbach, *Dealers' Financial Services*

Mary Ellen Rider, *University of Nebraska*

Eloise Lorch Rippie, *Iowa State University*

Edmund L. Robert, *Front Range Community College*

Clarence C. Rose, *Radford University*

David E. Rubin, *Glendale Community College*

Michael Rupured, *University of Georgia*

Peggy Schomaker, *University of Maine*

Barry B. Schweig, *Creighton University*

Elaine D. Scott, *Bluefield State University*

James Scott, *Southwest Missouri State University*

Wilmer E. Seago, *Virginia Tech University*

Kim Simons, *Madisonville Community College*

Marilyn K. Skinner, *Macon Technical Institute*

Rosalyn Smith, *Morningside College*

Horacio Soberon-Ferrer, *University of Florida*

Edward Stendard, *St. John Fisher College*

Mary Stephenson, *University of Maryland–College Park*

Eugene Swinnerton, *University of Detroit Mercy*

Lisa Tatlock, *The Master's College*

Francis C. Thomas, Port Republic, *New Jersey*

Stephen Trimby, *Worcester State College*

John W. Tway, *Amber University*

Shafi Ullah, *Broward Community College*

Dick Verrone, *University of North Carolina–Wilmington*

Jerry A. Viscione, *Boston College*

Stephen E. Wagner, Attorney at Law, Blacksburg, *Virginia*

Rosemary Walker, *Michigan State University*

Grant J. Wells, *Michigan State University*

Jon D. Wentworth, *Southern Adventist University*

Dorothy West, *Michigan State University*

Gloria Worthy, *State Technical Institute-Memphis*

Rui Yau, *South Dakota State University*

Alex R. Yguado, *L.A. Mission College*

Robert P. Yuyuenyongwatana, *Cameron University*

Martha Zenns, *Jamestown Community College*

Larry Zigler, *Highland College*

Virginia S. Zuiker, *University of Minnesota*

This 11th edition also has benefited from the contributions of some of the best personal finance experts in the United States, who have shared some specialized expertise by contributing to a series of boxes titled "Advice from a Pro...":

Dennis R. Ackley, *Ackley & Associates*

Jan D. Andersen, *California State University, Sacramento*

Sophia Anong, *Virginia Tech*

Lorie Broberg, *Oglala Lakota College*

Anthony J. Campolo, *Columbus State Community College*

Brenda J. Cude, *University of Georgia*

William Dean, *Southern University*

Lorraine R. Decker, *Decker & Associates Inc.*

Karen Drage, *Eastern Illinois University*

Patti Fisher, *Virginia Tech*

Jonathan Fox, *The Ohio State University*

Carol S. Fulmer, *The University of Alabama*

Jordan E. Goodman, *MoneyAnswers.com*

Holly Hunts, *Montana State University*

Alena C. Johnson, *Utah State University*

Hyungsoo Kim, *University of Kentucky*

Joan Koonce, *University of Georgia*

Frances C. Lawrence, *Louisiana State University*

Irene Leech, *Virginia Tech*

Dana Wolff, *Southeast Technical Institute*

Lori Lothringer, *Metropolitan Community College*

Allen Martin, *California State University–Northridge*

Diann Moorman, *University of Georgia*

Aimee D. Prawitz, *Northern Illinois University*

Kathleen Prochaska-Cue, *University of Nebraska–Lincoln*

Ann Ranczuch, *Monroe Community College*

Jamie Richter, *Northern Illinois University*

Michael Ruff, *Monroe Community College*

Michelle Singletary, *The Washington Post*

Donald Stuhlman, Wilmington College, *Delaware*

Sherry Tshibangu, *Monroe Community College*

Robert O. Weagley, *University of Missouri–Columbia*

Jon Wentworth, *Southern Adventist University*

We definitely wish to thank the many students who had the opportunity to read, critique, and provide input for various components of the *Personal Finance* project. Please keep sending us your e-mails.

This edition of *Personal Finance* benefited enormously from the editorial efforts of Clara Goosman. In addition to being a fine manager and editor, she brought much insight, creativity, intelligence, and wisdom to the project. Linda Bradley's accuracy check efforts were incomparable. Holly Henjum and Devanand Srinivasan did a superlative job supervising the production of this edition with its challenging format.

A project of this dimension could never have been completed without the patience, support, understanding, and sacrifices of our friends and families during the book's development, revision, and production. Tom Garman, professor emeritus and fellow at Virginia Tech University, lives in The Villages, Florida, and stays in contact with his children and their spouses and significant others: Dana, Julia, Tom, Scott, David, Alieu, Isatou, Kumba, Alimatou, and Ousman. Thanks are owed to all. Tom also credits the mentors in his life—Ron West, Bill Boast, Bill McDivitt, and John Binnion—for guiding him along the way, particularly through their noble examples of compassion, commitment, and excellence. He also thanks Gerry Chambers for her laughter, love, and support, which guarantees that the fourth quarter of his life will be blessed with happiness. Ray Forgue, retired from University of Kentucky, lives in Easley, South Carolina, with his wife Snooky and her son, Stuart, and proudly watches over his son Matthew and daughter Amy and Snooky's children Dru and Seth as they continue their working careers. Ray wishes to thank his mother, Mary, and brothers Bob, Gary, Joe, and Dave for their patience over the years as he spent time during vacation and holiday visits working on this book. Special thanks to Snooky, whose assistance on the first edition of *Personal Finance* continues to shine through to this current edition.

Finally, we wish to say "thank you" to the hundreds of personal finance instructors around the country who have generously shared their views, in person and by letter and e-mail, on what should be included in a high-quality textbook and ancillary materials. Some of you thankfully have written five or six times. You demand the best for your students, and we've listened. *Personal Finance* is your book! The two of us and the superlative team of people at Cengage Learning have tried very hard to meet your needs in every possible way. We hope we have exceeded your expectations. Why? Because we share the belief that students need to study personal finance concepts thoroughly and learn them well so that they will be truly successful in their personal finances.

E. Thomas Garman
ethomasgarman@yahoo.com

Raymond E. Forgue
perfinypm@yahoo.com

P.S. Dear students: If you are going to save any of your college textbooks, be certain to keep this one because the basic principles of personal finance are everlasting. Also, you might want to present the book as a gift to a significant other, spouse, sibling, or parent.

PART

1

Understanding Personal Finance

YOU MUST BE KIDDING, RIGHT?

Lauren Crawford invests $250 a month in her 401(k) retirement account, which earns an 8 percent annual return. After 35 years, how much money will she have in the account over and above the amounts she will contribute through the years?

A. $105,000

B. $210,000

C. $468,000

D. $573,000

The answer is C, $468,000 ($573,000 − $105,000). Lauren will contribute $105,000 ($3000 [$250 × 12] × 35). Lauren makes the big money ($468,000) off "the annual compounding of money," not just on the amounts she puts into her retirement plan each month ($105,000). It's all about the magic of compound interest!

LEARNING OBJECTIVES

After reading this chapter, you should be able to:

1 Use the building blocks to achieving financial success.

2 Understand how the economy affects your personal financial success.

3 Apply economic principles when making financial decisions.

4 Perform time value of money calculations in personal financial decision making.

5 Make smart decisions about your employee benefits.

6 Identify the professional qualifications of providers of financial advice.

WHAT DO YOU RECOMMEND?

Se Ri Pak, age 23, recently graduated with her bachelor's degree in library and information sciences. She is about to take her first professional position as an archivist with a large civil engineering firm in a rapidly expanding area in California. While in school, Se Ri worked part time, earning about $8000 per year. For the past two years, she has managed to put $1000 each year into an individual retirement account (IRA). Se Ri owes $15,000 in student loans on which she is obliged now to begin making payments. Her new job will pay $55,000. Se Ri may begin participating in her employer's 401(k) retirement plan immediately, and she can contribute up to 6 percent of her salary to the plan. Her employer will contribute 1/2 of 1 percent for every 1 percent that Se Ri contributes.

qingqing/Shutterstock.com

What do you recommend to Se Ri on the importance of personal finance regarding:

1. Participating in her employer's 401(k) retirement plan?

2. Understanding the effects of her marginal tax rate on her financial decisions?

3. Considering the current state of the economy in her personal financial planning?

4. Using time value of money considerations to project what her IRA might be worth at age 63?

5. Using time value of money considerations to project what her 401(k) plan might be worth when she is age 63 if she were to participate fully?

financial literacy
Knowledge of facts, concepts, principles, and technological tools that are fundamental to being smart about money.

personal finance
The study of personal and family resources considered important in achieving financial success; it involves how people spend, save, protect, and invest their financial resources.

financial responsibility
Means that you are accountable for your future financial well-being and that you strive to make wise personal financial decisions.

The 2007/2009 housing/credit/stock market collapse and economic crisis was of historic proportions. Nine million people in the United States had their jobs disappear. Many people of your parents' ages saw the value of their homes shrink 25 to 50 percent while at the same time half of their retirement funds evaporated. Consumer confidence dropped to an all-time low. Today's ensuing slow recovery is fraught with fear and anxiety about personal finances.

Can you successfully manage your personal finances in such an era of economic turbulence? Yes. But it will be challenging. Many experts today argue that we need to consume less, pay off our credit cards, and save and invest more to get ourselves out of this economic mess. This is good advice for your future. You can and will learn how to do these things because your long-term financial success depends upon it. The economy is going to be bumpy for the next few years. Yet many opportunities will arise for you to take smart actions to help assure your future financial success. You are fortunate to be reading this book as it provides prudent guidance for every step of the way.

Your **financial literacy** is your knowledge of facts, concepts, principles, and technological tools that are fundamental to being smart about money. Financial literacy empowers you. It improves your ability to handle day-to-day financial matters, helps you avoid the consequences of poor financial decisions that could take years to overcome, and helps you make informed and confident personal money decisions.

Personal finance is the study of personal and family resources considered important in achieving financial success; it involves how people spend, save, protect, and invest their financial resources. Topics in personal finance include financial and career planning, budgeting, tax management, cash management, credit cards, borrowing, major expenditures, risk management, investments, retirement planning, and estate planning. A solid understanding of personal finance topics offers you a better chance of success in facing the financial challenges, responsibilities, and opportunities of life. Such successes might include paying minimal credit costs, legally reducing your income taxes, purchasing automobiles at low prices, financing housing on excellent terms, buying appropriate and fairly priced insurance, selecting successful investments, planning for a comfortable retirement, and passing on your estate with minimal transfer costs. The best of all the successes is the sense of freedom from financial worries that comes with effectively planning your personal finances.

Financial responsibility means that you are accountable for your future financial well-being and that you strive to make good decisions in personal finance. Studying personal finance will help you avoid financial mistakes and show you how to take advantage of financial opportunities. The biggest barrier to achieving financial success is to live like you are rich *before* you are.

At the beginning of each chapter, we provide a short case vignette titled "What Do You Recommend?" Each story focuses on the financial challenges that can be experienced by someone who has not learned about the material in that chapter. You will be asked to think about what advice you might give the person as you study the chapter. Then at the end of each chapter, you will again be asked to provide more informed advice based on what you have learned. You will be much better informed then!

The goal of this book is to provide you access to up-to-date information and rational suggestions to empower you to be able to make informed decisions about spending, managing money, maintaining creditworthiness, purchasing insurance, and saving and investing. Good decision making means you will control your personal financial destiny and be successful.

THE BUILDING BLOCKS TO ACHIEVING PERSONAL FINANCIAL SUCCESS

Today's marketplace provides a constant barrage of messages suggesting that you can spend and borrow your way to financial success, security, and wealth. These messages are very enticing for those starting out in their financial lives. In truth, overspending and overuse of consumer credit seriously *impede* financial success.

Many people think that being wealthy is a function of how much you earn or inherit. In reality, it is much more closely related to your ability to understand the trade-offs and decisions that generate wealth for you. A **trade-off** is giving up one thing for another. For example, it is wise to give up some current spending in order to enjoy a financially comfortable future, which should allow you to drive the vehicles you desire, enjoy the vacations you want, and take pleasure in a financially stress-free retirement.

You have to do only a *few* things right in personal finance during your lifetime, as long as you don't do too many things wrong. Personal finance is not rocket science. You can succeed very well in your personal finances by making appropriate plans and taking sensible actions to implement those plans.

Start by Spending Less So You Can Save and Invest More

First, recognize that financial objectives are rarely achieved without forgoing or sacrificing current **consumption** (spending on goods and services). This restraint is accomplished by putting money into **savings** (income not spent on current consumption) for use in achieving future goals. Some savings are actually **investments** (assets purchased with the goal of providing additional income from the asset itself). By saving and investing, people are much more likely to have funds available for future consumption. If you save for tomorrow, you will be happier today *and* tomorrow.

Effective financial management often separates the *haves* from the *have-nots*. The haves, observes Virginia Tech professor Celia Hayhoe, are those people who learn to live on less than they earn and are the savers and investors of society. The have-nots are the spenders who live paycheck to paycheck, usually with high consumer debt. To succeed in personal finance, you should follow the adage to "Spend some and save some."

Saving for future consumption represents a good illustration of the human desire to achieve a certain **standard of living**. This standard is what an individual or group earnestly desires and seeks to attain, to maintain if attained, to preserve if threatened, and to regain if lost. Our standards include our wants and needs—our comforts and luxuries too. At any particular time, individuals actually experience their **level of living**. In essence, your standard of living is where you would like to be, and your level of living is where you actually are.

Plan for Financial Success and Happiness

Financial success is the achievement of financial aspirations that are desired, planned, or attempted. Success is defined by the person who seeks it. Some define financial success as being able to actually live according to one's standard of living. Many seek **financial security**, which provides the comfortable feeling that your financial resources will be adequate to fulfill any needs you have as well as most of your wants. Others want to be **wealthy** and have an abundance of money, property, investments, and other resources.

Financial happiness encompasses a lot more than just making money. It is the experience you have when you are satisfied with your money matters. People who are happy about their finances are likely to be spending within a budget and taking steps to achieve their goals, and this happiness spills over in a positive way to feelings about their overall enjoyment of life. Financial happiness is in part a result of practicing good financial behaviors. Examples of such behaviors include paying bills on time, spending less than

FINANCIAL POWER POINT

To Succeed Financially Do What Your Grandparents Did

To succeed in life financially, people today can do what their grandparents did. This includes a willingness to postpone gratification, invest for the future, work harder than the next person, and hold your kids to the highest expectations.

Figure 1-1   **Building Blocks to Achieving Financial Success**

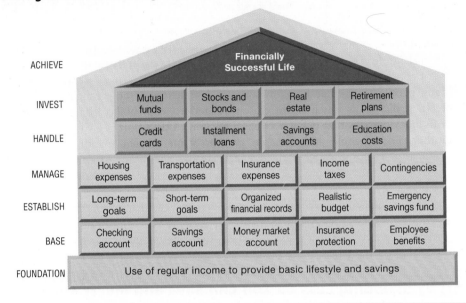

DID YOU KNOW?

The Five Fundamental Steps in the Financial Planning Process

There are five fundamental steps to the personal financial planning process: (1) Evaluate your financial condition relative to your education and career choice; (2) define your financial goals; (3) develop a plan of action to achieve your goals; (4) implement your plan; and (5) review your financial progress and make changes as appropriate. As indicated in step 5, this process is revisited periodically, ideally every year, and whenever your life takes a meaningful turn such as a new job, marriage, birth of a child, or even after a sad event such as a divorce or death of a family member.

you earn, knowing where your money goes, and investing some money for the future. The more good financial behaviors you practice, the greater your financial happiness. In fact, simply setting financial goals contributes to financial happiness.

Your Building Blocks of Financial Success

Bridging the gap between one's level of living and one's desired standard of living involves learning about how to achieve financial success. Figure 1-1 shows how the building blocks of a financially successful life fit together. Financial success and happiness come from using the building blocks of personal finance, such as having a foundation of regular income to provide basic lifestyle and savings, and establishing a financial base using employee benefits and checking and savings accounts. Other building blocks include setting financial goals, controlling expenditures, managing income taxes, handling credit cards, and investing in mutual funds and retirement plans. All of these factors are examined in the remaining chapters of the text.

 Concept Check 1.1

1. Describe financial success.

2. What is financial happiness?

3. What are the building blocks to achieving financial success?

THE ECONOMY AFFECTS YOUR PERSONAL FINANCIAL SUCCESS

 LEARNING OBJECTIVE ❷

Understand how the economy affects your personal financial success.

Your success in personal finance depends in part on how well you understand the economic environment; the current stage of the business cycle; and the future direction of the economy, inflation, and interest rates.

How to Tell Where We Are in the Business Cycle

An **economy** is a system of managing the productive and employment resources of a country, state, or community. The U.S. federal government attempts to regulate the country's overall economy to maintain stable prices (low inflation) and stable levels of employment (low unemployment). In this way, the government seeks to achieve sustained **economic growth**, which is a condition of increasing production (business activity) and consumption (consumer spending) in the economy—and hence increasing national income. Government policies also affect the economy. For example, tax cuts keep money in consumers' pockets, money that they are then likely to spend. Tax increases, in contrast, depress consumer demand.

The Business Cycle

Growth in the U.S. economy varies over time. The **business cycle** (also called the **economic cycle**) is a process by which the economy grows and contracts over time. It can be depicted as a wavelike pattern of rising and falling economic activity in which the same pattern occurs again and again over time. As illustrated in Figure 1-2, the phases of the business cycle are expansion (when the economy is increasing), peak (the end of an expansion and the beginning of a contraction), contraction (when the economy is falling), and trough (the end of a contraction and beginning of an expansion).

The preferred stage of the economic cycle is the **expansion phase**, where production is at high capacity, unemployment is low, retail sales are high, and prices and interest rates are low or falling. Under these conditions, consumers find it easier to buy homes, cars, and expensive goods on credit, and businesses are encouraged to borrow to expand production to meet the increased consumer demand. The stock market also rises because investors expect higher profits in the future.

As the demand for credit increases, short-term interest rates rise because more borrowers want money. Consumers and businesses purchase more goods, exerting upward pressure on prices. Eventually, prices and interest rates climb high enough to stifle consumer and business borrowing, send stock prices down, and choke off the expansion. The result is a period of negligible economic growth—perhaps a slight downturn—or even a decline in economic activity.

The Great Recession

In such situations, the economy often contracts and moves toward a **recession**. During recessions, consumers become pessimistic about their future buying plans. The typical U.S. recession is marked by an average economic decline of 2 percent that lasts for ten

economic growth
A condition of increasing production (business spending) and consumption (consumer spending) in the economy and hence increasing national income.

business cycle/economic cycle
Business cycles can be depicted as a wavelike pattern of rising and falling economic activity; the phases of the business cycle include expansion, peak, contraction (which may turn into recession), and trough.

recession
A recurring period of decline in total output, income, employment, and trade, usually lasting from six months to a year and marked by widespread contractions in many sectors of the economy.

Business Cycle Phases

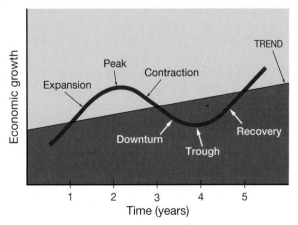

Figure 1-2

months with an average unemployment rate exceeding 6 percent. There have been five recessions since 1980. The federal government's Business Cycle Dating Committee of the National Bureau of Economic Research officially defines a recession as "a period of falling economic activity spread across the economy, lasting more than a few months, normally visible in real gross domestic product, real income, employment, industrial production, and wholesale-retail sales." The committee determined that the recession now popularly known as the Great Recession began in December 2007 and ended in June 2009, as a recovery began that month. The recession lasted 18 months, which makes it the longest of any recession since World War II.

The 5.1 percent economic decline during the Great Recession of 2007/2009 was the worst since the 1929–1933 Great Depression. The American economy was characterized by extremely high unemployment (over 10 percent), horrendous stock market declines (over 50 percent), and sharply falling housing prices (25 to 65 percent). One effect of the economic turmoil is **deleveraging**, meaning that instead of normal economic times when credit usage grows, it in fact shrinks. When businesses and consumers use less debt, home and car sales decline and so do jobs.

deleveraging
A time period when credit use shrinks in an economy instead of expanding as during normal economic times.

The Great Recession caused nine million adults in the United States to become unemployed, and 50 percent of the jobs lost were in manufacturing and construction. Half of all American workers suffered job losses, pay cuts, or reduced hours at work, or were forced into part-time employment. Surveys show that over 60 percent of those between age 50 and 61 have had to delay their retirements. Research suggests that the Great Recession destroyed 20 percent of American's wealth (e.g., home values and investments). Nationally, residential real estate values plunged about 35 percent. To reduce the likelihood of another such calamitous recession, the mission of the newly created Financial Stability Oversight Council is to build a warning system to identify financial companies in need of government intervention before they collapse and negatively impact the American economy.

double dip recession
This occurs when the economy has a recession and then, soon after emerging from the recession with a short period of growth, quickly falls back into recession.

Double Dip Recession Some fear that continued downward pressure on prices from weak wages and weak demand may result in a **double dip recession**. This occurs when the economy has a recession and then, soon after emerging from the recession with a short period of growth, quickly falls back into recession.

The Economic Future … Eventually … Will Be Expansion Despite the severity or length of any recession, eventually the economic contraction ends, and consumers and businesses become more optimistic. The economy then moves beyond the trough toward recovery and expansion, where levels of production, employment, and retail sales begin to improve, allowing the overall economy to experience some growth from its previously weakened state. The entire business cycle typically takes about six years.

Politicians and economic advisors struggle with which path to take to create economic growth. Most of the world has followed the Keynesian economic theory since the 1930s, which is to increase demand with stimulus spending even if it creates large temporary deficits. The logic is that when consumers and businesses spend less, the economy will be depressed unless the government spends more. Such spending creates additional economic growth that results in increased tax revenues, thus creating budget surpluses that can be used to pay down the debts.* Nations and political leaders today are differing in how to handle the current economic troubles, as some are choosing to slash public outlays. Concerns about the austerity approach are that it will lead to lower demand, lower growth, lower tax revenues, stock market declines, and an even higher national debt, as has occurred in Greece, Ireland, Portugal, Spain, and Great Britain.

More than 11 million new jobs will have to be created just to get the U.S. economy back to where it was when the Great Recession started. The Congressional Budget Office says that the U.S. economy must create 150,000 new jobs per month, or over 1 million annually to hold the unemployment rate constant. The 2007 to 2009 contraction of the economy will have costly aftereffects in the United States for years to come, including the *new normal* of slow job growth, slimmer paychecks, fewer credit cards, less consumer spending, and higher savings.

---

* The last budget surpluses in the United States were during the last two years of the Clinton presidency (1999 and 2000) due to restrained spending and increases in revenues from higher income tax rates and increased Social Security taxes on payrolls. Every year since then Congress has authorized more spending than projected revenue.

For the many who are unemployed (about 12 million), about 9 million who work part-time because they cannot find full-time employment, and 2.5 million who have given up looking for work, however, it feels like the recession has never ended. These people are describing reality because for many Americans life is not getting better. And many workers who have jobs still fear losing them. These indeed are times of austerity, and this will not change until demand and economic growth picks up.

The Congressional Budget Office says that given the severity of the Great Recession, it could take until 2016 or 2017 for unemployment to get back to the more typical 5 or 6 percent and see the economy return to a healthy growth rate of 3+ percent annually. The U.S. economy has to grow around 2.5 percent a year just to keep up with rising productivity and population growth, and thus to keep unemployment from rising. History shows that it takes 2 extra points of economic growth per year (hence a rate of growth of 4.5 or 5.5 percent) to knock the unemployment rate down 1 percent. The United Nations says it will take substantive economic growth to create 14 million new jobs in industrialized countries in Europe and Asia to get back to the level of employment in those countries when the Great Recession began. No one sees that happening soon.

FINANCIAL POWER POINT

Continued Instability in Financial Markets

During sluggish economic times, consumer confidence may slide, unemployment may rise, and the stock market may decline 5 percent in a week or just a day or two; however, this does not mean that people should stop saving and investing for their futures. Every generation has faced similar uncertainties. You should be optimistic about the long-term economic future and make decisions that are best for your personal finances.

How to Tell the Future Direction of the Economy

To make sound financial decisions, you need to know where we are in the business cycle, how well the economy is doing, and where the economy might be headed. You can do this by paying attention to some economic statistics that are regularly reported in the news as well as on cable TV business shows. Your knowledge can help guide your long-term financial strategy. An **economic indicator** is any economic statistic, such as the unemployment rate, GDP, or the inflation rate (terms discussed in the next few paragraphs), that suggests how well the economy is doing and how well the economy might be doing in the future.

economic indicator
Any economic statistic, such as the unemployment rate, GDP, or the inflation rate, that suggests how well the economy is doing now and how well it might be doing in the future.

Look at Procyclic Indicators
A **procyclic** (or **procyclical**) economic indicator is one that moves in the same direction as the economy. Thus if the economy is doing well, this number typically is increasing; however, if we are in a recession, this indicator is decreasing. Examples of procyclic indicators are retail sales (consumer spending accounts for about 70 percent of the U.S. economy), industrial production, new orders for durable goods (like household appliances), number of employees on nonagricultural payrolls, and the gross domestic product.

The best understood example of a procyclic economic indicator is the **gross domestic product (GDP)**, which is the broadest measure of the economic health of the nation because it reports how much economic activity (all goods and services) has occurred within the U.S. borders. The government regularly announces the rate at which the GDP has grown during the previous three months (www.bea.gov/newsreleases/rels.htm). In the United States, an annual rate of 2 percent or less is considered very low growth (not even enough to create jobs for new college graduates), and 3 percent is considered growth occurring at a safe speed that is not likely to induce excessive inflation. A rate of 4 percent or higher starts to worry economists and investors. The United States needs a GDP growth rate of about 2.6 percent just to keep unemployment from rising and much faster economic growth, such as a growth rate of 4 or 5 percent, to bring the unemployment rate significantly down.

gross domestic product (GDP)
The nation's broadest measure of economic health; it reports how much economic activity (all goods and services) has occurred within the U.S. borders during a given period.

Look at Countercyclic Indicators
A **countercyclic** (or **countercyclical**) economic indicator is one that moves in the opposite direction from the economy. For example, the unemployment rate is countercyclic because it gets larger as the economy gets worse. Similarly, the prices of gold and silver rise as the economy gets worse.

Look at Leading Indicators
Leading economic indicators are those that change before the economy changes; thus they help predict how the economy will do in the future. The stock market is a leading economic indicator because it usually begins to decline shortly before the overall economy slows down. Then the stock market advances

leading economic indicators
Statistics that change before the economy changes, thus helping predict how the economy will do in the future, such as the stock market, the number of new building permits, and the consumer confidence index.

before the economy begins to pull out of a recession. Other examples of leading economic indicators are the number of new building permits, existing home sales, home prices, jobless claims (average number of weekly first-time filings for unemployment benefits), the Standard & Poor's 500 Stock Index, and the consumer confidence index.

The **consumer confidence index** is a widely watched leading economic indicator that gauges how consumers feel about the economy and their personal finances. It gives a sense of consumers' willingness to spend (www.conference-board.org). Growing confidence suggests increased consumer spending. Consumers worried about the future postpone purchases, and the reduced spending acts as a drag on the economy.

The **index of leading economic indicators (LEI)** is a composite index, reported monthly by the Conference Board, that suggests the future direction of the U.S. economy (www.conference-board.org). The LEI averages ten components of growth from different segments of the economy, such as building permits, factory orders, and new private housing starts. Leading economic indicators are very important to investors as they help predict what the economy will be like in the future.

The Future Direction of Inflation, Prices, and Interest Rates

Inflation and interest rates typically move in the same direction. **Inflation** is a steady rise in the general level of prices. Inflation is measured by the changing cost over time of a "market basket" of goods and services that a typical household might purchase. Inflation often occurs when the supply of money (or credit) rises faster than the supply of goods and services available for purchases. It also may be attributed to excessive demand or sharply increasing costs of production.

Deflation Is a Reality Once expectations of inflation get too low, people anticipate falling prices. **Deflation** is a broad, sustained decline in prices of goods and services and contraction in the aggregate money supply that is hard to stop once it takes hold. This occurs when consumers refuse to spend, corporations flush with cash delay expansion plans and hold back on investments, and banks sit on cash rather than lend. This collapsed demand results in lower corporate profits, declining home values, rising unemployment, and lower incomes. The value of assets falls while debt payments become difficult. Deflationary pressures exist today in the United States and several other countries. Starting in the 1990s, the Japanese economy (the world's third largest) suffered through a decade-long period of deflation and recession, and after 20 years, the country continues to struggle with deflation.

Deflation occurred in the United States through 2009 as prices declined 0.34 percent during the year, and prices continued to decline during several months of 2010. Continued deflation in the United States is possible. When faced with deflation, government policymakers often embark on massive spending programs to stimulate economic growth. A lack of spending ensures a continuing stagnant economy, horribly high unemployment rates, no newly created jobs for school graduates, and political instability that is sometimes accompanied by civil unrest. Deficit spending, of course, creates high national liabilities. History shows that the strongest deficit reducer is a strong rise in gross domestic product because it produces accompanying increases in tax revenues.

Inflation Is the More Typical Economic Condition Inflation is the more typical condition in an economy, and is beneficial in moderation as it encourages job creation and economic growth. Workers may ask for higher wages, thereby adding to the cost of production. In response to the increases in the costs of labor and raw materials, manufacturers will charge more for their products. Lenders, in turn, will require higher interest rates to offset the lost purchasing power of the loaned funds. Consumers will lessen their resistance to price increases because they fear even higher prices in the future. In times of moderate to high inflation, buying power declines rapidly, and people on fixed incomes suffer the most. (A very negative complication of inflation that sometimes occurs is **stagflation**, which is the condition of stagnant economic growth and high unemployment accompanied by rising prices.)

index of leading economic indicators (LEI)
A composite index reported monthly by the Conference Board that suggests the future direction of the U.S. economy.

inflation
A steady and sustained rise in general price levels across economic sectors; measured by the changing cost over time of a "market basket" of goods and services that a typical household might purchase.

deflation
A broad, sustained decline in prices of goods and services that is hard to stop once it takes hold, causing less consumer spending, lower corporate profits, declining home values, rising unemployment, and lower incomes.

Here Is How Inflation Affects Your Income and Consumption When prices are rising, an individual's income must rise at the same rate to maintain its **purchasing power**, which is a measure of the goods and services that one's income will buy. From an income point of view, inflation has significant effects. Consider the case of Scott Marshall of Chicago, a single man who took a job in retail management three years ago at a salary of $50,000 per year. Since that time, Scott has received annual raises of $1000, $1200, and $1500, but he still cannot make ends meet because of inflation. Although Scott received raises, his current income of $53,700 ($50,000 + $1000 + $1200 + $1500) did not keep pace with the annual inflation rate of 3.0 percent ($50,000 × 1.03 = $51,500; $51,500 × 1.03 = $53,045; $53,045 × 1.03 = $54,636). If Scott's own cost of living rose at the same rate as the general price level, in the third year he would be $936 ($54,636 − $53,700) short of keeping up with inflation. He would need $936 more in the third year to maintain the same purchasing power that he enjoyed in the first year.

Personal incomes rarely keep up in times of high inflation. Your **real income** (income measured in constant prices relative to some base time period) is the more important number. It reflects the actual buying power of the **nominal income** (also called money income) that you have to spend as measured in current dollars. Rising nominal income during times of inflation creates the illusion that you are making more money, when in actuality that may not be true.

To compare your annual wage increase with the rate of inflation for the same time period, you first convert your dollar raise into a percentage, as follows:

$$\text{Percentage change} = \frac{\text{nominal income after raise} - \text{nominal income last year}}{\text{nominal income last year}} \times 100 \quad \textbf{(1.1)}$$

For example, imagine that Charlie Goosman, a single parent and assistant manager of a convenience store in Windermere, Florida, received a $1600 raise to push his $37,000 annual salary to $38,600. Using Equation (1.1), Charlie calculated his percentage change in personal income as follows:

$$\frac{(\$38,600 - \$37,000)}{\$37,000} \times 0.043 \times 100 = 4.3\%^*$$

After a year during which inflation was 4.0 percent, he did better than the inflation rate because his raise amounted to 4.3 percent. Measured in real terms, Charlie's raise was 0.3 percent (4.3 − 4.0). In dollars, his real income after the raise can be calculated by dividing his new nominal income by 1.0 plus the previous year's inflation rate (expressed as a decimal):

$$\text{Real income} = \frac{\text{nominal income after raise}}{1.0 + \text{previous inflation rate}} \quad \textbf{(1.2)}$$

$$\frac{\$38,600}{1 + 0.040} = \$37,115$$

Clearly, a large part of the $1600 raise Charlie received was eaten up by inflation. To Charlie, only $115 ($37,115 − $37,000) represents real economic progress, while $1485 ($1600 − $115) was used to pay the inflated prices on goods and services. The $115 real raise is equivalent to 0.31 percent ($115 ÷ $37,000) of his previous income, reflecting the difference between Charlie's percentage raise in nominal dollars and the inflation rate.

Here Is How Inflation Is Measured The U.S. Bureau of Labor Statistics measures inflation on a monthly basis using the **consumer price index (CPI)**. The CPI is a broad measure of changes in the prices of all goods and services purchased for consumption by urban households. The prices of more than 400 goods and services (a "market basket") sold across the country are tracked, recorded,

purchasing power
Measure of the goods and services that one's income will buy.

real income
Income measured in constant prices relative to some base time period. It reflects the actual buying power of the money you have as measured in constant dollars.

nominal income
Also called money income; income that has not been adjusted for inflation and decreasing purchasing power.

ADVICE FROM A PRO

Seven Money Mantras for a Richer Life

1. *It's not an asset if you are wearing it!*
2. *Is this a need or is it a want?*
3. *Sweat the small stuff.*
4. *Cash is better than credit.*
5. *Keep it simple.*
6. *Priorities lead to prosperity.*
7. *Enough is enough!*

Michelle Singletary
Nationally syndicated *Washington Post* columnist ("The Color of Money") and author of *Spend Well, Live Rich: How to Get What You Want with the Money You Have.*

Reprinted with permission of the author.

consumer price index (CPI)
A broad measure of changes in the prices of all goods and services purchased for consumption by urban households.

---

* This equation shows how the percentage change is calculated for any difference between two measurements. Divide the difference between measurement 1 and measurement 2 by the value of measurement 1. For example, a stock selling for $65 per share on January 1 and for $76 on December 31 of the same year would have risen 16.92 percent during the year: [($76 − $65) ÷ $65 = 0.1692 or 16.92%.]

weighted for importance in a hypothetical budget, and totaled. In essence, the CPI is a cost of living index. The index has a base time period—or starting reference point—from which to make comparisons. The 1982 to 1984 time period represents the base period of 100. For example, if the CPI were 221 on January 1, 2012, the cost of living would have risen 121 percent since the base period [$(221 - 100) \div 100 = 1.21$ or 121%]. Similarly, if the index rises from 221 to 225 on January 1, 2013, then the cost of living will have increased by 1.8 percent over the year [$(225 - 221) \div 221 = 0.018$ or 1.8%].

When prices rise, the purchasing power of the dollar declines, but not by the same percentage. Instead, it falls by the *reciprocal amount* of the price increase (the counterpart ratio quantity needed to produce unity). In the preceding illustration where prices increase between 2012 and 2013, prices rose 1.8 percent, whereas the purchasing power of the dollar declined 1.78 percent over the same period. [The previous year base of 221 divided by the index of 225 equals 0.9822; the reciprocal is 0.0178 ($1 - 0.9822$), or 1.78%.]

Inflation pushes up the costs of the products and services we consume. If automobile prices rose 20 percent over the past five years, for example, then it will take $28,800 now to buy a car that once sold for $24,000. Conversely, the purchasing power of the car-buying dollar has fallen to 83.3 percent of its original power ($24,000 \div $28,800) five years ago. If your market basket of goods and services differs from that used to calculate the CPI, you might have a very different **personal inflation rate** (the rate of increase in prices of items purchased by a particular person). Inflation pushes up the cost of borrowing, so monthly car payments and home mortgage rates increase when inflation rises.

You Can Track the Federal Funds Rate to Forecast Interest Rates and Inflation

One of the mandates of the Federal Reserve Board (an agency of the federal government commonly referred to as the **Fed**) is to "promote maximum employment and price stability." You can forecast interest rates and inflation by paying attention to changes in the **federal funds rate**, which is the short-term rate at which depository institutions lend balances at the Federal Reserve to other depository institutions overnight. Because it is set by the Fed and regularly reported by the news media, the federal funds rate is a benchmark for business and consumer loans and an indication of future Fed policy. When the economy slows down too much and inflation is low, the Fed reduces the federal funds rate, and in turn, lenders reduce their rates for short-term loans, thereby making it less costly to borrow and spend. In effect, the Fed pumps up the economy to spur business activity. The Fed's perfect outcomes are inflation at 2 percent or a bit lower, inflation at 3 percent or a bit lower, and unemployment at 5 percent or a bit higher. Recent Fed forecasts are for low inflation and high unemployment for the next few years.

When the Fed believes the economy is growing too fast, it raises the federal funds rate to increase borrowing costs in an effort to reduce borrowing. This usually curtails inflationary pressures and slows down the economy.

Here Is How Inflation Affects Your Borrowing, Saving, and Investing

Interest is the price of money. During times of high inflation, interest rates on new loans for cars, homes, and credit cards rise. Even though nominal interest rates for savers rise as well, the increases do not provide "real" gains if the inflation rate is higher than the interest rate on savings accounts or certificates of deposit.

Smart investors recognize that the degree of inflation risk is higher for long-term lending (5 or 20 years, for example) than for short-term lending (such as a year) because the likelihood of error when estimating inflation increases when lots of time is involved. Therefore, long-term interest rates are generally higher than short-term interest rates. Similarly, stock market investors are negatively affected when inflation causes businesses to pay more when they borrow, thereby reducing their profits and depressing stock prices. When inflation is at 5 percent annually, a dollar of profit that a company will earn a year from now will be worth only 95 cents in today's prices. If instead inflation were only 2 percent, that dollar would be worth 98 cents today. Such differences add up

Fed
The Federal Reserve Board, an agency of the federal government.

federal funds rate
The short-term rate at which depository institutions lend balances at the Federal Reserve to other depository institutions overnight.

interest
The price of borrowing money.

to significant amounts over many years. Throughout your financial life, you will want to factor the impact of inflation into your financial decisions in an effort to reduce its negative effects.

In summary, to assess the economic outlook for the United States, watch these indicators: (1) jobs (unemployment rate changes); (2) housing sales (new and existing); (3) consumer spending (retail sales and autos); (4) business spending (capital investment); and (5) inflation (changes in consumer price index).

Use Economic Information in Your Financial Decision Making A point at which the economy is in the trough of a recession may be an excellent time to invest in stocks because the economy will soon expand and stock prices will

The Fed meets regularly to discuss the economy and review federal interest rates.

rise. If economic indicators suggest that the economy is growing steadily, this may be a good time to invest in common stock and mutual funds as values are likely to continue to increase. If the economy begins to show clear signs of a slowdown, it may be a good time to invest in fixed-interest securities because interest rates are sure to fall as the government lowers its own interest rates to try to help stimulate the economy. Also, this may be a good time to sell stocks as values are likely to decline as the economy slows.

Concept Check 1.2

1. Summarize the phases of the business cycle.

2. Describe two statistics that help predict the future direction of the economy.

3. Give an example of how inflation affects income and consumption.

DID YOU KNOW?

Turn Bad Habits into Good Ones

Do You Do This?	Do This Instead!
Ignore news about the economy	Watch business news on cable television
Buy lots of extra features on products	Use marginal costs in buying decisions
Focus only on take-home pay	Sign up for employer tax-advantaged saving plans
Don't know how much to save for retirement	Calculate future values
Have not yet started to invest for retirement	Begin investing as soon as possible
Pay out-of-pocket expenses for health care	Use employer's cafeteria benefits plan for expenses
Get financial advice from friends	Seek advice of fee-only financial planner

THINK LIKE AN ECONOMIST WHEN MAKING FINANCIAL DECISIONS

Understanding and applying basic economic principles will affect your financial success. The most important of these are opportunity costs, marginal utility and costs, and marginal income tax rate.

Consider Opportunity Costs When Making Decisions

opportunity cost
The opportunity cost of any decision is the value of the next best alternative that must be forgone.

The **opportunity cost** of a decision is the value of the next best alternative that must be forgone. Examples of personal opportunity costs are time, effort, and health, and examples of financial opportunity costs are interest, safety, and liquidity. A simple example of opportunity costs in personal finance is spending money on current living expenses which, of course, reduces the amount you can save and invest. Also, buying on credit results in monthly payments later, which reduces the amount of income available for future spending or saving.

Using the concept of opportunity costs in your thinking allows you to address the personal consequences of choices because every decision inevitably involves trade-offs. For example, suppose that instead of reading this book you could have gone to a movie or watched television, but mainly you wanted to sleep. The lost benefit of that sleep— the next best alternative—is the opportunity cost when you choose to read. Knowing the opportunity cost of alternatives aids decision making because it indicates whether the decision made is truly the best option.

In personal finance, opportunity cost reflects the best alternative of what one could have done instead of choosing to spend, save, or invest money. For example, by deciding to put $2000 into a stock mutual fund for retirement rather than keeping the funds readily available in a savings account, you are giving up the option of using the money for a down payment on a new automobile. Keeping the money in a savings account has the opportunity cost of the higher return on investment that the stock mutual fund might pay. This opportunity to earn a higher rate of return is a primary consideration when making low-risk investment decisions.

Other challenging opportunity cost decisions are renting versus buying housing, buying a new or used car, buying or leasing a vehicle, working or borrowing to pay for college, purchasing life insurance or not, and starting early or late to save and invest for retirement. Another opportunity cost decision often is returning to college for a graduate degree.

If these costs are underestimated, then decisions will be based on faulty information, and judgments may prove wrong. Properly valuing the costs and benefits of alternatives represents a key step in rational decision making. The opportunity cost mathematics of the rent versus buy decision is illustrated later in Chapter 9.

FINANCIAL POWER POINT

Save $4.66 for Every $1 Not Saved Earlier

If you want to retire at age 63, you will have to save about $4.66 beginning at age 40 to make up for every dollar you did not save at age 20.

Identify Marginal Utility and Costs in Your Decision Making

Utility is the ability of a good or service to satisfy a human want. A key task in personal finance is to determine how much utility you will gain from a particular decision. For example, if you decide to spend $90 on a ticket to a concert, you might begin by thinking about what you might gain from the expenditure. Perhaps you'll enjoy a nice evening, good music, and so on.

marginal utility
The extra satisfaction derived from gaining one more incremental unit of a product or service.

Marginal utility is the extra satisfaction derived from having one more incremental unit of a product or service. **Marginal cost** is the additional (marginal) cost of one more incremental unit of some item. When known, this cost can be compared with the marginal utility received. Thinking about marginal utility and marginal cost can help in decision making because it reminds us to compare only the most important variables. It requires that we examine what we will really gain if we also experience a certain extra cost.

marginal cost
The additional (marginal) cost of one more incremental unit of some item.

To illustrate this idea, assume that you consider spending $150 instead of $90 (an additional $60) for a front-row seat at the concert. What marginal utility will you gain from that decision? Perhaps an ability to see and hear more or the satisfaction of having one of the best seats in the facility. You would then ask yourself whether those extra benefits are worth 60 extra dollars. In practice, people are inclined to seek additional utility as long as the marginal utility exceeds the marginal cost.

In another example, imagine that two new automobiles are available on a dealership lot in Ferndale, Michigan, where chemical engineer Charlene Hicks is trying to make a purchase decision. Both vehicles are similar models, but from different manufacturers. The first, with a sticker price of $29,100, has a moderate number of options; the second, with a sticker price of $30,800, has numerous options. Marginal analysis suggests that Charlene does not need to consider all of the options when comparing the vehicles. Instead, the concept of marginal cost says to compare the benefits of the additional options with the additional costs—$1700 in this instance ($30,800 − $29,100). Charlene need decide only whether the additional options are worth $1700.

Factor Your Marginal Income Tax Rate When Making Financial Decisions

When making financial decisions, consider the economic effects of paying income taxes. Of particular importance is the **marginal tax rate**, which is the tax rate at which your last dollar earned is taxed. As income rises, taxpayers pay progressively higher marginal income tax rates. Financially successful people often pay U.S. federal income taxes at the 25 percent, or higher, marginal tax rate. For example, if Juanita Martinez, an unmarried office manager working in Atlanta, Georgia, has a taxable income of $66,000 and receives a $1000 bonus from her employer, she has to pay an extra $250 in taxes on the bonus income ($1000 × 0.25 = $250). Juanita also has to pay state income taxes of 6 percent, or $60 ($1000 × 0.06 = $60), and Social Security taxes of 7.65 percent, or $76.50 ($1000 × 0.0765 = $76.50). Therefore, Juanita pays an effective marginal tax rate of nearly 40 percent (25% + 6% + 7.65% = 38.65%), or $386.50, on the extra $1000 of earned income.

> **marginal tax rate**
> *The tax rate at which your last dollar earned is taxed.*

People who pay high marginal tax rates can do better by making tax-exempt investments, such as buying bonds issued by various agencies of states and municipalities. For example, Serena Miller, a married chiropractor with two children from Prescott, Arizona, currently has $5000 in utility stocks earning 5 percent, or $250 ($5000 × 0.05), annually. She pays $62.50 in federal income tax on that income at her 25 percent marginal tax rate ($250 × 0.25), leaving her with $187.50 after taxes. Alternatively, a tax-exempt $5000 state bond paying 4 percent will provide Serena with a better after-tax return, $200.00 instead of $187.50. That is, she would receive $200.00 tax free from the state bond ($5000 × 0.04) compared with $187.50 ($250 − $62.50) after taxes on the income from the stocks.

The Very Best Kind of Income Is Tax-Exempt Income The very best kind of income, as this discussion implies, is **tax-exempt income**, which is income that is totally and permanently free of taxes. By legally avoiding paying one dollar in income taxes, you gain by not paying that dollar in taxes and, therefore, you receive the alternative use for that dollar. You also benefit by not having to earn another dollar to replace the one that might have been paid in taxes.

> **tax-exempt income**
> *Income that is totally and permanently free of taxes.*

The Second Best Kind of Income Is Tax-Sheltered Income The second-best kind of income for individuals is **tax-sheltered (or tax-deferred) income**—that is, income that is exempt from income taxes in the current year but that will be subject to taxation in a later tax year. Figure 1-3 shows that tax-sheltered returns on savings and investments provide much greater returns than returns on which income taxes have to be paid because more money remains available to be invested. In addition, tax-sheltered funds grow more rapidly because compounding (the subject of the next section in this chapter) is enhanced when larger dollar amounts continue to grow especially during the latter years of an investment. Realize, of course, that eventually one must pay income taxes on the income deferred.

> **tax-sheltered (tax-deferred) income**
> *Income exempt from income taxes in the current year but that will be subject to taxation in a later tax year.*

Figure 1-3

Tax-Sheltered Returns are Greater than Taxable Returns

In the illustration, the annual return is 8 percent and the annual contribution is $2000.

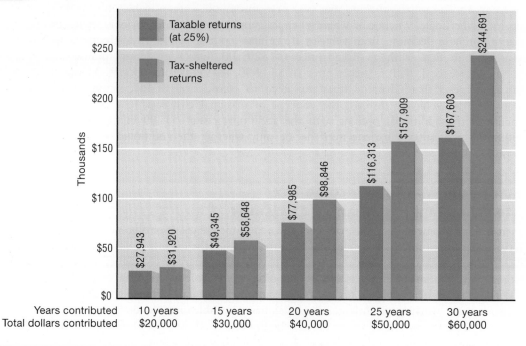

| Years contributed | 10 years | 15 years | 20 years | 25 years | 30 years |
| Total dollars contributed | $20,000 | $30,000 | $40,000 | $50,000 | $60,000 |

Legend: Taxable returns (at 25%); Tax-sheltered returns

Values shown: $27,943 / $31,920 (10 years); $49,345 / $58,648 (15 years); $77,985 / $98,846 (20 years); $116,313 / $157,909 (25 years); $167,603 / $244,691 (30 years)

 Concept Check 1.3

1. Define *opportunity cost* and give an example of how opportunity costs might affect your financial decision making.

2. Explain and give an example of how marginal analysis makes some financial decisions easier.

3. Describe and give an example of how income taxes can affect financial decision making.

LEARNING OBJECTIVE 4

Perform time value of money calculations in personal financial decision making.

time value of money
A method by which one can compare cash flows across time, either as what a future cash flow is worth today (present value) or what an investment made today will be worth in the future (future value). Also, the cost of money that is borrowed or lent; it is commonly referred to as interest and adjusts for the fact that dollars to be received or paid out in the future are not equivalent to those received or paid out today.

PERFORM TIME VALUE OF MONEY CALCULATIONS

A dollar in your pocket today is worth more than a dollar to be received five years from now. Why? Time is money.

The **time value of money** (TVM) is perhaps the single most important concept in personal finance. TVM is the cost of money that is borrowed or lent, and it is commonly referred to as interest. TVM adjusts for the fact that dollars to be received or paid out in the future are not equivalent to those received or paid out today. It is easy to understand that a dollar received today is worth more than a dollar received five years from now because today's dollar can be saved or invested and earn some kind of return, such as interest, so that in five years you expect it to be worth more than a dollar. The time value of money involves two components: future value and present value. And the good news is that TVM calculations require only basic math functions and can be easily performed by anyone.

There Are Only Two Common Questions About Money

To illustrate the time value of money, two questions in personal finance are commonly asked:

1. What will an investment (or a series of investments) be worth after a period of time? This question asks for a future value, which is referred to as compounding.

2. How much has to be put away today (or as a series of investments) to provide some dollar amount in the future? This question asks for a present value, which is referred to as discounting.

As you can see from these two questions, comparisons between time periods cannot be made without making adjustments to money values. Accordingly, time value of money calculations compare future and present values by taking into account the interest rate (or investment rate of return) and the time period involved.

Simple Interest The calculation of interest involves (1) the dollar amount, called the **principal**, (2) the rate of interest earned on the principal, and (3) the amount of time the principal is invested. One way of calculating interest is called **simple interest** and is illustrated by the **simple interest formula** where

principal
The original amount invested.

$$i = prt \text{ where}$$
$$p = \text{the } principal \text{ set aside}$$
$$r = \text{the } rate \text{ of interest} \qquad (1.3)$$
$$t = \text{the } time \text{ in years that the funds are left on deposit}$$

If someone saved or invested $1000 at 8 percent for four years, he would receive $320 in interest ($1000 × 0.08 × 4) over the four years.

Compounding Is the Basis of All Time Value of Money Considerations

But something is missing in the simple interest calculation. The simple interest formula assumes that the interest is withdrawn each year and only the $1000 stays on deposit for the entire four years, and thus interest is not added to the principal. Most people do not invest this way. Instead, they leave the interest earned in the account so that it will earn additional interest. This earning of interest on interest is referred to as **compound interest**. It arises when interest is added to the principal, so that from that moment on the interest that has been added also itself earns interest. This addition of interest to the principal is called **compounding**. The effect of compounding depends on the frequency with which interest is compounded and the periodic interest rate that is applied. Compound interest is always assumed in time value of money calculations.

Compounding is the best way to build investment values over time. Because of compounding, money grows much faster when the income from an investment is left in the account. In fact, the deposit of $1000 in our example would grow to $4,661 after 20 years (the calculation is described in the following paragraph). Many of the techniques for building wealth that we describe in this book are based on compounding. The way to build wealth is to make money on your money, not simply to put money away. Yes, you need to put money away first, but compounding over time is what really builds wealth.

Compounding serves as the basis of all time value of money considerations. To see how this works, let us look again at our example in which $1000 is invested at 8 percent for four years. Here is how the amount invested (or principal) would grow using compounding:

compound interest
Compound interest is earning of interest on interest and arises when interest is added to the principal so that, from that moment on, the interest that has been added also earns interest.

compounding
The addition of interest to principal; the effect of compounding depends on the frequency with which interest is compounded and the periodic interest rate that is applied.

At the end of year 1, the $1000 would have grown to $1080 [$1000 + ($1000 × 0.08)].

At the end of year 2, the $1080 would have grown to $1166.40 [$1080 + ($1080 × 0.08)].

At the end of year 3, the $1166.40 would have grown to $1259.71 [$1166.40 + ($1166.40 × 0.08)].

At the end of year 4, the $1259.71 would have grown to $1360.49 [$1259.71 + ($1259.71 × 0.08)].

Due to the effects of compounding, this investor would have earned an additional $40.49 ($360.49 – $320). While this amount might not seem like much, realize that a $1000 investment for a longer period—say, 40 years—earning 8 percent interest would grow to $21,724.52, providing $20,724.52 in interest over that time period. Simple interest would have resulted in only $3200 in interest ($1000 × 0.08 × 40). The benefit of compounding over that time period is an additional $17,524.52 in interest ($20,724.52 – $3200).

The results are even more dramatic if $1000 is invested at the end of each year for 40 years. The total at the end of 40 years would be $259,056, with $219,056 representing the interest on the invested funds. This illustration suggests one of the cardinal rules of personal financial planning: Getting rich is not a function of investing a lot of money. It is the result of investing regularly for long periods of time. The greatest investment strategy of all is compounding. Only through compounding will you attain the serious growth of your wealth over time.

There Are Only Two Types of Time Value of Money Calculations

Essentially there are two types of time value of money calculations: (1) converting present values to future values (as illustrated in the preceding example) and (2) converting future values to present values. Within each type, the calculations differ slightly depending on whether a lump sum is involved or whether a series of future payments (an **annuity**) is involved.

Calculating Future Values

Future value (FV) is the valuation of an asset projected to the end of a particular time period in the future. You can calculate the future value of a lump sum or the future value of a series of deposits.

Future Value of a Lump Sum   Equation (1.4) can be used to calculate the future value of a lump sum:

$$FV = (\text{Present value of sum of money})(i + 1.0)^n \quad \textbf{(1.4)}$$

where i represents the interest rate and n represents the number of time periods. Applying this formula to our earlier example of investing $1000 at 8 percent for four years, we obtain

$$\$1360.49 = (\$1000)(1 + 0.08)^4$$

or

$$\$1360.49 = (\$1000)(1.08)(1.08)(1.08)(1.08)$$

While mathematically correct, these calculations can be cumbersome when using long time periods. Table 1-1 provides a quick and easy way to determine the future dollar value of an investment. For the preceding example, use the table in the following

annuity
A stream of payments to be received in the future.

future value
The valuation of an asset projected to the end of a particular time period in the future.

Table 1-1

Future Value of $1 After a Given Number of Periods

Periods	1%	2%	3%	4%	5%	6%	7%	8%	9%	10%
1	1.0100	1.0200	1.0300	1.0400	1.0500	1.0600	1.0700	1.0800	1.0900	1.1000
2	1.0201	1.0404	1.0609	1.0816	1.1025	1.1236	1.1449	1.1664	1.1881	1.2100
3	1.0303	1.0612	1.0927	1.1249	1.1576	1.1910	1.2250	1.2597	1.2950	1.3310
4	1.0406	1.0824	1.1255	1.1699	1.2155	1.2625	1.3108	1.3605	1.4116	1.4641
5	1.0510	1.1041	1.1593	1.2167	1.2763	1.3382	1.4026	1.4693	1.5386	1.6105
6	1.0615	1.1262	1.1941	1.2653	1.3401	1.4185	1.5007	1.5869	1.6771	1.7716
7	1.0721	1.1487	1.2299	1.3159	1.4071	1.5036	1.6058	1.7138	1.8280	1.9487
8	1.0829	1.1717	1.2668	1.3686	1.4775	1.5938	1.7182	1.8509	1.9926	2.1436
9	1.0937	1.1951	1.3048	1.4233	1.5513	1.6895	1.8385	1.9990	2.1719	2.3579
10	1.1046	1.2190	1.3439	1.4802	1.6289	1.7908	1.9672	2.1589	2.3674	2.5937

The Importance of Higher Yields and More Time (Future Value of a Single Investment of $10,000)

Figure 1-4

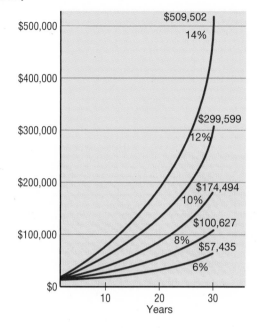

manner: Go across the top row to the 8 percent column. Read down the 8 percent column to the row for four years to locate the factor 1.3605 (at the intersection of the dark brown column and row). Multiply that factor by the present value of the cash asset ($1000) to arrive at the future value ($1360.50).

Appendix A.1 provides an even more complete table for calculating the future value of lump-sum amounts. Figure 1-4 demonstrates the importance of higher yields and longer time horizons by showing the effects of various compounded returns on a $10,000 investment. The $10,000 will grow to $57,435 in 30 years with an interest rate of 6 percent. Compounding $10,000 at 10 percent yields $174,494 over the same time period; at 14 percent, it yields a whopping $509,502! For practice you might want to confirm these results using Appendix A.1.

Rule of 72 Illustrated

Figure 1-5

The **rule of 72** is a handy formula for figuring the number of years it takes to double the principal using compound interest. You simply divide the interest rate that the money will earn *into* the number 72.

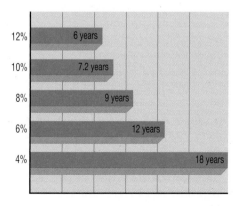

rule of 72
A formula for figuring the number of years it takes to double the principal using compound interest; simply divide the interest rate that the money will earn into the number 72.

Figure 1-6

Future Value of $2000 Annual Investments

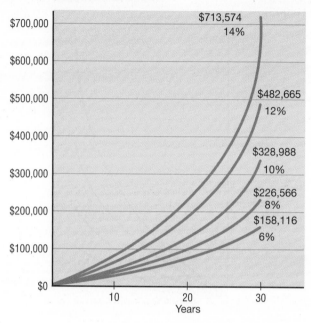

Future Value of a Stream of Payments (an Annuity) People often save for long-term goals by putting away a series of payments. Appendix A.3 provides a complete table for calculating the future value of a stream of deposited amounts, referred to as an annuity. Figure 1-6 graphically demonstrates the effects of various compounded returns on a $2000 annual investment made at the end of each year. The $2000 will grow to $91,524 in 20 years (read across the interest rate row in Appendix A.3 to 8 percent and then down the column to 20 years to obtain the factor of 45.762 to multiply by $2000) and to $226,566 in 30 years at an 8 percent rate. Compounding $2000 at 10 percent yields $114,550 in 20 years and $328,988 over 30 years; at 14 percent, it becomes $713,574 after 30 years! For practice you might want to confirm these results using Appendix A.3.

Finding Present Values Is Called Discounting

present value
The current value of an asset (or stream of assets) that will be received in the future; also known as discounted value.

Present value (or **discounted value**) is the current value of an asset (or stream of assets) that will be received in the future. **Discounting** is the process of reducing future values to present values. You can calculate the present value of a lump sum to be received in the future or the present value of a series of payments to be received in the future.

Present Value of a Single Lump Sum The present value of a lump sum is the current worth of an asset to be received in the future. Alternatively, it can be thought of as the amount you would need to set aside today at a given rate of interest for a given time period so as to have some desired amount in the future. Suppose you want to have $20,000 for the down payment on a new home in ten years. What would you need to set aside today to reach this goal if you could invest your money and receive a 7 percent return? Using Appendix A.2 you could look across the interest rate rows to 7 percent and then down to ten years to obtain the factor of 0.5083. Multiplying $20,000 by this factor reveals that $10,166 set aside today would allow you to reach your goal. (Note the connection here to the rule of 72: 7 percent divided into 72 is approximately 10.28, meaning that the investment would double in about 10.28 years. Indeed, $10,166 would approximately double to $20,000 in ten years.)

Present Value of a Stream of Payments (an Annuity) The present value of an annuity is the current worth of a stream of payments to be received in the future. Alternatively, it can be thought of as the amount you would need to set aside today at a given rate of interest for a given time period so as to receive that stream of payments. Suppose you want to have $30,000 per year for 20 years during your retirement. What amount would you need to have invested at retirement to reach this goal if you could invest your money and receive a 7 percent return? Using Appendix A.4 you could look across the interest rate rows to 7 percent and then down to 20 years to obtain the factor of 10.5940. Multiplying $30,000 by this factor reveals that $317,820 (10.5940 × $30,000) set aside at retirement would fund this stream of payments. Note the beauty of compound interest in this result. It takes only $317,820—not $600,000—to fund a $30,000 per year retirement for 20 years if you can earn 7 percent on your financial nest egg.*

Concept Check 1.4

1. Explain the difference between simple interest and compound interest, and describe why that difference is critical.

2. What are the two components used when figuring the time value of money?

3. Use Table 1-1 to calculate the future value of (a) $2000 at 5 percent for four years, (b) $4500 at 9 percent for eight years, and (c) $10,000 at 6 percent for ten years.

FINANCIAL POWER POINT

Web Calculators

Present and future value calculations can be readily performed on the Internet. Among the best calculators are those found at the following websites:

USA Today (www.usatoday.com/money/ perfi/calculators/calculator.htm)
Financial Calculators (www.fincalc.com/)
KJE (www.dinkytown.net/)
Bankrate.com (www.bankrate.com/ calculators.aspx)
CNNMoney (http://cgi.money.cnn.com/ tools/)
moneychimp (www.moneychimp.com/ calculator/compound_interest_ calculator.htm)

MAKE SMART MONEY DECISIONS AT WORK

Smart decisions about your employee benefits can increase your actual income by thousands of dollars each year. To do so wisely, select among employer-sponsored cafeteria plans; health care; flexible spending accounts; life, disability, and long-term care insurance; and retirement. These decisions often require you to calculate the tax-sheltered aspects of the employee benefits. Your benefits package might also include dental and vision care, child care, elder care, subsidized food services, and an educational assistance program, and these too will require smart financial decisions.

An **employee benefit** is compensation for employment that does not take the form of wages, salaries, commissions, or other cash payments. Examples include paid holidays, health insurance, and a retirement plan. The value of employee benefits often amounts to 30 percent or more of one's salary. Some employee benefits are tax sheltered, such as flexible spending accounts and retirement plans. **Tax sheltered** in this situation means that the employee avoids paying current income taxes on the value of the benefits received from the employer. The taxes may be postponed, or deferred, until a later date (usually a good idea)—perhaps until retirement, when the individual's income tax rate might be lower.

Choosing Tax-Free Cafeteria Plan Benefits

A **cafeteria plan** is a type of employee benefit plan where employees choose their benefits from a "menu" of taxable cash and one or more qualified nontaxable benefits, thereby providing a funding mechanism by which employees may pay for the benefits they choose on a pretax basis. For example, an employer might offer $4000 annually to each employee to spend on benefits. The plan might offer health insurance, life insurance, sick leave or disability benefits, medical expense reimbursement, vacation days, dependent care, adoption assistance, and orthodontia treatments. Employees choose the

 LEARNING OBJECTIVE ❺

Make smart decisions about your employee benefits.

employee benefit
Compensation for employment that does not take the form of wages, salaries, commissions, or other cash payments.

cafeteria plan (flexible benefits plan)
A type of employee benefit plan where employees choose their benefits from a "menu" of taxable cash and one or more qualified nontaxable benefits, thereby providing a funding mechanism by which employees may pay for the benefits they choose on a pretax basis.

---

* If you are using a financial calculator for time value of money calculations, see "How to Use a Financial Calculator" on the *Garman/ Forgue* companion website, or you can use the present and future value calculators also found on the *Garman/Forgue* companion website, www.cengagebrain.com.

benefits they want; thus, they have some choice in designing their own benefits package by selecting different types and/or levels of benefits that are funded with nontaxable employer dollars. A cafeteria plan is sometimes called a flexible benefits plan.

Making Decisions About Employer-Sponsored Health Care Plans

health care plan

An employee benefit designed to pay all or part of the employee's medical expenses.

Many employers offer employees a choice of **health care plans**. Employees usually can make a decision to change health plans once a year as well as when one's family situation changes, such as getting married. The premium for an unmarried employee could be $5000 to $10,000 annually depending upon the amount of coverage provided. Fortunately, the premiums for employees are often either paid for entirely or subsidized by the employer. For example, some employers pay the first $3000 of annual premiums for employee health care coverage and require that employees pay the remainder.

Partly because of soaring costs of health care coverage, employers often offer multiple choices. These may include an expensive traditional health plan, perhaps with a $9000 annual premium, that offers comprehensive coverage requiring little out-of-pocket spending by the employee. Also frequently available is a less expensive **high-deductible health care plan (HDHP)**, which has lower premiums and higher deductibles than a traditional health plan. It is a form of catastrophic coverage. A policy with perhaps a $3500 premium will require larger out-of-pocket health care spending by the employee. The *deductible* is the amount paid to cover expenses before benefits begin.

high-deductible health care plan (HDHP)

A plan that requires individuals to pay a higher deductible to cover medical expenses before insurance plan payments begin; chosen to save money on premiums.

Younger employees, particularly those who are typically healthy, often select high-deductible plans to save on the cost of premiums. For example, if an employer pays only the first $3000 in health care premiums for employees, an employee selecting the high-cost plan described previously has to pay $6000 ($9000 premium − $3000 employer contribution) annually, or $500 a month in premiums. This contrasts with only a $500 total annual premium for employees who select the high-deductible plan ($3500 premium − $3000 employer contribution). The maximum out-of-pocket limit for HDHPs is $5950 for self-only coverage and $11,900 for self-and-family coverage, after which the policy is supposed to pay for all health expenses.

health savings account (HSA)

Special savings account intended for people who have a high-deductible health care plan (with annual deductibles of at least $1000 for individuals and $2000 for families).

Some employers also offer **health savings accounts (HSAs)**. This special savings account is intended for people who have a high-deductible health care plan (with annual minimal plan deductibles of at least $1200 for individual coverage (but limited to $3050) and $2400 for self-and-family coverage (but limited to $6150). Employees make tax-deductible contributions to a savings account to be used for eligible expenses. Employers may also contribute. The employee invests HSA funds, and the money in the account grows tax free. Withdrawals are made to pay for medical expenses. The limits on contributions to an HSA are $3050 per year for individuals and $6150 for families. The money in the account remains there even if you don't spend it within a certain time period.

tax advantages

Advantages bestowed by legislation that reduce a tax on some preferred activity, such as employee participation in an employer's cafeteria plan, health savings account, or retirement plan.

Regulations of the Internal Revenue Service permit a number of **tax advantages**. These are benefits bestowed by legislation that reduce a tax on some preferred activity. Examples for employees are participation in an employer's cafeteria plan, health savings account, and retirement plan. Because many workers have an effective marginal tax rate (discussed earlier in the chapter) of nearly 40 percent, that same percentage can be *saved* or not spent by giving it to the government in taxes. The worker who contributes $3050, for example, to a health savings account saves approximately $1220 ($3050 × 0.40), further reducing his or her health care expenses.

Making Decisions About Employer's Flexible Spending Accounts

flexible spending account (FSA)

An employer-sponsored account that allows employee-paid expenses for medical or dependent care to be paid with an employee's pretax dollars rather than after-tax income.

A **flexible spending account (FSA)** is an employer-sponsored account that allows employee-paid expenses for medical or dependent care to be paid with an employee's pretax dollars rather than after-tax income. Under a typical FSA, the employee agrees to have a certain amount deducted from each paycheck, and that amount is then deposited in a separate account called a flexible spending account. As eligible expenses are incurred, the employee requests and receives reimbursements from the account.

DID YOU KNOW?

Examples of Good Financial Behaviors

Good financial behaviors to follow include these:

1. *Develop a plan for financial future.*
2. *Start or increase savings.*
3. *Follow a budget or spending plan.*
4. *Keep personal debts to a minimum.*
5. *Pay credit card bills in full each month.*
6. *Control and/or reduce living expenses.*
7. *Comparison shop for purchases.*
8. *Use a credit/budget counselor if debt becomes unmanageable.*

9. *Contemplate how economic events affect personal financial decision making.*
10. *Use a financial planner when faced with complicated financial questions.*
11. *Set aside an emergency fund sufficient to live on for three to six months.*
12. *Contribute to a flexible spending account at work.*
13. *Calculate how much money is needed for retirement.*
14. *Sign up to participate in employer's retirement plan.*
15. *Save and invest amounts sufficient to fund a financially successful retirement.*

Funds in a dependent care FSA account may be used to pay for the care of a dependent younger than age 13 or the care of another dependent who is physically or mentally incapable of caring for himself or herself and who resides in the taxpayer's home. Funds in a health care FSA account may be used to pay for qualified, unreimbursed out-of-pocket expenses for health care, but they may not be used for over-the-counter medicines unless specifically prescribed by a doctor.

The tax advantage of an FSA occurs because the amounts deducted from the employee's salary avoid federal income tax, Social Security taxes, and, in most states, state income taxes. Since many workers have an effective marginal tax rate (discussed earlier in the chapter) of nearly 40 percent, that same percentage can be *saved* or not spent by giving it to the government in taxes. Thus a person with a $50,000 salary who contributes $3000 to an FSA account could save perhaps $1200 ($3000 × 0.40) in taxes not paid.

Paying the FSA types of expenses with **pretax dollars** (money income that has not been taxed by the government) lowers taxable income and decreases take-home pay, and it increases effective take-home pay because of reimbursements. There are no standard limits, although most employers cap the maximum somewhere below $5000. Beginning in 2013, FSA contributions will be limited to $2500 each year with annual inflation increases.

pretax dollars
Money income that has not been taxed by the government.

Before enrolling in an FSA, you need to estimate your expenses carefully so that the amount in the FSA does not exceed anticipated expenses. According to Internal Revenue Service (IRS) regulations, unused amounts are forfeited and are not returned to the employee—a condition called the "use it or lose it" rule. However, employers may offer a 2½-month grace period during which time you can continue to spend the previous year's FSA money. Many employers offer debit cards that withdraw money directly from an employee's FSA. Only about 20 percent of eligible employees participate in flexible spending accounts, even though doing so saves money.

Making Decisions About Participating in Employer Insurance Plans

Life, disability, and long-term care insurance coverage is often available through employers. While the premiums charged for the group of employees for life insurance are rarely as low as those available in the general marketplace, some employers pay for part or all of employees' premiums. Coverage is typically one or two times the employee's salary. So, always sign up for free or subsidized life insurance at work. The premiums for disability and long-term care insurance are often less expensive when purchased through one's employer rather than in the general marketplace. See Chapters 10, 11, and 12 to begin to purchase any needed insurance coverage.

Making Decisions About Participating in Your Employer's Retirement Plan

More than half of all workers are covered by an employer-sponsored, defined-contribution retirement plan, also called a **tax-sheltered retirement plan**. These include 401(k) plans and similar 403(b) and 457 plans, as discussed in Chapter 17, Retirement Planning. Employer-sponsored retirement plans provide four distinct advantages.

First Advantage: Tax-Deductible Contributions

Tax-sheltered retirement plans provide tremendous tax benefits compared with ordinary savings and investment plans. Because pretax contributions to qualified plans reduce income, the current year's tax liability is lowered. The money saved in taxes can then be used to partially fund a larger contribution, which creates even greater returns. The 401(k) plan lets the IRS help employees finance their retirement plans because of the income taxes saved.

As Table 1-2 illustrates, you can save substantial sums for retirement with minimal effects on your monthly take-home pay. For example, a married man like Hongbok Lee of Macomb, Illinois, with a monthly taxable income of $4000 paying taxes at the 25 percent marginal tax rate who forgoes consumption and instead places $500 into a tax-sheltered retirement plan every month reduces monthly take-home pay from $3175 to $2800, or $375—that is certainly not an enormous amount. The net effect is that it costs that person only $375 to put away that $500 per month into a retirement plan. The immediate "return on investment" equals a fantastic 25 percent ($125 ÷ $500). In essence, the taxpayer puts $375 into his or her retirement plan and the government contributes $125. (Without the plan, the taxpayer would pay the $125 directly to the government.) A taxpayer paying a higher marginal tax rate realizes even greater gains. Because a substantial part of your contributions to a tax-sheltered retirement plan comes from money that you would have paid in income taxes, it costs you less to save more.

Second Advantage: Employer's Matching Contributions

To encourage saving for retirement, many employers offer a match. This is the amount an employer contributes to a worker's retirement account. Employers often match all or part of their employees' contributions, perhaps up to 6 percent of salary. An employee who saves $375 might receive an additional $375 a month from his/her employer. That's a 100 percent return on the employee's $375!

FINANCIAL POWER POINT

You Do Have a Promising Financial Future

The pessimism associated with recent stock market crashes and economic turmoil is not your future. You are still in college. You have many years ahead in which to save, cautiously use credit, and invest wisely for your long-term future. Don't let the economic shocks of the recent past alter your belief in the future. You will do very well financially by putting into practice what you learn in this book.

Table 1-2

It Costs Only $375 a Month (or $4500) to Save $6000 a Year for Retirement

Monthly Salary	$4000	Monthly Salary		$4000
Pretax retirement plan contribution	0	Pretax retirement plan contribution		500
Taxable income	4000	Taxable income		3500
Federal taxes*	682	Federal taxes		557
Monthly take-home pay	3318	Monthly take-home pay		2943
		Cost to put away $500 per month ($2800 − $2943)		245
Amount put away for retirement	0	Annual amount put away for retirement		6000

* From Chapter 4; 25 percent income tax rate, single.

Third Advantage: Tax-Deferred Growth Because interest, dividends, and capital gains from qualified plans are taxed only after funds are withdrawn from the plan, investments in tax-sheltered retirement plans grow tax free. The benefits of tax deferral can be substantial.

For example, if a person in the 25 percent tax bracket invests $2000 at the end of every year for 30 years and the investment earns an 8 percent taxable return compounded annually, the fund will grow to $158,116 at the end of the 30-year period. If the same $2000 invested annually were instead compounded at 8 percent within a tax-sheltered program, it would grow to $226,566! The higher amount results from compounding at the full 8 percent and not paying any income taxes. (Figure 1-6 on page 20 illustrates these differences in returns.) Indeed, when the funds are finally taxed upon their withdrawal some years later, the taxpayer may be in a lower marginal tax bracket.

Careful planning can result in a much more comfortable life when you retire.

Fourth Advantage: Starting Early Really Pays Off Big Recall the rule of 72, which can be used to calculate the number of years it would take for a lump-sum investment to double. A 9 percent rate of return doubles an investment every eight years. Waiting eight years to begin saving (starting at age 31 instead of 23) results in the loss of one doubling. Unfortunately, it is the *last* doubling that is lost, as illustrated in Table 1-3. In that example, $48,000 ($96,000 − $48,000) is lost due to a hesitancy to invest $3000. That is a tremendously negative opportunity cost for waiting eight years to start.

The gains are awesome when you start early and make regular, continuing investments instead of delaying. For example, a worker who starts saving $25 per week in a qualified retirement plan at age 23 will have about $616,390 by age 65, assuming an annual rate of return of 9 percent. Waiting until age 33 to start saving, instead of beginning at age 23, results in a retirement fund of *only* about $242,230. The benefit of starting to

Starting to Save Early Versus Starting Late				**Table 1-3**
Starting Earlier		**Starting Later**		
Age	$ Value	Age	$ Value	
23	$ 3,000	23	$ 0	
31	6,000	31	3,000	
39	12,000	39	6,000	
47	24,000	47	12,000	
55	48,000	55	24,000	
63	$ 96,000	63	$ 48,000	

Starting to save $3000 eight years earlier (age 23 instead of 31) earns the investor an extra $48,000 ($96,000 − $48,000) assuming a compound growth rate of 9 percent.

DID YOU KNOW?

Sean's Success Story

Sean appears in every chapter of this book. Sean always makes good decisions in personal finance, and he aims to be financially successful and happy. Following graduation during his first year of work as a public relations analyst earning $60,000, Sean signed up for his employer's low-premium, high-deductible health care plan. Within his employer cafeteria benefits plan, he chose the tax-free options of excellent vacation days, maximum sick leave and disability benefits, and a dollar limit of medical expense reimbursements. Sean did some future value calculations on the cost of his eventual retirement and then filled out the forms to contribute the maximum

possible to his 401(k) retirement plan ($3000), and since he is in the 25 percent tax bracket, he saved $750 ($3000 × 0.25) in income taxes. His $3000 was fully matched by his employer, thus giving him $6000 to invest within his retirement plan. Since he expects the economy to expand in the coming years, Sean concluded this was an excellent time to invest in stocks as values will probably rise, so he put the full $6000 into those kinds of investments. Sean decided that when his retirement account reaches $50,000 (probably in about five years with continuing contributions and values growing at 8 percent), he will contact a fee-only financial planner for investment advice.

---

invest early is $374,160 ($616,390 − $242,230). And the total extra dollars invested over the ten years was a mere $13,000! Putting in $13,000 early results in an extra $374,160. This effect occurs because most of the power of compounding appears in the last years of growth.

 Concept Check 1.5

1. Summarize the benefits of participating in a high-deductible health care plan at work.

2. Create a math example of why many employees participate in a tax-sheltered employee benefit plan, such as an HSA or 401(k) plan.

3. List two ways you can maximize the benefits from a tax-sheltered retirement program.

DID YOU KNOW?

Examples of Bad Financial Behaviors

Poor financial behaviors to avoid include the following:

1. *Purchasing something expensive that was wanted but not needed*
2. *Reaching the maximum limit on a credit card*
3. *Spending more money than available*
4. *Making a credit purchase after running out of money*
5. *Obtaining a cash advance on a credit card after running out of money*
6. *Using a cash advance on one credit card to pay another*
7. *Receiving an overdue notice from a creditor*
8. *Paying a credit card bill late*
9. *Paying a service charge for paying a utility bill late*
10. *Making a vehicle loan/lease payment late*
11. *Paying rent/mortgage late*
12. *Borrowing money from a coworker*
13. *Obtaining a cash advance from an employer*
14. *Borrowing from 401(k) retirement plan at work*
15. *Taking an old employer's 401(k) money in cash when changing jobs*
16. *Using a debit card (or writing a check) with insufficient funds, incurring hefty overdraft fees*

WHERE TO SEEK EXPERT FINANCIAL ADVICE

At various points in their lives, many people rely on the advice of a professional to make financial plans and decisions. Often this consultation is focused on a narrow area of their finances. Professional financial advisers, such as a family lawyer, tax preparer, insurance agent, credit counselor, or stockbroker, can be helpful. Too often, however, these people are not impartial because they are salespeople for specific financial services. Be aware that they typically want to sell you something rather than having your best interests at heart.

People often find it helpful to obtain the services of more broadly qualified financial experts. A **financial planner** is an investment professional who evaluates the personal finances of an individual or family and recommends strategies to set and achieve long-term financial goals. A good financial planner should be able to analyze a family's total needs in such areas as investments, taxes, insurance, education goals, and retirement and pull all of the information together into a cohesive plan. The planner may help a client select and prioritize goals and then rearrange assets and liabilities to fit the client's lifestyle, stage in the life cycle, and financial goals. When appropriate, planners should make referrals to outside advisers, such as attorneys, accountants, trust officers, real estate brokers, stockbrokers, and insurance agents. Effective financial advice helps you make better day-to-day financial decisions so you have more to spend, save, invest, and donate.

You can check the background of the planner you are considering. Self-regulatory organizations and government agencies are available to help.

- The Certified Financial Planner Board of Standards ([888] 237-6275; www.cfp.net) assists those searching for a CFP as well as accepts complaints.

- The National Association of Insurance Commissioners ([816] 842-3600; www.naic.org) directs inquiries to the appropriate state agency where you can check on planners who also sell insurance products.

- The Financial Industry Regulatory Authority (301) 590-6500 www.finra.org) regulates U.S. security firms.

- The National Association of Personal Financial Advisors ((847) 483-5400; www.napfa.org) sets standards for CFPs who call themselves fee-only financial planners.

- The Securities and Exchange Commission ([800] 732-0330; www.sec.gov) regulates investment advisers and all securities dealers.

LEARNING OBJECTIVE 6

Identify the professional qualifications of providers of financial advice.

financial planner
An investment professional who evaluates the personal finances of an individual or family and recommends strategies to set and achieve long-term financial goals.

ADVICE FROM A PRO

Questions to Ask a Financial Planner

Financial planners will influence your life and your future, so be sure to ask them these questions:

1. *What experience do you have, such as work history and companies with which you have been associated?*

2. *Am I permitted a no-cost, initial consultation, and how much time is allowed?*

3. *What are your qualifications to practice financial planning, such as education, formal training, licenses, and credentials, and who can vouch for your professional reputation including some of your long-term clients?*

4. *Will you be the only person working with me or will an associate be involved in evaluating and updating the plan you suggest, and how often are formal reviews held with the client?*

5. *How do you evaluate investment performance, and how often?*

6. *What process do you follow to identify a client's financial goals and may I see representative examples of financial plans, monitoring reports, and portfolios or actual case studies of your clients?*

7. *How much do you charge, what is your fee structure, how are you personally compensated, and if you earn commissions, how are they earned and from whom?*

8. *To whom would I take a complaint, if I had one?*

9. *Do you adhere to a fiduciary standard when working with your clients?*

10. *Can I have a written agreement that details the points above and the services to be provided?*

Joan Koonce
University of Georgia

DID YOU KNOW?

What You Want from a Financial Advisor

The shape of the relationship between you and your financial advisor should be clear from the beginning. It should be spelled out in writing, and both you and the advisor should have a copy of the document. This is known as an **investment policy statement**, and it details your investment philosophy, your financial situation, and the risks you are willing to take, as well as what the advisor will do for you. It provides a road map of how he/she will guide the investing of your money.

investment policy statement
A written document that spells out the relationship between an investor and his or her financial advisor and guides how the advisor will invest the person's money; it should detail the person's investment philosophy, financial situation, and the risks he or she is willing to take, as well as what tasks the advisor will perform.

How Financial Planners Are Compensated

One way or another, you will pay to get financial advice—commissions, fees, both—so assess the total costs up front as well as the opportunity costs. Financial planners earn their income in one of four ways:

1. **Commission-only financial planners and brokers** live solely on the commissions they receive on the financial products (such as investments or insurance) they sell to their clients. In this case, the plan will be "free," but a commission will be paid to the adviser by the source of the financial product, such as an insurance company or mutual fund. Advantage: Save money if you make only a few transactions.
2. **Fee-based financial planners** charge an up-front fee for providing services and charge a commission on any securities trades or insurance purchases that they conduct on your behalf. Advantage: Unlimited consultations with broker.
3. **Fee-offset financial planners** charge an annual or hourly fee. That fee will be reduced by any commissions earned off the purchase of financial products sold to the client. Advantage: Fee will be reduced as you trade investments.

Table 1-4

Financial Planner Professional Certifications

Many financial planners have voluntarily undergone training and satisfied various qualifications for particular professional certifications. Related work experience is often required.

Certification	Description	Contact Information
Accredited Estate Planner	Estate planning	(866) 226-2224 www.naepc.org
Certified Financial Planner (CFP®)	Best-known financial planning certification	(800) 322-4237 www.cfp.net
Chartered Financial Consultant (ChFC®)	Financial planning in insurance	(888) 263-7265 www.theamericancollege.edu
Chartered Life Underwriter (CLU®)	Life insurance	(888) 263-7265 www.theamericancollege.edu
Certified Public Accountant (CPA)	Income tax and estate planning	(888) 777-7077 www.aicpa.org
Personal Financial Specialist (PFS)	Personal finance credential for CPAs	(888) 777-7077 www.aicpa.org
Certified Trust and Financial Advisor (CTFA)	Trusts and taxes	(202) 663-5092 www.aba.com
Accredited Financial Counselor (AFC)	Financial counseling and money management	(614) 485-9650 www.afcpe.org
Chartered Mutual Fund Counselor (CMF®)	Mutual funds	(800) 237-9990 www.cffp.edu
Registered Investment Adviser (RIA)*	Investment adviser	(202) 551-6999 www.sec.gov
National Association of Personal Financial Advisors	Truly comprehensive, strictly fee-only	847-483-5400 www.napfa.org

* As investment advisors who are overseen by the Securities and Exchange Commission, RIAs are compelled to "act in the best interests of their customers." A different and much less stringent standard exists for all other stockbrokers and financial advisors. The latter, for example, may recommend some stocks or mutual funds investments that are suitable or appropriate even if another choice may be better or cheaper.

4. **Fee-only financial planners** earn no commissions and work solely on a fee-for-service basis—that is, they charge a specified fee (typically $50 to $200 per hour or 1 percent of the client's assets annually) for the services provided. They usually need five or more one-hour appointments to analyze a client's financial situation and to present a thorough plan. Fee-only planners do not sell financial products, such as stocks or insurance. As a result and unlike other financial planners/brokers, they do not recommend products that earn them a commission. Finding a true fee-only financial planner is challenging. Advantage: Receive unbiased advice.

Remember, it's your money and your financial future. So when you use the services of a financial planner, don't be intimidated. Ask the hardest questions and don't leave the planner's office until you understand the answers.

 Concept Check 1.6

1. What are the four ways financial planners may be compensated?

2. Describe two professional certification programs for financial planners.

DO IT NOW!

You know more about personal finance after reading this chapter, so get started right now by:

1. *Searching the Internet to identify the current stage in the business cycle;*

2. *Visiting www.bls.gov to determine the current inflation rate;*

3. *Going to www.conference-board.org to assess expectations for economic growth for the next 12 months.*

WHAT DO YOU RECOMMEND NOW?

Now that you have read the chapter on the importance of personal finance, what do you recommend to Se Ri in the case at the beginning of the chapter regarding:

1. Participating in her employer's 401(k) retirement plan?

2. Understanding the effects of her marginal tax rate on her financial decisions?

3. Considering the current state of the economy in her personal financial planning?

4. Using time value of money considerations to project what her IRA might be worth at age 63?

5. Using time value of money considerations to project what her 401(k) plan might be worth at age 63 if she were to participate fully?

BIG PICTURE SUMMARY OF LEARNING OBJECTIVES

LO1. Use the building blocks to achieving financial success.

Financial success and happiness come from using the building blocks of personal finance, such as having a foundation of regular income to provide basic lifestyle and savings, and establishing a financial base using employee benefits and checking and savings accounts. Other building blocks include setting financial goals, controlling expenditures, managing income taxes, handling credit cards, and investing in mutual funds and retirement plans.

LO2. Understand how the economy affects your personal financial success.

Using your knowledge of where we are in the business cycle and tracking a few economic statistics will guide you to make appropriate adjustments in your long-term financial strategy. Also recognize how inflation and deflation will affect your finances.

LO3. Apply economic principles when making financial decisions.

Understanding and applying the basic economic principles of opportunity cost, marginal utility and cost, and marginal income tax rate will affect your financial success. The opportunity cost of a decision is the value of the next best alternative that must be forgone. Marginal cost is the additional (marginal) cost of one more incremental unit of some item. When known, this cost can be compared with the marginal utility received. One's marginal tax rate is the tax rate at which your last dollar is taxed.

LO4. Perform time value of money calculations in personal financial decision making.

Dollars to be received or paid out in the future are not equivalent to those received or paid out today. A dollar received today is worth more than a dollar received a year from now because today's dollar can be saved or invested; by next year, you expect it to be worth more than a dollar. The time value of money involves two components: future value and present value.

LO5. Make smart decisions about your employee benefits.

Smart decisions can increase your actual income by thousands of dollars each year. You need to select wisely among choices within employer-sponsored cafeteria plans; health care; flexible spending accounts; life, disability, and long-term care insurance; and retirement. These decisions often require you to calculate the tax-sheltered aspects of the employee benefits.

LO6. Identify the professional qualifications of providers of financial advice.

When choosing a financial planner, know that many professional designations are meaningful in this field, such as CFP® and ChFC®. Costs may be charged on a fee-only, commission-only, fee-based, or fee-offset basis.

LET'S TALK ABOUT IT

1. **Economic Growth.** How might some of the federal government's recent efforts to help stimulate economic growth affect consumers?

2. **The Business Cycle.** Where is the United States in the economic cycle now, and where does it seem to be heading? List some indicators that suggest in which direction it may move.

3. **Great Recession.** What do you think about long-term impacts of the Great Recession of 2008/2009 on consumer spending, savings rates, and employment?

4. **Personal Finance Mistakes.** What are some common mistakes that people make in personal finance? Which three might be the worst, and why?

5. **Federal Reserve.** Describe some economic circumstances that might persuade the Federal Reserve to increase short-term interest rates.

6. **Opportunity Costs.** People regularly make decisions in personal finance that have opportunity costs. List three financial decisions you have made recently and identify the opportunity cost for each.

DO THE MATH

1. **Future Value.** As a graduating senior, Gwen Kumora of Manhattan, Kansas, is eager to enter the job market at an anticipated annual salary of $34,000. Assuming an average inflation rate of 3 percent and an equal cost-of-living raise, what will Gwen's salary be in ten years? In 20 years? (Hint: Use Appendix A.1 or calculations on the *Garman/Forgue* companion website.) To make real economic progress, how much of a raise (in dollars) does Gwen need to receive next year?

2. **Present and Future Values.** Rachael Berry, a freshman horticulture major at the University of Minnesota, has some financial questions for the next three years of school and beyond. Answers to these questions can be obtained by using Appendix A or the *Garman/Forgue* companion website.

(a) If Rachael's tuition, fees, and expenditures for books this year total $12,000, what will they be during her senior year (three years from now), assuming costs rise 4 percent annually? (Hint: Use Appendix A.1 or the *Garman/Forgue* companion website.)

(b) Rachael is applying for a scholarship currently valued at $5000. If she is awarded it at the end of next year, how much is the scholarship worth in today's dollars, assuming inflation of 3 percent? (Hint: Use Appendix A.2 or the *Garman/Forgue* companion website.)

(c) Rachael is already looking ahead to graduation and a job, and she wants to buy a new car not long after her graduation. If after graduation she begins an investment program of $2400 per year in an investment yielding 6 percent, what will be the value of the fund after three years? (Hint: Use Appendix A.3 or the *Garman/Forgue* companion website.)

(d) Rachael's Aunt Karroll told her that she would give Rachael $1000 at the end of each year for the next three years to help with her college expenses. Assuming an annual interest rate of 2 percent, what is the present value of that stream of payments? (Hint: Use Appendix A.4 or the *Garman/Forgue* companion website.)

3. **Present and Future Values.** Using the present and future value tables in Appendix A, the appropriate calculations on the *Garman/Forgue* companion website, or a financial calculator, calculate the following:

(a) The future value of $400 in two years that earns 5 percent.

(b) The future value of $1200 saved each year for ten years that earns 7 percent.

(c) The amount a person would need to deposit today with a 5 percent interest rate to have $2000 in three years.

(d) The amount a person would need to deposit today to be able to withdraw $6000 each year for ten years from an account earning 6 percent.

(e) A person is offered a gift of $5000 now or $8000 five years from now. If such funds could be

expected to earn 8 percent over the next five years, which is the better choice?

(f) A person wants to have $3000 available to spend on an overseas trip four years from now. If such funds could be expected to earn 7 percent, how much should be invested in a lump sum to realize the $3000 when needed?

(g) A person who invests $1200 each year finds one choice that is expected to pay 9 percent per year and another choice that may pay 10 percent. What is the difference in return if the investment is made for 15 years?

(h) A person invests $50,000 in an investment that earns 6 percent. If $6000 is withdrawn each year, how many years will it take for the fund to run out?

4. **Inflation.** Ginny's salary a year ago was $42,000. If inflation during the year was 3.5 percent, how much of a decline in her purchasing power occurred? Also, what would be her purchasing power if deflation of 1 percent occurred?

5. **Employee Benefits Decision.** Ramon signed up for his employer's cafeteria plan primarily because he can use the money to pay for unreimbursed medical expenses for himself and his disabled son. Since Ramon pays income taxes at the 25 percent rate, how much will he save in income taxes by participating in the program this year in the amount of $3000?

6. **Use the Rule of 72.** Using the rule of 72, calculate how quickly $1000 will double to $2000 at interest rates of 2 percent, 4 percent, 6 percent, 8 percent, and 10 percent.

FINANCIAL PLANNING CASES

CASE 1

Reasons to Study Personal Finance

Lindsey Beliveau of DeKalb, Illinois, is a senior in college, majoring in sociology. She anticipates getting married a year or so after graduation. Lindsey has only one elective course remaining and is going to choose between another advanced class in sociology and one in personal finance. As Lindsey's friend, you want to persuade her to take personal finance. Give some examples of how Lindsey might benefit from the study of personal finance.

CASE 2

A Closer Look at Financial Success

You have been asked to give a brief speech on how to achieve financial success. Define financial success

and financial happiness, and summarize the building blocks to achieving financial success.

CASE 3

Julia Price Thinks About the Economy

Throughout this book, we will present a continuing case about Julia Price. Following is a brief description about her. Six years ago, Julia graduated with a degree in aeronautical engineering and went to work as an engineer in Alabama. Last year she moved to Seattle, Washington, to start a job as a mid-level systems engineer on jet aircraft, and some of her design and coordination responsibilities include Defense Department projects. Julia thinks that the economy is going to get much worse in the next 12 to 24 months, probably with prices declining (deflation). Offer your opinions about her thinking.

BE YOUR OWN PERSONAL FINANCIAL MANAGER

1. **Practice Employment Decisions.** Assume you earn $40,000 annually and your employer offers (a) a flexible spending account to which you can contribute a maximum of $3000 this year, and (b) a 401(k) retirement account to which you may also contribute up to $3000. Your 401(k) contribution will be matched 50 percent by your employer. Assuming you can only afford to contribute $3000 to these benefits, explain what you would do with your $3000. Write an explanation of your decision and a table similar to Table 1-2 (on page 24) to support your thinking.

2. **Track the Economy.** Complete Worksheet 1: Tracking the Economy from "My Personal Financial Planner" to write up your findings on current data as well as your projections one and two years in the future.

3. **Future Values of a Lump Sum.** Complete Worksheet 2: Calculating the Future Value of a Lump Sum from "My Personal Financial Planner" for the following three questions: (a) $10,000, 2 years, 6%; (b) $22,500, 20 years, 8%; (c) $5000, 10 years, 7%. Fill out the worksheet including the last two columns.

4. **Future Value of an Annuity.** Complete Worksheet 3: Calculating the Future Value of an Annuity from "My Personal Financial Planner" for the following three questions: (a) $3000 annually, 5 years, 6%; (b) $1000 annually, 20 years, 8%; (c) $5000 annually, 30 years, 7%. Fill out the worksheet including the last two columns.

5. **Present Value of a Lump Sum.** Complete Worksheet 4: Calculating the Present Value of a Lump Sum from "My Personal Financial Planner" for the following three questions: (a) lump sum needed $10,000, 5 years, 6%; (b) lump sum needed $250,000, 30 years, 8%; (c) lump sum needed $30,000, 10 years, 7%. Fill out the worksheet including the last two columns.

6. **Present Value of an Annuity.** Complete Worksheet 5: Calculating the Present Value of an Annuity from "My Personal Financial Planner" for the following three questions: (a) withdraw $12,000 annually for 5 years at 6%; (b) withdraw $2000 annually for 15 years at 8%; (c) withdraw $3000 annually for 10 years at 7%. Fill out the worksheet including the last two columns.

ON THE 'NET

Go to the Web pages indicated to complete these exercises.

1. **Inflation.** Visit the Bureau of Labor Statistics Consumer Price Index homepage at www.bls.gov/cpi/ and link to information for various areas of the country and metropolitan areas of various sizes. Describe how prices have been changing for your area and city size during the past year.

2. **Future Direction of the Economy.** Visit the Conference Board website, http://www.conference-board .org/data/consumerconfidence.cfm, for the latest information on the consumer confidence index and the index of leading economic indicators. What do the indexes say about the direction of the economy over the next six months to one year?

3. **Economic Trends.** Scan the top four economic trends at the Economic Policy Institute (http://www.epi .org/) for insights on the future of the economy.

4. **Financial Planners' Code of Ethics.** Visit the website of the Financial Planning Association at www .fpaforfinancialplanning.org/AboutFPA/CodeofEthics/. Read through the code of ethics for members of the organization. What does the code tell you about the members?

5. **Financial Planning Careers.** Visit the website of the Certified Financial Planner Board of Standards at www.cfp.net and read about "Becoming a Certified Financial Planner™ Professional." Summarize your findings.

ACTION INVOLVEMENT PROJECTS

1. **Interview a Financial Planner.** Use the Internet and/or Yellow Pages to find a fee-only or fee-based financial planner in your community and telephone that person to ask if he/she would agree to an interview. Take the list of questions in the box "Advice from a Pro ... Questions to Ask a Financial Planner" on page 27 and use it as an outline for your interview. Ask the professional to pick the three questions that he/she considers the most important. Write a summary of your findings.

2. **Smart Money Decisions at Work.** Survey three employed relatives or friends to determine whether or not they take advantage of certain employee benefits at work, such as a cafeteria plan, health care plan, high-deductible health care plan, health savings account, flexible spending account, life insurance, and tax-sheltered retirement plan. Make a written summary of your findings.

3. **Opportunity and Marginal Costs.** Survey three relatives or friends and ask about their decision-making process when they most recently bought a vehicle. Find out if they thought about the opportunity costs when making the purchase. Also ask if they used marginal costs in their thinking. Make a written summary of your findings.

4. **Research Future Direction of the Economy.** Survey five people to determine their opinions on the direction of the economy over the next 12 months. Even though they may not know the meaning of these exact terms, ask about their perceptions on such indicators as the (a) gross domestic product, (b) consumer confidence, (c) inflation and deflation, (d) interest rates, and (e) federal fund rate. Make a table that summarizes your findings.

Visit the Garman/Forgue companion website at **www.cengagebrain.com**.

YOU MUST BE KIDDING, RIGHT?

Karl Springsteen is contemplating going to graduate school at night for a master's degree so he can advance his career and earn more than his current $44,000 salary income. He is a sales account manager for a health care organization, and he has a small business maintaining aquariums for medical offices and other small offices. How much more income can Karl expect over an anticipated 40-year career if he obtains the advanced degree?

A. $100,000

C. $600,000

B. $300,000

D. $900,000

The answer is C, $600,000. Over a 40-year working career, a person with a postgraduate degree can expect to earn more than $3 million, and this is about $600,000 more than a person with a bachelor's degree will earn. Getting an advanced degree is no guarantee of additional income, but the likelihood of such a reality is high!

LEARNING OBJECTIVES

After reading this chapter, you should be able to:

❶ Identify the key steps in successful career planning.

❷ Analyze the financial and legal aspects of employment.

❸ Practice effective employment search strategies.

© PETER DAZELEY/GETTY IMAGES

WHAT DO YOU RECOMMEND?

Ashley Linkletter, age 21, expects to graduate next spring with a bachelor's degree in business administration. Ashley's grades are mostly Bs and As, and she has worked part time throughout her college career. Ashley is vice president of the Student Marketing Association on her campus. She would like to work in management or marketing for a medium- to large-size employer. Because she loves the outdoors, Ashley thinks she would prefer a job in the Northwest, perhaps in northern California, Oregon, or Washington.

What would you recommend to Ashley on the importance of career planning regarding:

iStockphoto.com/Nyul

1. Clarifying her values and lifestyle trade-offs?

2. Enhancing her career-related experiences before graduation?

3. Creating career plans and goals?

4. Understanding her work-style personality?

5. Identifying job opportunities?

career
The lifework chosen by a person to use personal talent, education, and training.

You *can* control much of your financial future with effective career planning. A **career** is the lifework chosen by a person using his or her personal talent, education, and training. **Career planning** can help you identify an employment pathway that aligns your interests and abilities with the tasks and responsibilities expected by employers. Career planning has always been important, but with today's high level of unemployment and slow economy, it is absolutely crucial. You must plan your career, rather than wait to see what unfolds for you.

career planning
Finding employment that will use your interests and abilities and that will support you financially.

Your focus should not be simply a "job" but a career. The general progression of one's career will include a number of related jobs. Indeed, the average tenure at a job for U.S. workers is about three years. A career translates into a base of income, employee benefits, additional educational experiences, advancement opportunities, and a secure financial future. Career planning is a high-priority, do-it-yourself project, allowing you to take control of where you are going and how you are going to get there.

DEVELOPING YOUR CAREER PLAN

LEARNING OBJECTIVE

Identify the key steps in successful career planning.

career plan
A plan that identifies employment that interests you; fits your abilities, skills, work style, and lifestyle; and provides strategic guidance to help you reach your career goal.

Your **career plan** provides a strategic guide for your career through short-, medium-, longer-, and long-term goals as well as future education and work-related experiences. You can't advance very far in planning your financial life without also planning a career that will earn you an adequate income. A career that suits you will give you opportunities to display your abilities in jobs you find satisfying while providing balance between work and your personal life.

During sluggish economic times, you may need to modify any high expectations. Neither the pay nor the geographic location opportunities for employment may be quite what you expect. Realize, too, that the rest of your life will not be determined by your first professional job. No matter what job you choose, consider it a chance to do the required tasks effectively and learn more about yourself and your career field.

Career planning doesn't stop when you take your first career job. Rather, career planning is a continuous process that lasts throughout your life. Every time your life circumstances change, you will likely reconsider your career plan. Figure 2-1 provides an illustration of the steps in career planning. Your career plan begins with an assessment of your values and interests. Then you identify one or more career fields that match those values and interests. Next, you should review your abilities, experiences, and education and match them against requirements for the fields chosen to determine what education and experiences you need to obtain. As your education progresses, you will want to take advantage of networking opportunities and align yourself with tomorrow's employment trends. At graduation, you will be ready to begin your career.

Clarify Your Values and Interests

Thinking about and discovering what you want out of life gives you guidance for what to do to lead a satisfying life. Understanding yourself enables you to select a career path that best suits you.

Figure 2-1

Steps in Career Planning

1. Assess values and interests.
2. Identify one or more appropriate and desirable career fields.
3. Match your abilities, experiences, and education with your chosen career field.
4. Take advantage of networking opportunities.
5. Align yourself with tomorrow's employment trends.
6. Finalize your plan and begin your career.

Values are the principles, standards, or qualities considered worthwhile or desirable. Values provide a basis for decisions about how to live, serving as guides we can use to direct our actions. For something to be a value, it must be prized, publicly affirmed, chosen from alternatives, and acted upon repeatedly and consistently. Values are not right or wrong, or true or false; they are personal preferences.

People may place value on family, friends, helping others, religious commitment, honesty, pleasure, good health, material possessions, financial security, and a satisfying career. Examples of conflicting values are family versus satisfying career, privacy versus social networking, and material possessions versus financial security. When you make important decisions, you might be wise to think carefully to clarify your values before taking action. Consider making a list of your ten most important values.

Your **professional interests** are topics and activities about which you have feelings of curiosity or concern. Interests engage or arouse your attention. They reflect what you like to do. Interests, including occupational interests, are likely to vary over time.

You might consider making a list of your top ten interests. On that list will probably be some things you enjoy but have not done recently. Because of conflicting interests and alternative claims on your time, you cannot pursue all your interests. It is important in career planning to evaluate your interests; if you plan your career with your interests in mind, you will increase the likelihood of career satisfaction.

Interest inventories are measures that assist people in assessing and profiling the interests and activities that give them satisfaction. They compare how your interests are similar or dissimilar to the interests of people successfully employed in various occupations; the theory behind these interest inventories is that individuals with similar interests are often attracted to the same kind of work. These inventories can help you identify possible career goals that match your strongest personal interests.

The Strong Interest Inventory assessment is considered by many to be the gold standard of career exploration tools. The opportunity to take one or more interest inventory assessments, usually for free or at a nominal cost, is available at most colleges and state-supported career counseling facilities. These assessments can also be completed online for a fee. (See, for example, www.discoveryourpersonality.com/Strong.html and www.careercc.com/career_assessment.shtml.)

Identify One or More Desired Career Fields

The workplace has changed dramatically. People used to take a single job and remain at the same company until they retired. Now, people change jobs five to ten times during their working years. You are not likely to remain with one employer for a lifetime let alone ten years. You probably will completely change careers two or three times.

Thinking about a career goal helps you focus on what you want to do for a living. A **career goal** can be a specific job (e.g., cost accountant, teacher, human resources manager) or a particular field of work (e.g., health care, communications, construction). It helps guide you to do the kind of work you want in life rather than drift from job to job. You should focus on a series of jobs that form a career ladder. A **career ladder** typically describes the progression from entry level positions to higher levels of pay, skill, responsibility, or authority. Formulating a career goal requires thinking about your interests, skills, and experiences and learning about different careers and employment trends. The process of establishing a career goal motivates you to consider career possibilities that you may not have thought of otherwise.

To create a career goal, explore the jobs, careers, and trends in the employment marketplace that fit your interests and skills. Ask people you trust about their careers. Search websites such as those for the *Occupational Outlook Handbook* (www.bls.gov/oco/) and the *Occupational Outlook Quarterly* (www.bls.gov/opub/ooq/ooqhome.htm). Research the education requirements.

values
The principles, standards, or qualities that you consider desirable.

professional interests
Long-standing topics and activities that engage your attention.

interest inventories
Scaled surveys that assess career interests and activities.

career goal
Identifying what you want to do for a living, whether a specific job or field of employment.

career ladder
Describes the progression from entry level positions to higher levels of pay, skill, responsibility, or authority.

To decide on a career is a process. Selecting a career field involves making decisions about costs and benefits and lifestyle trade-offs.

Costs and Benefits When making career choices, you must weigh the benefits against the costs. The benefits could include a big salary, likelihood of personal growth and job advancements, and high job satisfaction. For some, the pluses might include the psychic benefit of a prestigious job with a high income. The costs might include living in a less desirable geographic area and climate, being too far from friends and family, sitting at a desk all day, working long hours, and doing too much travelling.

lifestyle trade-offs
Weighing the demands of particular jobs with your social and cultural preferences.

Lifestyle Trade-offs A **lifestyle trade-off** is weighing the demands of particular jobs with your social and cultural preferences When considering any career, think about what lifestyle trade-offs are important to you. For example, if access to big-name live entertainment, museums, and artistic activities is important, then working and living in a rural area may not be appropriate. If you like to visit new places, you may choose a career that involves frequent travel.

Consider the following lifestyle options in your decision making:

- Urban/rural setting
- Close/far from work
- Own/rent housing
- City/suburban life
- Warm/cold climate
- Near/far from relatives
- Constant/variable climate

In addition, employers in certain careers provide more support for working parents. Employer-subsidized child care and flexible work hours might be available at a "family-friendly" workplace.

DECISION-MAKING WORKSHEET

Career Field Research

Selecting a career field should be based on solid research. It helps to have a set of questions prepared in advance. Use this worksheet to gather data about one or more career fields and use the results to compare fields against your values and interests. Various sources of data for your research are located throughout this chapter.

Career field	Research results
General nature of work performed	
Working conditions such as typical hours, degree of travel required, physical activities, and work locations and surroundings	
Educational level, certifications, and training required for an entry-level position	
Typical career ladder including any geographical relocations that are likely to be required as one advances up the ladder	
Educational level, certifications, and training required for career advancement	
Earnings initially and as career progresses	
Typical employee benefits provided	
Career field outlook in terms of employment growth and likely technological advances	

These are all quality-of-life issues, your quality of life. The challenges are greater for dual-career couples because they must communicate effectively when considering the impact of one person's career decisions on the other. (Chapter 5 offers some tips on communication skills.) Remember, you always have the freedom to change your life and career objectives as you learn more about yourself and the world of work.

Review Your Abilities, Experiences, and Education

Reviewing your abilities, aptitudes, experiences, and education is a key step in career planning. The purpose is to see how well they match up with your career-related interests.

Abilities and Aptitudes Your **professional abilities** are the qualities that allow you to perform job-related tasks physically, mentally, artistically, mechanically, or financially. Most of us think of *ability* as a word describing how well we do something, a proficiency, dexterity, or technique, particularly one requiring use of the mind, hands, or body. Other examples of abilities include being skilled in working with people, being able to easily meet the public, and being good at persuading people.

Employer surveys indicate that the single most important ability needed for career success in the twenty-first century is computer skills. Also very highly ranked are communication skills and honesty/integrity. Consider making a list of your top ten abilities.

Aptitudes are the natural abilities and talents that people possess. Aptitudes suggest that you have a tendency or inclination to learn and develop certain skills or abilities. Are you good with numbers? Do you find public speaking easy to do? Do you enjoy solving problems? What are your natural talents? Consider making a list of your top ten aptitudes.

Experiences College graduates have much more going for them than a degree and a string of part-time job experiences. Reviewing your experiences is a step in career planning. Evaluate what you have been doing in your life, including jobs and internships, participation in student organizations and community and church groups, leadership on school projects, and volunteer activities.

Those still in college can enhance their résumés by learning as much as possible in school, participating in clubs and other student organizations (including volunteering for committees and campus projects), getting involved in a faculty research project, and attending off-campus professional meetings related to their major. Academic advisers can provide suggestions.

Employers want workers with good writing and public speaking talents, strong computer skills, fluency in a second language, and an understanding of global commerce and industry. Experiences that use and develop these traits are a big plus for job seekers.

Education and Professional Training Going to college is excellent preparation for your career and your life. But college may not have provided you with all the skills and abilities to be successfully employed. A review of your abilities, experiences, and education may suggest you need to seek additional education and professional training.

Know Your Preferred Work-Style Personality Every job requires the worker to function in relation to data, people, and things

professional abilities
Job-related activities that you can perform physically, mentally, artistically, mechanically, and financially.

aptitudes
The natural abilities and talents that individuals possess.

© Masterfile

Career planning should reflect your lifestyle preferences.

ADVICE FROM A PRO

Competencies of Successful People

People who are successful in their chosen careers, with their finances, and/or in life in general often possess and exhibit certain competencies.

1. *Set goals in the various aspects of life and track progress toward attaining goals.*

2. *Use organizational tools such as lists as well as time management techniques.*

3. *Exhibit integrity.*

4. *Understand their motives and behave ethically.*

5. *Make a quality effort every time.*

6. *Accept accountability for their decisions and actions.*

7. *Exhibit good written and oral communication skills.*

8. *Demonstrate strong computer skills.*

9. *Are open to new ideas.*

10. *Adapt easily to change.*

11. *Share knowledge to assist and mentor others.*

12. *Acquire advanced education and technical training and are life-long learners.*

13. *Take on new assignments and capitalize on the new skills learned.*

14. *Anticipate problems and work proactively to implement solutions.*

15. *Work well in teams and know when to lead and when to follow.*

16. *Project an image consistent with organizational values.*

17. *Understand the operations, structure, and culture of the organization.*

18. *Are loyal to and supportive of the company and boss.*

Caroline S. Fulmer
The University of Alabama
Certified Leadership Trainer for the Achieve Global Corporation

---

work-style personality
Your own ways of working with and responding to job requirements, surroundings, and associates.

in differing work environments and corporate cultures. Your **work-style personality** is a unique set of ways of working with and responding to your job requirements, surroundings, and associates. When making a career selection, you must balance your work-style personality against the demands of the work environment.

You can begin by rating each work value as shown in the Decision-Making Worksheet "What Is Your Work-Style Personality?" Next, go back to the list and circle the activities that you prefer to do most often. Armed with this information, you can now more clearly decide on careers that are most suitable for you.

Take Advantage of Networking

professional networking
Making and using contacts with individuals, groups, and other firms to exchange career information.

Professional networking is the process of making and using contacts, such as individuals, groups, or institutions, to obtain and exchange information in career planning. Use social-networking sites, including Facebook and LinkedIn. Every person you know or meet is a possible useful contact.

Networking requires that you make a conscious effort to use people you know and meet to maximize your job search process. Networking involves utilizing your social contacts, taking advantage of casual meetings, and asking for personal referrals. Most of your contacts will not be able to hire you, but they could refer you to the person who can, or they may be able to give you useful information about a potential employer.

Maintain a continually growing list of people who are family, neighbors, friends, college associates, coworkers, previous supervisors, teachers, professors, alumni, business contacts, and others you know through civic and community organizations such as churches and business and social groups. Take note of where your contacts work and what types of jobs they have. Ask these people for 10 to 20 minutes of their time so you can seek information and suggestions from them. Perhaps meet at their workplaces (where you might meet other potential networking contacts), and afterward send them thank-you notes.

As many as three-quarters of all job openings may never be listed in want ads, so the people in your network become a vital source of information about employment opportunities. For this reason, expanding the number of people in your network is advantageous; some of the people you know will also likely share their networking contacts. Networking is the number one way people are successful in their job search.

DECISION-MAKING WORKSHEET

What Is Your Work-Style Personality?

It would be useful for you to consider a number of work values critical to the process of career selection, particularly in the areas of work conditions, work purposes, and work relation-ships. Rate how you value the following work values as either very important in your choice of career, somewhat important, or unimportant.

Work-Style Factor	Your Rating of Importance		
	Very Important	**Somewhat Important**	**Unimportant**
1. Work Conditions			
Independence and autonomy			
Time flexibility			
Change and variety			
Change and risk			
Stability and security			
Physical challenge			
Physical demands			
Mental challenge			
Pressure and time deadlines			
Precise work			
Decision making			
2. Work Purposes			
Truth and knowledge			
Expertise and authority			
Esthetic appreciation			
Social conditions			
Material gain			
Achievement and recognition			
Ethical and moral			
Spiritual and transpersonal			
3. Work Relationships			
Working alone			
Public contact			
Close friendships			
Group membership			
Helping others			
Influencing others			
Supervising others			
Controlling others			

For additional values clarification, go back to the list and *circle the activities* that you want to do more often. The goal is to match your highest work-style values to career choices with similar work-style requirements.

Source: Adapted from D. C. Borchard, J. J. Kelly, and N. P. K. Weaver, *Your Career: Choices, Chances, Changes* (Dubuque, IA: Kendall/Hunt, 1990), Chapter 11.

Align Yourself with Tomorrow's Employment Trends

Right now, you may be focused on school—graduating and getting a good job. But you also need to find out where the jobs will be in the future. The job market today is rapidly changing—a result of economic downturns, corporate restructuring, company downsizing, and globalization—and the career path you are considering now may not continue to be a good choice in the years ahead.

What, then, are the trends in employment? The aging U.S. population will create jobs in the service industries of finance, insurance, health care, recreation, and travel.

Table 2-1

Projected High-Wage, High-Growth Occupations

Job Title	Employment in 2014	Median Annual Income
Accountants/auditors	1,440,000	$ 76,000
Advertising promotions managers	77,000	$ 95,000
Air traffic controllers	28,000	$153,000
Business operations specialists	396,000	$ 79,000
Child and social workers	324,000	$ 51,000
Compensation benefits managers	70,000	$100,000
Computer system analysts	640,000	$100,000
General and operations managers	2,100,000	$115,000
Human resource managers	72,000	$122,000
Industrial engineers	205,000	$ 98,000
Market research analysts	227,000	$ 81,000
Marketing managers	228,000	$153,000
Media and communications	46,000	$ 61,000
Medical/health service managers	305,000	$102,000
Property association managers	454,000	$ 60,000
Public relations specialists	231,000	$ 66,000
Sales managers	403,000	$122,000
Technical writers	62,000	$ 81,000
Training and development specialists	261,000	$ 74,000

Source: Bureau of Labor Statistics, Table 15, High-wage, high-growth occupations, by educational attainment cluster and earnings; authors' income projections to 2014.

Jobs are gravitating to existing population centers, particularly in warmer climates that have superior transportation systems. Jobs in manufacturing are largely going overseas to Mexico, Asia, Europe, and other countries, with the U.S. job market primarily demanding highly skilled workers in the service industries.

Strong job growth is projected for the twenty-first century in computer technology, business services, social services, child care, wholesale and retail sales, food services, hospitality, retirement facilities, health care, travel, and human resources. All require good communication skills. High-demand occupations tend to pay high salaries and offer career advancement opportunities. They often require good computer skills. Table 2-1 shows the projected job growth in high-wage, high-growth occupations in the United States.

Finalize Your Career Plan and Begin Your Career

As you near graduation, you will be ready to develop a formal career plan. Figure 2-2 provides an illustrative career plan. Your career plan should be realistic and flexible. Your career interests and goals will change over time, especially as you continue your education, gain work experience, and see how your friends fare with their jobs and avocations. Teaching music education might be your first career, but you may eventually realize that the accompanying small income could keep you on a tight financial budget forever. This issue might encourage you to consider a total career change—perhaps to sales in the music industry or a related field, where incomes are higher.

Some people go the other way. For example, after some years in the field of accounting, you might change career goals and go to work in your longtime interest area of horticulture, which pays less. Your interests might evolve over time as well. For example, a person with a full-time job in retail store management might decide to turn a hobby of gun collecting into selling guns as an online business. Staying in a career path but changing jobs occurs, too. For example, some hospital nurses decide after a few years that they have made a wrong career choice. While the job pays well, it

FINANCIAL POWER POINT

The Three Rules of Career Success

It has been said that a golfer needs to concentrate on 48 things when hitting the ball. Career advice is almost as complicated, and millions of words have been written about how to succeed in a career. But experts say you should focus on just three things.

1. *Competence: Be as good at your job as possible.*

2. *Confidence: Be able to formulate and communicate your ideas in a way that inspires others.*

3. *Caring: Put the interests of your company, coworkers, and customers ahead of your own.*

Career Goals and Plans for Harry Johnson

Figure 2-2

Harry Johnson began his working career following graduation from college by obtaining employment with a small commercial interior design firm. He has an undergraduate degree from a university accredited by the American Society of Interior Designers. He is happy that his first professional job is in his major field of interest.

Initial career goal: To become an interior designer. To design, plan, and supervise commercial/contract design projects.

Long-term career goal (20-plus years): Own or become a partner in a medium- to large-size commercial/contract interior design firm.

Short-term plans and goals in career establishment stage (3 to 6 years): Gain work experience in current job; receive employer compliments on quality of work; obtain continuing education credits for professional growth and development; secure higher-level design responsibilities, such as lead professional design team; volunteer for committee responsibilities in local and state professional associations; obtain substantial increases in income; receive promotions; learn operational aspects and marketing of the company.

Medium-term plans and goals in professional growth stage (7 to 12 years): Be promoted to the level of senior designer; consider going to work for another employer as a senior designer and, if necessary, move to another community; volunteer for higher-level service in professional associations; obtain a master of fine arts degree in interior design; become assistant to the firm's general manager.

Longer-term plans and goals in advancement stage (13 to 20 years): Become general manager of commercial design firm; seek out potential partners and sufficient financing to either buy out or start up a medium-size design firm.

---

involves shift work and very long days. Those who want to remain in the nursing profession may decide to leave the hospital setting and go to work for a nursing home or college health facility.

Technology has made it possible for many people to work at home online, as 1 in 15 workers has such an alternative work arrangement. Some people work off site for an employer, telecommuting (or teleworking) and perhaps spending one day every two weeks at the company office. Other people are self-employed entrepreneurs who run micro businesses. A good computer and software make it possible. Many excellent job opportunities exist. For ideas on working at home, see the Small Business Administration (www.sba.gov), National Association for the Self-Employed (www.nase.org), and Service Corps of Retired Executives (www.score.org).

Assessing yourself and your career plans every few years is important to achieving success in your working life. What do you find satisfying and not so satisfying? Honest answers will help you, particularly as your interests evolve. Your work experiences should hone your abilities and skills. Learning new skills on the job is common, and if that is not happening in a job, move on and change employers and perhaps careers.

DID YOU KNOW?

Your Worst Financial Blunders in Career Planning

Based on others' financial woes you will make mistakes career planning when you:

1. *Neglect to fully research a company before going for an interview.*

2. *Fail to match your interests and preferred work style with the requirements of the career.*

3. *Disregard networking by not getting involved in career-related professional associations.*

✔ **Concept Check 2.1**

1. Distinguish between a job and a career.

2. How do your values affect your trade-offs in career planning?

3. What can be done to enhance your abilities and experiences without working in a job situation?

4. What are the components of career plans and goals?

FINANCIAL AND LEGAL ASPECTS OF EMPLOYMENT

This section examines financial and legal aspects of employment to consider when analyzing your career plans, and it includes the Run the Numbers worksheet "Assessing the Benefits of a Second Income."

Place Dollar Values on Employee Benefits

employee benefits

Forms of remuneration provided by employers to employees that result in the employee not having to pay out-of-pocket money for certain expenses; also known as nonsalary benefits.

Employee benefits are tremendously important to employees, especially when comparing the benefits provided by one employer with another. **Employee benefits** (or **nonsalary benefits**) are forms of remuneration provided by employers to employees that result in the employee not having to pay out-of-pocket money for certain expenses. Examples include paid vacations, health care, paid sick leave, child care, tuition reimbursement, and financial planning services.

The topic of "making smart money decisions at work" was examined in Chapter 1, which provided details on selecting among employee benefits such as health care plans (including health savings accounts), flexible spending plans (such as dependent and health care FSA accounts), insurance (such as life, disability, and long-term care), and employer retirement plans. Review that section whenever appropriate.

You can place a monetary value on each employee benefit that is available. Some nonsalary benefits might not be applicable, such as child care if you are single. Others are super valuable, such as a health plan, since a policy purchased in the private market for a single person might have a premium of $5000 a year. To put monetary values on employee benefits, you may (1) place a market value on the benefit or (2) calculate the future value of the benefit.

Place a Market Value on the Benefit   If instead of enjoying a certain employee benefit, you had to pay out-of-pocket dollars for it, you can easily determine its market value. Private child care might cost $300 a week in your community; thus, when child care is provided free from your employer, that is a whopping $15,000 ($300 × 50 weeks) saved annually. Actually, it is more because you would likely have to earn perhaps $22,000 to have

DID YOU KNOW?

Value of Additional Education

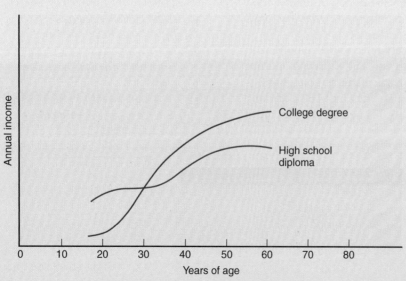

Income over the Life Cycle According to Age and Education

Income varies over the life cycle. Higher incomes typically go to those with more education or more specialized education. Adults with a bachelor's degree earn an average of $56,000 compared with $34,000 for high school graduates and $82,000 for those with advanced degrees, reports the U.S. Census Bureau.

These differences can add up over the years. A recent high school graduate with a current income of $27,000 will earn a cumulative $2,036,000 over a 40-year working career. A person with a new bachelor's degree earning $44,000 now will gross $3,300,000; and a person with a recent master's degree and a current income of $52,000 will receive a cumulative income of $3,900,000 over a 40-year working career. (The figures are based on 3 percent annual income increases in Appendix A.3)

DID YOU KNOW?

You May Give Up $200,000 If You Cash Out Your 401(k) Account When Changing Employers

When changing jobs, nearly half of workers unwisely cash out all the money in their employer-sponsored retirement plan instead of leaving it with the old employer, transferring it to a new employer's 401(k) plan, or moving it to an IRA rollover account. If an individual has $50,000 in a 401(k) account and cashes it out, that person gives up $233,000 in future dollars over the following 20 years.

	If you cash out $50,000:	If you roll over $50,000:
20% federal income tax withholding	−$10,000	
5% additional tax (in 25% tax bracket)	−$ 2,500	
10% early-withdrawal penalty	−$ 5,000	
5% state/local income tax	−$ 2,500	
Total withdrawn	−$20,000	+$50,000
Money spent on new car, TV, home repair, vacation, etc.	−$30,000	Money invested in another tax-deferred retirement account that earns 8 percent annually
Total	−$50,000	+$50,000
Additional investment actions taken	None	None
Investment balance after 20 years	$ 0	$233,050

$15,000 left over after paying $7000 in income and Social Security taxes. An employer-provided paid-for life insurance policy with a face value of $50,000 might cost $600 if you had to buy it yourself.

Calculate the Future Value of the Benefit The best income is income that is never taxed, called tax-exempt income. Chapter 1 examined this topic. Many employee benefits are of this type, and that's great from your personal finance perspective. Future value calculations come into play when you are trying to place a value on an employee benefit that is tax sheltered. Such income is exempt from income taxes in the current year but is subject to taxation in a later tax year.

An employer that provides a 401(k) retirement plan offers a valuable benefit. If an employer provides a match of $1200 a year to the regular contributions of the employee, for example, those $1200 contributions will eventually be the worker's money. And it will grow free of income taxes until the funds are withdrawn. Over 20 years, the annual employer contributions of $1200 grow to more than $44,000 (using Appendix A.3). That's a good employee benefit!

Know Your Legal Employment Rights

You have legal rights both during the hiring process and after you are hired. When selecting employees, employers may not discriminate based on gender, race, color, national origin, age, marital status, pregnancy, or mental or physical disabilities (if the person can perform the essential job tasks). Laws in many states and cities also prohibit discrimination against gays and lesbians in the hiring process.

Once hired, you have many rights. Employers must do the following:

- Pay the minimum wage established by federal, state, or local laws
- Provide unemployment insurance
- Provide workers' compensation benefits for job-related injuries or illness
- Pay Social Security taxes to the government, which are then credited to the employee's lifetime earnings account maintained by the Social Security Administration

RUN THE NUMBERS

Assessing the Benefits of a Second Income

A second income might add surprisingly little to your total earnings because of all the costs associated with earning it. In this example, a nonworking spouse is considering a job that pays $30,000 annually. The total accurate net amount of the extra $30,000 income is a mere $9205, thus adding only $767 ($9205/12 = $767) a month to total earnings.

1. **Second Income**

Annual earnings	$30,000
Value of benefits (life insurance)	300
Total 1	$30,300

2. **Expenses**

Federal income taxes (25% rate × $30,000)	$ 7,500
State/local income taxes (6% rate × $30,000)	1,800
Social Security taxes (7.65% × $30,000)	2,295
Transportation and commuting (50 weeks @ $40)	2,000
Child care (8 months after-school only)	3,200
Lunches out (50 weeks, twice a week at $10)	1,000
Work wardrobe (including dry cleaning)	1,200
Other work-related expenses (magazines, dues, gifts)	300
Take-out food for supper (too tired to cook; $100 per month)	1,200
Guilt complex purchases (to make up for time lost with others)	600
Total 2	$21,095

3. **Net Value of Second Income**

Total of 1 from above	$30,300
Subtract total of 2 from above	21,095
Total accurate net amount of second income	$ 9,205

The law requires that hourly employees be paid overtime for extra work hours put in beyond the standard 40-hour workweek. (Salaried employees are not paid overtime, and the vast majority of college graduates have salaried jobs.) In addition, a woman cannot be forced to go on maternity leave before she wants to do so if she does choose to take leave. You have the rights not to be unfairly discriminated against or harassed and to be employed in a safe workplace.

DID YOU KNOW?

What to Do When You Lose Your Job

Even in the best of economic times, about 5 or 6 percent of the workforce is unemployed, but in times when the unemployment rate is 8 or 9 percent, finding another job can be extremely difficult. What should you do when you are laid off?

1. ***Think of yourself as being employed.*** Your job is to find a new job. Set a work schedule for yourself and a location from which to do the work.

2. ***Get your finances in order.*** Determine how much money you have and the level of benefits you might be able to receive. Determine how long you can continue to pay your bills in the usual fashion.

3. ***Tap into your network.*** Let people know that you are looking for work. Rebuild your network if necessary. Build contacts with other unemployed persons in your field so that you can share successful and unsuccessful strategies.

4. ***Take a hard look at the prospects for a possible rebound of employment opportunities in your career***

field. Some of the jobs lost in the recent economic turmoil are the result of temporary sluggishness in an industry. Others will never come back.

5. **Get retrained.** This is especially important if your career field will see permanent reductions in the needed level of workers. Local community colleges may be especially focused on retraining programs and have financial assistance programs in place to help you.

6. **Be prepared to move.** Not all areas of the country are as bad off as the worst hit areas. And some areas are poised

to rebound faster. Areas with strong public schools and colleges, highly educated workers, and emerging high-tech and information-age industries will rebound first.

7. **Don't be afraid to be a temp.** Many firms will hire temporary workers at first when recovering so that they can quickly downsize if necessary. When the recovery really takes hold, they will look first to hire the temporary workers into their permanent work force.

You have the right to take leave for personal or family medical problems, pregnancy, or adoption. You also have the right to privacy in such personal matters. When you leave an employer, you have the right to continue your health insurance coverage, perhaps for as long as 18 months, by paying the premiums yourself. If you believe you have been wronged, you can assert your legal rights.

 Concept Check 2.2

1. Summarize how education level and age affect income.

2. What two techniques can be used to place monetary values on employee benefits?

3. Choose three career advancement tips and explain how each one might apply in someone's personal situation.

résumé
Summary record of your education, training, experience, and other qualifications.

EFFECTIVE EMPLOYMENT SEARCH STRATEGIES

Once you have undertaken some career planning, you will want to get a job in your preferred career field. This is a process that takes much effort. A successful job search might require 25 to 30 hours per week of your time. Your résumé, cover letter, and interview skills must all be geared to marketing yourself as the best person for the job. Effective search strategies follow.

Assemble an Attention-Getting Résumé

The Internet is a valuable resource for you in all aspects of career planning, including preparing a résumé. A **résumé** is a summary record of your education, training, experience, and other qualifications. It is often submitted with a job application. Your résumé, usually one or two pages in length, should be carefully written and contain zero errors or inconsistencies in message, content, and appearance. A survey of top executives reveals that 75 percent will not even consider an applicant whose résumé has one or more typos.

Its primary function is to provide a basis for screening people out of contention for jobs. When you supply a résumé, you are providing documentation for some kind of subjective evaluation against unknown criteria. Large employers, recruiters, and local and national websites screen résumés, and computer software is frequently used to scan them instead of humans. Use keywords from the job description such as "Microsoft Office" so the scanning process picks them up.

DID YOU KNOW?

Prospective Employers Can Check Your Credit Report

Thirteen percent of employers obtain the credit reports of prospective job candidates. A lousy credit history can suggest a lot about a person's inability to manage important tasks. Federal law requires (1) that individuals are aware that consumer credit reports may be used for employment purposes and must agree to such use and (2) that individuals are to be notified promptly if information in a consumer report may result in a negative employment decision. Over 20 states prohibit employers from using credit reports when hiring.

You should focus your résumé on experiences that are most relevant to the position you aspire to hold. When it is necessary to technically fulfill a requirement in the employment process, tailor a special edition of your résumé to fit that special set of circumstances. Résumés are usually presented in a **chronological format** (information in reverse order with the most recent first), **skills format** (aptitudes and qualities), or **functional format** (career-related experiences). See Figures 2-3, 2-4, and 2-5 for sample résumés. The most common mistake in a résumé is to fill it up with a long list of functions and responsibilities that you had in your previous jobs instead of evidencing the specific accomplishments that made a difference in the companies for which you worked.

Colleges have career centers with sample résumés and professional staff who can offer personal advice. You can also find examples of résumés on the Internet. Monster .com has 500,000 online résumés, and ResumeMailman.com forwards résumés to recruiters. Simply posting your résumé on an Internet site or sending out résumés is not conducting a significant job search. Realize, of course, that your current employer can view your résumé if it is posted on the Internet.

chronological format
Résumé that provides your information in reverse order, with the most recent first.

skills format
Résumé that emphasizes your aptitudes and qualities.

functional format
Résumé that emphasizes career-related experiences.

Target Your Preferred Employers

A key step in the job search process is to think about both the industries in which you would prefer employment and which employers might be best for you. If, for example, you want to work in the health care industry, you must visit the websites of health trade

Figure 2-3

Sample Chronological Résumé

CHRISTOPHER GORDON

SCHOOL ADDRESS:
2824 West Street
Ames, IA 50211
(401) 555-1212
E-mail: cgordon@yahoo.com

HOME ADDRESS:
3055 Vallejo Street, Apt.12
Denver, CO 80303
(303) 333-4141

CAREER OBJECTIVE	Entry-level position as a metallurgical engineer.
EDUCATION	Bachelor of Science, Metallurgical Engineering, Iowa State University, Ames, IA, June 2010.
	Associate of Arts, Kishwaukee Community College, Malta, IL, June 2006.
EXPERIENCE	August 2008–May 2010 (academic year, part time), Iowa State University, Ames, IA, Research Assistant to Professor John Binnion on metals and plastics, conducted research, performed statistical analyses, wrote reports, led group of interns.
	Summer 2008 and Summer 2007 (full time), EMD Electro-Motive Division, Metallurgical Engineering Department, Chicago, IL, Internship (paid), tested materials, prepared reports, participated in team efforts.
	September 2004–April 2005, Volunteer, Village Nursing Home, Denver, CO, updated some resident activities, organized weekend volunteers.
CAMPUS ACTIVITIES	2008–2010, Associate Editor college newspaper, Iowa State Progress; 2008, Vice President, ISU Metallurgical Society; 2006–2008, Hispanic Club; 2006–2008, Singer, University Chorale; 2006, Tutor for College of Engineering computer laboratory; 2007–2008, attended two national conferences of American Society for Metals International.
HONORS	Etta Mae Johnson Scholarship (2008); College of Engineering Academic Scholarship (2007); Most Valuable Member, ISU Metallurgical Society (2007); Julie Lynn Marshall Scholarship (2005).
REFERENCES	Available upon request.

Sample Functional Résumé

Figure 2-4

Jennifer Elizabeth Anklin
12144 Southwest 174th Loop
Tupelo, MS 38803
School: (662) 844-5698
Home: (662) 921-1213
Eanklin@hotmail.com

CAREER OBJECTIVE
Public relations or communications department with opportunities to learn.

EDUCATION
Bachelor of Science, University of Georgia, Consumer Economics and Housing with a minor in communications, Athens, GA, May 2010; Associate of Arts, Mississippi Valley Community College, Booneville, MS, August 2007.

CAREER-RELATED EXPERIENCES
Organized breakfast meetings, supervised new members, updated membership records, organized annual auction, created administrative procedures, Chamber of Commerce, Athens, GA, part time, 2008–10.
Maintained inventory records, monitored reordering systems, JC Penney Company, Athens, GA, part time, 2007–08.
Updated merchandising records, redesigned sales floor layout, Johnson's Shoes, Booneville, MS, part time, 2005–07.
Overseas experience building a school in Botswana.
Translated Spanish and French for Atlanta Translation Services.

CAMPUS CAREER-RELATED ACTIVITIES
Vice president, Sales and Merchandising Club; Treasurer, Aces Chorale Club; Secretary, National Honor Society; Secretary, Alpha Kappa Alpha Sorority; Co-coordinator Speaker's Committee, Consumer Club; Debate Club; attended SOCAP meetings in Atlanta; intramural hockey; campus church choir.

COMPUTER SKILLS
Microsoft Office, Corel WordPerfect Office, Corel Paint Shop Pro X, Adobe Acrobat, Dazzle Video Creator, QuickBooks Pro, Computer Assisted Design, Macromedia, FrontPage.

HONORS
Hanna Pallagrosi Academic Scholarship; Modu Samega-Janneh Service Award, College of Family and Consumer Sciences, University of Georgia; Highest Monthly Sales Award, JC Penney; Employee of the Month (twice), JC Penney.

REFERENCES
Furnished upon request.

Sample Skills Résumé

Figure 2-5

Joshua Fredrickson
2122 South 141th Street West, Apt. 340
San Antonio, TX 78204
School: (210) 207-5454
Home: (210) 419-1445
JFredrickson@hotmail.com

CAREER OBJECTIVE:
Professional position in human development with administrative responsibilities.

EDUCATION:
Master of Science, 2010, University of Texas at San Antonio, Human Development, San Antonio, TX; Bachelor of Science, 2007, University of Texas at San Antonio, Education and Human Development, San Antonio, TX; Associate of Arts, 2005, San Antonio College, San Antonio, TX.

CAREER-RELATED LEADERSHIP EXPERIENCES
- Organized and coordinated student session at national Family Relations Conference
- Hosted student session at Texas Family Relations Conference
- Led departmental graduate student study committee
- Treasurer of honor society Kappa Omicron Nu
- Organized speaker series for Kappa Omicron Nu
- Chaired Graduate Student Recruitment committee
- Vice President Study Body, San Antonio College
- Volunteer coordinator for neighborhood Meals-on-Wheels for adults

CAREER-RELATED WORK EXPERIENCE
- Administered intake procedures at Humanas Family Center
- Updated record-keeping systems for Humanas Family Center
- Planned learning activities for Gonzales Child Center
- Supervised parental security for Gonzales Child Center
- Presented research paper at Texas Family Relations Conference
- Attended two state Texas Family Relations Conferences
- Attended University of Utah summer seminar on human development
- Planned curriculum updates for Alamo Elder Center
- Trained and managed interns at campus family counseling center

CAREER-RELATED COMPUTER SKILLS
Word, Excel, Corel Graphics, Adobe Acrobat, SPSS, SAS.

HONORS
Henry B. Gonzales Public Service Scholarship, Lane Johnson Memorial Scholarship, Outstanding Member of Kappa Omicron Nu.

DID YOU KNOW?

Résumé Dos and Don'ts

When preparing your résumé, it is important to include key phrases for skills, traits, and technical expertise that a potential employer will identify as desirable. This is especially important when computer software is used to scan résumés. However, some phrases have become so commonplace that they have lost their impact. Following are examples of passé phrases and what to write instead:

• **Possess organizational skills:** describe a specific example of how a process you developed improved efficiency.

• **Bottom-line oriented:** provide an example of an effort you led that saved the company money.

• **Team player:** describe a team effort that you led or participated in that was particularly successful.

• **Results-oriented:** describe a problem you solved.

• **Effective presentation and communication skills:** describe a written or oral communication that you developed and bring an example to your interview.

• **Strong work ethic:** describe a particular project or new skill that you engaged in after-hours or on the weekend.

• **Meets or exceeds expectations:** identify a particular award or commendation that recognized your extra efforts.

• **Seeking a challenge:** identify a way you can help the company succeed.

ADVICE FROM A PRO

Career Advancement Tips

The essence of career advancement is to build your job-related knowledge and skills for the future by learning. You do not want to fall behind your coworkers and those who work for other employers, as they may be your future job market competitors. Change jobs when appropriate to obtain a different or better position that advances your career, or when deemed necessary to entirely alter your career. To advance in your career, consider the following:

• **Mentors.** Ask one or two people to serve as your mentors, people with whom you can regularly discuss your career progress. A mentor is an experienced person, often a senior coworker, who offers friendly career-related advice, guidance, and coaching to a less experienced person.

• **Traits.** Exhibit passion, self-discipline, confidence, and determination in your everyday responsibilities. Arrive early and stay late even if only for 10 to 15 minutes.

• **Volunteer.** Volunteer for new assignments.

• **Training.** Sign up for employer-sponsored seminars and training and certification opportunities.

• **Conferences.** Attend meetings and conferences in your field. Become a member of your local professional association and become active in its leadership.

• **College Courses.** Take advanced college courses and complete a graduate degree.

• **Professional Reading.** Stay alert to what is happening in your career field by reading professional and trade publications.

• **Current Events.** Be up to date on current events and business and economic news by reviewing websites and reading newspapers, news magazines, and business periodicals.

• **Nonwork Activities.** Be actively involved in something besides work, such as coaching children's athletics, playing softball, singing in a choral group, or teaching reading to illiterate adults.

Dana Wolff
Southeast Technical Institute

associations and various health care firms. Learn as much as you can about the health care industry. How broad is the industry? What types of companies are at the retail level? At the wholesale level? What kinds of firms provide services to the industry? Which companies are the largest? Which have the fastest growth rates? Which employers have employment facilities in geographic areas that are of interest to you? What are the leading companies? Which are the "employers of choice" that are family friendly or offer especially good benefits? What are the employee benefits at different companies? Knowing the industry and specific employers of interest to you tells you who to target for employment in your career path.

Identify Specific Job Opportunities

The next step is to identify specific job openings that fit your skill set and provide opportunities for advancement in your career. Use the resources below, and keep track of your job search progress using the Decision-Making Worksheet "Keeping Track of Your Job Search." Recall that networking was identified earlier as an important step in career planning. Networking is one of the best ways to identify job opportunities, as many jobs are not posted in newspaper want ads.

The Internet If you do not use the Internet in your job search, you are not likely to get the best job for your talents. You can use the Internet to obtain career advice, review job opportunities by industry and company, and conduct specialized job searches. You also can review résumés, create your résumé, create a cover letter, and post your résumé. The Internet allows you to review salary information, calculate living costs in different communities, and research career fairs. Just about all your search information on the Web can be saved for your future use.

The Internet is robust with helpful resources for job seekers. Check out these websites:
www.jobbankinfo.org
www.careerbuilder.com
www.careerjournal.com
www.flipdog.com
www.getthejob.com
www.jobster.com
www.monster.com
www.nationjob.com
www.Plaxo.com
www.resumemachine.com
www.rileyguide.com
www.Twitter.com

Career Fairs Career fairs are university-, community-, and employer-sponsored opportunities for job seekers to meet with perhaps hundreds or even thousands of potential employers over one or more days. Here you can schedule brief screening interviews with a dozen or more employers in a single day. Career fairs are advertised in local newspapers, on television, and on the Internet. Search "career fairs" on the Internet as well as at CareerBuilder.com and NationalCareerFairs.com.

career fairs
University-, community-, and employer-sponsored events for job seekers to meet with many employers quickly to screen potential employers.

Classified Advertisements Advertisements in newspapers and professional and trade publications—as well as their Internet equivalents—continue to be important in the job search process. They should not be your only focus, however. Larger newspapers, such as the *Atlanta Constitution* and *Chicago Daily News*, advertise jobs in large geographic areas. Others such as the *New York Times* and *Wall Street Journal* have jobs for the whole country. And others like the *Financial Times* (www.ft.com/jobs) describe overseas opportunities. Specialized trade publications and their Internet websites, in fields such as advertising (*Advertising Age*) and accounting (*Journal of Accountancy*), list numerous job openings. For other fields, see http://dir.yahoo.com/News_and_Media/Journals/.

Employment Agencies An **employment agency** is a firm specializing in locating employment positions for certain types of employees, such as secretaries, salespeople, engineers, managers, and computer personnel. Most employment agencies are paid fees by organizations that hire them to find new employees. Others charge the job hunter fees, sometimes very high amounts. Governments also have state or city employment offices that offer free services.

employment agency
Firm that locates employment for certain types of employees.

DECISION-MAKING WORKSHEET

Keeping Track of Your Job Search

The job search process involves a tremendous number of details. Below is a list of task areas in worksheet format that you can use to help keep track of your job search progress. Create lots of columns to the right so you can input important information, such as dates when you completed each effort.

	Date Done	Date to Do More
1. Identify your values.		
2. Decide on economic, psychic, and lifestyle trade-offs.		
3. Clarify career-related interests.		
4. Review abilities, experiences, and education.		
5. Identify employment trends.		
6. Create career goals and plans.		
7. Target preferred employers.		
8. Analyze your work-style personality.		
9. Compare salary and living costs in different cities.		
10. Place values on employee benefits.		
11. Create an expanding list of networking contacts.		
12. Obtain excellent letters of reference.		
13. Compile revealing personal stories.		
14. Assemble a résumé.		
15. Assemble a cover letter.		
16. Identify job opportunities:		
a. Career fairs		
b. Classified advertisements		
c. Employment agencies		
d. Internet		
17. Interviewing		
a. Research the company.		
b. Create responses for anticipated interview questions.		
c. Create positive responses to list of negative questions.		
d. Evaluate your interview performance.		
18. Send a thank-you note.		
19. Accept the job.		

Write an Effective Cover Letter

cover letter
A letter of introduction sent to a prospective employer to get an interview.

A **cover letter** is a letter of introduction sent to a prospective employer designed to express your interest in obtaining an interview. An effective cover letter helps introduce and sell you to the prospective employer. The cover letter should be specifically written for each position for which you are applying. See Figure 2-6 for an example. Expand upon a couple of details from your résumé, explaining how your talents and experience can benefit the employer. Communicate your enthusiasm for the job. When appropriate, mention a networking contact.

Address your cover letter, written on high-quality paper, to a specific person and request a brief meeting. If the hiring manager's name is not in the job announcement, telephone the employer and speak with a receptionist in the correct department. Be candid about your reason for needing a specific person's name. Your letter should try to secure a face-to-face meeting to obtain more information and gather impressions. End the letter with a sentence stating that you will be telephoning or e-mailing within two weeks to reassert your interest in the position. Then, do so!

If you don't hear back, send another hard copy of your resume and cover letter and attach a handwritten note that says, "Second submission. I'm very interested."

Sample Cover Letter

Figure 2-6

June 23, 2010

Mrs. Juanita M. Pena, President
Pena Public Relations Agency, Inc.
4235 International Blvd NW
Atlanta, GA 30303

Dear Mrs. Pena:

We met briefly in Atlanta at last January's luncheon meeting of the Society of Consumer Affairs Professionals in Business. My professor at that time, Julia Marlowe, introduced us and stated that your company was "undoubtedly one of the most successful creative agencies" in the Atlanta community.

My work experience in public relations and sales, academic background in consumer economics and communications, and research about your firm has led me to the conclusion that I am very interested in seeking employment in your organization. Also, a former employee of yours, Amanda Allyson, now with Hewitt Advertising, told me that you were a fine boss and encouraged me to join your fast-growing company.

My abilities to research, organize, communicate, and lead can provide Pena Public Relations with a person with multiple skills who can adapt to fast-changing needs. My strengths include fluency in three languages, serious computer skills, technical writing, persuasion, and ease in meeting new people. Attending two colleges and living in three states has broadened my perspectives as has studying public relations from the consumer perspective. See my enclosed résumé for more details.

I look forward to the opportunity to meet with you to better communicate my qualifications and evaluate how they might fit the Pena Public Relations Agency. You may contact me at (662) 921-1213 or Eanklin@hotmail.com. Also, I will telephone you in two weeks.

Sincerely,

Jennifer Elizabeth Anklin
Jennifer Elizabeth Anklin
12144 Southwest 174th Loop
Tupelo, MS 38803

Enclosure

Obtain Strong Reference Letters

College students too often simply ask a couple of professors they like to write them a letter of recommendation. Professors typically give their best judgments in these letters. This may include identifying some student weaknesses as well as strengths. Students who ask for a letter from an instructor who does not know them well also risk receiving a bland, boilerplate, or average kind of reference. Always provide a résumé to professors from whom you request letters as well as a copy of the job description for the position.

Ask only those professors who know you and your schoolwork well. Approach them with a request similar to "Are you willing to give me a positive letter of recommendation? I need one that points out my better qualities and performance here at college." If the instructor hesitates too long or gives you some negative feedback, consider asking a different professor for a recommendation. If your recommenders are willing to give you a separate copy of their letters, you will have them in your personal files for future use.

Formally Apply for the Job

You can't get a job without applying for it. Personalize your cover letter and résumé to fit the specific job of interest. Send it to the prospective employer. Many large employers prefer to receive job inquiries via the Internet, often through their website. If so, follow the application instructions to the letter. Other employers prefer a written letter and résumé. It's often smart to do both.

If you have not received a response to a job inquiry within two or three weeks, send a follow-up inquiry by adding a brief new opening sentence to your cover letter and send the revised letter with your résumé. When employers express interest in you as a prospective employee, they may request that you complete their official job application form. Be accurate in your responses.

DID YOU KNOW?

Sean's Success Story

Sean began his college career without a specific major in mind, although he knew he was interested in working with people. During his sophomore year, Sean took a class in public relations. He enjoyed the class immensely and realized that the public relations field fit his interests, abilities, and aptitudes. He declared a major in communications and talked to his advisor about jobs he could take to help him understand the field better and make good contacts for the future. Sean volunteered at his local chamber of commerce and signed up for an internship at a public relations firm in his senior year. At graduation, he mapped out a career plan and soon found a job in a small public relations firm that would help him learn all of the various aspects of running such a firm. Sean has been with the company for two years and was promoted to project manager. His long-term goal is to one day own his own public relations firm.

DID YOU KNOW?

How to Stay Positive in a Weak Job Market

Today's weak job market is causing financial strains for many and can delay career advancement. It has psychological impacts as well. These strategies can help you cope.

1. *Stay physically active and eat well. Exercise and staying fit have both physical and psychological benefits.*

2. *Be up front about your anxiety, frustration, stress, and even fear. Share your concerns with others from time to time.*

3. *Maintain a positive frame of mind. Delays are not permanent and the market will turn around.*

4. *Stay involved in your professional network.*

5. *Volunteer both for the good you will be doing and for the possibilities for networking it provides.*

job interview
Formal meeting between employer and potential employee to discuss job qualifications and suitability.

Interview for Success

The interview is the single most important part of your search for employment. A **job interview** is a formal meeting to discuss an individual's job qualifications and suitability for an employment position. When you are invited for an interview, be prepared. Projecting a positive attitude will help. Don't volunteer information in an interview that might hurt you, but respond to questions accurately. Misrepresenting facts, making even small distortions, will cast doubt on everything in your résumé and on everything you said in the interview. Malcolm Gladwell, author of *Blink*, argues that when you meet someone for the first time, "your mind takes about two seconds to jump to a series of conclusions." It is not intuition or a snap judgment; it is rapid rational thinking. Your appearance, smile, handshake, first few sentences, and tone of voice send critically important information to the interviewer. Practice your "blink" before every interview. (See www.gladwell.com/blink/.)

Do Some Research Before the Interview Before the interview, research the company. Try to know more about it than the interviewer. Learn how the company makes money, its operations and history, profitability, expansion plans, and other recent developments. Also research the company's competitors and the industry. You can find details on the Internet as most companies have websites. Know what the company is good at and how this relates to your skills. Be familiar with the job description. Find out what it is like to work at the specific company. When you do a background check on companies, you can seek out candid posts from current or former employees about salaries, company culture, and lousy bosses. However, be wary about unsubstantiated information. See Jobster (www.jobster.com), LinkedIn (www.linkedin.com), and Vault (www.vault.com).

Prepare Responses for Anticipated Interview Questions
Your responsibilities during the interview are to remain calm, reveal your personality, be honest, convey your best characteristics, handle questions well, and communicate your enthusiasm about the job. Always answer in a controlled manner. During the interview, be confident that you are the best person for the job and project yourself accordingly.

Job interviewers seem to ask similar questions. You should prepare in advance an articulate response for the following inquiries:

1. Tell me about yourself.
2. How would your instructors and previous employers describe you?
3. What did you like the most about college, and the least?
4. Tell me what you know about our company.
5. Why are you interested in working for this company?
6. What unique abilities and experiences qualify you for the job?
7. Describe some of your strengths and weaknesses.
8. What experiences have you had working with teams and coordinating such efforts?
9. Give an example of an ethical challenge you faced and tell how you handled it.
10. Relate a time when you were faced with a very difficult problem and how you handled it.
11. Describe the supervisors who motivated you to do your best work.
12. What were some of the best and worst aspects of your last job?
13. What do you do in your leisure time?
14. Describe your career plans for five and ten years from now.

Create Positive Responses to Negative Questions Be prepared to "turn any negative into a positive" when asked such questions. One popular negative question, of course, is, "What are your weaknesses?" Interviewers who ask these types of questions want to determine whether the applicant possesses certain qualities such as honesty, self-awareness, humility, sincerity, zest, and skill in managing shortcomings and mistakes. Denying weakness or being evasive means you don't get the job.

Practice your interview skills beforehand. Practice your responses, especially to negative questions. Perhaps make a videotape of a mock interview, and after evaluating your performance, do it again.

Compile Revealing Personal Stories Assemble some personal stories about yourself that reveal some of your better characteristics. You could have five or more interviews for a single job, and during the interview process, you are expected to talk about yourself. Therefore, prepare by writing down some concise stories or statements, perhaps about the time you took over caregiver duties for your siblings while your mother was hospitalized, or facilitated resolving some internal conflicts among the officers in your student club, or assisted a high school teacher to coordinate and supervise 20 students on a field trip, or worked 14 straight hours at Walmart during a weather emergency. Preparing as many as a dozen stories will give you many ways to talk about your positive qualities without just saying, "I'm good." Everyone says that! Communicate that message about yourself in part by telling stories to illustrate your better qualities.

Prepare Questions to Ask the Interviewer A key to success in any interview is to show your enthusiasm and interest in the position and organization. Compliment the interviewer's company based on some facts learned in your pre-interview research. Prepare some questions to ask, perhaps about future company plans, company policies, employee benefits, specific duties, and job expectations. You may want to inquire about the corporate culture, too. Write down your questions so you will have your thoughts clear in your mind.

Personality Tests One-third of employers give job candidates personality tests assessing team orientation, strengths important to a job, emotional intelligence, motivation, and true work-style inclinations. Don't try to game the employer by telling them what they want to hear—the "right" answer. Being honest confirms what the prospective employer already knows about you. Earlier in the chapter you were advised to take

DID YOU KNOW?

How to Interview over a Meal

More people lose a job interview over lunch than during the formal interview because they fail to realize that going to lunch is a continuation of the interview rather than a social situation. Employers want to hire people with some degree of refinement, people who will mix well with clients and executives. It is smart to engage in conversation over a meal, of course, but let the boss do most of the talking. Good etiquette tips include the following:

- Order something that is less expensive than what the host has ordered.
- Keep your elbows off the table.
- Break (don't cut) your bread or roll before buttering.
- Use the bread knife (the small knife to the left of your plate).

- Use the small fork outermost from the plate for the first course.
- Don't salt and pepper your meal before tasting it.
- Cut your meat one bite at a time.
- Don't talk with food in your mouth.
- Don't order beer, wine, or liquor.
- Avoid ordering soup or pastas because they can be too messy.
- Be extremely polite and respectful of the servers.
- Never complain about a meal.
- Leave it to your host to signal the server.
- If confused, be patient and follow the lead of the host.
- Leave your napkin on your chair when excusing yourself.
- When the meal is over, thank the host and state that you want the job.

some personality inventories on your own. That earlier preparation can help you be more effective should an employer want you to take such tests.

Be Ready for Telephone Interviews Present yourself in a professional manner when returning a telephone call or engaging in an interview. Have a pen or pencil and paper handy. Be aware of distractions in your surroundings, such as traffic noise. If necessary, arrange to call the interviewer back when you find a quiet place. Speak clearly, and eliminate the "uhs" and "ums." The interviewer will notice if you take a sip of coffee or a bite out of a bagel. Try to eliminate as many annoyances as possible to improve your chances of getting the job. Professional recruiters estimate that perhaps only 20 percent of college seniors adequately prepare for their campus interviews.

After the Interview, Evaluate It and Send a Thank-You Note After a job interview, take a few minutes to objectively evaluate your performance. Write down any questions you were asked that were different from what you expected and make some notes about ways to improve in your next interview. The more interviews you have, the better you will be able to present yourself. Also, immediately mail a thank-you note expressing your appreciation for the opportunity to interview and restate your interest in the position. Only e-mail a thank-you note if you are sure that method will be acceptable to the interviewer.

Negotiate and Accept the Job

Wait until after the job has been firmly offered to discuss salary. Do not be the first to give a definitive dollar amount. Ask for the salary range for the position. Your objective in negotiating is to obtain a salary 20 percent above the highest figure because you are an exceptional candidate and you will perform at the highest level anticipated. Don't sell yourself short.

Focus on both gross and net pay. A gross income of $37,000 shrinks to about $30,000 after subtracting federal income, Social Security, and Medicare taxes. Additional deductions for contributions for medical care, retirement, and flexible benefits may drop the take-home pay to $27,000, or $2250 a month. You can then add back the value of employer-paid benefits such as a retirement plan.

Comparing salary offers from employers located in different cities can be tricky without sufficient information on the approximate cost of living in each community. Sometimes those costs vary drastically. Information from the Internet reveals, for example, that life in a high-cost city such as Seattle is more expensive than life in a lower-cost city such as Portland, Oregon. The data are reported in index form, with the "average cost" community being given a rating of 100.

The following example demonstrates how to compare salary offers in two cities. Assume the Seattle (city 1) index is 138, and Portland's (city 2) is 114. You want to compare the buying power of a salary offer of $52,000 in Portland with a $65,000 offer in Seattle. The costs can be compared using Equations (2.1) and (2.2).

$$\text{Salary in city } 1 \times \frac{\text{index city } 2}{\text{index city } 1} = \text{equivalent salary in city } 2$$

$$\text{Seattle salary of } \$65,000 \times \frac{114}{138} = \$53,695 \text{ in buying power in Portland}$$

(2.1)

Thus, the $65,000 Seattle salary offer would buy $53,695 of goods and services in Portland, an amount more than the Portland offer of $52,000. All things being equal (and they are both nice cities), the Seattle offer is slightly better ($53,695 − $52,000 = $1,695).

To compare the buying power of salaries in the other direction, reverse the formula:

$$\text{Salary in city } 2 \times \frac{\text{index city } 1}{\text{index city } 2} = \text{equivalent salary in city } 1$$

(2.2)

$$\text{Portland salary of } \$52{,}000 \times \frac{138}{114} = \$62{,}947 \text{ in buying power in Seattle}$$

Thus, the $52,000 Portland offer can buy only $62,947 of goods and services in Seattle—an amount less than the $65,000 Seattle salary offer. All things being equal, the Seattle offer is still better. For fairer comparisons, add the value of employee benefits and redo the calculations. Note that non-salary benefits are typically 25 to 30 percent of the salary for persons with a college degree.

You may compare salary figures and the cost of living in different communities at the following websites (most use the ACCRA Cost of Living data [www.coli.org/]):

- CityRating.com (www.cityrating.com/costofliving.asp).
- CNNMoney.com (http://cgi.money.cnn.com/tools/costofliving/costofliving.html)
- Moving.com (www.moving.com/find_a_place/relosmart/rs.asp)
- Realtor.com (www.homefair.com/homefair/readart.html?art=bc_research)
- Salary.com (http://swz.salary.com/costoflivingwizard/layoutscripts/coll_start.asp)

Be comfortable with silence, and wait for a response. If the offer is less than what you were expecting, explain that point. Be firm but amicable. This will enhance the employer's respect for you. Tell the employer that you are not willing to start at the bottom or middle of the salary ladder. Reiterate your two or three strongest selling points. Be certain to make a short list of these points beforehand. If the employer states that the offer is final, reply that you need a day or two to think it over. Never turn down an offer until you are absolutely positive you must do so.

DID YOU KNOW?

How to Get a Raise

Find out what people in your field earn by talking with others, reviewing trade publications, and checking online at sites such as Glassdoor.com, vault.com, payscale.com, salary.com, and HotJobs.com. Then talk with your boss and write down well-defined, achievable, and measurable goals that you can work toward. This may occur during a formal annual review. Document your accomplishments in writing and keep records. Throughout the year, perhaps on a quarterly basis, discuss these with your boss. Do so in brief sit-down meetings rather than in brief hallway conversations.

Schedule a meeting with your boss before the scheduled time for the annual personnel review. Avoid mentioning how much you need a big raise and focus on your performance. If the boss cannot give you all the money you deserve, ask for a bigger bonus, enhanced health or retirement benefits, a more flexible work schedule, a change in work hours, permission to occasionally telecommute, or more vacation time.

Seattle has a lot to offer, but it comes at a price.

DID YOU KNOW?

Deciding Where and Whether to Relocate for a Job

Comparing salary offers among various cities where you might work is only part of the decision where and whether to relocate. Here are some resources for other important aspects of the decision:

The cost of housing—www.domania.com and www.zillow.com

Quality of life issues—money.cnn.com/best/bplive and www.homefair.com
Quality of schools—www.schoolmatters.com
Moving costs—www.relocation.com/library/moving_calculator.html

DID YOU KNOW?

Turn Bad Habits into Good Ones

Do You Do This?	*Do This Instead!*
Avoid getting to know your professors	Visit one professor in his/her office on a regular basis
Ignore student professional associations	Join and take a leadership role in at least one association
Still use an old résumé	Update your résumé annually
Simply change the name/address when writing a cover letter	Write a new cover letter for each job application
Plan to move back to your hometown after graduation	Explore employment opportunities in several new cities
Focus primarily on gross pay when deciding on a job opportunity	Factor take-home pay, employee benefits, and cost of living into your job decisions

If the terms are right, accept the job. Give your new employer your acceptance orally as well as in writing. Obtain a letter confirming your acceptance of the job at the agreed-upon salary with benefits such as moving expenses, flexible hours, and extra vacation days.

Periodically Update Your Career Plan

Getting that first job does not mean that your career planning efforts are over. Indeed, they have only just begun. You already know that employers formally evaluate their employees on a regular basis. You should do the same for your career plan. You want to assess whether you are progressing satisfactorily toward the goals you set earlier. This progress can be affected by changes you have undergone personally, the duties you have been asked to perform on your job, the nature of your chosen industry, and new opportunities that have emerged in the marketplace. At a minimum you should go back through the six career planning steps outlined earlier in this chapter on an annual basis.

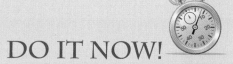

DO IT NOW!

You know more about personal finance after reading this chapter, so get started right now by:

1. *Preparing or updating your résumé.*
2. *Contacting your school's placement office to explore careers in your field.*
3. *Visiting one of your professors to seek a mentoring relationship.*

✓ Concept Check 2.3

1. Explain how networking can be used to one's advantage in career planning.

2. Offer suggestions on correctly assembling a résumé and cover letter, and explain how the two documents differ.

3. Explain how to compare salary and living costs in different cities.

4. Summarize the best methods to identify job opportunities.

5. List five suggestions for interviewing with success.

WHAT DO YOU RECOMMEND NOW?

Now that you have read the chapter on the importance of career planning, what do you recommend to Ashley in the case at the beginning of the chapter regarding:

1. Clarifying her values and lifestyle trade-offs in career planning?
2. Enhancing her career-related experiences before graduation?
3. Creating career plans and goals?
4. Understanding her work-style personality?
5. Identifying job opportunities?

BIG PICTURE SUMMARY OF LEARNING OBJECTIVES

LO1. **Identify the key steps in successful career planning.**

Career planning is identifying an employment pathway that aligns with your interests and abilities and that is expected to provide the lifestyle and work style you find enjoyable and satisfying. It includes defining your values, making lifestyle trade-offs, clarifying career-related interests, reviewing your talents, understanding employment trends, creating career goals, and targeting preferred employers.

LO2. **Analyze the financial and legal aspects of employment.**

The financial side of career planning includes comparing salary and living costs in different cities and placing values on employee benefits.

LO3. **Practice effective employment search strategies.**

Smart job search strategies include networking, obtaining excellent reference letters, compiling revealing stories, assembling a résumé and cover letter, identifying job opportunities, and interviewing for success.

LET'S TALK ABOUT IT

1. **Interviewing Tips.** List three interviewing tips for new college graduates looking for employment during sluggish economic times.

2. **Interview Mistakes.** Thinking about some common mistakes that people make in job interviews, which five are the worst? Make a list of ten things people should do to improve success in an interview.

3. **Career Trade-offs.** People regularly make decisions in career planning that have trade-offs. List three career decisions that people are likely to face, and identify some economic, psychic, and lifestyle trade-offs for each.

4. **Keeping Track Topics.** Review the task areas in the Decision-Making Worksheet "Keeping Track of Your Job Search," and identify what you think are the five that likely are the most difficult for people to accomplish. For each of the five, offer a suggestion that might help people accomplish the task.

DO THE MATH

1. **Economic Trade-off of Graduate School.** Delores Sotomajor hopes to earn an extra $600,000 over her remaining 40-year working career by going to night school to obtain a master's degree. If her income projection is correct, that's an average of $15,000 more income a year. Delores's employer is willing to pay $45,000 toward the $60,000 schooling costs, so she must pay out $15,000 of her own money.

   (a) What is the forgone lost future value of her $15,000 over the 40 years at 6 percent? (Hint: See Appendix A.1.)

   (b) What would be the forgone lost future value of $60,000 over 40 years if Delores had to pay all the costs for her master's degree? (Hint: See Appendix A.1.)

2. **Comparing Salary Offers.** Using Equations (2.1) or (2.2), if the cost-of-living index was 132 for Chicago and 114 for San Antonio, compare the buying power of a $50,000 salary in Chicago with a $47,000 offer in San Antonio.

3. **Future Value of Employer's Match.** Johann Winkle's employer makes a matching contribution of $1200 a year to his 401(k) retirement account at work. If the dollar amount of the employer's contribution increases 4 percent annually, how much will the employer contribute to the plan in the twentieth year from now? (Hint: See Appendix A.1.)

4. **Cashing Out 401(k) Plan.** Betty Amarrada has accepted a new job and is thinking about cashing out the $30,000 she has built up in her employer's 401(k) plan to use to buy a new car. If, instead, she left the funds in the plan and they earn 7 percent annually for the next 30 years, how much would Betty have in her plan? (Hint: See Appendix A.1.)

FINANCIAL PLANNING CASES

CASE 1

Harry and Belinda Johnson Consider Inflation and Children

Throughout this book, we will present a continuing narrative about Harry and Belinda Johnson. Following is a brief description of the lives of this couple.

Harry graduated with a bachelor's degree in interior design last spring from a large Midwestern university near his hometown. Belinda has a degree in information technology from a university on the West Coast and is employed in a medium-size public relations firm. Harry and Belinda both worked on their school's student newspapers and met at a conference during their junior year in college. They were married last June and live in an apartment in Kansas City. They will face many financial challenges over the next 20 years, as they buy their first home, decide on life insurance needs, begin a family, change jobs, and invest for retirement.

   (a) Harry receives $3000 in interest income annually from a trust fund set up by his deceased father's estate. The amount will never change. What will be the buying power of $3000 in ten years if inflation rises at 3 percent a year? (Hint: Use Appendix A.2.)

   (b) Belinda and Harry have discussed starting a family but decided to wait for perhaps five years in order to get their careers off to a good start and organize their personal finances. They also know that having children is expensive. They figure that the extra expense of a child would be about $5000 annually until high school graduation. How much money will they likely cumulatively spend on a child over 18 years assuming a 3 percent inflation rate? (Hint: Use Appendix A.3.)

CASE 2

Victor and Maria Hernandez Consider a Career Change

Throughout this book, we will present a continuing narrative about Victor and Maria Hernandez. Following is a brief description of the lives of this couple.

Victor and Maria, both in their late 30s, have two children: John, age 13, and Joseph, age 15. Victor has had a long sales career with a retail appliance store. Maria works part time as a medical records assistant. Victor is somewhat satisfied with his career but has always wondered about a career as a teacher in a public school. He would have to take a year off work to go to college to obtain his teaching certificate, and that would mean giving up his $43,000 salary for a year. Victor expects that he could earn about the same income as a teacher.

(a) What would his annual income be after 20 years as a teacher if he received an average 5 percent raise every year? (Hint: Use Appendix A.1.)

(b) Victor could earn $4000 each year teaching during the summers. What is the accumulated future value of earning those annual amounts over 20 years assuming a 5 percent raise every year? (Hint: Use Appendix A.3.)

CASE 3

Julia Price's Career Plans Change

Julia has recently undergone a severe career crisis. After nearly ten years as a professional engineer, her position was phased out by her company due to a loss of government contracts, and she has been offered a position in the marketing department. The new job will require that she interact with purchasing agents for various companies that are current and potential customers of her company. The job pays more but will require considerable travel. She will be using her engineering background, but the primary tasks all will relate to presenting herself and her company in the best possible light to these other firms. Julia thinks she should take the marketing job offer and make a personal commitment to doing it for one year and, if she does not truly enjoy the work, seek a new engineering job within her company or at another employer. Offer your opinions about her thinking.

CASE 4

Matching Yourself with a Job

After completing his associate of arts degree four months ago from a community college in Ashland, Kentucky, Jimmy Jackson has answered more than a dozen advertisements and interviewed several times in his effort to get a sales job, but he has had no success. Jimmy has never done sales work before, but he did take some business classes in college, including "Personal Selling." After some of the interviews,

Jimmy telephoned some of those potential employers only to find that even though they liked him, they said they typically hired only those people with previous sales experience or who seemed to possess terrific potential.

(a) If Jimmy actually were well suited for sales, which work values and work-style factors do you think he would rate as "very important"?

(b) What would you recommend to Jimmy regarding how to find out about the depth of his interest in a sales career?

(c) Assuming Jimmy has appropriate personal qualities and academic strengths to be successful in a sales career, what additional strategies should he consider to better market himself?

CASE 5

Career Promotion Opportunity

Nina and Ting Guo of Lima, Ohio, have been together for eight years, having married just after completing college. Nina has been working as an insurance agent ever since. Ting began working as a family counselor for the state of Illinois last year after completing his master's degree in counseling. Recently Nina's boss commented confidentially that he was going to recommend Nina to be the next person promoted, given a raise of about $15,000, and relocated to the home office in St. Louis, Missouri. Nina thinks that if offered the opportunity she would like to take it, even if it means that Ting will have to resign from his new job.

(a) What suggestions can you offer Nina when she gets home from work and wants to discuss with her husband her likely career promotion?

(b) What lifestyle factors and costs and benefits issues should Nina and Ting probably discuss?

BE YOUR OWN PERSONAL FINANCIAL MANAGER

1. **Work-Style Personality.** Do you know your preferred work-style personality? Take the time to complete the worksheet on page 41 or you can use Worksheet 6: What Is My Work-Style Personality from "My Personal Financial Planner."

   MY PERSONAL FINANCIAL PLANNER

2. **Values Clarification.** Go online and do a Web search for "values clarification assessment" to bring up a long list of possible values clarification exercises. Complete one or more exercises and then compare the results to

what you have been thinking in terms of your academic major in college and possible careers.

3. **Career Field Exploration.** Visit the Career Guide to Industries at www.bls.gov/oco/cg to determine the earnings, benefits, and employment outlook for a position in a career field that interests you. Complete Worksheet 7: Career Field Research from "My Personal Financial Planner" to write up your results including an assessment of how well

   MY PERSONAL FINANCIAL PLANNER

your work-style personality and values fit the career field that you researched.

4. **Compare Salary Offers.** Use two actual salary offers or two desired offers in two cities of your choosing to compare the salary offers based on the different costs of living in the two cities. See Worksheet 8: Comparing Salary Offers in Two Different Cities from "My Personal Financial Planner" as a guide for your analysis.

MY PERSONAL FINANCIAL PLANNER

5. **Assess the Benefits of a Second Income.** Using real or example data, assess the benefits of a second income for a dual-earner household in your salary range. Use the example provided in the text on page 46 or Worksheet 9: Assessing the Benefits of a Second Income from "My Personal Financial Planner" for your assessment.

MY PERSONAL FINANCIAL PLANNER

ON THE 'NET

Go to the Web pages indicated to complete these exercises. You can also go to the *Garman/Forgue* companion website at www.cengagebrain.com for an expanded list of exercises. Under General Business, select the title of this text. Click on the Internet Exercises link for this chapter.

1. **Research the Occupational Outlook Handbook.** Go to the website for the *Occupational Outlook Handbook* at www.bls.gov/oco/home.htm. Select two occupational areas that are of interest to you, and for each, determine the likely starting salary, career path, future salary expectations, and demand for people with the skills appropriate for the occupation.

2. **Research the National Unemployment Rate.** Go to the website for the Bureau of Labor Statistics' assessment of the labor outlook in the United States at www.bls.gov/bls/employment.htm. Browse through

the information provided to determine the current national unemployment rate for the nation as a whole and for a city or area of interest to you. Compare current statistics with those of one year ago and with projections for five and ten years in the future.

3. **Research a Career of Interest.** Check the U.S. Department of Labor's Career Guide to Industries at www.bls.gov/oco/cg to learn about the earnings, benefits, educational requirements, and employment outlook for a career of interest to you. Make a written summary of your findings.

4. **Check Out Income Levels.** Are your current perceptions about the income level typical for various career fields correct? Visit www.payscale.com and research salary data on five to seven fields including your own.

ACTION INVOLVEMENT PROJECTS

1. **Interview a Human Resource Manager.** Use the Internet and/or Yellow Pages to find a local company that employs people in your prospective career field. Request an interview with the human resource manager. Ask about salary levels, employee benefits, and the career ladder. Make a written summary of your findings.

2. **Prepare a Résumé and Cover Letter.** Using the newspaper want ads or Monster.com find a job listing for a position in your career field. Prepare a résumé and cover letter for the job. Take the job listing and

documents to your faculty advisor and ask him or her for feedback.

3. **Where Do You Want to Live?** It is highly likely that one of the best job opportunities for you at graduation will require that you move away from your hometown and/or where you went to college. While that new location is unknown now, it is not too early to begin thinking of where you might need and/or want to live. Use the list of websites in the box on page 58 to answer the four questions covered in the box for five different cities. Make a table that summarizes your findings.

Visit the Garman/Forgue companion website at **www.cengagebrain.com**.

Financial Statements, Tools, and Budgets

3

YOU MUST BE KIDDING, RIGHT?

The median net worth of American families is $95,000, and the mean amount is $453,000. (Those with high net worth pull the mean above the median.) What are the median and mean figures for families headed by a person less than 35 years of age?

A. $17,000 and $90,000

C. $48,000 and $180,000

B. $31,000 and $130,000

D. $61,000 and $199,000

The answer is A, $17,000 median and $90,000 mean. Median net worth goes up with age. It is $85,000 for families ages 35 to 44, $180,000 for ages 45 to 54, and $160,000 for ages 55 to 64. It's all about saving money and building wealth over time!

LEARNING OBJECTIVES

After reading this chapter, you should be able to:

1 Identify your financial values, goals, and strategies.

2 Use balance sheets and cash-flow statements to measure your financial health and progress.

3 Evaluate your financial strength and progress using financial ratios.

4 Collect and organize the financial records necessary for managing your personal finances.

5 Achieve your financial goals through budgeting.

WHAT DO YOU RECOMMEND?

Robert and Nicole Patterson, both age 26, have been married for four years and have no children. Robert is a licensed electrician earning $46,000 per year, and Nicole earns $41,000 annually as a middle-school teacher. Robert would like to go to half time on his job and return to school on a part-time basis; he is one year short of finishing his bachelor's degree in engineering. His education expenses would be about $10,000 per year, which could be partially covered by student loans. He has not yet discussed his plans with Nicole.

Robert and Nicole have recently started saving for retirement through their employment and have set aside some savings for emergencies. They have substantial credit card debt and are still paying off their student loans. The couple rents a two-bedroom apartment. Robert always thought it smart to save all of their receipts, bank statements, and other financial documents. His system for organizing their records is very simple; each month he puts everything in a manila envelope and then puts the 12 envelopes into a box at the end of the year.

Robert knows that his educational plans will have financial implications for the couple. He wants to factor these financial issues into his discussion with Nicole about his plans. To this point, they have never developed financial statements or explicit financial goals.

What do you recommend to Robert for his talk with Nicole on the subject of financial planning regarding:

1. Determining what they own and owe?

2. Better understanding their patterns of family income and expenditure?

© 2010 Jupiterimages Corporation

3. Using the information in Robert's newly prepared financial statements to summarize the family's financial situation?

4. Setting financial goals?

5. Evaluating their financial progress?

6. Setting up a record-keeping system to better serve their needs?

7. Starting a budgeting process to guide saving and spending?

Half of all adults say they do not budget. Four in ten say they are living beyond their means and rate themselves as fair or poor in managing money. To maintain a desired lifestyle, they spend every dollar they earn. They live paycheck to paycheck, and they often turn to credit cards. These people are incompetent in money matters, and their choices will forever make them the "have nots" in society rather than the "haves." Clearly, living above your means can lead to financial ruin at a young age. However, this does not have to happen to you!

This chapter provides the nitty-gritty details on how to go about becoming financially successful. You can attain your financial goals by setting goals and strategies that are consistent with your values, even during times of economic austerity. Along the way, you follow your spending plan, take appropriate actions to achieve results, and regularly measure your financial strength and progress. No matter what your previous financial background and experiences, applying the knowledge within this chapter will help you enjoy financial decision making and successfully manage your money.

FINANCIAL VALUES, GOALS, AND STRATEGIES

Identifying your financial values and goals sets the stage for financial success. Values and goals keep a balance between spending and saving and help you stay committed to your financial plans. Once goals are set, you can develop the strategies necessary for their achievement. **Financial planning**, the process of developing and implementing a coordinated series of financial plans, can help you achieve financial success. By planning your finances, you seek to manage your income and wealth so that you reach your financial goals.

Figure 3-1 provides an overview of effective personal financial planning, and Table 3-1 illustrates one couple's overall financial plan. Your managerial efforts push you toward

LEARNING OBJECTIVE

Identify your financial values, goals, and strategies.

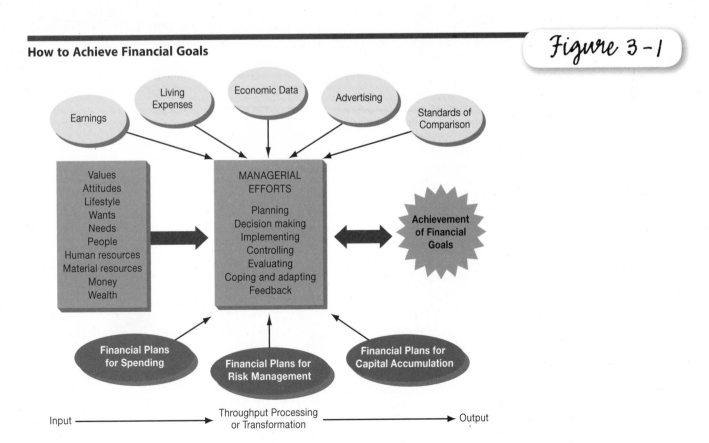

How to Achieve Financial Goals

Figure 3-1

Table 3-1

Financial Plans, Goals, and Objectives for Harry (Age 23) and Belinda (Age 22) Johnson, Prepared in February 2012

Financial Plan Areas	Long-Term Goals and Objectives	Short-Term Goals and Objectives
FOR SPENDING		
Evaluate and plan major purchases	Purchase a new car in two years.	Begin saving $200 a month for a down payment for a new car.
Manage debt	Keep installment debt under 10 percent of take-home pay.	Pay off charge cards at end of each month and do not finance any purchases of appliances or other similar products.
FOR RISK MANAGEMENT		
Medical costs	Avoid large medical costs.	Maintain employer-subsidized medical insurance policy by paying $135 monthly premium.
Property and casualty losses	Always have renter's or homeowner's insurance.	Make semiannual premium payment of $220 on renter's insurance policy.
	Always have maximum automobile insurance coverage.	Make premium payments of $440 on automobile insurance policy.
Liability losses	Eventually buy $1 million liability insurance.	Rely on $100,000 policy purchased from same source as automobile insurance policy.
Premature death	Have adequate life insurance coverage for both as well as lots of financial investments so the survivor would not have any financial worries.	Maintain employer-subsidized life insurance on Belinda. Buy some life insurance for Harry. Start some investments.
Income loss from disability	Buy sufficient disability insurance.	Rely on sick days and seek disability insurance through private insurers.
FOR CAPITAL ACCUMULATION		
Tax fund	Have enough money for taxes (but not too much) withheld from monthly salaries by both employers to cover eventual tax liabilities.	Confirm that employer withholding of taxes is sufficient. Have extra money withheld to cover additional tax liability because of income on trust from Harry's deceased father.
Revolving savings fund	Always have sufficient cash in local accounts to meet monthly and annual anticipated budget expense needs.	Develop cash-flow calendar to ascertain needs. Put money into revolving savings fund to build it up quickly to the proper balance. Keep all funds in interest-earning accounts.
Emergency fund	Build up monetary assets equivalent to three months' take-home pay.	Put $150 per month into an emergency fund until it totals one month's take-home pay.
Education	Maintain educational skills and credentials to remain competitive. Have employer assist in paying for Belinda to earn a master of business administration (MBA). Have Harry complete a master of fine arts (MFA), possibly a PhD in interior design.	Both take one graduate class per term.
Savings	Always have a nice-size savings balance. Regularly save to achieve goals. Save a portion of any extra income or gifts. Save $26,000 for a down payment on a home to be bought within five years.	Save enough to pay cash for a good-quality DVD player. Pay off Visa credit card balance of $390 soon. Begin saving $400 per month for a down payment on a new home.
Investment	Own substantial shares of a conservative mutual fund that will pay dividends equivalent to about 10 percent of family income at age 45. Own some real estate and common stocks.	Start investing in a mutual fund before next year.
Retirement	Retire at age 60 or earlier on income that is the same as the take-home pay earned just before retirement.	Establish individual retirement accounts (IRAs) for Harry and Belinda before next year. Contribute the maximum possible amount to employer-sponsored retirement accounts.
Estate planning	Provide for surviving spouse.	Each spouse makes a will.

achieving financial success. The couple has made plans in 15 specific areas spread across three broad categories: (1) spending, (2) risk management, and (3) capital accumulation.

Values Define Your Financial Success

Your **values** provide the underlying support and rationale for your financial and lifestyle goals. Your values are your fundamental beliefs about what is important, desirable, and worthwhile. They serve as the basis for your goals. All of us differ in the ways we value education, spiritual life, health, employment, credit use, family life, and many other factors. Personal financial goals grow out of these values because we inevitably consider some things more important or desirable than others. We express our values, in part, by the ways we spend, save, invest, and donate our money.

One major benefit of financial planning is using money wisely. People who are smart about personal finance typically value saving some of their income. They adhere to the personal finance philosophy of "Pay myself first." If you earn money, shouldn't you be "paid" first? Successful money managers do this instead of spending it all or, even worse, spending even more than they earn by using lots of credit. They establish a current spending level based on the necessities of life. They set aside money for future spending, such as for a vehicle purchase, home, child's education, vacation home, and living expenses during the years of retirement.

Financial Goals Follow from Your Values

Successful financial planning evolves from your financial goals. **Financial goals** are the specific long-, intermediate-, and short-term objectives to be attained through financial planning and management efforts. Financial and lifestyle goals should be consistent with your values. To serve as a rational basis for financial actions, they must be stated explicitly in terms of purpose, dollar amounts, and the projected dates by which they are to be achieved.

Set Specific Goals Setting goals helps you visualize the gap between your current financial status and where you want to be in the future. Make a list of your goals. Examples of general financial goals include finishing a college education, paying off debts (including education loans), meeting financial emergencies, taking a vacation, owning a home, accumulating funds to send children through college, owning your own business, creating peace of mind, ensuring family harmony, and having financial independence at retirement.

None of these goals, however, is specific enough to guide financial behavior. Specific goals should be measurable, attainable, relevant, and time-related. Saving for retirement should begin with a calculation of how much money you will need in retirement (see Chapter 17), and saving for retirement should start soon after you begin a full-time job. Saving for a child's education should begin when your first child is born, if not earlier.

Put Target Dates on Your Financial Goals Setting target dates for financial goals is important for success. Consider the example of Heather Vogel, a dance instructor from Champaign, Illinois. Heather has just made the last $347 payment on her four-year car loan. She does not like being in debt, so she does not want to take out such a large loan again. Heather would like to put at least part of the money she has been paying monthly for the loan into a savings account, which would allow her to replace her current vehicle in five years. Heather figures that it would take about $22,500 to buy a similar inexpensive high-mileage vehicle in five years. She assumes she could earn a 2 percent return on her savings and, using Appendix A.3, has determined that she would need to save $4323 per year ($22,500 ÷ 5.2040 for five years at 2 percent interest), or roughly $360 per month.

values
Fundamental beliefs about what is important, desirable, and worthwhile.

financial goals
Specific objectives addressed by planning and managing finances.

FINANCIAL POWER POINT

Turn Your Goals into Reality

The path toward turning a wish into reality begins with writing it down. If buying a condo is your goal, tape a photograph of a beautiful one onto your refrigerator. Then tell others about your financial goal. The constant reminders will help you make it into a reality.

Heather's thinking offers a good example of how financial goal setting works. She recognized the value she put on staying out of debt and proceeded to the general goal of trying to pay cash for her next car. After determining an overall dollar amount needed, she broke that amount down into first annual and then monthly amounts. For only $13 more per month than she has been paying on her loan ($360 – $347), Heather will be able to pay cash for her next car. This is the sacrifice she is willing to make to avoid using credit to buy a vehicle in the future.

Prioritize Your Goals   Once your financial goals are clearly identified, you can decide which are the most important. You simply prioritize the list by making trade-offs on what you can do with your finances in the near term as well as in the more distant future.

Financial Goals Require Wealth-Building Principles

Following are several wealth-building principles that may help you achieve your financial goals:

1. Set clear financial goals both in the short and long term.
2. Save by paying yourself first out of your paycheck.
3. Pay credit card balances in full each month.
4. Spend less than you earn.
5. Participate in the retirement plan at work.
6. Take full advantage of your employer's match on retirement savings.
7. Buy a home for the tax advantages.
8. Pay off your home before retirement.
9. Be patient when investing for the long term.
10. Live every day knowing that your financial future is under control.

Financial Strategies Guide Your Financial Success

financial strategies
Pre-established action plans implemented in specific situations.

Financial strategies are pre-established plans of action to be implemented in specific situations. Heather Vogel implemented a very effective strategy in the preceding example. That is, when a loan has been repaid, start a savings program with the same monthly payment amount. Saving may be easier for Heather if she arranges for the amount she'd like to save to be automatically deposited from her paycheck into her savings account. Another effective savings strategy is to arrange for one-half of every raise to go into savings before you become accustomed to the additional income.

Heather's actions have nothing to do with her earning more money. Many people falsely think that being wealthy is a function of how much you earn or inherit. Accumulating wealth is much more related to your ability to understand trade-offs among current and future wants and make the sacrifices that will save money and generate wealth for you. In Heather's case, all that remains for her to do is to put the strategy into action. She can then review her strategy annually and adjust it as necessary to keep pace with her shifting circumstances.

DID YOU KNOW?

Money Topics to Discuss with Your Partner

Personal finances are complex enough for just one person, but when two people join their financial lives together, things can get very complicated. When you find the right partner, it is smart to do the following:

- **Change beneficiaries.** Life insurance policies, retirement accounts, and mutual fund accounts all have beneficiaries (the people who will receive the funds at your death) named when you set them up. (See Chapters 12, 15, 17, and 18.)

- **Coordinate employee benefits.** Couples often have two incomes today, so each has a menu of employee benefits from which to choose. As a result, one spouse may drop a benefit that is being received via the other's plan. For example, if one partner receives family coverage for health care for free or at a low monthly cost, perhaps the other can drop that aspect of his or her own plan. One spouse might then be able to add another benefit at no cost, such as paid education expenses. Your employee benefits officer can help you decide which options to select.

- **Update life insurance coverage.** Focus on term life insurance for the bulk of your needs. (See Chapter 12.)

- **Review auto and homeowner's insurance coverages.** Also inventory your personal property. (See Chapter 10.)

- **Update names with government agencies.** If one or both partners' names are changed as a result of your new status, you need to notify the Social Security Administration and driver's licensing office of that change. You will need to show your marriage certificate as proof of the change.

- **Close redundant bank accounts.** Reducing the number of accounts that each partner brings into the marriage can save money on account fees. Decide which accounts are "yours mine, or ours." (See Chapters 5 and 6 for more on managing accounts.)

- **Get out of debt.** One or both of you may bring debts into the new family. Because a couple can live together a little more cheaply than two individuals who live apart, funds can be freed up to pay off credit card, student, and other loans. This debt reduction has an added benefit: It sets the stage for getting a mortgage to buy your first home. (See Chapters 6, 7, and 9.)

- **Decide on how to manage money.** Decide on who pays what bills and makes investment decisions. Decide on whether or not each person will have individual control over certain money. Decide on who pays for the debt that precedes the relationship. Decide on who pays for gift giving. Decide on what money tasks you will do together, such as establishing annual financial goals, making purchases with debt, and agreeing on which expenditures require joint agreement, like an expense over $300. (See Chapter 5 for how to effectively discuss money matters.)

- **Save for retirement separately.** Day-to-day living expenses will go down somewhat when you team up as a couple. Use some of that money to allocate additional amounts to your individual retirement plans. (See Chapter 17.)

- **Update estate transfer plans.** With a new "number one" in your life, you should change (or set up) your will, durable power of attorney, living will, and health care proxy. (See Chapter 18 for more information on these documents.)

 Concept Check 3.1

1. Summarize the financial planning process.

2. Explain the relationships among financial values, goals, and strategies.

FINANCIAL STATEMENTS MEASURE YOUR FINANCIAL HEALTH AND PROGRESS

Financial statements are compilations of personal financial data that describe an individual's or family's current financial condition. They present a summary of assets and liabilities as well as income and spending of an individual or family. The two most useful statements are the balance sheet and the cash-flow statement.

A **balance sheet** (or **net worth statement**) describes an individual's or family's financial condition on a specified date (often January 1) by showing assets, liabilities, and net worth. It provides a current status report and includes information on what you own, what you owe, and what the net result would be if you paid off all of your debts. It answers the question "Where are you financially right now?"

A **cash-flow statement** (or **income and expense statement**) lists and summarizes income and expense transactions that have taken place over a specific period of time, such as a month or a year. It tells you where your money came from and where it went. It answers the question "Where did your money go?"

 LEARNING OBJECTIVE **2**

Use balance sheets and cash-flow statements to measure your financial health and progress.

financial statements
Snapshots that describe an individual's or family's current financial condition.

balance sheet (or net worth statement)
Snapshot of assets, liabilities, and net worth on a particular date.

cash-flow statement (or income and expense statement)
Summary of all income and expense transactions over a specific time period.

The Balance Sheet Is a Snapshot of Your Financial Status Right Now

To benchmark where you are on the wealth-building scale, determine your net worth. If you are indeed serious about your financial success, then you will sit down soon with pencil and paper or at your computer to see exactly where you stand. You do so by preparing your balance sheet, which summarizes the value of what you own minus what you owe. Your balance sheet should be updated at least once each year so that you can assess your progress. Net worth grows slowly, but it definitely increases over time. If you are successful in your career and follow the basic principles outlined in this book, there is no reason why you cannot have a net worth of $1 million, or $2 million or more, later in your life. Net worth typically peaks for people in their 60s and declines thereafter as they live off their financial nest egg in retirement.

Components of the Balance Sheet A balance sheet consists of three parts: assets, liabilities, and net worth. Your **assets** include everything you own that has monetary value. Your **liabilities** are your debts—amounts you owe to others. Your **net worth** is the dollar amount left when what is owed is subtracted from the dollar value of what is owned—that is, if all the assets were sold at the listed values and all debts were paid in full. Your net worth is the true measure of your financial wealth.

What Is Owned—Assets Are "The Things You Own" The assets section of the balance sheet lists items valued at their **fair market value**—what a willing buyer would pay a willing seller, not the amount originally paid or what it might be worth a year from now. It is useful to classify assets as monetary, tangible, or investment assets.

Monetary assets (also known as **liquid assets** or **cash equivalents**) include cash and low-risk near-cash items that can be readily converted to cash with little or no loss in value such as checking and savings accounts. They are primarily used for maintenance of living expenses, emergencies, savings, and payment of bills.

Tangible (or **use** or **lifestyle**) assets are personal property whose primary purpose is to provide maintenance of one's everyday lifestyle. Tangible assets, such as furniture and vehicles, generally depreciate in value over time.

Investment assets (also known as **capital assets**) include tangible and intangible items that have a relatively long life and high cost and that are acquired for the monetary benefits they provide, such as generating additional income and appreciation (or increasing in value). Examples include stocks and bonds. Investment assets generally appreciate and are dedicated to the maintenance of one's future level of living.

Following are some examples of each kind of asset.

Monetary Assets

- Cash (including cash on hand, checking accounts, savings accounts, savings bonds, certificates of deposit, and money market accounts)
- Tax refunds due
- Money owed to you by others

Tangible Assets

- Automobiles, motorcycles, boats, bicycles
- House, condominium, mobile home
- Household furnishings and appliances
- Personal property (jewelry, furs, tools, clothing)
- Other "big ticket" items

Investment Assets

- Stocks, bonds, mutual funds, gold, partnerships, art, IRAs
- Life insurance and annuities (cash values only)
- Real property (and anything fixed to it)
- Personal and employer-provided retirement accounts

---

assets
Everything you own that has monetary value.

liabilities
What you owe.

net worth
What's left when you subtract liabilities from assets.

monetary assets/liquid assets/ cash equivalents
Assets that can be used as cash.

tangible (use) assets
Personal property used to maintain your everyday lifestyle.

investment (capital) assets
Tangible and intangible items acquired for their monetary benefits.

What Is Owed—Liabilities Are "The Money You Owe" The liabilities section of the balance sheet summarizes debts owed, including both personal and business-related debts. The debt could be either a **short-term** (or **current**) **liability**, an obligation to be paid off within one year, or a **long-term** (or **noncurrent**) **liability**, debts that do not have to be paid in full until more than a year from now. To be accurate, record debt obligations at their current payoff amounts (excluding future interest payments). Following are some examples of items to include in the liabilities section of a balance sheet, with some suggested subheadings.

short-term (current) liability
Obligation paid off within one year.

long-term (noncurrent) liability
Debt that comes due in more than one year.

Short-Term (or Current) Liabilities
- Personal loans owed to other people
- Credit card and charge account balances
- Other open-end credit obligations
- Professional services unpaid (doctors, dentists, chiropractors, lawyers)
- Taxes unpaid
- Past-due rent, utility bills, and insurance premiums

Long-Term Liabilities
- Automobile loans
- Real estate mortgages
- Home equity (second mortgage) loan
- Consumer installment loans and leases (although a lease is technically not a debt)
- Education loans
- Margin loans on securities

Net Worth—What Is Left Is "A Measure of Your Financial Worth"
Net worth is determined by subtracting liabilities from assets, as indicated in Equation (3.1), the *net worth formula:*

$$\text{Assets} - \text{liabilities} = \text{net worth} \quad \textbf{(3.1)}$$

or

$$\text{What is owned} - \text{what is owed} = \text{net worth}$$

This formula assumes that if you converted all assets to cash and paid off all liabilities, the remaining cash would be your net worth. For example, if your items of value had a fair market value of $8000 and the amount you owe to others is $4500, your net worth, or wealth, is $3500 ($8000 – $4500). Figure 3-2 shows household net worth figures by age group. Calculating your net worth will give you a reading on where you stand and point out any trouble spots on your balance sheet. College students typically have more debts than assets; thus they are technically **insolvent** because they have a negative net worth. When students graduate and take on full-time jobs, typically their balance sheets change dramatically after a few years.

insolvent
When a person owes more than he or she owns and the person has a negative net worth.

Sample Balance Sheet The total assets on a balance sheet must equal the total liabilities plus the net worth. Both sides must balance, which is the source of the name "balance sheet." You decide how much detail to include to show your financial condition accurately on a given date. The balance sheet shown in Table 3-2 (page 73) reflects the degree of detail and complexity that might be included for a couple with two children (Victor and Maria Hernandez).

Strategies to Increase Your Net Worth
You can increase your net worth by increasing assets, decreasing liabilities, or doing both. One way to increase assets and net worth is to cut back on spending. Perhaps consider

Figure 3-2

Net Worth by Age

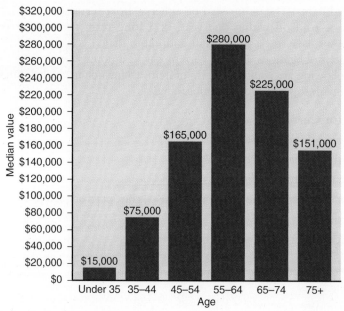

Source: Base data from Survey of Consumer Finances. Authors' estimates for 2012.

FINANCIAL POWER POINT

Income Does Not Create Wealth

People do not get wealthy by earning an income. Real wealth comes from increases in the value of assets over time such as the growth of investments within a 401(k) retirement program.

income
Total income received such as reported on a cash-flow statement.

expenses
Total expenditures made in a specified time such as reported on a cash-flow statement.

surplus (or net gain or net income)
When total income exceeds total expenses such as reported on a cash-flow statement.

deficit (or net loss)
When expenses exceed income such as reported on a cash-flow statement.

cash basis
Only transactions involving actual cash received or cash spent are recorded.

forgoing the cup of coffee or soda you buy each day as you head to class, as any decrease in spending leaves money in the bank as an asset. Reducing expenses on high-cost items such as housing and transportation will have an even greater effect on assets. A second way to increase net worth is to increase income to build assets or pay down debts. For example, as you earn more money, perhaps consider saving most of the difference between your new income and your old income rather than using the added money for more spending. Paying off debt, especially high-interest credit card balances, increases net worth.

The Cash-Flow Statement Tracks Where Your Money Came From and Went

The cash-flow (or income and expense) statement summarizes the total amounts that have been received and spent over a period of time, usually one month or one year. It shows whether you were able to live within your income during that time period. It reflects the flow of funds in and out.

A cash-flow statement includes three sections: **income** (total income received); **expenses** (total expenditures made); and **surplus** (or **net gain** or **net income**), when total income exceeds total expenses, or **deficit** (or **net loss**), when expenses exceed income. Such statements are usually prepared on a **cash basis,*** meaning the only transactions recorded are those involving actual cash received or cash that was spent.

Income/Cash Coming In: Where Your Money Comes From You may think of income as simply what is earned from salaries or wages, but there are other types of income that you should include on a cash-flow statement, such as the following:

- Bonuses and commissions
- Child support and alimony

---

* An alternative method is **accrual-basis budgeting** that recognizes earnings and expenditures when money is earned and expenditures are incurred, regardless of when money is actually received or paid.

**Balance Sheet for a Couple with Two Children—
Victor and Maria Hernandez, January 1, 2012**

Table 3-2

ASSETS			
Monetary Assets			
	Cash on hand	260	0.07%
	Savings account	1,500	0.40%
	Victor's checking account	2,700	0.72%
	Maria's checking account	3,300	0.89%
	Tax refund due	700	0.19%
	Rent receivable	660	0.18%
	Total Monetary Assets	$ 9,120	2.45%
Tangible Assets			
	Home	176,000	47.23%
	Personal property	9,000	2.42%
	Automobiles	11,500	3.09%
	Total Tangible Assets	$196,500	52.73%
Investment Assets			
	Fidelity mutual funds	4,500	1.21%
	Scudder mutual fund	5,000	1.34%
	Ford Motor Company stock	2,800	0.75%
	New York 2018 bonds	1,000	0.27%
	Life insurance cash value	5,400	1.45%
	IRA accounts	34,300	9.21%
	Real estate investment	114,000	30.59%
	Total Investment Assets	$167,000	44.82%
	Total Assets	$372,620	100.00%

LIABILITIES			
Short-Term Liabilities			
	Dentist bill due	120	0.03%
	Credit card debt	1,545	0.41%
	Total Short-Term Liabilities	$ 1,665	0.45%
Long-Term Liabilities			
	Sales finance company: auto	7,700	2.07%
	Savings bank: real estate	92,000	24.69%
	Total Long-Term Liabilities	$ 99,700	26.76%
	Total Liabilities	$101,365	27.20%
	Net Worth	$271,255	72.80%
	Total Liabilities and Net Worth	$372,620	100.00%

- Public assistance
- Social Security benefits
- Pension and profit-sharing income
- Scholarships and grants
- Interest and dividends received (from savings accounts, investments, bonds, or loans to others)
- Income from the sale of assets
- Other income (gifts, tax refunds, rent, royalties, capital gains)

Expenses/Cash Going Out: Where Your Money Goes All expenditures made during the period covered by the cash-flow statement should be included in the

fixed expenses
Expenses that recur at fixed intervals.

variable expenses
Expenses over which you have substantial control.

expenses section. The number and type of expenses shown will vary for each individual and family. Many people categorize expenses according to whether they are fixed or variable.

Fixed expenses are usually paid in the same amount during each time period; they are typically inflexible and often contractual. Examples of such expenses include rent payments and automobile installment loans. It usually takes quite an effort to reduce a fixed expense.

Variable expenses (or **flexible expenses**) are expenditures over which an individual has considerable control. Food, entertainment, and clothing are variable expenses, for example. Some categories, such as savings, can be listed twice, as both fixed and variable expenses. The following are examples of fixed and variable expenses that you might include in a cash-flow statement:

Fixed Expenses

- Savings and investments
- Retirement contributions (employer's plan, IRA)
- Housing (rent, mortgage, loan payment)
- Automobile (installment payment, lease)
- Insurance (life, health, liability, disability, renter's, homeowner's, automobile)
- Installment loan payments (appliances, furniture)
- Taxes (federal income, state income, local income, real estate, Social Security, Medicare, personal property)

Variable Expenses

- Meals (at home and away)
- Utilities (electricity, water, gas, telephone)
- Transportation (gasoline and maintenance, licenses, registration, public transportation, tolls)
- Medical expenses
  - Child care (nursery, baby-sitting)
  - Clothing and accessories (jewelry, shoes, handbags, briefcases)
  - Snacks (candy, soft drinks, other beverages)
  - Education (tuition, fees, books, supplies)
  - Household furnishings (furniture, appliances, curtains)
  - Cable television (beyond basic services)
  - Personal care (beauty shop, barbershop, cosmetics, dry cleaner)
  - Entertainment and recreation (hobbies, socializing, health club, downloads/tapes/CDs, movie rentals, movies)
  - Charitable contributions (gifts, church, school, charity)
  - Magazine subscriptions
  - Vacations and long weekends
  - Credit card payments
  - Savings and investments
  - Miscellaneous (postage, books, magazines, newspapers, personal allowances, domestic help, membership fees)

When reducing variable expenses, perhaps continue to enjoy café lattes and make bigger budget cuts elsewhere.

There is no rigid list of categories to be used in the expenses section, but you do need to classify all of your expenditures in some way. Rather than just use fixed and variable expenses categories, you might also separate expenditures into savings/investments, debts, insurance, taxes, and household expenses. The more specific your categories, the deeper your understanding of your outlays.

Cash Surplus (or Cash Deficit) The surplus (deficit) section shows the amount of cash remaining after you have itemized income and subtracted expenditures from income, as illustrated by the following calculations using Equation (3.2), the *surplus/deficit formula*. (A business would call this amount its net profit or net loss.)

$$\text{Surplus (deficit)} = \text{total income} - \text{total expenses}$$

or $\$1100 \text{ surplus} = \$12{,}500 - \$11{,}400$ (3.2)

$(\$800 \text{ deficit}) = \$14{,}900 - \$15{,}700$

A surplus demonstrates that you are managing your financial resources successfully and do not have to use savings or borrow money to make financial ends meet. When the calculation shows a surplus, that amount is then available (in your checking and savings accounts) to spend, save, invest, or donate. A surplus is not really cash lying around on the kitchen table; it is the cash value reflected in the accounts on your balance sheet. Figure 3-3 shows the typical personal financial situation over the life cycle in present value dollars, from the wealth accumulation years through retirement.

Sample Cash-Flow Statements Table 3-3 shows the cash-flow statement for a couple with two children (Victor and Maria Hernandez). It vividly highlights the additional income needed to rear children and shows the increased variety of expenditures that characterize a family's (rather than an individual's) lifestyle. As a person earns more income, the cash-flow statement usually becomes more involved and detailed.

Personal Finance over the Life Cycle

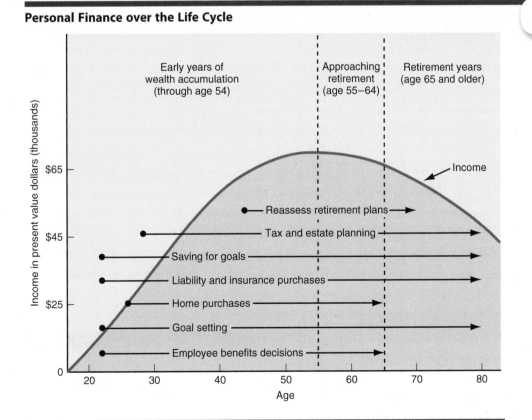

Figure 3-3

Table 3-3

Cash Flow Statement for a Couple with Two Children—Victor and Maria Hernandez, January 1, 2011–December 31, 2011

	Dollars	Percent
INCOME		
Victor's gross salary	63,180	70.99%
Maria's gross salary	15,500	17.42%
Interest and dividends	1,800	2.02%
Bonus	600	0.67%
Tax refunds	200	0.22%
Net rental income	7,720	8.67%
Total Income	89,000	100.00%
EXPENDITURES		
Fixed Expenses		
Mortgage loan payments	14,400	16.18%
Real estate taxes	2,400	2.70%
Homeowner's insurance	1,200	1.35%
Automobile loan payments	4,400	4.94%
Automobile insurance and registration	2,190	2.46%
Life insurance premiums	1,200	1.35%
Medical insurance (employee portion)	2,980	3.35%
Emergency fund savings	2,400	2.70%
Revolving savings fund	1,800	2.02%
Federal income taxes	11,300	12.70%
State income taxes	4,200	4.72%
City income taxes	1,600	1.80%
Social Security taxes	6,020	6.76%
Personal property taxes	950	1.07%
Retirement IRAs	6,000	6.74%
Total Fixed Expenses	$63,040	70.83%
Variable Expenses		
Food	4,900	5.51%
Utilities	2,100	2.36%
Gasoline and maintenance	3,100	3.48%
Medical expenses	3,400	3.82%
Medicines	1,750	1.97%
Clothing and upkeep	1,950	2.19%
Church	2,400	2.70%
Gifts	1,400	1.57%
Personal allowances	2,400	2.70%
Children's allowances	2,080	2.34%
Miscellaneous	480	0.54%
Total Variable Expenses	$25,960	29.17%
Total Expenses	$89,000	100.00%
SURPLUS (DEFICIT)	$ 0	0.00%

 Concept Check 3.2

1. Distinguish between the balance sheet and cash-flow statement.

2. How should assets and liabilities be valued for the balance sheet?

3. Distinguish between fixed and variable expenses.

TRACK YOUR FINANCIAL STRENGTH AND PROGRESS USING RATIOS

Financial ratios are numerical calculations designed to simplify the process of evaluating your financial strength and the progress of your financial condition. Ratios serve as tools or yardsticks to develop saving, spending, and credit-use patterns consistent with your goals. Calculators for these ratios can be found on the *Garman/Forgue* companion website.

financial ratios
Calculations designed to simplify evaluation of financial strength and progress.

Liquidity Ratio: Do I Have Enough Liquidity to Pay for Emergencies?

Liquidity is the speed and ease with which an asset can be converted to cash. You can use the **liquidity ratio** to determine the number of months that you could continue to meet your expenses using only your monetary assets if all income ceases. A high ratio is desirable. For example, compare the monetary assets on the balance sheet for Victor and Maria Hernandez in Table 3-2 ($9120) with their monthly expenses in Table 3-3 ($89,000 ÷ 12 = $7417) using Equation (3.3):

liquidity
Speed and ease with which an asset can be converted to cash.

liquidity ratio
Number of months you could meet expenses using only monetary assets if all income were to cease.

$$\text{Basic liquidity ratio} = \frac{\text{monetary (liquid) assets}}{\text{monthly expenses}}$$

$$= \frac{\$9120}{\$7417} \qquad (3.3)$$

$$= 1.23$$

$$= 1.23 \text{ ratio or 1 and 2/10ths of a month}$$

This financial ratio suggests that the Hernandezes may have insufficient monetary assets, unable to support them for much longer than one month (1.23 months) if they are faced with a loss of income. Experts recommend that people have monetary assets equal to three to six months' expenses in emergency cash reserves. Surveys reveal that half of American families say they could not come up with $2000 without selling some of their possessions. The exact amount of monetary assets necessary depends on your family situation and your job. A smaller amount may be sufficient for your needs if you have adequate income protection through an employee benefit program, are employed in a job that is definitely not subject to layoffs, or have a partner who works for money income. Households dependent on the income from a self-employed person with fluctuating income need a larger emergency cash reserve.

Asset-to-Debt Ratio: Do I Have Enough Assets to Meet My Debt Obligations?

The **asset-to-debt ratio** compares total assets with total liabilities. It provides you with a broad measure of your financial liquidity. This ratio measures solvency and ability to pay debts, as shown in Equation (3.4). A high ratio is desirable. Calculations based on the figures in the Hernandezes' balance sheet (Table 3-2) show that the couple has ample assets compared with their debts because they own items worth more than three times what they owe. (Reversing the mathematics shows that they owe less than one-third of what they own.)

asset-to-debt ratio
Compares total assets with total liabilities.

$$\text{Asset-to-debt ratio} = \frac{\text{total assets}}{\text{total debt}}$$

$$= \frac{\$372,620}{\$101,365} \qquad (3.4)$$

$$= 3.676 \text{ or a 3.7 to 1 ratio}$$

If you owe more than you own, then you are technically insolvent. While your current income may be sufficient to pay your current bills, you still do not have enough assets to cover all of your debts.

Debt Service-to-Income Ratio: Is My Total Debt Burden Too High?

The **debt service-to-income ratio** provides a view of your total debt burden by comparing the dollars spent on gross annual debt repayments (including rent or mortgage payments) with gross annual income. A ratio of 0.36 or less is desirable. Using data in Table 3-3,

debt service-to-income ratio
Compares dollars spent on gross annual debt.

Equation (3.5) shows that the Hernandezes' $18,800 in annual loan repayments ($14,400 for the mortgage loan and $4400 for the automobile loan) amount to 21.12 percent of their $89,000 annual income. Their ratio indicates that their gross income is adequate to make debt repayments, including housing costs, and implies that they usually have some flexibility in budgeting for other expenses. This ratio should decrease as you grow older.

$$\text{Debt service-to-income ratio} = \frac{\text{annual debt repayments}}{\text{gross income}}$$
$$= \frac{\$18,800}{\$89,000} \qquad \textbf{(3.5)}$$
$$= 21.12\%$$

Debt Payments-to-Disposable Income Ratio: Is My Nonmortgage Debt Too Stressful?

debt payments-to-disposable income ratio
Divides monthly disposable income into monthly debt repayments.

disposable income
Amount of income remaining after taxes and withholding; estimates funds available for debt repayment.

The **debt payments-to-disposable income ratio** divides monthly disposable personal income (not gross income) into monthly debt repayments (excluding mortgage debt). **Disposable income** is the amount of your income remaining after taxes and withholdings for such purposes as insurance and union dues. It estimates funds available for debt repayment. A ratio of 14 percent or less is desirable. A debt payments-to-disposable income ratio of 16 percent or more is considered problematic because the person is making high debt payments and quickly would be in serious financial trouble if a disruption in income occurred.

In the Hernandezes' case, their disposable monthly income from Table 3-3 is $5743 ($89,000 − $11,300 {federal income taxes} − $4200 {state income taxes} − $1600 {city income taxes} − $2980 {medical insurance premiums} / 12). Their monthly debt repayments from Table 3-3 are $366.67 ($4400 ÷ 12). The result using Equation (3.6) for the Hernandez family is a very small debt payments-to-disposable income ratio of 6.38 percent. Note that they have zero credit card debt.

$$\text{Debt payments-to-disposable income ratio} = \frac{\text{monthly nonmortgage debt repayments}}{\text{monthly disposable income}}$$
$$= \frac{\$366.67}{\$5743} \qquad \textbf{(3.6)}$$
$$= 6.38\%$$

Investment Assets-to-Total Assets Ratio: Am I Saving/Investing Enough?

investment assets-to-total assets ratio
Compares investment asset value with total assets.

The **investment assets-to-total assets ratio** compares the value of your investment assets with your total assets. This ratio reveals how well an individual or family is advancing toward their financial goals for capital accumulation, especially as related to retirement. A ratio of 50 percent or higher is desirable. A ratio of 10 percent might be appropriate for people in their 20s, 11 to 30 percent for those in their 30s, and above 30 percent for people in their 40s. Inserting the data from the balance sheet in Table 3-2 into Equation (3.7) shows that the Hernandezes have a ratio of 0.448, or 44.8 percent. As you can see, nearly half of their total assets is made up of investment assets (including the rental property that was Victor's mother's home before she died and left it to him); this ratio is a typical proportion for this stage in their lives.

$$\text{Investment assets-to-total assets ratio} = \frac{\text{investment assets}}{\text{total assets}}$$
$$= \frac{\$167,000}{\$372,620} \qquad \textbf{(3.7)}$$
$$= 0.448 \text{ or } 44.8\%$$

Other Ways to Assess Financial Progress

You can use other data from your balance sheet and cash-flow statement to help analyze your finances. Consider the assets listed on the balance sheet for Victor and Maria

Hernandez in Table 3-2. Do they have too few monetary assets compared with tangible and investment assets? Experts recommend that 15 to 20 percent of your assets be in monetary form and that this proportion increase as you near retirement. Do you have too much invested in one asset, or have you diversified, like the Hernandezes? Have your balance sheet figures changed in a favorable direction since last year? Is a growing proportion of your income coming from your investments? Are you making progress toward your financial goals? If not, ask: "Am I spending money where I really want to?," "In which categories can I reduce expenses?," and "Could I increase income?"

 Concept Check 3.3

1. Distinguish between the liquidity ratio and the asset-to-debt ratio.

2. Distinguish between the debt service-to-income ratio and the debt payments-to-disposable income ratio.

3. What can changes over time in your investment assets-to-total assets ratio tell you about your progress in reaching financial goals?

DID YOU KNOW?

Turn Bad Habits into Good Ones

Do You Do This?	*Do This Instead!*
Spend all your income	Save 10 percent or more
Overspend	Utilize a budget to control spending
Keep losing financial records	Create a record-keeping system
Do not know how much you owe	Make a balance sheet
Can't pay for auto insurance premium or vacation	Save for large irregular expenses
Run out of money every few months	Create a cash-flow calendar

---

COLLECT AND ORGANIZE YOUR FINANCIAL RECORDS TO SAVE TIME AND MONEY

Financial records are documents that evidence financial transactions, such as bills, receipts, credit card receipts and statements, bank records, tax returns, brokerage statements, and paycheck stubs. Your financial records will help determine where you are, where you have been, and where you are going financially. They also help you save money as well as make money. Good records enable you to review the results of financial transactions as well as permit other family members to find them in an emergency. Organized records help you take advantage of all available tax deductions when filing income taxes and provide you with more dollars to spend, save, invest, or donate.

Table 3-4 shows categories of financial records and the contents that might be included in each. Some records may be safely stored at home in a fire-resistant file cabinet or a safe. Other records should be kept in a **safe-deposit box**. Safe-deposit boxes are secured lock boxes available for rent ($50 to $250 per year) in banks. Two keys are used to open such a box. The customer keeps one key, and the bank holds the other. Many people keep duplicates of important records at their workplace or with relatives because the likelihood of records at both locations being stolen or destroyed simultaneously is very small. You can purge or shred some of your records when you no longer need them,

 LEARNING OBJECTIVE 4

Collect and organize the financial records necessary for managing your personal finances.

financial records
Documents that evidence financial transactions.

Table 3-4

Financial Records: What to Keep and Where

Category	Contents	
	In Home Files and Fireproof Home Safe	**In Safe-Deposit Box**
Financial plans/budgeting	Financial plans Balance sheets and cash-flow statements Current budget List of safe-deposit box contents Names and contact information for financial advisers	Names and contact information for financial advisers Copy of written financial plans, goals, and budgets
Career and employment	Current résumé College transcripts Letters of recommendation Employee benefits descriptions Written career plans	Employer retirement plan correspondence
Banking and financial services	Checkbook, unused checks, and canceled checks List of locations and account numbers for all bank accounts Checking and savings account statements Locations and access numbers for safe-deposit boxes Account transaction receipts	List of financial institutions and account numbers for all financial services accounts Certificates of deposit
Taxes	Copies of all income tax returns, both state and federal, for the past three years, including all supporting documentation Receipts for all donations of cash or property Log of volunteer expenses Receipts for property taxes paid	Copies of all income tax filings, both state and federal, for the past three years Records of securities purchased and sold
Credit	Utility and telephone bills Monthly credit card statements Receipts of credit payments List of credit accounts and telephone numbers to report lost/stolen cards Unused credit cards Credit reports and scores	List of credit accounts and telephone numbers to report lost/stolen cards Loan discharge notice when it is paid off Credit card bills for seven years if they support tax deductions
Housing, vehicles, and consumer purchases	Copies of legal documents (leases, mortgage, deeds, titles) Property appraisals and inspection reports Home repair/home improvement receipts Warranties Owner's manuals for purchases Auto registration records Vehicle service and repair receipts Receipts for important purchases	Original legal documents (leases, mortgage, deeds, titles) Copies of property appraisals Vehicle purchase contracts (until vehicle is sold) Photographs or videos of valuable possessions

	Contents	
Category	**In Home Files and Fireproof Home Safe**	**In Safe-Deposit Box**
Insurance	Original insurance policies List of insurance policies with premium amounts and due dates Premium payment receipts Calculation of life insurance needs Insurance claims forms and reports Medical records for family, including immunization records and list of prescription drugs	List of all insurance policies with company and agent names and addresses and policy numbers Listing with photographs or videotape of personal property
Investments	Records of stock, bond, and mutual fund transactions and certificate numbers Mutual fund statements Statements from brokers Reports from financial planner Company annual reports Retirement plan quarterly and annual reports Documents on business interests Written investment philosophy Written investment strategies	Contact information for all investment needs Stock and bond certificates Rare coins, stamps, and other collectibles
Retirement	Pension and retirement plan information Retirement statements Copies of all retirement plan transactions Copy of Social Security card Trust agreements Information on Social Security	Extra copy of all retirement plan transactions and statements Social Security statements (newest one)
Estate planning	Copy of current will Copies of advance directives (wills, living wills, medical powers of attorney, durable powers of attorney with originals with physician/attorney) Copies of trust documents (originals with executor, trustees/attorney)	Copy of will (original of all estate planning documents should be placed in attorney's office)
Personal information	Copy of birth certificate and marriage license Religious documents Copy of divorce decree, property settlement, and custody agreement Receipts for alimony and child support payments Custodial information for your children, relatives, and/or elderly parent	Passports while not being used Military and adoption papers Originals of birth, marriage, death certificates Originals of Social Security cards Originals of divorce decrees, property settlements, and custody agreements Master list of all important documents and their location Flash drive or CD containing soft copies of many financial records (update once a year)

such as non–tax-related checks and credit card receipts more than a year old, out-of-date warranties, expired insurance policies for which there will be no claims, records from automobiles you no longer own, and financial reports when supplanted with updated summary information.

 Concept Check 3.4

1. List some advantages of keeping good financial records.

2. Name three financial records that might best be kept in a safe-deposit box.

ADVICE FROM A PRO

Get-Tough Ways to Cut Your Spending

If you always run out of money before the month is over, you need to take some drastic steps to get your finances under control. Consider the following:

1. *Stop paying bank fees by maintaining minimum balances and eliminating overdrafts.*

2. *Stop making ATM withdrawals.*

3. *Stop getting cash back from debit or credit card purchases to use for pocket money.*

4. *Spend only cash or money that you have, and leave debit and credit cards at home.*

5. *Stop using credit cards.*

6. *Refinance credit card debt at a credit union.*

7. *Do not eat out.*

8. *Cut back on excessive telephone use.*

9. *Don't pay for entertainment; rather do activities that are free.*

10. *Reduce or stop spending on luxuries such as clothing, movies, entertainment, memberships, hobbies, CDs, DVDs, and expanded cable channels.*

11. *Drop landline telephone service and use only a cell phone.*

12. *Find cheaper auto insurance.*

13. *Increase your 401(k) retirement contribution as it reduces income taxes.*

14. *Change income tax withholding to increase take-home pay.*

15. *Use a list when shopping, and stick to it.*

16. *Avoid shopping malls and discount stores.*

17. *Sell an asset, especially one that requires additional expenses, such as a boat or second car.*

18. *Build up an emergency fund of savings even if it means temporarily decreasing retirement-plan contributions.*

19. *Only buy used items.*

20. *Make Christmas a "nonspend" holiday.*

21. *Move to lower-cost housing.*

22. *Increase income by working overtime or finding a second job.*

Alena C. Johnson
Utah State University

REACHING YOUR GOALS THROUGH BUDGETING: YOUR SPENDING/SAVINGS ACTION PLAN

 LEARNING OBJECTIVE **5**

Achieve your financial goals through budgeting.

Your financial success is largely a matter of choice, not a matter of chance. Your budget is where you make and implement those choices. Your budget is your plan for spending and saving. Budgeting forces you to consider what is important in your life, what things you want to own, how you want to live, what it will take to do that, and, more generally, what you want to achieve in life. The budgeting process gives you control over your finances, and it empowers you to achieve your financial goals while simultaneously (and successfully) confronting any unforeseen events. In short, budgeting answers the question, "What is my spending/savings action plan?" An advantage of budgeting is that it reduces stress because making and following a budget helps you get more of what you want.

Some people do all their budgeting mentally—and do so successfully. Good for them! Many of us, however, need to see the actual numbers on paper or on a computer screen. A **budget** is a paper or electronic document used to record both planned and actual income and expenditures over a period of time. Your budget represents the major mechanism through which your financial plans are carried out and goals are achieved. Figure 3-4 illustrates how to think about financial statements and budgeting. The cash-flow statement focuses on *where you have been* financially, the balance sheet shows *where you are* financially at the current time, and the budget indicates *where you want to go* in the future. Creating and following a spending plan has three stages: before, during, and after.

Action Before: Set Financial Goals

Before establishing your budget, take action to set financial goals. **Long-term goals** are financial targets or ends that an individual or family wants to achieve perhaps more than five years in the future. Such goals provide direction for overall financial planning as well as shorter-term budgeting. An example of a long-term goal is to create a $1 million retirement fund by age 60. Goals must be specific. They should contain dollar-amount targets and target dates for achievement.

If you have a small income or large debts, it may be unrealistic to think of long-term goals until any current financial difficulties are resolved. You may be unable to do much more than take care of immediate necessities, such as housing expenses, food, and utility bills. In such instances, you need to focus on short-term efforts to improve your financial situation. You may need to focus on paying down debt, not adding to it.

Establishing unrealistic short-term goals sets up a high likelihood of failure. Instead, set financial targets that are almost too easy to meet. For example, you may want to save $350 per month to use as a down payment on a home in five years. That may seem like a lot. Start perhaps painlessly by saving $100 per month for a few months. Then put away $150 for two months, $200 for two months, then $250, then $300, and finally $350 so that by the end of the first year you are on target.

Intermediate-term goals are financial targets that can be achieved between one year and perhaps three to five years. Examples of intermediate-term goals are creating an emergency fund amounting to three months of income within four years, saving $22,500 within three years for a down payment on a home, taking a $4000 vacation to China in two years, paying off $8000 in credit card debt in one and a half years, and paying off a $12,000 college loan in five years. **Short-term goals** are financial targets or ends that can be achieved in less than a year, such as finishing college, paying off an auto loan, increasing savings, purchasing assets (i.e., vehicle, furniture, television, stereo, clothes), reducing high-interest debt, taking an annual vacation, attending a wedding, buying life insurance, and making plans for retirement.

FINANCIAL POWER POINT

The Secret to Successful Budgeting

If you have some money in emergency savings, perhaps $500 or $2000, you probably will always have enough money to pay for vehicle repairs and unexpected travel, thus you never will have to pay with plastic for things that are not in your budget.

budget
Paper or electronic document used to record both planned and actual income and expenditures over a period of time.

long-term goals
Financial targets to achieve more than five years in the future.

intermediate-term goals
Financial targets that can be achieved within one to five years.

short-term goals
Financial targets or ends that can be achieved in less than a year.

About Financial Statements and Budgets

Figure 3-4

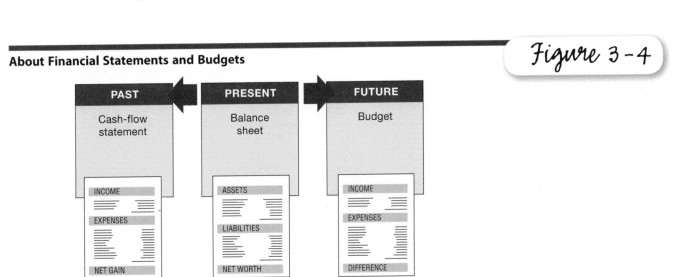

You need to be as clear as possible about what your financial goals are. The goals worksheet in Figure 3-5 provides examples of how much to save to reach long-, intermediate-, and short-term goals. People can view such savings as a fixed expenditure (such as withholding from a paycheck to contribute to an employer's retirement plan or to transfer to a savings account). Other savings may be a variable such as saving what is left over after all expenditures are made.

Prioritizing your goals makes sense. But what are your most important goals? One certain priority should be to pay off high-interest credit cards as soon as possible. Another is to contribute as much as you can afford to a retirement plan. Many college graduates buy a new car soon after getting their first job to celebrate having "made it." Before you're lured into following suit, give careful consideration to your priorities and remember that every action carries not only the dollar cost of the action taken but also the opportunity cost of the alternatives forgone. To achieve your long-term goals, you may have to sacrifice by deferring some of your short-term desires.

Here are suggestions for successful budgeting: (1) Keep it simple, (2) make it personal, (3) keep it flexible, and (4) be positive. A smart thing to do is to list the benefits to yourself that will occur when you reach a particular financial goal. You are likely to achieve a financial goal when you are convinced that it is your own goal, when you make

Figure 3-5 Goals Worksheet for Harry and Belinda Johnson

Date worksheet prepared January 1, 2012

1 LONG-TERM GOALS	2 AMOUNT NEEDED	3 MONTH & YEAR NEEDED*	4 MONTHS TO SAVE	5 DATE START SAVING	6 MONTHLY AMOUNT TO SAVE (2 ÷ 4)
European vacation	$3,000	Aug. 2015	30	Feb. '13	$100
Down payment on new auto	5,000	Oct. 2016	45	Jan. '13	111

Date worksheet prepared January 1, 2012

1 INTERMEDIATE-TERM GOALS	2 AMOUNT NEEDED	3 MONTH & YEAR NEEDED*	4 MONTHS TO SAVE	5 DATE START SAVING	6 MONTHLY AMOUNT TO SAVE (2 ÷ 4)
Down payment on home	$18,900	Dec. 2017	60	Jan. '12	$315

Date worksheet prepared January 1, 2012

1 SHORT-TERM GOALS	2 AMOUNT NEEDED	3 MONTH & YEAR NEEDED*	4 MONTHS TO SAVE	5 DATE START SAVING	6 MONTHLY AMOUNT TO SAVE (2 ÷ 4)
House fund	$3,600	Dec. '12	12	Jan. '12	315
Holiday vacation	1,200	Dec. '12	12	Jan. '12	100
Summer vacation	1,200	Aug. '12	6	Mar. '12	100
Anniversary dinner party	500	June '12	5	Jan. '12	50

*Goals requiring five years or more to achieve require consideration of investment return and after-tax yield, which will be presented in Chapter 4.

an emotional commitment to the goal, when your short-term goals lead to your long-term goals, and when you can visualize receiving the benefits of your goals.

Action Before: Make and Reconcile Budget Estimates

Before the month begins, you identify how you are spending money now in the process of making and reconciling budget estimates of income and expenditures. Here you resolve conflicting needs and wants by revising estimates as necessary. You can't have everything in life—especially this month—even though you might want it.

Make Budget Estimates **Budget estimates** are the projected dollar amounts in a budget that one plans to receive or spend during the period covered by the budget. Begin by estimating total gross income from all sources, and review take-home pay and then discretionary income. For example, Jonny Deppe's annual gross income is $60,000, and after employer withholdings for taxes, insurance premiums, and union dues, his **take-home pay** (also called **disposable income**) is $48,000. This is the money available for spending, saving, investing, and donating. Focus also on your **discretionary income**. This is the money left over once the necessities of living are covered, such as paying for housing, food, and other necessities. It is usually the money that is really "controllable" and often makes up the bulk of money available to pay for one's variable expenses. After Jonny pays his rent, food, utilities, and car payment, his discretionary income is $18,000.

Table 3-5 presents budget estimates for a college student, a single working person, a young married couple, a married couple with two young children, and a married couple with two college-age children. The college student's budget requires monthly withdrawals of previously deposited savings to make ends meet. The single working person's budget allows for an automobile loan, but not much else. The young married couple's budget permits one automobile loan, an investment program, contributions to individual retirement accounts, and significant spending on food and entertainment. The budget of the married couple with two young children allows for only an inexpensive automobile loan payment even though one spouse has a part-time job to help with the finances. The budget of the married couple with two college-age children permits a home mortgage payment, ownership of two paid-for automobiles, savings and investment programs, and a substantial contribution for future college expenses.

It is essential to make reasonable budget estimates. If you have seven holiday gifts to buy and expect to spend $50 for each, it's easy to make an estimate of $350. If you want to go out to dinner once each week with a friend at $50 per meal, estimate an expense of $200 per month. Avoid using unrealistically low figures by simply being fair and honest in your estimates. Then add up your totals.

Revise Budget Estimates to Create a "Balanced Budget"

When trying to make your spending conform with your budget goals, sometimes you will find the math is alarming! When initial expense estimates exceed income estimates, three choices are available: (1) earn more income, (2) cut back on expenses, or (3) try a combination of more income and fewer expenses. The process of reconciling needs and wants is a healthy exercise. It helps identify your priorities by telling you what is important in your life at the current time, and it identifies areas of sacrifice that you might make. Revising your short-term financial goals may also be required.

You must reconcile conflicting wants to revise your budget until total expenses do not exceed income. You have no choice! Perhaps you can change some "must have" items to "maybe next year" purchases. Perhaps you can keep some quality items but reduce their quantity. For example, instead of $200 for four meals for you and a friend at restaurants each month, consider dining out twice each month at $60 per meal. You'll save

budget estimates
Projected dollar amounts to receive or spend in a budgeting period.

take-home pay/disposable income
Pay received after employer withholdings for taxes, insurance, and union dues.

discretionary income
Money left over after necessities such as housing and food are paid for.

DID YOU KNOW?

Financial Software Tools to Manage Your Money

Financial software and planning tools, including many on the Internet, make managing your money—including record keeping—a snap. Financial software offers many benefits. Laborious calculations are sharply reduced, banking transactions can be performed with automatic updating of financial records. The balance sheet and cash-flow statements are automatically updated when transactions occur.

Some comprehensive Web portals on personal finances are Yahoo! Finance (www.finance.yahoo.com), MSN Money Central (http://money.msn.com//), and Quicken.com (www.quicken.intuit.com/). You will find all kinds of easy-to-use financial tools, including bill paying, banking, vehicle loan rate comparisons, mortgage shopping, online tax preparation, stock screening, stock quotes, online brokers, retirement calculators, and breaking news stories. Other excellent sites are *Money* (http://money.cnn.com/), *The Motley Fool* (www.Fool.com), *Kiplinger's Personal Finance Magazine* (www.Kiplinger.com), *USA Today* (www.USAToday.com), and *Yahoo!* (www.Yahoo.com).

Table 3-5

Sample Monthly Budgets for Various Family Units

Classifications	College Student	Single Working Person	Young Married Couple	Married Couple with Two Young Children	Married Couple with Two College-Age Children
INCOME					
Salary	300	2,800	2,200	3,500	4,400
Salary	0	0	2,100	860	1,600
Interest and dividends	5	15	15	15	80
Loans/scholarships	300	0	0	0	0
Savings withdrawals	570	0	0	0	500
Total Income	$1,175	$2,815	$4,315	$4,375	$6,580
EXPENSES					
Fixed Expenses					
Retirement contributions	$ 0	$ 20	$ 360	$ 180	$ 340
IRA	0	20	160	180	200
Savings (withheld)	0	20	20	10	100
Housing	350	750	900	1,100	1,300
Health insurance	0	0	60	150	140
Life and disability insurance	0	0	20	60	40
Homeowner's or renter's insurance	0	0	40	60	80
Automobile insurance	0	80	90	60	140
Automobile payments	0	280	345	220	0
Loan 1 (TV and stereo)	0	80	80	40	0
Loan 2 (other)	0	40	40	0	50
Federal and state taxes	30	455	715	600	710
Social Security taxes	23	210	330	305	385
Real estate taxes	0	0	0	0	40
Investments	0	0	60	100	300
Total fixed expenses	$ 403	$1,955	$3,220	$3,065	$3,825
Variable Expenses					
Other savings	$ 0	$ 60	$ 150	$ 0	$ 0
Food	180	230	270	340	350
Utilities	40	80	90	140	145
Automobile gas, oil, maintenance	0	90	110	90	100
Medical	10	30	40	70	50
Child care	0	0	0	260	0
Clothing	20	50	60	50	40
Gifts and contributions	10	20	40	60	80
Allowances	20	75	60	100	180
Education	400	0	0	0	1,500
Furnishing and appliances	10	10	30	20	20
Personal care	10	45	25	30	30
Entertainment	40	120	100	60	120
Vacations	17	30	40	30	60
Miscellaneous	15	20	80	60	80
Total variable expenses	$ 772	$ 860	$1,095	$1,310	$2,755
Total Expenses	$1,175	$2,815	$4,315	$4,375	$6,580

$80 a month and still have two really nice meals. Your actions on money matters override your words, so act accordingly.

Eventually you will finalize your "balanced budget" by making sure planned income equals or exceeds projected expenses.

Unfinished Business Estimates for Harry and Belinda Table 3-6 presents the projected annual budget for Harry and Belinda Johnson and reflects their efforts to reconcile their budget estimates. Wisely Harry and Belinda are "paying themselves first." They plan to save $100 a month in a savings/emergency fund, put away $300 per month to save to buy their own home, and contribute to both their retirement plans at work. However, the Johnsons have failed to complete their budget because their total planned expenses are $1310 more than their total planned income. The Johnsons have a little way to go to fully reconcile their annual budget estimates.

Action Before: Plan Cash Flows

Before the month begins, you plan your cash flows or where the money will go. Income usually remains somewhat constant month after month, but expenses do rise and fall, sometimes sharply. As a result, people occasionally complain that they are "broke, out of money, and sick of budgeting." This challenge can be anticipated by using a cash-flow calendar and eliminated by using a revolving savings fund.

Cash Flow Calendar for Harry and Belinda Johnson The budget estimates for monthly income and expenses in Table 3-6 have been recast in summary form in Table 3-7, providing a **cash-flow calendar** for the Johnsons. This is a very useful budgeting tool. Annual estimated income and expenses are recorded in this calendar for each budgeting time period in an effort to identify surplus or deficit situations. In the Johnsons' case, planned annual expenses still exceed income. The couple starts out the year with five months of income meeting expenses, and then they face planned monthly deficits for the remainder of the year.

Effective management of cash flow can involve curtailing expenses during months with financial deficits, increasing income, using savings, or borrowing. If you borrow money and pay finance charges, the credit costs will further increase your monthly expenses.

Revolving Savings Fund for Harry and Belinda Johnson For this reason alone, it is smart to "borrow from yourself" by using a **revolving savings fund**. This is a variable expense classification budgeting tool into which funds are allocated in an effort to create savings that can be used to balance the budget later so as to avoid running out of money. Establishing such a fund involves planning ahead—much like a college student does when saving money all summer (creating a revolving savings fund) to draw on during the school months. You establish a revolving savings fund for two purposes: (1) to accumulate funds for large nonmonthly irregular expenses, such as automobile insurance premiums, medical costs, holiday gifts, and vacations; and (2) to meet occasional deficits due to income fluctuations.

Table 3-8 shows the Johnsons' revolving savings fund. When preparing their budget, the Johnsons realized that in June, November, and December they were going to have significant deficits. Thus they decided to begin setting aside $250 per month to cover the June deficit, so by June they had $1250 in their revolving savings fund to cover that amount. Continued use of the revolving savings fund helped them meet the November deficit as well.

Harry and Belinda Argue About Budgeting Alternatives The Johnsons will still be $1530 short in December. Lacking that much money, the couple has a number of alternatives: (1) reduce some planned spending throughout the year to create sufficient surpluses, (2) use some of Harry's trust fund interest income to cover the deficit,

FINANCIAL POWER POINT

Cut the Dollars Not the Pennies

Experts say that you should not cut out the occasional café lattes to manage your money better. Instead of making penny cuts, enjoy the coffee and then make real dollar cuts elsewhere in your spending such as in housing, cars, preschool, child care, and health care. And cut back on the credit card charges. Other experts disagree and instead recommend that to really find money in your budget, you should cut back on all such miscellaneous treats.

cash-flow calendar
Budget estimates for monthly income and expenses.

revolving savings fund
Variable budgeting tool that places funds in savings to cover emergency or higher-than-usual expenses.

Table 3-6

2012 Annual Budget Estimates for Harry and Belinda Johnson

	Jan.	Feb.	Mar.	Apr.	May	June	July	Aug.	Sept.	Oct.	Nov.	Dec.	Yearly Total	Monthly Totals
INCOME														
Harry's salary	3,250	3,250	3,250	3,250	3,250	3,250	3,250	3,250	3,250	3,250	3,250	3,250	39,000	3,250.00
Belinda's salary	4,750	4,750	4,750	4,750	4,750	4,750	4,750	4,750	4,750	4,750	4,750	4,750	57,000	4,750.00
Interest	12	12	13	13	14	14	15	15	15	16	16	16	171	14.25
Trust	0	0	0	0	0	0	0	3,000	0	0	0	0	3,000	250.00
TOTAL INCOME	$8,012	$8,012	$8,013	$8,013	$8,014	$8,014	$8,015	$11,015	$8,015	$8,016	$8,016	$8,016	$ 99,171	$8,264.25
EXPENSES														
Fixed Expenses														
Rent	1,100	1,100	1,100	1,100	1,100	1,100	1,200	1,200	1,200	1,200	1,200	1,200	13,800	1,150.00
Health insurance	200	200	200	200	200	200	250	250	250	250	250	250	2,700	225.00
Life insurance	15	15	15	15	15	15	15	15	15	15	15	15	180	15.00
Home purchase fund	300	300	300	300	300	300	300	300	300	300	300	300	3,600	300.00
Renter's insurance	0	0	0	0	0	220	0	0	0	0	0	0	220	18.33
Automobile insurance	0	0	0	0	0	850	0	0	0	0	0	850	1,700	141.67
Auto loan payments	497	497	497	497	497	497	497	497	497	497	497	497	5,964	497.00
Student loan	300	300	300	300	300	300	300	300	300	300	300	300	3,600	300.00
Savings/emergencies	100	100	100	100	100	100	100	100	100	100	100	100	1,200	100.00
Harry's retirement plan	195	195	195	195	195	195	195	195	195	195	195	195	2,340	195.00
Belinda's retirement	190	190	190	190	190	190	190	190	190	190	190	190	2,280	190.00
Cable TV and Internet	120	120	120	120	120	120	120	120	120	120	120	120	1,440	120.00
Federal income taxes	1,210	1,210	1,210	1,210	1,210	1,210	1,210	1,210	1,210	1,210	1,210	1,210	14,520	1,210.00
State income taxes	400	400	400	400	400	400	400	400	400	400	400	400	4,800	400.00
Social Security	535	535	535	535	535	535	535	535	535	535	535	535	6,420	535.00
Auto registration	0	0	0	0	0	0	0	0	0	0	300	0	300	25.00
Total fixed expenses	$5,162	$5,162	$5,162	$5,162	$5,162	$6,232	$5,312	$5,312	$5,312	$5,312	$5,612	$6,162	$ 65,064	$5,422.00
Variable Expenses														
Savings/investments	0	0	0	0	0	0	0	2,000	0	0	0	0	2,000	166.67
Revolving savings fund	250	250	250	250	250	0	240	0	200	190	0	0	1,880	156.67
Food (groceries)	440	440	440	440	440	440	440	440	440	440	440	440	5,280	440.00
Food (out)	300	300	300	300	300	300	300	300	300	300	300	300	3,600	300.00
Utilities	125	150	150	150	100	100	100	100	100	125	125	150	1,475	122.92
Cell phones	75	75	75	75	75	75	75	75	75	75	75	75	900	75.00
Gas and maintenance	120	120	120	120	120	120	120	120	120	120	120	120	1,440	120.00
Doctor and dentist bills	100	100	100	100	100	100	100	100	100	100	100	100	1,200	100.00
Medicines	60	60	60	60	60	60	60	60	60	60	60	60	720	60.00
Clothing and upkeep	170	170	170	170	170	170	170	170	170	170	170	170	2,040	170.00
Church and charity	100	100	100	100	100	100	100	100	100	100	100	100	1,200	100.00
Gifts	80	80	110	75	140	20	20	60	60	50	400	300	1,395	116.25
Public transportation	60	60	60	60	60	60	60	60	60	60	60	60	720	60.00
Personal allowances	720	720	720	720	720	720	720	720	720	720	720	720	8,640	720.00
Entertainment	150	150	150	150	150	150	150	150	150	150	150	150	1,800	150.00
Holiday vacation	0	0	0	0	0	0	0	0	0	0	0	600	600	50.00
Summer vacation	0	0	0	0	0	0	0	1,200	0	0	0	0	1,200	100.00
Anniversary party	0	0	0	0	0	500	0	0	0	0	0	0	500	41.67
Miscellaneous	100	75	46	81	67	67	48	48	48	44	44	39	707	58.92
Total variable expenses	$2,850	$2,850	$2,851	$2,851	$2,852	$2,982	$2,703	$ 5,703	$2,703	$2,704	$2,864	$3,384	$ 37,297	$3,108.08
TOTAL EXPENSES	$8,012	$8,012	$8,013	$8,013	$8,014	$9,214	$8,015	$11,015	$8,015	$8,016	$8,476	$9,546	$102,361	$8,530.08
Difference (available for spending, saving, and investing)	$ 0	$ 0	$ 0	$ 0	$ 0	−1,200	$ 0	$ 0	$ 0	$ 0	−460	−1,530	−3,190	
Revolving savings withdrawals	0	0	0	0	0	1200	0	0	0	0	460	220	1,880	
Uncovered shortfall	$ 0	$ 0	$ 0	$ 0	$ 0	$ 0	$ 0	$ 0	$ 0	$ 0	$ 0	$1,310	$ 1,310	

Cash-Flow Calendar for Harry and Belinda Johnson

Table 3-7

Month	1 Estimated Income	2 Estimated Expenses	3 Surplus/ Deficit (1-2)	4 Cumulative Surplus/ Deficit
January	$ 8,012	$ 8,012	0	0
February	8,012	8,012	0	0
March	8,013	8,013	0	0
April	8,013	8,013	0	0
May	8,014	8,014	0	0
June	8,014	9,214	−1,200	−1,200
July	8,015	8,015	0	−1,200
August	11,015	11,015	0	−1,200
September	8,015	8,015	0	−1,200
October	8,016	8,016	0	−1,200
November	8,016	8,476	−460	−1,660
December	8,016	9,546	−1,530	−3,190
Total	$99,171	$102,361	−$3,190	

(3) dip into their emergency savings in December, and/or (4) utilize credit cards to get through the end-of-year expenses. Ideally, the Johnsons want to have sufficient emergency funds by the end of the year to establish their revolving savings fund for the following 12 months.

The Johnsons disagree about their budget priorities. Belinda wants to spend less on food out and to open a credit card account to pay for the deficits later in the year, while Harry wants to spend less on clothing and entertainment and to skip their planned anniversary dinner party. They both wonder how they can earn so much money and still have such challenging budgeting problems. The Johnsons might benefit by considering the suggestions in Chapter 5 (see pages 161–163) on how to talk with a significant other about financial matters. The Johnsons need to discuss their spending priorities and make decisions so they can reconcile their budget estimates for the year.

Action During Budgeting Period: Control Spending

Budget controls are techniques to maintain control over personal spending so that planned amounts are not exceeded. They give feedback on whether spending is on target and provide information on overspending, errors, emergencies, and exceptions or omissions. Following are several examples of budget controls:

Budget for Shopping Trips Set a budget for every shopping trip, and don't spend a penny more.

Record the Purpose of Expenditures Checks contains a space to record the purpose of expenditures. The check stub or register also provides a place to record explanations of expenditures. If you use automatic teller machines (ATMs) to withdraw cash or use debit cards to pay for day-to-day expenditures, record these withdrawals in the check register *immediately*. Retain the paperwork and write the purpose of each expense on the back of each. Deposit all checks received to your checking account without receiving a portion in cash; if you need cash, write a check or make an ATM withdrawal. If you get cash back when using a credit card, be sure to record why on the receipt.

Table 3–8   Revolving Savings Fund for Harry and Belinda Johnson

Month	Large Expenses	Amount Needed	Deposit into Fund	Withdrawal from Fund	Fund Balance
January		$ 0	$ 250	$ 0	$ 250
February		0	250	0	500
March		0	250	0	750
April		0	250	0	1,000
May		0	250	0	1,250
June	Party and insurance premiums	1,200	0	1,200	50
July		0	240	0	290
August		0	0	0	290
September		0	200	0	490
October		0	190	0	680
November	Holiday gifts	460	0	460	220
December	Holiday gifts and vacation	1,530	0	220	0
Total		$3,190	$1,880	$1,880	−$1,310

Keep Track of Credit Transactions People often do not record their credit transactions until they receive a statement. Then it is easy to continue buying on credit without recognizing the amount of indebtedness until the statement arrives. You should record each credit transaction when it occurs. If you spend $40 on clothing using a credit card, record the expenditure as clothing expenditure and reduce the amount you have remaining to spend for the month in that category.

DID YOU KNOW?

Secrets of Super Savers

How do some people enjoy the good life and still find ways to save 20 to 30 percent or more of their incomes? Like most people, such supersavers have home mortgages, pay tuition bills, and take vacations. And they have peace of mind about their finances because they have built up a sizeable cushion of savings and investments. They follow several rules to seriously save:

- Be goal oriented about savings and investments.
- Ignore impulse spending ("Do I *really* need it?") and choose to postpone buying anything expensive for X months.
- Avoid debt (auto loans and installment loans for computers, TVs, and furniture) and using credit cards so you will not spend money you don't have.

- Cut back on spending on expensive items such as homes (not the largest in the neighborhood) and cars (drive older ones), and enjoy vacations that are not too pricey.
- Choose to spend wisely on everyday expenses by comparison shopping, clipping coupons, buying cheaper goods and services, and being careful about entertainment expenses.
- Track spending by writing down every purchase.
- Make savings automatic by diverting the maximum contribution to your employer's retirement plan, and sign up for automatic transfers from a checking to a savings account as well as to a brokerage account, a 529 plan, a Roth IRA, and/or a high-yield savings account.
- Save more as income rises.

To help keep to a budget, use your check register to keep track of purchases.

Monitor Unexpended Balances to Control Overspending The number one method to control overspending is to monitor unexpended balances in each of your budget classifications. You can accomplish this task by using a budget design that keeps a declining balance, as illustrated by parts (a) and (b) of Figure 3-6. Other budget designs, such as those shown in parts (c) and (d) of Figure 3-6, need to be monitored differently. As illustrated in parts (c) and (d) of the figure, simply calculate subtotals every week or so, as needed, during a monthly budgeting period. You can also track your spending online.

Justify Exceptions to Avoid Lying to Yourself Budget exceptions occur when budget estimates in various classifications differ from actual expenditures. Exceptions usually take the form of overexpenditures, but can also occur in the over- or underreceipt of earnings. Simply spending extra income instead of recording it is not being honest with yourself. Recording the truth—by writing a few words to explain the exception—gives you the information to control your finances. If the exception is an expenditure, then immediately determine how to make up for the overexpenditure by reducing other expenses in your spending plan.

Use a Subordinate Budget A subordinate budget is a detailed listing of planned expenses within a single budgeting classification. For example, an estimate of $1200 for a vacation could be supported by a subordinate budget as follows: motels, $700; restaurants, $300; and entertainment, $200.

Use the Envelope System for the Strongest Control The envelope system of budgeting entails placing exact amounts of money into envelopes for purposes of strict budgetary control. Here you place money equal to the budget estimate for the various expenditure classifications in envelopes at the start of a budgeting period and write the classification name and the budget amount on the outside of each envelope. As expenditures are made, record them on the appropriate envelope and remove the proper amounts of cash. When an envelope is empty, funds are exhausted for that classification. Of course, you must safeguard your cash.

budget exceptions
When budget estimates differ from actual expenditures.

subordinate budget
Detailed listing of planned expenses within a single budgeting classification.

envelope system
Placing exact amounts into envelopes for each budgetary purpose.

FINANCIAL POWER POINT

Mobile Apps and Online Personal Finance Software Tools

You can manage your personal finances by going online or using your smartphone. Try these excellent mobile apps to manage your spending, banking, and credit cards: EasyMoney (www.handy-apps.com/main/EasyMoney.aspx), Mint (www.mint.com/features/anywhere/), Pageonce (www.pageonce.com), PocketMoney (http://pocketmoney.com/), and ProOnGo (http://proongo.com/). The best online software tools are Buxfer (www.buxfer.com/), Mint (www.mint.com), and YodleeMoneyCenter (www.yodlee.com).

Figure 3-6   Record-Keeping Formats

(a)

Food Budget: $90			
DATE	ACTIVITY	AMOUNT	BALANCE
2-6	Groceries	$20	$70
2-9	Dinner out	18	52
2-14	Groceries	11	

(b)

DATE	ACTIVITY	AMOUNT BUDGETED	EXPENDITURES	BALANCE
2-1	Budget estimate	$90		$90
2-6	Groceries		$20	70
2-9	Dinner out		18	52
2-14	Groceries		11	41
2-20	Groceries		25	16
2-28	February Totals	$90	$74	$16

(c)

DATE	ACTIVITY	Food Budget: $90	Clothing Budget: $30	EXPENDITURES Auto Budget: $60	Rent Budget: $275	Savings Budget: $60	Utilities Budget: $40	TOTAL Budget: $680	REMARKS
2-1	Gasoline			10				10	
2-6	Groceries	20						20	Had friends over
2-8	Gasoline			17				17	Good price
2-9	Dinner out	18						18	
2-14	Groceries	11						11	Pepsi on sale
2-15	Subtotals	/49		/27				/76	

(d)

			INCOME Salary	Other	TOTAL	EXPENDITURES Food	Clothing	Auto	Rent	Savings	Utilities	TOTAL	REMARKS
	Estimates		700	40	740	90	30	60	275	60	40	680	
	Balance forwarded from January		—	—	—	6	—	14	—	—	2	28	
	Sum		700	40	740	96	30	74	275	60	42	708	
DATE	ACTIVITY	CASH IN											
2-1	Paycheck	700	700										
2-1	Texaco-gasoline							10				10	
2-6	Safeway-groceries					20						20	Had friends over
2-8	7/11-gasoline							17				17	Good price
2-9	Dinner out-pizza					18						18	
2-14	Giant-groceries					11						11	Pepsi on sale
2-15	Subtotals	/700				/49		/27				/76	
2-16	Cell phone										41	41	
2-28	Totals	700		40	740	83	28	27	275	60	41	660	Good month

Action After: Evaluate Budgeting Progress to Make Needed Changes

Evaluation occurs at the end of each budgeting cycle. The purpose is to determine whether the earlier steps in your budgeting efforts have worked, and it gives you feedback to use for the next budget cycle. You review by comparing actual amounts with budgeted amounts, evaluating whether your objectives were met, and assessing the success of the overall process as well as your progress toward your short- and long-term goals. The evaluation process helps you to make any needed changes.

In some budget expenditure classifications, the budget estimates rarely agree with the actual expenditures—particularly in variable expenses. A **budget variance** is the difference between the amount budgeted and the actual amount spent or received. The remarks column, as illustrated in parts (c) and (d) of Figure 3-6, can help clarify why variances occurred. Overages on a few expenditures may cause little concern. If large variances have prevented you from achieving your objectives or making the budget balance, then take some action. Serious budget controls might have to be instituted or current controls tightened.

Whatever your goals, it feels good when you make progress toward them, and it is thrilling to achieve them. If you did not achieve some of your objectives, you can determine why and then adjust your budget and objectives accordingly. It is okay to revise your plans. Suppose at the end of the month Jackie Chen finds that he is unable to set aside a planned amount of $250 in monthly savings. By evaluating his budget, perhaps Jackie will find that unexpected emergency repairs to a broken window led him to spend more than budgeted for the month. Because Jackie understands why the objective was

FINANCIAL POWER POINT

Before You Buy

If you want to *save $1,000* this year, ask yourself these questions before you buy!

Source: Created by the LFE Institute, a corporate skills-based financial literacy curriculum developer. Copyright © LFE Institute, www.lfeinstitute.com.

budget variance

Difference between amount budgeted and actual amount spent or received.

DID YOU KNOW?

Save Money When Shopping by Using Coupons, Facebook, Twitter, and Smartphone Apps

You can save hundreds of dollars every year by taking advantage of coupons and discounts and using phone apps. There is nothing wrong with getting a "$25-off coupon at Ruby Tuesdays," a "$5-off coupon for Pepsi or Coke at Walgreens," or "$50 off a smartphone." Discounts are available, so try the following:

- Take advantage of Facebook or Twitter to sign up for coupons and discounts by linking your favorite brands.

- Receive daily coupon notices on local deals at Groupon.com and Livingsocial.com.

- Use your smartphone to check out ShopSavvy's app that scans an item barcode, sees who has it for less, and locates those sellers; in addition, it can send price alerts when items drop below the prices you've already seen.

- Utilize the Google Shopper app, which uses your smartphone's camera to recognize products by cover art, barcode scanning, voice, and text, and then provides reviews and specs. Also try Coupon Sherpa for your Android or iPhone.

- Search for air, car rental, and hotel coupon codes at Promotional/Codes.com or CouponWinner.com.

- Try out "price comparison" search engines such as PriceGrabber.com and Nextag.com.

- Redeem Sunday newspaper coupons that provide discounts for hundreds of products.

- Stop by the U.S. Post Office for an envelope of coupons if you are moving from one address to another.

- Take grocery store coupons attached to products, on tear pads, and on bottle necks as well as from cashiers upon checkout.

- Go online to obtain coupons and do so by setting up a separate e-mail account for coupons and then registering at the sites. Examples are Restaurant.com, Coupons.com, CoolSavings.com, SmartSource.com, GroceryCoupons.com, CouponMom.com, RetailMeNot.com and GrocerySmarts.com.

- Go to the websites for local radio stations, where they may have downloadable coupons for local restaurants and entertainment venues.

- Purchase valid coupons on eBay for only 10 to 25 cents on the dollar.

record keeping
Recording sources and amounts of dollars earned and spent.

net surplus
Amount remaining after all budget classification deficits are subtracted from those with surpluses.

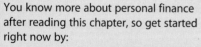
not achieved, he can set his sights on reaching the goal during the next budgeting time period.

Record Keeping In the process of budgeting, **record keeping** is the process of recording the sources and amounts of dollars earned and spent. Recording the estimated and actual amounts for both income and expenditures helps you monitor your money flow. Keeping track of income and expenses is the only way to collect sufficient information to evaluate how close you are to achieving your financial objectives. For those who keep records on paper, Figure 3-6 shows four samples of self-prepared record-keeping formats that vary in complexity. Most people record earnings and expenditures when they occur. When writing in the "activity" and "remarks" columns in your record, be descriptive because you may need the information later.

Adding Up Actual Income and Expenditures After the budgeting period has ended—usually at the beginning of a new month—you need to add up the actual income received and expenditures made during that period. You can perform this calculation on a form for each budget classification, as shown in parts (a) and (b) of Figure 3-6 or on a form with all income and expenditure classifications, as in parts (c) and (d) of Figure 3-6. Such calculations indicate where you may have overspent within your budget categories. If you are new at budgeting, do not be too concerned about overspending; it occurs in some classifications almost always, only to be balanced by underspending in other categories. Use such information to refine your budget estimates in the future. In three or four months, you will be able to estimate your expenses much more accurately. The *Garman/Forgue* companion website provides budgeting software as well as numerous other templates, calculators, and worksheets that you can use in your own personal financial planning.

What to Do with Budgeted Money Left Over at the End of the Month At the end of the budgeting time period, some budget classifications may still have a positive balance. For example, perhaps you estimated the electric bill at $100, but it was only $80. You may then ask, "What do I do with the $20 surplus?" You also may ask, "What happens to budget classifications that were overspent?"

People handle the **net surplus** (the amount remaining after all budget classification deficits are subtracted from those with surpluses) in any of the following ways:

- Carry the surpluses forward
- Put surpluses into a revolving savings fund
- Build a cash reserve by depositing surpluses in a savings account
- Pay down credit card debt
- Put surpluses toward a mortgage or other loan
- Invest in a retirement account
- Spend surpluses like "mad money" on anything you want

The budgeting form in part (d) of Figure 3-6 (page 92) allows for carrying balances forward to the next period. Some people carry forward deficits, with the hope that having less available in a budgeted classification the following month will motivate them to keep expenditures low. Because variable expense estimates are usually averages, it is best not to change the estimate based on a variation that occurs over just one or two months. If estimates are too high or low for a longer period, you will want to make adjustments.

Using financial software for budgeting takes the drudgery out of making and using a spending plan. And it gets to be easy after a few months. Budgeting can help you succeed financially.

✔ Concept Check 3.5

1. Identify two actions that should be performed before establishing a budget.

2. What are budget estimates? Offer some suggestions on how to go about making budget estimates for various types of expenses.

3. Distinguish between a cash-flow calendar and a revolving savings fund, and tell why each is important.

4. Offer three suggestions for effective budget controls.

WHAT DO YOU RECOMMEND NOW?

Now that you have read the chapter on financial planning, what do you recommend to Robert for his talk with Nicole on the subject of financial planning regarding:

1. Determining what they own and owe?

2. Better understanding their patterns of family income and expenditure?

3. Using the information in Robert's newly prepared financial statements to summarize the family's financial situation?

4. Setting financial goals?

5. Evaluating their financial progress?

6. Setting up a record-keeping system to better serve their needs?

7. Starting a budgeting process to guide saving and spending?

BIG PICTURE SUMMARY OF LEARNING OBJECTIVES

LO1. Identify your financial values, goals, and strategies.
By identifying your financial values, goals, and strategies, you can always keep a balance between spending and saving and stay committed to your financial success. You may create financial plans in three broad areas: plans for spending, plans for risk management, and plans for capital accumulation.

LO2. Use balance sheets and cash-flow statements to measure your financial health and progress.
Financial statements are compilations of personal financial data designed to furnish information on money matters. The balance sheet provides information on what you own, what you owe, and what the net result would be if you paid off all your debts. The cash-flow

statement lists income and expenditures over a specific period of time, such as the previous month or year.

LO3. Evaluate your financial strength and progress using financial ratios.
Financial ratios are numerical calculations designed to simplify the process of evaluating your financial strength and the progress of your financial condition. Ratios serve as tools or yardsticks to develop saving, spending, and credit-use patterns consistent with your goals.

LO4. Collect and organize the financial records necessary for managing your personal finances.
Your financial records will help determine where you are, where you have been, and where you are going financially. They also help you make money.

LO5.   **Achieve your financial goals through budgeting.** Budgeting is all about logical thinking about your finances. Budgeting forces you to consider what is important in your life, what things you want to own, how you want to live, what it will take to do that, and, more generally, what you want to achieve in life. A budget is a process used to record both projected and actual income and expenditures over a period of time, and it represents the major mechanism through which your financial plans are carried out and goals are achieved.

LET'S TALK ABOUT IT

1. **Families.** During sluggish economic times, the federal government's budgeting priority is to spend much more money than it takes in. What happens to families that try that, and why?

2. **Your Values.** What are your three most important personal values? Give an example of how each of those values might influence your financial plans.

3. **Cash Flow.** College students often have little income and many expenses. Does this reduce or increase the importance of completing a cash-flow statement on a monthly basis? Why?

4. **Financial Ratios.** Of the financial ratios described in this chapter, which two might be most revealing for the typical college student? Which two are the most revealing for a retiree?

5. **Why Budget.** Do you have a budget? Why or why not? What do you think are the major reasons why people do not make formal budgets?

6. **Control Spending.** What can a person do to control spending to better achieve financial success?

7. **Budgeting Mistake.** What is the biggest budget-related mistake that you have made? What would you do differently?

DO THE MATH

1. **Ratio Analyses for Victor and Maria.** Review the financial statements of Victor and Maria Hernandez (Table 3-2 and Table 3-3) and respond to the following questions:

   (a) Using the data in the Hernandezes' balance sheet, calculate an investment assets-to-net worth ratio. How would you interpret the ratio? The Hernandez family appears to have too few monetary assets compared with tangible and investment assets. How would you suggest that they remedy that situation over the next few years?

   (b) Comment on the couple's diversification of their investment assets.

   (c) Calculate the asset-to-debt ratio for Victor and Maria. How does this information help you understand their financial situation? How do their total assets compare with their total liabilities?

   (d) The Hernandezes seem to receive most of their income from employment rather than investments. What actions would you recommend for them to remedy that imbalance over the next few years?

   (e) The Hernandezes want to take a two-week vacation next summer, and they have only eight months to save the necessary $2400. What reasonable changes in expenses might they consider to increase net surplus and make the needed $300 per month?

2. **Ratio Analyses.** Use the following balance sheet and cash flow statement information to answer the questions below. Liquid assets: $10,000; home value: $210,000; monthly mortgage payment: $1300; investment assets: $90,000; personal property: $20,000; total assets: $330,000; short-term debt: $5500 ($250 a month); long-term term debt: $170,000 ($2100 a month); total debt: $175,500; monthly gross income: $9000; monthly disposable income: $6800; monthly expenses: $6000. Calculate the following:

   (a) Liquidity ratio

   (b) Asset-to-debt ratio

   (c) Debt service-to-income ratio

   (d) Debt payments-to-disposable income ratio

   (e) Investment assets-to-total assets ratio

3. **Cash Flow Surplus/Deficit.** Johan Sebastion earns $40,000 a year. He pays 30 percent of his gross income in federal, state, and local taxes. He has fixed expenses in addition to taxes of $1200 per month and variable expenses that average $900 per month. What is his net cash flow (surplus or deficit) for the year?

4. **Construct Financial Statements.** John Green has been a retail salesclerk for six years. At age 35, he is divorced with one child, Amanda, age 7. John's salary is $36,000 per year. He regularly receives $400 per month for child support from Amanda's mother. John invests $100 each month ($50 in his mutual fund and $50 in U.S. savings bonds). Using the following information, construct a balance sheet and a cash-flow statement for John.

ASSETS	Amount
Vested retirement benefits (no employee contribution)	$3,000
Money market account (includes $150 of interest earned last year)	5,000
Mutual fund (includes $200 of reinvested dividend income from last year)	4,000
Checking account	1,000
Personal property	5,000
Automobile	3,000
U.S. savings bonds	3,000

LIABILITIES	Outstanding Balance
Dental bill (pays $25 per month and is included in uninsured medical/dental)	$ 450
Visa (pays $100 per month)	1,500
Student loan (pays $100 per month)	7,500

ANNUAL EXPENSES	Amount
Auto insurance	$ 780
Rent	9,100
Utilities	1,200
Phone	680
Cable	360
Food	3,000
Uninsured medical/dental	1,000

ANNUAL EXPENSES	Amount
Dry cleaning	480
Personal care	420
Gas, maintenance, license	2,120
Clothes	500
Entertainment	1,700
Vacations/visitation travel	1,300
Child care	3,820
Gifts	400
Miscellaneous	300
Taxes	6,400
Health insurance	2,440

5. **Budgeting and Income Projections.** Sharon and Dick DeVaney of Monument, Colorado, have decided to start a family next year, so they are looking over their budget (illustrated in Table 3-5 as the "young married couple"). Sharon thinks that she can go on half-salary ($1050 instead of $2100 per month) in her job as a graduate assistant for about 18 months after the baby's birth; she will then return to full-time work.

(a) Looking at the DeVaneys' current monthly budget, identify categories and amounts in their $4315 budget where they realistically might cut back $1050. (Hint: Federal and state taxes should drop about $290 as their income drops.)

(b) Assume that Sharon and Dick could be persuaded not to begin a family for another two to three years until Sharon finishes graduate school. What specific budgeting recommendations would you give them for handling (i) their fixed expenses and (ii) their variable expenses to prepare financially for an anticipated $1050 loss of income for 18 months as well as the expenses for the new baby?

(c) If the DeVaneys' gross income of $4315 rises 3 percent per year in the future, what will their income be after five years? (Hint: See Appendix A.1 or the *Garman/Forgue* companion website.)

FINANCIAL PLANNING CASES

CASE 1

The Financial Statements of Harry and Belinda Johnson Suggest Budgeting Problems

Harry graduated with a bachelor's degree in interior design last spring from a large Midwestern university near his hometown. Belinda has a degree in information technology from a university on the West Coast and is employed in a medium-size public relations firm. Harry and Belinda both worked on their schools' student newspapers and met at a conference during their junior year in college. They were married last June and live in an apartment in Kansas City. They will face many financial challenges over the next 20 years, as they buy their first home, decide on life insurance needs, begin a family, change jobs, and invest for retirement.

Harry works at a medium-size interior design firm and, during the last half of 2011, earned a gross salary of $3100 per month. He also receives $3000 in interest income per year from a trust fund set up by his deceased father's estate; the trust fund will continue to pay that amount until 2020. Belinda works as a salesperson for a regional stock brokerage firm.

She earned a salary of $4750 per month during 2011. Belinda has many job-related benefits, including life insurance, health insurance, a retirement plan, and a credit union. Harry anticipates a raise of $150 a month in his salary by next January, and because of the sluggish economy, Belinda expects no raise whatsoever. The Johnsons live in an apartment located approximately halfway between their places of employment; however, their rent will increase by $100 a month next July. Harry drives about ten minutes to his job, and Belinda travels about 15 minutes via public transportation to reach her downtown job. Harry and Belinda's apartment is very nice, but small, and it is furnished primarily with furniture given to them by their families. Soon after starting their first jobs, Harry and Belinda decided to begin their financial planning. Fortunately each had taken a college course in personal finance. After initial discussion, they worked together for two evenings to develop the two financial statements presented below.

(a)   Briefly describe how Harry and Belinda probably determined the fair market prices for each of their tangible and investment assets.

(b)   Using the data from the cash-flow statement developed by Harry and Belinda, calculate a liquidity ratio, asset-to-debt ratio, debt service-to-income ratio, debt payments-to-disposable income ratio, and investment assets-to-total assets ratio. What do these ratios tell you about the Johnsons' financial situation? Should Harry and Belinda incur more debt, such as credit cards or a new car loan?

(c)   The Johnsons enjoy a high income because both work at well-paying jobs. They have spent parts of three evenings over the past several days discussing their financial values and goals together. As shown in the upper portion of Figure 3-5, they have established three long-term goals: $3000 for a European vacation to be taken in 2015, $5000 needed in October 2016 for a down payment on a new automobile, and $18,900 for a down payment on a home to be purchased in December 2017. As shown in the lower portion of the figure, the Johnsons did some calculations to determine how much they had to save for each goal—over the near term—to stay on schedule to reach their long-term goals as well as pay for two vacations and an anniversary party. After developing their balance sheet and cash-flow statement (shown below), the Johnsons made a budget for the year (shown in Table 3-6 on page 88). They then reconciled various conflicting needs and wants until they found that total annual income was close to the total of planned expenses. Next, they created a revolving savings fund (Table 3-8) in which they were careful to include enough money each month to meet all of their short-term goals. When developing their cash-flow calendar for the year (Table 3-7), they noticed a problem: substantial cash deficits toward the end of the year. In fact, despite their projected high income, they anticipate a deficit of $1530 for the year. To solve this problem, they do not anticipate increasing their income, using savings, or borrowing. Instead, they are considering modifying their needs and wants to reduce their budget estimates to the point where they would have a positive balance for the year. Make specific recommendations to the Johnsons on how they could make reductions in their budget estimates. Do not offer suggestions that would alter their new lifestyle drastically, as the couple would reject these ideas.

Balance Sheet for Harry and Belinda Johnson

January 1, 2012
ASSETS

Monetary Assets		
Cash on hand	1,178	5.48%
Savings (First Federal Bank)	890	4.14%
Savings (Far West Savings Bank)	560	2.60%
Savings (Homestead Credit Union)	160	0.74%
Checking (First Federal Bank)	752	3.50%
Total monetary assets	$ 3,540	16.45%
Tangible Assets		
Automobile (3-year-old Toyota)	11,000	51.13%
Personal property	2,300	10.69%
Furniture	1,700	7.90%
Total tangible assets	$15,000	69.72%
Investment Assets		
Harry's retirement account	1,425	6.62%
Belinda's retirement account	1,550	7.20%
Total investment assets	$ 2,975	13.83%
Total Assets	$21,515	100.00%
LIABILITIES		
Short-Term Liabilities		
Visa credit card	390	1.81%
Target credit card	45	0.21%
Dental bill	400	1.86%
Total short-term liabilities	$ 835	3.88%
Long-Term Liabilities		
Vehicle loan (First Federal Bank)	3,800	17.66%
Student loan (Belinda)	8,200	38.11%

January 1, 2012

	Dollars	Percent
Total long-term liabilities	$12,000	55.78%
Total Liabilities	$12,835	59.66%
Net Worth	$ 8,680	40.34%
Total Liabilities and Net Worth	$21,515	100.00%

Cash-Flow Statement for Harry and Belinda Johnson July 1–December 31, 2011 (First Six Months of Marriage)

Cash Flow	Dollars	Percent
INCOME		
Harry's gross income ($3100 × 6)	18,600	37.11%
Belinda's gross income ($4750 × 6)	28,500	56.86%
Interest on savings account	24	0.05%
Harry's trust fund	3,000	5.99%
Total Income	$50,124	100.00%
EXPENDITURES		
Fixed Expenses		
Rent	6,600	13.17%
Renter's insurance	220	0.44%
Automobile loan payments	2,980	5.95%
Automobile insurance	850	1.70%
Health insurance (withheld from salary)	1,200	2.39%
Student loan payments	3,600	7.18%
Life insurance (withheld from salary)	90	0.18%
Cable TV and Internet	720	1.44%
Health club	420	0.84%
Savings/emergencies	600	1.20%
Harry's retirement plan (6% of salary)	1,115	2.22%
Belinda's retirement plan (4% of salary)	1,140	2.27%
Federal income tax (withheld from salary)	4,600	9.18%
State income tax (withheld from salary)	1,600	3.19%
Social Security (withheld from salary)	3,600	7.18%
Automobile registration	300	0.60%
Total Fixed Expenses	$29,635	59.12%
Variable Expenses		
Food (groceries)	2,600	5.19%
Food (out)	1,800	3.59%
Utilities	750	1.50%
Cell phones	450	0.90%
Gasoline and maintenance	700	1.40%
Doctor's and dentist's bills	710	1.42%
Medicines	350	0.70%
Clothing and upkeep	1,200	2.39%
Church and charity	1,200	2.39%
Gifts	1,070	2.13%
Public transportation	720	1.44%
Personal allowances	4,160	8.30%
Entertainment	960	1.92%
Vacation (holiday)	600	1.20%
Vacation (summer)	1,200	2.39%

Cash Flow	Dollars	Percent
Miscellaneous	480	0.96%
Total Variable Expenses	$18,950	37.81%
Total Expenses	$48,585	96.93%
SURPLUS (DEFICIT)	$ 1,539	3.07%

CASE 2

Victor and Maria Hernandez

Victor and Maria, both in their late 30s, have two children: John, age 13, and Joseph, age 15. Victor has had a long sales career with a major retail appliance store. Maria works part-time as a medical records assistant. The Hernandezes own two vehicles and their home, on which they have a mortgage. They will face many financial challenges over the next 20 years, as their children drive, go to college, and leave home and go out in the world on their own. Victor and Maria also recognize the need to further prepare for their retirement and the challenges of aging.

Victor and Maria spent some time making up their first balance sheet, which is shown in Table 3-2. Victor and Maria are a bit confused about how various financial activities can affect their net worth.

(a) Assume that their home is now appraised at $192,000 and the value of their automobile has dropped to $9500. Calculate and characterize the effects of these changes on their net worth on their asset-to-debt ratio.

(b) If Victor and Maria take out a bank loan for $1545 and pay off their credit card debts totaling $1545, what effects would these changes have on their net worth?

(c) If Victor and Maria sell their New York 2018 bond and put the cash into the savings account, what effects would this have on their net worth and liquidity ratio?

CASE 3

Julia Price Thinks About Financial Statements, Tools, and Budgets

Julia graduated six years ago in aeronautical engineering and changed jobs once. Her income is more than sufficient for her needs. Julia contributes the maximum into her employer's retirement account and additionally saves about $400 a month. She has only about $1000 in credit card debt and makes a monthly car payment of $520. With such a strong financial position, she thinks it would be a waste of time to prepare financial statements and create a budget. Offer your opinions about her thinking.

CASE 4

Budget Control for a Recent Graduate

Mike Staten, a political scientist from Worcester, Massachusetts, graduated from college eight months ago and is having a terrible time with his budget. Mike has a regular monthly income from his job and no really large bills, but he likes to spend. He exceeds his budget every month, and his credit card balances are increasing. Choose three budget control methods that you could recommend to Mike, and explain how each one could help him gain control of his finances.

CASE 5

A Couple Creates an Educational Savings Plan

Stanley Marsh and Wendy Testaburger of South Park, Colorado, have two young children and have been living on a tight budget. Their monthly budget is illustrated in Table 3-5 on page 86 as the "married

couple with two young children." Wendy and Stanley are nervous about not having started an educational savings plan for their children. Wendy has just begun working on a part-time basis at a local accounting firm and earns about $860 per month; this income is reflected in the Marsh-Testaburgers' budget. They have decided that they want to save $200 per month for the children's education, but Wendy does not want to work more hours away from home.

(a) Review the family's budget and make suggestions about how to modify various budget estimates so that they could save $200 per month for the education fund.

(b) Briefly describe the effect of your recommended changes on the Marsh-Testaburgers' lifestyle.

BE YOUR OWN PERSONAL FINANCIAL MANAGER

1. **Financial Plan.** Use Table 3-1 on page 66 as a guide to making your financial plans, goals, and objectives for spending, risk management, and capital accumulation. Write up your findings.

2. **Balance Sheet.** Use Table 3-2 on page 73 as a guide to create a balance sheet or complete Worksheet 10: My Balance Sheet from "My Personal Financial Planner" to create your own detailed annual balance sheet. Write up your findings.

3. **Cash-Flow Statement.** Use Table 3-3 on page 76 as a guide to create a cash-flow statement or complete Worksheet 11: My Cash-Flow Statement from "My Personal Financial Planner" to create your own cash-flow statement. Write up your findings.

   MY PERSONAL FINANCIAL PLANNER

4. **Evaluate Your Financial Ratios.** Use the financial ratios on pages 77–78 to help evaluate your personal financial condition or complete Worksheet 12: My Financial Ratios from "My Personal Financial Planner" to record your financial ratios.

   MY PERSONAL FINANCIAL PLANNER

5. **Categorize Your Financial Records.** Review Table 3-4 "Financial Records: What to Keep and Where" on pages 80–81 to develop a system for your own records or complete Worksheet 13: My Financial Records from "My Personal Financial Planner" to record what records will be placed in your home file, safe-deposit box, or another place.

   MY PERSONAL FINANCIAL PLANNER

6. **Monthly Saving to Reach Your Goals.** Use Figure 3-5 "Goals Worksheet for Harry and Belinda Johnson" on page 84 as a guide to develop your own personal savings goals or complete Worksheet

   MY PERSONAL FINANCIAL PLANNER

14: Monthly Savings to Reach My Financial Goals from "My Personal Financial Planner" to record the dollar amount, time, and interim short-term goals.

7. **Nonmonthly Expenses.** Complete Worksheet 15: Determining Monthly Budget Amounts for My Nonmonthly Expenses from "My Personal Financial Planner" to carefully plan for your nonmonthly expenses over the year.

   MY PERSONAL FINANCIAL PLANNER

8. **Revolving Savings Fund.** Review Table 3-8 "Revolving Savings Fund for Harry and Belinda Johnson" on page 90 to develop a plan for yourself or complete Worksheet 16: My Revolving Savings Fund from "My Personal Financial Planner" to record how you can save to pay for irregular expenses throughout the year.

   MY PERSONAL FINANCIAL PLANNER

9. **Create Your Budget.** Use Table 3-6 on page 88 as a guide to create a 12-month budget or complete Worksheet 17: My Budget from "My Personal Financial Planner" to do so.

   MY PERSONAL FINANCIAL PLANNER

10. **Control Spending with Budget Worksheets.** Complete Worksheet 18: My Budget Category Ledger Worksheets from "My Personal Financial Planner" to create a system to monitor and control spending.

    MY PERSONAL FINANCIAL PLANNER

11. **Organize Your Financial Records.** Use Table 3-4 on pages 80–81 as a guide to helping you get your financial records in order. Write down some notes about your thinking on what documents you will need and where to keep them.

    MY PERSONAL FINANCIAL PLANNER

MY PERSONAL FINANCIAL PLANNER

ON THE 'NET

Go to the Web pages indicated to complete these exercises. You can also go to the *Garman/Forgue* companion website at www.cengagebrain.com for an expanded list of exercises. Under General Business, select the title of this text. Click on the Internet Exercises link for this chapter.

1. **Online Calculators.** Visit *Kiplinger's Personal Finance Magazine* website at www.kiplinger.com. There you will find a link to a long list of calculators that can be used in various present and future value calculations. Select four that you believe would be particularly useful in the aspects of personal financial planning that were discussed in this chapter.

2. **Family Budgets of Others.** Visit the website for the Economic Policy Institute at www.epi.org/content/budget_calculator/ where you can find an example of a family budget for many areas of the United States. Calculate the budget for an area of interest to you. How useful do you think such a calculator would be for a family interested in developing its own budget?

3. **Input Your Budget and Compare to Your Projected Expenditures.** Visit the website www.kiplinger.com/tools/budget/ and use the budgeting worksheet and input your projected monthly living costs in various categories. First, enter your estimates in the "Projected" column and print the page. Over the following month, keep track of your expenditures in these same categories, perhaps in a small notebook, and then re-enter both sets of numbers in the worksheet, and compare your projections to what you actually spent.

4. **Can You Make It Through the Month?** "Spent" is an online game that simulates the struggles of homelessness. Accept the challenge and take 10 minutes to play Spent (http://playspent.org/).

ACTION INVOLVEMENT PROJECTS

1. **Money Discussion Topics.** Use the list in the box "Did You Know? Money Topics to Discuss with Your Partner" as a guide to interview three married couples, asking them which of the topics they discussed with their partners within the first year of marriage. Make a table that summarizes your findings.

2. **Financial Mistakes.** Survey five people to learn about their financial mistakes in life. Ask each person to cite two financial mistakes he/she has made. Make a table that summarizes your findings.

3. **Short-Term Financial Goals.** Survey five people to ascertain their financial goals. Ask each person, "What are your top two short-term financial goals?" Make a table that summarizes your findings.

4. **Long-Term Financial Goals.** Survey five people to ascertain their financial goals. Ask each person, "What are your top three long-term financial goals?" Make a table that summarizes your findings.

Visit the Garman/Forgue companion website at **www.cengagebrain.com**.

PART 2

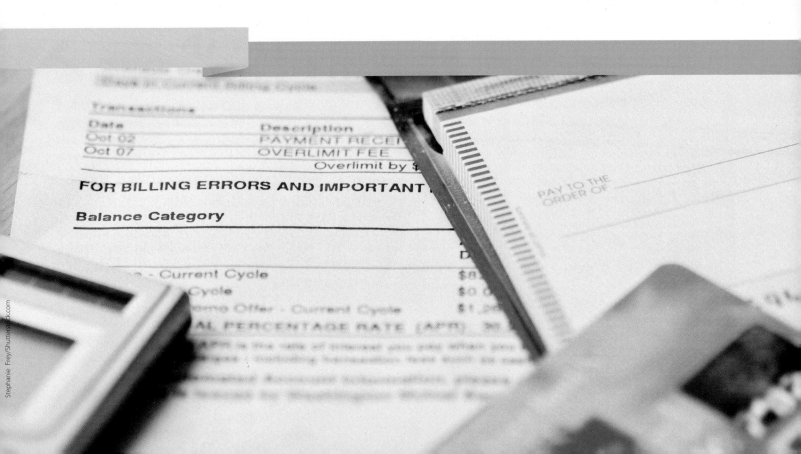

Managing Income Taxes

YOU MUST BE KIDDING, RIGHT?

Bharat Persaud's employer gave him a $2000 bonus last year, and when Bharat was filling out his federal income tax form, he discovered that $1000 of it moved him from the 15 percent marginal tax rate to 25 percent. How much tax will Bharat pay on the $2000?

A. $150

B. $180

C. $250

D. $400

The answer is D. The federal marginal tax rate is applied to your last dollar of earnings. The first $1000 of Bharat's bonus is taxed at the marginal tax rate of 15 percent ($150), but the second $1000 is taxed at 25 percent ($250). Be aware of your marginal tax rate!

LEARNING OBJECTIVES

After reading this chapter, you should be able to:

1 Explain the nature of progressive income taxes and the marginal tax rate.

2 Differentiate among the eight steps involved in calculating your federal income taxes.

3 Use appropriate strategies to avoid overpayment of income taxes.

© PETER DAZELEY/GETTY IMAGES, INC.

WHAT DO YOU RECOMMEND?

Tom Edgar and Gerry Szpanka plan to get married in two years. Tom earns $44,000 per year managing a fast-food restaurant. He also earns about $10,000 per year selling jewelry that he designs at craft shows held monthly in various nearby cities. Right after they get married, Tom plans to go back to college full time to finish the last year of his undergraduate degree. Gerry earns $58,000 annually working as an institutional sales representative for an insurance company. Both Tom and Gerry each contribute $100 per month to their employer-sponsored 401(k) retirement accounts. Tom has little additional savings, but Gerry has accumulated $18,000 that she wants to use for a down payment on a home. Gerry also owns 300 shares of stock in an oil company that she inherited four years ago when the price was $90 per share; now the stock is worth $130 per share. Tom and Gerry live in a state where the state income tax is 6 percent.

What would you recommend to Tom and Gerry on the subject of managing income taxes regarding:

1. Using tax credits to help pay for Tom's college expenses?

2. Determining how much money Gerry will realize if she sells the stocks, assuming she pays federal income taxes at the 25 percent rate?

3. Buying a home?

4. Increasing contributions to their employer-sponsored retirement plans?

5. Establishing a sideline business for Tom's jewelry operation?

Managing your money effectively includes efforts to avoid paying unnecessary sums to the government in taxes. These efforts will provide you with more money to do with what you want. "The avoidance of taxes is the only intellectual pursuit that carries any reward," wrote economist John Maynard Keynes.

You should pay your income tax liabilities in full, but that's all—there is no need to pay a dime extra. To achieve this goal, you need to adopt a **tax planning** perspective designed to reduce, defer, or eliminate some income taxes. To get started, you should recognize that you pay personal income taxes only on your **taxable income**. This amount is determined by subtracting various exclusions, adjustments, exemptions, and deductions from total income, with the result being the income upon which the tax is actually calculated. Details for these calculations are provided later. For now, simply remember that the main idea in managing income taxes is to reduce your taxable income as much as possible while maintaining a high level of total income. The result will lower your actual tax liability. By carefully analyzing and managing the subject of income taxes to your advantage, you can avoid overpayment of income taxes. Then you will have more money available every year to manage, spend, save, invest, and donate—activities that are the focus of the remainder of this book.

tax planning
Seeking legal ways to reduce, eliminate, or defer income taxes.

taxable income
Income upon which income taxes are levied.

LEARNING OBJECTIVE **1**

Explain the nature of progressive income taxes and the marginal tax rate.

taxes
Compulsory government-imposed charges levied on citizens and their property.

marginal tax bracket (MTB)/ marginal tax rate
One of six income-range segments at which income is taxed at increasing rates. Also known as marginal tax rate.

marginal tax rate
The tax rates that apply to income in each tax bracket range. Also known as marginal tax bracket.

indexing
Yearly adjustments to tax brackets that reduce inflation's effects on tax brackets.

PROGRESSIVE INCOME TAXES AND THE MARGINAL TAX RATE

Taxes are compulsory charges imposed by a government on its citizens and their property. The U.S. Internal Revenue Service (IRS) is the agency charged with the responsibility for collecting federal income taxes based on the legal provisions in the *Internal Revenue Code*.

The Progressive Nature of the Federal Income Tax

Taxes can be classified as progressive or regressive. The federal personal income tax is a **progressive tax** because the tax rate progressively increases as a taxpayer's taxable income increases. A higher income implies a greater ability to pay. As Table 4-1 shows, the higher portions of a taxpayer's taxable income are taxed at increasingly higher rates under the federal income tax. A **regressive tax** operates in the opposite way. That is, as income rises, the tax demands a decreasing proportion of a person's income. An example is a state sales tax, since a rate of perhaps 5 percent might have to be paid by everyone regardless of income.

The Marginal Tax Rate Is Applied to the Last Dollar Earned

The **marginal tax bracket (MTB)** is one of the six income-range segments that are taxed at increasing rates as income goes up. These rates are also called the **marginal tax rate**. The tax rates apply only to the income in each tax bracket range. Recall from Chapter 1 that the marginal tax rate is applied to your last dollar of earnings. Depending on their income, taxpayers fit into one of the brackets (as shown in Table 4-1) and, accordingly, pay at one of those marginal tax rates: 10 percent, 15 percent, 25 percent, 28 percent, 33 percent, or 35 percent. These marginal tax rates apply for tax years 2011 and 2012, unless Congress takes action to extend them. Each year, dollar amounts for the taxable income brackets are adjusted to reduce the effects of inflation in a process called **indexing**. This keeps taxpayers from being forced to pay more taxes as they receive raises simply to keep up with inflation. More income, even taxable income, is a good thing.

Your marginal tax rate is perhaps the single most important concept in personal finance. It tells you the portion of any extra taxable earnings—from a raise, investment income, or money from a second job—you must pay in income taxes. Correspondingly, it measures the tax reduction benefits of a tax-deductible expense that allows you to

Table 4-1

The Progressive Nature of the Federal Income Tax

Segment of Taxable Income	Marginal Tax Rate*
First $8,500	10%
Over $8,500 but not over $34,500	15%
Over $34,500 but not over $83,600	25%
Over $83,600 but not over $174,400	28%
Over $174,400 but not over $379,150	33%
Over $379,150	35%

* Tax rates for single taxpayer.

reduce your taxable income. Consider this example of how the marginal tax rate might apply. Susan Bassett is from Syracuse, New York (see Figure 4-1). Because of provisions in the tax laws, part of her $60,000 income ($9500 [$3700 + $5800]) is not taxed, the next $8500 is taxed at 10 percent, the next $26,000 is taxed at 15 percent, and the remaining $16,000 of Susan's $60,000 income is taxed at 25 percent. Thus, Susan is in the 25 percent marginal tax bracket because the *last* dollar that she earned is taxed at that level. Her tax liability is $8750 based on her $60,000 in income.

All tax information cited in this chapter is for income tax returns filed in 2012 for tax year 2011, unless otherwise noted. The mathematics shown in Figure 4-1 are based either on the **IRS tax table** (used for tax returns with incomes up to $100,000) or the **tax-rate schedules** (used for tax returns with incomes above $100,000).

Use Your Marginal Tax Rate to Help Make Financial Decisions

The marginal tax rate can affect many financial decisions that you make. Consider, for example, what happens if you are in the 25 percent marginal tax bracket and you make a $100 tax-deductible contribution to a charity. The charity receives the $100, and you deduct the $100 from your taxable income. This deduction results in a $25 reduction in your federal income tax ($100 × 0.25). In effect, you give only $75 (not $100) because the government, in effect, "gives" $25 to the charity.

Your Effective Marginal Tax Rate Is Higher

The **effective marginal tax rate** describes a person's total marginal tax rate on income after including federal, state, and local income taxes as well as Social Security and Medicare taxes. To determine your effective marginal tax rate on income, add all of these other taxes to your federal marginal tax rate. For example, a single taxpayer earning a

effective marginal tax rate
The total marginal rate reflects all taxes on a person's income, including federal, state, and local income taxes as well as Social Security and Medicare taxes.

Figure 4-1

How Your Income Is Really Taxed (Example: Susan Bassett with a $60,000 Gross Income)

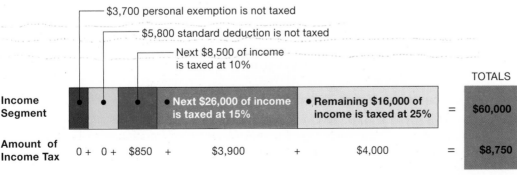

Susan's marginal tax rate is 25%.

DID YOU KNOW?

How to Determine Your Marginal Tax Rate

You can determine your marginal tax rate by following this example.

1. *Robert Heatherton is single and has a taxable income of $27,825, and looking at the illustrated tax table (Table 4-3 on page 118), he finds his tax on that amount of income ($3479).*

2. *Add $100 to that income for a total of $27,925, and find the tax on that amount ($3764).*

3. *Calculate the difference between the two tax amounts ($3764 – $3749). The extra $15 in taxes from a $100 increase in income reflects a federal marginal tax rate of 15 percent.*

average tax rate
Proportion of total income paid in income taxes.

LEARNING OBJECTIVE ②

Differentiate among the eight steps involved in calculating your federal income taxes.

total income
Compensation from all sources.

earned income
Compensation for performing personal services.

taxable income between $34,500 and $83,600 will pay federal income taxes at a marginal rate of 25 percent, a combined Social Security and Medicare tax rate of 7.65 percent, a state income tax rate of 6 percent, and a city income tax rate of 4 percent. These taxes result in an effective marginal tax rate of 43 percent (25 + 7.65 + 6 + 4 = 42.65, rounded to 43). Many employed taxpayers pay an effective marginal tax rate of 43 percent.

Your Average Tax Rate Is Much Lower than Your Marginal Rate

Many people wonder what proportion of their total income they pay in income taxes. Your **average tax rate** gives the answer to this question. For example, the average tax rate on Susan Bassett's total income (the illustration in Figure 4-1) is 14.5 percent ($8750 ÷ $60,000). This is somewhat more than the 9.2 percent average rate for all U.S. taxpayers (and you, too, will learn how to bring down your tax liability). The average federal tax rates in the United States are among the lowest in the world.

 Concept Check 4.1

1. Distinguish between a progressive and a regressive tax.

2. What is a marginal tax bracket, and how does it affect taxpayers?

3. Explain why some taxpayers have a marginal tax rate as high as 43 percent.

EIGHT STEPS IN CALCULATING YOUR INCOME TAXES

There are eight basic steps in calculating federal income taxes:

1. Determine your total income.
2. Determine and report your gross income after subtracting exclusions.
3. Subtract adjustments to income.
4. Subtract either the IRS's standard deduction amount for your tax status or your itemized deductions.
5. Subtract the value of your personal exemptions.
6. Determine your preliminary tax liability.
7. Subtract tax credits for which you qualify.
8. Calculate the balance due the IRS or the amount of your refund.

Figure 4-2 graphically depicts these eight steps in the overall process of federal income tax calculation. The idea is to reduce your income so that you pay the smallest amount possible in income taxes. You do so by reducing total income by removing nontaxable income and then subtracting exclusions, deductions, exemptions, and tax credits, as indicated in the unshaded boxes in Figure 4-2.

1. Determine Your Total Income

Practically everything you receive in return for your work or services and any profit from the sale of assets is considered income, whether the compensation is paid in cash, property, or services. Listing these earnings will reveal your **total income**—compensation from all sources—and much of it, but not all, will be subject to income taxes.

For most people, **earned income** is compensation for performing personal services. It is reported to them annually on a Form W-2, Wage and Tax Statement. Employers

The Steps in Calculating Your Income Taxes

Figure 4-2

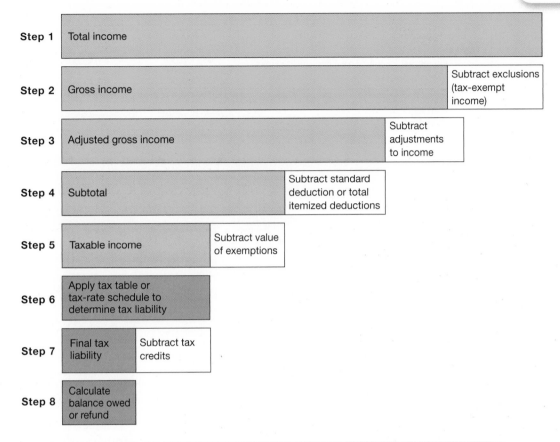

must provide W-2 information (see Figure 4-3) by January 31 of the year following the earned income. If you also receive income from interest or dividends or other sources, you will receive a Form 1099-INT or 1099-DIV, providing appropriate details. The IRS also receives the information on Form 1099, which it uses to check the income you report.

Making Tax Payments The federal income tax is a "pay as you go" tax. Through **payroll withholding**, an employer takes a certain amount from an employee's income as a prepayment of an individual's tax liability for the year and sends those dollars to the IRS, where they are credited to that particular taxpayer's account. People who are self-employed or who receive substantial income from an employer that is not required to practice payroll withholding, such as lawyers, accountants, consultants, and owners of rental property, must pay estimated taxes. They are required to estimate their tax liability and pay their **estimated taxes** in advance in quarterly installments on April 15, June 15, September 15, and the following year's January 15.

payroll withholding
The IRS requirement that an employer withhold a certain amount from an employee's income as a prepayment of that individual's tax liability for the year. It is sent to the government where it is credited to the taxpayer's account.

Income to Include The following types of income are included when you report your income to the IRS:

- Wages and salaries
- Commissions
- Bonuses
- Professional fees earned
- Hobby income
- Tips earned
- Severance pay

estimated taxes
People who are self-employed or receive substantial income from an employer that is not required to practice payroll withholding (such as lawyers and owners of rental property) are required by the IRS to estimate their tax liability and pay their taxes in advance in quarterly installments.

Figure 4-3 **W-2 Tax Form**

a Control number	22222	OMB No. 1545-0008		
b Employer identification number (EIN) 37-12345678			1 Wages, tips, other compensation 65,000.00	2 Federal income tax withheld 10,400.00
c Employer's name, address, and ZIP code Financial Knowledge Communications 1245 Oak Street Oak Park, IL 60302			3 Social security wages 65,000.00	4 Social security tax withheld 4,030.00
			5 Medicare wages and tips 65,000.00	6 Medicare tax withheld 94.25
			7 Social security tips	8 Allocated tips
d Employee's social security number 123-45-6789			9 Advance EIC payment	10 Dependent care benefits
e Employee's first name and initial Last name Suff. Yasuo Konami			11 Nonqualified plans	12a
			13 Statutory employee ☐ Retirement plan ☐ Third-party sick pay ☐	12b
			14 Other	12c
				12d
f Employee's address and ZIP code				

15 State Employer's state ID number IL 37-1411 9877	16 State wages, tips, etc.	17 State income tax 1,950.00	18 Local wages, tips, etc.	19 Local income tax	20 Locality name

Form **W-2** Wage and Tax Statement
Copy 1—For State, City, or Local Tax Department

Department of the Treasury—Internal Revenue Service

- Fair value of anything received in a barter arrangement
- Forgiven or cancelled debt (unless borrower is insolvent or bankrupt)
- Alimony received
- Scholarship and fellowship income spent on room, board, and other living expenses
- Grants and the value of tuition reductions that pay for teaching or other services
- Annuity and pension income received
- Withdrawals and disbursements from retirement accounts, such as an individual retirement account (IRA) or 401(k) retirement plan (discussed in Chapter 17, "Retirement Planning")
- Military retirement income
- Social Security income (a portion is taxed above certain income thresholds)
- Disability payments received if you did not pay the premiums
- Damage payments from personal injury lawsuits (punitive damages only)
- Value of personal use of employer-provided car
- State and local income tax refunds (only if the taxpayer itemized deductions during the previous year)
- Employee productivity awards
- Awards for artistic, scientific, and charitable achievements unless assigned to a charity
- Prizes, contest winnings, and rewards
- Gambling and lottery winnings
- All kinds of illegal income
- Fees for serving as a juror or election worker
- Unemployment benefits
- Net rental income
- Royalties
- Investment, business, and farm profits
- Interest income (this includes credit union dividends)

- Dividend income (including mutual fund capital gains distributions even though they are reinvested)

Capital Gains and Losses Are Taxed at Special Low Rates An **asset** is property owned by a taxpayer for personal use or as an investment that has monetary value. Examples of assets include stocks, mutual funds, bonds, land, art, gems, stamps, coins, vehicles, and homes. The net income received from the sale of an asset above the costs incurred to purchase and sell it is a **capital gain**. A **capital loss** results when the sale of an asset brings less income than the costs of purchasing and selling the asset. Capital gains and losses on investments must be reported on your tax return. Capital gains from the sale or exchange of property held for *personal use*, such as on a vehicle or vacation home, must be reported as income, but losses on such property are not deductible. There is no tax liability on any capital gain until the stock, bond, mutual fund, real estate, or other investment is sold. A **short-term gain (or** *loss*) occurs when you sell an asset that you have owned for one year or less; it is taxed at the same rates as **ordinary income**, which is all income other than capital gains. A **long-term gain (or** *loss*) occurs when you sell an asset that you have owned for more than one year (at least a year and a day), and it is taxed at special low rates. The long-term capital gains rate for taxpayers below the 25 percent bracket is zero percent, and the rate is 15 percent for those in the 25 percent bracket and above.

Capital losses may be used first to offset capital gains. If there are no capital gains, or if the capital losses are larger than the capital gains, you can deduct the capital loss against your other income, but only up to a limit of $3000 in one year. If your net capital loss is more than $3000, the excess may be carried forward to be deducted in the next tax year, again up to an annual $3000 maximum.

— important

capital gain
The net income received from the sale of an asset above the costs incurred to purchase and sell it.

long-term gain/loss
A profit or loss on the sale of an asset that has been held for more than a year.

Dividend Income Is Taxed at Special Low Rates Dividends paid out of current or accumulated earnings of a corporation are taxable, and shareholders are annually sent tax forms that explain what income is taxable and what is not. Dividends in the form of shares of stock are generally not taxable.

Dividends from most domestic corporations and many foreign companies are treated as "qualified dividends," meaning they are subject to the same favorable rates as capital gains. The rate for taxpayers below the 25 percent bracket is zero percent, and the rate is 15 percent for those in the 25 percent bracket and above. Form 1099-DIV is sent to appropriate taxpayers in January of the following year, and the amount that qualifies appears in box 1b.

Dividends from the following financial institutions are actually interest reported to taxpayers on Form 1099-INT: dividends from credit unions, cooperative banks, savings and loan associations, building and loan associations, and mutual savings banks. They are subject to ordinary income taxes. Dividends received from a life insurance policy are actually a refund of your premium and are not taxed.

FINANCIAL POWER POINT

Mortgage Debt Forgiveness

The law says that if before the end of 2012, you sold your home for less than you owed, restructured your mortgage, or had your home foreclosed where part of the debt was canceled, that amount generally will not be treated as income.

2. Determine and Report Your Gross Income After Subtracting Exclusions

Gross income consists of all income (both earned and unearned) received in the form of money, goods, services, and property before exclusions and deductions that a taxpayer is required to report to the IRS. To determine gross income, you need to determine which kinds of income are not subject to federal taxation and, therefore, need not be reported as part of gross income. These amounts are called **exclusions**.

Income to Exclude The more common exclusions (some are subject to limits) are as follows:

- Gifts
- Inherited money or property
- Income from a carpool

gross income
All income in the form of money, goods, services, and/or property.

exclusions
Income not subject to federal taxation.

- Income from items sold at a garage sale for a sum less than what you paid
- Cash rebates on purchases of new cars and other products
- Tuition reduction, if not received as compensation for teaching or service
- Federal income tax refunds
- State and local income tax refunds for a year in which you claimed the standard deduction
- Scholarship and fellowship income spent on course-required tuition, fees, books, supplies, and equipment (degree candidates only)
- Withdrawals from state-sponsored Section 529 plans (prepaid tuition and savings) used for education
- Prizes and awards made primarily to recognize artistic, civic, charitable, educational, and similar achievements
- Return of money loaned
- Withdrawals from medical savings accounts used for qualified expenses
- Earnings accumulating within annuities, cash-value life insurance policies, Series EE bonds, and qualified retirement accounts
- Interest income received on tax-exempt government bonds issued by states, counties, cities, and districts
- Life insurance benefits received
- Combat zone pay for military personnel
- Welfare, black lung, workers' compensation, and veterans' benefits
- Value of food stamps
- First $500,000 ($250,000 if single) gain on the sale of a principal residence
- Disability insurance benefits if you paid the insurance premiums
- Social Security benefits (except for high-income taxpayers)
- Rental income from a vacation home if not rented for more than 14 days
- First $5000 of death benefits paid by an employer to a worker's beneficiary
- Travel and mileage expenses reimbursed by an employer (if not previously deducted by the taxpayer)
- Employer-provided per diem allowance covering only meals and incidentals
- Amounts paid by employers for premiums for medical insurance, workers' compensation, and health and long-term care insurance
- Moving expense reimbursements received from an employer (if not previously deducted by the taxpayer)
- Employer-provided payments of $230 per month for free parking, transit passes, and commuter van pooling and $20 per month for qualifying bicycle cost reimbursements
- Value of premiums for first $50,000 worth of group-term life insurance provided by an employer
- Employer payments (up to $5000) for dependent care assistance (for children and parents)
- Benefits from employers that are impractical to tax because they are so modest, such as occasional supper money and taxi fares for overtime work, company parties, holiday gifts (not cash), and occasional theater or sporting events
- Employer contributions for employee expenses for education (up to $5250 annually; applies to expenses in 2011 and 2012), long-term care, moving, pension, adoption, health care, life and disability insurance, and health and medical savings accounts
- Employee contributions to flexible spending accounts

- Reimbursements from flexible spending accounts
- Interest received on Series EE and Series I bonds used for college tuition and fees
- Child support payments received
- Property settlement in a divorce
- Compensatory damages in physical injury cases

3. Subtract Adjustments to Income

In the process of determining your taxable income, you make **adjustments to income** (or **adjustments**). These are allowable subtractions from gross income, and include items such as moving expenses to a new job location (including college graduates who move to take their first job as long as it is at least 50 miles from their old residence); higher-education expenses for tuition and fees (up to $4000 [through 2011]); student loan interest for higher education, including that paid by a parent ($2500 maximum); military reservists' travel expenses (for more than 100 miles); contributions to qualified personal retirement accounts (IRA and 401[k] accounts) and health savings accounts; alimony payments; interest penalties for early withdrawal of savings certificates of deposit; expenses of up to $250 for teachers and other school professionals incurred for books, supplies, computer equipment, and supplementary materials used in the classroom (expires at end of 2011); and certain expenses of self-employed people (such as health insurance premiums). Adjustments are subtracted from gross income to determine **adjusted gross income (AGI)**. Subtracting adjustments to income from gross income results in a subtotal.

To illustrate the value of adjustments to income, consider that John Edwards from Columbia, South Carolina, has a gross income of $50,000. This past year he spent $1200 moving to Nashville, Tennessee, for a new job, and he also paid $2000 in higher-education expenses working on a graduate degree. The $3200 in adjustments reduces his gross income to $46,800, and therefore John saves $800 in income taxes because he is in the 25 percent marginal tax bracket.

Adjustments are called **above-the-line deductions** because they may be subtracted from gross income even if itemized deductions are not claimed. Adjustments may be taken regardless of whether the taxpayer itemizes deductions or takes the standard deduction amount (discussed next).

adjustments to income
Allowable subtractions from gross income.

> College adjustments

adjusted gross income (AGI)
Gross income less any exclusions and adjustments.

above-the-line deductions
Adjustments subtracted from gross income whether taxpayer itemizes deductions or not.

ADVICE FROM A PRO

A Sideline Business Can Reduce Your Income Taxes

A sideline business can open many doors to tax deductions. We would never recommend spending money for a tax deduction; however, if you're going to spend the money anyway, you should do everything you can to make it tax deductible.

By having your own business, every dollar you spend attempting to make a profit becomes tax deductible. While no deduction is allowed for personal expenses, you can deduct expenses for auto, travel, office, office equipment (e.g., desk, chair, computer), contributions to self-funded retirement accounts, health insurance premiums, educational expenses, entertainment, business gifts, and more. You can deduct salaries of employees, even if they are your children, other relatives, or friends.

The business does not have to be your primary employment. If you lose money in the business, you can deduct those losses from your other income. The IRS says that you must do what a "reasonable business person" would do to make a profit. If you do not meet that test, the IRS will classify the operation as a hobby business, require you to report the income, and disallow the deductions.

Anthony J. Campolo
Columbus State Community College

Table 4-2   Tax-Rate Schedules

Single

If taxable income is over—	But not over—	The tax is:
$ 0	$ 8,500	10% of the amount over $0
$ 8,500	$ 34,500	$850.00 plus 15% of the amount over $8,500
$ 34,500	$ 83,600	$4,750.00 plus 25% of the amount over $34,500
$ 83,600	$174,400	$17,025.00 plus 28% of the amount over $83,600
$174,400	$379,150	$42,449.00 plus 33% of the amount over $174,400
$379,150	No limit	$110,016.50 plus 35% of the amount over $379,150

Married Filing Jointly

If taxable income is over—	But not over—	The tax is:
$ 0	$ 17,000	10% of the amount over $0
$ 17,000	$ 69,000	$1,700.00 plus 15% of the amount over $17,000
$ 69,000	$139,350	$9,500.00 plus 25% of the amount over $69,000
$139,350	$212,300	$27,087.50 plus 28% of the amount over $139,350
$212,300	$379,150	$47,513.50 plus 33% of the amount over $212,300
$379,150	No limit	$102,574.00 plus 35% of the amount over $379,150

4. Subtract Either the IRS's Standard Deduction for Your Tax Status or Your Itemized Deductions

itemized deductions
Tax-deductible expenses.

standard deduction
Fixed amount that all taxpayers may subtract from their adjusted gross income if they do not itemize their deductions.

filing status
Description of a taxpayer's marital status on the last day of the tax year.

Taxpayers may reduce income further by the amount of the standard deduction. Or they can list their **itemized deductions**, which are specific items that may be used to directly reduce income. They can use either method, but not both. You want to use the larger of the two. The **standard deduction** is a fixed amount that all taxpayers (except some dependents) who do not itemize deductions regardless of their actual expenses may subtract from their adjusted gross income. In effect, it consists of the government's permissible estimate of any likely tax-deductible expenses these taxpayers might have. Two out of three taxpayers take the standard deduction.

The standard deduction amount depends on **filing status**, a description of your marital status on the last day of the year. A return can be filed with a status of a single person, a married person (filing separately or jointly), a head of household, or qualifying widow or widower. Certain tax benefits apply to each filing status. For example, the standard deduction amounts are $5800 for single individuals and twice as much, $11,600, for married people filing jointly.

Four **additional standard deductions** are permitted for certain people. They are allowed to deduct some or all of a standard deduction. Those who are age 65 or older and/or blind may claim an extra amount ($1450 for singles and $1150 for married) beyond taking their standard deduction.

Taxpayers whose tax-deductible itemized deductions exceed the standard deduction amount may deduct the larger amount instead of taking the standard deduction. For example, single people might list all of their possible tax deductions and find that they total $6000, which is more than the standard deduction amount of $5800 permitted for single taxpayers. The tax form lists the following six classifications of itemized deductions:

1. Medical and Dental Expenses
2. Taxes You Paid
3. Interest You Paid
4. Gifts to Charity
5. Casualty and Theft Losses

6. Job Expenses and Most Other Miscellaneous Deductions

Examples of deductions in each of these categories follow.

1. Medical and Dental Expenses (Not Paid by Insurance) in Excess of 7.5 Percent of Adjusted Gross Income*

- Medicine and drugs
- Insurance premiums for medical, long-term care, and contact lenses
- Medical services (doctors, dentists, nurses, hospitals, long-term health care)
- Sterilizations and prescription contraceptives
- Costs of a physician-prescribed course of treatment for obesity
- Expenses for prescription drugs/programs to quit smoking

Charitable contributions are typically tax deductible.

- Medical equipment and aids (contact lenses, eyeglasses, hearing devices, orthopedic shoes, false teeth, wheelchair lifts)
- Fees for childbirth preparation classes
- Costs of sending a mentally or physically challenged person to a special school
- Home improvements made for the physically disabled (ramps, railings, widening doors)
- Travel and conference registration fees for a parent to learn about a child's disease
- Transportation costs to and from locations where medical services are obtained, using a standard flat mileage allowance

2. Taxes You Paid

- Real estate property taxes (such as on a home or land)
- Personal property taxes (such as on an automobile or boat when any part of the tax is based on the value of the asset)
- State, local, and foreign income taxes
- State and local sales taxes may be taken in lieu of the itemized deduction for state and local income taxes (through 2011)

3. Interest You Paid

- Interest paid on home mortgage loans
- "Points" treated as a type of prepaid interest on the purchase of a principal residence
- "Points" paid when refinancing a home mortgage (portion deducted over life of the loan)
- Interest paid on home-equity loans
- Interest paid on loans used for investments
- Private mortgage insurance premiums if a homebuyer did not make at least a 20 percent down payment on a residence (through 2011)

---

* This 7.5 percent floor rises to 10 percent in 2013.

4. Gifts to Charity

- Cash contributions to qualified organizations such as churches, schools, and charities (receipt required for $250 or more)
- Noncash contributions at **fair market value** (what a willing buyer would pay to a willing seller); IRS says that personal property must be in "good used condition or better" to qualify
- Mileage allowance for travel and out-of-pocket expenses for volunteer charitable work
- Charitable contributions made through payroll deduction
- Contributions to charity up to $100,000 from one's individual retirement account (IRA) for those age 70½ or older (expires at end of 2011)

5. Casualty and Theft Losses (Not Paid by Insurance) in Excess of 10 Percent of Adjusted Gross Income

- Casualty losses (such as from storms, vandalism, and fires) in excess of $100
- Theft of money or property in excess of $100
- Mislaid or lost property if the loss results from an identifiable event that is unexpected or unusual (such as catching a diamond ring in a car door and losing the stone)

6. Job Expenses and Most Other Miscellaneous Deductions in Excess of 2 Percent of Adjusted Gross Income (Partial Listing)

- Union or professional association dues and membership fees
- Subscriptions to magazines, journals, and newspapers used for business or professional purposes
- Books, software, tools, and supplies used in a business or profession
- Cost of computers and cell phones required as a condition of your job
- Clothing and uniforms not suitable for off-the-job usage as ordinary wearing apparel (protective shoes, hats, safety goggles, gloves, uniforms), laundering and cleaning
  - Unreimbursed employee business expenses (but only a portion of the cost of meals and entertainment), including long-distance telephone calls, cleaning and laundry, and car washes (of business vehicle)
  - Investment-related expenses (e.g., computer software, fees for online trading, adviser fees, investment club expenses, IRA fees, safe-deposit box rental, subscriptions to investment magazines and newsletters, tax preparation fees)
  - Legal fees that pertain to tax advice in a divorce or alimony payments
  - Travel costs between two jobs, using a flat mileage allowance
  - Job-related car expenses (but not commuting to a regular job), using a flat mileage allowance or actual expenses
  - Commuting costs to a temporary workplace
  - Commuting costs that qualify as a business or education expense
  - Medical examinations required (but not paid for) by an employer to obtain or keep a job
  - Appraisal fees for charitable donations or casualty losses
  - Education expenses if required to keep your job or improve your job or professional skills (but not if the training readies you for a new career)

DID YOU KNOW?

Keep Your Tax Records a Long Time

You should never discard records relating to home purchases, contributions to retirement accounts, and investments. Because you have the burden of proving that the numbers you provided to the IRS are accurate, when in doubt about keeping a tax record, do not throw it out. Being able to prove your deductions is crucial to keeping more of your money. If it suspects fraud, the IRS can ask you for proof years later, any time in the future.

DID YOU KNOW?

The Best Tax Guides and Software

Your Federal Income Tax: For Individuals, Publication 17, is the IRS's detailed 100-plus-page book for preparing your income taxes. All federal income tax forms, regulations, guides, and answers to frequently asked questions can be obtained from the IRS at (800) TAX-3676, or at www.irs.gov. The IRS help line is (800) TAX-1040. Most taxpayers can obtain free tax preparation from the Volunteer Income Tax Assistance (VITA) program (www.vita-volunteers.org/index.htm, or call (800) 906-9887).

Tax guides that offer advice on how to reduce income taxes and computer software to assist in filling out your return are available online or at bookstores. A good and readable tax guide is the annual *J. K. Lasser's Your Income Tax* (www.jklasser.com/WileyCDA/Section/id-310351.html).

Popular computer software programs to help prepare income tax returns include H&R Block's TaxCut (www.hrblock.com/tax-software/index.html), Quicken's TurboTax (http://turbotax.intuit.com/), and TaxACT (www.taxact.com). Over 60 percent of taxpayers pay someone to prepare the return.

- Job-hunting expenses for typing, printing, résumé advice, career counseling, want ads, telephone calls, mailing costs, job placement agency fees, and travel for seeking a job in your current career field

- 50 percent of food and 100 percent of transportation and entertainment costs for job hunting (which does not have to be successful) in your current career

- 100 percent of gambling losses that offset reported gambling income (not subject to 2% AGI floor)

- 100 percent of business expenses for workers with disabilities (not subject to 2% AGI floor)

Given the considerable number of deductions listed here and numerous others for which you might qualify, it makes sense to take time to estimate how much you can count up in possible itemized deductible expenses. If the amount exceeds the standard deduction amount or is even close, go back and carefully itemize deductions and deduct the larger amount.

5. Subtract the Value of Your Personal Exemptions

An **exemption** (or *personal exemption*) is a legally permitted amount deducted from adjusted gross income based on the number of people supported by the taxpayer's income. A **dependent** is a relative or household member for whom an exemption may be claimed. Thus, exemptions may be claimed for the taxpayer and qualifying dependents, such as a spouse (if filing jointly), children, parents, and other dependents earning less than a specific income and for whom the taxpayer provides more than half of their financial support. For example, a husband and wife with two young children would have four exemptions.

A person can serve as an exemption on only one tax return—his or her own or another person's (usually a parent). Each exemption reduces taxable income by $3700. The value of an exemption is phased out for those with higher incomes. If you are claimed as a dependent on a parent's return, you may not claim a personal exemption for yourself, as only one person receives the exemption.

exemption (or personal exemption)
Legally permitted amount deducted from AGI based on the number of people that the taxpayer's income supports.

dependent
A relative or household member for whom an exemption may be claimed on one's income taxes.

6. Determine Your Preliminary Tax Liability

The steps detailed to this point have explained how to determine your taxable income. Taxable income is calculated by taking the taxpayer's gross income, subtracting the adjustments to income, subtracting the amount permitted for the number of exemptions allowed, and subtracting either the standard deduction or total itemized deductions.

The amount of taxable income is then used to determine taxpayers' preliminary tax liability via the tax tables or tax-rate schedules for their filing status (such as single or married filing jointly). The following examples illustrate how to determine tax liability. Table 4-3 shows segments of the tax table.

Table 4-3

Tax Table*

If Taxable Income Is		Your Tax Is	
At Least	**But Less Than**	**Single**	**Married Filing Jointly**
20,200	20,250	2,609	2,183
20,250	20,300	2,616	2,191
23,550	23,600	3,111	2,686
23,600	23,650	3,119	2,694
26,050	26,100	3,486	3,061
26,100	26,150	3,494	3,069
26,300	26,350	3,524	3,099
26,350	26,400	3,531	3,106
27,100	27,150	3,644	3,219
27,150	27,200	3,651	3,226
27,750	27,800	3,741	3,316
27,800	27,850	3,749	3,324
27,850	27,900	3,756	3,331
27,900	27,950	3,764	3,339
33,950	34,000	4,671	4,246
34,000	34,050	4,679	4,254
39,900	39,950	6,106	5,139
39,950	40,000	6,119	5,146
41,300	41,350	6,456	5,349
41,350	41,400	6,469	5,356
49,100	49,150	8,406	6,519
49,150	49,200	8,419	6,526
49,450	49,500	8,494	6,571
49,500	49,550	8,506	6,579
53,000	53,050	9,381	7,104
53,050	53,100	9,394	7,111
53,100	53,150	9,406	7,119
60,000	60,050	11,131	8,154
60,050	60,100	11,144	8,161
74,100	74,150	14,656	10,781
74,150	74,200	14,669	10,794
90,200	90,250	18,880	14,806
90,250	90,300	18,894	14,819

* These segments of the tax table are derived from IRS tax-rate schedules.

1. A married couple filing jointly has a gross income of $50,000, adjustments of $4700, two exemptions ($3700 each), and itemized deductions of $8285. They take the standard deduction of $11,600 because their itemized deductions do not exceed that amount.

Gross income	$50,000
Less adjustments to income	−4,700
Adjusted gross income	45,300
Less standard deduction for married couple	−11,600
Subtotal	33,700
Less value of two exemptions	−7,400
Taxable income	26,300
Tax liability (from Table 4-3)	$ 3,099

2. A single person has a gross income of $56,000, adjustments of $4050, one exemption, and itemized deductions of $8400. She subtracts her itemized deductions because the amount exceeds the $5800 standard deduction value.

Gross income	$56,000
Less adjustments to income	−3,950
Adjusted gross income	52,050
Less itemized deductions	−8,400
Subtotal	43,650
Less value of one exemption	−3,700
Taxable income	39,950
Tax liability (from Table 4-3)	$ 6,119

3. A married couple with a gross income of $137,000 has adjustments of $4000, two exemptions, and itemized deductions of $9800. The standard deduction value for a married couple is taken because it exceeds the itemized deductions.

Gross income	$137,000
Less adjustments to income	−4,300
Adjusted gross income	133,300
Less standard deduction	−11,600
Subtotal	121,700
Less value of two exemptions	−7,400
Taxable income	114,300
Tax liability (from Table 4-2)*	$ 20,750

*The tax liability is calculated from the tax-rate schedules in Table 4-2 because the taxable income exceeds $100,000. The tax liability is computed on taxable income as follows: $114,000 − $69,000 = $45,000 × 0.25 = $11,250 + $9,500 = $20,750.

DID YOU KNOW?

About the Alternative Minimum Tax

The **alternative minimum tax (AMT)** was created in 1969 to effectively take back some of the tax breaks allowed for regular tax purposes for very high–income taxpayers who previously were entirely escaping paying income taxes through legal means. Some high-income taxpayers are pushed into paying the higher AMT tax instead of the regular tax when claiming excess itemized deductions, certain tax-exempt interest, and/or a substantial number of exemptions. When the value of those benefits is added back to one's income, it may result in an AMT calculation that exceeds one's regular tax. About four million taxpayers pay the AMT tax rate at 26 or 28 percent, which typically amounts to an additional tax liability of about $3900.

7. Subtract Tax Credits for Which You Qualify

You may be able to lower your preliminary tax liability through tax credits. A **tax credit** reduces the amount of tax for which you are liable. Unlike a tax deduction, which reduces the amount of income subject to tax, a tax credit is a dollar-for-dollar subtraction from your tax liability. A $1000 tax deduction saves $250 in taxes if you are in the 25 percent bracket, but a $1000 tax credit saves you $1000.

You may take tax credits regardless of whether you itemize deductions. A **nonrefundable tax credit** may reduce your tax liability to zero (0), but not below. Thus if the nonrefundable credit amount exceeds the tax you owe, you are not given a refund of the difference. A **refundable tax credit** can reduce your tax liability to below zero (0), and the excess amount will be refunded. Credits are often subject to income limits, meaning that high-income taxpayers may not be eligible for a particular credit. The tax credits described below, unless noted, expire at the end of 2012. Congress, of course, could take action to extend them.

American Opportunity Tax Credit The **American Opportunity Tax Credit** provides an up to $2500 per student tax credit to help defray college expenses for the first four years of postsecondary education. The tax credit is for 100 percent of qualified tuition, fees, books, and course materials paid by the taxpayer during the taxable year not to exceed $2000, plus 25 percent of the next $2000 in qualified tuition, fees, and course materials. The maximum total credit is $2500. The money must have been spent for qualified tuition and expenses for textbooks, supplies, equipment, and student activity fees if required as a condition of enrollment. The credit can be claimed in two taxable years for individuals enrolled on at least a half-time basis during any part of the year. Forty percent of the credit is refundable.

Lifetime Learning Credit The **lifetime learning credit** (nonrefundable) may be claimed every year for tuition and related expenses paid for all years of postsecondary education undertaken to acquire or improve job skills. The expenses for one or more courses may be for yourself, your spouse, or your dependents. The student need not be pursuing a degree or other recognized credential. This credit amounts to 20 percent of the first $10,000 paid, for a maximum of $2000 for all eligible students in a family. There is no limit on the number of years the credit may be taken for the student. The Lifetime Learning and American Opportunity credits may not be claimed for the same student expenses for the same tax year.

Earned Income Credit The **earned income credit (EIC)** (or **earned income tax credit [EITC]**) is refundable, and it may be claimed not only by workers with a qualifying child but also, in certain cases, by childless workers. The maximum credit is $464 with no qualifying children, $3,094 with one child, $5112 with two children, and $5751 with three or more children. For married taxpayers with one child, the credit begins to phase out if adjusted gross income is $36,052.

Child and Dependent Care Credit The **child and dependent care credit** (nonrefundable) is for workers who pay employment-related expenses if the care for children under age 13 and/or other dependents gives them the freedom to work. Depending on your income, the credit may be up to 35 percent of qualifying care expenses of up to $3000 for one dependent and of up to $6000 of care expenses for two or more dependents. If your credit exceeds your tax liability, the credit is limited to the liability, but part or all of the credit may be refundable as an "additional child tax credit," which is discussed next.

Child Tax Credit Taxpayers can claim a **child tax credit** (CTC) of up to $1,000 per child under age 17. This refundable credit is also known as the **additional child tax credit**. Those who claimed the child portion of the child and dependent care tax credit and found that that credit exceeded their tax liability may be eligible for a credit of $1000 or more using Form 8812. This affects about 11 million families.

Adoption Credit An **adoption tax credit** (refundable) of up to $13,360 is available for the qualifying costs of an adoption.

---

tax credit
Dollar-for-dollar decrease in tax liability; also known as credit.

nonrefundable tax credit
A tax credit that can reduce one's tax liability only to zero; however, if the credit is more than the tax liability, the excess is not refunded.

refundable tax credit
A tax credit that can reduce one's income tax liability to below zero with the excess being refunded to the taxpayer.

American Opportunity Tax Credit
A partially refundable tax credit of up to $2500 a year to help defray college expenses for the first four years of postsecondary education.

lifetime learning credit
A nonrefundable tax credit that may be claimed every year for tuition and related expenses paid for all years of postsecondary education undertaken to acquire or improve job skills.

earned income credit (EIC)
A refundable tax credit that may be claimed by workers with a qualifying child and in certain cases by childless workers.

child and dependent care credit
A nonrefundable tax credit that may be claimed by workers who pay employment-related expenses for care of a child or other dependent if that care gives them the freedom to work, seek work, or attend school full time.

DID YOU KNOW?

Nearly Half of Households Pay No Income Tax

The Tax Policy Center reports that 47 percent of all households paid no federal income tax in a recent year, and this is up from the usual 38 percent. Thus millions of Americans paid nothing toward our national defense, highways, or federal parks. Their incomes were either too low, or the households qualified for enough credits, deductions, and exemptions to eliminate their tax liability. Most of those who escape federal income taxes still pay other taxes, including federal payroll taxes that fund Social Security and Medicare; federal and state excise taxes on gasoline, telephone services, tires, aviation, alcohol, and cigarettes; and state and/or local income taxes, property taxes, and sales taxes.

FINANCIAL POWER POINT

Don't Owe the IRS? File a Return to Obtain a Refundable Tax Credit

Claiming a credit may allow you to get money from the government even though you owed no income taxes for the year. To get a refundable tax credit, you must file a return. Double check to determine if you qualify for the earned income credit, additional child tax credit, or American Opportunity Tax Credit.

Mortgage Interest Credit A **mortgage interest tax credit** (nonrefundable) of up to $2000 for mortgage interest paid may be claimed under special state and local government programs that provide a "mortgage credit certificate" for people who purchase a principal residence or borrow funds for certain home improvements. The home must not cost more than 90 to 110 percent of the average area purchase price.

Retirement Savings Contribution Credit A nonrefundable **retirement savings contribution credit** (also known as a **saver credit**) of up to $1000 is available. For single individuals, a 50 percent credit applies on the amount saved (up to $2000) if AGI does not exceed $17,000; a 20 percent rate applies if AGI does not exceed $18,250; and a 10 percent rate applies if AGI does not exceed $28,250. For married persons, the AGI thresholds are $34,000, $36,500, and $56,500.

Elderly or Disabled Tax Credit. Individuals who are age 65 or older or who are permanently and totally disabled may claim a nonrefundable federal tax credit that can be as much as $1125.

Energy-Saving Vehicle Credit The up-to-$750 nonrefundable credit for buying certain plug-in vehicles expires at the end of 2011. Some states offer additional tax credits.

Energy-Saving Home Improvements Credit If you bought or upgraded energy-saving home improvements, such as heating and cooling equipment, windows, solar panels, skylights, solar water heaters, fuel cell equipment, or insulation, you may qualify for up to a nonrefundable $500 credit (through 2011).

8. Calculate the Balance Due the IRS or the Amount of Your Refund

tax refund
Amount the IRS sends back to a taxpayer if withholding and estimated payments exceed the tax liability.

If the amount withheld (shown on your W-2 form) plus any estimated tax payments you made is greater than your final tax liability, then you are entitled to receive a **tax refund**.

DID YOU KNOW?

Sean's Success Story

Sean is one smart fellow. After learning a lot about how to avoid income taxes, he took action. Sean made a down payment and bought a foreclosed home with a $120,000, 6 1/2 percent mortgage. The nearly $9000 in interest (from Table 9-4 on page 270) and $1500 property taxes together put him well over the $5800 standard deduction threshold. Therefore, he can take all kinds of additional deductions on his tax return, such as cash and noncash charitable contributions, mileage allowance and out-of-pocket expenses for volunteer charitable work, personal property taxes on his auto and boat, expenses for business magazines and newspapers to better manage his investments, and software to help prepare his income taxes. He started to contribute the maximum $3000 annually to his retirement account. Sean is researching all the tax credits to determine if he qualifies for any of them.

If the amount is less than your final tax liability, then you have a **tax balance due**. If you owe money, you pay by check, money order, or credit card. The IRS imposes a convenience fee of 2.5 percent of the amount charged on a credit card.

Which Tax Form Do You Use to File?

To file your income tax return, you record all your tax information on the correct tax form and submit it to the Internal Revenue Service by mail or online. Use the IRS tax form that is appropriate for your circumstances:

- **Form 1040EZ.** You are single or married, under age 65, and have no dependents; your income consists of less than $100,000 in wages, salary, and tips, and no more than $1500 in interest; and you do not claim any tax credits or adjustments or itemize deductions.

- **Form 1040A.** Your income is less than $100,000 and you use the standard deduction and/or take adjustments to income or tax credits.

- **Form 1040.** You itemize your deductions and you do or do not make contributions to a qualified retirement plan or take adjustments to income or tax credits. Figure 4-4 shows a completed 1040 Form for a taxpayer.

- **Form 1040X.** You are eligible for a deserved refund or refundable tax credit, or you want to correct any tax filing mistake(s) or claim overlooked deductions for any of the past three years.

File on Time and Check the Status of Your Refund

You should file your return on time—usually by April 15—to avoid a penalty. If you owe the IRS and you are broke, you can borrow to pay the taxes or contact the IRS about setting up an installment plan to repay the debt within three years.

Taxpayers hear from the IRS within three weeks if they have failed to sign the return, neglected to attach a copy of the Form W-2, made an error in arithmetic, or figured the tax incorrectly. Once taxpayers file their federal return, they can track the status of their refunds by using the "Where's My Refund?" tool, located on the front page of www.irs.gov.

File Your Income Taxes Electronically for Free and Get Your Refund Within Ten Days

Over 70 percent of taxpayers file electronic returns. To file your income taxes online by yourself, visit the website of the Internal Revenue Service (www.irs.gov) and click on "IRS E-file." Alternatively, you may choose to click on "IRS Free File" because it provides options for free brand-name tax software or online fillable forms plus free electronic filing for most taxpayers. E-filers may request that their refund be deposited directly into their bank account, and it usually will be deposited within ten days of filing.

 Concept Check 4.2

1. Give five examples of income that must be included in income reported to the Internal Revenue Service.

2. How are long-term and short-term capital gains treated differently for income tax purposes?

3. Give five examples of income that is excluded from IRS reporting.

4. List three examples of adjustments to income.

5. Distinguish between a standard deduction and a personal exemption.

6. What advice on filing a Form 1040X can you offer someone who did not file a federal income tax return last year or in any one of the past three years?

7. List five examples of tax credits.

Figure 4-4   **Federal Income Tax Form 1040 (Yasuo Konami)**

Form **1040**   Department of the Treasury—Internal Revenue Service
U.S. Individual Income Tax Return   (99)   IRS Use Only—Do not write or staple in this space.

	For the year Jan. 1–Dec. 31, 2010, or other tax year beginning , 2010, ending , 20	OMB No. 1545-0074

Name, Address, and SSN

See separate instructions.

PRINT CLEARLY

Your first name and initial: **Yasuo**   Last name: **Konami**

Your social security number: **123 45 6789**

If a joint return, spouse's first name and initial   Last name

Spouse's social security number

Home address (number and street). If you have a P.O. box, see instructions. **3333 Third Avenue**   Apt. no. **12**

City, town or post office, state, and ZIP code. If you have a foreign address, see instructions. **Oak Park, IL 60302**

▲ Make sure the SSN(s) above and on line 6c are correct.

Checking a box below will not change your tax or refund.

Presidential Election Campaign ▶ Check here if you, or your spouse if filing jointly, want $3 to go to this fund . . . . . . ▶ ☐ You ☐ Spouse

Filing Status

Check only one box.

1 ☒ Single
2 ☐ Married filing jointly (even if only one had income)
3 ☐ Married filing separately. Enter spouse's SSN above and full name here. ▶
4 ☐ Head of household (with qualifying person). (See instructions.) If the qualifying person is a child but not your dependent, enter this child's name here. ▶
5 ☐ Qualifying widow(er) with dependent child

Exemptions

6a ☒ **Yourself.** If someone can claim you as a dependent, **do not** check box 6a . . . . .
b ☐ Spouse . . . .

Boxes checked on 6a and 6b: **1**

c **Dependents:**

(1) First name Last name	(2) Dependent's social security number	(3) Dependent's relationship to you	(4) ✓ if child under age 17 qualifying for child tax credit (see page 15)
			☐
			☐
			☐
			☐

If more than four dependents, see instructions and check here ▶ ☐

No. of children on 6c who:
• lived with you
• did not live with you due to divorce or separation (see instructions)
Dependents on 6c not entered above

d Total number of exemptions claimed . . . .

Add numbers on lines above ▶ **1**

◀ Report number of exemptions

Income

Attach Form(s) W-2 here. Also attach Forms W-2G and 1099-R if tax was withheld.

If you did not get a W-2, see page 20.

Enclose, but do not attach, any payment. Also, please use Form 1040-V.

7	Wages, salaries, tips, etc. Attach Form(s) W-2	7	65,000 —
8a	**Taxable** interest. Attach Schedule B if required	8a	200 —
b	**Tax-exempt** interest. **Do not** include on line 8a . . .	8b	
9a	Ordinary dividends. Attach Schedule B if required	9a	
b	Qualified dividends	9b	
10	Taxable refunds, credits, or offsets of state and local income taxes	10	
11	Alimony received	11	
12	Business income or (loss). Attach Schedule C or C-EZ . . .	12	
13	Capital gain or (loss). Attach Schedule D if required. If not required, check here ▶ ☐	13	
14	Other gains or (losses). Attach Form 4797	14	
15a	IRA distributions . 15a	b Taxable amount . . .	15b	
16a	Pensions and annuities 16a	b Taxable amount . . .	16b	
17	Rental real estate, royalties, partnerships, S corporations, trusts, etc. Attach Schedule E	17	
18	Farm income or (loss). Attach Schedule F	18	
19	Unemployment compensation	19	
20a	Social security benefits 20a	b Taxable amount . . .	20b	
21	Other income. List type and amount	21	
22	Combine the amounts in the far right column for lines 7 through 21. This is your **total income** ▶	22	65,200 —

◀ Report income here

Adjusted Gross Income

23	Educator expenses	23	
24	Certain business expenses of reservists, performing artists, and fee-basis government officials. Attach Form 2106 or 2106-EZ	24	
25	Health savings account deduction. Attach Form 8889 .	25	
26	Moving expenses. Attach Form 3903	26	
27	One-half of self-employment tax. Attach Schedule SE .	27	
28	Self-employed SEP, SIMPLE, and qualified plans . .	28	
29	Self-employed health insurance deduction	29	
30	Penalty on early withdrawal of savings	30	
31a	Alimony paid b Recipient's SSN ▶	31a	
32	IRA deduction	32	4,000 —
33	Student loan interest deduction	33	1,100 —
34	Tuition and fees. Attach Form 8917	34	
35	Domestic production activities deduction. Attach Form 8903	35	
36	Add lines 23 through 31a and 32 through 35	36	5,100
37	Subtract line 36 from line 22. This is your **adjusted gross income** . . . . . ▶	37	60,100

◀ Subtract adjustments to income

For Disclosure, Privacy Act, and Paperwork Reduction Act Notice, see separate instructions.   Cat. No. 11320B   Form **1040**

Form 1040 (2010)

Page **2**

Tax and Credits	38	Amount from line 37 (adjusted gross income)	38	60,100 —
	39a	Check if: ☐ **You** were born before January 2, 1946, ☐ Blind. **Total boxes** ☐ **Spouse** was born before January 2, 1946, ☐ Blind. **checked ▶** 39a ☐		
	b	If your spouse itemizes on a separate return or you were a dual-status alien, check here ▶ 39b ☐		6,950 —
Standard Deduction for— • People who checked any box on line 39a, 39b, or 39c **or** who can be claimed as a dependent, see page 34. • All others: Single or Married filing separately, $5,800 Married filing jointly or Qualifying widow(er), $11,600 Head of household, $8,450	40	**Itemized deductions** (from Schedule A) **or** your **standard deduction** (see instructions) .	40	53,150 —
	41	Subtract line 40 from line 38	41	
	42	**Exemptions.** Multiply $3,650 by the number on line 6d	42	3,700 —
	43	**Taxable income.** Subtract line 42 from line 41. If line 42 is more than line 41, enter -0-	43	49,450 —
	44	**Tax** (see instructions). Check if any tax is from: **a** ☐ Form(s) 8814 **b** ☐ Form 4972 .	44	8,494
	45	**Alternative minimum tax** (see instructions). Attach Form 6251	45	
	46	Add lines 44 and 45 . . . . ▶	46	
	47	Foreign tax credit. Attach Form 1116 if required	47	
	48	Credit for child and dependent care expenses. Attach Form 2441	48	
	49	Education credits from Form 8863, line 23	49	
	50	Retirement savings contributions credit. Attach Form 8880	50	
	51	Child tax credit (see instructions)	51	
	52	Residential energy credits. Attach Form 5695 . . .	52	
	53	Other credits from Form: **a** ☐ 3800 **b** ☐ 8801 **c** ☐	53	
	54	Add lines 47 through 53. These are your **total credits**	54	
	55	Subtract line 54 from line 46. If line 54 is more than line 46, enter -0- . . ▶	55	
Other Taxes	56	Self-employment tax. Attach Schedule SE	56	
	57	Unreported social security and Medicare tax from Form: **a** ☐ 4137 **b** ☐ 8919	57	
	58	Additional tax on IRAs, other qualified retirement plans, etc. Attach Form 5329 if required .	58	
	59	**a** ☐ Form(s) W-2, box 9 **b** ☐ Schedule H **c** ☐ Form 5405, line 16 . .	59	
	60	Add lines 55 through 59. This is your **total tax** . . . . ▶	60	
Payments	61	Federal income tax withheld from Forms W-2 and 1099 . .	61	10,400 —
	62	2011 estimated tax payments	62	
	63	Making work pay credit. Attach Schedule M	63	
If you have a qualifying child, attach Schedule EIC.	64a	**Earned income credit (EIC)**	64a	
	b	Nontaxable combat pay election 64b		
	65	Additional child tax credit. Attach Form 8812	65	
	66	American opportunity credit from Form 8863, line 14 . .	66	
	67	First-time homebuyer credit from Form 5405, line 10 . . .	67	
	68	Amount paid with request for extension to file	68	
	69	Excess social security and tier 1 RRTA tax withheld . . .	69	
	70	Credit for federal tax on fuels. Attach Form 4136 . . .	70	
	71	Credits from Form: **a** ☐ 2439 **b** ☐ 8839 **c** ☐ 8801 **d** ☐ 8885	71	
	72	Add lines 61, 62, 63, 64a, and 65 through 71. These are your **total payments** . . ▶	72	10,400
Refund	73	If line 72 is more than line 60, subtract line 60 from line 72. This is the amount you **overpaid**	73	
	74a	Amount of line 73 you want **refunded to you.** If Form 8888 is attached, check here . ▶ ☐	74a	1,906 —
Direct deposit? ▶ See instructions.	b	Routing number	▶ c Type: ☐ Checking ☐ Savings	
	d	Account number		
	75	Amount of line 73 you want **applied to your 2012 estimated tax** ▶ 75		
Amount You Owe	76	**Amount you owe.** Subtract line 72 from line 60. For details on how to pay, see instructions ▶	76	
	77	Estimated tax penalty (see instructions)	77	

Third Party Designee	Do you want to allow another person to discuss this return with the IRS (see instructions)? ☐ **Yes.** Complete below. ☐ **No**
	Designee's name ▶ _____ Phone no. ▶ _____ Personal identification number (PIN) ▶ _____

Sign Here
Joint return? See page 12. Keep a copy for your records.

Under penalties of perjury, I declare that I have examined this return and accompanying schedules and statements, and to the best of my knowledge and belief, they are true, correct, and complete. Declaration of preparer (other than taxpayer) is based on all information of which preparer has any knowledge.

Your signature	Date	Your occupation	Daytime phone number
Yasuo Konami	04-15-12	Media Specialist	630 555-1234
Spouse's signature. If a joint return, **both** must sign.	Date	Spouse's occupation	

Paid Preparer Use Only

Print/Type preparer's name	Preparer's signature	Date	Check ☐ if self-employed	PTIN
Firm's name ▶			Firm's EIN ▶	
Firm's address ▶			Phone no.	

Form **1040**

♲ *Printed on recycled paper*

Callout boxes (right margin):
- Take itemized deductions or standard deduction
- Subtract value of exemptions
- Taxable income
- Calculate tax liability
- Report tax credits here
- Subtract tax credits
- Calculate balance owed or refund
- Do not forget to sign your return

STRATEGIES TO REDUCE YOUR INCOME TAXES

While the U.S. tax laws are strict and punitive about compliance (although the IRS audits less than 0.5 percent of all returns), they remain neutral about whether the taxpayer should take advantage of every "break" and opportunity possible. The strategies described here will enable you to reduce your tax liability.

Practice Legal Tax Avoidance, Not Tax Evasion

Tax evasion involves deliberately and willfully hiding income, falsely claiming deductions, or otherwise cheating the government out of taxes owed. It is illegal. A waiter who does not report tips received and a babysitter who does not report income are both evading taxes, as is a person who deducts $150 in charitable contributions but who does not actually make the donations.

Tax avoidance means reducing tax liability through legal techniques. It involves applying knowledge of the tax code and regulations to personal income tax planning. Tax evasion results in penalties, fines, interest charges, and a possible jail sentence. In contrast, tax avoidance boosts your income because you pay less in taxes; as a result, you will have more money available for spending, saving, investing, and donating.

tax evasion
Deliberately and willfully hiding income from the IRS, falsely claiming deductions, or otherwise cheating the government out of taxes owed; it is illegal.

tax avoidance
Reducing tax liability through legal techniques.

FINANCIAL POWER POINT

File IRS Form 1040X to Obtain Refunds for Previous Years

Anyone who was eligible for a refundable tax credit may file an **amended return** to receive it retroactively for the previous three tax years using Form 1040X. Use this easy-to-complete form to obtain a deserved refund or correct any tax filing mistakes on an original or previously filed return.

amended return
A special tax return form (Form 1040X) that may be filed to obtain a deserved refund or correct any tax filing mistakes on an original or previously filed return for the previous three years.

opportunity cost
Most valuable alternative that must be sacrificed to satisfy a want or need.

Realize That a Dollar Saved from Taxes Is Really Two Dollars—or More

These three reasons ought to motivate you to find legal ways to reduce your tax liability.

1. **The opportunity cost.** As noted in Chapter 1, the most valuable alternative that must be sacrificed to satisfy a want is called an **opportunity cost**. An opportunity cost is measured in terms of the value of this forgone option, and it is reflected by the cost of what one must do without or what one could have bought instead. By paying $1 in taxes, you lose the alternative use of that dollar.
2. **Earning another dollar to replace one given to the IRS.** If you pay a dollar too much in taxes, you may need to earn another dollar to replace it. A dollar saved in taxes, therefore, may be viewed as two dollars in your pocket.
3. **Earnings on a dollar not given to the IRS.** If the two dollars saved are invested, the earnings from that investment further expand your savings.

Strategy: Reduce Taxable Income via Your Employer

It may seem illogical to suggest that to lower your tax liability you should reduce your income. But it is not. The objective is to reduce *taxable* income. Reducing your federal taxable income also will reduce the personal income taxes imposed by state and local governments. Three useful ways of reducing taxable income are premium-only plans, dependent care flexible spending accounts, and defined-contribution retirement plans. Employees often are already paying for these expenses out of their own pockets with after-tax dollars; thus, it is wise to participate in plans that allow people to reduce taxes on money they are already spending.

Contributions to these employer-sponsored plans are usually free of federal, state, and Social Security and Medicare taxes. The amount withheld to pay for the benefit is deducted from a worker's salary before taxes are calculated. In effect, the IRS subsidizes or helps pay for part of your planned expenses. If your effective marginal tax rate is 43 percent, that is how much savings you obtain by participating. So if you contribute $5000 in pretax income per year to one or more employer-sponsored plans, you immediately save $2150 ($5000 × 0.43) because you do not have to pay that amount to the IRS.

Premium-Only Plan Many large employers offer a **premium-only plan (POP)** that allows employees to withhold a portion of their pretax salary to pay their premiums for employer-provided health benefits. Benefits could include health, dental, vision, and disability insurance. Amounts withheld are not reported to the IRS as taxable income. For example, if Nhon Ngo, a restaurant manager in Dallas, has $40 per month ($480 annually) withheld through his employer to pay for his share of the employer-sponsored health insurance premium, he saves over $206 ($480 × 0.43 [effective marginal tax rate]) a year because he does not have to send that amount to the government in taxes.

Transportation Reimbursement Plan A **transportation reimbursement plan** is a similar pretax program. This employer plan allows you the opportunity to save money by using payroll deduction with pretax salary dollars to pay for work-related transportation expenses, such as transit passes, van-pool commuting, and qualified parking. If Nhon contributes $600 in pretax income to his employer's transportation plan, he saves $258 ($600 × 0.43).

Flexible Spending Account An attractive benefit for employees who pay for child care or provide care for a parent is a salary reduction plan known as a **flexible spending account (FSA)** (also called an *expense reimbursement account*). An FSA allows an employee to fund qualified medical and dental expenses on a pretax basis through salary reduction to pay for out-of-pocket unreimbursed expenses for health care (soon to be limited by law to $2500 a year) and dependent care (maximum $5000 annually) that are not covered by insurance. Examples are annual deductibles, office copayments, orthodontia, prescriptions, and over-the-counter drugs for which one has a doctor's prescription. The salary reductions are not included in the individual's taxable earnings reported on Form W-2, and reimbursements from an FSA account are tax free.

Suppose Nhon in the preceding example has $1200 annually withheld through his employer to be used to pay out-of-pocket medical expenses (e.g., eyeglasses, chiropractors, physician copayments) plus another $3000 to pay out-of-pocket expenses for dependent care of his child. Nhon's $4200 ($1200 + $3000) in FSA withholdings reduces his costs by $1806 ($4200 × 0.43).

FSAs are subject to a **use-it-or-lose-it rule**, which means that any unspent dollars in the account at the end of the year are forfeited and not returned to the employee. The IRS allows a 2 1/2-month additional "grace period" if one's employer allows such an extension. As a result, you should make conservative estimates of your expenses when you elect your FSA choices. For example, if you had $1000 withheld for medical expenses but spent only $700 over the year, the balance of $300 will go back to your employer, not to you.

Defined-Contribution Retirement Plan Contributing money to a qualified employer-sponsored retirement plan reduces income taxes. A **defined-contribution retirement plan** (described in Chapters 1 and 17) is an IRS-approved retirement plan sponsored by an employer to which employees may make pretax contributions that lower their tax liability. The most popular plan is known as a **401(k) retirement plan**, although other variations exist as well.

The amount of money that an employee contributes to his or her individual account via salary reduction does not show up as taxable income on the employee's W-2 form. For example, if you contribute $2000 to your employer's retirement plan and you are in the 25 percent tax bracket, this immediately saves you $500 ($2000 × 0.25) that you will not have to pay in taxes.

An extra benefit of a defined-contribution retirement plan is that employers often offer full or partial **matching contributions** to employees' accounts up to a certain proportion. For example, if you invest $2000 into your 401(k) plan and your employer matches half of what you contribute, that is an immediate return of 50 percent ($1000 ÷ $2000) on your investment! The employer's "match" is essentially free money.

All of the dollars in a qualified retirement plan are likely to be invested in mutual funds where they will grow free of income taxes. Income taxes must eventually be paid when withdrawals are made, presumably during retirement when the marginal tax rate will be lower than during one's working years.

flexible spending account (FSA) (or expense reimbursement account)
An IRS-approved plan for employers that allows an employee to fund qualified medical expenses on a pretax basis through salary reduction to pay for out-of-pocket unreimbursed expenses for health and dependent care that are not covered by insurance.

use-it-or-lose-it rule
An IRS regulation requiring that unspent dollars in a flexible spending account at the end of a calendar year be forfeited, unless the employer allows a 2 1/2-month grace period for spending the funds.

defined-contribution retirement plan
IRS-approved retirement plan sponsored by employers that allows employees to make pretax contributions that lower their tax liability.

matching contributions
Employer programs that match employees' 401(k) contributions up to a particular percentage.

Strategy: Prune Taxable Investments

If you have some investments in your portfolio that have lost value, you may want to sell them before the end of the tax year. Then you can use those capital losses to offset any capital gains earned this year from other investments. If you do not have gains to offset, you can deduct up to $3000 in losses against your regular income. Another strategy is to donate stocks that have appreciated in value to charity. In addition to obtaining the substantial charitable tax deduction, you avoid having to pay taxes on the gain.

Strategy: Make Tax-Sheltered Investments

after-tax dollars
Money on which an employee has already paid taxes.

Investments are often made with **after-tax dollars**, which means that the individuals earned the money and paid income taxes on it. Then they take their after-tax money and invest it. The returns earned from these investments typically again result in taxable income. Investment alternatives are examined in Chapters 13 through 16.

tax-sheltered investments
Investments that yield returns that are tax advantaged.

Tax laws encourage certain types of investments or other taxpayer behaviors by giving them special tax advantages over other activities. As a result, numerous **tax-sheltered investments** exist. The tax laws allow certain income to be exempt from income taxes in the current year or permit an adjustment, reduction, deferral, or elimination of income tax liability. When making investment decisions, investors should consider tax-sheltered investments.

Some of the best tax-sheltering opportunities are offered to people who wish to save and invest for their retirement. Retirement accounts are not investments themselves but rather the "housing" for tax-advantaged investments. Several additional tax-sheltered opportunities exist that can help reduce one's tax liability.

pretax income
The amount of income withheld from a worker's salary before taxes are calculated.

Invest with Pretax Income
Making an investment contribution with **pretax income** means that you do not have to pay taxes this year on the income. For example, Elizabeth Johnson made a $1000 contribution into an individual retirement account (IRA) that qualified as an adjustment to income. Elizabeth's $1000 will not count as taxable income this year. This will save her $250 ($1000 × 0.25), assuming she pays income taxes at the 25 percent rate. Instead of paying the $250 in taxes on the $1000 in income, she can invest the $1000 in a stock mutual fund (discussed in Chapter 15) within her IRA account. Elizabeth's $1000 includes $250 that otherwise would have gone to the government in taxes. This tax shelter is available with most retirement accounts. In effect, investing with pretax income is an interest-free deferral of income taxes to another year, $250 in this case, to fund one's investment.

tax deferred
Income, dividends, or capital gains that are allowed to grow without taxes until distributions are taken.

Make Your Investments Grow Tax Deferred
When income, dividends, or capital gains are **tax deferred**, the investor does not pay the current-year tax liability and instead shifts the income and any tax liability to a later year. For example, if Adam Reynolds received $10,000 in net profit from his real estate investments, he would owe $2500 in income taxes this year assuming he pays at the 25 percent marginal tax rate. If his investments were either in tax-deferred alternatives or made within tax-deferred accounts, the law allows the taxes to be paid sometime in the future (or perhaps never at all). This benefit is substantial. Investments can grow faster because the money that would have gone to the government in taxes every year can remain in the investment to accumulate. The tax-free growth of such investments is called **tax-deferred compounding**.

Assume that Kyle Broflovski, who pays combined federal and state income taxes at the 30 percent rate, opens two mutual fund accounts: a regular taxable investment account and a tax-sheltered IRA investment account. Kyle puts $1000 into each account. One year later, each account is worth $1090. The extra $90 in each case represents investment growth derived from interest, dividends, and capital gains. The $90 increase in the regular taxable account is considered taxable income. If Kyle took out $27 to pay the tax liability, that would leave a net amount of $1063 in the account. In contrast, the whole $90 increase in the tax-sheltered account can stay there and continue to grow at a pretax annual rate of return rather than an after-tax rate. This means that the extra $27 in the tax-sheltered account is an asset that Kyle can keep out of Uncle Sam's reach for years and years; it can be invested and reinvested again and again. By the time income taxes must finally be paid—probably during retirement—Kyle might be in a lower tax bracket. In effect, the government "loans" tax-free money to Kyle to help fund his retirement plan.

Seven Examples of Tax-Sheltered Investments Numerous tax-sheltered investments exist. Seven popular ones follow.

INDIVIDUAL RETIREMENT ACCOUNTS The amount contributed (up to $5000 annually) to an **individual retirement account (IRA)** is considered an adjustment to income, which reduces your current-year income tax liability. Investments inside the IRA (such as stocks and stock mutual funds) accumulate tax deferred. Income taxes are owed on any eventual withdrawals, likely during retirement. This type of IRA is also known as a traditional individual retirement account.

ROTH IRA ACCOUNTS Contributions (up to $5000 annually) to a **Roth IRA** accumulate tax free and withdrawals are tax free. There is no tax break on contributions, as they are made with after-tax money. This is an excellent investment vehicle for people with a long-term investment horizon who want to save for retirement more money than they can through an employer-sponsored retirement plan. IRAs are examined in Chapter 17.

COVERDELL EDUCATION SAVINGS ACCOUNTS Contributions of up to $2000 per year of after-tax money may be made to a **Coverdell education savings account (also known as an *education savings account*** and formerly known as an "education IRA") to pay future education costs. Earnings accumulate tax free, and withdrawals for qualified expenses are tax free. The money can be used to pay for public, private, or religious school expenses, from kindergarten through trade school or college, including tuition, fees, room and board, tutoring, uniforms, home computers, Internet access and related technology, transportation, and extended day care.

QUALIFIED TUITION PROGRAMS There are two types of **qualified tuition programs**, and these are known as **529 plans**. Under the **prepaid educational service plan**, an individual purchases tuition credits today for use in the future. Also known as a state-sponsored **prepaid tuition plan**, this program allows parents, relatives, and friends to purchase a child's future college education at today's prices by guaranteeing that amounts prepaid will be used for the future tuition at an approved institution of higher education in a particular state. The funds may be used to pay for tuition only—not room, board, or supplies.

The second qualified (IRS Section 529) tuition program, called a **college savings plan**, is set up for a designated beneficiary. You may contribute up to $12,000 per year per child of after-tax money to a 529 college savings plan. Withdrawals are tax free if made for qualified education expenses such as tuition, room, and board. If one child does not go to college, the funds may be transferred to another relative. One may contribute to both a Section 529 plan and a Coverdell education savings account for the same beneficiary in the same year.

GOVERNMENT SAVINGS BONDS Series EE and Series I **government savings bonds** are promissory notes issued by the federal government. The income is exempt from state and local taxes. You may defer the income tax until final maturity (30 years) or report the interest annually. Reporting the interest in a child's name is advisable especially when it can be offset totally by the child's standard deduction. You may exclude accumulated interest from bonds from income tax in the year you redeem the bonds to pay qualified educational expenses. (See Chapter 14 for more information on these and similar bonds.)

TAX-EXEMPT MUNICIPAL BONDS Tax-exempt **municipal bonds** (also called **munis**) are long-term debts issued by local governments and their agencies that are used to finance public improvement projects. Interest is free from federal and state taxes if the bond is purchased in one's state of residence. Taxpayers in higher-income brackets (28 percent or more) often take advantage of these kinds of investments. (See Chapter 14.) Smart investors choose the bonds that pay the better return after payment of income taxes. The formula to decide whether a taxable investment or nontaxable investment is better for you appears in the box "How to Compare Taxable and After-Tax Yields."

DID YOU KNOW?

Top 1% of Income Earners Are Doing Well

IRS data show that the top 1 percent of taxpayers earned 20 percent of all the income reported, and they paid 38 percent of federal individual income taxes.

FINANCIAL POWER POINT

Create Future Tax-Free Income with Your Refund

You can instruct the IRS to deposit your tax refund directly into a Roth IRA. An IRA account can be opened online in minutes without making an initial deposit. All the money will grow tax free, and future withdrawals will be tax free too.

individual retirement account
Investment account that reduces current year income, and the funds in the account accumulate tax free.

Roth IRA
An individual retirement account of investments made with after-tax money; the interest on such accounts is allowed to grow tax free, and withdrawals are also tax free.

Coverdell education savings account (or education savings account)
An IRS-approved way to pay the future education costs for a child younger than age 18 whereby the earnings accumulate tax free and withdrawals for qualified expenses are tax free.

DID YOU KNOW?

How to Compare Taxable and After-Tax Yields

Investors may choose to put their money into vehicles that provide taxable income, such as stocks, corporate bonds, and stock mutual funds. Taxpayers also have the opportunity to lower their income tax liabilities by investing in tax-exempt municipal bonds, money market funds that invest in municipal bonds, and other tax-exempt ventures. (These investment alternatives are discussed in Chapter 14.)

Because of their tax-exempt status, these investments offer lower nominal returns than taxable alternatives. But after considering the effects of taxes, the actual return to an investor on a tax-exempt investment may be higher than the after-tax yield on a taxable corporate bond.

To find out whether a taxable investment pays a higher after-tax yield than a tax-exempt alternative, the investor must determine the after-tax yield of each alternative. The **after-tax yield** is the percentage yield on a taxable investment after subtracting the effect of federal income taxes that will need to be paid on the investment. The after-tax yield on a tax-exempt investment is the same as the nominal yield because you do not have to pay income taxes on income from this kind of investment. So the question is, "How does the investor calculate the after-tax yield on a taxable investment?"

When you know the taxable yield, use Equation (4.1) to determine the equivalent after-tax yield on a taxable investment. Only then can you decide which investment is better. For example, suppose Bobby Bigbucks pays income taxes at

the 35 percent combined federal and state marginal tax rate and is considering buying either a municipal bond that pays a 3.5 percent yield or a taxable corporate bond that pays a 5.7 percent yield. Equation (4.1) calculates the equivalent after-tax yield on the corporate bond:*

$$
\begin{aligned}
\text{After-tax yield} &= \text{taxable yield} \\
&\quad \times (1 - \text{federal marginal tax rate}) \\
&= 5.7 \times (1.00 - 0.35) \qquad \textbf{(4.1)}^{\dagger} \\
&= 5.7 \times 0.65 \\
&= 3.71
\end{aligned}
$$

The answer is 3.71 percent. Thus, a 5.7 percent taxable yield is equivalent to an after-tax yield of 3.71 percent. Eureka! Now Bobby knows that he should buy the corporate bond paying 5.7 percent because its after-tax yield of 3.71 percent is higher than the 3.5 percent paid by the municipal bond. These differences may look small, and they are, but over time they add up. For example, the extra 0.21 percent (3.71 – 3.50) yield on a $20,000 bond investment for 20 years amounts to $840 [$20,000 × 0.0021 × 20 (bond interest is not compounded)]. That's real money![†]

The higher your federal tax rate, the more favorable tax-exempt municipal bonds become as an investment compared with taxable bonds. The tax-exempt status of municipal bonds does not apply to capital gains. When you sell an investment for more than what you paid for it, you will owe federal income taxes on the capital gain.

* This and similar equations can be found and used on the *Garman/Forgue* companion website.

† The formula can be reversed to solve for the equivalent taxable yield when one knows the tax-exempt yield. To continue the example, the return for Bobby on a 3.71 percent tax-exempt bond is equivalent to a taxable yield of 5.7 percent [3.71 ÷ (1.00 – 0.35)]. If Bobby finds a tax-exempt bond paying more than 3.71 percent, he should consider buying it.

after-tax yield
The percentage yield on a taxable investment after subtracting the effect of federal income taxes that will need to be paid on the investment.

Here is an example to illustrate the benefits of municipal bonds. Assume that Lauren Rider, a retiree living in Lincoln, Nebraska, currently has $100,000 in a certificate of deposit earning 2.5 percent, or $2500 annually ($100,000 × 0.025). She pays $625 in tax on this income at her 25 percent federal marginal tax rate ($2500 × 0.25), leaving her a net after-tax return of $1875. Investing in a tax-exempt $100,000 municipal bond paying 2.0 percent would provide Lauren with a better after-tax return. She would receive $2000 ($100,000 × 0.02) tax free from a municipal bond, compared with $1875 ($2500 – $625) after taxes on the certificate of deposit. The increase in her after-tax income would be $125 ($2000 – $1875).

CAPITAL GAINS ON HOUSING A big tax shelter is available to homeowners when they sell their homes. Those with appreciated principal residences are allowed to avoid taxes on capital gains of up to $500,000 if married and filing jointly and on gains up to $250,000 if single. The home must have been owned and used as the taxpayer's private residence for two out of the five years immediately prior to the date of the sale.

DID YOU KNOW?

About the Flat Tax, Value-Added Tax, and Tax Reform Proposals?

Politicians and pundits are talking about tax reform. Many want to eliminate certain tax deductions and simplify the tax code. This is difficult to do since the vested interests that obtained a deduction in the first place will fight to keep it. Thus they will want Congress to continue to allow deductions for things like interest paid on home loans, interest on loans for investing, payment of property taxes, contributions to retirement plans, transportation reimbursements from employers, tax credit for child and dependent care, and deductions for flexible spending accounts. Who wants to give up "their" tax deduction?

Some call for a **flat tax** as a substitute for our current tax system. This is an income tax having but a single rate for all

taxpayers regardless of income level and type. Economists suggest that a single rate, perhaps 22 percent, might replace the revenue currently derived from the present multiple tax rates. For most taxpayers, this would be a tax increase.

An oft-suggested addition to our current income tax system is a federal **value-added tax (VAT)**, which is essentially a federal retail sales tax. It is a tax, perhaps 10 percent, on the estimated "value added" to a product or material at each stage of manufacture or distribution; thus it is a form of consumption tax paid by consumers. Even thought a VAT must be paid to the government by every company that handles a product from raw material to finished goods, businesses actually pay nothing since they receive tax credits for all the VAT they pay to suppliers. Over 40 industrialized countries have VATs.

Capital gains on the profitable sale of a home may be avoided by many sellers.

flat tax
An income tax having but a single rate for all taxpayers regardless of income level and type.

value-added tax
A federal retail sales tax on the estimated "value added" to a product or material at each stage of manufacture or distribution.

Strategy: Defer Income

Another way to reduce income tax liability is to defer income. You won't have to pay taxes on income earned after December 31st until the springtime of 15 months in the future. This goal is achieved by purposefully making arrangements to receive some of this year's income in the next year, when your marginal tax rate might be lower, perhaps only 25 percent rather than 28 percent. A 3 percent tax savings (paying at the 25 percent rate rather than 28 percent) on $2000 of income is $60 ($2000 × 0.03), enough to pay for a good meal in a restaurant. Your employer might be willing to give you a bonus or

ADVICE FROM A PRO

Buy a Home to Reduce Income Taxes

Hanna Pallagrosi of Rome, New York, took a sales position at a retail chain store two years ago, where she earned a gross income of $46,736. Hanna wisely made a $1000 contribution to her IRA. Her itemized deductions came to only $3800, so she took the standard deduction and personal exemption amounts. The result was a tax liability of $5525. Hanna was not happy about paying what she thought was a large tax bill that year.

Gross income	$46,736
Less adjustment to income	−1,000
Adjusted gross income	45,736
Less value of one exemption (old figure)	−3,650
Subtotal	42,086
Less standard deduction (old figure)	−5,700
Taxable income	36,386
Tax liability (from old tax table not shown)	$ 5,525

Last year, Hanna did not receive a raise. Nonetheless, Hanna continued to contribute $1000 into her IRA. To reduce her federal income taxes, she also became a homeowner after using some inheritance money to make the down payment on a condominium. During the year, she paid out $9126 in mortgage interest expenses and $1995 in real estate taxes. After studying various tax publications, Hanna determined that she had $3814 in other itemized deductions that, when combined with the interest and real estate taxes, totaled $14,935. These deductions reduced Hanna's tax liability dramatically.

Gross income	$46,736
Less adjustment to income	−1,000
Adjusted gross income	45,736
Less itemized deductions	−14,935
Subtotal	30,801
Less value of one exemption	−3,700
Taxable income	27,101
Tax liability (from Table 4-3)	$ 3,651

Hanna correctly concluded that the IRS "paid" $1575 ($5525 − $3650) toward the purchase of her condominium and her living costs because she did not have to forward those dollars to the government. An additional benefit for Hanna is that she now owns a home whose value could appreciate in the future. Buying a home can reduce one's income taxes.

Frances C. Lawrence
Louisiana State University

commission check in January rather than in December, and those who are self-employed can ask clients and customers to wait until January to pay their bills.

You might expect to be in a lower tax bracket in the following year because you anticipate fewer sales commissions or know that you will not work full time (for example, if you return to school, have a child, or decide to travel). Retired people may be able to postpone withdrawals of income from retirement plans, and entrepreneurs may delay billing customers for work.

Strategy: Accelerate Deductions

This strategy allows you to lower your taxable income sooner rather than later, which is usually a good idea. Many people find that they do not have enough itemized deductions to exceed the standard deduction amount. By shifting the payment dates of some deductible items, you can increase your deductions. For example, if a single person has about $5500 of deductible expenses this year, she could prepay some items in December to push the total over the $5800 threshold and benefit by taking the excess deductions now. The next year, she can take the standard deduction amount instead of itemizing.

accelerating deductions

A technique to save on income taxes by prepaying tax-deductible expenses a year in advance so as to increase one's itemizations higher than the standard deduction threshold and taking the standard deduction in the following year.

This process is known as **accelerating deductions**. Items that may be prepaid include medical expenses, dental bills, real estate taxes, state and local income taxes, the January payment of estimated state income taxes, personal property taxes that have been billed (e.g., on autos and boats), dues in professional associations, and charitable contributions. You may mail the payments or charge them on credit cards by December 31.

Strategy: Take All of Your Legal Tax Deductions

Although you should not spend money just to create a tax deduction, you are encouraged to take all of the deductions to which you are entitled. One way to increase itemized deductions, for example, is to purchase a home with a mortgage loan. The large amounts of money homeowners expend for both interest and real estate taxes are

DID YOU KNOW?

Consider the Tax Consequences of Managing Income Taxes

This is an example of how one couple—model taxpayers—took numerous tax deductions to reduce their income taxes. Ron and Marilyn West of Longmont, Colorado, have a complex income tax return because they have both made it a habit to learn about tax-saving strategies and to take advantage of them whenever possible. The Wests have a son in elementary school and a daughter in college; Ron's disabled mother, who requires in-home nursing care, lives in their home as well. Because Marilyn went to work immediately after high school, she only recently started taking college classes at night. Last year, she spent $1000 on night-school tuition.

Part of the Wests' income comes from tax-exempt sources. The table shows their total income and demonstrates how they arrived at a very low final tax liability. The couple has taken advantage of applicable exclusions, adjustments, deductions, exemptions, and credits. Their deductions and tax credits, typical for a couple with three dependents, result in a tax liability of only $2789. The marginal tax rate for the West family is 15 percent. Their average tax rate for all income is 2.8 percent ($2789 ÷ $100,550). For a family with such a substantial income, they have been extremely successful in lowering their tax liability.

	Dollars	
Total Income		
Ron's salary (self-employed)	$54,200	
Marilyn's salary	35,570	
Marilyn's year-end bonus	1,000	
State income tax refund (itemized last year)	180	
Interest on savings account	350	
Interest on tax-exempt state bonds	2,000*	
Gift from Marilyn's mother	2,500*	
Carpool income (Ron's van pool)	250*	
Reimbursements from flexible spending accounts	4,500*	
Total all income		$100,550
*Minus Excludable Income		
($2000 + $2500 + $250 + $4500 from above)		−$ 9,250
Gross Income		$ 91,300
Adjustments to Income		
Contribution—Ron's retirement account	$ 4,000	
Contribution—Marilyn's IRA	2,500	
Flexible spending account for health care	500	
Flexible spending account for dependent care	4,000	
College tuition and fees (daughter)	3,000	
Minus Adjustments to Income		−14,000
Adjusted Gross Income (AGI)		$ 77,300
Deductions		
Medical expenses (includes long-term care premiums)	6,900	
Exclusion (7.5% of AGI)	−5,798	
Total net medical expenses	$ 1,102	
Taxes		
Real property	2,800	
Personal property (vehicles)	210	
Total deductible taxes	$ 3,010	
Interest Expenses		
Home mortgage interest	10,800	
Home-equity loan interest	460	
Total deductible interest expenses	$11,260	
Contributions		
Church	1,200	
Other qualified charities	486	
Charitable travel	90	
Total deductible contributions	$ 1,776	

(continues on next page)

Total Income		Dollars
Casualty or Theft		
Lost diamond ring (uninsured)	8,100	
Insurance reimbursement	−0	
Reduction	−100	
Exclusion (10% of AGI)	−7,730	
Total deductible casualty loss	$ 270	
Miscellaneous		
Union dues (Ron)	480	
Safe-deposit box	30	
Unreimbursed job expenses	460	
Cost of Ron looking for a new job	900	
Investment publications	60	
Financial planning tax advice	150	
Tax publications	40	
Subtotal	2,120	
Less 2% of AGI	−1,546	
Total net miscellaneous deductions	$ 820	
Total Itemized Deductions		−17,746
Minus Exemptions (5 @ $3,700)		−18,500
Taxable Income		$ 41,300
Tax Liability (from Table 4-3)	$ 5,349	
Tax Credits		
Hope Scholarship credit (Marilyn)	−1,000	
Dependent care credit (Ron's mother)	−960	
Child tax credit (son)	−600	
Minus total tax credits		−2,560
Final Tax Liability		$ 2,789

DID YOU KNOW?

Your Worst Financial Blunders in Managing Income Taxes

Based on others' financial woes, you will make mistakes in personal finance when you:

1. *Turn all their income tax planning over to someone else.*

2. *Overwithhold income to receive a refund next year.*

3. *Ignore the impact of income taxes in their personal financial planning.*

deductible. Plus, if your property taxes and interest exceed the standard deduction amount, then you are able to take additional deductions that were ineligible because of the threshold.

Here are some other approaches to increase your deductions and keep more tax dollars in your pocket. Assume you are in the 15 percent marginal tax bracket and itemize deductions. Cash contributions made to people collecting door to door or at a shopping center during holidays are deductible, even though receipts are not given. Fifty dollars in contributions deducted can save you $7.50 in taxes. Instead of throwing out an old television set, donate it. An $80 charitable contribution for a TV will save you $12 in taxes. These amounts may sound like "small change," but lots of little tax deductions can quickly add up to more than $100, and that's real money!

Expenses for business-related trips can be a fruitful area for tax deductions. If you are in the 15 percent tax bracket and take one business trip per year, perhaps incurring $400 in deductible expenses, you will save another $60 in taxes, assuming your miscellaneous deductions already exceed 2 percent of your AGI. The IRS also permits tax deductions for the costs expended on occasional job-hunting trips. In other words, depending on your tax bracket, the U.S. government pays the bill for 15 or 25 percent of such expenditures.

Strategy: Shift Income to a Child

A parent who runs his or her own business may pay a child up to $9500 ($3700 [value of exemption] + $5800 [value of standard deduction]) in earned income, assuming no other income to the child before any income tax liability occurs for the child. Thus, the

DID YOU KNOW?

Turn Bad Habits into Good Habits

Do You Do This?	*Do This Instead!*
Did not file an income tax return assuming your employer withheld sufficient funds	File a return to obtain amounts overwithheld
Pay too much in income taxes	Use the strategies in this chapter to reduce your tax liability
Wish you could itemize instead of using the standard deduction	Buy a home so you can deduct mortgage interest and property taxes as well as take other deductions
Forget to take certain tax credits in the last three years	File 1040X amended returns to claim the credits and obtain the refunds
Neglect to save for retirement	Save money by contributing to a qualified retirement plan
Let a tax preparer fill out your income tax forms every year	Get smart about how to reduce your income tax liability and use software and do your own taxes

parent can deduct the payments as business expenses, and the child owes no tax on the $9500 income.

A parent also can shift income-generating investment assets to the name of a child who then may receive as much as $950 in tax-free investment income (known by the IRS as **unearned income**). The next $950 is taxed at the child's rate. If a child is under age 19 (or up to 24 for full-time students), the amount above $1900 is taxed as though it were the income of the parent. This is called the **kiddie tax**.

Strategy: Buy and Manage a Real Estate Investment

Tax losses are paper losses in the sense that they may not represent actual out-of-pocket dollar losses. They are created when deductions generated from an investment (such as depreciation and net investment losses) exceed the income from an investment.

Taxpayers are allowed to deduct certain real estate losses against ordinary taxable income, such as salary, interest, dividends, and self-employment earnings. Deductions are allowed for real estate investors who (1) have an adjusted gross income of $150,000 or less and (2) actively participate in the management of the property. Here the investor may deduct up to $25,000 of net losses from a "passive investment," such as real estate, against income from "active" sources, such as salary. For example, a residential real estate investment property might generate an annual cash income $1000 greater than the out-of-pocket operating costs associated with it. However, after depreciation expenses on the building are taken as a tax deduction, the resulting $1500 tax loss may then be used to offset other income. This tax break begins to phase out for those with higher incomes. (For more details, see Chapter 16, "Real Estate and High-Risk Investments.")

DO IT NOW!

You know more about personal finance after reading this chapter, so get started right now by:

1. *Projecting your taxable income and total withholding for this year.*

2. *Estimating your federal tax liability based on your income projection using this year's tax tables or schedules.*

3. *Revising your W-4 form with your employer as necessary to withhold more if you estimate owing more in taxes or to withhold less to get an immediate raise in take-home pay if you expect a refund.*

unearned income
Investment returns in the form of rents, dividends, capital gains, interest, or royalties.

tax losses
Paper losses that may not represent actual losses created when deductions generated from an investment exceed income from the investment.

✔ Concept Check 4.3

1. Distinguish between two types of tax-sheltered investment returns.

2. Explain how to reduce income taxes via your employer, and name three employer-sponsored plans to do so.

3. Summarize the differences between an individual retirement account (IRA) and a Roth IRA.

4. Identify three strategies to avoid overpayment of income taxes (different from above), and summarize the essence of each.

WHAT DO YOU RECOMMEND NOW?

Now that you have read the chapter on managing income taxes, what advice can you offer Tom and Gerry in the case at the beginning of the chapter regarding:

1. Using tax credits to help pay for Tom's college expenses?

2. Determining how much money Gerry will realize if she sells the stocks, assuming she pays federal income taxes at the 25 percent rate?

3. Buying a home?

4. Increasing contributions to their employer-sponsored retirement plans?

5. Establishing a sideline business for Tom's jewelry operation?

BIG PICTURE SUMMARY OF LEARNING OBJECTIVES

LO1. **Explain the nature of progressive income taxes and the marginal tax rate.**

The federal personal income tax is a progressive tax because the tax rate increases as a taxpayer's taxable income increases. The marginal tax rate is applied to your last dollar of earnings. Your effective marginal tax rate is probably 43 percent.

LO2. **Differentiate among the eight steps involved in calculating your federal income taxes.**

There are eight steps in calculating your income taxes. Certain types of income may be excluded. Regulations permit you to subtract adjustments to income, exemptions, deductions, and tax credits before determining your final tax liability.

LO3. **Use appropriate strategies to avoid overpayment of income taxes.**

You can reduce your tax liability by following certain tax avoidance strategies, such as putting your money in tax-sheltered investments, reducing taxable income via your employer, and investing pretax money for tax-deferred compounding. Other strategies are to postpone income, accelerate deductions, take all your legal deductions, and buy and manage a real estate investment.

LET'S TALK ABOUT IT

1. **During Sluggish Economic Times.** Congress recently reduced taxes on middle- and high-income taxpayers with the expectation that they will spend most of that money and help create more economic growth. Is this a good idea or bad, and why?

2. **Filing a Tax Return.** Many college students choose not to file a federal income tax return, assuming that the income taxes withheld by employers "probably" will cover their tax liability. Is such an assumption correct? What are the negatives of this practice if the employers withheld too much in income taxes? What are the negatives if the employers did not withhold enough in income taxes? Will any tax credits be lost?

3. **Fairness of Capital Gains.** Long-term capital gains are taxed at a rate of 15 or 5 percent, or zero (0). What is your opinion on the fairness of these lower capital gains tax rates as compared with the marginal rates applied to income earned from employment that range as high as 35 percent?

4. **Reporting Cash Income.** Some college students earn money that is paid to them in cash and then do not include this as income when they file their tax returns. What are the pros and cons of this practice?

5. **Sideline Business.** Identify one possible sideline business that you might engage in to reduce your income tax liability.

6. **Tax Credits.** Name three tax credits that a college student might take advantage of while still in school or during the first few years after graduation.

7. **Reduce Tax Liability.** Identify five strategies to reduce income tax liability that you will likely take advantage of in the future.

DO THE MATH

1. **Find Tax Liability.** What would be the tax liability for a single taxpayer who has a gross income of $29,700? (Hint: Use Table 4-3, and don't forget to first subtract the value of a standard deduction and one exemption.)

2. **Marginal Tax Rate.** What would be the marginal tax rate for a single person who has a taxable income of (a) $20,210, (b) $27,800, (c) $26,055, and (d) $90,230? (Hint: Use Table 4-2.)

3. **Calculate Tax Liability.** Find the tax liabilities based on the taxable income of the following people: (a) married couple, $74,125; (b) married couple, $53,077; (c) single person, $27,880; (d) single person, $53,000. (Hint: Use Table 4-3.)

4. **Use Tax Table.** Joseph Addai determined the following tax information: gross salary, $59,550; interest earned, $90; IRA contribution, $1000; personal exemption, $3700; and itemized deductions, $3950. Calculate Joseph's taxable income and tax liability filing single. (Hint: Use Table 4-3.)

5. **Use Tax Rate Schedule.** Anthony Clark determined the following tax information: salary, $144,000; interest earned, $2000; qualified retirement plan contribution, $7000; personal exemption, $3700; itemized deductions, $9000. Filing single, calculate Anthony's taxable income and tax liability. (Hint: Use Table 4-2.)

FINANCIAL PLANNING CASES

CASE 1

The Johnsons Calculate Their Income Taxes

Several years have gone by since Harry and Belinda graduated from college and started their working careers. They both earn good salaries. They believe that they are paying too much in federal income taxes. The Johnsons' total income last year included Harry's salary of $63,000 and Belinda's salary of $84,000. She contributed $3000 to her 401(k) for retirement. She earned $400 in interest on savings and checking and $3000 interest income from the trust that is taxed in the same way as interest income from checking and savings accounts. Harry contributed $3000 into a traditional IRA.

(a) What is the Johnsons' reportable gross income on their joint tax return?

(b) What is their adjusted gross income?

(c) What is the total value of their exemptions?

(d) How much is the standard deduction for the Johnsons?

(e) The Johnsons are buying a home that has monthly mortgage payments of $3000, or $36,000 a year. Of this amount, $32,800 goes for interest and real estate property taxes. The couple has an additional $14,000 in itemized deductions. Using these numbers and Table 4-3, calculate their taxable income and tax liability.

(f) Assuming they had a combined $18,000 in federal income taxes withheld, how much of a refund will the Johnsons receive?

(g) What is their marginal tax rate?

(h) Based on gross income, what is their average tax rate?

(i) List three additional ways that the Johnsons might reduce their tax liability next year.

CASE 2

Victor and Maria Reduce Their Income Tax Liability

The year before last, Victor earned $51,000 from his retail management position and Maria began working full-time and earned $45,000 as a dental hygienist. After they took the standard deduction and claimed four exemptions (themselves plus their two children), their federal income tax liability was about $12,000. After hearing from friends that they were paying too much in taxes, the couple vowed to try to never again pay that much. Therefore, the Hernandezes embarked on a yearlong effort to reduce their income tax liability. This year they tracked all of their possible itemized deductions, and both made contributions to qualified retirement plans at their places of employment.

(a) Calculate the Hernandezes' income tax liability for this year as a joint return (using Table 4-3) given the following information: gross salary income (Victor, $56,000; Maria, $51,000); state income tax refund ($400); interest on checking and savings accounts ($250); holiday bonus from Maria's employer ($375); contributions to qualified retirement accounts ($5000); itemized deductions (real estate taxes, $2600; mortgage interest, $6300; charitable contributions, $2500); and exemptions ($3700 each) for themselves and their two children.

(b)   List five additional strategies that Victor and Maria might consider for next year's tax planning to reduce their tax liability.

CASE 3

Julia Price Thinks About Reducing Her Income Taxes

Julia does well financially because she earns a good salary as an engineer, is somewhat frugal, and is making the maximum contribution to her employer-sponsored retirement plan. After reading about ways to decrease her income tax liability, she has some thoughts. Buying a home is an option, but Julia is worried about additional declines in housing prices. As an accomplished sculptural artist, she is thinking about creating a sideline business to sell some of her work and convert some everyday expenses into business expenses. She is considering taking a tax-deductible job-hunting trip and then stretching the trip into a vacation. Also on her possibilities list is to start a master's degree program in engineering to enhance her skills. Finally, Julia figures she could contribute $200 a month to a Roth IRA account. Offer your opinions about her thinking.

CASE 4

A New Family Calculates Income and Tax Liability

Geri Nichols and her two children, Austin and Alexandra, moved into the home of her new husband, Glenn Sandler, in Ames, Iowa. Geri is employed as a union organizer, and her husband manages a vegetarian food store. The Nichols-Sandler family income consists of the following: $40,000 from Geri's salary; $42,000 from Glenn's salary; $10,000 in life insurance proceeds from a deceased aunt; $140 in interest from savings; $4380 in alimony from Geri's ex-husband; $14,200 in child support from her ex-husband; $500 cash as a Christmas gift from Glenn's parents; $90 from a friend who rides to work in Geri's vehicle; and a $1600 tuition-and-books scholarship Geri received to go to college part time last year.

(a)   What is the total of the Nichols-Sandler reportable gross income?

(b)   After they put $5600 into qualified retirement plan accounts last year, what is their adjusted gross income?

(c)   How many exemptions can the family claim, and how much is the total value allowed the household?

(d)   How much is the allowable standard deduction for the household?

(e)   Their itemized deductions are $13,100, so should they itemize or take the standard deduction?

(f)   What is their taxable income for a joint return, and what is their marginal tax rate?

(g)   What is their final federal income tax liability? (Hint: Use Table 4-2.)

(h)   If Geri's and Glenn's employers withheld $6300 for income taxes, does the couple owe money to the government or do they get a refund? How much?

CASE 5

Taxable Versus Tax-Exempt Bonds

Art Williams, radio station manager in Franklin County, New Jersey, is in the 25 percent federal marginal tax bracket and pays an additional 5 percent in taxes to the state of New Jersey. Art currently has more than $20,000 invested in corporate bonds bought at various times that are earning differing amounts of taxable interest: $10,000 in ABC earning 5.9 percent; $5000 in DEF earning 5.5 percent; $3000 in GHI earning 5.8 percent; and $2000 in JKL earning 5.4 percent. What is the after-tax return of each investment? To calculate your answers, use the after-tax yield formula (or the reversed formula) on page 128, or the *Garman/Forgue* companion website.

CASE 6

Taxable Versus Nontaxable Income

Identify each of the following items as either part of taxable income or an exclusion, adjustment, or an allowable itemized deduction from taxable income for LaDainian Tomison and Megan Smithfield, a married couple from San Diego:

(a)   LaDainian earns $45,000 per year.

(b)   LaDainian receives a $1000 bonus from his employer.

(c)   Megan receives $40,000 in commissions from her work.

(d)   Megan receives $300 in monthly child support.

(e)   LaDainian pays $200 each month in alimony.

(f)   LaDainian contributes $2000 to his retirement account.

(g)   Megan inherits a car from her aunt that has a fair market value of $3000.

(h)   Megan sells the car and donates $1500 to her aunt's church.

(i)   LaDainian receives a $5000 gift from his mother.

BE YOUR OWN PERSONAL FINANCIAL MANAGER

1.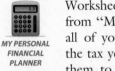
MY PERSONAL FINANCIAL PLANNER
   Keep Track of Your Sources of Income. Complete Worksheet 19: My Sources of Taxable Income from "My Personal Financial Planner" to record all of your various income sources throughout the tax year so that you will not forget to report them to the Internal Revenue Service. Record the names of the income sources in the spaces provided. Record the amounts in the appropriate spaces.

2.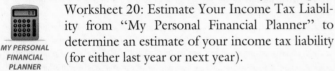
MY PERSONAL FINANCIAL PLANNER
   Estimate Your Income Tax Liability. Complete Worksheet 20: Estimate Your Income Tax Liability from "My Personal Financial Planner" to determine an estimate of your income tax liability (for either last year or next year).

3.
MY PERSONAL FINANCIAL PLANNER
   Should You File an Income Tax Return to Obtain a Refund? Complete Worksheet 21: Determining Whether I Should File for a Refund from "My Personal Financial Planner." Even if you are not required to file a return perhaps because you did not earn enough money, you should file if you have a refund coming—that is, if you had more taxes withheld from your paychecks than you ultimately owed. Follow the steps to make the determination.

4.
MY PERSONAL FINANCIAL PLANNER
   Strategies to Reduce Your Income Tax Liability. Complete Worksheet 22: Strategies to Reduce My Income Tax Liability from "My Personal Financial Planner." There are several ways to reduce your income tax liability. For each strategy that might be of interest, make checkmarks to identify what characteristics you like about each and which strategies you might follow during your tax-paying life.

ON THE 'NET

Go to the Web pages indicated to complete these exercises. You can also go to the *Garman/Forgue* companion website at www.cengagebrain.com for an expanded list of exercises. Under General Business, select the title of this text. Click on the Internet Exercises link for this chapter.

1. **IRS Publication 17.** Go to the Internal Revenue Service website address www.irs.gov/publications/p17/index.html. There you will find the IRS's entire Publication 17 online. This is the government's detailed explanation of all aspects of federal income taxes where you can look up almost any possible tax question. Summarize your observations about this publication.

2. **Estimate Your Tax Refund.** Visit the website for TurboTax at http://turbotax.intuit.com/tax-tools/calculators/taxcaster/?s=1 and use "TaxCaster" to estimate your tax refund. Fill in a few numbers and get an answer.

3. **Estimate Your Income Taxes.** Go to the website of Financial Calculators by KJE Computer Solutions, popularly known as the provider of DinkyTown calculators, at www.dinkytown.net/java/Tax1040.html. After you enter your filing status, income, deductions, and credits, it will estimate your income taxes.

4. **Check Taxes in Your State to Determine Your Effective Tax Rate.** Visit Bankrate.com's website www.bankrate.com/finance/taxes/check-taxes-in-your-state.aspx. There you will find a map of states. Click to find your state income tax, if applicable. What is your combined federal and state marginal tax rate? Add in another 7.65 percent for Social Security and Medicare taxes to determine your effective marginal tax rate.

5. **States Without Income Taxes.** Check the Internal Revenue Service website www.irs.gov/efile/article/0,,id=130684,00.html to see which states do not have state income taxes. What other types of taxes do you think those states have to raise revenue to pay for schools, police, courts, and other state government services?

ACTION INVOLVEMENT PROJECTS

1. **Telephone the Internal Revenue Service.** Dial 1 (800) TAX-3676 (or 1 (800) 829-3676) to pose a question for an IRS spokesperson. Think of a question before you call. Perhaps it has to deal with whether or not you qualify for a specific tax credit, can deduct expenses for a sideline business, or can make Roth IRA contributions. Write a summary of your findings.

2. **Tax Reform Proposals.** Type "tax reform" into your browser and skim read what you find of interest on three websites. Write a summary of your findings and include your views of what reform(s) you might prefer.

3. **Who Pays Income Taxes?** Type "income taxes, who pays" into your browser and skim read what you find of interest on three websites. For starters, you will discover that about half of all Americans do not pay any federal income taxes at all and that the top 5 percent of earners pay over half of all personal income revenues. Write a summary of your findings.

4. **Tax Bills Lowest Since 1950s.** Read the USA Today article on taxes in the United States at www.usatoday .com/money/perfi/taxes/2010-05-10-taxes_N.htm. In addition, search the Web for a more recent report on the same topic and write a summary of your findings.

5. **Corporate and Individual Tax Rates Around the World.** Comparing taxes on individuals and businesses around the world is extremely challenging. Some countries have a value-added tax paid by consumers. Many countries provide health care to citizens, while people in other countries have to pay health care premiums. Review the table provided by Worldwide-Taxes.com at www.worldwide-tax.com/#partthree, and write a brief summary of your impressions.

6. **Corporate Tax Avoidance.** Search the Web to try to discover how many billions the large multinational corporations in the United States do or do not pay in income taxes in this country. Include Glenn Beck and Jon Stewart in your searches. Write a summary of your findings.

Visit the Garman/Forgue companion website at **www.cengagebrain.com**.

Managing Checking and Savings Accounts

5

YOU MUST BE KIDDING, RIGHT?

Patti Patterson realized about two weeks ago that she had misplaced her debit card. At first she was not worried because she reasoned that it had to be somewhere at home. Last week she received her savings account statement. She looked at her statement today and found that $200 had been withdrawn from her account on five different occasions ($1000 total). She immediately called her bank to report the fraudulent withdrawals. How much of this money will Patti lose because of the unauthorized withdrawals?

A. $0   C. $500

B. $50   D. $1000

The answer is C, $500. Because Patti waited more than two days after realizing the card was lost to report it to her financial institution, federal law states that she is liable for the first $500 in unauthorized uses. If she had notified the bank within two days, her loss would have been only $50. If Patti failed to notify her bank of the loss within 60 days, the law states that she would lose all of the money taken fraudulently. It's smart to immediately report a lost debit card!

LEARNING OBJECTIVES

After reading this chapter, you should be able to:

1. Identify the tools of monetary asset management and sources of such financial services.

2. Earn interest and pay no or low fees on your checking accounts.

3. Make the best use of the benefits of savings accounts.

4. Explain the importance of placing excess funds in a money market account.

5. Describe electronic money management, including your legal protections.

6. Discuss your personal finances and money management more effectively with loved ones.

© PETER DAZELEY/GETTY IMAGES, INC.

WHAT DO YOU RECOMMEND?

Mark Rosenberg and Trina Adams are to be married in two months. Both are employed full time and currently have their own apartments. Once married, they will move into Trina's apartment because it is larger. They plan to use Mark's rent money to begin saving for a down payment on a home to be purchased in four or five years. Mark has a checking account at a branch of a large regional commercial bank near his workplace where he deposits his paychecks. He also has three savings accounts—one at his bank and two small accounts at a savings and loan association near where he went to college. Mark pays about $30 per month in fees on his various accounts. In addition, he has a $10,000 certificate of deposit (CD) from an inheritance; this CD will mature in five months. Trina has her paycheck directly deposited into her share draft account at the credit union where she works. She has a savings account at the credit union as well as a money market account at a stock brokerage firm that was set up years ago when her father gave her 300 shares of stock. She also has $9300 in an individual retirement account invested through a mutual fund.

What would you recommend to Trina and Mark on the subject of managing checking and savings accounts regarding:

1. Where they can obtain the services that they need for managing their monetary assets?

2. Their best use of checking accounts and savings accounts as they begin saving for a home?

3. The use of a money market account for managing their monetary assets?

4. Their use of electronic banking?

5. How they can best discuss the management of their money and finances?

Your financial success will depend in part on how well you manage your **monetary assets**. These assets were defined in Chapter 3 as cash and low-risk, near-cash items that can be readily converted to cash with little or no loss in value. If you are a typical college student, your monetary assets are the largest component of your net worth and are the major focus of the activities you consider "personal finance." As a result of Americans' "borrow and spend" mentality for many years and the subsequent Great Recession, times have changed. We as a society seem to be moving to a new era of austerity, one that watches money more carefully and saves more. In such times, the management of monetary assets takes on much greater importance. The personal savings rate in the United States now exceeds 6 percent after languishing below 1 percent for years.

People use monetary assets in one of three ways. First, they spend them. They buy food, clothing, entertainment, and a long list of products and services. Spending usually requires cash or the use of a check or a debit card to access funds in a checking account. (Using credit is covered in Chapters 6 and 7.) Checking accounts are appropriate places to keep money that you will spend within the next three to six months or so. The second way that people use monetary assets is to set aside funds to meet needs that will occur six months to five years in the future. You could keep these funds in a checking account, but savings accounts pay more interest. With savings accounts, the focus is on holding money safely until needed in the future. The money in most checking and savings accounts is fully insured by the federal government. The third way that people use monetary assets is to make investments. Here the goal is to earn a better return on your money for the long term. Investments are the best places to put money you will not need for 5, 10, or even 20 years in the future. The magic of the world of investments is that over long periods of time, it is quite possible to watch your money triple or quadruple over the original amount invested. Investments are examined in Chapters 13 through 17.

WHAT IS MONETARY ASSET MANAGEMENT?

Monetary asset (cash) management encompasses how you handle all of your monetary assets, including cash on hand, checking accounts, savings accounts and certificates of deposit, and money market accounts. The goal is to maximize interest earnings and to minimize fees while keeping funds safe and readily available for living expenses, emergencies, and saving and investment opportunities. Successful monetary asset management allows you to earn interest on your money while maintaining reasonable liquidity and safety. **Liquidity** refers to the speed and ease with which an asset can be converted to cash. Your funds are safe when they are free from financial risk.

The Three Tools of Monetary Asset Management

As illustrated in Figure 5-1, monetary asset management relies on three major tools:

1. Low-cost, interest-earning checking accounts from which to pay ongoing, current living expenses.
2. Interest-earning savings accounts in local financial institutions in which you deposit funds for upcoming expenditures or to accumulate funds for future investments.
3. Money market accounts in local financial institutions or other financial services providers. These accounts pay higher interest rates than checking and savings accounts. They have limited check-writing privileges and, thus, are a cross between a checking and a savings account.

---

monetary assets
Cash and low-risk, near-cash items that can quickly be converted into cash.

YOUR NEXT 5 YEARS

In the next five years, you can start achieving financial success by doing the following related to checking and savings accounts:

1. *Use a free, interest-earning checking account for your day-to-day spending needs.*
2. *Start now to build an emergency fund sufficient to cover three months of living expenses.*
3. *Use a pay-yourself-first approach as you begin to build other savings through high-interest accounts.*
4. *Use investment vehicles for wants that will not occur until five or more years in the future.*
5. *Use all your checking and savings accounts appropriately by never overdrawing the accounts and by reconciling them monthly.*

LEARNING OBJECTIVE ❶

Identify the tools of monetary asset management and sources of such financial services.

monetary asset (cash) management
How you handle your monetary assets.

liquidity
Ease with which an asset can be converted to cash.

FINANCIAL POWER POINT

Lifeline Banking May Save You Money

College students who are financially independent of their parents may qualify for a very low-cost lifeline banking account.

Figure 5-1

Three Tools of Monetary Asset Management (with Illustrative Interest Rates Earned on Deposited Funds in Addition to the Rate on a Checking Account)

Checking account	Savings account	Money market account
• NOW checking (pays interest)	• Statement savings ($+1/4\%$) • Certificate of deposit ($+1/3\%$ to $+2\%$)	• Money market deposit account ($+1/3\%$) • Super NOW ($+2/5\%$) • Money market mutual fund ($+1/2\%$ to $+3/4\%$) • Asset management account ($+1/2\%$ to $+3/4\%$)

Who Provides Monetary Asset Management Services?

financial services industry
Companies that provide monetary asset management and other services.

The **financial services industry** comprises companies that provide checking, savings, and money market accounts and possibly credit, insurance, investment, and financial planning services. These companies include depository institutions such as banks and credit unions, stock brokerage firms, mutual funds, financial services companies, and insurance companies. Table 5-1 matches these various types of firms with the financial products and services that they offer. As you can see, there is considerable overlap. For example, State Farm, which most people recognize as an insurance company, also owns a mutual fund and a bank.

depository institutions
Organizations licensed to take deposits and make loans.

Depository Institutions
Depository institutions are organizations licensed to take deposits and make loans. They all can offer some form of government account insurance on their customers' deposits and are government regulated. They offer a wide range of financial services. Examples of depository institutions are commercial banks,

Table 5-1

Today's Providers of Monetary Asset Management Services

Providers	What They Sell	Examples of Well-Known Company Names
Depository institutions (banks, mutual savings banks, and credit unions)	Checking, savings, lending, credit cards, investments, and trust advice	Citibank, Chase, Bank of America, Wells Fargo
Mutual funds	Money market mutual funds, tax-exempt funds, bond funds, and stock funds	Fidelity, T. Rowe Price, Vanguard
Stock brokerage firms	Securities investments (stocks and bonds), mutual funds, and real estate investment trusts	Schwab, Fidelity
Financial services companies	Checking, savings, lending, credit cards, securities investments, real estate investments, insurance, accounting and legal advice, and financial planning	American Express, A. G. Edwards, Raymond James
Insurance companies	Property and liability, health and life insurance, credit services, financial planning services	Allstate, Aetna, State Farm

savings banks, and credit unions. Although each is a distinct type of institution, people often call them all simply *banks*.

Commercial banks are corporations chartered under federal and state regulations. They offer numerous consumer services, such as checking, savings, loans, safe-deposit boxes, investment services, financial counseling, and automatic payment of bills. **Savings banks** (or **savings and loan associations–S&Ls**) focus primarily on accepting savings and providing mortgage and consumer loans. They offer checking services through interest-earning NOW accounts (discussed later in this chapter). Savings banks generally pay depositors an interest rate about 0.10 to 0.20 percentage points higher than the rate found at commercial banks. Accounts in federally chartered commercial banks and savings banks are insured against loss by the **Deposit Insurance Fund (DIF)** of the **Federal Deposit Insurance Corporation (FDIC)**, which is an agency of the federal government. The regulator of these banking entities is the **Office of the Comptroller of the Currency**.

A **credit union (CU)** also accepts deposits and makes loans. Credit unions operate on a not-for-profit basis and are owned by their members. The members/owners of the credit union all share some common bond, such as the same employer, church, trade union, fraternal association, or neighborhood. People in the family of a member are also eligible to join. Federally chartered credit unions have their accounts insured through the **National Credit Union Share Insurance Fund (NCUSIF)**, which is administered by the National Credit Union Administration (NCUA). State-chartered credit unions are often insured by NCUSIF, and most others participate in private insurance programs. Credit unions usually pay higher interest rates and charge lower fees than commercial banks or savings banks.

A **mutual savings bank (MSB)** is similar to a savings bank in that it also accepts deposits and makes housing and consumer loans. State laws permit these banks to operate in only 17 states, primarily those in the eastern United States. They are called "mutual" because the depositors own the institution and share in the earnings. Generally, MSBs have the FDIC's DIF coverage. Like savings banks, they offer interest-earning checking accounts.

credit union (CU)
Member-owned, not-for-profit insured financial institutions that provide checking, savings, and loan services to members.

Deposit Insurance Protects Your Money   Deposits in depository institutions are insured against loss of both the amount on deposit and the accrued interest by various insurance funds. Not a single depositor has lost a dime of insured funds since the inception of deposit insurance during the Great Depression of the 1930s. This **federal deposit insurance** for your deposits at any one institution works as follows:

1. The maximum insurance on all of your single-ownership (individual) accounts (held in your name only) is $250,000.
2. The maximum insurance on all of your joint accounts (accounts held with other individuals) is $250,000.
3. The maximum insurance on all of your retirement accounts is $250,000.
4. A maximum of $250,000 in insurance per beneficiary is available on **payable at death accounts** (accounts set up so that the funds go to a designated person[s] upon the death of the account holder).

federal deposit insurance
Insures deposits, both principal amounts and accrued interest, up to $250,000 per account for most accounts.

Thus, individuals might have several increments of insurance for their accounts at any one institution. Funds on deposit at other institutions will also have these same limits. So if you had $140,000 in individual accounts at each of two different institutions, you would have a total of $280,000 of deposit insurance.

Other Financial Services Providers   Depository institutions are not the only providers of monetary asset management services. Mutual funds, stock brokerage houses, and insurance companies provide some cash management services as well. The one service they do not provide are government-insured checking and savings accounts; however, many of these companies also own banks and thus do provide insured deposits through their banking entities.

mutual funds
Investment companies that raise money by selling shares to the public and then invest that money in a diversified investment portfolio.

Mutual funds are investment companies that raise money by selling shares to the public and then invest that money in a diversified portfolio of investments. Most have created cash management accounts to provide a convenient and safe place to keep money while awaiting alternative investment opportunities. Money deposited in a mutual fund is not insured by the federal government, although some mutual fund companies purchase insurance privately for the noninvestment portions of customers' accounts. Mutual funds are the subject of Chapter 15.

Stock brokerage firms are licensed financial institutions that specialize in selling and buying stocks, bonds, and other investments and providing advice to investors. They earn commissions based on the buy and sell orders that they process. Stock brokerage firms typically offer cash or mutual fund accounts into which clients may place money while waiting to make investments. The noninvestment portion of an account (for example, cash held in the account prior to making an investment) is insured by the Securities Investor Protection Corporation, a nongovernment entity.

Insurance companies provide property, liability, health, life, and other insurance products. Many offer monetary asset services, such as money market accounts. Some also offer vehicle loans and credit cards.

 Concept Check 5.1

1. Identify the primary goals of monetary asset management.

2. Explain the circumstances when it would be appropriate to have funds in a checking account, a savings account, or in investments.

3. Describe the primary differences between depository institutions and other financial services providers.

4. Describe your insurance protections when you have funds on deposit in a depository institution.

FINANCIAL POWER POINT

Press "Credit" When Using Your Debit Card

Debit card fees are now much more common when you make purchases with the card. Press the "credit" key instead and sign your name on the receipt and no fee will be charged.

LEARNING OBJECTIVE 2

Earn interest and pay no or low fees on your checking accounts.

checking accounts
At depository institutions, allow depositors to write checks against their deposited funds, which transfer deposited funds to other people and organizations.

interest-earning checking account
Any account on which you can write checks that pays interest.

TOOL #1— INTEREST-EARNING CHECKING ACCOUNTS

A **checking account** at a depository institution allows you to write checks against amounts you have on deposit. Checks transfer your deposited funds to other people and organizations. Checking accounts also can be accessed by using a **debit card** (or **check card**) in an automated teller machine (ATM) or a point-of-sale (POS) terminal at a retail store. When you use a debit card, funds are instantaneously removed from your account. You can also access your checking account via telephone or home computer. Whenever you deposit money into, withdraw funds from, or make any payment out of a checking account, make sure you record the transaction with its date, amount, and purpose, and calculate the new balance in the **check register**. This section examines the types of checking accounts available and checking account charges, fees, and penalties.

Types of Checking Accounts

Checking accounts may or may not pay interest. Interest-paying accounts with no or very low fees are available since all depository institutions offer some form of **interest-earning checking account** (also called a **negotiable order of withdrawal [NOW] account**).

A **share draft account** is the credit-union version of a NOW account. Costs for a share draft account are typically lower than those for a checking account at a bank or savings bank. NOW accounts and share draft accounts may pay higher interest rates on larger balances (such as amounts above $1000). The combination of a base rate and a higher rate is called **tiered interest**. For example, an account might pay 0.30 percent on the first $2000 and 0.50 percent on any additional funds in the account.

tiered interest
Common type of NOW account that pays lower interest on smaller deposits and higher interest on larger balances.

A **lifeline banking account** offers access to certain minimal financial services that every consumer needs—regardless of income—to function in our society. An applicant's income and net worth determine acceptance into a lifeline program. The cost of lifeline banking accounts is extremely low, often about $5 per month, and they do not pay interest.

Checking Account Minimum-Balance Requirements

Most interest-earning checking accounts have a minimum-balance requirement that, if not met, will result in the assessment of a monthly fee. In addition, interest earned is usually not paid for a month when the account falls below the minimum. An account with no minimum-balance requirement is preferable. Checking account users should consider the amount of interest that will be lost and the fees that will be imposed.

Decision making becomes more challenging when the institution offers an interest-earning account in combination with either a minimum- or average-balance requirement. With a **minimum-balance account**, the customer must keep a certain amount (perhaps $500 or $700) in the account throughout a specified time period (usually a month or a quarter) to avoid a flat service charge (usually $5 to $15). A fee is assessed whenever the triggering event occurs—that is, when the balance drops below the specified minimum. With an **average-balance account**, a service fee is assessed only if the average daily balance of funds in the account drops below a certain level (perhaps $800 or $1000) during the specified time period (usually a month or a quarter).

minimum-balance account
Checking account that requires customers to keep a certain minimum amount for a specified time period to avoid fees.

average-balance account
Checking account for which service fees are assessed if the account's average daily balance drops below a certain level during a specified time.

You should reconcile your bank accounts monthly.

© 2010 JGI/Tom Grill/Jupiterimages Corporation

FINANCIAL POWER POINT

Free Checking Is Not Really Free

Lots of banks offer "free" checking accounts. What this means is that there is no **minimum-balance requirement** or monthly maintenance fee on the account and no fee for writing too many checks. However, there will be fees for writing checks when there are insufficient funds in the account, using another bank's ATM, inactivity on the account, and other events. If you are charged an unexpected fee, consider challenging it. Tell the bank you are unhappy and considering moving the account.

DID YOU KNOW?

What Happens When You Write a Check?

When you write a check, you either simultaneously make a copy that serves as your record that the check was written or make a note of the transaction in your check register. When the check is paid by your bank, it is said to have **cleared** the bank. The check itself is treated in one of two ways. First, in the traditional method, a **canceled check** is sent to your bank so that the funds can be paid to whomever you had written the check. Second, in the method now most commonly used, the check is scanned by the receiving bank (or even the business to which you gave it) and an electronic **substitute check** is created and transmitted immediately to your bank. As a result, the check can clear your bank in a matter of minutes or hours. Your checking account statement will indicate which checks cleared via a substitute check. Substitute checks are an acceptable version of the original check written by you. Under

the Check Clearing for the 21st Century Act, your bank must quickly correct any errors in the processing of your check if the substitute check and the original check are both paid by your bank. Check your statement each month to ensure that this type of error has not occurred.

A **stop-payment order** tells your bank not to honor a check when it's presented for payment. To issue such an order, you can telephone your bank and stop payment on the check. In any event, a stop-payment order works only if the check has not yet cleared. And with electronic processing, check clearing can occur in a matter of minutes, as can debit card transactions. Be aware that if the verbal stop-payment order is not followed up with a written instruction to the bank, the person or merchant to whom the check was written can *still* cash the check after 14 days. Even with a written request, the check can be cashed after six months unless the order has been renewed.

stop-payment order
Notifying your bank not to honor a check when it's presented for payment.

In addition to monthly fees, institutions may assess many other fees. People interested in getting their money's worth in banking would be wise to avoid as many of the charges shown in Table 5-2 as possible.

DID YOU KNOW?

About Payment Instruments for Special Needs

There are four types of payment instruments that you might find useful from time to time.

Traveler's Checks

Traveler's checks are issued by large financial institutions (such as American Express, Visa, and Carte Blanche) and sold through various outlets. They are accepted almost everywhere. Purchasers typically pay a fee of 1 percent of the amount of the traveler's checks written in specific U.S. denominations ($10, $20, $50, and $100) and in many foreign currencies. All traveler's check companies guarantee replacement of lost checks if their serial numbers are identified.

Money Orders

A **money order** is a checking instrument bought for a particular amount with a fee assessed based on the amount of the

order. Many financial institutions, including retailers such as Wal-Mart and the U.S. Postal Service, sell money orders.

Certified Checks

A **certified check** is a personal check drawn on your account on which your financial institution imprints the word *certified*, signifying that the account has sufficient funds to cover its payment. The financial institution simultaneously places a hold on that amount in the account until the check clears. The fee for a certified check is $5 to $15.

Cashier's Checks

Some payees insist on receiving payment in the form of a **cashier's check** drawn on the account of the financial institution itself and, thus, backed by the institution's finances. To obtain such a check, you would pay the financial institution the amount of the cashier's check and pay a fee of $5 to $15.

Costs and Penalties on Checking and Savings Accounts

Table 5-2

Account Activity	Reasons for Assessing Costs or Penalties	Assessed on Checking or Savings
Automated teller machine (ATM) transactions	A customer's account is assessed a fee (often $1 to $3) for each transaction on an ATM; an additional fee may be charged for using an ATM not owned by the financial institution.	Checking, savings
Telephone, computer, or teller information	Fees are assessed for access or requests for account information by telephone, by computer, or in person (often $2 per transaction) after a number of free requests (perhaps three) have been made.	Checking, savings
Maintenance fees on a minimum-balance account (often waived if paychecks are directly deposited electronically)	The account balance falls below a set minimum amount, such as $300. A set fee of $10 to $20 per month is often charged.	Checking
Maintenance fees on an average-balance account (often waived if paychecks are directly deposited electronically)	The average daily account balance for the month falls below a set amount, such as $500. The cost is usually based on a set fee, a scaled amount (the more the account falls below the average, the greater the cost), or a percentage of the amount the account falls below the average.	Checking
Stop-payment order	A customer asks the financial institution to not honor a particular check; the fee is $25 to $30 per check.	Checking
Bad check "bounced" for insufficient funds	Charges of $25 to $40 or more are assessed for each check written or deposited to your account marked "insufficient funds."	Checking
Early account closing	Charges are assessed if a customer closes an account within a month or quarter of opening it. Charges range from $10 to $20.	Checking, savings
Delayed use of funds	Amounts deposited by check cannot be withdrawn until rules allow it.	Checking, savings
Inactive accounts	A monthly penalty may be assessed for inactive accounts (ones with no activity for six months to a year), sometimes $10 monthly.	Checking, savings
Excessive withdrawals	Some savings institutions assess a penalty ($2 to $5) when withdrawals exceed a certain number per month.	Savings
Early withdrawal	Amounts withdrawn before the end of a quarter earn no interest for that quarter.	Savings
Deposit penalty	Deposits made during the current quarter earn no interest until the beginning of the next quarter.	Savings

 Concept Check 5.2

1. Distinguish between an interest-paying checking account and a lifeline account.

2. What is meant by *free* checking?

3. List three checking account fees or penalties that you could easily avoid by using your account appropriately.

FINANCIAL POWER POINT

How to Obtain Free Checking

New federal laws have made it more difficult for banks to make high profits from overdraft and other fees. As a result, banks are cutting back on eligibility for free checking accounts. Most, however, will provide free checking if you have your paycheck directly deposited into the account.

TOOL #2—SAVINGS ACCOUNTS

The second tool of monetary asset management is a **savings account**. A savings account provides you with a readily accessible source of emergency cash and a temporary holding place for funds in excess of those needed for daily living expenses. Funds on deposit in a savings account are considered time deposits rather than **demand deposits** (another term for checking accounts). **Time deposits** are savings

 LEARNING OBJECTIVE **3**

Make the best use of the benefits of savings accounts.

ADVICE FROM A PRO

Endorse Your Checks Properly

Endorsement is the process of writing on the back of a check to legally transfer its ownership, usually in return for the cash amount indicated on the face of the check. Choosing the proper type of endorsement can protect you from having the check cashed by someone else against your wishes.

A check with a **blank endorsement** contains only the payee's signature on the back. Such a check immediately becomes a bearer instrument, meaning that anyone who attempts to cash it very likely will be allowed to do so, even if the check has been lost or stolen. You would be wise to never make a blank endorsement prior to depositing or cashing a check.

A **special endorsement** can be used to limit who can cash a check; to make this kind of endorsement, you write the phrase *Pay to the order of [name]* on the back along with your signature. A special endorsement can easily be put on a check that you want to sign over to another person. Such a "two-party check" is hard to cash other than by depositing it in an account at a financial institution.

A **restrictive endorsement** uses the phrase *For deposit only* written on the back along with the signature. It authorizes the financial institution to accept the check only as a deposit to an account. No one else can cash such a check. Checks deposited by mail should always be endorsed this way. In addition, you can include the name of the financial institution and the account number as part of the endorsement to make it even more restrictive.

Kathleen Prochaska-Cue
University of Nebraska–Lincoln

---

that are expected to remain on deposit in a financial institution for an extended period. Institutions have a rule requiring that savings account holders give 30 to 60 days' notice for withdrawals, although this restriction is seldom enforced. Some time deposits are **fixed-time deposits**, which specify a period that the savings *must* be left on deposit, such as six months or three years; certificates of deposit (CDs) fit this description. Savings accounts pay interest, although the rate of return is low. The benefit is that the money is safe (free from financial risk). The amount of interest you will earn depends on the frequency of compounding, the amount of money on deposit, and the interest rate. All other things being equal, accounts with the most frequent compounding earn the most interest.

Statement Savings Accounts

The typical savings account offered by depository institutions is the **statement savings account** (also called a passbook savings account). Statement savings accounts permit frequent deposits or withdrawals of funds. No fees are assessed as long as a low minimum balance ($25 to $100) is maintained. Statement savings account holders are provided with printed receipts to document their account transactions, and transactions usually can be accessed through ATMs online. The process for opening a savings account is similar to that for a checking account.

Certificates of Deposit

A **certificate of deposit (CD)** is an interest-earning savings instrument purchased for a fixed period of time. The required deposit amounts range from $100 to $100,000, while the time periods range from seven days to eight years. The interest rate in force when the CD is purchased typically remains fixed for the entire term of the deposit. Depositors collect their principal and interest when the CD expires. Interest rates on longer-term CDs are usually higher than the comparable rates on shorter-term instruments. Certificates of deposit are insured through the FDIC or the NCUSIF if purchased through an insured depository institution.

FINANCIAL POWER POINT

Using Checking Accounts in Budgeting

Copies of your written checks, your check register, and your debit card receipts are very useful in budgeting as they provide a record of money spent. Keep track of all checks written and retain all debit card receipts until you can verify their accuracy in your account statement.

certificate of deposit (CD)
An interest-earning savings instrument purchased for a fixed period of time.

Not All CDs Are the Same   CDs differ in the details of how they work. **Variable-rate certificates of deposit** (or **adjustable-rate CDs**) are also available. These instruments pay an interest rate that is adjusted (up or down) periodically. Typically, savers are allowed to "lock in," or fix, the rate at any point before their CDs mature. This variability detracts from the main virtue of the fixed-rate CD—predictability. The best variable-rate CDs have a guaranteed minimum interest rate. **Bump-up CDs** allow savers to bump up the interest rate once to a higher market rate, if available, and to add up to 100 percent of the initial deposit whenever desired. Beware that some so-called CDs, especially those with high interest rates, are actually "investment certificates." They are not insured and can be recalled by the financial institution and reissued at a lower interest rate prior to their maturity. Always ask "Is this a CD or an investment certificate?" If it's a CD, then verify that information.

You have no reason to restrict yourself to a nearby institution when searching for the highest CD yields. CD yields are updated weekly at www.bankrate.com. You might also check with a stock broker about a **brokered certificate of deposit** as these occasionally pay higher yields. Most CDs enjoy the added protection of federal deposit insurance.

Money withdrawn from a CD before the end of the specified time period is subject to interest penalties. For certificates held less than one year, the depositor may lose as much as three months' interest; on certificates held more than a year, the depositor may be penalized up to six months' interest. If the penalty exceeds the interest amount, you will get back less than you deposited. Consequently, before putting money into a CD, make sure that it is appropriate to tie up your funds in this way. If you feel you might need some of your funds early, consider laddering several smaller CDs rather than buying just one.

Ladder Your CDs to Lower Interest-Rate Risk   Most people who place money in CDs like them because the funds are insured and, thus, have no risk. But that is not exactly true. You see, when you put money in a CD, you have locked in an interest rate. There is a risk if rates in general go up while your money is in the CD. Why? Because you are stuck earning at the lower rate. Or if rates come down, you will have to renew at the lower rate when the CD matures. The uncertainty about changing rates is referred to as **interest-rate risk**. Laddering is a technique that smoothes out the fluctuations in interest rates and lowers this risk.

Here's how laddering works. Let's say you have $10,000 you would like to put into a CD. To start, simply go to www.bankrate.com and find the best rate you can get at the time. Then you purchase five CDs: CD #1 for $2000 for a one-year term, CD #2 for $2000 for a two-year term, CD #3 for $2000 for a three-year term, CD #4 for $2000 for a four-year term, and CD #5 for $2000 for a five-year term. If you want to have fewer rungs on the ladder, simply divide your initial funds by three or four rather than five.

As the CDs mature, you renew each of them for five years. After five years, you continue to have one CD mature each year, and you renew at the highest current market rate you can find (you do not have to stay with the same financial institution). As interest rates fluctuate over time, you always have some CDs at lower rates and some at higher rates. As a result, you are always earning an average rate overall, thus avoiding the possibility of having all of your money accruing very low rates. And you always will be able to access at least some of your money within a relatively short time frame.

How to Save

Americans have the lowest savings rates among the major countries of the world, even though they sharply increased their personal saving since the beginning of the Great Recession. When asked, they typically complain that "there simply is no money left over at the end of the month." In a sense, such comments are correct, but these people are thinking about savings in the wrong way.

Wise individuals take a different approach. They follow the adage **"pay yourself first,"** which means to treat savings as the first expenditure

pay yourself first
Treating savings as the first expenditure after—or even before—getting paid rather than simply the money left over at the end of the month.

FINANCIAL POWER POINT

How to Find a Better Bank

The largest and most well-known national banks have some of the worst fee assessments. Check out small local banks, credit unions, and online banks that meet your needs at www.icba.org, www.creditunion.coop, and www.bankrate.com. Make sure the institution provides federally insured accounts.

after—or even before—getting paid. Build savings into your budget right from the beginning. In this way, you can effectively build funds to provide for large, irregular expenditures and unforeseen expenses, meet short-term goals, and save for retirement, a down payment on a home, or a child's college education. Saving is not glamorous; slow and steady wins the race.

Your first savings goal is to accumulate enough money to cover living expenses (perhaps 70 percent of gross income) for three to six months. This money will serve as an **emergency fund** in case of job layoff, long illness, or other serious financial calamity. For a person with a $60,000 gross annual income, a three-month emergency fund might be $10,500 ($60,000 ÷ 12 = $5000; $5000 × 0.70 = $3500 for each month). People who should consider keeping more funds available—perhaps income to cover six months to a year of living expenses—are those who depend heavily on commissions or bonuses or who own their own businesses.

Most people do not have a sufficient emergency savings fund. Instead, they rely on credit cards when an emergency or unforeseen need arises. This is an unwise way to manage one's finances. Creating an emergency savings fund can be done by breaking the total needed into monthly savings targets and then setting aside the money until the goal is reached. Other savings goals can be saved for using techniques discussed in Chapter 3. If you have more than one or two goals, you can set up savings or investment accounts for each goal. In this way, you can keep track of your progress and keep money separately identified.

FINANCIAL POWER POINT

Be a Regular Saver

Be smart! Start saving regularly when you are young. Divide long-term goals into short-term benchmarks. Then when sufficient amounts are accumulated, move the funds from savings into higher-yielding savings instruments or investments.

DID YOU KNOW?

How to Reconcile Your Bank Accounts

It is a very good idea to maintain records of the activities occurring in your various banking accounts. You should record all checks written, debit card transactions, and deposits in your check register as they take place. It is also a good idea to go online every few days to confirm deposit and withdrawal (or checking) transactions.

You also should conduct an **account reconciliation** in which you compare your records with your bank's records, checking the accuracy of both sets of records and identifying any errors. The best time to do so is when you receive your monthly account statement from your bank. Account reconciliation is a three-step process:

1. *Bring your own records up to date.*

2. *Bring the bank's records up to date.*

3. *Reconcile the results from Steps 1 and 2.*

If the revised balance in your records and the revised balance from the bank statement differ, you will need to find where the error occurred. First, check the additions and subtractions in your records. Next, make sure that all previous entries in your records are properly reported on the account statement.

Looking for errors when Steps 1 and 2 yield differing results is a necessary but tedious task. Fortunately, it is less likely to be necessary today because of electronic banking. Many people go online frequently to check their balances and review their account activity for accuracy. In this way, they can catch errors early and are always very confident that their balances are exactly as shown in their own records. Here is a table you can use to guide your reconciling efforts.

STEP 1: Bring Your Own Records Up to Date	Amount
1. Enter balance from your check register.	$
2. Add deposits not yet recorded.	$
3. Subtract checks and other withdrawals not yet recorded.	$
4. Subtract bank fees and charges included in the monthly statement and not yet recorded.	$
5. Add interest earned.	$
ADJUSTED CHECKBOOK REGISTER BALANCE	

STEP 2: Bring the Account Statement Up-to-Date	
1. Enter ending balance from bank statement.	$
2. Add deposits made since bank statement closing date.	$
3. Subtract outstanding checks written since bank statement closing date.	$
ADJUSTED BANK STATEMENT BALANCE	$

STEP 3: Compare adjusted checkbook register balance and adjusted bank statement balance. If the two balances do not match, identify where the error occurred.

Savings Account Interest

The calculation of interest to be paid on deposits in financial institutions is primarily based on four variables:

1. Amount of money on deposit
2. Method of determining this balance
3. Interest rate applied to the balance
4. Frequency of compounding (such as annually, semiannually, quarterly, monthly, or daily)

The Truth in Savings Act requires depository institutions to disclose a uniform, standardized rate of interest so that depositors can easily compare various checking and savings options that pay interest. This rate, called the

FINANCIAL POWER POINT

Use a Savings Calculator

A very easy-to-use savings calculator can be found at http://cgi.money.cnn.com/tools/moneygrow/moneygrow_101.jsp. You can determine how much to save to reach your goal or find out what your savings will be worth at a future date.

DID YOU KNOW?

The Tax Consequences of Saving for Children's College

A long-term goal of many families is saving for their children's college education. The five best ways follow:

Put Money in a Section 529 College Savings Plan. Named after the related section of the Internal Revenue Service Code, many states have established a **Section 529 college savings plan**. Deposits into a 529 plan are not deductible, but withdrawals for qualified educational expenses are tax free. Section 529 plans offer two options: prepaid tuition or an investment plan. A state-sponsored prepaid tuition plan allows parents, relatives, and friends to purchase a child's future college education at today's prices by guaranteeing that today's payment will be used for the future tuition payments at an approved institution of higher education in a particular state. In a 529 investment plan, the state offers an investment program usually through a mutual fund from which the funds can be drawn when the child is in college.

Put Money in a Coverdell Education Savings Account (ESA). Nondeductible contributions up to a maximum of $2000 per year may be made to a **Coverdell education savings account** (formerly known as an education IRA) to pay the future education costs for a child younger than age 18. The money and earnings on the account can be withdrawn later tax free to pay for public, private, or religious school expenses, K–12 (expires in 2011), trade school, or college, including tuition, fees, tutoring, uniforms, home computers, educational computer software, and room and board.

Put Money for College in a Custodial Account. A **custodial account** is one opened in the name of a child younger than age 14 under the provisions of the Uniform Gifts to Minors Act (or Uniform Transfers to Minors Act). These funds can be used for college expenses. Taxpayers in the 10 percent and 15 percent tax brackets are able to sell assets, such as stocks or mutual funds, without paying any capital gains taxes.

Note that the so-called **kiddie tax** rule applies to unearned income (such as interest and dividends) of a minor child. This rule limits the ability of children to have their unearned income taxed at a child's low tax rate (presumably lower than the parent's tax rate). For children younger than

age 18, the first $950 of unearned income (the income earned from an investment) earned on custodial account assets is tax free to the child. The next $950 is taxed at the child's tax rate. Unearned income in excess of $1900 is taxed at the parent's (likely higher) rate. When children reach age 18, they will pay tax solely based on their own income tax bracket. Assets held in a custodial account for a long time should not be sold until the individual reaches age 18. At that point, the kiddie tax rules will no longer apply and, assuming the child falls into one of the two lowest tax brackets. Thus, he or she will qualify for the 0 percent tax rate on capital gains, making the profit free of federal taxes.

Discount bonds (also called **zeroes** or **zero coupon bonds**) are municipal, corporate, and government bonds that pay no annual interest. Discount bonds are sold to investors at sharp discounts from their face value and may be redeemed at full value upon maturity. For example, a $100 **Series EE savings bond** sold by the federal government can be purchased for $50, one-half its face amount. The interest, which is usually compounded semiannually, accumulates within the bond itself, and the return to the investor comes from redeeming the bond at its stated face value at the maturity date.

Parents can invest in discount bonds through a custodial account to help pay for a child's college education. The phantom income "paid" to the child is generally so small that little, if any, income taxes are due each year as the interest accrues. An advantage of Series EE savings bonds is that taxes on the interest that accrues each year are deferred until redemption. And the interest is tax free at redemption if the proceeds are used to fund the child's college education.

Put Money in a Roth IRA. Contributions to a Roth IRA account and the earnings within it accumulate tax free, and withdrawals are entirely free of tax after age 59½. Withdrawals before age 59½ are subject to the IRS's early distribution 10 percent withdrawal penalty. Before age 59½, the contributions to a Roth IRA account, but not the *earnings*, can be used for college expenses (or any purpose) without incurring the penalty. Withdrawals of deposits in a traditional IRA for college expenses also avoid the 10 percent penalty, but income taxes are due on the amounts withdrawn.

annual percentage yield (APY)
Return on total interest received on a $100 deposit for 365-day period, given the institution's simple annual interest rate and compounding frequency.

grace period
Period (in days) for which deposits or withdrawals can be made without any penalty.

annual percentage yield (APY), is a percentage based on the total interest that would be received on a $100 deposit for a 365-day period given the institution's annual rate of simple interest and frequency of compounding. The more frequent the compounding, the greater the effective return for the saver. The institution must use the APY as its interest rate in advertising and in other disclosures to savers.

Wise money managers select the savings option that pays the highest APY and avoid institutions that assess excessive costs and penalties. Given the same APY, savers should choose an institution that compounds interest daily. Comparison shopping could easily earn you an extra $10 to $20 each year on a $1500 savings account balance. Smart savers also consider the fees and penalties outlined in Table 5-2 when deciding where to open a savings account.

An account with a grace period provides the depositor with a small financial benefit. A **grace period** is the period (in days) during which deposits or withdrawals can be made and still earn interest from a given day of the interest period. For example, if deposits are made by the tenth day of the month, interest might be earned from the first day of the month. For withdrawals, the grace period generally ranges from three to five days. Thus, if a saver withdrew money from an account within three to five days of the end of the interest period, the savings might still earn interest as if the money remained in the account for the entire period.

 Concept Check 5.3

1. Describe reasons to keep money in a savings account rather than a checking account.

2. Distinguish between statement savings accounts and CDs.

3. Explain the benefits of a pay-yourself-first approach to saving.

4. Describe how you can use information about APY to your advantage.

TOOL #3—MONEY MARKET ACCOUNTS

LEARNING OBJECTIVE   4

Explain the importance of placing excess funds in a money market account.

Most people use checking and savings accounts as the cornerstones of their monetary asset management efforts. When income begins to exceed expenses on a regular basis, perhaps by $300 or $500 each month, a substantial amount of excess funds can quickly build up. Although this situation is a comfortable one, it is wise from a monetary asset

ADVICE FROM A PRO

Protect Yourself from Overdraft Fees

An **overdraft** occurs any time you write a bad check or use a debit card when there are insufficient funds in the account. If funds to cover the usage are not available, the bank will charge you a fee of perhaps $25 or even $40, and the merchant to whom a **bad check** was written will charge you a similar fee. The fees could total $80 for one bad check or overdraft!

It is easy to fall victim to these charges if you are not careful. One reason is that banks can choose the order in which they process checks/debits. Let's say you write a large check one day. The next day you use your debit card for three small purchases and the check shows up at your bank for payment. There might be enough money in your account to cover the three small items but not the check. The bank can choose to process the check first. You are now overdrawn and the three debit card items are overdrafts, as well. You now have four overdrafts. If the bank had cleared the debits first you would only have had one overdraft.

Almost $40 billion dollars in overdraft fees were collected by banks in a recent year. Such fees are one of their biggest profit centers. Don't be part of this equation. Your bank offers three ways to avoid overdraft fees:

1. ***Automatic funds transfer agreement.*** *The amount necessary to cover an overdraft will be transmitted from your savings account to your checking account, as long as you keep sufficient funds in your savings account. An automatic funds transfer agreement is the least expensive of these three alternatives.*

2. ***Automatic overdraft loan agreement.*** *The needed funds will be automatically loaned to you by your bank if you have an overdraft line of credit or will be charged as a cash advance to your Visa or MasterCard credit account with the same bank. Note that the loan may be advanced in fixed increments of $100. If you need only $10, for example, you will consequently be responsible for paying interest on amounts not needed. A cash advance fee of $10 or more may also be assessed by the credit card company.*

3. ***"Opt-in" overdraft/bounce protection.*** *The bank will honor overdrafts up to a certain limit, such as $1000, by loaning the money to the account holder. In return, the customer must pay a $25 to $40 fee for each overdraft. Then, the customer must repay the funds usually within less than one month. With some plans, the money is repaid as soon as money is put back in the account. The new Dodd-Frank Wall Street Reform and Consumer Protection Act requires that you "opt in" for this protection. Think twice before you do so. Many new users of checking accounts rack up high levels of fees because they do not really understand this protection. Opting in means that the bank will not alert or stop*

you when you use your debit card or write a check when there are insufficient funds. Use of a debit card for $3.50 for a drink and some chips could trigger a fee ten times as high. You must keep track of your own account balance and ensure that you have enough in your account each and every time you access the funds. Opting in is a high-risk and high-cost way to cover overdrafts. You should be able to get by with options 1 or 2 above. If you do want to opt in, read the rules of the plan before you make the decision.

Of the billions of dollars in overdraft fees assessed each year, most were to young and low-income customers. Will you be a victim? The choice is yours. Consider these ways to deal with overdrafts listed from best to worst:

Ways to cover your overdrafts	Examples of possible cost for EACH overdraft. You should know what YOUR bank charges
Practice good account management	$0; you have no overdrafts
Automatic funds transfer agreement	$0 to $5 transfer fee
Overdraft line of credit	$15 annual fee + 18% APR
Automatic overdraft loan from a credit card	$3 to $10 cash-advance fee + 18% APR
"Opt-in" overdraft/ bounce protection	$20 to $30
Bounced check	$40 to $60 ($25 to $40 bank fee + $20 to $30 merchant fee)

Patti Fisher, Sophia Anong, and Irene Leech
Virginia Tech

---

management point of view to move some of the excess funds into an account that pays more interest.

A **money market account** is any of a variety of interest-earning accounts that pays relatively high interest rates (compared with regular savings accounts) and offers some limited check-writing privileges. A money market account provides both checking and savings tools at a higher interest rate than other accounts. Such accounts are offered by banks, savings banks, credit unions, stock brokerage firms, financial services companies, and mutual funds. The types of money market accounts are super NOW accounts, money market deposit accounts, money market mutual funds, and asset management accounts.

money market account
Interest-earning accounts that pay relatively high interest rates and offer limited check-writing privileges.

FINANCIAL POWER POINT

Interest Is Taxable

Any interest earned on your checking and savings accounts must be reported as income on your federal and state income tax returns. Your financial institutions should send you a **Form 1099** statement that reports your interest income for the previous year; that information also is sent to the IRS. Failure to receive a Form 1099 does not absolve you of the requirement to report the earnings.

Super NOW Accounts

A **super NOW account** is a government-insured money market account offered through depository institutions. It takes the form of a high-interest NOW account with limited checking privileges (usually a maximum of six checks per month). The initial minimum deposit typically ranges from $1000 to $2500. If the average balance falls below a specified amount (such as $1000), the account reverts to earning interest at the lower rate offered on a regular NOW checking account. Depositors can withdraw their funds (using checks or a debit card or electronically) at any time without penalty.

DID YOU KNOW?

Turn Bad Habits into Good Ones

Do You Do This?	*Do This Instead!*
Ignore your account statements	Read each statement for completeness and accuracy
Talk about money only when there is a problem	Schedule regular "money talks" with your family
Pay fees every month for checking	Explore low- or no-fee accounts at a credit union
Overdraw your checking account	Keep track of your balance online and reconcile your account monthly
Keep most of your money in your checking account	Earn higher returns in a savings account, CD, or money-market account

FINANCIAL POWER POINT

Appoint a Financial Backup

If you are single, keep a close family member or friend apprised of the basics of your finances so that should something happen to you, that person could step in as necessary to handle your finances.

money market deposit account (MMDA)
Government-insured money market account with minimum-balance requirements and tiered interest rates.

money market mutual fund (MMMF)
Money market account in a mutual fund rather than at a depository institution.

asset management account (AMA, all-in-one account, or central asset account)
Multiple-purpose, coordinated package that gathers most monetary asset management vehicles into a unified account and reports activity on a single monthly statement to the client.

Money Market Deposit Accounts

A **money market deposit account (MMDA)** is also a government-insured money market account offered through a depository institution. It has minimum-balance requirements and tiered interest rates that vary with the size of the account balance. Institutions are allowed to establish fees for transactions and account maintenance, and account holders typically are limited to three to six transactions each month. Often the customer must deposit $1000 to open an account. If the average monthly balance falls below a certain amount, such as $2500, the entire account earns interest at the lower rate of a regular NOW account. MMDAs generally pay slightly higher interest rates than super NOW accounts.

Money Market Mutual Funds

A **money market mutual fund (MMMF)** is a money market account in a mutual fund investment company (rather than at a depository institution). It pools the cash of thousands of investors and earns a relatively safe and high return by buying debts with very short-term maturities (always less than one year). Interest is calculated daily, and an investor can withdraw funds at any time. Money market mutual funds typically pay the highest rate of return that can be earned on a daily basis by small investors.

MMMFs require a minimum deposit ranging from $500 to $1000. Dozens of mutual fund companies offer unlimited check writing with no minimums on check amounts. Electronic transfers are permitted, but ATMs cannot be used because MMMFs are not depository institutions. Although MMMFs are not insured by any federal agency, they are considered extremely safe. Some funds buy only debts of the U.S. government and therefore are virtually risk free. To open an MMMF account, you can contact a mutual fund company; more details are provided in Chapter 15.

Asset Management Accounts

An **asset management account (AMA**; also known as an **all-in-one account**) is a multiple-purpose, coordinated package that gathers most of the customer's monetary asset management vehicles into a unified account and reports them on a single monthly statement. Included in this package might be transactions in a money market mutual fund and in checking, credit card, debit card, loan, and stock brokerage accounts. Also known as **central asset accounts**, AMAs are offered through depository institutions, stock brokerage firms, financial services companies, and mutual funds. Such an account enables you to conduct all of your financial business with one institution. Typically,

DID YOU KNOW?

How Ownership of Accounts (and Other Assets) Is Established

When you open a new account, you will be asked to sign a signature card that can be used to verify the signatures of the owners of the account. Accounts can be owned either individually or jointly.

An **individual account** has one owner who is solely responsible for the account and its activity. At the death of the individual owner, the account becomes part of his or her estate and will go to heirs in accordance with the owner's will. If desired, individual accounts can be set up with a payable at death designation whereby a person is named in the account to receive the funds upon the death of the individual owner. This allows that person to gain quick access to the funds after the owner's death but does not give the person any rights to the account while the owner is still alive.

A **joint account** has two or more owners, each of whom has legal rights to the funds in the account. The forms of joint ownership discussed here apply to all types of property, including automobiles and homes, as well as checking and savings accounts. Three types of joint ownership exist:

1. *Joint tenancy with right of survivorship* (also called simply *joint tenancy*) is the most common form of joint ownership, especially for husbands and wives. In this case, each person owns the whole of the asset and can dispose of it without the approval of the other(s). With accounts at financial institutions, the financial institution will honor checks or withdrawal slips possessing any of the owners' signatures. An advantage of a joint account is that in case of death of one of the owners, the property continues to be owned by the surviving account holder(s).

2. *Tenancy in common* is a form of joint ownership in which two or more parties own the asset, but each retains control over a separate piece of the property rights. In most states, the ownership shares are presumed to be equal unless otherwise specified. When one owner dies, however, his or her share in the asset is distributed to his or her heirs according to the terms of a will (or if no will exists, according to state law) instead of automatically going to the other co-owners.

3. *Tenancy by the entirety*, which is recognized in about 30 states, is restricted to property held between a husband and a wife. Under this arrangement, no one co-owner can sell or dispose of his or her portion of an asset without the permission of the other. This restriction prevents transfers by one owner without the knowledge of the other.

Dual-earner couples often prefer to own some property together and some property separately. If you own a business and default on a loan, for example, your creditors usually cannot attach your home if it is in your spouse's name. Nonworking spouses, however, should get their name on all deeds and investments; in the event of divorce, courts typically award property to the people who legally own it. In **community property states**—in which most of the money and property acquired during a marriage is legally considered the joint property of both spouses—the rights of both husbands and wives are equally protected. (These jurisdictions include Arizona, California, Idaho, Louisiana, Nebraska, Nevada, New Mexico, Puerto Rico, Texas, Washington, and Wisconsin.)

$10,000, spread across all subaccounts, is required to open an AMA. Some AMAs assess an annual fee, usually $100. Notice that this would be a 1 percent fee on a $10,000 deposit ($100 ÷ $10,000) that reduces your return by 1 percentage point. AMAs usually have other features that attract investors as well—for example, free credit and debit cards, a rebate of 1 percent on credit card purchases, free traveler's checks, inexpensive term life insurance, and an investment advisory newsletter.

 Concept Check 5.4

1. Explain the benefits of opening a money market account.

2. Distinguish between a super NOW account and a money market account.

3. Identify the feature of depository institution accounts not available with money market mutual funds.

4. List some benefits of an asset management account.

FINANCIAL POWER POINT

It Is Easy to Find a Money Market Mutual Fund

You can find money market mutual funds (MMMFs) easily online. Some of these MMMFs are managed by American Century (www.americancentury.com), Dreyfus (www.dreyfus.com), Fidelity (www.fidelity.com), Vanguard (www.vanguard.com), and T. Rowe Price (www.troweprice.com).

ELECTRONIC MONEY MANAGEMENT

LEARNING OBJECTIVE 5

Describe electronic money management, including your legal protections.

Monetary asset management can be summed up today with the phrase "paper, plastic, or neither." "Paper" comprises the traditional cash- and check-based systems. "Plastic" is the use of a debit or other type of card to access your funds. "Neither" is the use of your computer or smartphone to access and use your accounts. The use of smartphones in banking is growing rapidly and consumers should be very careful as the transactions and other information transmitted is highly susceptible to interception by hackers and electronic eavesdroppers.

Most major banks now provide access to their banking services via websites. "Internet banks" operate entirely online, and they often pay the highest interest rates. **Electronic money management** occurs whenever transactions are conducted without using paper documents. Most of these activities involve **electronic funds transfers (EFTs)**, in which funds are shifted electronically (rather than by check or cash) among your various accounts and to and from other people and businesses.

electronic funds transfers (EFTs)
Funds shifted electronically (rather than by check or cash) among various accounts or to and from other people and businesses.

Electronic Money Management Can Be Easy but Is Not Always Free

There are costs assessed with the use of some electronic banking.

An **ATM transaction fee** may be assessed for using an ATM. Fees may be levied by your financial institution as well as by the institution that provides the ATM if you are using an ATM linked to a national network. For example, you might pay your institution $1 to $3 and another $1 to $3 (or more) to the machine provider. Making frequent, small withdrawals can be expensive: a $2 ATM fee is just 1 percent of a $200 withdrawal but is 10 percent of a $20 withdrawal.

ATM transaction fee
Payments levied each time an automated teller machine (ATM) is used.

Transaction fees of $1 to $3 also may be assessed whenever you make a purchase via a POS terminal at a retail store. This is most likely to happen when you use a PIN

DID YOU KNOW?

Using "Plastic" in Monetary Asset Management

There are many types of plastic devices used to access your money.

1. **ATM cards** *allow you to withdraw money from or transfer money among your checking and savings accounts at an automatic teller machine. You must use a personal identification number (PIN) to use the card.*

2. **Debit cards** *do ATM cards one better—you can also use them to make purchases via a point-of-sale (POS) terminal at retail outlets. Using a debit card to make a purchase immediately transfers money from your account. You typically use a PIN or provide your signature when using a debit card. Over one-half of all card transactions are now made with debit cards. Some merchants will also provide a discount when you use a debit, rather than credit, card. It pays to ask!*

3. **Stored-value cards** *contain a magnetic strip or bar code that encrypts the amount of money stored via the card. Some stored-value cards can be "reloaded" with additional funds. Colleges often use this type of card for student meal plans and other spending both on and off campus. Stored-value cards are much like a mini-checking account you can*

use wherever the card is accepted. A gift card is an example of a stored-value card. There are risks associated with gift cards since many have an expiration date (no shorter than five years after purchase for cards purchased after August, 2010) and an inactivity fee if there is no activity within a 12-month time period, and should the retail company go bankrupt or close in your area, the cards may be impossible to redeem.

4. **Electronic benefits transfer (EBT) cards** *are used by the government to pay military personnel and provide Social Security and other government benefits. They are much like a stored-value card, but the holder does not "load" the card—the payer does so, and sends the card to the recipient.*

5. **Credit cards** *allow you to make purchases or obtain cash with credit from the bank or retailer that issued the cards. These are debts that must be paid back, often with interest. In some states, merchants are allowed to charge a higher rate when a credit card is used for some purchases, such as for gasoline.*

Regardless of the type of card you are using, you should always make a photocopy of both sides of your card for use should the card ever be lost or stolen.

number. Such a usage is called an "online" transaction and occurs when you hit the "debit" button on the terminal. You can usually avoid the fee if you hit "credit" instead and the transaction becomes an "off-line" transaction. Rather than use your PIN, you sign for the purchase. The transaction is still a debit transaction but is processed in a way that costs less for your bank. You also have additional legal protections for "off-line" transactions as discussed later.

Fees can be assessed for other uses of electronic money management. Some banks charge for online banking services such as bill paying and verification of your account balances. Often the fees for these services are a fixed monthly rate for all usage that may be cheaper than writing checks and mailing payments. These paper-based services are often free. You can avoid almost all such fees by shopping for an account that matches your banking habits. Otherwise you will waste money on unnecessary banking fees.

Using Electronic Banking Safely

Federal and state regulations have been adopted to provide protections for the use of debit cards and other electronic banking. The Electronic Funds Transfer Act is the governing law, and the Federal Reserve Board's Regulation E provides specific guidelines on ATM and debit card liability. Cards can be issued only if the card cannot be used until validated and the user is informed of his or her liability for unauthorized use as well as other terms and conditions. When you sign up for electronic banking services, the depository institution must inform you of your rights and responsibilities in a written **disclosure statement**.

Users must be provided with written receipts when using an ATM or POS terminal. These receipts show the amount of the transaction, the date on which it took place, and other pertinent information. General protection of a customer's account takes the form of a **periodic statement** sent by the financial institution that shows all electronic transfers to and from the account, fees charged, and opening and closing balances. Smart users of electronic banking services and electronic funds transfers (EFTs) regularly compare the information on this periodic statement with their written receipts.

Fixing Errors If you find an error in your periodic statement, notify the issuing organization in writing as soon as possible. Use the notification procedures found in the disclosure statement accompanying your monthly statement. If the institution needs more than ten business days to investigate and correct a problem, generally it must return the amount in question to your account while it conducts the investigation.

If an error did occur, the institution must permanently correct it promptly. If the institution decides that no error occurred, it must explain its decision in writing and let you know that it has deducted any amount temporarily credited during the investigation. In such a case, the institution must honor withdrawals against the credited amount for

---

FINANCIAL POWER POINT

Reduce and Avoid ATM Fees

Minimize your ATM fees by making a few large withdrawals rather than more frequent small withdrawals. Avoid fees altogether by using your own bank's ATMs.

FINANCIAL POWER POINT

Use Direct Deposit to Save Money and Time

Many financial institutions offer no-fee checking accounts to customers who have their paychecks electronically sent from their employer via **direct deposit**. In addition, the institution may charge a lower interest rate on loans and credit card accounts for customers who use direct deposit.

---

periodic statements
Monthly reports that show all electronic transfers to and from accounts, fees charged, and opening and closing balances.

DID YOU KNOW?

Sean's Success Story

Sean's good efforts at establishing an emergency fund and regularly saving $300 or more per month have enabled him to build a cash reserve in excess of $14,000. He initially kept the funds in his checking and savings accounts but realized that the earnings off those funds were minimal, and there was always the temptation to dip into the funds for an occasional splurge. He decided to buy two $5000 CDs, one with a one-year maturity and another with a two-year maturity. He also opened up a money market account with $2000, leaving the remaining $2000 in his savings account for emergencies.

FINANCIAL POWER POINT

Use a Complicated PIN

Your personal identification numbers (PINs) "unlock" your accounts. You should write them down in case you forget them, but never keep the written record with the card. Do not use easily guessed PINs such as your birth date (112391) or repeated digits (444333). Use as complicated a PIN as your bank will allow.

card registration service
Firm that will notify all companies with which you have debit and credit cards if your cards are lost or stolen.

five days, allowing you time to deposit additional funds. You may ask for copies of the documents on which the institution relied in its investigation and again challenge the outcome if you believe that a mistake was made.

Protections for Lost Cards The sooner you report the loss of an ATM or debit card, the more likely you will be to limit your liability if someone uses the card without your permission. Cardholders are liable for only the first $50 of unauthorized use if they notify the issuing company within two business days after the loss or theft of their card or PIN. Note that fraudulent "online" debit card transactions using a PIN are *not* afforded this protection! After two days, cardholder liability for unauthorized use rises to $500. Some issuers, including Visa and MasterCard, have voluntarily waived enforcement of this liability. However, you risk unlimited loss for the card's misuse if, within 60 days after the institution sends your financial statement to you, you do not report an unauthorized transfer or withdrawal. Thus, you could lose all of the money in your account. These regulations apply to debit cards and other cards used to make electronic funds transfers (EFTs).

Note that the protections offered for fraudulent use of debit cards are not as strong as when your credit card is used fraudulently. It may be wiser to use a credit card for certain transactions, especially those made online. States may have laws that provide additional protection for consumers in EFT transactions.

Most homeowner's and renter's insurance policies (discussed in Chapter 10) already cover your liability for theft of both debit and credit cards. If you are not currently protected, such insurance coverage generally can be added. Many companies sell similar insurance as a separate policy for an annual premium of $30 to $60. In addition, some firms sell a **card registration service** that will notify all companies with which you have debit and credit cards in the event of loss. For $30 to $60 per year, you need make only one telephone call to report all card losses. Of course, you can also notify debit and credit card companies yourself at no cost.

Protect Your Privacy Yourself Having the law and insurance on your side when banking electronically or online is a good thing, but it is better to not have problems in the first place. Most victims of identity theft are between the ages of 20 and 29. Here are some tips for reducing the risk:

- Study your statements. Ask about anything that looks unusual or the least bit in error. A small $1 charge to a debit or credit card is a red flag that someone is checking to see if an account number is valid and hoping that you won't notice. Big charges come later.

- Never bank via computer on a wireless system away from home. Use your wireless system at home only if it is thoroughly protected.

- Be cautious about social networking and job search sites. Would you put personal information on a poster outside your home? Do not do so where all the world can see on the Web.

- Never provide account information if you get an unsolicited e-mail from your bank. It's likely from a scam artist, not the bank.

- When finished banking via computer, always hit the log off button at the top of the page and then close the browser window.

- Avoid using someone else's computer to manage your account. If you do, shut down the computer completely when finished.

- Regularly change your passwords and keep them to yourself.

- Keep your financial papers away from the eyes of roommates and houseguests.

- Buy a shredder and use it.

- Make and save paper copies of all your electronic transactions until you can verify their accuracy on your next account statement.

Concept Check 5.5

1. Distinguish among credit cards, debit cards, and a stored-value card.

2. List the steps you should take if you find an error in your periodic statement regarding an electronic transaction.

3. Summarize the rules that apply if you lose your ATM or debit card and it is used without your authorization.

DID YOU KNOW?

How to Protect Against the Privacy Risks from Using Your Cell Phone to Manage Money

More and more people today are using their cell phones and PDAs for managing money and transferring personal financial data. It is now even possible to deposit checks using a telephone application (app) and your phone's camera feature. Yet many fail to consider that the data stored in the device is ripe for identity theft. The data can fall into the wrong hands if the phone is lost, stolen, or simply replaced. Here are some things you can do to protect yourself.

1. *Do not store ID numbers and passwords* in your phone.

2. *Use complex passwords* of eight or more characters including symbols, numbers, and both upper- and lowercase letters. Change passwords every few months.

3. *Use the blocking mechanism* such as a password (and make it complex) provided with your device.

4. *Erase the flash-chip memory* using the "hard reset" function (or destroy the chip and/or SIM card) when discarding, trading-in, or recycling your phone.

THE PSYCHOLOGY OF MONEY MANAGEMENT

A common cause of tension in personal relationships is conflict over money. Some people seem unable to work together to perform even the fundamental tasks of managing money, such as reconciling the checking account, creating a workable budget, and paying bills on time. Often one of the partners brings a great deal of debt to a relationship. Other couples get into financial trouble because they use credit too often. Mutual trust in money matters can be developed—and must be—to have happy relationships and achieve financial success.

LEARNING OBJECTIVE 6

Discuss your personal finances and money management more effectively with loved ones.

Managing Money and Making Financial Decisions Are Different

Managing money includes such tasks as handling the checkbook, overseeing the budget, and doing the household shopping. Couples should agree on who will carry out these day-to-day chores and then carry through on their responsibilities. Financial experts recommend that each person in a relationship keep some money of his or her own. For dual-earning couples, this can be accomplished by setting up three checking accounts: a discretionary account for each individual (two accounts) and a third, joint account. Then clearly specify the budget categories related to each account. Each partner can then feel that he or she has access to money that the other partner does not control. These feelings of autonomy encourage independence and self-control in a relationship rather than dependency on the other person.

While managing family money is a significant task, decision making is where most disagreements arise. Shared decision making is the best model when defining goals and setting up a budget; when contemplating any major expense, such as buying

DID YOU KNOW?

The Financial Side of Popping the Question

Before you pop the question, or say "YES!" if asked, stop to consider the following questions. If you haven't discussed them or, worse, have been afraid to bring them up, perhaps it is time to take a big step back before you take the big step forward.

1. *Do you know how much your sweetie owes, to whom, and his/her plan for paying the debts off and when?*

2. *Have you seen each other's credit report and know each other's credit score?*

3. *Do you know what type of wedding you would like (and your sweetie would like), how much it would cost, and from where the money will come?*

4. *Do you have any concerns about how your sweetie spends money, and have you discussed the concerns and resolved them to your joint satisfaction?*

5. *Do you budget? Does your sweetie budget? Have you discussed your budgets?*

And for those of you who are thinking that these questions aren't important because you plan to live together before marriage, you should think again. Money issues are the number one problem area for both cohabiting couples and newlyweds.

DID YOU KNOW?

Your Worst Financial Blunders in Managing Checking and Savings Accounts

Based on others' financial woes, you will make mistakes in personal finance when you:

1. *Keep too much money in a checking account where it earns very little interest.*

2. *Fail to reconcile your accounts on a regular basis.*

3. *Keep money matters and worries to yourself.*

automobiles and housing; and when conferring on key topics such as insurance, estate planning and investments, and long-term financial plans.

Opposites Do Seem to Attract

In most areas of personality, the old adage that opposites attract does not hold up to reality. But the adage seems to be true for financial issues. The theory is that people look for someone who does not exhibit their own tendencies because they feel somewhat guilty about their financial shortcomings. Spenders know that they overdo this tendency, and knowing that it can be harmful, look for someone who tends to be more frugal. The key is to bring the patterns out in the open and to discuss them honestly without blaming or defending. Getting both partners to work a bit on their own tendency brings each closer to the middle and a more mutually acceptable pattern of money management.

People Connect Strong Emotions to Money

People often attach a number of emotions to money, including freedom, trust, self-esteem, guilt, indifference, envy, security, comfort, power, and control. They bring with them the patterns, beliefs, and attitudes that were prevalent in their family of origin. It is essential to recognize the importance of these emotions. Many people want to hold on to their fiscal autonomy as long as possible, and they may be embarrassed to inquire about how much others—even loved ones—spend, earn, or owe. For many people, money is an area of self-suspected incompetence. Author Judith Viorst suggests that becoming responsible and adept at managing one's financial matters represents a true passage into adulthood. This evolution involves communicating effectively with others on money matters. Addressing questions openly and calmly helps keep emotions in check. Separately writing down the answers to the following questions and then bringing the answers to the table in a meeting can be an effective way to discuss money matters.

1. What is my biggest money worry today?
2. What are we doing well financially?
3. Is there an issue in our finances that I would like to understand better?
4. If we needed to cut back our spending, what three areas are off limits and what three are fair game?
5. What money issues do we avoid and how can we bring them out into the open?

DID YOU KNOW?

How to Develop Money Sense in Children

A major theme of this chapter is that checking and savings accounts and investments are an integral part of reaching your financial goals. By progressively building savings funds, you can achieve financial success. Parents can help children develop money sense by providing them with opportunities to manage their own money while still young and guiding this behavior toward appropriate patterns. Financially clueless parents beget financially clueless children. Do not let that be you. Do the following to increase your children's ease in handling money:

1. *Give an allowance.* *Even children as young as 5 years old should have some money of their own. An allowance should be the source of these funds in the preteen years. The amounts of allowance should fit the family income level. Allowances are a means for teaching money management.*

2. *Encourage work.* *Once children reach their preteen years, there are many opportunities to earn their own money. When children see what it takes to make money, it is easier for them to know the real cost of spending.*

3. *Set reasonable limits.* *Children should be given age-appropriate limits for spending in various categories and should be required to save a portion, perhaps 50 percent, of their money. However, parents should not stop children from "wasting their money" or bail them out of every mistake. We learn best from experience, not from what someone else tells us is best.*

4. *Teach them to make good choices through increasingly complex activities.* *The dollar amounts and the areas of discretionary spending can increase as the child becomes older. A 7-year-old might be allowed to spend his or her own money on toys, snacks, and gifts to charity at church or school. A 14-year-old might be allowed to buy meals and clothing as well. More responsibility and autonomy should be given only as the child exhibits the ability to handle less complicated tasks.*

5. *Help them learn to wait.* *Children should have autonomy over at least some of their own money. But the remainder, perhaps 50 percent, should be saved. Then when children desire some high-cost item, they can see that saving for a while can help them reach their goal.*

6. *Talk about family finances with children.* *In many families, money matters are a taboo subject. Children need to see that parents must work at managing the family finances. They should know what it costs to raise a family and to make ends meet. Otherwise, kids will grow up with unrealistic expectations and behaviors that will be passed on to their children.*

7. *Be a role model.* *Children learn more from what they see than what they are told. Avoid borrowing money from children. They will learn that credit is easy. And, certainly, pay them back on time if you do borrow. Otherwise, they will think they can borrow without paying back. Save money yourself, and tell your children that saving means that you can't have something you, or they, want right away.*

How to Talk About Financial Matters

Discussions about money matters are not always easy. Some people who are entirely rational about other issues are unpredictable or even careless in money matters. Adults need to accept that honest differences may exist among people and respect these values. The following ideas will help you discuss money with more confidence and candor.

Get to Know Yourself The first step in learning to talk with others about financial matters is to understand your own approach to money. Consider the emotions described earlier to help get you started. It is constructive to discuss any differences in how you view yourself as compared with how your partner views you. Write these down.

Focus on Commonalities Successful communication about money requires that the effort be aimed toward agreeing on common goals and reaching a consensus of opinion without substantially compromising the views of others.

Learn to Manage Financial Disagreements Give all family members time to express their views when discussing financial matters. Each also needs to listen to what others are saying and feeling. If talking proves too difficult, have each person separately write down his or her concerns. By swapping notes, ideas and concerns can be shared. Schedule a time and place for financial talks, decide on agenda items, and leave other conflicts outside the door.

Recall from Chapter 3 that Harry and Belinda Johnson had a significant disagreement when setting up their budget to allow for their anniversary party and spending for

© 2010 Jupiterimages Corporation

Each member of the family should be aware of and involved with important financial decisions.

holiday gifts at the end of the year. As a result, they ended up with a draft budget that did not balance for the year as planned expenses exceeded anticipated income. They agreed to disagree and postponed difficult decisions that will need to be made on how to cover their shortfalls. They will need to do better in the future.

Use Positive "I" Statements   Messages focusing on "I" describe the behavior in question, the feelings you experienced because of the behavior, and any tangible effect on you. For example, a spouse might say, "I feel upset when we use credit cards because I do not know where we will find the money to pay the bills at the end of the month." "I" messages say three things: what (the behavior), I feel (feelings), and because (reason). Using "I" messages helps build stronger relationships because they tell the other person "I trust you to decide what change in behavior is necessary." Beware of "I" statements that begin with "I need you to...." "You" statements are blaming statements, such as "You always ...," "You never ...," and "If you don't, I will...." These statements have a high probability of being condescending to other people, of making them feel guilty, and of implying that their needs and wants are not as important as yours.

Be Honest and Talk Regularly   Achieving consensus requires that each person be honest when talking about money matters. It further demands that couples regularly talk about finances. Perhaps begin by deciding to talk about money matters for only ten minutes at a time. Also be prepared to compromise. When you make decisions together, act on them. Focus attention on current financial activities and issues as well as long-term financial planning. Use these discussions to forge overall long-term strategies for dealing with your family finances. Once the proper base has been established, short-term issues are more likely to fall into place.

Complications Brought by Remarriage

Remarriage merges financial histories, values, and habits as well as households. Some remarried couples—and those choosing to live together following a previous relationship—may have substantial combined incomes bolstered by child-support payments from a former spouse. In many cases, at least one person may be paying (instead of receiving) alimony and child support. When "his," "her," and "our" children are included in the household, living expenses can be quite steep. Special concerns for blended families include determining who assumes financial responsibility for biological offspring and stepchildren; handling resentment over alimony and child-support payments; and managing unequal assets, incomes, responsibilities, and debts. Even gift giving can become a quandary. These challenges can be mitigated with effective communication.

Many remarried people use "his" and "hers" funds and require the legally responsible parent owing financial support to a previous spouse or to children to make such payments out of his or her own money. Professor Jean Lown of Utah State University suggests that, "What is best is what the couple can agree on."

 Concept Check 5.6

1. Explain why it is difficult for many people in relationships to talk about money matters.

2. Identify four ways you could more effectively communicate about money matters.

3. List four things that parents can do to help their children be better money managers.

DO IT NOW!

Avoid Overdraft Fees

You know more about personal finance after reading this chapter, so get started right now by:

1. *Finding out what type of overdraft protection you have, if any, on your checking accounts.*

2. *Signing up for automatic funds transfer to be used first if you make an overdraft.*

3. *Making sure that your bank will block use of your debit card if there are insufficient funds in the account at the time of the usage.*

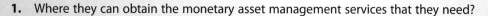

WHAT DO YOU RECOMMEND NOW?

© 2010 Hola Images/Jupiterimages Corporation

Now that you have read the chapter on managing checking and savings accounts, what would you recommend to Mark Rosenberg and Trina Adams in the case at the beginning of the chapter regarding:

1. Where they can obtain the monetary asset management services that they need?

2. Their best use of checking accounts and savings accounts as they begin saving for a home?

3. The use of a money market account for their monetary asset management?

4. Their use of electronic banking in the future?

5. How they can best discuss the management of their money and finances?

BIG PICTURE SUMMARY OF LEARNING OBJECTIVES

LO1. **Identify the tools of monetary asset management and sources of such financial services.**

Maximizing interest earnings and minimizing fees on savings and checking accounts is the goal of monetary asset management. The five primary providers of monetary asset management services include depository institutions (such as banks and credit unions),

stock brokerage firms, mutual funds, financial services companies, and insurance companies.

LO2. **Earn interest and pay no or low fees on your checking accounts.**

The first tool of monetary asset management is an interest-earning checking account that is used to pay monthly living expenses. When setting up an account, consider charges, fees, and penalties.

LO3.   Make the best use of the benefits of savings accounts.
Your second tool of monetary asset management is a savings account in which you can place funds not needed for six months to five years into the future. Some longer-term savings instruments such as certificates of deposit (CDs) allow you to safely earn even higher returns if you are willing to forgo liquidity.

LO4.   Explain the importance of placing excess funds in a money market account.
Your third tool of monetary asset management is a money market account. When your income begins to exceed expenses on a regular basis, it is wise to move excess funds into such an account, which typically pays a higher interest rate. The funds can be left in the account while you consider other investment options. Money market accounts include super NOW accounts, money market deposit accounts, money market mutual funds, and asset management accounts.

LO5.   Describe electronic money management, including your legal protections.
Electronic money management occurs whenever banking transactions are conducted via computers without the customer using paper documents. Electronic banking includes the use of automatic teller machines (ATMs), point-of-sale (POS) terminals, debit cards, and stored-value cards. The Electronic Funds Transfer Act protects consumers who use electronic money management.

LO6.   Discuss your personal finances and money management more effectively with loved ones.
Recognize the psychological and emotional aspects of money and identify your own approaches to money. Communicate openly and frequently about money matters by using "I" statements.

LET'S TALK ABOUT IT

1.   **Bank Account Fees.** Describe some examples of checking and savings account transactions that result in assessment of fees or penalties. Which are the least and most avoidable?

2.   **Avoiding Overdraft Fees.** You know someone who recently had $90 in overdraft fees for three small debit card transactions. Explain to him why such high fees resulted from such small transactions and the relative benefits of having an automatic funds transfer agreement versus an automatic overdraft loan agreement versus overdraft protection.

3.   **Forms of Account Ownership.** When would you recommend using an individual account, a joint tenancy with right of survivorship account, and a tenancy by the entirety account for your monetary assets?

4.   **Opting in.** Many people desire protection from the possibility of overdrawing their checking account. Banks make it easy by allowing you to opt into overdraft protection. Explain how this and other overdraft protections work and why the true cost of opting in may exceed the benefits.

5.   **Earning Higher Interest on Your Savings.** When might it be appropriate for you to save via a certificate of deposit versus a money market account?

6.   **Lost/Stolen Debit Cards.** What should you do if your ATM or debit card is lost or stolen? Why?

7.   **Talking About Money.** Have you ever had a disagreement with a friend or family member over a money issue? How might you communicate differently now?

8.   **Money Issues for Young Couples.** Review the questions for those contemplating marriage that are listed on page 160. Discuss the importance of these questions. Most couples do not discuss these issues early in a relationship. Why do you think that is so, and what do you think you will do should the challenge arise for you?

DO THE MATH

1.   **Invest Now or Later?** Twins Barbara and Mary are both age 27. Beginning at age 27, Barbara invests $2000 per year for ten years and then never sets aside another penny. Mary waits ten years and then invests $2000 per year for the next 30 years. Assuming they both earn 7 percent, how much will each twin have at age 67? (Hint: Use Appendixes A.1 and A.3 or visit the *Garman/Forgue* companion website.)

2.   **The Benefit of a Higher APY.** Caryn Thornton, age 18, recently received an inheritance of $50,000 from her grandmother's estate. She plans to use the money for the down payment on a home in ten years when she

finishes her education. Right now the funds are in a savings account paying 1.0 percent APY. How much would she have in ten years if instead she purchased a ten-year CD paying 4.0 percent? (Hint: Use Appendix A.1 or visit the *Garman/Forgue* companion website.)

3. **Reconciling a Checking Account.** Andrew Parker has a checking account at the credit union affiliated with his university. Illustrated below are his check register and monthly statement for the account. Reconcile the checking account and answer the following questions.

   (a) What is the total of the outstanding checks?

   (b) What is the total of the outstanding deposits?

   (c) Why is there a difference between the uncorrected balance in the check register and the balance on the statement?

   (d) What is the updated and correct balance in the check register to the right?

Account Name	Andrew Parker	Period of Activity	11/2/11– 12/01/11
Account #	**123-45678**		

Summary of Your Activity This Month

Date	Activity	Amount	Balance
11/02			$ 412.66
11/04	Debit Card POS Transaction	$17.46 ✓	395.20
11/09	Check #237	33.33 ✓	361.87
11/12	Direct Deposit	W 876.99 ✓	1238.86
11/13	Debit Card POS Transaction	84.56 ✓	1154.30
11/13	EFT	22.00 ✓	1132.30
11/15	Check #238	645.00 ✓	487.30
11/23	Debit Card POS Transaction	68.87	418.43
11/27	Debit Card POS Transaction	43.00 ✓	375.43
11/28	Deposit	200.00 ✓	575.43
11/30	Check #239	125.00 ✓	450.43
11/30	Service Charge	4.50	445.93
11/30	ATM Withdrawal	100.00 ✓	345.93
12/01	Check #240	46.00	299.93

Date	Check #	Payee/ Payor	For	Amount	Balance
11/01					$ 412.66
11/03	Debit Card ✓	CVS	Cold Meds	$ 17.46	395.20
11/05	237 ✓	Univ. Book-store	Of Mice and Men	33.33	361.87
11/12	Deposit ✓	PNC Bank	Payday-Yeah!	876.99	1238.86
11/12	238 ✓	ABC Property Mgmt.	Rent	645.00	593.86
11/13	Debit Card ✓	Kroger's	Groceries	84.56	509.30
11/13	Electronic Payment ✓	Maysville Water	Water Bill	22.00	487.30
11/23	Debit Card	Kroger's	Groceries	67.88	419.42
11/23	Debit Card ✓	Applebee's	Dinner with Karen	43.00	376.42
11/27	Deposit ✓	Mom	For Utilities	200.00	576.42
11/27	239 ✓	Duke Power	Electric/ Heat Bill	125.00	451.42
11/27	240 ✓	Conoco	Gas	46.00	405.42
11/30	Debit Card ✓	ATM With-drawal	Carry Around Money	100.00	305.42
12/01	241	Comcast	Cable Bill	53.88	252.54

4. **Saving for College.** You want to create a college fund for a child who is now 3 years old. The fund should grow to $30,000 in 15 years. If an investment available to you will yield 6 percent per year, how much must you invest in a lump sum now to realize the $30,000 when needed? (Hint: Use Appendix A.2 or visit the *Garman/Forgue* companion website.)

5. **Saving for Retirement.** You plan to retire in 40 years. To provide for your retirement, you initiate a savings program of $4000 per year yielding 7 percent. What will be the value of the retirement fund after 40 years? (Hint: Use Appendix A.3 or visit the *Garman/Forgue* companion website.)

FINANCIAL PLANNING CASES

CASE 1

How Should the Johnsons Manage Their Cash?
In January, Harry and Belinda Johnson had $3540 in monetary assets (see page 99): $1178 in cash on hand; $890 in a statement savings account at First Federal Bank earning 1.0 percent interest compounded daily; $560 in a statement savings account at the Far West Savings and Loan earning 1.1 percent interest compounded semiannually; $160 in a share account at the Smith Brokerage Credit Union earning a dividend of 1.3 percent compounded quarterly; and $752 in their non–interest-earning regular checking account at First Interstate.

(a) What specific recommendations would you give the Johnsons for selecting checking and savings accounts that will enable them to effectively use the first and second tools of monetary asset management?

(b) Their annual budget, cash-flow calendar, and revolving savings fund (see Tables 3-6, 3-7, and 3-8 on pages 88–90) indicate that the Johnsons will have additional amounts to deposit in the coming year. What are your recommendations for the Johnsons regarding use of a money market account? Why?

(c) What savings instrument would you recommend for their savings, given their objective of saving enough to purchase a new home? Support your answer.

(d) If the Johnsons could put most of their cash on hand ($1000) into a money market account earning 1.4 percent, how much would they have in the account after one year?

(e) Recall from Chapter 3 that Harry and Belinda had significant disagreements regarding their anniversary dinner and holiday gift spending and ended up not having a draft balanced budget for the year. Provide some advice for the couple about how to resolve or, better, prevent such disagreements in the future.

CASE 2

Victor and Maria Hernandez Need to Save Money Fast

The Hernandez family is experiencing some financial pressures, even though the couple has a combined income of $66,000. Also, their eldest son, Joseph, will start college in only three years. Maria is contemplating going to work full time to add about $25,000 to the family's annual income.

(a) How will this change in income affect the family's emergency fund needs?

(b) How much should they save annually for the next three years if they want to build up Joseph's college fund to $20,000, assuming a 3 percent rate of return and ignoring taxes on the interest? (Hint: Use Appendix A.1 or visit the *Garman/Forgue* companion website.)

(c) Given their 25 percent marginal tax rate, what is the Hernandezes' after-tax return and how would that affect the amount they would need to save each year?

(d) What savings options are open to the Hernandezes that could reduce or eliminate the effects of taxes on their savings program?

CASE 3

Julia Price Thinks About Using Checking and Savings Accounts

Julia's six-figure salary has allowed her to build up a considerable cash reserve of over $20,000. She initially had basic checking and savings accounts. She also has a credit card with her bank that she uses to make most of her purchases, thereby earning reward points. She is careful to pay the account balance in full each month. Over time, she purchased several CDs. About three years ago, she also opened a money market deposit account at her bank in which she keeps almost $10,000. Last week she got a call from the bank suggesting that she open a cash management account to coordinate her accounts and maximize her overall earnings. She is hesitant to do so as she feels her current arrangement meets her needs. Offer your opinions about her thinking.

CASE 4

Use of a Computer Banking Service

Trent Searle, a service station owner from Moscow, Idaho, pays a $10 monthly fee for home banking so he can pay all his bills online though his bank. His friend Scott Simpson feels that Trent is wasting his money on the service. Trent has service station income of $3000 per month, plus other earnings from some investments. In addition, he is part owner of an apartment complex, which gives him approximately $1000 per month in income. He always tries to put his excess earnings into solid investments so that they might bring future income and security.

(a) What specific computer banking services would help a person such as Trent?

(b) Justify Trent's paying the $10 monthly fee for computer banking.

CASE 5

A Lobbyist Considers Her Checking Account Options

Shudan Lee, a lobbyist for the textile industry living in Richardson, Texas, has had a no-interest checking account at a commercial bank for three years. The bank requires a minimum balance of $500 to avoid an account charge, and Shudan has always maintained this balance. Recently, she heard that a nearby savings and loan association is offering NOW accounts paying 1.5 percent interest on the average daily balance of the account. This institution requires a minimum balance of $300, but a forfeiture of monthly interest occurs if the account falls below this minimum. Given her past habits at the commercial bank, Shudan feels that the new $300 minimum would be easy to maintain. She is seriously thinking about moving her money to the NOW account.

(a) What is the main reason Shudan should move her checking account?

(b) What should Shudan know about the differences among NOW accounts offered at various financial institutions?

(c) If Shudan maintained an average balance of $1000 in a NOW checking account earning 1.5 percent interest, how much interest would she have earned on her money after one year? (Hint: Use Appendix A.1 or visit the *Garman/Forgue* companion website. Do not forget to subtract Shudan's initial lump-sum deposit from the derived answer.)

(d) How much more would Shudan have earned in one year if she decided to invest in a money market mutual fund paying 2 percent interest instead of the NOW account? (Hint: Use

Appendix A.1 or visit the *Garman/Forgue* companion website.)

CASE 6

Deciding Among the Tools of Monetary Asset Management

Kwaku Addo, a registered dietician from Columbia, Missouri, earns $4200 per month take-home pay and has the funds directly deposited in his checking account. He spends only about $3500 per month, and the excess funds have been building up in his account for about one year.

(a) What other types of accounts are available to Kwaku?

(b) How might he manage his accounts to earn as much interest as possible and keep his money safe?

(c) How might he use electronic money management to accomplish these tasks?

BE YOUR OWN PERSONAL FINANCIAL MANAGER

MY PERSONAL FINANCIAL PLANNER

1. **Checking and Savings Accounts.** Create a table outlining the rates, rules, and fees of your checking and savings accounts. Use Table 5-2 on page 147 as a guide for the types of information to include. Assess the appropriateness of the accounts for you and shop for more appropriate accounts if necessary using Worksheet 23: Selecting a Checking Account That Meets My Needs from "My Personal Financial Planner" as a guide for your selection process.

2. **Keep Your Accounts Current.** Go online every few days to monitor checking account activity. Use the "Did You Know?" box on page 150 or Worksheet 24: Reconciling My Checking Account from "My Personal Financial Planner" to help reconcile your account monthly.

3. **Protect Your Privacy.** Confirm the existence and amount of each transaction in your checking and

savings accounts soon after receiving your account statements. Report any discrepancies immediately.

4. **Prepare for Possible Identity Theft.** Create a table listing all of your checking, savings, and credit card accounts. For each, list the account number and customer service address and telephone number. Store the document in a safe location for easy access should you find that any unauthorized use has occurred or that the account "plastic" has been lost or stolen.

5. **Talk About Money.** If married or cohabiting, schedule a regular time to discuss finances with your partner. Use the material on pages 160–163 as a guide for the topics and tone of the discussions. To get your conversation started, you might pose the following questions: If we unexpectedly received $10,000 tax free, what would we do with it? If we had to cut our spending by 10 percent, where would we make the reductions?

ON THE 'NET

Go to the Web pages indicated to complete these exercises.

1. Visit the website for the Federal Reserve Board, where you will find articles (www.federalreserve.gov/consumer info/bankaccountservices.htm) on checking accounts. Browse through the articles to find five things you could

do that would help you get the most out of your checking account.

2. Visit the website for Bankrate.com at www.bankrate .com/brm/rate/chk_sav_home.asp for information about checking accounts. Use the search box to find articles on "Check 21," which governs check clearing

and processing. How might the rules of Check 21 affect your use of your checking account?

3. Visit the Bankrate.com website at www.bankrate.com/brm/rate/deposits_home.asp, where you will find information about rates of return on certificates of deposit. What is the best rate for a one-year CD and a five-year CD in a large city near your home (look in the state, then the city)? How do these rates compare with the average rates nationally and the highest rates nationally?

4. Visit the website for FDIC at www.fdic.gov/. Use the search box to find articles on "internet bank." Read the article titled "Safe Internet Banking." After reading the information, make a list of important positive and negative aspects of Internet banking. Is Internet banking right for you?

ACTION INVOLVEMENT PROJECTS

1. **Checking Accounts Where You Live.** Select five banks, savings banks, or credit unions in your community. Contact each to gather information on the types of checking accounts they offer and the basic rules of the accounts, including overdraft protections, fees, and interest rates. Make a table that summarizes your findings and identify one institution that best meets your needs.

2. **Account Monitoring.** Survey five of your friends about their patterns of monitoring their checking and savings accounts. Compare what they do to your own pattern.

3. **Debit and ATM Activity.** Survey five of your friends about the patterns and amounts of their typical debit and ATM card usage. Compare their patterns to your own and those recommended in this chapter.

4. **Money Talk.** Survey five couples in long-term relationships to ascertain their patterns of money talk. Ask each the following questions: "What are the areas of your finances that are easiest to discuss?" "What are your areas of most difficulty?" "How do you resolve disagreements?" Make a table that summarizes your findings and identify one institution that best meets your needs.

Visit the Garman/Forgue companion website at **www.cengagebrain.com**.

Building and Maintaining Good Credit

6

YOU MUST BE KIDDING, RIGHT?

People with no prior credit history or one that shows poor repayment patterns in the past often wonder if they will ever be able to get credit, especially in a sluggish economy when credit is difficult to obtain. Simply put, why would any lender want to trust them? Which of the following is true about the availability of credit for people in such situations?

A. No one will ever grant them credit.

B. If they wait a few years, the situation could change.

C. If they keep searching, they will find a lender that will treat them like everyone else.

D. Credit is relatively easy to obtain even today.

The answer is B. When credit is tight, it is difficult for people with poor or no credit to obtain credit. When credit availability eases, certain lenders will accept such applicants, although they will charge high interest rates. Building and maintaining a good credit history will always get you low interest rates!

LEARNING OBJECTIVES

After reading this chapter,
you should be able to:

1. Explain reasons for and against using credit.

2. Establish your own debt limit.

3. Achieve a good credit reputation.

4. Describe the common sources of consumer credit.

5. Identify signs of overindebtedness and describe the options that are available for debt relief.

© PETER DAZELEY/GETTY IMAGES, INC.

WHAT DO YOU RECOMMEND?

Carrie Savarin, age 25, is a nurse practitioner with the local health department in Philadelphia, PA. She earns $65,000 per year, with about $9000 of her income coming from overtime pay. Her disposable income is about $3300 per month. Her employer provides a qualified tax-sheltered retirement plan to which Carrie contributes 4 percent of her salary and for which she receives an additional 4 percent matching contribution from her employer. (She could contribute up to 6 percent with an equal employer match.) Carrie has $19,000 in outstanding student loans on which she will pay $354 per month over the next five years, and her total credit card debt is $3000 on which she has been paying $120 per month. Otherwise, she is debt free. Carrie would like to purchase a new or late-model used car to replace the car she has been driving since her senior year in high school. She has $2000 to use as a down payment.

Barry Austin Photography/Getty Images

What would you recommend to Carrie on the subject of building and maintaining good credit regarding:

1. Factors she should consider regarding her ability to take on additional debt?

2. The impact of her current debt on her ability to obtain a loan to buy a vehicle?

3. Where she might obtain financing for a vehicle loan?

4. The effect of taking on a loan on her overall financial planning?

Your financial success depends heavily on your ability to make the sacrifices necessary to spend less than you earn. This also suggests that you must use credit wisely. You should use credit only when necessary, pay low interest rates, make payments on time, and repay debts as quickly as possible. This can be challenging during difficult economic times when credit is less available and employment opportunities are limited, but advice is sound in good times and bad.

The term **credit** describes an arrangement in which goods, services, or money is received in exchange for a promise to repay at a future date. Most commonly, consumer credit takes the form of a **loan** that is repaid in equal payments over a set period of time or **credit cards**, which allow repeated use of credit as long as regular, monthly payments are maintained.

In 2007, American household debt reached 130 percent of income, the highest in history. Now, five years later, consumers have deleveraged by cutting back on their use of credit and paying down existing debts. They are saving more and the savings rate is now over 6 percent. This move to deleverage was a wise one on an individual basis and one that is recommended in good times and bad. One of the positive aspects of the troubled economy was the message it sent that too much debt can be very dangerous for individuals and families.

There are valid reasons for using credit but only when you can do so wisely. The failure to fully understand the nature of credit can come back to haunt us when things do not go as planned. Two keys are to set reasonable debt limits for yourself and know the best sources of credit. Doing so can prevent debt problems in the future.

YOUR NEXT 5 YEARS

In the next five years, you can start achieving financial success by doing the following related to building and maintaining good credit:

1. *Protect your credit reputation as carefully as you would safeguard your personal reputation.*

2. *Determine your own debt limit rather than relying on a lender before deciding to take on any debt.*

3. *Obtain copies of your credit bureau reports regularly, and challenge all errors or omissions you find.*

4. *Never cosign a loan for anyone, including relatives.*

5. *Always repay your debts in a timely manner.*

REASONS FOR AND AGAINST USING CREDIT

Credit represents a form of trust established between a lender and a borrower. If the lender believes that a prospective borrower has both the ability and the willingness to repay money, then credit will be extended. The borrower is expected to live up to that trust by repaying the lender. For the privilege of borrowing, a lender requires that a borrower pay interest and sometimes other charges.

You can distinguish between good and bad uses of credit. Among the good uses are a mortgage loan to buy a home, a loan to open a business, and student loans. These purposes have benefits because the funds are invested in ways that can have a long-term payoff. Bad uses of credit include using a credit card to support a lifestyle that you cannot otherwise afford and borrowing for daily expenses or overly expensive and otherwise unaffordable vehicles and homes.

Good Uses of Credit

Credit can be used in very positive ways to enhance personal financial planning. Following are some of the good reasons people use credit:

1. **For convenience.** Using credit cards simplifies the process of making many purchases. It provides a record of purchases, and it can be used as leverage if disputes later arise. Convenience use of credit is common. For example, many of us now use credit cards at the grocery store and the gas station. Convenience use is justified *only* if the card balance is paid in full each month, however. You do not want to be paying for today's restaurant meal for months or years in the future.

2. **For emergencies.** Consumers use credit to pay for unexpected expenses such as emergency medical services and automobile repairs.

3. **To make reservations.** Most motels, hotels, and car rental agencies require some form of deposit to hold a reservation. A credit card number can serve as such a deposit, allowing guaranteed reservations to be made over the telephone. In many

LEARNING OBJECTIVE ❶

Explain reasons for and against using credit.

credit
An arrangement in which goods, services, or money is received in exchange for a promise to repay at a future date.

loan
Consumer credit that is repaid in equal amounts over a set period of time.

credit cards
Cards that allow repeated use of credit as long as the consumer makes regular monthly payments.

credit card blocking
Hotels or other service providers use a credit card number to secure reservations and charge the anticipated cost of services.

cases, the hotel will notify the credit card issuer to put a hold on your account for the anticipated total amount of the charge. This common practice is called **credit card blocking**.

4. **To own expensive products sooner.** Buying "big ticket" items such as a home or automobile on credit allows the consumer to enjoy immediate use of the product. Many expensive items would not be purchased (or would be bought only after several years of saving) without the opportunity to pay for them over time. The expected life of the product should be at least as long as the repayment period on the debt.

5. **To take advantage of free credit.** Merchants sometimes offer "free" credit for a period of time as an inducement to buy. Free credit, however, should not be used to buy a more expensive item than you can afford. Known as "same as cash" or "interest-free" plans, these programs allow the buyer to pay later without incurring finance charges. The free credit lasts for a defined time period, but interest may be owed for the entire time period if the buyer pays even one day after the allotted free-credit period ends.

6. **For protection against rip-offs and frauds.** Internet and telephone purchases made on a credit card can be contested with the credit card issuer under the guidelines of the Fair Credit Billing Act (FCBA) as discussed more fully in Chapter 7. The protections afforded by the FCBA are not available when using a debit card.

7. **To obtain an education.** The high cost of education has forced many students to use student loans. This may be one of the better uses of credit, as the borrower is investing in himself or herself to raise the quality of life and/or income in the future. But the level of debt should be compared to the projected extra income provided by the education to be obtained.

FINANCIAL POWER POINT

Debt Reduces Your Ability to Save and Invest

Saving and investing over long periods of time is the key to building wealth. Taking on excessive debts early in life will seriously compromise your goal of being financially successful.

The Downside of Credit

Despite its benefits, the use of credit has a downside. Negative aspects include interest costs, the potential for overspending, credit's negative effect on your financial flexibility, and concerns about privacy.

1. **Use of credit reduces financial flexibility.** The greatest disadvantage of credit use comes from the loss of financial flexibility in personal money management. As the old German proverb states, "He who borrows sells his freedom." The money that you pay each month on your debts is money you could have spent elsewhere on other opportunities. Credit use also reduces your future buying power, as the money you pay out on a loan includes a finance charge as well as the principal. In fact, credit can be seen as a promise for you to "work for the creditor" in the future to pay off your debt. People rarely go through life without taking on debt from time to time. But carrying debt into retirement is not a smart move. Mortgage debt reduces significantly the flexibility you will need at that time in your life, so make paying off your home before retirement an important financial priority.

2. **It is very tempting to spend more money.** A major disadvantage of credit is that its use can lead to overspending. Using a credit card to buy $425 worth of new clothes and paying $25 per month for 20 months (a total of $500: $425 + $75 interest charge) may seem less painful than paying cash for a planned purchase of only $300 worth of clothes. The problem is this: Once you begin carrying credit card debt, it may seem easier to buy more on credit, especially if you have more than three or four cards—as is typical for U.S. credit card holders. This tendency to spend more is why sellers promote buying on credit so heavily.

3. **Avoid becoming a "financially overstretched" American.** Consumers with monthly nonmortgage debt repayments amounting to 15 percent of monthly take-home pay or more are considered to be precariously in debt. They teeter on the brink of disaster. By not paying bills on time, they run a high risk of a poor credit reputation, damage to employment prospects, an increase in rates paid for insurance,

and the loss of items purchased. During the recent economic meltdown, many people who were precariously in debt could not weather the loss of income as a result of layoffs and other financial setbacks. Some were victims of **predatory lending** when greedy or deceptive lenders took advantage of their lack of understanding of credit matters. For example, many homebuyers ended up with mortgage payments they could not afford, due to confusing and misleading terms and conditions as well as outright fraud. Predatory mortgage lending resulted in many homes being sold to people who could not truly afford to make the monthly payments. This contributed to the subsequent national crisis of mortgage foreclosures.

4. **Interest itself is costly. Interest** represents the price of credit. It is the "rent" you pay while you use someone else's money. When stated in dollars, interest makes up part of the **finance charge**, which is the total dollar amount paid to use credit (including interest and any other required charges such as a loan application fee). The Truth in Lending Act requires lenders to state the finance charge both in dollars and as an **annual percentage rate (APR)**. The APR expresses the cost of credit on a yearly basis as a percentage rate. For example, a single-payment, one-year loan for $1000 with a finance charge of $140 has a 14 percent APR.

Knowing the APR simplifies making comparisons among credit arrangements. The lower the APR, the lower the true cost of the credit. The APR can be used to compare credit contracts with different time periods, finance charges, repayment schedules, and amounts borrowed. Many states have **usury laws** (sometimes called **small loan laws**) that establish the maximum loan amounts, interest rates, and credit-related fees for different types of loans from various sources. These maximum rates can vary from 18 percent to as much as 54 percent. The laws of the state in which the lending institution is located apply, rather than the laws of the state in which the borrower lives. These regulations apply to the annual fee, late payment fee, and other fees charged on a bank credit card.

interest
In this context, interest is the "rent" you pay for using credit.

finance charge
Total dollar amount paid to use credit.

annual percentage rate (APR)
Expresses the cost of credit on a yearly basis as a percentage rate.

Concept Check 6.1

1. Which two good uses of credit seem most reasonable to you? Which do not?

2. Explain the two downsides of credit that would be most worrisome for you.

3. Distinguish between the APR and the finance charge on a debt.

SET YOUR OWN DEBT LIMIT

You should set your **debt limit**, which is the overall maximum you believe you should owe based on your ability to meet the repayment obligations. Most people's debt limit is and should be lower than what lenders are willing to offer. Lenders are willing to take chances that some borrowers will not repay, knowing that some of the interest paid by other borrowers will cover the unpaid debts. In fact, this was one of the issues that led to the recent credit crisis. Lenders for several years were very willing to lend, and many people assumed that if the lender thought they could repay that in fact they could. They were wrong. You should not take such a chance when making your own credit decisions.

When considering a new loan, many people simply look at the monthly payment required. This view is very shortsighted and shows a key misunderstanding of how credit works. For example, it is easy to get a low monthly payment simply by lengthening the time period over which the loan will be repaid. You should assess your overall debt obligations before taking on any additional debt. There are three ways to determine your debt limit:

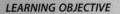
LEARNING OBJECTIVE

Establish your own debt limit.

debt limit
Overall maximum you believe you should owe based on your ability to meet repayment obligations.

ADVICE FROM A PRO

Guard Your Privacy

Identity theft is the most common form of consumer fraud in the United States. It occurs whenever someone else uses your personal information, such as a credit card number, to steal from merchants, from credit card companies, or from you. Armed with very little personal information, a clever thief can borrow someone's credit identity and run up thousands of dollars in debt. To protect your privacy, follow these guidelines:

- Keep account access information private from family members other than a spouse or parent. Much identity theft is actually perpetrated by family members, or often a temporary visitor or guest who digs into files or papers left exposed to view.

- Offer no personal information (such as your address, telephone number, or Social Security number) to merchants when using a credit card. If the merchant requires identification beyond the credit card (for example, a driver's license), do not allow such information to be written down or photocopied.

- Save all purchase and ATM receipts, and regularly check them against statements from creditors and sellers.

- Do not give out your credit card or checking account number on the telephone to anyone you do not know or did not telephone directly yourself.

- Never give your **card verification value** over the phone or online to a merchant unless you initiated the contact with the merchant. This is the three- or four-digit code in the signature strip on the back of a credit card.

- Review your credit bureau report at least once each year through www.annualcreditreport.com.

- Report lost or stolen credit cards and suspicious billing information without delay, especially if you make Internet purchases.

- If your credit card is lost or stolen, or if you ever suspect fraudulent use of an account, contact one of the national credit bureaus because any one of them can put a "fraud alert" on your file at all three companies. Fraud alert messages notify potential credit grantors to verify your identification before extending credit in your name.

- Tell all of your financial services companies (banks, lenders, insurance companies) that you want to opt out of any information-sharing programs they maintain with affiliated or external companies.

- Never respond to e-mail messages from your bank stating that your account may have been compromised and you need to provide account information such as account numbers and passwords even if the e-mail message looks authentic. Your bank will never ask you for this type of information in an e-mail.

- Immediately change the marital status linked to your credit card account if you become married, separated, or divorced.

- Shred all credit card statements containing account numbers.

- Place a **security freeze** on your credit report, which is an effective way to prevent unauthorized credit accounts from being opened in your name. With a freeze, you tell the credit bureaus not to release your financial records to anyone without your consent. You are issued a personal identification number (PIN) to give your authorization. In most states there is a nominal charge for this service.

Karen Drage
Eastern Illinois University

1. Debt payments-to-disposable income method
2. Ratio of debt-to-equity method
3. Continuous-debt method

Method 1: Debt Payments-to-Disposable Income

debt payments-to-disposable income method
Percentage of disposable personal income available for regular debt repayments aside from set obligations.

disposable income
Amount of income remaining after taxes and withholding for such purposes as insurance and union dues.

To use the **debt payments-to-disposable income method**, you first need to decide the percentage of your disposable personal income that can be spent for regular debt repayments, excluding the first mortgage loan on a home and credit card charges that are paid in full each month. **Disposable income** is the amount of your income remaining after taxes and withholding for such purposes as insurance and union dues. Table 6-1 shows some monthly debt-payment limits expressed as a percentage of disposable personal income. As the table indicates, with monthly payments representing 15 to 18 percent of monthly disposable personal income, a borrower is precariously overindebted and fully extended; taking on additional debt would be unwise. This means that someone with an average income and an expensive car loan might not be able to afford to carry any credit card balances that carry over from month to month.

Debt-Payment Limits as a Percentage of Disposable Personal Income*

Table 6-1

Percent	Current Debt Situation	Borrower's Feelings	Take on Additional Debt?
0	No debt at all	No stress about personal finances	Taking on some consumer debt is fine
10 or less	Little debt	Borrower feels no stress from debt repayment obligations	More debt could be undertaken cautiously
11 to 14	Safe debt limit but fully extended financially	Borrower is moderately stressed about pressure from debt repayment obligations	Should not acquire more debt, and a debt-consolidation loan from a credit union may be a good option
15 to 18	Precariously overindebted	Borrower starts to feel seriously stressed about debts and hopes no emergency arises	Absolutely should not take on more debt
19 to 28	Seriously overindebted	Borrower feels overwhelming stress and is desperate about debts	Contact a nonprofit credit counseling company
29+	Excessively overindebted	Borrower feels hopeless or knows his or her debts are so large that he or she is doomed to financial failure	Contact a bankruptcy attorney

*Excluding home mortgage loan repayments and convenience credit card purchases to be repaid in full when the monthly bill arrives

Once you decide the percentage that is appropriate for you, you can compare it with your **debt payments-to-disposable income ratio** as discussed in Chapter 3. In that chapter, we calculated a debt payments-to-disposable income ratio for the Hernandez family of 9.32 percent. As indicated by Table 6-1, they could take on new debt—but only cautiously.

Table 6-2 shows the effects on a budget of increasing debts. In the table, after deductions, disposable personal income amounts to $2200 per month. Current budgeted expenses (totaling the full $2200) are allocated in a sample distribution throughout the various categories. As you can see, increasing debt payments from $0 to $550 per month (for example, to buy a new automobile or home entertainment system on credit) has dramatic effects on this budget.

A responsible financial manager must decide where to cut back to meet monthly credit repayments. As the debt load grows, each 5 percentage point increase makes it much more difficult to "find the money" and make the cutbacks. In this case, the borrower reduced expenditures on savings and investments immediately and then finally reduced the amount in this category to $50. Food was cut back, but only slightly. Utilities, automobile insurance, and rent are relatively fixed expenses; as a consequence, it is difficult to reduce these amounts without moving or buying a less expensive car. Entertainment expenses were steadily reduced, and newspapers and magazines were eliminated altogether.

Where would you make reductions? Spending a few minutes changing the figures in Table 6-2 will give you an idea of your priorities and the size of the debt limit that you might establish. Note that the debt payments-to-disposable income method focuses on the amount of monthly debt repayment—not the total debt. As a result, it also would be wise to consider the length of time that the severe financial situation caused by high debt payments might last. You could get yourself into financial trouble for many years.

Method 2: Ratio of Debt to Equity

Another method for determining your debt limit involves calculating the ratio of your consumer debt to your assets. In Chapter 3, we performed such an analysis for the Hernandez family when we calculated their asset-to-debt ratio. The **debt-to-equity ratio** is similar except that it uses the **equity** in a person's assets (the amount by which the value of those assets exceeds debts), excluding the value of a primary residence and the first mortgage on that home. This ratio recognizes that mortgage debt does not get people into trouble. In fact, mortgage debt is backed up by excellent collateral—one's own home.

From Table 3-2 on page 73, we see that the Hernandez family has assets of $196,620 ($9120—monetary assets; $20,500—tangible assets less the value of their

debt-to-equity ratio
Ratio of your consumer debt to your assets.

Table 6-2   Effects of Increasing Debt Payments on a Budget*

Gross income	$34,000
Deductions for taxes, 401(k), insurance	$ 7,600
Disposable personal income	$26,400
Monthly disposable income	$ 2,200

	No Debt	10% Debt	15% Debt	20% Debt	25% Debt
Rent	$ 700	$ 700	$ 700	$ 700	$ 700
Savings and investments	250	180	120	80	50
Food	280	250	240	220	210
Utilities (telephone, electricity, heat)	130	130	130	120	120
Insurance (automobile, renter's, and life)	80	80	80	80	80
Transportation expenses	100	90	90	80	80
Charitable contributions	60	50	50	40	40
Entertainment	140	120	110	100	80
Clothing	50	40	30	20	20
Vacations and long weekends	60	50	40	40	30
Medical/dental expenses	60	50	50	50	50
Newspapers and magazines	40	30	30	30	0
Cable TV	50	50	40	40	30
Personal care	30	20	20	20	20
Gifts and holidays	40	30	30	30	30
Health club	60	60	60	60	60
Miscellaneous	70	50	50	50	50
Debt repayments	0	220	330	440	550
TOTAL	$2,200	$2,200	$2,200	$2,200	$2,200

*One person's decisions on where to cut back expenses to make increasing monthly debt payments.

home; and $167,000—investment assets). Their debts (excluding their home mortgage) total $9365 ($120 + $1545 + $7700). With $9365 in debts and $196,620 in assets, the Hernandezes have equity of $187,255 ($196,620 − $9365), or a debt-to-equity ratio of 0.05 ($9365 ÷ $187,255).

The ratio of debt-to-equity method provides a quick idea of one's financial solvency. The larger the ratio, the riskier the likelihood of repayment. A ratio in excess of 0.33 is considered high. The Hernandezes are well under that limit, unlike the result found by calculating their debt payments-to-disposable income ratio. This contrast occurs primarily because of their real estate investment asset, on which they have no debt.

Method 3: Continuous Debt

Another approach for determining your debt limit is the **continuous-debt method**. If you are unable to get completely out of debt every four years (except for a mortgage loan), you probably lean on debt too heavily. You could be developing a credit lifestyle in which you will never eliminate debt and will continuously pay out substantial amounts of income for finance charges—likely $1200 or more per year, and that is like throwing away $100 every month for absolutely nothing!

Dual-Earner Households Should Set a Lower Debt Limit

Having two incomes in a household has its benefits. Two people, each of whom earns $36,000 per year, will gross $72,000, with a disposable personal

FINANCIAL POWER POINT

Are You Worried About Your Debts?

If you are worried about your debts, then you should be. Your own gut feeling is often the best indicator of carrying too much debt.

DID YOU KNOW?

How to Manage Student Loan Debt

Total student loan debt outstanding now exceeds $850 million, more than that owed on all credit cards combined. The average student with loan debt owes more than $24,000 at graduation. Large student loan debts make it far more challenging to meet other financial goals such as buying a home and saving for retirement. Strive to keep your student debt load down. Here are some tips for managing the student debt you do accrue:

1. ***Choose the most advantageous repayment pattern allowed.*** *The standard repayment plan for student loan debt calls for equal monthly installments paid over ten years, but to pay the debt off faster, you can establish a graduated repayment plan whereby the payments are lower in the early years but then increase in later years.*

2. ***Pay electronically.*** *Make arrangements to have the monthly payment transferred electronically out of a checking account and you can receive a small reduction in the interest rate.*

3. ***Make your repayments on time, every time.*** *In some programs, if you make the first 48 payments on time, the interest rate will be reduced by 1 or 2 percentage points. Failing to repay in a timely manner can have dire consequences,*

including forfeiture of federal and state income tax refunds, as well as Social Security and veterans' benefits.

4. ***Consolidate your student loans.*** *Consolidating your education loans means that all your existing loans are paid off and one new loan is created. This strategy may allow for a much more convenient repayment schedule. The interest rate may be lower, and the amount of time for repayment may be longer, resulting in a lower monthly payment under the new loan. Loans can be consolidated through a private bank or through one of two government programs: Sallie Mae (www.salliemae.com) or Federal Direct Consolidation Loans (www.loanconsolidation.ed.gov).*

5. ***If necessary, sign up for the Federal government's income-based repayment plan.*** *If your student loan debt is very high compared to your salary, you may qualify for a plan that has low payments and the remaining debt is forgiven after 25 years if you have made payments consistently up to that point. See http://studentaid.ed.gov/. You may also qualify for reduced payments if you work in a public-service job, in an underserved profession, or for a national service organization such as AmeriCorps. Go to www.finaid.org/loans/forgiveness.phtml.*

income of around $54,000, or $4500 monthly. It may seem that the couple can afford a much higher level of debt than before the incomes were combined. While the guidelines given in Table 6-1 are realistic, they would allow a doubling of debt payments if the addition of a second earner doubled household earnings.

Jose Luis Pelaez/Getty Images

Two incomes should not mean a double debt limit.

Many young couples adopt a lifestyle based on two incomes. Their spending grows in tandem with their rising incomes. After a while, they are spending and borrowing to the limit. This situation cannot go on forever, of course. Eventually they may begin to feel financially stressed and wonder, "How can we be so broke when we make so much money?" When a child comes along or one partner loses a job or overtime pay, they may quickly get into deep financial trouble as debts that had been manageable with two incomes quickly become overwhelming. Bad economic times can have devastatingly negative financial impacts on families who have taken on too much debt. Couples would be wise to set a debt limit based on the higher of their two incomes and use the second income to build savings accounts and make investments early in their lives together. That will truly protect their future financial security. This is one of the smartest financial actions a couple can make—saving and investing extra money early in a relationship.

 Concept Check 6.2

1. Distinguish among the debt payments-to-disposable income, ratio of debt-to-equity, and continuous-debt methods for setting your debt limit.

2. What are the threshold levels for both the debt payments-to-disposable income and ratio of debt-to-equity methods that would indicate that a person is carrying too much debt?

3. Discuss how dual-earner households should consider their ability to carry additional debt.

DID YOU KNOW?

Turn Bad Habits into Good Ones

Do You Do This?	Do This Instead!
Ignore the list of transactions in your credit card account statements	Inspect your statements for signs of identity theft
Assume your credit bureau files are correct and up to date	Check your file with alternating bureaus every four months
Borrow from your own bank when you need new credit	Shop around for the best credit terms and lowest APR
Assume you are doing fine if you can make your monthly debt payments	At least once a year, calculate your debt limit using appropriate ratios

OBTAINING CREDIT AND BUILDING A GOOD CREDIT REPUTATION

 LEARNING OBJECTIVE 3

Achieve a good credit reputation.

Credit is widely and readily available to most of us today. It is not unusual for a customer to walk into a retail store such as Target or Home Depot and be offered a credit card account that can be used immediately. However, if the applicant has not used credit previously (no credit), or has bounced a lot of checks, or has failed to honor credit agreements in the past (bad credit), an offer of credit is typically not extended. Your success in obtaining credit hinges on an understanding of the credit approval process and having a good credit reputation.

The Credit Approval Process

To obtain credit, you must first complete a credit application. Based on the information in this application, the lender will investigate your credit history. The information is then evaluated (sometimes instantly via computer), and the lender decides whether to extend credit. When an application is approved, the rules of the account are contained in the credit agreement.

You Apply for Credit A **credit application** is a form or interview that requests information that sheds light on your ability and willingness to repay debts. This information helps lenders make informed decisions about whether they will be repaid by borrowers. Answering questions completely and honestly both on an application form and during an interview (if any) is important. If inconsistencies arise during the lender's subsequent investigation of the applicant's credit history, the lender could refuse the request for credit or charge a higher interest rate. At the time of application, always ask for a copy of the rules governing the account, including the APR and various repayment terms. However, these terms are not final and can change when the actual decision to lend is made. That is why you should read all credit contracts before signing.

Approximately 15 percent of all people who apply for credit are denied. Half of the unsuccessful applicants have no established **credit history** (a continuing record of a person's credit usage and repayment of debts) or their credit history contains negative information. A bad credit history is like having high blood pressure—you may not know you have a problem until something bad happens, such as when your loan application is rejected.

credit application
Form or interview that provides information about your ability and willingness to repay debts.

credit history
Continuing record of a person's credit usage and repayment of debts.

DID YOU KNOW?

Unfair Credit Discrimination Is Unlawful

The Equal Credit Opportunity Act (ECOA) prohibits certain types of **unfair discrimination** (making distinctions among individuals based on unfair criteria) when granting credit. Under this law, a lender must notify an applicant within 30 days about the lender's acceptance or rejection of a credit application. The ECOA also requires the creditor to provide the applicant with a written statement, if requested, detailing the reasons for refusing credit. Rejecting a credit application due to poor credit history is legal. Conversely, it is illegal to reject applicants on the basis of gender, race, age, national origin, religion, or receipt of Social Security income or public assistance. Credit applications cannot ask for information that could be used in a biased manner, such as marital status and childbearing plans. (Applicants may offer such information voluntarily,

however.) If discrimination is proved in court, the lender may be fined as much as $10,000. Always request that a lender who turns you down for credit provide you with the credit score it used in the decision and the name of the credit bureau that provided the score.

A creditor cannot require an applicant to disclose income from alimony, separate maintenance payments, or child support payments. If the borrower wants this income to be counted during the lender's evaluation of the application, the creditor can consider whether that income stream is received consistently. Information about a spouse or former spouse may not be requested unless the spouse will use the account, it is a joint account, or repayment of debts will rely on the spouse's income or other financial support. The law requires that credit granted in both spouses' names be used to build a credit history for the parties as a couple as well as for each individual spouse.

The Lender Obtains Your Credit Report Upon receiving your completed credit application, the lender conducts a **credit investigation** and compares the findings with the information on your application. The goal of the investigation is to assess the applicant's creditworthiness. Lenders want to know the applicant's prior credit usage and repayment patterns, income, length of employment, and home ownership status.

To conduct its investigation, the lender obtains a **credit report** from a **credit bureau** that keeps records of many borrowers' credit histories. Lenders pay a fee for each credit report requested. Credit bureaus compile information from merchants, utility companies, banks, court records, and creditors. Most of the more than 2000 local credit bureaus in the United States belong to national groups that collectively have access to the credit histories of more than 170 million adults. There are three

credit report
Information compiled by a credit bureau from merchants, utility companies, banks, court records, and creditors about your payment history.

credit bureau
Firm that collects and keeps records of many borrowers' credit histories.

major national credit-reporting bureaus: Experian, TransUnion, and Equifax. A lender may consult one or all of the bureaus when you apply for credit.

The Lender Also Obtains Your Credit Score All three of the major credit-reporting bureaus also calculate and report credit scores to lenders. Lenders use a **credit score** (also known as **risk score**) in which a statistical measure is used to rate applicants on the basis of various factors deemed relevant to creditworthiness and the likelihood of repayment. You also have the right to know your scores, although you may have to pay a fee to do so. The most well-known score is the FICO score developed by Fair Isaac Corporation. The FICO score ranges from 300 to 850. Another commonly used score is the Vantage Score developed by all three national credit bureaus. Vantage scores can range from 501 to 990 and also include a letter grade from A to E. Borrowers with C or better are deemed to be most worthy of credit. Lenders are free to use whatever scoring system they prefer.

credit score (risk score)
Statistical measure used to rate applicants based on various factors deemed relevant to creditworthiness and the likelihood of repayment.

DID YOU KNOW?

Making Sense of Credit Scores

Although the credit-scoring systems in use today go by a number of brand names, the most widely used is the **FICO score** developed by Fair Isaac Corporation (www.myfico.com). Because your credit file and the method of calculating the score may differ at each of the three major credit bureaus, your credit score at each may differ as well. (See "Access Your Credit Bureau File for Free" on page 181.) Your credit scores are vitally important because they dictate whether you will be granted credit and at what interest rates. Under the Fair and Accurate Credit Transactions Act of 2003, credit bureaus must provide consumers with their credit scores upon request. A nominal fee ($8 to $12) is charged for a credit score report. However, if you are denied credit altogether or at less than favorable rates you must be told why, and if the reason was your credit score you may request a credit score report at no charge.

Credit scores are produced via complex statistical models that correlate certain borrower characteristics with the likelihood of repayment. The exact methodologies employed in the models, though similar, are closely held secrets. The factors used in the FICO score system are shared openly by Fair Isaac Corporation on the company's website:

1. **Payment history.** Are you late with your payments? How late? How often? On how many of your accounts?

2. **Amounts owed.** What is the balance on each of your credit obligations? (Even if you pay in full each month, there might be a balance on a given date.) How do the amounts owed vary on various types of accounts, such as credit cards versus loans? How many accounts have balances? Are you maxed out or nearly so on your cards, regardless of the dollar amount of your balances? (Credit scores are negatively affected if you have a balance on any card in excess of 30 percent of the credit limit on that card.) On loans, how much of the original loan is still owed?

3. **Length of credit history.** How long have you had each account? How long has it been since you used the accounts?

4. **Taking on more debt.** How many new accounts do you have? How long has it been since you opened a new

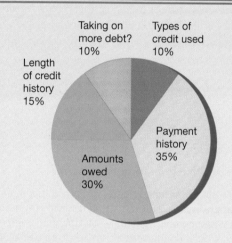

account? How many recent inquiries have been made by lenders to which you have made application? If you had a period of poor credit usage in the past, for how long have you been in good standing?

5. **Types of credit used.** Do you have a good mix of credit usage, with reliance on multiple types depending on the purpose of the credit (for example, not using a credit card to buy a boat)? How many accounts in total do you have?

About one-fourth of consumers have a FICO score below 620, making it nearly impossible to get a loan from all but the most expensive types of lenders. The FICO website provides suggestions on how to improve your FICO score. For example, if you are maxed out on two cards and have low balances on others, you might shift some of the large balances to other cards so that you owe no more than 30 percent of the debt limit on any of your cards. This percentage, known as the **credit utilization ratio**, contributes almost one-third of the weight of your credit score. If you have many dormant accounts, you could close some of them. This is especially important if you plan to apply for a mortgage in the next year or so as mortgage lenders do look at your total available credit whether it is being used or not. The chart above indicates the relative importance of each of the five factors in the development of FICO scores.

The Lender Decides Whether to Accept the Application and Under What Terms The approval or rejection of credit is based on the lender's judgment of the willingness and ability of the applicant to repay the debt. If the application is accepted, a contract is created that outlines the rules governing the account. For credit cards, this contract is called a **credit agreement**. For loans, the contract is called a **promissory note** (or simply, the **note**).

The actual lender always makes the decision about whether to grant credit. Credit scoring simply allows lenders to categorize credit users according to the perceived level of risk. Under the concept of **tiered pricing**, lenders may offer lower interest rates to applicants with the highest credit scores while charging steeper rates to more risky applicants. The difference in rates is modest except for those with scores below 620. People with such low credit scores can often find some lender that will say yes. However, the interest rates will be much higher. To get the lowest rates possible, you should always make sure that your credit bureau file is accurate before filling out a credit application.

Your Credit Reputation

The information about you that is contained in credit bureau files is one of the most important aspects of your financial life. It is used not only when lenders decide whether to approve your applications for credit but also when you apply for a job, insurance, and rental housing. Thus, it is important that you build a good credit reputation and confirm that the information in your file is as accurate and up to date as possible.

Build a Strong Credit History Some people who are new to the world of credit wonder whether they will ever get credit when they need it. They will if they establish a good credit history. This is what is meant when someone is said to have "good credit." The following steps can help you have "good credit":

1. **Establish both a checking account and a savings account.** Lenders see people who can handle these accounts as being more likely to manage credit usage properly.
2. **Have your telephone and other utilities billed in your name.** The fact that you can maintain a good payment pattern on your utility bills indicates that you can manage your money wisely and will do the same with your credit repayments.
3. **Request, acquire, and use an oil-company credit card.** These cards are easy to obtain. If one company refuses, simply apply to another company, as companies' scoring systems differ. Use the credit sparingly, and repay the debt promptly.
4. **Apply for a bank credit card.** Your own bank is the best place to start your search for a credit card. If not successful there, you usually can find some bank that will issue you a card (search at www.bankrate.com). The credit limit may be low (perhaps $500) and the APR high (perhaps 27 percent), but at least the opportunity exists to establish a credit history. Later, you can request an increase in the credit limit and a lower APR.
5. **Ask a bank for a small, short-term cash loan.** Putting these borrowed funds into a savings account at the bank will almost guarantee that you will make the required three or four monthly payments. In addition, the interest charges on the loan will be partially offset by the interest earned on the savings.
6. **Pay off student loans.** Some have their first exposure to credit through the student loans they use to attend college. Paying off these loans quickly through a series of regular monthly payments can show prospective lenders that you are a responsible borrower.

Access Your Credit Bureau File for Free Federal law requires credit bureaus to provide consumers with their credit reports upon request. You can obtain one report for free each year from each of the national credit bureaus. In addition, consumers must

credit agreement
Contract that stipulates repayment terms for credit cards.

promissory note (note)
Contract that stipulates repayment terms for a loan.

FINANCIAL POWER POINT

Closing Accounts Does Not Help Your Credit Score

Many people think that closing credit card accounts will help a credit score. This is not usually the case unless you have a large number of accounts that you do not use. When accounts are closed, it reduces the ratio between what you owe to the total amount of credit available on all credit cards, and that smaller window of credit available reduces your credit score. Also, credit scores are higher when accounts have been open for longer periods of time. Therefore, if you feel you must close accounts, close your newest accounts, not the oldest. Also take care to ensure that closing accounts does not raise your credit utilization ratio above 30 percent.

© 2011 Central Source LLC

Each member of the family should be aware of and involved with important financial decisions.

be notified if merchants report negative information to a credit bureau. You should request a report periodically (certainly every year) and whenever you move, have a change in family status (marry, get divorced, or become widowed), resolve any credit billing errors or disputes (to ensure that negative information is not in your file), or plan to sign up for new credit in the next few months.

Only One Website Is Truly Free To obtain a free credit report, simply contact www.annualcreditreport.com. This is the *only* site that links you directly to the mechanism for obtaining a free report.

Avoid Other Websites If you contact one of the sites with similarly worded names or directly contact one of the three major credit-reporting bureaus, you will be enticed to sign up for a **credit-reporting service**. Such services allow you to access your report as often as daily and obtain your credit score, supposedly for free for a month or two. However, these offers are **negative option plans**. You may be automatically signed up for a plan costing as much as $100 or more per year and your membership renews automatically unless you notify them that you want it to end at the end of the free period. This is a bad deal, especially when you can obtain the information in your files for free.

Actually, You Can Obtain a Free Report Every Four Months The free annual credit report law allows you to check your credit for free every four months. How? By staggering your requests across the three national bureaus.* For example, in January you can request a report from Experian through www.annualcreditreport.com. Then, in May you can order a report from TransUnion. In September you can request a report from Equifax. Then in January, it's back to Experian. Because the bureaus all gather information from essentially the same sources, you can have some confidence that what appears on one file will be present in the others. If you find an error, contact all three to make the correction.

Here's How to Fix Errors in Your Report When you obtain your report, you should thoroughly inspect it for accuracy. If you find an error, the **Fair Credit Reporting Act (FCRA)** allows you to challenge the error as it requires that reports contain accurate information. It also requires that only bona fide users be permitted to review your file for approved purposes. The FCRA governs both lenders and credit bureaus.

FINANCIAL POWER POINT

Your Credit Score Is Based on Your Credit Report

The importance of the accuracy of the information in your credit bureau file is emphasized by the fact that your credit score is determined solely by that information. Make sure your credit bureau files are accurate and be as concerned about your credit score as you are about your GPA.

Fair Credit Reporting Act (FCRA)
Requires that credit reports contain accurate, relevant, and recent information and that only bona fide users be permitted to review a file for approved purposes.

---

* The major credit bureaus often sell lists of consumer names in their files (but not each person's specific credit history information) for credit card marketing purposes. To have your name withheld for two years from this practice, call (888) 567-8688 or go online at www.optoutprescreen.com.

If you find an error or omission in a credit report from a particular credit bureau, you should immediately take steps to correct the information since the FCRA is partially enforced by consumers. Here's how to assert your rights:

1. Simultaneously notify both the credit bureau and the original lender of the error and ask for confirmation. State that you wish to exercise your right to a reinvestigation under FCRA. Specifically, you should ask the bureau to "reaffirm" the item.

2. The bureau and lender must reinvestigate the information within 45 days. If the bureau cannot complete its investigation within 45 days, it must drop the information from your credit file.

3. If the information was erroneous, it must be corrected. If a report containing the error was sent to a creditor investigating your application within the past six months, a corrected report must be sent to that creditor.

4. If the credit bureau refuses to make a correction (perhaps because the information was "technically correct"), you may wish to provide your version of the disputed information (in 100 words or less) by adding a **consumer statement** to your credit bureau file. This statement will be included with any credit reports by that bureau.

5. Also obtain a report from the other two bureaus to ensure that the error does not also appear in their files. If an error appears, correct it beginning at step #2.

6. Negative information in your file is generally not reportable after a period of seven years except for bankruptcy data, for which the time limit is ten years.

consumer statement
Your version of a credit issue that shows up on your credit report when the credit bureau refuses to drop a disputed claim.

DID YOU KNOW?

The Effects of Divorce on Your Credit

The breakup of a marriage affects the creditworthiness of both partners. The Federal Trade Commission offers the following suggestions for individuals seeking a divorce.

Pay careful attention to credit accounts held jointly, including mortgages, second mortgages, and credit cards. The behavior of one divorcing spouse will continue to affect the other individual as long as the accounts are held in both names. One party could make credit card charges, for example, and refuse to pay the debt, leaving the financial burden on the other party. When possible, ask creditors to close joint accounts and reopen them as individual accounts. Never accept a creditor's verbal assurance, either over the telephone or in person, that an account has been closed. Always insist on

written confirmation, including the effective date of the account closure.

When debts were accumulated in both names, a divorce decree has no legal effect on who technically owes which debts. Creditors can legally collect from *either* of the divorcing parties. If the person absolved of responsibility for the debt under the divorce decree is forced by a creditor to pay off the account, he must then go to court to seek enforcement of the divorce decree and collect reimbursement from the former spouse.

Both before and after a divorce, get a copy of your credit report from each of the three credit bureaus. Check them for accuracy and challenge any problem areas, such as accounts that continue to be shown in both names.

✔ Concept Check 6.3

1. Summarize the basic steps that occur when someone applies for credit.

2. What is a credit history, and what role do credit bureaus play in the development of your credit history?

3. What is a credit score, and what five major factors go into its calculation?

4. Identify five actions you can take to build a good credit reputation.

5. Summarize the protections provided under the Fair Credit Reporting Act.

SOURCES OF CONSUMER LOANS

Today's consumers have many sources of consumer loans from which to choose. Most consumer lending occurs through depository institutions and sales finance companies. Other sources include consumer finance companies, stockbrokers, and insurance companies. Table 6-3 shows the interest rates charged and example payment amounts and finance charges from these various sources of consumer loans.

Depository Institutions Lend Money to Their Customers

Depository institutions include commercial banks, mutual savings banks, savings banks, and credit unions (see Chapter 5 for more-detailed descriptions of these institutions). They tend to make loans to their own customers and to noncustomers with good credit histories. Depository institutions offer highly competitive rates, partly because the funds loaned are obtained primarily from their depositors. The interest rate commonly ranges from 9 to 18 percent. Research indicates that many people who go elsewhere for loans actually meet the qualifications for depository institution lending and end up paying a higher interest rate than necessary.

Sales Finance Companies Lend Money to Purchasers of Consumer Products

sales finance company

Seller-related lender whose primary business is financing sales for its parent company.

A **sales finance company** is a seller-related lender (such as GMAC Financial Services for General Motors Corporation and Ford Motor Credit) whose primary business is financing the sales of its parent company. Such firms specialize in making purchase loans, often with the item being bought serving as the collateral for the loan. Because the seller often works in close association with the sales finance company, credit can be approved on the spot.

Sales finance companies require collateral and deal only with customers who are considered medium to good risks. Thus, their interest rates are often competitive with those offered by depository institutions. Their interest rates may be even lower than those offered by other sources if the seller subsidizes the rate to encourage sales—as with the special low-APR financing often offered on new cars, for example. Most new-car loans today are made by sales finance companies.

Consumer Finance Companies Make Small Cash Loans

consumer finance company/ small-loan company

Firm that specializes in making relatively small secured or unsecured loans that require monthly installment payments.

A **consumer finance company** specializes in making relatively small loans and is, therefore, also known as a **small-loan company**. These lenders range from the well-recognized CitiFinancial and Beneficial Finance Corporation to many local neighborhood lenders. Such companies make both secured and unsecured loans and require

Table 6-3   Estimating What It Costs to Borrow Money

Lender	Annual Percentage Rate	Two-Year Loan Monthly Payment	Two-Year Loan Finance Charge	Five-Year Loan Monthly Payment	Five-Year Loan Finance Charge
Life insurance company	4	$43.42	$ 42.19	$18.42	$104.99
Sales finance company	6	44.32	63.68	19.33	159.80
Credit union	8	45.23	85.52	20.28	216.80
Commercial bank	10	46.14	107.36	21.25	275.00
Mutual savings bank	10	46.14	107.36	21.25	275.00
Savings and loan association	10	46.14	107.36	21.25	275.00
Bank credit card	18	49.92	198.08	25.39	523.40
Consumer finance company	24	52.87	268.88	28.77	726.20

Credit costs money. Just how much can be seen by considering the cost of borrowing $1000 for two years and for five years from various sources at various interest rates.

repayment on a monthly installment basis. They focus mainly on the **subprime lending** market. This market focuses on lending to people who normally would not qualify for credit with FICO scores of less than 620. The interest rates they charge are higher than those available from depository lenders because consumer finance companies focus on borrowers with low credit scores.

DID YOU KNOW?

About Alternative Lenders

A number of avenues through which to obtain credit are available that may not look like credit. Credit can come from unusual sources, including payday lenders, rent-to-own stores, and pawnshops.

Payday lenders (which are illegal in some states) are businesses that grant credit when they honor a personal check but agree not to deposit the check for a week or longer. The fees for check cashing are sometimes 20 percent or more of the amount of the check, pushing the APR (if the check is held for later deposit) to several hundred percent or higher.

A **rent-to-own program** provides a mechanism for buying an item with little or no down payment by renting it for a period of time, after which it is owned. Furniture, appliances, and electronic entertainment items are commonly sold via the rent-to-own approach. This form of credit is often used by people who believe they cannot qualify for credit purchases. These programs have two big drawbacks for consumers. First, the renter does not own the item until the final payment is made. Paying late or stopping payments will cause the products to be seized with no allowance being made for the previous "rental" payments. Second, the actual cost for renting items is often exorbitantly high. For example, a TV worth $300 might be rented for $15 per week for one year, producing a finance charge of $480 (52 × $15 – $300).

A **pawnshop** is a lender that offers single-payment loans, often ranging from $100 to $500, for short time periods (typically two to six months), after the borrower turns over an item of personal property to the pawnshop. The dollar amount loaned is typically equal to one-third or less of the value of the item pawned. In most states, a borrower need merely turn over the item, present identification, and sign on the dotted line. The pawnshop owner can legally sell the item if the borrower fails to redeem the property by paying the amount due, plus interest, within the time period specified. The pawnshop commonly charges an interest rate of about 5 percent per month plus a 2 percent monthly storage fee; thus, the annual combined "interest" amounts to 84 percent [(5 + 2) × 12]. Clearly, pawnshops represent the lender of last resort for borrowers.

Approximately one-fifth of all loans granted by consumer finance companies are for the purpose of debt consolidation. Other common uses of such loans are for travel, vacations, education, automobiles, and home furnishings. Some small-loan companies specialize in making loans by mail. They advertise in newspapers and magazines and on the Internet to attract borrowers, who complete a credit application and receive approval via mail.

Stockbrokers Lend Money to Their Clients

People build significant assets in investment accounts that may be earmarked for their children's college education, their own retirement, or other purposes. If you have a margin account (see Chapter 14), you can borrow from your stockbroker using your investments as collateral. Although many people prefer not to tap into these investment funds directly, it may be possible to borrow from or against these accounts. In addition, it may be possible to borrow from certain employer-sponsored, tax-sheltered retirement accounts (see Chapter 17), depending on the rules of the plan. Care must be taken to ensure that the loan plus interest is repaid so that the savings goal can still be met. Tax consequences may arise if retirement account loans are not repaid. (See Chapter 17 for details.)

Insurance Companies Lend Money to Their Policyholders

Insurance companies, such as State Farm or Allstate, offer car loans and credit cards to their policyholders. They may make these loans out of their own funds or have bank

DID YOU KNOW?

About the CARD Act

In 2009, Congress passed the Credit Card Accountability, Responsibility, and Disclosure Act (CARD Act). The law regulates the rules used by lenders and how they must disclose those rules to borrowers. It covers consumer products like credit cards and mortgages, including what fees, penalties, and interest rates are fair. The CARD Act does not apply to credit cards held by businesses.

subsidiary companies set up to handle such loans. Insurance companies loan only to their customers with high credit scores. They can be a low-cost source from which to borrow money.

Policyholders who have cash-value life insurance policies can obtain loans based on the cash values built up in their policies. (This topic is examined in Chapter 12.) An advantage to borrowing on a cash-value life insurance policy is that the interest rates are low, ranging from 4 to 6 percent even though the policyholders actually are borrowing their own money. Many people fail to pay back such loans because no fixed schedule of repayment is established and insurance companies do not pressure borrowers to repay the debt. If the insured person dies before repaying the loan, the life insurance company will deduct the amount of the loan from the amount that would otherwise be paid on the policy.

Choose Your Source of Credit Wisely

As you have read above, you have many sources from which to borrow. Most borrowers want to hear a quick "yes" when they apply for credit, and that goal can be made easier by applying to lenders who are willing to grant credit to almost anyone. But this is not the wisest approach for two reasons. First, lenders who make borrowing easy charge higher interest rates. Second, such lenders grant credit to people with low credit scores. When you borrow from such lenders, the credit scoring system assumes you are doing so because you cannot get credit from lenders with higher standards. The result is that your credit score goes down when you borrow from consumer finance companies, debt consolidators, and payday lenders. Figure 6-1 provides a graphical representation of various lenders with those with the highest standards at the top of the pyramid and those with the lowest standards at the bottom. Always try to borrow from lenders as high on the pyramid as possible given your credit score.

Figure 6-1   The Credit Pyramid

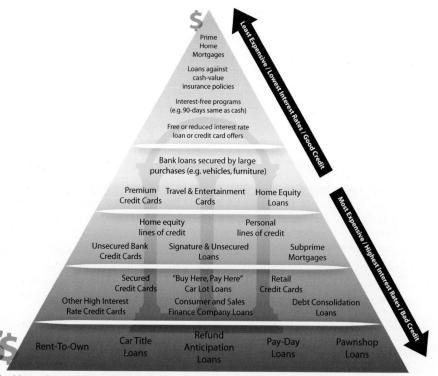

Source: Michael Rupured, © 2008 University of Georgia Cooperative Extension. Used by permission.

Concept Check 6.4

1. List the four types of depository institutions that are sources of credit for consumers.

2. Distinguish between a sales finance company and a consumer finance company.

3. Summarize how stockbrokers and insurance companies serve as sources of consumer credit.

4. Explain where you would go to obtain credit at the lowest cost.

DID YOU KNOW?

Sean's Success Story

Sean's success as a personal financial manager is reflected in his debt situation. While in college, Sean worked part-time for his living expenses and only used student loans to pay for his tuition and fees. He had a credit card that provided cash-back rewards. He used the card for all of his expenses and paid the balance in full each month. He used the cash-back amount each year to help pay for a road trip during spring break. During his senior year, Sean checked his credit report with all three national bureaus. He found one or two mistakes in each and had the errors corrected. He now checks one of the files every four months. Sean has been considering the purchase of a new vehicle so he purchased his FICO score and was pleased to see that the score was above 700, indicating that he would qualify for a loan at the lowest possible rates. He plans to seek preapproval from at least three sources including his credit union before visiting a dealership. Sean's approach to building and maintaining good credit will benefit him for years to come.

DEALING WITH OVERINDEBTEDNESS

People become **overindebted** when their excessive personal debts make repayment difficult and cause financial distress.

Ten Signs of Overindebtedness

1. **Not knowing how much you owe.** Have you lost track of how much you owe? Do you avoid reality by not adding up the total? Are you afraid to add up how much debt you have?

2. **Running out of money.** Are you using credit cards on occasions when you previously used cash? Are you borrowing to pay insurance premiums, taxes, or other large, predictable bills? Are you borrowing to pay for regular expenses such as food or gasoline? Do you try to borrow from friends and relatives to carry you through the month?

3. **Paying only the minimum amount due.** Do you pay the minimum payment—or just a little more than the minimum—on your credit cards instead of making large payments to more quickly reduce the balance owed?

4. **Exceeding debt limits and credit limits.** Are you spending more than 14 percent of your take-home pay on nonmortgage credit repayments? Do you sometimes reach the maximum approved credit limits on your credit cards?

5. **Requesting new credit cards and increases in credit limits.** Have you applied for additional credit cards to increase your borrowing capacity? Have you asked for increases in credit limits on your current credit cards? Have you obtained a cash advance on one credit card to make the payment on another card?

 LEARNING OBJECTIVE 5

Identify signs of overindebtedness and describe the options that are available for debt relief.

overindebted
When one's excessive personal debts make repayment difficult and cause financial distress.

6. **Paying late or skipping credit payments.** Are you late more than once a year in paying your mortgage, rent, car loan, or utility bills? Do you frequently pay late charges? Are you juggling bills to pay the utilities, rent, or mortgage? Are creditors sending overdue notices?

7. **Taking add-on loans.** Taking **add-on loans**, also called **flipping**, occurs when you refinance or rewrite a loan for an even larger amount before it has been completely repaid. Suppose that a loan of $1000 has been repaid down to $400. You decide to refinance the debt balance of $400 by borrowing $2000 and using the additional $1600 ($2000 – $400) for other purposes.

8. **Using debt-consolidation loans.** Are you borrowing, perhaps from a new source, to pay off old debts? Such action may temporarily reduce pressure on your budget, but it also indicates that you are overly indebted.

9. **Experiencing garnishment. Garnishment** is a court-sanctioned procedure by which a portion of the debtor's wages are set aside by the debtor's employer to pay debts. Wages and salary income, including that of military personnel, can be garnished. The Truth in Lending Act prohibits more than two garnishments of one person's paycheck. The total amount garnished cannot represent more than 25 percent of a person's disposable income for the pay period or more than the amount by which the weekly disposable income exceeds 30 times the federal minimum wage (whichever is less). In addition, the law prohibits garnishment from being used as grounds for employment discharge.

10. **Experiencing repossession or foreclosure. Repossession** is a legal proceeding by which the lender seizes an asset (called **foreclosure**, if the property is a home) for nonpayment of a loan. When a lender repossesses property, the borrower may still owe on the debt because of a deficiency balance. A **deficiency balance** occurs when the sum of money raised by the sale of the repossessed collateral fails to cover the amount owed on the debt plus any repossession expenses (collection, attorney, and court costs) paid by the creditor.

Consider the tale of Betty Peterson, a staff sergeant in the army from San Diego, California, whose husband lost his civilian job. In an attempt to reduce expenditures, Betty voluntarily turned her Chevrolet HHR back to the finance company while still owing $11,000 on the debt. A month later, she was notified that the vehicle had been sold at auction for $7800; the proceeds were reduced to only $7100, however, due to collection and selling costs of $500 and attorney fees of $200. Betty was billed for a deficiency balance of $3900 ($11,000 – $7100). She would have been much better off had she sold the vehicle herself, as vehicles at auction usually sell for much less than their book values.

Federal Law Regulates Debt Collection Practices

The federal **Fair Debt Collection Practices Act (FDCPA)** prohibits third-party debt collection agencies from using abusive, deceptive, and unfair practices in the legitimate effort to collect past-due debts. **Debt** (or **credit**) **collection agencies** are firms that specialize in making collections that could not be obtained by the original lender. In some cases, they assist the original lender (for a fee); in other cases, they take over (purchase) the debt and become the creditor. When a debtor offers to make payment for several debts, the FDCPA requires that the amount paid must be applied to whichever debts the debtor desires. Banks, dentists, lawyers, and others who conduct their own collections (second-party collectors) are exempt from the provisions of the FDCPA. Nevertheless, many states have enacted similar laws that govern these second-party collectors.

Collection agencies are prohibited from telephoning the debtor at unusual hours, making numerous repeated telephone calls during the day, not applying payments to amounts under dispute, using deceptive practices (such as falsely claiming that their representatives are attorneys or government officials), making threats, or using abusive

---

garnishment
Court-sanctioned procedure by which a portion of debtors' wages are set aside by their employers to pay debts.

repossession/foreclosure
Legal proceeding by which the lender seizes an asset.

deficiency balance
Occurs when money raised by the sale of repossessed collateral doesn't cover the amount owed on the debt plus any repossession expenses.

FINANCIAL POWER POINT

Old Debts May Never Die

It is not uncommon for a credit collector to contact someone who thought a debt was written off by a lender and demand repayment. Always insist on written evidence of the debt. Also find out if your state's statute of limitations has run out before paying anything. One dollar of repayment will start the clock ticking again, because if you make a partial payment you reaffirm the debt as valid.

Fair Debt Collection Practices Act (FDCPA)
Prohibits third-party debt collection agencies from using abusive, deceptive, or unfair practices to collect past-due debts.

debt collection agency
Firm that specializes in collecting debts that the original lender could not collect.

language. They also cannot telephone a debtor's employer. Even with these limitations, collection agencies can be irritatingly persistent when collecting past-due accounts. If the collection effort is not successful, as a last resort the creditor may take the debtor to court to seek a legal judgment against the debtor; this judgment may be collected by repossessing some of the debtor's property or garnishing wages.

Steps to Take to Get Out from Under Excessive Debt

Even the most well-meaning credit user can become overextended as a result of illness, unemployment, or divorce. What should you do if you realize that you are overly indebted?

1. **Determine your account balances and the payments required.** Find out exactly what it would take to pay off your balances today. This amount is not the same as the total of your remaining payments and probably includes penalties and late charges if you have been unable to keep up with your payments. Also ask your lenders to give you a monthly payment dollar amount needed to pay off the debts by the date previously agreed.

2. **Focus your budget on debt reduction.** Calculate the percentage of your budget necessary to make the payments on your debts, and then add 5 percent. Use this extra money to help pay your creditors by applying the extra money to the debt with the highest APR. The sacrifices required will pay off in the long run. Remember, paying off debts provides a higher "rate of return" than money in savings and investments, so "invest" your money in debt repayment first.

3. **Contact your creditors.** Try to work out a new payment plan with your creditors. Many lenders, including those that finance automobiles, may let you skip a payment. They want to see you solve your financial problems so you can avoid bankruptcy. Creditors are more likely to work with borrowers who come to them first rather than after collection efforts begin.

4. **Take on no new credit.** Return your credit cards to the issuer or lock them up so that you cannot use them. Disciplined action to reduce debt should show results in only a few months. If progress does not occur, seek professional help.

5. **Refinance.** Determine whether some loans can be refinanced to obtain a lower interest rate, especially mortgage loans. (See Chapter 9 for details.) Even if you refinance, keep making the same payment so you will pay the new loan off more quickly. Consumers who have difficulty making credit repayments may resort to a **debt-consolidation loan**, through which the debtor exchanges several smaller debts with varying due dates and interest rates for a single large loan. Obtaining a debt-consolidation loan might be appropriate for someone who has acquired too much debt, but you should avoid the temptation to use this strategy simply to lower your total monthly payments. However, it is a smart move to use debt consolidation to lower APRs on existing debt.

6. **Avoid bad help.** Many companies claim that they want to help people in debt. A **credit repair company** (also known as a **credit clinic**) is a firm that offers to help improve or fix a person's credit history for a fee. Experts say that none are reputable. Visit bbb.org for the reputation of any credit repair company you are considering. Credit repair companies cannot charge a fee until your debt is reduced, settled, or renegotiated.

   In reality, no company can remove or "fix" accurate but negative information in anyone's credit history. You can improve your future credit history by making on-time repayments. And you can correct errors in your credit bureau files on your own for free with little effort.

7. **Find good help.** You may be able to obtain free budget and credit advice from your employer, credit union, or labor union. Also, many banks and consumer finance companies offer advice to help financially distressed debtors, as do nonprofit **credit counseling agencies (CCAs)**. Such an agency can make arrangements with unsecured creditors to collect payments from overly indebted consumers to

debt-consolidation loan
A loan taken out to pay off several smaller debts.

credit repair company (credit clinic)
Firm that offers to help improve or fix a person's credit history for a (usually hefty) fee.

credit counseling agency (CCA)
Agency that can arrange payment schedules with unsecured creditors for overly indebted consumers and can provide individuals with credit counseling.

FINANCIAL POWER POINT

Debt Management Plans and Your Credit Score

Entering into a debt management plan will not lower your credit score. However, the credit score is not the only factor that lenders use when judging creditworthiness. Some lenders will look on a debt management plan unfavorably and deny credit or charge higher APRs for people who have been on a plan, compelling those people to search more extensively for good credit terms.

debt management plan (DMP)
Arrangement whereby the consumer provides one monthly payment (usually somewhat smaller than the total of previous credit payments) that is distributed to all creditors.

repay debts, and it can provide individuals with credit counseling, assistance with financial problems, educational materials on credit and budgeting, and a **debt management plan (DMP)**. A DMP is an arrangement whereby the consumer provides one monthly payment (usually somewhat smaller than the total of previous credit payments) that is distributed to all creditors. Creditor concessions, such as reduced interest rates, may also allow debtors to repay what they owe more quickly than would otherwise be possible. Credit counseling services are provided at a nominal cost on a face-to-face basis, online, or via the telephone. Seek an agency that is a not-for-profit agency that has 501(c)3 status from the IRS and that will do a full budget review for you. Make sure the agency is a member of the Association of Independent Consumer Credit Counseling Agencies ([800] 450-1794; www.aiccca.org) or the National Foundation for Credit Counseling ([800] 388-2227; www.nfcc.org). Contact the Better Business Bureau for a reputation report as well.

Bankruptcy as a Last Resort

bankruptcy
Constitutionally guaranteed right that permits people (and businesses) to ask a court to find them officially unable to meet their debts.

discharged debts
Debts (or portions thereof) that are excused as a result of a bankruptcy.

Chapter 13 of the Bankruptcy Act (wage earner or regular income plan)
Designed for individuals with regular incomes who might be able to pay off some or all of their debts given certain court protections.

When debts are so overbearing that life seems really bleak—a situation that may be aggravated by recent unemployment, illness, disability, death in the family, divorce, or small-business failure—many people consider filing a petition in federal court to declare bankruptcy. **Bankruptcy** is a constitutionally guaranteed right that permits people (and businesses) to ask a court to find them officially unable to meet their debts. Federal laws allow bankruptcy for consumers in two forms: Chapter 13 and Chapter 7. Under each, the court will designate some debts as **discharged debts** that are excused. Some debts are never excused through bankruptcy. These include education loans that have come due within the previous seven years, fines, alimony, child support, income taxes for the most recent three years, and debts for causing injury while driving under the influence of alcohol or drugs. Bankruptcy is not a do-it-yourself project. Use a lawyer who specializes in consumer bankruptcies.

Before you can file for bankruptcy under either Chapter 7 or Chapter 13, you must complete credit counseling with an agency approved by the United States Bankruptcy Trustee's office. The purpose of this counseling is to give you an idea of whether you really need to file for bankruptcy or whether an informal repayment plan would get you back on your economic feet. Once your bankruptcy case is over, you'll have to attend another counseling session, this time to learn personal financial management. Only after you submit proof to the court that you have fulfilled this requirement can you get a bankruptcy discharge wiping out your debts.

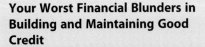

DID YOU KNOW?

Your Worst Financial Blunders in Building and Maintaining Good Credit

Based on others' financial woes, you will make mistakes in personal finance when you:

1. *Fail to regularly check the accuracy of your credit bureau files.*

2. *Let a lender's willingness to grant credit be an indicator that you can afford to repay the debt.*

3. *Pay more than 14 percent of your disposable income toward nonmortgage debt payments.*

Chapter 13—Regular Income Plan Chapter 13 of the Bankruptcy Act (also known as the **wage earner** or the **regular income plan**) is designed for individuals with regular incomes who might be able to pay off some or all of their debts given certain protections of the court. Under this plan, the debtor submits a debt repayment plan to the court that is designed to repay as much of the debt as possible, typically in three to five years. After the debtor files a petition for bankruptcy, the court issues an **automatic stay**—a court order that temporarily prevents all creditors from recovering claims arising from before the start of the bankruptcy proceeding. This action protects the debtor from collection efforts by creditors, including garnishments. Typically, no assets may be sold by the debtor or repossessed by the lender after a stay is granted.

After the court notifies all creditors of the petition for bankruptcy, a hearing is scheduled. With the help of a **bankruptcy trustee** (an agent of the bankruptcy court), who verifies the accuracy of a bankruptcy petition at a hearing and who distributes the assets according to a court-approved plan, the proposed repayment plan is reviewed (and modified, if necessary) and finally approved by the court. The debtor must then follow a strict budget while repaying the obligations. During this time, the bankrupt person cannot obtain any new credit without the permission of the trustee.

DID YOU KNOW?

How Long You Should Wait Before Declaring Bankruptcy

The thought of declaring bankruptcy is so onerous that many people wait too long to seek its protection. Both Chapter 7 and 13 bankruptcies allow debtors to keep a portion of their assets. For example, 401(k) retirement accounts are protected from creditors in bankruptcy. If a debtor begins taking money out of a retirement plan when faced with mounting debt and ultimately must declare bankruptcy, the debtor would have used up an asset that could have been 100% protected had he or she filed sooner. If the only way you can pay your debts is to tap your retirement plan, you should consult a lawyer about whether the time already has come to seek bankruptcy protection.

If the debtor makes all scheduled payments, he or she is discharged of any remaining amounts due that could not be repaid within the repayment period.

Chapter 7—Immediate Liquidation Plan Chapter 7 of the Bankruptcy Act, also called **straight bankruptcy**, provides for an immediate liquidation of assets. This option is permitted when it would be highly unlikely that substantial repayment could ever be made. Petitioners seeking to file Chapter 7 must pass a "means" test. Those who fail this test because their income is too high must file Chapter 13 instead.

When Chapter 7 is allowed, most of the bankrupt person's assets are given over to the bankruptcy trustee. Any assets that serve as collateral for loans are turned over to the appropriate secured creditors. Most of the remaining assets are sold, and the proceeds of the sales are distributed to the unsecured creditors of the bankrupt person. A debtor may choose to sign a reaffirmation agreement and become legally obligated again to pay all or a portion of a debt that would have been discharged in the bankruptcy case, such as for a vehicle. Any leftover debt is usually discharged by the court when the debtor emerges from bankruptcy. State and federal laws govern what assets the debtor can keep. In general, bankrupt people are allowed to keep a small amount of equity in their homes, an inexpensive automobile, and limited personal property.

Bankruptcy should be used as a last resort rather than as a quick fix or cure-all for overuse of credit. Bankruptcy remains on one's credit record for ten years. Because employers, landlords, and creditors check credit reports, people who have declared bankruptcy typically face years of trouble when renting housing, obtaining home loans, and getting credit cards. Discharged debtors usually emerge with little, if any, debt and a much improved net worth and a poor credit score. They also cannot use Chapter 7 bankruptcy again for at least six years. Therefore, some creditors will lend to such individuals, but at much higher interest rates than usual.

Chapter 7 of the Bankruptcy Act (straight bankruptcy)
Provides for the liquidation of assets with proceeds applied to paying off excusable debts to the degree possible.

DO IT NOW!

You know more about personal finance after reading this chapter, so get started right now by:

1. *Obtaining a free copy of your credit report (www.annualcreditreport.com) from one of the three national credit bureaus.*

2. *Confirming the accuracy of the report and, if there are errors or omissions, challenging them with all three bureaus.*

3. *Repeating steps two and three every four months, staggering the bureaus to ensure that each request is free.*

 Concept Check 6.5

1. Identify four signs of overindebtedness.

2. List the major provisions of the Fair Debt Collection Practices Act.

3. What services are provided by a credit counseling agency and how might a debt management plan work to provide relief for someone who is having debt problems?

4. Distinguish between Chapter 7 and Chapter 13 bankruptcy and explain who might be forced to use Chapter 13 rather than Chapter 7.

WHAT DO YOU RECOMMEND NOW?

Now that you have read this chapter on building and maintaining good credit, what would you recommend to Carrie Savarin regarding:

1. Factors she should consider regarding her ability to take on additional debt?

2. The impact of her current debt on her ability to obtain a loan to buy a vehicle?

3. Where she might obtain financing for a vehicle loan?

4. The effect of taking on a loan on her overall financial planning?

BIG PICTURE SUMMARY OF LEARNING OBJECTIVES

LO1. **Explain reasons for and against using credit.**
People borrow for a variety of reasons—for example, to deal with financial emergencies, to have goods immediately, and to obtain discounts in the future. Perhaps the greatest disadvantage of using credit is the ensuing loss of financial flexibility in personal money management. The annual percentage rate (APR) provides the best approximation of the true cost of credit.

LO2. **Establish your own debt limit.**
It is important to establish your own debt limit. Three methods can be used: the debt payments-to-disposable income method, the ratio of debt-to-equity method, and the continuous-debt method.

LO3. **Achieve a good credit reputation.**
In the process of opening a credit account, the lender investigates your credit history, obtains a credit score (such as a FICO score) from a credit bureau, and then determines whether to grant credit and under what conditions.

LO4. **Describe the common sources of consumer credit.**
Major sources of consumer loans include depository institutions (commercial banks, savings and loan associations, and credit unions), sales finance companies, and consumer finance companies. Loans are also available through insurance companies and stockbrokers. Depository institutions typically offer the best interest rates, although sales finance companies sometimes offer low rates to increase sales of the products being financed. In any case, only those people with high credit scores qualify for the best rates from any source.

LO5. **Identify signs of overindebtedness and describe the options that are available for debt relief.**
Among the signals of being overly indebted are exceeding credit-limit guidelines and running out of money too often. People experiencing serious financial difficulties can obtain professional assistance through nonprofit credit counseling agencies or by contacting an attorney about bankruptcy.

LET'S TALK ABOUT IT

1. **Good Versus Bad Debt.** If there is such a thing as good debt, what types of debt do you consider to be "good"? What types do you consider to be "bad"?

2. **Your Creditworthiness.** What aspects of your financial life make you creditworthy? What aspects would make it difficult for you to obtain credit?

3. **Assessing Your Debt Load.** How might students judge whether they are taking on too high a level of student loan debt?

4. **Where Could I Borrow for a Vehicle?** If you wanted to borrow money to buy a new or used car, where would you turn? Why?

5. **Your Privacy.** Are you concerned that the major national credit bureaus may have files containing information about you? What do you think about the process required to correct errors in those files?

6. **Easy Credit.** Is it too easy for college students to get credit cards? Do you know anyone who has gotten into financial difficulty because of overuse of credit cards?

7. **Feelings About Bankruptcy.** How do you feel about bankruptcy? When might bankruptcy be justified in your opinion? When might it not be justified?

DO THE MATH

1. **Taking Out a Motorcycle Loan.** Martin Jones is single and recently graduated from law school. He earns $9000 per month, an awesome salary for someone only 26 years old. However, he has $1400 withheld for federal income tax, $540 for state income taxes, $686 for Social Security taxes, and $230 for health insurance every month. He has outstanding student loans of almost $80,000 on which he pays about $900 per month and a 0% auto loan payment of $300 on a Chevrolet Cobalt he purchased new during law school. He is considering taking out a loan to buy a BMW motorcycle.

   (a) What is Martin's debt payments-to-disposable income ratio?

   (b) Based on your answer to (a), how would you advise Martin about his plan?

2. **Buying a Vacation Home.** Carmen and Juan Montoya have just finished putting their three daughters through college. As empty-nesters, they are considering purchasing a vacation home on a nearby lake because prices have dropped in recent years. The house might also serve as a retirement home once they retire in 12 years. The Montoyas' net worth is $283,000 including their home worth about $265,000 on which they currently owe $143,000 for their first mortgage. Their outstanding debts in addition to their mortgage include

$12,500 on one car loan, $13,700 on a second car loan, and a $25,500 second mortgage on their home taken out to help pay for college expenses.

   (a) Calculate the Montoyas' debt-to-equity ratio.

   (b) Advise them as to the wisdom of borrowing for a vacation home at this time.

3. **A Recent Graduate's Debt Status.** Karla Menken recently graduated with a degree in food science and now works for a major consumer foods company earning $43,000 per year with about $36,000 in take-home pay. She rents an apartment for $1040 per month. While in school, she accumulated about $38,000 in student loan debt on which she pays $385 per month. During her last fall semester in school, she had an internship in a city about 100 miles from her campus. She used her credit card for her extra expenses and has a current debt on the account of $8000. She has been making the minimum payment on the account of about $320. She has assets of $14,000.

   (a) Calculate her debt payment-to-disposable income ratio.

   (b) Calculate her debt-to-equity ratio.

   (c) Comment on Karla's debt situation and her use of student loans and credit cards while in college.

FINANCIAL PLANNING CASES

CASE 1

The Johnsons Attempt to Resolve Their Credit and Cash-Flow Problems

Harry and Belinda have a substantial annual joint income—more than $95,000, in fact. Nevertheless, they expect to experience some cash-flow deficits during several months of the upcoming year (see Tables 3-6 and 3-7 on pages 88–89).

To resolve this difficulty, the couple is considering opening a credit card account and using it exclusively for those expenditures that will cause the deficits they face. They could also open a line of credit that would allow them to borrow money by simply going online and having money placed in their checking account.

   (a) What are the advantages and disadvantages of the Johnsons opening these accounts?

   (b) What financial calculations should Harry and Belinda undertake to see whether they could afford to borrow more money at this time?

(c) What might Harry and Belinda do before applying for credit to ensure that they will pay the lowest interest rate possible?

CASE 2

Victor and Maria Advise Their Niece

Victor and Maria have always enjoyed a close relationship with Maria's niece Teresa, who graduated from college with a pharmacy degree. Teresa recently asked Maria for some assistance with her finances now that her education debts are coming due. She owes $19,000 in student loans and earns $44,000 per year in disposable income. Teresa would like to take on additional debt to furnish her apartment and buy a better car.

(a) What advice might Maria give Teresa about managing her student loan debt?

(b) If next year Teresa were to consolidate her loans into one loan at 8 percent interest, what advice might Maria give regarding Teresa's overall debt limit using both the debt payments-to-disposable income method and the continuous-debt method? (Hint: Use Table 6-3 on page 184 or visit the *Garman/Forgue* companion website to calculate monthly payments for various time periods.)

CASE 3

Julia Price Thinks About a Loan to Buy a Ski Boat

Julia has been thinking about the purchase of a boat. As a teenager, she was an avid water skier at her parents' summer home. Now that she has moved away, she wants to renew her hobby at a lake nearby. Julia recently received a raise of $200 per month and plans to visit a dealership nearby to see what kind of boat she can buy with that level of payment. Based on the information in this chapter, including Table 6-3, offer your opinions about her thinking.

CASE 4

Reducing Expenses to Buy a New Car

Courtney Bennett recently graduated from college and accepted a position in Manhattan, Kansas, as an assistant librarian in the public library. Courtney has no debts, and her budget is shown in the first column of Table 6-2. She now faces the question of whether to trade in her old car for a new one requiring a monthly payment of $330. Taking the role of a good friend of Courtney, suggest how Courtney might cut back on her expenses so that she can afford the vehicle.

(a) What areas might be cut back?

(b) How much in each area might be cut back?

(c) After finishing your analysis, what advice (and possibly alternatives) would you offer Courtney about buying the new car?

CASE 5

Preparation of a Credit-Related Speech

Jacob Marchese of Auburn, Alabama, is the credit manager for a regional chain of department stores. He has been asked to join a panel of community members and make a ten-minute speech to graduating high-school seniors on the topic "Using Credit Wisely." In the following outline that Jacob has prepared, provide him with some suggested comments.

(a) What is consumer credit?

(b) Why might graduates use credit?

(c) How can graduates use credit wisely?

CASE 6

Debt Consolidation as a Debt Reduction Strategy

Justin Granovsky, an assistant manager at a small retail shop in Detroit, Michigan, had an unusual amount of debt. He owed $5400 to one bank, $1800 to a clothing store, $2700 to his credit union, and several hundred dollars to other stores and individuals. Justin was paying more than $460 per month on the three major obligations to pay them off when due in two years. He realized that his take-home pay of slightly more than $2100 per month did not leave him with much excess cash. Justin discussed an alternative way of handling his major payments with his bank's loan officer. The officer suggested that he pool all of his debts and take out an $11,000 debt-consolidation loan for seven years at 14 percent. As a result, he would pay only $206 per month for all his debts. Justin seemed ecstatic over the idea.

(a) Is Justin's enthusiasm over the idea of a debt-consolidation loan justified? Why or why not?

(b) Why can the bank offer such a "good deal" to Justin?

(c) What compromise would Justin make to remit payments of only $206 as compared with $460?

(d) If you assume that the debt-consolidation loan will cost more in total interest, what would be a justification for this added cost?

BE YOUR OWN PERSONAL FINANCIAL MANAGER

1. **Your Credit Report.** Visit the website for obtaining a free credit report at www.annualcreditreport.com to order a copy of your credit report. Check the accuracy of the report and follow the directions provided to correct any errors. If no report is available on you, it should be because you have never used credit. If you have used credit and there is no report, you should notify the credit bureaus of this error.

2. **Set Your Debt Limit.** Based on your personal balance sheet and cash-flow statement, calculate your debt payments-to-disposable income and debt-to-equity ratios. Do you feel that you are overly indebted by these measures? Also consider the continuous-debt method in your considerations. Use Worksheet 25: The Effect of Taking on Additional Debt on My Financial Ratios from "My Personal Financial Planner" to determine if you could take on any debt at this time.

3. **List Your Outstanding Installment Loans.** Make an inventory of your installment loans including each loan's purpose, to whom the debt was owed, payoff date, monthly payment, and monthly due date using Worksheet 26: My Installment Loan Inventory from "My Personal Financial Planner."

4. **Protect Your Privacy.** A lost or stolen debit or credit card can cost you money and time. Using your credit report and other information from various billing statements, compile a list of all your debit and credit accounts including the telephone number and address of where to send notification if the card is lost or stolen.

5. **List Your Student Loans.** Make an inventory of your student loans including source, amounts currently owed, current APR, when payments must begin, approximate monthly payment, and the maximum number of years you will have to repay the loan using Worksheet 27: My Student Loan Inventory from "My Personal Financial Planner."

ON THE 'NET

Go to the Web pages indicated to complete these exercises.

1. Visit the website for the Federal Reserve Board at www.federalreserve.gov/consumerinfo/default.htm. Locate its online copy of the *Consumer Handbook on Credit Protection Laws.* Identify one additional protection not discussed in this book that is provided by each of the following laws: the Fair Credit Billing Act, the Equal Credit Opportunity Act, and the Fair Credit Reporting Act.

2. Visit the website for Fair Isaac Corporation at www.myfico.com/CreditEducation/. Read up on how credit scoring works. Identify three actions you could take to improve your credit score.

3. Visit the website for Experian at http://www.experian.com/consumer-products/vantage-score.html. Read about how the Vantage Score differs from other credit scores. Also determine the relative importance of various credit history items.

ACTION INVOLVEMENT PROJECTS

1. **Understanding Credit Applications.** Drop by a local bank or credit union and ask for an application for a credit card. Read through the items of information that are requested in the application. Why do you think that the lender asks for the information requested? Do you think the lender would view the information that you would provide positively?

2. **Good Uses of Credit.** Survey five of your friends about their perceptions of when it is appropriate to use credit. Compare their views to your own.

3. **The Downside of Credit.** Survey five of your friends about their three most negative aspects of using credit. Compare their three aspects to your own three negative aspects and those listed in this chapter.

4. **Perceptions of Bankruptcy.** Survey five of your friends about their feelings about and understanding of bankruptcy. Do their feelings conflict with yours? Is their understanding of bankruptcy accurate?

Visit the Garman/Forgue companion website at **www.cengagebrain.com**.

YOU MUST BE KIDDING, RIGHT?

College students who have a credit card in their own name (and most do) have an average debt of about $4000 at graduation. If they maintain that level of debt for ten years, how much total interest will they pay over that decade?

A. $4800

B. $6000

C. $7200

D. $8400

The answer is C. A credit card with an 18 percent APR (typical for college students) translates to a 1.5 percent rate per month (18% ÷ 12). The $4000 debt multiplied by this rate equals $60 ($4000 × 0.015) per month in interest. And $60 multiplied by 120 months equals $7200. You must pay more than the required minimum monthly amount plus any new charges in order to reduce a credit card debt. Otherwise you will pay many thousands of dollars in interest and be in debt for years and years!

LEARNING OBJECTIVES

After reading this chapter, you should be able to:

❶ Compare the common types of consumer credit, including credit cards and installment loans.

❷ Describe the types and features of credit card accounts.

❸ Manage your credit card accounts to avoid fees and finance charges.

❹ Describe the important features of consumer installment loans.

❺ Calculate the interest and annual percentage rate on consumer loans.

WHAT DO YOU RECOMMEND?

Darrell Cochrane, a 31-year-old optician in St. Augustine, Florida, made $42,000 last year. Darrell avoided using credit and credit cards until he was 28 years old, when he missed three months of work due to a water-skiing accident. He made ends meet by obtaining two bank credit cards that, because of his lack of a credit history, carry 19.6 and 24 percent annual percentage rates (APRs). Darrell now has 11 credit card accounts open: five bank cards and six retail store cards. He uses them regularly, presenting whatever card a store will honor. He owes $13,000 on the 24 percent APR card and $4400 on the 19.6 percent APR card. His other three bank cards carry APRs of 11 percent, 12 percent, and 15 percent, and he owes $500 to $700 on each one. For the past year, Darrell has been making only the minimum payments on his bank cards. His retail cards all carry APRs in excess of 21 percent. Although he has managed to keep from running a balance on those cards during most months, occasionally these accounts have balances as well.

© Michael Newman/Photo Edit

What would you recommend to Darrell on the subject of credit cards and consumer loans regarding:

1. His approach to using credit cards, including the number of cards he has?

2. Estimating the credit card interest charges he is paying each month?

3. How he might lower his interest expense each month?

4. Consolidating his credit card debts into one installment loan?

YOUR NEXT 5 YEARS

In the next five years, you can start achieving financial success by doing the following related to credit cards and consumer loans:

1. *Pay all your credit card balances in full each month, or no longer than two or three months later.*

2. *Move credit card balances you do carry to lower-interest accounts and never make convenience purchases on the accounts on which you carry a balance.*

3. *Check your monthly billing statements against your receipts for accuracy every month and challenge all discrepancies.*

4. *Use student loans for direct education expenses only rather than to maintain a better lifestyle.*

5. *Choose installment loans based on the lowest annual percentage rate (APR) rather than monthly payment and years to repay.*

LEARNING OBJECTIVE

Compare the common types of consumer credit, including credit cards and installment loans.

installment credit (closed-end credit)
Credit arrangement in which the borrower must repay the amount owed plus interest in a specific number of equal payments.

open-ended (revolving) credit
Arrangement in which credit is extended in advance of any transaction so that borrowers do not need to reapply each time they need to use credit.

credit limit
Maximum outstanding debt that a lender will allow on an open-ended credit account.

You cannot borrow your way to financial success. For proof ask some of the millions of Americans who have been unable to pay their credit card bills or had their homes foreclosed because of the sluggish U.S. economy and job losses. Using any kind of credit requires deliberate thinking and planning. You need to first consider whether the reason you are borrowing is sound and then decide in advance how you will repay the debt. This is especially true for credit cards. Credit card usage can be managed so that you pay no interest at all. But this can occur only if you pay your balance in full every month. Planning how to repay an installment loan is also important because you commit to making a series of monthly payments for one to seven or more years. Smart borrowers understand the mathematics behind the calculation of the finance charges on these installment loans. Smart borrowers always focus on the **annual percentage rate (APR)** when comparing among various sources of credit. The APR is the cost of credit on a yearly basis stated as a percentage rate.

TYPES OF CONSUMER CREDIT

Consumer credit is nonbusiness debt used by consumers for expenditures other than home mortgages. (Borrowing for housing has investment aspects that result in a separate classification as discussed in Chapter 9.)

There are two types of consumer credit: installment credit and noninstallment credit.

- With **installment credit** (also called **closed-end credit**), the borrower must repay the amount owed plus interest in a specific number of equal payments, usually monthly. For example, an $18,000 automobile loan might require monthly payments of $356 for 60 months at 7 percent interest.

- **Noninstallment credit** includes single-payment, open-ended credit, and service credit. **Single-payment loans** are the easiest of the three to understand. As an example, a borrower might take out a loan of $2000 at 12 percent interest for one year. If so, a single payment of $2240 ($2000 + $240 interest; $2000 × 0.12) would be due at the end of one year.

With **open-ended credit** (also called **revolving credit**), credit is extended in advance of any transaction so that the borrower does not need to reapply each time credit is desired. Credit cards are an example of open-ended credit. Any amounts owed will be repaid in full in a single payment or via a series of equal or unequal payments, usually made monthly. The borrower can use the account as long as the total owed does not exceed his or her **credit limit**. This credit limit is set by the lender and is the maximum outstanding debt allowed on the credit account. Credit limits vary with the perceived creditworthiness of the borrower.

Open-ended credit can be used to make purchases and, in some cases, to obtain cash advances. It is the most convenient type of credit, and it is also the most abused. Many open-ended accounts—but not all—use a credit card. A **credit** (or **charge**) **card** is a plastic card identifying the holder as a participant in the charge account plan of a lender, such as a retailer or financial institution.

Cash advances may be obtained at any financial institution that issues the type of card (Visa, MasterCard, Discover, and so on) being used. A cash advance is a cash loan from a credit card account. In most cases, the borrower receives cash, such as from an ATM. Alternatively, the funds may be transferred electronically into the cardholder's checking account.

A **personal line of credit** is a form of open-ended credit that allows the borrower access to a prearranged revolving line of credit provided by the lender (usually a commercial bank, savings bank, credit union, or brokerage firm). The essence of a line of credit is that borrowers can obtain a cash advance when needed and not have to reapply for a loan each time they need money. Like credit card accounts, a personal line of credit includes a credit limit and a flexible repayment schedule. Some people also use the equity in their home as collateral for a line of credit. This arrangement is referred to as a **home-equity line of credit**.

   Service credit is granted to consumers by public utilities, physicians, dentists, and other service providers that do not require full payment when services are rendered. For example, your electric company allows you to use electricity all month and then sends you a bill that may not be due for 10 to 15 days. Service credit usually carries no interest, although penalty charges and interest may apply if payments are made late. Service may eventually be cut off for continued slow payment or nonpayment of the debt.

 Concept Check 7.1

1. Distinguish between installment credit and open-ended credit.

2. Explain the basic features of revolving credit.

3. Describe how someone might use a personal line of credit.

CREDIT CARD ACCOUNTS PROVIDE INSTANT ACCESS TO CREDIT

Once a credit card account is opened, it can be used at any time. Credit card accounts allow the borrower to pay the balance in full at any time or carry over a balance owed from month to month (travel and entertainment cards are an exception). If a balance is carried over, a **minimum payment** must be made each month to cover interest and a small payment on the amount owed (the **principal**). If at least the minimum payment amount is not received by the **due date** (the specific day by which the credit card company should receive payment from you), the cardholder must pay a **late payment fee** and may be declared in **default**. Default occurs when a borrower has failed to make a payment of principal or interest when due or failed to meet any other requirement of a credit agreement.

   About two-thirds of American adults have a credit card account, and just over one-half pay their balances in full in any given month. Those who maintain balances can do so for years, even as other charges are added to the same account. As long as the total debt remains below the credit limit, the user may continue to make charges against the account. When desired, a borrower may ask a creditor to increase his or her credit limit.

 LEARNING OBJECTIVE **2**

Describe the types and features of credit card accounts.

minimum payment
Payment that must be made to a credit account each month to cover interest and a portion of the amount owed.

principal
Total amount owed on a credit account not including interest.

Types of Credit Card Accounts

Credit card accounts include bank credit cards, retail credit cards, and travel and entertainment accounts (such as American Express's familiar "green card").

Bank Credit Cards A **bank credit card account** is an open-ended credit account at a financial institution allowing the holder to make purchases on credit almost anywhere. Visa, MasterCard, Discover, and Optima are the most commonly recognized bank card names. However, the actual lender is the bank, savings bank, or credit union through which the card is offered. Visa, MasterCard, and the like are simply service providers that maintain the electronic network through which transactions are communicated. Participating merchants pay transaction fees (typically 1¼ to 5 percent) to these companies based on the dollar amounts charged. Virtually all financial institutions offer bank credit cards, as do a number of consumer products companies, such as AT&T, Allstate Insurance, and Verizon. These companies contract with Visa, MasterCard, and a bank to offer these **cobranded credit cards**.

   Many bank credit card issuers periodically send **cash advance** (or **convenience**) **checks** to their cardholders. Of course, these instruments are not genuine checks but simply a check-equivalent way to take a cash advance. Customers can use these "checks" to make payments to others or themselves. If such a payment is used to make a payment

bank credit card account
Open-ended credit account with a financial institution that allows the holder to make purchases almost anywhere.

cash advance (or convenience) checks
A check-equivalent way to take a cash advance on a credit card.

FINANCIAL POWER POINT

Cash Advances Are Very Expensive

Obtaining money via a credit card cash advance may seem easy. It is also very expensive. First, there is a transaction fee. It is usually a percentage of the amount taken (3 to 5 percent is common), but there is often a minimum amount that makes the percentage much higher on small advances. Then there is the interest that begins to accrue immediately even if you are not carrying a balance on the card. Plus, the interest rate on cash advances is often higher than for purchases.

balance transfer
Full or partial payment on the balance of one credit card using a cash advance from another.

retail credit cards
Allow customers to make purchases on credit at any of the outlets of a particular retailer.

DID YOU KNOW?

There Will Soon Be a Computer in Your Card

Credit card issuers are rolling out technology that will give your credit card computing power. These cards have small chips embedded in the plastic, giving you more options when you use your card. For example, you may be able to choose whether the transaction will be charged directly to your checking account like a debit card or to your credit card. These new cards may be used overseas without problems, in contrast to today's credit cards. An added benefit of these cards is enhanced identity theft protections as they are much harder to use by someone other than the genuine account holder.

on another credit card, it represents a **balance transfer**. Cash advances and balance transfers are extremely lucrative for lenders. They can require an initial up-front fee based upon the amount borrowed. Then the interest clock starts ticking on the date of the loan at rates that are typically higher than for regular uses of the card, such as making purchases. If you receive convenience checks but do not want to use them, either put them in a safe place or destroy them immediately because they easily could be used fraudulently by someone else.

Some bank credit cards are a form of **prestige card**, often with a precious metal in the brand name such as "gold," "silver," or "platinum." These accounts require that the user possess higher credit qualifications and offer enhancements such as free traveler's checks and higher credit limits. Prestige cards may carry higher annual fees.

Some Visa and MasterCard credit cards are identified as **affinity cards**— that is, standard bank cards with the logo of a sponsoring organization imprinted on the face of the card. The issuing financial institution often donates a portion of the annual fee and a small percentage of the amounts charged (perhaps 0.25, 0.5, or 1 percent) to the sponsoring organization. Sponsors may include charitable, political, sports, or other organized groups, such as the Sierra Club or Mothers Against Drunk Driving. Supporters of the sponsoring organization may be motivated to use an affinity card because the organization receives money from each transaction. Creditors rightly calculate that fewer delinquencies will occur among the particular group of people, so they can afford to transfer some dollars to the named organization.

Retail Credit Card Accounts A **retail credit card** allows a customer to make purchases on credit at any of the outlets of a particular retailer or retail chain. Examples of credit card accounts at retail stores include those offered by JCPenney, Best Buy, and Shell Oil. Many retailers have alliances with a financial institution to offer a bank credit card that carries the retailer's logo and can also be used anywhere the bank credit card can be used.

Some smaller retail establishments offer open-ended accounts that do not use a credit card as the vehicle for using the account. With these retail charge accounts, customers simply ask to have the purchase put on their account for repayment at a later date. Repayment may be required in full monthly or allowed to be spread over time.

Travel and Entertainment Cards Travel and entertainment (T&E) cards are similar to bank credit cards in that they allow holders to make purchases at numerous businesses. The entire balance charged must be repaid within 30 days, however. The best-known T&E cards are those issued by American Express and Diners Club International. Such cards are often used by businesspeople for food and lodging expenses while traveling. They are somewhat more difficult to obtain than bank cards because applicants must have higher-than-average incomes to qualify for an account; in addition, applicants must pay an annual membership fee of $150 or more. T&E cards are not accepted at nearly as many outlets as are bank credit cards.

Common (But Not Always Beneficial) Aspects of Credit Card Accounts

Federal law requires credit card lenders to disclose all the rules governing the account to borrowers before they sign up for any card. Some of that information must be displayed in a uniform manner, as illustrated in the sample credit card disclosure box in Figure 7-1 The remainder of the information appears in the credit agreement (contract). Credit card issuers are free to change some of the rules on an account at any time as long as they notify the account holder of the change at least 45 days in advance. This notification is usually included as an insert in the monthly bill for the account. You can avoid any penalties imposed by the new rules by paying off the account or by closing it. If you cannot pay the bill in full, you will be

DID YOU KNOW?

How to Close a Credit Card Account Correctly

Credit card accounts are open-ended credit and, therefore, can remain open for decades even if you never use the card or stop using it at some point. Accounts are not closed if you cut up the cards. The lender must be formally notified of your request before the account will be officially closed. Here's what to do:

1. *Pay off your balance in full.* Accounts cannot be truly closed until they are paid off. You can, however, ask an issuer to stop honoring a card.

2. *Obtain the customer service telephone number* for the lender from your most recent monthly statement. If you do not have a recent bill, obtain a copy of your credit report, which will list the contact information for the lender.

3. *Contact the lender* to request the address to which you should send your cancellation request. It will not be the same address to which you send your monthly payment. Confirm that there is no longer a balance owed as some-

times a very small amount of interest may still be owed for the last month when an account is paid off.

4. *Send a written request* to close the account and request that the creditor send a confirmation that the account is, indeed, closed.

5. *Obtain a copy of your credit report*, after 90 days, from one of the three national credit bureaus (pay if necessary). If the account shows as closed, obtain free copies from the other two bureaus as confirmation at the next opportunity. If the account shows as still open at the first bureau, ask for a reinvestigation and also obtain copies from the other two bureaus to ensure the account shows as closed appropriately.

Note that you cannot close an account on which you currently owe a balance. You can, however, ask the lender to no longer honor the card. Many people think that closing a credit card account will help their credit score. Generally this is not true as it raises the ratio between the amount of credit card debt you can carry and the amount you do carry.

---

obligated to adhere to the new rules until you close the account. This section outlines some of the more important aspects of credit card accounts.

Some Credit Card Offers Come Preapproved Companies interested in expanding their base of credit customers sometimes pay credit bureaus to prescreen their files and identify people who pass certain tests of creditworthiness. A company may then send applications for credit to the prescreened people. Some consumers will have been preapproved as part of this process, so they merely need to sign the notice to open the account. It is important to understand that being preapproved means only that you will be granted credit. Both the credit card debt limit and APR will be determined after you apply for an account.

Annual and Transaction Fees Can Be Avoided Some bank credit card lenders assess **annual fees** ranging from $25 to $75 (or more). In addition, lenders may charge a **transaction fee** (a small charge levied each time a card is used). The card illustrated in Figure 7-1 assesses transaction fees for cash advances and balance transfers. Some lenders even charge a fee for printing the monthly credit bill. Most fees are not required to be included in the APR calculation because they cannot be known in advance. As you can see, an apparently low-rate card may turn into a high-cost card when all fees are considered.

annual fees
Charges levied against cardholders for the privilege of having an open account but that are not included in the advertised APR.

transaction fee
Charge levied against cardholders per use of the card that is not included in the APR advertised.

Liability for Lost or Stolen Cards Is Limited The Truth in Lending Act limits a cardholder's **credit card liability** for lost or stolen credit cards. Under the law, if you notify the card issuer within two days of a loss or theft, you are not legally responsible for any fraudulent usage of the card. After two days, your maximum liability for fraudulent usage of the card (including telephone calling cards) prior to your notification is $50. You are not responsible for any fraudulent usage after you notify the issuer of the loss. Although your financial liability is low, many companies nevertheless specialize in selling credit card insurance (for an annual premium ranging from $15 to $49) that will pay creditors for the first $50 of unauthorized use of an insured person's lost or stolen credit cards. Such insurance is profitable for the sellers but an unnecessary expense for you. If you are insistent and perhaps talk with a credit card company supervisor, most will waive the

FINANCIAL POWER POINT

Opt Out to Avoid Unwanted Credit Card Offers

Federal law states that consumers have the right to opt out of receiving unsolicited credit card offers. To put a stop to the mailings using the official system, dial (888) 5-OPT-OUT or visit www.optoutprescreen.com.

Figure 7-1

Sample Credit Card Disclosure Box

Federal law requires that key pieces of information be disclosed in direct-mail advertising and when applying for credit cards and any time the rules of an account are changed. An example of this required disclosure is provided here. To search for the best offers on credit cards, you can visit www.bankrate.com or www.cardtrack.com.

Interest Rates and Interest Charges	
Annual Percentage Rate (APR) for Purchases	**2.9%** introductory APR for first 6 months.
	After that, your APR will be **19.2%**. This APR will vary with the market based on the Prime Rate.
APR for Balance Transfers	**0%** introductory APR on balance transfers requested within 6 billing cycles of account opening.
	After that, your APR will be **19.2%**. This APR will vary with the market based on the Prime Rate.
APR for Cash Advances	**21.99%**
	This APR will vary with the market based on the Prime Rate.
Penalty APR and When It Applies	Up to **27.99%**, based on your credit worthiness.
	This APR may be applied to your account if you:
	1. Make a late payment;
	2. Go over your credit limit;
	3. Make a payment that is returned; or
	4. Do any of the above on another account you have with us.
	This APR will vary with the market based on the Prime Rate.
	How Long Will the Penalty APR Apply? If your APRs are increased for any of these reasons, the Penalty APR will no longer apply to existing balances if you make the next six consecutive payments when due. The Penalty APR will apply to other balances indefinitely.
How to Avoid Paying Interest on Purchases	Your due date is at least 23 days after the close of each billing cycle. We will not charge you interest on purchases if you pay your entire balance by the due date each month.
Minimum Interest Charge	If you are charged interest, the charge will be no less than $2.00.
For Credit Card Tips from the Federal Reserve Board	To learn more about factors to consider when applying for or using a credit card, visit the website of the Federal Reserve Board at http://www.federalreserve.gov/creditcard.
Fees	
Annual Fee	$0
Transaction Fee: • Balance Transfer	Either **$10** or **4%** of the amount of each transfer, whichever is greater. (During the first six billing cycles after account opening, either **$10** or **3%** of the amount of each transfer, whichever is greater.)
• Cash Advance	Either **$10** or **4%** of the amount of each cash advance, whichever is greater.
• Foreign Transaction	**3%** of each transaction in U.S. dollars.
Penalty Fees • Late Payment	$25
• Over the Credit Line	**The amount charged in excess of the limit or $25; whichever is less.**
• Returned Payment	$25

How We Will Calculate Your Balance: We use a method called "average daily balance (including new purchases)."

Loss of Introductory APR: We may end your Introductory APR and apply the Penalty APR if you make a late payment.

Variable APRs for each billing period are based on the Prime Rate published in *The Wall Street Journal* 2 days before the Closing Date of the billing period. If the Prime Rate increases, variable APRs will increase. In that case, you may pay more interest and have a higher Minimum Payment Due.

$50 fee for unauthorized use as a gesture of goodwill to keep you as a good customer. You also should realize that most homeowner's and renter's insurance policies will pay the $50 fee you might be charged for unauthorized use of a lost or stolen credit card.

DID YOU KNOW?

Credit Card Rules Can Change at Any Time

When you open a credit card account, the account rules and interest rate are determined based on two groups of factors. The first consists of items related to your credit history and information in your application form. The second group relates to conditions in the economy as a whole and the policies of the issuer of the card.

Over time, these sets of information can change, and as a result, the card issuer may wish to make amendments to the interest rate, credit limit, and other card rules or features. By law, it can do so with 45 days of advance notice. Interest rates cannot be changed on existing balances; therefore, the issuer must give you the option of rejecting or accepting a change. If you reject the change, the card will be blocked for further usage, and you may repay any balance according to the old rules. Once you have repaid the balance owed, your card is cancelled. If you accept the changes, they will take effect 45 days after notification.

Late-Payment, Bounced-Check, and Over-the-Limit Fees Are Very Costly The dollar amount of fees assessed by credit card issuers continue to go up every year. Late-payment fees of up to $25 (perhaps $35 for a second offense within six months) are often applied when the borrower fails to make a payment by the due date. Most card issuers assess a similar charge if you write a bad check when making your monthly payment. Many credit card issuers charge a significant over-the-limit fee (again up to $25 or $35 for a second offense within six months) when the cardholder exceeds his or her credit limit. These fees can only be assessed if the cardholder agrees to allow the lender to accept over-the-limit usage. If this agreement has not been given, over-the-limit usage will be blocked. Each of these fees is much higher than necessary in terms of the actual cost to the lender for these rule violations. Indeed, they represent a significant source of profits for credit card issuers. The account illustrated in Figure 7-1 assesses a maximum fee of $25 for each of these offenses.

Teaser Interest Rates May Be Appealing Some cards carry a temporarily low **introductory rate** (**teaser rate**) to entice borrowers to apply for an account. Teaser rates must stay in effect for six months after the account is opened unless the cardholder violates a rule of the account such as being late with a payment by more than 60 days. Teaser APRs of 0 to 3.9 percent are common. In Figure 7-1, the teaser rate is 2.9 percent for purchases and 0.0 percent for cash advances. The APR typically reverts to a much higher fixed or variable interest rate (19.2% in the example in Figure 7-1) after the introductory period ends. Some credit card borrowers take advantage of teaser rates by opening new accounts regularly and transferring the balances from other accounts to the new account to take advantage of the low introductory rate despite the high balance transfer fee that might exist. Customers with a good credit history can use this technique several times in succession.

Default Rates Are Extremely High If the borrower makes a late payment even once during the introductory period, usually the introductory rate will be rescinded and the regular rate on the account will be applied. A more serious downside to most credit card accounts is the assessment of a **default rate** (or **penalty APR**). A default rate is a high APR that is assessed whenever a borrower fails to uphold certain rules of the account, such as being more than 60 days late or not staying within the specified credit limit. The disclosure notice in Figure 7-1 indicates that if you are late making a payment even once during the introductory period, you will not only lose the teaser rate but also see a default rate of up to 27.99 percent APR. By law, default rates must be reviewed after six months and rescinded if all payments have been made on time in that period.

FINANCIAL POWER POINT

The Card You Use Might Save You Money

Merchants are allowed to give discounts when you pay cash or use a debit card rather than a Visa or MasterCard. If the availability of such a discount is not obvious, just ask. You could save 2 to 3 percent on a purchase.

FINANCIAL POWER POINT

Rewards Cards Do Not Always Make Sense

Rewards cards tend to have higher APRs, so it makes no sense to use a rewards card if you are going to carry a balance on such a card.

introductory rate
A temporarily low initial interest rate to entice borrowers to apply for a credit card.

default rate
A high APR that is assessed whenever a borrower fails to uphold certain rules of the account, such as making on-time payments or staying within the specified credit limit.

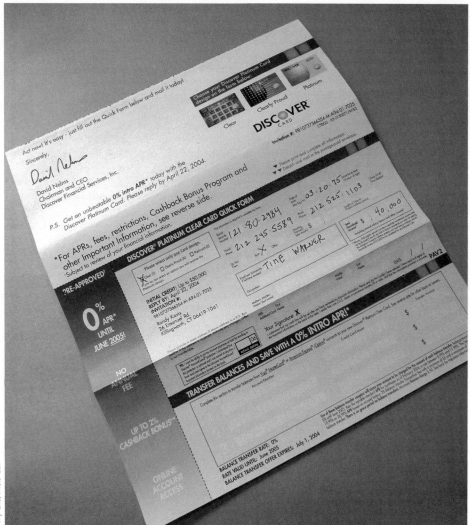

Extremely low APRs are usually temporary. Read the rules of your account carefully.

Amy Etra/Photo Edit

variable interest rate cards
Have rates that change monthly or annually according to general changes in the economy as a whole.

Variable Interest Rates Can Easily Go Up Credit card accounts (and installment loans) carry either fixed or variable interest rates. **Variable interest rates** go up and down, usually monthly or annually, often according to changes in interest rates in the economy as a whole. The example in Figure 7-1 has a variable interest rate with the prime rate used as a base rate. The **prime rate** is a key measure of interest rates in the economy, and its fluctuations drive the changes in rates for all types of variable-rate credit. In recent years, the prime rate has ranged from 3 to 4 percent. As indicated in Figure 7-1, the card company uses the prime rate as published in *The Wall Street Journal* to determine interest rates for purchases, cash advances, and balance transfers on the card.

Credit Card Insurance Is Overpriced Many lenders encourage borrowers to sign up for **credit life insurance** that pays the unpaid balance of a loan—to the lender—in the event of the borrower's death. Credit life insurance is grossly overpriced (and very profitable) and is a cost that can be avoided. The same can be said for **credit disability insurance**, which repays the outstanding loan balance if the borrower becomes disabled (with "disability" usually being very narrowly defined), and credit unemployment insurance.

DID YOU KNOW?

Secured Credit Cards Can Be a Very Bad Deal

A **secured credit card** (also called a **collateralized credit card**) is backed by collateral in the form of a savings account opened at the financial institution that issues the card. Banks offering secured credit cards typically charge an application fee and require the applicant to make a deposit of $500 to $1000 into a savings account. The person then receives a credit limit in the same amount on a bank credit card. The savings balance cannot be withdrawn as long as the card is available for use. The deposit is refunded (with a small amount of interest) when the credit card balance is paid off and the account closed. Most people do not need a secured credit card, but those who have no alternative should consider obtaining one from a reputable institution, as scams abound in this market. Fees to open these accounts can be as high as 50 percent of the credit limit.

Concept Check 7.2

1. Distinguish among bank credit cards, retail credit cards, and travel and entertainment cards.

2. What are the differences and similarities between a cash advance and a balance transfer using a bank credit card?

3. Describe the positive and negative aspects of having a variable interest rate on a credit card.

4. What is a default rate and how might a cardholder come to have to pay this interest rate?

5. Briefly describe five common fees assessed on credit card accounts and how they can be avoided.

FINANCIAL POWER POINT

About 1 in 20 Credit Card Accounts Are in Default

Due to their ease of use, credit cards are the primary source of consumer debt other than home mortgages. Typically, about 5 percent of all credit card accounts are more than 30 days past due.

YOU MUST MANAGE YOUR CREDIT CARDS WISELY

LEARNING OBJECTIVE ❸

Manage your credit card accounts to avoid fees and finance charges.

Credit cards can be a positive tool in personal financial management—but only when used appropriately. To do so, you must understand and monitor your credit statements, correct any billing errors quickly, and verify the computation of any finance charges that accrue. Your goal should be to use the credit card in a manner that avoids *all* fees, including finance charges. This means paying your balance in full every month. Otherwise, credit card debt is the most expensive form of debt used by most people. As one expert observed, "You want to earn a 21% risk-free return on your money? Pay off your credit cards."

If you do not manage your credit cards wisely, you will unnecessarily pay hundreds or even thousands of dollars every year in interest, penalties, and fees to credit card companies. You also may mess up your credit rating and, as a result, will wind up paying higher interest rates than normal for all your credit transactions including vehicle and

ADVICE FROM A PRO

Control and Reduce Your Credit Card Debt

If your credit card debt rises to a hard-to-manage level, consider the following suggestions:

1. *Immediately stop* using your credit cards, and do not open new credit accounts or accept any new credit offers.

2. *Gather your most recent credit card statements*, sit down with pencil and paper, and write down the balance of each debt and the interest rate. Then set a payoff date and calculate the monthly payment you will need to pay off the debt by that date using a calculator like the ones found at www.bankrate.com or http://money.cnn.com.

3. *Consider transferring existing balances* on high-interest rate accounts to an account with a lower interest rate. Use caution, however, because brief introductory periods, transaction fees, and penalties may eliminate any potential savings.

4. *Pay the minimum amount due* on your cards with low interest rates, and pay as much as possible on the cards with the highest interest rates. Continue to do so until all of your debts are paid off.

5. *Evaluate* all of your budgeted expenditures and plan to devote the largest possible amounts toward paying off your credit card balances.

6. *Work overtime* or take another job. Devote any extra income, such as a tax refund, toward paying these debts.

7. *Consider seeking assistance* from a nonprofit credit counseling agency if after three to six months you are not making good progress toward paying off your credit card balances. It can negotiate with your creditors to lower your payments and interest rates and to reduce or eliminate late fees and over-the-limit charges.

Lorie Broberg
Oglala Lakota College

home purchases. You might even miss out on a job opportunity because some employers turn down applicants who have poor credit histories.

Credit Statements

Active charge account holders receive a monthly **credit statement** (also called a **periodic statement**) that summarizes the charges, payments, finance charges, and other activity on the account. The significant features of credit statements are the billing date, due date, transaction and posting dates, grace period, minimum payment, and credit for merchandise returns and billing errors obtained. You also need to know how to correct errors in your credit statements. Figure 7-2 shows an example monthly statement for a credit card.

Billing Date The **billing date** (sometimes called the **statement date** or **closing date**) is the last day of the month for which any transactions are reported on the statement. In Figure 7-2, this date is 3/22/2012. Any transactions or payments made after this date will be recorded on the following month's credit statement. The statement is mailed to the cardholder a day or so after the billing date. The billing date is generally the same day of each month, and the time period between billing dates is referred to as the **billing cycle**.

Due Date The due date is the specific day by which the credit card company should receive payment from you. In Figure 7-2, this date is 4/20/12. The period between the billing date and the due date represents the time allowed for statements and payments to be mailed and for the borrower to make arrangements to pay. Federal law states that bills must be mailed to cardholders at least 21 days before payments are due. The account illustrated in Figure 7-2 has a 29-day grace period. If payment is received later than the due date, a credit bureau may be notified of slow payment. If no payment is received, the company may begin collection efforts, but commonly, companies will simply carry the balance over to the next month.

By law, card issuers can charge a late payment penalty of no more than $25 or the amount of the late payment if it is lower than $25. In the example statement, a late fee of $25 was added. More vigorous collection efforts will occur if the next month's payment is also missed. Your due date must be the same each month, and if it falls on a weekend or holiday, you have until the following business day to pay. Payments received by 5 p.m. on the due date are considered to be on time.

Transaction and Posting Dates The date on which a credit cardholder makes a purchase (or receives a credit, as described later in this chapter) is known as the **transaction date**. In the past, several days would pass before the credit card company was informed of the transaction and the charge was posted to the account (on the posting date). With the increased use of magnetic strip readers at retailers, however, these dates may be concurrent, with both matching the date on which the clerk or the customer "swipes" the card through the reader. Interest is charged from the posting date unless a grace period is offered; some lenders charge interest from the transaction date.

Grace Period A **grace period** is the time period between the posting date of a transaction and the due date, within which any new credit card purchases made during the billing cycle will avoid finance charges (also see Figure 7-1). Most cards provide a grace period only if the previous month's total balance was paid in full and on time. About one-third of cardholders pay their bills in full by the due date and receive, in effect, an interest-free loan on their new purchases during the next billing cycle. It is a smart financial move to use one credit card for convenience items that are paid in full each month and another credit card for items for which paying off the balance each month is not possible. Use a no-annual-fee card for the convenience purchases and a low-APR card for purchases for which you carry a balance. Avoid cards that do not offer a grace period. In Figure 7-2, the cardholder has a previous unpaid balance, $535.07, and was charged interest on the unpaid balance as well as on the new charges made within the billing cycle, starting from the date they were posted to the account. Thus, this example lacks a grace period because of the unpaid balance on the card.

Sample Statement for a Bank Credit Card Account

Figure 7-2

XXX Bank Credit Card Account Statement
Account Number XXXX XXXX XXXX XXXX
February 21, 2012 to March 22, 2012

Summary of Account Activity

Previous Balance	$535.07
Payments	–$450.00
Other Credit	–$0.00
Purchases	+$529.57
Balance Transfers	+$785.00
Cash Advances	+$318.00
Past Due Amount	$0.00
Fees Charged	**+$69.45**
Interest Charged	**+$11.05**
New Balance	$1,798.14
Credit limit	$2,000.00
Available credit	$201.86
Statement closing date	3/22/2012
Days in billing cycle	30

Questions?

Call Customer Service	1-XXX-XXX-XXXX
Lost or Stolen Credit Card	1-XXX-XXX-XXXX

Payment Information

New Balance	$1,798.14
Minimum Payment Due	$53.00
Payment Due Date	4/20/12

Late Payment Warning: If we do not receive your minimum Payment by the date listed above, you may have to pay a $25 late fee and your APRs may be increased up to the Penalty APR of 28.99%

Minimum Payment Warning: If you make only the minimum payment each period, you will pay more in interest and it will take you longer to pay off your balance. For example:

If you make no additional charges using this card and each month you pay...	You will pay off the balance shown on this statement in about...	And you will end up paying as estimated total of...
Only the minimum payment	10 years	$3,284
$62	3 years	$2,232 (Savings = $1,052)

If you would like information about credit counseling services, call 1-800-XXX-XXXX

Please send billing inquiries and correspondence to:
PO Box XXXX, Anytown, Anystate XXXXX

Notice of Changes to Your Interest Rates

You have triggered the Penalty APR of 28.99%. This change will impact your account as follows:

Transactions made on or after 4/9/12: As of 5/10/12, the Penalty APR will apply to these transactions. We may keep the APR at this level indefinitely.

Transactions made before 4/9/12: Current rates will continue to apply to these transactions. However, if you become more than 60 days late on your account, the Penalty APR will apply to those transactions as well.

Important Changes to Your Account Terms

The following is a summary of changes that are being made to your account terms. For more detailed information, please refer to the booklet enclosed with this statement.

These changes will impact your account as follows:

Transactions made on or after 4/9/12: As of 5/10/12, any changes to APRs described below will apply to these transactions.

Transactions made before 4/9/12: Current APRs will continue to apply to these transactions.

If you are already being charged a higher Penalty APR for purchases: In this case, any changes to APRs described below will not to go into effect at this time. These changes will go into effect when the Penalty APR no longer applied to your account.

Revised Terms, as of 5/10/12	
APR for Purchases	16.99%

Transactions

Reference Number	Trans Date	Post Date	Description of Transaction or Credit	Amount
5884186PS0388W6YM	2/22	2/23	Store #1	$146.19
854338203FS8OO0Z5	2/25	2/25	Pymt Thank You	–
564891561545KOSHD	2/25	2/26	Store #2	$247.36
1542202074TWWZV48	2/26	2/26	Cash Advance	$318.00
4545754784KOHUIOS	2/27	3/1	Balance Transfer	$785.00
2564561023184102315	2/28	3/1	Store #3	$ 34.32
045148714518979874	3/4	3/5	Store #4	$ 29.45
0547810544898718AF	3/15	3/17	Store #5	$ 72.25

Fees

Reference Number	Trans Date	Post Date	Description	Amount
9525156489SFD4545Q	2/23	2/23	Late Fee	$25.00
84151564SADS874H	2/27	2/27	Balance Transfer Fee	$23.55
256489156189451516L	2/28	2/28	Cash Advance Fee	$20.90
			TOTAL FEES FOR THIS PERIOD	**$69.45**

Interest Charged

Interest Charge on Purchases	$ 6.40
Interest Charge on Cash Advances	$ 4.65
TOTAL INTEREST FOR THIS PERIOD	**$11.05**

2012 Totals Year-to-Date	
Total fees charged in 2012	$90.14
Total interest charged in 2012	$18.27

Interest Charge Calculation

Your **Annual Percentage rate (APR)** is the stated interest rate on your account.

Type of Balance	Annual Percentage Rate (APR)	Balances Subject to Interest Rate	Interest Charge
Purchases	14.99% (V)	$512.14	$6.40
Cash Advances	21.99% (V)	$253.50	$4.65
Balance Transfers	0.00%	$637.50	$0.00

(V) = Variable Rate

FINANCIAL POWER POINT

Special Rules for Credit Card Applicants Age 18 to 20

Under the 2009 Credit Card Accountability, Responsibility and Disclosure (CARD) Act, when a person age 18 to 20 applies for a credit card, the lender must verify that the person has sufficient independent income or require a cosigner.

minimum payment amount
Lowest allowable monthly payment required by the lender.

FINANCIAL POWER POINT

How Your Credit Card Payment Is Applied

Under the Credit Card Accountability, Responsibility and Disclosure (CARD) Act, whenever you make more than a minimum payment on your credit card account, the lender must apply any excess above the minimum payment to the portion of the card debt that carries the highest APR.

credit receipt
Written evidence of any items returned that notes the specific amount and date of the transaction.

periodic rate
The APR for a charge account divided by the number of billing cycles per year (usually 12).

average daily balance
Sum of the outstanding balances owed each day during the billing period divided by the number of days in the period.

Minimum Payment Amount To meet their obligations, borrowers must make a **minimum payment amount** monthly that is no smaller than the amount required by the creditor. In Figure 7-2, the cardholder has two options: pay the total amount due ($1784.53) or make at least the minimum payment of $53. If the borrower pays the full amount due, finance charges on new purchases in the next billing cycle generally can be avoided. If a partial payment, such as the "total minimum payment due" of $53, is made, additional finance charges will be assessed and will be payable the following month.

The Credit Card Accountability, Responsibility and Disclosure Act requires that your credit card statement include the number of months it will take to pay off your card balance if you make only the minimum payment with no additional charges. In the example, it would take ten years to pay off the balance with the minimum payment, resulting in additional interest of almost $1500 ($3284.00 − $1784.53). In contrast, making a payment of $62 per month with no additional charges would reduce the payoff period to only three years and save $1052 in interest charges. Since the inclusion of this information on credit card statements in 2010, median credit card balances have declined over 20 percent, demonstrating that people who are informed about all those potential interest dollars make better repayment decisions. You, too, should pay close attention to this information when deciding what payment amount to make on your credit cards.

Transaction Fees Credit card companies usually charge transaction fees whenever the card is used for a balance transfer or cash advance. In the example in Figure 7-2, both of these fees are assessed because these types of transactions occurred during the billing cycle. Fees for purchase transactions are much less common, although they are more typical if the card is used in another country.

Credit for Merchandise Returns and Errors If you return merchandise bought on credit, the merchant will issue you a **credit receipt**—written evidence of the items returned that notes the specific amount of the transaction. In essence, the amount of the merchandise credit is charged back to the credit card company and eventually to the merchant. A credit may also be granted by the credit card company when a billing error has been made (discussed in the next section) or when an unauthorized transaction appears. Credits obtained in the current month should appear on the next monthly statement as a reduction of the total amount owed. The credit statement in Figure 7-2 shows a $13.45 credit.

Computation of Finance Charges

Companies that issue credit cards must tell consumers the APR applied as well as the method used to compute the finance charges. The APR then translates into a **periodic rate**, which is the APR for a charge account divided by the number of billing cycles per year (usually 12). For example, a periodic rate of 1½ percent per month would result from an APR of approximately 18 percent (actually a bit higher because of compounding); both figures must be disclosed. Typically, the finance charge is calculated by first computing the **average daily balance**—the sum of the outstanding balances owed each day during the billing period divided by the number of days in the period. The periodic rate is then applied against that balance. For example, a card with an 18 percent APR, a 1½ percent periodic rate, and an average daily balance of $1000 would have a finance charge for the month of $15 ($1000 × 0.015). Note that in the examples in Figure 7-1 and Figure 7-2, differing APRs apply for purchases, balance transfers, and cash advances. This is the typical arrangement on credit cards today.

How Credit Card Average Daily Balances Are Calculated

Three methods are commonly used to calculate the average daily balance on a credit card billing statement:

ADVICE FROM A PRO

Avoid the Minimum Payment Trap

Do you currently have balances outstanding on your credit cards? If so, how long have you carried those balances? If you open an account in college and already have an unpaid balance of $2500 upon your graduation at age 22, you may find that the balance will not drop below $2500 for many years. This situation occurs when you continue to make purchases with the card but continue to send in only the required minimum payment amount. If $2500 is still owed on the account years later, then you have permanent debt. In essence, you have never repaid the college charges. With an 18 percent APR, the finance charges on a principal of $2500 for 15 years will total $6750 (0.18 × $2500 × 15), almost three times as much as the debt itself!

The outlook is similarly bleak if you discontinue using the card for new purchases but still remit only the required minimum repayment amount. Credit card issuers often require a minimum monthly payment as low as 3 or 3½ percent of the outstanding balance. This tiny payment requirement is mathematically guaranteed to keep the user in debt for many, many years. To illustrate, a minimum payment of $75 (3 percent) on an outstanding balance of $2500 with a 1½ percent monthly periodic rate results in only one-half of the payment ($37.50 = $2500 × 0.015) going to reduce the actual debt (the principal). The other $37.50 is used to pay the monthly interest. At this rate of repayment, it will take more than six years to repay the $2500.

A ploy that card issuers frequently use is to allow cardholders to "skip a payment"—in essence, to make "a zero-dollar minimum payment." Interest will continue to accrue for the month during which no payment is made. This practice increases the total amount owed because the unpaid interest simply adds to the unpaid balance.

Such offers for a "low" or "zero-dollar" minimum payment illustrate the minimum payment trap. To avoid paying credit card charges for six to ten years, or even longer, you must make much larger monthly payments that go toward retiring your credit card balances. Better still, ask yourself—no, ask yourself twice—"Do I really need to charge it?" And remember, focusing solely on the minimum payment hides the numbers that really matter: how much you owe and at what rate.

Donald Stuhlman
Wilmington College, Delaware

1. **Average daily balance excluding new purchases.** The cardholder pays interest only on any balance left over from the previous month.
2. **Average daily balance including new purchases with a grace period.** The balance calculation includes the balance from the previous month and any new charges made during the billing cycle. The grace period allows for the exclusion of new charges made during the billing cycle only if the balance from the previous billing cycle was zero.
3. **Average daily balance including new purchases with no grace period.** The balance from the previous month and any new charges made during the billing cycle are included in the balance calculation, even if the previous month's balance was paid in full.

The following chart illustrates how finance charges vary for a hypothetical situation in which a borrower charges $1000 per month and pays only the minimum payment, except for every third month when the balance is paid in full. Executing this scheme four times over the course of a year would result in the finance charges shown in the chart under the two most common ways of computing the average daily balance and for low-, average-, and high-interest cards.

	Annual Percentage Rate		
	12.0%	**17.3%**	**19.8%**
Average daily balance (excluding new purchases)	$40.00	$ 57.60	$ 66.00
Average daily balance (including new purchases with a grace period)	$80.00	$115.20	$132.00

Fair Credit Billing Act (FCBA)
Helps people who wish to dispute billing errors on revolving credit accounts.

How to Correct Errors on Your Credit Card Billing Statement

The **Fair Credit Billing Act (FCBA)** helps people who wish to dispute billing errors on revolving credit accounts. In effect, the FCBA permits a **chargeback**; that is, the amount of the transaction is charged back to the business where the transaction originated.

chargeback
The amount of the transaction is charged back to the business where the transaction originated in the case of a dispute or challenge by the cardholder.

FINANCIAL POWER POINT

Billing Errors Are Way Too Common

The University of Michigan's Survey of Consumers shows that nearly one in six households reported an error on their credit card accounts.

Withholding payment to a credit card company is permitted when the cardholder alleges that a mathematical error has been made in a billing statement, when fraudulent use of the card appears to have occurred, or when (within certain reasonable limitations) a **goods and services dispute** asserts that the charges were for faulty, damaged, shoddy, defective, or poor-quality goods and services and you made a good-faith effort to try to correct the problem with the merchant. For goods and services disputes, the FCBA applies only to charges of more than $50 made in your home state or within 100 miles of your current mailing address. Most lenders apply the spirit of the FCBA to any goods and services disputes, regardless of the geographic distances involved.

Your Time Limits You must make your billing error complaint within 60 days after the date on which the first bill containing the error was mailed to you. The lender then has 30 days to acknowledge your notification and, within 90 days, must either correct the error permanently, return any overpayment (if requested), or provide evidence of why it believes the bill to be correct (such as a copy of a charge slip you supposedly signed).

dunning letters
Notices that make insistent demands for repayment.

Lender Responsibilities While the dispute is being investigated, creditors cannot assess interest on or apply penalties for nonpayment of the disputed amount, send **dunning letters** (notices that make insistent demands for repayment), or send negative information about your account to a credit bureau without stating that "some items are in dispute." A lender that does not follow the procedures correctly cannot collect the first $50 of the questioned amount, even if the bill was correct. Back interest and penalties may be charged if the disputed item is proved to be legitimately owed.

Your Action Steps Take several actions when disputing an item on a billing statement:

Shoppers frequently rely on purchase loans when buying big ticket items such as furniture and TVs.

1. **Notify the merchant** involved of the error. Although the FCBA does not apply to merchants, it is often the merchant that caused the error and who is in the best position to clear up the error. Be sure to tell the merchant that you also are asserting your rights under the FCBA with the card issuer.

2. **Send a written notice** of the error to the credit card issuer. The notice must be in writing to qualify for the protections provided under the FCBA. Instead of sending the notice to the same address where repayments are normally remitted, examine the billing statement thoroughly, looking for an address under the heading "Send Inquiries to" or something similar. If the error is an "unauthorized use," make sure you indicate this as these disputes have added protections.

3. **Provide photocopies** (not originals) of any necessary documentation. Keep the originals to challenge any finding by the company that no error occurred.

4. **Withhold payment for disputed items.** If possible, pay the remaining amount owed in full to isolate a disputed item. Under the provisions of the FCBA, the card company must immediately credit your account for the amount in dispute.

5. **Review your credit bureau file** after the dispute has been settled to ensure that it does not include information regarding your refusal to repay the disputed amount.

Concept Check 7.3

1. Describe how the finance charge is typically calculated on a credit card account.

2. What is the major benefit of having a credit card with a grace period?

3. Briefly summarize the steps you should take if you find an error on your credit card account billing statement.

UNDERSTANDING CONSUMER INSTALLMENT LOANS

Consumers obtain installment credit in two ways. With a **cash loan**, the borrower receives cash and then uses it to make purchases, pay off other loans, or make investments. With a **purchase loan** (also called **sales credit**), the consumer makes a purchase on credit with no cash transferring from the lender to the borrower. Instead, the funds go directly from the lender to the seller. For example, a car buyer might obtain a purchase loan from the Ford Motor Credit to buy a new Ford Edge. With some purchase loans, the lender is the seller. For all consumer loans, the borrower will sign a formal **promissory note** (a written installment loan contract) that spells out the terms of the loan.

LEARNING OBJECTIVE **4**

Describe the important features of consumer installment loans.

promissory note
Written installment loan contract that spells out the terms of the loan.

Installment Loans Can Be Unsecured or Secured

Credit can either be unsecured or secured. An **unsecured loan** is granted solely based on the good credit character of the borrower. Sometimes unsecured loans are called **signature loans** because they are backed up by only the borrower's signature. Because unsecured loans carry higher risk than secured debts, the interest rate charged on them is substantially higher.

A **secured loan** requires a cosigner or collateral. A **cosigner** agrees to pay the debt if the original borrower fails to do so. Being a cosigner is a major responsibility because a cosigner has the same legal obligations for repayment as the original borrower does. In case of default, a lender will go after the party—either the borrower or the cosigner—from whom it is more likely to collect the funds. Remember that when people require a cosigner, it means that the lender feels that the borrower is not creditworthy on his or her own, and that judgment is usually quite correct. A good rule in life is to never cosign for a loan, even for relatives.

unsecured loan/signature loan
Loan granted based solely on borrower's good creditworthiness.

secured loan
Loan that is backed by collateral or a cosigner.

DID YOU KNOW?

Sean's Success Story

Sean has been very careful about his use of credit since he graduated and began working full time for a marketing firm. He purchased a two-year-old used car soon after taking his job. He shopped thoroughly for the lowest APR and, so far, has made all of his payments on time. He also has three credit cards. One is a rewards card that he uses for most of his day-to-day spending, and he pays the card balance off in full every month. He has used his rewards bonuses to buy several cameras that he uses in his photography hobby. Sean has a second card that he uses when he travels on business. This is also a

rewards card, and it provides air miles that he has used for personal travel. He pays this card off with his travel reimbursement checks from his employer. He doesn't use his third card very often as it is used to charge items that he figures that he might not be able to pay in full when the monthly bill is received. Sean is careful to make certain that he pays off the card balance before using it again for another purchase. He also does not carry this card with him so that he must return home before fully deciding to take on more debt that he cannot repay in full when the bill is received.

A loan secured with collateral means that the lender has a security interest in the property that is pledged as collateral. For example, the vehicle itself is the collateral on an automobile loan. The item of collateral does not necessarily need to be the property purchased with the loan. Typically, the lender records a lien in the county courthouse to make the security interest known to the public. A **lien** is a legal right to seize and dispose of (usually sell) property to obtain payment of a claim. When the loan is repaid, the lien will be removed. (The borrower should double check to make sure this removal occurs.)

In the event that the borrower fails to repay a loan, the creditor can exercise the lien and seize the collateral through repossession, sometimes without notice. Almost all credit contracts contain an **acceleration clause** stating that after a specific number of payments are unpaid (often just one), the loan is considered in default and all remaining installments are due and payable upon demand of the creditor. These clauses protect the lender's interest but can prove very difficult for borrowers. Don't be fooled if you miss a payment and the lender does not exercise the acceleration clause immediately: It can do so at any time after default occurs. Do not ignore a warning letter from a creditor!

Purchase Loan Installment Contracts

Two kinds of contracts are used when purchasing goods with an installment loan:

- **Installment purchase agreements** (also called **collateral installment loans** or **chattel mortgage loans**), in which the title of the property passes to the buyer when the contract is signed

- **Conditional sales contracts** (also known as **financing leases**), in which the title does not pass to the buyer until the last installment payment has been paid

An installment purchase agreement provides a measure of protection for the borrower, as the creditor must follow all legal procedures required by state law when repossessing the property. Some state laws permit the lender to take secured property back as soon as the buyer falls behind in payments, possibly by seizing a car right from a person's driveway.

 Concept Check 7.4

1. Describe how a cash loan and a purchase loan differ.

2. Distinguish between a secured and an unsecured loan.

3. Describe when a lender might enforce an acceleration clause on a loan and explain the impact of such an action by the lender.

4. Differentiate between an installment purchase agreement and a conditional sales contract.

CALCULATING INTEREST ON CONSUMER LOANS

The federal **Truth in Lending Act (TIL)** requires lenders to disclose to credit applicants both the interest rate expressed as an APR and the finance charge. Always inquire about the APR if it is not readily apparent, and use it to compare rates from other lenders to obtain the best deal. The finance charge is the cost of credit expressed in dollars. The finance charge plus the original amount borrowed must be paid. It has been said that the hardest thing to do is to "make twelve easy payments."

Calculating an Installment Loan Payment

Installment credit typically comes with a **fixed interest rate**, meaning that the rate will not change over the life of the loan. Lenders often offer **variable-rate loans** (also called

---

lien
A legal right to seize and dispose of (usually sell) property to obtain payment of a claim. Once the loan is paid, the lien is removed.

acceleration clause
Part of a credit contract stating that after a specific number of payments are unpaid (often just one), the loan is considered in default, and all remaining installments are due and payable upon demand of the creditor.

 LEARNING OBJECTIVE **5**

Calculate the interest and annual percentage rate on consumer loans.

Truth in Lending Act (TIL)
Requires lenders to disclose to credit applicants both the interest rate expressed as an annual percentage rate (APR) and the finance charge.

Monthly Installment Payment (Principal and Interest) Required to Repay $1000*

Table 7-1

APR[†]	Number of Monthly Payments						
	12	24	36	48	60	72	84
5	$85.61	$43.87	$29.97	$23.03	$18.87	$16.10	$14.13
6	86.07	44.32	30.42	23.49	19.33	16.57	14.61
7	86.53	44.77	30.88	23.95	19.80	17.05	15.09
8	86.99	45.23	31.34	24.41	20.28	17.53	15.59
9	87.45	45.68	31.80	24.88	20.76	18.03	16.09
10	87.92	46.14	32.27	25.36	21.25	18.53	16.60
11	88.38	46.61	32.74	25.85	21.74	19.03	17.12
12	88.85	47.07	33.21	26.33	22.24	19.55	17.65
13	89.32	47.54	33.69	26.83	22.75	20.07	18.19
14	89.79	48.01	34.18	27.33	23.27	20.61	18.74
15	90.26	48.49	34.67	27.83	23.79	21.14	19.27
16	90.73	48.96	35.16	28.34	24.32	21.69	19.86
17	91.20	49.44	35.65	28.85	24.85	22.25	20.44
18	91.68	49.92	36.15	29.37	25.39	22.81	21.02
19	92.16	50.41	36.66	29.90	25.94	23.38	21.61
20	92.63	50.90	37.16	30.43	26.49	23.95	22.21

* To illustrate, assume an automobile loan of $14,000 at 8 percent for five years. To repay $1000, the monthly payment is $20.28; therefore, multiply $20.28 (8% row and 60-month column) by 14 to give a monthly payment of $283.92. For amounts other than exact $1000 increments, simply use decimals. For example, for a loan of $14,500, the multiplier would be 14.5.

† For fractional interest rates of 5.5, 6.5, 7.5, and so on, simply take a monthly payment halfway between the whole-number APR payments. For example, the payment for 48 months at 9.5 percent is $25.12 ($25.36 − $24.88 = $0.48; $0.48 ÷ 2 = $0.24; $0.24 + $24.88 = $25.12).

adjustable-rate loans) to borrowers. When the loan rate varies, the monthly payment will go up or down, allowing the loan to be paid off by the same date as originally established in the contract.

To help you figure out the required monthly payment for different loan amounts, Table 7-1 shows various monthly installment payments used to repay a $1000 loan at commonly seen APR interest rates and time periods. For loans of other dollar amounts, divide the borrowed amount by 1000 and multiply the result by the appropriate figure from the table. For example, an automobile loan for $12,000, financed at 10 percent interest, might be repaid in 36 equal monthly payments of $387.24 ($32.27 × 12). A loan for $3550 at 16 percent for 24 months will require monthly payments of $173.81 ($48.96 × 3.550).

The finance charge must include all mandatory charges to be paid by the borrower. In addition to interest, lenders may charge fees for a credit investigation; a loan application; or credit life, credit disability, or credit unemployment insurance. When fees are required, the lender must include them in the finance charge in dollars as part of the APR calculations. When the borrower elects these options voluntarily, the fees are not included in the finance charge and APR calculations, even though they raise the actual cost of borrowing.

It is easy to calculate the finance charge on a consumer loan. First, multiply the monthly payment by the number of months and subtract the original amount borrowed. In the 36-month automobile loan example given earlier, the finance charge would be $1940.64 [($387.24 × 36) − $12,000]. Second, add any other mandatory charges.

Calculation of the Finance Charges and APR for Installment Loans

Interest accounts for the greatest portion of the finance charge. Three methods are used to calculate interest on installment and noninstallment credit: the declining-balance (sometimes called the simple-interest) method, the add-on interest method, and the discount method. The add-on method predominates at banks, savings banks, and consumer finance companies for installment loans for automobiles, furniture, and other credit requiring collateral. The declining-balance method is widely used by credit unions to

variable-rate (adjustable-rate) loans
Loans for which the interest rate varies with the monthly payment going up or down, allowing the loan to be paid off by the original end date.

calculate interest on loans. The declining-balance method is always used for credit cards and for most home mortgages.

The following discussion illustrates the calculation of the APR for installment loans using each of the three methods.

The Declining-Balance Method Is Fair to Both Lender and Borrower

declining-balance method
Interest calculation method in which interest is assessed during each billing period (usually each month) based on the outstanding balance of the installment loan that billing period.

With the **declining-balance method**, the interest assessed during each payment period (usually each month) is based on the current outstanding balance of the installment loan. The lender initially calculates a schedule (such as that given in Table 7-2) to have the balance repaid in full after a certain number of months. The borrower may vary the rate of repayment by making payments larger than those scheduled or may repay the loan in full at any time.

Here is an illustration of the declining-balance method for an installment loan. As shown in Table 7-2, at the end of the first month, a periodic interest rate (the monthly rate applied to the outstanding balance of a loan) of 1½ percent (18 percent annually divided by 12 months) is applied to the beginning balance of $1000, giving an interest charge of $15. Of the first monthly installment of $91.68, $15 goes toward the payment of interest and $76.68 ($91.68 – $15.00) goes toward payment of the principal.

For the second month, the outstanding balance is reduced to $923.32 ($1000 – $76.68). Since the balance is $78.68 lower, the interest portion of the payment drops to $13.85 (0.015 × $923.32). Because the declining-balance method applies the periodic interest rate to the outstanding loan balance, the APR and the simple interest rate will differ only if fees (such as an application fee) boost the finance charge. (This method of paying off a loan, called **amortization**, is also discussed in Chapter 9 when we examine home mortgage loans.) Note that declining-balance loans carry no prepayment penalties.

amortization
Loan repayment method in which part of the payment goes to pay interest and part goes to repay principal. Extra payments toward principal shorten the life of the loan and decrease the total amount of interest paid.

The Add-On Method Favors the Lender

add-on interest method
Interest is calculated by applying an interest rate to the amount borrowed times the number of years to arrive at the total interest to be charged.

The add-on method is a widely used technique for computing interest on installment loans. With this method, the interest is calculated and added to the amount borrowed to determine the total amount to be repaid. Equation (7.1) is used to calculate the dollar amount of interest. Note that the interest rate used in this equation for the add-on method is an add-on rate and should not be confused with the APR.

With the **add-on interest method**, interest is calculated by applying an interest rate to the amount borrowed times the number of years. The add-on interest formula given in Equation (7.1) is used as follows:

$$I = PRT \quad (7.1)^*$$

Table 7-2

Sample Repayment Schedule for $1000 Principal Plus Interest Using the Declining-Balance Method (1½ Percent per Month)

Month	Outstanding Balance	Payment	Interest	Principal	Balance
1	$1,000.00	$91.68	$15.00	$76.68	$923.32
2	923.32	91.68	13.85	77.83	845.49
3	845.49	91.68	12.68	79.00	766.49
4	766.49	91.68	11.50	80.18	686.31
5	686.31	91.68	10.29	81.39	604.92
6	604.92	91.68	9.07	82.61	522.31
7	522.31	91.68	7.83	83.85	438.46
8	438.46	91.68	6.58	85.10	353.36
9	353.36	91.68	5.30	86.38	266.98
10	266.98	91.68	4.00	87.68	179.30
11	179.30	91.68	2.69	88.99	90.31
12	90.31	91.66	1.35	90.31	0

where

      I = Interest or finance charges
      P = Principal amount borrowed
      R = Rate of interest (simple, add-on, or discount rate)
      T = Time of loan in years

For example, assume that Megan Broman of New York City borrows $2000 for two years at 9 percent add-on interest to be repaid in monthly installments. Using Equation (7.1), her finance charge in dollars is $360 ($2000 × 0.09 × 2). Adding the finance charge ($360) to the amount borrowed ($2000) gives a total amount of $2360 to be repaid. When this amount is divided by the total number of scheduled payments (24), we find that Megan must make 24 monthly payments of $98.33.

Calculating the APR When the Add-On Method Is Used

Add-on rates and APRs are not equivalent. This is because the add-on calculation assumes the original debt is owed for the entire period of the loan. But of course the debt does go down as the debt is repaid. In the example just given, Megan does not have use of the total amount borrowed for the full two years. Equation (7.2) shows the n-ratio method of estimating the APR on her add-on loan.

$$\begin{aligned}\text{APR} &= \frac{Y(95P + 9)F}{12P(P + 1)(4D + F)} \quad\quad (7.2)^* \\ &= \frac{(12)(95 \times 24 + 9)(360)}{12(24)(24 + 1)[(4 \times 2000) + 360]} \\ &= \frac{(12)(2289)(360)}{(288)(25)(8360)} \\ &= \frac{9{,}888{,}480}{60{,}192{,}000} \\ &= 16.4\% \end{aligned}$$

where

      APR = Annual percentage rate
      Y = Number of payments in one year
      F = Finance charge in dollars (dollar cost of credit)
      D = Debt (amount borrowed or proceeds)
      P = Total number of scheduled payments

Using Equation (7.2), the APR is 16.4 percent. Note that the APR is approximately double the add-on rate because, on average, Megan has use of only half of the borrowed money during the entire loan period.

The Rule of 78s Determines the Prepayment Penalty When an Add-On Loan Is Repaid Early

Most installment loan contracts that use the add-on method include a **prepayment penalty**—a special charge assessed to the borrower for paying off a loan early. Prepayment penalties take into consideration the reality that borrowers should pay more in interest early in the loan period when they have the use of more money and increasingly less interest as the debt shrinks over time. With an add-on method loan, however, the interest is spread evenly across all payments rather than declining as the loan balance falls. If an add-on method loan is paid off early, the lender will use some penalty method to compensate for the lower interest component applied in the early months.

prepayment penalty
Special charge assessed to the borrower for paying off a loan early.

* Calculations involving Equation (7.1) and (7.2) can be performed on the *Garman/Forgue* companion website.

DID YOU KNOW?

Turn Bad Habits into Good Ones

Do You Do This?	*Do This Instead!*
Skim read your credit card billing statements	Read each statement for completeness and accuracy
Pay with whatever card you pull out first from your wallet or purse	Never make purchases that you plan to pay off with a credit card on which you carry a balance
Make only the minimum payment on your credit card	Set a date for paying off that card balance in full and make the payments required to meet your goal
Ignore the potential to earn rewards on your credit cards	Open an account that provides rewards and make day-to-day purchases paying balances in full when billed
Focus on the size of the monthly payment when you take out loans	Focus on the annual percentage rate and length of loan

rule of 78s method/sum of the digits method for calculating prepayment penalties
A common method of calculating the prepayment penalty on a loan that uses the add-on method for calculating the interest.

DO IT NOW!

You know more about personal finance after reading this chapter, so get started right now by:

1. *Making a list of all your debts currently outstanding, the amounts owed, to whom, and at what interest rates.*

2. *Projecting any money you will borrow between now and graduation.*

3. *Using the calculator at www.bankrate .com/brm/popcalc2.asp to determine your monthly payments if you were to pay off your total debt owed at graduation within 3 years, 5 years, and 10 years.*

discount method of calculating interest
Interest is calculated based on a discount rate multiplied by the amount borrowed and by the number of years to repay. Interest is then subtracted from the amount of the loan and the difference is given to the borrower. In this method, interest is paid up front before any part of the payment is applied to the principal.

The **rule of 78s method** (also called the **sum of the digits method**) is the most widely used method of calculating a prepayment penalty. Its name derives from the fact that, for a one-year loan, the numbers between 1 and 12 for each month add up to 78 ($12 + 11 + 10 + 9 + 8 + 7 + 6 + 5 + 4 + 3 + 2 + 1$). For a two-year loan, the numbers between 1 and 24 would be added, and so on for loans with longer time periods.

To illustrate the use of the rule of 78s method, consider the case of Devin Grigsby from West Lafayette, Indiana. He borrowed $500 for 12 months plus an additional $80 finance charge and is scheduled to pay equal monthly installments of $48.33 ($580 ÷ 12). Assume Devin wants to pay the loan off after only six months. He might assume—incorrectly—that he would owe only $250 more because after six months he had paid $250 (one-half) of the $500 borrowed and $40 (one-half) of the finance charge, for a total of $290 in payments ($48.33 × 6). Actually, Devin still owes $268.46, including a prepayment penalty of $18.46. To calculate this amount using the rule of 78s method, the lender adds together all of the numbers between 12 and 7 (12 for the first month, 11 for the second, and so on for six months): $12 + 11 + 10 + 9 + 8 + 7 = 57$. The lender assumes that during the first six months $58.46 [(57 ÷ 78) × $80]— not $40—of the finance charges was received from the $290 in payments Devin had made on the loan.* Consequently, only $231.54 ($290.00 − $58.46) was paid on the $500 borrowed, leaving $268.46 ($500.00 − $231.54) still owed, for a prepayment penalty of $18.46 ($268.46 − $250.00).

With the Discount Method, Interest Is Paid Up Front

The discount method is sometimes used by creditors to compute the interest on an installment loan. With the **discount method**, the interest is calculated based on a discount rate that is multiplied times the amount borrowed and multiplied by the number of years to repay. The interest is then subtracted from the amount of the loan, and only the difference is given to the borrower. Thus, the interest is paid up front. When this method is applied to our earlier example involving Megan Broman, she would receive only $1640 [$2000 − ($2000 × 2 × 9%)] at the beginning of the loan period. Her monthly payment would be $83.33 ($2000 ÷ 24). Using Equation (7.2), the APR would be 19.8 percent (the APR rises because only $1640 is obtained while $2000 is repaid).

---

* If the loan was paid off after one month, the amount of interest paid is assumed to be 12/78 of the $80 finance charge, or $12.31. For a loan paid in full after two months, the amount of interest paid is assumed to be 23/78 of the total (12/78 for month 1 plus 11/78 for month 2), or $23.59.

Concept Check 7.5

1. Explain how the interest is calculated on a consumer loan that uses the declining-balance method.

2. Summarize how interest is calculated on a consumer loan that uses the add-on method.

3. What is the effect of the rule of 78s when a borrower repays an add-on method loan early?

4. Explain how the interest is calculated on a consumer loan that uses the discount method.

WHAT DO YOU RECOMMEND NOW?

Now that you have read this chapter on credit cards and consumer loans, what would you recommend to Darrell Cochrane regarding:

1. His approach to using credit cards, including the number of cards he has?

2. Estimating the credit card interest charges he is paying each month?

3. How he might lower his interest expense each month?

4. Consolidating his credit card debts into one installment loan?

BIG PICTURE SUMMARY OF LEARNING OBJECTIVES

LO1. Compare the common types of consumer credit, including credit cards and installment loans.

Borrowers can use both installment and noninstallment credit. Open-ended credit is an example of noninstallment credit. It permits the customer to gain repeated access to credit without having to fill out a new application each time money is borrowed. The consumer may choose either to repay the debt in a single payment or to make a series of payments of varying amounts. Bank credit cards and travel and entertainment credit cards are the most commonly used open-ended credit accounts.

LO2. Describe the types and features of credit card accounts.

Credit card borrowers must adhere to all the rules of the account or risk being charged a number of punitive fees such as late-payment and bounced-check fees. Borrowers also need to be wary of default rates, which may raise the APR on the account for any violation of the account rules. Some lenders apply default rates if the borrower falls behind in payments on other accounts, even if the borrower is in good standing on the lender's own account.

LO3.   Manage your credit card accounts to avoid fees and finance charges.

As required by the CARD Act, credit card statements provide a monthly summary of account activity, the calculation of any finance charges, and how long it will take to pay off the card balance if you only pay the minimum payment required. Credit card issuers compute finance charges by multiplying the average daily balance by the periodic interest rate.

LO4.   Describe the important features of consumer installment loans.

Consumer loans, also called installment loans, have several features that distinguish them from credit card accounts. Loans usually have a fixed payment for a fixed number of months. Once the loan is paid off, the account is closed and a new account would need to be opened if the person wanted to take out another loan.

LO5.   Calculate the interest and annual percentage rate on consumer loans.

Both the declining-balance and add-on methods are used to calculate the interest on installment loans, although the annual percentage rate (APR) formula gives the correct rate in all cases. With declining-balance loans, the dollar amount of interest incorporated in each monthly payment declines as the loan balance declines.

LET'S TALK ABOUT IT

1. **Borrowing in Tough Economic Times.** The great recession of 2007-09 was made more difficult for many people because of their high debt loads. How has your perception of carrying credit card debt, student loans, and other borrowing changed as a result of today's sluggish economy?

2. **What Type of Borrowing Might Be Best?** If you wanted to borrow money to study abroad for a semester and could pay it back within two years after returning, would you prefer a single-payment loan, an installment loan, or a cash advance on a credit card? Why?

3. **Are Rebates a Good Idea?** Some credit cards offer a 1 percent or higher rebate for all purchases made on the card. How would you feel about using such a card to get those rebates with the intention of paying the balance off in full each month?

4. **Default Rates.** Do you feel that the much higher default interest rates are justified if you are not repaying a credit card on time? Does your opinion differ if the default rate was applied because you were behind on another account with that lender and not on the account charging the default rate?

5. **The Declining Balance Method.** How do you feel about the fact that interest costs are higher in the early months of a declining-balance loan than they are in the later months?

6. **The Rule of 78s.** Are prepayment penalties such as that applied with the rule of 78s justified? Why or why not?

DO THE MATH

1. **Monthly Payments and Finance Charges.** Kimberly Jensen and Rebecca Parker of Mankato, Minnesota, are both single. The pair share an apartment on the limited resources provided through Kimberly's disability check from Social Security and Rebecca's part-time job at a grocery store. The two grew tired of their old furniture and went shopping. A local store offered credit at an APR of 16 percent, with a maximum term of four years. The furniture they wish to purchase costs $2800, with no down payment required. Using Table 7-1 or the *Garman/Forgue* companion website, make the following calculations:

   (a) What is the amount of their monthly payment if they borrow for four years?

   (b) What are the total finance charges over that four-year period?

   (c) How would the payment change if Kimberly and Rebecca reduced the loan term to three years?

   (d) What are the total finance charges over that three-year period?

   (e) How would the payment change if they could afford a down payment of $500 with four years of financing?

   (f) What are the total finance charges over that four-year period given the $500 down payment?

   (g) How would the payment change if they could afford a down payment of $500 with three years of financing?

   (h) What are the total finance charges over that three-year period given the $500 down payment?

2. **Average Daily Balance and Finance Charges.** Talika Sampson, an antiques dealer from Wilmington, North Carolina, received her monthly billing statement for April for her MasterCard account. The statement indicated that she had a beginning balance of $600, on day 5 she charged $150, on day 12 she charged $300, and on day 15 she made a $200 payment. Out of curiosity, Talika wanted to confirm that the finance charge for the billing cycle was correct.

   (a) What was Talika's average daily balance for April without new purchases?

   (b) What was her finance charge on the balance in part (a) if her APR is 19.2 percent?

   (c) What was her average daily balance for April with new purchases?

   (d) What was her finance charge on the balance in part (c) if her APR is 19.2 percent?

3. **Average Daily Balance.** Elizabeth Mountbatten, a biologist from Lexington, Kentucky, is curious about the accuracy of the interest charges shown on her most recent credit card billing statement, which appears in Figure 7-2 on page 207. Use the average daily balances provided to recalculate the interest charges and compare the result with the amount shown on the statement.

4. **Comparing APRs.** Timothy Sprater of Elko, Nevada, has been shopping for a loan to buy a new car. He wants to borrow $18,000 for four or five years. Timothy's credit union offers a declining-balance loan at 9.1 percent for 48 months, resulting in a monthly payment of $448.78. The credit union does not offer five-year auto loans for amounts less than $20,000, however. If Timothy borrowed $18,000, this payment would strain his budget. A local bank offered current depositors a five-year loan at a 9.34 percent APR, with a monthly payment of $376.62. This credit would not be a declining-balance loan. Because Timothy is not a depositor in the bank, he would also be charged a $25 credit check fee and a $45 application fee. Timothy likes the lower payment but knows that the APR is the true cost of credit, so he decided to confirm the APRs for both loans before making his decision.

   (a) What is the APR for the credit union loan?

   (b) Use the n-ratio formula to confirm the APR on the bank loan as quoted for depositors.

   (c) What is the add-on interest rate for the bank loan?

   (d) What would be the true APR on the bank loan if Timothy did not open an account to avoid the credit check and application fees?

5. **Rule of 78s.** Aaron Carson of Hays, Kansas, obtained a two-year installment loan for $1500 to buy some furniture eight months ago. The loan had a 12.6 percent APR and a finance charge of $204.72. His monthly payment is $71.03. Aaron has made eight monthly payments and now wants to pay off the remainder of the loan. The lender will use the rule of 78s method to calculate a prepayment penalty.

   (a) How much will Aaron need to give the lender to pay off the loan?

   (b) What is the dollar amount of the prepayment penalty on this loan?

FINANCIAL PLANNING CASES

CASE 1

The Johnsons' Credit Questions

Harry and Belinda need some questions answered regarding credit. Their three-year-old car has been experiencing mechanical problems lately. Instead of buying a new set of tires, as planned for in March, they are considering trading the car in for a newer used vehicle so that Harry can have dependable transportation for commuting to work. The couple still owes $3600 to the bank for their current car, or $285 per month for the remaining 18 months of the 48-month loan. The trade-in value of this car plus $1000 that Harry earned from a freelance interior design job should allow the couple to pay off the auto loan and leave $1250 for a down payment on the newer car. The Johnsons have agreed on a sales price for the newer car of $14,250. The money planned for tires will be spent for other incidental taxes and fees associated with the purchase.

   (a) Make recommendations to Harry and Belinda regarding where to seek financing and what APR to expect.

   (b) Using the *Garman/Forgue* companion website or the information in Table 7-1, calculate the monthly payment for a loan period of three, four, and five years at 8 percent APR. Describe the relationship between the loan period and the payment amount.

   (c) Harry and Belinda have a cash-flow deficit projected for several months this year (see Table 3-6 and Table 3-7 on pages 88–89). Suggest how, when, and where they might finance the shortages by borrowing.

CASE 2

Victor and Maria Have a Billing Dispute

Maria Hernandez was reviewing her recent bank credit card account statement when she found two charges that she and Victor could not have made. The charges were for rental of a hotel room and purchase of a meal on the same day in a distant city. These charges totaled $219.49 out of the couple's $367.89 balance for the month.

(a) What payment should Maria make on the account?

(b) How should she notify her credit card issuer about the unauthorized use?

(c) Once the matter is resolved, what should Maria do to ensure that her credit history is not negatively affected by this error?

CASE 3

Julia Price Thinks About Her Use of Credit Cards

Julia has been thinking about how she uses credit cards. She has two bank cards and three store cards. The APRs on the cards range from 10.5 to 24.9 percent, with the store cards being among the highest. She uses the cards often and picks whatever card she comes to first in her wallet. Most months she pays the balance off in full. However, sometimes she is unable to pay the balance on one or more of the cards, and so she only pays the minimum balance. Julia feels she is doing her best on managing her cards but wants to do better. She is thinking about using just one of her bank cards for any purchases that she thinks she will be unable to pay at the end of the month. Offer your opinions about her thinking.

CASE 4

A Delayed Report of a Stolen Credit Card

Angela Craycraft of Fairbanks, Alaska, took her sister-in-law Mariah Johnson out for an expensive lunch. When it came time to pay the bill, Angela noticed that her Visa credit card was missing, so she paid the bill with her MasterCard. While driving home, Angela remembered that she had last used the Visa card about a week earlier. She became concerned that a sales clerk or someone else could have taken it and might be fraudulently charging purchases on her card.

(a) Summarize Angela's legal rights in this situation.

(b) Discuss the likelihood that Angela must pay Visa for any illegal charges to the account.

CASE 5

Clauses in a Car Purchase Contract

Virginia Rowland is a dentist in Jackson, Mississippi, who recently entered into a contract to buy a new automobile. After signing to finance $18,000, she hurriedly left the office of the sales finance company with her copy of the contract. Later that evening, Virginia read the contract and noticed several clauses—an acceleration clause, a repossession clause, and a rule of 78s clause. When she signed the contract, Virginia was told these standard clauses should not concern her.

(a) Should Virginia be concerned about these clauses? Why or why not?

(b) Considering the rule of 78s clause, what will happen if Virginia pays off the loan before the regular due date?

(c) If Virginia had financed the $18,000 for four years at 7 percent APR, what would her monthly payment be, using the information in Table 7-1 or on the *Garman/Forgue* companion website?

BE YOUR OWN PERSONAL FINANCIAL MANAGER

1. 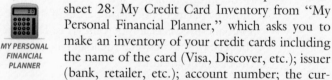 **List Your Credit Card Accounts.** Complete Worksheet 28: My Credit Card Inventory from "My Personal Financial Planner," which asks you to make an inventory of your credit cards including the name of the card (Visa, Discover, etc.); issuer (bank, retailer, etc.); account number; the current APRs for purchases, balance transfers, and cash advances; outstanding balance, if any; usual due dates; and phone numbers to use if the card is lost/stolen or there is a billing error.

2. 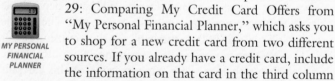 **Shop for a New Credit Card.** Complete Worksheet 29: Comparing My Credit Card Offers from "My Personal Financial Planner," which asks you to shop for a new credit card from two different sources. If you already have a credit card, include the information on that card in the third column in the worksheet. Determine whether your current card is the best of the three, or if you have no current card, choose among the two you have researched.

3. **Monitor Your Credit Card Statements.** Review your most recent credit card statements for accuracy. List the steps you would take if you found an error in the statement.

4. **Compare Hypothetical Vehicle Loans.** Assume you have decided to buy a used car by borrowing $6000 and you have offers for loans at 6, 8, and

MY PERSONAL FINANCIAL PLANNER

10 percent and each can be for 3, 4, or 5 years. Complete Worksheet 30: Monthly Installment Loan Payment Calculator from "My Personal Financial Planner" to determine the monthly payment for each of the six loan arrangements. Which loan is most attractive to you and why?

ON THE 'NET

Go to the Web pages indicated to complete these exercises.

1. **Review Current Market Interest Rates.** Visit the website for Bankrate.com at www.bankrate.com, where you will find information on bank credit card interest rates around the United States. View the information for the lenders in a large city nearest your home. How does the information compare with the interest rates charged on your own credit card account(s)? How do the rates in the city you selected compare with those found elsewhere in the United States?

2. **Explore the Impact of Varying Interest Rates and Time Periods on a Loan Payment Amount.** Visit the website for Interest.com at www.interest.com/auto.

There you will find an auto loan calculator that determines the monthly payment for any declining-balance loan given a specified time period, interest rate, and loan amount. Assume you wish to borrow $12,000 to buy a car. Vary the time period and interest rate of the loan to see how these variations affect your monthly payment.

3. **How Long Will It Take to Pay Off Your Credit Card?** Do you owe money on one or more credit cards? Visit the Bankrate.com website at www.bankrate.com and click on "More calculators" to find a calculator that will tell you how long it will take to pay off your balances given various monthly payment amounts.

ACTION INVOLVEMENT PROJECTS

1. **Comparing Credit Card Offers.** Select two local retailers, a local bank, and a local credit card and request credit card applications. Compare the applications for the types of information they require. Compare the APRs offered among the cards and others that you may already hold. Make a table that summarizes your findings and write some brief reactions to what you found.

2. **Credit Card Repayment Patterns.** Survey five of your friends about their patterns of using their credit card accounts including their choice to make the minimum payment rather than pay off the balance in full each month. Compare what they do to your own pattern and write a summary of your findings.

3. **Credit Card Billing Errors.** Survey five of your friends about experiences they have had concerning a billing error on their credit cards. Compare the steps they took to resolve the error(s) with those recommended in this chapter. Write a summary of your findings.

4. **Installment Loan Interest Methods.** Visit a bank and a credit union in your community and your own bankers. Tell them that you are considering taking out a loan to purchase a vehicle. Inquire whether they offer declining-balance or add-on method loans and which approach they would recommend. Compare the responses to the information provided in this chapter and write a summary of your findings.

Visit the Garman/Forgue companion website at **www.cengagebrain.com**.

8

Vehicle and Other Major Purchases

YOU MUST BE KIDDING, RIGHT?

When Dora Marquez graduated from college three years ago, she really wanted a fully equipped Honda Civic. Her monthly payment would be about $350 per month, about $70 more than she could afford. To help Dora meet her budget, the dealer suggested that she lease the vehicle and offered a 42-month lease option at $270 per month with a driving maximum of 12,000 miles per year. The contract had a $0.30 per mile fee at the end of the lease for any excess mileage. Now, with six more months on her lease, Dora is already 1500 miles over the 42,000 (3.5 × 12,000) mileage limit in her contract. What is Dora's best option at this point?

A. Turn back the vehicle now and pay the $450 (1500 × $0.30) for excess mileage.

B. Try to cut back on her driving to minimize her excess mileage fee, which could be higher than $2500 if she keeps driving at the same rate as she has been.

C. Stop driving the car and pay $450 for excess mileage when she turns it back at the end of the lease.

D. Continue driving the vehicle and buy it at the end of the lease by paying the residual value agreed upon when she entered into the contract.

The answer is D. None of the other options is financially practical. Dora learned a hard lesson. Leases may have a lower monthly payment but have hidden costs that often are not known until the very end of the contract!

© PETER DAZELEY/GETTY IMAGES, INC.

LEARNING OBJECTIVES

After reading this chapter, you should be able to:

❶ Explain the three steps in the planned buying process that occur prior to interacting with sellers.

❷ Describe the process of comparison shopping.

❸ Negotiate and decide effectively when making major purchases.

❹ Use effective complaint procedures.

WHAT DO YOU RECOMMEND?

David and Lisa Cosgrove of Tacoma, Washington, are in their early 40s and have three children. They own three vehicles. Lisa drives an almost-new Toyota Camry; David uses a five-year-old Ford pickup; and Amber, the couple's 17-year-old daughter, drives a ten-year-old Dodge. Recently, a fire in their garage destroyed both the Dodge and the Camry. The Cosgroves received an insurance settlement of $21,900 on Lisa's car, although the loan payoff amount was $22,800. Amber's Dodge was not insured for fire. The couple wants to obtain replacement cars that are similar to those destroyed.

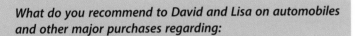

What do you recommend to David and Lisa on automobiles and other major purchases regarding:

1. How to search for two vehicles to replace those destroyed?

2. Whether to replace Lisa's vehicle with a new or used vehicle?

3. Whether to lease or buy a vehicle?

4. How to decide between a rebate and a special low APR financing opportunity if they decide to purchase a new vehicle for Lisa?

5. How to negotiate with the sellers of the vehicles?

 **LEARNING OBJECTIVE ❶**

Explain the three steps in the planned buying process that occur prior to interacting with sellers.

need
Item thought to be necessary.

want
Item not necessary but desired.

Planned buying entails thinking about the details of a purchase from the initial desire to buy to your satisfaction after the purchase. You should use planned buying principles any time, but they are especially important when you are buying a car or making other "big ticket" purchases. The seven distinct steps that lead you through the planned buying process are illustrated in Figure 8-1. Steps 1, 2, and 3 occur before you interact with sellers: determining your needs and wants, performing preshopping research, and fitting a purchase into your budget. Comparison shopping and other interactions with sellers comprise the fourth step in the buying process. Steps 5 and 6—negotiating and making the decision—follow. The seventh and final step—evaluation of the decision—is taken after making the purchase. After reading this chapter, you will understand enough about the planned buying process to save money when buying expensive goods while still meeting your needs and many of your wants.

DO YOUR HOMEWORK BEFORE YOU BUY

Let's look now at the first three steps, all of which should occur before you actually interact with sellers. They are, in a sense, the homework you do when preparing to buy.

Wants Versus Needs

A **need** is something thought to be a necessity; a **want** is unnecessary but desired. In truth, very few needs exist, yet in everyday language, people talk often of "needing" certain things. Avoid calling something a need because this may make it no longer open to careful consideration. Instead, consider all purchase options to be wants even though some wants are more important than others. The most important can be determined by prioritizing your wants. This approach allows for consideration of the benefits and costs of each want. Costs should include opportunity costs as measured by some other want or goal that will become less attainable if a given want is satisfied. For example, buying a car with a retractable sunroof might mean that you cannot afford to purchase one with a remote start feature.

Setting priorities becomes difficult when a decision is complex such as when buying a car or home. Consider the case of Sharon Wilson, a physical therapist from St. Paul, Minnesota. Sharon has been late to work several times in the past few months because her 12-year-old car has been having too many mechanical problems. Sharon wants to avoid being late. But how? Should she buy a new car or a used car, lease a new car, repair

Figure 8-1   **The Steps in Planned Buying**

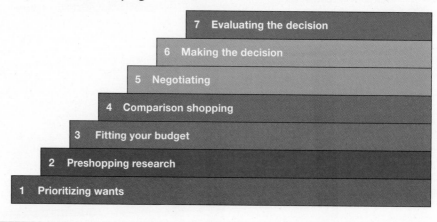

her current car, or take the bus to work? After considering these options, Sharon decided to buy a new car. Now she must determine which features are of high or low priority. To do so, Sharon developed the worksheet shown in Figure 8-2. Such a worksheet makes it easier to formalize her wants.

Get Smart with Preshopping Research

Smart shoppers learn as much as they can about a product or service before buying. This process starts with **preshopping research**—gathering information before actually beginning to interact with sellers. Manufacturers, sellers, and service providers are all important sources of information about products and services during preshopping research. Two other sources are friends and consumer magazines. If you know someone who drives a car you're considering, ask that person's opinion of it.

What Do You Really Know About the Product? You can also
research a car in *Consumer Reports*, a magazine that objectively tests and reports on numerous product categories. Monthly issues of *Consumer Reports* generally provide a two- to five-page narrative analyzing the products and summarizing the information in chart form. *Consumer Reports Buying Guide*, which is published every December, lists facts and figures for all kinds of products. And each year, the April issue of *Consumer Reports* is devoted entirely to the purchase of automobiles. All this and more can be seen at www.ConsumerReports.org.

FINANCIAL POWER POINT

Avoid Impulse Buying

Buying too quickly without fully considering priorities and alternatives is called **impulse buying**. It wastes money, and impulse buyers often do not buy what they really want.

impulse buying
Buying too quickly without fully considering priorities and alternatives.

preshopping research
Gathering information before actually beginning to interact with sellers.

Priority Worksheet (for Sharon Wilson)

Figure 8-2

AUTOMOBILE FEATURE	PRIORITY LEVEL		
	1	2	3
Adaptive cruise control (uses radar to keep a safe distance)		✔	
Air conditioning	✔		
Aluminum wheels		✔	
Automatic transmission	✔		
Backing-up cross-path monitoring		✔	
Blind-spot monitoring			✔
Capless fuel filler	✔		
4-wheel ABS		✔	
4-wheel drive		✔	
Keyless locking system			✔
Lane departure warning			✔
Leather seats	✔		
"MyFord" type infotainment system		✔	
Pedestrian detection			✔
Power windows	✔		
Pass-through rear seat		✔	
Satellite radio	✔		
Seat belt tightening when braking		✔	
Sun/moon roof			✔
Top-level sound system	✔		

manufacturer's suggested retail price (MSRP)
The retail price set by the manufacturer and posted on the federally required side window sticker.

dealer invoice price (or base invoice price)
The amount the automaker charges the dealership for new vehicles at the time the dealer buys them; it does not reflect some discounts that the dealer gets.

DID YOU KNOW?

When People Trade in Their Cars

Surveys show that about 15 percent of vehicle owners replace their cars before they have 100,000 miles, more than half get another vehicle when the old one has between 100,000 and 250,000 miles on the odometer, and about one-quarter wait for 250,000 or more miles.

Gauge Environmental Impact Many products such as vehicles, electronic equipment and household appliances have an impact on the environment. This factor is part of many people's purchase decisions and relevant information is often available. For example, government-required window stickers on new vehicles, starting with the 2013 model year, will include both estimated annual fuel costs and the vehicle's overall environmental impact. The labels will also compare vehicles across classes so potential buyers can make informed decisions.

What Price Should You Expect to Pay? Advertising is often a key source of information about prices. You can also obtain price information through catalogs, on the telephone, and over the Internet. This situation differs for big-ticket items. While the prices of furniture, appliances, and vehicles may be advertised, that price is rarely the lowest price you can expect to pay. This is because sellers of big-ticket items typically have the authority to negotiate an even lower price, if necessary, to make a sale. During sluggish economic times, you can really bargain for a deal. You should have a clear understanding what price to expect to pay before going out to shop. Otherwise, you risk negotiating a price higher than necessary.

Break the Dealer's Code on New Vehicle Prices You will see two prices when you walk into a dealer's showroom: (1) manufacturer's suggested retail price, and (2) dealer invoice price. Both are artificial numbers; thus your negotiation effort should not be to get close to the dealer invoice price but to a lower *real price* you may decide to pay. The **manufacturer's suggested retail price (MSRP)** is the retail price set by the manufacturer and posted on the federally required side window sticker. The dealership wants you to pay full MSRP plus any miscellaneous charges.

The **dealer invoice price** (or **base invoice price**) is the amount the automaker charges the dealership for new vehicles at the time the dealer buys them; it does not reflect some discounts that the dealer gets. The invoice price typically has some additional charges tacked on by the dealer, which are attempts to generate additional revenue.

Find Real Price Information on New and Used Vehicles Edmunds.com reports that the average price for new cars and trucks is over $29,000. Smart buyers can research the average retail and wholesale prices on new and used vehicles by visiting the websites for Edmunds (www.edmunds.com), Kelley Blue Book (www.kbb.com), or the National Automobile Dealers Association (http://www.nadaguides.com).

Know the Value of Your Trade-in Vehicle When buying vehicles, it is common, but not always advantageous, to trade in an old model when buying a new one. Vehicle buyers should know the true value of any vehicle they will trade in. Using the websites mentioned earlier, you can find the likely trade-in value of your vehicle (the wholesale price) as well as the amount you could sell it for yourself (the retail price). Armed with this information, you can more effectively negotiate a good trade-in allowance on your existing vehicle with a dealer. If you don't get a good offer on your vehicle from the dealer, shop at another dealer or consider selling it yourself.

Can I Afford It?

When considering a big-ticket item everyone wonders, "Can I afford it?" An unaffordable cash purchase can wreck your budget for one or two months. However, the negative effects of an ill-advised credit or lease contract may last for years.

A Car Buying Illustration One way to view the cost of a major expenditure is to consider the cost per use of the product. For example, Paul Lenz, an autoworker from Dothan, Alabama, is considering buying a high-quality video camera. He has researched several models in the $700 to $750 price range. Paul figures that he would use the camera about 20 times per year and knows that the average video camera lasts about seven years, giving him 140 uses. Dividing this figure into the price of a $700 model yields a cost per use of $5 ($700 ÷ 140), excluding the cost of videotapes and maintenance. It might be possible for Paul to save money by renting or borrowing a camera when he needs one. Or he could buy a less expensive camera.

To see how this process works with a more expensive purchase, consider how Sharon Wilson (see Table 8-1) might fit a new car into her budget. She estimates that the dealer invoice price of the car she wants will be about $28,000. This is the price for the car she wants, not including her highest-priority wants. These options will likely add about $3300 more to the dealer invoice price: air conditioning, $700; automatic transmission, $600; leather seats, $700; capless fuel filler, $100; power windows, $400; top-level sound system, $600; and satellite ratio, $200. Buying a car with these features will run the cost to $31,300 ($28,000 + $3300 for the options). She expects to use $3500 from her savings account as a down payment, receive $2000 for trading in her old car, and borrow the remaining amount. The actual price she will pay for the car will depend on her ability to negotiate the final price down from the dealer invoice price. From her preshopping research, Sharon knows that the final agreed upon price should be about 12 percent less than the dealer invoice price. Sharon figures she should be able to negotiate the price of the purchase down by at least 10 percent from $31,300 to $28,170 ($31,300 − $3130 [$31,300 × 0.10]).

Time invested in preshopping research pays off in better purchase decisions.

Table 8-1

Fitting a Vehicle Payment into a Monthly Budget (Sharon Wilson's $2440 Disposable Income)

	Prior Budget	Possible Cutbacks	New Budget
Food	$ 350	$ −30	$ 320
Clothing/laundry	120	−50	70
Vehicle maintenance/ repairs/tires	80	−30	50
Auto insurance	80		80
Gasoline	160	−20	140
Housing	800		800
Utilities	150		150
Telephone	70		70
Entertainment	150	−50	100
Gifts	50	−10	40
Church and charity	60		60
Personal care	100	−20	80
Savings	200	−100	100
Miscellaneous	70	−20	50
TOTAL	**$2,440**	**$ −330**	**$2,110**
Car payment			707
TOTAL WITH CAR PAYMENT	**$2,300**	**$ −330**	**$2,887**

FINANCIAL POWER POINT

How Many Hours of Work Will This Item Cost?

When buying a new vehicle, computer, television, or any big-ticket item, divide the cost of the item by your hourly take-home pay. For example, if you divide the cost of an $1100 personal computer by $10 take-home pay ($15 − taxes), that tells you that you must work 110 hours to pay for it.

DID YOU KNOW?

How to Buy a Safe Car

The following pointers may help you buy a safer vehicle:

- **Check government safety test results.** The federal government crash-tests motor vehicles to analyze their safety. For results on various makes and models, call the National Highway Traffic Safety Administration (NHTSA) "auto hotline" at (800) 424-9393 or visit www.safercar.gov.

- **Consider a vehicle with extra airbags.** Almost all cars have driver and passenger front-seat airbags. For added protection, consider models that also provide head, side-tubular, knee, rear-curtain, seat-belt, and/or rear-seat-center airbags.

- **Check on recalls.** When buying a used car, visit www.nhtsa.gov to see whether the vehicle has been recalled. If so, confirm that the repairs have been made to the car you're considering; if not, buy elsewhere. Dealers are required to fix for free vehicles recalled for safety reasons.

The final cost Sharon will pay depends on (1) the price she actually pays for the car, (2) the amount of the down payment, (3) the time period for payback of the loan, (4) the amount she receives in trade for her old car, and (5) the interest rate on the vehicle loan. Assuming a car price of $28,170 and another $830 for sales tax and title fees to register the vehicle, Sharon will need to finance about $29,000 ($28,170 + $830). The monthly payment over 48 months for an 8 percent loan could be about $707 a month (from Table 7-1 on page 213 [$24.41 × 29]).

Fit the Vehicle Payment into a Monthly Budget The next challenge is to determine if a possible vehicle payment is truly affordable. Sharon tried to fit the $707 car payment into her budget as shown in Table 8-1.

Table 8-1 shows Sharon's monthly budget. She started with the fact that her take-home pay of $2440 is totally committed, including $200 in monthly savings. So she juggled the numbers to see if she could finance a new car and found she could only find $330. That's far short of the $707 needed for a monthly payment. By taking out a longer, 60-month 8 percent loan, she could reduce her payments to about $588 per month (29 × $20.28 from Table 7-1 on page 213). Sharon's alternatives are to make more cutbacks in her budget, work overtime, or get a part-time job. Or she could forget the new car entirely and look for a used vehicle that is affordable.

 Concept Check 8.1

1. What is planned buying?

2. Distinguish between *needs* and *wants*, and explain why it may be better to act as if no needs exist.

3. Describe the types of information you need to be your own expert when making big-ticket purchases.

4. Summarize the process to determine whether you can afford a particular purchase.

USE COMPARISON SHOPPING TO FIND THE BEST BUY

Comparison shopping is the process of comparing products or services to find the best buy. A **best buy** is a product or service that, in the buyer's opinion, represents acceptable quality at a fair or low price for that level of quality. Purchasing the product with the lowest price does not necessarily ensure a best buy because quality and features count, too.

Prices on big-ticket items such as autos, furniture, appliances, and electronic equipment are rarely the same from seller to seller and vary from week to week. You can begin your comparison shopping online, but most likely you will need to visit different stores to see the products. Experts recommend that consumers use the **"rule of three"** when shopping at stores. This means comparing at least three alternatives before making a decision.

Compare Financing Options

Neither the lowest interest rate nor the smallest payment means the best credit plan. Better credit terms are frequently available at lenders not associated with sellers. Your bank and credit union lend money to make purchases for vehicles and household appliances. Also check out websites such as bankrate.com or interest.com.

Beware, Beware Beware of taking out a longer loan on a vehicle purchase, such as for five or more years, because the value of your car may be less than the amount you owe. This is known as being **upside down** because you have negative equity. If you default on the loan or sell the vehicle, you will have to make up the difference. Rolling the negative equity forward into the car financing of the next vehicle purchase means that the amount will be added to the price of the new car.

When talking with sellers, consider "same as cash" offers on furniture, appliances, and electronics that allow you to delay interest or payment for, perhaps, 90 days to one year. If the product is paid off during this time period, you will not incur any finance charges. Be wary, however, because interest will be charged retroactively if a payment is late or if the purchase isn't fully paid off during the required time period.

When shopping for an automobile, do not give out your Social Security number or allow the dealer to photocopy your driver's license before you go on a test drive. With that information, the dealer could access your credit report and estimate how much you can afford to pay and your ability to obtain financing elsewhere.

What Is a Fair Interest Rate? A borrower with a high credit score who can get a 1 percentage point reduction in interest for a $15,000 loan over 48 months can save hundreds of dollars in interest paid over the life of the loan. Interest rates for all types of loans, including vehicle loans, can be found at www.bankrate.com. Buyers should obtain multiple quotes from banks and credit unions. When shopping for a major purchase, ask your local bank or credit union for a **loan preapproval** before you visit sellers. This pre-shopping step will let you know how much you can borrow and at what interest rate.

Choose Between a Low Interest Rate and a Rebate A source of loans for new vehicles is sales financing arranged through the dealer or manufacturer. The interest rate on this credit is often low when manufacturers or dealers want to generate additional sales volume.

Many sellers also offer rebates to encourage people to buy. With a **rebate**, the seller refunds a portion of the purchase price of the product either as a direct payment or a credit against future purchases (often through a gift card). Vehicle manufacturers offer rebates of $1000 to $5000 to purchasers of new vehicles as a way to generate more sales volume or to move slow-selling models. In most cases, the buyer must choose between the rebate and a low APR loan offer also being offered by the manufacturer. Many people choose to borrow the full price elsewhere and receive the rebate in cash. In effect, this option means that they are borrowing more money than the vehicle actually costs. Plus, the buyers also lose out on the opportunity for the low APR offer.

The Run the Numbers worksheet on page 230 provides a way to calculate whether a rebate or low APR financing is the better option. If you do decide to take the rebate on a new vehicle, you should apply the money to the down payment on the vehicle or pay extra on the first monthly payment on the loan. Rebates are common when purchasing products such as vehicles, cell phones, and computers. The most current details on manufacturers' rebates to both consumers and auto dealers can be found at Edmunds.com (www.Edmunds.com).

Compare Leasing to Buying

Leasing a new vehicle is an increasingly attractive option to people who are in the market for a car. About 20 percent of the new cars "sold" each year are actually leased. It is even possible to lease used cars. Is leasing a better deal than financing? You cannot answer this question until you understand some basics and risks of leasing.

When **leasing** a vehicle or any other product, you are, in effect, renting the product while the ownership title remains with the lease grantor. Regulation M issued by the Federal Reserve Board governs lease contracts. A requirement of this regulation is a mandatory disclosure of pertinent information about the lease that the consumer is considering. The disclosure form must summarize the offer of the **lessor** (leasing agency) to the **lessee**

comparison shopping
Process of comparing products or services to find the best buy.

best buy
Product or service that, in the buyer's opinion, represents acceptable quality at a fair or low price for that quality level.

upside down
A situation where the owner of a financed asset owes more than it is worth, thus creating negative equity.

loan preapproval
Oral commitment from a bank or credit union agreeing to furnish credit for a purchase; lets buyers know how much they can borrow and at what interest rate.

FINANCIAL POWER POINT

People Waste Rebates

Only about half of people who buy manufacturers' products that offer rebates actually take the time to complete and mail in the forms to obtain the money. The rate is even lower on items costing less than $50. Advice: Complete and mail the form as soon as you return home with the purchase.

rebate
A partial refund of a purchase price offered as an inducement to buy.

leasing
Renting a product while ownership title remains with the lease grantor.

RUN THE NUMBERS

Choosing Between Low-Interest-Rate Dealer Financing and a Rebate

Advertisements for new vehicles often offer low APRs for dealer-arranged loans. A cash rebate of $1000 to $3000 (or more) off the price of the car may be offered as an alternative to the low interest rate. If you intend to pay cash, then the cash rebate obviously represents the better deal. But which alternative is better when you can arrange your own financing?

To compare the two APRs accurately, you must add the opportunity cost of the forgone rebate to the finance charge of the dealer financing. The worksheet provides an example of this process. Suppose a dealer offers 2.9 percent financing for three years with a $907 finance charge; alternatively, you can receive a $3000 rebate if you arrange your own financing. The price of the car before the rebate is $22,000. Assume you can make a $2000 down payment and that you can get a 6.5 percent loan on your own. This worksheet can be found on the *Garman/Forgue* companion website, or you can find similar worksheets at www.bankrate.com and at www.kiplinger.com.

The lower of the values obtained in steps 3 and 4 is the better deal. In this instance, the financing that you arranged on your own is more attractive. In fact, any loan you arrange that carries an APR lower than 12 percent compares favorably with the dealer-arranged financing in this case.

Step	Example	Your Figures
1. Determine the dollar amount of the rebate.	$3000	_____
2. Add the rebate amount to the finance charge for the dealer financing (dollar cost of credit).	+$ 907	_____

3. Use the formula from Chapter 7 (Equation [7.2] on page 215 and replicated here as Equation [8.1]) to calculate an adjusted APR for the dealer financing.

$$APR = \frac{Y(95P + 9)F}{12P(P + 1)(4D + F)} \quad (8.1)$$

where

APR = Annual percentage rate
Y = Number of payment periods in one **year**
F = **Finance** charge in dollars
D = **Debt** (amount borrowed)
P = Total number of scheduled **payments**

$$APR = \frac{(12)[(95 \times 36) + 9]($3000 + $907)}{12 \times 36(36 + 1)[(4 \times $20,000) + ($3000 + $907)]} \quad = 12\%$$

4. Write in the APR that you arranged on your own.   6.5%   _____

(consumer). The information in this form should be compared with the actual lease contract prior to signing to ensure that the lease signed is actually what was agreed upon verbally.

Leasing Terminology   Five terms are important in leasing:

gross capitalized cost (gross cap cost)
Includes vehicle price plus the cost of any extra features such as insurance or maintenance agreements.

adjusted capitalized cost (adjusted cap cost)
Subtracting the capitalized cost reductions from the gross capitalized cost.

residual value
Projected value of a leased asset at the end of the lease time period.

1. **The gross capitalized cost (gross cap cost)** includes the price of the vehicle plus what the lessee paid to finance the purchase plus any other items the lessee agreed to pay for over the life of the lease, including insurance or a maintenance agreement.
2. **Capitalized cost reductions (cap cost reductions)** are monies paid on the lease at its inception, including any down payment, trade-in value, or rebate.
3. **The adjusted capitalized cost (adjusted cap cost)** is determined by subtracting the capitalized cost reductions from the gross capitalized cost.
4. **The residual value** is the projected value of a leased asset at the end of the lease time period.
5. **The money factor** (or **lease rate** or **lease factor**) measures the rent charge portion of your payment. Although the money factor is sometimes described by dealers as a figure for comparing leases, lease forms must carry the following disclosure about the money factor: "This percentage may not measure the overall cost of financing this lease."

Rule number one when considering leasing: Always negotiate the purchase price before discussing a lease! Leasing requires an initial outlay of cash to pay for the first month's lease payment and a security deposit. Payments are based on the capitalized cost of the asset minus any capitalized cost reductions and the residual value. This difference represents the cost of using the asset during the lease period; when divided by the number of months in the contract, it serves to establish the base for the monthly lease payment. (Some new vehicles are offered with single-payment leases in which the entire difference between the capitalized cost and residual value is paid up front.) With monthly payment leases, the payments are lower than monthly loan payments for equivalent time periods because you are paying for only the reduction in the asset's value—not its entire cost. To compare the costs of leasing versus buying, use the Run the Numbers worksheet, "Comparing Automobile Financing and Leasing." Also see www.leasecompare.com.

Open- and Closed-End Leases A lease may be either open end or closed end. In an **open-end lease**, you must pay any difference between the projected residual value of the vehicle and its actual market value at the end of the lease period. When a vehicle depreciates more rapidly than expected, the holder of an open-end lease has to pay extra money when the lease expires. For example, a vehicle with an $11,000 residual value but a $10,250 market value would require an end-of-lease payment of $750 ($11,000 − $10,250). The Consumer Leasing Act limits this end-of-lease payment to a maximum of three times the average monthly payment.

Most vehicle leases are closed-end leases. In a **closed-end lease** (also called a **walkaway lease**), the holder pays no charge if the end-of-lease market value of the vehicle is lower than the originally projected residual value. However, closed-end leases may carry some type of end-of-lease charge if the vehicle has greater than normal wear or excess mileage. For example, a four-year closed-end lease might require a $0.30 per mile **excess mileage charge** in excess of 55,000 miles. If you actually drove the vehicle

closed-end lease/walkaway lease
Agreement in which the lessee pays no charge if the end-of-lease market value of the vehicle is lower than the originally projected residual value.

excess mileage charge
Fees assessed at the end of a lease if the vehicle was driven more miles than originally specified in the lease contract.

RUN THE NUMBERS

Comparing Automobile Financing and Leasing

This worksheet can be used to compare leasing and borrowing to buy a vehicle. Remember that the cost of credit is the finance charge—the extra that you pay because you borrowed. Leases also carry costs, but they are hidden in the contract. Indeed, some may remain unknown until the end of the lease period. These lease costs, which are indicated by an asterisk (*), are negotiable and are defined in the text. Ask the dealer for the price of each item, as these fees must be disclosed by dealers. Then complete the worksheet and compare the dollar cost of leasing with the finance charge on a loan for the same time period.

To make the comparison accurately, you must know the underlying price of the car as if you were purchasing it. Often you are not offered this value with a lease arrangement, so you should always negotiate a price for the vehicle before mentioning your interest in leasing.

Shop for a lease through dealers and independent leasing companies because costs vary widely. This worksheet can be found on the *Garman/Forgue* companion website, or you can find similar worksheets at www.bankrate.com (search for "calculators") or www.kiplingers.com/tools.

Step	Example	Your Figures
1. Monthly lease payment (36 payments of $375, for example)	$13,500	_____
2. Plus acquisition fee* (if any)	300	_____
Plus disposition charge* (if any)	300	_____
Plus estimate of excess mileage charges* (if any)	0	_____
Plus projected residual value of the vehicle	4,500	_____
3. Amount for which you are responsible under the lease	18,600	_____
4. Less the adjusted capitalized cost (gross capitalized cost* less the capitalized cost reductions*)	16,000	_____
5. Dollar cost of leasing to be compared with a finance charge if you purchased the vehicle	2,600	_____

balloon automobile loan
A loan that has a low monthly payment similar in amount to that required if the vehicle had been leased and with a large final payment similar in amount to the residual value under a lease.

60,000 miles during the four years, you would be charged an extra $1500 [$0.30 × 5000 (60,000 − 55,000)].

With either an open- or closed-end lease, you may purchase the vehicle at the end of the lease period. With an open-end lease, you would pay the actual cash value. With a closed-end lease, you would pay the residual value.

Lots of Leasing Fees Other charges are possible with a lease. An **acquisition fee** is either paid in cash or included in the gross capitalization cost. It pays for a credit report, application fee, and other paperwork. A **disposition fee** is assessed when you turn in the vehicle at the end of the lease and the lessor must prepare it for resale. An **early termination charge** may also be levied if you decide to end the lease prematurely. Be wary of a lease with an early termination charge, even if you do not plan to end the lease early, because termination also occurs when a leased vehicle is traded in or is totally wrecked or stolen. Make sure you obtain a written disclosure of these charges well before you actually make your decision. The **early termination payoff** is the total amount you would need to repay if you end the lease agreement early; it includes both the early termination charge and the unpaid lease balance. In its early years, your lease may be financially upside down, which means that you owe more on the vehicle than it is worth.

Be Cautious About Leasing Getting a good deal on a leased vehicle can be very complicated. Therefore, be cautious if you talk about buying all through the negotiation process only to be offered a lease at the last minute. Because the monthly charge will be lower, you may be tempted to sign a deal that actually costs considerably more. In addition, make sure all oral agreements related to trade-in value, mileage charges, and rebates are included in the lease contract.

Avoid Balloon Loans One option for people considering a lease is a balloon automobile loan. You can arrange this type of financing through your bank or credit union. With a **balloon automobile loan**, you actually buy the vehicle with the last monthly payment equaling the projected residual value of the vehicle at the end of the loan period. This arrangement effectively lowers all the other earlier monthly payments to make them more competitive with lease payments. When the final balloon payment is due, perhaps $1000 to $7000, the borrower generally has three options:

1. Sell the car and pay the balloon payment with the proceeds (with luck, the vehicle will sell for a high enough amount).
2. Pay the balloon payment and keep the vehicle.
3. Return the vehicle to the lender to cover the balloon payment.

Be Cautious About "Gap" Insurance New cars and low-mileage used cars depreciate (go down in value) very quickly after purchase, often as much as 25 percent after leaving the dealer's lot. If you take out a vehicle loan with a low down payment, it is possible that the value of the vehicle will go down faster than the amount owed. As a result, you can owe more on the vehicle than it is worth. This situation is referred to as being "upside down" and can last for up to two years after the initial purchase.

Being upside down can be a big problem when a newer vehicle is totaled in an accident. In such cases, the insurance company will reimburse for the value of the vehicle, not the amount owed on the loan. Many car dealers sell **gap insurance** that pays off the remainder of the loan if the insurance payment is insufficient to do so. While gap insurance is attractive, it is very profitable for the dealer and not such a good deal for the buyer. You should consider the possibility of being upside down as a sign that you are not making a large enough down payment or that you are buying a vehicle that is too expensive for you.

Compare Warranties

Warranties are an important consideration in comparison shopping. Almost all products have **warranties**—assurances by sellers that goods are as promised and that certain steps will be taken to rectify problems—even if only in the form of implied warranties. The longer the warranty is and the more it covers, the better the warranty.

Implied and Express Warranties Under an **implied warranty**, the product sold is warranted to be suitable for sale (a **warranty of merchantability**) and to work effectively (a **warranty of fitness**) whether or not a written warranty exists. Implied warranties are required by state law. To avoid them, the seller can state in writing that the product is sold **as is**. If you buy any product "as is," you have no legal recourse if it fails to perform, even if the salesperson made verbal promises to take care of any problems. Used cars are often sold as is.

Written and oral warranties are called **express warranties**. Companies that offer written express warranties must do so under the provisions of the federal Magnuson-Moss Warranty Act if the product is sold for more than $15. This law provides that any written warranty offered must be classified as either a full warranty or a limited warranty.

Full and Limited Warranties A **full warranty** includes three stringent requirements:

1. A product must be fixed at no cost to the buyer within a reasonable time after the owner has complained.
2. The owner will not have to undertake an unreasonable task to return the product for repair (such as ship back a refrigerator).
3. A defective product will be replaced with a new one or the buyer's money will be returned if the product cannot be fixed after a reasonable number of attempts.

A **limited warranty** includes less than a full warranty. For example, it may offer only free parts, not labor. Note that one part of a product could be covered by a full warranty (perhaps the engine on a lawnmower) and the rest of the unit by a limited warranty. Read all warranties carefully, and note that both full and limited warranties are valid for only a specified time period.

Extended Warranties (Service Contracts) Are Overpriced

An **extended warranty** (or **service contract**) is an agreement between the contract seller (the dealer, manufacturer, or an independent company) and the buyer of a product to provide repair or replacement for covered components of the product for some specified time period. Extended warranties are sometimes given names such as **maintenance agreement** or **buyer protection plan**. These service contracts are purchased separately from the product itself (such as a vehicle, appliance, or electronics equipment). The cost is paid either in a lump sum or in monthly payments.

Extended warranties are not insurance but act similarly. For example, a 40-inch high-definition television could have an extended warranty that promises to fix anything that goes wrong during the third and fourth years of ownership; the manufacturer's warranty covers the first two years. This contract might cost $120 for each year, or $10 per month.

Although buying an extended warranty might provide peace of mind, it is unwise financially because it makes little economic sense to insure against risks that can, if necessary, be paid for out of current income or savings. Plus extended warranties are horribly overpriced. More than 80 percent of all service contracts are never used, and total payouts to consumers to make repairs amount to less than 10 percent of all money spent on the contracts. More than half the profits of some electronics dealers come from extended warranty sales, not the products themselves.

Extended warranties are not a good choice when buying electronics because the products rarely have problems beyond the warranty period. Products that do seem to break down frequently are cell phones, laptops, treadmills, and elliptical trainers. Buy a service contract only from the actual manufacturer or dealer that sold the item. These contracts are prevalent in the vehicle, appliance, and electronics markets because of the high profits involved and the persuasiveness of salespeople, who typically earn an extra high commission on the sale of an extended warranty.

warranty
Sellers' assurances that goods are as promised and that certain steps will be taken to rectify problems if they arise.

as is
Way for the seller to get around legal requirements for warranties; the buyer takes all risk of nonperformance or other problems despite any salesperson's verbal assurances.

full warranty
Warranty that meets three stringent promises: the product must be fixed at no cost to the buyer within a reasonable time, the owner will not have to undertake an unreasonable task to return the product for repair, and a defective product will be replaced with a new one or the buyer's money will be returned if the product cannot be fixed.

limited warranty
Any warranty that offers less than the three conditions for full warranty.

extended warranty/service contract/maintenance agreement/buyer protection plan
Agreement between the seller and buyer of a product to repair or replace covered product components for some specified time period; purchased separately from the product itself.

Automobile manufacturers and dealers offer service contract plans; in addition, a number of independent companies offer service contracts for new vehicles. A deductible of about $100 usually must be paid with each use of the contract. Repairs are usually covered and may include preventive maintenance for covered components. The cost for an extended warranty averages $1800, and $800 of that is dealer profit, with $250 going to the salesperson. Sellers can afford to be more generous on a deal if they know that most of the money will be made back on the service contract. About one-third of people buy an extended warranty on their new vehicles, and three-fourths of those who haggled over price got a discount.

 Concept Check 8.2

1. What is the goal of comparison shopping?

2. Explain why lease payments for a new vehicle are lower than loan payments for the same vehicle.

3. Describe the relationships among capital cost, capital cost reductions, and residual value in a lease.

4. Explain the difference between an implied warranty and an express warranty. How do they relate to the term *as is*?

5. What is an extended warranty? What is a disadvantage of such a contract?

ADVICE FROM A PRO

Tips for Buying Online

People use the Internet to shop for appliances, vehicles, furniture, and other big-ticket items. Here's how you can become a better online shopper:

1. **Use only secure sites.** *A secure site will feature a key or lock symbol on its screens or have a URL starting with "https" ("s" for secure). Sites displaying the VeriSign symbol must meet certain security standards.*

2. **Only do business** *with sellers for which you have complete contact information, including a "snail mail" (postal) address and telephone number. To avoid bogus websites, verify any bargain website deal at the company's headquarters.*

3. **Review shipping policies** *and costs as well as return policies before placing your order.*

4. **Do not use your regular e-mail address.** *Set up a separate address at Yahoo!, Gmail, or other provider and use it solely for online transactions. This will reduce the spam coming into your everyday e-mail account.*

5. **Never use a debit card** *for online purchasing. When the debit card transaction is executed, your cash is immediately transferred from your account to the seller's account. Using a credit card allows you to request a chargeback (see Chapter 7) from the credit card company.*

6. **Use only one particular credit card** *for online purchases. This practice will serve you well if your account number is stolen. In such a case, you can notify the one credit card issuer of the theft and block the card's future use without affecting your other accounts.*

7. **Print and keep copies** *of all purchase documents, warranties, credit card authorizations, and shipping notices.*

8. **Check the site's privacy policy.** *Sites that display the TRUSTe symbol or Better Business Bureau Online seal have agreed to meet certain privacy standards.*

9. **Opt out** *of any list sharing that the seller might conduct with other merchants.*

Brenda J. Cude
University of Georgia

 LEARNING OBJECTIVE **3**

Negotiate and decide effectively when making major purchases.

NEGOTIATE EFFECTIVELY

Negotiating and decision making follow comparison shopping in the buying process. If you move through these steps too quickly, you may pay too much even when you have done a great job with your preshopping research and comparison shopping. Sellers of such products sell every day, and they are highly skilled; in contrast, consumers are amateurs when it comes to buying big-ticket items. Smart shoppers learn to negotiate.

Successful Negotiators Are Armed with Information

Negotiating (or **haggling**) is the process of discussing the actual terms of an agreement with a seller. Consumers skip this step when making day-to-day purchases because prices in most stores are firm. With high-priced items—especially appliances, furniture, fine jewelry, and vehicles—there is an opportunity, and often an expectation, that offers and counteroffers will be made before arriving at the final price.

Negotiating is challenging for consumers when buying vehicles because many variables must be considered, including the price of the vehicle, the trade-in value (if any), the possibility of a rebate, the prices of options, the interest rate, and possibly a service contract. The dealer can appear to be cooperative on one aspect and make up the difference elsewhere. The key to successful negotiation is to be armed with accurate information on all variables, especially the price, interest rate, trade-in value, and dealer holdbacks.

negotiating/haggling
Process of discussing actual terms of agreement with a seller, usually on higher-priced items.

Always obtain a firm price for a vehicle before negotiating financing or a trade-in.

Discover the Dealer Holdback Consumers have caught on to the fiction of new-car prices and now focus on the **dealer invoice price** or **seller's cost**, which reflects the price the dealer has been billed from the manufacturer. But this may not be the price the dealer truly will have to pay when the vehicle is sold. This occurs because manufacturers often offer a **dealer holdback** (or **dealer rebate**) to dealers. A dealer holdback is a percentage of the total MSRP that the manufacturer holds and then gives back to the dealer, often at the end of the year or quarter. Potential buyers often do not know about holdbacks. Here the dealer can hold back a sum of money from (instead of paying to) the manufacturer, thereby providing the dealer with additional profit on the vehicle.

Because of holdback incentives, dealers can sell a vehicle at or below dealer invoice price and still make a good profit. For example, a vehicle might have a sticker price of $27,890, an invoice price of $24,600, and a dealer holdback of 5 percent, or $1230. A negotiated price of $24,500 will still net the dealer a profit of $1130 [$1230 − ($24,600 − $24,500)]. Remember both the MSRP and dealer invoice price

dealer invoice price/seller's cost
Reflects the price the dealer has been billed from the manufacturer.

dealer holdback/dealer rebate
A percentage of the total MSRP that the manufacturer holds and then gives back to the dealer, often at the end of the year or quarter.

are artificial numbers set by the manufacturer and dealer to allow lots of room to negotiate a profitable price to the seller. For this reason, do not hesitate to negotiate for a price that is below the dealer invoice price. Visit www.edmunds.com and www.truecar.com for a listing of current dealer holdback offers on various makes and models of vehicles.

new-vehicle buying service
No-fee organization that arranges discount purchases for new-car buyers who are referred to nearby participating automobile dealers that have agreed to charge specific discount prices.

Negotiate Your Price   The complexity and uncertainty involved in negotiating the price of a new vehicle have inspired the development of special services intended to assist buyers. A **new-vehicle buying service** is a no-fee organization that arranges discount purchases for buyers of new cars who are referred to nearby participating automobile dealers that have agreed to charge specific discount prices. After you sign up, a local dealer will call you to offer a no-haggle price, which is often within 4 percent of the dealer invoice price. The buying service earns its income by collecting a finder's fee from the dealer. **Professional shoppers**, in exchange for a fee (perhaps $150 to $450) based on the dealer invoice price, will find the best available price from a nearby dealer and finalize the sale. Alternatively, for a lower fee (perhaps $100 to $200), they will obtain price quotes so you can finalize the deal yourself. The following websites offer more information about these services:

- www.autobytel.com
- www.autos.msn.com
- www.carbargains.com
- www.carsala.com
- www.carsdirect.com
- www.autoadvisor.com

DID YOU KNOW?

Hard-Sell Stuff Your Car Doesn't Need

Many new car dealers pad your final cost and their profits by offering a lot of last-minute options, sometimes even without the customer's approval. Often the option is already on the vehicle, so if you don't want it you have to come back later after they remove it. Options you may do without include underside rust protection, cloth seat fabric guard, on-board navigation system, Bluetooth technology, exterior paint sealant, upgraded stereo system, satellite reception, rear-seat video, CD changer, alarms, exterior trim package, vehicle ID window etching, and an extended warranty. "Just say no" is good advice. Even if you want an option or two, resist the dealer's high-pressure sales efforts because you may get a better deal through other sources.

When negotiating a vehicle purchase, the key is to obtain a firm price from a dealer for the vehicle and optional equipment desired before discussing *any other* aspects of the deal. Rule number one in auto buying: Do not mention financing or a trade-in until you have pinned the salesperson down to a price! You will know from your preshopping research and comparison shopping what a good price for the vehicle in question would be.

Start your bargaining from this low price rather than the asking price or dealer invoice price on the vehicle. Obtain prices from three or more dealers and then let each know that you have done so and whether or not their price is low compared with the others. The dealer will then have the chance to reduce the asking price to meet the competition. This smart strategy pressures the dealer to meet your needs rather than the other way around.

Negotiate Your Interest Rate   Negotiating the interest rate, or APR, on a vehicle loan is not only possible but also essential to getting a good deal overall. Most vehicle borrowers accept that the dealer-arranged financing is the best the dealer can find. Buyers often do not know that the dealer benefits from having the borrower agree to a higher rate. Here is how the process works. The dealer asks the buyer to complete a loan application. The application is submitted to one or more lenders with whom the dealer has a pre-existing affiliation. The lenders will assess the application and, if approved, suggest an APR. However, if the dealer suggests and gets an acceptance for a higher rate by the buyer (perhaps by saying that the buyer's credit score is low), the dealer (and salesperson) receives a higher fee for arranging the higher APR loan. In this way, the dealer can make money even if the profit off the sale of the vehicle itself is minimal. This is why it is so important to have a good credit history, know your credit score, and arrange the best financing you can on your own and accept the dealer financing only if it can beat your deal.

Negotiate Your Trade-in Getting a good deal on a vehicle purchase typically requires one more negotiation—your trade-in. You can pay a low price for the car you are buying, arrange a low-rate loan, and still not have a good deal if you do not receive what your trade-in is worth. Success here depends on knowing the value of your vehicle as a trade-in based on your preshopping research. The same online sources you used to get that information also have information on the average price at which similar vehicles are selling via private individuals. While it is true that trade-in values are usually lower than private sale values, you also have the costs of selling and the time involved if you decide not to accept the dealer's offer for your vehicle.

Trade-ins are another way for a seller to make more money on the transaction. In one common sales technique, called **high-balling**, a dealer offers a trade-in allowance that is much higher than the vehicle is worth. This apparent generosity may look very good to a buyer. But beware; the dealer is likely making up for this elsewhere, possibly in a higher-than-necessary price for the purchased vehicle. You will not know whether you are being high-balled unless you know the value of your trade-in.

high-balling
Sales tactic in which a dealer offers a trade-in allowance that is much higher than the vehicle is worth.

Play "Good Cop–Bad Cop" When Buying a Vehicle Many people are uncomfortable negotiating with sellers. Sellers understand this and are very good at putting people at ease with friendly talk and a supportive tone. But underneath, they are all business. How should you play the game? If you are a good negotiator, bring a friend along to be the friendly good cop while you focus on the deal and ask the hard questions. If you dislike negotiating, you can be the good cop, while your friend can ask the hard questions and focus on getting a good deal.

Make the Decision at Home Using a Decision-Making Grid

It is unwise to make buying decisions for expensive purchases inside a retail store or showroom. By waiting until you get home to make the final decision, you are free of pressure from a salesperson and free of your own need to "get it over with." After taking some time to rationally consider all of the consequences of the purchase, you can return to the dealer's showroom and close the sale.

A **decision-making grid** allows you to visually and mathematically weigh the decision you are about to make. Table 8-2 depicts a grid for someone deciding among three different washing machines. The first task in developing such a grid is to determine the various attributes for making the decision. In Table 8-2, these factors include price, durability, and styling. Each attribute is assigned a weight that reflects the importance each has in the mind of the purchaser. Each alternative under consideration is then given a score (from 1 to 10 in this case) that indicates how well it performs on that attribute.

Decision-Making Grid (Illustrated for a Washing Machine)

Table 8-2

Attribute	Weight (W)	Alternative A Rating (R)*	Alternative A Weighted Rating $W \times R$	Alternative B Rating (R)*	Alternative B Weighted Rating $W \times R$	Alternative C Rating (R)*	Alternative C Weighted Rating $W \times R$
Price	30%	9	2.7	7	2.1	5	1.5
Durability	25%	6	1.5	8	2.0	10	2.5
Features	20%	6	1.2	8	1.6	10	2.0
Warranty	15%	6	0.9	10	1.5	8	1.2
Styling	10%	10	1.0	6	0.6	8	0.8
TOTAL	**100%**		**7.3**		**7.8**		**8.0**

* Using a 10-point scale where 10 is the highest score.

The rating (R) is multiplied by the weight (W) to obtain a weighted score. The total of the weighted scores for each alternative can then be compared with the totals for the other choices to determine which one "wins." In Table 8-2, Alternative C, which has a total score of 8.0, scores the best.

A grid of this type helps bring objectivity to your decision-making process and can be of benefit, especially when buying big-ticket items. In addition to this numeric evaluation, you may consider other factors in your decision, such as seller reputation.

Finalizing a Car Deal

After negotiating a good deal and making your final decision, it would be nice if you could simply return to the dealer and sign the necessary papers. But even then there is opportunity for the dealer to push for a little more profit. One technique that is used at this point is called **low-balling**. This involves quoting and getting a verbal agreement from a buyer for an artificially low price. Then the salesperson attempts to raise the already negotiated price when it comes time to finalize the written contract. For example, after agreeing on the price of a vehicle with a buyer, the salesperson states that, as a formality, the approval of a manager is necessary. While the buyer is dreaming of driving home in the new car, the salesperson and the manager are talking about how much more they can get for the vehicle. When the salesperson returns, he or she indicates that there is a problem. Perhaps the trade-in value is too high, or the dealer invoice price can't be discounted by quite as much as planned, or the price of a certain option has increased. In reality, of course, low-balling is simply a ruse to allow the dealer to get more money. Smart buyers stand firm and insist on the deal that had been negotiated; otherwise, they walk out the door.

Finally, it is time to sign the papers. Commonly at this point the salesperson turns the buyer over to another member of the sales team whose specific job it is to have all the papers signed to finalize the sale, the loan, and the transfer of the title and registration of the vehicle. Sign only a **buyer's order** that names a specific vehicle and all charges, and do so only after the salesperson and sales manager have signed *first*. Then verify that all aspects of the deal are as originally agreed, sign your name, and drive away in your new vehicle.

The So-Called Buyer's Remorse "Legal Right" Is a Myth

Buyer's remorse is a myth pertaining to the buyer's supposed legal right to change his or her mind and return a vehicle after signing a purchase contract. This is a popular misconception—that consumers always have what is referred to as a three-day "cooling-off period," or three days to decide whether the consumer wants to honor a signed contract.

low-balling
A sales tactic where the seller quotes an artificially low price to obtain a verbal agreement from a buyer and then attempts to raise the negotiated price when it comes time to finalize the written contract.

buyer's order
Written offer that names a specific vehicle and all charges; only sign such offers after the salesperson and sales manager have signed first.

buyer's remorse
A myth pertaining to the buyer's supposed legal right to change his or her mind and return a vehicle after signing a purchase contract.

ADVICE FROM A PRO

How to Buy a Used Vehicle

Most consumer-buying experts recommend purchasing late-model used cars to get the most from your car-buying dollar. You need to be careful when buying a used vehicle, however. Following are some basic steps that can help you get a good vehicle for the money:

1. **Decide how much you can afford to spend.** Decide in advance how much you can afford.

2. **Decide which features and options you want.** Decide on features based on what is important to you. Are you concerned most about safety? Comfort? Ease of operation? Rank the features you want such as power steering, air con-

ditioning, or aluminum wheels. Consider choosing an older model to obtain the features you value without spending too much more.

3. **Search for reliable makes and models in your price range.** The Internet is an excellent source of used-car pricing information. You should consult the most recent April issue of Consumer Reports for its lists of recommended used vehicles in various price ranges.

4. **Start your search.** Start with online sources and also use classified advertisements in your local newspaper and used-vehicle advertising publications.

5. **Select quality source.** New-car dealerships tend to offer the nicer, more reliable, and more expensive used vehicles.

Used-car dealerships tend to have the worst quality. Private individuals deserve your attention because if they are not lying, they usually own the vehicle and know its history. Used cars sold by rental agencies such as Hertz and Avis can be good choices because the cars have been regularly maintained.

6. ***Quickly rule out the unworthy.*** *Immediately rule out any vehicle that seems to have a problem or raises a question in your mind. Do the same for sellers who do not seem cooperative. Too many vehicles are available to waste your time considering poor-quality vehicles or wrestling with uncooperative sellers.*

7. ***Check your selections carefully.*** *Inspect your final choices inside and out. Take along a friend who is knowledgeable about cars if you are not car savvy. Ask for maintenance records including the name, address, and phone number of the previous owner and give that person a telephone call. Have your mechanic examine the vehicle. Although the examination may cost $50 to $75, it could help you avoid purchasing a vehicle with problems and save many dollars in repair bills later.*

8. ***Obtain the vehicle's history.*** *A **vehicle history report**, available from carfax.com, lists ownership history, odometer readings, accident reports, flood damage, total-loss information, and any title fraud. It is provided free from most sellers. Also check the government's information on fraud and theft at www.vehiclehistory.gov.*

9. ***Negotiate and decide.*** *Never pay the asking price for a used vehicle. Get all verbal promises and guarantees in writing. If a seller will not put his or her words in writing, shop elsewhere. Finally, return to the quiet of your home to consider your alternatives and to make your final decision. If necessary, put down a small refundable deposit to hold the vehicle for a day or two while you make your decision.*

Aimee D. Prawitz and Jamie A. Richter
Northern Illinois University

Evaluate Your Decision

The planned buying process comes full circle when you evaluate your decision. The purpose of this step is to think about where things went well and where they went less smoothly. The lessons learned will prove useful when you make a similar purchase in the future. Sometimes the buying process turns out so successful that you may want to compliment the seller.

 Concept Check 8.3

1. List some of the complexities in vehicle buying and offer your advice on how to get a best buy.

2. What three aspects of a vehicle purchase should be negotiated? In what order?

3. Why should you make major purchase decisions at home?

4. Summarize how to use a decision-making grid.

FINANCIAL POWER POINT

Purchase Used Cars and Drive Them Forever

The best way to buy vehicles with the lowest overall cost is to buy late-model used cars and drive them for ten or more years or 200,000 miles, whichever comes first. New cars lose 25 percent of their value in the first year and 40 to 45 percent by the end of the second year.

DID YOU KNOW?

Sean's Success Story

When shopping for a new car, Sean ran the numbers on leasing versus buying only to determine that he really could not afford the kind of vehicle he truly wanted. Therefore, he decided to buy a used car. He found a luxurious two-year-old Ford with only 21,000 miles on the odometer and bargained the price down to $19,000; thus, he avoided two years of heavy depreciation. Sean searched online for financing deals and then discovered an excellent rate at a nearby credit union. He paid the $5 credit union membership fee and deposited $5 to open an account, and they gave him a loan over 36 months. Sean considered buying an extended warranty but decided it would be too expensive and he didn't know the reputation of the seller. He has had the car for over two years now, and it has proved to be a reliable vehicle.

UTILIZE EFFECTIVE COMPLAINT PROCEDURES

Despite your efforts to make good consumer buying decisions, not all purchases turn out as well as you want. You may want to try to return goods, get out of a contract, file a complaint, or seek to right a wrong using an alternative dispute resolution program or using small claims court.

Use the Cooling-Off Rule to Cancel a Contract

If you buy something at a store and later change your mind, you may or may not be able to return the merchandise. However, if you buy an item in your home or at a location that is not the seller's permanent place of business, you may have that option. The Federal Trade Commission's (FTC's) **cooling-off rule** gives you three days to cancel a contract of $25 or more after signing it for a sale made anywhere other than a seller's normal place of business. The right to cancel for a full refund extends until midnight of the third business day after the sale.

The FTC's cooling-off rule applies to sales at the buyer's home, workplace, or dormitory, or at facilities rented by the seller on a temporary or short-term basis, such as hotel or motel rooms, convention centers, fairgrounds, and restaurants. The rule applies even when you invite the salesperson to make a presentation in your home. The cooling-off rule does not apply to sales made entirely by mail or telephone, sales that are needed to meet an emergency, or to real estate, insurance, or securities.

Under the rule, the salesperson must tell you about your cancellation rights at the time of sale. The salesperson also must give you two copies of a cancellation form (one to keep and one to send) and a copy of your contract or receipt. The contract or receipt should be dated, show the name and address of the seller, and explain your right to cancel. The contract or receipt must be in the same language that is used in the sales presentation. The best way to avoid problems is to read the contract carefully and to fully inspect a new or used product or service before taking ownership. Various states have cooling-off rules that sometimes apply even longer cancellation periods to specific types of sales, such as dancing lessons, buying clubs, and timeshares.

Sometimes you may want to complain about the product or service so as to obtain **redress**—that is, to right the wrong. This process should start with the actual seller, as indicated in Table 8-3. Seeking redress through the first three channels in the complaint procedures as shown in the table can rectify almost all consumer complaints.

Levels to Bring Your Complaint	Channels for Complaint
1. Local business 2. Manufacturer 3. Self-regulatory organizations 4. Consumer action agencies 5. Small-claims or civil court	Salesperson → supervisor → manager/owner Consumer affairs department → president/chief executive officer Better Business Bureau → trade associations → mediation/arbitration panels Private consumer action groups → media action lines → government agencies Small-claims court → civil court

Complaint Procedure (Levels and Channels of Complaining) *Table 8-3*

Mediation and Arbitration

Alternative dispute resolution programs are industry- or government-sponsored programs that provide an avenue to resolve disputes outside the formal court system. Vehicle manufacturers utilize these programs as part of their warranty procedures. **Mediation** is a procedure in which a neutral third party works with the parties involved in the dispute to arrive at a mutually agreeable solution. In **arbitration**, a neutral third party hears (or reads) the claims made and the positions taken by the parties to the dispute and then issues a ruling that is binding on one or both parties.

Lemon Laws and Small-Claims Courts

All states have new-vehicle **lemon laws** that provide guidelines for arbitrators to use to order a dealer's buyback of a "lemon." A common definition of a lemon in these laws is a vehicle that was in the shop for repairs four times for the same problem in the first year after purchase. (For the specific definition in your state, visit www.carlemon.com.) To enforce a lemon law, the buyer must go through the warranty process specified in the owner's manual. Eventually, if the problem is not resolved, an arbitration hearing will be held through which the owner can request a buyback. Some states have also enacted used-vehicle lemon laws.

Sometimes your best efforts at redress may not prove successful. As a result, you might consider taking legal action in **small-claims court**. In this state court, civil matters are often resolved without the assistance of attorneys (in some states, attorneys are actually prohibited from representing clients in small-claims courts). Small-claims courts usually place restrictions on the maximum amount under dispute, typically ranging from $500 to $2500, for which a claim may be made in those courts. To file a small-claims court action, contact your local county courthouse and ask which court hears small claims.

alternative dispute resolution programs
Industry- or government-sponsored programs that provide an avenue to resolve disputes outside the formal court system.

lemon laws
State laws that provide guidelines for arbitrators to use to order a dealer's buyback of a "lemon" as defined under the law—commonly a car that has been in the shop four or more times to fix the same problem.

small-claims court
State courts in which civil matters are often resolved without attorney assistance.

DO IT NOW!

You know more about personal finance after reading this chapter, so get started right now by:

1. *Setting up a filing system for the warranty information and receipts for all products you own that have a warranty.*
2. *Decide on a big-ticket item you would like to own in the near future and create a decision-making worksheet for it similar to Table 8-2, using your criteria and weights.*

Concept Check 8.4

1. Outline the steps to go through to seek redress.
2. Summarize the FTC's cooling-off rule to cancel a contract.
3. Distinguish between mediation and arbitration.
4. How do lemon laws work?

WHAT DO YOU RECOMMEND NOW?

Now that you have read this chapter on vehicle and other major purchases, what do you recommend to David and Lisa Cosgrove regarding:

1. How to search for two vehicles to replace those destroyed?

2. Whether to replace Lisa's vehicle with a new or used vehicle?

3. Whether to lease or buy a vehicle?

4. How to decide between a rebate and a special low APR financing opportunity if they decide to purchase a new vehicle for Lisa?

5. How to negotiate with the sellers of the vehicles?

BIG PICTURE SUMMARY OF LEARNING OBJECTIVES

LO1. Explain the three steps in the planned buying process that occur prior to interacting with sellers.

The planned buying process includes three steps that occur prior to interacting with sellers: prioritizing wants, obtaining information during preshopping research, and fitting the planned purchase into the budget. These steps represent the homework needed when preparing to buy.

LO2. Describe the process of comparison shopping.

To interact effectively with sellers, you should comparison shop to find the best buy. When purchasing vehicles and other big-ticket items, this shopping process includes comparing prices, financing arrange-

ments, leasing options, warranties, and extended warranties.

LO3. Negotiate and decide effectively when making major purchases.

Negotiating with sellers involves obtaining a fair price, low-cost financing, and a high trade-in allowance. After negotiating, the final decision should be made at home.

LO4. Use effective complaint procedures.

When the buying process has not gone well, you can use a variety of effective complaint procedures including the FTC's cooling-off rule, mediation, arbitration, lemon laws, or a small-claims court to try to resolve the situation.

LET'S TALK ABOUT IT

1. **Steps in the Planned Buying Process.** Do you think all of the steps in the planned buying process are used when buying simple everyday products (such as a loaf of bread or a half-gallon of milk), or are they used only when buying big-ticket items?

2. **Positives and Negatives of Leasing.** What benefits do you see in leasing a vehicle? What negatives exist when leasing?

3. **A Bad Purchase Decision.** What is the worst purchase decision you have ever made? What step(s) in the planned buying process could you have done better in that situation?

4. **Do You Complain?** When was the last time you were seriously dissatisfied with a purchase? Did you complain? Why or why not? If you complained, what was the outcome?

DO THE MATH

1. **Future Value on Cost of Extended Warranty.** Jackie Jones of Blacksburg, Virginia, is considering paying $150 a year for an extended warranty on several of her major appliances. If the appliances are expected to last for five years and she can earn 2 percent on her savings, what would be the future value of the amount she will pay for the extended warranty?

2. **Value of Shopping Carefully.** Jimmy Johnson of Dallas, Texas, is a good shopper. He always comparison shops and uses coupons every week. Jimmy figures he saves at least $40 a month as a result. Assuming an interest rate of 2 percent, what is the future value of this amount over ten years?

3. **Buy Versus Lease.** Amanda Forsythe of Tampa, Florida, must decide whether to buy or lease a car she has selected. She has negotiated a purchase price of $24,700 and could borrow the money to buy from her credit union by putting $3000 down and paying $515 per month for 48 months at 6.5 percent APR. Alterna-

tively, she could lease the car for 48 months at $310 per month by paying a $3000 capital cost reduction and a $350 disposition fee on the car, which is projected to have a residual value of $8100 at the end of the lease. Use the Run the Numbers worksheet on page 230 to advise Amanda about whether she should buy or lease the car.

4. **Rebate Versus Low Interest Rate.** Kyle Parker of Fayetteville, Arkansas, has been shopping for a new car for several weeks. So far, he has negotiated a price of $27,000 on a model that carries a choice of a $2500 rebate or dealer financing at 2 percent APR. The dealer loan would require a $1000 down payment and a monthly payment of $564 for 48 months. Kyle has also arranged for a loan from his bank with a 7 percent APR. Use the Run the Numbers worksheet on page 230 to advise Kyle about whether he should use the dealer financing or take the rebate and use the financing from the bank.

FINANCIAL PLANNING CASES

CASE 1

The Johnsons Decide to Buy a Car

After three years of riding a bus to work, Belinda finds that she can no longer do so because her employer moved to a location that is not convenient for public transportation. Thus the Johnsons are in the market for another car. Harry and Belinda estimate that they could afford to spend about $10,000 on a good used car by making a down payment of $2000 and financing the remainder over 24 months at $355 per month.

(a) Make suggestions about how the $355 might be integrated into the Johnsons' budget (Table 3-5 on page 86) by making reductions in certain expense categories.

(b) If they cannot make room in their budget for a $355 monthly car payment, would you recommend they finance a vehicle for 36 or 48 months? Why or why not?

(c) Which sources of used cars should they consider? Why?

(d) Assume that the Johnsons have narrowed their choices to two cars. The first car is a three-year-old Chevrolet Malibu with 24,000 miles; it is being sold for $10,000 by a private individual. The seller has kept records of all maintenance and

repairs. The second car is a three-year-old Ford Fusion with 28,000 miles, being sold by a used-car dealership. Harry contacted the previous owner and found that the car was given in trade on another car about three months ago. The previous owner cited no major mechanical problems but simply wanted a bigger car. The dealer is offering a written 30-day warranty on parts only. The asking price is $10,400. Which used car would you advise the Johnsons to buy? Why?

(e) Would you recommend that they purchase or lease a low-priced new vehicle instead of buying a used vehicle? Why or why not?

CASE 2

Victor and Maria Hernandez Buy a Third Car

The Hernandezes' older son, Hector, has reached the age at which it is time to consider purchasing a car for him. Victor and Maria have decided to give Maria's old car to Hector and buy a later-model used car for Maria.

(a) What sources can Victor and Maria use to access price and reliability information on various makes and models of used cars?

(b) What sources of used cars might be available to Victor and Maria, and what differences might exist among them?

(c) How might Victor and Maria check out the cars in which they are most interested?

(d) What strategies might Victor and Maria employ when they negotiate the price for the car they select?

CASE 3

Julia Price Wants to Drive a BMW

It has been almost 15 years since Julia graduated with a major in aeronautical engineering, and now she makes a ton of money working as a middle manager for a large engineering defense contracting company. While she is not very thrifty, she does like a good deal, especially on expensive purchases. Julia recently compared new models of the BMW 749I Series, Jaguar XF, Audi S6, and Infiniti M56. She checked out reviews in *Consumer Reports* and other magazines and test drove each vehicle. After deciding on the BMW, Julia shopped online for dealers beyond her community. Julia thinks that she will save about $3800 if she buys her car and an extended warranty on it from a dealer located 40 miles from her home instead of her hometown seller. She is not sure whether she should take advantage of the dealer's 3 percent financing versus a $4000 rebate, take the rebate and get a 6 percent loan from a nearby credit union, or lease the vehicle. Offer your opinions about her thinking.

CASE 4

Purchase of a New Refrigerator

Gary Joseph, a financial consultant from Spokane, Washington, is remodeling his kitchen. Gary, who lives alone, has decided to replace his refrigerator with a new model that offers more conveniences. He has narrowed his choices to two models. The first is a basic 16-cubic-foot model with a bottom freezer for $799. The second is a 25.4-cubic-foot model with side freezer for $999. Additional features for this model include icemaker, textured enamel surface, and ice and water dispenser. Gary's credit union will lend him the necessary funds for one year at a 12 percent APR on the installment plan. Following is his budget, which includes $2140 in monthly take-home pay.

Food	$ 300
Entertainment	120
Clothing	60
Gifts	$ 70
Charities	75
Car payment	330
Personal care	60
Automobile expenses	120
Savings	130
Housing	825
Miscellaneous	50
Total	**$2,140**

(a) What preshopping research might Gary do to select the best brand of refrigerator?

(b) Using the information in Table 7-1 on page 213 or the *Garman/Forgue* companion website, determine Gary's monthly payment for the two models.

(c) Fit each of the two monthly payments into Gary's budget.

(d) Advise Gary to help him make his decision.

CASE 5

A Dispute over New-Car Repairs

Christopher Hardison, a high school football coach from Oklahoma City, Oklahoma, purchased a new SUV for $28,000. He used the vehicle often; in fact, in less than nine months, he had put 14,000 miles on it. A 24,000-mile, two-year warranty was still in effect for the power-train equipment, although Christopher had to pay the first $100 of each repair cost. After 16,500 miles and in month 11 of driving, the car experienced some severe problems with the transmission. Christopher took the vehicle to the dealer for repairs. A week later he picked the car up, but some transmission problems remained. When Christopher took the car back to the dealer, the dealer said that no further problems could be identified. Christopher was sure that the problem was still there, and he was amazed that the dealer would not correct it. The dealer told him he would take no other action.

(a) Was Christopher within his rights to take the car back for repairs? Explain why or why not.

(b) What logical steps might Christopher follow if he continues to be dissatisfied with the dealer's unwillingness or inability to repair the car?

(c) Should Christopher seek any help from the court system? If so, describe what he could do without spending money on attorney's fees.

BE YOUR OWN PERSONAL FINANCIAL MANAGER

1. **Can You Afford a Vehicle Payment?** Review Table 8-1, "Fitting a Vehicle Payment into a Monthly Budget," and reflecting upon your own likely financial situation following graduation, write down a few notes explaining how following such an approach might be appropriate for you.

2. **Priority Worksheet.** Review Figure 8-2, "Priority Worksheet (for Sharon Wilson)," to help you think through the options that you desire in a new vehicle. Tentatively decide on the top five options you would prefer on a new vehicle and write up your findings or complete Worksheet 29: My Top Priority Motor Vehicle Features from "My Personal Financial Planner" to establish your priorities.

MY PERSONAL FINANCIAL PLANNER

3. **Comparing Vehicle Purchase Contracts.** To avoid simply focusing on one or two aspects of buying a vehicle, such as the monthly payment or the trade-in value, complete Worksheet 30: Comparing Vehicle Purchase Contracts from "My Personal Financial Planner" to help you focus on effectively comparing what is important to you.

MY PERSONAL FINANCIAL PLANNER

4. **Lease or Buy a Vehicle?** Review the Run the Numbers worksheet, "Comparing Automobile Financing and Leasing," on page 231 to help to decide which choice is better for you or complete Worksheet 31: Should I Lease or Buy a Vehicle? from "My Personal Financial Planner."

MY PERSONAL FINANCIAL PLANNER

5. **Rebate or Low-Rate Financing?** Review the Run the Numbers worksheet, "Choosing Between Low-Interest-Rate Dealer Financing and a Rebate," on page 230 to help to decide which alternative is better for you when you can arrange your own financing or complete Worksheet 32: Should I Take a New Vehicle Rebate or Low-Rate Financing Offer? from "My Personal Financial Planner."

MY PERSONAL FINANCIAL PLANNER

6. **Major Purchase Decision-Making Grid.** Review Table 8-2, "Decision-Making Grid (Illustrated for a Washing Machine)," on page 237 and think about a purchase you might make. Then complete Worksheet 33: Decision-Making Worksheet for a Major Product Purchase from "My Personal Financial Planner" and insert the weighted scores you think appropriate.

MY PERSONAL FINANCIAL PLANNER

7. **Sample Complaint Letter.** Review Table 8-3, "Complaint Procedure (Levels and Channels of Complaining)," to draft a letter to seek redress for a deficient product or service you may have had in the past using Worksheet 34: Sample Product or Service Complaint Letter from "My Personal Financial Planner" as a guide.

MY PERSONAL FINANCIAL PLANNER

ON THE 'NET

Go to the Web pages indicated to complete these exercises. You can also go to the *Garman/Forgue* companion website at www.cengagebrain.com for an expanded list of exercises. Under General Business, select the title of this text. Click on the Internet Exercises link for this chapter.

1. **Keys to Vehicle Leasing.** Visit the website of the Federal Reserve Board at www.federalreserve.gov/pubs/leasing where you will find a link titled "Keys to Vehicle Leasing" that expands on the information in this book. Use this information to generate a list of pros and cons of leasing versus purchasing a vehicle. By clicking on "sample leasing form" on this Web page, you can view and print a copy of the required vehicle leasing disclosure form.

2. **Car Buying Advice.** Visit the website of *Consumer Reports* magazine at www.consumerreports.org and click on the "Cars" tab and then see the "Car Buying Advice" section. There you will find lots of information on how to buy cars as well as reliability data. In what

ways are the strategies similar and in what ways do they differ from the tips offered in this book for buying a used car?

3. **Consumer Protection Organizations.** Search Google for "consumer protection organizations" that assist consumers with complaints. Create a table showing your findings for five organizations, and include the name, telephone number, Web address, main purpose, and types of problems addressed for each.

4. **Visit Edmunds.com.** Go online to Edmunds.com and search the site carefully. Write a report of your findings.

5. **Value of Used Cars.** Visit the website for the Kelly Blue Book at www.kbb.com to determine the market price of three used cars that might be of interest to you. Determine their "used car retail value," "trade-in value," and "private party value." Why do the three values differ?

ACTION INVOLVEMENT PROJECTS

1. **Needs and Wants.** Using Figure 8-2 as a guide, make a list of the options in the first column that you would want if you could have any car you wanted. Realizing that getting all the options would be a dream (these are wants), go back to the list, move the priority level on certain items, and move the checkmarks to the second or third priorities. Your needs should now be in column one with wants in the other columns.

2. **Price Available Vehicles.** Telephone three new car dealers to determine if they have a particular make and model of vehicle that is of interest to you, for example, a two-year-old Toyota Prius. Inquire about number of vehicles available of the make and model of interest, colors, options of interest, and asking prices. Make a table of your findings.

3. **Compare Financing Terms.** Telephone two new car dealers to determine some financing details on used vehicles. Inform the dealers that your FICO credit score is above 750 and that you want to finance $12,000 after making a $4000 down payment. Find out the interest rate, number of years one could finance, and the monthly payments. Make a table of your findings.

Visit the Garman/Forgue companion website at **www.cengagebrain.com**.

Obtaining Affordable Housing

9

YOU MUST BE KIDDING, RIGHT?

Horst Brandt recently bought a new home and borrowed $230,000 at 5.75 percent interest for 30 years. His monthly payment for interest and principal will be $1342. A friend suggested that Horst should have easily been able to find a loan at 5.5 percent with a monthly payment of $1306. Horst dismissed his friend's comments, arguing that the difference in the monthly payments was no big deal. His friend replied, "Horst, it's not the monthly payment, it's the interest." How much more in interest will Horst pay over the life of the loan because he took a loan with the higher rate?

A. $3000

B. $6000

C. $9000

D. $13,000

The answer is D. Horst will be making a higher payment each and every month for 30 years. While the difference in the monthly payment seems small [$36 ($1342 − $1306) per month in this example], even a small difference in the interest rates on mortgage loans can add up to thousands of dollars in extra interest over the life of the loan. That is why searching for the lowest possible interest rate is so important when borrowing to buy a home!

LEARNING OBJECTIVES

After reading this chapter, you should be able to:

1. Decide whether renting or owning your home is better for you.

2. Explain the up-front and monthly costs of buying a home.

3. Describe the steps in the home-buying process.

4. Distinguish among the conventional and alternative ways of financing a home and list the advantages and disadvantages of each.

5. Identify the key considerations when selling a home.

WHAT DO YOU RECOMMEND?

Libby Clark has worked for a major consumer electronics retailer since graduating from college. The company has operations across the country with regional headquarters in Atlanta, Denver, Minneapolis, and Boston. She has been based in the Atlanta area for the past three years, and given the recent declines in home prices there, she has begun to think about buying a home rather than renting her townhouse apartment. Then, last month, Libby was promoted to deputy regional director for the Denver office. The promotion represents a key step for becoming a regional director in four or five years. Regional directors may or may not be promoted from within their current region.

AP Photo/Paul Sakuma

What do you recommend to Libby on the subject of buying a home regarding:

1. Buying or renting housing in the Denver area?

2. Steps she should take prior to actively looking at homes?

3. Finding a home and negotiating the purchase?

4. The closing process in home buying?

5. Selecting a type of mortgage to fit her needs?

6. Things to consider regarding the sale of her new home should she ultimately be promoted to a position in another of the four regions?

You probably are renting housing right now because about 90 percent of all younger people rent. In contrast, approximately 80 percent of people aged 55 to 64 are homeowners. Given these statistics, it is likely that you eventually will want to seriously consider buying a home. At that point, you should mathematically evaluate the financial benefits of renting versus buying and take a good hard look at what it really costs to buy a home.

Is a home an investment or just a place to live? Housing values typically increase less than 4% annually or less than half what usually is earned on a diversified portfolio of stocks and bonds. However, home prices have declined 20 to 50 percent in most markets since 2006.

If you decide to buy, you will likely obtain a **mortgage loan**—a loan to purchase real estate in which the property itself serves as collateral. There are many types of mortgage loans, and you will need to fully understand your mortgage options before you obligate yourself for up to 30 years.

The recent explosion in mortgage foreclosures and resulting decline in housing prices occurred partly because millions of Americans took out complicated mortgages that they did not understand. Many mortgages that seemed affordable at first turned out later to be unaffordable as the monthly repayment amounts increased because the contracts allowed for rising interest rates. The resulting rising payments and declining home values have been a disaster for millions of homeowners, especially for those who lost their jobs. In addition, other buyers speculated by investing in housing, expecting values to continue to rise during and beyond the housing boom of the 2000s. You should know that a rule of all investing is that spectacular gains cannot continue forever. Furthermore, millions of others who were trying to sell their homes in the distressed market wound up losing money in the process. So knowing how to buy housing is not enough! You must also understand the process of selling a home.

YOUR NEXT 5 YEARS

In the next five years, you can start achieving financial success by doing the following related to obtaining affordable housing:

1. *Read your leases and other real estate contracts thoroughly before signing.*

2. *Save the money for a down payment within a tax-sheltered Roth IRA account.*

3. *Get your finances in order before shopping for a new home by reducing debt, budgeting better, and clearing up anything that keeps you from having a high credit score.*

4. *Buy a home as soon as it fits your budget and lifestyle so you can take advantage of special income tax deductions and price appreciation over time.*

5. *If you make a down payment of less than 20 percent on a home, cancel private mortgage insurance as soon as the equity in your home pushes the loan-to-value ratio down to 80 percent.*

SHOULD YOU RENT OR BUY YOUR HOME?

Whether to rent or buy depends on your preferences and what you can afford. In the short run, renting is usually less expensive than buying. In the long run, the opposite is usually true.

Rented Housing May Be Less Expensive at First

People may choose to rent their housing for many reasons. For some, the large down payment and high monthly loan payments are barriers to buying a home. Some may simply prefer the easy mobility of renting or want to avoid many of the responsibilities associated with buying. Prospective renters need to consider the monthly rental fees, damage and security deposits, the lease agreement and restrictions, and tenant rights.

Rent, Deposit, and Related Expenses
Rent is the cost charged for using an apartment or other housing space. It is usually due on a specific day each month, with a late penalty being assessed if the tenant is tardy in making the payment. Other fees could be assessed for features such as use of a clubhouse and pool, exercise facilities, cable television, and space for storage and parking.

A **damage deposit** is an amount given in advance to a landlord to pay for repairing the unit beyond the damage expected from normal wear and tear. It is often charged before the tenant moves in, is often equal to one month's rent, and is refundable if at the end of the lease the tenant leaves the home in good condition. You may also be required to pay a **security deposit** to provide some assurance that you will not move without paying your rent. Again, this amount is often equal to the last month's rent payment. It too is refundable. Thus, an apartment with a monthly rent of $800 might require payment of $800 for the first month's rent, an $800 security deposit, and an $800 damage deposit for a total of $2400.

mortgage loan
Loan to purchase real estate in which the property itself serves as collateral.

rent
Cost charged for using an apartment or other housing space.

lease
In this context, a contract specifying both tenant and landlord legal responsibilities.

subleasing
An arrangement in which the original tenant leases the property to another tenant.

Written Lease Contracts Protect All Parties A **lease** is a contract specifying the legal responsibilities of both the tenant and the landlord. It identifies the amount of rent and security deposit, the length of the lease (typically one year), payment responsibility for utilities and repairs, penalties for late payment of rent, eviction procedures for nonpayment of rent, and procedures to follow when the lease ends. Leases often state whether the security deposit accumulates interest, how soon the unit must be inspected for cleanliness after the tenant vacates the premises, and when the security deposit (or the balance) will be forwarded to the tenant. Without a written lease, any or all of these terms can be subject to misunderstanding.

Two types of leases generally govern tenant–landlord relationships. The first provides for **periodic tenancy** (for example, week-to-week or month-to-month residency), where the agreement can be terminated by either of the parties if they give proper notice in advance (for example, one week or one month). Without such notice, the agreement stays in effect. This arrangement also typically applies in situations in which no written lease is established. The second type of lease provides for **tenancy for a specific time**, usually for one year. When this period expires, the agreement terminates unless prior notice is given by both parties that the agreement will be renewed.

Lease agreements may contain a variety of restrictions that are legally binding on tenants. For example, pets may or may not be permitted; when they are permitted, landlords often require a large security deposit. Excessive noise from home entertainment systems or parties may be prohibited as well. To protect other renters from overcrowding, a clause may limit the number of overnight guests.

An important restriction applies to **subleasing** (wherein an original tenant leases the property to another tenant). Here a tenant who moves before the lease expires may need to obtain the landlord's permission before someone else can take over the rental unit. The new tenant may even have to be approved, and the original tenant will retain some financial liability until the term of the original lease expires.

Tenants Have Rights Even in the Absence of a Written Lease

Tenants have a number of legal rights under laws in most states and many local communities. Some important rights are as follows:

- Prohibitions against **harassment** (rent increases, eviction, or utility shutoff) for reporting building-code violations or otherwise exercising a tenant's legal rights.

- Assurances of some legally prescribed minimum standard of **habitability** for items such as running water, heat, and a working stove and the safety of access areas such as stairways.

- The right to make minor repairs and deduct the cost from the tenant's next rent payment. This right is subject to certain restrictions, such as giving sufficient prior written notification to the landlord.

- Prompt return of a security deposit, with limits placed on the kinds of deductions that can be made. Landlords must explain specific reasons for deductions. Some state laws require that interest be paid on security deposits.

- The right to file a lawsuit against a landlord for nonperformance. Such suits can be brought in a small-claims court.

Owned Housing May Be Less Expensive in the Long Term

Americans have historically chosen single-family dwellings to satisfy their owned-housing desires. Other alternatives are popular, too, such as condominiums, cooperatives, manufactured housing, and mobile homes.

Single-Family Dwellings A **single-family dwelling** is a housing unit that is detached from other units. Buyers have many choices available for both new and existing homes with varying floor plans and home features. Some people prefer the modern kitchens and other features found in newer homes; others prefer the larger rooms, higher ceilings, and completed landscaping of older homes.

single-family dwelling
Housing unit that is detached from other units.

Condominiums and Cooperatives The terms **condominium** and **cooperative** describe forms of ownership rather than types of buildings. These forms of ownership typically cost less than single-family dwellings, offer recreation facilities, and have few if any maintenance obligations.

With a **condominium** (or **condo**), the owner holds legal title to a specific housing unit within a multiunit building or project and owns a proportionate share in the common grounds and facilities. The entire complex is run by the owners through a **homeowners association**. Besides making monthly mortgage payments, the condominium owner must pay a monthly **homeowners association fee** that is established by the homeowners association. This fee covers expenses related to the management of the common grounds and facilities and insurance on the building. Some areas of concern for condominium owners include potential increases in homeowner's fees and limited resale appeal of the unit. Condo market prices are much more volatile than for single-family dwellings as condos don't increase as much in value as single-family dwellings. In addition, during a housing downturn, their values decline more than single-family homes.

condominium (condo)
Form of ownership with the owners holding legal title to their own housing unit among many, with common grounds and facilities owned by the developer or homeowners association.

Be sure to factor homeowners association fees into the monthly income needed to purchase a condominium.

With a **cooperative** (or **co-op**), the owner holds a share of the corporation that owns and manages a group of housing units. The value of this share is equivalent to the value of the owner's particular unit. The owner also holds a proportional interest in all common areas. A monthly fee for the cooperative covers the same types of items as does a condominium fee and also includes an amount to cover the professional management of the complex as well as payments on the cooperative's mortgage debt. (The pro rata share for interest and property taxes is deductible on each shareholder's income tax return.)

cooperative (co-op)
Form of ownership in which the owner holds a share of the corporation that owns and manages a group of housing units as well as common grounds and facilities.

Manufactured Housing and Mobile Homes **Manufactured housing** consists of fully or partially factory-built housing units designed to be transported (often in portions) to the home site. Final assembly and readying of the housing for occupancy occurs at the home site. **Mobile homes**, in contrast, are fully factory-assembled housing units that are designed to be towed on a frame with a trailer hitch. Mobile homes depreciate in value every year just like automobiles.

So Who Pays More—Renters or Owners?

According to conventional wisdom, homeowners enjoy a financial advantage over renters when total housing costs are calculated over many years. Renters generally pay out less money in terms of annual cash flow, but owners receive annual income tax advantages and they usually see increases in the value of their homes over time that can improve their financial situation. However, as evidenced by events of the past few years, there is no guarantee that housing values will increase in a uniform fashion over the years; they might even decline. In some markets, home prices are inflated. Ask your real estate agent for the **price-to-rent ratio** in your community. This ratio shows the average home price divided by annual rent in a community. Higher numbers, such as those above the national average of 15, mean that home values are high relative to the cost of renting. (See Chapter 16 for more information on price-to-rent ratios.)

Your goal in buying a place to live should not be driven by dreams of possible financial gain. Buying is still a smart move, but you must crunch the numbers to be absolutely certain the housing you choose is purchased at the right price and is affordable. Affordability must include not only the monthly payment but other additional homeownership expenses such as homeowners association fees.

Based on Initial Cash Flow, Renters Appear to Win The Run the Numbers worksheet "Should You Buy or Rent?" on page 253 illustrates a comparison between a small condominium and an apartment with similar space and amenities. For the apartment, rent would total $1000 per month. Assume you could buy the condominium for $180,000 by using $36,000 in savings as a down payment and borrowing the remaining $144,000 for 30 years at 6.0 percent interest. As the worksheet shows, renting would have a cash-flow cost of $11,640 after a reduction for the interest that could be earned on your savings (after taxes). Buying requires several expenses beyond the monthly mortgage payment, including a monthly $150 homeowner's fee ($1800 annually) in our example. In this case, the cash-flow cost of buying is $16,485, or $4,845 more than renting.

After Taxes and Appreciation, Owners Usually Win To make the comparison more accurate, you must also consider the tax and appreciation aspects of the two options. If you rent, you would pay $180 ($720 × 0.25) in income taxes on the interest on the amount in your savings account ($36,000) not used for a down payment. If you buy the condominium, $1768 of the $10,360 in annual mortgage loan payments during the first year will go toward the principal of the debt, and the remainder—$8592 ($10,360 – $1768)—will go toward interest. Both mortgage interest and real estate property taxes qualify as income tax deductions. If you are in the 25 percent marginal tax bracket, your taxes would be reduced by $2148 ($8592 × 0.25) as a result of deducting the mortgage interest and by $750 ($3000 × 0.25) as a result of deducting the real estate tax. In effect, every time you make a payment you will get some of it back from the government.

Condominiums also have a likelihood of appreciation, or increase, in the home's value. A very conservative assumption would be that the condominium will increase in value by 1 percent per year. A home valued at $180,000 would, therefore, be worth $181,800 ($180,000 × 1.01) after one year, a gain of $1800. In this case, buying is financially better than renting by approximately $1801 ($11,820 – $10,019).

RUN THE NUMBERS

Should You Buy or Rent?

This worksheet can be used to estimate whether you would be better off renting housing or buying. If you are renting an apartment and planning to buy a house, qualitative differen-

ces will enter into your decision. This worksheet will put the financial picture into focus. A similar worksheet can be found on the Ginnie Mae website at www.ginniemae.gov/rent_vs _buy/rent_vs_buy_calc.asp?Section=YPTH.

	Example Amounts		Your Figures	
	Rent	Buy	Rent	Buy
Annual Cash-Flow Considerations				
Annual rent ($1000/month) or mortgage payments ($863.35/month)*	$ 12,000	$ 10,360	____	____
Property and liability insurance	360	725	____	____
Private mortgage insurance	N/A	0	N/A	____
Real estate taxes	0	3,000	____	____
Maintenance	0	600	____	____
Other housing fees	0	1,800	____	____
Less interest earned on funds not used for down payment (at 2%)	720	N/A	____	N/A
Cash-Flow Cost for the Year	**$11,640**	**$ 16,485**	____	____
Tax and Appreciation Considerations				
Less principal[†] repaid on the mortgage loan	N/A	1,768	N/A	____
Plus tax on interest earned on funds not used for down payment (25% marginal tax bracket)	180	N/A	____	N/A
Less tax savings due to deductibility of mortgage interest[‡] (25% marginal tax bracket)	N/A	2,148	N/A	____
Less tax savings due to deductibility of real estate property taxes (25% marginal tax bracket)	N/A	750	N/A	____
Less appreciation on the dwelling (2.5% annual rate)	N/A	1,800	N/A	____
Net Cost for the Year	**$11,820**	**$ 10,019**	____	____

*Calculated from Table 9-4 on page 270
†Calculated according to the method illustrated in Table 9-2 on page 268
‡Mortgage interest tax savings equal total mortgage payments minus principal repaid multiplied by the marginal tax rate.

Note that the calculations above compare somewhat equivalent housing types. The process is more complicated when you want to compare renting an apartment with buying a house. You definitely should still do the math but recognize that you are comparing unlike properties. It is probable that you will find that buying a home is significantly more expensive than renting for the first few years. But if you stay in the home for five to seven years or longer, the financial situation improves for the homeowner, especially for one with a fixed interest rate loan. This assumes you do not pay too much for it in the first place.

People who bought homes in the mid-2000s hoping to **flip** them for a quick profit sometimes found the opposite to be true. They lost money when they had to sell at a price lower than desired because the market was flooded with too many properties for sale. The same thing happened to people who bought homes they could not afford while hoping that an increase in value would allow them to refinance for better terms after a couple of years. Worst off were people who bought homes with little or no down payment. When the value of their homes decreased, they found themselves horribly **upside down** (also known as **under water**) meaning that they owed more than the homes were worth. Many are under water $50,000, $100,000, or more.

DID YOU KNOW?

Walking Out on a Mortgage Is a Bad Idea

As troubles continue in today's economy, numerous borrowers are deciding to take a **strategic default**. Here they simply choose to stop paying on their mortgage. This may be attractive because most mortgages are **nonrecourse loans**. With such loans, the lender has no recourse to go after other assets if the foreclosed home brings an insufficient amount to cover the outstanding debt when sold at auction. Nonetheless, a strategic default looks very bad on one's credit history. There also is a moral issue here.

DID YOU KNOW?

About Buying a Foreclosed Property

A major reason for the declines in home prices in recent years is the large number of foreclosed properties on the market. If there are four homes for sale in a neighborhood and one is a foreclosure residence, prices on the other three properties are typically lowered to the value of the one in foreclosure. Foreclosure properties can be found on such websites as www.Foreclosure.com, www.Foreclosures.com, and www.RealtyTrac.com, which charge monthly subscription fees for access to their databases. If interested in buying such a property you must know how foreclosure works. Here are the three stages of foreclosure:

1. ***Preforeclosure.*** *Preforeclosure is the time between when the homeowner has been notified by the lender that he or she is in default and when the lender has filed a notice of foreclosure with the local county clerk where the property is located. To purchase such a property, you would negotiate a price directly with the owner who may or may not know that foreclosure is imminent. The owner may be willing to take a price lower than the market value especially if the offer is above the mortgage balance. Here the owner can get out of the loan and avoid foreclosure and perhaps still recoup some money. Time is of the essence at this stage as the actual foreclosure can take place in as little as 30 days.*

2. ***Foreclosure Auction.*** *Once foreclosure occurs, the bank will attempt to sell the home at a **foreclosure auction**. Most of the people bidding on these homes are professionals as the buyer must come up with the cash immediately. In many instances, the bids are too low and the lender rejects them all.*

3. ***Short Sale.*** *If the auction produces no bids sufficiently high to pay off the outstanding debt, the lender typically takes ownership of the property. The lender then will attempt to sell the property on its own or through a real estate agent. This is known as a **short sale** because the lender will accept less than the full mortgage amount. The process for purchasing a property in a short sale requires that offers are taken to the lender for approval. Lenders are tough negotiators as they want to get as much money as possible for the property but may be willing to waive closing costs and other fees, making the overall cost more affordable. The lender agrees to absorb the loss, although he or she might demand the homeowner make some kind of payment or share the loss.*

There are some potential pitfalls when buying a foreclosed residence. The property is likely to need repairs, so insist upon a professional home inspection. Also, taxes and other assessments may be owed. You should hire a real estate attorney to help when making an offer and for the closing.

foreclosure

Process in which the lender sues the borrower to prove default and asks the court to order the sale of the property to pay the debt.

Any slip-up in making mortgage payments results in **foreclosure**. This is a process in which the lender sues the borrower to prove default and asks the court to order the sale of the property to pay the debt. Ironically, home buyers are finding home prices substantially lower today than a few years ago, so these may be good times to do some careful shopping to buy a home.

Concept Check 9.1

1. Explain the purpose and value of a lease for both the renter and the landlord.

2. Distinguish between periodic tenancy and tenancy for a specific time when renting housing.

3. Identify three ways that home buyers can save on their income taxes.

4. Illustrate how housing buyers can pay less than renters when taxes and appreciation of housing values are considered.

WHAT DOES IT COST TO BUY A HOME?

 LEARNING OBJECTIVE 2

Explain the up-front and monthly costs of buying a home.

Buying housing represents the largest outlay of funds over most people's lifetime. Some of these costs occur up front. The largest of these is usually the down payment. Others, such as the mortgage payment, occur monthly. A few items, such as real estate property taxes, require both an initial outlay and recurring monthly payments. Table 9-1 illustrates these outlays for the purchase of a $185,000 home with $25,000 down financed

Illustrated Up-Front and Monthly Costs When Buying a Home (Purchase Price of a Home, $185,000 with $25,000 Down; Closing on July 1)

Table 9-1

Home-Buying Costs	At Closing	Monthly
Payments Required Up Front		
Down payment	$ 25,000	
Points (1)	1,600	
Attorney's fee	500	
Title search	200	
Title insurance (to protect lender)	320	
Title insurance (to protect buyer)	320	
Loan origination fee	800	
Credit reports	75	
Home inspection	400	
Deed recording fees	250	
Appraisal fee	250	
Termite and radon inspection fee	130	
Lot survey fee	100	
Home title transfer fee	1,600	
Notary fee	150	
Payments Required Monthly		
Principal and interest (from Table 9-3 for a $160,000 loan for 30 years at 6.0%)		$ 959.28
Mortgage insurance		53.33
Warranty insurance		30.00
Payments Required Up Front and Then Monthly		
Property taxes ($2160 for the entire year, $1080 for first half-year, then $180 monthly)	1,080*	180.00
Homeowner's insurance ($1200 for the entire year; $600 for first half-year, then $100 monthly)	600†	100.00
Subtotal	**$33,375**	**$1,322.61**
Less amount owed by seller	−1,080*	
Total	**$32,295**	**$1,322.61**

*Would be received from seller, who legally owes these taxes, and then deposited in escrow account to be available when the tax bill comes due at the end of the year.
†Would be paid to escrow account to be available when the premium for the next year is due.

by a 30-year mortgage at 6.0 percent interest. (We have used a 6.0 percent rate for illustration purposes. Rates may be lower or higher depending on your credit score and market conditions.) This same example is used repeatedly throughout this chapter to illustrate the costs of home buying as it is near the median price for first-time buyers in metropolitan areas.

Pay Up-Front Costs at the Closing

First-time home buyers are faced with high initial costs when buying a home. These include the down payment and closing costs. **Closing costs** include fees and charges other than the down payment and may vary from 2 to 5 percent of the mortgage loan amount. The down payment and closing costs must be paid at a meeting called the **closing** at which ownership of the property is transferred. All the parties to the purchase, sale, and the mortgage loan are represented at the closing. Up-front costs are indicated in green in Table 9-1.

closing costs
Include fees and charges other than the down payment and may vary from 2 to 5 percent of the mortgage loan amount.

The Down Payment The **down payment** on a home is simply the portion of the purchase price that is not borrowed. The buyer actually writes a check to the seller for that amount. In this example, we assume that the prospective homeowner has $25,000 to use as a down payment on a $185,000 home and will, thus, need to borrow $160,000.

down payment
Portion of the purchase price that is not borrowed.

point/interest point
Fee equal to 1 percent of the total mortgage loan amount.

Points A **point** (or **interest point**) is a fee equal to 1 percent of the total loan amount. Any charges for points must be paid in full when the home is bought, although sometimes they can be added to the amount borrowed. Lenders use points to increase their income return on loans. For example, a lender might advertise a loan as having an interest rate 0.25 percentage point below prevailing rates but then charge 1 point. Any points are, in effect, prepaid interest and compensate the lender for having a low interest rate. In our example, the lender charged 1 point on the $160,000 loan, resulting in a charge of $1600. By law, interest points must be included when calculating the APR for the loan because they really are interest. Interest points are deductible on federal income tax returns.

Attorney Fees Home buyers should hire an attorney to review documents and advise and represent them prior to and during closing. Attorney fees commonly amount to 0.5 percent of the purchase price of the home, although some attorneys do this work for a flat fee ($500 in our example).

title
Legal right of ownership interest to real property.

deed
Written document used to convey real estate ownership.

Title Search and Insurance The **title** to real property is the legal right of ownership interest. In real estate transactions, the title is transferred to a new owner through a **deed**, which is a written document used to convey real estate ownership.

Four types of deeds are used:

1. A **warranty deed** is the safest, as it guarantees that the title is free of any previous mortgages.
2. A **special warranty deed** guarantees only that the current owner has not placed any mortgage encumbrances on the title.
3. A **quitclaim deed** transfers whatever title the current owner had in the property with no guarantee.
4. A **deed of bargain and sale** conveys title with or without a guarantee that the seller had an ownership interest.

title insurance
Protects the lender's interest if the title search is later found faulty.

A title search and the purchase of title insurance protect the buyer's title to the property. Your attorney or title company will conduct a **title search** by inspecting court records and prepare a detailed written history of property ownership called an **abstract**. The seller normally pays the fees for this process ($200 in our example). Lenders often require buyers to purchase **title insurance** because it protects the lender's interest if the title is later found faulty. Premiums for title policies vary among title companies. The one-time charge at closing may amount to 0.20 percent of the amount of the loan for each policy ($320 [$160,000 × 0.002] in our example). Homeowners who wish to insure their own interest must purchase a separate title insurance policy (another $320 in our example).

home inspection
Conducted to ensure that the home is physically sound and that all operating systems are in proper order.

appraisal fee
Fee charged for a professionally prepared estimate of the fair market value of the property by an objective party.

Miscellaneous Fees When a prospective mortgage borrower applies for a loan, the lender may charge a **loan origination fee** at the closing to process the loan ($800 or half of a point in our example). In addition, credit reports ($75 in our example) are needed before a home buyer can obtain a loan—and the borrower pays the fee for this report as well. Another important up-front cost is the **home inspection** ($400 in our example) conducted to ensure that the home is physically sound and that all operating systems are in proper order. Title and deed recording fees ($250 in our example) are charged to transfer ownership documents in the county courthouse. An **appraisal fee** ($250 in our example) may be required to obtain a professionally prepared estimate of the fair market value of the property by an objective party. If you are charged an appraisal fee, you have the right to receive a copy of the appraisal. Occasionally, termite and radon inspections ($130 in our example) are required by local laws, and these are a good idea even when not required. A **survey** ($100 in our example) is sometimes required to certify the specific boundaries of the lot. Finally, separate **notary fees** ($150 in our example) may be charged for the services of those legally qualified to certify (or notarize) signatures. Some communities also charge a **home title transfer fee**, which is simply a tax imposed to support community services such as police, fire, and schools.

Your Monthly Costs Include Both Principal and Interest

Once a home is purchased, the monthly costs can consume as much as 30 or 40 percent of your disposable income. These costs include the portion of your monthly payment that goes to principal (the amount you owe) and interest. Additional monthly costs can include mortgage insurance, home warranty insurance, property taxes, and homeowner's insurance. Monthly costs are indicated in blue in Table 9-1.

Mortgage Principal and Interest A mortgage loan requires repayment of both principal (P) and interest (I), which are the first two letters of the acronym **PITI**, which real estate agents and lenders often use to indicate a mortgage payment that includes principal, interest, real estate taxes, and homeowner's insurance. In the example in Table 9-1, the mortgage payment for principal and interest on a 30-year mortgage for $160,000 at 6.0 percent is $959.28. (Later in this chapter, you will learn how the P and I components for any mortgage loan are calculated).

PITI

Elements of a monthly real estate payment consisting of principal, interest, real estate taxes, and homeowner's insurance.

Mortgage Insurance Lenders today expect a 70 to 80 percent **loan-to-value (LTV) ratio** when a home is purchased. The LTV ratio is simply the loan amount divided by the value of the home (the purchase price initially). An 80 percent LTV ratio translates into a 20 percent down payment, an amount that is difficult to come by for most first-time buyers.

loan-to-value (LTV) ratio

Original or current outstanding loan balance divided by the home value.

Special Insurance Programs for Those Who Can Only Afford a Low Down Payment Fortunately, a number of special programs allow for lower down payments for many types of home buyers and especially first-time buyers. When a buyer makes a lower down payment that results in an LTV higher than that desired by the lender, the lender requires that the borrower purchase mortgage insurance.

FINANCIAL POWER POINT

Joint Ownership Is Best When Couples Buy a Home

Married couples and unmarried persons buying a home together should generally put the ownership in both names using joint tenancy with right of survivorship. If one of the parties dies, the other will have clear title to the entire property.

Mortgage insurance insures the difference between the amount of down payment required by the lender's desired LTV ratio and the actual, lower down payment. In this way, the lender is assured of payment of the loan balance if the home were later repossessed for default and sold for less than the amount owed. Mortgage insurance may be obtained from several sources and can be canceled when the LTV ratio reaches the desired percent as the loan is paid down. You can obtain mortgage insurance from the following sources.

- **Private Mortgage Insurance. Private mortgage insurance (PMI)** is obtained from a private company. The largest private mortgage insurer is the Mortgage Guaranty Insurance Corporation (MGIC, pronounced "magic"). The cost of PMI varies from 0.25 to 2.0 percent of the debt, depending on the degree to which the loan-to-value ratio exceeds the lender-desired percentage. In our example, the loan-to-value ratio is 86.5 percent ($160,000 ÷ $185,000), and the lender required 80 percent (20 percent down). As a result, the annual private mortgage insurance premium is 0.4 percent of the mortgage loan (0.004 × $160,000) and is $640, or $53.33 per month ($640 ÷ 12).

   Instead of making monthly payments for PMI, it may be possible to obtain lender-paid mortgage insurance. In such a case, the lender pays the mortgage insurance premium and, in return, charges a higher interest rate on the loan of perhaps an additional ¼ to ¾ of a percentage point. In this way, the mortgage insurance premium is tax deductible because it represents part of the interest payments. But in this case, the insurance cannot be canceled when the LTV ratio hits the desired percentage without completely refinancing the loan.

- **FHA Mortgage Insurance.** To encourage lending, the **Federal Housing Administration (FHA)** of the U.S. Department of Housing and Urban Development (HUD) insures loans that meet its standards. FHA-insured loans can allow you to borrow with as little as 3.5 percent down plus a 1.75 percent up-front charge. The maximum amount of the loan varies by geographic region, but the lowest maximum is in the range of $275,000. To obtain such mortgage insurance, the borrower must be creditworthy and the home must meet the FHA's minimum-quality standards.

mortgage insurance

Insures the difference between the amount of down payment required by an 80 percent LTV ratio and the actual, lower down payment.

private mortgage insurance (PMI)

Mortgage insurance obtained from a private company.

Federal Housing Administration (FHA)

An arm of the U.S. Department of Housing and Urban Development (HUD) that insures loans that meet its standards to encourage home ownership.

(For information on HUD mortgage programs, visit www.hud.gov/buying/index.cfm.) FHA mortgage insurance premiums may be paid as a single up-front, lump-sum payment or may be financed and paid in monthly amounts in the same way as private mortgage insurance.

- **VA Mortgage Insurance.** The federal **Department of Veterans Affairs (VA)** promotes home ownership among military veterans (active-duty, reserve, and National Guard veterans may qualify) by providing the lender with a guarantee against buyer default. In effect, the VA (www.homeloans.va.gov) guarantee operates much like FHA or private mortgage insurance—that is, the lender is guaranteed a portion of the loan's value in the event that the home must be repossessed and sold.

- **State/Local Mortgage Assistance Program.** Many state and local governments provide support for first-time home buyers through various housing agencies. These supports often take the form of special low down payment loan programs, forgivable down payment loans, and certain guarantees that encourage lenders to accept lower than usual down payments or mortgage interest rates. First-time buyers should always explore such opportunities in their communities. Lenders in your area can provide you with information about programs that target these special-needs groups. Or go to www.hud.gov/buying/localbuying.cfm for links to programs in each state.

Home Warranty Insurance　All homes for sale carry some type of implied warranty (see Chapter 8). In most states, home sellers must complete and sign a form required by state law to verify the condition of home features and major mechanical equipment at the time of sale. A seller who knowingly hides serious defects might be liable, but the buyer may have to hire an attorney and sue to prove this point. Also, many new-home builders provide an express warranty good for one year on the new homes they sell.

DID YOU KNOW?

The New Realities of Home Buying

The bursting of the housing bubble, the sluggish economy of the early 2010s, and government efforts to revive the economy with low interest rates have combined to create a new, and in some ways unprecedented, environment for first-time home buyers. Key features of this new environment include two factors that work in favor of first-time buyers and two that work against them.

1. ***Historically low interest rates.*** *Interest rates of around 4.5 percent for the most qualified borrowers result in extremely low monthly payments compared to more typical economic times. At 7 percent, the monthly payment on a $150,000, 30-year loan is $998 for principal and interest. That same loan at 4.5 percent would require a payment of $760. Home loan payments today are affordable for many first-time buyers.*

2. ***A buyer's market.*** *With so many homes on the market, sellers are forced to take less money for their properties, resulting in good deals for buyers.*

3. ***Tougher lending standards.*** *Mortgage lenders are much more careful when approving first-time mortgage loan applicants. Home lenders only approve loans today to those with high credit scores and a good earnings history. If you have never had a mortgage before, the lender may require clear indicators that your income will continue to be sufficient to cover your payments. The lender will want a higher front- and back-end ratio and will require that you have been at the same job for one, or even two, years. Many first-time buyers have trouble meeting these standards.*

4. ***Higher down payments.*** *First-time buyers could easily find loans with just 5 percent down. Now, lenders are being much more careful and holding the line on the traditional 20 percent down payment requirement. It used to be that affording the monthly payment was the biggest barrier for first-time buyers. Now, it is the affordability of the required down payment.*

Home warranty insurance, another option for the homeowner, operates much like a service contract (also discussed in Chapter 8). Insurance companies sell this type of insurance on existing homes through real estate agents and builders. The example in Table 9-1 has a $30-per-month home warranty insurance protection. Typically, the homeowner must pay the first $100 to $500 of any repair.

Taxes and Insurance Are Paid Both Up Front and Monthly

Some home-buying costs do not fit neatly into an up-front or monthly pattern. This is because they are billed annually. Property taxes and homeowner's insurance are examples. **Taxes** (*T*) and **insurance** (*I*) represent the last two letters of PITI. To ensure that these are paid when due, the lender usually requires that monthly installments be paid into an escrow account. An **escrow account** is a special reserve account at a financial institution in which funds are held until they are paid to a third party. When the insurance and tax bills are due, the lender pays them out of the escrow account.

escrow account
Special reserve account at a financial institution in which funds are held until they are paid to a third party—in this case, for home insurance and for property taxes.

Real Estate Property Taxes **Real estate property taxes** (the T in PITI) must be paid to local governments and may range from 1 to 4 percent of the value of the home. The total property tax ($2160 in our example) is due once each year when the government sends out its tax bill. However, if a buyer takes possession during the tax year, the buyer must pay the taxes accrued so far into the escrow account at the closing ($1080, or 6 × $180 here) to ensure that sufficient funds will be available when the bill comes due at the end of the year. Then the monthly amount ($180 in our example) is paid thereafter into the escrow account. (Because it is the seller who really owed the taxes for the six months prior to the sale, the seller will pay the buyer $1080 on the day of the closing.)

Real estate property taxes are based on the value of buildings and land. To calculate these taxes, local government officials first establish a **fair market value** for the owner's home and land. Next, the **assessed value** of the property is calculated. A home with a fair market value of $160,000, for example, might have an assessed value of $120,000. Some government officials establish the assessed value of a property as the same as the actual fair market value. Although you can do little to influence the tax rate on real estate property, you can claim that the assessed valuation of your home is too high. If your appeal is successful, your tax bill will be lowered accordingly. About one-half of all appeals succeed in today's market with lower property values.

Homeowner's Insurance Lenders always require homeowners to insure the home itself in case of fire or other calamity. Both the home and its contents can be covered in a typical homeowner's insurance policy (the second I in PITI). (Chapter 10 covers this information in detail.) The annual premium for such insurance must be paid each year in advance ($1200 in this example). Lenders require prepayment of the estimated insurance premium each month ($100 here) into the escrow account. In our example illustrated in Table 9-1, the purchaser must be prepared to pay one-half year's premium ($600 here) on the closing day so that there will be sufficient funds in the account to pay the next year's full premium in six months when it is due.

Decide Based on All Costs

The wise financial planner will carefully estimate all initial and monthly costs of housing. Focusing only on the down payment and the monthly payment for principal and interest does not tell the whole story. In our example, the borrower put only 13.5 percent of the purchase price ($25,000 ÷ $185,000) as a down payment but, with points and other up-front costs, actually had to come up with 17.46 percent ($32,295 ÷ $185,000) at the closing. Thus, the closing costs represented almost 4 percent (17.46% – 13.5%) of the purchase price. Similarly, the monthly payment for principal and interest was $959.28, but the actual monthly outlay will be $1322.61, an increase of 39 percent [($1322.61 – $959.28) ÷ $959.28]. This is the real dollar amount that buyers must fit into their budget when trying to determine whether they can afford to buy a home.

Concept Check 9.2

1. What is the standard down payment amount on a mortgage loan?

2. If you make a down payment that is lower than standard, identify the extra cost you will be required to pay.

3. Why do lenders use points in home loans, and who is responsible for paying points?

4. Explain why the down payment and mortgage principal and interest understate the actual up-front and monthly costs of home ownership.

5. When should you request that private mortgage insurance be canceled if such insurance was required at the time of purchase of a home?

6. Identify the components of PITI.

THE STEPS IN HOME BUYING

LEARNING OBJECTIVE ❸

Describe the steps in the home-buying process.

The steps in the home-buying process closely resemble the planned buying steps outlined in Chapter 8. It may take several weeks or months to find a home that represents a good value and another three to five months to actually move into the home. Special attention will need to be paid to the seven steps outlined in Figure 9-1.

Figure 9-1

Steps in the Process of Buying a Home

You should plan on it taking about 6 months to buy a home from the time you begin your efforts until you actually move in.

6 months before moving in	**1. Get your finances in order.** • Ensure that your credit bureau file is accurate and request any updates or corrections as necessary. • Estimate all your expected monthly housing costs. • Adjust your budget to fit the costs expected.
3 to 5 months before moving in	**2. Prequalify for a mortgage.** • Shop for best rates. • Estimate affordability using front- and back-end ratios. • Consult several lenders and mortgage brokers.
2 to 4 months before moving in	**3. Search for a home online and in person.**
2 months before moving in	**4. Agree to terms with a seller.** • Negotiate a price with the seller and give the seller earnest money. • Have your lawyer go over the purchase contract with you. • Sign the purchase contract with the seller. • Have the home inspected by someone you hire.
1 to 2 months before moving in	**5. Obtain a mortgage loan. Decide on the best type of mortgage loan for you.** • Formally apply for a mortgage from the desired lender. • Consider locking-in an interest rate if rates are likely to go up before the closing. • Arrange for a lawyer to help you go over the contract and the good-faith estimate of closing costs.
2 to 4 weeks before moving in	**6. Prepare for the closing.** • Make moving arrangements. • Activate all utilities. • Initiate the change of address process.
The Big Day	**7. Attend the closing.** • Correct any errors in the contract or uniform settlement statement. • Sign your name. Write the big checks. • Celebrate!!!!

1. Get Your Finances in Order

You need to be financially ready to buy a home. Three tasks ease the process: doing a credit checkup, accurately estimating all monthly housing costs, and fitting projected housing costs into your budget.

Clean Up Your Credit History Your credit history can make or break your chances of buying the home of your dreams. Obtain copies of your credit report and your credit scores from all three major credit reporting agencies (lenders use all three) about six months in advance of buying housing; you can then clear up any errors before the loan application process begins. See Chapter 6, pages 178 to 183 for the steps to take to correct errors in your credit report and how to do so for free. Most people can improve their credit scores by correcting errors and rearranging credit accounts. See www.myfico .com/CreditEducation/ImproveYourScore.aspx for suggestions.

Use Internet Resources to Estimate Your Monthly Housing Costs It is vital to have an accurate estimate of what you will have to pay on a monthly basis for your new home. And it is not enough to just estimate the amount of the payment for principal and interest on your mortgage loan. Other costs must be considered, too. You should include all likely components of the monthly payment into your budget: the principal and interest, property taxes, homeowner's insurance, mortgage insurance, and perhaps a home warranty fee. You should also consider any additional costs you might pay for utilities. Heating, air conditioning, electric, and water are all areas for which homeowners generally pay more than renters. Estimating a 50 percent increase from what you are currently spending might be appropriate. Resources are available on the Internet to help estimate housing costs. See www.bankrate.com, www.hud.com, and www.realtor.com.

1. Start by choosing the type of home you would like to own and the neighborhood in which you would like to live.
2. Go to the www.realtor.com website to search for housing that matches your interests. You will be able to estimate the selling price of similar housing and, by subtracting your available down payment amount, estimate the amount you will need to borrow.
3. Go to the www.bankrate.com website to estimate the current interest rates on mortgage loans in your market.
4. Use the calculator at www.bankrate.com to estimate the monthly payment for a loan of the amount you need at the prevailing interest rates.
5. Add an additional 30 to 40 percent (it was 39 percent in the Table 9-1 example) to the monthly payment on the loan itself for such things as homeowner's insurance, property taxes, maintenance, and upkeep.

Fit the Housing Costs into Your Budget Once you have an estimate of the monthly costs associated with buying a home, you will need to see how these costs fit into your budget. You can follow a similar process as outlined in Chapter 8 on pages 224 to 228 to fit your payment into your budget. Some mortgages are set up for lower payments initially with possible (for adjustable-rate loans) and planned (for some loans tailored for first-time buyers) increases in the monthly payment. You will need to anticipate these and factor them into your budget to ensure that you will be able to afford any payment increases that could occur in the future. If your budget cannot accommodate your estimate of monthly costs, you may need to revise your goals by downsizing the type of home you desire or choosing housing in another neighborhood. Then readjust the estimate of your monthly housing costs and fit these revised numbers into your budget.

2. Prequalify for a Mortgage

It is really smart to begin looking into whether you will qualify for a mortgage loan given the price range of homes that you like and your intended down payment. You also need to make a preliminary decision about the time period of the

FINANCIAL POWER POINT

Combining Incomes to Buy a Home

A young couple that buys a home based on their combined income is locked into a full-time, dual-income lifestyle to pay the loan. Family obligations or a job loss may later disrupt their willingness or ability to continue that lifestyle. Instead, base your housing affordability on just one income or on part-time work for the second person.

loan and the choice between a fixed or variable interest rate (topics covered later in this chapter). A primary goal is to find the lowest APR for loans available. A good place to start is with the financial institutions in which you have your checking and savings accounts. In addition, you can search for low-rate loans at www.bankrate.com. Helpful information can be found at the websites for the U.S. Department of Housing and Urban Development (www.hud.gov/buying) and the Federal National Mortgage Association (www.homepath.com).

DID YOU KNOW?

The Income Needed to Qualify for a Mortgage

The table below gives you a quick idea of how much income you need to buy a home at a certain price using a front-end ratio of 28 percent. The illustration is for a 30-year loan with a 20 percent down payment. For each home price, the top figure in each row shows the monthly payment for principal, interest, real estate taxes, and homeowner's insurance for the interest rates; the bottom figure shows the required gross annual income to qualify for the loan. For example, a 6 percent loan on a $180,000 home requires a monthly payment of $1088 plus an income of $46,600 to qualify. Taxes and insurance are assumed to be 1.5 percent of the purchase price (divided by 12 months). Visit the *Garman/Forgue* companion website to perform these calculations for a variety of home prices and interest rates.

Interest Rate	Price of Home						
	$120,000	**$150,000**	**$180,000**	**$210,000**	**$240,000**	**$270,000**	**$300,000**
4.5	636	795	954	1,114	1,272	1,432	1,591
	27,300	34,100	40,900	47,700	54,600	61,400	68,200
5.0	665	832	998	1,164	1,331	1,497	1,663
	28,500	35,700	42,800	49,900	57,000	64,200	71,300
5.5	695	869	1,043	1,216	1,390	1,564	1,737
	29,800	37,200	44,700	52,100	59,600	67,000	74,500
6.0	725	907	1,088	1,269	1,451	1,634	1,814
	31,100	38,900	46,600	54,400	62,200	70,000	77,700
6.5	757	946	1,135	1,324	1,514	1,703	1,892
	32,400	40,600	48,700	56,800	64,900	73,000	81,100
7.0	789	986	1,183	1,380	1,577	1,775	1,971
	33,800	42,300	50,700	59,200	67,600	76,100	84,500

Once you have an idea of the interest rate you might pay, you can consult lenders to determine whether you would actually qualify for a mortgage in the amount you would like. Lenders use two rules of thumb to estimate the maximum affordability of housing expenses: the front-end ratio and the back-end ratio.

front-end ratio
Compares the total annual PITI expenditures for housing with the loan applicant's gross annual income to assess the borrower's ability to pay the mortgage.

- The **front-end (maximum allowable monthly housing expense) ratio** compares the total annual expenditures for housing (the principal and interest on the mortgage plus the real estate taxes and insurance) with the loan applicant's gross annual income. Generally, the total annual expenditures should not exceed 25 to 29 percent of gross annual income. Applying a 28 percent front-end ratio, a young couple with a combined gross annual income of $84,000 could qualify for a mortgage requiring total annual expenditures of less than $23,520 (0.28 × $84,000), or $1960 per month.

back-end ratio
Compares the total of all monthly PITI expenditures plus auto loans and other debts with gross monthly income.

- The **back-end (maximum allowable monthly housing expense and long-term debt) ratio** compares the total of all monthly debt payments (for the mortgage, real estate taxes, and insurance, plus auto loans and other debts) with gross monthly income. Generally, lenders require that monthly debt payments do not exceed 33 to 41 percent of gross monthly income. Applying a back-end ratio of 38 percent, the same couple could qualify for any loan that does not result in total monthly debt repayments exceeding $2660 (their monthly income of $7000 [$84,000 ÷ 12] × 0.38). During the housing boom of the mid-2000s, some lenders allowed people to buy homes with back-end ratios as high as 50 percent. Such practices were ripe for disaster, as recent history has shown. You should never rely on what a lender says you can afford. If you think you will lose sleep at night because of a high mortgage payment, you should instead buy a home that costs less.

About 10 percent of all mortgage loans today are arranged through a mortgage broker. A **mortgage broker** is an individual or company that acts as an intermediary between borrowers and lenders. In other words, a broker helps lenders find borrowers and borrowers find lenders. Either the lender or the borrower may pay the fee charged by the broker. If the lender pays this fee, the broker legally represents the lender. If the borrower pays it, the broker legally represents the borrower. Thus, if you want the broker to work to find you the lowest possible rate, you should be prepared to pay for the service.

mortgage broker
Individual or company that acts as an intermediary between borrowers and lenders.

DID YOU KNOW?

About Parental Help for Making a Down Payment

Many young, first-time home buyers look to family members, usually parents, to help them make the required down payment. If the assistance is a gift to be paid at the closing, the lender will usually require a gift letter with the mortgage application stating that the funds will truly be a gift and from the giver's own funds. Loans from parents are more complicated. The lender will require that the loan terms be put in writing and the payment amounts will be included when determining mortgage affordability. The IRS will be involved as well. Inter-

est paid to the down payment lender will be considered taxable income for the lender. If there is no interest or the rate is below current market interest rates, and the buyer's tax return is audited, the IRS will determine the **imputed interest** amount that would otherwise have been paid, and that amount will be taxable for the lender. Interest paid by the borrower will not be tax deductible unless the down payment loan is secured by a lien on the home. Mortgage lenders will rarely agree to have a second lien holder, however.

3. Search for a Home Online and in Person

Searching for a home requires a commitment of time. You do not want to be impulsive when you will be committing yourself to many thousands of dollars of expense. You can find housing in any number of ways, but the Internet is most helpful. You can narrow your choices to excellent prospects without ever leaving home. Simply go to www.realtor.com and search for homes in your community. You will be able to see floor plans, photos, descriptions of features and condition, and price-related information. Once you have found some homes you would like to see, you can contact the seller or the real estate agent handling the properties.

4. Agree to Terms with the Seller

Once you have your finances in order and have received assurances that you can qualify for a mortgage, you can start looking for a home in earnest. Sellers generally put a price on the property that is 5 to 15 percent higher than the amount that they actually expect to receive. Therefore, you may want to make an offer to buy that is somewhat lower than the asking price. Perhaps $5000 to $15,000 or more is at stake here. Some buyers today make very low offers, perhaps 20 to 25 percent less than the asking price, and hope that a distressed seller will sell. However, the difference between median asking and sales prices is around $5000.

FINANCIAL POWER POINT

Keep Your Debts Low if You Want to Buy a Home

A student loan, car loan, or credit card payments can easily disqualify a potential home buyer based on the back-end ratio. If you plan on buying a home some day, you need to be very careful about taking on too much debt while in school and after graduation.

Make an Offer to Buy The written offer to purchase real estate is called a **purchase offer** (or an **offer to purchase**). Of course, you will specify a price, but other aspects of the sale may be included in your offer as well. Examples of conditions include successful

purchase offer/offer to purchase
Written offer to purchase real estate.

DID YOU KNOW?

How to Search for a Home

You can be a more effective home shopper if you do the following:

- **Make a list** in advance of special features or "must have" items that you are looking for in your new home.

- **Drive around the neighborhood** before you visit a property. Get out of the car and listen. Are there industrial noises or excessive highway noises? Any pet noises from the neighbors? Then ask the real estate agent and/or seller about any aspects that are of interest to you such as types of neighbors and availability of parks and schools.

- **Look at only two or three properties** in one day at most. Looking at too many homes at one time can be confusing and exhausting.

- **Bring a notepad and tape measure** with you. Make sketches of the floor plans that you like. Bring along a camera or video equipment.

- **Obtain written information** describing details about the home. Ask about special home features, utility costs (you can confirm these with the utility company), and any recent improvements and repairs.

- **Check for slope and sags** by rolling a small rubber ball along floors, countertops, and door frames.

- **Walk around the outside of the property** to assess the external condition of the home and yard. Look for signs of water damage to the home or drainage issues in the yard.

DID YOU KNOW?

Sean's Success Story

Sean knew that he could not afford to buy a home for a few years after he took his first job after college. Nonetheless, he began saving for this goal by using direct deposit to put 5 percent of his salary into a savings account set up exclusively as a home-buying savings fund. At the end of each year, he used the funds to buy certificates of deposit designed to mature six years after his graduation. Now after six years, he has a fund exceeding $20,000 and has begun taking steps to buy a condominium. Sean's first step was to obtain his credit reports and credit score to ensure that his financial history was accu-

rate. He then contacted several lenders to determine the interest rate and monthly payment he could expect on a property costing about $200,000. His good credit allowed him to be preapproved at that amount so he reworked his budget to see if he could afford the required monthly payment including an estimate for homeowner's insurance and property taxes. He was happy to see that he could do so. He has begun shopping for condos in the $180,000 range to give him a budget cushion once mortgage payments begin. Sean is excited about buying his first home.

earnest money
Funds given to the seller as a deposit to hold the property until a purchase contract can be negotiated.

termite and radon inspections; a home inspection of the plumbing, heating, cooling, and electrical systems; and inclusion of the living room drapes and kitchen and other appliances. When you make an offer, you need to give the seller some **earnest money** as a deposit; 1 or 2 percent of the purchase price should be sufficient to show your good faith when making an offer to purchase the seller's property. This money is returned if the seller rejects the offer.

Respond to a Counteroffer Most home sellers do not accept the first offer from a prospective buyer. Instead, they usually make a **counteroffer**, which is a legal offer to sell (or buy) a home at a different price and perhaps with different conditions from those outlined in the original offer. You can assume that a seller who is willing to make a counteroffer may also be willing to sell at a slightly lower price. Thus, if you make a counteroffer falling between the two prices, a sale will usually result. Of course, if you push the seller too far, you risk having the seller back out of the negotiations altogether.

Negotiate a Price and Sign a Purchase Contract A **purchase contract** (or **sales contract**) is the formal legal document that outlines the actual agreement that results from the real estate negotiations. It includes the final negotiated price and a list of conditions that the seller has agreed to accept. When the purchase contract is signed, the seller keeps the earnest money as a deposit. If at this point you simply change your mind about buying, you will forfeit your earnest money and may be sued for damages.

purchase contract/sales contract
Formal legal document that outlines the actual agreement that results from the real estate negotiations.

DID YOU KNOW?

The Role of Real Estate Agents

A **real estate broker (agent)** is a person licensed by a state to provide advice and assistance, for a fee, to buyers or sellers of real estate. Real estate brokers who are members of the National Association of Realtors often use the registered trademark of **Realtor**® to describe themselves. Brokers typically earn a commission of 5 to 7 percent on the sale price of a home. The seller—not the buyer—usually pays this commission. **Flat-fee brokers**, who charge a flat fee for their services rather than a percentage-based commission, are also available in most real estate markets.

Almost any agent can show you housing that is **listed** (under contract with the seller and the broker) by the realty firm. In addition, many communities have a **multiple-listing (or open-listing) service**, which is an information and referral network among real estate brokers allowing properties listed with a particular broker to be shown by all other brokers.

Buyers should understand that a real estate agent can play three possible roles. The **listing agent** is the party with whom the seller signs the listing agreement. Listing agents advertise the property, show it to prospective buyers, and assist the seller in negotiations. They receive a commission

when the home is sold and owe the seller undivided loyalty. A **selling agent** is any real estate agent that seeks out buyers for a home. Listing agents also play this role, but any real estate agent can search for buyers to whom to sell a property.

Most home buyers use a real estate agent in their search for a home. They should understand that the agent's legal obligation is to the party who will pay his or her fee or commission—generally the seller! Buyers should be wary of this potential conflict of interest and hire their own broker if they need such services. That is, home buyers who want an agent to represent their interests should obtain the services of a **buyer's agent**. This person serves as the buyer's representative in the real estate negotiations and transaction. You can find reputable buyer's agents at www.rebac.net or www.naeba.org.

Why is the distinction among the three types of agents important? Consider the example of a buyer who has asked a selling agent to help him find a home. During negotiations, the potential buyer decides to offer $175,000 for a property with an asking price of $189,000 but tells the selling agent that he would be willing to go as high as $180,000. The selling agent would then be legally obligated to tell the seller about this $180,000 figure.

As a potential buyer, you want to make sure that your earnest money is protected by including one or more **contingency clauses** in the purchase contract. These clauses specify that certain conditions must be satisfied before a contract is binding. One recommended clause would stipulate that the seller must refund the earnest money if the buyer cannot obtain satisfactory financing within a specified time period, usually 30 days. Other important contingency clauses should allow the buyer to opt out of the deal if the appraisal comes in below the agreed upon price or the home fails to pass certain aspects of the home inspection (for example, the inspection uncovers a major structural defect).

real estate broker
Person licensed by a state to provide advice and assistance, for a fee, to buyers or sellers of real estate.

contingency clauses
Specify that certain conditions must be satisfied before a contract is binding.

5. Formally Apply for a Mortgage Loan
Only after you sign a purchase contract do you formally apply for a mortgage loan on the specific home you have selected. The potential lender usually approves or turns down this request within a few days.

When you apply for a mortgage, the lender must mail you a **good-faith estimate** within three days of your application. All lenders must use the same format for this document as shown at www.hud.gov/offices/hsg/ramh/res/gfestimate.pdf. The good-faith estimate lists all the costs associated with the loan, including the annual percentage rate, application and processing fees, and any other charges that must be paid when the deal is legally consummated. Table 9-1 provides an example of the type of information in the good-faith estimate.

good-faith estimate
Lender's list of all the costs associated with the loan, including the annual percentage rate (APR), application and processing fees, closing costs, and any other charges that must be paid when the deal is legally consummated.

DID YOU KNOW?

Your Credit Score Affects the Mortgage Rate You Pay

Mortgage lenders charge interest rates based on your credit score. Here are illustrative FICO credit scores and the corresponding mortgage loan interest rates.

Credit Score	APR
760–850	4.8%
700–759	5.0%
680–699	5.2%
660–679	5.4%
640–659	5.8%
620–639	6.4%
Below 620	It is unlikely that a loan could be obtained and, if so, only in the subprime market.

Loan applicants whose scores are lower than desired are turned down. At that point the borrower may seek a lender in the **subprime market**, which serves higher-risk applicants with credit scores below 620. Borrowers who are placed in this market are often happy to have obtained a loan. However, such loans carry higher interest rates than normal and have terms and conditions that can lead to future repayment difficulties. Some subprime borrowers actually may qualify for loans at standard rates if they take steps to improve their credit scores and search more extensively.

The exact interest rate on your mortgage may be the current rate at the time of application or the rate in force at the time of closing. If you expect rates to rise between the time you apply for the loan and the actual closing, you may wish to pay a small fee to obtain a **mortgage lock-in**. This agreement includes a lender's promise to hold a certain interest rate for a specified period of time, such as 60 days. It may be part of, but is not the same as, a **loan commitment** (or **loan preapproval**), which is a lender's promise to grant a loan.

loan commitment/loan preapproval
Lender's promise to grant a loan.

6. Prepare for the Closing

After you have obtained a mortgage, you are not yet finished. Of course, you will want to do all the usual tasks associated with moving: giving notification of your change of address, hiring a moving company (or not), and getting your utilities shut off at your old residence and on at your new one are examples. However, there are two very important additional steps to take that can save you thousands of dollars and many headaches.

Hire Your Own Inspector Recall that you should always have a contingency clause included in your purchase contract so that you can back out of the deal if the house fails to pass the home inspection. The licensed or certified inspector should look for termite infestation, wood rot, and radon gas as well as examine the general condition of the home, including heating/cooling, plumbing, and electrical. You should pay the inspector yourself ($250 to $350 is the typical fee) and should not choose one based on the recommendation of the seller's real estate agent. You want an independent person who is well qualified to look out for your interests. If the inspector finds problems, you can negotiate with the seller for an adjustment in the purchase price of the home or, in severe cases, use the contingency clause to back out of the deal.

FINANCIAL POWER POINT

Protect Your Credit Score While Waiting for Your Mortgage to Close

In the weeks leading up to the closing for a home purchase, it may be tempting to begin buying furniture, appliances, outdoor equipment, and other costly items for the home. Think twice if doing so means racking up high balances on your credit cards. Your mortgage lender will raise your interest rate if you significantly change your credit score before closing.

Hire an Attorney The good-faith estimate that you receive is a legal document outlining your entire up-front and monthly home-buying costs. Hiring an attorney to go over the estimate and your purchase contract to ensure that everything is in order is money well spent. Many of the closing costs are negotiable, and your attorney can advise on how to keep these costs to a minimum. If you are buying a home that was previously foreclosed, it is absolutely critical that you hire an attorney well experienced in these transactions. Some unfortunate buyers of foreclosed properties have later found serious defects in their titles as well as claims against the home.

7. Sign Your Name on Closing Day

To complete the sale, the buyer, the seller, and their chosen representatives generally gather in the lender's office for the closing. At the closing, all required documents are signed and payments are made. A key document is the **uniform settlement statement**, which lists all of the costs and fees to be paid at the closing. You have the right to see this statement one business day before the closing so that you can avoid surprises and can compare the fees with the good-faith estimate provided earlier. Challenge any discrepancy.

 Concept Check 9.3

1. Distinguish between the two rules of thumb that lenders use to assess housing affordability.

2. What services does a mortgage broker offer?

3. What services do real estate agents provide for buyers?

4. Why should a buyer be cautious about working with a seller's agent?

5. Explain the benefits of having contingency clauses in a home purchase agreement.

uniform settlement statement
Lists all of the costs and fees to be paid at the closing.

Buyers Have a Right to Full Disclosure on Closing Costs

Federal law governs the information about closing costs that must be disclosed to real estate purchasers when you apply for a mortgage, at least one day prior to the closing, and again at the closing. You should negotiate every closing cost item because these costs average about $4000 on a median-priced home. A full description of the required disclosures can be found by going to www.hud.gov and searching for the keyword "RESPA" to learn more about your rights under the Real Estate Settlement Procedures Act.

FINANCING A HOME

People often rent housing for five years or more while they save enough to make a down payment to purchase a home. Some couples postpone having children, while other people cut back on entertainment and vacations and put off making major purchases. Before buying, you must become knowledgeable about mortgage loans and learn how they are used to purchase a home.

 LEARNING OBJECTIVE 4

Distinguish among the conventional and alternative ways of financing a home and list the advantages and disadvantages of each.

The Mathematics of Mortgage Loans

Mortgage loans are available from depository institutions (described in Chapters 5 and 7) and mortgage finance companies. In exchange for the loan, the lender (**mortgagee**) has a **lien** on the real estate—that is, the legal right to take and hold property or to sell it in the event the borrower (**mortgagor**) defaults on the loan.

The term *mortgage* receives its name from the concept of amortization, which is the process of gradually paying off a loan through a series of periodic payments to a lender. Each payment is allocated in two ways:

1. **A portion goes** to pay the simple interest on outstanding debt for that month multiplied by the periodic (monthly) interest rate.
2. **The remainder goes** to repay a portion of the principal, which is the debt remaining from the original amount borrowed.

As the principal is paid down, increasingly smaller portions of the payments will be required to pay interest while the portion of the payments devoted to the principal will grow larger. These changes in the allocation of each payment are illustrated in Figure 9-2.

Note the slow decline in the amount of each monthly payment going toward interest. A high proportion of each monthly payment during the early years of a mortgage loan is allocated to interest. This is because the outstanding debt remains very high. Table 9-2 shows the interest and principal payment amounts for the first three months of a $160,000, 30-year, 6.0 percent mortgage loan. For the first month, $800 goes for interest costs, and only $159.28 goes toward retirement of the principal of the loan. Table 9-3 provides a partial **amortization schedule** for the same loan. When you take out a mortgage loan, you will receive a full amortization schedule for each month of the

amortization schedule
List that shows all the monthly payments, the portions that will go toward interest and principal, and the debt remaining after each payment is made throughout the life of the loan.

Figure 9-2

Change in Principal and Interest Components of the Monthly Payment on a $160,000 Mortgage Loan at 6.0 Percent Interest Rate for 30 Years

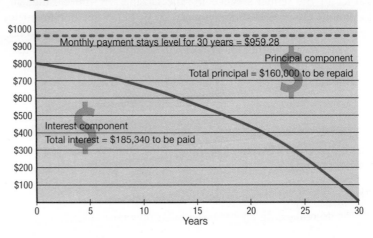

Table 9-2

Amortization Effects of Monthly Payment of $959.28 on a $160,000, 30-Year Mortgage Loan at 6.0 Percent

First Month		
	$160,000 × 6.0% × ¹⁄₁₂ =	$800.00 Interest payment
	$959.28 − 800.00 =	$159.28 Principal repayment
	$160,000 − 159.28 =	$159,840.72 Balance due
Second Month		
	$159,840.72 × 6.0% × ¹⁄₁₂ =	$799.20 Interest payment
	$959.28 − 799.20 =	$160.08 Principal repayment
	$159,840.72 − 160.08 =	$159,680.64 Balance due
Third Month		
	$159,680.64 × 6.0% × ¹⁄₁₂ =	$798.40 Interest payment
	$959.28 − 798.40 =	$160.88 Principal repayment
	$159,680.64 − 160.88 =	$159,519.76 Balance due

homeowner's equity
Dollar value of the home in excess of the amount owed on it.

loan listing all the monthly payments, the portions that will go toward interest and principal, and the debt remaining after each payment is made.

It takes many years of monthly payments to significantly reduce the outstanding balance of the loan. At any point, the amount that has been paid off (including the down payment) plus any appreciation in the value of the home represents the **homeowner's equity** (the dollar value of the home in excess of the amount owed on it). Figure 9-3 illustrates the buildup of equity in a home that results from reductions in the amount owed and the growth in the home's value. Note that the bulk of the increase in equity is a result of increases in the market value of the home. You want to buy a home based on its features and location, not as an investment. Nonetheless, equity buildup over the long run is a definite plus. If desired, additional payments can be directed toward the principal at any time to reduce the amount owed, increase equity, and reduce the eventual total amount of interest paid on the loan. The equity portion of a mortgage payment is a type of forced savings and helps explain why homeowners typically have a higher net worth than renters.

Three Factors That Affect the Mortgage Payment

Three factors affect the monthly payment on a mortgage loan: the amount borrowed, the interest rate charged, and the length of maturity of the loan.

Partial Amortization Schedule for a $160,000, 30-Year (360-Payment) Mortgage Loan at 6.0 percent

Table 9-3

Payment Number (Month)	Monthly Payment Amount	Portion to Interest	Portion to Principal Repayment	Total of Payments to Date	Outstanding Loan Balance
1	$959.28	$800.00	$159.28	$ 959.28	$159,840.72
2	959.28	799.20	160.08	1,918.56	159,648.94
3	959.28	798.40	160.88	2,877.84	159,472.20
12	959.28	791.02	168.26	11,511.36	158,035.18
24	959.28	780.64	178.64	23,022.72	155,949.18
60	959.28	745.50	213.78	57,566.80	148,886.97
120	959.28	670.93	288.35	115,113.60	133,897.16
180	959.28	570.34	388.95	172,670.40	113,678.15
240	959.28	434.65	524.63	230,227.20	86,405.74
300	959.28	251.63	707.65	287,784.00	49,619.34
360	959.28	4.77	954.51	345,340.80	0

Change in Loan Balance and Owner's Equity for a $185,000 Home Purchased with $25,000 Down at a 6.0 Percent Interest Rate for 30 Years (Assumes a 3% Annual Market Price Increase)

Figure 9-3

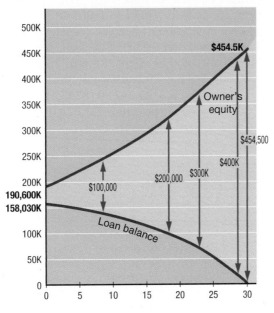

1. Amount Borrowed The payment schedule illustrated in Table 9-4 gives the monthly payment required for each $1000 of a mortgage loan at various interest rates. Using this table, you can calculate the monthly payment for mortgage loans of different amounts. For example, the $160,000 mortgage loan described earlier (6.0 percent for 30 years) costs $5.9955 per $1000 per month. Thus, 160 × $5.9955 equals $959.28.

Making a down payment that is larger than required lowers the borrower's monthly payments. For example, a down payment of 30 percent, or $55,500, would lower the monthly payment on the loan to $776.42 [$5.9955 × ($185,000 − $55,500) ÷ 1000].

Table 9-4

Estimating Mortgage Loan Payments for Principal and Interest (Monthly Payment per $1000 Borrowed)

	Payment Period (Years)			
Interest Rate (%)	15	20	25	30
4.0	$7.3969	$6.0598	$5.2783	$4.7742
4.5	7.6499	6.3265	5.5583	5.0669
5.0	7.9079	6.5996	5.8459	5.3682
5.5	8.1708	6.8789	6.1409	5.6779
6.0	8.4386	7.1643	6.4430	5.9955
6.5	8.7111	7.4557	6.7521	6.3207
7.0	8.9883	7.7530	7.0678	6.6530

Note: To use this table to figure a monthly mortgage payment, divide the amount borrowed by 1000 and multiply by the appropriate figure in the table for the interest rate and time period of the loan. For example, a $160,000 loan for 30 years at 6.0 percent would require a payment of $959.280 [($160,000 ÷ 1000) × 5.9955]; over 20 years, it would require a payment of $1146.29 [($160,000 ÷ 1000) × 7.1643]. For calculations for different interest rates, visit the *Garman/Forgue* companion website.

A smaller loan also carries lower total interest costs and may qualify for an interest rate that is perhaps 0.5 percentage points lower. In that case, the payment for the same loan would amount to only $735.29 [$5.6779 × ($185,000 − $55,500) ÷ 1000].

2. Interest Rate   The higher the interest rate, the higher the monthly payment on a mortgage loan (see Table 9-4). For example, a $959.28 monthly payment is required for a $160,000 mortgage loan taken out for 30 years at 6.0 percent. If the interest rate were 7.0 percent, the monthly mortgage payment would be $1064.48 (160 × $6.6530), an increase of over $100. The effects are even greater when you consider the total of all the monthly payments and the total interest paid over the life of the loan. The 6.0 percent loan will have total payments of $345,340.80 (360 × $959.28) with total interest of $185,340.80 ($345,340.80 − $160,000.00). For the 7.0 percent loan, total payments are $383,212.80 (360 × $1064.48), and total interest is $223,212.80 ($383,212.80 − $160,000.00). Thus, the added cost for the 30-year loan at 7.0 percent is $37,872 over the life of the loan.

ADVICE FROM A PRO

Cancel Private Mortgage Insurance as Soon as Possible

Most first-time home buyers cannot make the standard loan-to-value ratio of 80 percent (20 percent down) and must buy private mortgage insurance. As the borrower makes mortgage payments over time, the amount of principal remaining to be paid will decline until eventually the 80 percent threshold is reached. At that point, the lender must notify the borrower of the opportunity to drop the PMI. And, by law, the lender must terminate the PMI when the loan-to-value ratio reaches 78 percent based on the market value of the home at the beginning of the mortgage.

But there is no need to wait that long. As illustrated in Figure 9-3, a borrower might start out owing $160,000 or 86.5 percent of the value of the home. It takes about five and one-half years to reach the 80 percent threshold ($148,000 =

0.80 × $185,000) simply by making loan payments. The good news is that the value of the home may increase faster than the loan principal declines. In the example in Figure 9-3, the 80 percent threshold will be reached in about three years because of the rising value of the home. When that threshold is attained, the borrower can ask the lender to cancel the PMI. Lenders usually require an appraisal of the property before doing so, but the cost of the appraisal (perhaps $300) represents money well spent. It is a smart move to make such a request, and it is even smarter to continue making the same monthly payment on the mortgage after the PMI is removed. The extra amount will be applied to the principal of the loan, thereby paying it off even sooner.

Michael Ruff and Sherry Tshibangu
Monroe Community College, Rochester, NY

3. Length of the Loan Table 9-5 illustrates the relationships among maturity length, monthly payment, and interest cost for a $100,000 loan at various interest rates. A longer term of repayment results in a smaller payment (for loans with the same interest rate). More total interest is paid over the longer repayment time period despite the lower monthly payment. For example, the monthly payment on a 5.5 percent loan is $688 for 20 years but only $568 for 30 years. When the loan is paid back in 20 years, the total interest costs are much lower ($65,100 rather than $104,400, for a savings of $39,300).

Some borrowers choose a mortgage loan with a comparatively short 15-year maturity. The advantages include a faster buildup of equity, lower total interest, and a quicker payoff of the loan. These advantages can also be gained with a 20- or 30-year mortgage by simply paying additional amounts toward the principal during the time period of the loan. It is wise to take a longer repayment period even if you plan to pay off the loan in 15 (or fewer) years. With that strategy, the faster payoff is optional rather than mandatory.

The Conventional Mortgage and Adjustable Mortgage Loans

A **conventional mortgage** is a fixed-rate, fixed-term, fixed-payment mortgage loan. Borrowers like conventional mortgages because they are so predictable. For example, a $160,000 loan could be granted at a 6.0 percent annual interest rate over a period of 30 years with a fixed monthly payment of $959.28. The payment is the same for month after month and year after year. Most borrowers see a conventional fixed-rate loan as the best possible choice because the amount of all future payments is known in advance.

With an **adjustable-rate mortgage (ARM)**—sometimes called a **variable-rate mortgage**—the borrower's interest rate fluctuates according to some index of interest rates based on the rising or falling cost of credit in the economy. With an ARM, the risk of interest rate changes is assumed by the borrower, not the lender. As a consequence, the monthly payment could increase or decrease, usually on an annual basis, but sometimes monthly. Borrowers with ARMs should always determine the "worst case" scenario for interest rate increases under their loan contract and calculate the monthly payment that would result.

ARM rates are usually 1 to 3 percentage points below conventional mortgage rates. Lenders sometimes offer an even lower **teaser rate** to entice people to borrow using an ARM. Such a loan will carry an interest rate for the first year or so that may be 1 to 3 percentage points below the regular ARM loan rates, a substantial savings over a conventional mortgage. Borrowers using an ARM with a teaser rate must be prepared for the higher monthly payments that will occur when interest rates rise in the future. If you do not feel you can afford even a minimal increase in the rate, you should not take out this type of loan, or any of the following alternative mortgages that can easily result in negative amortization.

conventional mortgage
A fixed-rate, fixed-term, fixed-payment mortgage loan.

adjustable-rate mortgage (ARM)/variable-rate mortgage
Mortgage in which the borrower's interest rate fluctuates according to some index of interest rates based on the rising or falling cost of credit in the economy—thus transferring interest rate risk to the borrower.

teaser rate
Low interest rate that lenders sometimes use to lure buyers; these rates will be low for the first year or so and then will rise to more realistic rates.

Monthly Payment and Total Interest to Repay a $100,000 Loan

Table 9-5

Length of Loan	Interest Rate (%)				
	5.0	**5.5**	**6**	**6.5**	**7**
30 years	$ 537	$ 568	$ 600	$ 632	$ 665
	93,300	104,400	116,000	127,500	139,400
25 years	585	614	644	675	707
	75,500	84,200	93,200	102,500	112,100
20 years	660	688	716	745	775
	58,400	65,100	71,800	78,800	86,000
15 years	791	817	844	871	899
	42,300	47,100	51,900	56,800	61,800

Note: Figures are rounded. The top figure in each pair is the monthly payment, and the bottom figure is the total interest paid to the nearest $100.

You can use this table to estimate the monthly payment and total interest on any loan at these same interest rates. Simply divide the amount of the loan by $100,000 and multiply that figure by the amounts shown in the table. For example, the loan of $160,000 at 6.0% for 30 years illustrated in this chapter has a monthly payment of $960 (1.6 × $600) and total interest of $185,600 (1.6 × $116,000). Note that these figures differ slightly from those earlier due to rounding.

FINANCIAL POWER POINT

Should You Use a Fixed or Adjustable Rate Loan?

With mortgage rates at their lowest point in years, borrowers are wise to look for a fixed-rate loan. The key is to know where rates are likely to be headed in the future. If up, go fixed. If down, go adjustable.

negative amortization
Occurs when monthly payments are actually smaller than necessary to pay interest on the loan, which will result in a rising principal loan balance.

interest-only mortgage
Mortgage in which the borrower pays only the interest on the mortgage in monthly payments for a fixed term, then either refinances the principal, pays off the principal, or starts paying the higher monthly payment with the principal payments added in.

Most ARMs have **interest-rate caps** that limit the amount by which the interest rate can increase (perhaps no more than 2 percent per year and no more than 5 percent over the life of the loan). This may not seem like much, but if the 6 percent loan we have been using as an example in this chapter were to go up the full 5 points after ten years because of rising inflation, the new payment would be almost $1300, which would be $340, or 35 percent more than the original $959 payment. While such an increase is unlikely, it could happen under the terms of the agreement. **Payment caps**, however, limit the amount by which the payment can vary on an ARM. Having a loan with a payment cap but without an equivalent interest-rate cap is an invitation to **negative amortization**, which occurs when monthly payments are actually smaller than necessary to pay the interest. This practice will result in a principal loan balance that rises rather than falls. Payment caps are an invitation to financial disaster.

Many variations of ARMs exist. One, the **option ARM** mortgage, was a contributor to the housing foreclosure crisis. Option ARMs give the borrower the option of paying the standard payment, an interest-only payment, or (even worse) a less-than-interest payment resulting in negative amortization. Many people took out option ARMs that had artificially low teaser rates for the first years of the loan. Then, perhaps after four years, the rate would reset to market rates with a new monthly payment perhaps $200 or more above the earlier payments. Millions of mortgages that started as affordable became unaffordable and went into foreclosure after the rates reset.

Alternative Mortgage Loans

Most alternative lending approaches aim to keep the monthly payment as low as possible, especially in the early years of the loan. This also permits borrowers to purchase larger, more expensive homes than they might be able to afford with a conventional loan. Do not take out an alternative loan to buy a home unless you are positive you can afford it. Remember that in recent years, millions of Americans made the wrong decision by taking out these types of loans and then defaulted.

Interest-Only Mortgage With an **interest-only mortgage** loan, you pay only the interest on the mortgage in monthly payments for a fixed term. No monthly payment is made on the debt itself. After the end of that term, usually five to seven years, you can refinance, pay the balance in a lump sum, or start paying off the principal with a

DID YOU KNOW?

The Tax Consequences of Buying a Home

Home ownership makes you eligible for three big tax breaks.

1. ***Mortgage interest and real estate taxes are tax deductible on federal (and most state) income tax returns.*** *These amounts often exceed the IRS's standard deduction (see Chapter 4). You can then take advantage of even more deduction opportunities that are available to taxpayers who itemize.*

2. ***You can save the funds to buy a home in a tax-sheltered account.*** *Individuals can use Roth IRAs (see Chapter 17) to save for retirement. Once the account is five years old, as much as $10,000 may be withdrawn tax free and penalty free, provided that a qualifying, first-time home buyer uses the funds for home-buying costs. This mechanism even allows parents or grandparents to make withdrawals*

from their Roth IRAs to help young family members buy their first home.

3. ***The profits made by selling a home can be tax free.*** *If you sell a home for more than you originally paid, you have a* **capital gain***. Gains are ordinarily taxable, but homeowners can avoid paying taxes on gains by buying a home that is more expensive, thus rolling the gain into the new home. Also, capital gains of up to $500,000 if married and filing jointly and up to $250,000 if single may be avoided. To qualify, the home must have been owned and used as the principal residence for two of the last five years prior to the date of the sale. In the first few years of home ownership, any appreciation likely will be offset by the anticipated sales commission. This explains the advice that you should not buy a home unless you know you will live in it for three years.*

commensurate jump in the monthly payment. The obvious lure of an interest-only mortgage is its lower monthly payment. However, if the value of the home were to decrease, negative amortization would occur, possibly leading to the borrower becoming upside down on the mortgage.

Graduated-Payment Mortgage With a **graduated-payment mortgage**, smaller-than-normal payments are required in the early years, but payments gradually increase to larger-than-normal payments in later years. The interest rate is fixed, but payments early in the life of the mortgage may be lower than necessary to pay even the interest, resulting in possible negative amortization. Graduated-payment mortgages are attractive to buyers who expect substantial increases in their income in the future. You should be very certain of such increase before you think about using a graduated payment mortgage

graduated-payment mortgage
Mortgage in which the borrower pays smaller-than-normal payments in the early years but payments gradually increase to larger-than-normal payments in later years.

Lender Buy-Down Mortgage With a **lender buy-down mortgage**, a base interest rate is set for the loan that is perhaps 0.5 percentage points higher than the interest rate for a conventional mortgage. For the first year, the borrower pays a rate 2 percentage points below the base rate. In the second year, the rate is 1 point below the base rate. In the third and future years, the base rate would be changed. These changes are known in advance and are contractual. First-time home buyers often use buy-down mortgages to take advantage of lower monthly payments in early years of the loan. The borrower must be confident that these increases will fit into their planned budget before considering this type of mortgage.

Rollover (Renegotiable-Rate) Mortgage A **rollover mortgage** consists of a series of short-term loans for two- to five-year time periods but with total amortization spread over the usual 25 to 30 years. The loan is renewed for each time period at the market interest rates that prevail at the time of the renewal. The beginning interest rate on rollover mortgages can be deceptively attractive for a first-time home buyer. Interest rates are low in today's market; thus there is only one way interest rates can go in the future—up.

Shared-Appreciation Mortgage With a **shared-appreciation mortgage**, the lender offers an interest rate about one-third less than the market rate. In exchange, the lender gains the right to receive perhaps one-third of any appreciation in the home's value when the home is sold or ten years after the time of the loan.

biweekly mortgage
A form of growing-equity mortgage (GEM) that calls for payments of half of the normal payment to be made every two weeks; the borrower thus makes 26 payments a year and reduces the principal amount by one full payment each year; this reduces the mortgage term to about 20 years on a 30-year mortgage.

Growing-Equity Mortgage The **growing-equity mortgage (GEM)** is meant for people who design their loan in advance to reduce interest costs by paying off the mortgage loan early. One form of GEM is the **biweekly mortgage**, which calls for payments to be made every two weeks that represent half of the normal monthly payment.

DID YOU KNOW?

Turn Bad Habits into Good Ones

Do You Do This?	*Do This Instead!*
Think a verbal lease for renting is just fine	Get all terms in writing
Move into an apartment without inspecting for defects and damages	Make a written list of all defects and damages at both move-in and move-out
Make your rent payment late from time to time	Make all payments on time; your landlord may report patterns to a credit bureau
Hope, rather than plan, to buy a home	Start saving for a down payment as soon as you get a job after graduation
Want a home just like your parents' home	Recognize that buying a small starter home is just fine

The borrower, therefore, makes 26 payments per year. For example, a $160,000, 6 percent, 30-year loan requires a $959.28 monthly payment for a total of $11,511.36 (12 × $959.28) paid in one year. On a biweekly basis with payments of $479.64 ($959.28 ÷ 2), the total amount paid each year would be $12,470.64 ($479.64 × 26). The difference of $959.28 ($12,470.64 − $11,511.36) is equivalent to one extra monthly payment per year and is applied to the principal of the loan. Under the biweekly repayment plan, a loan may be repaid in approximately 20 years, rather than the 30 years dictated by the monthly payment plan.

Setting up a loan as a GEM from the beginning forces you to make the agreed-upon additional payments. However, almost all mortgages use the declining-balance method of calculating interest (see Chapter 7), thus permitting payment of additional amounts toward principal at any time. Thus, you can voluntarily pay additional amounts on the principal without being locked into it as you would with a growing equity mortgage. For example, even paying an additional $70 (or $1030) per month on the preceding loan would allow the loan to be paid off in just over 25 years and would save over $36,000 in interest costs.

Assumable Mortgage With an **assumable mortgage**, the buyer pays the seller a down payment generally equal to the seller's equity in the home and takes responsibility for the mortgage loan payments for the remaining term of the seller's existing mortgage loan. The buyer's goal is to obtain the loan at the original interest rate, which should be below current market rates. This approach will work only if the original mortgage loan agreement does not include a **due-on-sale clause**. Such a clause requires that the mortgage loan be fully paid off if the home is sold. It can impose a burden on the seller because it prohibits a buyer from assuming the mortgage loan.

Seller Financing **Seller financing** occurs whenever the seller of a home agrees to accept all or a portion of the purchase price in installments rather than as a lump sum. Usually seller financing is a short-term arrangement, however, with payments based on amortization occurring over perhaps 20 years and a balloon payment due after perhaps five years. That is, all principal not paid after five years would be due at once. At that time the buyer might seek a conventional loan.

---

assumable mortgage
Buyer pays the seller a down payment generally equal to the seller's equity in the home and takes responsibility for the mortgage loan payments for the remaining term of the seller's existing mortgage loan.

due-on-sale clause
Requires that the mortgage loan be fully paid off if the home is sold. It can impose a burden on the seller because it prohibits a buyer from assuming the mortgage loan.

DID YOU KNOW?

About Second Mortgage Loans

People whose home has increased significantly in value or who have paid down most of the mortgage principal have equity in their homes. They can use a second mortgage to borrow based on this home equity, with the property serving as collateral for both the first and second mortgage loans. A **second mortgage** is an additional loan on a residence besides the original mortgage. In case of default, the amount owed on the original mortgage must be paid first. Because of this additional risk, the interest rate on a second mortgage is often 2 to 5 percentage points higher than current market rates for first mortgages.

Historically, people have used second mortgages to pay for major remodeling projects, finance college costs for children, pay off medical bills, or start a business. Today, some people use these funds for everyday living expenses, an unwise practice dubbed "eating one's house."

Two types of second mortgages exist:

- The **home-equity installment loan**, where a specific amount of money is borrowed for a fixed time period with fixed monthly payments.

- The **home-equity line of credit**, where a maximum loan amount is established and the loan operates as open-ended credit, much like a credit card account. These line-of-credit loans often have variable interest rates and flexible repayment schedules.

The credit limit on a second mortgage loan is usually set at 80 to 90 percent of the home's appraised value minus the amount owed on the first mortgage. For example, a person with a home appraised at $200,000 with a balance owed of $100,000 on a first mortgage might be allowed to take out a $60,000 second mortgage [($200,000 × 0.80) − $100,000].

In most seller financing, the buyer obtains the title to the property when the deal is closed and the contract is signed. In contrast, a **land contract** (or **contract for deed**) brings greater risk for the buyer because all terms in the contract (including payment of the debt) must be satisfied before transfer of title will occur. As a result, if you move before paying off the contract in full, you forfeit all money paid in installments to the seller and any appreciation in the home's value. You build no equity until the contract is completed.

land contract/contract for deed
Brings greater risk for the buyer because all terms in the contract (including payment of the debt) must be satisfied before transfer of title will occur.

Reverse Mortgage

A **reverse mortgage**, also known as a **home-equity conversion loan**, allows a homeowner older than age 61 to borrow against the equity in a home that is fully (or close to fully) paid for and to receive the proceeds in a lump sum or a series of monthly payments. The contract allows the person to continue living in the home. Essentially, the borrower trades his or her equity in the home in return for the funds. The most likely prospects for such loans are elderly people who have paid off their mortgages but are strapped for income. The mortgage does not have to be paid back until the last

reverse mortgage/home-equity conversion loan
Allows a homeowner older than age 61 to continue living in the home and to borrow against the equity in a home that is fully paid for and to receive the proceeds in a series of monthly payments, often over a period of 5 to 15 years or for life.

RUN THE NUMBERS

When You Should Refinance Your Mortgage

It is sometimes advantageous to refinance an existing mortgage when interest rates decline. In **mortgage refinancing**, a new mortgage is obtained to pay off and replace an existing mortgage. Most often it is undertaken to lower the monthly payment on the home by taking out a loan with a lower interest rate.

The example here illustrates how to determine whether refinancing your mortgage is a wise choice. The original mortgage for $160,000 was obtained seven years ago at a 5.5 percent interest rate for 30 years. The monthly payment is $908. After seven years, the principal owed has declined to $142,100. If interest rates for new mortgages have declined to 4.5 percent, the owner could take out a new mortgage at the lower rate for a monthly payment of $827. Borrowing $142,100 for 23 years at 4.5 percent saves approximately $81 per month ($908 – $827). However, refinancing may have

some up-front costs, including a possible prepayment penalty on the old mortgage and closing costs for the new mortgage. The question then becomes, will these costs exceed the monthly savings gained with a lower payment?

The following worksheet provides a means for estimating whether refinancing offers an advantage. It compares the future value of the reduced monthly payments (line 5) with the future value of the money used to pay the up-front costs (estimated here at 2%) of refinancing (line 8). The homeowner would need to estimate the number of months he or she expects to own the home after refinancing. Given an estimate of four years in this example, the net savings would be $977 (subtracting line 8 from line 5), and refinancing would benefit the owner. In this example, planning to live in the home only three more years would result in it not being financially advantageous to refinance. A similar worksheet can be found at http://www.bankrate.com/calculators/mortgages/refinance-calculator.aspx.

Decision Factor	Example	Your Figures
1. Current monthly payment	$ 908	_____
2. New monthly payment	827	_____
3. Monthly savings (line 1 – line 2)	81	_____
4. Additional years you expect to live in the house	4	_____
5. Future value of an account balance after 4 years if the monthly savings were invested at 3% after taxes (using the calculator on the *Garman/Forgue* companion website)	4,175	_____
6. Prepayment penalty on current loan (0%)	0	_____
7. Points and fees for new loan (2%)	2,842	_____
8. Future value of an account balance after 4 years if the prepayment penalty and closing costs ($4263) had been invested instead at 3% after taxes (using the calculator on the *Garman/Forgue* companion website)	3,198	_____
9. Net saving after 48 months (line 5 – line 8)	$ 977	_____

It may also be possible to borrow more than the current balance on the existing loan, thereby utilizing some of the equity built up in the home. Borrowers refinancing for more than the amount owed should understand that rebuilding the equity to its previous level may take many years. And it is dangerous because if home prices decline the borrower will owe more on the home than it is worth.

FINANCIAL POWER POINT

Be Cautious About Tapping Your Equity to Pay Other Debts

Homeowners sometimes refinance a mortgage at an amount higher than they actually owe on the house. They use the excess to pay off credit card debts and vehicle loans or buy large-screen TVs. This, of course, reduces the equity in their homes. If the home declines in value, the homeowner will experience negative equity, and if the homeowner sells the home, he or she will owe money to the lender. Because many people borrowed against the equity in their homes and then saw home prices decline an average of 35 percent nationally since 2007, today four out of every five homeowners owe more than their property is worth. Spending one's home equity is financially dangerous.

LEARNING OBJECTIVE ⑤

Identify the key considerations when selling a home.

FSBO

For sale by owner; commonly pronounced "fizbo"; home sold directly by the homeowner to save on sales commission paid to a real estate broker.

surviving owner sells the house, moves out permanently, or dies. For more information on reverse mortgages, go to http://www.hud.gov/offices/hsg/sfh/hecm/rmtopten.cfm.

✔ **Concept Check 9.4**

1. Explain why the portions of a monthly mortgage payment that are allocated toward interest and toward principal will vary as the loan is repaid.

2. Distinguish between a conventional mortgage loan and an adjustable-rate loan.

3. Identify the two ways that home buyers build equity in their property.

4. Define negative amortization and describe one way that it might occur on a variable-rate loan.

5. Specify one advantage and one disadvantage of an interest-only mortgage loan.

SELLING A HOME

While most of this chapter deals with buying a home, important considerations also arise when you are selling a home. It is extremely important to do minor painting, cleaning, and repairing before listing your home for sale. Sellers also are required by law to disclose known defects in the home to the real estate agent and to potential buyers.

Should You List with a Broker or Try to Sell a Home Yourself?

Knowing that the sales commission to a broker on a $200,000 home could be $12,000 provides motivation for some homeowners to consider selling their homes themselves. The key to success in a **FSBO** (for sale by owner; commonly pronounced "fizbo") is to

© 2011 Jupiterimages Corporation

FSBOs can save a home seller money but usually take longer to sell.

FINANCIAL POWER POINT

How to Sell a Home in a Lousy Market

What if you want to sell your home in a declining market with lots of foreclosed properties that have further depressed home values? Tell your real estate agent that you are willing to pay a commission of 8 or 9 percent rather than 6 percent. This will motivate the agent to show your home by bringing lots of people to see it. The agent's broker will also insist that all his or her agents show the property because the broker will earn more money too. The extra you pay in commission (about $4000 on a $200,000 house) is probably much less than the money you would lose if you reduce your asking price.

know what price to ask for your home. Asking too little could cost you much more than the commission paid to a broker. Setting the price too high keeps potential buyers away.

Many homeowners begin by contacting a few real estate agents to get their opinions on how much the home is worth. Agents are often quite willing to give their opinions because the homeowner might list the home with them if it does not sell quickly. Placing a for-sale sign on your lawn and spending about $500 on advertising the property should keep your telephone ringing for a few months with inquiries.* If your home does not sell, you might want to list it with a broker.

Brokers require that homeowners sign a **listing agreement** permitting them to list the property exclusively or with a multiple-listing service. A multiple-listing service may work best because it allows every broker in the community to show and sell the home. Brokers "qualify" prospective buyers—distinguishing between serious buyers and people who are just looking or cannot afford the home. If your broker cannot find a buyer within 60 days, consider signing an agreement with another broker who might prove more aggressive in advertising and selling your property. If a sale occurs (or begins) during the time period of the listing agreement, you must pay a commission to the broker for any sale to a buyer not listed as an exception in the listing agreement.

Selling Carries Its Own Costs

The largest selling cost is the **broker's commission**. These commissions often amount to 6 percent of the selling price of the home. Some sellers are unaware that brokers may negotiate their commission. Smart sellers also pay for a title search, a professional appraisal, and their own home inspection as well.

Most mortgage loans are paid off before maturity because people move and sell their homes. Mortgage loan contracts sometimes have a clause that specifies a **prepayment fee** or penalty, which can range from 1 to 3 percent of the original mortgage loan. On a $160,000 mortgage loan, for example, the charge might vary from $1200 to $4800. Usually, the penalty is only for an early payoff in the first few years of the loan.

Local communities may assess **real estate transfer taxes**. These taxes are paid by the seller and also possibly the buyer. The tax is based on the purchase price of the home or the equity the seller has in the home. These tax rates can be as high as 2 or 4 percent, that is, $4000 or $8000 on a $200,000 home. When paid by the seller, they may affect the offer that the seller is willing to accept for the home.

Be Wary of Seller Financing

Some sellers who have experienced trouble when marketing their homes have successfully resorted to many variations of seller financing, although

listing agreement
Agreement that brokers require homeowners to sign that permits the broker to list the property exclusively or with a multiple-listing service.

broker's commission
Largest selling cost in selling a home; these commissions often amount to 6 percent of the selling price of the home.

real estate transfer taxes
Community-assessed taxes paid by the seller and also sometimes by the buyer based on the purchase price of the home or the equity the seller has in the home.

DID YOU KNOW?

Your Worst Financial Blunders in Obtaining Affordable Housing

Based on others' financial woes, you will make mistakes in personal finance when you:

1. *Take out a mortgage loan that you really cannot afford.*

2. *Pay too much for a home and/or at too high an interest rate.*

3. *Fail to request that private mortgage insurance be canceled when the loan-to-value ratio drops to 80 percent.*

---

* For more information on selling your own home, visit www.fsbo.com, http://wiki.fool.com/Discount_broker, or www.forsalebyowner.com.

DO IT NOW!

You know more about personal finance after reading this chapter, so get started right now by:

1. *Talking to family members or friends who have bought a home to obtain their insights into the process including any not-so-pleasant surprises.*

2. *Exploring the housing market at www.realtor.com for the geographic area where you might live if you get a job offer in that location.*

3. *Setting a reasonable goal for a down payment amount and calculating how much you would have to save per month to reach it at http://www .bankrate.com/calculators/savings/ saving-goals-calculator.aspx.*

difficulties can arise with these options. Suppose you have a home worth $200,000 with a mortgage loan balance of $90,000 and equity of $110,000. The buyer assumes the existing mortgage loan, puts up $40,000 in cash, and takes out a second mortgage from *you* to repay the $70,000 over five years. At closing, the broker receives a commission of $12,000, and you come away with only $28,000 cash—a small sum to use in making a down payment on another home. Also, seller financing carries a risk that the buyer may not be able to make the second mortgage payments to you and could potentially default on the loan.

✓ Concept Check 9.5

1. List some disadvantages of trying to sell a home yourself.

2. List one advantage and one disadvantage of using a real estate broker to sell a home.

3. Describe two costs associated with selling a home in addition to the real estate commission.

AP Photo/Paul Sakuma

WHAT DO YOU RECOMMEND NOW?

Now that you have read the chapter on buying housing, what do you recommend to Libby Clark regarding:

1. Buying or renting housing in the Denver area?

2. Steps she should take prior to actively looking at homes?

3. Finding a home and negotiating the purchase?

4. The closing process in home buying?

5. Selecting the type of mortgage to fit her needs?

6. Things to consider regarding the sale of her home should she ultimately be promoted to a position in another of the four regions?

BIG PICTURE SUMMARY OF LEARNING OBJECTIVES

LO1. Decide whether renting or owning your home is better for you.

When choosing housing, renters must consider the costs of rent, a security deposit, and related items. Home buyers can choose among single-family dwellings, condominiums, cooperative housing, manufactured housing, and mobile homes. Renters generally pay out less money in terms of cash flow in the short run, whereas owners enjoy tax advantages and generally see an increase in the market value of their homes, making them better off financially in the long run.

LO2. Explain the up-front and monthly costs of buying a home.

Home buyers understand that they will make a down payment and then make monthly principal and interest payments on their mortgage. What many don't understand is that closing costs for interest points and other aspects of the purchase can add 5 percent or more to the amount needed up front at the closing. Similarly, monthly charges for private mortgage insurance (PMI), homeowner's insurance, and real estate property taxes can add 25 percent or more to their monthly payment for principal and interest.

LO3. Describe the steps in the home-buying process.

The home-buying process includes (a) getting your finances in order, (b) prequalifying for a mortgage, (c) searching for a home online and in person, (d) agreeing to terms with a seller, (e) obtaining a mortgage loan, (f) preparing for the closing, and (g) signing your name on closing day.

LO4. Distinguish among the conventional and alternative ways of financing a home and list the advantages and disadvantages of each.

Mortgage loans for homes are amortized. Amortization is the process of gradually paying off a mortgage through a series of periodic payments to a lender, with a portion of each payment going toward the principal and another portion going toward the interest owed. Conventional mortgages and adjustable-rate mortgages are the most common types of housing loans. Numerous alternative types of mortgages are available that have reduced the importance of the long-term, fixed-rate mortgage loan and that provide new ways to keep the monthly payment as low as possible.

The mathematics of buying a home shows how loan payments are calculated and how the portion of each monthly payment that goes toward interest declines, resulting in the portion that goes toward the principal increasing with each subsequent payment.

LO5. Identify the key considerations when selling a home.

When selling a home, it is wise to consider the pros and cons of listing with a real estate broker versus selling the home yourself, the transaction costs of selling, and the pitfalls of seller financing.

LET'S TALK ABOUT IT

1. **The Housing Collapse.** How have the recent foreclosure crisis and collapse in home values affected your thinking about buying a home someday?

2. **Renting Versus Buying.** What do you see as the advantages and the disadvantages for you of renting or buying housing at the current time? How might your feelings change in the future, such as within five years?

3. **Feelings About Long-Term Debt.** In the early years of the standard 30-year mortgage loan, as little as 10 percent of the monthly payment actually goes toward repaying the debt. As a result, it takes many, many years for the loan balance to come down to any significant extent. Explain how that affects your feelings about taking on such a long-term obligation.

4. **Who Can Help You.** What experts could you turn to for assistance during the home-buying and loan application processes? What conflicts of interest most concern you?

5. **Alternative Mortgages.** Would you prefer a conventional mortgage, an adjustable-rate mortgage, or one of the other alternatives described in this chapter to finance a home purchase? Why?

6. **Negotiating the Purchase of a Home.** Some closing costs on a home purchase are negotiable. Would you feel comfortable entering into a discussion of these items? Why or why not?

DO THE MATH

1. **Deciding to Buy.** Walter and Marcie Jensen of Atlanta, Georgia, both of whom are in their late 20s, currently are renting an unfurnished two-bedroom apartment for $880 per month, plus $130 for utilities and $34 for insurance. They have found a condominium they can buy for $170,000 with a 20 percent down payment and a 30-year, 5 percent mortgage. Principal and interest payments are estimated at $730 per month, with property taxes amounting to $150 per month and a homeowner's insurance premium of $720 per year. Closing costs are estimated at $3200. The monthly homeowners association fee is $275, and utility costs are estimated at $160 per month. The Jensens have a combined income of $57,000 per year, with take-home pay of $4100 per month. They are in the 15 percent tax bracket, pay $225 per month on an installment loan (ten payments left), and have $39,000 in savings and investments outside of their retirement accounts.

    (a)   Can the Jensens afford to buy the condo? Use the results from the *Garman/Forgue* companion website or the information on page 262 to support your answer. Also, consider the effect of the purchase on their savings and monthly budget.

    (b)   Walter and Marcie think that their monthly housing costs would be lower the first year if they bought the condo. Do you agree? Support your answer. Assume that they currently have $7000 in tax deductible expenses.

    (c)   If they buy, how much will Walter and Marcie have left in savings to pay for moving expenses?

    (d)   Available financial information suggests that mortgage rates might drop over the next few months. If the Jensens wait until the rates drop to 4.0 percent, how much will they save on their monthly mortgage payment? Use the information in Table 9-4 or the *Garman/Forgue* companion website to calculate the payment.

2. **Mortgage Affordability.** Seth and Cassie Moore of Baltimore, Maryland, have an annual income of $78,000 and want to buy a home. Currently, mortgage rates are 6 percent. The Moores want to take out a mortgage for 30 years. Real estate taxes are estimated to be $4800 per year for homes similar to what they would like to buy, and homeowner's insurance would be about $1500 per year.

    (a)   Using a 28 percent front-end ratio, what are the total annual and monthly expenditures for which they would qualify?

    (b)   Using a 36 percent back-end ratio, what monthly mortgage payment (including taxes and insurance) could they afford given that they have an automobile loan payment of $470, a student loan payment of $350, and credit card payments of $250? (Hint: Subtract these amounts from the total monthly affordable payments for their income to determine the amount left over to spend on a mortgage.)

    (c)   If mortgage interest rates are around 5 percent and the Moores want a 30-year mortgage, use the information in the Did You Know box on page 262 to estimate how much they could borrow given your answer to part a. (Hint: Subtract the monthly real estate taxes and homeowner's insurance from your part a answer first.)

3. **Rent Versus Buy.** Phillip Guadet of Monroe, Louisiana, has been renting a small, two-bedroom house for several years. He pays $900 per month in rent for the home and $300 per year in property and liability insurance. The owner of the house wants to sell it, and Phillip is considering making an offer. The owner wants $130,000 for the property, but Phillip thinks he could get the house for $125,000 and use his $25,000 in 3 percent certificates of deposit that are ready to mature for the down payment. Phillip has talked to his banker and could get a 4.5 percent mortgage loan for 25 years to finance the remainder of the purchase price. The banker advised Phillip that he would reduce his debt principal by $2200 during the first year of the loan. Property taxes on the house are $1800 per year. Phillip estimates that he would need to upgrade his property and liability insurance to $800 per year and would incur about $1500 in costs the first year for maintenance. Property values are increasing at about 2.5 percent per year in the neighborhood. Phillip is in the 25 percent marginal tax bracket.

    (a)   Use Table 9-4 to calculate the monthly mortgage payment for the mortgage loan that Phillip would need.

    (b)   How much interest would Phillip pay during the first year of the loan?

    (c)   Use the Run the Numbers worksheet, "Should You Buy or Rent?" on page 253 to determine whether Phillip would be better off buying or renting.

4. **Refinancing a Mortgage.** Kevin Tutumbo of Rochester Hills, Michigan, has owned his home for 15 years and expects to live in it for five more years. He originally borrowed $105,000 at 6 percent interest for 30 years to buy the home. He still owes $65,750 on the loan. Interest rates have since fallen to 5.0 percent, and

Kevin is considering refinancing the loan for 15 years. He would have to pay 2 points on the new loan with no prepayment penalty on the current loan.

(a) What is Kevin's current monthly payment?

(b) Calculate the monthly payment on the new loan.

(c) Advise Kevin on whether he should refinance his mortgage using the Run the Numbers worksheet, "When You Should Refinance Your Mortgage" on page 275.

FINANCIAL PLANNING CASES

CASE 1

The Johnsons Decide to Buy a Home

Belinda Johnson's parents and maternal grandmother have combined their finances and presented Harry and Belinda with $35,000 with which to purchase a home. The Johnsons have shopped and found a house in a new housing development that they like very much. They could either borrow from the developer or obtain a loan from one of three other mortgage lenders. The financial alternatives and data for the home are summarized in the table below.

(a) Which plan has the lowest total up-front costs? The highest?

(b) What would be the full monthly payment for PITI and PMI for each of the options?

(c) If the Johnsons had enough additional cash to make the 20 percent down payment, would you recommend lender 1 or lender 2? Why?

(d) Assuming that the Johnsons will need about $3000 for moving costs (in addition to closing costs), which financing option would you recommend? Why?

Financing Details on a Home Available to the Johnsons

Price: $190,000. Developer A will finance the purchase with a 10 percent down payment and a 30-year, 5 percent ARM loan with 2 interest points. The initial monthly payment for principal and interest is $917.96 ($171,000 loan after the down payment is made; 171 × $5.3682). After one year, the rate rises to 5.5 percent, with a principal plus interest payment of $961.15. At that point, the rate can go up or down as much as 2 percent per year, depending on the cost of an index of mortgage funds. There is an interest-rate cap of 5 percent over the life of the loan. Taxes are estimated to be about $1800, and the homeowner's insurance premium should be about $700 annually. A mortgage insurance premium of $88 per month must be paid monthly on the two 10 percent down options.

Home: Price, $190,000; Taxes, $1800; Insurance, $700

	Developer A	Lender 1	Lender 2	Lender 3
Loan term and type	30-year ARM*	30-year CON†	15-year CON	20-year REN‡
Interest rate	5.0%	5.5%	6%	5.5%
Down payment	$ 19,000	$ 38,000	$ 38,000	$ 19,000
Loan amount	171,000	152,000	152,000	171,000
Points	3,420	1,520	0	5,130
Principal and interest payment	917.96	863.04	1282.66	1176.29
PMI	88	0	0	88

*Adjustable-rate mortgage
†Conventional.
‡Renegotiable every five years.

CASE 2

Victor and Maria Hernandez Learn About Real Estate Agents

Victor and Maria have been thinking about selling their home and buying a house with more yard space so that they can indulge their passion for gardening. Before they make such a decision, they want to explore the market to see what might be available and in what price ranges. They will then list their house with a real estate agent and begin searching in earnest for a new home.

(a) What services could a real estate agent provide for the couple, and what types of agents could represent them as they sell their current home?

(b)   A friend has advised them that they really need a buyer's agent for the purchase of a new home. Explain to the Hernandezes the difference between buyer's and seller's agents.

CASE 3

Julia Price Contemplates Buying a Home

Julia has been thinking about buying a home. For several months, she has been watching real estate shows on television and visiting open houses in her community. She thinks it is time to take the plunge and buy a much larger home since she can genuinely afford it. She also thinks that housing prices will rise substantially in the next five years. She has explored the interest rates currently being charged for mortgages and has calculated the amount of money she can afford to pay given her income. She is thinking that her next step would be to call a real estate agent and begin looking in earnest. Offer your opinions about her thinking.

CASE 4

Michael and Jonathan Weigh the Benefits and Costs of Buying Versus Renting

Michael Higginbottom and Jonathan Van Ness of Logan, Utah, are trying to decide whether to rent or purchase housing. Both men are single. Michael favors buying and Jonathan leans toward renting, and both seem able to justify their particular choice. Michael thinks that the tax advantages are a very good reason for buying. Jonathan, however, believes that cash flow is so much better when renting. See whether you can help them make their decision.

(a)   Does the home buyer enjoy tax advantages? Explain.

(b)   Discuss Jonathan's belief that cash flow is better with renting.

(c)   Suggest some reasons why Michael might consider renting rather than purchasing housing.

(d)   Suggest some reasons why Jonathan might consider buying rather than renting housing.

(e)   Is there a clear-cut basis for deciding whether to rent or buy housing? Explain why or why not.

CASE 5

Emma Chooses Among Alternative Mortgage Options

Emma Rafferty of Long Beach, California, has examined several options for new home financing. She has been favoring alternative mortgage plans because of their lower mortgage rates.

(a)   What broad concerns are present with alternative mortgages?

(b)   What financing option would you suggest for Emma, assuming she is able to use any type of mortgage available? Why?

(c)   How would you advise Emma if she were considering using an option ARM mortgage to buy her home?

CASE 6

Jeremy Decides to Sell His Home Himself

Jeremy Jorgensen of Tucson, Arizona, is concerned about the costs involved in selling his home, so he has decided to sell his home himself rather than pay a broker to do it.

(a)   How would you advise Jeremy if he asked you whether he should sell the house himself or list with a broker? Explain your answer.

(b)   Would Jeremy really save money by selling his home himself if he considers his time as part of his costs? Why or why not?

(c)   Can you suggest any ways that Jeremy might reduce his selling costs without doing the selling himself? Explain.

BE YOUR OWN PERSONAL FINANCIAL MANAGER

1.
Are You Ready to Buy a Home? Review the material in the Run the Numbers worksheet "Should You Buy or Rent?" on page 253. Then using dollar amounts that fit your situation, complete Worksheet 37: Should I Rent or Buy Housing from "My Personal Financial Planner."

MY PERSONAL FINANCIAL PLANNER

2.   **Save to Buy a Home.** Review the material on "Setting Financial Goals" on page 83–85 and on "How to Save" on page 149–150 and then complete Worksheet 14: Monthly Savings Needed to Reach My Goals from "My Personal Financial

MY PERSONAL FINANCIAL PLANNER

Planner," which allows you to determine the monthly savings amount you would need to reach a goal of having a down payment on a home.

3.
Can You Afford a Mortgage? Review the material on "The Income Needed to Qualify for a Mortgage" on page 262. Then using dollar amounts that fit your situation, complete Worksheet 38: Income Needed to Qualify for a Mortgage from "My Personal Financial Planner." What price range of home could you afford given the results of your analysis?

MY PERSONAL FINANCIAL PLANNER

4. **Shop for a Mortgage.** If you are ready to buy a home, review the material on "The Conventional Mortgage and Adjustable Mortgage Loans" and "Alternative Mortgage Loans" on pages 271–273. Then using that information complete Worksheet 39: Mortgage Shopping Worksheet from "My Personal Financial Planner" to begin your search for a mortgage.

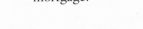
MY PERSONAL
FINANCIAL
PLANNER

5. **Should You Refinance Your Mortgage?** Do you have an existing mortgage? Review the material on "When You Should Refinance Your Mortgage" on page 275. Then using dollar amounts that fit your situation, complete Worksheet 42: Should I Refinance My Mortgage? from "My Personal Financial Planner."

MY PERSONAL
FINANCIAL
PLANNER

ON THE 'NET

To complete these exercises, go to the *Garman/Forgue* companion website at www.cengagebrain.com. Under General Business, select the title of this text. Click on the Internet Exercises link for this chapter, and answer the questions that appear on the Web page.

1. **Current Interest Rates.** Visit the website for Bankrate .com (www.bankrate.com/mortgage.aspx), where you will find information on mortgage interest rates around the United States. View the information for the lenders in a large city near your home. How does the information compare with the interest rates on your own credit card account(s)? How do the rates in the city you selected compare with other rates found in the United States?

2. **Can You Afford to Buy?** Visit the website for the U.S. Department of Housing and Urban Development, where you will find a calculator (www.ginniemae.gov/ 2_prequal/intro_questions.asp?Section=YPTH) that helps you determine the amount you can afford for the pur-

chase of a home given your income and funds available for a down payment, closing costs, and other home-buying expenses. Enter the data requested for your current situation. What does the calculator tell you about your housing affordability? Change the entered data for some point in the future when you project a better financial situation for yourself. How do the results change?

3. **Searching for a Home to Buy.** Visit the website for the National Association of Realtors (www.realtor .com), where you can search for owned housing in various locales around the United States. Look for housing in your community. Were you able to find housing that meets your price range and other criteria? Also search for similar housing in the San Diego, California (high-cost) and Syracuse, New York (low-cost) metropolitan areas. Compare these cost results with the housing found in your area.

ACTION INVOLVEMENT PROJECTS

1. **Do Some Home Shopping.** Realtors often open homes for sale to the public on Sunday afternoons. Spend an afternoon looking at housing that is for sale in a neighborhood near your campus. Gather the information sheets that are provided at the homes and take notes during your visits. Prepare a brief report that summarizes what you have learned about housing costs, features, and locations in the community.

2. **Comparing Leases.** Survey five of your friends who live in rental housing about their feelings about written leases. For those who have written leases, compare several for the rights and responsibilities of tenants outlined in the leases. Write a summary of your findings.

3. **Assess the Real Estate Market.** Make an appointment to talk with a real estate agent in your community. Ask

whether home sales are slow or brisk, how long it typically takes for buyers to find a desirable home, whether home values are rising or declining, and tips the agent would give to people in your situation who hope to own their own homes one day. Write a summary of your findings.

4. **See How Others Go About Buying a Home.** Ask friends and relatives for the names of one or two people who have bought a home in recent years. Contact the home buyers and ask them for an interview in person or over the phone to discuss how they went about buying a home and their feelings about how the process turned out for them. Compare their procedures and experiences with what you have learned in this chapter.

PART

3

10

Managing Property and Liability Risk

YOU MUST BE KIDDING, RIGHT?

Tiffany Blake recently caused an automobile accident when she had a blowout on the freeway. The cost of repairs to Tiffany's car will be $13,200, which exceeds the car's $12,500 fair market value. The damage to the other two vehicles was $17,800 and $6400, respectively. Fortunately, no one was injured in the accident. On the advice of her insurance agent, Tiffany had purchased an auto insurance policy with a $500 collision deductible and liability limits of $25,000/$50,000/$15,000. What dollar amount of her losses will be covered by her policy?

A. $12,700   C. $36,200

B. $27,000   D. $37,400

The answer is B. The company will pay her $12,000 after her $500 deductible for the loss of her vehicle. The company will also pay $15,000 for the damage to the other vehicles as that is the limit for property damage liability under her policy. Tiffany will be personally responsible for the remainder since like most people, she did not carry sufficient liability protection.

LEARNING OBJECTIVES

After reading this chapter, you should be able to:

❶ Apply the risk-management process to address the risks to your property and income.

❷ Explain how insurance works to reduce risk.

❸ Design a homeowner's or renter's insurance program to meet your needs.

❹ Design an automobile insurance program to meet your needs.

❺ Describe other types of property and liability insurance.

❻ Summarize how to make an insurance claim.

© PETER DAZELEY/GETTY IMAGES, INC.

WHAT DO YOU RECOMMEND?

George and Emily Chandler of Athens, Georgia, recently had a fire in their garage that destroyed two of their cars and did considerable damage to the garage and to the outside of their home. After receiving their reimbursements from their homeowner's and automobile insurance policies, the Chandlers realized that they were seriously underinsured. One vehicle was not insured for fire, and the insurance on their dwelling amounted to only 60 percent of its current replacement value.

What do you recommend to George and Emily about managing property and liability risk regarding:

1. The risk-management steps they should take to update their insurance coverages?

2. The relationship between severity and frequency of loss when deciding whether to buy insurance?

3. Adequately insuring their home?

4. The use of deductibles and policy limits to keep their automobile insurance premiums at a manageable level while still maintaining vital coverage?

property insurance
Protection from financial losses resulting from the damage to or destruction of your property or possessions.

liability insurance
Protection from financial losses suffered when you are held liable for others' losses.

 LEARNING OBJECTIVE   1

Apply the risk-management process to address the risks to your property and income.

risk
Uncertainty about the outcome of a situation or event.

risk management
Process of identifying and evaluating purely risky situations to determine and implement appropriate management.

Up to this point, this book has focused on ways to manage your money and strategies for using financial resources to achieve your personal goals. But it is just as important to protect your resources and assets from the possibility of financial loss from accidents, acts of nature, illness or injury, and death. Uninsured and underinsured losses often result in people declaring personal bankruptcy. An uninsured loss can lead to overuse of credit that then snowballs out of control. Today many people are experiencing such difficulties during these challenging economic times. You can manage the risk of such losses through the use of insurance. This chapter focuses on property and liability losses that occur from accidents and acts of nature. Chapter 11 focuses on losses related to illness or injury, and Chapter 12 looks at losses related to death.

The items you own and your day-to-day activities expose you to two types of losses. First, your property might be damaged. **Property insurance** protects you from financial losses resulting from the damage to or destruction of your property or possessions. Second, you might be held responsible **(legally liable)** for losses suffered by others. **Liability insurance** protects you from financial losses suffered by others for which you are legally liable. The most commonly purchased forms of property and liability insurance are insurance for your home and its contents and insurance for your use and ownership of vehicles.

RISK AND RISK MANAGEMENT

People Often Misunderstand the Concept of Risk

Risk is uncertainty about the outcome of a situation or event. It arises out of the possibility that the outcome will differ from what is expected. In the area of financial losses, risk consists of uncertainty about both whether the financial loss will occur and how large it might be. There are two types of risk. **Speculative risk** exists in situations where there is potential for gain as well as for loss. Investments such as those made in the stock market involve speculative risk. **Pure risk** exists when there is no potential for gain, only the possibility of loss. Fires, automobile accidents, illness, and theft are examples of events involving pure risk. Insurance only addresses pure risk.

Many people think of "odds" or games of chance when they hear the word risk. In fact, risk and chance are different concepts. The difference between the two is subtle but very important. An event with a 95 percent chance of occurring is highly likely to occur. Thus, both uncertainty and risk are low. An event with a 0.000001 percent chance of occurring is highly likely *not* to occur. Thus, both uncertainty and risk are low. When an event has a moderate chance of occurring—5 percent, for example—the uncertainty and risk are relatively high because it is difficult to predict the one person in 20 who will experience the event. In such cases, insurance often represents a wise choice for reducing risk.

Apply the Five-Step Risk-Management Process

Risk management is the process of identifying and evaluating situations involving pure risk to determine and implement the appropriate means for its management. The goal is to minimize any risk or potential for risk through advance planning. Risk management entails making the most efficient arrangements *before* a loss occurs. Risk management is an essential part of personal financial management because it preserves the benefits of all your other financial planning efforts. Risk management usually requires the purchase of insurance, although insurance is only one of the ways to handle risk, and it is not always the best choice.

The risk-management process involves five steps; Table 10-1 outlines these steps in the risk-management process.

The Risk-Management Process

Table 10-1

	Possessions	Activities	Accompanying Perils
Step 1 *Identify sources of risk.*	Vehicle House Jewelry	Driving Smoking Traveling	Accident Fire Theft
Step 2 *Estimate risk and potential losses.*	(a) Determine the likely frequency of losses associated with each exposure. (b) Determine the potential severity and magnitude of losses associated with each exposure.		
Step 3 *Choose how to handle risk.*	(a) Avoid risk. (b) Retain risk. (c) Control losses. (d) Transfer risk. (e) Reduce risk.		
Step 4 *Implement the risk-management plan.*	(a) Refrain from certain activities. (b) Take extra precautions. (c) Buy insurance.		
Step 5 *Evaluate and adjust the program.*			

Step 1: Identify Sources of Risk   Sources of risk, called **exposures** are the items you own and the activities in which you engage that expose you to potential financial loss. Owning and/or driving an automobile are common exposures. To determine your exposures to risk, you should take an inventory of what you own and what you do.

Your exposures fall into five categories:

1. You may suffer a loss to your property, such as can happen during a house fire.
2. You could be held legally responsible for losses suffered by others such as if you cause an automobile accident.
3. You may become ill or be injured and have costs associated with health care.
4. You may suffer a loss of income as a result of illness or accident.
5. Your family may incur expenses and suffer a loss of income as a result your death.

You also need to identify the perils that you face. A **peril** is any event that can cause a financial loss. Fire, wind, theft, vehicle collision, illness, and death are all examples of perils.

peril
Any event that can cause a financial loss.

Step 2: Estimate Risk and Potential Losses   Once you identify your exposures to risk, you estimate both loss frequency and loss severity. **Loss frequency** refers to the likely number of times that a loss might occur over a period of time. **Loss severity** describes the potential magnitude of the loss(es).

Many people wonder whether they should buy insurance when loss frequency is low, for example, if they are young and healthy or if they live in a safe neighborhood. This is not a good way to think about potential losses because they still could occur, and if loss frequency is low, the insurance premium would be small. Figure 10-1 illustrates the relationship between loss severity and loss frequency in risk management.

What is much more important is loss severity. "How much might I lose?" is the question you should ask. When considering possible property losses, you simply make an estimate of the value of the property. Liability losses are more complicated because the severity of the loss depends on the circumstances of the person you harm. For example,

Figure 10-1

The Relationship Between Severity and Frequency of Loss

	HIGH SEVERITY	LOW SEVERITY
LOW FREQUENCY	Purchase insurance to cover the potentially large losses. Their infrequency will make premiums affordable.	Consider retaining risk because the frequency and severity of loss are both low.
HIGH FREQUENCY	Purchase insurance. Loss control efforts can be useful in reducing the necessarily high premiums.	Retain risk but also budget for losses that are likely to be frequent.

if you caused an accident that permanently disabled a young heart surgeon with three small children, you would be liable for the surgeon's care, lost earnings over his or her lifetime, and future care and education of the children. A loss of several million dollars is not out of the question in such a situation.

Step 3: Choose How to Handle Risk　The risk of loss may be handled in five ways: risk avoidance, risk retention, loss control, risk transfer, and risk reduction. Each strategy may be appropriate for certain circumstances, and the mix that you choose will depend on the source of the risk, the size of the potential loss, your personal feelings about risk, and the financial resources you have available to pay for losses.

- **Risk avoidance**. The simplest way to handle risk is to avoid it. With this approach, you would refrain from owning items or engaging in activities that expose you to possible financial loss. For example, choosing not to own an airplane or not to sky-dive limits your exposure. Avoiding risk is not always practical, however.

- **Risk retention**. A second way to handle risk is to retain or accept it. The risk that the shrubbery around your house might die during a dry spell is such a retained risk. Conscious risk retention plays an important role in risk management. For example, you can use a **deductible clause** in an insurance policy to retain an initial portion of the risk. In this way, you pay the first few dollars of a loss (perhaps $200 or $500) before the insurance company will reimburse for a loss. Risk retention due to ignorance or inaction is unwise. For example, many people foolishly put off the purchase of life insurance after having children because they consider it to be a morbid, unpleasant task.

- **Loss control**. Loss control, the third method of handling risk, is designed to reduce loss frequency and loss severity. For example, installing heavy-duty locks and doors will reduce the *frequency* of theft losses. Installing fire alarms and smoke detectors cannot prevent fires but will reduce the *severity* of losses from them. Insurance companies often require loss-control efforts or give discounts to policyholders who implement them.

- **Risk transfer**. A fourth way to handle risk is to transfer it. In a risk transfer, an insurance company agrees to reimburse you for a financial loss. For example, a professional football team's star running back might take out an insurance policy on his legs. In this case, the uncertainty is simply transferred from the running back or his team to an insurance company. Insurance represents one method of transferring risk, although not all risk transfers can be classified as insurance because insurance goes beyond merely transferring risk to the actual reduction of risk.

- **Risk reduction**. The fifth way to handle risk is to reduce it to acceptable levels. Insurance is used by policyholders when they arrange for all or a portion of their risk to be covered by an insurance company, thereby reducing their personal level of risk.

risk retention

Accepting that some risks simply arise in the course of one's life and consciously retaining that risk.

deductible clause

Requires that the policyholder pays an initial portion of any loss.

loss control

Designing specific mechanisms to reduce loss frequency and loss severity.

risk reduction

Includes mechanisms, such as insurance, that reduce the overall uncertainty about the magnitude of loss.

Step 4: Implement the Risk-Management Program

The fourth step in risk management is to implement the risk-handling methods you have chosen. For most households, this means buying insurance to transfer and reduce risk. This involves selecting types of policies and coverage, dollar amounts of coverage, and sources of insurance protection.

People often wonder what types of insurance to buy and how many dollars of coverage to choose. You should use the maximum possible loss as a guide for the dollar amount of coverage to buy. This way of thinking makes use of the **large-loss principle**, which states "insure the risks that you cannot afford and retain the risks that you can reasonably afford." In other words, pay for small losses out of your own pocket and purchase as much insurance as necessary to cover

Renters need insurance too.

large, catastrophic losses that will ruin you financially. The example earlier of an auto accident that injures a heart surgeon would bring you such ruin because you would be held responsible for those losses. Consequently, you would want high dollar amounts of liability coverage on your auto insurance.

large-loss principal
A basic rule of risk management that encourages us to insure the risks that we cannot afford and retain the risks that we can reasonably afford.

Step 5: Evaluate and Adjust the Program

The final step in risk management entails periodic review of your risk-management efforts. The risks people face in their lives change continually. Therefore, no risk-management plan should be put in place and then ignored for long periods of time. For certain exposures, such as ownership of an automobile, an annual review is appropriate. For areas involving life insurance, a review should occur about once every three to five years or whenever family structure and employment situations change. The necessary adjustments should be implemented promptly to reflect changes over your life cycle. Many people foolishly keep existing policies that no longer fit their needs (too little or too much coverage) simply because they buy once and then ignore their insurance needs for years.

✔ Concept Check 10.1

1. Distinguish between pure risk and speculative risk.

2. Explain the distinctions between risk and odds.

3. Distinguish among the five common risk exposures that most people face.

4. Describe the five steps of risk management.

5. Based on likelihood of loss and severity of loss, explain why one is more important when deciding whether to buy insurance.

FINANCIAL POWER POINT

Buy—Don't Be Sold—Insurance

Always remember that your goal is to "buy" the insurance you need at a fair price. Do not let yourself be "sold" more or less insurance coverage than you need at excessive prices. Visit www.insquote.com and www.insure.com once you have decided what insurance you need.

UNDERSTANDING HOW INSURANCE WORKS

LEARNING OBJECTIVE 2

Explain how insurance works to reduce risk.

insurance
Mechanism for transferring and reducing pure risk through which a large number of individuals share in the financial losses suffered by members of the group as a whole.

premium
Comparatively small, predictable fee with which individuals or companies can replace an uncertain—and possibly large—financial loss.

insurance policy
Contract between the person buying insurance (the insured) and the insurance company (the insurer).

hazard
Any condition that increases the probability that a peril will occur.

Insurance is a mechanism for transferring and reducing pure risk through which a large number of individuals share in the financial losses suffered by members of the group as a whole. Insurance protects each individual in the group by replacing an uncertain—and possibly large—financial loss with a certain but comparatively small fee. This fee, called the **premium**, has four components:

1. The individual's share of the group's losses
2. Insurance company reserves set aside to pay future losses
3. A proportional share of the expenses of administering the insurance plan
4. An allowance for profit (when the plan is administered by a profit-seeking company)

Insurance premiums are usually assessed on an annual, semiannual, or quarterly basis, and the coverage is paid for in advance. You generally will be charged an extra fee if you choose to make the payments monthly.

The **insurance policy** is the contract between the person buying insurance (the **insured**) and the insurance company (the **insurer**). It contains language that describes the rights and responsibilities of both parties. Most people do not take the time to read and understand their insurance policies. As a result, insurance remains one of the least understood purchases people make. You can do a much better job of managing your risks if you understand the basic terms and concepts used in the field of insurance.

Hazards Make Losses More Likely to Occur

A **hazard** is any condition that increases the probability that a peril will occur. Driving under the influence of alcohol represents an especially dangerous hazard. Three types of hazards exist:

- A **physical hazard** is a particular characteristic of the insured person or property that increases the chance of loss. An example of a physical hazard is high blood pressure in a person covered by health insurance.
  - A **morale hazard** exists when a person is indifferent to a peril. For example, a morale hazard exists if the insured party, knowing that theft insurance will pay for the loss, becomes careless about locking doors and windows.
  - A **moral hazard** exists when an insured person wants a peril to occur so that he or she can collect on an insurance policy.

Insurance companies often limit or deny coverage if a loss occurs as a result of a morale or moral hazard.

Only Certain Losses Are Insurable

Certain minimum requirements must be met for a loss to be considered insurable—in particular, the loss must be fortuitous, financial, and personal. **Fortuitous losses** are unexpected in terms of both their timing and their magnitude. A loss caused by a lightning strike and fire to your home is fortuitous; a loss caused by a decline in the market value of your home is not because it is reasonable to expect home values to rise and fall over time. A **financial loss** is any decline in the value of income or assets in the present or future. Financial losses can be measured objectively in dollars and cents. When you become sick, you suffer as a result of the discomfort, inconvenience, lost wages, and medical bills. Insurance will cover only the lost wages and medical bills, however, because these losses—but not the others—can be objectively measured. Finally, **personal losses** can be directly suffered by specific individuals or organizations rather than society as a whole.

The Principle of Indemnity Limits Insurance Payouts

principle of indemnity
Insurance will pay no more than the actual financial loss suffered.

The **principle of indemnity** states that insurance will pay *no more* than the actual financial loss suffered. For example, an automobile insurance policy will pay only the actual cash value of a stolen automobile. This principle prevents a person from gaining financially from a loss (certainly a moral hazard). The principle of indemnity does not guarantee that insured losses will be totally reimbursed. Every policy includes **policy limits** which specify the maximum dollar amounts that will be paid under the policy. As a result, insurance purchasers must carefully select policy limits sufficient to cover their potential losses.

How to Pay Less for Insurance and Still Maintain Sufficient Coverage

Some features of insurance policies can lower your premiums without significantly reducing the protection offered. These features include deductibles, coinsurance, hazard reduction, and loss reduction.

1. **Pay the first few dollars of a loss yourself.** A **deductible** is an initial portion of any loss that must be paid before the insurance company will provide coverage. For example, automobile collision insurance often includes a $500 deductible and that means that the first $500 of loss to the car must be paid by the insured. The insurer then pays the remainder of the loss, up to the limits of the policy. You usually have a choice of deductible amounts, and the higher the deductible, the more you will save on your premium. This is because the insurance company will have fewer small losses to pay.

policy limits
Specify the maximum dollar amounts that will be paid under the policy.

2. **Pay a share of any loss yourself. Coinsurance** is a method by which the insured and the insurer share proportionately in the payment for a loss. For example, health insurance policies commonly require that the insured pay 20 percent of a loss and the insurer pay the remaining 80 percent. Substantial premium reductions can be realized through coinsurance, but you must be prepared to pay your share of losses. The following **deductible and coinsurance reimbursement formula** can be used to determine the amount of a loss that will be reimbursed when the policy includes a deductible and a coinsurance clause:

coinsurance
Method by which the insured and the insurer share proportionately in the payment for a loss.

$$R = (1 - CP)(L - D) \quad \textbf{(10.1)}$$

where

R = Reimbursement
CP = Coinsurance percentage required of the insured
L = Loss
D = Deductible

As an example, assume you have a health insurance policy with a $100 deductible per hospital stay and a 20 percent coinsurance requirement. If the hospital bill is $1350, the reimbursement will be $1000, calculated as follows:

$$R = (1.00 - 0.20)(\$1350 - \$100)$$
$$= (0.80)(\$1250)$$
$$= \$1000$$

3. **Reduce the chances that a loss will occur. Hazard reduction** is action taken by the insured to reduce the probability of a loss occurring. Insurance companies often offer reduced premiums to insureds who practice hazard reduction—for example, to nonsmokers.

4. **Reduce the dollar amount of a loss. Loss reduction** is action taken by the insured to lessen the severity of loss if a peril occurs. Smoke alarms and fire extinguishers in the home are examples of loss reduction efforts. These items will not prevent fires, but their use may lead to less severe damage. Many insurers offer reduced premiums to policyholders who practice loss reduction.

Risk Is Reduced for the Insurer Through the Law of Large Numbers

Insurance consists of two basic elements: the reduction of risk and the sharing of losses. When you buy insurance, you exchange the uncertainty of a potentially large financial

DID YOU KNOW?

How to Read an Insurance Policy

Insurance policies do not invite casual reading. Consequently, many people fail to thoroughly examine their policies until a loss occurs, only to find that they had misunderstood the terms of the agreement. You can avoid such problems by systematically reading a policy before you purchase it, focusing on eight points:

1. **Perils covered.** *Some policies list only the perils that are covered; others cover all perils except those listed. The definition of certain perils may differ from that used in everyday language.*

2. **Property covered.** *Like perils, the property covered under a policy may be listed individually, or only the excluded property may be listed. When the property is listed individually, any new acquisitions must be added to the policy.*

3. **Types of losses covered.** *Three types of property losses can occur: (a) the loss of the property itself, (b) extra expenses that may arise because the property is rendered unusable for a period of time, and (c) loss of income if the property was used in the insured's work.*

4. **People covered.** *Insurance policies may cover only certain individuals. This information usually appears on the first page of the policy but may be changed subsequently in later sections.*

5. **Locations covered.** *Where the loss occurs may have a bearing on whether it will be covered. It is especially important to know which locations are not covered.*

6. **Time period of coverage.** *Policies are generally written to cover specific time periods. Restrictions may exclude coverage during specific times of the day or certain days of the week or year.*

7. **Loss control requirements.** *Insurance policies often stipulate that certain loss control efforts must be maintained by the insured. For example, coverage for a vehicle may be denied if the owner knowingly allows it to be driven by an unlicensed person.*

8. **Amount of coverage.** *All insurance policies specify the maximum amount the insurer will pay for various types of losses.*

The information on these eight points may be spread throughout a policy. In fact, coverage that appears to be provided in one location actually may be denied elsewhere. Carefully review the entire policy to determine the protection it provides. If necessary, phone the salesperson or company to obtain clarification.

---

law of large numbers
As the number of members in a group increases, predictions about the group's behavior become increasingly accurate.

FINANCIAL POWER POINT

Check Up on Your Company and Agent

Insurance companies must have the financial strength to pay losses as promised. You can assess your company's financial strength at www.standardandpoors.com by clicking on "Ratings" and then "Insurance." Always seek out an agent who has the appropriate professional designations—chartered life underwriter (CLU) in life insurance and chartered property and casualty underwriter (CPCU) in automobile and homeowner's insurance.

loss for the certainty of a fixed insurance premium, thereby reducing your risk. As Yogi Berra once said "It is tough to make predictions, especially about the future." But predictions are much easier for an insurance company than for an individual. This is because risk is reduced for the insurer through the **law of large numbers**: As the number of members in a group increases, predictions about the group's behavior become increasingly more accurate. This greater accuracy decreases uncertainty and, therefore, risk.

To illustrate, consider a city of 100,000 households in which the probability of a fire striking a household is 1 in 1000, or 0.1 percent. Thus, 100 home fires are likely to occur each year in this community. If we focus on groups of 100 households at a time, we cannot predict very accurately whether a fire will strike a house in a given group. Some groups might have two or three fires, while others might experience none. If we combine all the households into one group, however, we can more accurately predict that 100 fires will occur ($100,000 \times 0.001$). Even if 103 fires occurred, our prediction would be in error by only a small percentage. Insurance companies, which may have millions of customers, can be even more accurate in their group predictions.

Each Person Benefits Even If the Person Does Not Suffer a Loss

Individual insurance purchasers benefit regardless of whether they actually suffer a loss because of the reduction of risk. This is the essence of insurance. Reduced risk gives one the freedom to drive a car, own a home, and plan financially for the future with the knowledge that some unforeseen event will not result in financial disaster.

DID YOU KNOW?

How Companies Select Among Insurance Applicants

The purchase of insurance begins with an offer by the purchaser in the form of a written or oral policy application. The insurer typically issues a temporary insurance contract, called a **binder**, which is replaced at a later date with a written policy. The application then goes through a process of **underwriting**—that is, the insurer's procedure for deciding which insurance applicants to accept. To describe the process of underwriting, it is necessary to first understand how insurance rates are set.

An **insurance rate** is the price charged for each unit of insurance coverage. Rates represent the average cost of providing coverage to various **classes of insureds**; these classes consist of insureds who share similar characteristics. For example, automobile insurance policyholders may be classified by age, gender, marital status, and driving record, as well as by the make and model of vehicle that they drive.

When underwriters receive an application, they assign the applicant to the appropriate class. They then determine whether the rates established for that class are sufficient to

provide coverage for that applicant. Underwriters divide insurance applicants into four groups:

*   *Preferred* applicants have lower-than-average loss expectancies and save money because they typically qualify for lower premiums.

*   *Standard* applicants have average loss expectancies for their class and pay the standard rates.

*   *Substandard* applicants have higher-than-average loss expectancies and may be charged higher premiums and have restrictions placed on the types or amounts of coverage they may purchase.

*   *Unacceptable* applicants have loss expectancies that are much too high and are rejected.

You can save money by confirming with your agent that you have been placed in the proper class for premium-determination purposes. Verifying that you are in the proper class is also important because a claim may be denied if premiums were based on an inappropriate classification.

Who Sells Insurance?

Sellers of insurance, called **insurance agents**, represent one or more insurance companies. They have the power to enter into, change, and cancel insurance policies on behalf of these companies. Two types of insurance agents exist: independent agents and exclusive agents.

Independent insurance agents are independent businesspeople who act as third-party links between insurers and insureds. Such agents earn commissions from the companies they represent and will place each insurance customer with the company that they believe best meets that customer's particular needs.

Exclusive insurance agents represent only one insurance company for a specific type of insurance. They are employees of the insurance company they represent. Life insurance, for example, is often sold through exclusive insurance agents.

Direct sellers are companies that market their policies through salaried employees, mail-order promotions, newspapers, the Internet, and even vending machines. Any type of insurance can be sold directly

Each type of seller presents both advantages and disadvantages. Independent agents may provide more personalized service and can select among several companies to meet a customer's needs. Exclusive agents can provide personalized service as well but are limited to the policies offered by the one company they represent and their sales commissions tend to be low. For people who know what coverage they need, the lowest-cost insurance premiums can be found with direct sellers.

insurance agent
Representative of an insurance company authorized to sell, modify, service, and terminate insurance contracts.

direct sellers
Companies that market insurance policies through salaried employees, mail-order promotions, newspapers, the Internet, and even vending machines.

 Concept Check 10.2

1. Define *insurance.*

2. Distinguish among the three types of hazards.

3. Why is the principle of indemnity so important to insurance sellers?

4. Identify four key points to review when reading an insurance policy.

5. Summarize how to use deductibles, coinsurance, hazard reduction, and loss reduction to lower the cost of insurance.

6. Differentiate among independent agents, exclusive agents, and direct sellers.

HOMEOWNER'S INSURANCE

Design a homeowner's or renter's insurance program to meet your needs.

homeowner's insurance
Combines liability and property insurance coverages that homeowners and renters typically need into single-package policies.

named-perils policies
Cover only losses caused by perils that the policy specifically mentions.

all-risk (open-perils) policies
Cover losses caused by all perils other than those that the policy specifically excludes.

homeowner's general liability protection
Applies when you are legally liable for another person's losses, other than those that arise out of use of vehicles or your professional duties.

basic (homeowner's insurance) form (HO-1)
Named-perils policy that covers 11 property-damage–causing perils and provides three areas of liability-related protection: personal liability, property damage liability, and medical payments.

Whether you own or rent housing, you face the possibility of suffering property and liability losses. **Homeowner's insurance** combines the liability and property insurance coverages needed by homeowners and renters into a single-package policy. Four types of homeowner's insurance are available for people who own houses, another type for the owners of condominiums, and one other type for those who rent housing.

Coverages

The standard homeowner's insurance policy is divided into two sections.

Property Coverage Section I provides protection for various types of property damage losses, including the following: (1) damage to the dwelling, (2) damage to other structures on the property—referred to as **appurtenant structures**, (3) damage to personal property and dwelling contents, and (4) expenses arising out of a loss of use of the dwelling (for example, food and lodging). Additional coverages are usually provided for such items as debris removal, trees and shrubs, and fire department service charges.

An important variable related to Section I of a policy involves the number of loss-causing perils that are covered. **Named-perils policies** cover only those losses caused by perils that are specifically mentioned in the policy. **All-risk** (or **open-perils**) policies cover losses caused by all perils other than those specifically *excluded* by the policy. All-risk policies provide broader coverage because hundreds of perils can cause property losses, but only a few would be excluded. Common exclusions are flood, earthquake, and mold unless caused by some nonexcluded event such as burst water pipes. Coverage for excluded perils can often be purchased for an additional premium if desired. In coastal states or those prone to earthquakes, your policy may require a higher deductible if you suffer a loss due to these perils.

Liability Coverage Section II deals with liability insurance. Whenever homeowners are negligent or otherwise fail to exercise due caution in protecting visitors, they may potentially suffer a liability loss. **Homeowner's general liability protection** applies when you are legally liable for the losses of another person. Homeowners often wish to take responsibility for the losses of another person regardless of the legal liability. Consider, for example, a guest's child who suffers burns from touching a hot barbecue grill. **Homeowner's no-fault medical payments protection** will pay for bodily injury losses suffered by visitors regardless of who was at fault. In the preceding example, such coverage would help pay for the medical treatment of the visitor's burns. **Homeowner's no-fault property damage protection** will pay for property losses suffered by visitors to your home. An example of such a loss might be damage to a friend's leather coat that was chewed by your dog.

Types of Homeowner's Insurance Policies

Six distinct types of homeowner's insurance policies exist: HO-1 through HO-4, HO-6, and HO-8. Each is a standardized package of protections designed to cover the perils that commonly affect homeowners and renters. They are described in detail in Table 10-2 and more generally in the sections that follow. The same terms and identifying numbers are generally used by most insurance companies.

Basic Form (HO-1) The **basic form (HO-1)** is a named-perils policy that covers 11 property-damage–causing perils and provides three areas of liability-related protection: personal liability, property damage liability, and medical payments. The most common perils that can cause property damage—fire and lightning, windstorm, theft, and smoke—are covered in the basic homeowner's policy. People who have finished basements (perhaps a TV room or spare bedroom) should purchase additional sewer backup coverage, as this possibility is not one of the 11 named perils.

Broad Form (HO-2)
The **broad form (HO-2)** is a named-perils policy that covers 18 property-damage–causing perils and provides protection from the three liability-related exposures.

Special Form (HO-3)
The **special form (HO-3)** provides open-perils protection for four types of property losses: losses to the dwelling, losses to other structures, landscaping losses, and losses generating additional living expenses. Contents and personal property are covered on a named-perils basis for 17 of the 18 common homeowner's perils (the exception is glass breakage). In terms of liability protection and in all other respects, the coverage under HO-3 is the same as under HO-2.

Renter's Contents Broad Form (HO-4)
The **renter's contents broad form (HO-4)** is a named-perils policy that protects the insured from losses to the contents of a dwelling rather than the dwelling itself. It covers 17 perils and provides liability protection. HO-4 is ideal for renters because it provides protection from losses to dwelling contents and personal property and provides for additional living expenses if the dwelling is rendered uninhabitable by one of the covered perils. Although insurance is relatively inexpensive, only one-fourth of all renters carry HO-4 protection.

Condominium Form (HO-6)
The **condominium form (HO-6)** is a named-perils policy protecting condominium owners from the three principal losses they face: losses to contents and personal property, losses due to the additional living expenses that may arise if one of the covered perils occurs, and liability losses. (The building itself is insured by the management of the condominium.) Two additional coverages are included in the HO-6 policy as necessary to meet the specific needs of the condominium unit owner. The first is protection against losses to the structural alterations and additions that condominium owners sometimes make when they remodel their units. The second is supplemental coverage for the dwelling unit to protect the condominium owner if the building is not sufficiently insured.

Older Home Form (HO-8)
The replacement value of an older home may be much higher than its market or actual cash value. The **older home form (HO-8)** is a named-perils policy that provides actual-cash-value protection on the dwelling. It does not provide that the dwelling be rebuilt to the same standards of style and quality, as those standards may be prohibitively expensive today. Instead, the policy provides that the dwelling be rebuilt to make it serviceable.

Buying Homeowner's Insurance
Four questions must be answered when buying a homeowner's policy.

1. How much coverage will you need to replace the dwelling itself?
2. How much coverage will you need on the contents and personal property?
3. How much protection will you need for items such as jewelry, money, guns, or antiques that have specific limits?
4. How much coverage will you need for liability protection?

How Much Coverage Is Really Needed on Your Dwelling?
If you own your home, your first step is to determine the dwelling's replacement value. You could either use the services of a professional liability appraiser and/or consult with your insurance agent to determine replacement value. Note that over one-half of the homes in the United States are said to be underinsured.

Homeowner's insurance policies usually contain a **replacement-cost requirement** that stipulates that a home *must* be insured for 80 percent of its replacement value (some companies require 100 percent). Thus, a home with a replacement value of $200,000 would need to be insured for $160,000 (or perhaps $200,000), and this amount would

special (homeowner's insurance) form (HO-3)
Provides open-perils protection (except for the commonly excluded perils of war, earthquake, and flood) for four types of property losses.

renter's contents broad form (HO-4)
Named-perils policy that protects the insured from losses to the contents of a rented dwelling rather than to the dwelling itself.

FINANCIAL POWER POINT

Renter's Insurance Is Not Expensive

Renter's insurance can cost as little as $20 per month, and discounts are available if you buy from the same company that provides your auto coverage.

replacement-cost requirement
Stipulates that a home must be insured for 80 percent of its replacement value (some companies require 100 percent) in order for any loss to be fully covered.

Table 10-2   Summary of Homeowner's Insurance Policies

	HO-1 (Basic Form)	HO-2 (Broad Form)	HO-3 (Special Form)
Perils covered (descriptions are given below)	Perils 1–11	Perils 1–18	All perils except those specifically excluded for buildings; perils 1–18 on personal property (does not include glass breakage)
House and any other attached buildings	Amount based on replacement cost, minimum $15,000	Amount based on replacement cost, minimum $15,000	Amount based on replacement cost, minimum $20,000
Detached buildings (appurtenant structures)	10 percent of insurance on the home (minimum)	10 percent of insurance on the home (minimum)	10 percent of insurance on the home (minimum)
Trees, shrubs, plants, etc.	5 percent of insurance on the home, $500 maximum per item	5 percent of insurance on the home, $500 maximum per item	5 percent of insurance on the home, $500 maximum per item
Personal property	50 percent of insurance on the home (minimum)	50 percent of insurance on the home (minimum)	50 percent of insurance on the home (minimum)
Loss of use and/or additional living expense	10 percent of insurance on the home	20 percent of insurance on the home	20 percent of insurance on the home
Credit card, forgery, counterfeit money	$1000	$1000	$1000

Liability coverage/limits
    (for all policies)

Comprehensive personal liability	$100,000
No-fault medical payments	$1000
No-fault property damage	$500

Special limits of liability

For the following classes of personal property, special limits apply on a per-occurrence basis (e.g., per fire or theft): money, coins, bank notes, precious metals (gold, silver, etc.), $200; computers, $5000; securities, deeds, stocks, bonds, tickets, stamps, $1000; watercraft and trailers, including furnishings, equipment, and outboard motors, $1000; trailers other than for watercraft, $1000; jewelry, watches, furs, $1000; silverware, goldware, etc., $2500; guns, $2000.

List of perils covered
1. Fire, lightning
2. Windstorm, hail
3. Explosion
4. Riots
5. Damage by aircraft
6. Damage by vehicles owned or operated by people not covered by the homeowner's policy
7. Damage from smoke
8. Vandalism, malicious mischief
9. Theft
10. Glass breakage
11. Volcanic eruption
12. Falling objects (external sources)
13. Weight of ice, snow, sleet
14. Collapse of building or any part of building (specified perils only)
15. Leakage or overflow of water or steam from a plumbing, heating, or air-conditioning system
16. Bursting, cracking, burning, or bulging of a steam or hot water heating system, or of appliances for heating water
17. Freezing of plumbing, heating, and air-conditioning systems and home appliances
18. Injury to electrical appliances and devices (excluding tubes, transistors, and similar electronic components) from short circuits or other accidentally generated currents

HO-4 (Renter's Contents Broad Form)	HO-6 (For Condominium Owners)	HO-8 (For Older Homes)
Perils 1–9, 11–18	Perils 1–18	Perils 1–11
10 percent of personal property insurance on additions and alterations to the apartment	$1000 on owner's additions and alterations to the unit	Amount based on actual cash value of the home
Not covered	Not covered (unless owned solely by the insured)	10 percent of insurance on the home (minimum)
10 percent of personal property insurance, $500 maximum per item	10 percent of personal property insurance, $500 maximum per item	5 percent of insurance on the home, $500 maximum per item
Chosen by the tenant to reflect the value of the items, minimum $6000	Chosen by the homeowner to reflect the value of the items, minimum $6000	50 percent of insurance on the home (minimum)
20 percent of personal property insurance	40 percent of personal property insurance	20 percent of insurance on the home
$1000	$1000	$1000

This table describes the standard policies. Specific items differ from company to company and from state to state. When you want a limit that exceeds the standard limit for your company, you usually can increase the limit by paying an additional premium.

be the maximum that the insurance company would be obligated to pay for a total loss (after payment of the deductible by the policyholder). If you fail to meet your replacement-cost requirement, you will not be considered fully insured and must coinsure partial losses as well. The amount of reimbursement for partial losses will be calculated using the **replacement-cost-requirement formula**:

$$R = (L - D) \times [I \div (RV \times 0.80 \text{ or } 1.00)] \quad \textbf{(10.2)}$$

where

R = Reimbursement payable
L = Amount of loss
D = Deductible, if any
I = Amount of insurance actually carried
RV = Replacement value of the dwelling

Consider the example of Chris Shearer from Las Cruces, New Mexico, who owns a home with a replacement value of $200,000 with a $500 deductible. Chris had insured his home for $144,000, even though the policy required coverage of 80 percent of the replacement cost. Last month a fire in his home caused damage amounting to $80,500. Applying Equation (10.2), Chris's calculations are as follows:

$$R = (\$80,500 - \$500) \times [\$144,000 \div (\$200,000 \times 0.80)]$$
$$= \$80,000 \times (\$144,000 \div \$160,000)$$
$$= \$80,000 \times 0.90$$
$$= \$72,000$$

As this calculation shows, Chris will be reimbursed for only $72,000 of his loss. His failure to insure his house for 80 percent of its replacement cost, or $160,000 ($200,000 × 0.80), means he will be covered for only 90 percent ($144,000 ÷ $160,000) of its value, and he must pay 10 percent of any partial loss—in this case, $8000. Three out of four homes in the United States are underinsured by an average of 35 percent.

Meeting an 80 percent replacement-cost requirement enables you to avoid coinsurance on small losses but might still result in inadequate coverage on large losses that, though rare, exceed the policy limit. Thus, it is wise to insure your dwelling for 100 percent of its replacement cost. However, you will also want to increase your limits each year to keep up with inflation in housing construction costs. To do so, you can sign up for **inflation guard protection** to have your insurance company increase your coverage automatically each year.

DID YOU KNOW?

What's Covered While You Are Away at College

College students often wonder about what kind of insurance coverage they have while they are attending school away from home. Students who have moved into their own residence to live year-round need to buy their own renter's and automobile insurance policies. This is because the family's homeowner's and auto coverages will only apply if the student (1) lives in a dorm or fraternity/sorority house or (2) lives off campus in what is clearly a temporary arrangement (that is, the student returns home during semester breaks and over the summer).

If you are covered by your family's policies, here are some guidelines to remember:

1. *Property stored away from home is often only covered for up to 10 percent of the coverage on the home. If the family home is insured for $150,000, for example, then $15,000 of*

coverage applies—and this is probably adequate for most students. Remember, however, this is a family total. If three siblings are away at school simultaneously, it may be inadequate. Additional coverage can be purchased through your homeowner's insurance agent.

2. *Expensive items such as jewelry or computers are subject to specific limits in the homeowner's insurance policy. Purchase additional protection for these items if necessary.*

3. *Auto insurance rates are based on where the vehicle is garaged (or parked) at night. The insurance agent should be notified if a covered vehicle is used while away at school. It is better to pay a slightly higher rate than to face denial of coverage for a loss because of misinformation. A discount is common for a college student listed on a parent's policy if the student does not have a car at school and the school is at least 100 miles from the parent's home.*

---

actual cash value (of personal property)
Represents the purchase price of the property less depreciation.

DID YOU KNOW?

How to Insure High-Value Items

Some high-value items of personal property are subject to specific item limits in the standard homeowner's policy. For example, the typical policy provides maximum coverages of $200 for cash, $5000 for personal computers, and $1000 for jewelry. This is because most people do not have such items above these values and do not need higher levels of coverage. If your inventory reveals a higher valuation on such items, you can simply ask your company for extra coverage and pay the higher premium required. Think of it as super-sizing your policy.

contents replacement-cost protection
Option sometimes available in homeowner's insurance policies (including the renter's form) that pays the full replacement cost of any personal property.

How Much Coverage Is Needed on Your Personal Property?

Making a **personal property inventory** of, and placing a value on, all the contents of your home are time-consuming but important tasks. Table 10-3 shows the inventory and valuation for the contents of and personal property in a typical living room. You should conduct such an inventory for each room, the basement, garage, shed, and yard possessions. When totaled, these values will enable you to select proper policy coverage limits. Most homeowner's policies are designed to automatically cover contents and personal property for up to 50 percent of the coverage on the home. For example, if your home is insured for $240,000, you would have $120,000 in personal property insurance. If you need more coverage, simply notify your agent.

Notice that Table 10-3 lists three estimates for the value of the contents of a room: the purchase price, the actual cash value, and the replacement cost. Historically, property insurance policies paid only the **actual cash value** of an item of personal property, which represents the purchase price of the property less depreciation. The **actual-cash-value (ACV) formula** is:

$$ACV = P - [CA \times (P \div LE)] \quad \textbf{(10.3)}$$

where

P = Purchase price of the property
CA = Current age of the property in years
LE = Life expectancy of the property in years

Consider the case of Marianna Kinard, a music teacher from Orangeburg, South Carolina, whose nine-year-old heating/air-conditioning unit was struck by lightning. The unit cost $2400 when new and had a total life expectancy of 12 years. Its actual cash value when it was struck by lightning was:

$$ACV = \$2400 - [9 \times (\$2400 \div 12)]$$
$$= \$2400 - (9 \times \$200)$$
$$= \$600$$

Marianna could not replace the unit for $600. A more realistic replacement cost might be $3000. **Contents replacement-cost protection** is an option sometimes

Personal Property Checklist: Living Room

Table 10-3

Item	Date Purchased	Purchase Price	Actual Cash Value	Replacement Cost
Furniture				
Sofa	8/07	$ 750	$ 375	$ 950
Chair	11/05	250	100	375
Lounger	12/08	575	300	695
Ottoman	12/08	100	50	120
Bookcase	4/10	275	225	300
End table (two)	7/11	300	250	300
Appliances				
TV	1/11	550	500	600
DVD	6/10	400	300	400
Wall clock	7/05	60	10	100
Furnishings				
Carpet	6/04	375	50	600
Painting	12/08	125	225	225
Floor lamp	4/06	150	50	225
Art (three items)	10/10	600	600	800
Table lamp	4/06	75	40	100
Table lamp	5/10	125	100	135
Throw pillows	7/07	45	20	60
TOTAL		**$ 4,755**	**$ 3,195**	**$ 5,985**

available in homeowner's insurance policies that pays the full replacement cost of any personal property. The standard limitation that applies to contents (50 percent of insured value of the dwelling) remains in effect if contents replacement-cost protection is purchased. The overall limit on contents may need to be raised, as it is easy to reach the 50 percent figure when replacement-cost valuation is used.

How Much Coverage Is Needed for Liability Losses? Newly written standard homeowner's policies provide $300,000 ($100,000 for older policies unless amended) of personal liability coverage, $1000 of no-fault medical expense coverage, and $500 of no-fault property damage coverage. It is smart to apply the large-loss principle here and increase the policy limits for all three of these coverages (or consider an umbrella liability policy discussed later). The extra cost is small because the odds of these larger losses are low.

FINANCIAL POWER POINT

Stay Out of the Doghouse

Over one-third of homeowner's insurance liability claims are associated with dog bites. Make sure your insurance company knows that you have a dog. And raise your liability limits for better protection.

 Concept Check 10.3

1. Describe the types of losses covered under the property insurance portion of a homeowner's policy.

2. Give three examples of liability protection under homeowner's insurance policies.

3. List the six types of homeowner's insurance policies (HO-1 through HO-4, HO-6, and HO-8).

4. Identify four types of personal property for which the covered loss is limited to a specific dollar amount under standard homeowner's insurance policies (see Table 10-2).

5. List the three questions you should ask yourself when determining the policy limits for a homeowner's insurance policy.

AUTOMOBILE INSURANCE

automobile insurance
Combines the liability and property insurance coverages that most car owners and drivers need into a single-package policy.

Driving a car is the largest single exposure to catastrophic losses for most Americans. A split-second error in driving judgment or bad luck can result in many tens of thousands of dollars of automobile-related property damage and personal injury losses. **Automobile insurance** combines the liability and property insurance coverages needed by automobile owners and drivers into a single-package policy. It is illegal to operate a motor vehicle without assuming financial responsibility for any losses you might cause; therefore, most states require automobile owners to purchase automobile insurance to meet this responsibility (although there are millions of illegally uninsured drivers on the roads).

Losses Covered

Automobile insurance combines four distinct types of coverage: (1) liability insurance, (2) medical payments insurance, (3) protection against uninsured and underinsured motorists, and (4) insurance for physical damage to the insured automobile. Each coverage has its own policy limits, conditions, and exclusions. Table 10-4 summarizes the coverage provided by automobile insurance policies for people not specifically excluded in the policy.

automobile bodily injury liability
Occurs when a driver or car owner is held legally responsible for bodily injury losses that other people, including pedestrians, suffer.

automobile property damage liability
Occurs when a driver or car owner is held legally responsible for damage to others' property.

Coverage A—Liability Insurance Liability insurance covers the insured when he or she is held responsible for losses suffered by others. Two types of liability can arise out of the ownership and operation of an automobile. **Automobile bodily injury liability** occurs when a driver or car owner is held legally responsible for bodily injury losses suffered by other people, including pedestrians. **Automobile property damage liability** occurs when a driver or car owner is held legally responsible for damage to the property of others. Such damage can include damage to another vehicle, a building, or roadside signs and utility poles.

Table 10-4   Summary of Automobile Insurance Coverages

Section	Type of Coverage	People Covered	Property Covered	Recommended Limits
A	LIABILITY INSURANCE (1) Bodily injury liability	Relatives living in insured's household driving an owned or nonowned automobile	Not applicable	At least legally required minimums or $250,000/$500,000, whichever is greater
	(2) Property damage liability	Relatives living in insured's household driving an owned or nonowned automobile	Automobiles and other property damaged by insured driver while driving	At least legally required minimum or $100,000, whichever is greater
B	MEDICAL PAYMENTS	Passengers in insured automobile or nonowned automobile driven by insured family member	Not applicable	$50,000 or higher
C	UNINSURED AND UNDERINSURED	Anyone driving insured car with permission and insured family members driving nonowned automobiles with permission	Not applicable	$50,000/$100,000 or higher, if available
D	PHYSICAL DAMAGE (1) Collision	Anyone driving insured car with permission	Insured automobile	Actual cash value less deductible
	(2) Comprehensive	Not applicable	Insured automobile and its contents	Actual cash value less deductible

The most common type of automobile insurance policy is the **family auto policy (FAP)**. A FAP covers the vehicle owner, relatives living in the vehicle owner's household, and people who have the owner's permission to drive the vehicle. In addition, any other vehicle that the owner borrows with permission is similarly covered for all family members.

The policy limits for FAPs are quoted as **split liability limits**, usually three numbers such as 100/300/50, with each number representing a multiple of $1000 (Figure 10-2). The first number gives the maximum that will be paid for liability claims for *one* person's bodily injury losses resulting from an automobile accident ($100,000 in our example). The second number indicates the overall maximum that will be paid for bodily injury liability losses to *any number* of people resulting from an automobile accident ($300,000 in our example). The third number specifies the maximum that will be paid for property damage liability losses resulting from an accident ($50,000 in our example).

In some policies, the liability limits are stated as a **single liability limit** such as $250,000. Under such policies, all property and bodily injury liability losses resulting from an accident would be paid until the limit is reached. These policies are referred to as **personal auto policies (PAPs)**. Family members of the vehicle owner may or may not be covered under a PAP when driving the vehicle, depending on the policy provisions.

Liability insurance covers only the insured for losses suffered by others. It does not pay for bodily injury losses suffered by the insured or for property damage to the insured's car. Injured passengers of an at-fault driver may collect under the driver's liability coverage, but only after exhausting the coverage provided under medical payments (discussed later) and only after reimbursement is made to people injured in other vehicles or as pedestrians. Driving a rental car exposes you to the same potential liabilities as driving your own vehicle. If you have automobile liability insurance, such liabilities will usually be covered while you drive a rented car. Check your coverage before you rent a car so you can avoid buying overpriced insurance from the rental agency.

FINANCIAL POWER POINT

Bodily Injury Losses Can Be Very High

A one-day stay in a hospital intensive care unit can cost upwards of $50,000. An accident with several severe injuries can result in losses in excess of $300,000. When buying a policy, remember to select high liability limits as they are a must.

Automobile Liability Insurance Policy Limits

Figure 10-2

Automobile liability insurance limits may be quoted as split liability limits:

100/300/50

$100,000	$300,000	$50,000
Per-person bodily injury limit specifying that $100,000 is the most that will be paid for any **one person's** bodily injury liability losses from an accident.	Per-accident bodily injury limit specifying that $300,000 is the most that will be paid for **all** bodily injury liability losses from an accident.	Per-accident property damage liability limit specifying that $50,000 is the most that will be paid for **all** property damage liability losses from an accident.

OR

They may be quoted as a single liability limit:

$250,000

Per-accident limit for all liability losses specifying $250,000 as the most that will be paid in liability losses arising out of one accident.

Drivers need to make sure they have sufficient liability coverage in the event of an accident—the person at fault is typically responsible for all damages.

automobile medical payments insurance
Insurance that covers bodily injury losses suffered by the driver of the insured vehicle and any passengers, regardless of who is at fault.

personal injury protection (PIP)
Medical payments coverage for the driver and any passengers for bodily injury losses as well as possibly lost wages and rehabilitation expenses common in no-fault accident states.

subrogation rights
Allow an insurer to take action against a negligent third party (and that party's insurance company) to obtain reimbursement for payments made to an insured.

Coverage C—uninsured and underinsured motorist insurance
Coverage that an insured can purchase as part of automobile insurance that covers the insured in an accident when an uninsured or underinsured driver is at fault.

Coverage B—Medical Payments Insurance **Automobile medical payments insurance** covers bodily injury losses suffered by the driver of the insured vehicle and any passengers regardless of who is at fault. Medical losses occurring within one year and as a direct result of an accident will be reimbursed up to the limits of the policy. Automobile medical payments insurance also covers insured family members who are injured while passengers in any car or who are injured by a car when on foot or riding a bicycle. Medical payments coverage is subject to a single policy limit, which is applied per person, per accident.

In such states that have adopted some type of no-fault automobile insurance, insureds collect first (and possibly *only*) from their own insurance companies for bodily injury losses resulting from an automobile accident. In these states, the medical payments coverage, which is often referred to as **personal injury protection (PIP)** covers the driver and any passengers for bodily injury losses as well as possibly lost wages and rehabilitation expenses. Under medical payments or PIP, drivers and their injured passengers collect directly from the driver's insurance. If the driver was not at fault, then the driver's insurer pays the claims and subsequently may choose to exercise subrogation rights against the at-fault party. **Subrogation rights** allow an insurer to take action against a negligent third party (and that party's insurance company) to obtain reimbursement for payments made to an insured. Subrogation rights are limited in no-fault states.

Coverage C—Uninsured and Underinsured Motorist Insurance Sometimes the driver at fault in an automobile accident carries no insurance or has insufficient liability insurance coverage. To protect against such uncovered losses, an insured can purchase uninsured and underinsured motorist insurance as part of his or her own automobile insurance policy. When the medical payments coverage is exhausted, the uninsured and underinsured motorist coverage will provide protection. **Uninsured motorist insurance** protects the insured and the insured's passengers from bodily injury losses (and, in a few states, property damage losses) resulting from an automobile accident caused by an uninsured motorist. It provides protection above that extended under the automobile medical payments insurance. **Underinsured motorist insurance** protects the insured and his or her passengers from bodily injury losses (and, in some cases, property damage losses)

FINANCIAL POWER POINT

Save Money the Right Way on Auto Insurance

The two ways to save money on auto insurance are to raise your deductible and lower your liability limits. Raising your deductible is the smarter move. Choosing lower limits is unwise, as you will be personally liable if an accident exceeds those limits.

DID YOU KNOW?

Turn Bad Habits into Good Ones

Do You Do This?	*Do This Instead!*
Assume your parents' homeowner's policy covers you at school	Confirm that you are correct and, if not, buy your own renter's policy
Base your potential auto liability losses on your own financial status	Estimate the maximum loss others could suffer if you caused an accident
Base your insurance decisions on how much coverage will cost	Base your decisions on the potential losses you could suffer
Buy low limits on your liability coverages	Buy higher limits or an umbrella liability policy
Buy policies with the lowest possible deductible	Raise the deductibles on your policies and apply the savings toward higher limits

when the at-fault driver has insurance but that coverage is insufficient to reimburse the losses.

The limits for uninsured motorist insurance are quoted in a manner similar to that for automobile liability insurance. For example, uninsured motorist protection with limits of 50/100 would provide a maximum of $50,000 for any one injured person and a maximum of $100,000 for multiple bodily injury losses in the same accident. Most states require insurers to offer uninsured and underinsured motorist insurance. Such insurance is a smart risk-management choice and carries a very low premium—often less than $50 per year.

Coverage D—Physical Damage Insurance A number of perils can cause property losses to an insured automobile. **Automobile physical damage insurance** provides protection against losses caused by damage to your car from collision, theft, and

DID YOU KNOW?

Quick and Easy Steps Can Cut Your Insurance Bill

There is no point in paying more for insurance than necessary. Here are some suggestions for achieving this goal.

Select Appropriate Coverages and Limits. Buy only needed coverages, and select policy limits appropriate for the largest potential losses.

Retain Risks That Are Affordable. Retain risks that you can afford—by raising a deductible, for example—and only insure against losses that would be financially unaffordable.

Take Advantage of Discounts. Most insurance companies offer discounted premiums for policyholders who buy multiple policies (for example, both automobile and homeowner's insurance) from them.

Engage in Loss Control. Many companies charge lower premiums to policyholders who take steps to reduce the probability or severity of loss. For example, discounts are available if you install dead-bolt door locks or a fire extin-

guisher in your home. Ask your agent what you need to do to qualify.

Shop Around for the Lowest-Cost Coverage. Insurance premiums from one company can be twice as much as those charged by another company and for essentially the same coverage, so considerable savings can be realized by seeking quotes from multiple agents and direct sellers. To obtain a quote, simply telephone an agent or direct seller and provide some basic descriptive information. You can also use a Web-based quote service such as www.insure.com or www.insquote.com.

Become Insurance Wise. The insurance regulatory agency in your state (to find yours, visit www.naic.org/state_web _map.htm) may publish helpful insurance buyer's guides that discuss how to buy specific types of insurance, compare premiums, and rate the companies providing such insurance. In addition, *Consumer Reports* magazine periodically publishes feature articles that discuss insurance.

collision insurance
Reimburses insureds for losses to their vehicles resulting from a collision with another car or object or from a rollover.

comprehensive automobile insurance
Protects against property damage losses to an insured vehicle caused by perils other than collision and rollover.

DID YOU KNOW?

You Can Change Insurers at Any Time

You do not have to wait until renewal time to change insurance companies. If shopping around reveals that you can save money and/or improve your coverage with a new company, consider doing so right away. Contact the new company first to ensure that you have been accepted and then contact the old company. You will receive a refund of the unused premium less a minor processing charge when you cancel.

DID YOU KNOW?

Buying Insurance Based Only on Price Is a Recipe for a Financial Disaster

Insurance companies sometimes suggest that you can simply tell them what you want to pay and that they will tailor a plan for you. While this is true, there is no guarantee that the coverage they will sell you at that price will fit your needs or is even a good deal. The best approach is to determine the coverage you need and then shop around for the best deal on that coverage.

other perils. The most common peril is, of course, a collision with another vehicle or an object. The next most common peril is theft.

Collision insurance reimburses an insured for losses resulting from a collision with another car or object or from a rollover. The insurer pays the cost of repairing or replacing the insured's car, regardless of who is at fault. When the other driver is at fault, subrogation rights may allow the insurer to obtain reimbursement through that driver's property damage liability protection. Collision insurance is written with a deductible that usually ranges from $100 to $1000. If you carry collision insurance coverage on your own car, you are generally covered when you drive someone else's car with that person's permission. Most automobile insurance policies provide for collision coverage on rental cars if such coverage applies to your owned vehicle. Again, check with your agent before you rent a car.

Comprehensive automobile insurance protects against property damage losses caused by perils other than collision and rollover. Covered perils include fire, theft, vandalism, hail, and wind, among many others. Comprehensive insurance is written on an open-perils basis, and it often includes a deductible ranging from $100 to $500.

When you have a loss that qualifies under collision and comprehensive insurance, an estimate of the repair cost will be made. If this estimate exceeds the value that the insurance company puts on the vehicle, the lower of the two figures is paid, less any deductible. Insurance companies set vehicle values based on the average current selling price of vehicles of the same make, model, and age and the vehicle's mileage and condition prior to the occurrence of the damage.

Other Valuable Protections Three other low- or no-cost, but helpful, coverages are available to automobile insurance buyers. **Towing coverage** pays the cost of having a disabled vehicle transported for repairs. It usually pays only the first $25 or $50 per occurrence but will cover any towing need—not just assistance needed due to an accident. **Rental reimbursement coverage** provides a rental car when the insured's vehicle is being repaired after an accident or has been stolen. It often has a daily payout limit of $20 to $30 and, therefore, may provide only part of the funds needed to obtain replacement transportation. Coverage for injuries suffered by cats or dogs traveling with you is offered at no cost by some companies. The maximum reimbursement is typically $500 or $1000 per animal.

Buying Automobile Insurance

The smart risk manager will shop carefully for automobile insurance because of its high cost. The task is to select the proper automobile insurance program while keeping premiums as low as possible. Because coverages are fairly standardized and premiums vary widely, comparison shopping for premium prices often saves hundreds of dollars.

The first step toward designing an adequate automobile insurance program involves identifying the types of losses that might occur. This task is easy because the standard policies cover most of the losses that you can reasonably expect to face as a result of owning and driving a vehicle.

Next, you must determine the amount of coverage you need. At a minimum, you must conform to the financial responsibility requirements mandated by your state. Because medical expenses and automobile repair costs can be enormous, it is wise to buy high liability limits. Limits of at least $250,000/$500,000/$100,000 are commonly recommended. Similarly high limits for uninsured and underinsured motorist coverage are advisable. Limits recommended for automobile medical expense coverage are a minimum of $100,000 per person.

It may be tempting to decline some of the coverages provided in a policy to reduce the overall premium. For example, lower premiums may be obtained by eliminating collision coverage, as the charge for such coverage typically represents 30 to 40 percent of the total automobile insurance premium. This cost-saving strategy is recommended only for cars having a book value of less than $2000. Elimination of other nonessential coverages (for example, comprehensive or uninsured/underinsured motorist insurance) would yield little savings while sharply reducing protection.

 Concept Check 10.4

1. Identify the four types of automobile insurance coverage.

2. Explain the meaning of the numbers 100/200/75.

3. Identify who is protected by medical payments coverage.

4. Distinguish between collision and comprehensive insurance.

5. Explain why selecting a policy with a high deductible and high liability limits is better than one with a low deductible and low liability limits.

DID YOU KNOW?

The Best Way to Title Vehicles

Couples may be tempted to put major assets in both their names, and sometimes this is the best way to go. For automobiles, however, the decision is complicated. The owner of a vehicle is legally liable for accidents caused by the driver. If both partners own an automobile, both could be sued. Thus, it is smart to title an automobile in only one name. For couples with two vehicles, each should be owned separately.

BUY SPECIALIZED PROTECTION FOR OTHER LOSS EXPOSURES

Some people need protection against property and liability losses that are not covered by homeowner's or automobile insurance policies.

 LEARNING OBJECTIVE **5**

Describe other types of property and liability insurance.

Comprehensive Personal Liability Insurance

Owning a home and driving a car are not the only sources of potential liability you may face. Consider the case of Will Crain, a pharmacist from Missoula, Montana. While climbing in a restricted area, he accidentally loosened some rocks, which fell down the slope and seriously injured hikers below. Because Will was in a restricted area and had failed to warn the hikers of his presence, he was held liable for their injuries and ordered to pay a court judgment of $178,000. Recall that the standard homeowner's insurance policy provides comprehensive personal liability insurance up to a specified limit, usually $100,000. Individuals who lack such coverage can purchase a separate **comprehensive personal liability policy**. Those with homeowner's (including renter's) insurance who desire higher limits should ask their insurance agent to raise the limits on their existing policy.

Flood and Earthquake Insurance

Standard homeowner's insurance policies exclude losses caused by flood and earthquakes. This is because these types of losses are subject to **adverse selection**. This means that people who are most likely to suffer such losses know that they are and those that are least likely know that, too. As a result, only those people with high probabilities of loss will want to buy the coverage, thereby violating the law of large numbers. But if you live in a flood-prone area or earthquake zone, your risk of loss should be addressed. The **National Flood Insurance Program** is a federal government program that makes flood insurance available in counties where flood is common. **Earthquake insurance** can be purchased only from a private insurance company either as a separate policy or as an **endorsement** (an addition to a standard policy) to an existing homeowner's or renter's insurance policy.

endorsement
An addition to a standard insurance policy designed to expand coverage for a special area of need.

Professional Liability Insurance

Professionals such as physicians, lawyers, and accountants can be held legally liable for losses suffered by their patients or clients. **Professional liability insurance** (sometimes called **malpractice insurance**) protects individuals and organizations that provide professional services when they are held liable for the losses of their clients. Policy limits, deductibles, premiums, and other characteristics of such policies vary widely depending

professional liability insurance/ malpractice insurance
Protects individuals and organizations that provide professional services when they are held liable for their clients' losses.

RUN THE NUMBERS

Buying Automobile Insurance

Even though automobile insurance premiums can vary by hundreds of dollars annually among companies, only four in ten consumers shop around when they buy or renew coverage. It is especially important to re-shop for automobile insurance after you have had an accident or major ticket or purchased a vehicle. Insurance companies differ in how they handle these changes and a new company might be a better option for you.

You can use the following worksheet to record automobile insurance premium quotations obtained from insurers. Remember to add surcharges for previous claims and other factors as well as to subtract discounts for which you might qualify. If you must join an organization (for example, the American Automobile Association) to obtain coverage from an insurer, add the membership fees to the final premium.

Coverage Type	Coverage†/Amount of Deductible	Premium* Company A (example)	Company B (your figures)	Company C (your figures)
A. Liability insurance				
Bodily injury	250/500	$ 132	___	___
Property damage	100	58	___	___
B. Medical payments/ personal injury protection				
Medical payments	100	$ 51	___	___
PIP (no-fault states)	N/A	N/A	N/A	N/A
C. Uninsured/underinsured motorist protection				
Uninsured motorist	50/100	$ 28	___	___
Underinsured motorist	50/100	$ 17	___	___
D. Physical damage protection				
Collision coverage	$100 deductible	$ 126	___	___
	$200 deductible	111	___	___
	$500 deductible	88	___	___
	$1,000 deductible	62	___	___
Comprehensive	no deductible	59	___	___
	$100 deductible	41	___	___
	$200 deductible	34	___	___
	$500 deductible	24	___	___
Total premium		438	___	___
Plus surcharges		N/A	___	___
Less discounts		33	___	___
Final premium*		**$405**	___	___

*Premium for six months for a midsize car in a medium-size city based on a $200 collision deductible and a $100 comprehensive deductible.
†Multiples of $1000.

on the profession involved. Professional liability policies are written with policy limits of $250,000 or more. A $1 million professional liability policy written for a marriage counselor may cost as little as $300 per year; in contrast, some surgeons pay $60,000 or more per year for professional liability insurance.

umbrella (excess) liability insurance
Catastrophic liability policy that covers liability losses in excess of those covered by any underlying homeowner's, automobile, or professional liability policy.

Umbrella Liability Insurance

It is possible to lose one's entire life savings as a result of a single liability loss. **Umbrella (or** excess) liability insurance is a catastrophic liability policy that covers liability losses in excess of those covered by any underlying homeowner's, automobile, or professional liability policy. Such policies provide two benefits. First, the types of losses covered are broader than those recognized by more narrowly defined policies. Second, these policies

DID YOU KNOW?

How Automobile Insurance Would Apply to an Accident

Just how the myriad provisions in an automobile insurance policy apply to a specific accident mystifies many people. As a result, the claims process may generate considerable dissatisfaction after an accident. The example given here and outlined in the following chart is intended to clarify the application of the multiple coverages and limits.

In September of last year, Donna Redman, a college student from Macomb, Illinois, caused a serious accident when she failed to yield to an approaching vehicle while attempting to make a left turn. Donna suffered a broken arm and facial cuts, resulting in medical costs of $1254. Her passenger, Philip Windsor, was seriously injured with head and neck wounds requiring surgery, a two-week hospital stay, and rehabilitation. Philip's injuries generated medical costs of $17,650. The driver of the other car, John Monk, suffered serious back and internal injuries and facial burns that resulted in some disfigurement. His medical care costs totaled $22,948. His passenger, Annette Monk, suffered cuts and bruises requiring minor medical care at a cost of $423.

Both cars were completely destroyed in the accident. Donna's 10-year-old Buick was valued at $2150. John's Mazda Miata was valued at $19,350. The force of the impact spun John's car around, causing it to destroy a traffic-signal control box (valued at $3650).

Both Donna and John were covered by family automobile policies with liability limits of $20,000/$50,000/$15,000 and medical payment limits of $5000 per person and $100 collision coverage deductibles. In total, Donna had to pay $11,048 out of her own pocket, as the policy limits were exceeded by John's medical costs and the property damage. If she had taken out a single-limit personal automobile policy for $65,000 (the total of her $50,000 per-accident bodily injury liability and $15,000 per-accident property damage liability), then she would have incurred no out-of-pocket liability losses.

An additional point needs to be raised concerning situations in which an accident victim suffers serious, permanent injuries that are not fully reimbursed by the insurance policy protecting the driver at fault. In our example, John suffered very painful injuries resulting in permanent disfigurement. He may wish to sue Donna for his pain and suffering and for his unpaid medical expenses. If he were to file such a suit, Donna would be provided with legal assistance by her insurance company. Any judgment that exceeds the policy limits (remember that Donna's per-person policy limit has already been reached) will be Donna's responsibility, however. Both Donna and John were terribly underinsured.

Donna Redman's Accident: Who Pays What?

Coverage	Donna's Policy	John's Policy
Liability (limits) (multiples of $1000):	(20/50/15)	(20/50/15)
Bodily injury:		
John Monk	$ 20,000	
Annette Monk	423	
Philip Windsor	12,650	
Property damage:		
John Monk's car	15,000	
Medical payments (limits):	($5,000)	($5,000)
John Monk	5,000*	
Annette Monk	5,000*	
Donna Redman	1,254	
Philip Windsor	5,000	
Collision coverage (limits):	(ACV, $100 deductible)	(ACV, $100 deductible)
Donna's car	2,050	
John's car	19,250*	
Donna's out-of-pocket expenses:		
John Monk's bodily injury	2,948	
John Monk's car	4,350	
Traffic-signal control box	3,650	
Collision insurance deductible	100	
TOTAL	**$11,048**	

*Included in Donna's column because John's company filed a claim against Donna by exercising its subrogation rights.

DID YOU KNOW?

Sean's Success Story

Sean's success as a personal financial manager is reflected in his tangible assets. He owns a two-year-old luxury vehicle and a motorcycle. He has all the latest home entertainment equipment in his condo in an upscale neighborhood. He also has substantial coin and stamp collections as both hobbies and investments. He recently undertook a thorough risk-management process to assess his exposures to risk and assess the ways to best address the risks he faces. As a result, he bought additional insurance to cover his personal property and stamps and coins. He also raised his automobile insurance deductible to $1000 and used the savings to raise his liability limits to 250/500/100. He also purchased a $2 million umbrella liability policy. Sean feels more secure now and plans to reassess his risk-management efforts every year.

provide for high dollar amounts of coverage over and above the basic policies. To be covered for these higher limits, you must carry the basic coverages as well.

Figure 10-3 shows how umbrella policies work. In this example, the insured has an automobile insurance policy with total liability limits of $130,000 (the total liability coverage for one accident is $100,000 per bodily injury plus $30,000 for property damage), a homeowner's insurance policy with liability protection of $100,000, and a $150,000 professional liability insurance policy. If the insured bought an

Figure 10-3   How Umbrella Liability Policies Work

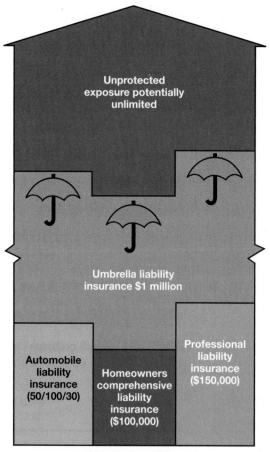

Types of Exposures

DID YOU KNOW?

About Wedding Insurance

The cost of a large wedding can be $30,000 or more. Much of that amount must be paid up front. If either party backs out, there is not much you can do. But what if something happens and the wedding must be postponed? There is insurance for such situations. Wedding insurance generally covers situations such as these: (1) a member of the immediate families dies or becomes ill (pre-existing illness is excluded); (2) a guest is injured; (3) caterers fail to provide a service; (4) clothing providers and photographers do not deliver their services; and (5) gifts are stolen or damaged. It is a good idea to use a credit card for many of the expenses because of the dispute protections provided for credit card purchases (see Chapter 7) that are not available for debit, check, or cash purchases.

umbrella policy with a $1 million limit and then experienced a $750,000 professional liability loss, the umbrella policy would provide protection of $600,000 after the professional liability policy limits were exceeded. Umbrella policies are relatively low in cost when purchased to supplement basic policies (perhaps $150 to $200 per year for an additional $1 million of protection) and protect against virtually all liability exposures that a person might face.

Floater Policies

Floater policies provide all-risk protection for accident and theft losses to movable property (such as cameras, sporting equipment, MP3 players, and clothing) regardless of where the loss occurs. Floater protection for personal property is part of the standard homeowner's insurance policy. Property owned for business purposes is excluded. This means that a mechanic's tools, a lawyer's books, and a karaoke DJ's equipment, for example, would not be covered. A separate floater policy would be required.

Many items of personal property are transported in automobiles and kept at temporary residences such as motel rooms. Automobile insurance policies do not cover portable personal property. If it is covered under a homeowner's policy at home, however, personal property will be covered elsewhere under the floater protection provided by the homeowner's policy. For example, a compact disc player permanently installed in a car would not be considered portable and thus would be covered by the automobile policy. If it can be removed for use indoors, the CD player would be covered under the homeowner's (or renter's) policy.

floater policies
Provide all-risk protection for accident and theft losses to movable property regardless of where the loss occurs.

✔ Concept Check 10.5

1. Explain how purchasing an umbrella liability insurance policy applies the large-loss principle.

2. Are you preparing for a professional career that might expose you to liability losses? How might you protect yourself from such losses?

3. Give two examples of someone who might want to purchase a floater insurance policy.

HOW TO COLLECT ON YOUR PROPERTY AND LIABILITY LOSSES

The direct benefit of owning insurance becomes evident when a loss occurs and it is time to file a claim. Even when you have a legitimate claim, however, you may want to consider whether you should do so. A small claim might be best ignored.

LEARNING OBJECTIVE **6**

Summarize how to make an insurance claim.

ADVICE FROM A PRO

Applying the Large-Loss Principle to Property and Liability Insurance

You should always select insurance coverage limits for the highest possible loss. Although rare, such losses can destroy your financial future. That thinking underlies the large-loss principle discussed earlier. Here is how to apply the principle to property and liability insurance.

For your personal property insurance, you should select limits that equal the value of the property involved. A $240,000 home should be insured for $240,000. Better yet, you can add **extended-replacement coverage**, which covers the difference if the price to rebuild exceeds your dwelling limit. Select all-risk policies rather than named-peril policies. Yes, the cost may be high, but the loss of your property would be much worse.

The purchase of an umbrella liability policy is the best way to apply the large-loss principle to liability insurance.

Never buy the legal minimums for auto insurance. Causing an accident that destroys one newer-model vehicle can exceed most state minimum limits.

You can afford to apply the large-loss principle through the use of higher deductibles. Ask yourself: "What is the largest loss I can afford to cover myself?" Then choose the highest deductible that does not exceed what you can afford to cover. The money saved by selecting a higher deductible can be used to pay for higher policy limits. For example, on a 100/300/50 auto policy with a $100 deductible, you can save as much as $300 per year by simply raising the deductibles to $1000! Then you can apply some of those savings to buy a $1,000,000 umbrella policy to protect yourself from a catastrophe.

Jan D. Andersen PhD
Emeritus Associate Professor
California State University, Sacramento

Recall that insurance is for the losses you cannot afford. Filing frequent claims (or even notifying the agent of a loss) can result in an increase in your rates. One claim probably will not cause a problem. Having a second claim within a two-year period may be looked at negatively. Of course, if you have a large claim, you would want to file for its recovery. Here are the four steps that you should take when you have a loss.

1. Contact Your Insurance Agent

The first step—contacting your agent—should be taken as soon as possible, but only after you have decided that you will ultimately file a claim. Follow the agent's instructions regarding who to contact next (including filing a written police report) and what to do to minimize the magnitude of the loss. Then keep the company informed of everything relevant to the loss, even if it requires daily or weekly contact until the claim is settled. The tenacious claimant is likely to collect fully on a loss.

DID YOU KNOW?

Your Worst Financial Blunders in Managing Property and Liability Risk

Based on others' financial woes, you will make mistakes in personal finance when you:

1. *Buy only the legal minimum coverage on the liability insurance on your vehicle.*

2. *Fail to keep good records (e.g., lists, photos, receipts) that could serve to document insured property losses.*

3. *Pay high premiums because you select low deductibles on property insurance for your home and car.*

2. Document Your Loss

You carry the burden of proof whenever a property or liability loss occurs. Adequate documentation of the circumstances and the amount of the loss is essential. In the absence of such documentation, the insurance company will generally interpret the situation in the manner most favorable to its interests, not yours.

The best way to document a theft, fire, or other personal property loss is with pictures. Photograph or videotape all valuable property in your home when you purchase it or when you obtain insurance coverage. Write the date of purchase, price paid, description, model name and number, and serial number (if any) of the property on the back of the photograph or verbally record it on the videotape. Prepare a list describing any items not photographed or videotaped. Keep such records in a safe-deposit box, in a file cabinet at work, or with a relative. If a loss occurs, present a *copy* of your documentation to the agent or insurance company.

You should always file a police report if you become involved in an automobile accident. Insureds also should prepare a narrative giving the time and place of the accident, the direction of travel and estimated speed of the cars involved, the road and weather conditions, and the behavior of all parties involved. Include a diagram of the accident scene showing the location of the vehicles before, during, and after the time of impact, plus the locations of traffic lights and signs and any landmarks (for example, road construction or repairs). If possible, obtain the names and contact information for witnesses. Police reports are also advisable (and often required) when filing a theft claim of any type.

3. File Your Claim

An **insurance claim** is a formal request to the insurance company for reimbursement for a covered loss. All of the documentation and information will be requested by the insurance agent or a **claims adjuster** (the person designated by the insurance company to assess whether the loss is covered and to determine the dollar amount that the company will pay). Insurance companies require that claims be made in writing, although the adjuster may assist you in completing the necessary forms.

4. Sign a Release

Part of the final step in the claims-settlement process is to sign the **release** which is an insurance document affirming that the dollar amount of the loss settlement is accepted as full and complete reimbursement and that the insured will make no additional claims for the loss against the insurance company. Signing the release absolves the insurance company of any further responsibility for the loss. Resist the temptation to sign a release until you are sure that the full magnitude of the loss has become evident.

 Concept Check 10.6

1. What is the best way to establish documentation for potential losses to your personal property?

2. Describe what you should do to file a claim most effectively when involved in an automobile accident.

3. Describe the term *release* and explain why signing a release too soon might work to your disadvantage.

FINANCIAL POWER POINT

Getting Started on Your Personal Property Inventory

The tangible assets listed on your balance sheet can serve as a starting point when developing your personal property inventory. Then take photos of the items and document the purchase price and date of the purchase.

DO IT NOW!

You know more about personal finance after reading this chapter, so get started right now by:

1. *Identifying your exposures to risk and the magnitude of the losses that could occur.*

2. *Assessing your automobile insurance coverage and making changes as necessary.*

3. *Buying renter's insurance if you rent your housing.*

insurance claim
Formal request to the insurance company for reimbursement for a covered loss.

claims adjuster
Person designated by the insurance company to assess whether the loss is covered and to determine the dollar amount that the company will pay.

release
Insurance document affirming that the dollar amount of the loss settlement is accepted as full and complete reimbursement.

WHAT DO YOU RECOMMEND NOW?

Now that you have read the chapter on risk management and property liability insurance, what would you recommend to George and Emily in the case at the beginning of the chapter regarding:

1. The risk-management steps they should take to update their insurance coverages?

2. The relationship between severity and frequency of loss when deciding whether to buy insurance?

3. Adequately insuring their home?

4. The use of deductibles and policy limits to keep their automobile insurance premiums at a manageable level while still maintaining vital coverage?

BIG PICTURE SUMMARY OF LEARNING OBJECTIVES

LO1.   Apply the risk-management process to address the risks to your property and income.

Personal financial managers practice risk management to protect their present and future assets and income. Risk management entails identifying the sources of risk, evaluating risk and potential losses, selecting the appropriate risk-handling mechanism, implementing and administering the risk-management plan, and evaluating and adjusting the plan periodically.

LO2.   Explain how insurance works to reduce risk.

Insurance is a mechanism for reducing pure risk by having a larger number of individuals share in the financial losses suffered by all members of the group. It is used to protect against pure risk but cannot be used to protect against speculative risk, which carries the potential for gain as well as loss. Likewise, insurance cannot be used to provide payment in excess of the actual financial loss suffered. Insurance consists of two elements: the reduction of pure risk through application of the law of large numbers, and the sharing of losses.

LO3.   Design a homeowner's or renter's insurance program to meet your needs.

Homeowner's insurance is designed to protect homeowners and renters from property and liability losses. Six types of homeowner's insurance are available, including one geared toward renters. Homeowner's policies can be purchased on a named-perils or an open-perils basis.

LO4.   Design an automobile insurance program to meet your needs.

Automobile insurance is designed to protect the insured against property and liability losses arising from use of a motor vehicle. These policies typically provide liability insurance (both bodily injury and property damage liability), medical payments or personal injury protection insurance, property insurance on your car, and underinsured and uninsured motorist insurance. The most commonly purchased type of automobile insurance is the family automobile policy. The premium for automobile insurance is based on the characteristics of the insured driver, including age, gender, marital status, and driving record.

LO5.   Describe other types of property and liability insurance.

Other important types of property and liability insurance include floater policies (to protect personal property regardless of its location), professional liability insurance, and umbrella liability insurance.

LO6.   Summarize how to make an insurance claim.

The insured is responsible for documenting and verifying a loss. Photographs or videotapes of the insured property are ideal for documenting claims made under a homeowner's insurance policy. A police report provides the best documentation for claims made under an automobile insurance policy.

LET'S TALK ABOUT IT

1. **Insurance Underwriting.** How do you feel about being grouped into classes in the insurance underwriting process? Do you feel that insurance companies should treat all people alike?

2. **Actual Cash Value.** Many people complain that property insurance policies should pay more than what the insurance companies say is the actual cash value of the property, such as for a used motor vehicle that is in near-perfect condition. How do you feel about this issue, and what would happen if insurance companies were more generous in their reimbursements?

3. **Auto Liability Limits.** Do you know the liability limits on the automobile insurance policy under which you are covered? Are the limits appropriate?

4. **Personal Property Protection.** Is your personal property, such as furniture and computer, covered under a homeowner's or renter's insurance policy? If not, why not? If so, what are the policy limits?

5. **Auto Insurance Claims.** What experiences have you or a family member had with the automobile insurance claims process? What if anything might have been done differently or better?

DO THE MATH

1. **How Much of Fire Loss Will Be Covered?** Toula and Ian Miller of St. Clairsville, Ohio, recently suffered a fire in their home. The fire, which began in a crawl space at the back of the house, caused $24,000 of damage to the dwelling. The garage, valued at $8400, was totally destroyed but did not contain a car at the time of the fire. Replacement of the Millers' personal property damaged in the home and garage amounted to $18,500. In addition, $350 in cash and a stamp collection valued at $3215 were destroyed. While the damage was being repaired, the Millers stayed in a motel for one week and spent $1350 on food and lodging. The house had a value of $95,000 and was insured for $68,400 under an HO-3 policy with a $250 deductible. Use Table 10-2 to answer the following questions. (Hint: You must first determine whether the Millers have adequate dwelling replacement coverage and, if not, what percentage of the necessary 80 percent coverage they do have. The resulting answer will determine the percentage of the loss to the dwelling covered, and consequently the amount to be reimbursed by the insurance company.)

   (a) Assuming that the deductible was applied to the damage to the dwelling, calculate the amount covered by insurance and the amount that the Millers must pay for each loss listed: the dwelling, the garage, the cash and stamp collection, and the extra living expenses.

   (b) How much of the amount of the personal property loss would be covered by the insurance policy? Paid for by the Millers?

   (c) Assuming that they have contents replacement-cost protection on the personal property, what amount and percentage of the total loss must be paid by the Millers?

2. **Sufficient Dwelling Coverage?** Adam Barrow of Columbia, Missouri, has owned his home for ten years. When he purchased it for $178,000, Adam bought a $160,000 homeowner's insurance policy. He still owns that policy, even though the replacement cost of the home is now $300,000.

   (a) If Adam suffered a $20,000 fire loss to the home, what percentage and dollar amount of the loss would be covered by his policy?

   (b) How much insurance on the home should Adam carry to be fully reimbursed for a fire loss?

3. **Coverage on a One-Vehicle Accident.** Bill Converse of Pomona, California, recently slid off a gravel road and struck a tree. Bill's vehicle suffered $7500 in damage. The vehicle has a book value of $6000. Bill carried collision insurance with a $500 deductible. How much will Bill be reimbursed by his policy?

4. **How Much of a Major Auto Accident Loss Will Be Covered?** Ashley Diamond of Laramie, Wyoming, drives an eight-year-old Toyota valued at $9600. She has a $75,000 personal automobile policy with $10,000 per-person medical payments coverage and both collision ($200 deductible) and comprehensive coverage. David Smith of Fort Collins, Colorado, drives a four-year-old Chevrolet Malibu valued at $9500. He has a 25/50/15 family automobile policy with $20,000 in medical payments coverage and both collision ($100 deductible) and comprehensive insurance. Late one evening, while he was driving back from Rocky Mountain National Park, David's car crossed the centerline of the road, striking Ashley's car and forcing it into a ditch. David's car also left the road and did extensive damage to the front of a roadside store. The following table indicates the damages and their dollar amounts.

Item	Amount
Bodily injuries suffered by Ashley	$ 6,800
Bodily injuries suffered by Fran, a passenger in Ashley's car	28,634
Ashley's car	9,600
Bodily injuries suffered by David	2,700
Bodily injuries suffered by Cecilia, a passenger in David's car	12,845
David's car	9,500
Damage to the roadside store	14,123

Complete the following chart and use the information to answer these questions:

(a) How much will Ashley's policy pay Ashley and Fran?

(b) Will subrogation rights come into play? In what way?

(c) How much will David's bodily injury liability protection pay?

(d) To whom and how much will David's property damage liability protection pay?

(e) To whom and how much will David's medical protection pay?

(f) How much reimbursement will David receive for his car?

(g) How much will David be required to pay out of his own pocket?

David Smith's Accident: Who Pays What?

Coverage	David's Policy	Ashley's Policy
Liability (limits)	—	—
Bodily injury		
Ashley	—	—
Fran	—	—
Cecilia	—	—
Medical payments (limits)	—	—
David	—	—
Ashley	—	—
Fran	—	—
Cecilia	—	—
Collision coverage (limits)	—	—
David's car	—	—
Ashley's car	—	—
David's out-of-pocket expenses	—	—
Fran's bodily injury	—	—
Excess property damage losses	—	—
Collision insurance deductible	—	—
TOTAL	—	—

FINANCIAL PLANNING CASES

CASE 1

The Johnsons Decide How to Manage Their Risks

Six years have passed since the Johnsons were married, and their financial affairs have become much more complicated. Both Harry and Belinda are earning about 30 percent more at work. They have purchased a $140,000 condominium that has added about $400 per month to their housing expense. And they have purchased a second car for $3200. As a result of these changes, Harry and Belinda realize that they now face greater risks in their financial affairs. They have decided to review their situation with an eye toward managing their risks more effectively. Use Table 10-1, their net worth and income and expense statements at the end of Chapter 3 (on pages 98–99), and other information in this chapter to answer the following questions:

(a) What are Harry and Belinda's major sources of risk from home and automobile ownership, and what is the potential magnitude of loss from each?

(b) Given the choices listed in Step 3 of Table 10-1, how should the Johnsons handle the sources of risk listed in part a?

CASE 2

The Hernandezes Consider Additional Liability Insurance

Victor and Maria's next-door neighbor, Jasmine Saunders, was recently sued over an automobile accident and eventually was held liable for $437,000 in damages. Jasmine's automobile policy limits were 100/300/50. Because of the shortfall, she had to sell her house and move into an apartment. Victor and Maria are now concerned that a similar tragedy might potentially befall them. They have a homeowner's policy with $100,000 in comprehensive personal liability coverage and an automobile policy with 50/100/25 limits, and Maria has a small ($100,000) professional liability policy for her dental hygiene practice.

(a) How might Victor and Maria more fully protect themselves through their homeowner's and automobile insurance policies?

(b) What additional benefits would they receive in buying an umbrella liability policy?

CASE 3

Julia Price Thinks About Managing Her Property and Liability Risk

Julia has always tried to keep her insurance spending under control by purchasing low limits on her policies. Now that her assets and income have grown, she is beginning to reconsider the wisdom of this approach when buying insurance. Julia knows she has a lot more to lose in terms both of property and liability exposures. Last week, she called her insurance agent to discuss raising her policy limits on her homeowner's and automobile insurance policies. The agent suggested she consider an umbrella liability policy. Julia still wants to be frugal and is considering simply raising the limits on the policies she already has rather than obtaining another policy. Offer your opinions about her thinking.

CASE 4

The Princes' Auto Insurance Is Not Renewed

Mark and Kelly Prince of Jacksonville, Florida, face a crisis. Their automobile insurance company has notified them that their current coverage expires in 30 days and will not be renewed. Mark and the Princes' younger son each had a minor, at-fault accident during the past year. Their children are otherwise good drivers, as are both parents. The Princes are confused because they know families whose members have much worse driving records but still have insurance.

(a) Explain to Mark and Kelly why their policy might have been canceled.

(b) Use the box on page 305 to give Mark and Kelly some pointers on how to save money when shopping for a new auto insurance policy.

CASE 5

A Student Buys Insurance for a Used Car

Makiko Iwanami, a student from Osaka, Japan, is in one of your classes. She is considering the purchase of a used car and has been told that she must buy automobile insurance to register the car and obtain license plates. Makiko has come to you for advice, and you have decided to focus on three aspects of automobile insurance.

(a) Explain how liability insurance works in the United States. Advise Makiko about which liability insurance limits she should select.

(b) Makiko is especially impressed that automobile insurance includes medical payments coverage because she has no health insurance. Explain why the medical payments coverage does not actually solve her health insurance problem, and describe the type of coverage it provides.

(c) Makiko plans to pay cash for the car and doesn't want to spend more than $5000. Outline the coverage provided by collision insurance and factors that might make such coverage optional for Makiko.

CASE 6

An Argument About the Value of Insurance

You have been talking at a party to some friends about insurance. One young married couple in the group believes that insurance is almost always a real waste of money. They argue, "The odds of most bad events occurring are so low that you don't need to worry." Furthermore, they say, "Buying insurance is like pouring money down a hole; you rarely have anything to show for it in the end." Based on what you have learned from this chapter, how might you argue against this couple's point of view?

CASE 7

Abigail Contemplates a New Homeowner's Insurance Policy

Abigail Elizabeth Proctor of Medford, Oregon, recently bought a home for $200,000. The previous owner had a $160,000 HO-1 policy on the property, and Abigail can simply pay the premiums to keep the same coverage in effect. Her insurance agent called her and cautioned that she would be better off to upgrade the policy to an HO-2 or HO-3 policy. Abigail has turned to you for advice. Use the information in Table 10-2 to advise her.

(a) What additional property protection would Abigail have if she purchased an HO-2 policy?

(b) What additional property protection would Abigail have if she purchased an HO-3 policy?

(c) What property protection would remain largely the same whether Abigail had an HO-1, HO-2, or HO-3 policy?

(d) Advise Abigail on what differences in liability protection, if any, exist among the three policies.

BE YOUR OWN PERSONAL FINANCIAL MANAGER

1. **Property Loss Exposures.** Use Worksheet 43: My Home Inventory from "My Personal Financial Planner" to develop a list of your personal property items, including items you keep at school and those at other locations such as the home of a family member. Use Table 3-2 on page 73 and Table 10-3 on page 301 as guides for the types of information to include. Assess the appropriateness of insurance to protect these items from loss.

MY PERSONAL FINANCIAL PLANNER

2. **The Risk-Management Process.** Build upon your list of property loss exposures to develop a complete risk-management assessment. Use Table 10-1 on page 289 as a guide and use Worksheet 44: My Insurance Inventory from "My Personal Financial Planner" to record the results of your efforts.

MY PERSONAL FINANCIAL PLANNER

3. **Evaluate Your Need for Homeowner's or Renter's Insurance.** Determine whether or not you are currently covered by a homeowner's or renter's insurance policy. If you are, determine whether the policy is adequate for your needs. If you are not, decide what coverage levels you will need.

4. **Evaluate Your Automobile Insurance.** If you drive a vehicle owned by a family member or yourself, you are covered by the insurance policy on that vehicle. Use Table 10-4 on page 302 as a guide to assess the coverage under that policy. Determine whether the policy adequately protects you from loss, and if not, identify what changes you want to make in the policy.

5. **Shop for Automobile Insurance.** Use the Run the Numbers worksheet on page 308 or Worksheet 45: My Comparison of Auto Insurance Providers from "My Personal Financial Planner" to shop for vehicle insurance based on your analysis in item 4 above. Use your current policy for Company A in the worksheet. Then contact two additional companies to obtain quotes on similar coverage to determine whether you are receiving a good value for your current policy or would benefit from switching companies.

MY PERSONAL FINANCIAL PLANNER

ON THE 'NET

Go to the Web pages indicated to complete these exercises. You can also go to the *Garman/Forgue* companion website at www.cengagebrain.com for an expanded list of exercises. Under General Business, select the title of this text. Click on the Internet Exercises link for this chapter.

1. **Minimum Liability Limits.** Visit the website for the National Association of Insurance Commissioners at www.naic.org/state_web_map.htm, where you will find a map where you can link to the Insurance Commission in your state. Determine the minimum automobile insurance liability limits in your state. How well-insured do you feel someone would be if he or she carried only these minimums?

2. **Insurance Buyer's Guides.** Visit the website for the National Association of Insurance Commissioners, where you will find a map at www.naic.org/state_web_map.htm through which you can link to your state insurance regulator's website. If available in your state, obtain an insurance buyer's guide for automobile and homeowner's insurance that describes policy provisions and compares insurance rates. Use these rate comparisons to select two automobile insurance companies that would be appropriate for your needs. Write or telephone the companies to obtain specific premium quotations for the desired insurance protection. Do the same for single-family dwelling, condominium, or renter's insurance, depending on your circumstances.

3. **Safe Cars Save Money.** Visit the website for the Insurance Institute for Highway Safety at www.iihs.org/ratings/default.aspx. For your own vehicle and one or two you would like to own, check how the vehicles stack up against the competition in terms of injury protection.

ACTION INVOLVEMENT PROJECTS

1. **The Benefits of Renter's Insurance.** Identify three to five of your friends who currently live in rental housing. Ask them if they are covered by a renter's insurance policy. If not, ask them why they have not decided to buy such coverage. If they are covered, ask them to give their assessment of the costs and benefits of having a policy.

2. **Independent Versus Exclusive Insurance Agents.** Interview two insurance agents, one who is an independent agent and one who is an exclusive agent. Ask each to describe the benefits to a customer who buys insurance from that type of agent.

3. **Automobile Insurance Claims.** Interview three or four people who have been involved in an automobile insurance accident. Ask them to summarize the claims process as they experienced it and how they now view the process compared to what they expected.

Visit the Garman/Forgue companion website at **www.cengagebrain.com**.

YOU MUST BE KIDDING, RIGHT?

Amber Parker is a 32-year-old married mother with two children, ages 3 and 4. She used to work out of her home as a medical transcriptionist for a local hospital that offered a health care plan. Last year Amber suffered severe head injuries in a bicycling accident. Amber's wounds have healed and she has regained her ability to speak but is not yet able to walk on her own or use her hands and arms very well. Amber is recuperating at home but requires a daily paid caregiver to assist with her personal needs. Her children now go to daycare, and it may be five years before she can work again. Which of the following aspects of her injury were covered by Amber's health care plan?

A. Her hospital stay and surgery

B. Her at-home custodial care

C. The cost of daycare for her children

D. Her lost income

The answer is A. Having a health care plan is a must. But your protection is incomplete until you have addressed the need for rehabilitation and custodial care as well as for the potential lost income from a period of disability!

LEARNING OBJECTIVES

After reading this chapter, you should be able to:

❶ Identify ways that people can manage the financial burdens resulting from illness or injury.

❷ Distinguish among the types of protection for direct health expenses.

❸ Describe the benefits and limitations of health care plans.

❹ Develop a plan to protect your income when you cannot work due to disability.

❺ Explain how to protect yourself from the expenses for long-term care.

WHAT DO YOU RECOMMEND?

Danielle DiMartino is a 36-year-old single mother with two children, ages 10 and 14. Her 10-year-old daughter has a history of ear infections that require doctor's office visits four or five times per year. Danielle's 71-year-old mother lives with the family for financial reasons; she has hereditary high blood pressure and high cholesterol as well as diabetes. Danielle's mother has enrolled in Medicare Parts A and B.

Danielle's employer pays all or a portion of the cost for a health care plan to cover the company's workers, their spouses, and their dependents. Danielle has four options: (1) the basic HMO managed by a local university medical school/hospital with no additional cost for Danielle, but with additional cost of $122 per month to cover her children, (2) a health insurance plan with a PPO at that same medical center for an additional cost of $245 per month, (3) a traditional health insurance plan that provides access to virtually all health care providers in her community for $455 per month, and (4) a high-deductible plan with a $5000 deductible at no additional cost. Danielle's employer offers no disability income or long-term care group plan. She does receive ten sick days per year, which can accumulate if not taken. Danielle has accumulated 30 days.

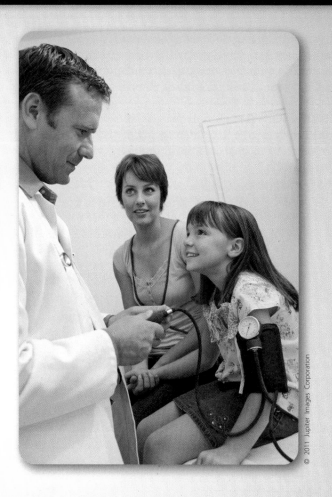

What do you recommend to Danielle DiMartino on the subject of managing health expenses regarding:

1. Choosing among the four alternatives available to her?
2. Danielle's concerns about providing for her mother's health care needs?
3. Danielle's need for disability income insurance?
4. How Danielle can cover her long-term care risk?

Few things in life are more important than your good health. When illness or injuries do strike, three possible issues may affect your finances. First there are the direct costs of the required health care, such as the cost of hospital stays, surgeries, and visits to a physician's office. Second, there are the costs of your rehabilitation and custodial care, such as a stay in a nursing home. And third, there is the potential for lost income when you cannot work due to illness or injury.

This chapter looks at the ways you can address these three financial concerns. You should not take them lightly. Health care costs can quickly wipe out all your assets. Also, you should know that medical-related debts are the number one cause of personal bankruptcy.

ADDRESSING THE FINANCIAL BURDENS OF ILLNESS OR INJURY

On average, more than $8000 is spent on health care for each American every year. About 85 percent of Americans are covered by a health care plan that will pay a portion of these costs. You can obtain protection as an individual or as a member of a group. A **group health plan** is sold collectively to an entire group of people rather than to individuals. The health care plan offered by an employer or to students enrolled in a particular college is an example of a group plan.

Years ago, most workers could rely on their employer to provide them with a health care plan. But employers that offer plans can spend over $10,000 in premiums per covered worker, and the high cost has resulted in employers scaling back their assistance in paying for such plans. As a result, workers who are covered by a health care plan pay about 15 percent of the monthly costs of the plan itself with these costs up about 50 percent over the last 5 years. In addition, workers are paying a higher share of the health care expenses that are covered by the plan when illness strikes.

Each of the three types of losses resulting from illness or injury can be addressed in multiple ways. Of course, you can pay all of your own expenses. That is not always possible or smart. We provide a summary of your options here and in Table 11-1.

1. Covering Your Direct Health Care Costs

Direct health care can be paid for by a traditional health insurance, health maintenance organization (HMO), or a high-deductible health care plan (each is defined later). These three types of plans may cover as much as 90 to 100 percent of one's costs and comprise the plans typically offered by employers. Purchased by an individual, these plans can cost $600 or more per month for an individual and $1200 or more monthly for family coverage.

Fifty million people age 65 or over are enrolled in the **Medicare** program, which is the federal government's single-payer health care program for the elderly. Medicare is divided into two parts. **Medicare Part A** is the hospitalization portion of the program; it requires no premium. Most people do not pay a monthly Part A premium because they or a spouse has 40 or more quarters of Medicare-covered employment. **Medicare Part B** is the supplementary health expense insurance portion for outpatient care, doctor office visits, or certain other services of the Medicare program; it requires payment of a monthly premium (approximately $115). Both components require patients to pay a portion of their costs. Medicare also includes an optional prescription coverage plan under **Medicare Part D**. Participants pay the first $310 of prescription costs annually plus copays for each prescription and must make much higher payments if they spend more than $2850 on prescriptions.

LEARNING OBJECTIVE ❶

Identify ways that people can manage the financial burdens resulting from illness or injury.

group health plan
Sold collectively to an entire group of people rather than to individuals, such as the group health care policies offered by employers.

FINANCIAL POWER POINT

Group Health Plans Are Best

Participating in a group plan is desirable for three reasons: First, group health coverage costs less than an individual plan. Second, employers often pay all or the major portion of the cost. Third, people who have existing health problems are less likely to be rejected because of their condition.

Table 11–1   Types of Protection from Health-Related Expenses

	Types of Expense				
	Direct Health Care			**Rehabilitative and Custodial Care**	**Lost Income**
Provider of Coverage?	• Health maintenance organizations (HMOs) • Medicare for those age 65 and over • Medicaid for low-income/low-wealth individuals	• Traditional health insurance • Medicare for those age 65 and over • Medicaid for low-income/low-wealth individuals	• Consumer-driven health insurance plans	• Long-term care insurance • Medicaid for low-income/low-wealth individuals	• Disability income insurance • Social Security for eligible workers and their families
Services Covered?	Provide hospital, surgical, and medical services directly through their own hospital and physicians or under contract with such providers	Reimburses or pays for hospital, surgical, medical, and other health care costs	Reimburse or pay for hospital, surgical, medical, and other health care costs that exceed a high deductible of $5000 or more	Reimburses for costs associated with custodial care (not direct medical care)	Provides a monthly income to replace that lost when the insured is unable to work due to accident or injury
Payment Mode?	Charge a monthly fee on a prepaid basis	Charges monthly premiums for the insurance coverage	Charge monthly premiums for the insurance coverage	Charges monthly or annual premiums	Charges a monthly premium
Purchased By?	Individuals or by employers as an employee benefit	Individuals or by employers as an employee benefit	Individuals or by employers as an employee benefit	Individuals	Individuals or by employers as an employee benefit

Medicare
The federal government's health care program for the elderly.

Medicaid
A government health care program for low-income people funded jointly by the federal and state governments.

long-term care insurance
Provides reimbursement for costs associated with custodial care in a nursing facility or at home.

Medicare Advantage Plans are offered by private companies (insurers or HMOs) approved by Medicare and they combine Parts A and B into one plan. Choosing a Medicare Advantage Plan typically results in lower **out-of-pocket costs**. Out-of-pocket costs are simply any dollar amounts for care that people covered by health care plans must pay themselves.

Low-income individuals and families may qualify for **Medicaid**, a government health care program funded jointly by the federal and state governments. Eligibility for Medicaid is based on household income and net worth. Beginning in 2014, households with incomes below 133 percent of the poverty threshold will be eligible for Medicaid. One in six Americans is covered by Medicaid or the **S-CHIP program**, which is a government program similar to Medicaid that covers children whose parents are middle income but do not have access to a private health care plan. There are no premiums.

2. Covering Your Rehabilitative and Custodial Care Costs

Accident victims, people with chronic disease, and the elderly often have needs that go beyond direct health care. At one extreme is the need for a stay in a nursing home and at the other might be a short period of time during which a patient receives rehabilitation. Health care plans tend to cover only "medically necessary" care, not rehabilitation and custodial needs. **Long-term care insurance** provides reimbursement for costs associated with custodial care in a nursing facility or at home. A key feature of Medicaid is its coverage of long-term custodial care. Elderly who have "spent down" their assets on long-term care expenses may be eligible to receive Medicaid reimbursement for a portion of these costs. Those in the greatest need for long-term care insurance tend to be those in the middle-income range. They often lack the financial resources to pay for nursing home care (perhaps $6000 per month) and have too high an income to qualify for Medicaid.

3. Covering Your Lost Income

Anyone with a job can lose income when he or she becomes sick or is injured. Many employers offer sick days and other time off that can be used as necessary. Some employers may offer **disability income insurance** that replaces a portion of the income lost when you cannot work because of illness or injury. These plans come in two forms. A **short-term disability income insurance plan** replaces a portion of one's income for a short period of time, perhaps up to two years. Short-term plans are sometimes partially paid for by the employer. Employers may also offer a group **long-term disability income insurance plan** for coverage periods of five or more years. The employee is usually required to pay the full premium for such coverage. If your employer does not offer either of these plans, you may buy them on your own.

Workers who are eligible can collect **Social Security Disability Income Insurance** benefits from the federal government if their disability is total (meaning they cannot work at any job) and is expected to last one year (or until death if that is anticipated within one year). The amount of these benefits is based on the worker's average lifetime earnings subject to Social Security tax and, thus, might not be sufficient to adequately support young workers and their families.

Older workers who become disabled may have another option available. Many have built up considerable funds in a tax-sheltered retirement account. These funds can be utilized to replace lost income when disabled.

 Concept Check 11.1

1. List three ways that group health plans are better than individually purchased plans.

2. Identify the five mechanisms available to help people pay for direct health care costs.

3. Explain why someone might want to purchase long-term care insurance.

4. Explain how someone might replace the income lost due to illness or injury.

SOURCES OF PROTECTION FROM DIRECT HEALTH CARE COSTS

A **health care plan** is a generic name for any program that pays or provides reimbursement for direct health care expenditures. When a health plan is available as an employee benefit, the employer typically pays the cost for the worker (and possibly other members of the worker's immediate family) for the lowest-cost plan the employer offers. Employees can choose a higher-priced option or add family members to the coverage by paying an additional charge. New employees generally must make a choice among the available plans within the first few days of being hired.

Health Maintenance Organizations

Health maintenance organizations (HMOs) provide a wide array of health care services, including hospital, surgical, and preventive health care. Some HMO plans require a small copayment of $5 to $25 for each office visit or prescription. A goal of HMOs is to catch any medical problem early, which helps keep overall costs low by reducing the probability of subsequent high-cost medical treatment. HMO plans are available to groups and individuals.

FINANCIAL POWER POINT

Three Ways to Obtain Health Care Benefits

Health benefits can come from three sources. First, your employer might provide them as an employee benefit. Second, you might qualify for a government program. Three, you can buy protection as an individual.

disability income insurance
Insurance that covers a portion of the income lost when you cannot work because of illness or injury.

Social Security Disability Income Insurance
Under this government program, eligible workers can receive some income if their disabilities are total, meaning that they cannot work at any job.

LEARNING OBJECTIVE

Distinguish among the types of protection for direct health expenses.

health care plan
Generic name for any program that pays or provides reimbursement for direct health care expenditures.

health maintenance organizations (HMOs)
Health insurance plans that provide a broad range of health care services for a set monthly fee on a prepaid basis.

New employees often must choose from among a menu of health care plans soon after being hired.

managed care plans
Any health care plan that controls the conditions under which health care can be obtained.

DID YOU KNOW?

The Essence of Health Care Reform

The health care reform law that passed in 2010, formally known as the Patient Protection and Affordable Health Care Act, began taking effect that same year with numerous provisions being phased into effect through 2014 and beyond. Provisions of the law that took effect by December 31, 2011, are included in this chapter. Table 11-2 summarizes those provisions and others scheduled to go into effect after January 2012. To stay updated as the requirements of the act evolve, go to www.healthcare.gov/law/introduction/index.html.

FINANCIAL POWER POINT

The Difference Between Health Insurance and HMOs

Health insurance pays for or reimburses you for your care. HMOs actually provide your health care.

HMOs Provide Prepaid Health Care The monthly fee, or premium, charged by an HMO is actually a prepayment for your health care. The fee is based on the health services that the average plan member would tend to use. HMOs do not put dollar limits on how much health care can be used. Instead, they list the types of health care they will provide under the contract.

How HMOs Work HMO subscribers are assigned a **primary-care physician** by the HMO or choose one from a list of physicians employed by the HMO. The primary-care physician usually must order all procedures and approve referrals to specialized health care providers (for example, a cardiologist) within the HMO. HMOs are one of several types of **managed care plans**. Such plans seek to control the conditions under which health care can be obtained. Examples of controls include preapproval of hospital admissions, restrictions on which hospital or doctor can be used, and mandates regarding the type of procedures that will be employed to treat a specific health problem. If the HMO itself does not provide a particular type of care, the primary care physician refers the patient to a local hospital or clinic for those services. One HMO variation is the **individual practice organization (IPO)**, a structure in which the HMO contracts with—rather than hires—groups of physicians. These physicians maintain their own offices in various locations around a community and serve as the primary-care physicians and specialists for the HMO.

Traditional Health Insurance

Health insurance provides protection against direct medical expenses resulting from illness and injury. It may cover hospital, surgical, and other medical expenditures. These coverages can be purchased separately, but most consumers and employers prefer **comprehensive health insurance** because it combines these protections into a single policy. Unlike with HMOs, where you are paying for health care in advance, health insurance is based on the concept of reimbursement for losses, with the patient choosing the type of care based on the advice of his or her physician. For this reason, health insurance plans are often referred to

Provisions of the Patient Protection and Affordable Health Care Act

Table 11-2

Topic	Description	Effective Date
Coverage for those who cannot obtain insurance	Establishes temporary insurance programs to allow employers to provide health care plans for retirees over age 55 who are not eligible for Medicare. Establishes temporary insurance programs for individuals with pre-existing conditions who have been uninsured for at least six months. These programs will phase out when required coverage and federal subsidies begin in 2014.	June 2010
Coverage for young adults	Allows children to stay on parents' policies until age 26.	September 2010
Insurance company rates	Health plans required to spend a minimum of 80% of premiums on medical claims. States and federal officials required to review premium increases of health care providers.	September 2010
Mandatory coverage requirements	Requires plans to cover, at no additional charge, most preventive care. Significantly reduces the denial of coverage for children age 18 and under with pre-existing conditions. Prohibits nongroup plans from canceling coverage.	September 2010
Maximum payouts	Companies no longer allowed to set a maximum lifetime payout amount under newly written health care policies.	September 2010
Disclosure of health care employee benefits	Employers required to report the value of health benefits on W-2 form (but this is not taxable income).	January 2011
Long-term care insurance	Under the CLASS (Community Living Assistance Services and Support) program, employed, working-age adults will have the opportunity to enroll in a long-term care plan through their employer.	October 2012
Pre-existing conditions	Prohibits the denial of coverage for persons with pre-existing conditions.	January 2014
Shopping for health care plans	A state-based health care exchange will be created to provide a marketplace where uninsured individuals and small business can comparison shop for health care plans.	January 2014
Required coverage and federal subsidies	Most Americans will be required to buy a health care plan or pay fines of $95 ($285 per family) or 1 percent of taxable income, whichever is greater. Fines will increase in 2015 and 2016 and be adjusted upward for inflation thereafter. Those who qualify based on income will be eligible for federal income tax credits for the cost of buying a health care plan.	January 2014
Maximum payouts	Companies no longer allowed to set a maximum annual payout amount under newly written health care policies.	January 2014

as **indemnity plans** or **fee-for-service plans** because they compensate the insured for the cost of care received.

Health insurance plans often identify a **preferred provider organization (PPO)**. A PPO is a group of health care providers (doctors, hospitals, and other health care providers) who contract with a health insurance company to provide services at a discount. This discount is then passed along to the policyholders in the form of reductions or elimination of deductibles and coinsurance requirements if they choose the PPO providers for their health care.

Consider the case of Dru Cameron, who works in the field of international marketing. Her firm's health insurance plan has contracted with a PPO representing a local university's teaching hospital and its affiliated physicians. Because Dru chose the university hospital for treatment of a broken ankle, she saved $150 on the $250 deductible and did not have to pay the usual 20 percent coinsurance share of office visit charges. She gave

comprehensive health insurance
Insurance that provides protection against financial losses resulting from hospital, surgical, and medical expenditures.

preferred provider organization (PPO)
Group of health care providers (doctors, hospitals, and other health care providers) who contract with a health insurance company to provide services at a discount.

consumer-driven health care
An approach to health care protection in which the consumer elects a health care plan with a high deductible and high overall policy limits.

high-deductible health care plan (HDHP)
Can either be traditional health insurance or an HMO that follows the consumer-driven health care philosophy by charging relatively high deductibles.

up the right to go to her family doctor, who is not a PPO member, although she could still see that physician for other health care needs in the future.

A **provider-sponsored network (PSN)**, also called a **provider-sponsored association**, is a group of cooperating physicians and hospitals who have banded together to offer a health insurance contract. Such networks operate primarily in rural areas, where access to HMOs may be limited. As a group, the members of the PSN coordinate and deliver health care services and manage the insurance plan financially. They contract with outside providers for health services that are not available through members of the group.

Consumer-Driven Health Care

Consumer-driven health care is an approach to health care protection where the consumer elects a health care plan with a high deductible and high overall policy limits. The principle behind consumer-driven health care is that when consumers are spending more of their own health care dollars initially, they will become knowledgeable and informed patients/employees and will spend their own money more carefully than they would spend an employer's or health plan's funds. Sellers of these products say that they give the individual the opportunity and responsibility to manage their health care costs. The higher out-of-pocket spending by consumers will encourage them to shop around, compare prices, pick and choose among options, and all the other things consumers normally do when making expensive purchases. In return, the consumer receives a high level of protection from a catastrophic, high-cost disease or injury.

High-Deductible Health Care Plan A **high-deductible health care plan (HDHP)** is a tax-exempt account created to pay for qualified medical expenses of the account holder and his or her spouse/dependents. Consumers and employers are attracted to HDHPs because the premium costs for such plans are lower than premiums for more comprehensive plans. Under HDHPs, the individual pays a smaller premium each month and, in return, the individual has a higher deductible and higher out-of-pocket expenses until catastrophic coverage begins. The minimum deductible for these plans is $1200 ($2400 for a family) but can be as high as $5000 per year. One-half of employees who are offered a high-deductible plan by their employers take it.

The plans have an annual out-of-pocket limit of $5950 for an individual or $11,900 for a family and then the catastrophic coverage kicks in. High-deductible plans have much lower premiums than other plans because consumers pay a much larger portion of their health care bills. People who must buy their own health care plan, especially

DID YOU KNOW?

How Medicare and Medicaid Differ

Medicare is for older Americans. It is funded by means of the Medicare payroll tax. This tax for most American workers is 1.45 percent of earned income. Both employees and employers pay the 1.45 percent. Beginning in 2013, high-income workers will pay a 2.35 percent Medicare tax. This affects individuals earning more than $200,000 and families earning more than $250,000; unearned income will be taxed at a 3.8 percent rate. Medicare's primary beneficiaries include people age 65 and older who are eligible for Social Security retirement benefits. Medicare is divided into two parts. Medicare

Part A is the hospitalization portion of the program; it requires no premium. Medicare Part B is the supplementary health expense insurance portion for outpatient care, doctor office visits, or certain other services of the Medicare program; it requires payment of a monthly premium.

Medicaid is for the poor, and their eligibility is based on household income and net worth. The health services provided through this program generally include hospital, surgical, and medical care. In some states, dental care for children may be covered as well. Costs are shared by federal and state governments.

younger workers, often find the lower premiums for a high-deductible plan attractive. You are required to have an HDHP in order to establish a health savings account, discussed next.

Health Savings Accounts The question, then, is how to afford the high out-of-pocket cost when health care is needed. The answer is with a **health savings account (HSA).** An HSA is a tax-deductible savings account into which individuals and/or their employers can deposit tax-sheltered funds to use later to pay medical bills including the deductibles and other out-of-pocket costs required by a high-deductible plan. The maximum annual savings deposit is $5950 for an individual or $11,900 for a family plan.

Health Reimbursement Arrangements Another consumer-driven health care program is a **health reimbursement arrangement (HRA).** An HRA consists of funds set aside by employers to reimburse employees for qualified medical expenses. Thus, the employer helps employees pay their medical bills. An HRA is funded solely by an employer. There is no limit on the employer's contributions, which are excluded from an employee's taxable income.

Flexible Spending Arrangements A flexible spending arrangement (FSA) is an employer-sponsored account that allows employee-paid expenses for medical or

health savings account (HSA)
Tax-deductible savings accounts into which individuals or employers can deposit tax-sheltered funds to pay medical bills.

health reimbursement account (HRA)
Funds that employers set aside to reimburse employees for qualified health expenses.

ADVICE FROM A PRO

Be Smart When Shopping for an Individual Health Plan

Shopping for an individual health care plan (a plan that is not provided through a group) requires a comparison of the many options available. You should focus your attention on three areas: (1) the cost, (2) the company, and (3) the plan itself. Be wary of policies that emphasize that they are "affordable" as it usually means that the coverage is very limited.

The Cost

A sound health insurance plan, when purchased outside of a group, can easily cost more than $1000 per month for a typical family of four. Obviously, comparison shopping is essential. When you apply for an individual health care plan, the company's decision whether to accept you is based on a number of underwriting factors, including your age, gender, occupation, family and personal health history, and physical condition. Each of these factors has a bearing on the likelihood of health-related expenditures and, therefore, the cost. You can access the cost of individual plans in your state at www.healthcare.gov.

   Medical information bureaus (similar to credit bureaus) maintain files on insurance applicants.* Both medical and non-medical information is maintained in these files. If you are charged more or turned down for credit or insurance because of information in such a file, you should know your consumer rights. If you were denied coverage or charged extra, you have the right to be told that the information came from a medical information bureau. You can then request a copy of the report to verify the accuracy of the information.

The Company

It is important to choose a financially sound health care company. Wise financial planners always ask about the percentage of premiums collected by an insurance company that is subsequently paid out to reimburse the losses of the participants. The **claims ratio (payout ratio)** formula is

$$\text{Claims ratio} = \frac{\text{losses paid}}{\text{premiums collected}} \quad (11.1)$$

   Top companies typically have claims ratios that exceed 90 percent. At the other extreme are companies (especially those that sell hospital indemnity and dread disease insurance by mail, the Internet, over the telephone, or through newspaper inserts) that have claims ratios of less than 25 percent. The lower the claims ratio, the lower the return (the actual benefits) to the policyholder on the premium dollar paid.

The Plan

The smart way to compare health care plans is to set some criteria in advance for judging whether a policy provides the needed coverage. The plans that do provide the needed coverage (and have high claims ratios) can then be compared on a price basis. Individual plans can have gaping holes in coverage, and no plan should be purchased "sight unseen." If an agent or company will not allow you to study a plan for a few days, buy your policy elsewhere. Do not rely solely on agent promises. Review the policy yourself.

Holly Hunts
Montana State University

* To obtain a copy of your report ($8 or free within 30 days of an adverse report), write the Medical Information Bureau at P.O. Box 105, Essex Station, Boston, MA 02112; call (617) 426-3660 for an application; or visit www.mib.com/html/request_your_record.html.

FINANCIAL POWER POINT

What If Your Employer Does Not Offer a Health Care Plan?

The 20 million workers whose employers do not offer a health care plan might select a high-deductible health care plan in conjunction with a health savings account. The monthly premium might be as low as $200.

dependent care to be paid with an employee's pretax dollars rather than after-tax income. Under a typical FSA, the employee agrees to have a certain amount deducted from each paycheck, and that amount is then deposited in a separate account called a flexible spending account. As eligible expenses are incurred, the employee requests and receives reimbursements from the account.

Here is how these three plans might fit together for an employee working for an employer that offers a choice of health care plans. The worker might choose the high-deductible plan from the options provided. The employee could then set up an HSA to set aside funds to pay the high deductible required by the HSA with the employer possibly providing funds for the HSA, as well.

What if you have no access to an employer-provided health care plan? In this case you could buy a high-deductible plan on your own and set up an HSA to set aside funds to pay the high deductible and other costs associated with the HSA.

 Concept Check 11.2

1. Distinguish between health maintenance organizations (HMOs) and traditional health insurance.

2. Identify two benefits of selecting a preferred provider organization (PPO) when seeking health care.

3. Explain the linkage between high-deductible health care plans and health savings accounts (HSAs) and health reimbursement accounts (HRAs).

YOUR HEALTH PLAN BENEFITS AND LIMITS

LEARNING OBJECTIVE 3

Describe the benefits and limitations of health care plans.

certificate of insurance
Document or booklet that outlines group health insurance benefits.

You can save yourself considerable confusion, delay, and money if you understand your health plan benefits before illness or injury strikes. If you have a group plan, you will receive a **certificate of insurance** that outlines your benefits. If you have purchased a plan on your own, you should become familiar with your health insurance policy or your HMO contract. Here are some questions to ask yourself and background information to understand what you find in these documents.

What Types of Care Are Covered?

dental expense insurance
Insurance that provides reimbursement for dental care expenses.

The typical health care plan covers hospital room and board expenses, surgical procedures both as an inpatient and outpatient, prescription drugs, diagnostic tests, visits to the doctor's office, and many other aspects of health care. Dental and vision care are generally not covered. You can buy separate **dental expense insurance** (possibly as a group plan through your employer) to provide reimbursement for dental care expenses. Orthodontic treatment is typically excluded. High deductibles and coinsurance requirements and low policy limits can make dental plans less beneficial than they might appear. **Vision care insurance** provides reimbursement for eye examinations and purchase of glasses and contact lenses. Vision care insurance is typically written on a group basis as an employee benefit. For an individual, vision care insurance is probably not a good buy because the highest expenses for eye care arise out of diseases and injuries to the eyes, which would be covered under basic health care plans.

pre-existing conditions
Medical conditions or symptoms that the plan participant knew about or had diagnosed within a certain time period before the plan effective date.

Health plans contain provisions that exclude coverage for certain **pre-existing conditions**. These are health conditions or symptoms that were known to the participant or diagnosed within a certain time period, usually one or two years, before the effective date of the plan. Pre-existing conditions can be excluded for a period of time after a plan goes into effect or, possibly, permanently. Group plans exclude fewer

What Happens to Your Health Plan When You Graduate?

College students may continue to stay on a parent's health care coverage while they are full-time students. Under the Patient Protection and Affordable Health Care Act, young adults can stay on (or be added to) a parent's plan until their 26th birthday whether in college or not. They do not need to live with or be financially dependent on the parent and can even be married. The only exception is that if a parent's employer-based plan that was in place before the law took effect excluded children, it may continue to do so.

pre-existing conditions than individual plans. The health care reform law, the Affordable Care Act, requires that starting in 2014, people with pre-existing conditions can no longer be denied health care coverage. Until then, people who have a health condition and who have been uninsured for at least six months may be able to obtain coverage via a high-risk pool administered by the federal government or their particular state (see http://naschip.org/portal). Plans may also dictate waiting periods for specific types of expenses. For example, maternity benefits often have a one-year waiting period.

Who Is Covered?

Health care plans can be written to cover an individual, a family, or a group. Few misunderstandings arise when an individual is the focus of the coverage, but family policies can be more complex. Generally, a family consists of a parent or parents and dependent children. Are children who are born while the plan is in effect automatically covered from the moment of birth? What about stepchildren? At what age are children no longer covered? These questions must be answered to ensure that all family members receive adequate protection.

When Does Coverage Begin and End?

Individual and group health care plans are usually written on an annual basis. An annual plan beginning on January 1 will start at 12:00 a.m. that day and end at 11:59 p.m. on December 31. Any illness that begins during the year will be covered. But will coverage continue if the plan expires while you are in the hospital? The answer is usually yes. Similarly, a surgical procedure performed after a plan expires but for an illness or injury for which treatment was originally begun during the plan period may be covered.

FINANCIAL POWER POINT

Making Changes in Your Group Plan

When you work for an employer that offers a group health plan, you must wait until the next **open-enrollment period** to make changes in coverage or switch among alternative plans. Open-enrollment periods occur once each year in October and last for about one month. Open-enrollment period requirements are generally waived for such family changes as births, adoptions, divorce, and marriage.

You Do Not Need to Buy Accident and Dread Disease Health Insurance

Accident and dread disease health insurance are often purchased by people who have no other health care plan or fear that their health care plan will fall short of their needs. Buying these policies is unwise. **Accident insurance** pays a specific amount per day—for example, $100 for a hospital stay arising out of an accident—or a specific amount for the loss of certain limbs or body parts—for example, $2000 for the loss of a finger or an arm. **Dread disease insurance** provides reimbursement for medical expenses arising out of the occurrence of a specific disease, such as cancer. These plans are typically highly overpriced and provide benefits much less generous than implied in sales promotions. Since the average daily cost for a hospital stay is more than $1200, these policies cover very little.

DID YOU KNOW?

Dual-Income Couples Should Coordinate Their Employee Health Care Benefits

Dual-income households often have overlapping health care benefits. For example, both Harry and Belinda Johnson's employers provide partially subsidized family health insurance plans as employee benefits. The Johnsons chose to be covered under Belinda's policy because it provides more protection and is less expensive. Belinda's coverage is fully paid for, and she can add Harry to the plan for only $125 per month.

Harry's employer offers a flexible approach toward providing employee benefits. Employees are provided with $800 per month to be used for any of the employee benefits available from a menu of benefits offered by the employer. If Harry chose his employer's health care plan, he would need to pay

$375 of the $800 for this benefit. He could use the remaining $425 for life insurance, dental insurance, disability income insurance, or an additional contribution into his 401(k) plan. Harry has decided to forgo his health insurance and will pay the extra $125 to be covered under Belinda's plan. As a result, he has $675 ($800 − $125) available for other options. Harry decided to sign up for disability and dental expense insurance and have the remainder go into his 401(k) plan.

With a group, all employees are usually covered, but new members may have to endure a waiting period before receiving protection. If the group includes the employees of a business, different protection may be offered for full-time and part-time employees. The family of the group member may be covered, but, once again, the definition of "family" must be understood.

---

guaranteed renewable policies
Policies that must be continued in force as long as the policyholder pays the required premium.

deductibles
Clauses in health care plans that require you to pay an additional portion of health expenses annually before receiving reimbursement.

copayment
A variation of a deductible that requires you to pay a specific dollar amount each time you use your benefits for a specific covered expense item.

Health care plans must be renewed each year. If you are in a group plan, you can renew your participation during the plan's open-enrollment period. Renewal of individual plans is handled in one of three ways. **Optionally renewable policies** may be canceled or changed by the plan provider but only at the time of expiration and renewal, often with 30 days' notice. **Guaranteed renewable policies** must be continued in force as long as the policyholder pays the required premium. Premiums may change but only if the change applies to an entire class of participants rather than to an individual participant. Guaranteed renewability is recommended for health care plans and long-term care insurance. **Noncancelable policies** must be continued in force without premium changes up to age 65 as long as the participant pays the required premium. Noncancelable policies are recommended when buying disability income insurance.

How Much Must You Pay Out of Your Own Pocket?

Health care plans contain provisions that specify the level of coverage for your expenses and the portion that you must pay yourself.

You Pay a Deductible Annually Deductibles are clauses in health care plans that require you to pay an initial portion of medical expenses annually before receiving reimbursement. A deductible of $200 per year, for example, would mean that the patient must pay the first $200 of the medical costs for the year. Family plans generally include a deductible for each family member (again, perhaps $200 per year) with a maximum family deductible (perhaps $500 per year). Once the deductible payments for individual family members reach the maximum family deductible ($500 in this example), further individual deductibles will be waived.

You Make a Copayment When Services Are Used A **copayment**, which is a variation of a deductible, requires you to pay a specific dollar amount each time you have a specific covered expense item. A copayment is often required for visits to the doctor's office and prescription drugs. For example, you might have to pay $25 for each prescription, with the insurer paying the remainder. A copayment differs from a deductible in that it might require that you pay $35 for each office visit even after the deductible is met.

FINANCIAL POWER POINT

All Health Care Plans Have a Grace Period

Health plans contain provisions for a grace period (typically 30 days), which prevents the lapse of a policy if a payment is late. The policy remains fully in force during the grace period but only if the insured pays the premium before the end of the grace period.

DID YOU KNOW?

Practicing a Healthy Lifestyle Can Reduce the Cost of Your Health Care Plan

Health care plans have always charged more (or even denied coverage) for people with pre-existing health conditions. Nowadays, health care plans are giving discounts to people who maintain a healthy lifestyle.

Most common are discounts for nonsmokers. Discounts are also offered those who drink alcohol in moderation, exercise regularly, and meet good health-risk assessment targets for weight, blood pressure, and cholesterol levels. Maintaining good health also pays off financially due to reduced chronic disease in later years, resulting in a longer and more productive career and a healthier retirement.

You Pay a Coinsurance Percentage of Your Charges A **coinsurance clause** requires you to pay a proportion of any loss suffered. The typical share is 80/20, with the insurer paying the larger percentage. Usually, a coinsurance cap limits the annual out-of-pocket payments required of the patient when meeting the coinsurance. The following example illustrates how a deductible of $250 and an 80/20 coinsurance provision with a $1000 coinsurance cap work together to determine the coverage for an $8760 health care bill. Because the deductible is the responsibility of the insured party, the patient pays the first $250. The coinsurance ratio is applied to the remaining $8510 ($8760 − $250) until the portion paid by the patient reaches the coinsurance cap. Thus, $1000 is covered by the insured and $4000 by the insurer. The additional expenses of $3510 ($8510 − $1000 − $4000) are covered 100 percent by the insurance company up to the overall limits of coverage (perhaps $100,000). In this example, the insured party will pay $1250 ($250 deductible + $1000 coinsurance) and the insurer will pay $7510 ($4000 coinsurance + $3510 remaining charges).

coinsurance clause
Requires the insured to pay a proportion of any loss suffered.

You Pay the Remainder After Policy Limits Are Reached Policy limits specify the maximum dollar amounts that a health insurance plan will pay to reimburse a covered loss. To illustrate policy limits for a health insurance plan, we will consider the case of Karl Gruenfeld, an unmarried medical technologist from Council Bluffs, Iowa.

- **Item limits** specify the maximum reimbursement for a particular health care expense. Karl's policy contains a $75 maximum per X ray. Karl was undergoing treatment for lung cancer in early 2011 and then had a heart attack later that same year. During the year, he incurred X-ray expenses of $2880 (24 sets of X rays at $120 each). The policy will pay $1800 (24 × $75) of this expense, and Karl must pay the remaining $1080.

- **Daily limits** are common in low-cost and supplemental hospital insurance plans. A frequently cited limit is $1000 per day. This may seem adequate, but the average for a hospital bill is over $1200 per day and $2500 for intensive-care units, and these figures only include the hospital expense portion of the total health care bill.

- **Episode limits** specify the maximum payment for health care expenses arising from a single episode of illness or injury, with each episode being considered separately. Karl's policy contains an episode limit of $600,000 for all covered expenses. The cost of Karl's cancer treatments amounted to over $550,000 (including the covered portion of the X rays). His policy will pay all of these charges. In September, Karl suffered a heart attack with various expenses amounting to $175,000. His policy will pay these expenses in full because the heart attack is considered a separate episode rather than a continuation of the first, which would have put him over the $600,000 limit.

item limits
Specify the maximum reimbursement for a particular health care expense.

Disputes may arise over whether a recurrence of an illness represents a separate episode. A **recurring clause** clarifies conditions under which a recurrence of an illness is considered a continuation of the first episode or a separate episode. If the recurrence is considered a separate episode, the deductible may need to be paid, but

coordination-of-benefits clause
Prevents an individual from collecting insurance benefits that exceed the loss suffered by noting the order in which plans will pay if the insured individual is covered by multiple plans.

premium conversion plans
With premium conversion, the employee's share of the premiums is paid with pretax dollars; those amounts are not included when the employer reports the employee's income to the IRS.

flexible spending arrangements
Employer arrangements that allow employees to place a portion of their salary into an account that is used to pay some of their health care expenditures, including employee-paid health plan premiums.

reimbursement will be available up to the full episode limit. If the recurrence is considered a continuation of the original episode, the second deductible will not apply, but the loss may exceed the episode limit.

- **Annual limits** specify the maximum payment for covered expenses occurring within one year. Consider Karl's cancer treatments and heart attack. If his policy had contained a $750,000 annual limit as was allowed in 2011, Karl would have used $725,000 ($550,000 + $175,000) of this amount and would have only $25,000 ($750,000 − $725,000) remaining for the year. Under the Affordable Care Act, annual limits must be at least $2 million in 2012, and all such limits will be prohibited in 2014 and beyond.

Coordination of Benefits A **coordination-of-benefits clause** prevents you from collecting insurance benefits that exceed the loss suffered. Such a clause designates the order in which plans will pay benefits if multiple plans apply to a loss. The primary plan is the first applied to any loss when more than one plan provides coverage. If it fails to reimburse 100 percent of the loss, then any secondary (or excess) plans will be applied in order until the loss is fully paid or until benefits are exhausted, whichever occurs first.

DID YOU KNOW?

The Tax Consequences of Managing Health Expenses

The Internal Revenue Code allows several avenues for reducing income taxes when you spend your own money on health care plan premiums and health care expenses:

1. Many employees may save on taxes when they use **premium conversion plans** to pay their health care insurance premiums (discussed in Chapter 1). With premium conversion, the employee's share of the premiums is paid with pretax dollars; those amounts are not included when the employer reports the employee's taxable income to the IRS.

2. Many employers offer **flexible spending arrangements**, allowing employees to place a portion of their salary into

an account that is used to pay some of their health care expenditures, including employee-paid health plan premiums (discussed in Chapter 1). Flexible spending accounts are a "use it or lose it" proposition, and annual contributions will be capped at $2500 beginning in 2013. Thus, you should set aside only an amount that you are sure you will use.

Health care expenditures (including a portion of certain long-term care insurance premiums) can be used as itemized deductions on one's income tax return. Self-employed people may deduct (as a business expense, not an itemized deduction) the cost of health care plan premiums for themselves and their dependents.

ADVICE FROM A PRO

Maintain Your Health Care Plan Between Jobs

What happens when you no longer work for an employer that offers a group health care plan and you want to continue the coverage? You can assert your **COBRA rights** (Consolidated Omnibus Budget Reconciliation Act of 1985). These rules allow you to remain a member of a group health plan for as long as 18 months if you worked for an employer with more than 20 workers. COBRA applies to you and to any of your dependents who had been covered under the employer's plan. COBRA rights apply to your dependents for 36 months. These rights

must be exercised within 60 days after the termination of employment, and you must pay the full premiums (including both the employee's and the employer's portions) plus a 2 percent administrative fee.

Eligibility to remain under the group plan eventually will run out. Federal law also mandates **guaranteed portability** that allows you to convert your group coverage to individual coverage within 180 days before COBRA ends, if that is part of the employer's plan originally or as amended. Your individual policy premiums will be higher, but the waiting period and pre-existing condition provisions will not apply.

You might be tempted to go without coverage for a time because of the high cost of converting your previous plan, you expect to have a job soon that will provide coverage, or simply because you are healthy and expect to stay that way. This latter reason is shortsighted because young people do get sick or are injured. For example, young adults are at higher risk for automobile injuries, and your car insurance will cover only a small portion of your medical bills if you are seriously injured in an accident. So what should you do?

Buy short-term health insurance. These plans can be paid for monthly for a term of six months or a year and may be renewable. Coverage for a premium of perhaps $200 per month may be available. These plans are not as compre-hensive, of course, but they cover the basics. Select a plan with a high limit and a high deductible to be covered for a serious illness. You can pay for routine doctor's office visits out of pocket.

Going without health insurance has an added risk. If you develop a serious medical condition while uninsured, it will be considered a pre-existing condition and make coverage difficult or impossible to obtain in the future. Bottom line . . . stay insured. You can search for plans in your locality at http://finder.healthcare.gov.

William Dean
Southern University, Baton Rouge, Louisiana

 Concept Check 11.3

1. What are pre-existing conditions, and how do they affect coverage under health plans?

2. Distinguish among a deductible, a copayment, and coinsurance.

3. Explain COBRA rights and portability rights that apply when you leave a job that has a group health care plan.

4. Distinguish among item limits, episode limits, and annual limits as used in health care plans.

5. Distinguish among optionally renewable, guaranteed renewable, and noncancelable health care plans.

6. List three ways you can save on taxes when paying for health care or insurance.

PROTECT YOUR INCOME DURING DISABILITY

A number of resources are available for income protection during a period of disability. Many U.S. workers have sick-pay benefits that can help ease the burden of a short period of disability, such as four weeks. Disability income insurance is probably the most over-looked type of insurance, though it is vitally important for all workers. For example, a 22-year-old without dependents would probably need no life insurance but would likely need disability insurance for support during a period of disability. While employer-based retirement plans provide benefits to workers who become disabled while still employed, such benefits plans fall far short of fully meeting the needs of workers who have accumulated little or no retirement savings.

COBRA rights
The Consolidated Omnibus Budget Reconciliation Act of 1985 allows a former employee to remain a member of a group health plan for as long as 18 months if the employee worked for an employer with more than 20 workers.

guaranteed portability
Provision that allows an individual to convert group coverage to individual coverage within 180 days before COBRA ends.

What Is Your Level of Need?

The first question to ask when contemplating disability income insurance is, "How much protection do I need?" The dollar limits on disability income policies are written either in increments of $100 per month or as a percentage of monthly income. Policy coverage is limited to 60 to 80 percent of the insured's after-tax earnings. Note that the government's Social Security disability income program may provide $14,000 to $28,000 annually in tax-free income to the family of a fully insured disabled worker. See Appendix B at the end of the book or the *Garman/Forgue* companion website for an illustration of how to estimate these benefits, or visit www.ssa.gov/top10.html.

Determining the amount of additional protection needed is challenging because some sources of help may not actually be available for all disabilities. It is smart to

 LEARNING OBJECTIVE 4

Develop a plan to protect your income when you cannot work due to disability.

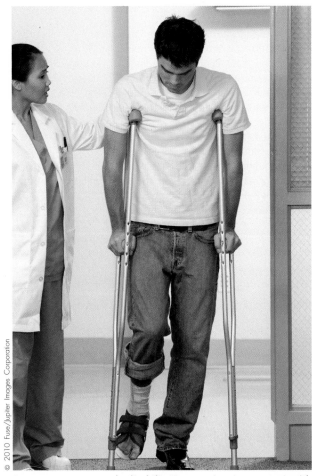

A young person needs disability income insurance even with no dependents.

complete the calculations in the Run the Numbers feature, "Determining Disability Income Insurance Needs." You can use the figure obtained in the worksheet as a starting point when shopping for disability income insurance protection.

RUN THE NUMBERS

Determining Disability Income Insurance Needs

The determination of disability insurance needs begins with your current monthly after-tax income. From this figure, subtract the amounts you would receive from Social Security disability and other sources of disability income. The resulting figure will provide an estimate of extra coverage needed.

Decision Factor	Example	Your Figures
1. Current monthly after-tax income	$2,100	_____
2. Minus previous established disability income protections	+ $ 750	_____
(a) Monthly Social Security disability benefits	_____	_____
(b) Monthly benefit from employer-provided disability insurance	600	_____
(c) Monthly benefit from private disability insurance	_____	_____
(d) Monthly benefit from other government disability insurance	_____	_____
Total Subtraction	−1,350	_____
3. Estimated monthly disability income insurance needs	$ 750	_____

What Disability Income
Insurance Policy Provisions Best Meet Your Need?

Once you have estimated your level of need, you can begin your search for a disability income insurance policy. Look first for the major policy provisions, discussed in the following paragraphs, that meet your needs. Disability income insurance policies are complicated so avoid relying on the verbal assurances of the agent selling the policy, do your own analysis, and seek the advice of a financial planner.

Waiting Period The **waiting period (elimination period)** in a disability income policy is the time period between the onset of the disability and the date that disability benefits begin. Because disability income benefits are paid monthly, the first check will not arrive until 30 days after the end of the waiting period.

Benefit Period The **benefit period** in a disability income policy is the maximum period of time for which benefits will be paid. It begins when the elimination period ends. The benefit period is usually stated in years but may instead state a specific age when benefits will cease. Most disability income policies will not pay past age 65.

Degree of Disability Policies can be written on an "own-occupation" or "any-occupation" basis. An **own-occupation policy** will provide benefits if you can no longer perform the occupation you had at the time you became disabled. An **any-occupation policy** will provide full benefits only if you cannot perform any occupation. In effect, an any-occupation policy is an income replacement policy, as it makes up a portion of the difference between what you were earning prior to becoming disabled and what you can earn while disabled. Own-occupation policies are more generous and, therefore, cost more. Some policies provide own-occupation coverage during the first two years of a disability, and then switch to an any-occupation basis with income replacement for the remaining years of the benefits. Such **split-definition policies** are likely to provide benefits for rehabilitation and retraining at insurance company expense.

A **residual clause** is a feature of own-occupation policies that allows for some reduced level of disability income benefits when a partial—rather than full—disability occurs. Consider the case of Françoise LaDeux, a criminal lawyer in Providence, Rhode Island, who purchased a disability policy offering a benefit of $3000 per month. Françoise later developed multiple sclerosis and was forced to cut back her workload by 50 percent, thereby taking a 50 percent pay cut. Her disability policy had a residual clause, so she received $1500 (0.50 × $3000) per month during her disability.

FINANCIAL
POWER POINT

Disability Income Insurance Can Be More Important Than Life Insurance

At age 22, a person's chances of becoming disabled for at least three months are seven times greater than his or her chances of dying. Disability income insurance is more important for young, single adults than life insurance.

waiting period
The time period between the onset of a disability and the date that disability benefits begin.

benefit period
The maximum period of time for which benefits will be paid under a disability income or other insurance policy.

any-occupation policy
Provides full benefits only if the insured cannot perform any occupation.

residual clause
Feature of own-occupation policies that allows for some reduced level of disability income benefits when a partial—rather than full—disability strikes.

DID YOU KNOW?

Sean's Success Story

Early in his working life, Sean recognized that financial success is not simply a matter of making more money and building assets. He also focused on protecting his assets and income through the purchase of insurance. Sean has always been healthy but knew that illness and accidents happen all the time. His first step was to sign up for the health care plan offered by his employer. He selected the high-deductible plan to keep his costs under control and signed up for a health savings account

to accumulate funds for his out-of-pocket health care expenses. In addition, Sean used a premium conversion option to pay his portion of the plan's cost on a pretax basis, and he set up a flexible spending arrangement with his employer. Sean also considered the risk of being unable to work due to illness or injury. Fortunately his employer offered a group disability income insurance plan, and Sean signed up for the plan and selected a 120-day waiting period and a ten-year benefit that would pay 60 percent of his salary should he not be able to work.

DID YOU KNOW?

Workers' Comp Pays If You Are Hurt on the Job

If you are injured on the job or become ill as a direct result of your employment, state law requires your employer to pay any resulting medical costs. **Workers' compensation insurance** covers employers for liability losses for injury or disease suffered by employees that result from employment-related causes. The benefits to the employee include health care, recuperative care, replacement of lost income, and, if necessary, rehabilitation. Thus, workers' compensation insurance covers the full range of health-related losses. Because only those losses resulting from work-related accidents are covered and benefits are limited, workers' compensation can only supplement your total health insurance plan.

Social Security rider

Provides an extra dollar amount of protection if a person fails to qualify for Social Security disability benefits (70 percent of all applicants are rejected).

A Social Security Rider Provides Additional Protection If you have figured your disability income insurance needs assuming that you would receive Social Security benefits, you will find yourself with inadequate protection if your Social Security application is denied (70 percent of all applicants are rejected). To provide an extra dollar amount of protection if you fail to qualify for Social Security disability benefits, a **Social Security rider** may be added to your policy. Consider the case of Karen Gifford, a florist from Urbana, Illinois. Karen determined that her disability insurance needs would be $1400 per month after assuming that she would receive $1000 from Social Security if she were to become disabled. She could have purchased a $2400-per-month policy and removed all uncertainty, but the premium would have been more than she could afford. Instead, she bought a $1400 policy with a $1000 Social Security rider for a premium savings of 30 percent.

Cost-of-Living Adjustments You are wise to seek out a policy with a **cost-of-living clause**, which will increase your benefit amount to keep up with inflation. You might also consider buying a policy that limits benefits to a percentage of income rather than a specific dollar amount per month. With such a policy, your potential monthly benefit would increase automatically as your income increases.

DID YOU KNOW?

Turn Bad Habits into Good Ones

Do You Do This?	*Do This Instead!*
Simply assume your health care plan provides the coverage you want	Read the plan documents and make the changes desired
Pay all of your medical expenses with after-tax dollars	Sign up for a premium conversion plan for your health insurance payments, a flexible savings arrangement, and a health savings account to save on taxes
Ignore the potential for lost income if you became sick or injured	Explore the purchases of disability income insurance through your employer or on your own.
Go without a health care plan if a group plan is not available through your or a family member's employer	Buy a short-term plan until such time as a group plan becomes available
Ignore your employer's open-enrollment period	Use open enrollment to reassess all of your employee benefits including those related to health care

Concept Check 11.4

1. Explain how you determine your level of need for disability income insurance.

2. Identify the major policy provisions to consider when purchasing disability income insurance.

3. Distinguish between any-occupation and own-occupation disability income insurance plans.

4. Describe how you might adjust the waiting period on a disability income insurance policy in order to affordably obtain a longer benefit period.

DID YOU KNOW?

Higher Deductibles and Longer Waiting Periods Can Protect You from Catastrophe

Recall from Chapter 10 that it is smart to insure against the losses you cannot afford and handle more affordable losses on your own. This large-loss principle should be your guide for health-related risks as well. Here is how to apply it:

1. *If you do not have access to a health care plan at work and have limited resources to buy a health care plan on your own, you can use a high-deductible health care plan in conjunction with a health savings account (HSA) (see page 327). This will affordably protect you against catastrophic direct medical costs.*

2. *Select a long benefit period for both your disability income and long-term care insurance needs. For an equivalent dollar amount, you can buy many more years of protection by extending the waiting period only slightly as illustrated graphically here.*

For $X you might buy a plan with a short waiting period (WP) and a short benefit period (BP):

WP	BP	Coverage Has Run Out

Even better, for the same $X you might buy a plan with a slightly longer waiting period (WP) and a much longer benefit period (BP):

WP	BP	Coverage Has Run Out

PLANNING FOR LONG-TERM CUSTODIAL CARE

Many health care episodes include a period of time when the patient no longer needs skilled medical care but does need assistance to a degree that requires confinement in a nursing home or special help at home. This need is especially prevalent with the extremely elderly and patients with certain conditions such as Alzheimer's disease. Such costs are not covered by HMOs, health insurance, or Medicare because the care is usually considered "not medically necessary" by these providers. Elderly who have spent down their assets then may be eligible to receive Medicaid reimbursement for a portion of their custodial long-term and nursing home care. But for others, a long-term care policy may be an important part of one's health care planning.

Factors to assess when considering a long-term care policy include the following:

1. **The degree of impairment required for benefits to begin.** Insurance companies use the inability to perform a certain number of **activities of daily living (ADLs)** as a criterion for deciding when the insured becomes eligible for long-term care benefits. Typically, a

DID YOU KNOW?

Your Worst Financial Blunders in Managing Health Expenses

Based on others' financial woes, you will make mistakes in personal finance when you:

1. *Go unprotected for health care when you change jobs.*

2. *Duplicate employer-provided health care protection with your employed spouse.*

3. *Ignore your need for disability income insurance.*

activities of daily living (ADLs)
Insurance companies use the inability to perform a certain number of such activities as a criterion for deciding when the insured becomes eligible for long-term care benefits.

skilled nursing care
Intended for people who need intensive care, that is, 24-hour-a-day supervision and treatment by a registered nurse under the direction of a doctor.

benefit amount
Long-term care plans are generally written to provide a specific dollar benefit per day of care.

FINANCIAL POWER POINT

Who Most Needs Long-Term Care Insurance

Low-wealth, low-income individuals can be covered for long-term care expenses under the Medicaid program. Those who have accumulated retirement nest eggs approaching $500,000 generally can afford the cost of long-term care. It is those in the middle who most need long-term care insurance.

DO IT NOW!

You know more about personal finance after reading this chapter, so get started right now by:

1. *Learning exactly what group health care coverage you actually do have through your job, your school, and/or your family.*

2. *Investigating the possibility of saving on income taxes via a premium conversion plan, flexible spending arrangement, or health savings account (HSA).*

3. *Identifying one behavior that you engage in that could lead to health problems later in life and taking steps to reduce its impact.*

policy pays benefits when a person cannot perform two or three ADLs without assistance. The ADLs commonly used in this type of decision making are bathing, bladder control, dressing oneself, eating without assistance, toileting (moving on and off the toilet), and transferring (getting in and out of bed). Because bathing is often one of the first ADLs that is lost, a policy that does not list bathing as a criterion makes it more difficult to reach the threshold at which benefits become available.

2. **The level of care covered.** The levels of nursing home care are usually categorized three ways. **Skilled nursing care** is intended for people who need intensive care, meaning 24-hour-a-day supervision and treatment by a registered nurse, under the direction of a doctor. **Intermediate care** is appropriate for people who do not require around-the-clock nursing but who are not able to live alone. **Custodial care** is suitable for many people who do not need skilled nursing care but who nevertheless require supervision (for example, help with eating or personal hygiene). Insurance companies' definitions of these levels of care may differ and must be considered when policies are evaluated. Although the largest expenses related to long-term care result from a stay in a nursing home, many people are able to remain in their homes with the assistance of visiting nurses, therapists, and even housekeepers. Long-term care policies can be written to cover such in-home care.

3. **The person's age.** The younger the person is when the policy is purchased, the lower the premium as the odds of needing care increase with age. The trade-off lies between buying young and paying premiums for many years versus waiting to purchase a policy, at which time it may be difficult to afford coverage because of pre-existing conditions and consequently high policy costs.

4. **The benefit amount.** Long-term care plans are generally written to provide a specific dollar benefit per day of care. If the cost per day for nursing homes in your geographic area is typically $140, you might buy a policy for $110 per day, thereby coinsuring for a portion of the expenses.

5. **The benefit period.** Although it is possible to buy a policy with lifetime benefits, this option can be very expensive. The average nursing home stay is about two and one-half years. A policy with a three-year limit might cost one-third less than a policy with a lifetime benefit period.

6. **The waiting period.** Policies can pay benefits from the first day of nursing home care or they can include a waiting period. Selecting a 30-day or 90-day waiting period can significantly reduce premiums.

7. **Inflation protection.** If a policy is purchased prior to age 60, the buyer faces a significant risk in that inflation may render the daily benefit woefully inadequate when care is ultimately needed. Some policies increase the daily benefit by 4 or 5 percent per year to adjust for inflation, but this protection adds considerably to the premium. The younger your age when a policy is purchased, the more you need inflation protection.

✔ Concept Check 11.5

1. Describe the protections provided by long-term care insurance.

2. Distinguish between the benefit period and the waiting period for a long-term care policy.

3. List three aspects of long-term care insurance that affect the cost of a policy.

WHAT DO YOU RECOMMEND NOW?

Now that you have read the chapter on health care planning, what do you recommend to Danielle DiMartino in the case at the beginning of the chapter regarding:

1. Choosing among the four alternatives available to her?

2. Danielle's concerns about providing for her mother's health care needs?

3. Danielle's need for her own disability income insurance?

4. How Danielle can cover her long-term care risk?

© 2011 Jupiter Images Corporation

BIG PICTURE SUMMARY OF LEARNING OBJECTIVES

LO1. Identify ways that people can manage the financial burdens resulting from illness or injury.

Health-related losses include the cost of direct health care, the cost of rehabilitation and custodial care, and the lost income when one is ill or injured. Protection from the costs of direct health care is provided by a health care plan. Long-term care insurance can protect you from rehabilitation and custodial care costs. Disability income insurance can replace income lost while disabled.

LO2. Distinguish among the types of protection for direct health expenses.

HMOs, traditional health insurance, and consumer-driven health plans address the need for direct health care. HMOs provide health care on a prepaid basis. Health insurance will reimburse you or pay your medical bills directly. Consumer-driven health care plans require that consumers pay a higher portion of the costs out of pocket. Health savings accounts provide a tax-sheltered way to save up the funds to pay these costs. Health reimbursement accounts allow an employer to help pay these costs for an employee.

LO3. Describe the benefits and limitations of health care plans.

Health care policies contain language that outlines coverage in general and, more important, describes the limitations and conditions that determine the level of protection afforded under the plan. Some of the more important plan provisions include what types of care are covered, who is covered under the plan, and the time period for the coverage. Important limitations on coverage include deductibles and copayments, coinsurance requirements, and policy limits.

LO4. Develop a plan to protect your income when you cannot work due to disability.

Disability income insurance replaces a portion of the income lost when you cannot work as a result of illness or injury. The amount you need is equal to your monthly after-tax income less any benefits to which you are entitled (for example, Social Security). By selecting among various policy provisions, you can tailor a policy that fills any gaps in your existing disability protection.

LO5. Explain how to protect yourself from the expenses for long-term care.

Long-term care insurance provides a per-day dollar reimbursement when the insured person must stay in a nursing home or other long-term care facility. It is not designed to provide health care protection, as that coverage is available through other plans such as an HMO, private insurance, or Medicare/Medicaid. Medicaid does provide long-term care benefits, but Medicare does not.

LET'S TALK ABOUT IT

1. **Your Health Care Plan.** Are you covered by a health care plan? If so, what do you see as the largest potential for losses if you become ill or injured? How well do you understand the plan?

2. **HMOs Versus Health Insurance.** HMO plans and health insurance plans take different approaches to health care. What are the major differences between the two types of plans? Which plan would you prefer for your own health care protection?

3. **Long-Term Care Insurance.** Are you covered by a long-term care insurance plan? What would happen if you became so incapacitated that such care was necessary? What could you do?

4. **Disability Income Insurance.** Are you covered by disability income insurance? What would happen if you were unable to work for two or three years because of illness or injury?

5. **Patient Protection and Affordable Health Care Act.** Much controversy remains about the health care reform law. Many of the provisions are already in effect, and others are scheduled to be in effect soon (see "Did You Know? The Essence of Health Care Reform"). Do you support the law? If not, which provisions (listed in Table 11-2), if any, would you like to see eliminated?

DO THE MATH

1. **Health Care Coverage Amounts.** Christina Haley of San Marcos, Texas, age 61, recently suffered a severe stroke. She was in intensive care for 12 days and was hospitalized for 18 more days. After being discharged from the hospital, she spent 45 days in a nursing home for medically necessary nursing and rehabilitative care. Christina had a comprehensive health insurance plan through her employer. The policy had a $1000 deductible, a $50,000 episode limit, and a $250,000 annual limit with an 80/20 coinsurance clause with a $2000 coinsurance cap. Christina's policy covered the medically necessary services performed in a nursing home setting. Her total bill was $125,765.

   (a) How much of Christina's expenses was paid by her insurance policy?

   (b) How much did Christina pay?

2. **Health Care Coverage Amounts.** Michael Howitt of Berkley, Michigan, recently had his gallbladder removed. His total bill for this event, which was his only health care expense for the year, came to $13,890. His health insurance plan has a $500 annual deductible and an 80/20 coinsurance provision. The cap on Michael's coinsurance share is $2000.

   (a) How much of the bill will Michael pay?

   (b) How much of the bill will be paid by Michael's insurance?

FINANCIAL PLANNING CASES

CASE 1

The Johnsons Consider Buying Disability Insurance

Although Belinda's employer offers a generous employee benefit program, it does not provide disability income protection other than 8 sick days per year, which may accumulate to 20 days if Belinda does not use them. Harry also has no disability income insurance. Although both have worked long enough to qualify for Social Security disability benefits, Belinda has estimated that Harry would receive about $640 and she would receive about $800 per month from Social Security. Harry and Belinda realize that they could not maintain their current living standards on only one salary. Thus, the need for disability income insurance has become evident even though they probably cannot afford such protection at this time. In fact, they chose not to purchase the disability waiver of premium option when they purchased their life insurance. Advise them on the following points:

(a) Use the Run the Numbers worksheet on page 334 to determine how much disability insurance Harry and Belinda each need. Use the December salary figures from Table 3-6 on page 88. To determine the amount of taxes and Social Security paid by each, assume that Harry, whose salary represents approximately 40 percent of their total income, paid a comparable percentage of the taxes.

(b) Use the information on pages 333–337 to advise the Johnsons about their selections related to the following major policy provisions:

1. Elimination period

2. Benefit period

3. Residual clause

4. Social Security rider

5. Cost-of-living adjustments

CASE 2

The Hernandezes Face the Possibility of Long-Term Care

Victor Hernandez recently learned that his uncle has Alzheimer's Disease. While discussing this tragedy with Maria, he realized that two of his grandparents probably had the disease, although no formal diagnosis was ever made. As a result, Victor and Maria have become interested in how they might protect themselves from the financial effects of long-term health care.

(a) What factors should the Hernandezes consider as they shop for long-term care protection?

(b) Victor is still in his 40s. How does his age affect their decisions related to long-term care protection?

CASE 3

Julia Price Assesses Her Health Care Plan

Julia is about to change jobs. Her new employer offers several different health care plans including a traditional fee-for-service plan with a PPO, an HMO, and a high-deductible health care plan. Her employer will pay the first $300 per month for any plan she chooses. This means that Julia will have to pay the remainder of the premium for the plan plus the deductible and coinsurance and copayments. These costs are higher than they were at her previous employer, and she is concerned about the added expenses. After talking with the employee benefits office at the new firm, she is considering saving money by opting for the high-deductible plan and signing up for a health savings account, a premium conversion plan, and a flexible spending arrangement. Offer your opinions about her thinking.

CASE 4

A New Employee Ponders Disability Insurance

Jim Napier of Indiana, Pennsylvania, recently took a new job as a manufacturer's representative for an aluminum castings company. While looking over his employee benefits materials, he discovered that his employer would provide 10 sick days per year, and he can accumulate these to a maximum of 60 sick days if any go unused in a given year. In addition, his employer provides a $1000-per-month, short-term, one-year total disability policy. When he called the employee benefits office, Jim found that he might qualify for $500 per month in Social Security disability benefits if he became unable to work. Jim earns a base salary of $2000 per month and expects to earn about that same amount in commissions, for an average after-tax income of $3100 per month. After considering this information, Jim became understandably concerned that a disability might destroy his financial future.

(a) What is the level of Jim's short-term, one-year disability insurance needs?

(b) What is the level of Jim's long-term disability insurance needs?

(c) Help Jim select from among the important disability insurance policy provisions to design a disability insurance program tailored to his needs.

CASE 5

A CPA Selects a Health Care Plan

Your friend Taliesha Jackson of Stillwater, Oklahoma, recently changed to a new job as a CPA in a moderate-size accounting firm. Knowing that you were taking a personal finance course, she asked your advice about selecting the best health insurance plan. Her employer offered five options. In addition, she could open a flexible spending arrangement and pay any premiums she must pay through a premium conversion plan:

- **Option A:** A comprehensive health insurance plan with a $500 annual deductible and an 80 percent/20 percent coinsurance clause with a $2000 out-of-pocket limit. The policy has a $500,000 lifetime limit. Taliesha must pay $60 per month toward this plan.

- **Option B:** Same as option A except that a PPO is associated with the plan. If Taliesha agrees to have services provided by the PPO, her annual deductible drops to $100 and the coinsurance clause is waived. As an incentive to get employees to select option B, Taliesha's employer will provide dental expense insurance worth about $40 per month.

- **Option C:** A comprehensive health insurance plan with a $200 annual deductible and a 90 percent/10 percent coinsurance clause with a $1000 out-of-pocket limit. This has a $1 million lifetime limit. Taliesha must pay $150 per month toward the cost of this plan.

- **Option D:** Membership in an HMO. Taliesha will have to contribute $40 extra each month if she chooses this option.

- **Option E:** A high-deductible health plan at no monthly cost to Taliesha. The annual deductible is $3000. There is a 90 percent/10 percent coinsurance provision. The annual out-of-pocket maximum is $5000. Her employer offers a $1000 health reimbursement account, and if she chooses, Taliesha can set up an HSA to help her pay her expenses during the year.

(a) To help her make a decision, Taliesha has asked you to list two positive points and two negative points about each plan. Prepare such a list.

(b) Why might Taliesha's employer provide an incentive of dental insurance if she chooses option B?

(c) Which plan would you recommend to Taliesha? Why?

BE YOUR OWN PERSONAL FINANCIAL MANAGER

1. **How Do You Pay for Your Health Care?** Make a list of the health care services that you used last year and estimate the cost of each of those services. Then indicate how these costs were paid, whether by yourself, by a health plan, or shared. Write a summary of what you have learned about how your health care expenses are paid.

2. **Analyze Your Health Care Plan!** Obtain a copy of your health insurance policy or the explanation of benefits brochure if you are covered by a group plan. Analyze the plan by focusing on the types of care covered, persons covered, its deductibles, coinsurance and copay amounts, dollar limits, and any restrictions on providers of your health care.

3. **What Level of Social Security Disability Benefits Is Available to You?** Visit the website for the Social Security Administration and use its online calculator at www.ssa.gov/planners/benefitcalculators.htm to determine whether you are currently eligible to receive Social Security disability insurance benefits if you become disabled and the projected level of those benefits.

MY PERSONAL FINANCIAL PLANNER

4. **Calculate Your Need for Disability Income Insurance.** Use the Run the Numbers worksheet and material on page 334 or Worksheet 46: Determining My Disability Income Insurance Needs from "My Personal Financial Planner" to estimate the amount you would need to replace should you become disabled.

5. **Explore Your Options for Saving on Taxes via Your Health Care Plan.** Are you currently employed and eligible to participate in an employer-sponsored health care plan? Use the material on pages 326–328 and 332 to assess the opportunities you have to make use of premium conversion, a flexible spending account, high-deductible health care plan, and a health savings account to lower your after-tax cost of health care.

ON THE 'NET

Go to the Web pages indicated to complete these exercises. You can also go to the *Garman/Forgue* companion website at www.cengagebrain.com for an expanded list of exercises. Under General Business, select the title of this text. Click on the Internet Exercises link for this chapter.

1. **Assessing the Quality of a Health Care Plan.** Visit the website for the National Committee for Quality Assurance at www.ncqa.org, where you will find a link to its "report cards" on quality and accreditation status of health plans. If you are covered by a health plan, search for information on your plan. If you are not covered or if data are not available on your plan, select a major city and obtain the report on a plan in that city. What information, criteria, and other data in the report might assist you in assessing the quality of any plan?

2. **Understanding Health Care Reform.** Visit the website for U.S. Department of Health and Human Services at www.healthcare.gov/law/introduction/index.html for information on the health care reform law. What provisions in the law will be most beneficial to you in your current life situation? How might the law affect you once you graduate?

3. **Benefiting from Long-term Care Insurance.** Visit the website for U.S. Department of Health and Human Services at www.longtermcare.gov and read its information on long-term care insurance. How might such protection fit into your risk-management program or that of your family?

ACTION INVOLVEMENT PROJECTS

1. **Views Concerning Having Health Care Protection.** Talk to five fellow students who are not taking your personal finance class. Ask them to explain their feelings about their health care plan if they have one and about not having protection if they do not. Then ask them how they plan to meet their health care needs once they graduate. Make a table that summarizes your findings.

2. **What Is It Like to Choose Among an Employer's Health Care Options?** Survey three individuals or couples who are covered by a group health care plan at work. Ask them how they went about making the choice among the plans the employer offered. Include a discussion of how they approach the same decisions when the open-enrollment period occurs with the plan each October. Write a summary of their responses and how their experiences affected your thinking about an employer-provided plan.

3. **Applying the Large-Loss Principle to Health Care Planning.** The large-loss principle says that one is better off paying a higher initial portion of any loss and expanding the coverage for the largest and most catastrophic losses. In health care planning, this would mean selecting a high-deductible health care plan for your direct health care expenses and a longer waiting period and longer benefit period for your disability

income and long-term care insurance plans. Talk to three students in your personal finance class on their views of this approach. Also talk to three people outside of your class who are covered by a health care plan for their views. Write a summary of the responses of these two groups and how their views affect your own thinking about the large-loss principle.

4. **Addressing the Need for Disability Income Insurance.** Talk to a family member who has gone through the process of deciding about disability income insurance. Ask what motivated him or her to decide to buy or not buy such insurance. Also ask about which aspects were the most difficult part of the process. Write a summary of the responses and how your family member's efforts, or lack thereof, affect your thinking about disability income insurance.

5. **Planning for Long-Term Care.** Talk to a family member who has had to decide how to meet the long-term care needs of a loved one. Ask what aspects were the most difficult part of the process. Also ask your family member how going through the process affected his or her thinking about planning for their own long-term care needs. Write a summary of your family member's responses and how his or her efforts, or lack thereof, affect your thinking about long-term care.

Visit the Garman/Forgue companion website at **www.cengagebrain.com**.

YOU MUST BE KIDDING, RIGHT?

Michelle and Jason Bailey are in their early 30s and expecting their first child next month. Each earns about $40,000 per year. Currently, they have $20,000 life insurance policies on each of their lives with the other named as the beneficiary. They bought these policies a few years ago to pay for death-related expenses if tragedy struck. With the baby coming, they are thinking about buying $300,000 in life insurance coverage on each of their lives so the proceeds could be used to replace the income lost if one of them died. How much will Michelle and Jason each pay for this additional protection?

A. About $25 per month   C. About $100 per month

B. About $50 per month   D. About $200 per month

The answer is A. Term life insurance for people in their 30s costs about $1 per $1000 of coverage per year. Thus, Michelle and Jason could each buy this insurance for $300 each or about $25 per month—a small price to pay for the security provided. Always buy inexpensive term life insurance so that you replace the lost income needed by your dependents if you were to pass away!

LEARNING OBJECTIVES

After reading this chapter, you should be able to:

1. Understand the reasons why you might need life insurance and calculate the appropriate amount of coverage.

2. Distinguish among types of life insurance.

3. Explain the major provisions of life insurance policies.

4. Apply a step-by-step strategy for implementing a life insurance plan.

© PETER DAZELEY/GETTY IMAGES, INC.

WHAT DO YOU RECOMMEND?

Karen Bridgeman, age 28, and her husband Will, age 30, are planning to start a family in the next year. Both have small cash-value life insurance policies ($25,000 and $50,000, respectively) that their parents purchased when they were children. Karen is a real estate attorney and earns $90,000 per year. She plans to continue working after having a child. Karen's employer offers a 401(k) plan into which she contributes a maximum of 6 percent of her salary each year matched by her employer one-half of 1 percent for each 1 percent that Karen contributes. Her employer does not offer employer-paid life insurance. Will is a high-school teacher and track coach and makes $49,000 per year. His employer pays the full cost of his retirement pension plan. An optional supplemental retirement plan is available into which Will can contribute 5 percent of his salary, but he has not done so as yet. Will has an employer-provided life insurance policy equal to twice his annual salary. Will and Karen have no other life insurance.

Junial/Dreamstime

What do you recommend to Karen and Will on the subject of life insurance planning regarding:

1. Their changing need for life insurance once they have a child?

2. What types of life insurance they should consider and whether they should purchase multiple policies?

3. Coordinating their retirement savings and other investments with their life insurance program?

4. Shopping for life insurance?

YOUR NEXT 5 YEARS

In the next five years, you can start achieving financial success by doing the following related to life insurance planning:

1. *Calculate your life insurance needs every three years or when major life events occur, such as the birth of a child.*

2. *Comparison-shop for term life insurance on the Internet to obtain the lowest possible rates.*

3. *Employ the principle of "buy term life insurance and invest the rest" with guaranteed renewable term life insurance.*

4. *Partially fund your tax-sheltered retirement plan with the money saved by purchasing term rather than cash-value insurance.*

5. *Protect against health-related premium increases by selecting guaranteed renewable term policies and cash-value policies that have a guaranteed insurability option.*

 LEARNING OBJECTIVE 1

Understand the reasons why you might need life insurance and calculate the appropriate amount of coverage.

life insurance
An insurance contract that promises to pay a dollar benefit to a beneficiary upon the death of the insured person.

final expenses
One-time expenses occurring just prior to or after a death.

FINANCIAL POWER POINT

Buying Life Insurance Versus Investing

Most college students will live into their 80s, although about 20 percent will die before retirement. Use life insurance to protect against an early death and make investments to prepare for a long life.

George Burns once observed, "If you live to be one hundred, you've got it made. Very few people die past that age." But for most of us, death will come earlier even if we do not know when. With the uncertainty of when death will occur comes financial risk. Two financial problems arise because you cannot know how long you will live. The first problem is the risk of living too long. This is the possibility that you will outlive your savings during retirement. Life insurance is not the best way to address the living-too-long problem. Instead, you should invest through tax-sheltered retirement savings plans (discussed in Chapter 17). The second problem is the risk of dying too soon. This is the possibility that you might die before adequately providing for the financial well-being of loved ones, especially your spouse and children. **Life insurance** protects your loved ones against the possibility that you may die too soon. As you will see, term life insurance does this best.

Most Americans either do not buy life insurance at all or purchase insufficient coverage. The need for life insurance is greatest in the child-rearing years because the income of one or more adults is needed to support a child financially. This often requires insurance coverage in the amount of $250,000, $500,000, or even $1,000,000. As children grow up, they need fewer years of financial support, and the necessity of life insurance on the income earner begins to decline. And eventually, the children leave home. In due course, the need for life insurance is eliminated because sufficient funds should be available for survivors through savings and investments that build up over time, primarily through a retirement plan.

Americans tend to buy the wrong type of life insurance—cash-value—when term insurance policies cost about 80 percent less. The smartest financial strategy is to use the money saved by buying term insurance to invest in a tax-sheltered retirement plan. This approach is referred to as "buy term and invest the rest."

HOW MUCH LIFE INSURANCE DO YOU NEED?

The primary reason for buying life insurance is to allow your family members to continue with their lives free from the financial burdens that your death would bring. Income can be made available for spouse and children. Insurance proceeds can safeguard home ownership. Future college or other educational plans can remain intact. The bottom line? Your purchase of life insurance is to benefit your loved ones, not yourself. So if you are young, unmarried, and childless, you don't need life insurance.

What Financial Needs Must Be Met upon Your Death?

Financial losses that arise from dying too soon include expenditures for final expenses; the lost income of the deceased; and funds for a readjustment period, debt repayment, and possibly education expenses for a surviving spouse and children.

Final-Expense Needs **Final expenses** are one-time expenses occurring just prior to or after a death. The largest of these expenses is for the funeral and burial or cremation of the deceased, which could cost as little as $1000 or as much as $10,000. Travel expenses for family members to attend a funeral can be quite high, as can food and lodging expenses for mourners. Severe and costly disruptions of family life can last for months. There also are costs associated with settling the estate of the deceased, and these can be paid for with life insurance proceeds.

Income-Replacement Needs Once someone else becomes financially dependent on you, your income will be the major financial loss resulting from your premature death. Included in this lost income is the value of any essential employee benefits, such as health care benefits for your dependents. Dual-earner families who depend on both incomes to maintain the desired level of living should plan on protecting both sources of income.

Readjustment-Period Needs Families often need a period of readjustment after the death of a loved one. This period may last for several months to two or three years and may have financial consequences that require substantial life insurance proceeds. For example, the death of a parent with young children may require the surviving spouse to forgo employment for a while. Similarly, a surviving employed spouse may need to take time off from working—perhaps a year or two—to obtain further education.

Debt-Repayment Needs Some people want to buy enough additional life insurance to pay off all installment loans, credit cards, and the outstanding balance on the home mortgage. This is an understandable motivation, but a family that has bought sufficient life insurance for the replacement of lost income probably will not need to make specific insurance provisions for the repayment of most debts. It is sometimes helpful, however, to buy a small amount of additional life insurance to pay off all debts other than the mortgage in order to simplify the finances of the survivors.

College-Expense Needs Many families with small children already have a college savings plan in place. Adequate replacement of lost income should allow for continuation of the plan. Most families use current income to help pay their children's college expenses, and therefore, the death of a family income provider may impede the ability to meet this need. The solution is to earmark a dollar amount of life insurance proceeds for future college expenses. A suggested amount would be the current cost of tuition and room and board and expenses for four years at a desired institution.

Other Special Needs Many families have special needs that must be considered in the life insurance-planning process. For example, a family might have a child with special needs who will require medical or custodial care as an adult. Wealthier families might need extra life insurance to pay federal estate taxes and state inheritance taxes (covered in Chapter 18).

There Are Three Ways You Can Meet the Need

There are three ways you can meet your need for protection from losses described earlier: existing assets, government benefits, and life insurance.

1. Existing Assets Can Help Meet the Need Over time, individuals and families usually acquire at least a minimal amount of savings and investments. The funds held in savings accounts, certificates of deposit, stocks, bonds, and mutual funds often are specifically earmarked for some special goal, such as retirement, travel, or college for children. In the event of a premature death, they could be used to pay final and readjustment expenses as well as to replace lost income, even though it might be wiser to retain these funds for their originally intended purposes. Retirement funds of the deceased, such as 401(k) plans and IRAs (discussed in Chapter 17), are additional resources. Younger families should be wary of using funds in retirement accounts for living expenses after the death of an income provider because this may jeopardize the surviving spouse's retirement.

2. Government Benefits May Help Meet Some of the Needs Widows, widowers, and their dependents may qualify for various government benefits—most notably **Social Security survivor's benefits**, which are paid to a surviving spouse with children or to the children directly if there is no surviving spouse. The level of benefits depends on income earned during the lifetime of the deceased. (Details on estimating Social Security benefits are provided in Appendix B and on the *Garman/Forgue* companion website.) If eligible, a family can receive as much as $28,000 per year, but these benefits generally cease when the youngest child reaches age 18. About 6.4 million

FINANCIAL POWER POINT

Husbands and Wives Need Their Own Life Insurance Plans

Husbands and wives should integrate their life insurance plans, but both need individual policies. This is true even if one partner makes the bulk of the family income. The cost of replacing the household labor of a stay-at-home spouse should be included in life insurance planning.

Social Security survivor's benefits
Government program benefits paid to a surviving spouse and children.

Adequate life insurance can ensure that important goals, such as paying for a child's education, are met should a parent die.

beneficiary
Person who receives life insurance proceeds, as per the policy.

needs-based approach
A superior method of calculating the amount of insurance needed that considers all of the factors that might potentially affect the level of need.

Americans receive Social Security survivor's benefits, including 2 million children who receive an average of $750 a month.

3. Life Insurance Can Close Any Remaining Gap in Needs

Life insurance is the simplest form of insurance because it protects against only one peril—death. The benefit the policy will pay in cash is known in advance. This payment to the **beneficiary** (the person named in the policy to receive the funds) will occur within a few days once a death certificate is presented to the insurance company. Insurance proceeds are not subject to income taxes and beneficiaries may use the funds in any way they wish. However, if the funds are put in the bank or invested in some way, any interest or dividends earned will be subject to income taxation.

Employers often provide life insurance to their employees as an employee benefit; the amount is often one or two times the employee's salary. In addition, some people have existing life insurance that was purchased for them as children or that they purchased previously. These coverages can reduce the need for additional life insurance purchases.

What Dollar Amount of Life Insurance Do You Need?

Determining the magnitude of the losses resulting from a premature death can be complicated. Two methods are commonly used: a multiple-of-earnings approach and a needs-based approach. The needs-based approach is more accurate and reflects the changes in family status, income, assets, and age that will occur over your life cycle.

The Multiple-of-Earnings Approach Uses Flawed Logic

The **multiple-of-earnings approach** estimates the amount of life insurance needed by multiplying your income by some number, such as 5, 7, or 10. Thus, someone with an annual income of $40,000 would need $200,000 to $400,000 in life insurance. Life insurance agents often suggest this simple approach.

Another multiple-of-earnings approach is to use the interest factors from Appendix A-4 for an expected investment rate of return and a given number of years of need. The logic here is that at death, the survivor could invest the funds received from the life insurance policy on the person who has died to provide a flow of income for the number of years desired. For example, parents who wish to provide their family with income of $40,000 for 20 years at a real rate of return of 3 percent (after inflation and taxes) would need to have about $600,000 ($40,000 × 14.8775) of life insurance protection on their lives.

The multiple-of-earnings approach has shortcomings. It addresses only one of the factors affecting life insurance needs—income-replacement needs—and does not take into consideration such factors as age, family situation, and other assets that could cover the lost income.

The Needs-Based Approach Is the Best Method

The **needs-based approach** for estimating life insurance needs considers all of the factors that might potentially affect the level of need. It improves upon the calculations of the multiple-of-earnings approach by including a more accurate assessment of income-replacement needs and incorporates factors that add to and reduce the level of need. The Run the Numbers worksheet, "The Needs-Based Approach to Life Insurance," illustrates calculations made via the needs-based approach. You would be wise to calculate your current needs for life insurance and then to revisit those calculations every three years and when changes occur in your employment or family situation or your health status.

RUN THE NUMBERS

The Needs-Based Approach to Life Insurance

This worksheet provides a mechanism for estimating life insurance needs using the needs-based approach. The amounts needed for final expenses, income replacement, readjustment needs, debt repayment, college expenses, and other special needs are calculated and then reduced by funds available from government benefits and any current insurance or assets that could cover the need. This worksheet is also available on the *Garman/Forgue* companion website.

Factors Affecting Need	Example	Your Figures
1. Final-expense needs Includes funeral, burial, travel, and other items of expense just prior to and after death	$ 12,000	$ _____
2. Income-replacement needs Multiply 75 percent of annual income * by the interest factor from Appendix A-4 that corresponds to the number of years that the income is to be replaced and the assumed after-tax, after-inflation rate of return. ($36,000 × 19.6004 for 30 years at a 3% rate of return)	+ 705,614	+ _____
3. Readjustment-period needs To cover employment interruptions and possible education expenses for surviving spouse and dependents	+ 19,000	+ _____
4. Debt-repayment needs Provides repayment of short-term and installment debt, including credit cards and personal loans	+ 10,000	+ _____
5. College-expense needs To provide a fund to help meet college expenses of dependents	+ 75,000	+ _____
6. Other special needs	+ 0	+ _____
7. Subtotal (combined effects of items 1–6)	+ $821,614	+ _____
8. Government benefits Present value of Social Security survivor's benefits and other benefits Multiply monthly benefit estimate by 12 and use Appendix A-4 for the number of years that benefits will be received and the same interest rate that was used in item 2. ($2725 × 12 × 11.9379 for 15 years of benefits and a 3% rate of return)	− 390,369	− _____
9. Current insurance assets	− 98,000	− _____
10. Life insurance needed	$ 333,245	$ _____

*Seventy-five percent is used because about 25 percent of income is used for personal needs.

Calculating Life Insurance Needs for a Couple with Small Children

Consider the example of Zoel Raymond, a 35-year-old factory foreman from Holyoke, Massachusetts, who has a spouse (age 30) and three sons (ages 8, 7, and 3 years). Zoel earns $48,000 annually and desires to replace his income for 30 years, at which time his spouse would be approaching retirement. The "Example" column of the Run the Numbers worksheet, "The Needs-Based Approach to Life Insurance," expands on the situation faced by Zoel.

1. **Final-expense needs.** Zoel estimates his final expenses for funeral, burial, and other expenses at $12,000.
2. **Income-replacement needs.** Zoel's income of $48,000 is multiplied by 0.75 and the interest factor of 19.6004. This factor was used because Zoel decided that it would be best to replace his lost income for 30 years or until Mary, his wife, reached age 60 and passed through the Social Security blackout period. Zoel and Mary are moderate-risk investors and believe that she could earn a 3 percent after-tax, after-inflation rate of return on life insurance proceeds. Income-replacement needs based on these conditions amount to $705,614.

FINANCIAL POWER POINT

Life Insurance Can Provide a Flow of Future Income

Having the right amount of life insurance will allow your family to invest the proceeds received and then make withdrawals to replace the income you could have provided for them had you lived.

FINANCIAL POWER POINT

Social Security Survivor Benefits Have a Blackout Period

Once the youngest child reaches age 18, a surviving spouse enters the **Social Security blackout period** and is ineligible for Social Security survivor benefits. The blackout period ends when the surviving spouse reaches age 60. The surviving spouse may then collect survivor's benefits until age 62, and then may begin collecting Social Security retirement benefits based on his or her own or the deceased spouse's retirement account, whichever provides the higher payment.

3. **Readjustment-period needs.** Mary is a reporter for a local newspaper, earning an annual income of $38,000. Allocating $19,000 for readjustment-period needs would allow her to take a six-month leave of absence from her job or meet other readjustment needs.

4. **Debt-repayment needs.** Zoel and Mary owe $10,000 on various credit cards and an auto loan. They also owe about $128,000 on their home mortgage. Mary would like to pay off all debts except the mortgage debt if Zoel dies. The mortgage debt would be affordable if Zoel's income were adequately replaced.

5. **College-expense needs.** Zoel estimates that it would currently cost $25,000 for each of his sons to attend the local campus of a public university. If he dies, $25,000 of the life insurance proceeds could be invested for each son. If invested appropriately, the funds should grow at a rate sufficient to keep up with increasing costs of a college education.

6. **Other special needs.** Zoel and Mary do not have any unusual needs related to life insurance planning, so they entered zero for this factor.

7. **Subtotal.** The Raymonds total items 1 through 6 on the worksheet and determine that the family's financial needs arising out of Zoel's death would amount to $821,614. Although this sum seems large to them, they have access to two resources that can reduce this figure, as indicated in items 8 and 9.

8. **Government benefits.** Zoel estimates that his family would qualify for monthly Social Security survivor's benefits of $2725, or $32,700 a year.* These benefits would be paid for 15 years, until his youngest son turns 18. The present value of this stream of benefits is $390,369 (from Appendix A-4), assuming a 3 percent return for 15 years.

9. **Current insurance and assets.** Zoel has a $50,000 life insurance policy purchased five years ago. His employer also pays for a group policy equal to his $48,000 gross annual income. Zoel's major assets include his home and his retirement plan. Because he does not want Mary to have to liquidate these assets if he dies, he includes only the $98,000 insurance coverage in item 9.

10. **Life insurance needed.** After subtracting worksheet items 8 and 9 from the subtotal, Zoel estimates that he needs an additional $333,245 in life insurance. This amount may large, but Zoel can meet this need through term life insurance for as little as $30 per month.

Because Mary earns an income that is about 80 percent of Zoel's, her life insurance needs may be about 20 percent lower. To determine the specific amount, the couple must complete a worksheet for her as well. Next, the Raymonds will need to decide what type of life insurance is best and from whom to buy the additional life insurance needed. These topics are covered later in this chapter.

Calculating Life Insurance Needs for a Young Professional Irene Leech of Lynchburg, Virginia, recently graduated with a degree in tourism management and has accepted a position paying $43,000 per year. Irene is single and lives with her sister. She owes $14,500 on a car loan and $21,800 in education loans. She has about $7000 in the bank. Among her employee benefits is an employer-paid term insurance policy equal to her annual salary.

Irene has been approached by a life insurance agent who used the multiple-of-earnings approach to suggest that she needs $215,000 in life insurance, or about five times her income. Does she? If you apply the needs-based approach to Irene's situation, you will see the following:

---

* Your personal Social Security benefits can be estimated by requesting a Social Security Statement from the Social Security Administration (www.ssa.gov). Appendix B also provides estimates.

- Irene estimates her final expenses at $10,000, which she entered for item 1. Because Irene has no dependents, she needs no insurance for income-replacement needs, readjustment-period needs, college-expense needs, or other special needs.

- Items 2, 3, 5, and 6 in the needs-based approach worksheet on page 349 are zero because Irene has no dependents.

- Irene's survivors will not qualify for any government benefits, so item 8 will also be zero.

- Irene would like to see her $14,500 automobile loan and $21,800 education loans repaid in the event of her death. She feels better knowing that her younger sister could inherit her car free and clear. She entered $36,300 for item 4.

- Irene has combined life insurance and assets of $50,000, so she entered that amount for item 8.

The resulting calculations show that Irene needs no additional life insurance ($10,000 + $36,300 − $50,000 = −$3700). The agent suggested that Irene buy now while she is young and rates are low. This, too, is not a smart approach because you should not buy life insurance simply to lock in low rates. That would be like buying car insurance before you own a car. Unless you have a personal or family-based medical history that might interfere with the purchase of life insurance when needed later, you, like Irene, should wait until you actually need life insurance before buying a policy.

 Concept Check 12.1

1. Distinguish between the dying-too-soon problem and the living-too-long problem and the best ways to address each.

2. List five types of needs that can be addressed through life insurance.

3. Explain why the multiple-of-earnings approach is less accurate than a needs-based approach to life insurance planning.

4. Identify two periods in a typical person's life cycle when the need for life insurance is low and one when it is high.

THERE ARE ONLY TWO BASIC TYPES OF LIFE INSURANCE

Many people are confused by the wide variety of life insurance plans available. But, in reality, there are only two types of life insurance: term life insurance and cash-value life insurance. **Term life insurance** is often described as "pure protection" because it pays benefits only if the insured person dies within the time period (term) covered by the policy. The policy must be renewed if coverage is desired for another time period. In this way, it acts much like car or homeowner's insurance. All the other life insurance policies are variations of **cash-value life insurance**. These policies pay benefits at death (like term policies) but also include a savings/investment element that can provide benefits to the policyholder prior to the death of the insured person. Thus, they include a **cash value** that represents the value of the investment element in the life insurance policy. Because of its investment aspect, many people automatically believe cash-value life insurance is the better option, but this is false. Cash-value life insurance costs much more than term insurance, and there are much better options for investing than life insurance, as you will learn in upcoming chapters.

Term Life Insurance Is Pure Protection

Term life insurance contracts are most often written for time periods (or terms) of 1, 5, 10, or even 20 years. If the insured survives the specified time period, the beneficiary receives no monetary benefits. Term insurance can be purchased in contracts with face amounts in

 LEARNING OBJECTIVE 2

Distinguish among types of life insurance.

term life insurance
"Pure protection" against early death; pays benefits only if the insured dies within the time period (term) that the policy covers.

cash-value life insurance
Pays benefits at death and includes a savings/investment element that can provide a reduced level of benefits to the policyholder prior to the death of the insured person.

face amount
Dollar value of protection as listed in the policy and used to calculate the premium.

guaranteed renewable term insurance
Protects you against the possibility of becoming uninsurable.

level-premium term insurance
Term policy with long term under which premiums remain constant. Also called guaranteed level-premium term insurance.

convertible term insurance
Offers policyholders the option of exchanging a term policy for a cash-value policy without evidence of insurability.

multiples of $1000, usually with a minimum face amount of $50,000. The **face amount** is the dollar value of life insurance protection as listed in the policy and used to calculate the premium. Variations on term life insurance include decreasing term insurance, guaranteed renewable term insurance, convertible term insurance, and credit (term) life insurance.

Unless otherwise stipulated by the original contract, you must apply for a new contract and may be required to undergo a medical examination to renew the policy. The premium will increase with each renewal, reflecting your increasing age and greater likelihood of dying while the new policy remains in force. For example, a $100,000 five-year renewable term policy for a man age 25 might have an annual premium of $100; at age 35, the policy might cost $135; and at age 45, it might cost $220. Term policies are much less expensive than a new cash-value policy at any given age because they do not include a savings/investment element. If you have a health problem, you may be denied a new policy or be required to pay much higher premiums.

Guaranteed Renewable Term Insurance   Proving insurability at renewal may be difficult if you develop a health problem during the time period of a term policy. To avoid this dilemma, term life insurance policies are usually written as **guaranteed renewable term insurance**. The guarantee protects you against the possibility of becoming uninsurable. The number of renewals you can make without proving insurability may be limited to two or three, and a maximum age may be specified for these renewals (usually 65 or 70 years). Unless you are positive that you will not need a renewal, guaranteed renewable term insurance is recommended.

Level-Premium Term Insurance   You can avoid term insurance premium increases as you grow older in part by buying **level-premium (or guaranteed level-premium) term insurance**, which is a term policy with a long time period (perhaps 5, 10, or 20 years). Under such a policy, the premiums remain constant throughout the entire life of the policy. Premiums charged in early years are higher than necessary to balance out the lower-than-necessary premiums in later years covered by the policy. Premiums on policies written for ten or more years usually remain constant for a five-year interval, and then might increase to a new constant rate for another five- or ten-year interval. Such level-premium policies may include a **re-enter provision**, requiring proof of good health at the beginning of each five-year interval. If health status changes, the insured must re-enter the policy at a higher rate than originally anticipated. Avoid policies with such a provision, especially if you anticipate needing coverage beyond the initial level-premium interval.

Decreasing Term Insurance   With **decreasing term insurance**, the face amount of coverage declines annually, while the premiums remain constant. The owner chooses an initial face amount and a contract period, after which the face amount of the policy gradually declines (usually each year) to some minimum (such as $50,000) in the last year of the contract. For example, a woman age 35 might buy a 30-year $200,000 decreasing term policy that declines by $5000 each year. The major benefit of decreasing term policies is that they more closely fit changing insurance needs, which typically decline as a person ages.

Convertible Term Insurance   **Convertible term insurance** offers the policyholder the option of exchanging a term policy for a cash-value policy without evidence of insurability. Usually, this conversion is available only during the first five years of the policy. Some policies provide for an automatic conversion from term to cash-value insurance after a specific number of years.

There are two ways to convert a term policy to a cash-value policy. First, you can simply request the conversion and begin paying the higher premiums required for the cash-value policy. The savings/investment element of the cash-value policy will begin accumulating as of the date of the conversion. Second, you can pay the company the cash value that would have built up had the policy originally been written on a cash-value basis. Although this lump sum may be a considerable amount, it does represent an asset for the policyholder. Furthermore, the new premiums will be based on your age at the time that you bought the original term policy, which may result in lower premiums.

Group Term Life Insurance **Group term life insurance** is issued to people as members of a group rather than as individuals. Most such policies are written for a large number of employees, with premiums being paid in full or in part by the employer. Group life insurance premiums are average rates based on the characteristics of the group as a whole. If you are insured under a group plan, you need not prove your insurability, and if you leave the group, you can usually convert it to an individual policy without proof of insurability. Such convertibility represents a major benefit for people whose health status makes individual life insurance unaffordable or unattainable.

Credit and Mortgage Term Life Insurance **Credit term life insurance** will pay the remaining balance of a loan if the insured dies before repaying the debt. **Mortgage life insurance** specifically focuses on the repayment of mortgage debt. In essence, both of these types of term insurance are decreasing term insurance with the creditor named as beneficiary. These products are grossly overpriced, and the only people who should consider their purchase are those who are truly uninsurable because of a serious health condition. Most people are insurable and can obtain term life coverage for a minimal cost, so they do not need credit or mortgage term life insurance.

Cash-Value Life Insurance Has a Savings Element

Cash-value life insurance pays benefits upon the death of the insured and also incorporates a savings/investment element. This cash value belongs to the owner of the policy rather than to the beneficiary (although they can be the same person). While the insured is alive, the owner may obtain the cash value by borrowing it from the insurance company or by surrendering and canceling the policy. Cash-value insurance is referred to as **permanent insurance** because it does not need to be renewed and because coverage is maintained for the entire life of the insured as long as premiums are paid. The annual premiums for cash-value policies usually remain constant.

The premiums for newly written cash-value policies are always higher than those for term policies providing the same amount of coverage. This difference arises because only a portion of the premium is used to provide the death benefit; the remainder is used to keep the premium level and to build the cash value. Figure 12-1 illustrates the premium differences between cash-value and term life insurance policies.

Comparison of Premium Dollars for Cash-Value and Term Life Insurance

Figure 12-1

Cash-Value Policy

| Premium to pay for insurance protection, sales commissions, and company expenses | | Premium to provide for the building of cash value plus related company expenses |

Term Policy

| Premium to pay for insurance protection, sales commissions, and company expenses | | Dollars not spent on life insurance and available to invest |

Figure 12-2

The Fundamental Nature of Cash-Value Life Insurance

The $100,000 death benefit (face value) paid to the beneficiaries comprises a decreasing amount of life insurance and the policyholder's returned built-up cash values.

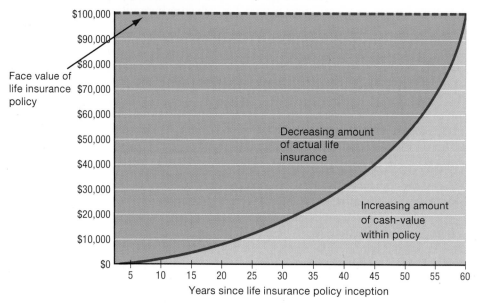

Cash-value life insurance represents a combination of decreasing term insurance and an investment account that adds up to the face amount of the policy. Figure 12-2 illustrates this concept. Initially, for example, you might have $100,000 of insurance and no savings. Several years later, you might have built up $2000 in savings within the policy. In the event of your death, your beneficiary would collect $100,000, of which $2000 would be your own money. If you lived long enough, the cash value could equal—and might surpass—the $100,000 figure. In effect, your beneficiary would then collect your "savings account" rather than an insurance payment.

Even though the cash value of a life insurance policy accumulates throughout your life, only the face amount of the policy will be paid upon your death. In many ways, cash-value policies represent a kind of forced saving that allows funds to build up while you buy life insurance.

whole life insurance
Form of cash-value life insurance that provides lifetime life insurance protection and expects the insured to pay premiums for life. Also called straight life insurance.

Whole Life Insurance
Whole, or straight, life insurance is the most popular form of cash-value life insurance, and it provides lifetime life insurance as the premiums are paid every year the person is alive. The policy remains in effect and does not need to be renewed as long as the premiums are paid on time.

Limited-Pay Whole Life Insurance
Limited-pay whole life insurance is whole life insurance that allows premium payments to cease before you reach the age of 100. Two common examples are **20-pay life policies**, which allow premium payments to cease after 20 years, and **paid-at-65 policies**, which require payment of premiums only until the insured turns 65. Although premiums need be paid only for the specified time period, the insurance protection lasts for your entire life.

limited-pay whole life insurance
Whole life insurance that allows premium payments to cease before the insured reaches the age of 100.

The annual premiums for limited-pay insurance policies are higher than those for whole life insurance policies because the insurance company has fewer years to collect premiums. Limited-pay policies are said to be **paid up** when the owner can stop paying premiums. An extreme version of limited-pay life insurance is **single-premium life insurance**, in which the premium is paid once in the form of a lump sum.

paid up
Point at which the owner of a whole life policy can stop paying premiums.

Adjustable Life Insurance
The three cornerstones of cash-value life insurance are the premium, the face amount of the policy, and the rate of cash-value accumulation. **Adjustable life insurance** allows you to modify any one of these three components,

with corresponding changes occurring in the other two. These changes may be made without providing new proof of insurability. For example, you might feel that the birth of more children has increased your need for life insurance. Adjustable life insurance would allow you to increase the face amount. In return, your premiums could increase, the cash-value accumulation could slow, or some combination of the two could apply.

Modified Life Insurance Modified life insurance is whole life insurance for which the insurance company charges reduced premiums in the early years and higher premiums thereafter. The premiums are lower in early years because some of the protection during the early years is provided by term insurance. The period of reduced premiums can vary from one to five years. Modified life insurance is primarily designed for people whose life insurance needs are high (young parents, for example) but who cannot immediately afford the premiums required for a cash-value policy. Because modified life insurance uses term insurance in the early years, it accumulates cash value extremely slowly.

Endowment Life Insurance Endowment life insurance pays the face amount of the policy either upon the death of the insured or at some previously agreed-upon date, whichever occurs first. The date of payment, called the endowment date, is commonly some specified number of years after issuance of the policy (for example, 20 or 30 years) or some specified age (such as 65). New endowment policies are no longer being written. After existing policies "endow" and are converted to cash, this type of policy will disappear.

Some Cash-Value Life Policies Earn a Variable Return

The rate at which the cash value accumulates in a cash-value policy depends on the rate of return earned. All of the cash-value policies described earlier earn a guaranteed minimum rate of return, often 3 or 4 percent. Thus, they are known as **fixed-rate policies**. Some policies, however, have a guaranteed minimum rate of return but pay a higher **current rate** depending on the success of the investments made by the insurance company. Table 12-1 illustrates these rates. An understanding of these policies requires an examination of the premium, the cost of the insurance protection portion, the rate of return on the invested funds, and the company's expense charges.

Universal Life Insurance Universal life insurance provides both the pure protection of term insurance and the cash-value buildup of whole life insurance, along with variability in the face amount, rate of cash-value accumulation, premiums, and rate of

universal life insurance
Provides the pure protection of term insurance and the cash-value buildup of whole life insurance, along with face amount variability, rate of cash-value accumulation, premiums, and rate of return.

Cash-Value Buildup—Guaranteed Versus Current Rates *

Table 12-1

Policy Year	"Guaranteed" Cash-Surrender Value (4.0% rate)	"Current Rate" Cash-Surrender Value (7.6% rate)
1	$ 0	$ 0
2	0	236
3	585	886
4	1,280	1,577
5	1,993	2,377
6	2,723	3,187
7	3,470	4,212
8	4,234	5,258
9	5,016	6,302
10	5,816	7,419
15	10,089	14,748
20	14,738	25,812
25	19,888	39,419

* Figures are illustrative for a $50,000 universal life policy; the annual premium is $684.

ADVICE FROM A PRO

Don't Be Fooled by "Vanishing-Premium" or "Return-of-Premium" Policies

Life insurance agents often pitch **vanishing-premium life insurance**, which is designed to allow policyholders to cease making premium payments after just a few years. In these plans, cash-value accumulations are used to pay premiums that no longer must be paid. While attractive at first glance, these policies contain a significant hazard. If the growth in cash-value accumulations proves insufficient to pay the premium, the owner of the policy will be billed for the premium shortfall—possibly after many years of having not paid premiums. Always assume any life insurance charge that can be imposed will be imposed.

A similar type of plan is called a **return-of-premium policy**. Here the policy promises to return all the premiums paid if the insured person maintains the policy and lives past a certain number of years—usually 30. These policies cost more so that the extra funds can be invested to provide for the return of premiums. Insurance companies promote these policies as a way to avoid "wasting" your money. In reality, what they are trying to do is entice you to keep the policy in effect for a long time even if you do not need the coverage anymore. Instead buy term insurance and decide for yourself when it is best to drop a policy.

Hyungsoo Kim
University of Kentucky, Lexington, Kentucky

---

return. Initially, the purchaser selects a face amount, and the company quotes an annual premium. The annual premium goes into the cash-value fund, from which the company deducts the cost of providing the insurance protection and charges for company expenses. As time goes by, the owner of the policy may reduce or increase the premium, with corresponding changes occurring in the insurance protection or amount added to cash value. If premiums drop below the amount necessary to cover the insurance protection and expenses, funds are removed from the cash-value account to cover the shortfall.

Essentially, universal life insurance combines annual term insurance with an investment program. Universal life policies are usually available in initial face amounts of $100,000 or more. The rate of return is tied to some interest rate prevailing in the financial markets or is dictated by the insurance company. The rate of return often exceeds those available under fixed-rate cash-value policies.

Variable Life Insurance

Variable life insurance allows you to choose the investments made with your cash-value accumulations and to share in any gains or losses. The face amount of your policy and the policy's cash value may rise or fall based on changes in the rates of return on the invested funds. The face amount of the policy usually will not drop below the originally agreed-upon amount, however. Instead, the cash value will fluctuate. If you are unfamiliar with markets for corporate stocks and bonds and mutual funds, however, you should probably avoid variable life insurance. Many variable life insurance policies contain provisions calling for the payment of fees and sales charges before the policyholder can share in any investment returns. Variable life insurance policies are complicated and should be read and analyzed very carefully before purchase.

variable-universal life insurance

Form of universal life insurance that gives the policyholder some choice in the investments made with the cash value accumulated by the policy. Also called flexible-premium variable life insurance.

Variable-Universal Life Insurance

Variable-universal life insurance is a form of universal life insurance that gives the policyholder some choice in the investments made with the cash value accumulated by the policy. It is sometimes called **flexible-premium variable life insurance**. It is a popular type of cash-value life insurance because it most closely embodies the philosophy of "buy term and invest the difference." (Actually buying a term policy and putting your premium savings into investments is the wiser approach as transaction costs are much lower.) Because you select the investment vehicles (a combination of stocks, bonds, or money market mutual funds), you can potentially realize a higher rate of return than is possible under other cash-value policy types. With this flexibility comes the risk of a lower rate of return, of course. As a result, variable-universal life policies usually provide no minimum guaranteed rate of return. Table 12-2 summarizes the features of term life insurance, cash-value insurance with a fixed return, and cash-value insurance with a variable return.

Comparisons of Three Popular Life Insurance Policies

Table 12-2

Feature	Term Insurance	Cash-Value Life Insurance	
		Whole Life Insurance	**Variable Life Insurance**
Cash-value accumulation	None	Fixed rate of accumulation	Variable accumulation as premium and interest rates vary
Rate of return paid on cash accumulations	Not applicable	Fixed	Variable with interest rates in the economy or as specified by company
Face amount	Fixed or declining during term of the policy; changeable at renewal	Fixed	Variable
Premiums	Low, with increases at renewal	High and fixed	High, but variable within limits
Cost of the death benefit portion	Low, with interest at renewal	Unknown	Known, but can vary and may hide some expense charges
Company expense charges	Low, but unknown; hidden in premium	Unknown; hidden in premium	Known; may be high

Variable-universal life insurance also carries higher commissions and is more likely to require annual fees than other forms of life insurance. A 2 percent annual fee would change a policy with an annual return of 5 percent on its investments to one with a net 3 percent return. You should also compare the policy's investment component with alternative investments. (Investments are covered in Chapters 13 to 16.)

 Concept Check 12.2

1. Distinguish between term life insurance and cash-value life insurance.
2. Explain why the premiums for term insurance are so much lower than those of cash-value life insurance.
3. Describe the benefit of buying guaranteed renewable term insurance.
4. Explain why the amount of "insurance" declines over time under a cash-value life insurance policy.
5. Distinguish between cash-value life insurance with a fixed return and with a variable return.

UNDERSTANDING YOUR LIFE INSURANCE POLICY

A **life insurance policy** is the written contract between the insurer and the policyholder. It contains all of the information relevant to the agreement. Several parties will be named in the life insurance contract (policy). The **owner, or policyholder**, retains all rights and privileges granted by the policy, including the right to amend the policy and the right to designate who receives the proceeds. The **insured** is the person whose life is insured. In addition to the beneficiary, the owner will name a **contingent beneficiary** who will become the beneficiary if the original beneficiary dies before the insured. Although the owner and the insured are often the same person, it is possible for four different people to play all these roles.

Policy Terms and Provisions Unique to Life Insurance

Life insurance policies define the terminology used in the policy and outline the basic provisions of such insurance. This information serves to clarify the meaning of the policy and the protection afforded the insurer and the policyholder.

 LEARNING OBJECTIVE 3

Explain the major provisions of life insurance policies.

owner/policyholder
Retains all rights and privileges granted by the policy, including the right to amend the policy and the right to designate who receives the proceeds.

insured
Individual whose life is insured.

DID YOU KNOW?

How Insurance Policies Are Organized

All insurance policies have five basic components including declarations, insuring agreements, exclusions, conditions, and endorsements. In order of their usual location in the policy, these five elements contain information as follows:

1. *Declarations* provide the basic descriptive information about the insured person or property, the premium to be paid, the time period of the coverage, and the policy limits. Also included may be promises by the insured to take steps to control the losses associated with a specific peril. For example, a life insurance purchaser may promise not to smoke in exchange for paying a discounted premium. The information in the declarations is used to help determine the premium and for identification purposes.

2. *Insuring agreements* are the broadly defined coverages provided under the policy. The insurer makes these promises in return for the premium paid by the insured. For example, in life insurance, the insurer promises to pay the death benefit amount to the beneficiary in the event of the insured's death. In automobile insurance, the insuring agreements will often include definitions of a motor vehicle or insured premises to clarify the promises made.

3. *Exclusions* narrow the focus and eliminate specific coverages broadly stated in the insuring agreements. The insurer makes no promise to pay for these exceptions and special circumstances. For example, suicide is commonly excluded during the first two years of a life insurance policy. A common automobile insurance exclusion denies coverage under a family policy if the car is used primarily for business purposes. People who do not understand the exclusions in their policies may believe they are covered for a loss when, in fact, they are not.

4. *Conditions* impose obligations on both the insured and the insurer by establishing the ground rules of the agreement. For example, they might include procedures for making a claim after a loss, rules for cancellation of the policy by either party, and procedures for changing the terms of the policy. The insured who fails to adhere to the procedures or obligations described in the conditions may be denied coverage when a loss occurs.

5. *Endorsements* (or *riders* as they are sometimes called in life insurance) are amendments and additions to the basic insurance policy that can both expand and limit coverage to accommodate specific needs. When the terms of an endorsement or rider differ from the terms of the basic policy, the endorsement will be considered valid. Endorsements may be requested at any time during the life of the policy to expand coverage, raise the policy limits, and make other changes.

The Application The **life insurance application** is the policyholder's offer to purchase a policy. It provides information and becomes part of the life insurance policy (the contract). Any errors or omissions in the application may allow the insurance company to deny a request for payment of the death benefit.

Lives Covered Most life insurance policies cover the life of a single person—the insured. It is also possible to cover two or more people with one policy, however. **First-to-die policies** cover more than one person but pay only when the first insured dies. These policies are less costly than separate policies written on each person, but the survivor then has no coverage after the first person dies. An alternative is the **survivorship joint life policy**, which pays when the last person covered dies.

The Incontestability Clause Life insurance policies generally include an **incontestability clause** that places a time limit—usually two years after issuance of the policy—on the right of the insurance company to deny a claim. This clause addresses the problems arising out of erroneous statements in the application.

incontestability clause
Places a time limit on the right of the insurance company to deny a claim.

The Suicide Clause Life insurance policies generally include a **suicide clause** that allows the life insurance company to deny coverage if the insured commits suicide within the first few years after the policy is issued. If the specified number of years (usually two) has elapsed, the full death benefit will be paid. If not, only the premiums paid up to that point will be refunded.

insurance dividends
Surplus earnings of the insurance company when the difference between the total premium charged exceeds the cost to the company of providing insurance.

Cash Dividends **Insurance dividends** are defined by the Internal Revenue Service as a return of a portion of the premium paid for a life insurance policy; they are not considered taxable income. They represent the surplus earnings of the company when the difference between the total premium charged exceeds the cost to the company of providing insurance. Policies that pay dividends are called **participating policies**, and policies that do not pay dividends are called **nonparticipating policies**. Both term and cash-value policies may pay dividends. Owners of participating policies may receive dividends as a cash payment, leave them with the insurance company to earn interest, or use the dividends to purchase small amounts of additional paid-up life insurance.

participating policies
Life insurance policies that pay dividends.

Death Benefit The **death benefit** of a life insurance policy is the amount that will be paid upon the death of the insured person.

death benefit
Amount that will be paid to the beneficiary when the insured dies.

The amount of the death benefit may be either higher or lower than the face amount. It can be higher due to such items as earned dividends not yet paid or premiums paid in advance. Or it can be lower due to outstanding policy loans or unpaid premiums. Consider a $100,000 participating whole life policy with annual premiums of $1380. If the insured died halfway through the policy year, with an outstanding cash-value loan of $5000 and earned but unpaid dividends of $4000, the death benefit would be $99,690, calculated as follows:

$100,000	Face amount
4,000	Unpaid dividends
+ 690	Premiums paid in advance (one-half year)
$104,690	Subtotal
− 5,000	Outstanding cash-value loan
$ 99,690	Death benefit

Grace Period Prompt payment of the premium is crucial to the continuation of coverage provided by any insurance policy. A **lapsed policy** is one that has been terminated because of nonpayment of premiums. More than one-half of all whole life policies lapse within ten years of being issued. If your life insurance policy lapses, you must prove insurability and pay any missed premiums, plus interest, to be reinstated. Alternatively, you might pay a higher premium for a new policy, reflecting your current age.

To help prevent a lapse, state laws generally require that cash-value and multiyear term policies include a **grace period**, that is, a period of time (usually 30 days following each premium due date) during which an overdue premium may be paid without a lapse of the policy. During the grace period, all provisions of the policy remain intact, but only if payment is made before the grace period ends. Assume, for example, that payment was due but not paid on January 1. If the insured were to die on January 15, the policy could be reinstated as long as payment was made by January 30, given a 30-day grace period. It also may be possible to "buy back" a lapsed cash-value policy by paying any missed premiums and the cash value that would have accumulated while the policy was lapsed.

grace period
Period of time during which an overdue premium may be paid without a lapse of the policy.

DID YOU KNOW?

Turn Bad Habits into Good Ones

Do You Do This?	Do This Instead!
Assume that you have life insurance set up by your parents	Confirm that you are covered and for how much
Put off thinking about life insurance because you are young	Determine the dollar amount of insurance that you need and buy insurance to cover any shortfall
Assume a cash-value life insurance policy is the best way to buy life insurance	Explore term life insurance as the lowest cost and most appropriate means of protection
Rely on a life insurance agent to determine how much and what type of insurance to buy	Make your own assessments based on your income and family obligations

Multiple Indemnity A **multiple indemnity clause** provides for a doubling or tripling of the face amount if death results from certain specified causes. It is most often used to double the face amount if death results from an accident. Such a clause is often included automatically as part of the policy at no extra cost, but sometimes a charge is assessed. If you are adequately insured, a multiple indemnity clause is unnecessary.

Settlement Options Allow the Beneficiary to Decide How to Receive the Death Benefit

Settlement options are the choices that the life insurance beneficiary or policyholder has in determining how the death benefit payment will be structured. The owner may choose the option before death, or the beneficiary may select the option after the insured's death. Each option's appropriateness depends on the beneficiary's financial situation. The five settlement options are as follows:

1. **Lump sum.** The death benefit may be received as a lump-sum cash settlement immediately after death. This is often the best approach to take because the beneficiary can invest the proceeds and earn a return higher than the insurance company would pay.
2. **Interest income.** The beneficiary can receive the annual interest earned from the death benefit. For example, the beneficiary would receive $4000 each year from a $100,000 death benefit earning 4 percent interest. The $100,000 principal would remain intact and would continue to earn interest until the death of the beneficiary, when it becomes part of his or her estate.
3. **Income of a specific amount.** The beneficiary may receive a specific amount of income per year from the death benefit. Under this option, payments cease when the death benefit and interest are exhausted. For example, a $100,000 death benefit earning 4 percent interest would provide a $15,000 annual income for approximately eight years.*
4. **Income for a specific period.** The beneficiary may receive an income from the death benefit for a specific number of years. For example, a widow with small children may choose to receive an income for 18 years. The insurance company would calculate a level of income that would allow for equal proceeds each year, with all funds, including interest, being exhausted at the end of the 18th year.
5. **Income for life.** The beneficiary may elect to receive an income for life. In such a case, the insurance company would use the life expectancy of the beneficiary to calculate the level of income that would allow for equal annual payments so that funds would be exhausted by the expected date of the beneficiary's death. If the beneficiary lives longer than expected, the income payments would continue.

Policy Features Unique to Cash-Value Life Insurance

Cash-value life insurance policies carry special features that all relate to the cash values built up in the policies.

The Policy Illustration Prior to death, you may cash in the policy for the accumulated cash value, which cancels your insurance coverage, or you may borrow all or part of the cash value. You must repay the amount borrowed with interest, and any amount owed will be subtracted from the face amount of the policy if you die while the debt remains outstanding.

Cash-value life insurance policies generally provide a **policy illustration** that charts the projected growth in the cash value for given rates of return. Two rates are usually quoted: the **guaranteed minimum rate of return** (the minimum rate that, by contract, the company is legally obligated to pay) and the **current rate** (the rate of return recently paid by the company to policyholders). Agents typically emphasize the current rate, perhaps by presenting a table that illustrates the rate of cash-value accumulation resulting from the two rates. Table 12-1 (on page 355) provides an example of a policy illustration. Note the differences in the two cash-value columns in Table 12-1—you can readily understand why the agent would emphasize the current rate. Policy illustrations can easily be made to look much more optimistic than it is reasonable to expect. Only after the policy is

---

* This option and options 4 and 5 are variations of an annuity and are covered further in Chapter 17.

in force for perhaps 10 to 20 years can an accurate picture be drawn. For this reason, it is smart to periodically ask your agent for an **in-force illustration** that shows the cash-value status of the policy and projections for the future given the current rate of return at the time of the illustration (rather than the rate used at the inception of the policy).

Policy illustrations can be helpful in many cases, but they can also be written in such a way as to make the policy look better than it really is. Asking a few pertinent questions can help cut through some of the misconceptions:

1. Is the "current rate" illustrated actually the rate paid recently? What was the current rate in each of the past five years?
2. What assumptions have been made regarding company expenses, dividend rates, and policy lapse rates?
3. Does all of my cash value earn a return at the current rate? (If not, the current rate is misleading.)
4. Is the illustration based on the "cash surrender value" or the "cash value"? (The cash surrender value is usually the lower value and reflects what will actually be paid if the policy is cashed in.)

Nonforfeiture Values **Nonforfeiture values** are amounts stipulated in a life insurance policy that protect the cash value, if any, in the event that the policyholder chooses not to pay or fails to pay the required premiums. The policy owner can receive the accumulated cash-value funds in one of three ways. First, he or she may simply surrender the policy and receive the **cash surrender value**, which represents the cash value minus any surrender charges. Second, the policy owner may continue the policy with the original face amount but for a time period shorter than the original policy. Third, the policy may be continued on a paid-up basis, with a new and lower face amount being established based on the amount that can be purchased with the accumulated funds. Table 12-3 illustrates the nonforfeiture values for a paid-at-65 cash-value policy. Note that a cash-value policy has very little cash surrender value unless you have held it for ten years or more.

Policy Loans The owner of a cash-value policy may borrow all or a portion of the accumulated cash value. Interest rates charged for the loan will range from 2 to

nonforfeiture values
Amounts stipulated in a life insurance policy that protect the cash value, if any, in the event that the policyholder chooses not to pay or fails to pay required premiums.

cash surrender value
Represents the cash value of a policy minus any surrender charges.

Cash-Value Life Insurance Nonforfeiture Values *Table 12-3*

	A	B		C
(Policyholder can choose A, B, or C.)				
Policy Year	**Cash or Surrender Value***	**Period of $10,000 Term Insurance**		**Face Value of Term Insurance Paid Up for Life**[†]
		Years	**Days**	
0	$ 0	0	0	$ 0
2	0	0	0	0
3	60	2	81	240
4	190	7	35	720
5	310	10	282	1,140
10	1,000	19	351	3,160
15	1,790	22	346	4,900
20	2,690	23	122	6,410
30	4,350	21	228	8,260
35	5,390	20	286	9,140
40	6,520	For life	—	10,000
45	7,110	For life	—	10,000

For a $10,000, paid-at-65, limited-payment, cash-value life insurance policy for a male aged 25; the annual premium is $180.

*The policy has a back-end load that reduces the buildup of cash value in early years.
†Much lower commissions tend to be charged on term insurance policies.

automatic premium loan
Provision that allows any premium not paid by the end of the grace period to be paid automatically with a policy loan if sufficient cash value or dividends have accumulated.

waiver of premium
Sets certain conditions under which an insurance policy would be kept in full force by the company without the payment of premiums.

guaranteed insurability (guaranteed purchase option)
Permits the cash-value policyholder to buy additional stated amounts of cash-value life insurance at stated times in the future without evidence of insurability.

8 percent, depending on the terms of the policy. In addition, the interest rate earned on the remaining cash value typically reverts to the guaranteed minimum rate while the loan remains outstanding. As a result, the cash value ultimately accumulated may be significantly reduced.

An **automatic premium loan** provision allows any premium not paid by the end of the grace period to be paid automatically with a policy loan if sufficient cash value or dividends have accumulated. In the first few years of a policy, this provision may not offer much benefit because cash value and dividends accumulate slowly. Eventually these funds may grow enough to pay premiums for a considerable length of time, thereby effectively preventing the lapse of the policy.

Many life insurance companies make a policy's death benefit available to an insured who is terminally ill through a **living benefit clause** that allows the payment of all or a portion of the death benefit prior to death if the insured contracts a terminal illness. This allows the policy to offer, in effect, long-term health care protection. These early payments are not cash-value loans, so it is possible to obtain more than the cash value accumulated in the policy. In addition, **viatical companies** specialize in buying life insurance policies from insureds for $0.50 to $0.80 per $1 of death benefit in return for being named beneficiary on the policy.

Waiver of Premium A **waiver of premium** sets certain conditions under which an insurance policy would be kept in full force by the company without the payment of premiums. It usually applies when a policyholder becomes totally and permanently disabled, but it may also apply under other conditions, depending on the policy provisions. In effect, the waiver-of-premium option (for an extra cost) protects against the risk of becoming disabled and being unable to pay premiums. This option can be expensive and may account for as much as 10 percent of the policy premium. If you are adequately covered by disability income insurance (see Chapter 11), then you might want to avoid this option.

Guaranteed Insurability The **guaranteed insurability** (or **guaranteed purchase**) option permits the cash-value policyholder to buy additional stated amounts of cash-value life insurance at stated times in the future without evidence of insurability. This option differs from the guaranteed renewability option for term insurance in that it enables the owner to increase the face amount of the policy or to buy an additional policy. The policy might allow the exercise of these options when the insured turns 30, 35, or 40, or when he or she marries or has children. The added cost of this option is nominal and worthwhile.

 Concept Check 12.3

1. Distinguish among the owner, the insured, the beneficiary, and the contingent beneficiary of a life insurance policy.

2. Briefly describe each of the five components of all insurance policies.

3. Identify the five settlement options for the payment of the proceeds of a life insurance policy to its beneficiary.

4. Besides taking the cash value as a lump sum, what are four more ways a cash-value policyholder may take the proceeds of the policy at cancellation?

5. Distinguish between an automatic premium loan and a waiver-of-premium option in a life insurance policy.

6. Explain how guaranteed renewability for term life insurance and guaranteed insurability for cash-value insurance protect insured people who develop serious health conditions.

DID YOU KNOW?

About Life Insurance After Divorce

If you receive income from a former spouse through either alimony or child support, life insurance on that person is strongly advised. If a policy that was purchased while a couple was married remains in effect, it is wise to keep it. To be certain that the correct beneficiary is named, have that requirement stated in a court order and/or made part of the divorce decree, and require written confirmation from the insurance company that the beneficiary is appropriately noted. The custodial parent should then be named as owner of the policy, thereby preventing the noncustodial parent from making any changes in the policy. Noncustodial parents will also need life insurance on their former spouses because they will probably receive custody of the children if the former spouse dies and may need additional income to support the larger household.

YOUR STEP-BY-STEP STRATEGY FOR BUYING LIFE INSURANCE

Every year more than $150 billion of new life insurance is purchased in the United States. Does each individual really need life insurance? Was the policy purchased the right one, and was it purchased from a reputable company and agent? Did the buyer pay the right price?

LEARNING OBJECTIVE **4**

Apply a step-by-step strategy for implementing a life insurance plan.

First Ask Whether or Not, and for How Much, Your Life Should Be Insured

Anyone whose death will result in financial losses to others should be covered by life insurance unless other resources are sufficient to cover the losses. At a minimum, there will be final expenses such as for funeral and burial. Beyond that, the need depends on the person's family situation. Parents with minor children almost always need life insurance.

People who generally do not need life insurance include children and people with no dependents who have no desire to leave an estate. People who are sometimes unnecessarily insured include retirees who may have already built up assets sufficient to provide for income for survivors and to cover final expenses. The only way to really know how much additional life insurance you need is through the needs-based calculations covered earlier in this chapter. You should do this yourself and not rely on an insurance agent who has a vested interest in selling you some life insurance.

Next, Properly Integrate Your Life Insurance into Your Overall Financial Planning

Advertising and sales promotion literature for cash-value life insurance often pushes the idea that this type of insurance is a good investment and is appropriate as a retirement savings vehicle. Most independent personal finance experts would disagree strongly. Instead, they typically advise people to take a broader perspective and think of life insurance as just one facet of their financial plans. As mentioned at the beginning of this chapter, you should always think in terms of the two longevity risks: the risk of living too long and the risk of dying too soon. Investing through tax-sheltered retirement plans, not in expensive life insurance policies, most effectively solves the living-too-long problem. Inexpensive term life insurance most effectively solves the dying-too-soon problem.

Your need for life insurance will change significantly over the course of your life, and so should your life insurance plan. You should reassess your plan every two or three years and any time your family or employment situation changes. Keep these facts in mind:

FINANCIAL POWER POINT

Retirees Need Little or No Life Insurance

Life insurance needs typically decrease while assets increase over the course of one's life. At some point, savings and investments should exceed potential losses and eliminate the need for life insurance—especially after age 60. Stop paying the premiums and spend the money on something else.

- During childhood and while single, your need for life insurance is either nonexistent or very small because few, if any, other people rely on you for financial support.

- With marriage comes the increased responsibility for another person, although life insurance needs probably remain low because spouses usually have the potential to support themselves if the other partner were to die.

- The arrival of children, however, triggers a sharp increase in life insurance needs. Children often require as many as 25 years of parental support.

- As children grow older, the number of years of their remaining dependency declines, reducing the need for life insurance.

- Parents with grown children see a reduced need for life insurance because their retirement investment program will have grown large enough to cover the losses that death might bring.

- Retirement and widowhood reduce the need for life insurance or may even eliminate it altogether.

bikeriderlondon/Shutterstock.com

As a family ages, life insurance needs typically decrease.

Figure 12-3 depicts a life insurance and investment plan recommended over an individual's life cycle. This plan is built on two foundations: (1) the purchase of term insurance for the bulk of life insurance needs (because term insurance is more flexible than cash-value insurance and provides more protection for each premium dollar) and (2) a systematic, regular investment program.

DID YOU KNOW?

The Tax Consequences of Life Insurance

The proceeds of life insurance policies are not taxable income. Thus, a survivor who receives a $100,000 check from an insurance company keeps all the money. He or she can spend, save, invest, or donate the funds. Some people might be persuaded by an insurance agent to consider cash-value life insurance to be a smart tax-advantaged way to invest for retirement. While life insurance does have some tax-sheltering aspects because the cash value built up in the policy is not subject to income taxes, cash-value life insurance does not compare favorably with 401(k) retirement plans available through your employer or with an IRA (discussed in Chapter 17):

1. *The premiums paid on life insurance policies cannot be used to reduce taxable income; however, contributions to IRAs and 401(k) plans do offer this significant advantage.*

2. *The rate of return earned within cash-value life insurance policies has historically lagged well behind what can be achieved by a diversified portfolio of stock and bond mutual funds (discussed in Chapters 13–15 and 17).*

3. *The commissions and expense charges on cash-value life insurance are substantially higher than those associated with investing in no-load mutual funds. Hence the net cost of investing in mutual funds is far lower than buying cash-value life insurance. (See Chapter 15.)*

Conclusion: You should be contributing the maximum amount possible into available tax-sheltered retirement plans before you even begin to consider the purchase of cash-value life insurance as an appropriate way to save for retirement.

Wisely Using Life Insurance and Investments over the Life Cycle

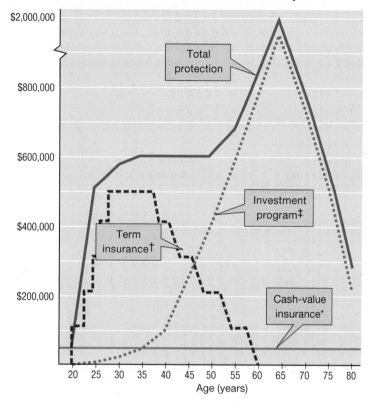

Figure 12-3

Note: *With a guaranteed insurability option and paid up at 65.
　†Term insurance policies.
　‡Includes vested employer-sponsored retirement (e.g., 401[k]) plans. (See Chapter 17.)

ADVICE FROM A PRO

Buy Term and Invest the Rest

Many people incorrectly think of life insurance as an investment and not as an expense. And the life insurance industry likes it that way. Be smart and spend as little money as possible to buy the coverage you need. One way to do this is to use the strategy to "buy term and invest the rest." If you invest the money difference between the cost of premiums for a term life insurance policy and the cost of premiums for a more expensive cash-value policy, you will always come out ahead financially over the long-term. To see why, consider the buildup of protection shown in the accompanying table for Seth Cameron, a 30-year-old art gallery administrator from New York City who is considering life insurance policies. Seth could pay an $870 annual premium to buy a $100,000 whole life policy. Alternatively, he could spend $130 for the first-year premium of a $100,000 five-year renewable term policy and invest the $740 difference ($870 − $130) in a mutual fund account and earn a 5 percent after-tax rate of return.

If Seth were to die tomorrow, the policy's beneficiary would receive both the $100,000 in insurance proceeds and the $740 in savings. After five years (age 35), Seth's annual $740 in savings would have grown to $4293; if he were to die at that time, the total death benefit would be $104,293. If Seth dies years into the future, the estate is even further ahead because of the growing principal in the account. By age 60, Seth's mutual fund investment would have grown to $58,052. If the fund earned higher than 5 percent annually, the amount would be much greater. By the time Seth reached age 60, the term insurance premiums would exceed the premiums for the cash-value policy. However, his need for life insurance would presumably be eliminated or greatly reduced at that point. If Seth's children were self-supporting by then, he could probably drop the term insurance policy altogether. Nevertheless, his mutual fund account would remain to provide a financial nest egg of $58,052 or more to his heirs.

(continues on next page)

With the "buy term and invest the rest" strategy, Seth would have been insured more than 30 years at total premium cost of just $7350. By contrast, the cash-value policy would have required total premiums of $26,100 ($870 × 30), and the policy's cash value at year 30 would be about $44,000.

For "buy term and invest the rest" to work, however, the difference between the term and cash-value policy premiums must, in fact, be invested on a regular basis. Many people say that they will invest this money but then fail to follow through on that promise. You can succeed with a little discipline. The easiest way to ensure that your money is actually invested is to set up an automatic investment program (AIP) in which a mutual fund is authorized to withdraw money from your checking account, perhaps monthly, to buy mutual fund shares. When you agree to invest the "difference" automatically, the strategy will work well for you. (See Chapters 13 and 15.)

Estate Buildup If a Term Life Insurance Buyer Invests the Difference

Age	Premium for Five-Year Renewable Term	Difference (Not Spent on Whole Life)	Total Investment and Earnings* at 5%	Total Estate
30	$130	$740	$ 740	$100,740
35	150	720	4,293	104,293
40	180	690	9,657	109,657
45	210	660	16,328	116,328
50	240	630	24,668	124,668
55	590	280	35,139	135,139
60			58,052	58,052

*This illustration makes the following assumptions: The whole life policy premium for the same $100,000 in coverage is fixed at $870 every year; the buyer pays the five-year renewable term premium at the beginning of each year; and the difference is invested. Those amounts stay in the investments account all year, as does the previous year's ending balance. Investments earn a compounded 5 percent after-tax annual rate of return. Upon the insured's death, the beneficiary would receive the $100,000 face amount of the term life insurance policy plus the amount built up in the investments account earning 5 percent.

Source: Jordan E. Goodman, "America's Money Answers Man" (www.MoneyAnswers.com), author of *Everyone's Money Book* and *Everyone's Money Book* series.

Your life insurance needs vary over your life cycle. A certain amount is permanent as it provides for funeral, burial, and other final expenses. This need fits well with the purchase of a permanent cash-value policy with a guaranteed insurability option, although some people prefer to buy term insurance for meeting this need. A $20,000 to $50,000 policy is sufficient. The remainder of your life insurance should consist of multiple term insurance policies that you start buying when you begin to have dependents. These should be five- or ten-year, level-premium, guaranteed renewable policies in increments of $100,000 or more. The policies should be layered so that you can drop policies as your need declines. By the time you reach retirement, you will have dropped all your term policies, and the cash-value policy can remain to pay final expenses or be cashed in to provide a little retirement income. Of course, this scenario requires that you implement an investment program to save for retirement. Chapters 13 through 17 cover investments and retirement planning in sufficient detail to provide you with the necessary tools to construct this program.

Decide Where and How to Buy Your Life Insurance

The most important feature of any life insurance company is its ability to pay its obligations. The company you choose must have the stability and financial strength to survive for the many years your policy will remain in force. Ratings of the financial strengths of insurance companies are available from A.M. Best Company (www.ambest.com) and Standard & Poor's (www.standardandpoors.com).

You Can Get a Great Price Buying Life Insurance Online Smart personal financial managers take a do-it-yourself approach to life insurance. They regularly calculate their needs and decide what types of insurance to buy and cancel in what increments. This allows them to use a **premium quote service** that offers computer-generated comparisons among 20 to 80 different companies. Premium quote services can be found at www .insure.com, www.quotescout.com, and www.accuquote.com. These websites also offer online life insurance needs calculators and a wealth of information on life

premium quote service
Offers computer-generated comparisons among 20 to 80 different companies.

layering term insurance policies
Purchasing level-premium term policies so that coverage grows when you need it most and then can be decreased as your needs change.

DID YOU KNOW?

How to Layer Your Term Insurance Policies for Only $60 per Month

Trying to meet one's life insurance needs with just one or two life insurance policies is not the best way to obtain protection over the life cycle. Life insurance needs fluctuate over one's lifetime, and you will need flexibility. Your life insurance needs are low (burial, debt repayment) until the moment when your first child is born or adopted. Then the need can easily spike up to $200,000 or $500,000 (or more). This need will remain high until the youngest child is approximately 10 years old and then will decrease until your retirement age. You can meet the bulk of this need by **layering term insurance policies** so that coverage grows and then can be decreased as your needs change.

An example is provided in the following chart. It assumes that the person is age 25 when a first child is born and age 30 when a last child is born. In this example, the parents buy several level-premium term policies near the birth of the first child, with the policies having differing time periods. They buy another policy when their last child is born and another as the first child gets close to college age. As the children go out on their own, some of the earliest policies expire, thereby reducing the overall amount of insurance as the parents' needs decline.

One benefit of layering is affordability. Based on premium rates for healthy nonsmokers, the cost for the plan illustrated here would never be more than $60 per month.

Age	Buy	Policies in Force at Each Age	Total Coverage at Each Age
25	Policy 1, $100,000, 30 years	#1, #2, #3	$450,000
	Policy 2, $150,000, 25 years		
	Policy 3, $200,000, 20 years		
30	Policy 4, $150,000, 25 years	#1, #2, #3, #4	600,000
35		#1, #2, #3, #4	600,000
40	Policy 5, $50,000, 20 years	#1, #2, #3, #4, #5	650,000
45		#1, #2, #4, #5	450,000
50		#1, #4, #5	300,000
55		#5	50,000
60			0

insurance from an unbiased perspective. In addition, all the major life insurance companies have an online purchase system. Term insurance is easiest to buy this way, but even cash-value insurance can be purchased online.

Or You Can Use a Local Insurance Agent

An **insurance agent** is a representative of an insurance company authorized to sell, modify, service, and terminate insurance contracts. In the United States, life insurance is typically sold through exclusive agents who represent only one company, although some independent agents represent more than one company.

The life insurance agent must be qualified to design a program tailored to your specific needs and should understand the dynamics of family relationships, which influence all life insurance needs. The agent should have earned a professional designation, such as chartered life underwriter (CLU). To earn the CLU, an agent must have three years of experience and pass a ten-course program in life insurance counseling. Some agents also may have earned the certified financial planner (CFP) or chartered financial consultant (ChFC) designation.

Your agent should be willing to take the time to provide personal service and to answer all of your questions about the policy both before and after you purchase it. Always ask an agent about the first-year commission on any policies you are considering. In addition, you should check your agent's reputation with your state's insurance and securities investment regulatory agencies.

FINANCIAL POWER POINT

State Insurance Departments Are a Good Consumer Resource

You can find information about life insurance companies through your state's insurance regulatory agency (www.naic.org/state_web_map.htm).

insurance agent
Representative of an insurance company who is authorized to sell, modify, service, and terminate insurance contracts.

DID YOU KNOW?

Sean's Success Story

Sean has always felt that life insurance planning is an important part of his overall financial well-being. When he graduated from college, his first job provided him with a term-life insurance policy equal to his annual salary. He calculated his need for life insurance and found that this amount was adequate. He has been in a steady relationship for almost two years and has begun to think about how his life insurance needs might change should he get married. Last week, he met with a life insurance agent who suggested that Sean buy a $50,000 whole life policy as a base of coverage on which he can build additional amounts through its guaranteed insurabil-

ity option. Sean obtained quotes on such a policy from two other companies and has decided to go with the plan his agent suggested. The annual premium on the policy is $587. Sean understands that additional increments of cash-value coverage will cost about the same premium, so he plans to rely on term life insurance as his needs grow in the next few years. He plans to buy multiple policies that he can add and discard in a layering process. The money he saves by purchasing term insurance will be invested in a Roth IRA retirement account that he can use to pay for his children's college or his own retirement when the time comes.

DID YOU KNOW?

About Life Insurance Sales Commissions

Sales commissions are paid to the selling insurance agent every year that a life insurance policy remains in force. Very low sales commissions tend to be charged on term insurance policies—often no more than 10 percent of the premium if the policy is purchased directly rather than through an agent.

In contrast, sales commissions typically represent as much as 90 percent of the first-year premium paid for a cash-value life insurance policy. Over the next several years, commissions drop considerably (perhaps declining annually to 50, 40, 30, 20, and eventually 10 percent) so that more of the premium each year builds cash value.

You can buy all types of life insurance policies with low sales commissions on the Internet as well as through fee-only financial planners and fee-for-service insurance agents. Cash-value policies sold with a low commission rate may have a surrender charge, which is a fee assessed if the policyholder withdraws some or all of the cash value accumulated. This charge is often highest in the early years of the policy but may be reduced or eliminated in later years. The policy illustrated in Table 12-1 has a surrender charge, for example. Ask about commissions and surrender charges whenever you shop for life insurance. Be wary of policies that have both high commissions and surrender charges.

Signs of an Unethical Life Insurance Agent

1. The agent pressures you to replace one cash-value policy, especially one that is several years old, with another.
2. The agent focuses strongly on the net cost of the policy or its so-called "vanishing" premiums rather than how the policy genuinely meets the needs of your family.
3. The agent suggests that the high current rate of return is all but guaranteed and unlikely to go down.
4. The agent says it is a good idea to borrow from a policy to make some other investment such as an annuity.
5. The agent pressures you to sign and pay for a policy without taking it home to read.
6. The agent asks that the first premium check be made out to the agent and not the company.

How to Compare Costs Among Policies

The price people pay for life insurance depends on their age, health, and lifestyle. Age is important, of course, because the probability of dying increases with age. A person who has a health problem such as heart disease or diabetes may pay considerably higher rates for life insurance or may not be able to obtain coverage at any price. People with hazardous occupations (police officers) or dangerous hobbies (skydivers) are often required to pay higher life insurance premiums as well. Life insurance companies typically offer their lowest prices to "preferred" applicants whose health status and lifestyle (for example, nonsmokers) suggest longevity. "Standard" and "impaired" applicants would pay more. Because companies differ in how they assign these labels to applicants, you should comparison-shop for the best treatment.

Term life insurance premiums are usually quoted in dollars per $1000 of coverage. Generally, the higher the face amount of the policy, the lower the rate per $1000. For example, a company might sell term life insurance for $1 per $1000 per year when purchased in face amounts of $100,000 or more and for $1.25 per $1000 per year for policies of less than $100,000. Policies with face amounts of $1 million can cost less than $0.50 per $1000 per year for people younger than age 35.

It is easy to pay too much for term life insurance, especially if you do not comparison-shop. The rates shown in Table 12-4 represent good values for term insurance. Note that smokers pay much higher premiums than nonsmokers because, as a group, smokers die ten years earlier than nonsmokers. Men pay more than women because they typically die three years earlier. Table 12-5 lists annual premiums that are near the average required for various types of insurance policies.

FINANCIAL POWER POINT

You May Have Ten Days to Cancel a New Policy

Most states require that sellers of life insurance and annuities give consumers a ten-day, **free-look provision** that allows them that period of time to study a newly written policy and, if desired, cancel it and receive a full refund. Contact www.naic.org to see if your state has such a requirement.

Fair Prices for Term Life Insurance*

Table 12-4

	(Authors' estimates based on Internet shopping on the major quote services)				
	Nonsmokers		**Smokers**		
Age	**Male**	**Female**	**Male**	**Female**	
18–30	$0.70	$0.67	$1.00	$0.95	
35	$0.83	$0.74	$1.25	$1.15	
40	$1.08	$1.00	$1.95	$1.60	
45	$1.67	$1.60	$2.80	$2.40	
50	$2.30	$2.20	$4.00	$3.25	

*Multiply the rate by each $1000 of coverage and add $60 for estimated administrative fees. For example, a fair annual premium for a $50,000 policy for a 36-year-old male nonsmoker might be $101.50 ($0.83 × 50 = $41.50; $41.50 + $60 = $101.50).

Typical Premiums* for Various Types of Life Insurance (Face Amount $100,000)

Table 12-5

Policy Type	Policy Year							
	1	**2**	**3**	**5**	**10**	**11**	**20**	**Age 65**
Annual renewable term (guaranteed renewability to age 70)	$ 80	$ 81	$ 82	$ 83	$ 90	$ 92	$110	$2,400
Decreasing term (over 20 years)	160	160	160	160	160	160	160	0
Convertible term (within 5 years)	170	170	170	170	940	940	940	940
Whole life	870	870	870	870	870	870	870	870
Universal life	590	590	590	590	680	730	760	790
Limited-pay life (paid at age 65)	920	920	920	920	920	920	920	0

*Premiums quoted are for a 21-year-old male nonsmoker.

DO IT NOW!

You know more about personal finance after reading this chapter, so get started right now by:

1. *Finding out if you currently have life insurance and, if so, what type you have.*

2. *Using the needs approach (a calculator can be found on this book's website) to determine your present need for additional life insurance.*

3. *Discussing the results of the above with your closest family members.*

Three Methods May Be Used to Compare Similar Life Insurance Policies The cost of insurance measured in dollars per $1000 is not an appropriate way to compare term with cash-value insurance or when examining different types of cash-value insurance. Three methods are used to compare similar policies:

1. **Net cost method.** The **net cost** of a life insurance policy equals the total of all premiums to be paid minus any accumulated cash value and accrued dividends. It is calculated for a specific point in time during the life of the policy—for example, at the end of the 10th or 20th year. The net cost is often a negative figure, giving a false impression that the policy will pay for itself. You should ignore net cost calculations provided by a life insurance agent.

2. **Interest-adjusted cost index method.** A **cost index** is a numerical method used to compare the costs of similar plans of life insurance. The **interest-adjusted cost index (IACI)** measures the cost of life insurance, taking into account the interest that would have been earned had the premiums been invested rather than used to buy insurance. The lower the IACI, the lower the cost of the policy. Ask for 5-, 10-, 20-, and 30-year IACI values as well because companies have been known to manipulate their dividend and cash-value accumulations to look especially good at the 20-year point. You should insist on being told the index before you agree to buy a policy, and you should shop elsewhere if the agent refuses, resists, or implies that the index has little value.

3. **Interest-adjusted net payment index method.** The IACI assumes that the policy will be cashed in and surrendered at the end of a certain period (usually 20 years) rather than remaining in force until the death of the insured. If the policy will remain in force until death, you can use the **interest-adjusted net payment index (IANPI)** to effectively measure the cost of cash-value insurance. The lower the IANPI, the lower the cost of the policy.

interest-adjusted net payment index (IANPI)
If a policy will remain in force until death, this method allows you to effectively measure the cost of cash-value insurance. The lower the IANPI, the lower the cost of the policy.

✓ Concept Check 12.4

1. List the benefits of buying term and investing the rest.

2. Identify the weaknesses of cash-value life insurance as a mechanism for saving for retirement.

3. Explain how the pattern of one's life insurance program should vary from young adulthood through retirement years.

4. Explain how you can benefit by layering your term insurance policies.

WHAT DO YOU RECOMMEND NOW?

Now that you have read the chapter on protecting loved ones through life insurance, what would you recommend to Karen and Will Bridgeman in the case at the beginning of the chapter regarding:

1. Their changing need for life insurance once they have a child?

2. What types of life insurance they should consider and whether they should purchase multiple policies?

3. Coordinating their retirement savings and other investments with their life insurance program?

4. Shopping for life insurance?

Junial/Dreamstime

BIG PICTURE SUMMARY OF LEARNING OBJECTIVES

LO1. **Understand the reasons why you might need life insurance and calculate the appropriate amount of coverage.**

Life insurance is designed to provide protection from the financial losses that result from death. The reasons to purchase life insurance change over the life cycle. The need for this type of protection is nonexistent or very small for children and single adults. Factors affecting life insurance needs include the need to replace income, final-expense needs, readjustment-period needs, debt-repayment needs, college-expense needs, availability of government programs, and ownership of other life insurance and assets. Two methods to calculate life insurance needs are the multiple-of-earnings approach and the needs-based approach. The needs-based approach is the more accurate of the two and should be conducted every three years or whenever your family situation changes.

LO2. **Distinguish among types of life insurance.**

Two basic types of life insurance exist: term life insurance and cash-value life insurance. Variations on term life insurance include decreasing term insurance, guaranteed renewable term insurance, convertible term insurance, and credit life insurance. Variations on cash-value insurance include whole life insurance, limited-pay life insurance, and universal and variable life insurance.

LO3. **Explain the major provisions of life insurance policies.**

A life insurance policy is a written contract between the insurance purchaser and the insurance company, spelling out in detail the terms of the agreement. When buying life insurance, you should pay attention to the policy's general terms and conditions, the special features of cash-value life insurance, and settlement options.

LO4. **Apply a step-by-step strategy for implementing a life insurance plan.**

Life insurance should be purchased to address the dying-too-soon problem. Your investments should manage the living-too-long problem. Addressing these two problems appropriately requires a small amount of cash-value life insurance, high amounts of term insurance while you are raising children, and a sound investment program to prepare for your retirement years. You should not purchase life insurance until you have determined the actual dollar amount and type of policy you need and compared premiums using various life insurance cost indices.

LET'S TALK ABOUT IT

1. **Thinking About Life Insurance.** What were your feelings about the need for life insurance before you read this chapter? What are they now? Have they been influenced by the recent poor economy?

2. **Are You Insured?** Are you covered by life insurance? If so, how much? Do you feel that you are over- or under-insured?

3. **Term Versus Cash-Value Insurance.** Why do you think people persist in buying cash-value life insurance when, in most cases, they would be better off buying term insurance and investing the money saved into a tax-sheltered retirement account?

4. **Life Insurance for Married Couples.** In many married-couple families, one of the spouses is the primary breadwinner, and the other focuses more on homemaking duties. In your view, how does such an arrangement affect the approach that should be taken for each spouse in terms of life insurance?

5. **Life Insurance for Unmarried Couples.** Many young people today choose to cohabitate rather than marry (at least for some time period). Should this affect their thinking about life insurance?

DO THE MATH

1. **Life Insurance Needs for a Young Single.** Andrew Blake of Tuscaloosa, Alabama, is single and has been working as an admissions counselor at a university for three years. Andrew owns a home valued at $156,000 on which he owes $135,000. He has a two-year-old vehicle valued at $12,500 on which he owes $8000. He has about $3800 remaining on his student loans. His retirement account has grown to $7800, and he owns some stock valued at $4400. He has no life insurance and is considering buying some. How much should he buy?

2. **Life Insurance Needs for a Young Married Couple.** Kyle and Laura Parker from Ypsilanti, Michigan, have been married for three years. They recently bought a home costing $212,000 using a $190,000 mortgage. They have no other debts. Kyle earns $42,000 per year, and Laura earns $41,000. Each has a retirement plan valued at approximately $10,000. They recently received an offer in the mail from their mortgage lender for a mortgage life insurance policy of $190,000. Their only life insurance currently is a $20,000 cash-value survivorship joint life policy. They each would like to provide the other with support for five years if one of them should die.

   (a) Assuming $10,000 in final expenses and $20,000 allocated to help make mortgage payments, calculate the amount of life insurance they need using the needs-based approach.

   (b) How would their needs change if Laura became pregnant?

3. **Borrowing from a Cash-Value Life Insurance Policy.** Lauren Crow of Riverside, California, has a $100,000 participating cash-value policy written on her life. The policy has accumulated $4700 in cash value; Lauren has borrowed $3000 of this value. The policy also has accumulated unpaid dividends of $1666. Yesterday Lauren paid her premium of $1200 for the coming year. What is the current death benefit from this policy?

FINANCIAL PLANNING CASES

CASE 1

The Johnsons Change Their Life Insurance Coverage

Harry and Belinda Johnson spend $15 per month on life insurance in the form of a premium on a $10,000, paid-at-65 cash-value policy on Harry. Belinda has a group term insurance policy from her employer with a face amount of $85,500 (1.5 times her annual salary). By choosing a group life insurance plan from his menu of employee benefits, Harry now has $39,000 (his annual salary) of group term life insurance. Harry and Belinda have decided that, because they have no children, they could reduce their life insurance needs by protecting one another's income for only four years, assuming the survivor would be able to fend for himself or herself after that time. They also realize that their savings fund is so low that it would have no bearing on their life insurance needs. Harry and Belinda are basing their calculations on a projected 4 percent rate of return after taxes and inflation. They also estimate the following expenses: $10,000 for final expenses, $6000 for readjustment expenses, and $5000 for repayment of short-term debts.

   (a) Should the $3000 interest earnings from Harry's trust fund be included in his annual income for the purposes of calculating the likely dollar loss if he were to die? (See the discussions about the Johnsons at the end of Chapter 2.) Explain your response.

   (b) Based on your response to the previous question, how much more life insurance does Harry need? Use the Run the Numbers worksheet on page 349 to arrive at your answer.

   (c) Repeat the calculations to arrive at the additional life insurance needed on Belinda's life.

   (d) How might the Johnsons most economically meet any additional life insurance needs you have determined they may have?

   (e) In addition to their life insurance planning, how might the Johnsons begin to prepare for their retirement years?

CASE 2

Victor and Maria Hernandez Contemplate Switching Life Insurance Policies

Victor and Maria Hernandez have a total of $200,000 in life insurance. Victor has a $50,000 cash-value policy purchased more than 20 years ago when the couple was first married and a $100,000 group term policy through his employer. Maria has a $50,000 group term insurance policy through her employer. The couple has been approached by a life insurance agent who thinks that they need to change their policy mix because, he says, they are inadequately insured. Specifically, the agent has suggested that Victor cash in his cash-value policy and buy a new variable-universal life insurance policy.

   (a) If Victor cashes in his policy, what options would he have when receiving the cash value?

   (b) Determine what the $16,000 in cash value in Victor's life insurance policy would be worth in 20 years if that sum were invested somewhere else and earned an 8 percent annual return. (Hint: Use the *Garman/Forgue* companion website.)

   (c) Would cashing in the policy be a wise decision? Why or why not?

   (d) As the Hernandezes' children are now grown and out on their own, and both Victor and

Maria are employed full time, give general reasons why Victor may need more or less insurance.

(e) Explain why it would be a bad idea for Victor to buy a variable-universal life insurance policy.

CASE 3

Julia Starts Thinking About Life Insurance

Julia Price is now in her late 30s and has always wanted children. She has arranged to adopt two siblings from overseas, ages 2 and 4. Julia is happy that she earns enough money to support the children adequately, but the agency sponsoring the adoption also requires that adoptive parents purchase sufficient life insurance. Julia currently has a $20,000 paid-up cash-value life insurance policy purchased by her parents when she was a child. In addition, Julia's employer provides term insurance that matches her salary as an employee benefit, $150,000 in her case. She talked with the agency, and they suggested that she buy a whole life insurance policy in the amount of $450,000 based on her current salary of $150,000. Julia isn't sure this is the way to go. For one thing, the policy would cost about $5000 per year. Further, she realizes that the amount the agency requires would not maintain the children's lifestyle for long and not be sufficient to help pay for their college educations. Julia is thinking that guaranteed renewable term insurance would be a better way to go. Offer your opinion about her thinking.

CASE 4

Life Insurance for a Newly Married Couple

Just-married couples sometimes overindulge in the type and amount of life insurance that they buy. John and Nicole Greenwood of Murfreesboro, Tennessee, took a different approach. Both were working and had a small amount of life insurance provided through their respective employee benefit programs: John, $40,000, and Nicole, $50,000. During their discussion of life insurance needs and related costs, they decided that if Nicole completed her master's degree in industrial psychology, she would have better employment opportunities. Consequently, they decided to use money they had available for additional life insurance to pay for Nicole's education. They both feel, however, that they do not want to have inadequate life insurance.

(a) In what way does Nicole's return to school alter the Greenwoods' life insurance needs?

(b) Would you agree that the amount of life insurance provided by the Greenwoods' respective employers is adequate while Nicole is in school? Explain your response.

(c) Summarize how the Greenwoods' life insurance needs might change over their life cycle.

CASE 5

Fraternity Members Contemplate Permanent Life Insurance

Zachary Chen is a college student from Prescott, Arizona. Soon to graduate, Zachary was approached recently by a life insurance agent, who set up a group meeting for several members of his fraternity. During the meeting, the agent presented six life insurance plans and was very persuasive about the benefits of a universal life insurance plan that his company calls Affordable Life II. Under the plan, the prospective graduate can buy $100,000 of permanent life insurance for a very low premium during the first five years and then pay a higher premium later when income presumably will have increased. Zachary was confused after the meeting, as were his friends. Armed with your knowledge from this personal finance book, you have been asked to respond to some of their questions.

(a) Do you think universal life insurance is a good deal for these people? Why or why not?

(b) How can the individual fraternity members decide how much life insurance they need?

(c) Life insurance cannot be as confusing as the agent made it seem. What clearer explanation would you give to the fraternity members?

(d) What type of life insurance, if any, would you advise for the fraternity brothers?

(e) How would they know if a life insurance policy is offered at a fair price?

CASE 6

A Married Couple with Children Address Their Life Insurance Needs

Joseph and Samantha Hensley of Rochester, Michigan, are a married couple in their mid-30s. They have two children, ages 5 and 3, and Samantha is pregnant with their third child. Samantha is a part-time book indexer who earned $15,000 after taxes last year. Because she performs much of her work at home, it is unlikely that she will need to curtail her work after the baby is born. Joseph is a family therapist; he earned $48,000 last year after taxes. Because both are self-employed, Samantha and Joseph do not have access to group life insurance. They are each covered by $50,000 universal life policies they purchased three years ago. In addition, Joseph is covered by a $50,000, five-year guaranteed renewable term policy, which will expire next year. The Hensleys are currently reassessing their life insurance program. As a preliminary step in their analysis, they have determined that Samantha's account with Social Security would yield the family about $1094 per month, or an annual benefit of $13,128, if she were to die. For Joseph, the figure would be $2072 per month, or an annual benefit of $24,864. Both agree that they would like to support each of their children to age 22, but to date, they have been unable to start a college savings fund. The couple estimates that it would cost $40,000 to put each child through a regional university in their state as measured in today's dollars. They expect that burial expenses for each spouse would total about $12,000, and they would like to have a lump sum of $50,000 to help the surviving spouse make payments on their home mortgage. They also feel that each spouse would want to take a six-month leave from work if the other were to die.

(a)   Calculate the amount of life insurance that Samantha needs based on the information given. Use the Run the Numbers worksheet on page 349 or the *Garman/Forgue* companion website. Assume a 3 percent rate of return after taxes and inflation and an income need for 22 years because the unborn child will need financial support for that many years.

(b)   Calculate the amount of life insurance that Joseph needs based on the information given. Use the Run the Numbers worksheet on page 349 or the *Garman/Forgue* companion website. Assume a 3 percent rate of return after taxes and inflation and an income need for 22 years because the unborn child will need financial support for that many years.

(c)   If Samantha and Joseph purchased term insurance to cover their additional needs, how much more would each need to spend on life insurance based on the information in Table 12-4?

BE YOUR OWN PERSONAL FINANCIAL MANAGER

1.   **Calculating Life Insurance Need.** Review the material in "How Much Life Insurance Do You Need?" on pages 346–351. Then using dollar amounts that fit your personal situation, complete Worksheet 47: Determining My Life Insurance Needs from "My Personal Financial Planner." If you are currently single and childless, for the purposes of this activity, assume that you are 30 years old, have two children under age 5, are married, and earn $60,000 per year and redo the estimate of need. How would having a family change your need for life insurance?

MY PERSONAL
FINANCIAL
PLANNER

2.   **Review Your Life Insurance Program.** Review the material in "There Are Only Two Basic Types of Life Insurance" and "Understanding Your Life Insurance Policy" on pages 351–362. Then examine any life insurance policies on your life. Given what you learn from those policies and your own need for life insurance as determined in item 1 above, decide on the amount and type(s) of additional life insurance you probably need and any appropriate policy features, such as who should own the policy(s) and be named as beneficiaries.

3.   **Name Your Beneficiary.** Review the information in "Understanding Your Life Insurance Policy" on pages 357–362. Then revisit the naming of the beneficiary on any policies currently in force on your life and make any changes desired. If you are not currently covered by an insurance policy, assume that you have taken a job after graduation and your employer offers free life insurance as an employee benefit. Who would you name as your beneficiary?

4.   **Life Insurance Settlement Options.** Review the material in "Settlement Options Allow the Beneficiary to Decide How to Receive the Death Benefit" on page 360. If you were the beneficiary on another person's life insurance policy in the amount of $100,000, how would you choose to receive the benefits if you were to receive the proceeds of the policy?

5.   **Life-Cycle Life Insurance Planning.** Review the information in "Next, Properly Integrate Your Life Insurance into Your Overall Financial Planning," including Figure 12-3. Then map out a plan for yourself that integrates life insurance and investments. The plan should protect you from both the dying-too-soon and living-too-long risks outlined on pages 363-366. Make appropriate assumptions for your plans regarding marriage and having children and project your plan out to age 65.

6.   **Set Up a Layered Term Insurance Program.** Review the material in the Did You Know? box titled "How to Layer Your Term Insurance Policies for Only $60 per Month" on page 367, and then complete Worksheet 48: Layering Term Insurance Policies from "My Personal Financial Planner," which allows you to set up a term insurance program until age 60. Use your current personal situation if you currently have dependents, or assume that you will earn an annual salary of $45,000 at age 25 and plan to have at least two children.

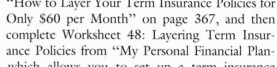
MY PERSONAL
FINANCIAL
PLANNER

ON THE 'NET

Go to the Web pages indicated to complete these exercises. You can also go to the *Garman/Forgue* companion website at www.cengagebrain.com for an expanded list of exercises. Under Economics and Business, select "Finance" and then "Personal Finance" and select the title of this text. Click on the Internet Exercises link for this chapter.

1. **Obtain a Quote on Your Life Insurance.** Visit the website for AccuQuote at www.accuquote.com to obtain a quote for the annual premium on a $200,000 guaranteed renewable, ten-year term policy for you. Then call a life insurance agent in your community to obtain a quote on the same term insurance coverage. How do the term rates quoted by your local agent compare with the rates found over the Internet? Also, ask for the quote on a $100,000 universal life policy with guaranteed insurability and waiver-of-premium options. Ask the agent to explain why the quotes for the two types of policies differ. Analyze his or her response based on what you learned in this chapter.

2. **Check an Insurance Company's Financial Strength.** Visit the website for A.M. Best Company at www.ambest.com/ratings and check the ratings for the insurance company recommended by the agent in Exercise 1 as well as the company with the lowest cost for term insurance that you found on the Web. What do the ratings tell you about the relative strengths of those companies?

3. **Determine Your Need for More Life Insurance.** Visit the Life and Health Insurance Foundation for Education website at www.lifehappens.org/life-insurance-needs-calculator. Calculate your current need for life insurance. Then recalculate your need for five years from now given your estimates of your income and family situation.

ACTION INVOLVEMENT PROJECTS

1. **Review Life Insurance Company Websites.** Visit the websites of four major life insurance companies. Focus on how their approaches to educating the public about life insurance are similar to or different from the information provided in this chapter. Write a summary of your findings.

2. **Talk to a Life Insurance Agent.** Visit a life insurance agent and ask for an assessment of your life insurance needs given your current life-cycle phase and situation. Compare the information you receive with what you have learned in this chapter and write a summary of your findings.

3. **How Others Approach the Need for Life Insurance.** Talk to three friends and/or relatives below age 30 who are married. Ask about their approach to life insurance and how they have gone about setting up a life insurance program. Write a summary of your findings and compare what they have done to what you would do if you were in a similar situation.

4. **Term Versus Cash-Value Life Insurance.** Talk to three of your friends or acquaintances who have never purchased life insurance. Explain to them the differences between term and cash-value life insurance. Then inquire about which type they would prefer to buy. Write a summary of your findings and compare their views with yours.

Visit the Garman/Forgue companion website at **www.cengagebrain.com.**

PART

4

YOU MUST BE KIDDING, RIGHT?

Twins Laura and Lauren Jackson have worked for the same employer for many years. They have always differed in their philosophies regarding investing for retirement. Laura invested $5000 for ten years starting at age 25 and never added any more money to the account. Lauren waited until age 35 to begin saving for retirement and she invested $5000 per year for 20 years, and she too never contributed more to her account. Assuming that they both earn an 8 percent annual return, how much more money will Laura have accumulated for retirement than Lauren by the time they reach age 65?

A. $144,000

B. $234,000

C. $494,000

D. $728,000

The answer is B, $234,000. Laura's account balance at age 65 is projected at $728,000 and Lauren's is $494,000. Even though Laura saved for only 10 years compared with Lauren's 20 years of saving, Laura's long-term investment approach had her starting to save for retirement early in her working career. Thus, she accumulated 47 percent more money than her sister ($234,000 ÷ $494,000). Starting early on long-term investment goals is a money-winning idea!

LEARNING OBJECTIVES

After reading this chapter, you should be able to:

❶ Explain how to get started as an investor.

❷ Identify your investment philosophy and invest accordingly.

❸ Describe the major factors that affect the rate of return on investments.

❹ Decide which of the four long-term investment strategies you will utilize.

❺ Create your own investment plan.

WHAT DO YOU RECOMMEND?

Jennifer and Janie are sisters, both in their 20s. Jennifer drives a leased BMW convertible, and she makes about $42,000, including tips, as a part-time bartender at two different restaurants. Although she has no employee benefits, she enjoys having flexible work hours so that she can go to the beach and the local nightspots. Currently, Jennifer has $10,000 in credit card debt. She has $1500 in a bank savings account, and two years ago she opened an individual retirement account (IRA) with a $1000 investment in a mutual fund. Her sister Janie drives a paid-for Honda Civic, pays her credit card purchases in full each month, and sacrifices some of her salary by putting $100 per month into her employer's company stock through her 401(k) retirement account. Over the past seven years, the stock price, which was once about $40, has risen to almost $70, and Janie's 401(k) plan is now worth about $16,000. Janie also has invested about $14,000 in aggressive-growth mutual funds, and she plans to use that money for a down payment on a home purchase. She earns $58,000 as a manager of a restaurant, plus she receives an annual bonus ranging from $2000 to $4000 every January that

she uses for a spring vacation in Mexico. Janie's employer provides many employee benefits.

What do you recommend to Jennifer and Janie on the subject of investment fundamentals regarding:

1. Getting more money to save and invest?
2. Prerequisites to investing for Jennifer?
3. Portfolio diversification for Janie?
4. Dollar-cost averaging for Jennifer?
5. Investment alternatives for Janie?

LEARNING OBJECTIVE

Explain how to get started as an investor.

investing
Putting saved money to work so that it makes you even more money.

securities
Assets suitable for investment, including stocks, bonds, and mutual funds.

stocks
Shares of ownership in a corporation.

portfolio
Collection of investments assembled to meet your investment goals.

FINANCIAL POWER POINT

Create Wealth from Investments, Not from Wages

For most people, it is difficult to accumulate wealth by saving out of earnings. Most wealth comes from investment growth. To create wealth, use your savings to invest in stocks, bonds, mutual funds, or real estate and/or start a business.

At many points in this book, we have encouraged you to set aside funds for the future, especially by accumulating funds through regular savings. This approach is a wise course of action, but building real wealth requires an additional consideration—earning a good rate of return on your money. The difference in the return is a major distinction between mere savings and investing.

For the past 25 years, one of the best ways to make money over the long term was to invest in stocks, bonds, and mutual funds that invest in those vehicles. Despite the recent economic meltdown and stock market declines as well as the subsequent bull market, this remains the best advice. The earning power of the U.S. and world economies, even with serious fluctuations, endures. This chapter (and the following three chapters) explains both why this is true and how to succeed during an economic recession; in sluggish, weak economic times; or in the course of a rapidly growing economy. Being clueless about investing is not an option for those who want to achieve financial success.

STARTING YOUR INVESTMENT PROGRAM

To help secure a desirable future lifestyle, you cannot spend every dollar that you earn today. Instead, you must sacrifice by setting aside some of your current income and investing it. You postpone the pleasure of using money for here-and-now consumption so you can have more in the future. To be financially successful, you are wise to start investing early in life, invest regularly, and stay invested. Why? Because, for every five years you delay investing, you will have to double your monthly investment amount to achieve the same goals. Remember: You—and no one else—are responsible for your own financial success.

Investing Is More Than Saving

Savings is the accumulation of excess funds by intentionally spending less than you earn. Investing is more. **Investing** is taking some of the money you are saving and putting it to work so that it makes you even more money. Your goals and the time it will take to reach those goals dictate the investment strategies you follow and the investment alternatives you choose.

The most common ways that people invest are by putting money into assets called **securities**, such as stocks, bonds, and mutual funds (often purchased through their employer-sponsored retirement accounts), and by buying real estate. **Stocks** are shares of ownership in a corporation, and bonds represent loans to companies and governments. All of your investment assets make up your **portfolio**, the collection of multiple investments in different assets chosen to meet your investment goals.

Suggestions on Your Readiness to Invest

Here are signs you are ready to begin an investment program. If you are not accomplishing these basic personal financial tasks, get your finances in order so you can get your investing program under way:

- **You live within your income.** If you find yourself constantly running short of cash toward the end of the month or if you make only minimum payments on your credit card balances, you need to institute budget controls so you can live within your income.

- **You are able to save regularly.** A good financial manager forgoes some spending to save regularly to build an emergency fund, acquire goods and services, and achieve other goals. You can't invest unless you have some savings with which to begin.

- **You use credit wisely.** Pay off any high-interest debt and pay credit card bills in full each month. Have a maximum credit limit sufficient to meet personal financial emergencies.
- **You carry adequate insurance.** Liability insurance protects your assets and lifestyle in the event you experience a loss and/or are sued. Health insurance is a must. Term life insurance protects the lifestyle of dependents.

Decide Why You Want to Invest

When you have reasons to invest, such as to buy a home or plan for a financially satisfying retirement, you will be more likely to consider investments as a high-priority category in your budget. People invest for five reasons:

- To achieve financial goals, such as taking a vacation, purchasing a new car, making a down payment on a home, financing a child's education, or starting a business
- To gain wealth and a feeling of financial security
- To increase current income
- To meet retirement income needs
- To maximize enjoyment of life

Where Can You Get the Money to Invest?

You must save money to have it for investing. Consider the following suggestions:

- **Pay yourself first.** Live within your means every time you receive income by earmarking in your budget some money for saving.
- **Save—don't spend—extra funds.** When unexpected money arrives, save part or all of it. Examples of extra money are a year-end employer bonus, a commission check, a salary raise, a gift of money, an inheritance, and an income tax refund. Also, when you have a surplus in a monthly budget category, save it.
- **Participate in your employer's retirement plan.** When your employer offers to match your contribution to a 401(k) retirement plan, invest at least enough to get the full match because it's free money.
- **Make saving automatic.** Have funds automatically transferred from your bank to a savings account or money market fund and arrange for preset transfers from your paycheck to your retirement plan.
- **Continue to make installment payments to yourself.** If you make installment repayments on a debt or lease, continue to make the "payments" (or part of the amount) to your savings account after the debt has been repaid.
- **Break a habit.** Put aside the money you would have spent on a former habit, such as buying lottery tickets, lattes at Starbucks, and enjoying pricey restaurant lunches.
- **Stop a cash leak.** Almost everyone's budget has a category or two that often involves overspending. Cutting back on entertainment or food or another cash leak may help you find some cash to invest.
- **Get a part-time job.** Save the after-tax money earned from an extra job.
- **Scrimp for one month.** To succeed, cut back and question every possible expense. Knowing that this level of frugality will end after 30 days will help motivate you.

What Investment Returns Are Possible?

Figure 13-1 shows the long-term rates of return on some popular investments. While stock market returns have averaged more than 10 percent over the long term, the returns in the 2001-2010 decade were extremely low and then sharply higher the last couple of years. Corporate profits—and investor's returns—are difficult to earn when the U.S. and most of the world's economies are struggling. During such challenging economic times, one's average investment returns from stocks are more likely to be 5 to 6 percent. This is likely to come from a 2 percent dividend yield for stocks and an

Figure 13-1

The Long-Term Rates of Return on Investments

(Annualized returns from 1926 through 2011)

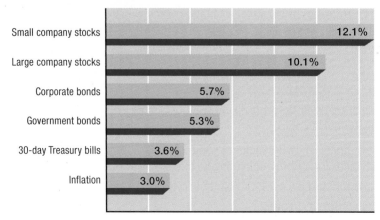

earnings growth rate of around 4 percent. Despite these "half-size returns," these are still good returns when inflation is low.

Since 1927, the worst 20-year performance for stocks was a gain of 3 percent annually. The return for the decade of 2000 to 2009 was -1 percent annually, primarily because of the horrible stock market of the Great Recession. Over the past 80 years, the chance of making money during any one year in the stock market has been 66 percent. Over five years, the probability increases to 81 percent; over ten years, it increases to 89 percent.

The scenario for long-term investors in the foreseeable future in the United States is unspectacular average equity return primarily owing to weak demand and sluggish economic growth. Some sectors and geographic regions in the world will continue to outperform others. During long periods of poor economic times, there are always periods of growth as well. Realize, too, that as the U.S. and other economies return to a mode of solid economic growth, the typical stock investor can once again expect average investment returns in excess of 10 percent annually. Also understand that the stock market always goes up in anticipation of the economy showing measurable growth. Thus, if you wait too long, you will miss the increase.

When people invest their money, they take a **financial risk** (also called **business risk**)—namely, the possibility that the investment will fail to pay any return to the investor. At the extremes, a company could have a very good year earning a considerable profit, or it could go bankrupt, causing investors to lose all of their money. Later in the chapter, we examine how investing poses a number of other kinds of risk.

Investors hope that their investments will earn them a positive **total return**, which is the income an investment generates from a combination of current income and capital gains. **Current income** is money received while you own an investment. It is usually received on a regular basis as interest, rent, or dividends. As we have noted elsewhere in the text, **interest** is the charge for borrowing money. Investors in bonds earn interest. **Rent** is payment received in return for allowing someone to use your real estate property, such as land or a building. A **dividend** is a portion of a company's earnings that the firm pays out to its shareholders. For example, Nina Henson from Oneonta, New York, purchased 100 shares of H&M stock at $45 per share ($4500) last year. The company paid dividends of $3 per share during the year, so Nina received $300 in cash dividends as current income.

A **capital gain** occurs only when you actually sell the investment; it results from an increase in the value of the initial investment. It is calculated by subtracting the total amount paid for the investment (including purchase transaction costs) from the higher price at which it is sold (minus any sales transaction costs). For example, if the price of

financial risk
Possibility that an investment will fail to pay a return to the investor.

total return
Income an investment generates from current income and capital gains.

current income
Money received while you own an investment; usually received regularly as interest, rent, or dividends.

interest
Charge for borrowing money; investors in bonds earn interest.

capital gain
Increase in the value of an initial investment (less costs) realized upon the sale of the investment.

H&M company stock rose to $52 during the year, Nina could sell it for a capital gain. If Nina paid a transaction cost of $1 per share at both purchase and time of sale, her capital gain would be $500 [($5200 − $100) − ($4500 + $100)].

Capital losses can occur as well. For most investments, a trade-off arises between capital gains and current income. Investments with potential for high capital gains often pay little current income, and investments that pay substantial current income generally have little or no potential for capital gains. Long-term investors are usually willing to forgo current income in favor of possibly earning substantial future capital gains.

The **rate of return, or yield**, is the total return on an investment expressed as a percentage of its price. It is usually stated on an annualized basis. For example, if Nina sells the H&M stock for $52 per share after one year, she will have a total return of $800 ($300 in dividends plus $500 in capital gains). Her yield would be 17.78 percent ($800 ÷ $4500).

capital loss
Decrease in paper value of an initial investment; only realized if sold.

rate of return/yield
Total return on an investment expressed as a percentage of its price.

✔ Concept Check 13.1

1. What should you do before you are ready to invest?

2. Identify three ways that you personally could find some money to invest in the next five years.

3. What are the two parts of an investor's total return?

LEARNING OBJECTIVE ❷

Identify your investment philosophy and invest accordingly.

IDENTIFY YOUR INVESTMENT PHILOSOPHY AND INVEST ACCORDINGLY

Achieving financial success requires that you understand your investment philosophy and adhere to it when investing. Thus, you also need to know about investment risk and what to do about it. Keep in mind the advice offered by investment guru Warren Buffett, "The first rule of investing is don't lose money; the second rule is don't forget Rule No. 1."

speculative risk
Involves the potential for either gain or loss; equity investments might do either.

investment risk
The possibility that the yield on an investment will deviate from its expected return.

How to Handle Investment Risk

Pure risk, which exists when there is no potential for gain, only the possibility of loss, was discussed in Chapter 10. Investments, in contrast, are subject to **speculative risk**, which exists in situations that offer potential for gain as well as for loss. **Investment risk** represents the uncertainty that the yield on an investment will deviate from what is expected. For most investments, the greater the risk is, the higher the potential return. This potential for gain is what motivates people to accept increasingly greater levels of risk, as illustrated in Figure 13-2. Nevertheless, many people remain seriously averse to risk.

Figure 13-2 also provides insight about possible investment choices. Don't be overwhelmed because all of these investments are explained in the following chapters. You *will* learn how to make informed investment decisions for yourself.

Risk-Free Investing Exists If you want a completely safe investment, you can invest in U.S. Treasury securities (discussed in Chapter 14), which are backed by the full faith and credit of the U.S. government. With this sort of investment, you lend your money to the federal government and it is later returned with interest. One form of Treasury securities is the short-term Treasury bill, or **T-bill**, which is a government IOU of one year or less. Because T-bills are risk-free investments, they pay too low a return for most people, perhaps only 0.25 or 0.35 percent. Some people, however, invest in T-bills to safeguard their money until it is invested at a later time.

FINANCIAL POWER POINT

Take a Risk-Tolerance Quiz

Find out how much risk you can comfortably tolerate by taking a risk-tolerance quiz at one of the following websites:

* Bankrate.com: www.bankrate.com/brm/news/investing/20011127a.asp

* MSN: www.moneycentral.msn.com/investor/calcs/n_riskq/main.asp

* Kiplinger: www.kiplinger.com/tools/riskfind.html

* Vanguard: https://personal.vanguard.com/us/FundsInvQuestionnaire

The Risk Pyramid Reveals the Trade-Offs Between Risk and Return

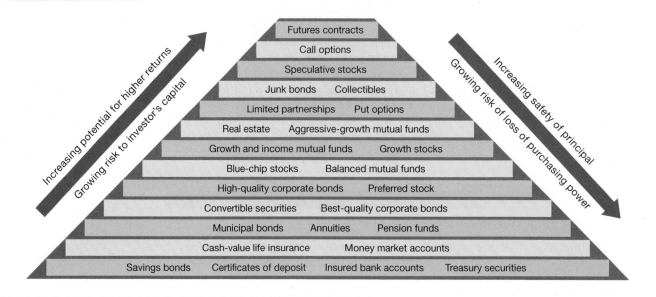

Investors Demand a Risk Premium Investors need the promise of a high return to warrant placing their money at risk in an investment. When making investments, people demand a **risk premium (or equity risk premium)** for their willingness to make investments for which there is no guarantee of future success. This risk premium constitutes the difference between a riskier investment's expected return and the totally safe return on the T-bill. The premium is the compensation needed to encourage risk-averse investors to invest in equities rather than keeping money in safer investments, like U.S. government securities.

If the expected return is 8 percent on stocks and 3 percent on ten-year Treasury securities, the risk premium is 5 percent. Industry experts figure that the amount of the risk premium for most investors is 3 to 5 percent, although the long-term average is 8 percent. Higher-risk investments carry higher-risk premiums.

risk premium (or equity risk premium)
The difference between a riskier investment's expected return and the totally safe return on the T-bill; this premium is the compensation needed to encourage risk-averse investors to invest in equities rather than keeping money in safer investments, like T-bills.

Ultraconservative Investors Are Really Just Savers

The world of investments offers many ways to save that present little or no risk of losing your principal and still earn respectable—albeit limited—returns. These financial vehicles include federally insured savings accounts, certificates of deposit, and EE bonds, as well as money market accounts. Ultraconservative investors, especially those who cannot sleep at night if they think their money is at risk, do not consider putting money into investments, choosing instead to stick with the safest options. Over the course of a year, an ultraconservative investor who places $1000 in one of these options will not lose a penny and will likely gain $15 to $20. In actuality, ultraconservative investors are not really investors. They are savers. As a result, they do not get ahead financially over the long term because taxes and inflation offset most, if not all, of their interest earnings. On the other hand, when asset values sharply decline, ultraconservative investors still have their money!

What Is Your Investment Philosophy?

Investors have to take risks that are appropriate to reach their financial goals. The task is to find the right balance and make choices accordingly. You must weigh the risks of an investment with the likelihood of not reaching your goal. Your **risk tolerance** is your willingness to weather changes in the values of your investments. This is not the same as your capacity to take risk. To be successful in investing, your tolerance for risk must be

risk tolerance
An investor's willingness to weather changes in security prices, that is, to weather market risk.

factored into your investment philosophy. If you lose sleep over your investments, you know it is time to reduce your risk and adjust your investment philosophy.

An **investment philosophy** is one's general approach to tolerance for risk in investments, whether it is conservative, moderate, or aggressive, given the financial goals to be achieved. The more risk you take, within reason, the more you can expect to earn and accumulate over the long term. However, just because you are comfortable with a risky portfolio does not mean that you actually need one. By the same token, you still need to be aggressive enough to meet your financial goals. Smart investors follow their investment philosophy without wavering; they do not change course unless their basic objectives change.

Are You a Conservative Investor?

If you have a **conservative investment philosophy**, you accept very little risk and are generally rewarded with relatively low rates of return for seeking the twin goals of a moderate amount of current income and preservation of capital. **Preservation of capital** means that you do not want to lose any of the money you have invested. In short, you could be characterized as an investor who is **risk averse**. A risk-averse investor is one who tends to dislike risk and is unable to put money into investments that seem risky, although he or she might take a risk if the promised return is high.

Conservative investors focus on protecting themselves. They do so by carefully avoiding losses and trying to stay with investments that demonstrate gains, often for long time periods (perhaps for five or ten years). Tactically, they rarely sell their investments. Investors who are approaching retirement or who are planning to withdraw money from their investments in the near future often adhere to a conservative investment philosophy.

Conservative investors typically consider investing in obligations issued by the government. Examples include Treasury bills, notes, and bonds (insured as to timely payment of principal and interest by the U.S. government), municipal bonds, high-quality (blue-chip) corporate bonds and stocks, balanced mutual funds (which own both stocks and bonds), certificates of deposit, and annuities. A **bond** is essentially a loan that the investor makes to a government or a corporation. Thus, a bond is a debt of the issuer. Over the course of a year, a conservative investor with $1000 could possibly lose $20 and is likely to gain $20 to $30.

Are You a Moderate Investor?

People with a **moderate investment philosophy** seek capital gains through slow and steady growth in the value of their investments along with some current income. They invite only a fair amount of risk of capital loss. Most have no immediate need for the funds but instead focus on laying the investment foundation for later years or building on such a base. Moderate investors are fairly comfortable during rising and falling market conditions. They remain secure in the knowledge that they are investing for the long term. Their tactics might include spreading investment funds among several choices and trading some assets perhaps once a year.

People seeking moderate returns consider investing in dividend-paying common stocks, growth and income mutual funds, high-quality corporate bonds, government bonds, and real estate. Over the course of a year, a moderate investor with $1000 could possibly lose $150 and is likely to gain $40 to $60.

Are You an Aggressive Investor?

If you choose to strive for a very high return by accepting a high level of risk, you have an **aggressive investment philosophy**. As such, you could be characterized as a risk seeker. Aggressive investors primarily seek capital gains. Many such investors take a short-term approach, remaining confident that they can profit substantially during major upswings in market prices.

People seeking exceptionally high returns consider investing in common stocks of new or fast-growing companies, high-yielding junk bonds, and aggressive-growth mutual funds. Such investors may put their money into limited real estate partnerships, undeveloped land, precious metals, gems, commodity futures, stock-index futures, and collectibles. Devotees of this investment philosophy sometimes do not spread their funds among many alternatives. Also, they may adopt short-term tactics to increase capital gains. For example, aggressive investors might place most of their investment funds in a single stock in the hope that it will rise 10 percent over 90 days, giving an annual yield

investment philosophy
Investor's general tolerance for risk in investments, whether it is conservative, moderate, or aggressive, given the investor's financial goals.

conservative investment philosophy (risk aversion)
Investors with this philosophy accept very little risk and are generally rewarded with relatively low rates of return for seeking the twin goals of a moderate amount of current income and preservation of capital.

risk averse
In investments, one who tends to dislike risk and is unable to put money into investments that seem risky, although he or she might take a risk if the promised return is high.

bond
A debt instrument issued by an organization that promises repayment at a specific time and the right to receive regular interest payments during the life of the bond; from the investor's standpoint, a loan that the investor makes to a government or a corporation.

moderate investment philosophy (risk indifference)
Investors with this philosophy accept some risk as they seek capital gains through slow and steady growth in investment value along with current income.

aggressive investment philosophy (risk seeker)
Investors with this philosophy primarily seek capital gains, often with a short time horizon.

An active investor keeps a close watch on the economy and financial markets.

active investor
An investor who wishes to manage his or her own account by carefully studying the economy, market trends, and investment alternatives; regularly monitoring these factors; and buying and selling three to four times a year to rebalance his or her portfolio.

market efficiency
The speed at which new information is reflected in investment prices suggesting that security prices are reflective of their true value at all times because publicly available information has driven market prices to the correct level.

passive investor
An investor who does not actively engage in trading securities or monitoring his or her investments; seeks to match the market return via mutual funds or other managed investments in the longer term.

of more than 30 percent. Those shares could then be sold and the money invested elsewhere.

Investment tactics for aggressive investors are discussed in Chapter 16. Aggressive investors must be emotionally and financially able to weather substantial short-term losses—such as a downward swing in a stock's price of 30 or 40 percent—even though they might expect that an upswing in price will occur in the future. Over the course of a year, an aggressive investor with $1000 could possibly lose $300 and could gain $100, $200, $300, or even more.

Should You Take an Active or Passive Investing Approach?

Another aspect of your personal investment philosophy is your level of involvement in investing. That is, do you want to be an active or passive investor?

Active Investing An **active investor** carefully studies the economy, market trends, and investment alternatives; regularly monitors these factors; and makes decisions to buy and sell, perhaps three or four or more times a year, with or without the advice of a professional. In addition, because the prices of many investments vary with certain news events, world happenings, and economic and political variables, active investors stay alert. Knowing what is going on in the larger world helps active investors understand when to buy or to sell investments quickly so as to reap profits and/or reduce losses.

Active Investing in an Efficient Market Market efficiency has to do with the speed at which new information is reflected in investment prices. The theory is that security prices are reflective of their true value at all times because publicly available information has driven market prices to the correct level.

Thus the typical person is challenged to find undervalued investments. When information is reported in the financial press, it is already too late for the typical investor to act and make a profit. And investors don't always even know which information is relevant. Therefore, individual investors cannot pursue an active investment strategy that beats the market as they are just as likely to invest in an overpriced security rather than one that is undervalued. Thus, the typical investor earns substantially less than average market returns. Not surprisingly, stock analysts and investment managers believe they can make better choices than the average investor in part because they can act on information more quickly than other investors. The reality, however, is that 60 to 80 percent of investment managers fail to beat the average returns of the stock market.

Passive Investing A **passive investor** does not actively engage in trading of securities or spend large amounts of time monitoring his or her investments. Such an individual may make regular investments in securities, such as mutual funds (described in Chapter 15), and his or her assets are rarely sold for short-term profits. Instead, passive investors simply aim to match the returns of the entire market. They ignore "hot" tips and the investment of the day touted in the financial press. They keep their emotions in check, and they earn higher returns than active investors over the long term. Most long-term investors utilize a passive approach.

So What Should You Do?

Once you have clarified your investment philosophy and how involved you want to be as an investor, you will be able to make future investing decisions with confidence and conviction. You will be able to show patience by following your long-term views rather than making emotional and wrong decisions—in other words, mistakes—about your money. The investments you choose and the returns earned are likely to match your investment philosophy.

Also important is the time horizon of the goal for which you are investing. When investing for a short-term goal, you would want to be very conservative to ensure that a sudden drop in the market would not jeopardize your reaching the goal before the market has time to recover. When investing for long-term goals, you can afford to be more aggressive. That is why the stock market is a good place to save for retirement. When you retire, you can leave a portion of your portfolio in stocks since you likely will still have 20 to 25 years before you need the last dollars in your nest egg.

Identify the Kinds of Investments You Want to Make

The investments you choose should match your interests. Before investing, think about lending versus owning, short term versus long term, and how to select investments that are likely to provide your desired potential total return.

Do You Want Lending Investments or Ownership Investments?
You can invest money in two ways, by lending or by owning. When you lend your money, you receive some form of IOU and the promise of repayment plus interest. The interest is a form of current income while you hold the investment.

You can lend by depositing money in banks, credit unions, and savings and loan associations (via savings accounts and certificates of deposit) or by lending money to governments (via Treasury notes and bonds as well as state and local bonds), businesses (corporate bonds), mortgage-backed bonds (such as Ginnie Maes), and life insurance companies (annuities). These lending investments, or **debts**, generally offer both a fixed maturity and a fixed income. With a **fixed maturity**, the borrower agrees to repay the principal to the investor on a specific date. With a **fixed income**, the borrower agrees to pay the investor a specific rate of return for use of the principal. Such investments allow lenders to be fairly confident that they will receive a certain amount of interest income for a specified period of time and that the borrowed funds will eventually be returned. Thus, the return is somewhat assured. No matter how much profit the borrower makes with your funds, the investing lender receives only the fixed return promised at the time of the initial investment. Lending investments rarely result in capital gains.

Alternatively, you may invest money through ownership of an asset. Ownership investments are often called **equities**. You can buy common or preferred corporate stock (to obtain part ownership in a corporation) in publicly owned companies, purchase shares in a mutual fund company (which invests your funds in corporate stocks and bonds), put money into your own business, purchase real estate, buy commodity futures (pork bellies or oranges), or buy investment-quality collectibles (such as rare antiques or stamps). Ownership investments have the potential for providing current income; however, the emphasis is usually upon achieving substantial capital gains.

Making Short-, Intermediate-, and Long-Term Investments
If you are investing for a short-term time horizon of less than a year or an intermediate-term of perhaps up to five years, you want to be confident that you preserve the value of what you have. After all, you don't want to lose money in an investment when you need to use that money for a near-term goal, such as college tuition, or be forced to sell an investment because you need cash in a hurry. People with a short or intermediate time horizon require investments that offer some predictability and stability. As a result, these investors are usually more interested in current income than capital gains.

If you are investing to achieve long-term goals, by contrast, you want your money to grow. Therefore, you are likely to keep your money in the same investments for 10 or 20 years. Long-term investors usually invite more risk by seeking capital gains as well as current income. Table 13-1 provides an overview of investments for various time horizons, and Table 13-2 on page 389 gives an overview of several investment alternatives.

Long-term investors seek growth in the value of their investments that exceeds the rate of inflation. In other words, they want their investments to provide a positive **real rate of return**. This is the return after subtracting the effects of both inflation and income taxes.

debts
Lending investments that typically offer both a fixed maturity and a fixed income.

fixed maturity
Specific date on which a borrower agrees to repay the principal to the investor.

fixed income
Specific rate of return that a borrower agrees to pay the investor for use of the principal (initial investment).

equities
Ownership equities such as common or preferred stocks, equity mutual funds, real estate, and so on that focus on capital gains more than on income.

real rate of return
Return on an investment after subtracting the effects of inflation and income taxes.

DID YOU KNOW?

Calculate the Real Rate of Return (After Taxes and Inflation) on Investments

1. *Identify the rate of return before income taxes.* Perhaps you think that a stock will offer a return of 10 percent in one year, including current income and capital gains.

2. *Subtract the effects of your marginal tax rate on the rate of return to obtain the after-tax return.* If you are in the 25 percent federal income tax bracket, the calculation is $(1 - 0.25) \times 0.10 = 0.075 = 7.5$ percent.

3. *Subtract the effects of inflation from the after-tax return to obtain the real rate of return on the investment after taxes and inflation.* If you estimate an annual inflation of 4 percent, the calculation gives 3.5 percent (7.5 percent − 4.0 percent). Thus, your before-tax rate of return of 10 percent provides a real rate of return of 3.5 percent after taxes and inflation.

Choose Investments for Their Components of Total Return

When investing, you want to build a portfolio of investments that will provide the necessary potential total return through current income and capital gains in the proportions that you desire. One stock might provide an anticipated cash dividend of 1.5 percent and an expected annual price appreciation of 6 percent, for a total anticipated return of 7.5 percent. Another choice offering the same projected total return might be a stock with expected annual cash dividends of 2.5 percent and capital gains of 5 percent.

 Concept Check 13.2

1. Summarize your investment philosophy and general approach to tolerance for risk.

2. Indicate whether you view yourself as an active or passive investor, and explain why.

3. Summarize why so many people are lousy investors and not very successful.

4. Summarize your personal views on lending or owning investments.

5. Which type of investment return—current income or capital gains—seems more attractive to you? Why?

Table 13-1

Investments for Various Time Horizons

Time Periods	Possible Investments
Less than 2 years	NOW checking account
	Savings account
	Money market account
	Certificates of deposit
	Treasury issues/corporate bonds maturing within 2 years
2 to 5 years	Corporate bonds maturing within 5 years
	Ginnie Mae bonds
	Stocks paying high dividends
	Balanced mutual funds
6 to 10 years	Stocks paying high dividends
	Ginnie Mae bonds
	Short-term bonds
	Long-term bonds
	Long-term certificates of deposit (CDs)
	Growth and income mutual funds
	Real estate
More than 10 years	Growth stocks
	Long-term bonds
	Precious metals
	Aggressive-growth mutual funds
	Real estate

RISKS AND OTHER FACTORS AFFECT THE INVESTOR'S RETURN

Because of the uncertainty that surrounds investments, people often follow a conservative course in an effort to keep their risk low. Being too conservative when investing means that they also risk not reaching their financial goals. To be a successful investor, you must understand the major factors that affect the rate of return on investments. Being informed, you can then take the appropriate risks when making investment decisions.

LEARNING OBJECTIVE   3

Describe the major factors that affect the rate of return on investments.

Random Risk Is Reduced by Diversification, Eventually

Random risk (also called unsystematic risk) is the risk associated with owning only one investment of a particular type (such as stock in one company) that, by chance, may do very poorly in the future because of uncontrollable or random factors, such as labor unrest, lawsuits, and product recalls. If you invest in only one stock, its value might rise or fall. If you invest in two or three stocks, the odds are lessened that all of their prices will fall. Such **diversification**—the process of reducing risk by spreading investment money among several investment opportunities—provides one effective method of managing random risk. The principle holds that when you own different types of investment assets in a portfolio, some assets should be rising when others are falling. It results in a potential rate of return on all of the investments that is lower than the potential return on a single alternative, but the return is more predictable and the risk of loss is lower. Diversification averages out the high and low returns.

Research suggests that you can cut random risk in half by diversifying into as few as five stocks or bonds; you can eliminate random risk by holding 15 or more stocks or bonds. Rational investors diversify so as to reduce random risk, and over the long term—as little as a decade—it works.

random/unsystematic risk

Risk associated with owning only one investment of a particular type (such as stock in one company) that, by chance, may do very poorly in the future due to uncontrollable or random factors that do not affect the rest of the market.

diversification

Process of reducing risk by spreading investment money among several investment opportunities.

Overview of Investment Alternatives

Table 13-2

This chapter provides background information to help you to initially assess which types of investments might best suit your needs. The next three chapters examine details of investment alternatives. After reading those chapters, you will have learned enough about investments to make informed decisions.

- **Stocks.** Shares of ownership in the assets and earnings of a business corporation. Examples: Blue-chip stocks (like Dow Chemical, ExxonMobil, and General Electric), well-known growth stocks (like Microsoft and McDonald's), lesser-known growth stocks (like American Greeting and Healthdyne), and income stocks (like water and electricity companies).
- **Bonds.** Interest-bearing negotiable certificates of long-term debt issued by a corporation, a municipality (such as a city or state), or the federal government. Examples: U.S. savings bonds, Series EE bonds, corporate bonds, high-yield corporate bonds, municipal bonds, and zero-coupon bonds.
- **Mutual funds.** An investment company that combines the funds of investors who have purchased shares of ownership in it and then invests that money in a diversified portfolio of stocks and bonds issued by other corporations or governments. Examples: Fidelity Growth Fund, Calvert Social Investment, and Vanguard Growth Index.
- **Real estate.** Property consisting of land; all structures permanently attached to that land; and accompanying rights and privileges, such as crop and mineral rights. Examples: residential housing units, commercial properties, residential lots, and raw land.
- **High-risk investments.** Alternatives that have the potential for significant fluctuations in return over short time periods, perhaps only days or weeks. Examples: collectibles (baseball cards, posters, sports jerseys, comic books, stamps, rare coins, antiques), precious metals and stones, and options and futures contracts.

**market risk/systematic risk/
undiversifiable risk**

*Risk that the value of an investment
may drop due to influences and events
that affect all similar investments.*

Market Risk and the Great Recession

Diversification among stocks or bonds cannot eliminate all risks. Some risk would exist even if you owned all of the stocks in a market because stock (and bond) prices in general move up and down over time. This movement results in **market risk** (also known as **systematic or nondiversifiable risk**). In this case, the value of an investment may drop due to influences and events that affect all similar investments. Examples include a change in economic, social, political, or general market conditions; fluctuations in investor preferences; or other broad market-moving factors, such as a recession or a terrorist attack. Market risk can be reduced, though only partially, by dividing your portfolio among several different markets. Normally, not all markets will decline at the same time, but it can happen, as it did between 2007 and 2009.

DID YOU KNOW?

What Happened to All the Money?

Many trillions of dollars in stock market value, money in 401(k) retirement accounts and college savings funds, and equity in homes disappeared between 2007 and 2009. The stock market crash and declining home prices means a lot of money no longer exists. Well, to be honest, it never existed because it was not money in the first place. Money is cash, and an investment or equity in a home is not cash until the asset is converted into cash. Potential money is not the same as cash.

Economists generally believe that all uncertainty can be reduced to measurable risk and that unregulated markets should be stable. However, the worldwide Great Recession demonstrates the ever-present possibility of a systemic mistake in the logic of efficient markets as all types of investments fell in unison. The collapse proves that once-in-a-lifetime financial disasters not only can occur but do, and the financial markets (e.g., credit, investment, and real estate) need better government regulation. The mission of the newly created Financial Stability Oversight Council is to build a warning system to identify financial companies in need of government intervention before they collapse and negatively affect the American economy.

U.S. and world markets are continuing to slowly recover in today's difficult economic environment. Over the short term, diversification cannot protect your investments against market declines, but at least some of your investments will hold their value or most of it. Market risk is the risk that remains after an investor's portfolio has been fully diversified within a particular market, such as stocks. Over the years, market risk has averaged about 8 percent. As a consequence of this risk, the return on any single securities investment (such as a stock), through no fault of its own, might vary up and down about 8 percent annually. The total risk in an investment consists of the sum of the random risk and the market risk.

Other Types of Investment Risks

A number of other investment risks affect investor returns:

- **Business failure risk. Business failure risk**, also called **financial risk**, is the possibility that the investment will fail, perhaps go bankrupt, and result in a massive or total loss of one's invested funds. Investigate thoroughly before investing. See Chapters 14, 15, and 16.

- **Inflation risk.** Inflation risk may be the most important concern for the long-term investor. **Inflation risk**, also called **purchasing power risk**, is the danger that your money will not grow as fast as inflation and therefore not be worth as much in the future as it is today. Over the long term, inflation in the United States has averaged 3.1 percent annually. Thus, the cumulative effects of inflation diminish your investment return. Historically, common stocks and real estate have reduced inflation risk, as values tend to rise with inflation over several years. However, houses, real estate, and other ownership investments are also subject to **deflation risk**. This is the chance that the value of an investment will decline when overall prices decline. Housing prices declined 30 to 50 percent in many communities in the United States between 2007 and 2011.

- **Time horizon risk.** The role of time affects all investments. The sooner your invested money is supposed to be returned to you—the **time horizon** of an investment—the less the likelihood that something could go wrong. The more time your money is invested, the more it is at risk. For taking longer-term risks, investors expect and normally receive higher returns.

- **Business-cycle risk.** As we discussed in Chapter 1, economic growth usually does not occur in a smooth and steady manner and this affects profits as well as investment returns. This is known as **business-cycle risk**. Instead, periods of expansion lasting three or four years are often followed by contractions in the economy, called recessions, that may last a year or longer. The profits of most industries follow the business cycle. Some businesses do not experience business-cycle risk because they continue to earn profits during economic downturns. Examples are gasoline retailers, supermarkets, and utility companies.

  Market-volatility risk. All investments are subject to occasional sharp changes in price as a result of events affecting a particular company or the overall market for similar investments, and this is **market-volatility risk**. For example, the value of a single stock, such as that of a technology company like Microsoft, might change 10 or even 30 percent in a single day. Also, all technology stocks could decline 2 or perhaps 5 percent if two or three competitors announce poor earnings. In an average year, the price of a typical stock fluctuates up and down by about 50 percent; thus, the price of a stock selling for $30 per share in January might range from $15 to $45 before the end of the following December. In difficult economic times, it is not unusual for overall stock market prices to fall (or rise) 3, 4, or 5 percent in a single day. Terrifying daily swings are likely to remain a constant during turbulent economic times. Such swings may be today's "new normal." Long-term investors, however, need not be overly concerned with such short-term fluctuations; simply stay invested.

- **Liquidity risk. Liquidity** is the speed and ease with which an asset can be converted to cash. You can convert your savings into cash instantly. You can sell your stocks and bonds in one day, although it may take four days to have the proceeds available in cash. **Liquidity risk** is the risk that a given security or asset cannot be traded quickly enough in the market to prevent a loss (or make the required profit). Real estate is **illiquid** because it may take weeks, months, or years to sell.

- **Reinvestment risk.** Reinvestment risk is the risk that the return on a future investment will not be the same as the return earned by the original investment.

- **Marketability risk.** When you have to sell a certain asset quickly, it may not sell at or near the market price. This possibility is referred to as **marketability risk**. Selling real estate in a hurry, for example, may require the seller to substantially reduce the price in order to sell to a willing buyer.

business-cycle risk
The fact that economic growth usually does not occur in a smooth and steady manner, and this impacts profits as well as investment returns.

market-volatility risk
The fact that all investments are subject to occasional sharp changes in price as a result of events affecting a particular company or the overall market for similar investments.

liquidity
The speed and ease with which an asset can be converted to cash.

liquidity risk
The risk that a given security or asset cannot be traded quickly enough in the market to prevent a loss (or make the required profit).

Transaction Costs Reduce Returns

Buying and selling investments may result in a number of transaction costs. Examples include "fix-up costs" when preparing a home for sale, appraisals for collectibles, and storage costs for precious metals. **Commissions** are usually the largest transaction cost in investments. These are fees or percentages of the units or selling price paid to salespeople, agents, and companies for their services—that is, to buy or sell an investment. The commission charged to buy an investment (one commission) and then later sell it (a second commission) is partially based on the value of the transaction. Typical ranges for commissions are as follows: stocks, 1.5 to 2.5 percent (although trades can be made on the Internet for less than $20); bonds, 0 to 2.0 percent; mutual funds, 0 to 8.5 percent; real estate, 4.5 to 7.5 percent; options and futures contracts, 4.0 to 6.0 percent; limited partnerships, 10.0 to 15.0 percent; and collectibles, 15.0 to 30.0 percent. Long-term investors in particular can substantially increase their investment returns by holding down transaction costs.

commissions
Fees or percentages of the selling price paid to salespeople, agents, and companies for their services in buying or selling an investment.

Leverage May Increase Returns

Another factor that can affect return on investment is **leverage**. In the leveraging process, borrowed funds are used to make an investment with the goal of earning a rate of return in excess of the after-tax costs of borrowing. Investing in real estate for its rental income provides an illustration of leverage, as shown in Table 13-3. Assume that a

leverage
Using borrowed funds to invest with the goal of earning a rate of return in excess of the after-tax costs of borrowing.

Table 13-3

Leverage Illustration: Buying Real Estate

	Pay Cash	Use Credit
Purchase price of office building	$ 300,000	$ 300,000
Amount borrowed	0	−270,000
Amount invested	300,000	30,000
Rental income ($2500 per month)	30,000	30,000
Minus tax-deductible interest (6.5%, 30-year loan on $270,000)	−0	−17,450
Net earnings before taxes	30,000	12,550
Minus income tax liability (25% bracket)	−7,500	−3,137
Rental earnings after taxes	$ 22,500	$ 9,413
	÷300,000	÷30,000
Percentage return on amount invested	7.5%	31.38%

person can buy a small office building either by making a $30,000 down payment and borrowing $270,000 or by paying $300,000 cash. If the rental income is $30,000 annually ($2500 per month) and the person pays income taxes at a 25 percent rate, a higher return can be obtained using credit to buy the building because the yield would be 31.38 percent versus a 7.5 percent yield when paying cash.

Leverage Can Enhance Capital Gains Leverage can prove particularly beneficial when substantial capital gains occur, as this strategy sharply boosts the return on the investment. Assume that at the end of one year, the value of the building described in the previous example has appreciated 7 percent and you could sell it for $321,000 (excluding commission costs). If you had purchased the property for $300,000 cash and then sold it for $321,000, the capital gain on the sale would be 7 percent (the $21,000 return divided by the $300,000 originally invested). If you had bought it using credit, the capital gain would be 70 percent (the $21,000 return divided by the $30,000 originally invested, ignoring transaction costs, taxes, and inflation).

Leverage Can Magnify Negative Returns Leverage has a potential negative side for individual investors as well. In the preceding example, if you used credit to purchase the property, you would need a minimum rental income of $20,479 (from Table 9-4 on page 270, 6½ percent interest on a 30-year loan) to make the mortgage loan payments. A few months of vacancy or expensive repairs to the building could result in a losing situation. Furthermore, any decline in value would be magnified when you use leverage. You can become financially overextended by using leverage for investments, a factor that you should not ignore.

 Concept Check 13.3

1. Distinguish between random risk and market risk.

2. Summarize three other risks that may affect investment returns.

3. Explain how transactions costs, leverage, and income taxes increase or decrease investment returns.

ESTABLISHING YOUR LONG-TERM INVESTMENT STRATEGY

 LEARNING OBJECTIVE ❹

Decide which of the four long-term investment strategies you will utilize.

Investing is not rocket science! Anyone reading this book and following its recommendations for making long-term investments can become a successful investor.

The Wisdom of Starting to Invest Early in Life

Table 13-4

Age	Early Investor*		Late Investor†	
	Cumulative Investment	**Account Value**	**Cumulative Investment**	**Account Value**
30	$ 2,000	$ 2,180	$ 0	$ 0
35	10,000	13,047	0	0
40	20,000	33,121	2,000	2,180
45	0	50,960	10,000	13,047
50	0	78,408	20,000	33,121
55	0	120,641	30,000	64,007
60	0	185,621	40,000	111,529
65	0	285,601	50,000	184,648

Conclusion: $20,000 gets the early investor $285,601; $50,000 gets the late investor only $184,648.

*The early investor invested $2000 at the beginning of every year from ages 30 to 39 (ten years of cumulative investing totaling $20,000), and the funds compounded at 9 percent annually.
†The late investor invested $2000 at the beginning of every year from ages 40 to 64 (25 years of cumulative investing totaling $50,000), and the funds compounded at 9 percent annually.

Long-Term Investors
Understand the Importance of Starting Early

Every chapter in this book contains illustrations of the importance of the time value of money. You are wise to start investing as early in life as possible. Delaying ten years before starting to save $2000 a year in a tax-deferred account that earns a 10 percent return can cost you $500,000! Saving $2000 a year between age 25 and 65 accumulates to $885,000, but if you don't start until age 35, you accumulate only $329,000. Thus the $20,000 that you did not invest between ages 25 and 35 will cost you $556,000 ($885,000 − $329,000) by the time you reach age 65. Another example of the wisdom of starting to invest early in life is shown in Table 13-4. Here the early investor starts to invest at age 30 but does so for only 10 years and stops, yet he or she is ahead of the late investor who waits to start until age 40 and invests for 25 years. It should be clear that small amounts of money invested early can snowball into a big investment account.

Long-Term Investors Understand Bull and Bear Markets

Long-term investors understand how the **securities markets** (places where stocks and bonds are traded) are performing as a whole. That is, are the markets moving up, moving down, or remaining stagnant?

securities markets
Places where stocks and bonds are traded (or in the case of electronic trading, the way in which securities are traded).

DID YOU KNOW?

Sean's Success Story

Sean's financial life continues successfully. Only six years past college graduation, he has a retirement plan at work now worth over $90,000. He continues to have an aggressive investment philosophy and is invested in six mutual funds through his job, which is similar to that shown in the upper row ("high risk/aggressive") of Figure 13-4 on page 401. After paying off his car three years ago, Sean continued to make payments to himself, thus building up his savings account as well, which now is over $20,000. He is worried about the economy even though it has been rising recently, so he is keeping those dollars out of the stock market for the time being. Sean's employer recently announced that employees may now contribute up to 8 percent of their salaries to their retirement plan, so he is going online this weekend to bump up his contribution from 6 percent.

bull market
Market in which securities prices have risen 20 percent or more over time.

Bull Markets Are Profitable for Investors A **bull market** results when securities prices have risen 20 percent or more over time. Historically, the more than 20 bull markets have seen an average gain of 136 percent. The bull market of the 1990s saw average annual returns of 18 percent.

Bear Markets Turn into Bull Markets A securities market in which prices have declined in value by 20 percent or more from previous highs, often over the course of several weeks or months, is called a **bear market**. Four bear markets have occurred since 1980, and the 2000-02 bear market was followed by another in 2007-09. The bear market that started in October 2007 saw stock prices decline 55 percent by March 2009. Then the optimistic bull buyers took over thinking that surely the U.S. economy had already reached rock bottom and that stock prices were certain to rise as the economy recovered. During the ensuing record-setting bull market stock prices had risen 70% in 9 months by December 2009, and values continued to climb another 30% by the summer of 2011.

The Lost Decade of the 2000s Between 2000 and 2010, stocks returned a dismal −1.7 percent per year. Historically, after coming out of deep economic slumps, stocks have been strong for the next decade. This economic recovery has been sluggish.

A *bull* in the market is a person who expects securities prices to go up; a *bear* expects the general market to decline. The origin of these terms is unknown, but some suggest that they refer to the ways that the animals attack: Bears thrust their claws downward, and bulls move their horns upward. Historically, bear markets last, on average, about 9 months; bull markets average 3.8 years in length. Economists argue that the serious shocks of the recent past should not alter investors' belief in the future.

bull market
Market in which securities prices have risen 20 percent or more over time.

bear market
Market in which securities prices have declined in value by 20 percent or more from previous highs, often over the course of several weeks or months.

Long-Term Investors Accept Substantial Market Volatility

Long-term investors must be able to withstand some **market volatility**, the likelihood of large price swings in their chosen securities. The price of a typical stock fluctuates up and down by about 50 percent every year due to the company's success (or lack of it) and various market conditions.

Benjamin Graham, investment sage and author of *The Intelligent Investor*, argues that the investor should be interested in the possibility of profiting from wide fluctuations in prices. The opportunity of volatility is to buy stocks wisely when they are underpriced and sell them wisely when they rise above that value. This is known as **value investing** (examined in Chapter 14). Staying focused on the value of an individual investment is more important than its price, particularly in times of market turmoil. Long-term investors who get scared during market downturns and withdraw most or all of their investing dollars miss out on the subsequent increase in prices during the next up market. Long-term investors must learn to accept market volatility by ignoring short-term market movements.

market volatility
The likelihood of large price swings in securities due to a company's success (or lack of it) and various market conditions.

Long-Term Investors Do Not Practice Market Timing

Market timers attempt to predict the short-term movements of various markets (or market segments) and, based on those predictions, move capital from one segment to another in order to capture market gains and avoid market losses. Essentially, market timers try to outguess the trend of stocks or other prices. For example, an investor worried about the future might sell his or her investments and move to cash. Another investor who anticipates increasing future stock prices might get 100% invested in stocks.

To succeed in timing the market, you need to know just the right time to buy and just the right time to sell, know what signals suggest you take action, and exhibit the discipline to do it. Market timers often sell at the first sign of trouble and then keep their money out of the market until better opportunities are apparent. If you try to time the market, you are just as likely to miss an upswing as you are to avoid a downswing. Here is some advice for those who want to time the market: Shift money into or out of your stock funds at your own peril, but if you do, be certain to do exactly the opposite of the average fund investor. Instead of trying to time the market, each investor should practice asset allocation and rebalance his or her portfolio at least once of year; these topics are examined later in this chapter.

market timers
Investors who attempt to predict the short-term movements of various markets (or market segments) and, based on those predictions, move capital from one segment to another in order to capture market gains and avoid market losses.

Research shows that most of the market's gains are realized in a few trading days that occur every now and then. If market timers are out of the market on those days, they lose. In times of rising markets, it is very easy for market timers to sell too early and, as a result, miss out on much larger profits as the bull market continues to push up prices even more. Those who sell after a sudden drop in investment value, a "down market," actually lock in their losses. And what do these investors do if the stock market drops even further? The bottom line is this: What contributes the most to successful investing is not timing, but time.

Individual investors typically earn only about half of what the stock market averages. Research from Dalbar documents that for the past 20 years the average stock fund investor had an annualized return of only 3.2 percent, compared with 8.2 percent for the Standard & Poor's 500-stock index. Outwitting the market is tough.

What causes lower returns? One cause is trading too much. The more you trade, the more likely you are to make a wealth-destroying mistake. Such investors also often sell winners too soon and keep losers too long. Furthermore, males are over-confident investors, and their investment returns trail those of females.

Emotion, not logic, often rules investing decisions. Investors often overreact when buying and selling as their thinking goes through alternating times of panic and euphoria. When plunging portfolio values become too much to bear, investors just want the pain to end so they sell, which presumably means big losses. This is "buying high and selling low," which is the opposite of what investors should do.

At the other extreme, when the market prices are rapidly rising, people are fooled into thinking that it is safe to invest more ("I've got to put more money in there") and lose their sense of caution because it must be safe if everyone else is buying. People look at behavior and assume it is based on knowledge, but often it's not. This is an illustration of **herd behavior**, which arises when investors decide to copy the observed decisions of other investors or movements in the markets rather than follow their own beliefs and information.

Herd behavior happens in part because people feel compelled to look at prices in the newspaper every day or watch the 24-hour financial news chatter, such as CNBC and CNN, whose TV talking heads spew financial factoids with minute-by-minute updates and sensationalize every blip in the stock markets. Such arcane and sometimes meaningless information creates anxiety or mania that can lead to bad decision making.

FINANCIAL POWER POINT

Out of the Market? You Missed a 45 Percent Gain

If you had been out of stocks during the market's ten best days in the past decade, according to Charles Schwab, you would have missed out on 45 percent of the gains.

Long-Term Investors Try to Avoid Herd Behavior

Acquiring more "facts" is not the same as gaining knowledge or expertise. Stay focused on your long-term investing strategy and make decisions accordingly; otherwise, your returns will be less than the averages.

herd behavior
When emotion, not logic, rules investing decisions and investors decide to copy the observed decisions of other investors or movements in the markets rather than follow their own beliefs and information.

There Are Only Four Strategies for Long-Term Investors

To succeed financially, you must establish your own long-term investment strategies. Fortunately, this is easy because there are only four strategies to follow, and they all hang together.

Strategy 1: Buy-and-Hold Anticipates Long-Term Economic Growth

Stocks have delivered an historic average return of over 10 percent over many, many years. Realize, however, that that return measures only what a buy-and-hold investor would earn by putting money in at the start of the period and keeping his or her money invested through good times and bad.

The secret to long-term investing success is benign neglect. Long-term investors need to relax with the confidence and knowledge that investing regularly and not trading frequently will create a substantial portfolio over time. Long-term investors do not follow or react emotionally to the day-to-day changes that occur in the market. Ignoring them is the best advice. Because most people are sensitive to short-term losses, daily monitoring could motivate one to make shortsighted buying and selling decisions. Selling high-quality assets in a bear market is a poor strategy because sellers lock in their losses, plus they fail to realize that bear markets are typically short in duration. It is smart to buy more shares when prices are lower during market downturns because rising prices in a bull market always follow a bear market.

buy and hold/buy to hold
Investment strategy in which investors buy a widely diversified mix of stocks and/or mutual funds, reinvest the dividends by buying more stocks and mutual funds, and hold onto those investments almost indefinitely.

Most long-term investors use the investment strategy **buy and hold** (also called **buy to hold**). That is, they buy a widely diversified mix of stocks and/or mutual funds, reinvest the dividends by buying more stocks and mutual funds, and hold on to those investments almost indefinitely. With this approach, the investor expects that the values of the assets will increase over the long run in tandem with the growth of the U.S. and world economies. The investments may pay some current income as well. The investor's emphasis is on holding the assets through both good and bad economic times with the confidence that their values will go up over the long term. This is a wise strategy.

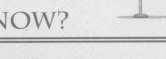

DID YOU KNOW?

The Stock Market Crash Affected Buy-and-Hold Investors

Buy-and-hold investors know that stock market swings are normal. They hold during times when stock prices are declining with confidence that returns come to those who wait. All stock investors got hurt during the recent economic turmoil, but buy-and-hold investors were negatively affected much less than others. One of the best time to invest for long-term investors is when the share prices of high-quality firms have been beaten down to affordable levels.

Some critics argue that "buy and hold" is a discredited concept, but they are wrong because this is still the best approach for investing over 20 years or longer. Long-term investors must have the patience and fortitude necessary to tolerate bear markets, no matter how severe.

Buy and hold does not mean buy and ignore. Investors are unwise to blindly hold on to an investment for years. Instead, review all holdings at least once a year to make sure that each remains a good investment. Questions to ask include: "Is the valuation too high?"; "Has the fundamental outlook of the company changed?"; "Does this asset still fit my investment plan?"; "Would I buy it today?" If necessary, sell the asset.

Strategy 2: Dollar-Cost Averaging Buys at "Below-Average" Costs
Dollar-cost averaging (or **cost averaging**) is a systematic program of investing equal sums of money at regular intervals regardless of the price of the investment. In this approach, the same fixed dollar amount is invested in the same stock or mutual fund at regular intervals over a long time. Since investments generally rise more than they fall, the "averaging" means that you purchase more shares when the price is down and fewer shares when the price is high. Most of the shares are, therefore, purchased at **below-average costs**.

dollar-cost averaging/cost averaging
Systematic program of investing equal sums of money at regular intervals, regardless of the price of the investment.

This strategy avoids the risks and responsibilities of investment timing because the stock purchases are made regularly (usually every month) regardless of the price. It also ignores all outside events and short-term gyrations of the market, providing the investor with a disciplined buying strategy. A well-diversified stock mutual fund would be an excellent choice for dollar-cost averaging.

below-average costs
Average costs of an investment if more shares are purchased when the price is down and fewer shares are purchased when the price is high.

Table 13-5 shows the results of dollar-cost averaging for a stock under varying market conditions (commissions are excluded). As an example, assume that you invest $300 into a stock every three months. Notice that dollar-cost averaging is successful in all three scenarios illustrated.

DOLLAR-COST AVERAGING IN A FLUCTUATING MARKET   To illustrate the effects of dollar-cost averaging, assume that you first invested funds during the "fluctuating market" shown in Table 13-5. Because the initial price is $15 per share, you receive 20 shares for your investment of $300. Then the market drops—an extreme but easy-to-follow example—and the price falls to $10 per share. When you buy $300 worth of the stock now, you receive 30 shares. Three months later, the market price rebounds to $15 and you invest another $300, receiving 20 shares. The price then drops and rises again.

average share price
Calculated by dividing the share price total by the number of investment periods.

You now own 120 shares, thanks to your total investment of $1500. The **average share price** is calculated by averaging the amounts paid for the investment: Simply divide the share price total by the number of investment periods. In this example, the average

Dollar-Cost Averaging for a Stock or Mutual Fund Investment

Table 13-5

	Fluctuating Market			Declining Market			Rising Market		
	Regular Investment	Share Price	Shares Acquired	Regular Investment	Share Price	Shares Acquired	Regular Investment	Share Price	Shares Acquired
	$ 300	$15	20	$ 300	$15	20	$ 300	$ 6	50
	300	10	30	300	10	30	300	10	30
	300	15	20	300	10	30	300	12	25
	300	10	30	300	6	50	300	15	20
	300	15	20	300	5	60	300	20	15
Totals	$1,500	$65	120	$1,500	$46	190	$1,500	$63	140
	Average share price: $13.00 ($65 ÷ 5)*			Average share price: $9.20 ($46 ÷ 5)*			Average share price: $12.60 ($63 ÷ 5)*		
	Average share cost: $12.50 ($1500 ÷ 120)†			Average share cost: $7.89 ($1500 ÷ 190)†			Average share cost: $10.71 ($1500 ÷ 140)†		

*Sum of share price total ÷ number of investment periods.
†Total amount invested ÷ total shares purchased.

share price is $13 ($65 ÷ 5). The **average share cost**, a more meaningful amount, is the actual cost basis of the investment used for income tax purposes. It is calculated by dividing the total amount invested by the total shares purchased. In this example, it is $12.50 ($1500 ÷ 120). Based on the recent price of $15 per share, each of your 120 shares is worth on average $2.50 ($15 − $12.50) more than you paid for it. Thus, your gain is $300 (120 × $2.50; or $15 × 120 = $1800, $1800 − $1500 = $300).

average share cost
Actual cost basis of the investment used for income tax purposes, calculated by dividing the total amount invested by the total shares purchased.

DOLLAR-COST AVERAGING IN A DECLINING MARKET   Markets may also decline over a time period. The "declining market" columns in Table 13-5 (representing a prolonged bear market of 15 months) show purchases of 190 shares for increasingly lower prices that eventually reach $5 per share at the bottom of the business cycle. In a declining market, if you keep investing using dollar-cost averaging, you will purchase a large volume of shares. If you sell when the market is down substantially, you will not profit. In this example, you have purchased 190 shares at an average cost of $7.89, and

ADVICE FROM A PRO

Use a Dividend-Reinvestment Plan to Dollar-Cost Average

More than 1000 well-known companies allow investors to purchase shares of stock directly from them without the assistance of a stockbroker and then to continue to invest on a regular basis without paying brokerage commissions. Such a program is known as a **dividend-reinvestment plan (DRIP)**. You simply sign up with the company, agreeing to buy a certain number of shares and to reinvest cash dividends into more shares of stock for little or no transaction fee. Investors' accounts are credited with fractional shares, too.

Walmart is illustrative. It requires a minimum investment of $250 and continuing investments of $50 thereafter. The enrollment fee is $20 plus $0.10 per share. Most companies

will buy back shares for a transaction fee of only $10. Companies offering DRIPs include Ameritech, ExxonMobil, Home Depot, Tenneco, Walmart, McDonald's, and Sears, Roebuck and Co. For a list of companies offering direct purchases, see the Securities Transfer Association at www.sharebuiler.com or the Direct Stock Purchase Plan Clearinghouse at www.dripinvestor.com/clearinghouse/home.asp.

Buying shares regularly through a DRIP is a great example of dollar-cost averaging. It allows you to take advantage of fluctuating stock prices by purchasing on a regular basis at below-average costs.

Jon Wentworth
Southern Adventist University, Collegedale, Tennessee

they now have a depressed price of $5. Selling at this point would result in a substantial loss of $550 [$1500 − (190 × $5)]. Dollar-cost averaging requires that you continue to invest if the longer-term prospects suggest an eventual increase in price.

DOLLAR-COST AVERAGING IN A RISING MARKET   During the "rising market" in Table 13-5, you continue to invest but buy fewer shares. The $1500 investment during the bull market bought only 140 shares for an average cost of $10.71. In this rising market, you profit because your 140 shares have a recent market price of $20 per share, for a total value of $2800 (140 × $20).

Almost anyone can profit in a rising market. If you use dollar-cost averaging over the long term, you will continue to buy in rising, falling, and fluctuating markets. The overall result will be that you buy more shares when the cost is down, thereby lowering the average share cost to below-average prices. The totals in Table 13-5, for example, reveal an overall investment of $4500 ($1500 + $1500 + $1500) used to purchase 450 shares (120 + 190 + 140) for an average cost of $10 per share ($4500 ÷ 450). With the recent market price at $20, you will realize a long-term gain of $4500 ($20 current market price × 450 shares = $9000; $9000 − $4500 invested = $4500 gain). Note that the dollar-cost averaging method would remain valid if the time interval for investing were monthly, quarterly, or even semiannually; benefits are derived from the regularity of investing.

DOLLAR-COST AVERAGING OFFERS TWO ADVANTAGES   First, it reduces the average cost of shares of stock purchased over a relatively long period. Profits occur when prices for an investment fluctuate and eventually go up. Although this approach does not eliminate the possibility of loss, it does limit losses during times of declining prices. And profits accelerate during rising prices. Second, dollar-cost averaging dictates investor discipline. This strategy of investing is not particularly glamorous, but it is the only approach that is almost guaranteed to make a profit for the investor. It takes neither brilliance nor luck, just discipline. People who invest through individual retirement accounts (IRAs), employee stock ownership programs, and 401(k) retirement plans (all discussed in Chapter 17) enjoy the benefits of dollar-cost averaging when they invest regularly. Dollar-cost averaging is a systematic strategy that will eventually get your portfolio where you want it to be.

Strategy 3: Portfolio Diversification Reduces Portfolio Volatility

Owning too much of any one investment creates too great a financial risk. Experts advise that you never keep more than 5 or 10 percent of your assets in one investment, including your employer's stock. Many workers who did not diversify properly have seen their retirement funds disappear or be drastically reduced in value when their employers' stocks plunged in price.

DID YOU KNOW?

The Tax Consequences in Investment Fundamentals

There are some favorable aspects to income taxes to think about when making investments.

1. **After-tax return.** *When comparing similar investments, your objective is to earn the best after-tax return. This return is the net amount earned on an investment after payment of income taxes. (See Equation 4.1 on page 128.)*

2. **Income versus capital gain.** *Current investment income, such as dividends and interest, is taxed at one's marginal tax bracket, likely 25 percent. Capital gains are taxed at special lower rates, likely at 10 or 15 percent.*

3. **Tax-deferred investments.** *The income and capital gains from investments within employer-sponsored retirement accounts are not subject to income taxes until the funds are withdrawn.*

4. **Tax-exempt income.** *Income earned from municipal bonds is exempt from income taxes.*

5. **Tax-exempt investments.** *The income and capital gains from investments within Roth IRA accounts are not subject to income taxes, unless the funds are removed from the account within five years of opening it.*

Diversification is the single most important rule in investing. **Portfolio diversification** is the practice of selecting a collection of different asset classes of investments (such as stocks, bonds, mutual funds, real estate, and cash) that are chosen not only for their potential returns but also for their dissimilar risk–return characteristics.

The goal of portfolio diversification is to create a collection of investments that will provide an acceptable level of return and an acceptable exposure to risk. This outcome can be achieved because asset classes typically react differently to economic and marketplace changes. The major benefit of having a diversified portfolio is that when one asset class performs poorly, there is a good chance that another will perform well, and vice versa.

For example, you might buy a number of mutual funds, perhaps including a balanced fund, an asset-allocation fund, a life-cycle fund, and an aggressive-growth fund. Similarly, you could invest in three or four stocks within an industry group, instead of just one, and then invest in several industry groups, plus invest in a bond mutual fund and a certificate of deposit.

As shown in Figure 13-3 diversification reduces portfolio volatility while averaging out an investor's return. If you were totally invested in the item that rose 13 percent, you would be happy; if you were totally invested in the one that declined 10 percent, you would be sad. Instead your diversified portfolio averaged 7.1 percent, which is a respectable return. Diversification lowers the odds that you will lose money investing and increases the odds that you will make money.

Examine the ending portfolio values in Table 13-6. They illustrate that the gains in the equity portion of a $200,000 portfolio evenly balanced between bonds and stocks and 10% cash are modest in a rising market (up 10% or $9000), and although losses in a declining market are substantial (down 50% or $45,000), they are not devastatingly horrible, as is the case in a portfolio that is too heavy in equities (minus $85,000). Diversification protects against such dire losses.

Strategy 4: Asset Allocation Keeps You in the Right Investment Categories for Your Time Horizon
As long as your investments are sensibly diversified, asset allocation, rather than your choice of specific securities, is the most important determinant of financial performance. Research shows that more than 90 percent of returns earned by long-term investors result from having one's assets allocated in a diversified portfolio. Thus you must strive to own the right asset categories at the right time.

Asset allocation, a form of diversification, is deciding on the proportions of your investment portfolio that will be devoted to various categories of assets. Asset allocation helps preserve capital by selecting assets so as to protect the entire portfolio from negative events while remaining in a position to gain from positive events. This strategy helps control your exposure to risk.

portfolio diversification
Practice of selecting a collection of different asset classes of investments (such as stocks, bonds, mutual funds, real estate, and cash) that are chosen not only for their potential returns but also for their dissimilar risk–return characteristics.

asset allocation
Form of diversification in which the investor decides on the proportions of an investment portfolio that will be devoted to various categories of assets.

Diversification Averages Out an Investor's Return

Figure 13-3

The chart below represents a hypothetical mix of winning and losing investments after one year. One investor, for instance, increased in value 8 percent; another declined 10 percent. While some investments lost value, over the year those losses were offset with the gains of others, and the overall portfolio earned a 7.1 percent average return.

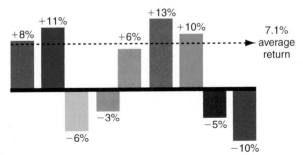

Table 13-6

Stock Market Turmoil Proves the Case for Diversification

Beginning Portfolio Values ($200,000 each)			Ending Portfolio Values	
Portfolio A—Balanced Between Bonds and Stocks			**Stocks Jump 10%**	**Stocks Crash 50%***
Cash	Bonds	Equities[†]		
10%	45%	45%		
$20,000	$90,000	$90,000	+$9,000	−$45,000
Portfolio B—Light on Bonds and Heavy on Equities				
Cash	Bonds	Equities[†]		
5%	10%	85%		
$10,000	$20,000	$170,000	+$17,000	−$85,000

*Decline from previous high in stock market prices during severe economic recession.
[†]Equity portion of portfolio rises or falls with changes in stock market prices.

To achieve an appropriate mix of growth, income, and stability in your portfolio, you need a combination of three investments: (1) stocks and/or stock mutual funds (equities), (2) bonds (debt), and (3) cash (or cash equivalents like Treasury securities). Asset allocation requires that you keep your equities, debt, and cash at a fixed ratio for long time periods, occasionally rebalancing the allocations, perhaps quarterly or annually, so as to continue to meet your investment objectives.

Your allocation proportions and investment choices need to reflect your age, income, family responsibilities, financial resources, risk tolerance, goals, retirement plans, and investment time horizon. You need not change the proportions of your asset allocation until your broad investment goals change—possibly not for another five or ten years. When your investment objectives change, perhaps because of marriage, birth of a child, child graduating from college, loss of employment, divorce, or death of a spouse, you may need to change your asset allocation as well. Otherwise, stay the course.

KNOW YOUR RISK TOLERANCE AND HOW MUCH TIME YOU HAVE TO INVEST   Figure 13-4 illustrates model portfolios that reflect varying degrees of risk tolerance and time horizons. A young, risk-tolerant, long-term investor with an aggressive investment philosophy might have a portfolio that is 100 percent in equities because equities offer the highest return over the long term. Younger investors also have ample time to ride out market fluctuations and make up any major losses. A moderate approach with a time horizon of six to ten years might have an equities-bond-cash portfolio of 60/30/10 percent.

REBALANCE YOUR INVESTMENTS AT LEAST ONCE A YEAR
Portfolio rebalancing is the process of bringing the different asset classes back into proper relationship following a significant change in one or more of them. You must reset your asset allocation to return your portfolio to the proper mix of stocks, bonds, and cash when they no longer conform to your plan. Here is why. Assume you have a moderate investment philosophy and started out with a 50/40/10 bond-equities-cash portfolio, as shown in Figure 13-5, and a year later, stock values increased to 49 percent of your portfolio's value while bonds dropped to 42 percent. The result: Your portfolio is now too heavy in stocks and too light in bonds. It is too risky. As shown in Figure 13-5, this suggests that you sell some of your equities and use the proceeds to buy more bonds, thus rebalancing your portfolio according to your previously determined asset allocations.

DID YOU KNOW?

Asset Allocation Rules of Thumb

Consider these two rules of thumb to guide the stock and bond allocation of your portfolio:

1. *The percent to invest in equities is 110 minus your age, multiplied by 1.25. For example, if you are 40 years old, calculate as follows: 110 − 40 = 70; 70 × 1.25 = 87.5. Therefore, a 40-year-old investor is advised to maintain a portfolio where 87.5 percent of the assets are in equities and 12.5 percent are in bonds (or cash equivalents).*

2. *The percent to invest in equities is found by subtracting your age from 120. Put the resulting number in the form of the percentage of your portfolio to invest in stocks. Put the remainder in bonds. So if you are age 30, put 90 percent (120 − 30) in stocks and 10 percent in bonds. Every year, subtract your age from 120 again and rebalance your portfolio as needed.*

Model Investment Portfolios and Appropriate Time Horizons

Figure 13-4

0–5 Years	6–10 Years	11+ Years	Risk Tolerance/ Investment Philosophy
10% Cash 30% Bonds 60% Equities	20% Bonds 80% Equities	100% Equities	High Risk/Aggressive
20% Cash 40% Bonds 40% Equities	10% Cash 30% Bonds 60% Equities	20% Bonds 80% Equities	Moderate Risk/Moderate
35% Cash 40% Bonds 25% Equities	20% Cash 40% Bonds 40% Equities	10% Cash 30% Bonds 60% Equities	Low Risk/Conservative

When rebalancing, you will be selling high and buying low—the goal of all investors. It is temperamentally difficult for investors to rebalance. They don't like to sell assets that have increased in value because they hope those values will continue to increase. Rebalancing is an appropriate form of market timing as it provides some of the benefits of market timing without the risk.

Employees who participate in their employer-sponsored retirement plan may have access to services to automatically rebalance their retirement assets. Instead of being a do-it-yourself investor, a worker can sign up for the services of a **limited managed account**. Once you have decided on your preferred asset allocation and signed a contract with a vender approved by your employer, the company sells and buys your mutual fund assets, usually quarterly, on your behalf to adjust your portfolio back to your specific standards. The service is free, or a nominal fee is charged.

limited managed account
An account at an investment firm whereby, for a fee, they sell and buy your mutual fund assets, usually quarterly, on your behalf to automatically rebalance your portfolio back to your specific standards.

Rebalancing Assets in Your Investment Portfolio

Figure 13-5

Day 1 — Beginning asset allocation of portfolio

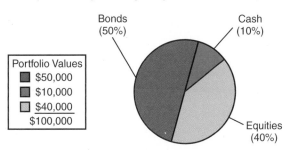

Bonds (50%) Cash (10%) Equities (40%)

Portfolio Values
- $50,000
- $10,000
- $40,000

$100,000

One year later — This allocation needs rebalancing to original percentages

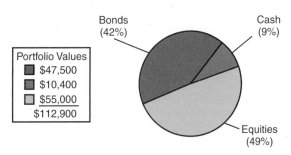

Bonds (42%) Cash (9%) Equities (49%)

Portfolio Values
- $47,500
- $10,400
- $55,000

$112,900

DID YOU KNOW?

Your Worst Financial Blunders in Investment Fundamentals

Based on others' financial woes, you will make mistakes in personal finance when you:

1. *Buy and sell more than you should.*
2. *Diversify less than you should.*
3. *Hold on to a bad investment long after evidence shows it was a bad decision.*

---

modern portfolio theory (MPT)
Goal is to identify the investor's acceptable level of risk tolerance and then find an optimal portfolio of assets that may reduce overall portfolio volatility while providing the highest expected returns for that level of risk.

Monte Carlo analysis
Technique that performs a large number of trial runs of a particular portfolio mix of investments, called simulations, to find an optimal allocation for a particular investor's goals and risk tolerance.

A sophisticated application of asset allocation can be accomplished using **modern portfolio theory (MPT)**. Here, the goal is to identify the investor's acceptable level of risk tolerance and then find an optimal portfolio of assets that may reduce overall portfolio volatility while providing the highest expected returns for that level of risk. A popular form of MPT is **Monte Carlo analysis**. This technique performs a large number of trial runs of a particular portfolio mix of investments, called simulations. It calculates hundreds or even thousands of possible investment combinations to determine the probability that a particular selection of investments will reach an investor's goal, such as a specific retirement income at a certain point in the future. Such MPT programs are often offered through employers as part of their 401(k) retirement plans. See Chapter 17 for more information.

 Concept Check 13.4

1. Summarize why smart people conclude that it is impossible to beat the average stock market returns, and then note why some market timers try anyway.

2. Summarize what the buy-and-hold strategy is all about.

3. Explain the concept of dollar-cost averaging including why one invests at below-average costs.

4. What is asset allocation and why does it work?

5. What is the goal of portfolio diversification and how is this accomplished?

ADVICE FROM A PRO

When to Sell an Investment

It is time to consider selling an investment when one of the following conditions has been met:

- Something significant about the company's business or its earnings has changed dramatically for the worse since you bought the company's stock.

- The stock is doing so well that it is overvalued, and the share price is much higher than what you believe the company is worth.

- The investment is performing poorly and causing you undue anxiety. The great financier Bernard Baruch advised, "Sell down to the level where you are sleeping well."

- You need cash for a worthwhile purpose, and this investment appears the most fully priced.

- The investment no longer fits your situation or goals, and you have a more promising place to invest your money.

Diann Moorman
University of Georgia

CREATING YOUR OWN INVESTMENT PLAN

To create an **investment plan**, which is a reflection of your investment philosophy and your logic on investing to reach specific goals, see the illustrated plan for Jamie Richter in Figure 13-6. You can begin creating your own investment plan by identifying your financial goals and explaining your investment philosophy as called for in Steps 1 and 2 in Figure 13-6.

LEARNING OBJECTIVE ❺

Create your own investment plan.

investment plan
An explanation of your investment philosophy and your logic on investing to reach specific goals.

Figure 13-6

Jamie Richter's Investment Plan

After some thinking and reading, Jamie, age 24, jotted down some investment plan notes.

> **1 – Investment philosophy:**
> Moderate; I am willing to accept some risk to achieve investment goals.

⬇

> **2 – Goals:**
> (a) Start saving for retirement; (b) Begin saving for down payment on a new car.

⬇

> **3 – Monthly amounts to invest:**
> $200 for retirement; $200 for down payment.

⬇

> **4 – Investment alternatives:**
> (a) Employer's stock; (b) 20 mutual funds offered by vendor, Fidelity, within employer's 401(k) plan; (c) Large mutual fund families, like Vanguard and T. Rowe Price; (d) Stocks of regional companies; (e) Certificates of deposit.

⬇

> **5 – Rationale for decisions:**
> Starting next month, begin investing in my employer's 401(k) plan to earn $100 monthly matching contributionas this gives me a 50 percent immediate return ($200 of my money plus $100 of my employer's money). For every dollar invested I will receive an immediate 50 percent return because my employer's policy is to match 401(k) contributions 50 cents on the dollar for the first 6 percent of earnings.
>
> Additional thoughts: (a) Employer's stock may be risky; (b) Really do not know much about local stocks; (c) Down payment funds go into money market account to accumulate and then earn higher rate on certificates of deposit.

⬇

> **6 – Key risk factors:**
> (a) Do not need retirement funds for 30 or more years, so I can invite more risk for a higher return; (b) I expect to need the down payment funds within 3 to 4 years, so the investment cannot be risky.

⬇

> **7 – Anticipated return:**
> (a) Hopefully 7 to 8 percent on the retirement investments; (b) For the down payment funds, hopefully 1 1/2 to 2 percent in a money market account, and perhaps 4 to 5 percent in a certificate of deposit.

⬇

> **8 – Actions to take:**
> (a) Fill out 401(k) forms in Human Resources Department to withhold $200 monthly and invest it in a mutual fund with an investment objective of moderate to high growth; (b) Open an account at large mutual fund company and automatically send $200 monthly from my banking account to a money market account until sufficient funds accumulate to buy a certificate of deposit.

DID YOU KNOW?

Turn Bad Habits into Good Ones

Do You Do This?	Do This Instead!
Make small contribution to employer's retirement plan	Contribute the maximum
Invest conservatively for retirement	Invest aggressively for long-term goals
Try to time investments to market ups and downs	Stay invested for the long term
Ignore transaction costs on investments	Hold down transaction costs
Invest mostly in employer's stock	Reduce holding to 10 percent

FINANCIAL POWER POINT

Create Your Financial Plan on the Web

To obtain an overall assessment of your financial progress and advice on how to achieve your goals, you may want to consult an online financial advisor to construct a financial plan. Prices vary from $250 to $500 or more. Check out Fidelity .com, Schwab.com, TRowePrice.com, and Vanguard.com. Answers to specific financial questions for $50 to $100 may be obtained on the Web and over the telephone from companies such as Myfinancialadvice.com.

To help in your thinking for Step 3 in Figure 13-6, review Table 13-1 for the time horizons of various investments. (Terms new to you are explained in the chapters that follow.) What are the time horizons for your investment goals? Are you building up an amount for a down payment on a home, creating a college fund for a child, or putting away money for retirement? Or are all three time horizons relevant? Keep in mind why you are investing and proceed accordingly. Now calculate the numbers. How much money do you need to achieve each goal, and by when? What is the total of your current investment assets? Do the math.

Step 4 in Figure 13-6 asks about investment alternatives. Review Figure 13-1 on the long-term rates of return on various investments and Table 13-2 for alternatives. Then examine Figure 13-2 because it shows the trade-offs between risk and return on investment alternatives. Next take a pencil and delete some investment choices that do not appeal to you or match your investment philosophy. You will be left with alternatives that better fit your investment goals, philosophy, and time horizon. Now you have an investment plan, so record your responses to Steps 5, 6, and 7. Then create a model investment portfolio appropriate for your life now using Figure 13-4 as a model. All that remains is to put your plan into action. That means filling out forms to open an investment account, selecting your investments, writing checks for your first investing dollars, and monitoring your investments. These topics are examined in the chapters that follow.

DO IT NOW!

You know more about personal finance after reading this chapter, so get started right now by:

1. *Saving even a small amount through a pay-yourself-first philosophy perhaps by signing up to automatically transfer some money every payday to a savings account.*

2. *Identifying the percentages you would allocate to stocks, bonds, and cash equivalents using an asset allocation strategy to save for retirement.*

3. *Visiting www.finance.yahoo.com every weekday for one month to become familiar with how and why the stock market moves from day to day.*

Concept Check 13.5

1. Review Tables 13-1 and 13-2 and Figures 13-1 and 13-2, and record in writing an investment plan to fund your retirement, presumably one of your own long-term goals.

WHAT DO YOU RECOMMEND NOW?

Now that you have read the chapter on investment fundamentals, what do you recommend to Jennifer and Janie on the subject regarding:

1. Getting more money to save and invest?

2. Prerequisites to investing for Jennifer?

3. Portfolio diversification for Janie?

4. Dollar-cost averaging for Jennifer?

5. Investment alternatives for Janie?

BIG PICTURE SUMMARY OF LEARNING OBJECTIVES

LO1. **Explain how to get started as an investor.**
Before investing, think about your goals, why you want to invest, and whether you are ready to invest. After you find the money to invest, contemplate the types of returns you might anticipate. Investors hope that their investments will earn them a positive total return, which is the income an investment generates from current income and capital gains.

LO2. **Identify your investment philosophy and invest accordingly.**
Achieving financial success requires that you understand your investment philosophy and adhere to it when investing. An investment philosophy is one's general approach to tolerance for risk in investments, whether it is conservative, moderate, or aggressive, given the financial goals to be achieved. You also need to know about investment risk and what to do about it. Before investing your money, you need to think about lending versus owning, short term versus long term, and how to select investments that are likely to provide your desired potential total return.

LO3. **Describe the major factors that affect the rate of return on investments.**
Because of the uncertainty that surrounds investments, people often follow a conservative course in an effort to keep their risk low. Being too conservative when investing means that they risk not reaching

their financial goals. To be a successful investor, you must understand the major factors that affect the rate of return on investments so you can then take the appropriate risks when making investment decisions. Key concepts include random and market risk and time horizon.

LO4. **Decide which of the four long-term investment strategies you will utilize.**
To succeed as an investor, you must establish your own long-term investment strategy. Most investors accept the fact that they cannot time the market with any consistency. Long-term investors are passive investors. They wisely ignore the ups and downs of the stock market and the business cycle and simply use the four investment strategies of diversification, buy and hold, dollar-cost averaging, and asset allocation.

LO5. **Create your own investment plan.**
An investment plan is an explanation of your investment philosophy and your logic on investing to reach specific goals. Steps include identifying your goals, contemplating which types of investments might best fit your investment goals, clarifying your investment philosophy, reviewing possible investments that match specific investment time horizons, calculating the numbers using appropriate time horizons, learning about investment alternatives, and narrowing down your choices.

LET'S TALK ABOUT IT

1. **Your Investing Success.** Describe your thoughts about the likelihood of your long-term investing success given the recent severe downturn in the economy and stock markets.

2. **Why to Invest.** Why should people invest? Give three reasons each for college students, young college graduates in their 20s, couples with young children, and people in their 50s.

3. **Market Risk.** What do you think is the likelihood of many more years of continuing high market risk and poor stock market returns due to sluggish economic growth?

4. **What Is Your Tolerance for Risk in Investing?** Is it the same as for other members of your class? Why or why not?

5. **Your Investment Philosophy.** Is your investment philosophy conservative, moderate, or aggressive? Give two reasons to support the adoption of your philoso-

phy. How does your view compare with the philosophies of other members of your class?

6. **Invest How Much?** Assume you have graduated from college and have a good-paying job. If you had to commit to investing regularly right now, how much money would you put away every month? Explain why. How does your view compare with the views of other members of your class?

DO THE MATH

1. **Annual Investments.** Michael and Jessica Mackewich, who live in Fresno, California, have as a new investment goal to create a college fund for their newborn daughter. They estimate that they will need $200,000 in 18 years. Assuming that the Mackewiches could obtain a return of 6 percent, how much would they need to invest annually to reach their goal? Use Appendix A-3 or the *Garman/Forgue* companion website.

2. **Number of Years.** Michael Marion's mother, who lives in New Port Richey, Florida, wants to help pay for her grandchild's education. How many years will it take her to reach her goal of $30,000 if she invests $1000 per year, earning 6 percent? Use Appendix A-3 or the *Garman/Forgue* companion website.

3. **Future Cost.** If one year of college currently costs $15,000, how much will one year cost Joshua Spindle's newborn daughter, Serena, in 18 years, assuming a 5 percent annual rate of inflation? Use Appendix A-1 or the *Garman/Forgue* companion website.

4. **Returns and Actions.** Samantha Rennakker from Collegedale, Tennessee, had $50,000 in investments at the beginning of the year that consisted of a diversified portfolio of stocks (40 percent), bonds (40 percent), and cash equivalents (20 percent). Her returns over the past 12 months were 13 percent on

stocks, 6 percent on bonds, and 4 percent on cash equivalents.

(a) What is Samantha's average return for the year?

(b) If Samantha wanted to rebalance her portfolio to its original position, what specific actions should she take?

5. **Early Investor Wins.** Eric and Adam, who are twins living in Rexburg, Idaho, took different approaches to investing. Eric saved $2000 per year for ten years starting at age 23 and never added any more money to the account. Adam saved $2000 per year for 20 years starting at age 35. Assuming that the brothers earned an 8 percent return, who had accumulated the most by the time they reached age 63? Use Appendix A-1 and Appendix A-3 or the *Garman/Forgue* companion website.

6. **Taxable or Tax-Free.** Ashley Rivera of Milford, Nebraska, has a choice of two investments: a $1000 tax-free municipal bond that pays 4.3 percent interest or a $1000 taxable corporate bond that pays 6.3 percent interest. Both bonds will mature in five years. If Ashley is in the 25 percent tax bracket, which bond should she choose? Use the information on page 128 or the *Garman/Forgue* website.

FINANCIAL PLANNING CASES

CASE 1

The Johnsons Embark on an Solid Investment Program

After nearly eight years of marriage, Harry and Belinda's finances have improved, even though they have incurred debts for an automobile loan and a condominium. Because they did not contribute very much to their retirement plans every year, Harry's account is currently worth only $28,000 and Brenda's is $31,000, but they do have $12,000 in investments outside their employers' retirement plans.

Therefore, the Johnsons have decided to seriously forgo some current spending for the next three

years to concentrate on getting a solid investment program under way while they still have two incomes available and before they start a family. They are willing to accept a moderate amount of risk and expect to invest between $600 and $800 per month over the next three years. Respond to the following questions:

(a) In what types of investments (choose only two) might the Johnsons place the first $2000? (Review Tables 13-1, 13-2, and 13-6 for ideas and available options, and consider the types of investment risks inherent in each choice.) Give reasons for your selections.

(b) In what types of investments might they place the next $4000? Why?

(c) What types of investments should they choose for the next $10,000? Why?

CASE 2

Victor and Maria Hernandez Try to Catch Up on Their Investments

The expenses associated with sending two children through college prevented Victor and Maria Hernandez from adding substantially to their investment program. Now that their younger son, Brian, has completed school and is working full time, they would like to build up their investments quickly. Victor is 47 years old and wants to retire early, perhaps by age 60. In addition to the retirement program at his place of employment, Victor believes that their investment portfolio, currently valued at $70,000, will need to triple to $210,000 by retirement time. He and Maria realize that they will have to sacrifice a lot of current spending to save and invest for retirement.

(a) What rate of return is needed on the $70,000 portfolio to reach their goal of $210,000 (assuming no additional contributions)? Use Appendix A-3 or visit the *Garman/Forgue* companion website.

(b) Victor and Maria think they will need a total of $400,000 for a retirement financial nest egg. Therefore, they will need to create an additional sum of $190,000 through new investments. Assuming an annual return of 8 percent, how much do the Hernandezes need to invest each year to reach their goal of $190,000? Use Appendix A-3 or visit the *Garman/Forgue* companion website.

(c) If they assume a 6 percent annual return, how much do the Hernandezes need to invest each year to reach their goal of $190,000? Use Appendix A-3 or visit the *Garman/Forgue* companion website.

CASE 3

Julia Price's Goal Is to Buy a Luxury Condominium

It has been about 20 years since Julia graduated with a major in aeronautical engineering, and she has been quite successful in her career and her personal finances. Accordingly she wants to sell her home and buy a luxury condominium. She has $40,000 in savings, and she figures that she can continue her savings and investment program for three more years before making a 20 percent down payment on a luxury condominium. The home that she wants to purchase is currently priced at $450,000. Julia thinks she should invest her $40,000 and additional savings during the next three years by using lending investments like certificates of deposit and bonds rather than owning stocks or stock mutual funds. Offer your opinions about her thinking.

CASE 4

A First-Time Investor Gets a Head Start

Jennifer Marsh, a recent dental school graduate from Indiana, Pennsylvania, is thinking about jump-starting a retirement savings plan by investing the $50,000 gift that her elderly uncle gave her. She also wants to invest $1000 a month for the next 25 years for retirement. Jennifer knows little about investments and does not seem to have a big desire to learn.

(a) What can you suggest to Jennifer about figuring out her investment philosophy? (Hint: Mention the information in Figure 13-2 in your response.)

(b) Would you recommend active or passive investing for her, and why?

(c) Should Jennifer be a lender or owner?

(d) Identify three risks to her retirement investments that Jennifer should try to avoid, and explain how she can avoid them.

(e) Select two of the four recommended investment strategies to recommend to Jennifer, and explain why she should follow them.

(f) If Jennifer's $50,000 is invested in a standard investment account and her $1000 monthly is invested in a tax-sheltered account, with each account growing at 8 percent annually for 25 years, how much money will she have accumulated? (Hint: Adjust the lump-sum investment for taxes.)

BE YOUR OWN PERSONAL FINANCIAL MANAGER

1. **Your Personal Risk Pyramid.** Review Figure 13-2, "The Risk Pyramid Reveals the Trade-Offs Between Risk and Return," and record your opinions on which types of risk you are probably willing to take over the next ten years in the world of investing by listing the names of the investments with which you would be comfortable.

2. **Readiness to Invest.** Review the section titled "Suggestions on Your Readiness to Invest" on pages 380–381 and then complete Worksheet 49: My Readiness-to-Invest Checklist from "My Personal Financial Planner," giving yourself grades for the various prerequisites to investing and setting dates for completion.

MY PERSONAL
FINANCIAL
PLANNER

3. **What Is Your Investment Philosophy?** Review the section titled "Identify Your Investment Philosophy and Invest Accordingly" on pages 383–386 and then complete Worksheet 50: My Investment Philosophy from "My Personal Financial Planner" to record various aspects of your approach to investing.

MY PERSONAL
FINANCIAL
PLANNER

4. **Your Long-Term Investment Strategies.** Complete Worksheet 51: My Preferred Long-Term Investment Strategies from "My Personal Financial

MY PERSONAL
FINANCIAL
PLANNER

Planner" by check marking the strategies you like and that you might follow during your investing life.

5. **Investment Goals and Time Horizons.** Review Table 13-1, "Investments for Various Time Horizons," on page 388 while reflecting on your anticipated personal financial life and complete Worksheet 52: My Investment Goals and Time Horizons from "My Personal Financial Planner." Record your short- and long-term investment goals and what investments you might consider to help achieve them.

MY PERSONAL
FINANCIAL
PLANNER

6. **Real Return on Investments.** Review the box "Did You Know? Calculate the Real Rate of Return (After Taxes and Inflation) on Investments" on page 388 and complete Worksheet 53: The Real Return on My Investments from "My Personal Financial Planner" by inserting some realistic numbers next to the examples.

MY PERSONAL
FINANCIAL
PLANNER

ON THE 'NET

Go to the Web pages indicated to complete these exercises.

1. **Investing Foolishly.** Visit the website for the Motley Fool at www.fool.com/how-to-invest/thirteen-steps/index.aspx?source=ifltnvsnv0000001. Read the article discussing the "13 Steps to Investing Foolishly." Which of the 13 steps were you aware of before reading this chapter? Which did you become aware of after reading this chapter and the article?

2. **Investing for Beginners.** Visit the About.com website for investment beginners at http://beginnersinvest.about.com/od/assetallocation1/a/aa102404.htm and read the article on asset allocation. Identify the asset allocation percentages with which you would feel most comfortable now. How might your views change in five years? Twenty years?

3. **Why Invest?** Visit the John Hancock website www.jhfunds.com/Article.aspx?ArticleID=%7B79432E5F-30DF-4624-94F8-FC319EA99D71%7D and read the article titled "Why Invest?" Compare what you read there with what is in this chapter.

4. **Herd Behavior.** Visit the website for Kiplinger.com at www.kiplinger.com/magazine/archives/dont-trust-the-crowd-.html. Read the article "Don't Trust the Crowd." What insights to herd investing did you learn that are different from those learned from this book?

5. **Pay Down Debt Before Investing.** Go to Bankrate.com's website www.bankrate.com/calculators/credit-cards/credit-card-payoff-calculator.aspx to enter your credit card debts and find out what it will take to pay them off.

ACTION INVOLVEMENT PROJECTS

1. **When to Invest.** The text outlines certain suggestions on readiness to invest on pages 380–381. Make a list of likely dates when you think you will have accomplished each (perhaps in one, two, or five years). Make a table of your results.

2. **Your Investment Strategy.** The text discusses four strategies for long-term investors on pages 392–402. Which one appeals to you most and why?

3. **Risk-Tolerance Quiz.** Go to two of the risk-tolerance quiz websites listed in "Financial Power Point: Take a Risk-Tolerance Quiz" on page 383 and offer some comments on how they differ.

4. **Current Investment Magazine Article.** Obtain a current issue of *Money* or *Kiplinger's Personal Finance* and summarize an article that offers suggestions on investing.

Investing in Stocks and Bonds

YOU MUST BE KIDDING, RIGHT?

Brothers Ricky and Marvin Morton differ in investment philosophies—Ricky is conservative and Marvin holds a moderate investing outlook. Their father left each of them $100,000 when he died ten years ago, and Ricky invested in common stocks while Marvin invested in corporate bonds. After ten years, how much more money is Ricky likely to have in his account than Marvin?

A. $35,000

B. $53,000

C. $163,000

D. $216,000

The answer is B, $53,000. One could typically expect to obtain a long-term average annual return of 8 percent on U.S. common stocks compared with 5 percent on corporate bonds. A $100,000 common stock portfolio that returned 8 percent annually would accumulate to $216,000 in ten years while a bond portfolio earning 5 percent annually over the same time period would grow to $163,000. Ricky's willingness to accept more risk by investing in common stocks may provide him with a balance bigger than his brother's by a whopping 32 percent!

LEARNING OBJECTIVES

After reading this chapter, you should be able to:

1 Explain how stocks and bonds are used as investments.

2 Classify common stocks according to their major characteristics.

3 Describe fundamental and numerical ways to evaluate stock values.

4 Use the Internet to evaluate common stocks in which to invest.

5 Summarize how stocks are bought and sold.

6 Describe how to invest in bonds.

© PETER DAZELEY/GETTY IMAGES, INC.

WHAT DO YOU RECOMMEND?

Caitlin Diaz, age 42, is a senior Web designer for a communications company in Lansing, Michigan. She earns $92,000 annually. From her salary, Caitlin contributes $200 per month to her 401(k) retirement account, through which she invests in the company's stock. Caitlin is divorced and has custody of her three children, 10-year-old twins and a 12-year-old. Her ex-husband pays $1500 per month in child support. Caitlin and her former spouse contribute $3000 each annually to a college fund for their children. Over the past 15 years, Caitlin has built a $300,000 stock portfolio after starting by investing the proceeds of a $50,000 life insurance policy following the death of her first husband. Currently, her portfolio is allocated 40 percent into preferred stocks (paying 4.5 percent); 30 percent into cyclical, blue-chip common stocks (P/E ratio of 14); 10 percent into Treasury bonds (paying 3.2 percent); 10 percent into municipal bonds (paying 2.2 percent); and 10 percent into AAA corporate bonds (paying 4.6 percent). Today's comparable corporate bonds pay 5 percent. Caitlin's total return in recent years has been about 6 percent annually. Her investment goals are to have sufficient cash to pay for her children's education and to retire in about 18 years.

What do you recommend to Caitlin on the subject of stocks and bonds regarding:

1. Investing for retirement in 18 years?

2. Owning blue-chip common stocks and preferred stocks rather than other common stocks given Caitlin's investment time horizon?

Golden Pixels LLC/Shutterstock.com

3. The wisdom of owning municipal bonds rather than corporate bonds?

4. The likely selling price of her corporate bonds, if sold today?

5. Investments that might be appropriate to fund her children's education?

To earn a larger return than offered by conservative investments, you must accept more risk. Historically, common stocks, for example, have earned substantially more than cash savings, often twice as much. When you invest in stocks and bonds, you can increase returns significantly while increasing risk only slightly. These investments belong in everyone's investment portfolio because they provide opportunities for conservative, moderate, and aggressive investors alike. Your task when selecting stocks and bonds is to find the right balance between safety and risk.

This is true despite the recent meltdown of U.S. and global stocks. During distressed economic times, the price of an individual stock might fall 5 or 10 percent or more in one day! Investors lock in losses *only* if they sell what they own. And keep in mind that prices might rebound the next day or week or month. The principles of long-term investing are valid because over time turbulent stock and bond markets calm down and provide investors fairly predictable returns. In fact, a good time to invest is when the share prices of high-quality firms have been beaten down to affordable levels. When the stock markets are down, that means they are "on sale" as prices are lower than usual.

You should realize that economic slumps eventually always spark a powerful market recovery. The typical post-recession rally in prices on the stock market is a 50 percent increase over the following 18 months. In fact, the bear stock market that started in October 2007 saw stock prices decline 55 percent by March 2009, and then the subsequent bull market nearly doubled prices by the summer of 2011. Investing is an act of faith and confidence in the future of the U.S. and global economies. History argues that by the time students in college are ready to retire, stock market prices will have tripled or quadrupled.

YOUR NEXT 5 YEARS

In the next five years, you can start achieving financial success by doing the following related to investing in stocks and bonds:

1. *Include stocks and bonds or mutual funds that own stocks and bonds in your investment portfolio.*

2. *Use fundamental analysis to determine a company's basic value before investing in any individual stock.*

3. *Resist putting money into so-called hot stocks.*

4. *Invest part of the conservative portion of your portfolio in TIPS (Treasury Inflation-Protected Securities) to beat inflation.*

5. *When you have children, use zero-coupon bonds to help save for their education.*

THE ROLE OF STOCKS AND BONDS IN INVESTMENTS

 LEARNING OBJECTIVE 1

Explain how stocks and bonds are used as investments.

Individual investors provide the money corporations use to create sales and earn profits. The investor shares in those profits. A **corporation** is a state-chartered legal entity that can conduct business operations in its own name. A **public corporation** is one that issues stock purchased by the general public and traded on stock markets such as the New York Stock Exchange. In contrast, the stock of a **privately held corporation** is held by a relatively small number of people and is not traded on a public stock exchange. The ability to sell shares of ownership to investors offers a corporation the opportunity to develop into a firm of considerable size. It can continue to exist even as ownership of its shares changes hands. AT&T, for example, has issued more than 4 million shares of stock.

A corporation's financial needs will vary over time. To begin its operations, a new corporation needs **start-up capital** (funds initially invested in a business enterprise). During its life, a corporation may need additional money to grow. To raise capital and finance its goals, it may issue three types of **securities** (negotiable instruments of ownership or debt): common stock, preferred stock, and bonds, which we mentioned in Chapter 13.

Common Stock

Stocks are shares of ownership in the assets and earnings of a business corporation. Each stock investor is a part owner in a corporation. **Common stock** is the most basic form of ownership of a corporation. For the investor, stocks represent potential income because the investor owns a piece of the future profits of the company. Investors usually have two expectations: (1) the corporation will be profitable enough that income will exceed expenses, thereby allowing the firm to pay **cash dividends** (a share of profits distributed

privately held corporation
One that issues stock purchased by a relatively small number of people and is not traded on a public stock exchange.

start-up capital
Funds initially invested in a business enterprise.

securities
Negotiable instruments of ownership or debt, including common stock, preferred stock, and bonds.

stocks
Shares of ownership in a business corporation's assets and earnings.

common stock
Most basic form of ownership of a corporation.

cash dividend
Cash profits that a firm distributes to stockholders.

market price
The current price of a share of stock that a buyer is willing to pay a willing seller.

stockholder/shareholder
Each person who owns a share of a company's stock holds a proportionate interest in firm ownership (a very small slice) and, therefore, in the assets and income of the corporation.

residual claim
Common stockholders have a right to share in the income and assets of a corporation after higher-priority claims are satisfied.

voting rights
Proportionate authority to express an opinion or choice in matters affecting the company.

preferred stock
Type of fixed-income ownership security in a corporation that pays fixed dividends.

cumulative preferred stock
Preferred stock for which dividends must be paid, including any skipped dividends, before dividends go to common stockholders.

convertible preferred stock
Can be exchanged at the option of the stockholder for a specified number of shares of common stock.

principal
Face amount of a bond, or price originally paid for a bond.

in cash); and (2) the **market price** of a share of stock, which is the current price that a buyer is willing to pay a willing seller, will increase over time. Stocks usually require a low minimum investment. Common stocks pay annual returns about twice as high as preferred stocks and bonds. Investors expect to earn annual returns of 8 percent or higher on average over time from the combination of dividends and capital gains.

Each person who owns a share of stock—called a **shareholder** or **stockholder**—has a proportionate interest in the ownership (usually a very small slice) and, therefore, in the assets and income of the corporation. This **residual claim** means that common stockholders have a right to share in the income and assets of a corporation only after higher-priority claims are satisfied. These higher-priority claims include interest payments to those who own company bonds and preferred stocks.

Stockholders have a **limited liability**, as their responsibility for business losses is limited to the amount invested in the shares of stock owned. These amounts may be small or large, but the most the shareholder can lose is the original amount invested. If the corporation becomes bankrupt, the common stockholder's ownership value consists of the amount left per share after the claims of all creditors are satisfied first. Each common stockholder has **voting rights**: the proportionate authority to express an opinion or choice in matters affecting the company. Stockholders vote to elect the company's **board of directors**. This group of individuals sets policy and names the principal officers of the company—**management**—who run the firm's day-to-day operations. The number of votes cast by each shareholder depends on the number of shares he or she owns. Stockholders attend an annual meeting or vote by *proxy*—shareholders' written authorization to someone else to represent them and to vote their shares at a stockholder's meeting.

Preferred Stock

Preferred stock is a type of fixed-income ownership security in a corporation. Owners of a preferred stock receive a fixed dividend per share that corporations are required to distribute before any dividends are paid out to common stockholders. They receive no extra income from the stock other than their fixed dividend, even when the firm is highly profitable. The regular dividend payments appeal to those who desire a reliable stream of income, such as retired investors. While the income stream may be consistent, the market price of preferred stock is sensitive to interest rates. Preferred stockholders rarely have voting privileges.

Sometimes a corporation decides not to pay dividends to preferred stockholders because it lacks profits or simply because it wants to retain and reinvest all of its earnings. When the board of directors votes to skip (*pass*) making a cash dividend to preferred stockholders, holders of **cumulative preferred stock** must be paid that dividend before any future dividends are distributed to the common stockholders. For example, assume that a company passes on the first two quarterly dividends of $2.25 each to preferred stockholders, who expect to receive $9 each year ($2.25 × 4 quarters). If the company prospers and wants to give a cash dividend to its common stockholders in the third quarter, it must first pay the passed $4.50 to the cumulative preferred stockholders. Furthermore, the usual third-quarter cash dividend of $2.25 has to be made to the preferred stockholders before the common stockholders can receive any dividends. In the case of **noncumulative preferred stock**, the preferred stockholders would have no claim to previously skipped dividends. **Convertible preferred stock**, a unique security occasionally sold by companies, can be exchanged at the option of the stockholder for a specified number of shares of common stock.

Bonds

Individuals who want to invest by loaning their money can do so by buying bonds and becoming a creditor (again very small) of the business. As we noted in Chapter 13, a **bond** is an interest-bearing negotiable certificate of long-term debt issued by a corporation, the U.S. government, or a municipality (such as a city or state). Bonds are basically IOUs. Corporations and governments often use the proceeds from bonds to finance expensive construction projects and to purchase costly equipment.

With bonds, investors lend the issuer a certain amount of money—the **principal**—with two expectations: (1) they will receive regular interest payments at a fixed rate of return for many years, and (2) they will get their principal returned at some point in the future, called the **maturity date**. The regular pattern of dividends appeals to those who desire a reliable stream of income. The market price of bonds is sensitive to interest rates.

An Illustration of Stocks and Bonds: Running Paws Cat Food Company

To better understand how a corporation finances its goals by issuing common and preferred stock while also paying returns for stockholders, consider the example of Running Paws Cat Food Company. When reading through the example, imagine that the numbers have many more zeros to better visualize a company the size of Google or Microsoft.

Running Paws Is Born Running Paws began as a small family business in Lincoln, Nebraska, started by Linda Webtek. She developed a wonderful recipe for cat food and sold the product through a local grocery store. As sales increased, Linda decided to incorporate the business, expand its operations, and share ownership of the company with the public by asking people to invest in the company's future. Running Paws issued 10,000 shares of common stock at $10 per share. Three friends each bought 2500 shares, and Linda signed over the cat food recipe and equipment to the corporation itself in exchange for the remaining 2500 shares. At that point, Running Paws had $75,000 in working capital (7500 shares sold at $10 each), equipment, a great recipe, and a four-person board of directors. Each of the directors worked for the firm, although they paid themselves very low salaries.

Running Paws Begins to Grow The sales revenues of a corporation like Running Paws are used to pay (1) expenses, (2) interest to bondholders, (3) taxes, (4) cash dividends to preferred stockholders, and (5) cash dividends to common stockholders, in that order. If money is left over after items 1 and 2 are paid, the corporation has earned a **profit**. If funds are available after item 3 is paid, the company has an **after-tax profit**. The average corporation pays out 40 to 60 percent of its after-tax profit in cash dividends to stockholders. The remainder, called **retained earnings**, is left to accumulate and finance the company's goals—often expansion and growth. In its early years, Running Paws retained all of its profits and distributed no dividends.

Common stockholders, such as the stockholders of Running Paws Cat Food Company, are not guaranteed dividends. However, most profitable companies do pay common stockholders a small dividend on a quarterly basis until increased earnings justify paying out a higher amount. Given that Running Paws retained all its earnings, you might wonder why people would invest in such a company. Two reasons explain the attraction. First, as a company becomes more efficient and profitable, cash dividends to common stockholders may not only begin but also become significant. Second, the market price of the stock may increase sharply as more investors become interested in the future profitability of a growing company. Common stock constitutes a share of ownership; thus as the company grows, the price of its common stock follows suit.

Increasing sales meant more production for Running Paws. Soon more orders were coming in from Chicago than the firm could handle. After three years, the owners of Running Paws decided to expand once again. They wanted to borrow an additional $100,000, but their business was so new and its future so uncertain that lenders demanded an extremely high interest rate. To raise the needed funds, the owners decided to issue 5000 shares of preferred stock at $20 per share, promising to pay a cash dividend of $1.80 per share annually, providing a 9 percent yield to investors. The

maturity date
Date upon which the principal is returned to the bondholder.

DID YOU KNOW?

Don't Get Scared Out of Buying Stocks and Bonds

Buying individual stocks and bonds feels risky to investors because the rate of return and value of these securities fluctuate up and down over time. Investment expert Peter Lynch says, "The real key to making money in stocks is not to get scared out of them." Investing based on the recent past is like driving a car while focused on the rear view mirror: stupid and dangerous. Therefore, remain optimistic about stocks and look for gains of 7 to 10 percent annually for the next 10 or 20 years. Instead of owning stocks directly, most investors often choose to invest in stocks and bonds indirectly through mutual funds, which is discussed in Chapter 15.

FINANCIAL POWER POINT

Assume Your Investments Earn 5 Percent to 6 Percent

When planning for long-term financial goals, assume your investments will conservatively earn 3 percent after inflation or at least 5 percent to 6 percent a year. Your investment returns could be higher.

profit
Money left over after a firm pays all expenses and interest to bondholders.

after-tax profit
Money left over after a firm has paid expenses, bondholder interest, and taxes.

retained earnings
Money left over after a firm has paid expenses, bondholder interest, taxes, preferred stockholder dividends, and common stockholder dividends.

pre-emptive right
Right of common stockholders to purchase additional shares before a firm offers new shares to the public.

preferred stock was sold to outside investors, but the original investors retained control of the company through their common stock.

Running Paws Becomes a National Company Following its pattern of expanding into new markets, Running Paws soon developed additional lines of cat food that sold well. With the proceeds from the sale of preferred stock, and after a new plant in Brooklyn, New York, opened, the income of the four-year-old business finally exceeded expenses, and it had a profit of $13,000. The board of directors declared the promised preferred stock dividend of $9000 (5000 preferred shares × $1.80) but no dividend for common stockholders. In the following year, net profits after taxes amounted to $28,000. Once again the board paid the $9000 dividend to preferred stockholders but retained the remainder of the profits to finance continued expansion and improved efficiency.

Then one of the original partners wanted to exit the business and needed to sell her 2500 shares of stock, for which she had originally paid $25,000. Because Running Paws was beginning to show some profits, two other private investors recommended by a local stockbroker made offers to purchase her shares. The shares were sold at $16 per share, with 1500 shares going to one investor and 1000 shares to another investor. Thus, this original investor gained $15,000 in price appreciation ($16 × 2500 = $40,000; $40,000 − $25,000 = $15,000) when she sold out. (The corporation did not profit from this transaction.) Now five owners of the common stock, including the two new ones, voted for the board of directors, with each share representing one vote.

During the sixth year, the company's sales again increased and its earnings totaled $39,000. This time the board voted $9000 for the preferred stockholders and $5000 ($0.50 per share) for the common stockholders but retained the remaining $25,000. With the $5000 distribution, the common stockholders finally began to receive cash dividends.

Even with its success, Running Paws faced another decision. To distribute its products nationally would require another $400,000 to $500,000 for expansion costs. After much discussion, the board voted to sell additional shares of stock and issue some bonds.

The company planned to sell 10,000 shares of common stock at $25 per share. This would dilute the owners' proportion of ownership by half. Common stockholders, however, have a **pre-emptive right** to purchase additional shares before new shares are offered to the public. Thus, each current stockholder retained the legal right to maintain proportionate ownership by being allowed to purchase more shares.

Bonds were sold, too.* Running Paws issued two hundred $1000 bonds with a coupon rate of 8 percent. After several months, all of the new stock and bond shares were sold. After brokerage expenses, the company netted more than $190,000 from the bonds to help finance the expansion. On the stock sales, various local stockbrokers took selling commissions totaling $16,000, leaving $234,000 available for the company to use for expansion. These and other investors will follow the progress of Running Paws and buy and sell shares accordingly. The company will not benefit from this trading. Running Paws and its shareholders will benefit from a rising stock price because ownership in a growing company becomes increasingly valuable. If Running Paws continues to prosper, its board of directors might work toward having its stock listed on a regional stock exchange (discussed later in this chapter) to facilitate trading of shares and to further enhance the company's image.

---

* Companies that need capital to begin or expand their operations sell new issues of stocks, bonds, or both to the investing public. New issues of stock are referred to as **initial public offerings (IPOs)**. **Investment banking firms** serve as intermediaries between companies issuing new stocks and bonds and the investing public.

Concept Check 14.1

1. Distinguish between common stocks and bonds.

2. How do public corporations use stocks and bonds?

3. Why do individuals invest in stocks and bonds?

THE MAJOR CHARACTERISTICS OF COMMON STOCKS

When thinking about investing in a stock it is helpful to begin by understanding two pieces of key information about how they are priced: price/earnings ratio and beta.

Understand a Stock's Price/Earnings Ratio and Beta

Price/Earnings Ratio The **price/earnings ratio (P/E ratio)** (or **multiple**) is the current market price of a stock divided by earnings per share (EPS) over the past four quarters. This ratio is the primary means of valuing a stock. It demonstrates how expensive the stock is versus the company's recently reported earnings, by revealing how much you are paying for each $1 of earnings. For example, if the market price of a share of Running Paws stock is currently $25 and the company's EPS is $1.60, the P/E ratio will be 16 ($25 ÷ $1.60 = 15.6, which rounds to 16). This value can also be called a 16-to-1 ratio or multiple, or a P/E ratio of 16. The P/E ratios of many corporations are widely reported on the Internet and in the financial section of newspapers. Stocks with low P/E ratios tend to have higher dividend yields, less risk, lower prices, and slower earnings growth.

To assess a company's financial status, you could compare that firm's P/E ratio with the P/E ratios for other similar stocks. The P/E ratios for corporations typically range from 5 to 25. The average P/E ratio is about 16, although it varies for different

LEARNING OBJECTIVE

Classify common stocks according to their major characteristics.

price/earnings (P/E) ratio (or multiple)
The current market price of a stock divided by earnings per share (EPS) over the past four quarters; used as the primary means of valuing a stock.

Being invested in the stock market is an excellent way to create wealth.

industries. Financially successful companies that have been paying good dividends through the years might have a P/E ratio ranging from 7 to 10. Rapidly growing companies would likely have a much higher P/E ratio—11 to 20. Speculative companies might have P/E ratios of 25 or 50 or even higher because they have low earnings now but anticipate much higher earnings in the future. Firms that are expected to have strong earnings growth generally have a high stock price and a correspondingly high P/E ratio. The P/E ratio tends to fall as uncertainty about future earnings rises, and vice versa.

Inverting the typical P/E ratio of 12 reveals that stocks have an **earnings yield** of 8.5 percent. In other words, each $100 of stocks is backed by $8.50 in expected earnings. During times of low interest rates, an 8.5 percent yield on stocks looks terrific.

Trailing and Projected Price/Earnings Ratios The standard P/E ratio is, in fact, called a **trailing P/E ratio** measure because it is calculated using recently reported earnings, usually from the previous four quarters. Investors need to focus on future prospects when analyzing the value of a stock. A **projected P/E** or **forward price/earnings ratio** divides price by projected earnings over the coming four quarters, an estimate available via online stock quote providers. The earnings yield, which is the inverse of the P/E ratio (Running Paws' earnings yield is 6.4 percent [$1.60 ÷ $25]), helps investors think more clearly about expectations for investments.

Use Beta to Compare a Stock to Similar Investments Beta is a number widely used by investors to predict future stock prices. The **beta value** (or **beta coefficient**) is a measure of an investment's volatility compared with a broad market index for similar investments over time. For large-company stocks, the S&P 500 Stock Index often serves as a benchmark. The average for all stocks in the market is a beta of +1.0, and a beta greater than 1.0 indicates higher-than-market volatility. Recall that market risk is assumed to be 8 percent; thus when the overall stock market increases 8 percent a stock with a 1.0 beta is likely to increase the same amount. Beta reports the relative history of an investment's up-and-down price changes.

Most stocks have positive betas between 0.5 and 2.0. A beta of less than 1.0 (0.0 to 0.9) indicates that the stock price is less sensitive to the market. This is because the price moves in the same direction as the general market, but not to the same degree. A beta of more than +1.0 to +2.0 (or higher) indicates that the price of the security is more sensitive to the market because its price moves in the same direction as the market but by a greater percentage. Higher betas mean greater risk relative to the market. A beta of zero suggests that the price of the stock is independent of the market, much like that of a risk-free U.S. Treasury security. You may look up betas for stocks at Quote.com (www.quote.com/beta/chart.action) and at Yahoo! Finance at http://screen.yahoo.com/stocks.html.

Cyclical and Countercyclical Stocks

The term **cyclical stock** describes the stock of a company whose profits are greatly influenced by changes in the economic business cycle. Such companies operate in consumer-dependent industries, such as automobiles, housing, airlines, retailing, and heavy machinery. The market prices of cyclical stocks mirror the general state of the economy and reflect the various phases of the business cycle. During times of prosperity and economic expansion, corporate earnings rise, profits grow, and stock prices climb; during a recession, these measures decline sharply. The stock of many firms characterized as blue-chip, income, growth, value, or speculative stocks can be described as cyclical stocks. Cyclical stocks have a beta of about 1.0.

A stock with a beta that is less than 1.0 is called a **countercyclical** (or **defensive**) **stock** because it exhibits price changes contrary to movements in the business cycle. These stocks perform well even in an environment characterized by weak economic activity and sliding interest rates. Cigarette smokers, for example, do not quit during a recession, and people usually continue to go to movies, consume soft drinks, purchase cat and dog food, buy electric utility service, and grocery shop. The prices of countercyclical stocks remain steady during an economic recession.

---

earnings yield
The earnings per share of a stock divided by its price; an inversion of the price/earnings ratio; helps investors more clearly see investment expectations.

trailing P/E ratio
Calculated using recently reported earnings, usually from the previous four quarters.

projected P/E ratio
Because investors need to look to the future rather than the past, this measure divides price by projected earnings over the coming four quarters. Also known as forward price/earnings ratio.

beta value/beta coefficient
A measure of stock volatility; that is, how much the stock price varies relative to the rest of the market.

cyclical stock
The stock of a company whose profits are greatly influenced by changes in the economic business cycle.

countercyclical (or defensive) stock
A stock that exhibits price changes contrary to movements in the business cycle.

Income Stocks

A company whose stock is classified as an **income stock** characteristically may not grow too quickly, but year after year pays a cash dividend higher than that offered by most companies. It does so because the firm has fairly high earnings and chooses to retain only a small portion of the earnings. To declare high cash dividends regularly, a company has to have a steady stream of profits. Stocks issued by telephone, electric, and gas utility companies fit this profile and are labeled income stocks. Investors in these companies usually are not very concerned with the P/E ratio or the growth potential of the price of the stock. The betas of such stocks are often less than 1.0. Individuals who desire some income from their portfolio are often attracted to income stocks.

Growth Stocks

The term **growth stock** describes the stock of a company that offers the promise of much higher profits tomorrow and has a consistent record of relatively rapid growth in earnings in all economic conditions. The return to investors from growth stocks comes primarily from increases in share prices. Such stocks typically pay low or no dividends because most of their earnings are retained to maintain company growth.

Well-Known Growth Stocks Stocks of companies that are leaders in their fields, that dominate their markets, and that have several consecutive years of above-industry-average earnings are considered **well-known growth stocks**. Investor awareness of such corporations is widespread, and expectations for continued growth are high. The P/E ratio is high, too. Many growth stocks have a glamorous reputation that improves or declines sharply in conjunction with the overall market and, therefore, have betas of 1.5 or more. Investors like well-known growth stocks because they typically pay some dividends and offer a good opportunity for price appreciation. In the past, well-known growth stocks have included those offered by Apple (AAPL), Genentech (DNA), Google (GOOG), Panera Bread (PNRA), Urban Outfitters (URBN), and Wells Fargo (WFC).

Lesser-Known Growth Stocks Because some **lesser-known growth stocks** are not as popular with investors, the P/E ratios for such firms are generally lower (although still high) than those of the more glamorous growth stocks. Often such firms represent regional businesses with strong earnings or companies that may be the third or fourth leading firm in an industry. In recent years, lesser-known growth stocks have included: Alamo Group (AG), Royal Caribbean (RCL), Bucyrus International (BUCY), Blackboard (BBBB), Maidenform Brands (MFB), Chipotle Mexican Grill (CMG), Quicksilver Resources (KWK), and Terex Corp (TEX). Their betas are usually 1.5 to 2.0 or higher.

Value Stocks

A **value stock** is one that tends to trade at a low price relative to its company fundamentals (dividends, earnings, sales, and so on) and thus is considered undervalued by a value investor. A **value investor** believes that the market isn't always efficient and that it is possible to find companies trading for less than they are worth. Value investors try to buy stocks when they are quoted below their fair value and sell them when they rise above that level.

Value stocks often operate within industries that benefit from a growing economy. Stocks that have a relatively high dividend yield, low price/sales ratio, and/or low P/E ratio are classified as value stocks. The low valuations that value stocks enjoy are often a result of some type of bad news (poor earnings report, bad press, legal issues, and so on). Although their stock prices may have changed, some past examples of value stocks have included Amgen (AMGN), AT&T (T), eBay (EBAY), Gap (GPS), Intel (INTC), and Target (TGT).

Speculative Stocks

The term **speculative stock** describes the stock of a company that has a potential for substantial earnings at some time in the future. These stocks are considered speculative

---

income stock
A stock that may not grow too quickly, but year after year pays a cash dividend higher than that offered by most companies.

growth stock
The stock of a company that offers the promise of much higher profits tomorrow and has a consistent record of relatively rapid growth in earnings in all economic conditions.

well-known growth stocks
Stocks of companies that are leaders in their fields, that dominate their markets, and that have several consecutive years of above-industry-average earnings.

value stock
A stock that tends to trade at a low price relative to its company fundamentals (dividends, earnings, sales, and so on) and thus is considered undervalued by a value investor.

DID YOU KNOW?

Reasons to Invest in Dividend-Paying Stocks

When you invest in companies that pay dividends, odds are that they will continue to pay the dividend even when the company is not doing well financially. Dividend-paying companies typically outperform other firms and provide a greater return than the return on the S&P 500 index. Firms that pay dividends typically boost them about 3.2 percent annually. When inflation is low a dividend of 2 to 4 percent is a decent return. Finally, dividend-paying companies are less volatile than other stocks with a beta of less than 1.0.

speculative stock
Stock of a company that has a potential for substantial earnings at some time in the future, although those earnings may never be realized.

because those earnings may never be realized. A speculative stock may have a spotty earnings record or be so new that no earnings pattern has emerged. Investors in these companies accept some risk because they expect the companies to be highly profitable in the future. They hope that the company will make a new discovery, invent a new product, or generate valuable information that later may push up the price of the stock, creating substantial capital gains.

Examples of speculative companies include computer graphics firms, Internet applications firms, small oil exploration businesses, genetic engineering firms, and some pharmaceutical manufacturers. For these firms, the P/E ratio fluctuates widely in tandem with the company's fortunes, and beta values exceeding 2.0 are common. For every speculative company that succeeds, many others do poorly or fail altogether. Although their stock prices may have changed, some past examples of speculative stocks have included Alimera Sciences (ALIM), Dendreon (DNDN), ICO Global Communications (ICOG), Polar Wireless (BCDD), and Star Scientific (CIGX).

A **penny stock** is one that sells for less than $1 per share, and there are about 5000. They are typically issued by new companies with erratic sales, few profits, and only some hope of success. Penny stocks are sometimes sold over the telephone by high-pressure salespeople to unsophisticated investors. Legitimate stocks or not, these are very speculative investments.

Tech Stocks

tech stocks
Stocks in the technology sector that offer technology-based products and services, biotechnology, Internet services, network services, wireless communications, and more.

Tech stocks are those in the technology sector. Technology firms are dominant in the stock market and include firms that offer technology-based products and services, biotechnology, Internet services, network services, wireless communications, and more. Some are large blue-chip firms, such as Amazon (AMZN), Microsoft (MSFT), and Cisco Systems (CSCO), while many are smaller companies, such as Research In Motion Limited (RIM), Tibco Software (TIBX), SanDisk (SNDK), and VMware (VMW).

Blue-Chip Stocks

blue-chip stocks
Stocks that have been around for a long time, have a well-regarded reputation, dominate its industry, and are known for being solid, relatively safe investments.

The term **blue-chip stocks** suggests a company that has been around for a long time, has a well-regarded reputation, dominates its industry (often with annual revenues of $1 billion or more), and is known for being a solid, relatively safe investment. Typically, blue-chip companies have a history of both good earnings and consistent cash dividends, and they grow at approximately the same rate as the overall economy. The term comes from poker, in which the highest chip denomination is colored blue.

Blue-chip stock shares are widely held by individual investors, mutual funds, and pension plans. The earnings of blue-chip companies (whose stocks are usually considered income stocks or well-known growth stocks) are expected to increase at a consistent but unspectacular rate because these highly stable firms are the leaders in their industries. Examples of such stocks are Walmart, Coca-Cola, Gillette, Berkshire Hathaway, and ExxonMobil. Investing in such companies is considered much less risky than investing in other types of firms.

Large-Cap, Small-Cap, and Midcap Stocks

large-cap stocks
Those public corporations that are capitalized by issuing $3 billion to $4 billion (or more) of stocks; most are considered blue-chip companies.

A company's size classification in the stock market is based on its **market capitalization**. This is the total value of a company's common stock shares determined at its current market price. **Large-cap stocks** are those of firms that have issued more than $10 billion of stocks. Most are considered blue-chip companies, too. Examples include Goodyear (GT), HJ Heinz (HNZ), Norfolk Southern (NSC), Procter & Gamble (PG), and Visa (V). Stocks of midsize and smaller firms often outperform large-cap stocks.

Midcap stocks are the stocks of those remaining companies that are quite substantial in terms of capitalization—perhaps $2 billion to $10 billion in size—but not among the very largest firms. Examples include Dolby Laboratories (DLB), Priceline.com (PCLN), Raymond James Financial (RJF), and WR Grace (XNYS). A **small-cap stock** is stock of a company that has a capitalization of $300 million to $2 billion. Examples include BJ's Restaurants (BJRI), Ethan Allen Interiors (ETH), Playboy Enterprises (PLA), and Village Super Market (VLGEA). **Microcaps** are firms with $50 to $300 million in capitalization. When the smaller firms achieve substantial increases in sales and earnings, their stock prices typically jump quite sharply. Examples are Frontier Oil (FTO), Gulfmark Offshore (GLF), and Meridian Bioscience (VIVO).

 Concept Check 14.2

1. Summarize the meanings of the terms *price/earnings ratio* and *beta*.

2. Distinguish between income stocks and growth stocks.

3. Explain how a value stock might or might not differ from a blue-chip stock or a tech stock.

HOW TO EVALUATE STOCK VALUES

How do you know whether buying a particular stock is a good idea? Or when you should sell shares that you hold? To get answers, first use fundamental research analysis, instead of technical analysis to evaluate a stock. Second, use numerical measures to evaluate stock values. And third, run the numbers to calculate a particular stock's potential rate of return.

Use Fundamental Analysis to Evaluate Stocks

The premise underlying **fundamental analysis** is that each stock has an intrinsic (or true) value based on its expected stream of future earnings. Most professional stock analysts and investors take this approach to investing as they research corporate and industry financial reports. Fundamental analysis suggests that you can identify some stocks that will outperform others given the state of the economy. The fundamental approach presumes that a stock's basic value is largely determined by its current and future earnings trends, assets and debts, products, competition, and management's expertise to assess its growth potential. The aim is to seek out sound stocks—perhaps even unfashionable ones—that are priced below what they ought to be.

An opposing and minority view on valuing common stocks is advocated by proponents of **technical analysis**, often newsletter authors. This method of evaluating securities analyzes statistics generated by market activity, such as past prices and volume. Technical analysts do not attempt to measure a security's intrinsic value but instead use charts, graphs, mathematics, and software programs to identify and predict future price movements. Technical analysis has proved to be of little value, although some novice investors may find technical analysts' logic appealing.

Fundamental analysis suggests that you should consider investing only in companies that will likely be industry leaders—not necessarily the largest firms and fastest-growing industries, but the pacesetters in terms of profitability. You should invest in a stock because you have good reasons related to earnings and profitability, such as a new division in a firm that soon is expected to be quite profitable, a firm is starting to outsell its competitors, product research looks promising, or the firm is a leader in an industry that will be a future driver of profits in the economy.

Corporate earnings are the profits a company makes during a specific time period. If a company cannot generate earnings now or in the future, stock market analysts and investors are not going to be impressed. As people reach this conclusion, there quickly will be more sellers than buyers of the company's common stock, and that will depress the stock's market price. Corporate earnings are at the core of fundamental analysis.

Earnings per Share
A company's **earnings per share (EPS)** is annual profit divided by the number of outstanding shares. It indicates the income that a company has available, on a per-share basis, to pay dividends and reinvest as retained earnings. The EPS is a measure of the firm's profitability on a common-stock-per-share basis, and it is helpful because investors can use it to compare financial conditions of many companies. The EPS is reported in the business section of many newspapers.

fundamental analysis
School of thought in market analysis that assumes each stock has an intrinsic (or true) value based on its expected stream of future earnings.

technical analysis
Method of evaluating securities that uses statistics generated by market activity, such as past prices and volume, over time to determine when to buy or sell a stock.

corporate earnings
The profits a company makes during a specific time period that indicate to many analysts whether to buy or sell a stock.

earnings per share (EPS)
A firm's profit divided by the number of outstanding shares.

In our example, assume that next year, after payment of $9000 in dividends to preferred stockholders, Running Paws had a net profit of $32,000. With 20,000 shares of stock, the company's EPS would be $1.60 ($32,000 ÷ 20,000).

price/sales ratio (P/S ratio)
Tells the number of dollars it takes to buy a dollar's worth of a company's annual revenues; calculated by dividing company's total market capitalization by its sales for the past four quarters.

Price/Sales Ratio The **price/sales ratio (P/S ratio)** indicates the number of dollars it takes to buy a dollar's worth of a company's annual revenues. The P/S is obtained by dividing a company's total market capitalization by its sales for the past four quarters. For example, if Running Paws Cat Food Company's common stock currently sells for $25 per share and 20,000 shares of the company's stock are outstanding, its total capitalization is $500,000. If company revenues (sales of cat food) were $750,000 over the past year, the stock's P/S would be 0.67 ($500,000 ÷ $750,000). Stock analysts suggest investors avoid companies with a P/S greater than 1.5 and favor those having a P/S of less than 0.75. Many investors ignore the P/S, but it works better than the highly acclaimed P/E ratio in predicting which companies provide the best return, as explained in James P. O'Shaughnessy's *What Works on Wall Street*.

Additional Numerical Measures to Evaluate Stock Prices

Several other numerical measures are used to evaluate stock performance. These numbers are readily available to investors on the Internet that will help you assess future stock prices.

cash dividends
Distributions made in cash to holders of common and preferred stock typically paid four times a year.

Cash Dividends Stocks usually pay dividends. **Cash dividends** are distributions made in cash to holders of stock. They are the current income that you receive while you own shares in the company. The firm's board of directors usually declares a dividend on a quarterly basis (four times per corporate year), typically at the end of March, June, September, and December. Dividends are ordinarily paid out of current earnings, but in the event of unprofitable times (low earnings or none), the money might come from cash reserves held by the company. Occasionally, a company will borrow to pay the dividend so as to maintain its reputation of consistently paying dividends. Later profits can be used to repay any funds borrowed for this purpose.

dividends per share
Translates the total cash dividends paid out by a company to common stockholders into a per-share figure.

Dividends per Share The **dividends per share** measure translates the total cash dividends paid out by a company to common stockholders into a per-share figure. For example, Running Paws might elect to declare a total cash dividend of $8000 for the year to common stockholders. In that case, cash dividends per share would amount to $0.40 ($8000 ÷ 20,000 shares).

dividend payout ratio
Dividends per share divided by earnings per share (EPS); helps judge the likelihood of future dividends.

Dividend Payout Ratio The **dividend payout ratio** is the dividends per share divided by EPS. It helps you judge the likelihood of future dividends. For example, imagine that Running Paws Cat Food Company earned $32,000 (after paying preferred stockholders), paid out a cash dividend of $8000 to company stockholders, and retained the remaining $24,000 to facilitate growth of the company. In this case, the dividend payout ratio equals 0.25 ($8000 ÷ $32,000). For that year, Running Paws paid a dividend equal to 25 percent of earnings.

Newer companies usually retain most, if not all, of their profits to facilitate growth. An investor interested in growth would, therefore, seek a company with a low payout ratio. The lower the payout ratio, the greater the likelihood that the company will grow, resulting in later capital gains for investors. Examples of companies that historically have a high payout ratio are AT&T (T), Chevron (CVX), Exelon (EXC), Home Depot (HD), Intel (INTC), Merck (MRK), Pfizer (PFE), and Verizon (VZ).

dividend yield
Cash dividend to an investor expressed as a percentage of the current market price of a security.

Dividend Yield The **dividend yield** is the cash dividend paid to an investor expressed as a percentage of the current market price of a security. For example, the $0.40 cash dividend of Running Paws divided by the current $25 market price for its stock reveals a dividend yield of 1.6 percent ($0.40 ÷ $25). Growth and speculative companies typically pay little or no cash dividends, so they have limited dividend yields. Such companies are attractive to investors who are interested in capital gains.

book value/shareholder's equity
Net worth of a company, determined by subtracting total liabilities from assets.

Book Value Book value (also known as **shareholder's equity**) is the net worth of a company, which is determined by subtracting the company's total liabilities from its assets. It theoretically indicates a company's worth if its assets were sold, its debts were paid off, and the net proceeds were distributed to the investors who own the outstanding shares of common stock.

Book Value per Share The **book value per share** reflects the book value of a company divided by the number of shares of common stock outstanding. Running Paws has a net worth of $230,000, which, when divided by 20,000 shares, gives a book value per share of $11.50.

Often little relationship exists between the book value of a company and its earnings or the market price of its stock. A stock's price usually exceeds its book value per share. The reason is that stockholders bid up the stock price because they anticipate earnings and dividends in the future and expect the market price to rise even more. When the book value per share exceeds the price per share, the stock may truly be underpriced.

Price-to-Book Ratio The **price-to-book ratio (P/B ratio)**, also called the **market-to-book ratio**, identifies firms that are asset rich, such as many banks, brokerage firms, and insurance companies. The P/B ratio is the current stock price divided by the per-share net value of the company's plant, equipment, and other assets (book value). It tells you the premium that you are paying for the net assets of the company.

In the Running Paws example, the book value per share of $11.50 would be divided into the recent price at which the stock was sold ($25 in this case); thus, the P/B ratio for Running Paws is 2.17. The current P/B ratio for most stocks lies between 2.1 and 1.0. The lower the ratio, the less highly a company's assets have been valued, indicating that the stock may be currently underpriced. If the ratio is less than 1, the assets may be utilized ineffectively. In such cases, an underperforming and undervalued company may become a target of a corporate takeover.

Calculating a Stock's Potential Rate of Return

There is but a single reason to make an investment: to obtain a positive return. So how do you determine the potential return on a stock investment?

Find Out the Alpha Statistic One indicator of return is an investment's **alpha statistic**, which quantifies the difference between an investment's expected return and its actual recent performance (outperforming or underperforming) given its risk. A stock or mutual fund with a positive alpha means the company did better than expected for its level of risk compared to a benchmark; a negative alpha indicates poor performance. Alphas for individual stocks, mutual funds, and other investments are available online through brokerage firms, advisory services, and mutual fund companies. Alphas are an important statistic, but they are based on past performance and, thus, provide only a guide for future performance.

Calculating a Potential Investment Return Takes Five Steps Although you cannot know the exact performance of any investment in advance, you certainly will want to pay no more than the "right price" for the investment given its potential rate of return. Calculating returns on a potential investment involves five steps. Armed with these data, you will be better positioned to make informed decisions:

1. Use beta to estimate the level of risk of the investment.
2. Estimate the market risk.
3. Calculate the required rate of return.
4. Calculate the potential rate of return on the investment.
5. Compare the required rate of return with the potential rate of return on the investment.

1. USE BETA TO ESTIMATE THE RISK OF THE INVESTMENT Beta is a useful piece of information when you want to estimate the rate of return you require on an investment in a stock, bond, or mutual fund before putting your money at risk. Betas for individual stocks, mutual funds, and other investments are available online from brokerage firms, advisory services, and investment magazines.

book value per share
Reflects the book value of a company divided by the number of shares of common stock outstanding.

DID YOU KNOW?

About Employee Stock Options

Many employers give stock options to attract and retain employees. An **employee stock option (ESO)** is a gift, like a bonus, from an employer to an employee that allows employees to benefit from the appreciation of their employer's stock without putting any money down. The company gives the employee the right and opportunity to "exercise" the option by buying the stock sometime in the future at an "exercise" or "striking" price established when the option was given. If the company prospers, when the employee eventually decides to exercise the options, the current share price may be much higher than the exercise price, thus allowing the employee to buy the shares at a considerable discount.

price-to-book ratio (P/B ratio)
Current stock price divided by the per-share net value of a firm's plant, equipment, and other assets (book value).

alpha statistic
Quantifies the difference between an investment's expected return and its actual recent performance (outperforming or underperforming) given its risk compared to a benchmark; positive values indicate better-than-market performance.

The following example illustrates how to use beta to estimate the amount of risk in an investment portfolio. Assume you are willing to accept more risk than the general investor and that you buy a stock with a beta of 1.5. If the average price of all stocks rises by 20 percent over time, the price of the stock you chose might rise by 30 percent, which is the beta of 1.5 multiplied by the increase in the market ($1.5 \times 20\%$). If the average price of all stocks drops in value by 10 percent, the price of the stock you chose might drop by 15 percent ($1.5 \times 10\%$).

2. ESTIMATE THE MARKET RISK To estimate the required rate of return on an investment, you need to quantify the market risk. **Market risk**, also known as **systematic risk**, which we discussed in Chapter 13, is the risk associated with the effects of the overall economy on securities markets. It often causes the market price of a particular stock or bond to change, even though nothing has changed in the fundamental values underlying that security. Historical records indicate that 8 percent represents a realistic estimate of market risk for U.S. stocks. Market risk was substantially higher during the recent turbulence in stock markets, and in the near term, it remains elevated.

3. CALCULATE YOUR REQUIRED RATE OF RETURN The return on short-term U.S. Treasury bills has historically exceeded the rate of inflation by a slight degree. Thus, when T-bills pay 2 percent interest, the inflation rate might hover around 1.7 percent. This circumstance provides almost no gain for the investor because both inflation and income taxes reduce the return to about zero. For this reason, investors often use the yield on Treasury bills as a base number that provides a zero **real rate of return**—that is, a zero return on investment after inflation and income taxes.

To calculate your required rate of return on an investment, multiply the beta value of an investment by the estimated market risk and then add the risk-free T-bill rate, as shown in Equation (14.1). For current T-bill rates, see www.treasurydirect.gov/indiv/products/prod_tbills_glance.htm and www.treasurydirect.gov/RI/OFBills. Use Equation (14.1) to determine an **estimate of the required rate of return on an investment**.

$$\text{Estimate of the required rate of return on an investment} = \text{T-bill rate} + (\text{beta} \times \text{market risk}) \quad \textbf{(14.1)}$$

estimate of the required rate of return on an investment
A calculation that multiplies the beta value of an investment by the estimated market risk and adds the risk-free T-bill rate that suggests to investors the return required to put their money at risk.

For example, assume you are considering investing in Running Paws Cat Food Company, which has a beta of 1.5. If you assume a market risk of 8 percent and the current T-bill rate is 2.0 percent, the total rate of return you will require on this investment is 14.0 percent $[2.0 + (1.5 \times 8.0)]$. Investors need the promise of a return higher than 14 percent to put their money at risk in this investment.

4. CALCULATE THE STOCK'S POTENTIAL RATE OF RETURN The **potential return** for any investment over a period of years can be determined by adding anticipated income (from dividends, interest, rents, or other sources) to the future value of the investment and then subtracting the investment's original cost. The investor using fundamental analysis can obtain the figures needed to construct the expected stream of future earnings for a company from a variety of sources. For example, you can use estimates for earnings and dividends gathered from large investment data firms such as Value Line or Standard & Poor's, an individual stock analyst's projections, figures from the company itself, or you can create your own numbers.

potential return
Determined by adding anticipated income (from dividends, interest, rents, or other sources) to the future value of investment and then subtracting the investment's original cost.

Add Up Projected Income and Price Appreciation. Table 14-1 illustrates how to sum up the projected income and price appreciation. You can convert these figures into a **potential rate of return** by calculating the approximate compound yield, as shown in Equation (14.2). This figure can then be compared with returns on other investments.

potential rate of return
A calculation of the approximate compound yield of an investment that sums up projected income and price appreciation, and the resulting figure may then be compared with returns on other investments.

Example: Running Paws Cat Food Company. Based on a recommendation from his stockbroker, Martin Crane, who lives in Seattle, is considering Running Paws Cat Food Company as a potential investment. Martin figures that the company's stock might provide a better return than inflation and income taxes for about five years. He has determined the following information about this stock investment: It is currently priced at $30 per share, its most recent 12-month earnings amounted to $2.40 per share, and the cash dividend for the same period was $0.66 per share.

End of Year	Earnings	Dividend Income
1	$2.76	$0.76
2	3.17	0.87
3	3.65	1.00
4	4.20	1.15
5	4.83	1.33
Total dividends		$5.11
Average annual dividend ($5.11 ÷ 5)		$1.02

One Investor's Projections of the Earnings and Dividends for Running Paws Cat Food Company

Table 14-1

Martin began the task of projecting the future value of one share of the stock by using the EPS information. He first calculated the P/E ratio to be 12.5 ($30 ÷ $2.40). Next, as illustrated in Table 14-1, Martin applied a 15 percent rate of growth estimate (the same rate that occurred in previous years, according to Running Paws' annual report) for the EPS for each year ($2.40 × 1.15 = $2.76; $2.76 × 1.15 = $3.17; and so forth). Using a P/E ratio of 12.5 (the same as the current ratio), Martin estimated the market price at the end of the fifth year to be $60.38 (12.5 × $4.83). This calculation gives a projected net appreciation in stock price over five years of $30.38 ($60.38 minus the current price of $30).

$$ACY = \frac{\text{average annual dividend} + \dfrac{\text{projected price of stock} - \text{current price of stock}}{\text{number of years projected}}}{\dfrac{\text{projected price of stock} + \text{current price of stock}}{2}} \quad \textbf{(14.2)}$$

$$= \frac{\$1.02 + \dfrac{\$60.38 - \$30.00}{5}}{\dfrac{\$60.38 + \$30.00}{2}}$$

$$= \frac{\$1.02 + \$6.08}{\$45.19}$$

$$= 15.7\%$$

To project the future income of the investment in Running Paws—the anticipated cash dividends—Table 14-1 shows that Martin estimated a 15 percent growth rate in the cash dividend ($0.66 × 1.15 = $0.76; $0.76 × 1.15 = $0.87; and so forth). Adding the projected cash dividends over five years gives a total of $5.11. Martin obtained the potential return for one share of Running Paws over five years by adding anticipated dividend income ($5.11) to the future value of the investment ($60.38) less its original cost ($30.00), for a result of $35.49 ($5.11 + $30.38). Thus, Martin has projected that $30 invested in one share of Running Paws will earn a potential total return of $35.49 in five years.

The question now becomes, what is the percentage yield for this dollar return? The **approximate compound yield (ACY)** provides a measure of the annualized compound growth of any long-term investment. You can determine this value by using Equation (14.2). The calculation requires use of an *annual average* dividend rather than the specific projected dividends. In this example, the annual average dividend of $1.02 is computed by dividing the $5.11 in dividend income by five years. Substituting the data from Table 14-1 into Equation (14.2) and using the average annual dividend figure results in an approximate compound yield of 15.7 percent on the potential investment in one share of Running Paws stock for five years. (This formula can be found on the *Garman/Forgue* companion website.)

approximate compound yield (ACY)

A measure of the annualized compound growth of any long-term investment stated as a percentage.

DID YOU KNOW?

Seven Questions Every Investor Needs to Answer

Before investing, investors ought to have written down responses to the following questions:

1. *My investment experience?*
2. *My investment philosophy (conservative, moderate, or aggressive)?*
3. *My investment goals?*
4. *My age and family responsibilities?*
5. *My net worth?*
6. *My income?*
7. *My investment time horizon?*

5. COMPARE THE REQUIRED RATE OF RETURN WITH THE POTENTIAL RATE OF RETURN ON THE INVESTMENT Now the moment of decision making is at hand. You compare the estimated required rate of return on an investment (given its risk) with the investment's potential projected rate of return. In our example involving Running Paws Cat Food Company, the risk suggested a required rate of return of 14.0 percent. The investment's potential rate of return was projected to be 15.7 percent, which suggests that Running Paws is a good buy for Martin at the current selling price of $30—that is, the stock is underpriced. Once armed with projected rate of return information for an investment, you can compare it with other investments.

 Concept Check 14.3

1. What is the focus of fundamental analysis?
2. Distinguish between EPS and the P/E ratio.
3. Summarize the differences among dividend payout ratio, dividends per share, and dividend yield.
4. Explain why individuals considering investing in stocks begin by thinking about the return on U.S. Treasury bills.
5. Explain how a stock with a beta of 1.0 differs from ones with a beta of 1.2 and 2.5.
6. Summarize the five steps in calculating the potential rate of return on a stock investment.

USE THE INTERNET TO EVALUATE AND SELECT STOCKS

An overwhelming amount of information is available on stock investments. With more than 8000 U.S. public companies to choose from and another 50,000 stocks in other countries, stock selection takes time. Hundreds of investment resources exist, including television and radio shows, books, websites, blogs, and newsletters. What approach should you take? Use the Internet because everything you need is online. The Internet is a source of up-to-the-minute, high-quality information on investments.

Begin by Setting Criteria for Your Stock Investments

The process of setting criteria for a stock investment starts with a review of your investment plan, as discussed in Chapter 13 and illustrated in Figure 13-6 on page 403. To make informed selections of the stock investments that match your investment goals, philosophy, and time horizon, begin by making decisions on criteria for your stock investments:

- What classifications of stocks are best suited for your goals?
- What market capitalization meets your desires?
- What specific numeric measures do you require on beta, sales, profitability, P/E ratio, dividends, payout ratio, and market price?
- What projected EPS growth do you require?
- Do you want to invest in an industry leader?

Investor Education Is Widely Available

Comprehensive investment websites provide updated news headlines; market overviews; market statistics; industry statistics; industry trends; corporate stock symbols; current stock market prices; specific company profiles, history, financials, prices, and outlook for

DID YOU KNOW?

How to Use Online Stock Calculators

You can perform almost any kind of mathematical calculation necessary in investing by using one of the online investment websites. For example, by using WalletPop.com (www.walletpop.com/calculators/stocks), you can get answers to these questions:

- *Which is better: income or growth stock?*
- *What is my current yield from dividends?*

- *How much do commissions and fees affect my stock's rate of return?*
- *What stock price will achieve my target rate of return?*
- *What is the return on my stock if I sell now?*
- *Should I wait a year to sell my stock?*
- *Should I sell my stock now and invest the money elsewhere?*

Although annual reports contain some important information, many are mainly marketing tools for the corporation.

the future; tips on how to build a portfolio; and stock-screening tools with search capabilities. Following are some popular websites for investing:

- The Motley Fool (www.fool.com)
- Morningstar (www.morningstar.com)
- *Kiplinger's Personal Finance* (www.kiplinger.com/personalfinance/)
- CNNMoney.com (www.money.cnn.com/pf/index.html)
- Yahoo! Finance (www.finance.yahoo.com/marketupdate?u)
- BusinessWeek.com (www.businessweek.com/finance/)
- SmartMoney.com (www.smartmoney.com/personal-finance/)
- AOL Money Basics (www.dailyfinance.com/?icid=navbar_Finance)
- NASDAQ (www.nasdaq.com)
- Zacks Investment Research (www.zacks.com)

Set Up Your Portfolio Online

You can set up a portfolio through an online brokerage account or by using any of several websites. For example, see Kiplinger at www.kiplinger.com/portfolio/portfolio.php and Yahoo! Finance (http://finance.yahoo.com/p?k=pf_1). Both let you insert the number of shares you own and at what price. The site then tracks stock quotes to update the value of your holdings.

Stock Screening

You can research stocks, bonds, and mutual funds by using **stock-screening tools** available on the Internet. Screening enables you to quickly sift through vast databases of numerous companies to find those that best suit your investment objectives. For example, you can use the Kiplinger screening tool to filter thousands of stocks using 27 search criteria, and you can use Kiplinger's or another company's tools to identify dividend-paying stocks, small companies, and growth companies. You simply set the standard for screening, such as high P/E ratios, and the program sorts out the investment choices, including five-year EPS growth projections by professional stock analysts. You may be surprised to find how easy it is to screen stocks. The following websites offer stock-screening tools:

- Kiplinger (www.kiplinger.com/tools/stockscreener/index.html)
- Morningstar (http://screen.morningstar.com/stockselector.html?hsection=toolcenterstsel)
- MSN Money (http://moneycentral.msn.com/investor/finder/customstocksdl.asp)
- MarketWatch (www.marketwatch.com/tools/stockresearch/screener//)

FINANCIAL POWER POINT

Buy Stocks in a Bad Market and Gain Tenfold Later

If you invest $3000 a year for ten years buying stocks cheap during a horrible stock market that earn a zero return and do not invest another dollar, your $30,000 will be worth ten times that amount, $302,000, by retirement if stock values increase a normal 8 percent annually for the next 30 years.

stock-screening tools
Enable you to quickly sift through vast databases of hundreds of companies to find those that best suit your investment objectives.

FINANCIAL POWER POINT

iPhone Apps for Investing

Vanguard's iPhone app users can access their stock brokerage accounts and mutual fund accounts, read market news, listen to podcasts, and watch videos. Scores of apps for investing are available including those from Chase, CNBC Real-Time, Mint, Morningstar, Bloomberg, Forbes, Wikinvest Portfolio Manager, and Yahoo!.

10-Q report
A report required by the SEC prepared by the company showing its financial results for the quarter, a discussion from management, a list of material events and other risk factors that have occurred, forecasts of the company's future, and notes of any significant changes or events in the quarter.

annual report
Legally required yearly report about financial performance, activities, and prospects sent to major stockholders and made available to the general public.

Get a Sense of the History of a Stock

You can study the price of stock movements over different time frames, including bull and bear markets, as well as make comparisons to various benchmarks such as the S&P 500 Index. See MarketWatch (http://big charts.marketwatch.com/historical//) and MoneyCentral (http://money central.msn.com/investor/research/welcome.asp).

Go to the Source for Company Information

The investor's section of a company's website contains a wealth of information, including historical data, current happenings, upcoming actions, and latest earnings results. Public companies must regularly report their financial status to the government and the public, and this type of information is available at the company website and through other links.

Corporate filings required by the Securities and Exchange Commission are available on the Internet from the Electronic Data Gathering and Retrieval (EDGAR) project (www.edgar-online.com). Top online sources for stock, bond, and mutual fund information include Morningstar (www.morningstar.com) and Bloomberg (www.bloomberg.com). Each public company has its own website that offers insights from management about the future of the firm, and it is easy to request a company's annual report.

Every company registered with the Securities and Exchange Commission (SEC) is required to file once each year to ensure public availability of accurate current information about the firm. The company summarizes its financial activities for the year. The **10-Q report** includes the financial results for the quarter, a discussion from management, a list of material events and other risk factors that have occurred (such as legal problems and loss of a large customer), a forecast of the company's future, and any significant changes or events in the quarter. A similar 10-K report is filed annually. You can obtain both 10-Q and 10-K reports from the SEC online (www.sec.gov). You can find executive compensation details on Form DEF 14A.

The company's **annual report** is mostly a numbers-free publication that looks like a slick marketing magazine. While annual reports do contain some summarized financial information, they serve more as promotional corporate brochures.

There are numerous websites that offer fundamental and technical analysis of stocks. The Motley Fool does so with humor.

When a company issues any new security, it files a **prospectus** with the SEC. This disclosure describes the experience of the corporation's management, the company's financial status, any anticipated legal matters that could affect the company, and potential risks of investing in the firm. The language is legalistic and full of technical jargon, but the interested investor may find it useful to sift through the details.

prospectus
Highly legalistic information presented by a firm to the SEC and to the public with any new issue of stock.

Use Security Analysts' Research Reports

Stock analysts working for independent stock advisory firms or stock brokerages write research reports on companies and industries, as illustrated in Figure 14-1 with a report from Standard & Poor's. Reports based on fundamental analysis are quite informative. The quality of advice is uneven, ranging from brilliant to pedestrian as analysts have a tendency to run with the herd and make similar recommendations. They often recommend buying certain stocks and rarely suggest selling. The prudent investor interprets "hold" recommendations as a signal to sell.

Read Research Firms

The two most popular firms that offer stock advisory research services on a subscription basis to individual investors are Morningstar (www.morning star.com) and Value Line (www.valueline.com). The cost for these services is in the hundreds of dollars per year. A Google search for "stock advisory newsletters" will reveal several dozen firms that offer guidance on stock selections, market updates, and investment advice. You may wish to avoid those that offer suggestions based on a "technical" or "chartist" approach to analyzing stocks rather than a mainstream approach that emphasizes fundamental research.

Be Aware of Economic Trends

Investors need to stay aware of trends in the general economy. You need to know the stage of the business cycle (recession or prosperity) and the current interest and inflation rates. You also need to understand how economic conditions are likely to change over the next 12 to 18 months. (This topic was examined in Chapter 1.) Economic information is available through almost all media:

- Search engines: Yahoo!, Google, and Momma
- Big newspapers: *USA Today, Los Angeles Times, The Wall Street Journal*
- Business news: *BusinessWeek, Fortune, Forbes, Financial World*
- Personal finance: *Money* magazine and *Kiplinger's Personal Finance*
- Investment sources: *The Wall Street Journal, Barron's, Investor's Business Daily, MarketWatch*
- News magazines: *U.S. News & World Report, Time*

FINANCIAL POWER POINT

Investment Blogs

There is a vast array of investment blogs. Many are rubbish; some seem useful. Some favorites include www.RandomRoger .blogspot.com, www.InventingMoney .blogspot.com, and www.AllFinancial Matters.com. See the Stock Market Blogs Resource Page (http://seekingalpha.com/ article/3033) for a list of the best blogs on the stock market.

FINANCIAL POWER POINT

Amateur Investors Have an Advantage over Big Stock Research Firms

Three to five years before analysts really start to follow such developments, local people can be among the first to see the company in which they work start to turn around. They also may see nearby businesses with bright futures.

Pay Attention to Securities Market Indexes

Reports on securities market indexes are provided around the clock in almost every media. "The Dow went up 300 points today." "The S&P 500 rose 168 points." When it is reported that "the Dow rose 110 points today in heavy trading," realize that these "points" are changes in the index, not actual dollar changes in the value of the stocks. A **securities market index** is an indicator of market performance. It measures the average value of a number of securities chosen as a sample to reflect the behavior of a more general market. Indexes aim to provide a comprehensive, unbiased, and stable barometer of a broad market. Investors use the indexes to determine trends to help in their decision making. Popular indexes include the following.

securities market index
Measures the average value of a number of securities chosen as a sample to reflect the behavior of a more general market.

Dow Jones Industrial Average (DJIA)
The most widely reported of all stock market indexes that tracks prices of only 30 actively traded blue-chip stocks, including well-known companies such as American Express and AT&T.

Dow Jones Industrial Averages   The **Dow Jones Industrial Average (DJIA)** is the most widely reported of all indexes. The most popular DJIA industrial average follows prices of only 30 actively traded blue-chip stocks, including well-known companies

Figure 14-1   Illustrative Stock Analyst's Report

Stock Report | February 26, 2011 | NNM Symbol: **GOOG** | **GOOG** is in the S&P 500

Google Inc

STANDARD &POOR'S

| S&P Recommendation **BUY** ★★★★☆ | Price $610.04 (as of Feb 25, 2011) | 12-Mo. Target Price $750.00 | Investment Style Large-Cap Growth |

UPDATE: PLEASE SEE THE ANALYST'S LATEST RESEARCH NOTE IN THE COMPANY NEWS SECTION

GICS Sector Information Technology
Sub-Industry Internet Software & Services

Summary The world's largest Internet company, Google specializes in online search and advertising.

Key Stock Statistics (Source S&P, Vickers, company reports)

52-Wk Range	$642.96– 433.63	S&P Oper. EPS 2011E	32.53	Market Capitalization(B)	$153.040	Beta	1.20
Trailing 12-Month EPS	$26.31	S&P Oper. EPS 2012E	35.72	Yield (%)	Nil	S&P 3-Yr. Proj. EPS CAGR(%)	22
Trailing 12-Month P/E	23.2	P/E on S&P Oper. EPS 2011E	18.8	Dividend Rate/Share	Nil	S&P Credit Rating	NA
$10K Invested 5 Yrs Ago	$16,164	Common Shares Outstg. (M)	321.5	Institutional Ownership (%)	80		

Price Performance

30-Week Mov. Avg. · · · 10-Week Mov. Avg. – – **GAAP Earnings vs. Previous Year** Volume Above Avg. STARS
12-Mo. Target Price — Relative Strength — ▲ Up ▼ Down ▶ No Change Below Avg. ☆

(chart spanning 2007 2008 2009 2010 2011)

Options: ASE, CBOE, P, Ph

Analysis prepared by **Scott H. Kessler** on January 24, 2011, when the stock traded at **$ 609.94.**

Highlights

We believe gross revenues will rise 15% in 2011, benefiting from more spending on Internet advertising, the appeal of search advertising, international expansion, and increasing traction for display and mobile advertising. We think the company continues to face challenges in some businesses and we believe uncertain economies pose difficulties, but we see GOOG as relatively well positioned.

We expect largely flat pro forma operating margins from 2010 to 2012, reflecting less reliance on large content partners and a focus on cost containment, offset by growth investments and a less favorable revenue mix. Although revenues have been adversely affected by currency fluctuations, we believe a hedging program has aided profits.

Our EPS estimates include notable expenses related to stock-based compensation. In July 2010, GOOG announced the proposed acquisition of ITA Software, a provider of airline travel data, information and solutions, for $700 million, to enhance its travel search offerings, but this transaction is still pending, in light of governmental review.

Investment Rationale/Risk

We believe competitive pressures and concerns about GOOG's size/power could detract from revenue growth. Nonetheless, its business model has been resilient, in our view. We are constructive on efforts to broaden its offerings, especially with Web applications (Apps) and mobile services, but we believe that in some cases GOOG paid excessive amounts to do so. In November 2006, GOOG acquired YouTube for $1.8 billion in stock, and in March 2008 it purchased DoubleClick for $3.2 billion.

Risks to our opinion and target price include possible market share losses, new offerings or partnerships that do not succeed or continue as some expect, and challenges related to legal/regulatory issues.

Peer analysis involving P/E and P/E-to-growth considerations yields an average value of around $800. Our DCF model assumes a WACC of 10.8%, five-year average annual FCF growth of 15%, and a perpetuity growth rate of 3%, and yields an intrinsic value of about $650. Our 12-month target price, weighting these inputs, leads to our 12-month target price of $750.

Qualitative Risk Assessment

LOW   MEDIUM   **HIGH**

Our risk assessment reflects what we see as the emerging nature and relatively low barriers to entry of the Internet segment, significant and mounting competition, substantial and increasing investment and related new offerings, and our view of somewhat lacking corporate governance practices.

Quantitative Evaluations

S&P Quality Ranking   NR

D | C | B- | B | B+ | A- | A | A+

Relative Strength Rank   MODERATE

50

LOWEST = 1   HIGHEST = 99

Revenue/Earnings Data

Revenue (Million $)

	1Q	2Q	3Q	4Q	Year
2010	6,775	6,820	7,286	8,440	29,321
2009	5,509	5,523	5,945	6,674	23,651
2008	5,186	5,367	5,541	5,701	21,796
2007	3,664	3,872	4,231	4,827	16,594
2006	2,254	2,456	2,690	3,206	10,605
2005	1,257	1,385	1,578	1,919	6,139

Earnings Per Share ($)

	1Q	2Q	3Q	4Q	Year
2010	6.06	5.71	6.72	7.81	26.31
2009	4.49	4.66	5.13	6.13	20.41
2008	4.12	3.92	4.06	1.21	13.31
2007	3.18	2.93	3.38	3.79	13.29
2006	1.95	2.33	2.36	3.29	9.94
2005	1.29	1.19	1.32	1.22	5.02

Fiscal year ended Dec. 31. Next earnings report expected: Mid April. EPS Estimates based on S&P Operating Earnings; historical GAAP earnings are as reported.

Dividend Data

No cash dividends have been paid.

Source: Google report, February 26, 2011. Reprinted by Standard & Poor's, a division of the McGraw-Hill Companies Copyright February 26, 2011.

such as American Express, AT&T, Caterpillar, Chevron, Coca-Cola, Merck, Walmart and Walt Disney. The average is calculated by adding the closing prices of the 30 stocks and dividing by a number adjusted for splits, spin-offs, and dividends.* The DJIA also produces a transportation average based on 20 stocks, a utility average based on 15 stocks, and a composite average based on all 65 industrial, transportation, and utility stocks.

Standard & Poor's 500 Index The popular **Standard & Poor's (S&P) 500 Index** reports price movements of 500 stocks of large, established, publicly traded firms. It includes stocks of 400 industrial firms, 40 financial institutions, 40 public utilities, and 20 transportation companies. Companies with the highest market values influence the index the greatest.

NASDAQ Composite Index The **NASDAQ Composite Index** takes into account virtually all U.S. stocks (about 3200) traded in the over-the-counter market in the automated quotations system operated by the National Association of Securities Dealers. It provides a measure of companies not as popular or as large as those traded on the NYSE, including price behavior of many smaller, more speculative companies, although some big companies (such as Cisco Systems, Intel, Microsoft, and Staples) are listed as well. It is often used as a benchmark for the performance of high-tech stocks.

Dow Jones Wilshire 5000 Index The **Dow Jones Wilshire 5000 Index** represents the total market value of virtually all the publically traded stocks in the United States. One point in the index is worth $1 billion; thus when the index is 11,220, that translates into a U.S. stock market valued at over $11 billion.

Russell 2000 Index The **Russell 2000 Index** is a small-cap stock market index of relatively small capitalized companies and is the most widely quoted measure of the overall performance of the small-cap to midcap company shares.

Foreign Stock Exchanges Stock exchanges are located in major cities throughout the world, including London, Sydney, Tokyo, Toronto, and Kuala Lumpur. U.S. investors often check the stock exchanges throughout the night to gain a hint of what might happen that day in the U.S. stock market.

Securities Exchanges (Stock Markets)

As we first noted in Chapter 13, a **securities exchange** (also called a **stock market**) is a market where agents of buyers and sellers can find each other easily by providing an orderly, open plan to trade securities. Each exchange has its own rules, is subject to government regulation, and provides constant supervision and self-regulation. The transactions were historically performed in an organized physical location, such as the New York Stock Exchange (NYSE, and also known as the "*Big Board*") and the American Stock Exchange, both in New York City. You may visualize a bustling exchange that ends the trading day with a bell. However, today most stock trading occurs in a fragmented collection of 50 trading platforms, and most transactions are performed electronically.

The market capitalization of the NYSE's 8000+ listed companies is over $12 trillion. The average daily trading value of securities is $150 billion. The NYSE is operated by Germany's Deutsche Boerse, which combines the world's two largest exchanges.

Regional stock exchanges are located in Boston, Chicago, Philadelphia, and San Francisco and newer exchanges exist like Direct Edge, in Jersey City, New Jersey, and BATS Exchange in Kansas City, Missouri. They are all called **organized exchanges**.

securities exchange/stock market
Market where agents of buyers and sellers can find each other easily by providing an orderly, open plan to trade securities.

organized exchanges
Actual physical location for a market, at which some securities prices are set by open outcry.

---

* A **stock split** occurs when the shares of a stock owned by existing shareholders are divided into a larger number of shares. This may be an indicator that management expects better profits in the years ahead. Many companies provide a cash dividend to stockholders, and sometimes companies declare a noncash dividend in the form of a **stock dividend**. Here the shareholder receives additional shares of the company's stock.

over-the-counter (OTC) marketplace
An electronic telecommunications network that facilities the buying and selling of securities that usually are not listed on the major exchanges through market makers.

broker/dealer
A brokerage firm representing a buyer that communicates with another brokerage firm that has the desired securities, thus in effect "making a market" for one or more securities.

market making
A broker/dealer who both buys and sells securities by maintaining an inventory of specific securities to sell to other brokerage firms and stands ready to buy reasonable quantities of the same securities at market prices.

electronic communications network (ECN)
A computer system that matches desired sellers and buyers of stocks outside of stock exchanges.

OTC Market and Electronic Communications Network

The **over-the-counter (OTC) marketplace** is an electronic telecommunications network that facilitates the buying and selling of securities that usually are not listed on the major exchanges through market makers. **Market makers** are brokerage firm dealers who are miles apart that execute trades and earn commissions using the bid-ask system. A vital part of the OTC market is that prices on stocks are provided through NASDAQ. In an OTC sale, a stockbroker at a brokerage firm representing a buyer communicates with another brokerage firm that has the desired securities. Hundreds of broker/dealers execute trades internally, filling orders out of their own inventory of stocks.

The second brokerage firm is more accurately known as a **broker/dealer** because, in addition to offering the usual brokerage services, it can "make a market" for one or more securities. That is, broker/dealers both buy and sell securities. **Market making** occurs when a broker/dealer attempts to provide a continuous market by maintaining an inventory of specific securities to sell to other brokerage firms and stands ready to buy reasonable quantities of the same securities at market prices. To avoid potential conflicts of interest with a client, whenever a stockbroker sells securities in which the brokerage firm has made a market, the buying investor must be informed of that fact.

An **electronic communications network (ECN)** is a computer system that matches desired sellers and buyers of stocks outside of stock exchanges. ECNs have lower transaction costs because they avoid the market makers and the bid-ask spread system. ECNs make up about 30 percent of NASDAQ trading and are used to execute some transactions on the NYSE and AMEX. ECNs are also used for after-hours trading as they operate 24 hours a day.

Looking Up a Stock Price

What affects the price of a stock the most is supply and demand. When more people want to buy, the price goes up. When more people want to sell, the price goes down. If you know the company's stock symbol (search Google for "stock symbols"), the current price of any stock may be obtained by inputting the company symbol into Google or any of the other popular investment websites, such as Yahoo! Finance, MSN Money, and MarketWatch.

The millions of daily buying and selling transactions involving stocks, bonds, and mutual funds are summarized in *The Wall Street Journal*, the most widely read financial newspaper in the United States. Many daily newspapers publish abbreviated information, and security prices are quoted and traded to two decimal points. Stock quotations that might appear in *The Wall Street Journal* for Walmart, a retailer, are illustrated in Figure 14-2.

Column 1: YTD % Change. The numbers in this column report the "year to date (YTD) as a percentage" change in the price (+8.6%) of Walmart stock since January 1 of the current calendar year.

Columns 2 and 3: 52 Weeks, High and Low. This column shows that Walmart stock traded at a high price of $63.08 and a low price of $41.50 during the previous 52 weeks, not including the previous trading day.

Column 4: Stock and Sym. This column gives the name of the stock (Walmart in this example) and its abbreviated trading symbol (WMT).

Column 5: Div. The dividend amount is based on the last quarterly declaration by the company. For example, Walmart last paid a quarterly dividend that, when converted to an annual basis, amounts to an estimated $0.28 annual dividend.

Column 6: Yld %. The figure in this column represents the yield as a percentage of dividend income, calculated by dividing the current price of the stock into the recent estimated dividend. The yield of the Walmart stock is 0.4 percent.

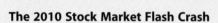

DID YOU KNOW?

How Stocks Are Quoted

Figure 14-2

1	2	3	4		5	6	7	8	9	10
YTD %CHG	52 WEEKS HI	LO	STOCK (SYM)		DIV	YLD %	PE	VOL 100S	LAST	NET CNG
+17.2	45.29	28.70	Walgreen	WAG	.14	.4	44	27540	39.45	+0.59
+ 3.7	20.56	14.00	WallaceCS	WCS	.66	3.4	17	714	19.70	+0.06
+ 0.1	34.50	23.00	WaddReed A	WDR	.35	1.1	25	2228	32.24	+0.04
+ 8.6	63.08	41.50	Walmart	WMT	.28	.4	42	104572	62.52	+0.82

+ 18.7	17.50	8.55♣	WacknhutCorr **WHC**		...	18	448	16.45	− 0.40
+ 0.1	34.50	23	WaddlReed A **WDR**	.35	1.1	25	2228	32.24	+ 0.04
+ 17.2	45.29	28.70	Walgreen **WAG**	.14	.4	44	27540	39.45	+ 0.59
+ 3.7	20.56	14	WallaceCS **WCS**	.66	3.4	17	714	19.70	+ 0.06
+ 8.6	63.08	41.50	WalMart **WMT**	.28	.4	42	104572	62.52	+ 0.82
+ 9.6	14.65	7.60	WalterInd **WLT**	.12	1.0	12	1625	12.40	− 0.10
+ 3.1	42.99	26.52	WashMut **WM** s	1.00f	3.0	11	45891	33.71	− 0.45
			WashMut PIES	4.00	5.4	...	14	74.10	− 0.40
			WashPost B **WPO**	5.60	.9	25	51	596.90	− 0.60
			WashREIT **WRE**	1.33	4.9	20	590	26.99	− 0.11
			WasteMgt **WMI**	.01	...	34	15675	27.46	− 0.52
			WtrPikTch **PIK**		...	11	51	9.48	+ 0.38
			WatersCp **WAT**		...	26	17787	32.76	+ 1.31
			Watsco WSO	**.12f**	**.7**	**19**	**3016**	**17.05**	**+ 1.46**
			WatsnPharm **WPI**		...	28	10379	30.22	+ 0.06
			WatsonWyatt A **WW**		...	18	3106	26.45	+ 0.95
			WattsInd A **WTS**	.24	1.5	16	3198	16.20	+ 0.45
			WausaMosin **WMO**	.34	2.9	62	1503	11.87	...
			Weatherford **WFT**		...	26	16527	46.09	− 0.40
			WeiderNutrtn A **WNI**	.15	8.6	dd	251	1.75	+ 0.01
			WeightWatchers **WTW** n		...	...	1128	35.82	+ 0.62
			WeingtnRlty **WRI**	3.33f	6.5	18	943	50.87	− 0.04
			WeisMkts **WMK**	1.08	3.8	18	121	28.09	− 0.01
[illegible]	[illegible]	[illegible]	Wellman **WLM**	.36	2.3	61	1194	15.90	− 0.11
+ 3.2	131.25	81.65♣	WelptHlth **WLP**		...	19	4837	120.59	+ 3.09
+ 12.8	51.71	38.25	WellsFargo **WFC**	1.04	2.1	25	45366	49.05	+ 0.16
+ 1.0	25.75	24.75	WellsFargo QUIPS **WPF** n		...	...	410	25.38	− 0.27
+ 9.6	32.78	20	Wendys **WEN**	.24	.8	19	5596	31.97	− 0.44
+ 6.9	63.25	45.10	Wendys TECONS	2.50	4.0	...	15	62.25	− 0.55
+ 44.0	**9.50**	**3.95**	**WescoInt WCC**		...	**17**	**240**	**7.13**	**+ 0.37**

Column 7: PE. This figure provides the P/E ratio based on the current price. The earnings figure used to calculate the price is not published in the newspaper but is the latest available. When Walmart's "last" or closing price of $62.52 is divided by earnings, it gives a P/E ratio of 42.

Column 8: Vol 100s. This figure indicates the total volume of trading activity for the stock measured in hundreds of shares. Thus, 10,457,200 shares of Walmart were traded on that day.

Column 9: Last. The price of the last trade of the day before the market closed for Wal-Mart was $62.52.

Column 10: Net Cng. The net change, +$0.82, represents the difference between the closing price (last) on this day and the closing price of the previous trading day. Today's Walmart closing (last) price of $62.52 was up $0.82 from the previous closing price, which must have been $61.70.

Using Portfolio Tracking to Keep Track of Your Investments

Keeping track of investments requires record keeping, particularly for income tax purposes. These tasks can be performed easily using a computer software program. **Portfolio tracking** automatically updates the value of your portfolio after you enter the symbols of the stocks you own and the number of shares held. Online portfolio tracking services also alert you to events that may affect your stocks. Tracking helps you stay on top of your holdings so you know which stocks are performing well, which are underperforming, and which might need to be sold. See MSN Money (http://moneycentral.msn.com/investor/home.aspx), E*Trade (https://us.etrade.com/e/t/home), Morningstar (www.morningstar.com), and InvestorGuide.com.

portfolio tracking
Automatically updates the value of your portfolio after you enter the symbols of the stocks you own and the number of shares held.

Concept Check 14.4

1. Give three examples of the types of website resources available to investors on the Internet.
2. List five places where you can obtain investment information on a specific stock.
3. Distinguish between the Dow Jones Industrial Average and the S&P 500.
4. Where can you go to look up stock symbols and prices?

BUYING AND SELLING STOCKS

LEARNING OBJECTIVE 5

Summarize how stocks are bought and sold.

stockbroker/account executive
Professional who is licensed to buy and sell securities on behalf of the brokerage firm's clients.

security's street name
Securities certificates kept in the brokerage firm's name instead of the name of the individual investor.

cash account
A brokerage account that requires an initial deposit (perhaps as little as $1000) and specifies that full settlement is due to the brokerage firm within three business days after a buy or sell order has been given.

discount brokers
Charge commissions to execute trades that are often 30 to 80 percent less than the fees charged by full-service brokers, but also offer fewer services.

Securities transactions require the use of a licensed broker serving as a middleman between the seller and the buyer and collecting a fee on each purchase or sale of securities. A **stockbroker** (also known as an **account executive**) is licensed to buy and sell securities on behalf of the brokerage firm's clients. You can buy or sell securities through an online or human stockbroker who works for a brokerage firm that has access to the securities markets. Brokerage firms often provide investors with investment advice.

As a matter of convenience and to facilitate resale, investors prefer to leave securities certificates in the name of their brokerage firm rather than take physical possession themselves. Securities certificates kept in the brokerage firm's name instead of the name of the individual investor are known as the **security's street name**.

Brokers have a duty to assess each client's suitability for particular investments. Regulations also require that they disclose when they are selling securities owned by the firm for which they work. Figure 14-3 shows the flow of securities transactions.

Discount, Online, and Full-Service Brokers

To trade securities, you will need a brokerage firm to act as your agent. You can open an account at a full-service general brokerage firm or a discount brokerage firm. The firm charges a commission for any trading it conducts on your behalf. You should make clear to the brokerage firm, in writing, your investment objectives and your desired level of risk. You can open an account rather easily at any brokerage firm. A **cash account** requires an initial deposit (perhaps as little as $1000) and specifies that full settlement is due to the brokerage firm within three business days after a buy or sell order has been given. After each transaction, your account is debited or credited, and written confirmation is immediately forwarded.

Discount Brokers   Many investors use **discount brokers** because they charge commissions to execute trades that are often 30 to 80 percent less than the fees charged by full-service brokers. These brokers feature low commissions because they have lower overhead. Most offer excellent research and investment tools. Transactions can be completed online as well as via a toll-free telephone number; investors can also obtain price quotes, check the status of their accounts, and transfer funds online or by phone. Examples of highly rated discount brokers are Fidelity, TD Ameritrade, Charles Schwab, USAA Brokerage Services, and Vanguard.

Figure 14-3   **Securities Transactions**

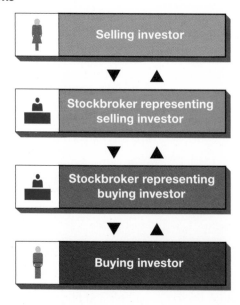

ADVICE FROM A PRO

Check the Background of Your Stockbroker or Investment Advisor

You can check the background of a stockbroker or a brokerage firm via the Financial Industry Regulatory Authority (FINRA) (www.finra.org/Investors/%20ToolsCalculators/BrokerCheck/index.htm). Some investors neglect to investigate a stockbroker or firm and lose money as a result. The broker may abscond with the investor's funds; at other times, the investor receives poor advice. Don't let it happen to you! Check out the Securities and Exchange Commission's website (www.sec.gov/investor/brokers/htm) to review criminal complaints and regulatory problems with any of 220,000 investment advisers.

Allen Martin, in memoriam
California State University–Northridge

Online Brokers Online **discount brokers** (also called Internet **or** electronic discount brokers) have reduced the cost of executing a trade to perhaps $20 or even $10 because their primary business is online trading. All the discount brokers noted are also online brokers. Additional highly rated online brokers are TD Ameritrade, E*Trade, Fidelity, Scott Trade, and Vanguard.

Online Day Trading Online **day trading** occurs when an investor buys and sells stocks quickly throughout the day with the hope that the price will move enough to cover transaction costs and earn some profits. Day traders do not own stocks overnight. Transactions are executed online because they can be done quickly with low commissions. Day trading is a risky practice. One of billionaire Warren Buffett's commandments for getting ahead in personal finance states, "You will lose money if you trade stocks actively."

Full-Service General Brokerage Firms A traditional **general brokerage firm** offers a full range of services to customers, including investment information and advice; research reports on companies, industries, general economic trends, and world events; an investment newsletter; recommendations to buy, sell, or hold stocks; execution of securities transactions by live brokers and online; and margin loans. Investors receive monthly statements summarizing all of the transactions in their account and commissions, dividends, and interest. Commissions and fees are higher than those of discount and online brokers; however, investors can discuss their investments with a qualified professional. Examples of highly rated full-service general brokerage firms are Edward Jones, Raymond James, UBS, Morgan Stanley Smith Barney, and Wells Fargo Advisors.

Broker Commissions and Fees

Brokerage firms receive a commission on each securities transaction to cover the direct expenses of executing the transaction and other overhead expenses. They have established fee schedules that they use when dealing with any except the largest investors. The fees reflect a commission rate that declines as the total value of the transaction increases. For example, in lieu of a minimum commission charge of $25, a brokerage firm might charge 2.8 percent on a transaction amounting to less than $800, 1.8 percent on transactions between $800 and $2500, 1.6 percent on amounts between $2500 and $5000, and 1.2 percent on amounts exceeding $5000.

Transaction costs are based on sales of **round lots**, which are standard units of trading of 100 shares of stock and $1000 or $5000 par value for bonds. An **odd lot** is an amount of a security that is less than the normal unit of trading for that particular security; for stocks, any transaction less than 100 shares is usually considered to be an odd lot. When brokerage firms buy or sell shares in odd lots, they may charge a fee of 12.5 cents (called an *eighth*) per share on the odd-lot portion of the transaction, which is called the *differential*.

The payment of commissions can quickly reduce the return on any investment. A purchase commission of 2 percent added to a sales commission of another 2 percent, for

online discount brokers
Such brokers, also called Internet or electronic discount brokers, have reduced the cost of executing a trade to perhaps $20 or even $10 because their primary business is online trading.

day trading
Occurs when an investor buys and sells stocks quickly throughout a day with the hope that prices will move enough to cover transaction costs and earn some profits.

general (full-service) brokerage firms
Offer a full range of services to customers, including investment advice and research.

round lots
Standard units of trading of 100 shares of stock and $1000 or $5000 par value for bonds.

odd lot
An amount of a security that is less than the normal unit of trading for that particular security; for stocks, any transaction less than 100 shares is usually considered to be an odd lot.

DID YOU KNOW?

Regulations Help Protect Against Investment Fraud

Public trust is vital to the success of the securities industry; without it, consumers will not invest. Regulation of securities markets aims to provide investors with accurate and reliable information about securities, maintain ethical standards, and prevent fraud against investors. This regulation occurs at four levels:

1. **Securities and Exchange Commission (SEC).** *The SEC is a federal government agency that focuses on ensuring disclosure of information about securities to the investing public and on approving the rules and regulations employed by the organized securities exchanges. The SEC requires registration of listed securities with appropriate and updated information. It also prohibits manipulative practices, such as using insider information for illegal personal gain or causing the price of a security to rise or fall for false reasons. All states require registration of securities sold within their states, and they, too, regulate the securities industry.*

2. **Self-Regulatory Agencies.** *The Financial Industry Regulatory Authority (FINRA) and other self-regulatory organiza-*

tions enforce standards of conduct for their members and their member organizations. They dictate rules for listing and for trading securities.

3. **Brokerage Firms.** *Individual brokerage firms have established standards of conduct for brokers that govern how they deal with investors.*

4. **Security Investors Protection Corporation (SIPC).** *The SIPC is a limited insurance program to protect the investing public when an SEC-registered brokerage firm goes bankrupt. Although investment losses are not covered, the SIPC protects each of an investor's accounts at a brokerage firm against financial loss as a result of unreturned securities and cash up to a total of $500,000, but no more than $100,000 in cash.*

5. **Financial Services Oversight Council (FSOC).** *The mission of the FSOC is to build a warning system to identify financial companies in need of government intervention before they collapse and negatively impact the American economy by causing another severe recession.*

---

example, means that the investor has to earn a 4 percent yield just to pay the transaction costs. Brokerage commissions typically range from $25 to 3 percent of the value of the transaction. The easiest way to hold down investing costs is to find a brokerage firm that charges low commissions.

How to Order Stock Transactions

Hundreds of millions of shares of securities are traded daily on the stock markets in the United States. Every trade brings together a buyer and a seller to complete the transaction at a given price.

The Process of Trading Stocks Assume you instruct brokerage firm A to purchase a certain number of shares at a specific price. The firm relays the buy order to its representative, who coordinates trading. Because the brokerage firm has a seat on the exchange, the buy order is then given to the brokerage firm's contact person at the exchange—a **floor broker**. This broker contacts a **specialist**, a person on the floor of the exchange who handles trades of that particular stock in an effort to maintain a fair and orderly market. The buy order is then filled, either by taking shares from the specialist's own inventory or by matching it with another investor's sell order.

Matched or Negotiated Stock Price Securities prices are either matched or negotiated.

MATCHED PRICE On the organized stock exchanges, a match must occur between the buyer's price and the seller's price for a sale to take place. Therefore, a specialist could hold a specific order for a few minutes, a few hours, or even a week before making a match. With actively traded issues, a transaction is completed in just a few minutes. A slower-selling security can be traded more quickly if an investor is willing to accept the current market price (as discussed later).

NEGOTIATED PRICE In the over-the-counter market, the final transaction price is negotiated because two prices are involved. The **bid price** is the highest price anyone has declared that he or she wants to pay for a security. Thus, it represents the amount a brokerage firm is willing to pay for a particular security. The **ask price** is the lowest price

floor broker
Brokerage firm's contact person at an exchange.

specialist
Person on the floor of an exchange who handles trades of a particular stock in an effort to maintain a fair and orderly market.

bid price
Declared highest price anyone wants to pay for a security.

ask price
Declared lowest price that anyone is willing to accept to sell a security.

anyone will accept at that time for a particular security. Thus, it represents the amount for which another brokerage firm is willing to sell a particular security.

The **spread** represents the difference between the bid price at which a broker/dealer will buy shares and the higher ask price at which the broker/dealer will sell shares. The spread can be as little as 5 cents per share, but it can range from 10 to 20 cents for OTC stocks. In addition to paying the ask price, investors typically pay a nominal sales commission to their stockbroker for executing the transaction.

If a buyer does not want to pay the asking price, he or she instructs the stockbroker to offer a lower bid price, which may or may not be accepted. If it is refused, the buyer might cancel the first order and raise the bid slightly in a second order in the hope that the owner will sell the shares at that price. Otherwise, the buyer may have to pay the full ask price to complete the deal. OTC trades usually occur at prices somewhere between the bid and ask figures.

Types of Stock Orders Basically, there are only two types of orders—buy and sell. The stockbroker will buy or sell securities according to prescribed instructions in a process called *executing an order*. Those instructions can place constraints on the prices at which those orders are carried out. Following are examples of instructions that may accompany stock orders.

MARKET ORDER A **market order** instructs the stockbroker to execute an order at the prevailing market price—that is, the current selling price of the stock. A stockbroker can generally conduct the desired transaction within a few minutes. The floor broker tries to match the instructions from many investors with the narrow range of prices available from the specialist. Traders on the floor of the stock market typically shout and signal back and forth as part of this effort to match buyers and sellers. Most trades are market orders.

LIMIT ORDER A **limit order** instructs the stockbroker to buy or sell a stock at a specific price. It may include instructions to buy at the best possible price but not above a specified limit, or to sell at the best possible price but not below a specified limit. A limit order provides some protection against buying a security at a price higher than desired or selling at a price deemed too low. The stockbroker transmits the limit order to the specialist. The order is executed if and when the specified price (or better) is reached and all other previously received orders on the specialist's book have been considered.

A disadvantage for buyers who place a limit order is that they might miss an excellent opportunity. For example, assume you place a limit order with your stockbroker to buy 100 shares of Running Paws common stock at $60.50 or lower. You have read in the newspaper that the stock has recently been selling at $61 and $61.25, and you hope to save $0.50 to $1.00 on each share. On that same day, the company announces publicly that it plans to expand into the dog food area for the first time. Investor confidence in the new sales effort pushes the price up to $70. If you had given your stockbroker a market order instead, you would have purchased 100 shares of Running Paws at perhaps $61.50, which would have given you an immediate profit of $850 ($70 − $61.50 = $8.50; $8.50 × 100 shares = $850) on an initial investment of $6150 ($61.50 × 100).

A disadvantage for sellers placing a limit order is that it could result in no sale if the price drops because of negative news. Assume that you bought stock at $50 that is currently selling at $58 and that you have placed a limit order to sell at a price of no less than $60 so as to take your profit. The price could creep up to $59 and then fall back to $48, however. In this event, you did not sell the securities because the limit order was priced too high, and they are now worth less than what you originally paid for them. A limit order is best used when you expect great fluctuations in the price of a stock and when you buy or sell infrequently traded securities on the over-the-counter market. Limit orders account for about one-third of all trades.

STOP ORDER (STOP-LOSS ORDER) A **stop order** instructs a stockbroker to sell your shares of stock at the market price if a stock declines to or goes below a specified price. It is often called a **stop-loss order** because the investor uses it to protect against a sharp drop in price and thus to stop a loss. The specialist executes the order as soon as the stop-order price is reached and a buyer is matched at the next market price.

As an example of how to stop a loss, assume you bought 100 shares of Running Paws stock at $70. You are nervous about the company's entry into the competitive dog

spread
Represents difference between the bid price at which a broker/dealer will buy shares and the higher ask price at which the broker/dealer will sell shares.

market order
Instructs the stockbroker to execute an order at the prevailing market price— that is, the current selling price of the stock.

limit order
Instructs the stockbroker to buy or sell a stock at a specific price.

stop order
Instructs a stockbroker to sell your shares of stock at the market price if a stock declines to or goes below a specified price.

food business, however, and you fear that it might lose money. As a consequence, you place a stop order to sell your shares if the price drops to $56, thereby limiting your potential loss to 20 percent ($70 − $56 = $14; $14 ÷ $70 = 0.20). Some months later, you read in the financial section of your newspaper that even after six months, Running Paws still has less than 1 percent of the dog food market. You call your stockbroker, who informs you that the price of Running Paws stock dropped drastically in response to the article, which was published in the previous day's *Wall Street Journal*. The broker reports that all of your shares were sold at $55, that the current price is $49, and that the sales transaction notice is already in the mail to your home. The stop order cut your losses to slightly more than 20 percent ($70 − $55 = $15; $15 ÷ $70 = 21.4 percent) and saved an additional loss of $6 ($55 − $49) per share. Thus, the stop order limited your loss to $1500 [(100 × $70 = $7000) − (100 × $55 = $5500)] instead of $2100 [(100 × $70 = $7000) − (100 × $49 = $4900)].

You can use a stop order to protect your profits, too. Assume you bought 100 shares of Alpo Dog Food Company at $60 per share, which now has a current selling price of $75. Your paper profit is $1500 ($75 − $60 = $15; $15 × 100 shares = $1500), less commissions. To protect part of that profit, you place a stop order with your stockbroker to sell at $65 if the price drops that low. If your stock is sold, you will have a real profit of $500 ($65 − $60 = $5; $5 × 100 shares = $500). If Alpo Dog Food stock climbs in price instead, perhaps in response to the bad news about Running Paws, the stop order would have cost you nothing. If the price does climb, you might replace the stop order with one having a higher price to lock in an even greater amount of profit.

TIME LIMITS Investors have several ways to place time limits on their orders to buy or sell stocks. A **fill-or-kill order** instructs the stockbroker to buy or sell the stock at the market price immediately or else cancel the order. A **day order** is valid only for the remainder of the trading day during which it was given to the brokerage firm. Unless otherwise indicated, any order received by a stockbroker is assumed to be a day order. A **week order** remains valid until the close of trading on Friday of the current week. A **month order** is effective until the close of trading on the last business day of the current month. An **open order**, also called a **good-til-canceled (GTC) order**, remains valid until executed by the stockbroker or canceled by the

DID YOU KNOW?

Your Worst Financial Blunders in Investing in Stocks and Bonds

Based on others' financial woes, you will make mistakes in personal finance when you:

1. *Invest in stocks that do not match your investment philosophy.*

2. *Fail to use fundamental analysis when making stock investments.*

3. *Buy stocks on margin or sell stocks short.*

DID YOU KNOW?

The Tax Consequences of Investing in Stocks and Bonds

The government encourages investing through tax policies that favor investors.

Dividends and Interest

Taxes are low on dividend income. Funds put into regular investment accounts represent "after-tax money" (you earn an income, you pay taxes on that income, and then you invest some of the remaining money). Taxes are due on any interest, dividends, and capital gains in the year in which the income is received. The IRS considers as interest income any increase in the par value on bonds, including TIPS bonds. Interest is taxable at the investor's marginal tax rate. Dividend income is taxed at a maximum rate of 15 percent for most people; a zero percent rate applies to lower-income taxpayers.

Capital Gains and Losses

Capital gains taxes are low. No tax liability is incurred for any capital gains until the stock, bond, mutual fund, real estate, or other investment is sold. When you sell an investment, such as a stock, the gain or loss is calculated by analyzing what you paid for the investment plus broker commissions and loads minus the selling price minus commissions or redemption fees. Short-term gains (for investments held one year or less) are taxed at the same rates as ordinary income. Long-term gains (for investments held at least a year and a day) are taxed at special rates: The maximum federal rate is 15 percent, and taxpayers in the 10 to 15 percent tax brackets pay a long-term capital gains tax of zero percent. Long-term capital gain rates for collectibles such as stamps and coins are 28 percent. Capital losses can be used to offset capital gains or even your regular income. See Chapter 4.

investor. If you give an order longer than a week in duration, you should carefully monitor events and then alter the order if the situation changes substantially.

Margin Buying and Selling Short Are Risky Trading Techniques

For investors interested in taking on additional risk, there are two advanced trading techniques, and both involve using credit: buying stocks on margin and selling short. Buying stocks on margin involves using a line of credit from a stockbroker, thereby enabling the investor to effectively control many more shares with a small amount of cash. Investors who sell shares of stock short are actually selling shares they do not own.

Margin Trading Is Buying Stocks on Credit

Some investors open a margin account with a brokerage firm in addition to their cash account so they can buy securities using credit. Opening a **margin account** requires making a substantial deposit of cash or securities ($2000 or more) and permits the purchase of other securities using credit granted by the brokerage firm. Using a margin account to purchase securities, or **margin buying**, allows the investor to apply leverage that magnifies returns. In essence, the investor borrows money from the brokerage firm to buy more stocks and bonds than would be possible with his or her available cash. Both brokerage firms and the Federal Reserve Board regulate the use of credit to buy securities.

The **margin rate** is the percentage of the value (or equity) in an investment that is not borrowed. The most recent requirement is 50 percent for common stock. Thus at least 50 percent of each dollar invested must be the investor's. The remainder may be borrowed from the broker. The securities purchased, as well as other assets in the margin account, are used as collateral.

BUYING ON MARGIN CAN INCREASE RETURNS Buying on margin is commonly used to increase the individual's return on investment. For example, assume that Greenfield Computer Company common stock is selling for $80 per share. You want to buy 100 shares, requiring a total expenditure of $8000. Using your margin account, you will make a cash payment of $4000 (0.50 × $8000), with the brokerage firm lending you the difference of $4000 ($8000 − $4000).

For the sake of simplicity, we will omit commissions from this example and assume that the brokerage firm lends the funds at 10 percent interest. Thus, your equity (market value minus amount borrowed) in the investment is $4000. If the price of Greenfield stock increases from $80 to $92 at the end of a year, you can sell your investment for gross proceeds of $9200, minus the amount invested ($4000), minus the amount borrowed ($4000), and minus the cost of borrowing ($4000 × 0.10 = $400), for a return of $800. Because you invested equity of only $4000 to obtain a profit of $800, you have earned a return of 20 percent ($800 ÷ $4000). If you had put up the entire $8000 and not bought on margin, your return on investment would have been only 15 percent ($9200 − $8000 = $1200; $1200 ÷ $8000 = 0.15). In this way, you can use credit to increase the rate of return on your own investment. Those with an aggressive investment philosophy might buy on margin because it gives them the opportunity to obtain a higher rate of return.

BUYING ON MARGIN CAN INCREASE LOSSES If the price of a security bought on margin declines, however, leverage can work against you. For example, if the price of the Greenfield stock bought at $80 dropped to $70 after a year, you would lose $10 per share on the 100 shares, for a total loss of $1000. Your gross proceeds from selling the stock would be only $7000. If you bought the stock on 50 percent margin, these proceeds are offset by the cost of the investment ($4000), the margin loan from the broker ($4000), and interest on the loan ($400), for a total deduction of $8400 and a net loss of $1400 ($7000 − $8400). Thus, a loss of $1400 on an investment of $4000 is a negative return of 35 percent (−$1400 ÷ $4000). The same $10 loss per share (from a price of $80 to $70 per share) would have been a negative loss of only 12.5 percent if the stocks were not bought on margin ($7000 − $8000 = −$1000; −$1000 ÷ $8000 = −0.125).

margin account
Account at a brokerage firm that requires a substantial deposit of cash or securities and permits the purchase of other securities using credit granted by the brokerage firm.

margin buying
Using a margin account to buy securities; allows the investor to apply leverage that magnifies returns—or losses.

margin rate
Set by the Fed, percentage of the value (or equity) in an investment that is not borrowed—recently 25 to 50 percent.

DID YOU KNOW?

How to Determine a Margin Call Stock Price

To determine the price at which a margin call for a stock will occur, use the formula given in Equation (14.3). This formula also appears on the *Garman/Forgue* companion website.

$$\text{Margin call} = \frac{\dfrac{\text{amount owed}}{\text{broker}} \div \left(1 - \dfrac{\text{margin call}}{\text{requirement}}\right)}{\text{number of shares bought}} \quad (14.3)$$

$$\$64 = \frac{\$4800 \div (1 - 0.25)}{100}$$

margin call

If a stock price declines to the point that the investor's equity is less than the required percentage, a representative of the brokerage firm makes a phone call and tells the investor to either put up more money or securities or face having the position bought on margin (liquidated).

buying long

Buying a security (especially on margin) with the hope that the stock price will rise.

selling short

Investors selling securities they do not own (borrowing them from a broker) and later buying the same number of shares of the security at a lower price (returning them to the broker).

covering a position

When an investor using a margin account buys back securities sold short or sells securities bought long.

A MARGIN CALL MAKES MATTERS EVEN WORSE When the price of a stock declines to the point where the investor's equity is less than the required percentage, the brokerage firm will make a telephone call to the investor. A representative of the firm will tell the investor to immediately either put up more collateral (money or other stocks) or face having the investment liquidated. This procedure is known as a **margin call**. If the investor fails to put up the additional cash or securities to maintain a required level of equity in the margin account, the broker will sell the securities at the market price, resulting in a sharp financial loss to the investor. The investor is required to repay the broker for any losses. The margin call concept protects the broker that has loaned money on securities.

Selling Short Is Selling Stocks Borrowed from Your Broker
Buying a security with the hope that it will go up in value—the goal of most investors—is called **buying long**. You might suspect, however, that the price of a security will drop. You can earn profits when the price of a security declines by **selling short**. In this trading technique, investors sell securities they do not own (borrowing them from a broker) and later buy the same number of shares of the security at a lower price (returning them to the broker). Thus, the investor earns a profit on the transaction. Brokerage firms require an investor to maintain a margin account when selling short because it provides some assurance that the investor can repay the firm for the borrowed stock, if necessary. As a result, some or all of an investor's funds deposited in a margin account are effectively tied up during a short sale. Many brokers hold the proceeds of a short sale, without paying interest, until the customer **covers the position** by buying it back for delivery to the broker.

AN EXAMPLE OF SHORT SELLING As an example, suppose you believe that the price of Greenfield stock will drop substantially over the next several months. You have heard that some top managers of the company may resign and that competitors are expected to introduce newer products. Accordingly, you instruct your broker to sell 100 shares of Greenfield at $80 per share ($80 × 100 = $8000). In this illustration, assume that you have a 50 percent margin requirement, which means you have committed $4000 (0.50 × $8000). The shares are actually borrowed by the broker from another investor or another broker. Several months later, Greenfield announces lower profits because of strong competition, and the share price drops to $70. Now you instruct your broker to buy 100 shares at the new price and use the purchased shares to repay the borrowed shares. You gain a profit of $1000 ($8000 − $7000), ignoring commissions, providing a return of 25 percent ($1000 ÷ $4000).

USING MARGIN TO SELL SHORT A very small price drop can provide big profits for the short-term investor who sells short *and* uses margin-buying techniques. As an example, imagine that you sell 100 shares of a $10 stock with a 50 percent margin requirement. The committed funds amount to $500 (0.50 × $1000). Even if the price of the stock declines by only $1, you still earn a significant profit: 100 shares sold at $10 equals $1000, minus 100 shares bought at $9 equals $900, for a profit of $100 and a return of 20 percent ($100 ÷ $500). The price could decline in only a day or two! This possibility of a fast, high return explains the allure of such investments.

Almost unlimited losses can occur with the use of margin to sell short if the price rises rather than falls. For example, if instead of declining, the price of the stock soars from $10 to $22, the loss will exceed the original investment: 100 shares sold at $10 equals $1000, minus 100 shares bought at $22 equals $2200, for a loss of $1200 and a negative return of 440 percent ($2200 ÷ $500). When the price of a security rises, short sellers are subject to margin calls.

Only a small proportion of investors sell stocks short because this approach is so risky. Selling short and buying on margin are techniques to be used only by sophisticated investors.

LEARNING OBJECTIVE **6**

Describe how to invest in bonds.

> ## ✓ Concept Check 14.5
>
> **1.** Summarize the differences among discount, online, and full-service brokers.
>
> **2.** Distinguish between round lot and odd lot broker's commissions.
>
> **3.** Summarize the differences among types of stock orders: market, limit, and stop order.
>
> **4.** Explain what buying on margin is and how it can go wrong for an investor.
>
> **5.** Explain what selling short is and how it can go wrong for an investor.

INVESTING IN BONDS

You should consider investing in bonds if you wish to receive periodic income from a portion of your investments. While bonds usually offer a lower return to investors than stocks, there are good reasons to include bonds in one's portfolio. The primary one is to reduce market risk. Others include obtaining a regular source of predictable although lower income, likelihood of profiting from possible future increases in the value of bonds, and matching some of one's assets to one's investment time horizon. A variety of bonds are available to the investor.

Investment-grade bonds offer investors a reasonable certainty of regularly receiving the periodic income (interest) and retrieving the amount originally invested (principal). Only about 8 percent of the 23,000 largest U.S. companies that issue bonds meet the highest investment-grade rating standards. Bonds are usually issued at a **par value** (also known as **face value**) of $1000. An investor typically earns a low to moderate return on bond investments, an appropriate yield when compared with the higher total returns earned on riskier stocks and stock mutual funds. Owning some bonds (or bond mutual funds) along with stocks and cash diversifies an investment portfolio.

Speculative-grade bonds pay a high interest rate. These are often called **junk bonds,** and they are long-term, high-risk, high-interest-rate corporate (or municipal) IOUs issued by companies (or municipalities) with poor or no credit ratings. The interest rates paid investors on junk bonds are 3.5 to 8 percentage points more than those of Treasury bonds. Also called **high-yield bonds,** they carry investment ratings that are below traditional investment grade and carry a higher risk of default (not repaying the bond investors). Keep in mind that higher returns require greater risk, as suggested in Figure 14-4. The **default rate** on high-quality bonds is less than 1 percent. The default rate on junk bonds typically is between 8 and 24 percent. For more information, see Bond Pickers (www.bondpickers.com) or www.defaultrisk.com or search Google using "high-yield bonds."

investment-grade bonds
Offer investors a reasonable certainty of regularly receiving periodic income (interest) and retrieving the amount originally invested (principal).

speculative-grade bonds
Long-term, high-risk, high-interest-rate corporate (or municipal) IOUs issued by companies (or municipalities) with poor or no credit ratings. Also called junk bonds or high-yield bonds.

DID YOU KNOW?

Websites for Bond Investors

Useful websites for bond investors include:

- *Bergen Capital BuySellBonds.com (www.buysellbonds.com/pages/index.html)*

- *JW Korth Shop-4-Bonds (www.shop4bonds.com)*

- *Securities Industry and Financial Markets Association (www.investinginbonds.com)*

- *Yahoo! Finance (http://finance.yahoo.com/bonds)*

Figure 14-4   **Higher Returns on Bonds Requires Greater Risk**

Higher yield = (Credit quality ↓) OR (Longer maturity ↑)

Individual investors usually avoid buying individual junk bonds because of the substantial financial risk involved with owning too few investments. Instead, they reduce risk by diversifying their investments through a "high-yield income" bond mutual fund (see Chapter 15) that has junk bonds in its portfolio.

Corporate, U.S. Government, and Municipal Bonds

Three types of bonds are available: corporate bonds, U.S. government securities, and municipal government bonds.

corporate bonds
Interest-bearing certificates of long-term debt issued by a corporation.

Corporate Bonds Pay Reasonable Returns   Corporate bonds are interest-bearing certificates of long-term debt issued by a corporation. They represent a needed source of funds for corporations. The dollar value of newly issued bonds is three times the dollar value of newly issued stocks. Because of tax regulations, corporations often finance major projects by issuing long-term bonds instead of selling stocks. One reason they do so is that payments of dividends to common and preferred stockholders are not tax deductible for corporations, unlike interest paid to bondholders. State laws require corporations to make bond interest payments on time. Therefore, companies in financial difficulty are required to pay bondholders before paying any short-term creditors.

Compared with other bonds, corporate bonds pay the highest interest rates. The default risk varies with the issuer. To help you in appraising the risks and potential rewards of bond investments, independent advisory services, such as Moody's Investors Service, Standard & Poor's, and Fitch, grade bonds for credit risk. These firms publish what they describe as unbiased ratings of the financial conditions of corporations and municipalities that issue bonds. A **bond rating** represents the opinion of an outsider on the quality—or creditworthiness—of the issuing organization. It reflects the likelihood that the issuing organization will be able to repay its debt. Ratings for each bond issue are continually re-evaluated, and they often change after the original security has been sold to the public. Investors have access to measures of the **default risk** (or **credit risk**), which is the uncertainty associated with not receiving the promised periodic interest payments as well as the principal amount when it becomes due at maturity. Bond rating directories are available in large libraries and online.

bond rating
An impartial outsider's opinion of the quality—or creditworthiness—of the issuing organization.

default risk/credit risk
Uncertainty associated with not receiving the promised periodic interest payments and the principal amount when it becomes due at maturity.

Table 14-2 shows the bond ratings used by Moody's and Standard & Poor's. The higher the rating, the greater the probable safety of the bond and the lower the default risk. The lower the rating of the bond, the higher the stated interest rate or the effective interest rate. When bonds are reduced in price from their face amount, more risk is involved. Higher ratings denote confidence that the issuer will not default and, if necessary, that the bond can readily be sold before its maturity date. Investment-grade corporate bonds may provide returns as much as 1.5 percentage points higher than the returns available on comparable U.S. Treasury securities.

U.S. Government Securities Represent Quality and Safety   U.S. Treasury securities are the world's safest investment because the government has never defaulted on its debt. U.S. Treasury securities are backed by the "full faith, credit, and taxing power of the U.S. government," and this all but guarantees the timely payment of principal and interest.

Treasury securities
Known as Treasuries, securities issued by the U.S. government, including bills, notes, and bonds.

U.S. government securities are classified into two groups: (1) Treasury bills, notes, and bonds and (2) federal agency issue notes, bonds, and certificates. Treasury bills, notes, and bonds are collectively known as **Treasury securities**, or **Treasuries**. The federal government uses these debt instruments to finance the public national debt.

Summary of Bond Ratings

Table 14-2

Ratings		Interpretation of Ratings
Moody's	**Standard & Poor's**	
Aaa Aa A	AAA AA A	High investment quality suggests ability to repay principal and interest on time. Aaa and AAA bonds are generally referred to as "gilt-edged" because issuers have demonstrated profitability over the years and have paid their bondholders their interest without interruption; thus, they carry the smallest risk.
Baa Ba	BBB BB B	Medium-quality investments that adequately provide security to principal and interest. They are neither highly protected nor poorly secured; thus, they may have some speculative characteristics. Bonds rated Baa and higher by Moody's and BBB and higher by S&P are investment-grade quality; Ba, BB, and lower-rated bonds are junk bonds.
B Caa Ca	CCC CC C	Lack characteristics of a desirable investment and investors have decreasing assurance of repayment as the rating declines. Elements of danger may be present regarding repayment of principal and interest.
C	DDD DD D	In default with little prospect of regaining any investment standing.

Treasury securities have excellent liquidity and are simple to acquire and sell. Previously issued marketable Treasury securities are bought and sold in securities markets through brokers. New issues can be purchased online using the Treasury Direct Plan (www.publicdebt.treas.gov), where they are stored electronically. Individuals may buy Treasury securities in amounts as small as $100.

The interest rates on federal government securities are lower than those on corporate bonds because they are virtually risk free. The possibility of default is near zero. Individuals with a conservative investment philosophy are often attracted to the certainty offered by U.S. government securities. Investors can purchase Treasury securities through their bank or broker or directly from the Treasury. Investors often buy Treasury issues to protect a portion of their assets and to diversify their portfolios. Although interest income is subject to federal income taxes, interest earned on Treasury securities is exempt from state and local income taxes.

TREASURY BILLS, NOTES, AND BONDS **Treasury bills**, or **T-bills**, are short-term government securities with maturities ranging from a few days to 52 weeks. Bills are sold at a discount from their face value (par). The difference between the original purchase price and what the Treasury pays you at maturity, the gain or "par," is interest. This interest is exempt from state and local income taxes but is reported as interest income on your federal tax return in the year the Treasury bill matures. Stated as an interest rate, the return on such investments is called a **discount yield**. For example, if you buy a $10,000 26-week Treasury bill for $9925 and hold it until maturity, your interest will be $75 for an annual return of approximately 1.5 percent. An investor can hold a bill until maturity or sell it before it is due. When a bill matures, the proceeds can be reinvested into another bill or redeemed and the principal will be deposited into the investor's checking or savings account. The minimum purchase of T-bills is now $100.

A **Treasury note** or **bond** is a fixed-principal, fixed-interest-rate government security issued for an intermediate or long term. Notes are issued for two, three, five, or ten years, and pay interest every six months. Treasury bonds have a maturity of 10 to

Treasury bills
Known as T-bills, U.S. government securities with maturities of one year or less.

discount yield
Difference between the original purchase price of a T-bill and what the Treasury pays you at maturity—the gain, or "par," is interest.

Treasury note/Treasury bond
Fixed-principal, fixed-interest-rate government security issued for an intermediate term or long term. Notes mature in ten years or less; bonds mature in more than ten years.

Reinvestment Risk

As we noted in Chapter 13, **reinvestment risk** (or **duration risk**) is the risk that the return on a future investment will not be the same as the return earned by the original investment in part because of falling interest rates. Also, because of inflation, the promised rate of interest will turn out to be worth less over time.

I bonds

Nonmarketable savings bonds backed by the U.S. government that pay an earnings rate that combines two rates: a fixed interest rate set when the investor buys the bond and a semiannual variable interest rate tied to inflation that protects the investor's purchasing power.

Treasury Inflation-Protected Securities (TIPS)

Marketable Treasury bonds whose value increases with inflation. These inflation-indexed $1000 bonds are the only investment that guarantees that the investor's return will outpace inflation.

zero-coupon bonds (zeros or deep discount bonds)

Municipal, corporate, and Treasury bonds that are issued at a sharp discount from face value and pay no annual interest but are redeemed at full face value upon maturity.

U.S. government savings bonds

Nonmarketable, interest-bearing bonds issued by the U.S. Treasury.

Series EE savings bonds

Nonmarketable, interest-bearing bonds issued by the federal government that are issued at a sharp discount from face value and pay no annual interest, and that may be redeemed at full value upon maturity.

30 years. Notes and bonds exist only as electronic entries in accounts. The interest rate on notes and bonds is typically higher than the rates for T-bills because the lending period is longer. Interest payments are to be reported as interest income on one's federal tax return in the year received. When the security matures, the investor is repaid the principal. Investors can hold a note or bond until maturity or sell it.

I bonds are nonmarketable savings bonds backed by the U.S. government that pay an earnings rate that is a combination of two rates: a fixed interest rate that is set when the investor buys the bond and a semiannual variable interest rate tied to inflation that protects the investor's purchasing power. They are sold at face value, such as $50 for a $50 bond. Interest stops accruing 30 years after issue, and I bonds pay off only when redeemed. If you redeem an I bond within the first five years, you will forfeit the three most recent months' interest; after five years, you will not be penalized. All earnings on savings bonds are exempt from both state and local income taxes, while federal taxes can be deferred until the bonds are either redeemed or reach final maturity. I bonds cashed in to pay education expenses are tax exempt.

Treasury Inflation-Protected Securities (TIPS) are marketable Treasury securities whose principal increases with changes in the Consumer Price Index (CPI). These inflation-indexed bonds are the only investment that guarantees that the investor's return will outpace inflation. TIPS bonds are sold in terms of 5, 10, and 30 years, and interest is paid to TIPS owners every six months until they mature. The interest rate is set when the security is purchased, and the rate never changes. The principal is adjusted every six months according to the rise and fall of the CPI; if inflation occurs and the CPI rises, the principal increases. The government sends the interest payment on the new principal to the investor's account. The fixed interest rate on TIPS is applied to the inflation-adjusted principal; so if inflation occurs throughout the life of a TIPS security, every interest payment will be greater than the one before it. The amount of each interest payment is determined by multiplying the inflation-adjusted principal by one-half the interest rate.

The inflation-adjusted amount added to the principal on a TIPS bond every six months is taxable, even though the investor does not receive the money until the bond matures. Thus, TIPS bonds pay "phantom taxable interest income," like **zero-coupon bonds** (described in the Advice from a Pro box on page 444), so the investor pays federal income taxes on the interest earned each year. The investor must use other funds to pay the taxes on that income. If the TIPS are owned in a retirement account, the returns are not taxable until withdrawn.

When TIPS mature, the federal government pays the inflation-adjusted principal (or the original principal if it is greater). Investors can hold a TIPS bond until it matures or sell it before it matures. The interest on TIPS bonds can be excluded from federal income tax when the bond owner pays tuition and fees for higher education in the year the bonds are redeemed.

U.S. government savings bonds are nonmarketable, interest-bearing bonds issued by the federal government and sold at face value. They are considered a low-risk savings product that earns interest while protecting one from inflation.

Series EE/E savings bonds are a secure savings product issued by the federal government that pays a fixed rate of interest for up to 30 years. The maximum amount of savings bonds you can buy in a single year is $5000. Electronic **EE savings bonds** are sold at face value in TreasuryDirect. Paper bonds are no longer available. EE savings bonds are sold at one-half of the face value and pay no annual interest, and they may be redeemed at full value upon maturity. For example, a $100 EE savings bond might be purchased for half of its face amount, $50. The interest, compounded semiannually, accumulates within the bond itself, and the return to the investor comes from redeeming the bond at its stated face value at the maturity date. Interest on Series EE bonds is exempt from state and local taxes. There is no federal income tax liability on the interest at redemption if the proceeds are used to fund the child's college education. (**Series HH savings bonds** [no longer sold] were originally issued at par and acquired only by exchanging Series EE bonds. Interest on Series HH bonds is exempt from state and local taxes.)

AGENCY BONDS PAY SLIGHTLY BETTER RETURNS THAN TREASURIES
More than 100 different bonds, notes, and certificates of debt are issued by various federal agencies that are government-sponsored enterprises but stockholder owned; these are **agency bonds**. Well-known examples of these agencies are Fannie Mae (Federal National Mortgage Association) and Freddie Mac (Federal Home Loan Mortgage Corporation), which together stand behind 40 percent of the outstanding investment-grade bonds. These are the two government-chartered agencies responsible in part for the housing and credit debacle that went bankrupt and today are substantially owned by the federal government. Fannie and Freddie service and continue to sell bonds, buy mortgages, and package home loans into securities.

> **agency bonds**
> *Bonds, notes, and certificates of debt issued by various federal agencies that are government-sponsored enterprises but stockholder owned, such as the Federal National Mortgage Association.*

Other government-chartered agencies that issue bonds include the Tennessee Valley Authority, Federal Farm Credit Banks, Federal Home Loan Banks, Government National Mortgage Association (Ginnie Mae), and Student Loan Marketing Association (Sallie Mae). Each security represents interest in a pool of mortgages that are sold to institutions and investors in units of $25,000, although they can also be purchased in smaller units through a mutual fund.

The assets and resources of the issuing agency back these bonds. Although the federal government does not guarantee the debt issued by such agencies, it did provide billions of dollars when Fannie Mae and Ginnie Mae faced default. Agency bonds are not as widely publicized as Treasury securities, yet they pay a yield two-tenths to four-tenths of one percentage point higher than the yield for comparable-term Treasury securities.

Municipal Government Bonds As we discussed in Chapter 4, **municipal government bonds** (also called **munis**) are long-term debts issued by local governments (cities, states, and various districts and political subdivisions) and their agencies. Their proceeds are used to finance public improvement projects, such as roads, bridges, and parks, or to pay ongoing expenses. Moody's Bond Record rates some 20,000 munis, and twice as many unrated securities exist. Bonds range in quality from AAA-rated state highway bonds to unrated securities issued by local governmental parking authorities.

> **municipal government bonds (munis)**
> *Long-term debts (bonds) issued by local governments (cities, states, and various districts and political subdivisions) and their agencies.*

The investor's interest income on municipal bonds is not subject to federal income taxes. This is because the U.S. Constitution requires that municipal bond interest be exempt from federal income tax. Because the interest income is tax free, municipal bonds are also known as **tax-free bonds** or **tax-exempt bonds**. Interest income on munis also is exempt from state and local income taxes when the investor lives in the state that issued the bond.

Municipal bonds offer a lower stated return than other bonds. However, if your marginal tax rate is higher than 25 percent, it generally makes economic sense to invest in municipal bonds because the after-tax return on a muni might be higher than that of a corporate bond. To compare the after-tax returns of investments, see page 128.

Capital gains on the sale of munis are taxable. Such gains may be realized when bonds are bought at a discount and then sold at a higher price or redeemed for full value at maturity. Bonds bought at a premium also may appreciate to produce a gain.

Unique Characteristics of Bonds
Bonds have certain characteristics that distinguish them from other investment alternatives.

Coupon Rate The bond's **coupon rate** (also known as the **coupon, coupon yield,** or **stated interest rate**) is the interest rate printed on the certificate when the bond is issued. It reflects the total annual fixed rate of interest that will be paid. For example, Leslie Sherman, a retired teacher from Waukesha, Wisconsin, bought a 20-year, $1000 Running Paws Cat Food Company bond last week with a coupon rate of 7 percent that promises to pay her $70 in interest annually (bonds pay interest in two semiannual

> **coupon rate/coupon/coupon yield/stated interest rate**
> *Interest rate printed on the certificate when the bond is issued.*

ADVICE FROM A PRO

Zero-Coupon Bonds Pay Phantom Interest

Zero-coupon bonds (also called **zeros** or **deep discount bonds**) are municipal, corporate, and Treasury bonds that pay no annual interest. They are sold to investors at sharp discounts from their face value and may be redeemed at full value upon maturity. For example, a 7 percent, $1000 zero-coupon bond to be redeemed in the year 2025 might sell today for $258. Zeros pay no current income to investors, so investors do not have to be concerned about where to reinvest interest payments. The semiannual interest accumulates within the bond itself, and the return to the investor comes from redeeming the bond at its stated face value at the maturity date. In this manner, zeros operate much like Series EE savings bonds and T-bills. The maturity date for a zero could range from a few months to as long as 30 years.

Parents often invest in zero-coupon bonds to help pay for their children's college education, and they wisely establish ownership of the zeros in the child's name. The phantom income "paid" to the child is generally so small that little, if any, income taxes are due. Treasury zeros, unlike other zeros, are not callable.

People planning for retirement often buy zeros because they know exactly how much will be received at maturity. Even though the investor receives no interest money until maturity, the investor still pays income taxes every year on the interest that accumulates within the bond. Investors can avoid income taxes altogether by buying zeros in a qualified tax-sheltered retirement plan account.

Anne Ranczuch
Monroe Community College, Rochester, New York

---

serial bonds
Bonds that are retired serially; that is, each bond is numbered consecutively and matures according to a prenumbered schedule at stated intervals.

sinking fund
Bond feature through which money is set aside with a trustee each year for repayment of the principal portion of the debt at maturity.

indenture
Written, legal agreement between bondholders and debtor that describes terms of the debt by setting forth the maturity date, interest rate, and other details.

secured bond
Pledges specific assets as collateral in indenture or has the principal and interest guaranteed by another corporation or government agency.

unsecured bond/debenture
Does not name collateral as security for debt; backed only by the good faith and reputation of the issuing agency.

registered bond
Bondholder's name is recorded so that checks or electronic funds transfers for payment of interest and principal can be safely forwarded when due.

installments—$35 in this instance). A disadvantage of bonds is that the investment does not provide the automatic benefit of compounding of interest; therefore, investors have no choice but to find other places to invest interest payments.

Serial or Sinking Fund The coupon rate of a bond remains the same until the maturity date, when the face amount is due and the debt is required to be paid off (or **retired**). Corporate bonds often mature in 20 to 30 years. Occasionally, bonds are retired serially; that is, each bond is numbered consecutively and matures according to a prenumbered schedule at stated intervals. These investments are known as **serial bonds**. Many bonds include a **sinking fund** through which money is set aside with a trustee each year for repayment of the principal portion of the debt. The details about each bond issue are contained in its **indenture**. This written, legal agreement between a group of bondholders (representing each bondholder) and the debtor describes the terms of the debt by setting forth the maturity date, interest rate, and other factors.

Secured or Unsecured Bonds are issued as either secured or unsecured. A corporation issuing a **secured bond** pledges specific assets as collateral in the indenture or has the principal and interest guaranteed by another corporation or a government agency. In the event of default, the trustee could take legal action to seize and sell such assets. In the event of bankruptcy, the claims of secured creditors are paid first.

An **unsecured bond** (or **debenture**) does not name collateral as security for the debt and is backed only by the good faith and reputation of the issuing agency. Although secured bonds might appear safer than unsecured bonds, this assumption may not be true. The strong financial reputations of many large corporations enable them to offer unsecured bonds that are safer than the secured bonds of many other companies. All federal government bonds are unsecured and are backed by the U.S. government.

Registered and Issued By law, all bonds issued now are **registered bonds**. This provides for the recording of the bondholder's name so that checks or electronic funds transfers for payment of interest and principal can be safely forwarded when due. The Internal Revenue Service is notified of the payments as well. A registered bond can be transferred only when the registered owner endorses the transaction.

Book Entry All bonds today are issued in **book-entry form**, which means that certificates are not issued. Instead, an account is set up in the name of the issuing organization or the brokerage firm that sold the bond, and interest is paid into this account when due. In the past, all corporations issued **bearer bonds** (also called **coupon bonds** because owners redeemed the coupons for interest). Some of these older bonds are still traded today.

Callable An issuer might desire to exercise a **call option** when interest rates drop substantially. For example, assume a company issues bonds paying a $70 annual dividend (7 percent coupon rate). When interest rates drop perhaps to 6 percent, the 7 percent bonds may represent too high a cost for borrowing to the corporation. If the bonds have a **callable** feature, according to dates and terms detailed in the indenture, the issuer can redeem the bonds before the maturity date. In such a case, the issuer repurchases the bond at par value or by paying a premium, often a partial year's worth of interest. Approximately 80 percent of long-term bonds are classified as callable.

Evaluating Bond Prices and Returns

Much of the economic turmoil in the U.S. and world investment markets emanated from the U.S. credit markets. Billions of dollars of credit securities were characterized as **toxic debt** as they were found to be backed by assets of dubious value and quickly became impossible to value or to sell without incurring tremendous losses. The bond rating companies of S&P, Moody's, and Fitch Ratings completely failed to properly evaluate and grade those securities in a reasonable and prudent manner. The resulting illiquidity in credit markets caused some institutions to go bankrupt, and confidence in the ratings companies deservedly declined. In addition, the prices of other bonds quickly soared or declined 25 percent or more. As markets continue to return to normal, investors can again utilize the standard factors to evaluate bond prices and potential returns: interest rates, premiums and discounts, current yield, and yield to maturity.

Interest Rate Risk Results in Variable Value A bond's price, or its value on any given day, is affected by a host of factors. These include its type, coupon rate, and availability in the marketplace; demand for the bond; prices for similar bonds; the underlying credit quality of the issuer; and the number of years before it matures. Most important, the price also varies because of fluctuations in current **market interest rates** in the general economy. The state of the economy and the supply and demand for credit affect market interest rates. These are the current long- and short-term interest rates paid on various types of corporate and government debts that carry similar levels of risk.

Long-Term Interest Rates Set by Investors plus Occasional Fed Interventions Long-term rates are largely set by bond investors' buying and selling decisions, primarily based on their expectations of future inflation. Short-term interest

book-entry form
Bond certificates are not issued; rather, an account is set up in name of the issuing organization or the brokerage firm that sold the bond, and interest is paid into this account when due.

call option
Stipulation in an indenture that allows issuer to repurchase the bond at par value or by paying a premium, often one year's worth of interest. Bonds are thus callable.

market interest rates
Current long- and short-term interest rates paid on various types of corporate and government debts that carry similar levels of risk.

DID YOU KNOW?

Turn Bad Habits into Good Ones

Do You Do This?	Do This Instead!
Invest only in certificates of deposit	Invest in common stocks and bonds
Listen to tips and invest in hot stocks	Invest only in stocks with good fundamentals
Invest in speculative stocks	Utilize no more than 10 percent of your funds for speculative stocks
Invest in fewer than five stocks	Invest in more or buy stock mutual funds
Ignore big changes in interest rates	Invest in bonds on interest rate shifts
Accept broker's advice on stock choices	Use the Internet to research stocks
Utilize full-service brokers exclusively	Buy and sell online to save on commissions
Buy on margin and sell short	Never buy on margin and sell short, as it is too risky
Avoid bonds as investments	Buy some TIPS bonds

DID YOU KNOW?

Sean's Success Story

Sean's success in investing through the years pushed the value of his portfolio to $140,000. His portfolio in 2006 matched his aggressive investment philosophy: cash (10%), bonds (10%), and equities (80%). However, his investments took a terrible hit during the bear market crash of October 2007. Because of defaults, his bond values dropped from $14,000 to $11,000. The equity portion of his portfolio, which was mostly high-tech, small-cap and microcap stocks and stock mutual funds, dropped 50 percent from $112,000 to $56,000.

The first thing Sean did was to spend less money on eating out, DVDs, and electronics to try and keep his net worth figure from dropping even further. He was scared but resisted the urge to sell low and get out of the market

completely; therefore, he stayed invested throughout that long year, which was depressing for almost all investors. By the following November, the equities in his portfolio rose almost 50 percent from $56,000 to $84,000. Even though these were still shaky economic times, Sean reinvested the proceeds in the market, and he will continue to invest regularly as the stock markets recover in the coming years with the slowly growing world economies. Thus by remaining invested as the market recovered, Sean recovered a good part of his losses, and his portfolio is down only about 10 percent from its high. During 2010 and 2011, Sean watched as stock market prices continued to climb upward, pretty much every month.

interest rate risk
Risk that interest rates will rise and bond prices will fall, thereby lowering the prices on older bond issues.

fixed yield
Interest income payment remains the same regardless of the bond's price.

variable value
Because interest rates change, bonds may trade at a premium (more than face value) or at a discount (less than par) so that the yield equals the current yield for bonds with similar maturities and risk levels.

rates are manipulated by the Federal Reserve Board, which is popularly known as the Fed. When inflation rises, the Fed often raises interest rates to discourage borrowing, which reduces consumer and business spending. When the economy slows, the Fed often lowers the interest rates on short-term Treasury issues in an attempt to stimulate economic activity by making it cheaper for companies to borrow and expand. On occasion, the Fed buys long-term mortgage securities and Treasury bonds and notes and related debt for autos and credit cards. The Fed has funneled cash into frozen credit markets to provide more liquidity, thus helping to lower long-term interest rates.

Pricing a Bond in Today's Market

As we noted in Chapter 13, **interest rate risk** is the risk that interest rates will increase and bond prices will fall, thereby lowering the prices on older bond issues. This decline in value ensures that an older bond and a newly issued bond will offer potential investors approximately the same yield. Bonds generally have a **fixed yield** (the interest income payment remains the same) but a **variable value**.

For example, assume you own a 30-year bond with a face value of $1000 paying a semiannual coupon interest rate of 6 percent that has 20 years remaining until maturity. If interest rates in the general economy jump to 8 percent after one year, no one will

DID YOU KNOW?

The Two Best Times to Invest in Bonds

1. *If interest rates are expected to rise,* probably because of the likelihood of increased inflation in the economy and expected actions of the Fed to increase interest rates, bond prices are sure to fall over time; therefore, you should invest only in short-term bonds. Take the small returns and then sell when it is time to invest those funds in equities.

2. *If interest rates are expected to decline,* probably because of the likelihood of a slowing economy and anticipating Fed actions to lower interest rates, bond prices will rise over time; therefore, you should purchase bonds with long maturities that are not callable. Later when interest rates go down, the price of your bonds will rise substantially.

want to buy your 6 percent bond for $1000 because it pays only $60 per year. If you want to sell it, the price of the bond will have to be lowered, perhaps to $802.80. The **value of bond (or bond selling price) formula**, Equation (14.4), shows the calculation involved. If rates on similar bonds are now at 8 percent, then the discount rate is 8 percent (or 4 percent twice a year for 40 payments). The task is to calculate the present value of the interest payments and the repayment lump sum. To do so, use Appendix A.2 and Appendix A.4 and look across the interest rows to 4% and down to 40 "n" periods.

Value of Bond = Present value of interest payments + present value of lump sum

$$= (\text{Annual interest payment}/2 \times \text{PVIFA}^{i,n}) + (\text{Lump sum} \times \text{PVIF}^{i,n})$$

where

i = new annual **interest** rate divided by 2

n = number of years to maturity times 2

$$= (\$60/2 \times \text{PVIFA}^{4\%,40}) + (\$1,000 \times \text{PVIF}^{4\%,40})$$

$$= (\$30 \times 19.7928) + (\$1,000 \times 0.2083)$$

$$= \$593.78 + \$208.30 = \$802.08$$

(14.4)

Conversely, if interest rates on newly issued bonds slip to 4 percent, the price of your 6 percent bond will increase sharply, perhaps to $1273.55. Thus, investors might be willing to pay a **premium** of $273.55 ($1273.55 – $1000), which is a sum of money paid in addition to a regular price, to buy your $1000 bond paying 6 percent when other rates are only 4 percent. Remember that bond yields and prices move in opposite directions—as one goes up, the other goes down.

premium
A sum of money paid in addition to a regular price.

The price of a bond is most volatile in the following circumstances: (1) when it was sold at less than face value when first issued, (2) when the stated rate is low, and (3) when the bond maturity time is long. The investor who holds a bond to maturity might ignore such information.

Premiums and Discounts

Premiums and Discounts When a bond is first issued, it is sold in one of three ways: (1) at its face value (the value of the bond stated on the certificate and the amount the investor will receive when the bond matures), (2) at a discount below its face value, or (3) at a premium above its face value. After a bond is issued, its market price changes in order to provide a competitive effective rate of return for anyone interested in purchasing it from the original bondholder.

As an example, assume that Running Paws Cat Food Company decided to issue 20-year bonds at 8.8 percent. While the bonds were being printed and prepared for sale, the market interest rate on comparable high-risk bonds rose to 9 percent. In this instance, Running Paws would sell the bonds at a slight discount to provide a competitive return. Discounts and premiums on bonds reflect changing interest rates in the economy and the number of years to maturity.

Current Yield The **current yield** equals the bond's fixed annual interest payment divided by its bond price. It is a measure of the current annual income (the total of both semiannual interest payments in dollars) expressed as a percentage when divided by the bond's current market price. When you buy a bond at par, its current yield equals its coupon yield. For example, a bond with a 5.5 percent coupon yield purchased at par for $1000 has a current yield of 5.5 percent. As bond prices fluctuate because of interest rate changes and other factors, the current yield also changes. For example, if Leslie paid $940 for a $1000 bond paying $55 per year, the bond's current yield is 5.85 percent, as shown by the **current yield formula**, Equation (14.5).

current yield
Equals the bond's fixed annual interest payment divided by its bond price.

$$\text{Current yield} = \frac{\text{current annual income}}{\text{current market price}}$$

$$= \frac{\$55}{\$940}$$

$$= 5.85\%$$

(14.5)

A bond's current yield is based on the purchase price, not on the prices at which it later trades. The current yields for many bonds based on that day's market prices are available online and are published in the financial section of many newspapers.

The total return on a bond investment consists of the same components as the return on any investment: current income and capital gains. In Leslie's case, she will receive $1000 at the maturity date (20 years from now), even though she paid only $940 for the bond; therefore, her anticipated total return (or effective yield) will be higher than the 5.85 percent current yield. How much higher is accurately revealed by the yield to maturity formula (discussed next).

yield to maturity (YTM)
Total annual effective rate of return earned by a bondholder on a bond if the security is held to maturity—takes into consideration both the price at which the bond sold and the coupon interest rate to arrive at effective rate of return.

Check Bond Performance Online

BondInfo (www.nasdbondinfo.com/asp/bond_search.asp) is where you will find bond indexes and tools to gauge overall market direction and to measure the performance of corporate bond holdings against the broader market of more than 30,000 corporate bonds.

Yield to Maturity   Yield to maturity (YTM) is the total annual effective rate of return earned by a bondholder on a bond if the security is held to maturity. The YTM is the internal rate of return on cash flows of a fixed-income security. The YTM reflects both the current income and any difference if the bond was purchased at a price other than its face value spread over the life of the bond. The market price of a bond equals the present value of its future interest payments and the present value of its face value when the bond matures.

Three generalizations can be made about the yield to maturity:

1. If a bond is purchased for exactly its face value, the YTM is the same as the coupon rate printed on the certificate.
2. If a bond is purchased at a premium, the YTM will be lower than the coupon rate.
3. If a bond is purchased at a discount, the YTM will be higher than the coupon rate.

For example, because Leslie bought her 20-year bond with a coupon rate of 5.5 percent at a discount for $940, her yield to maturity must be greater than the coupon rate because she will receive $60 more than she paid for the bond when she receives the $1000 at maturity. Exactly how much greater can be determined by calculating an approximate yield to maturity when contemplating a bond purchase because bonds that seem comparable may have different YTMs.

The **yield to maturity (YTM) formula**, Equation (14.6), which is duplicated on the *Garman/Forgue* companion website, factors in the approximate appreciation when a bond is bought at a discount or at a premium:

$$YTM = \frac{I + [(FV - CV)/N]}{(FV + CV)/2} \quad \text{(14.6)}$$

where

I = **Interest** paid annually in dollars
FV = **Face value**
CV = **Current value** (price)
N = **Number** of years until maturity

If Leslie paid $940 for a 20-year bond with a 5.5 percent coupon rate, the YTM is calculated as follows:

$$YTM = \frac{\$55 + [(\$1000 - \$940)/20]}{(\$1000 + \$940)/2}$$

$$= \frac{\$58}{\$970}$$

$$= 5.98\%$$

If you plan to buy and hold a bond until its maturity, you should compare YTMs instead of current yields when considering a purchase because YTMs fairly represent all factors. The current yield on a bond is not an effective measure of the total annual return to the investor; in fact, the fewer years until maturity, the worse an indicator it becomes. As just calculated, Leslie's 20-year bond with a coupon rate of 5.5 percent and a current yield of 5.85 percent has a YTM of 5.98 percent. If the same bond had been purchased with only ten years until maturity, the YTM would be 6.29 percent; with five years until maturity, the YTM would be 6.90 percent; and with two years until maturity, the YTM would be 8.76 percent. Exact YTMs are online and listed in detailed bond tables available at large libraries and at brokers' offices.

Six Decisions for Bond Investors Individuals interested in investing in bonds can review resources on the website of the Securities Industry and Financial Markets Association (www.investinginbonds.com). It offers a free, searchable database of the latest corporate, government, municipal, and mortgage-backed bond issues and prices. Bond investors must make six decisions:

1. **Decide on credit quality.** Consider Treasury/agency, investment-grade corporate and municipal, and below investment-grade corporate and municipal.

2. **Decide on maturity.** Consider the time schedule of your financial needs: short, medium, or long term. Bonds with a short maturity have the lowest current yield but excellent price stability. Medium maturity bonds pay close to the higher rates earned on long-term bonds and enjoy much greater price stability.

3. **Determine the after-tax return.** Assuming equivalent risk, choose the bond that provides the better after-tax return because tax-exempt securities may offer a higher after-tax return than taxable alternatives. To compare the after-tax return of investments, see page 128.

4. **Select the highest yield to maturity.** Given similar bond securities with comparable risk, maturity, and tax equivalency, investors are wise to choose the one that offers the highest yield to maturity, as calculated by Equation (14.6).

5. **Consider selling.** When interest rates have dropped, consider selling because you can profit when rate decreases push up the value of your bond. Consider selling also if the bond rating has seriously slipped because it could mean greater risk and possible default.

6. **Think about investing in bond mutual funds.** Consider whether it is smarter to invest in bond mutual funds rather than individual bonds. This topic is examined in Chapter 15.

FINANCIAL POWER POINT

Ladder Your Bond Investments

Laddering is a form of buy-and-hold investing in bonds. Here you purchase a collection of bonds with different maturities spread out to match your time horizon. For example, you could buy bonds that mature in 2, 4, 6, 8, 10, 12, 14, 16, 18, and 20 years. You would receive interest on some bonds every six months, and every two years you would get back the principal on a bond that matures.

DO IT NOW!

You know more about personal finance after reading this chapter, so get started right now by:

1. *Identifying three types of stocks (see pages 416–419) that are appropriate for your investment goals and selecting an example of each.*

2. *Following the price fluctuations of those stocks for two months.*

3. *Assessing after two months whether the changes in price you saw were due primarily to movements in the stock market as a whole (market risk) or aspects of the companies' own success.*

 Concept Check 14.6

1. Distinguish between investment- and speculative-grade bonds.

2. Give some reasons why individuals often invest in corporate bonds rather than Treasuries.

3. Summarize the differences among Treasury bonds, I bonds, and TIPS bonds.

4. Explain what interest rate risk is and tell what calculation individuals considering bond investments should use to avoid that problem when buying an existing bond.

Golden Pixels LLC/Shutterstock.com

WHAT DO YOU RECOMMEND NOW?

Now that you have read the chapter on stocks and bonds, what do you recommend to Caitlin Diaz in the case at the beginning of the chapter regarding:

1.   Investing for retirement in 18 years?

2.   Owning blue-chip common stocks and preferred stocks rather than other common stocks given Caitlin's investment time horizon?

3.   The wisdom of owning municipal bonds rather than corporate bonds?

4.   The likely selling price of her corporate bonds, if sold today?

5.   Investments that might be appropriate to fund her children's education?

BIG PICTURE SUMMARY OF LEARNING OBJECTIVES

LO1.   Explain how stocks and bonds are used as investments.

Individual investors provide the money corporations use to create sales and earn profits. The investor shares in those profits.

LO2.   Classify common stocks according to their major characteristics.

Common stocks may be broadly classified as either income or growth stocks. Other terms used to describe stocks are *blue chip, value, speculative,* and *tech.* Market capitalization is used to classify large-cap, midcap, and small-cap stocks.

LO3.   Describe fundamental and numerical ways to evaluate stock values.

The investor studies certain fundamental factors, such as the company's sales, assets, earnings, products or services, markets, and management, to determine a company's basic value. To do so, investors examine several revealing ratios such as price/earnings (P/E), price/sales (P/S), and dividend payout, as well as revealing numbers such as book value per share. Individuals also estimate the value of a company by using beta to compare its history and expected future profitability with those of competing stocks.

LO4.   Use the Internet to evaluate common stocks in which to invest.

Individuals begin evaluating stocks by setting criteria for a stock investment. This may involve using stock-screening software; obtaining security analysts' research reports, annual reports, 10-Q and 10-K reports, and prospectuses; acquiring economic and stock market data; and using portfolio-tracking services.

LO5.   Summarize how stocks are bought and sold.

Securities transactions require the use of a licensed broker serving as a middleman between the seller and the buyer. You can buy or sell securities online or through a live stockbroker who works for a brokerage firm that has access to the securities markets. Many individuals use discount and online brokers rather than full-service brokers. Types of stock orders include market, limit, and stop orders. Buying on margin and selling short are risky trading techniques.

LO6.   Describe how to invest in bonds.

Investment-grade bonds offer a reasonable certainty of regularly receiving the periodic income (interest) and retrieving the amount originally invested (principal). Junk bonds are available, too. Corporate bonds usually pay higher returns than government bonds. Interest rate risk results in variable value in bond investments.

LET'S TALK ABOUT IT

1.   **Investing Today.** What counsel can you offer long-term investors who are hesitant to invest in stocks and bonds in today's economy?

2.   **Three Good Companies.** Make a list of three products and services that you buy on a weekly or monthly basis and the companies that sell them. Offer your initial views on whether each company would be a good place to invest money.

3. **Two Useful Measures.** The text introduced a variety of ways to measure stock performance. Name two of those measures that you might use in your own decision making. Offer reasons for selecting those measures.

4. **Would You Buy?** You have just heard that Microsoft's stock price dropped $5. If you had the money, would you buy 100 shares? Give three reasons why or why not.

5. **Interesting Stock.** Review the three basic classifications of common stock and the other descriptive terms. Based on your personal comfort level for risk, which type of stock would be of interest to you? Give three reasons why.

6. **Sources of Information.** If you had an investment portfolio of stocks worth $20,000, identify three sources for information that you would likely use to keep abreast of current information affecting your investments.

7. **Potential Rate of Return.** Do you think anyone really calculates the potential rate of return on a particular investment? Should they? If so, offer a reason why.

8. **Invest Using Credit.** Buying on margin and selling short both involve using credit. Would you invest this way? Give two reasons why or why not.

9. **Interest in Bonds.** Do bonds interest you as an investment? Why or why not?

DO THE MATH

1. **Numerical Measures.** A stock sells at $15 per share.

    (a) What is the EPS for the company if it has a P/E ratio of 20?

    (b) If the company's dividend yield is 5 percent, what is its dividend per share?

    (c) What is the book value of the company if the price-to-book ratio is 1.5 and it has 100,000 shares of stock outstanding?

2. **Bond Selling Price.** What is the market price of a $1000, 8 percent bond if comparable market interest rates drop to 6 percent and the bond matures in 15 years?

3. **Market Price.** What is the market price of a $1000, 8 percent bond if comparable market interest rates rise to 10 percent and the bond matures in 14 years?

4. **Equivalent Taxable Yield.** For a municipal bond paying 5.4 percent for a taxpayer in the 25 percent tax bracket, what is the equivalent taxable yield? (Hint: See page 128.)

5. **Equivalent Taxable Yield.** For a municipal bond paying 5.7 percent for a taxpayer in the 33 percent tax bracket, what is the equivalent taxable yield? (Hint: See page 128.)

6. **Yield, Price, and YTM.** A corporate bond maturing in 15 years with a coupon rate of 9.9 percent was purchased for $980.

    (a) What is its current yield?

    (b) What will be its selling price in two years if comparable market interest rates drop 1.9 percentage points?

    (c) Calculate the bond's YTM using Equation (14.6) or the *Garman/Forgue* companion website.

7. **Yield, Price, and YTM.** A corporate bond maturing in 20 years with a coupon rate of 8.2 percent was purchased for $1100.

    (a) What is its current yield?

    (b) What will the bond's selling price be if comparable market interest rates rise 1.8 percentage points in two years?

    (c) Calculate the bond's YTM using Equation (14.6) or the *Garman/Forgue* companion website.

8. **Beta Calculations.** Michael Margolis is a single parent and motivational training consultant from Orem, Utah. He is wondering about potential returns on investments given certain amounts of risk. Michael invested a total of $6000 in three stocks ($2000 in each) with different betas: stock A with a beta of 0.8, stock B with a beta of 1.7, and stock C with a beta of 2.5.

    (a) If the stock market rises 12 percent over the next year, what will be the likely value of each investment?

    (b) If the stock market declines 8 percent over the next year, what will be the likely value of each investment?

9. **Investment Calculations.** Xiao and Shiao Jing-jian, newlyweds from Rockville, Maryland, have decided to begin investing for the future. Xiao is a 7-Eleven store manager, and Shiao is a high-school math teacher. The couple intends to take $3000 out of their savings for investment purposes and then continue to invest an additional $200 to $400 per month. Both have a

moderate investment philosophy and seek some cash dividends as well as price appreciation.

Calculate the five-year return on the investment choices in the table below. Put your calculations in tabular form like that shown in Table 14-1. (Hint: At the end of the first year, the EPS for Running Paws will be $2.40 with a dividend of $0.66, and the EPS for Eagle Packaging will be $2.76 with a projected dividend of $0.86.)

(a) Using the appropriate P/E ratios, what are the estimated market prices of the Running Paws and Eagle Packaging stocks after five years?

(b) Show your calculations in determining the projected price appreciations for the two stocks over the five years.

(c) Add the projected price appreciation of each stock to its projected cash dividends, and show the total five-year percentage returns for the two stocks.

(d) Determine the average annual dividend for each stock, and use these figures in calculating the approximate compound yields for each.

(e) Assume that the beta is 2.5 for Running Paws and 2.8 for Eagle Packaging. If the market went up 20 percent during the year, what would be the

likely stock prices for Running Paws and Eagle Packaging?

(f) Assume that inflation is approximately 4 percent and the return on high-quality, long-term corporate bonds is 8 percent. Given the Jing-jians' investment philosophy, explain why you would recommend (1) Running Paws, (2) Eagle Packaging, or (3) a high-quality, long-term corporate bond as a growth investment. Support your answer by calculating the potential rate of return using the information on pages 421 to 423 or by using the *Garman/Forgue* website. The Jing-jians are in the 25 percent marginal tax bracket.

	Running Paws	Eagle Packaging
Current price	$30.00	$48.00
Current earnings per share (EPS)	$ 2.00	$ 2.30
Current quarterly cash dividend	$ 0.15	$ 0.18
Current P/E ratio	15	21
Projected earnings annual growth rate	20%	20%
Projected cash dividend growth rate	10%	10%

FINANCIAL PLANNING CASES

CASE 1

The Johnsons Want Greater Yields on Investments

The investments of Harry and Belinda have done well through the years. While the cash portion of their portfolio has risen to $16,000, it is earning a minuscule 1 percent in a money market account;

thus they are seeking greater yields with bond investments. Examine the following table, which identifies eight investment alternatives, and then respond to the questions that follow. The coupon rates vary because the issue dates range widely, and market prices are above par because older bonds paid higher interest than today's issues.

Name of Issue	Bond Denomination	Coupon Rate Percent	Years Until Maturity	Moody's Rating	Market Price	Current Yield	YTM
Corporate ABC	$1000	7.0	4	Aa	$1400		
Corporate DEF	1000	7.5	20	Aa	1550		
Corporate GHI	1000	5.9	12	Baa	1250		
Corporate JKL	1000	7.8	5	Aaa	1500		
Corporate MNO	1000	6.1	15	B	1260		
Corporate PQR	1000	5.8	11	B	1200		
Treasury note	1000	7.9	3	—	1600		
Municipal bond	1000	4.1	20	Aa	1200		

(a) What is the current yield of each investment alternative? Use Equation (14.5) or visit the *Garman/Forgue* companion website. (Write your responses in the proper column in the table.)

(b) What is the yield to maturity for each investment alternative? (Write your responses in the proper column in the table.) You may calculate the YTMs by using Equation (14.6) or by visiting the *Garman/Forgue* companion website.

(c) Knowing that the Johnsons follow a moderate investment philosophy, which one of the six corporate bonds would you recommend? Why?

(d) Given that the Johnsons are in the 25 percent federal marginal tax rate, what is the equivalent taxable yield for the municipal bond choice? Should they invest in your recommendation in part (c) or in the municipal bond? Why? You may calculate the equivalent taxable yield using the information on page 128.

(e) Which three of the eight alternatives would you recommend as a group so that the Johnsons would have some diversification protection for their $16,000? Why do you suggest that combination?

CASE 2

Victor and Maria Hernandez Wonder About Investing

Victor and Maria have decided to increase their contribution to their investment portfolio since Victor is now age 59 and thinking about retiring in five years. For years, they have followed a moderate-risk investment philosophy and put their money in suitable stocks, bonds, and mutual funds. The value of their portfolio is now $320,000, and this is in addition to their paid-for rental property, which is worth $200,000. They plan to invest about $9000 every year for the next five years.

(a) Why should Victor and Maria consider buying common stock as an investment with the additional money?

(b) If Victor and Maria bought a stock with a market price of $50 and a beta value of 1.8, what would be the likely price of an $8000 investment after one year if the general market for stocks rose 10 percent?

(c) What would the same investment be worth if the general market for stocks dropped 10 percent?

CASE 3

Julia Price Seeks Rewards in the Bond Market

Julia's investments survived the Great Recession–related bear stock market declines because she was well diversified and was investing more heavily in bonds in the years preceding the decline. When it seemed like the coming recession was starting to look like a reality, Julia cashed out of some equities and moved most of that money into corporate bonds and Treasuries. As a result, over the past three years, the bond portion of her portfolio rose over

20 percent due to low inflation and declining interest rates. Instead of taking her capital gains by selling the bonds, she remains pessimistic about the economy and believes that interest rates will either remain low or drop a little more over the next year or two. Thus she is considering selling her remaining equities and investing those proceeds into the bond market. Offer your opinions about her thinking.

CASE 4

An Aggressive Investor Seeks Rewards in the Bond Market

Karry Varcoe works as a drug manufacturer's representative based in Newton, Iowa. She has an aggressive investment philosophy and believes that interest rates will drop over the next year or two because of an expected economic slowdown. Karry, who is in the 25 percent marginal tax rate, wants to profit in the bond market by buying and selling during the next several months. She has asked your advice on how to invest her $15,000.

(a) If Karry buys corporate or municipal bonds, what rating should her selections have? Why?

(b) Karry has a choice between two $1000 bonds: a corporate bond with a coupon rate of 5.1 percent and a municipal bond with a coupon rate of 3.2 percent. Which bond provides the better after-tax return? (Hint: See Equation [4.1] on page 128.)

(c) If Karry buys fifteen 30-year, $1000 corporate bonds with a 5.1 percent coupon rate for $960 each, what is her current yield? (Hint: Use Equation [4.1].)

(d) If market interest rates for comparable corporate bonds drop 1 percent over the next 12 months (from 5.1 percent to 4.1 percent), what will be the approximate selling price of Karry's corporate bonds in (c)? (Hint: Use the *Garman/Forgue* companion website.)

(e) Assuming market interest rates drop 1 percent in 12 months, how much is Karry's capital gain on the $15,000 investment if she sells? How much was her current return for the two semi-annual interest payments? How much was her total return, both in dollars and as an annual yield? (Ignore transaction costs.)

(f) If Karry is wrong in her projections and interest rates go up 1 percent over the year, what would be the probable selling price of her corporate bonds? (Hint: Use the *Garman/Forgue* companion website.) Explain why you would advise her to sell or not to sell.

CASE 5

Two Brothers' Attitudes Toward Investments

Kyle Broflovski, a guidance counselor in Freeport, Illinois, has purchased several corporate and government bonds over the years, and his total bond investment now exceeds $40,000. He prefers a variable-value investment with some inflation protection. His kid brother Ike, a highly paid physician, has more than $150,000 invested in various blue-chip income stocks in a variety of industries.

(a) Justify Kyle's attitude toward bond investments.

(b) Justify Ike's attitude toward stock investments.

(c) Explain why both brothers might be happy investing some of their money in TIPS bonds.

CASE 6

A College Student Ponders Investing in the Stock Market

Richard Ford of Jefferson City, Tennessee, has $5000 that he wants to invest in the stock market.

Richard is in college on a scholarship and does not plan to use the $5000 or any dividend income for another five years, when he plans to buy a home. He is currently considering a stock selling for $25 per share with an EPS of $1.25. Last year, the company earned $900,000, of which $250,000 was paid out in dividends.

(a) What classification of common stock would you recommend to Richard? Why?

(b) Calculate the P/E ratio and the dividend payout ratio for this stock. Given this information and your recommendation, would this stock be an appropriate purchase for Richard? Why or why not?

(c) Identify the components of the total return Richard might expect, and estimate how much he might expect annually from each component.

BE YOUR OWN PERSONAL FINANCIAL MANAGER

1. **Your Stock Preferences.** Complete Worksheet 54: My Preferences Among Stocks from "My Personal Financial Planner" by identifying, for each of the seven types of stock, those that are of interest to you, what you do or do not like about them, and those in which you might invest during your own investing life.

MY PERSONAL FINANCIAL PLANNER

2. **Compare Different Stocks as Investments.** Learn about the stocks of three publically traded companies of interest to you, perhaps General Motors, Ford Motor Company, and Google, by visiting the website for Kiplinger.com at www.kiplinger.com. Then complete Worksheet 55: Comparing Stocks as Investments from "My Personal Financial Planner" by recording for each company each of the several performance variables.

MY PERSONAL FINANCIAL PLANNER

3. **Preference Among Types of Bond.** Complete Worksheet 56: My Preference Among Bonds from "My Personal Financial Planner" by marking for each of the nine types one characteristic you do or do not like about each and which might be of interest to you as an investor.

MY PERSONAL FINANCIAL PLANNER

4. **Taxable Versus Tax-Free Income.** Complete Worksheet 57: Comparing Taxable and Tax-Free Income from "My Personal Financial Planner" by inserting a realistic rate of investment return

MY PERSONAL FINANCIAL PLANNER

and tax rate and then performing the appropriate calculations.

5. **Current Yield.** Complete Worksheet 58: The Current Yield on My Bond Investment from "My Personal Financial Planner" by inserting realistic different current market prices on two existing bonds (perhaps $980 and $910) and different annual interest payments (perhaps $70 and $80) for two bonds and calculating the current yields.

MY PERSONAL FINANCIAL PLANNER

6. **Present Value of a Bond.** Complete Worksheet 59: The Present Value on My Bond Investment from "My Personal Financial Planner" by going online to find the current market prices of two existing bonds, perhaps individual issues of General Motors and Ford Motor Company, and then inserting the following information in the places provided: annual interest payment and years to maturity. Look online elsewhere for a current market interest rate on comparable securities, or perhaps use 7%, and complete the calculations required.

MY PERSONAL FINANCIAL PLANNER

7. **Yield to Maturity on a Bond.** Complete Worksheet 60: The Yield to Maturity on My Bond from "My Personal Financial Planner" by going online to find the following information about two bonds: current market price, face value, number of years until maturity, and annual interest in dollars.

ON THE 'NET

Go to the Web pages indicated to complete these exercises.

1. **Latest Financial Information.** Go to Kiplinger.com and determine the top three news items related to personal investing. Note how you can use that information in making wise investment decisions.

2. **Stock Quotes.** Visit the website for Kiplinger.com at www.kiplinger.com, where you can find stock quotes for most publicly traded companies. Type in the symbols for the following companies: Coca-Cola (KO), Google (GOOG), Microsoft (MSFT), and Disney (DIS). Evaluate these four firms on the basis of EPS, dividend yield, and P/E ratio. What do these data suggest to you about the relative attractiveness of these companies for investors?

3. **Stock Screener.** Visit the website for Yahoo! Finance, where you can find a stock-screener utility at http://screen.yahoo.com/stocks.html. Search among the S&P 500 stocks for companies with a $50 minimum share price. How many companies meet this criterion? Select again using a P/E ratio from 0 to 20. How many companies meet this new criterion? Why is this list longer? Do you recognize any of the companies on either list?

4. **Online Trading.** Go to the website for E*Trade, an online brokerage firm (https://us.etrade.com/e/t/home). Find out what services they offer and learn about their investing and trading education.

5. **Recent Treasury Prices.** Visit the website for the U.S. Treasury Department at www.treasurydirect.gov and enter its Institutional section, where you will find the results of recent auctions for Treasury notes and bonds. What do the results of the auctions over the past year tell you about market expectations for movement of interest rates in the future? (Hint: Compare auction rates for bonds and notes with similar maturity periods.)

6. **Find Bond Ratings.** Visit the Standard and Poor's website at www.standardandpoors.com and look up the current bond ratings for General Motors and Ford Motor Company. Summarize your findings.

7. **Bond Calculator.** Go to Investopedia's Bond Calculator to input illustrative pricing data on bonds (www.investopedia.com/calculator/BondPrice.aspx). Write what you think of this tool.

8. **Beta Values.** Go to CalculatorEdge (www.calculatoredge.com/finance/betas.htm) and input basic information on any stock to calculate its beta. Use 2 percent or a lower figure as the risk-free interest rate.

ACTION INVOLVEMENT PROJECTS

1. **Answer Seven Questions.** Review the box "Did You Know? Seven Questions Every Investor Needs to Answer" and write down your responses to each question.

2. **Latest Stock Market Values.** Using a resource like *The Wall Street Journal* or the Internet in general, find the latest values for the following market indexes and indicate how each has performed over the past 12 months:

DJIA, S&P 500, NASDAQ Composite, Dow Jones Wilshire 5000 Index, and Dow Jones Wilshire 2000.

3. **Prices of Popular Stocks.** Find the latest values for the following stocks and indicate how each has performed over the past 12 months: American Express, AT&T, Caterpillar, Coca-Cola, Dell, Merck, Walmart, and Walt Disney.

Visit the Garman/Forgue companion website at **www.cengagebrain.com**.

YOU MUST BE KIDDING, RIGHT?

Twins Amanda and Daniel invest in mutual funds. Amanda majored in finance. For more than 20 years, she invested in managed funds, counting on intelligent professional financial advisers to select the winning companies more often than not. Daniel majored in English; he invested in unmanaged index funds that achieve the same return as a particular market index by buying and holding all or a representative selection of securities in the index. After 20 years of investing, what are the odds that Amanda's investment portfolio balance will be better than Daniel's?

A. zero

C. 20%

B. 10%

D. 30%

The answer is B or A but never C or D. Managed mutual funds generally do not earn returns for investors that exceed the overall market indexes. The fact is the average mutual fund manager earns a lower return at least 80 percent of the time. Finding a mutual fund investment manager who can consistently beat the market is very challenging!

LEARNING OBJECTIVES

After reading this chapter, you should be able to:

❶ Describe the features, services, and advantages of investing in mutual funds.

❷ Differentiate mutual funds by investment objectives.

❸ Summarize the fees and charges involved in buying and selling mutual funds.

❹ Establish strategies to evaluate and select mutual funds that meet your investment goals.

WHAT DO YOU RECOMMEND?

David and Sarah Gent, a couple in their early 30s, have a 2-year-old child and enjoy living in a moderately priced downtown apartment. David, a library director, earns $50,000 annually. Sarah earns $59,000 as a merchandise buyer for a specialty store. They are big savers: Together they have been putting $1000 to $2000 per month into CDs, and the couple now has a portfolio worth $120,000 paying about 3 percent annually. The Gents are conservative investors and want to retire in about 20 years.

What do you recommend to David and Sarah on the subject of investing through mutual funds regarding:

1. Redeeming their CDs and investing their retirement money in mutual funds?

2. Investing in growth and income mutual funds instead of income funds?

3. Buying no-load rather than load funds?

4. Buying target-date mutual funds instead of balanced mutual funds?

5. Buying mutual funds through their employers' 401(k) retirement accounts rather than saving through a taxable account as they have been doing?

LEARNING OBJECTIVE

Describe the features, services, and advantages of investing in mutual funds.

mutual fund
Investment company that pools funds by selling shares to investors and makes diversified investments to achieve financial goals of income or growth, or both.

net asset value (NAV)
Per-share value of a mutual fund.

Most investors prefer to avoid buying individual stocks and bonds because of the high financial risk associated with owning too few investments like two or three stocks or bonds. The average investor usually cannot accumulate a portfolio diversified enough to minimize the risk linked to the failure of a single holding. Investors often also lack both the ability and time required to research individual securities and manage such a portfolio. In an effort to avoid these problems, many people invest *in* the stock and bond markets *through* mutual funds, which typically buy hundreds of different stocks and bonds. Mutual funds make it easy and convenient for investors to open an account and continue investing. Half of all households invest through mutual funds.

WHY SHOULD YOU INVEST IN MUTUAL FUNDS?

A **mutual fund** is an investment company that pools funds obtained by selling shares to investors and makes investments to achieve the financial goal of income or growth, or both. Mutual funds invest in a diversified portfolio of stocks, bonds, short-term money market instruments, and other securities or assets.

The fund might own common stock and bonds in such companies as AT&T, IBM, Sears, or Running Paws Cat Food Company (our example from Chapter 14). The combined holdings are known as a **portfolio**, as we noted in Chapter 13 and as shown graphically in Figure 15-1. The mutual fund company owns the investments it makes and the mutual fund investors own the mutual fund company. Unlike corporate shareholders, holders of mutual funds have no say in running the company, although they have equity interest in the pool of assets and a residual claim on the profits.

The Net Asset Value Is the Price You Pay for a Mutual Fund Share

One measure of the investor's claim on assets is the net asset value. The **net asset value (NAV)** is the price one pays (excluding any transaction costs) to buy a share of a mutual fund. It is the per-share net worth of the mutual fund. It is calculated by summing the

---

Figure 15-1   **How a Mutual Fund Works**

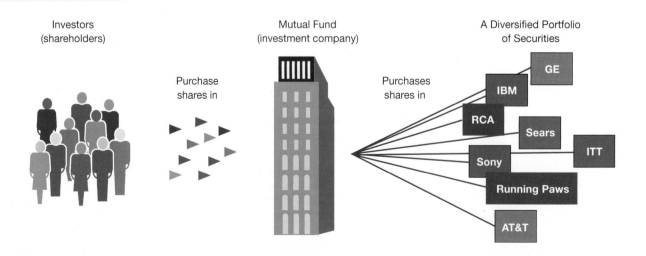

values of all the securities in the fund's portfolio, subtracting liabilities, and then dividing by the total number of shares outstanding.

$$\text{Net asset value} = \frac{\text{market value of assets} - \text{market value of liabilities}}{\text{number of shares}} \quad (15.1)$$

For example, a mutual fund has 10 million shares outstanding and a portfolio worth $100 million, and its liabilities are $5 million. The net asset value of a single share is

$$\text{Net asset value} = \frac{\$100,000,000 - \$5,000,000}{10,000,000} = \frac{\$95,000,000}{10,000,000} = \$9.50 \text{ per share}$$

The NAV rises or falls to reflect changes in the market value of the investments held by the mutual fund company. This value is calculated daily after the major U.S. stock exchanges close, and a new NAV is posted in the financial media. If the assets held in a mutual fund increase in value, the NAV will rise. For example, if a mutual fund owns IBM and General Electric common stocks and the prices of those stocks increase, the increased value of the underlying securities is reflected in the NAV of fund shares. The increase in NAV due to rising portfolio values is price appreciation. When investors sell shares at a net asset value higher than that paid when they purchased the shares (after transaction costs), they will have a capital gain.

Dividend Income and Capital Gains Distributions Result from the Mutual Fund's Earnings

A **mutual fund dividend** is income paid to investors out of profits that the mutual fund has earned from its investments. The dividend represents both ordinary income dividend distributions and capital gains distributions. **Ordinary income dividend distributions** occur when the fund pays out dividend income and interest (monthly, quarterly, or annually) it has received from securities it owns. **Capital gains distributions** represent the net gains (capital gains minus capital losses) that a fund realizes when it sells securities that were held in the fund's portfolio. Mutual funds distribute capital gains once a year, even though the gains occur throughout the year whenever securities are sold at a profit. When a fund pays out these distributions, the NAV drops by the amount paid. Figure 15-2 illustrates theses sources of mutual fund returns.

Capital Gains Can Result When You Sell Mutual Fund Shares

While you are invested in a mutual fund, the shares you own will provide you with current income, as described in the previous section. You can choose to take this income as it is earned or reinvest it by purchasing additional shares in the fund. But what happens if you want to sell some or all of your shares? In such a case, you would hope that the

mutual fund dividend
Income paid to investors out of profits earned by the mutual fund from its investments.

ordinary income dividend distributions
Distributions that occur when the fund pays out dividend income and interest (monthly, quarterly, or annually) it has received from securities held in the fund.

capital gains distributions
Distributions representing the net gains (capital gains minus capital losses) that a fund realizes when it sells securities that were held in the fund's portfolio.

Investor Returns from Mutual Funds

Figure 15-2

Sources of Investor Returns from Owning a Share in a Mutual Fund		
Current Income (returns received while you own a share)		**Capital Gains** (returns received when you sell your share)
Ordinary Dividend Income Distributions	Capital Gains Distributions	
The mutual fund receives dividends from the stocks and interest from the bonds it holds in its portfolio. These are passed on to you every three months (quarterly).	The mutual fund occasionally sells stocks and bonds in its portfolio. When it receives more from the sale than it paid for the securities, it achieves a capital gain. The gains are passed along to you each year (annually).	When you sell your share in the mutual fund, you receive the NAV of the share at its current market price. If that price is higher than the price you paid at purchase, you have a capital gain due to the increase in NAV. Your capital gain will be reduced by transaction costs.

shares have a higher value at the time of the sale than when you originally purchased the shares. If so, you earn a capital gain.

Advantages of Investing Through Mutual Funds

open-end mutual fund
Investment that issues redeemable shares that investors purchase directly from the fund (or through a broker for the fund).

The type of mutual fund that is the focus in this chapter is an **open-end mutual fund**. Accounting for more than 90 percent of all funds, open-end mutual funds issue redeemable shares that investors purchase directly from the fund (or through a broker for the fund) instead of purchasing from investors on a stock market. They are always ready to sell new shares of ownership and to buy back previously sold shares at the fund's current NAV. Open-end mutual funds, numbering more than 11,000, outnumber companies listed on the New York Stock Exchange (approximately 2800). Mutual funds offer a number of advantages to investors.

Diversification Mutual funds are broadly diversified in financial markets. They might own several hundred different securities, and all are represented in a single mutual fund share. The individual with $500 or $5000 to invest could never obtain such diversification. A diversified portfolio reduces the risk if a company or sector fails. **Random risk**, or **nonsystematic risk**, as we discussed in Chapter 1, is reduced. Recall that random risk arises when one owns only one investment of a particular type (such as stock in one company) that, by chance, may do very poorly in the future due to uncontrollable or random factors. Many investors find it easier to achieve diversification through ownership of mutual funds that own stocks and bonds rather than picking and then owning individual stocks and bonds.

Affordability Individuals can invest in mutual funds with relatively low dollar amounts for initial purchases, such as $250 or $1000. Subsequent purchases can be as little as $50.

fund investment advisers
Money managers, securities analysts, and traders of a mutual fund that have access to the best research; they select, buy, sell, and monitor the performance of the securities purchased; thus, they oversee the portfolio.

Professional Management Many investors lack the knowledge, time, and commitment to worry about which of their stocks and bonds to buy and sell. Mutual fund investors like the fact that professional investment advisers registered with the Securities and Exchange Commission (SEC) manage their investment portfolio. The fund management company may control many millions or billions of dollars of assets. The **fund investment advisers** have access to the best research, and they select, buy, sell, and monitor the performance of the securities purchased; they oversee the portfolio. Investment advisers use the most current information, analytical tools, and investment techniques available. Fund investment advisers (money managers, securities analysts, and traders) share the same investment objective as the individual investor: to make money by increasing the net asset value of the mutual fund.

redeems
When an investor sells shares.

Liquidity Mutual funds have good **liquidity**, a term we discussed in Chapter 5 and Chapter 13. You can very easily convert mutual fund shares into cash without loss of value because the investor sells (**redeems**) the shares back to the investment company. To do so, individuals simply pick up the telephone or go online. The price the investor gets depends on the value of the portfolio and the resulting NAV.

Low Transaction Costs Because mutual funds trade in large quantities of shares, they pay far less in brokerage commissions than individual investors. Lower transaction costs result in higher returns for investors. Individuals purchase mutual fund shares from the fund itself (or through a broker for the fund) instead of from other investors on a secondary market, such as the New York Stock Exchange or NASDAQ stock market. Shares bought and sold are at the NAV plus any fees and charges that the fund imposes, and these are often low. While some funds charge significant fees on purchases and redemptions, individuals need not invest in those funds.

Uncomplicated Investment Choices Selecting a mutual fund is easier than selecting specific stocks or bonds. Mutual funds state their investment objectives, allowing investors to select funds that almost perfectly match their own objectives. Identifying mutual funds that meet certain investment criteria can be done easily using mutual fund screening software. This topic is examined later in this chapter.

Unique Mutual Fund Services

Mutual funds offer a number of valuable services that are unique to this type of investment and that are helpful and appealing to investors.

Convenience Mutual funds are extremely convenient for investors. Funds make it easy to open an account and invest in and sell shares. Fund prices are widely quoted. Services include toll-free telephone numbers, detailed records of transactions, and various checking and savings alternatives. Funds handle all the paperwork and record keeping, including accounting for fractional shares, so it is simple for investors to calculate taxable gains and losses when shares are sold.

Ease of Buying and Selling Shares Opening an account with a mutual fund company is just as simple as opening a checking account. After sending the fund your initial investment, you can easily buy more shares. Any number of shares can be sold at any time, or you can simply ask that a specific dollar amount be taken out by selling the appropriate number of shares. Each share is redeemed at the closing price—that is, the NAV—at the end of the trading day. Shares can be bought and sold by communicating with the company via telephone, wire, fax, mail, or online.

Check Writing and Electronic Transfers Mutual funds often offer interest-earning money market mutual funds in which investors can accumulate cash, accept dividends, or hold their money while making decisions about investing. They can write checks from money market funds. A money market fund invests exclusively in cash and cash equivalents. Investors can electronically transfer funds to and from mutual funds and banks.

Distribution of or Automatic Reinvestment of Income and Capital Gains Unlike most other investments, mutual funds allow investors to choose to receive current income payments or have them automatically reinvested to purchase additional fund shares (often without paying any commissions). This is **automatic reinvestment**, and it produces the same effects as the compounding of interest because the investor earns money on past earnings. Fractional shares are acquired as needed. Automatic reinvestment is one of the most appealing aspects of mutual funds for investors. Most shareholders wisely reinvest their mutual fund income to keep all of their capital fully invested, as illustrated in Figure 15-3.

automatic reinvestment
Investor's option to choose to automatically reinvest any interest, dividends, and capital gains payments to purchase additional fund shares.

Telephone and Internet Exchange Privileges An **exchange privilege** (also called a **switching, conversion,** or **transfer privilege**) permits mutual fund shareholders to easily swap shares on a dollar-for-dollar basis for shares in another mutual fund managed by the same mutual fund family. Telephone and online transfers from one fund to another, such as moving money from a domestic stock fund to a Taiwan international fund, can be accomplished at no cost or for only a small charge, typically $5 or $10 per transaction, called an **exchange fee**. A **mutual fund family** is an investment management company that offers a number of different mutual funds to the investing public, each with its own investment objectives. There are more than 400 mutual fund families (see http://biz.yahoo.com/p/fam/a-b.html).

exchange privilege
Allowance for mutual fund shareholders to easily swap shares on a dollar-for-dollar basis for shares in another mutual fund within a mutual fund family. Also called switching, conversion, or transfer privilege.

exchange fee
Small amount charged to move money among funds within a mutual fund family.

Automatic Investment Funds often allow investors to make periodic monthly or quarterly payments using money automatically transferred from their bank accounts or paychecks to the mutual fund company. You can invest as little as $25 monthly or quarterly. This is an example of dollar-cost averaging. You can change your investment selections without penalty by contacting the fund. By regularly investing in mutual funds, you can build a substantial portfolio of assets over time.

mutual fund family
Investment management company that offers a number of different funds to the investing public, each with its own investment objectives or philosophies of investing.

Effortless Establishment of Retirement Plans Mutual funds are perhaps the best option available to people saving for retirement through 401(k) plans and IRAs (topics examined in Chapter 17). An employee can fill out a one-page form that directs his or her employer to transfer a specified dollar amount from every paycheck to a mutual fund to buy shares for a 401(k) plan. Individuals can fill out a one-page form to buy shares for their individual retirement accounts, too.

Beneficiary Designation When opening a mutual fund account, the investor must complete a form to designate a beneficiary in case of the investor's death. A **beneficiary designation** enables the shareholder to name one or more beneficiaries so that the proceeds go to them without going through probate. The delays and expenses of probate are discussed in Chapter 18.

beneficiary designation
Allowance of fund holder to name one or more beneficiaries so that the proceeds bypass probate proceedings if the original shareholder dies.

Figure 15-3

The Wisdom of Automatic Dividend Reinvestment

Reinvesting income greatly compounds share ownership. Figure 15-3 illustrates the positive results obtained by reinvesting dividends. The initial $10,000 investment in S&P 500 Index Fund grew to $64,060 over 20 years, instead of $38,090, because of the reinvestment of dividends. "More than 40% of the total return of the S&P 500 over the past 80 years has come from reinvested dividends. Therefore, I believe enrolling in an automatic reinvestment program is an easy (and painless) way of accumulating wealth over time," says Sam Stovall, Chief Investment Strategist of Standard & Poor's.

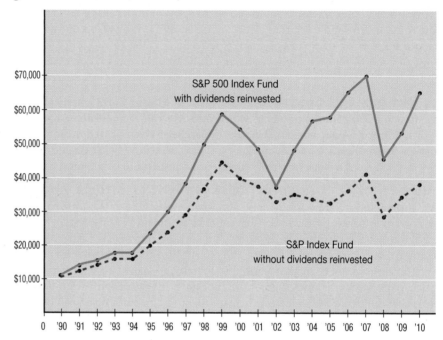

Source: Reprinted by permission of Standard & Poor's, a division of the McGraw-Hill Companies, Copyright 2011.

DID YOU KNOW?

Types of Investment Companies

The Investment Company Act of 1940 distinguishes among investment companies. Open-end mutual funds are by far the most widely owned investment companies. Four other types exist:

1. ***Closed-end mutual funds. Closed-end mutual funds*** *issue a limited and fixed number of shares at inception and do not buy them back. These companies operate with a fixed amount of capital. Closed-end shares are bought and sold on a stock exchange or in the over-the-counter market. After the original issue is sold, the price of a share depends primarily on the supply and demand in the market rather than the performance of the investment company assets. Closed-end shares are actively traded like common stocks and bonds, primarily on the New York Stock Exchange.*

2. ***Real estate investment trusts.*** *A special kind of closed-end investment company is a **real estate investment trust (REIT)**. REITs invest in a portfolio of assets as defined in the* trust agreement, such as properties, like office buildings and shopping centers (called an equity REIT), or mortgages (a mortgage REIT). Hybrid REITs invest in both. REITs have no predetermined life span. REIT shares are traded on stock exchanges, although many are illiquid investments.

3. ***Unit investment trusts.*** *A **unit investment trust (UIT)** is a closed-end investment company that makes a one-time public offering of only a specific, fixed number of units. A UIT buys and holds an unmanaged fixed portfolio of fixed-maturity securities, such as municipal bonds, for a period of time. This could be a few months or perhaps 50 years. Each unit represents a proportionate ownership interest in the specific portfolio of perhaps 10 to 50 securities. Sold by brokers for perhaps $250 to $1000 a unit, there is no trading of these securities, although brokers may repurchase and resell them.*

4. ***Exchange-traded funds.*** *An **exchange-traded fund (ETF)** is a basket of passively managed securities structured like*

an index fund (described later in this chapter) as it owns all or a representative set of securities that duplicate the performance of a market segment or index. In effect, ETFs ditch the fund manager and pass the savings on to the investor. There are ETFs for the S&P 500, called Spiders; the Dow Jones Industrial Average, called Diamonds; and Qubes based on the NASDAQ 100. There are over 900 ETFs, and their prices are set by market forces since they are listed on securities markets (primarily on the American Stock Exchange [AMEX]) and traded throughout the day by brokers. ETFs give investors an easy way to track an index without buying an index fund. ETFs are available for nearly every asset class, from stocks and bonds to industrial metals and commodities.

Multiple Ways to Withdraw Income Mutual funds offer **withdrawal options** (also called **systematic withdrawal plans**) to shareholders who want to receive income on a regular basis from their mutual fund investments. Once enrolled in a withdrawal plan, the minimum withdrawal amount is $50. The fund forwards the amounts to you (or to anyone you designate) at regular intervals (monthly or quarterly). You can make regular withdrawals by (1) taking a set dollar amount each month, (2) cashing in a set number of shares each month, (3) taking the current income as cash, or (4) taking a portion of the asset growth.

enhanced ETF (active ETF)
An exchange-traded fund that tracks an index but overinvests in companies with the greatest potential; thus, it is an actively managed ETF.

withdrawal options/systematic withdrawal plans
Arrangements with a mutual fund company for shareholders who want to receive income on a regular basis from their mutual fund investments.

Concept Check 15.1

1. Explain how net asset value is calculated and how it is used by mutual funds.

2. List five advantages of investing in mutual funds.

3. Name five services that are unique to mutual funds.

MUTUAL FUND OBJECTIVES

Most mutual funds are **managed funds**, meaning that professional managers are constantly evaluating and choosing securities using a specific investment approach. On a daily basis, active managers select the stocks and bonds in which to invest and sell them when they deem appropriate. The managers earn a fee for their services, and ultimately their choices are responsible for the performance of the fund.

Before investing in any specific mutual fund, you need to decide whether the fund's investment objectives are a good fit for your own investment philosophy and financial goals. The SEC requires funds to disclose their investment objective. Mutual funds may be classified in one of three categories: income, growth, and growth and income. Each type has different features, risks, and reward characteristics, and the name of a fund gives a clue to its objectives.

 LEARNING OBJECTIVE 2

Differentiate mutual funds by investment objectives.

managed funds
Funds that employ professional managers who constantly evaluate and choose securities to buy or sell, using a specific investment approach.

Income Objective

A mutual fund with an **income objective**, such as money market and bond funds, invests in securities that pay regular income in dividends or interest.

Money Market Funds Mutual fund companies and brokerage firms offer **money market funds (MMFs)**. They invest in highly liquid, relatively safe securities with very short maturities (always less than 60 days), such as CDs, government securities, and commercial paper (i.e., short-term obligations issued by corporations). To enhance liquidity, regulations require that MMFs keep 10 percent of their assets in cash or investments that can be converted easily to cash within one day. You can write checks or use an ATM card to access a money market fund account. Issuers keep the NAV (the price of each share of the fund) at $1.

As we discussed in Chapter 5, money market funds (and there are more than 1000 of them) pay a higher rate of return than accounts offered through banks and credit unions. They are considered extremely safe. **Tax-exempt money market funds** limit their investments to tax-exempt municipal securities with maturities of less than 60 days.

tax-exempt money market funds
Funds that limit their investments to tax-exempt municipal securities with maturities of 60 days or less.

government securities money market funds
Funds that appeal to investor concerns about safety by investing solely in U.S. Treasury bills and other short-term securities backed by the U.S. government.

bond funds
Fixed-income funds that aim to earn current income higher than a money market fund without incurring undue risk by investing in a portfolio of bonds and other low-risk investments that pay high dividends and offer capital appreciation.

The earnings are tax free to investors. **Government securities money market funds** appeal to investors' concerns about safety by investing solely in Treasury bills and other short-term securities backed by the U.S. government.

Bond Funds　Bond funds (also called **fixed-income funds**) aim to not incur undue risk while earning current income higher than a money market fund by investing in a portfolio of bonds and other investments, such as preferred stocks and common stocks that pay high dividends. They also earn some capital gains because bond fund prices fluctuate with changing interest rates. Bond funds are categorized by what they own and the maturities of their portfolio holdings.

- **Short-term corporate bond funds** invest in securities maturing in one to five years.
- **Short-term U.S. government bond funds** invest in Treasury issues maturing in one to five years.
- **Intermediate corporate bond funds** invest in investment-grade corporate securities with five- to ten-year maturities.
- **Intermediate government bond funds** invest in Treasuries with five- to ten-year maturities.
- **Long-term corporate bond funds** specialize in investment-grade securities maturing in 10 to 30 years.
- **Long-term U.S. government bond funds** invest in Treasury and zero-coupon bonds with maturities of ten years or longer.
- **Mortgage-backed funds** invest in mortgage-backed securities issued by agencies of the U.S. government, such as Fannie Mae (Federal National Mortgage Association) and Freddie Mac (Federal Home Loan Mortgage Corporation).
- **Junk bond funds** invest in high-yield, high-risk corporate bonds.
- **Municipal bond (tax-exempt) funds** invest in municipal bonds that provide tax-free income. Both investment-grade and high-yield municipal bond funds exist.
- **Single-state municipal bond funds** invest in debt issues of only one state.
- **World bond funds** invest in debt securities offered by foreign corporations and governments.

Growth Objective

A mutual fund that has a growth objective seeks capital appreciation. It invests in the common stock of companies that have above average growth potential, firms that may not pay a regular dividend but have the potential for large capital gains. Growth funds carry a fair amount of risk exposure, and this is reflected in substantial price volatility. Growth funds are categorized by what they own and their investment goals.

aggressive growth funds
Funds that invest in speculative stocks with volatile price swings, seeking the greatest long-term capital appreciation possible. Also known as maximum capital gains funds and capital appreciation funds.

growth funds
Funds that seek long-term capital appreciation by investing in common stocks of companies with higher-than-average revenue and earnings growth, often the larger and well-established firms.

growth and income funds
Funds that invest in companies that have a high likelihood of both dividend income and price appreciation; less risk-oriented than aggressive growth funds or growth funds.

value funds
Funds specializing in stocks that are fundamentally sound whose prices appear to be low (low P/E ratios) based on the logic that such stocks are currently out of favor and undervalued by the market.

　　Aggressive growth funds (also known as **maximum capital gains funds**) seek the greatest long-term capital appreciation. Also known as **capital appreciation funds**, they make investments in speculative stocks with volatile price swings. They may employ high-risk investment techniques, such as borrowing money for leverage, short selling, hedging, and options. Lots of buying and selling occurs to enhance returns.

　　Growth funds seek long-term capital appreciation by investing in the common stocks of companies with higher-than-average revenue and earnings growth, often the larger and well-established firms. Such companies (like Walmart, Microsoft, and Coca-Cola) tend to reinvest most of their earnings to facilitate future growth.

　　Growth and income funds invest in companies that have a high likelihood of both dividend income and price appreciation.

　　Value funds specialize in stocks that are fundamentally sound and whose prices appear to be low (low P/E ratios), based on the logic that such stocks are currently out of favor and undervalued by the market.

　　Large-cap funds invest in the stocks of companies with a market capitalization of more than $10 billion.

　　Midcap funds invest in the stocks of midsize companies with a market capitalization of $2 to $10 billion in size that are expected to grow rapidly.

Small-cap funds (or **small company growth funds**) invest in lesser-known companies with a market capitalization of $300 million to $2 billion in size that offer strong potential for growth.

Microcap funds invest in high-risk companies with a market capitalization of $50 to $300 million.

Sector funds concentrate their investment holdings in one or more industries that make up a targeted part of the economy that is expected to grow, perhaps very rapidly, such as energy, biotechnology, health care, and financial services.

Regional funds invest in securities listed on stock exchanges in a specific region of the world, such as the Pacific Rim, Australia, or Europe.

Precious metals and gold funds invest in securities associated with gold, silver, and other precious metals.

Global funds invest in growth stocks of companies listed on foreign exchanges as well as in the United States, usually multinational firms.

International funds invest only in foreign stocks throughout the world.

Emerging market funds seek out stocks in countries whose economies are small but growing. Fund prices are volatile because these countries tend to be less stable politically.

Growth and Income Objective

A mutual fund that has a combined growth and income objective seeks a balanced return made up of current income and capital gains. Such funds heavily invest in common

DID YOU KNOW?

About Absolute-Return Mutual Funds

An **absolute-return mutual fund** is a new and very complex investment that promises to deliver consistent returns in any market and avoid losses by employing investment management techniques that differ from traditional mutual funds, such as using short selling, futures, options, commodities, derivatives, arbitrage, leverage, and unconventional assets including foreign currencies. Most have the term "absolute return" in their names. Experts argue they are difficult to analyze since they are similar to hedge funds. Many argue that these funds may be promising more than they can deliver.

ADVICE FROM A PRO

Invest Only "Fun Money" Aggressively

Once the investor has his or her financial plan in place, taking on more risk is acceptable—but *only* within the limits of the individual's "fun money." **Fun money** is a sum of investment money that you can afford to lose without doing serious damage to your total portfolio. You might, for example, resolve to trade with a specific sum, such as $5000, or perhaps no more than 2 or 3 percent of your portfolio. Keep such fun money in a separate account from your long-term investments. Decide mentally that if and when the money is gone, it has been spent on an activity that you enjoyed trying, but accept that the money lost is lost forever. In particular, avoid the temptation to "throw good money after bad" in trying to recover your losses.

Speculative investing is not much different from gambling. The biggest danger of fun-money investing is that you might be successful. Success can give you the confidence—albeit perhaps false confidence—that you are a great investor. While you might be the next billionaire investor like Warren Buffett, such success is likely to tempt you to aggressively invest even more of the assets in your total portfolio. That approach can result in disaster.

Investing in aggressive growth mutual funds for some might be a lot of fun, particularly when the amount of money at stake is small. Over time, you will be best served by pursuing a disciplined investing plan with a focus on diversification. As financial columnist Jane Bryant Quinn observes, "The money you really need for life is better off in broadly diversified mutual funds, where a mistake is not forever."

Robert O. Weagley
University of Missouri–Columbia

DID YOU KNOW?

Stable-Value Funds Are Available Only Through Employers

Stable-value funds are available through employer-sponsored retirement plans. This is a different breed of fund. They get their name in part because they buy an insurance policy designed to allow the fund to redeem shares at a stable price regardless of overall market prices. This gives investors some assurance that the fund will be able to maintain the net asset value of the portfolio. Stable-value funds invest in high-

quality, intermediate-term bond funds, including **guaranteed investment contracts (GICs)** offered by insurance companies. A GIC guarantees the owner a fixed or floating interest rate for a predetermined period of time, and the return of principal is guaranteed. Over the past ten years, stable-value funds returned 5.0 percent annually compared to 2.6 percent for money market funds. GIC funds increased in value during the worst of the economic recession while virtually all others declined.

---

stocks. They seek a return not as low as offered by funds with an income objective but not as high as that offered by funds with a growth objective. They invite less risk than growth funds. There are a variety of growth funds.

Growth and income funds invest in companies expected to show average or better growth and pay steady or rising dividends.

Equity-income funds invest in well-known companies with a long history of paying high dividends as they emphasize income and capital preservation.

socially responsible funds
Funds that invest in companies that meet some predefined standard of moral and ethical behavior.

Socially responsible funds invest in companies that meet some predefined standard of moral and ethical behavior. Criteria could be progressive employee relations, strong records of community involvement, an excellent record on environmental issues, respect for human rights, and safe products (as well as no "sinful" products such as tobacco, guns, alcohol, gambling). See www.socialinvest.org for examples. Some of the best performing socially responsible funds are Parnassus Workplace, The Appleseed Fund, Azzard Ethical Mid Cap, Monetta Young Investor, and Ave Maria Opportunity.

balanced funds
Funds that keep a set mix of stocks and bonds, often 60 percent stocks and 40 percent bonds, in order to earn a well-balanced return of income and long-term capital gains.

Balanced funds (or **hybrid funds**) keep a set mix of stocks and bonds, often 60 percent stocks and 40 percent bonds, in order to earn a well-balanced return of income and long-term capital gains.

Blend funds invest in a combination of stocks and money market securities, but no fixed-income securities, such as bonds.

asset allocation funds
Investments in a mix of assets (usually stocks, bonds, and cash equivalents and sometimes international assets, gold, and real estate); they buy and sell regularly to reduce risk while trying to outperform the market.

Asset allocation funds invest in a mix of assets (usually stocks, bonds, and cash equivalents and sometimes international assets, gold, and real estate), and they buy and sell regularly to reduce risk while trying to outperform the market. The asset mix may be based on risk tolerance (aggressive, moderate, and conservative).

target-date retirement funds/ life-cycle funds
Asset allocation funds that offer investors premixed portfolios of stocks, bonds, and cash that investors of a certain age and risk tolerance might prefer, and they are often named for the year one plans to retire.

Target-date retirement funds (life-cycle funds) are asset allocation funds that offer investors premixed portfolios of stocks, bonds, and cash that investors of a certain age and risk tolerance might prefer. They are often named for the year one plans to retire, for example, the "Fidelity Freedom Fund 2030." These are targeted to people in their 30s, 40s, 50s, 60s, and 70s. Target-date funds shift assets from aggressive to moderate to a more conservative mix of securities as the retirement target date approaches. They seek to first grow and then preserve the portfolio assets. This is a no-hassle, "set-it-and-forget-it" approach to investing for retirement. Regulations require target-date funds to provide investors with information that shows the projected allocations over the life of the fund.

Mutual fund funds earn a return by investing in other mutual funds. This provides extensive diversification, but expenses and fees are higher than average.

unmanaged fund
Fund with very low management fees since managers do not evaluate or select individual securities; ETFs and index funds are examples.

An **index fund** is a mutual fund whose investment objective is to achieve the same return as a particular market index by buying and holding all or a representative selection of securities in it. Index funds are called **unmanaged funds** because their managers do not evaluate or select individual securities. An S&P 500 index fund would effectively mirror the companies in the index, which are primarily large-cap U.S. stocks. Annual management fees are extremely low, perhaps only 0.07 to 0.30 percent.

DID YOU KNOW?

ETFs Are Growing in Popularity

ETFs are simply mutual funds that trade on exchanges the way that stocks do. ETFs are growing in popularity in part because Vanguard and some other mutual fund companies have eliminated sales commissions on ETFs. One in four investors has ETFs in their portfolios partly because of the extremely low costs (0.36% annual management fee on average), which are lower than similar mutual funds (0.66% on average). The lowest annual fee of all ETFs (0.07 percent) is Vanguard Total Stock Market ETF (VTSAX), which tracks 3000 stocks, while Schwab's U.S. Broad Market ETF (SCHB) tracks 2500 stocks with an annual fee of 0.08 percent. An **enhanced ETF** is an exchange-traded fund that tracks an index but overinvests in companies with the greatest potential; thus it is an actively managed ETF.

 Concept Check 15.2

1. How can investors use a money market fund?

2. Distinguish among mutual funds with an income objective, growth objective, and growth and income objective, and give two examples of each.

3. Distinguish between asset allocation and target-date funds.

4. Explain why investors like index mutual funds.

MUTUAL FUND INVESTING FEES AND CHARGES

Individuals who invest through mutual funds pay transaction costs that often are less than those associated with buying individual stocks, bonds, and cash equivalent securities. **Shareholder fees** are charged directly to investors for specific transactions, such as purchases, redemptions, or exchanges. **Annual fund operating expenses** are the normal operating costs of the business that are deducted from fund assets before earnings are distributed to shareholders. The fees and charges associated with investing in mutual funds are many, and they can be confusing; some can be avoided.

FINANCIAL POWER POINT

ETFs and Index Funds Have the Lowest Fees

Both index funds and ETFs follow market benchmarks with very low fees (perhaps 0.07 to 0.30), and ETF management fees are usually lower than index funds. Very few individual investors or fund managers will do better than the indexes. Instead of looking for a needle in a haystack, why not buy the haystack?

LEARNING OBJECTIVE

Summarize the fees and charges involved in buying and selling mutual funds.

DID YOU KNOW?

Bond Funds Will Drop in Value

Extremely low interest rates—like those during and following an economic recession—are eventually replaced by rising interest rates because subsequent economic growth typically results in inflation. When interest rates go up, the value of a bond mutual fund decreases. Investors in bond funds actually own hundreds of individual bonds with varying maturity dates; thus, the bonds in a bond mutual fund have an average interest rate and average maturity.

If you own a bond fund and interest rates go up, beware. For every 1 percentage point change in interest rates, the value of the bond fund changes by the amount of the duration of maturity. For example, if a bond fund has an average duration of seven years and interest rates rise 1 percentage point, the value of the bond fund will drop by 7 percent. Should today's low interest rates rise 3 percent over the next few years, the net asset value of a bond mutual fund is likely to decline in value by 21 percent. This is a real possibility.

Load Versus No-Load Funds

All mutual funds are classified as either load or no-load funds. This refers to whether or not they assess a sales charge, or load, when shares are purchased.

Load Funds Always Charge Transaction Fees Funds that levy a sales charge for purchases are called **load funds**. Load funds are generally sold by stock brokerage firms, banks, and financial planners rather than marketed directly to investors by a mutual fund company. The load is the commission used to compensate brokers.

This commission, also called a **front-end load**, typically amounts to 3 to 8.5 percent of the amount invested; this reduces the amount available to purchase fund shares. For example, assume that you and your stockbroker have discussed the investment potential of the Conglomerate Cat and Dog Food Mutual Fund and you decide to invest $10,000. Because this load fund charges a commission of 8.5 percent (the maximum permitted by the SEC), the stockbroker receives $850 ($10,000 × 0.085). As a result, only $9150 of your money is actually available to purchase shares. Such a commission is much higher than stock transaction costs, which are usually 0.25 percent to 2 percent of the security's purchase price.

The sales charge may be shown either as the stated commission or as a percentage of the amount invested. The **stated commission** (8.5 percent in our example) is always somewhat misleading. The percentage of the amount invested is a more accurate figure because it is based on the actual money invested and working. A stated commission of 8.5 percent actually amounts to 9.3 percent of the amount invested: $10,000 − $9150 = $850; $850 ÷ $9150 = 9.3%. If you want to invest a full $10,000 in this load fund, you will need to pay out $10,930 [$10,930 − ($10,930 × 8.5%) = $10,000]. Investments of $10,000 or more often receive a discount on the load.

So-called **low-load funds** may carry a sales charge of perhaps 1 to 3 percent. These funds may also be sold by brokers and are sold via mail and sometimes through mutual fund retailers located in shopping centers. About half of all mutual funds levy a load.

No-Load Funds A no-load fund sells shares at the net asset value without the addition of sales charges. These mutual fund companies let people purchase shares directly from the mutual fund company without the services of a broker, banker, or financial planner. Interested investors simply seek out advertisements for these funds in financial newspapers, magazines, and the Internet and make contact through toll-free telephone numbers, online, or mail. The SEC does allow funds to be called "no-load" even though they assess a service fee of 0.25 percent or less when shares are purchased. Confusing!

Some No-Load Funds Assess 12b-1 Fees A **12b-1 fee** (named for the SEC rule that permits the charge) is an annual charge deducted by the fund company from a fund's assets to compensate underwriters and brokers for fund sales as well as to pay for advertising, marketing, distribution, and promotional costs. A 12b-1 fee is also known as a **distribution fee**. This fee also pays for **trailing commissions**, which is compensation paid to salespeople for months or years in the future. Although the funds do not call 12b-1 fees "loads" because they are not charged up front, they have the same effect as loads—that is, they reduce the investor's return, often dramatically. Over 60 percent of funds assess 12b-1 fees, including some no-load funds.

These **hidden fees** decrease a shareholder's earning power each year without being described as a sales commission. A 12b-1 fee is actually a "perpetual sales load" because it is assessed on the initial investment as well as on reinvested dividends, every year, forever. The SEC caps 12b-1 fees at 0.75 percent, although it also permits a 0.25 percent service fee, which brings the total cap to 1 percent. Some funds stop assessing 12b-1 fees after four to eight years.

Many No-Load Funds Also Assess Deferred Load and Redemption Fees Approximately 60 percent of no-load mutual funds (and many load funds) assess additional fees for transactions, such as deferred load and redemption charges. A **contingent deferred sales charge**, also known as a **back-end load**, is a sales commission that is imposed only when shares are sold. Deferred loads are often on a sliding scale. The fee may decline 1 percentage point for each year the investor owns the fund. For example, a fund might charge a 6 percent fee if an investor redeems the shares within one year of purchase, and then the fee declines on an annual basis, until it reaches zero after six years.

A **redemption charge** (or **exit fee**) is similar to a contingent deferred sales charge, although it is often much lower. A fund assesses such a charge to reduce excessive trading of fund shares. The fee is usually 1 percent of the value of the shares redeemed. It disappears after the investment has been held for six months or a year. Long-term investors should not shy away from funds with redemption fees that disappear after a year.

Mutual Fund Share Classes

A single mutual fund may be available to investors in more than one class of shares: Class A, B, or C. Classes A, B, and C all invest in the same portfolio of securities and have the same investment objectives but have different fee and expense patterns. Class A shares charge a front-end load. Class B shares, which are rarely promoted anymore, are sold on a no-load basis but with a 12b-1 fee and a contingent deferred sales charge. Class C shares also are sold on a no-load basis with a 12b-1 fee but have a redemption charge. Consequently, the performance results for each class will differ depending on how long you hold the shares.

How to Compare Mutual Fund Fees

To compare the costs of various funds and share classes for your expected holding period and estimated returns, see the Financial Industry Regulatory Authority's Mutual Fund Expense Analyzer (http://apps.finra.org/investor_Information/ea/1/mfetf.aspx). This tool estimates the value of the funds and impact of fees and expenses on your investment and also allows you to look up applicable fees and available discounts for thousands of funds.

The SEC requires that mutual funds provide investors with a summary prospectus— in plain English—of information needed to help make investment decisions, and it appears at the front of a fund's full prospectus. It must include a **standardized expense table** that describes and illustrates in an identical manner the effects of all of its fees and other expenses. Look for the fund's **expense ratio**, the expense per dollar of assets under management. Expense ratios average 1.45 percent for diversified stock funds and 0.25 percent for index funds.

What's Best: Load or No Load? Low Fee or High Fee?

The best choice is to invest in no-load mutual funds with low fees. Investors can almost guarantee a poorer return than others if they put their money into a load fund with high management fees. Experts agree that "If you pick your own funds, sales charges and high management fees are a total waste of money."

Sales Commissions Reduce Returns The sales commissions charged by load funds indisputably reduce total returns. When investment results are adjusted to account for the effects of sales charges, no-load mutual funds always have an initial advantage because the investor has more money at work.

12b-1 Fees Kill Long-Term Returns Annual 12b-1 charges are very costly over the long run. If you pay 1 percent per year in 12b-1 fees for a mutual fund in which you invest for ten years, you will be giving up nearly 10 percent of your investment amount in trailing commissions. Yikes!

Avoiding Large Management Fees Is Critical to Investment Success Independent research has found that over five-year periods, lower-cost funds always deliver returns better than those offered by higher-cost funds. Even a small difference in fees can seriously affect long-term returns. For example, a $50,000 portfolio earning an 8 percent annual

---

redemption charge/exit fee
Similar to a deferred load but often much lower; used to reduce excessive trading of fund shares.

standardized expense table
SEC-required information that describes and illustrates mutual fund charges in an identical manner so that investors can accurately compare the effects of all of a fund's fees and other expenses relative to other funds.

expense ratio
Expense per dollar of assets under management.

DID YOU KNOW?

How to Learn More About Mutual Funds

Information on mutual fund investing is vast, and current information about mutual funds is available from numerous sources.

Websites Focusing on Mutual Funds

- Yahoo! Finance (http://finance.yahoo.com/funds)
- The Motley Fool (www.foolfunds.com)
- *Kiplinger's Personal Finance* (www.kiplinger.com/guides/mutualfunds/)
- CNNMoney.com (http://money.cnn.com/pf/funds/index.html)
- BusinessWeek Online (www.businessweek.com/investor/funds.html)
- SmartMoney.com (www.smartmoney.com/investing/mutual-funds/)

Personal Finance Magazines

Kiplinger's Personal Finance, Money, BusinessWeek, Consumer Reports, Forbes, Fortune, and *Worth.* Comprehensive examinations of the performance of numerous mutual funds are fea-tured every year in the late August issue of Forbes, the October issue of *Money,* a late February issue of *BusinessWeek,* and the September issue of *Kiplinger's Personal Finance* magazine.

Financial Press

The Wall Street Journal, Barron's, Investor's Business Daily, and the business sections of newspapers such as *The New York Times* and *USA Today.*

Online News and Quote Services

CompuServe, Dow Jones News/Retrieval-Private Investor Edition, Farcast, Personal Journal, Quote.com, and Reuters Money Network.

Mutual Fund Investment Publications and Websites

Morningstar Mutual Funds, Morningstar No-Load Funds, Mutual Funds Update, Investment Companies Yearbook, IBC/Donoghue's Mutual Funds Almanac, Standard & Poor's, Lipper Mutual Fund Profiles, Moody's, and *The Value Line Mutual Fund Survey.* Dozens of newsletters that specialize in mutual funds are available, too. Morningstar (www.morningstar.com) and the Investment Company Institute (www.ici.org) provide information on thousands of funds. Some charge fees, and others are free.

---

return would grow to $176,182 in 20 years with a 1.5 percent management fee. By comparison, over the same time span, it would grow to $193,484 with a 1.0 percent fee and to $212,393 with a 0.5 percent fee. Over 30 years, the returns with these fee rates would be $330,718, $380,613, and $437,748, respectively. That's nearly a 33 percent greater long-term return for investing in a low-fee fund instead of a fund with high management fees. The positive impact of low management fees on your long-term investment returns are enormous.

 Concept Check 15.3

1. Give three examples of fees and charges associated with load funds.

2. Which is better for most investors, load or no-load funds?

3. Summarize the effects of loads and fees on investment returns.

HOW TO SELECT THE FUNDS IN WHICH YOU SHOULD INVEST

 LEARNING OBJECTIVE **4**

Establish strategies to evaluate and select mutual funds that meet your investment goals.

Selecting mutual funds in which to invest is usually a do-it-yourself effort. A tremendous amount of objective information is available to help potential investors evaluate and select funds. To explain the process of selecting funds, let's follow Jamie Richter's decision making. She is in her late twenties, lives in Sacramento, California, and earns $51,000 annually in her sales management job. Figure 15-4 illustrates the process of selecting mutual fund investments, and Table 15-1 contains performance data for a number of large-cap mutual funds from *Kiplinger's Personal Finance* magazine.

The Process of Selecting Mutual Funds

Figure 15-4

1. Review your investment policy	Conservative
	Moderate
	Aggressive
2. Review your investment goals	Goal
	Time horizon
	Return
	Taxes
3. Eliminate funds inappropriate for your investment goals	Income
	Growth
	Growth and income
	Specific fund types
4. Choose low load or no load	
5. Determine if investment advice is needed	For immediate investments
	For later portfolio review
6. Screen and compare funds that meet your investment criteria	Fund-screening tools
	Fees and charges
	Performance
	Services
7. Monitor your mutual fund portfolio	Portfolio monitoring on the 'Net
	Fund quotations in newspapers

Mutual Fund Performance

Table 15-1

20 Largest Stock Mutual Funds Ranked by Size

Rank/Name	Symbol	Assets† (in billions)	Total return through Jan. 7*			Max. sales charge	Toll-free number
			1 yr.	3 yrs.	5 yrs.		
1. American Gro Fund of America A@	AGTHX	$161.8	10.7%	−1.5%	1.9%	5.75%	800-421-0180
2. Vanguard Total Stck Mkt Idx Inv@	VTSMX	150.7	15.5	−0.1	2.5	none	800-635-1511
3. American EuroPacific Gro A@	AEPGX	109.0	6.6	−2.7	4.4	5.75	800-421-0180
4. Vanguard 500 Index Inv@	VFINX	102.6	13.5	−1.4	1.8	none	800-635-1511
5. American Cptl Wrld Gro & Inc A@	CWGIX	81.3	5.2	−3.9	3.8	5.75	800-421-0180
6. American Cptl Inc Builder A@	CAIBX	79.4	6.9	−2.7	3.8	5.75	800-421-0180
7. Fidelity Contrafund@	FCNTX	75.5	16.3	−0.2	4.3	none	800-544-9797
8. American Inc Fund of America A@	AMECX	68.1	10.8	0.3	3.9	5.75	800-421-0180
9. American Invstmt Co of America A@	AIVSX	62.1	9.2	−1.7	2.0	5.75	800-421-0180
10. Vanguard Emerging Mkts Stock Idx@	VEIEX	59.5	14.5	0.3	10.7	0.25ʳ	800-635-1511
11. Franklin Income A@	FKINX	57.8	11.8	2.7	5.6	4.25	800-632-2301
12. Vanguard Wellington@	VWELX	53.9	9.8	2.2	5.3	none	800-635-1511
13. American Washington Mutual A@	AWSHX	50.9	12.3	−2.2	1.7	5.75	800-421-0180
14. American Balanced A@	ABALX	50.5	11.6	1.5	3.6	5.75	800-421-0180
15. American Fundamental Inv A@	ANCFX	49.8	12.0	−1.7	3.8	5.75	800-421-0180
16. BlackRock Global Allocation A@	MDLOX	48.7	7.8	2.0	6.8	5.25ˢ	800-441-7762
17. American New Perspective A@	ANWPX	46.0	10.7	−0.7	5.0	5.75	800-421-0180
18. Dodge & Cox Intl Stock	DODFX	43.4	9.4	−3.1	3.8	none	800-621-3979
19. Dodge & Cox Stock	DODGX	43.0	11.9	−3.9	−0.3	none	800-621-3979
20. Fidelity Spartan 500 Index Inv@	FUSEX	40.9	13.6	−1.3	1.9	none	800-544-6666
S&P 500 WITH DIVIDENDS			13.6%	−1.3%	1.9%		
MSCI EAFE			5.5%	−5.9%	1.8%		

*Annualized for three and five years.
†For all share classes combined.
@Rankings exclude share classes of this fund with different fee structures or higher minimum initial investments.
ʳMaximum redemption fee.
ˢFront-end sales charge; redemption fee may apply. MSCI EAFE is MSCI's Europe, Australasia, Far East index.
Source: ©2011 Morningstar Inc.

FINANCIAL POWER POINT

Backward or Forward Mutual Fund Ratings

Many investors review Morningstar mutual fund ratings for guidance in selecting funds in which to invest. Five stars indicate the best and one star indicates the worst. (See www.morningstar.com or http://money.cnn.com/.) The star ratings are backward-looking, quantitative measures of past returns that are adjusted for risk, costs, and sales charges. Other fund analysts (*Kiplinger's Personal Finance* magazine, *Money* magazine, *Consumer Reports*, and other investment publications) offer forward-looking, subjective recommendations of funds that they think have the best chance at success.

The returns of mutual funds for the past 5 years illustrate sluggish economic growth and the 2007/2009 meltdown of stock market values. Returns greatly improved over the most recent year shown in the table. Investors should never choose a mutual fund based on the most recent 1-year return, but instead should consider the selection suggestions that follow.

Review Your Investment Philosophy and Investment Goals

Jamie began by reviewing her investment philosophy and financial goals. These topics were examined in Chapter 13. Jamie has a moderate investment philosophy, and she has a written investment plan (Figure 13-6 on page 403). The investment goal she is interested in investing for now is retirement, and her investment time horizon is the next 30 years or more. She anticipates an annual return of at least 7 to 8 percent. She does not care about income taxes because these investments will be made within Jamie's tax-deferred 401(k) retirement plan at work, where her earnings will grow tax free.

Jamie does not have any lump sums available in a savings or money market account to use for investing. To help fund her retirement plans, she decided to have $200 a month withheld from her paycheck to invest in a mutual fund with a growth investment objective. Jamie's employer's 401(k) plan offers about 20 funds as well as company stock.

Eliminate Funds Inappropriate for Your Investment Goals

Jamie began by reviewing all fund classifications (pages 463–467) and balancing the risks and returns of various funds as illustrated in Figure 15-5. She wants to eliminate mutual funds inappropriate for her retirement investment goal.

Figure 15-5   Balancing Risk and Returns on Mutual Funds

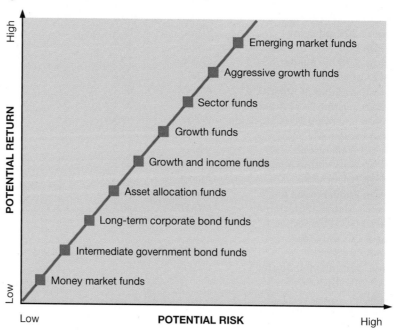

Note that increasing the potential for higher returns also increases the risk to the investor's capital.

DID YOU KNOW?

Turn Bad Habits into Good Ones

Do You Do This?	*Do This Instead!*
Have only a few investments like stocks and bonds	Diversify by investing in mutual funds
Find it difficult to reinvest dividends and interest	Invest in funds that reinvest automatically
Buy load funds or those with high 12b-1 fees	Invest in no-load funds or ETFs
Seem confused about the right funds in which to invest	Use a free online fund-screening tool
Find it difficult to monitor your investments	Manage your fund portfolio free online

Jamie recognizes that increasing the potential for higher returns also increases the risk to the investor's capital. Therefore, she eliminated the following types of funds: sector funds, emerging markets funds, and aggressive growth funds, as well as stock in the company where she works. She also realizes that investing too conservatively invites the risk of failure to achieve her goal of a financially successful retirement. Therefore, Jamie eliminated money market funds.

Create a Portfolio of Funds in Which to Invest

Instead of simply investing in "this and that" funds, Jamie smartly decided to create a portfolio of mutual funds tailored to her needs. At www.kiplinger.com/tools/investment-portfolio-finder/index.html she found 22 portfolios recommended by *Kiplinger's Personal Finance* editors and writers. They are customized for different situations and stages of life. On that website, she can get updated returns and track the performance of her investments with the benchmark portfolios.

Choose No-Load Funds with Low Management Fees

The sales commissions charged by load funds indisputably reduce total returns. Jamie reasoned that since no-load mutual funds have an initial advantage—the investor has more money at work—she preferred no-load funds. Because her $200 a month was going into investment for retirement, she also thought that 12b-1 fees would be very costly over the long term. For the same reason, she wanted to avoid high management fees. She did not care about back-end loads and exit fees, as these largely disappear over time. Jamie decided to invest in one or more no-load mutual funds with no or low 12b-1 fees and very low management expense ratios. Jamie will have to look up some of this information on the Internet since data in Table 15.1 is limited.

DID YOU KNOW?

Sean's Success Story

Sean's superb financial life continues. He increased his 401(k) contributions from 6 to 8 percent so the $90,000 in mutual funds in the account will total over $100,000 by December. That figure will be a milestone for Sean's retirement planning. While the return on his mutual fund portfolio was only 2 percent between 2007 and 2009, it did not decline and it went up over 10 percent in both 2010 and 2011. Furthermore, Sean figures that the stock market is bound to go up again as the economy grows and unemployment declines; therefore, he has decided to move his investments completely into stock mutual funds between January and March of next year. Sean figures that the market will continue to improve, so it will be best for him to soon be fully invested for the future.

Obtain Investment Information and Advice

Because Jamie is going to invest in no-load funds, she figured she did not need the services of a broker or financial adviser. Instead, she plans to use the tremendous resources that are available via the Vanguard website (www.vanguard.com)—information, education, and professional advice. Vanguard is the largest mutual fund in the country. Jamie's employer offers investing and retirement planning seminars and workshops provided by Ernst & Young, Vanguard, T. Rowe Price, and other companies. Significant others are welcome to attend. Employer-sponsored financial advice may cover an employee's entire financial situation, including debt reduction, college planning, spousal assets, real estate, and other investments. Once Jamie's retirement assets build up to a substantial amount, perhaps $50,000 or more, she might be wise to seek additional professional expert financial advice.

Jamie's employer offers retirement plan participants access to services that automatically rebalance their retirement assets known as a **limited management account**. For an annual fee of ½ of 1 percent of her retirement assets, the firm sells and buys her mutual fund assets on a quarterly basis to rebalance her portfolio back to her specific standards. A recent study found that of those employees who took advantage of limited management account guidance, the median annual return was almost two points higher than those who did not accept such help.

Screen, Compare, and Select Funds That Meet Your Criteria

When comparing the track records of mutual funds, there are a number of criteria to consider. These may include expenses; net asset value; minimum initial purchase; size of fund; ratings; past performance (perhaps one, three, five, and ten years); best and worst performance in up and down markets (volatility); fund manager tenure; and services. Jamie is interested in stock funds, international funds and global funds, low management fees, and no or low 12b-1 fees.

Jamie started searching for mutual fund investments at Vanguard (https://personal.vanguard.com/us/FundsMFSIntro?%20FROM=VAN), which is considered one of the best mutual fund selection websites, and she began by typing in the fund symbols in "search." A **fund screener** or **fund-screening tool** permits an individual to screen all of the mutual funds in the market. Other mutual fund screening tools are available at the following websites:

- Yahoo! Finance (http://finance.yahoo.com/funds)
- Kiplinger.com (www.kiplinger.com/tools/fundfinder/fundsearch.php)
- Fidelity (http://personal.fidelity.com/products/funds/mutual_funds_overview.shtml.cvsr)

---

limited management account

An account at an investment firm whereby, for a fee, they sell and buy your mutual fund assets, usually quarterly, on your behalf to automatically rebalance your portfolio back to your specific standards.

FINANCIAL POWER POINT

What to Look for When Investing in an Actively Managed Stock Mutual Fund

If you want to invest in an actively managed stock fund, screen for those with experienced managers (a decade or more of leadership), low annual expenses (below 1 percent a year), and a low annual turnover rate (since the average fund replaces nearly 100 percent of its stocks annually, eliminate funds with 25 percent or more turnover). You can run a screen at Morningstar.com.

---

fund screener/fund-screening tool

Permits investors to screen all of the mutual funds in the market to gauge performance.

DID YOU KNOW?

About Mutual Fund Volatility Ratings

Volatility characterizes a mutual fund's (or any security's) tendency to rise or fall in price over a period of time. A measure of volatility is the **standard deviation**, which gauges the degree to which a security's historical return rises above or falls below its own long-term average return—and therefore may be likely to do so again in the future. A standard deviation is a probability indicator, not an economic forecast. The bigger an investment's standard deviation, the more volatile its price may be in the future. High volatility suggests greater long-term rewards but a greater-than-normal risk of short-term losses during economic downturns. Other common measures of risk are beta, the Sharpe Ratio, and R-squared. Publications like *Kiplinger's Personal Finance* magazine, *Money*, *Morningstar*, and *U.S. News & World Report* provide volatility ratings for mutual funds.

DID YOU KNOW?

The Tax Consequences of Mutual Fund Investing

Ordinary income dividend distributions, capital gains distributions, and realized gains from the sale of mutual funds are generally subject to taxation.

- In regular investment accounts:

    - When you buy and hold mutual fund shares, you owe income taxes on any ordinary income dividends and on the fund's capital gains in the year you receive or reinvest them.

    - When you sell shares, you owe taxes on the capital gains earned on the difference between what you paid for the shares and the selling price (less transaction costs).

- Before purchasing a mutual fund toward the end of the year, like in December, determine whether the fund has already made its end-of-year capital gains distribution. If you buy the fund before the **record date** (the date established by an issuer to determine who is eligible to receive a dividend or distribution), you will receive the income but you also will owe capital gains taxes for the whole year. Buying after the record date avoids that tax because you will not receive the distribution.

- Interest from a tax-exempt municipal bond fund is exempt from federal income taxes.

- In retirement accounts (such as a 401[k] or traditional IRA account), taxes are deferred until withdrawn.

Jamie focused on large-cap funds, including those shown in Table 15-1. She researched funds using the Vanguard fund screener. She obtained online a profile prospectus from Vanguard on each of the funds she liked. A **profile prospectus** (or **fund profile**) describes the mutual fund, its investment objectives, and how it tries to achieve its objectives. Written in lay language, it offers a two- to four-page summary presentation of information contained in an SEC-required legal prospectus that answers 11 key investor questions, including risks, fees, and details about the fund's ten-year performance record.

profile prospectus/fund profile
Publication that describes the mutual fund, its investment objectives, and how it tries to achieve its objectives in lay terms rather than the legal language used in a regular prospectus.

After reading fund details, looking at the numbers, and comparing performance, Jamie decided to split her monthly $200 investment between Vanguard Total Stock Market Index (VTSMX) and Vanguard Emerging Markets Stock Index (VEIEX), partly because of their low to nil expense ratios. (In addition, any minimum initial investment fees are waived for investments via her employer's retirement plan.) Jamie thinks the fund managers will beat the average market returns, such as a S&P 500 index like Vanguard's 500 Index (VFINX). Jamie might be right, or she might be wrong.

The next step is for Jamie to contact the human resources department at her employer and sign the documents to withhold $200 a month from her paycheck and invest $100 into each of the two funds. Jamie also knows that for every dollar invested, she gets an immediate 50 percent return because her employer's policy is to match 401(k) contributions 50 cents on the dollar for the first 6 percent of earnings. Jamie's 401(k) balance in 12 months, therefore, will show $2400 in contributions and $1200 in employer matching contributions (that's an immediate 50 percent return on her $2400!), plus whatever gain occurs (hopefully not a loss) in NAV. Jamie's 401(k) balance next year is likely to be more than $3600. Chapter 17 examines retirement planning.

Monitor Your Portfolio of Mutual Fund Investments

Tracking your portfolio is imperative because investors do not want to keep an underperforming mutual fund in their portfolio

It is easy to research mutual funds on the Internet.

©iStockphoto.com/Sportstock

DID YOU KNOW?

Your Worst Financial Blunders in Investing Through Mutual Funds

Based on others' financial woes, you will make mistakes in personal finance when you:

1. *Buy funds with high fees and expenses.*

2. *Withdraw dividends rather than reinvesting.*

3. *Chase performance by investing in "hot" funds.*

for very long, assuming other similar funds are doing better. Detailed records are also useful when preparing income tax returns. If Jamie wants to invest outside of her 401(k) plan in the same or other no-load funds, she can purchase funds directly from mutual fund investment companies, such as family fund companies like Fidelity, T. Rowe Price, or any other mutual fund, like Gabelli, Neuberger, or Calvert.

Use Portfolio Monitoring on the Internet Monitoring a mutual fund portfolio is easy using any of the top-rated mutual fund websites cited earlier. For example, see Yahoo!'s portfolio manager capabilities at http://finance.yahoo.com/funds/monitoring_funds.

Check Fund Quotations in Newspapers You can check closing prices online any time on any of the financial websites cited earlier or read quotes in newspapers. See Figure 15-6 for an illustration. Newspapers' quotations for no-load mutual funds list the name of the fund followed by columns for its net asset value, net change from the previous day, and year-to-date percentage return. For example, within the group listing for Fidelity Investments mutual funds, the Balanced Fund (abbreviated as Balanc) has a net asset value (NAV) of $15.14, a change in the net asset value (NET CHG) of –$0.20 from the closing price of the previous trading day, and a year-to-date percentage return (YTD %RET) of 1.1 percent.

mutual fund bid price

Shareholders receive this amount per share when they redeem their shares, which is the same dollar amount as the NAV.

MUTUAL FUND BID PRICE In mutual funds, the NAV is also known as the **mutual fund bid price**. Shareholders receive this amount per share when they redeem their shares—that is, the company is willing to pay this amount to buy the shares back. Also, the NAV is the amount per share an investor will pay to purchase a fund, assuming it is a no-load fund. A no-load fund is indicated as such by the alphabetic letter n at the end of the fund's name.

mutual fund ask (or offer) price

Price at which an investor can purchase a mutual fund's shares; current NAV per share plus sales charges.

MUTUAL FUND ASK PRICE The **mutual fund ask price** (or **offer price**) is the price at which a mutual fund's share can be purchased by investors. It equals the current NAV per share plus sales charges, if any. If you wanted to buy or sell shares of Fidelity Balanced Fund, a no-load (note the superscript n in Figure 15-6) mutual fund, the price

Figure 15-6

How Mutual Funds Are Quoted

NAME	NAV	NET CHG	YTD %RET
Fidelity Invest			
Balanc^n	15.14	– 0.20	+ 1.1
Contra	43.67	– 0.45	– 11.2
MidCap^n	23.86	– 0.49	– 8.1
MagIn	107.84	– 2.46	– 8.9

Fidelity Invest

A Mgr	15.83	–0.24 – 4.3	Govtinc	9.82	+0.02 + 2.5
AggrGr r	22.68	–0.76 – 37.1	GroCo	55.13	–1.97 – 22.6
AggrInt	11.60	–0.15 – 12.8	GroInc	38.56	–0.69 – 7.9
AMgrAggr	11.73	–0.35 – 10.0	GroIncII	9.33	–0.18 – 8.7
AMgrGr	14.83	–0.29 – 6.8	HighInc r	8.81	–0.01 – 2.5
AMgrIn	11.38x	–0.11 – 0.4	Independnc	16.46	–0.60 – 25.0
Balanc	15.14	–0.20 + 1.1	IntBd	10.16	+0.02 – 4.4
BluCh	44.52	–1.34 – 13.6	IntGov	9.66	+0.02 + 3.6
Canad r	19.30	–0.21 – 8.2	IntGr	19.31	–0.26 – 15.0
CapAp	21.53	–0.57 – 3.1	IntlBnd	7.83	+0.04 – 4.2
ChinaReg	13.61	–0.08 – 7.4	InvGB	7.20	+0.01 + 3.7
Colnc r	7.35	–0.04 – 1.3	Japan r	11.86	–0.21 – 13.7
		–5.55 – 7.6	JpnSmCo r	7.64	–0.09 – 4.3
		–0.45 – 11.2	LargeCap	15.56	–0.41 – 12.3
		–0.28 – 5.2	LatinAm r	12.62	–0.13 – 3.4
		–0.29 – 0.5	LevCoSt	10.56	–0.15 + 4.9
		–0.35 – 12.1	LowP r	26.61	–0.29 + 15.1
		–0.29 – 5.2	MagIn	107.84	–2.46 – 8.9
		–0.39 – 11.2	MidCap	23.86	–0.49 – 8.1
		–0.68 – 3.9	MtgSec	10.78	+0.02 + 3.5
		–0.15 – 11.7	NewMkt r	11.38	–0.04 + 4.9
		–0.09 – 4.5	NewMill	27.27	–1.25 – 19.2
		–0.86 – 2.8	Nordic	19.60	–0.12 – 25.0
		–0.47 – 4.9	OTC	32.41	–1.42 – 21.0
		–0.21 – 18.8	Ovrse	29.16	–0.57 – 15.2
		–0.13 – 15.0	PcBas r	15.37	–0.27 – 11.1
		–4.03 – 8.2	Puritn	18.38	–0.19 – 0.9
		–0.33 – 1.2	RealE	19.49	–0.05 + 8.3
		–1.02 – 7.6	STBF	8.74	+0.02 + 4.4
		–0.06 – 10.3	SmallCap r	13.54	–0.20 + 0.2
		–0.40 – 8.4	SmCapSlc	15.06	–0.25 – 7.2
GNMA	10.79	+0.01 + 3.7	SE Asia r	10.68	–0.10 – 6.6
GloBal	15.90	–0.16 – 8.8	StratInc	9.13	+0.01 + 3.2

would be $15.14 per share. The funds listed without an *n* are load funds. The SEC requires that appropriate footnotes appear in newspaper listings of mutual funds to indicate other expenses and charges.

 Concept Check 15.4

1. Explain why it is important to review your investment philosophy and goals when selecting mutual fund investments.

2. Explain how you would eliminate funds inappropriate for your investment goals, given your situation and assuming you are working full time.

DO IT NOW!

You know more about personal finance after reading this chapter, so get started right now by:

1. *Identifying five services provided by mutual funds (see pages 460–463) that appeal to you.*

2. *Identifying three of your long-term financial goals and determining whether you would seek a fund with a growth objective or growth and income objective for each goal.*

3. *Selecting one mutual fund from those listed in Table 15-1 on page 471 to follow for one or two months, then reassessing your selection if warranted.*

WHAT DO YOU RECOMMEND NOW?

Now that you have read the chapter on mutual funds, what do you recommend to David and Sarah Gent in the case at the beginning of the chapter regarding:

1. Redeeming their CDs and investing their retirement money in mutual funds?

2. Investing in growth and income mutual funds instead of income funds?

3. Buying no-load rather than load funds?

4. Buying target-date mutual funds instead of balanced mutual funds?

5. Buying mutual funds through their employers' 401(k) retirement accounts, rather than saving through a taxable account as they have been doing?

© istockphoto.com/gchutka

BIG PICTURE SUMMARY OF LEARNING OBJECTIVES

LO1. Describe the features, services, and advantages of investing in mutual funds.

A mutual fund is an investment company that pools funds obtained by selling shares to investors and makes investments to achieve the financial goal of income or growth, or both. The net asset value (NAV) is the per-share value of the fund. Advantages of mutual funds include diversification, affordability, and professional management. Unique services include ease of buying and selling, check writing, and effortless establishment of retirement plans.

LO2. Differentiate mutual funds by investment objectives.

A mutual fund with an income objective invests in securities that pay regular income in dividends or interest. A fund that has a growth objective seeks capital appreciation. A fund that has a combined growth and income objective seeks a balanced return made up of current income and capital gains. The name of a fund, such as aggressive growth fund, gives a clue to its objectives. Index funds and ETFs are popular because they earn the same return as a particular market index.

LO3.   Summarize the fees and charges involved in buying and selling mutual funds.
Individuals who invest through mutual funds pay shareholder fees for specific transactions, such as purchases, redemptions, or exchanges. They also pay annual fund operating expenses that are deducted from fund assets before earnings are distributed to shareholders. Investors may be faced with load and

no-load funds, 12b-1 fees, and deferred load and redemption fees.

LO4.   Establish strategies to evaluate and select mutual funds that meet your investment goals.
The process of selecting mutual funds in which to invest is usually a do-it-yourself effort. The steps are (1) review investment philosophy, (2) review investment goals, (3) create a portfolio of funds in which to invest, (4) eliminate funds inappropriate for your investment goals, (5) choose no-load funds with low management fees, (6) obtain investment information and advice, (7) screen and compare funds that meet your investment criteria, and (8) monitor your mutual fund portfolio.

LET'S TALK ABOUT IT

1.   **Investing in Tough Economic Times.** Comment on this statement: "A great time to invest is during times of economic turmoil when assets are undervalued."

2.   **One Fund of Interest.** Review the objectives of mutual funds and the characteristics of various funds. Based on your investment philosophy and risk tolerance, which one type of fund would be of most interest to you if you were saving to buy a home several years from now? Give reasons why.

3.   **Two Funds.** Assume you graduated from college a few years ago, have a good job paying $55,000 annually, and want to invest $300 per month in mutual funds for retirement. Which combination of two or more mutual funds (see pages 463 to 467) would you think appropriate? Give reasons for each of your selections.

4.   **Spread Your Money into Funds.** Assume that your uncle gave you $50,000 to invest solely in mutual funds. Based on your point in the life cycle and your investment philosophy, identify your investment goals and explain how you would spread your money among different funds. (See pages 463–467.)

5.   **Good Choices.** Identify the types of mutual funds that would be good choices to meet the following investment objectives: emergency fund, house down payment, college fund for 2-year-old child, and retirement fund for a 25-year-old. (See pages 463 to 467.) Give two reasons why each of your recommendations would be appropriate.

6.   **Load or No-Load.** Which is a better choice for you, load or no-load mutual funds? Give some reasons.

DO THE MATH

1.   **Profits and Taxes.** Ten months ago, George Jetson, from Nacogdoches, Texas, invested $1000 by buying 100 shares of the Can't Lose Mutual Fund, an aggressive growth no-load mutual fund. George reinvested his dividends, so he now has 112 shares. So far, the NAV for George's investment has risen from $10 per share to $13.25.

     (a)   What is the percentage increase in the NAV of George's mutual fund?

     (b)   If George redeemed the first 100 shares of his mutual fund investment for $13.25 per share, what would be his capital gain over the amount invested?

     (c)   Assuming George pays income taxes at the 25 percent rate, how much income tax will he have to pay if he sells those first 100 shares?

2.   **Mutual Fund Sales.** Two years ago, Stephanie Johnason, from Berkeley, California, invested $1000 by buying 125 shares ($8 per share NAV) in the Can't Lose Mutual Fund, an aggressive growth no-load mutual fund. Last year, she made two additional investments of $500 each (50 shares at $10 and 40 shares at $12.50). Stephanie reinvested all of her dividends. So far, the NAV for her investment has risen from $8 per share to $13.25. Late in the year, she sold 60 shares at $13.25.

     (a)   What were the proceeds from Stephanie's sale of the 60 shares?

     (b)   To use the Internal Revenue Service's average-cost basis method of determining the average price paid for one share, begin by calculating the average price paid for the shares. In this instance, the $2000 is divided by 215 shares (125 shares +

50 shares + 40 shares). What was the average price paid by Stephanie?

(c) To finally determine the average-cost basis of shares sold, you multiply the average price per share times the number of shares sold—in this

case, 60. What is the total cost basis for Stephanie's 60 shares?

(d) Assuming that Stephanie has to pay income taxes on the difference between the sales price for the 60 shares and their cost, how much is this difference?

FINANCIAL PLANNING CASES

CASE 1

The Johnsons Decide to Invest Through Mutual Funds

After learning about mutual funds, the Johnsons are confident that they are a great way to invest, especially because of the diversification and professional management that funds offer. The couple has a financial nest egg of $9500 to invest through mutual funds. They also want to invest another $300 per month on a regular basis.

Although not yet completely firm, Harry and Belinda's goals at this point are as follows:

• They want to continue to build their retirement income to retire in about 36 years.

• They will need about $10,000 in six to eight years to use as supplemental income if Belinda has a baby and does not work for six months.

• They might buy a luxury automobile requiring a $10,000 down payment if they decide not to have a child.

Knowing that the Johnsons have a moderate investment philosophy, that they live on a reasonable budget, and that they have a well-established cash-management plan, advise them on their mutual fund investments by responding to the following questions:

(a) Some comparable mutual fund performance data on stock funds are shown in Table 15-1. Using only that information and assuming that you are recommending some funds for the Johnsons' retirement needs, which two funds would you recommend? Why?

(b) How would you divide the $9500 between the two stock funds? Why?

(c) How much of the $300 monthly investment amount would you allocate to each of the stock funds? Why?

(d) Assume that both funds increase in value over the next ten years. Another bear market then occurs, causing the NAVs to drop 25 percent

from the previous year. Would you recommend that the Johnsons sell their accumulated shares in the funds? Why or why not?

(e) Determine the value of the shares purchased with their $9500 original investment in ten years, assuming that the two funds' NAVs increase 8 percent annually for the ten years. (Hint: Use Appendix A.1 or the *Garman/Forgue* companion website.)

CASE 2

Victor and Maria Invest for Retirement

Victor and Maria Hernandez plan to retire in less than 15 years. Their current investment portfolio is distributed as follows: 40 percent in growth mutual funds, 40 percent in corporate bonds and bond mutual funds, and 20 percent in cash equivalents. They have decided to increase the amount of risk in their portfolio by taking 10 percent from their cash equivalent investments and investing in some mutual funds with strong growth possibilities.

(a) Of the stock mutual funds listed in Table 15-1, which two would you recommend to meet the Hernandezes' goals? Why?

(b) Would you recommend that the Hernandezes remain invested in those two funds during their retirement years? Why or why not?

CASE 3

Julia Price Is Going to Invest Big in Mutual Funds

It has been over 25 years since Julia graduated with a major in aeronautical engineering, and she has been quite successful in her career as well as in managing her personal finances. She has moved up the career ladder, earns a high salary, has $50,000 in equity in her condo, and has an investment portfolio valued at $300,000 that includes $200,000 in retirement assets through her employer's 401(k) plan. She wants to liquidate the entire $300,000 now invested in stocks, bonds, and gold into mutual funds. Julia is optimistic about the future of investing. After serious research, Julia has decided to invest $300,000 into ETFs and index mutual funds rather than actively managed funds. Offer your opinions about her thinking.

CASE 4

Matching Mutual Fund Investments to Economic Projections

Glenn Wickler, an automobile salesperson for the past ten years in Reno, Nevada, is divorced and contributes to the support of his two children. He is interested in investing in mutual funds. Glenn wants to put $20,000 of accumulated savings into a stock index mutual fund and then continue to invest $200 monthly for the foreseeable future, perhaps using the money for retirement starting in about 25 years. Glenn has limited his choices solely to the four mutual funds listed in Table 15-1.

(a)   In Table 15-1, note that there are two index funds based on the S&P 500 Index. Suggest a reason why Glenn should invest in one or the other, noting that the returns for the Vanguard 500 Index Fund slightly exceeded the Fidelity Spartan Index Fund.

(b)   Given that Glenn plans to invest $2400 annually for the next 25 years, which of the other two index funds (Vanguard Total Stock Market

Index Fund or Vanguard Emerging Markets Stock Fund) would you recommend, and why?

CASE 5

Selection of a Mutual Fund as Part of a Retirement Plan

Etta Mae Westbrook, a single mother of a 6-year-old child, works for a utility company in Chestertown, Maryland, and is willing to invest $3000 per year in a mutual fund. She wants the investment income to supplement her retirement pension starting in approximately 30 years, and she has a moderate investment philosophy. Etta is concerned about not investing too conservatively because she expects to live a long life, given that her eldest relatives lived well into their 80s and early 90s. Advise Etta Mae by responding to the following questions:

(a)   If Etta invests $3000 annually into two growth mutual funds, which two types would you recommend and why? See the list on page 465.

(b)   Alternatively, if Etta invests $3000 annually into two growth and income funds, which two would you recommend and why? See the list on pages 466–467.

(c)   Summarize why these four types of mutual funds might be suitable for Etta.

BE YOUR OWN PERSONAL FINANCIAL MANAGER

1.   **Your Mutual Fund Preferences.** Review the section "Mutual Fund Objectives" and then complete Worksheet 61: My Mutual Fund Preferences from "My Personal Financial Planner." For each of the types of mutual funds listed, identify which are of interest to you and one characteristic you like about them, and note those in which you might invest during your own investing life.

2.   **Comparing Mutual Fund Investments.** Learn about three stock mutual funds that might be of interest to you, such as Vanguard Target Retirement 2055 Fund (VFFVX), Vanguard Target Retirement 2050 Fund (VFIFX), and Spartan 500 Index – Investor Class (FUSEX), by going online. Then complete Worksheet 62: Comparing Mutual Funds as Investments from "My Personal Financial Planner" by recording the facts requested.

3.   **Calculating Mutual Fund Returns.** Use the information for the exercises immediately above and complete Worksheet 63: Calculating the Return on Mutual Fund Investments from "My Personal Financial Planner," which will help you determine the return from income and capital gains after you make some assumptions, such as a 5-year holding period and the like.

4.   **Evaluating My Investment Returns.** Complete Worksheet 64: Evaluating the Performance (Gain or Loss) of My Investments from "My Personal Financial Planner" using one example for which you make the assumptions. Perhaps you can use the Spartan 500 Index – Investor Class (FUSEX) in which you invested $3000 two years ago for $6.50 and its present price of $8.25.

ON THE 'NET

Go to the Web indicated to complete these exercises.

1.   **Which ETFs for You?** Visit the website for Vanguard Investments and read its section on exchange-traded funds (ETFs) (https://personal.vanguard.com/us/whatweoffer/etfs). Summarize why you think ETFs might or might not be a good investment for you.

2.   **Mutual Fund Information.** Visit the website for CNNMoney. Go to the page titled "What Is a Mutual Fund" at http://money.cnn.com/retirement/guide/investing_mutualfunds.moneymag/index.htm. Review the dozen or so short articles and compare what you read there with what you read in this chapter. List two things that are new to your understanding.

3.   **FINRA on Mutual Funds.** Visit the website for the Financial Industry Regulatory Authority (FINRA) at www.finra.org/Investors/SmartInvesting/ChoosingInvestments/MutualFunds/, where you will find a section titled "Choosing Investments: Mutual Funds." Review the several paragraphs there and compare what you read with what you read in this chapter. List two things that are new to your understanding.

ACTION INVOLVEMENT PROJECTS

1.   **Compare Socially Responsible Mutual Funds.** Go to the website of the Social Investment Forum and review the performance of several socially responsible mutual funds listed there (www.socialinvest.org/resources/mfpc). Summarize your thoughts on the investment returns of these types of funds.

2.   **Review Some Mutual Fund Portfolios.** Go to Kiplinger's portfolio builder at www.kiplinger.com/tools/investment-portfolio-finder/index.html and click on three of the illustrative portfolios that might fit your needs. Summarize your findings.

3.   **Using a Fund Screener.** Go to the fund screener of Yahoo! Finance (http://finance.yahoo.com/funds) and look up three funds of interest to you, perhaps using some of the names of funds you found in the exercise immediately above. Summarize your findings.

4.   **Monitoring a Mutual Fund Portfolio.** Go to Yahoo!'s portfolio manager website at http://finance.yahoo.com/funds/monitoring_funds and watch the video on portfolios. Also read the three short tutorial articles there. Describe your conclusions on using their portfolio manager system.

Visit the Garman/Forgue companion website at **www.cengagebrain.com**.

Real Estate and High-Risk Investments

YOU MUST BE KIDDING, RIGHT?

Friends Richard Belisle and Dave Sanders both have aggressive investment philosophies. Richard invests primarily in residential real estate, and Dave invests in commodities futures contracts. As longtime investors, they consider themselves experts, but occasionally, each has experienced financial losses. What are the odds that the typical investor will make money investing in commodities futures contracts?

A. 50%

B. 30%

C. 20%

D. 10%

The answer is D. Ninety percent of individual investors in futures contracts lose money. Funds used for these investments should be only those that one can afford to lose!

LEARNING OBJECTIVES

After reading this chapter, you should be able to:

1 Demonstrate how you can make money investing in real estate.

2 Recognize how to take advantage of beneficial tax treatments in real estate investing.

3 Calculate the right price to pay for real estate and how to finance your purchase.

4 Assess the disadvantages of investing in real estate.

5 Summarize the risks and challenges of investing in collectibles, precious metals, and gems.

6 Explain why options and futures are high-risk investments.

© PETER DAZELEY/GETTY IMAGES, INC.

WHAT DO YOU RECOMMEND?

Jamie Day, a 37-year-old marketing manager for a large corporation in Long Beach, California, earns $110,000 per year. She saves about $800 each month beyond her contributions to her employer's 401(k) retirement plan. Her total 401(k) holdings are worth $260,000.

Ever since her grandfather gave her some stocks as a child, Jamie has loved investing—and she has enjoyed a good track record with her efforts. Jamie is an active trader, often trading every three or four weeks, primarily in the oil, technology, and prescription drug industries. Every year, she has some losses as well as gains. Her private portfolio is currently worth $160,000. Jamie has never bought or sold options or futures contracts, but her stockbroker suggested that she consider them. Jamie also has a friend who owns several residential rental properties who has asked her to consider investing as her partner in her next real estate venture.

What do you recommend to Jamie on the subject of real estate and high-risk investments regarding:

1. Investing in real estate?

2. Putting some of her money in a high-risk investment, like collectibles or gold?

3. Investing in options and futures contracts?

real estate (or housing) bubble
Rapid and unsustainable increases in home prices followed by sharp declines in values.

high-risk/speculative investments
Present potential for significant fluctuations in return, sometimes over short time periods.

 LEARNING OBJECTIVE 1

Demonstrate how you can make money investing in real estate.

real estate
Property consisting of land, all structures permanently attached to that land, and accompanying rights and privileges, such as crops and mineral rights.

direct ownership
Results when investor holds the actual legal title to property.

A home tends to accomplish more than just putting a roof over your head. It is also an investment, because historically housing values have increased over the long term. A **real estate** (or **housing**) **bubble** for residential markets occurred in the United States between 2005 and 2007. The bubble saw rapid increases in home valuations until they were unsustainable. The real estate market crashed, and it has yet to recover! Home values plummeted 20, 40, or 50 percent or even more in some communities. The "for sale" prices on millions of foreclosed homes simultaneously pulled down the values of other homes. About 25 percent of all mortgage holders—11 to 15 million homeowners—owe more on their homes than they are worth. The results are that: (1) many people own homes that have declined in value, and (2) buying opportunities exist for new homeowners because prices are lower. Real estate today remains an investment option that is definitely riskier than in the past but nevertheless is one that can pay ample returns.

Investors who seek high returns and are willing to accept greater risks might consider owning tangible assets such as collectibles, precious metals, and gems for their investment potential. Another alternative is options and futures contracts. All these are referred to as **high-risk (speculative) investments** because they have the potential for significant fluctuations in return, sometimes over short time periods. They are suitable only for investors with an aggressive investment philosophy.

HOW TO MAKE MONEY INVESTING IN REAL ESTATE

Real estate investing is not the same as buying a home in which to live, which was the subject of Chapter 9. Investing in real estate can provide you with extra income now and give a boost to your future retirement plans. But you have to do a lot of things right. Real estate investing is not rocket science, but investors must be smart about taxes, financing, insurance, and community economics. Dealing with tenants requires a business attitude, not a willingness to view tenants as friends. Real estate investments are complex, and they are much riskier than investing in mutual funds and stocks.

Real estate is property consisting of land, all structures permanently attached to that land, and accompanying rights and privileges, such as crops and mineral rights. A real estate investment is termed **direct ownership** when an investor holds actual legal title to the property. For example, you can invest directly as an individual or jointly with other investors to buy properties designed for residential living, such as houses, duplexes, apartments, mobile homes, and condominiums. You also could invest in commercial properties designed for business uses, such as office buildings, medical centers, gas stations, and motels. You might buy raw land or residential lots, although they are extremely risky and often lose money for the investor.

Question 1: Can You Make Current Income While You Own?

The most important consideration for real estate investors in today's real estate market is not whether the price will rise enough in a few years to make a profit. The boom days of the housing bubble are gone! The focus for real estate investors now is whether the rental income will be sufficient to make ends meet while waiting for the property to increase in value.

If you invest in a property and you are paying out more than the rental income coming in, besides having a negative cash flow on the investment, you face two risks: (1) whether you can afford to continue paying out that money month after month and year after year, and (2) whether you can make up for these cash flow losses when the property sells, which you hope will be for more than you paid for it. Get either of these wrong, and you lose your invested money and maybe more.

Know the Price-to-Rent Ratio To measure the current income in a real estate market, investors can begin by using the **price-to-rent ratio**, which is the ratio of median residential real estate prices to the median annual rents that can be earned from the real estate. It measures what you can earn by owning the asset relative to what you pay for it. Nationally the price-to-rent ratio was 15 at the peak of the housing bubble; now it is 11. The ratio ranges from 7 to 35 depending on local market conditions—meaning how high housing prices are. For investors, the lower the price-to-rent ratio is in a given community and a particular property, the easier it should be to earn back your investment. For example, in San Jose, California, a condominium renting for $2600 a month might sell for the high price of $890,000 for a price-to-rent ratio of 28.5 (12 × $2600 = $31,200; $890,000/$31,200).

Price-to-rent ratio = Home price/annual rent

28.5 = ($890,000/$31,200 [$2,600 monthly rent × 12]) **(16.1)**

Alternatively, a home in Pittsburgh, Pennsylvania, might cost $165,000 and rent for $1200 a month, thus providing a price-to-rent ratio of 11.5 ($165,000/$14,400 [$1200 × 12]). Investing in rental property with a high ratio will provide a profit only with a future increase in its resale value, which may be difficult to achieve in today's economic times.

Current Income Results from Positive Cash Flow In real estate investing, current income takes the form of positive cash flow. For an income-producing real estate investment, you pay operating expenses out of rental income. If the property has a mortgage (a common occurrence), payments toward the mortgage principal and interest also must be made out of rental income. Operating expenses such as vacancies, taxes, mortgage payments, and repairs may eat up half or more of the rental income.

The amount of rental income you have left after paying all operating expenses is called **cash flow**. The amount of cash flow—obtained by subtracting any cash outlays from the cash income—depends on the amount of rent received, the amount of expenses paid, and the amount necessary to repay the mortgage debt. Investors usually prefer a positive cash flow to a negative cash flow because any shortages represent out-of-pocket expenses for the investor.

Many real estate investments will not generate an immediate positive cash flow, even though they may offer the likelihood of potential returns through price appreciation. However, home prices are still declining in some markets and are totally flat in others. Thus investors in today's challenging real estate market should be very cautious when considering whether they could manage a negative cash flow for a few years while waiting for capital gains to materialize upon selling the property, because they may not.

Calculate the Rental Yield Investors also calculate the **rental yield** on properties, as shown in Equation (16.2). This is a computation of how much income the investor might pocket from rent each year before mortgage payments as a percentage of the purchase price. Most properties yield about 4 percent of income annually, although the rental yield may be as little as 1 or 2 percent and as high as 8 or 9 percent. Less expensive properties often offer higher yields. The formula assumes half of rental income goes for expenses other than debt repayment.

$$\text{Rental yield} = \frac{(\text{rent} \div 2)}{\text{purchase price}} \quad \textbf{(16.2)}$$

	San Jose	Pittsburgh
Purchase price	$890,000	$165,000
Annual rent	31,200	14,400
Annual rent/2	15,600	7,200
Yield (annual rent/2/purchase price)	1.75%	4.36%

price-to-rent ratio
The ratio of median residential real estate prices to the median annual rents that can be earned from the real estate.

cash flow
Amount of rental income you have left after paying all operating expenses.

rental yield
A computation of how much income the investor might pocket from rent each year (before mortgage payments) as a percentage of the purchase price; divide the annual rent by 2 and then divide by the purchase price.

Question 2: Can You Profit When You Sell the Property?

The **capital gain** earned in a real estate investment comes from price appreciation. It is the amount above ownership costs for which an investment is sold. In real estate, ownership costs include the original purchase price as well as expenditures for any capital improvements made to a property prior to sale. **Capital improvements** are costs incurred in making changes in real property—beyond maintenance and repairs—that add to its value. Installing a pool and adding a room represent capital improvements.

Repairs are expenses (usually tax deductible against an investor's cash-flow income) necessary to maintain the value of the property. Repainting, mending roof leaks, and fixing plumbing are examples of repairs.

As an example, assume that Andrew Webb, an unmarried schoolteacher from Murray, Kentucky, bought a small rental house as an investment five years ago for $120,000 in cash that he received as an inheritance. He fixed some roof leaks (repairs) for $1000 and then added a new shed and some kitchen cabinets (capital improvements) at a cost of $10,000 before selling the property this year for $160,000. As a result, Andrew happily realized a capital gain of $30,000 ($160,000 minus the $120,000 purchase price minus $10,000 in capital improvements).

Historically, residential real estate values could generally be expected to increase 3 percent annually, about the rate of inflation or a little above. In some markets, prices may rise that much or more; however, prices have declined throughout the United States and fell dramatically in formerly hot real estate markets. In markets in which real estate is difficult to sell (too many properties on the market and too few buyers), perhaps because of continuing job losses in a sluggish regional economy, residential housing prices might decline 2 or 3 percent annually for a long time. That means continuing deflation in home prices in some markets year after year.

Profiting from capital gains may occur because of special circumstances. For example, there may be increased demand for housing due to construction of a new shopping mall or school or due to a new major employer coming to town. Or the asking price of a particular property might be sharply reduced because of a divorce or foreclosure or because the owners have moved.

If you cannot comfortably forecast the future of what you invest in, such as price appreciation on a property in a local housing market, you are speculating. Using a mortgage loan to invest in real estate invites more risk. While price appreciation is where the big profits are in real estate, you can reduce risk by investing in property for which the expected rental income exceeds projected mortgage payments, property taxes, and maintenance costs.

capital improvements
Costs incurred in making value-enhancing changes (beyond maintenance and repair) in real property.

repairs
Usually tax-deductible expenses necessary to maintain property value.

DID YOU KNOW?

Invest in Foreclosed Property Using a Short Sale

Foreclosure is the legal and professional procedure in which a mortgagee, or other lienholder, usually a lender, repossesses a home and sells it because the borrower has fallen behind in making payments on the loan. Prior to foreclosure, the homeowner has three options: (1) depart the property and try to repay the lender the deficiency, (2) declare bankruptcy, or (3) try to arrange a short sale. Sometimes the remaining balance owed on the home is more than the property is worth. Such homeowners are "upside down" or "under water" because they owe more than their property is worth. Unless the lender is willing to modify the terms of the loan, the lender then pursues the homeowner for the deficiency.

In a **short sale**, the lender accepts less than the full mortgage amount and often forgives whatever debt is left unpaid. The **deficiency amount** is the difference between the amount owed and what the bank collects at the short sale. When a bank agrees to a short sale, the homeowner hires an agent to find a buyer. New rules require lenders to provide preapproved terms for short sales; thus, an investor's bid is more likely to be accepted. Lenders agree to absorb the loss, although they might demand the homeowner make some kind of payment or share the loss. A debt that is forgiven may be subject to income taxes. A short sale may be a buying opportunity for investors, although negotiating with banks is likely to be a cumbersome and lengthy process.

Recognize That Leverage Can Increase the Return on Investment

As we noted in Chapter 13, **leverage** involves using borrowed funds to make an investment with the goal of earning a rate of return in excess of the after-tax costs of borrowing. Lenders often allow investors to borrow from 75 to 90 percent of the price of a property.

Suppose that Andrew, from the example given earlier, had made a down payment of $25,000 and borrowed the remainder, instead of paying cash for the house. What effect would this borrowing have on his return? In the first instance, Andrew paid $120,000 cash for the property and earned a 25 percent return on his investment ($30,000 ÷ $120,000) over the five-year period, or roughly 5 percent per year. In the second situation, using leverage, he would have an apparent return of 120 percent ($30,000 ÷ $25,000), or roughly 24 percent per year. The true return would be lower because of mortgage payments, interest expenses, property taxes, and repairs but would still be a double-digit return. Such a high potential return is what is so appealing to many real estate investors.

A slumping economy can lead to unfinished units and losses for real estate investors.

The **loan-to-value ratio** measures the amount of leverage in a real estate investment project. It is calculated by dividing the amount of debt by the value of the total original investment. For example, because his down payment was $25,000 on the $120,000 property, Andrew had a loan-to-value ratio of 79 percent ($95,000 ÷ $120,000), or 79 percent leverage.

loan-to-value ratio
Measures the amount of leverage in a real estate investment project by dividing the total amount of debt by the market price of the investment.

✓ Concept Check 16.1

1. What are the two key questions to consider before investing in real estate?

2. Distinguish between the price-to-rent ratio and the rental yield as measures of current income.

3. Give an example of how leverage can increase an investor's return in real estate.

TAKE ADVANTAGE OF BENEFICIAL TAX TREATMENTS

The U.S. Congress, through provisions in the Internal Revenue Code, encourages real estate investments by giving investors five special tax treatments.

LEARNING OBJECTIVE ❷

Recognize how to take advantage of beneficial tax treatments in real estate investing.

1. Depreciation Is a Tax Deduction

Investors in real estate become successful by understanding the "numbers" of real estate investing. For example, assume that Jisue Han, a lawyer from Keyser, West Virginia, invested $200,000 in a residential building ($170,000) and land ($30,000). She rents the property to a tenant for $24,000 per year. You might initially think that Jisue has to pay income taxes on the entire $24,000 in rental income. Wrong. IRS regulations allow taxpayers to deduct depreciation from rental income. **Depreciation** represents the decline in value of an asset over time due to normal wear and tear and obsolescence. A

depreciation
Decline in value of an asset over time due to normal wear and tear and obsolescence.

DID YOU KNOW?

Smart Steps to Protect Yourself Before Investing in Real Estate

1. Set up a limited liability corporation to own your real estate investments because it protects your personal assets in case someone is injured on your rental property and sues you.

2. Consider investing in properties only in locales where there are thriving businesses located near good schools, supermarkets, and public transportation.

3. Hire an accountant experienced in real estate investing.

4. Line up financing options before searching for properties.

5. Hire an inspector to inspect the physical condition of the property.

6. Hire a licensed contractor for plumbing, electrical, and expensive repair jobs rather than doing them yourself.

7. Consider hiring a management company to tend to your property; the cost is 5 to 10 percent of rental income.

8. Set aside $5000 as a contingency fund for unanticipated problems with real estate investment property.

proportionate amount of a capital asset representing depreciation may be deducted against income each year over the asset's estimated life. Land cannot be depreciated.

Jisue can deduct an equal part of the building's cost over the estimated life of the property. IRS guidelines provide that residential properties may be depreciated over 27.5 years, while nonresidential properties are allowed 39 years. Jisue calculates (from Table 16-1) the amount she can annually deduct from income to be $6182 ($170,000 ÷ 27.5). Table 16-1 shows the effects of depreciation on her income taxes, assuming Jisue pays income taxes at a combined federal and state rate of 36 percent. In this example, the depreciation deduction lowers taxable income on the property from $24,000 to $17,818 ($24,000 − $6182) and increases the return on the investment to 9.29 percent.

2. Interest Is a Tax Deduction

Real estate investors incur many business expenses in attempting to earn a profit: interest on a mortgage, real estate taxes, insurance, utilities, accounting and legal costs, management bills, homeowner's association fees, capital improvements, and repairs. The largest of these costs often is the interest expense, as properties are often purchased with a mortgage loan. Table 16-2 illustrates the effect of interest expenses on income taxes. To purchase her $200,000 investment property, assume Jisue borrowed $175,000 for 15 years at 5 percent with a monthly payment of $1383 (from Table 9-4 on page 270). After deducting annual depreciation of $6182 and interest expenses of $16,596, her taxable

Table 16-1

Depreciation Reduces Income Taxes and Increases Investor's Return

			Without Depreciation	With Depreciation
Total amount invested	$ 200,000	Gross rental income	$24,000	$24,000
Cost of land	− 30,000	Less annual depreciation expense	0	6,182
Cost of rental building	$ 170,000	Taxable income	24,000	17,818
Depreciation for 27.5 years	$ 6,182	Income taxes (36 percent combined federal and state tax rate)	8,640	6,414
		After-tax return	$15,360	$17,586
		After-tax yield (divide return by $200,000)	7.68%	8.79%

Additional Effect of Interest Paid on Income Taxes on Return

Table 16-2

Gross rental income	$24,000
Less annual depreciation deduction	−6,182
Subtotal	$17,818
Less interest expense for the year (5 percent $175,000 mortgage)	−16,596
Taxable income	$ 1,222
Cash flow after paying interest ($24,000 − $16,596)	7,404
Less income tax liability (0.36 × $1222)	−440
After-tax return ($7404 − $440)	$ 6,964
After-tax yield [$6964 ÷ ($200,000 − $175,000)]	27.8%

income is reduced to $1222. Because her income tax liability is only $440, Jisue's after-tax return of $6964 yields 27.8 percent on her leveraged investment.

Tax laws permit investors to deduct interest expenses (with the amount of the deduction allowed depending on the investor's marginal tax bracket). The interest deduction gives Jisue a cash flow after paying mortgage interest of $7404 ($24,000 − $16,596). In essence, the $16,596 in interest is paid with $5974 ($16,596 × 36 percent combined federal and state income tax rate) of the money that was not sent to the federal and state governments and $10,622 ($16,596 − $5974) of Jisue's money.

3. Capital Gains Are Taxed at Very Low Rates
Capital gains on real estate are realized through price appreciation. For most taxpayers, long-term capital gains are taxed at a rate of 15 percent.

4. Exchange of Properties Can Be Tax Free
Another special tax treatment results when a real estate investor trades equity in one property for equity in a similar property. If none of the people involved in the trade receives any other form of property or money, the transaction is considered a **tax-free exchange** (or a **1031 exchange**). If one person receives some money or other property, only that person has to report the extra proceeds as a taxable gain. For example, assume you bought a residential rental property five years ago for $220,000 and today it is worth much more. You trade it with your friend by giving $10,000 in cash for your friend's $280,000 single-family rental home. Your friend needs to report only the $10,000 as income this year. In contrast, you do not need to report your long-term gain, $50,000 ($280,000 − $10,000 − $220,000), until you actually sell the new property.

tax-free exchange
Arises when a real estate investor trades equity in one property for equity in a similar property and no other forms of property or money change hands.

5. Taxes Can Be Lower on Vacation Home Rental Income
If you rent out your vacation property for 14 or fewer days during the year, you can pocket the income tax free because the IRS does not want to hear about this gain. The home is considered a personal residence, so you can deduct mortgage interest and property taxes just as you would for your principal residence. (That same tax break is available for those who rent their primary home for 14 days or less, say for people attending a major sporting event in your city.)

If you limit your use to fewer than 15 days or 10 percent of the time it is rented, whichever is greater, you are a landlord and you have turned the endeavor into a business. Lots of days in excess of the 14-day limit spent maintaining the property and fixing it up do not count as personal days. You may deduct expenses attributable to the rental business, such as mortgage interest, property taxes, depreciation, utilities, repairs, insurance, advertising, homeowner's association fees, and property management fees, as well as auto and other travel expenses. If you actively participate in the management of the property (defined as approving new tenants, deciding on rental terms, or approving repairs and capital improvements), you can deduct rental expenses up to the level of rental income you report prorated for the number of days it was rented out. When your adjusted gross income (AGI) is less than $100,000, a maximum of $25,000 of rental-related losses may

DID YOU KNOW?

Vacation Condos Are Not Good Investments

Despite attractive prices that have declined one-third or more in resort areas, it is still almost impossible to make the "investment" numbers add up. Today you can rent a four-bedroom winter high-season vacation villa in Orlando for $80 a night that used to go for $2000 a week. For the typical condo landlord investor to profit, the property has to be rented for 26 to 30 weeks out of a year, and owners are competing on price against the hotel industry. Smart people rent vacation condos but never buy them. Vacationers realize it is easy to go online, review photos of condos, read the comments of previous renters, and call owners directly to negotiate a discounted price.

 LEARNING OBJECTIVE ❸

Calculate the right price to pay for real estate and how to finance your purchase.

discounted cash-flow method
Effective way to estimate the value or asking price of a real estate investment based on after-tax cash flow and the return on the invested dollars discounted over time to reflect a discounted yield.

be deducted each year to offset income from any source, including your salary. The $25,000 limit is gradually phased out as your AGI moves between $100,000 and $150,000. This ability to shelter income from taxes represents a terrific benefit for people who invest in real estate on a small scale.

✔ **Concept Check 16.2**

1. Summarize how depreciation is used to reduce the income from a real estate investment.

2. Briefly explain how the interest paid on the mortgage of a real estate investment reduces one's income taxes.

3. Summarize the special income tax regulations on renting out vacation homes.

PRICING AND FINANCING REAL ESTATE INVESTMENTS

Sure ways to go wrong in a real estate investment are to pay too much for the property and finance it incorrectly.

Pay the Right Price

The **discounted cash-flow method** is an effective way to estimate the present value or appropriate price of a real estate investment. It emphasizes after-tax cash flow and the return on the invested dollars discounted over time to reflect a discounted yield. Software programs are available online to calculate the discounted cash flows. You also can use Appendix A-2, as illustrated in Table 16-3.

To see how this method works, assume that you require an after-tax rate of return of 10 percent on a condominium advertised for sale at $210,000. You estimate that rents can be increased about 2 percent each year for five years. After all expenses are paid, you expect to have after-tax cash flows of $4000, $4100, $4200, $4300, and $4400 for the five years. Assuming some price appreciation, you anticipate selling the property for $230,000 after all expenses are incurred. How much should you pay now to buy the property?

Table 16-3 explains how to answer this question. Multiply the estimated after-tax cash flows and the expected proceeds of $230,000 to be realized on the sale of the property by the present value of a dollar at 10 percent (your required rate of return). Add the present values together to obtain the total present value of the property—in this case, $198,343. The asking price of $210,000 is too high for you to earn an after-tax return of 10 percent.

Table 16-3

Discounted Cash Flow to Estimate Price

	After-Tax Cash Flow	Present Value of $1 at 10 Percent*	Present Value of After-Tax Cash Flow
1 year	$ 4,000	0.9524	$ 3,809
2 years	4,100	0.9070	3,718
3 years	4,200	0.8638	3,627
4 years	4,300	0.8227	3,537
5 years	4,400	0.7835	3,447
Sale price of property in 5 years	$230,000	0.7835	180,205
Present value of property			$198,343

* From Appendix A-2

ADVICE FROM A PRO

Timesharing Is a Financial Disaster

Timesharing is the joint ownership or lease of vacation property through which the principals occupy the property individually for set periods of time. Timesharing is not an investment, although it is promoted as a way to simultaneously invest and obtain vacation housing. For $5000 to $20,000, buyers can purchase one or more weeks' use of luxury vacation housing furnished right down to the salt-and-pepper shakers. Timeshare owners pay an annual maintenance fee of perhaps $200 to $300 for each week of ownership. Maintenance fees increase every year, and occasionally there are special assessment fees.

With **deeded timesharing**, the buyer obtains a legal title or deed to limited time periods of use of real estate. Purchasers become secured creditors who are guaranteed continued use of the property throughout any bankruptcy proceedings. They really own their week (or two) of the property. **Nondeeded timesharing** is a legal right-to-use purchase of a limited, preplanned timesharing period of use of a property. It is a long-term lease, license, or club membership permitting use of a hotel suite, condominium, or other accommodation, and the right to use expires in 20 to 25 years. If the true owner

of the property—the developer—goes bankrupt, creditors can lock out the timeshare purchasers (technically they are tenants) from the premises.

It is very hard to sell a timeshare, and sales commissions of legitimate resellers are 30 percent of the price. The Resort Property Owners Association says that the average timeshare unit languishes on the market for 4.4 years before being sold. At any point in time, 60 percent of all timeshares are up for sale. Timeshare sellers rarely sell for 50 percent of their original investment in the sale. As one observer said, "If someone tries to sell you a timeshare, run!"

In good economic times or bad, you can find rental lodgings in the same area at a lower price than owning. The only good thing about owning a timeshare is that it forces you to take a yearly vacation, and the vacation will be at the same place regardless of where you live in the future. However, some timeshare plans allow owners to swap their property for others in distant locations.

Lori Lothringer
Metropolitan Community College, Omaha, Nebraska

Your choices are to negotiate the price down, accept a return of less than 10 percent, increase rents, hope that the sale price of the property will be higher than $230,000 five years from now, or consider another investment. The discounted cash-flow method provides an effective way to estimate real estate values because it takes into account the selling price of the property, the effect of income taxes, and the time value of money.

Financing a Real Estate Investment

Borrowing to finance a real estate investment is more expensive than borrowing to buy one's own home, often 0.5 to 1.5 percentage points above the rate for customary homebuyers. There is more risk because the investor does not live at the property. The minimum down payment for investors is often 20 or 25 percent. Most investors finance real estate investments with conventional fixed-rate, fixed-term mortgage loans, as described in Chapter 9, Obtaining Affordable Housing. An investor who puts down a substantial down payment might qualify for an adjustable rate mortgage loan.

To make a smaller down payment and get a lower mortgage rate, some real estate investors buy a home, live in it for a year, and then rent it out as an investment. Another way to finance a real estate investment is through **seller financing** (or **owner financing**). This occurs when a seller is willing to self-finance a loan by accepting a promissory note from the buyer who makes monthly mortgage payments. No lending agency is involved. Investing buyers pay higher interest rates for seller financing. The seller may accept little or no down payment in exchange for an even higher interest rate, perhaps 1½ to 2½ percent above conventional mortgage rates. Owner-financed deals can be transacted very quickly for investors.

A popular way to start in real estate investing is to purchase **sweat equity property**. With this approach, you seek a property that needs repairs but has good underlying value. You buy this fixer-upper at a favorable price and "sweat" by spending many hours cleaning, painting, and repairing it to rent or sell at a profit.

seller financing/owner financing
When a seller self-finances a buyer's loan by accepting a promissory note from a buyer, who makes monthly mortgage payments.

FINANCIAL POWER POINT

Find Out Home Prices

To find prices on homes anywhere in the country, check out Yahoo! Real Estate (http://realestate.yahoo.com/Homevalues), Zillow.com (www.zillow.com), Trulia.com (www.trulia.com/home_prices/), and Domania (www.domania.com). Just type in an address to obtain valuations.

sweat equity property
Property that needs repairs but that has good underlying value; an investor buys the property at a favorable price and fixes it up to rent or sell at a profit.

DID YOU KNOW?

Sean's Success Story

Sean got greedy and then got smart. He greedily invested too heavily in stock mutual funds and then, because of the gyrations in the stock market, got scared and pulled out by the end of the year with his portfolio down about 10 percent. He got smarter when he decided to no longer jump in and out of the market trying to make quick profits. Thus he has decided to invest his 401(k) funds in ETFs and mutual funds that pretty much track the broader indexes. In addition, Sean and his brother calculated the numbers on a real estate investment with a projected 7 percent annual return, so they made a down payment on a duplex that is close to an A-rated high school. The old renters have signed new leases, and the investment produces a positive cash flow.

LEARNING OBJECTIVE **4**

Assess the disadvantages of investing in real estate.

✓ Concept Check 16.3

1. Summarize how the discounted cash-flow method helps determine the right price to pay for a real estate investment.

2. Comment on the wisdom of buying a timeshare as an investment.

3. List three ways to finance a real estate investment.

DISADVANTAGES OF REAL ESTATE INVESTING

Real estate investing can be profitable. But it does have some significant disadvantages.

- **Business risk.** It is quite possible to lose money in real estate investments. A local recession, perhaps because a large employer moved away, can depress housing prices. Zoning changes can slash housing values. Rents cannot keep up with costs in communities in which industries and jobs are moving elsewhere or in deteriorating neighborhoods.

- **Foreclosures.** In communities where there are many foreclosures, other sellers have to lower their home prices to compete. This depresses the values of all comparable housing—no matter how wonderful the location or condition—thus making it more difficult for anyone to sell at a reasonable price.

- **Illiquidity.** Real estate is expensive, and the market for investment property is much smaller than the securities market. As a result, it is common to experience trouble in selling. It may take months or even a year or more to find a buyer, arrange the financing, and close the sale of a real estate investment.

- **Complexity.** Real estate investments require much more investigation than do most other investments. Numerous assumptions about financial details in the future also must be made.

- **Large initial investment.** Direct investment in real estate generally requires many thousands of dollars, often with an initial outlay of $15,000, $30,000, $50,000, or more.

- **Lack of diversification.** So much capital is required in real estate investing that spreading risk is almost impossible.

- **Dealing with tenants.** Someone has to screen rental applicants for their credit histories, criminal records, work references, and experience with previous landlords. State laws may make it impossible to evict a deadbeat tenant for several months. Picking the wrong tenants can quickly turn a real estate property into a financial loss.

- **Time-consuming management demands.** Managing a real estate investment requires time for conducting regular inspections of the property, dealing with insurance companies, making repairs, and collecting overdue rents.

- **Low current income.** Expenses may reduce the cash-flow return to less than 2 percent or even generate a net loss in a given year.

- **Unpredictable costs.** Estimating costs is problematic. Investors cannot control increasing real estate tax assessments or predict when a central air-conditioning unit might break down.

- **Interest rate risk.** When interest rates rise, fewer people can afford to buy homes, and this puts downward pressure on prices and rents.

- **Legal fees.** The services of a real estate attorney will be needed to help handle the real estate purchase, sale, building inspections, zoning issues, tenant problems, insurance disputes, accounting, and any liability issues. Title insurance is a critically important expense to investors, particularly when allegations suggest that lenders may or may not have properly inspected the seller's legal documents.

- **High transfer costs.** Substantial transfer costs, often representing 6 to 7 percent of the property's sale price, plus money for fix-up costs, may be incurred when real estate is bought or sold.

DID YOU KNOW?

The Tax Consequences of an Income-Producing Real Estate Investment

When you are considering a real estate investment, you use the investment amount (purchase price or down payment) to begin the process of estimating the likely rate of return. This calculation may then be compared with other investment alternatives. Because some of the many assumptions in real estate calculations could be incorrect, caution is warranted in real estate analyses.

The following table shows five-year estimates for a hypothetical residential property in Rapid City, South Dakota, located close to a well-respected high school with a purchase price of $200,000. The building will be purchased with a $150,000 mortgage loan, so the buyer has to make a $50,000 down payment plus pay $8000 in closing costs. The gross rental income of $18,000 annually is projected to rise at an annual rate of 5 percent, vacancies and unpaid rent at 10 percent, real estate taxes at 7 percent, insurance at 8 percent, and maintenance at 10 percent. Virtually the entire payment for the 30-year, $150,000, 6½ percent, fixed-rate mortgage loan is assumed to be interest during these early years. For income tax purposes, the land is valued at $20,000, and the building is

depreciated over 27.5 years. The amount of annual straight-line depreciation is calculated to be $6546 ($200,000 − $20,000 = $180,000; $180,000 ÷ 27.5 = $6546).

Note (in line D) how challenging it is to earn current income from rental properties. During the first two years, the total cash flow (line D) is projected to be positive ($976 and $652), but for the following three years, the cash flow is expected to be negative (−330, −$10, and −$305). However, because the income tax laws permit depreciation (line E, $6546) to be recorded each year as a real estate investment expense, even though it is not an out-of-pocket cost, the investor calculates a total taxable loss (line F) for each of the five years of expected ownership (−$5570 the first year). These losses can be deducted on the investor's income tax returns. Because the investor pays a 30 percent combined federal and state income tax rate, the loss results in a first-year annual tax savings of $1671 (line G). Therefore, instead of sending the $1671 to the government in taxes, the investor can use that amount to help pay the operating expenses of the investment. Consequently, the net cash-flow income (line D) of $976 is enhanced by tax savings (line G) of $1671 to result in a net cash-flow gain after taxes of $2647 ($1671 + $976).

Estimates for a Successful Real Estate Investment

	Year				
	1	**2**	**3**	**4**	**5**
A. Gross rental income	$18,000	$18,900	$19,845	$20,837	$21,879
Less vacancies and unpaid rent	1,800	1,890	1,985	2,084	2,188
B. Projected gross income	$16,200	$17,010	$17,860	$18,753	$19,691
C. Less operating expenses					
Principal and interest (P + I)	$11,376	$11,376	$11,376	$11,376	$11,376
Real estate taxes (T)	2,600	2,782	2,977	3,185	3,408
Insurance (I)	800	864	933	1,008	1,089
Maintenance	2,400	2,640	2,904	3,194	3,513
Total operating expenses	$17,176	$17,662	$18,190	$18,763	$19,386
D. Total cash flow	$ 976	$ 652	$ (330)	$ (10)	$ (305)
E. Less depreciation expense	(6,546)	(6,546)	(6,546)	(6,546)	(6,546)
F. Taxable income (or loss) (D − E)	$ (5,570)	$ (5,894)	$ (6,876)	$ (6,556)	$ (6,851)
G. Annual tax savings (30 percent marginal rate)	1,671	1,768	2,062	1,966	2,055
H. Net cash-flow gain (or loss) after taxes (G + D)	$ 2,647	$ 2,420	$ 1,732	$ 1,956	$ 1,750

Assume that the property appreciates in value at an annual rate of 4 percent and will be worth $243,330 (line K) in five years ($200,000 × 1.04 × 1.04 × 1.04 × 1.04 × 1.04). If it

is sold at this price, a 6 percent real estate sales commission of $14,599 ($243,330 × 0.06) would reduce the net proceeds to $228,731 ($243,330 − $14,599).

Now we can calculate the **crude annual rate of return** on the property, as shown in the second table. A crude rate of return is a rough measure of the yield on amounts invested that assumes that equal portions of the gain are earned each year. The total return in this example was substantial. The investor made out-of-pocket cash investments of $50,000 for the down payment and $8000 in closing costs, and we subtract the accumulated net cash flow (line N) of $10,505 (adding all the numbers across line H because the investor already has received that money) for a total investment (line O) of $47,495. The investor has a capital gain (line M) of $53,461. After dividing to determine the before-tax total return (line R) to obtain 112 percent, the crude annual rate of return (line S) is 22.4 percent annually over the five years (112 percent ÷ 5 years).

Crude Rate of Return on a Successful Real Estate Investment

Taxable cost

I.	Purchase price ($50,000 down payment; $150,000 loan)	$200,000
	Closing costs	8,000
	Subtotal	208,000
J.	Less accumulated depreciation	32,730
	Taxable cost (adjusted basis)	$175,270
Proceeds (after paying off mortgage)		
K.	Sale price	$243,330
	Less sales commission	14,599
	Net proceeds	$228,731
L.	Less taxable cost (J)	175,270
M.	Taxable proceeds (capital gain)	$ 53,461
Amount invested		
	Down payment	$ 50,000
	Closing costs	8,000
N.	Less accumulated net cash-flow gains	(10,505)
O.	Total invested	$ 47,495
Crude annual rate of return		
P.	Total invested	$ 47,495
Q.	Taxable proceeds (capital gain from M)	$ 53,461
R.	Before-tax total return ($53,461 ÷ $47,495)	112%
S.	Crude before-tax annual rate of return (112 percent ÷ 5 years)	22.4%

 Concept Check 16.4

1. Summarize why foreclosures and illiquidity are disadvantages in real estate investing.

2. Comment on why real estate investors often have time-consuming management demands.

INVESTING IN COLLECTIBLES, PRECIOUS METALS, AND GEMS

 LEARNING OBJECTIVE 5

Summarize the risks and challenges of investing in collectibles, precious metals, and gems.

speculator
An investor who buys in the hope that someone else will pay more for an asset in the not-too-distant future.

collectibles
Cultural artifacts that have value because of their beauty, age, scarcity, or popularity, such as antiques, stamps, rare coins, art, baseball cards, and so on.

Investors often think of assets as something they would like to own for the long term. When investing in collectibles, precious metals, and gems, the investor owns illiquid real assets, not intangible items represented by pieces of paper. While an asset may be bought for its long-term investment potential, profits might be earned in the short term. A **speculator** buys in the hope that someone else will pay more for an asset in the not-too-distant future. Speculators often buy or sell in expectation of profiting from market fluctuations. If you put money into these illiquid assets, limit your speculative investing to no more than 5 percent of your total investment portfolio, and buy only what you truly adore. But don't consider collectibles, precious metals, and gems as part of your savings plan for retirement. When investing for retirement you should use long-term strategies as outlined in Chapter 13, not speculate.

Collectibles

Collectibles are cultural artifacts that have value because of their beauty, age, scarcity, or popularity. They include baseball cards, posters, sports memorabilia, guns, photographs, paintings, prints, ceramics, comic books, watches, lunchboxes, matchbooks, glassware, spoons, stamps, rare coins, art, rugs, fine wine, cars, and antiques. The collectible markets are fueled by nostalgia, limited availability, and "what is hot to own today." Prices for collectibles often lag other investments and continue to lag. Collectibles won't beat the return of stocks over the long term, but they are lots of fun to own.

Making a Profit on Collectibles Is Not Easy One key to success in collectibles is to invest in quality—the higher the better. Think about the highest value collectibles as being equivalent to blue-chip stocks. Although buying collectibles can be fun and easy, turning a profit may not. The only return on collectibles occurs through price appreciation, and you must sell to realize a profit. That could be hard for you to do if the collectibles give you pleasure. If you sell, you will pay a 28 percent income tax rate on collectibles rather than a 15 percent tax on capital gains.

Items that are almost certain to lose value include those that are mass produced and marketed as collectibles or limited editions. You often see these kinds of collectibles advertised on television and in newspapers and magazines. Another risk is the wholesale-to-retail price spread, which could be 50 or 100 percent. If you buy from a dealer, you'll probably pay a markup of about 40 to 50 percent. You generally get more for your money buying at an auction. Prices on collectibles vary greatly from item to item and year to year. Markets are fickle. If the investor needs to convert the asset to cash, a sale may take days, weeks, or months, and the seller may be forced to accept a lower price. The collectibles industry is rife with forgeries, scams, and frauds, particularly in sports memorabilia.

Buying and Selling Collectibles on the Internet You can buy collectibles on the Internet, using eBay for example, purchasing in minutes what you might never have found even after searching for years in magazines, junk shops, flea markets, and auctions. Buying collectibles on the Internet is efficient and convenient, and it is easy to compare products and prices. It is hard to inspect the collectible before purchase, however. Search Google for "collectibles," but realize that this is a risky way to invest.

Gold and Other Precious Metals

There is an allure to owning gold. You can own and hold it with pride, and it is beautiful to look at. Gold is a uniquely private, personal, and portable way to hold some genuine wealth. For purposes of investing, however, gold does not generate current income while you own it. Its value is determined solely by supply and demand at the time of sale. Thus, investing in gold is speculating. Some other metals beside gold have a similar appeal to investors.

Fear Pushes Up Gold Prices Fear is what pushes up the price of gold. Some of the world's worried investors purchase gold reasoning that if their national economies crash they will be able to trade gold even if their country's paper currency is devalued. Those who buy gold are typically concerned about such things as high inflation, rising interest rates, countries seen as printing too much money, economic collapse, possible wars, excessive government borrowing, collapse of the credit system, and international trade wars. The fear that gripped investors around the globe since the beginning of the Great Recession has moved from the fringes of the investing world to the mainstream with "gold fever." Prices have soared, and gold hoarders, who are often criticized as crackpots, for a while appear to be smart speculators.

Gold Prices Were Stagnant but Recently Have Soared Back in 1976 when there were serious concerns about extremely high inflation in the United States, gold prices jumped from $100 an ounce to more than $800 by 1980, and then the price went to $400 before sliding sharply lower to $280 by 2001. This roller coaster ride has happened again. After 25+ years of little change, gold prices began to rise slowly until they hit $1000 in March of 2008 during the worst of the Great Recession and then sharply dropped to $700 a few months later. As the U.S. and world's economies continued to struggle and the dollar declined in value, gold prices climbed to over $1530 in 2011. For gold to get back up to its 1980 high of $800 when adjusted for inflation, it would have to close at $2250. So, in real terms, it is still not back to the high it reached 30 years ago.

While the increase over the past ten years in gold prices may make gold sound like an appealing speculative investment, consider further that if you bought $10,000 in gold

FINANCIAL POWER POINT

Search for Collectibles Prices at Christie's and Sotheby's Online

The giant auction houses of Christie's (www.christies.com) and Sotheby's (www.sothebys.com) offer big selections of prints, photographs, watches, wines, furniture, diamond jewelry, and other collectibles. Check out their catalogs and videos on their websites, and consider signing up for text messages and the ability to bid by phone or online.

in 1980, it would have been worth $10,600 in 2008. If you invested the same $10,000 in 1980 in a mutual fund that tracks the S&P 500, you would have over $200,000 by 2008. These are not the kind of data that a gold promoter wants investors to see.

Can the fear and greed of doomsayers, conspiracy theorists, and gold promoters keep gold prices rising, or is this the same kind of price bubble that happened in the U.S. housing market? Like any investment, gold is subject to a meltdown. Experts differ. Some say buy it as a long-term hedge against paper money losing value while others say sell before the bubble bursts. The smart investor proceeds with caution even when speculating.

You Can Invest in Gold in Several Ways

An initial investment in gold need not be expensive, although buying gold directly can be. There are many ways to invest in gold or other precious metals.

gold bullion
A refined and stamped weight of precious metal.

Gold Bullion   Gold bullion is often thought of as the large gold "bricks" that weigh about 28 pounds that people imagine are stored in Fort Knox. Each brick is worth more than $100,000 at today's prices. The term *bullion* simply means a refined and stamped weight of precious metal. Gold bullion is traditionally purchased and traded in 1- and 10-ounce gold bars. Gold as bullion is expensive to own. There are fees for refining, fabricating, and shipping bullion. A sales charge of 5 to 8 percent is common. There are storage costs. When gold is sold, the bank or dealer buying it from an investor may insist on reassaying its quality, yet another cost for the investor. The investor should purchase insurance against fire, theft, and fraud because such transactions are not regulated by the federal government.

Gold and other precious metals are highly volatile investments.

gold bullion coins
Various world mints issue these coins, which contain 1 troy ounce (31.15 grams) of pure gold.

Gold Bullion Coins   Some costs of investing in gold can be avoided by those wanting to take physical possession of gold bullion itself by owning modern **gold bullion coins**, each containing 1 troy ounce (31.15 grams) of pure gold issued by the various world mints. The most popular coins are the South African Krugerrand, Canadian Maple Leaf, and the U.S. Gold Eagle. Other gold bullion coins are available, including the Great Britain Sovereign, Australian Kangaroo Nugget, and Chinese Panda. Minimum orders are ten coins, and commissions are 2 to 4 percent both when buying and selling.

These gold bullion coins do not need to be tested for purity, are portable, and have worldwide liquidity. Investors need to store and insure their coins. Visit www.usmint.gov for a list of U.S. Gold Eagle dealers.

Collectible Gold Coins People who buy collectible gold coins buy them in part because of their intrinsic beauty and scarcity. Such investors face high markups, difficulty in grading coins (or must pay to hire a grading service), and costs for storage and insurance. Major coin graders include American Numismatic Association Certification Service (www.anacs.com), Numismatic Guaranty Corporation (www.ngccoin.com), and Professional Coin Grading Service (www.pcgs.com).

Gold Mining Stocks, Mutual Funds, and ETFs Investors wanting to capitalize on world crises, economic fears, and rising gold prices by investing in smaller amounts may choose to put speculative cash in the stocks of gold mining companies, in mutual funds that own gold companies, and in exchange-traded funds (ETFs). For example, you may have heard of the now defunct Homestake Gold Mine, one of the early enterprises associated with the Gold Rush of 1876 in the northern Black Hills of what was then Dakota Territory. Today, there are a handful of gold mining companies in the United States and dozens around the world.

Popular gold mutual funds include Van Eck International Investors (INIVX), USAA Precious Metals and Minerals (USAGX), Oppenheimer Gold & Special Metals A (OPGSX), and Vanguard Precious Metals and Mining (VGPM). Gold mutual fund prices can readily swing up or down 50 percent in three months. The largest gold exchange-traded fund (ETF) is SPDR Gold Shares (GLD). Other popular gold ETFs are iShares COMEX Gold Trust (IAU) and Market Vectors Gold Miners ETF (GDX).

Investing in Silver, Platinum, Palladium, and Rhodium

Some other metals also appeal to certain investors. Silver, platinum, palladium, and rhodium are metals used industrially and occasionally in jewelry. The values of these metals rise and fall with changes in demand. An investor might reason that since palladium is used in auto production that when demand in China and India for vehicles increases substantially, the price of the metal will soar. Prices can drop, too; silver declined 25 percent in 4 days last year. Illustrative ETFs in these precious metals include iShares Silver Trust (SLV), ETFS Physical Platinum (PPLT), and ETFS Physical Palladium Shares (PALL).

Precious Stones and Gems

Precious stones and gems, such as diamonds, sapphires, rubies, and emeralds, are also examples of high-risk investments. Investors purchase investment-grade gems as "loose gems" rather than as pieces of jewelry. Wholesale firms, not jewelers, sell the best-quality precious gems. The gem certification process may be touted as a science, but it is not; rather it is educated guesswork. Obtaining two assessments of a stone's quality, particularly on stones of less than 1 carat, is likely to result in a variation of 10 to 20 percent.

Novice investors often buy at retail and then wind up trying to sell at retail. This approach is the opposite of smart investing—that is, buying low and selling high. Sales commissions on precious stones are high, and reselling is very difficult. Losing 20 to 50 percent of one's investment upon selling is common.

 Concept Check 16.5

1. Identify one collectible that might be an interesting investment, and explain why it might be difficult to make a profit.

2. Explain why some investors buy gold and other precious metals, and tell why that type of investment might be appealing or unappealing to you.

3. Identify some risks of investing in precious stones and gems.

LEARNING OBJECTIVE

Explain why options and futures are high-risk investments.

option
Contract to buy or sell a financial asset at a specified point in the future at a specified price.

stock option
Security that gives the holder the right to buy or sell a specific number of shares (normally 100) of a certain stock at a specified (striking) price before a specified expiration date.

option writer
Agrees to sell an option contract that promises either to buy or to sell a specified asset for a fixed striking price.

option holder
Person who buys and then owns an option contract.

call option
Gives option holder the right to buy the optioned asset from the option writer at the striking price at any time before the expiration date.

put option
Gives option holder the right to sell the optioned asset to the option writer at the striking price at any time before the option expires.

INVESTING IN OPTIONS AND FUTURES CONTRACTS

Derivative securities are available for commodities, equities, bonds, interest rates, exchange rates, and indexes (such as a stock market index, consumer price index, and weather conditions). A **derivative** (or **derivative security**) is an instrument used by people to trade or manage more easily the asset upon which these instruments are based. Investors choose derivatives to either reduce risk by hedging against losses or taking on additional risk by speculating. The investor's returns are derived solely from changes in the underlying asset's price behavior. Two of the most common derivative instruments are options and futures contracts.

Options Allow You to Buy or Sell an Asset at a Predetermined Price

An **option** is a contract to buy or sell an asset at some point in the future at a specified price. The most common type of option is a **stock option**.* This security gives the holder (purchaser) the right, but not the obligation, to buy or sell a specific number of shares (normally 100) of a certain stock at a specified price (the **striking price**) before a specified date (the **expiration date**, typically three, six, or nine months).

Options Are Created by an Option Writer An **option writer** signs an option contract through a brokerage firm and promises either to buy or to sell a specified asset for a fixed striking price. In return, the option writer receives an **option premium** (the price of the option itself) for standing ready to buy or sell the asset at the wishes of the option purchaser. Once written and sold, an option may change hands many times before its expiration. The **option holder** is the person who actually owns the option contract. The original option writer always remains responsible for buying or selling the asset if requested by the holder of the option contract.

Two types of option contracts exist: calls and puts. A **call option** gives the option holder (buyer) the right, but not the obligation, to buy the optioned asset from the option writer at the striking price. A **put option** gives the option holder (buyer) the right, but not the obligation, to sell the optioned asset to the option writer at the

---

* Recall from Chapter 14 that some employers give stock options as a way to attract and retain employees. If the price of the underlying stock increases sufficiently, the employee can profit by exercising the option to buy the shares at the predetermined price and then quickly selling the shares at the higher current price.

DID YOU KNOW?

How to Make Sense of Option Contracts

An option is a contract that gives its holder the right, but not the obligation, to buy or sell an asset at a specified price.

The two principal players in the options game are the option writer and the option holder. Their relationships are summarized below.

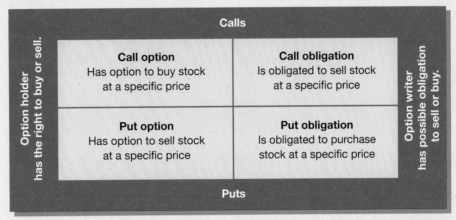

striking price. The Did You Know? box titled "How to Make Sense of Option Contracts" explains the relationships between option writers and option holders for both puts and calls.

Most option contracts expire without being exercised by the option holder, and the option writer is the only person to earn a profit. The profit results from the option premium charged when the option was originally sold. Buying and selling options are techniques used by both conservative and aggressive investors.

Conservative Writers Profit by Selling Covered Calls Selling calls can be a fairly safe way to generate income by conservative option writers who own the underlying asset (the stock). When they sell a call, it is described as a **covered option** because the writer owns the underlying stock. (If the writer does not own the asset, it is a **naked option**, a speculative position.) When used effectively by conservative option writers, calls can potentially pick up an extra return of perhaps 1 to 2 percent every three months and minimize risk at the same time. In effect, this conservative investor protects himself financially by hedging his investment against loss due to price fluctuation.

You can profit by selling a call on stock already owned, giving the buyer the right to purchase your shares at any time during a relatively short period at a fixed strike price. Here is an example.

Assume you have 1000 shares of ABC stock originally bought for $56 (total investment of $56,000) and you write a call to sell the shares at a strike price of $60. The option price is $2, so you gain an instant premium of $2000 (omitting commissions). Three scenarios are possible:

1. If the stock price does not change in three months, the call expires. As the covered call writer, you profit from the $2000 premium.
2. If the stock price rises to $65, the holder exercises the call and buys the stock at $60. Your profit is $6000 ($4000 from appreciation in the stock price from $56 to $60, plus the $2000 premium). You missed out on potentially greater profits, however, because you sold the stocks at the striking price of $60. Without the option, you could have sold the stock at $65 per share.

3. If the stock price drops to $50, the buyer of the call will not exercise it because the market price is less than the striking price. You keep the $2000 premium, which cuts your loss from $6000 to $4000 ($56 − $50 = $6; $6 × 1000 = $6000).

Conservative Investors Reduce Risks by Putting a Put on a Collar

Buying puts with a "collar" is a way to give up some potential gains on a stock one already owns in return for limiting losses. Puts allow the holder of the contract to sell an asset at a specific striking price for a certain time period, commonly three months. For example, if you own 1000 shares of ABC stock originally purchased at $56 per share (total investment of $56,000), you hope that the market price of the stock will go up. If it goes down instead, you may suffer a loss. To reduce this risk, you could buy a put for 1000 shares at a striking price close to the purchase price of the stock—for example, $52. The total price of the option contract might be $2000 ($2 per share). Three scenarios are possible:

1. If the stock price does not change in three months, the put expires, and you are out only the $2000.

2. If the stock price rises to $65, you allow the put to expire because it is greater than the striking price, and again you are out only the $2000. Alternatively, you could sell your shares at $65 and realize a profit of $7000 ($65 × 1000 = $65,000; $65,000 − $56,000 − $2000 = $7000).

3. If the stock price drops to $50, you would exercise the put and sell your stock at the striking price of $52, thereby hedging your loss from $6000 ($56 − $50 = $6; $6 × 1000 = $6000) to $4000 ($56 − $52 = $4; $4 × 1000 = $4000).

Speculative Investors Try to Profit with Options

Aggressive investors in the options market attempt to profit in two ways. First, because a market typically exists for each security for a period of three months, the investor can hope for an increase in the value of the option. For example, if the price of a stock is rising, the holder of a call option might sell it to another investor for a higher price than that originally paid. Second, the investor can exercise the option at the striking price, take ownership of the underlying securities, and sell them at a profit.

Investors take an extremely speculative position when they do not own the underlying asset, as when they sell naked calls or sell naked puts. Option traders can suffer considerable losses. For example, the writer of a put may incur a loss when the market price of an optioned asset drops below the striking price. The writer would be forced to buy the asset from the option holder at a price higher than the market price. Writing naked options is high-risk investing!

Speculative Investors Buy Calls to Create Tremendous Leverage

The lure of a call is that the option holder can control a relatively large asset with a small amount of capital for a specified period of time. If the market price of the asset rises to exceed the striking price plus the premium, the holder could make a substantial profit. For example, Jeremy Dietrich, a technology expert from St. Augustine, Florida, bought a stock option call on Coca-Cola Company (KO) in March when the stock was selling for $55 per share. The striking price is $60, the expiration date is the third Friday in March, and the price (premium) of the call is $2 per share. The option contract cost is $200 ($2 × 100 shares under his control). Jeremy hopes that the per-share price for Coca-Cola Company will rise. He prefers not to buy the stock outright because 100 shares of Coca-Cola Company would cost him a great deal more—$5500 ($55 × 100).

For Jeremy to break even on the call option deal, the price of Coca-Cola Company shares must rise to $62 before the call expires, as shown in Equation (16.3). If Jeremy exercises the call option, he can buy the stock at $60 from the option writer and sell it on the market for the current market price of $62 (ignoring commissions). In this instance, he earns $2 per share ($62 − $60), which offsets the $2 per share purchase price of the option. If the price of Coca-Cola Company stock rises to $65, Jeremy would make a $3 profit per share, for a total profit of $300. Based on his $200 investment, this gain amounts to a 150 percent return ($300 ÷ $200) earned over a short period. If the Coca-Cola Company stock price fails to reach $60 by late March, Jeremy's $200 in calls will expire with no value at all, and he will lose the amount he paid (invested) for the options.

ADVICE FROM A PRO

How to Calculate Breakeven Prices for Option Contracts

Investors need to know the **breakeven price** for option contracts. At this price, the cost of a contract is negated by a profit (or the cost is reduced by hedging a loss). The breakeven prices for two types of option contracts—puts and calls—are calculated using Equation (16.3) and Equation (16.4), respectively. If the striking price on a put option contract was $52 and the option contract cost $2000 and provided for the control of 1000 shares of stock, then the breakeven price of a share of the stock would be $50, as the calculation shows. If the striking price on a call was $60 and the option contract cost $200 and provided for the control of 100 shares of stock, then the breakeven price of a share of the stock would be $62.

$$\text{Puts breakeven price} = \text{striking price}$$
$$- \frac{\text{contract cost}}{\text{number of shares under control}} \quad (16.3)$$
$$\$50 = \$52 - \frac{\$2000}{1000}$$

$$\text{Calls breakeven price} = \text{striking price}$$
$$+ \frac{\text{contract cost}}{\text{number of shares under control}} \quad (16.4)$$
$$\$62 = \$60 + \frac{\$200}{100}$$

When calculating the breakeven prices for both puts and calls, it is critical to include all transaction costs in the contract cost. These costs include the option premium and perhaps sizable commissions paid to brokers. Commissions will be paid on the option contract itself, and subsequent commissions may be paid related to execution or sale of the option contract. In the preceding put example, a price below $50 triggers the sale of 1000 shares that will come at an additional, and perhaps unanticipated, commission cost. This possibility leads to some sage advice: When planning, always consider the full and subsequent costs of the deal.

Jonathan Fox
The Ohio State University

DID YOU KNOW?

About Hedge Funds

Hedge funds are freewheeling risky investment pools for the extremely wealthy that use unconventional investment strategies. They are global companies, beyond most of the regulations of the U.S. government. Hedge funds trade options and commodities, sell short, use leverage, risk arbitrage, buy and sell currencies, and invest in undervalued securities (poorly performing companies, those in bankruptcy, companies that may be merged).

Hedge funds can profit in times of market volatility as well as in a falling market. The investors are partners. Fees charged by the hedge fund manager are 2 to 5 percent of assets under management and 20 to 40 percent of the profits of the fund. None of the 8000 hedge funds can be offered or advertised to the general investing public in the United States. They are limited to "accredited investors and purchasers" who have incomes over $200,000 and a net worth over $1 million and who own more than $5 million in investments. Quite a few hedge funds have had catastrophic losses and have gone bankrupt.

Selling Options You would want to sell a put or a call when the option's market price has risen sufficiently due to changes in the market price of the underlying asset to ensure a profit. Alternatively, you might sell an option to prevent further losses if its market price is dropping.

Commodities Futures Contracts

futures contract
Type of exchange-traded standardized forward contract that specifies the size of the contract, quality of product to be delivered, and delivery date.

A **futures contract** is similar to an option in that it is a type of forward contract that is standardized (usually in terms of size of contract, quality of product to be delivered, and delivery date) and traded on an organized exchange. The difference is that futures contracts require the holder to buy the asset on the date specified. If the holder does not want to buy the asset, he or she must sell the contract to some other investor or to someone who wants to actually use the asset.

Futures contracts usually focus on agricultural, commercial, and mining products. Organized commodities markets include the New York Coffee and Sugar Exchange; New York Cocoa Exchange; CME Group (pigs, eggs, potatoes, and cattle); Chicago Board of Trade (corn, wheat, soybeans, soybean oil, oats, silver, and plywood); International Monetary Market (foreign currencies and U.S. Treasury bills); New York Commodity Exchange (gold and silver); and New York Mercantile Exchange (platinum).

Economic Need Creates Futures Markets Farmer Dave planting a 10,000-bushel soybean crop in Chana, Illinois, might want to sell part of it now to ensure the receipt of a certain price when the crop is actually harvested. Similarly, a food-processing company might want to purchase soybeans now to protect itself against sharp price increases in the future. And an orange juice manufacturer might want to lock in a supply of oranges at a definite price now rather than run the risk that a winter freeze might push up prices. These economic needs create futures markets.

Speculators May Trade in Futures Markets The speculative investor who buys or sells a commodity contract is hoping that the market price of the commodity will rise (or fall) before the contract matures, usually 3 to 18 months after it is written. Futures offer the potential for extremely high profits because all futures contracts by definition are highly leveraged. Depending on the commodity, the volatility of the market, and the brokerage house requirements, an investor can put up as little as 5 to 15 percent of the total value of the contract. Some contracts require a deposit of only $300. Commissions average about $20 for each purchase and sale.

To illustrate the use of leverage in buying futures contracts, assume that Danielle Anthony, a scuba-diving instructor from Union, New Jersey, purchases a wheat contract for 5000 bushels at $3.80 per bushel in July. The contract value is $19,000 ($3.80 × 5000), but Danielle puts up only $2500. Each $0.01 increase in the price of wheat represents a total of $50 profit to her ($0.01 × 5000). If the price rises $0.50 to reach $4.30 by late July, Danielle is "in the money" and will make $2500 ($0.50 × 5000 bushels) and double her investment by directing the futures exchange to close out her position. The theory is that she could buy the wheat for $3.80 per bushel (as stipulated in the contract) rather than the market price of $4.30 in late July. As an investor, Danielle does not actually want the wheat; she wants her profit by selling her contract. Another investor, perhaps a bread company, is likely to purchase that futures contract to obtain wheat at a below-market price.

The potential for loss exists, too. If the price drops $0.50 to reach $3.30, Danielle would lose $2500. If the price declines, the broker will make a margin call and ask Danielle to provide more money to back up the contract. If Danielle does not have these additional funds, the broker can legally sell her contract and "close out" the position, which results in a true cash loss for Danielle. Because of the risks involved, brokerage houses require their futures customers to have a minimum net worth of $50,000 to $75,000, exclusive of home and life insurance.

FINANCIAL POWER POINT

You Can Buy ETFs That Invest in Commodities

Investors can choose from over 75 exchange-traded funds (ETFs) that invest in commodities like corn, gold, silver, steel, nickel, and lithium. Most companies invest a small amount of their assets in future contracts and keep the remainder in Treasuries. Popular ETFs include iShares GSCI (GSG), Deutsche Bank Commodity Index (DBC), SPDR Gold Shares (GLD), and iShares Comex Gold (IAU).

DID YOU KNOW?

Sure Ways to Lose Money in Investing

If you don't know a lot about the specific investments you are considering, you are sure to lose money. You may lose a lot. If you are a long-term investor, avoid these risky investments.

- Margin trading
- Short selling

- Options (puts and calls)
- Commodity futures (pork bellies, oranges)
- Limited real estate partnerships
- Gold, precious metals, and gems
- Infomercial investment schemes
- Timeshares

Futures Are a Zero-Sum Game In each commodity transaction, a winner and a loser will emerge. A buyer of a futures contract benefits if the price of the commodity increases, but the seller suffers. When prices decline, the reverse is true. An estimated 90 percent of investors in the futures market lose money; 5 percent (mostly the professionals) make good profits from the losers; and the remaining 5 percent break even.

Investors need to be aware that they are dealing in very sophisticated markets when they trade in options or futures. Trading in futures is a **zero-sum game** in which the wealth of all investors remains the same; the trading simply redistributes the wealth among those traders. Each profit must be offset by an equivalent loss; therefore, the average rate of return for all investors in futures is zero. The return actually becomes negative if transaction costs are included. In the world of options and futures, losers outnumber winners. For decades, commodities futures have had the stigma of being little more than tools for gambling. Average investors do not belong in commodities.

zero-sum game
Situation in which the wealth of all investors remains the same; the trading simply redistributes the wealth among those traders. Each profit must be offset by an equivalent loss; therefore, the average rate of return for all investors in futures is zero.

DO IT NOW!

You know more about personal finance after reading this chapter, so get started right now by:

1. *Imagining what you would do if you came into $50,000 that you could invest without any concern about losing the money. Would you invest all or some of it in high-risk investments? Explain why or why not.*

2. *Searching your local newspaper for opportunities to buy a house as rental property, assuming that real estate is an*

option for this investment. Find out the price-to-rent ratio for an average home in your community and then estimate the asking price for a particular property, the rate of interest you could expect for a mortgage, the likely rent you could charge, and other factors.

3. *Then calculating the net present value of the property to determine the price you might offer for the property.*

 Concept Check 16.6

1. Distinguish between a call and a put for the options investor.

2. Summarize two ways a person with a conservative investment philosophy can profit in options.

3. Explain how a speculative options investor can lose a lot of money.

4. Offer reasons why futures contracts are not appropriate for the average investor.

WHAT DO YOU RECOMMEND NOW?

Now that you have read the chapter on real estate and high-risk investments, what do you recommend to Jamie on:

1. Investing in real estate?

2. Putting some of her money in a high-risk investment, like collectibles or gold?

3. Investing in options and futures contracts?

BIG PICTURE SUMMARY OF LEARNING OBJECTIVES

LO1. Demonstrate how you can make money investing in real estate.

The key questions for real estate investors are: "Can you make current income while you own the property?" and "Can you profit with capital gains when you sell the property?" To help find answers, investors calculate the price-to-rent ratio and rental yield. Recognize, too, that leverage can enhance real estate returns

LO2. Recognize how to take advantage of beneficial tax treatments in real estate investing.

The Internal Revenue Service offers investors five beneficial tax treatments, including depreciation, interest that is deductible, legally permitted tax-free exchanges of real estate, special tax breaks on renting and vacation homes, and very low tax rates on capital gains.

LO3. Calculate the right price to pay for real estate and how to finance your purchase.

The discounted cash-flow method is an effective way to estimate the value or asking price of a real estate investment. It takes into account the selling price of the property, the effect of income taxes, and the time value of money. There are various ways to finance a real estate investment, although a conventional mortgage loan is the most popular.

LO4. Assess the disadvantages of investing in real estate.

There are many disadvantages in real estate investing: large initial investment, lack of diversification, dealing with tenants, low current income, unpredictable costs, illiquidity, and high transfer costs.

LO5. Summarize the risks and challenges of investing in collectibles, precious metals, and gems.

When investing in collectibles, precious metals, and gems, the investor owns illiquid real assets, not intangible items represented by pieces of paper. The investor's only return comes from price appreciation, as they do not pay interest or dividends. While prices are set by supply and demand, promoters hype these high-risk investments. Changing investor tastes and rumors also influence prices. You should choose to invest, not speculate.

LO6. Explain why options and futures are high-risk investments.

Derivatives, such as options and futures, are instruments used by market participants to trade or manage more easily the asset upon which these instruments are based. While all types of investors can profit in options, only speculators with an aggressive investment philosophy should consider trading in futures. Most investors in derivatives lose money, and losses can accumulate quickly.

LET'S TALK ABOUT IT

1. **Invest in Real Estate.** Describe what would encourage you to invest in real estate given that in many communities prices have declined severely.

2. **Reasons to Invest.** Assume you have $30,000 in cash. Give reasons why you might want to invest that money in a real estate investment. Offer two reasons why others might not be willing to invest in real estate.

3. **Manage Tenants.** Do you think you could successfully deal with tenants and the management demands required in real estate investing?

4. **Disadvantages of Real Estate.** The text describes several disadvantages of real estate investments. Identify two that might stop you from investing in real estate. Identify ways to circumvent those two obstacles.

5. **Timeshare as an Investment.** Explain why timeshares should not be considered an investment. What are some reasons people buy timeshares?

6. **Invest in High Risk.** What percentage of your portfolio, if any, do you think should be invested in high-risk investments? Explain.

7. **Options and Futures.** Both options and futures are high-risk investments. Identify one that seems like an unwise idea, and explain why it is unappealing.

DO THE MATH

1. **Price-to-Rent Ratios.** Calculate the price-to-rent ratios for the following properties arranged by price of home followed by likely annual rental income: (a) $400,000/$40,000; (b) $300,000/$36,000; (c) $200,000/30,000.

2. **Return Using Leverage.** Donny bought a rental property for $300,000 cash and, one year later, sold it for $320,000. His brother Denny bought the building next door with only $60,000 of his own money and borrowed $240,000, and (after ignoring expenses) then sold it for $320,000. What is the rate of return for each investor?

3. **Real Estate Investment Returns.** Justin Nicholas, an electrician from Mattoon, Illinois, is interested in the numbers of real estate investments. He has reviewed the figures in Table 16-2 and is impressed with the potential 27.8 percent return after taxes. Justin is in the 25 percent marginal tax bracket. Answer the following questions to help guide his investment decisions:

   (a) Substitute Justin's 25 percent marginal tax bracket (his state has no state income tax) in Table 16-2, and calculate the taxable income and return after taxes.

   (b) Why does real estate appear to be a favorable investment for Justin?

   (c) What one factor might be changed in Table 16-2 to increase Justin's return?

   (d) Calculate the after-tax return for Justin, assuming that he bought the property and financed it with a 7 percent, $175,000 30-year mortgage with annual interest costs of $13,971.

4. **Vacation Condo Investment.** Elizabeth Bennett, a caterer from Itta Bena, Mississippi, is considering buying a vacation condominium apartment for $265,000 in Park City, Utah. Elizabeth hopes to rent the condo to others to keep her costs down. Answer the following questions to help Elizabeth with her decisions.

   (a) Elizabeth's $210,000, 30-year mortgage loan has a 6 percent interest rate and costs $15,108 annually (from Table 9-4 on page 270). She figures that $14,000 of her mortgage payments will go for interest during the first year. On top of that are monthly expenses for property taxes ($140), homeowner's insurance ($80), and homeowner's association fee ($100). Which of these costs will be tax deductible?

   (b) If Elizabeth is in the 30 percent combined federal and state marginal tax bracket, how much less in taxes will she pay if she buys this condo?

   (c) Given that she would like to personally use the condo for vacations totaling 10 to 12 days per year, how many days will Elizabeth have to rent it out before she would become eligible to deduct rental losses from her taxes?

   (d) Because Park City is primarily a winter ski resort, fewer condo renters can be found in the off season; therefore, Elizabeth is concerned about qualifying to deduct rental losses. Assuming she could rent the condo for $400 per day, summarize the IRS-approved rental alternative she could use to generate some tax-free income. Calculate the maximum amount of money Elizabeth could obtain using that plan.

   (e) Figure Elizabeth's annual net out-of-pocket cost to buy the condominium and rent it out minimally for tax-free income. List the costs and total on an annualized basis. Next, deduct the savings on income taxes as well as the presumed rental for the number of IRS-allowed days.

   (f) Using the figure derived in part (e), what would Elizabeth's out-of-pocket cost per day be to use the condo herself if she stayed there ten days each year? Fifteen days each year?

FINANCIAL PLANNING CASES

CASE 1

The Johnsons Consider a Real Estate Investment

Harry and Belinda Johnson are considering purchasing a residential income property as an investment. The Johnsons want to achieve an after-tax total return of 7 percent. They are considering a property with an asking price of $190,000 that should produce $27,000 in gross rental income and $15,000 in net operating income.

(a) Calculate the price-to-rent ratio on the property.

(b) Calculate the present value of after-tax cash flow for the property, assuming that the after-tax cash-flow numbers are $8000 for the first year, $8400 for the second year, $8800 for the third year, $9200 for the fourth year, and $9600 for the fifth year, and that the selling price of the property will be $210,000 in five years. Prepare your information in a format similar to Table 16-3, using Appendix A-2 or the *Garman/Forgue* companion website to discount the future after-tax cash flows to their present values.

(c) Give the Johnsons your advice on whether they should invest in the property at its current price of $190,000.

CASE 2

Victor and Maria Consider Hedging an Investment with Puts

Victor and Maria Hernandez invested in 200 shares of Pharmacia Corporation common stock at $93 per share. They purchased the stock because the company is testing a new drug that may represent a significant medical breakthrough. The stock's value has already risen $8 in three months, in anticipation of the U.S. Food and Drug Administration's approval of the new drug. Many observers believe that the price of the stock could reach $120 if the drug is successful. If it does not prove to be the breakthrough anticipated, the price of the stock could drop back to the $85 range, or even lower. The Hernandezes are optimistic but feel that they should hedge their position a bit. As a result, they have decided to purchase two nine-month Pharmacia 100-share puts for $3 per share at a striking price of $93 per share. Ignore commissions when answering the following questions.

(a) What price would the Pharmacia stock need to reach for the Hernandezes to break even on their investment?

(b) How much would the Hernandezes gain if they sold the stock for $102 six months from now?

(c) How much would the return be as a percentage on an annualized basis?

(d) If the price of the stock dropped to $85 in six months, how much would the Hernandezes lose?

CASE 3

Julia Price Tries High-Risk Investing

Julia continues to be a hard worker and, at age 50, has saved and invested wisely for her planned financially successful retirement. She has an extra $15,000 in a cash management account beyond what she needs for emergency savings. She rejected options and futures as too risky but is considering gold. Julia wonders if the price increases of the past decade will continue, and she has always thought about investing in antique furniture. Offer your opinions about her thinking.

CASE 4

Real Estate or Stocks?

Junhee Chang, a senior research analyst in St. Clairsville, Ohio, has bought and sold high-technology stocks profitably for years. Lately some of her stock investments have done poorly, including one company that went bankrupt. Emily, a longtime friend at work, has suggested that the two of them invest in real estate together because property values in some neighborhoods have been rising in anticipation of a large manufacturing company's plans to increase its workforce. Emily has looked at three small office buildings and some residential duplexes as possible investments.

(a) Contrast the wisdom of investing in commercial office buildings versus the attraction of investing in residential properties.

(b) List three of the advantages associated with real estate investments.

(c) List three things that can go wrong for real estate investors.

CASE 5

From Real Estate to Options and Futures

Brandon Williams and Jason Richardson, longtime partners in Lawton, Oklahoma, have bought and sold real estate properties for ten years. They have profited on many transactions, although they had some substantial losses last year. Their portfolio of real estate is worth about $4.7 million, on which they owe $2.9 million. Jason has read about investing in options and futures contracts, and last week, he talked with a stockbroker about the possibilities.

(a) Offer some reasons why Jason might gain by investing $100,000 or $200,000 in options and futures contracts.

(b) List some of the risks of options trading for Brandon and Jason.

(c) From an investor's point of view, contrast trading in futures contracts with buying highly leveraged real estate.

BE YOUR OWN PERSONAL FINANCIAL MANAGER

1. **Foreclosure and Short Sales.** Given that there are so many foreclosed homes on the market, tell why you might or might not be interested in buying one as an investment. Write a summary of your conclusions.

2. **Before Investing in Real Estate.** Review the information in the Did You Know? Box titled "Smart Steps to Protect Yourself Before Investing in Real Estate" and identify two suggestions that you definitely would follow if you invested in real estate. Write a summary of your conclusions.

3. **Disadvantages of Real Estate Investing.** Review the list in the "Disadvantages of Real Estate Investing" section and identify two disadvantages that you think might keep you from personally investing in real estate. Write a summary of your conclusions.

4. **Real Estate ETFs.** Go to the "Real Estate ETF" page for StockEncyclopedia.com (http://etf.stock-encyclope dia.com/category/real-estate-etfs-reits.html) and select five illustrative companies that sell REIT ETFs. Write a brief report comparing those five ETFs.

ON THE 'NET

1. **Research Home Prices.** To find prices on homes in your community, go to Yahoo! Real Estate (http://realestate.yahoo.com/Homevalues). Input addresses of homes on five nearby streets and summarize your price information findings.

2. **Research Mortgage Rates.** Find out current mortgage rates for 15-, 20-, and 30-year loans for both residential and investment loans. See LendingTree.com, Quickenloans.com, BankRate.com, and Loan.com. Write a brief report on your findings.

3. **Current Prices of Metals.** Find out the current prices of five popular metals, such as gold, silver, nickel, aluminum, cobalt, copper, lead, palladium, platinum, and silver, at websites like About.com (http://metals.about .com/cs/utilities/l/blprices.htm), Kitco (www.kitco.com /charts/), and USA Gold (www.usagold.com/gold price.html). Write a brief report on your findings.

4. **Price-to-Rent Ratios.** Visit the website for "20 Something Finance" and look at the table on price-to-rent ratios in various U.S. cities (http://20somethingfi nance.com/rent-or-buy-home/). Select a metropolitan area near you, record its price-to-rent ratio, and then give your opinion on whether prices will go up or down over the next two years.

5. **Gold ETFs.** Go online and search "gold prices per ounce" on Google or Bing. Click on five websites, including Wikipedia's "Gold ETFs," and review what is written, especially about predictions of future prices. Prepare a report summarizing your findings.

6. **Collectibles Websites.** Search the Internet for five websites featuring one type of collectible that interests you (such as coins, toys, watches, or sports memorabilia). Choose two websites and write a brief report comparing the types of information and features available for buyers of collectibles.

7. **Research Hedge Funds.** Go online and research two of the five largest hedge funds (JP Morgan Chase, Bridgewater Associates, Paulson & Co., Brevan Howard, and Soros Fund Management) by inserting "hedge fund" after the company name. Write a report comparing what services the two funds perform, participation requirements, and investment returns.

ACTION INVOLVEMENT PROJECTS

1. **Community Real Estate Prices.** Telephone two real estate brokers to determine if the prices of single-family dwellings in your community have been decreasing or increasing over the past four or five years, and ask why. Inquire about homes located near your college as well as those farther away from campus. Prepare a brief report of your findings including reasons for the change in prices.

2. **Invest in Commercial Real Estate.** Research current commercial properties for sale in your college community by reviewing the real estate section of newspapers. How many listings do you find? How many duplexes? How many small apartment buildings? Select one and prepare a report analyzing the property using the price-to-rent ratio and rental yield.

3. **Tax Consequences of Real Estate Investment.** Select a possible commercial real estate investment in your community and make a "first attempt" to prepare an analysis similar in format to that in the Did You Know? box titled "The Tax Consequences of an Income-Producing Real Estate Investment." Make any reasonable assumptions you desire and calculate the numbers. Prepare the table and a brief report of your findings.

Visit the Garman/Forgue companion website at **www.cengagebrain.com**.

PART

5

Kellis/Shutterstock.com

YOU MUST BE KIDDING, RIGHT?

Lindsey Jones is 27 years old, and she recently took a new job. Lindsey had accumulated $6000 in her previous employer's 401(k) retirement plan, and she withdrew it to help pay for her wedding. How much less money will Lindsey have at retirement at age 67 if she could have earned 8 percent on the $6000?

A. $6000

C. $96,000

B. $24,000

D. $130,000

The answer is D. Spending retirement money for discretionary purposes, instead of keeping it in a tax-deferred account where it can compound for many years, is unwise. The lesson is to keep your retirement money where it belongs!

LEARNING OBJECTIVES

After reading this chapter, you should be able to:

1. Estimate your Social Security retirement income benefit.

2. Calculate the amount you must save for retirement in today's dollars.

3. Understand why you should save for retirement within tax-sheltered retirement accounts.

4. Distinguish among the types of employer-sponsored tax-sheltered retirement plans.

5. Explain the various types of personally established tax-sheltered retirement accounts.

6. Make wise investment choices when deciding on how to invest for retirement.

7. Describe techniques for making your retirement money last.

WHAT DO YOU RECOMMEND?

Maryanne Johnson, age 32, worked for a previous employer for eight years. When she left that job, Maryanne left her retirement money in that employer's defined-contribution plan. It is now worth $120,000. After getting divorced and remarried four years ago, she has been working as an assistant food services manager for a large convention center in Indianapolis, Indiana, earning $80,000 per year. Maryanne contributes $267 each month (4 per-cent of her salary) to her account in her employer's 401(k) retirement plan. Her current employer provides a 100 per-cent match for the first 4 percent of Maryanne's salary contributions. Rules allow her to contribute a total of 8 percent on her own. Today, Maryanne's 401(k) account balance is $21,000. Her investments are equally divided among three mutual funds: a growth fund, a value fund, and an S&P index fund.

Maryanne's husband, Bob, is permanently disabled, and most of his medical expenses are paid for through Maryanne's health benefits at work. Bob receives $1000 per month in disability insurance benefits, and he earns about $5000 per year as a freelance cartoonist. Maryanne is hoping that she and Bob can retire when she is age 55.

What do you recommend to Maryanne and Bob on the subject of retirement and estate planning regarding:

1. The major steps in the process to determine the amount of Maryanne and Bob's retirement savings goal?

2. How Bob's net income could be invested in a personal tax-sheltered retirement account?

3. The kinds of investment accounts into which they might put additional money over the next 23 years if they determined they needed $1 million to meet their retire-ment savings goal?

4. The investment strategies that Maryanne and Bob might follow for accumulating their retirement funds?

YOUR NEXT 5 YEARS

In the next five years, you can start achieving financial success by doing the following related retirement planning:

1. *Save continuously within a tax-sheltered employer-sponsored retirement plan at least the amount required to obtain the full matching contribution from your employer.*

2. *Start saving early in life by diversifying through mutual funds and limit company stock to no more than 10 percent of your portfolio.*

3. *Accept enough risk to increase the likelihood that you will have enough money in retirement.*

4. *Contribute to Roth IRA accounts to supplement your employer-sponsored plans.*

5. *Keep your hands off your retirement money. Do not borrow it. Do not withdraw it. When changing employers, roll over the funds into the new employer's plan or a rollover IRA account.*

retirement
The time in life when the major sources of income change from earned income (such as salary or wages) to employer-based retirement benefits, private savings and investments, income from Social Security, and perhaps part-time employment.

Today's Americans are healthier, are better educated, will live longer, and have higher expectations than their counterparts from earlier generations. Enjoying financial security during your retirement years is not a matter of luck. It takes investment planning and action. The first rule of wise retirement investing is diversification. When the stock market crashed in 2008, millions of American investors lost 40 to 50 percent of their investment assets. The biggest declines occurred in portfolios that were not diversified. Those who had a well-diversified portfolio lost only about 20 percent and were in much better shape when the market started its rebound in 2009. As you get closer to retirement, about age 50, or 55, experts recommend that you begin orienting your portfolio toward safer, more conservative investment alternatives—but not too conservative.

By investing regularly for retirement, you can turn small monthly investments into hundreds, then thousands, and eventually a million dollars or more over the years. Saving and investing 10 percent of your pay starting at age 25 can provide a lump sum of $1,540,000 at age 65, while saving just 6 percent will provide only $924,000. Yet workers age 18 to 30 only set aside an average of 5.3 percent. These calculations are based on a salary of $40,000 with 3 percent annual pay increases and investments that earn an 8 percent annual return. While compiling such a seemingly enormous sum may seem like an impossible proposition today, you can and, indeed, need to do it.

Retirement is the time in life when the major sources of income change from earned income (such as salary or wages) to employer-based retirement benefits, private savings and investments, income from Social Security, and perhaps part-time employment. (See Figure 17-1.) Planning for retirement has changed dramatically over the years. Yesterday's employer-provided pensions were commonly a reward for 30-plus years of working for one employer, but they are no longer widely available. Instead, most employers today offer voluntary retirement plans to which employees may or may not choose to contribute. As a result, both the responsibility of investing funds for retirement and the risk of making poor investments with these funds has been shifted from the employer to the employee. Thus the fact is that you—and only you—are responsible for meeting your retirement needs.

To prepare for a financially successful retirement, you must build a sufficient amount of savings and investments to supplement other sources of income in retirement, such as **Social Security retirement benefits**. To succeed in this endeavor, you must make sound investment decisions regarding your retirement assets. You must start early to save for retirement through the various retirement plans and accounts that are available to you and adequately fund them through regular and consistent savings throughout your 30 or 40 years in the workforce. You can then let the magical powers of compounding fully fund your needs and wants during the latter third of your life.

Figure 17-1

Sources of Retirement Income

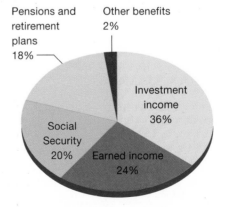

UNDERSTANDING YOUR SOCIAL SECURITY RETIREMENT INCOME BENEFITS

The Social Security program has become the most successful and popular domestic government program in U.S. history. Funding for Social Security benefits comes from a compulsory payroll tax split equally between employee and employer. Social Security taxes withheld from wages are called **FICA taxes** (named for the **Federal Insurance Contributions Act**). The amounts withheld are put into the Social Security trust fund accounts from which benefits are paid to current program recipients by the **Social Security Administration (SSA)**.

Your Taxes Support Social Security and Medicare Benefits

Wage earners pay both FICA and Medicare taxes to the SSA. The FICA tax is paid on wage income up to the **maximum taxable yearly earnings (MTYE)**, which comprises the maximum amount to which the FICA tax is applied. The MTYE figure—$106,800 for the most recent year—is adjusted annually for inflation. The FICA tax rate has been 12.4 percent, consisting of 6.2 percent paid by employees* and 6.2 percent paid by employers. Self-employed workers pay a FICA tax rate of 12.4 percent, twice that of wage earners, because they are their own employers.

Wage earners and their employers also pay a 1.45 percent **Medicare tax** on all earnings. The MTYE limit does not apply to the Medicare tax; thus the 1.45 rate applies to all employment income. Most workers pay 7.65 (6.2 + 1.45) percent of their earnings to the SSA. For example, a person earning $35,000 pays a combined FICA and Medicare tax of $2678 ($35,000 × 0.0765), and a person earning $110,000 pays $6622 ($106,800 × 0.062) plus $1595 ($110,000 × 0.0145), or a total of $8217.

It Takes a Minimum of Ten Years to Qualify for Social Security Retirement Benefits

The Social Security program covers nine out of every ten U.S. employees, although many employees of state governments are exempt and instead are covered by their state's plan. To qualify for Social Security retirement, survivors, or disability insurance benefits for you and your family, you must accumulate sufficient credits for employment in any work subject to the FICA taxes. The periods of employment in which you earn credits need not be consecutive. Military service also provides credits. You earn **Social Security credits** for a certain amount of work covered under Social Security during a calendar year. For example, workers receive one credit if they earned $1120 (for the most recent year) during any one of the four 90-day periods during the year and the annual maximum of four credits if they earned $4480 (4 × $1120). The dollar figure required for each credit earned is raised annually to keep pace with inflation.

The number of credits you have earned determines your eligibility for retirement benefits and for disability or survivors benefits if you become disabled or die. Table 17-1 shows the length-of-work requirements to receive various Social Security benefits. The SSA recognizes four statuses of eligibility.

1. Fully Insured Fully insured status requires 40 credits and provides the worker and his or her family with eligibility for benefits under the retirement, survivors, and disability programs. Once obtained, this status cannot be lost even if the person never works again. Although it is required to receive retirement benefits, "fully insured" status does not imply that the worker will receive the maximum benefits allowable.

---

*For 2011 only, Congress reduced the FICA tax rate paid by employees from 6.2% to 4.2%.

LEARNING OBJECTIVE **1**

Estimate your Social Security retirement income benefit.

FICA taxes
A 6.2 percent tax paid by both the worker and employer on the worker's employment income up to the maximum taxable yearly earnings.

maximum taxable yearly earnings (MTYE)
The maximum amount to which the FICA tax is applied.

FINANCIAL POWER POINT

Financing Social Security

Based on the Social Security Administration Trustees' best estimate, program costs will exceed tax revenues starting in 2016. Social Security's combined trust funds are projected to allow full payment of scheduled benefits until they become exhausted in 2037. While many young people doubt that Social Security will provide them with benefits, there are solutions. Simple fixes that actually will work and are favored by people of both parties and all age groups are to increase the wage cap, increase the payroll tax, and change the benefit formula.

Medicare tax
A 1.45 percent tax paid by both the worker and employer on all the worker's employment income.

Social Security credits
Accumulated quarterly credits to qualify for Social Security benefits obtained by paying FICA taxes.

fully insured Social Security status
Requires 40 credits and provides workers and their families with benefits under the retirement, survivors, and disability programs; once status is earned, it cannot be taken away even if the eligible worker never works again.

Table 17-1   Length-of-Work Requirements for Social Security Benefits

Types of Benefits	Payable to	Minimum Years of Work Under Social Security
Retirement and Survivors*	You, your spouse, child, dependent spouse 62 or older	10 years (fully insured status)
Full	Widow(er) 60 or older, disabled widow(er) 50–59, widow(er) if caring for child 18 years or younger, dependent children, dependent widow(er) 62 or older, disabled dependent widow(er) 50–61, dependent parent at 62	10 years (fully insured status)
Current	Widow(er) caring for child 18 years or younger, dependent children	1½ years of last 3 years before death (currently insured status)
Disability	You and your dependents	If younger than age 24, you need 1½ years of work in the 3 years prior to disablement; if between ages 24 and 31, you need to work half the time between when you turned 21 and your date of disablement; if age 31 or older, you must have 5 years of credit during the 10 years prior to disablement.
Medicare		
Hospitalization (Part A: automatic benefits)	Anyone 65 or older plus some others, such as the disabled	Anyone qualified for the Social Security retirement program is qualified for Medicare Part A at age 65; others may qualify by paying a monthly premium for Part A.
Medical expense (Part B: voluntary benefits)	Anyone eligible for Part A and anyone else 65 or older (payment of monthly premiums required)	No prior work under Social Security is required.

* A lump-sum death benefit no greater than $255 is also granted to dependents of those either fully or currently insured.

Source: U.S. Department of Health and Human Services.

FINANCIAL POWER POINT

You Do Not Want to Rely Solely on Social Security

If you invest wisely during your working years, Social Security is likely to provide less than 20 percent of your retirement income since you will have ample investment income. If you do not invest wisely, Social Security may provide 100 percent of your retirement income. Note however, that the actual dollar amount of Social Security income is the same in both cases. Retirees with the lowest levels of total income receive over 80 percent of their total retirement income from Social Security. Those with the highest levels receive less than 20 percent of total retirement income from Social Security. You want to be in the latter group.

2. Currently Insured To achieve **currently insured status**, six credits must be earned in the most recent three years. This status provides for some survivors or disability benefits but no retirement benefits. To remain eligible for these benefits, a worker must continue to earn at least six credits every three years or meet a minimum number of covered years of work established by the SSA.

3. Transitionally Insured **Transitionally insured** status applies only to retired workers who reach the age of 72 without accumulating 40 credits (ten years). These people are eligible for very limited retirement benefits.

4. Not Insured Workers younger than age 72 who have fewer than six credits of work experience are **not insured**.

You Can Obtain an Estimate of Your Social Security Retirement Benefits

The Social Security Administration makes available your **Social Security Estimate** that includes a record of your earnings history, a record of how much you and your various employers paid in Social Security taxes, and an estimate of the benefits that you and your family might be eligible to receive now and in the future. You can request a Social Security Estimate at www.ssa.gov/estimator/. The actual dollar amount of your eventual Social Security retirement benefits will be based on the average of the highest

35 years of earnings during your working years. In these calculations, your actual earnings are first adjusted, or **indexed**, to account for changes in average wages since the year the earnings were received. The SSA then calculates your average monthly indexed earnings during the 35 years in which you earned the most. The agency applies a formula to these earnings to arrive at your **basic retirement benefit** (or **primary insurance amount**). This is the amount you would receive at your **full-benefit retirement age**—currently 67 for those born in 1960 or later.

You have three options regarding when to begin receiving Social Security retirement benefits.

1. Begin Receiving Benefits at Your Full-Benefit Age
Once you have reached your full-benefit retirement age, you are eligible to receive your basic monthly retirement benefit. You can begin collecting these benefits even if you continue working full or part time. Your level of employment income will not affect your level of benefits, although it may affect the income taxes that you pay on your Social Security benefits (as discussed later in this chapter).

2. Begin Receiving Reduced Benefits at a Younger Age
You can choose to start receiving retirement benefits as early as age 62, regardless of your full-benefit retirement age. If you do so, however, your basic retirement benefit will be permanently reduced approximately 6 percent for each year you start early. Thus, if your full-benefit retirement age is 67, your benefits will be permanently reduced 30 percent (5 years × 6 percent). If you choose to take the earliest Social Security retirement benefits, you will be ahead financially if you do not survive to about age 80. Sixty percent of retirees elect to take their Social Security benefits early.

People considering early Social Security retirement benefits need to be aware that their checks will be further reduced if they have earned income above the annual limit ($14,160 for the most recent year). The reduction is a $1 reduction in benefits for every $2 in earnings. A person entitled to $1000 per month ($12,000 per year) in early retirement benefits who has an earned income of $15,000, for example, will be penalized $420 in benefits on the income above $14,160 ($15,000 − $14,160 = $840/2). It is possible to earn enough to completely eliminate your benefits, so the decision to take Social Security benefits early requires careful analysis.*

3. Begin Receiving Larger Benefits at a Later Age
You can delay taking benefits beyond your full-benefit retirement age. In such a case, your benefit would be permanently increased by as much as 8 percent per year. You can continue to work even

---

Social Security Estimate
On-line information that the Social Security Administration makes available to all workers, which includes earnings history, Social Security taxes paid, and an estimated benefit amount.

FINANCIAL POWER POINT

Periodically Verify the Accuracy of Your Social Security Statement Estimate

Each year you should obtain your Social Security Estimate. You should make sure that the SSA's records are up-to-date and accurate. You have only three years to correct any errors.

basic retirement benefit/ primary insurance amount
Amount of Social Security benefits a worker would receive at his or her full-benefit retirement age, which is 67 for those born after 1960.

full-benefit retirement age
Age at which a retiree is entitled to full Social Security benefits; 67 for those born in 1960 or later.

FINANCIAL POWER POINT

Online Calculators Can Help You Decide About Social Security Benefits at 62 or Later

You can compute your own retirement benefit estimate using a program that you can download to your computer from www.ssa.gov/OACT/ANYPIA/. You can do the calculations for an early, on-time or delayed beginning start date for receiving

Social Security retirement benefits to determine which option is best for you. Or go to Met Life's calculator to use their Social Security Decision Tool (www.metlife.com/individual/financial-tools/social-security-tool/index.html). This calculator takes into account your current age, how close you are from retirement, gender, and life expectancy.

---

* In the year you reach your full retirement age, you can earn up to $37,680 between January and your birthday without penalty. Above that amount, your Social Security check will be reduced by about 33 cents for every dollar earned. After full retirement age, there is no penalty for working. And the benefits aren't lost permanently. Once you reach full retirement age, your benefits may be recalculated to a higher amount to account for your increased earning record.

after you begin taking these delayed benefits. Again, your level of employment income will not affect your level of benefits, but it may affect the income taxes that you pay on your Social Security benefits.

Concept Check 17.1

1. List the financial planning actions that individuals must take during their working life to prepare for retirement, and comment on the cost of delaying saving for retirement.

2. Summarize how workers become qualified for Social Security benefits.

3. Distinguish between the benefits provided under Social Security for a worker who is fully insured and a worker who is currently insured.

4. How is the dollar amount of one's Social Security benefit determined?

5. Explain what happens if you choose to retire earlier than your full retirement age, which is probably 67.

LEARNING OBJECTIVE 2

Calculate the amount you must save for retirement in today's dollars.

**retirement savings goal/
retirement nest egg**
Total amount of accumulated savings and investments needed to support a desired retirement lifestyle.

HOW TO CALCULATE THE AMOUNT YOU MUST SAVE FOR RETIREMENT IN TODAY'S DOLLARS

To plan for a financially successful retirement, you first need to set a goal. Otherwise, as one of the most quoted figures in sports, baseball legend Yogi Berra, says, "If you don't know where you are going, you will end up somewhere else." Your **retirement savings goal**, or **retirement nest egg**, is the total amount of accumulated savings and investments needed to support your desired retirement lifestyle. Financial planners often say that people need 80 to 100 percent of their preretirement gross income (including Social Security benefits) to meet their expenses in retirement and maintain their lifestyle. This amount includes what you have to pay in income taxes. Achieving this goal will be a big challenge, but it is one you can meet successfully. As the American Savings Education Council says, "You have the power to choose today how you will spend your retirement tomorrow."

Setting a personally meaningful retirement goal helps motivate people to take the necessary saving and investing actions. If you begin to save and invest for retirement early in life, the compounding effect on money over time will make it fairly easy for you to reach your retirement savings goal. If you want to spend less than 15 minutes to get a basic idea of the savings you will need when you retire, see the one-page worksheet of the American Savings Education Council's Ballpark Estimate (www.choosetosave.org/ballpark/).

Projecting Your Annual Retirement Expenses and Income

Projecting your annual retirement expenses in current dollars and being knowledgeable about the sources of income that might support these expenditures lead logically to a key question that may be asked in several ways: "How much money must be set aside to provide that support?" or "What is my retirement savings goal?" or "How large a retirement nest egg do I need?" To calculate this amount, you can fill out the Run the Numbers worksheet, "Estimating Your Retirement Savings Goal in Today's Dollars" (page 518). Each spouse in a married couple should prepare a worksheet rather than combine income and savings amounts. You do not have to remain clueless about how much money you will need when you retire or how much you must save to get there. Simply do the math.

An Illustration of Retirement Needs

Consider the case of Erik McKartmann, aged 35 and single, the manager of a weight loss and fitness center in South Park, Colorado. Erik currently earns $50,000 per year. He has been contributing $165 per month ($1980 annually) into an IRA account he set up several years ago before beginning his current job. Erik hopes to retire at age 62.

1. Erik has chosen not to develop a retirement budget at this time. Instead, he simply multiplied his current salary by 80 percent to arrive at an estimate of the annual income (in current dollars) needed in retirement of $40,000 ($50,000 × 0.80). This amount was entered on line 1 of the worksheet. If Erik wants to increase the amount of dollars to support a higher retirement lifestyle, he can simply increase the percentage in the calculation.

2. Erik checked the Social Security Administration to estimate his benefits in today's dollars. At age 62, he could expect a monthly benefit of $1100 (in current dollars). Multiplying by 12 gave an expected annual Social Security benefit of $13,200 (in current dollars), which Erik entered on line 2 of the worksheet.

3. Line 3 of the worksheet, which calls for Erik's expected pension benefit, is appropriate for defined-benefit plans. After discussing his expected employer pension with the benefits counselor at work, Erik found that his anticipated benefit under the plan would amount to approximately $5800 annually, assuming that he remained with the company until his retirement, so he entered that figure on line 3.

4. Erik adds lines 2 and 3 to determine his total estimated retirement income from Social Security and his employer pension. The amount on line 4 would be $19,000 ($13,200 + $5800).

5. Subtracting line 4 from line 1 reveals that Erik would need an additional income of $21,000 ($40,000 − $19,000) in today's dollars from savings and investments to meet his annual retirement income needs.

6. At this point, Erik has considered only his annual needs and benefits. Because he plans to retire at age 62, Erik will need income for 20 years based on his life expectancy. (Of course, Erik could live well into his 80s, which would mean that he would need to save even more.) Using Appendix A-4 and assuming a return that is 3 percent above the inflation rate, Erik finds the multiplier 14.8775 where 3 percent and 20 years intersect. He then calculates that he needs an additional amount of $312,427 (14.8775 × $21,000) at retirement. That's a big number! And it is in current dollars. The number does not dissuade Erik from saving because he knows he has time and the magic of compounding on his side.

7. Erik's current savings and investments can be used to offset the $312,427 he will need for retirement. Erik has zero savings in his employer's 401(k) account; however, he does have some money invested in an IRA ($24,000), plus some other investments ($13,000). These amounts are totaled ($37,000) and recorded on line 7E.

8. If left untouched, the $37,000 that Erik has built up will continue to earn interest and dividends until he retires. Because he has 27 more years until retirement, Erik can use Appendix A-1 and, assuming a growth rate of 3 percent over 27 years, find the factor 2.2213 and multiply it by the total amount in line 7. Erik's $37,000 should have a future value of $82,188 at his retirement, so he puts this amount on line 8.

Understanding your Social Security and employer-based retirement benefits is a first step in retirement planning.

© 2010 Klaus Tiedge/Jupiter Images Corporation

DID YOU KNOW?

About Women and Retirement Planning

Women are less likely to get retirement benefits from their employers. This occurs, in part, because women are more likely to work for employers who do not offer a retirement plan. In addition, women often earn less than men; hence, because of their lower average incomes, women receive less Social Security income than men (about $900 per month compared with over $1100). Women live longer than men; therefore, women should consider saving more money for retirement than men.

9. Subtracting line 8 from line 6 reveals that Erik's retirement nest egg will need an additional $230,239 ($312,427 – $82,188) at the time of retirement.
10. Using Appendix A-3 and a growth rate of 3 percent over 27 years, Erik finds a factor of 40.7096. When divided into $230,239, it reveals that he needs savings and investments of $5656 per year until retirement.
11. Erik records his current savings and investments of $1980 per year on line 11.
12. Erik subtracts line 11 from line 10 to determine the additional amount of annual savings that he should set aside in today's dollars to achieve his retirement goal. His shortfall totals $3676 per year. By saving an extra $306 each month ($3676 ÷ 12), he can reach his retirement goal established in step 1.

RUN THE NUMBERS

Estimating Your Retirement Savings Goal in Today's Dollars

This worksheet will help you calculate the amount you need to set aside each year in today's dollars so that you will have adequate funds for your retirement. The example here assumes that a single person is now 35 years old, hopes to retire at age 62, has a current income of $50,000, currently saves and invests about $1980 per year, contributes zero to an employer-sponsored retirement plan, anticipates needing a

retirement income of $40,000 per year assuming a spending lifestyle at 80 percent of current income ($50,000 × 0.80), and will live an additional 20 years beyond retirement. Investment returns are assumed to be 3 percent after inflation—a reasonable but conservative estimate for a typical portfolio. The financial needs would differ if the growth rate of the investments was less than 3 percent. This approach simplifies the calculations and puts the numbers to estimate retirement needs into today's dollars. The amount saved must be higher if substantial inflation occurs.

		Example	Your Numbers
1.	Annual income needed at retirement in today's dollars (Use carefully estimated numbers or a certain percentage, such as 70% or 80%.)	$ 40,000	_____
2.	Estimated Social Security retirement benefit in today's dollars	$ 13,200	_____
3.	Estimated employer pension benefit in today's dollars (Ask your retirement benefit adviser to make an estimate of your future pension, assuming that you remain in the same job at the same salary, or make your own conservative estimate.)	$ 5,800	_____
4.	Total estimated retirement income from Social Security and employer pension in today's dollars (line 2 + line 3)	$ 19,000	_____
5.	Additional income needed at retirement in today's dollars (line 1 – line 4)	$ 21,000	_____
6.	Amount you must have at retirement in today's dollars to receive additional annual income in retirement (line 5) for 20 years (from Appendix A-4, assuming a 3% return over 20 years, or 14.8775 × $21,000)	$312,427	_____
7.	Amount already available as savings and investments in today's dollars (add lines 7A through 7D, and record the total on line 7E)		
	A. Employer savings plans, such as a 401(k), SEP-IRA, or profit-sharing plan	0	
	B. IRAs and Keoghs	$ 24,000	
	C. Other investments, such as mutual funds, stocks, bonds, real estate, and other assets available for retirement	$ 13,000	
	D. If you wish to include a portion of the equity in your home as savings, enter its present value minus the cost of another home in retirement	0	
	E. Total retirement savings (add lines A through D)	$ 37,000	_____
8.	Future value of current savings/investments at time of retirement (using Appendix A-1 and a growth rate of 3% over 27 years, the factor is 2.2213; thus, 2.2213 × $37,000)	$ 82,188	_____
9.	Additional retirement savings and investments needed at time of retirement (line 6 – line 8)	$230,239	_____
10.	Annual savings needed (to reach amount in line 9) before retirement (using Appendix A-3 and a growth rate of 3% over 27 years, the factor is 40.7096; thus, $230,239 ÷ 40.7096)	$ 5,656	_____
11.	Current annual contribution to savings and investment plans	$ 1,980	_____
12.	Additional amount of annual savings that you need to set aside in today's dollars to achieve retirement goal (in line 1) (line 10 – line 11)	$ 3,676	_____

DID YOU KNOW?

Online Retirement Calculators

There are dozens of online retirement calculators, mostly free, that take only minutes to complete. These are educational tools that help get you thinking and perhaps acting about saving and investing for retirement. A simple calculator, such as Fidelity's interactive website (http://personal.fidelity.com/planning/retirement/content/myPlan/index.shtml), can get you started.

A more comprehensive calculator, such as T. Rowe Price's (www.troweprice.com/ric), uses modern portfolio theory (as discussed in Chapter 13). It calculates a projected monthly income stream throughout retirement taking into account current and future savings in employer-sponsored retirement plans, as well as other retirement accounts and regular taxable accounts, Social Security, other sources of income, expected number of years in retirement, and investment strategy before and after retirement.

Research suggests that those who calculate how much they need to save often end up having a more financially successful retirement. In your assumptions, perhaps use a 5 percent long-term rate of return minus a 3 percent annual inflation rate, and try more than one calculator.

Following are some additional websites for retirement planning:

- *AARP (www.aarp.org/money/financial_planning/)*
- *CNNMoney.com (http://money.cnn.com/pf/retirement/)*
- *MSN Money (www.moneycentral.msn.com/retire/home.asp)*
- *The Motley Fool (www.fool.com/Retirement/ RetirementPlanning/RetirementPlanning01.htm)*
- *SmartMoney.com (www.smartmoney.com/retirement/)*
- *GenYWealth (www.genywealth.com/)*

Suggestions for Funding Erik's Retirement Goal

Erik needs to continue what he is doing—saving and investing—plus save a little more so he can enjoy his lifestyle when his full-time career ends. Erik should discuss with his benefits counselor how much he can save and invest via the company's new 401(k) program.

Erik needs to save more for retirement. He should contribute an additional $3676 per year, which is only another $306 per month, into his employer's 401(k) plan—that is, about 7.3 percent of his salary. To create an extra margin of safety, and if the rules of his employer's retirement plan permit it, he could save even more of his salary. His employer might also make a matching contribution (discussed later) of some of Erik's 401(k) contributions.

One of the reasons Erik needs to save more is that he plans to retire at age 62. If he were instead to plan to retire at 67 (his Social Security retirement age), he could save about $1500 less per year and have income until age 87 rather than 82. This is a decision he can defer until he gets older. If he is in good health at age 62, he can wait to retire. People routinely underestimate the number of years they will be retired. This is because their life expectancy at birth is not the same as their life expectancy as they get older.

ADVICE FROM A PRO

Buy Your Retirement on the Layaway Plan

The large retirement savings goal dollar amount scares some people. To allay such concerns, the following novel approach to thinking about retirement saving has been suggested. You can look at your retirement as something you "buy." The "retail price" is the retirement nest egg goal itself. From that amount, you can subtract "discounts" for anticipated income from Social Security, employer-sponsored retirement accounts, personal retirement accounts, and any other funds you expect to have accumulated. Then you identify the difference—the shortfall indicated on line 9 of the Run the Numbers worksheet—and buy it on a "layaway plan." The additional amounts you periodically save and invest are, therefore, the "layaway payments" with which you "buy" your retirement. This is smart thinking!

Dennis R. Ackley
Ackley & Associates, Kansas City, Missouri

You may have a life expectancy at birth of 77 years, but if you make it to age 70, your life expectancy is age 87. And that is simply the average; almost half of 70 year olds will make it to age 90.

The additional $3676 in current dollars assumes that the growth of Erik's investments will be 3 percent higher than the inflation rate. As his income goes up, Erik should continue saving about 7.3 percent of his income to reach his goal of retiring at age 62. In this way, he will have a larger amount of income at retirement, thereby replacing his higher level of employment income. Redoing the calculations every few years will help keep Erik informed and on track for a financially successful retirement.

LEARNING OBJECTIVE ③

Understand why you should save for retirement within tax-sheltered retirement accounts.

after-tax money
Funds put into regular investment accounts; subject to income taxes.

tax-sheltered retirement accounts
Retirement account for which all earnings from the invested funds are not subject to income taxes.

FINANCIAL POWER POINT

Cost of Delaying Saving for Retirement

Making steady contributions of $3000 every year to a tax-sheltered retirement account earning 8 percent annually for 30 years will accumulate to $340,000. Delaying ten years before beginning to save accumulates only $137,000. Thus, the ten early years of saving $3000 annually (only $30,000 in total) gives you an additional $203,000 for retirement!

pretax money
Investing before income taxes are calculated, thus gaining an immediate elimination of part of your income tax liability for the current year.

tax deferred
The individual does not have to pay current income taxes on the earnings (interest, dividends, and capital gains) reinvested in a retirement account.

✓ **Concept Check 17.2**

1. List the steps in the process of estimating your retirement savings goal in today's dollars.

2. In the text example, what can Erik do to save more for his retirement?

3. Give your impression of the idea of buying retirement on the "layaway plan."

INVESTING IN TAX-SHELTERED RETIREMENT ACCOUNTS MAKES IT EASIER TO REACH YOUR GOAL

The funds you put into regular investment accounts represent **after-tax money**. Assume, for example, that a person in the 25 percent tax bracket earns an extra $1000 and is considering investing those funds. She will pay $250 in income taxes on the extra income, which leaves only $750 in after-tax money available to invest. Furthermore, all earnings from the invested funds are also subject to income taxes each year as they are accrued. Matters are much different when you invest in **tax-sheltered retirement accounts**.

First Benefit:
Your Contributions May Be Tax Deductible

Contributions may be "deductible" from your taxable income in the year the contributions are made. In this situation, you pay zero taxes on the contributed amount of income in the current year. This means that you are investing with **pretax money**, and the salary amount you defer, or contribute, to a tax-sheltered retirement account comes out of your earnings before income taxes are calculated. Thus, you gain an immediate elimination of part of your income tax liability for the current year. The advantage of using tax-deductible contributions is illustrated in Table 17-2. The maximum contribution varies (discussed later) depending on the type of tax-sheltered account you are using.

Second Benefit: Tax-Deferred Earnings
Allow You to Accumulate Much More Retirement Money

Income earned on funds in tax-sheltered retirement accounts accumulates **tax deferred**. In other words, the individual does not have to pay income taxes on the earnings (interest, dividends, and capital gains) as they accrue as long as they are reinvested within the retirement account.

You will have much more money when it is time to retire if you use tax-sheltered accounts for your investing instead of personal taxable accounts. This is because your entire deposit goes into the account tax free and all of your investment earnings will remain in the account to grow. The following examples assume that a person who pays combined federal income taxes at a 25 percent rate invests $3000 per year for 35 years in a diversified

The Financial Benefits of 401(k) Participation

Table 17-2

Samantha Smarty participates in her employer's 401(k) retirement plan, and contributes $3600 of her $60,000 income. Since her contributions are tax deductible and she is in the 25 percent federal tax bracket, this reduces her federal income taxes by $900 ($9600 – $8700), and it takes another $200 off her state income tax liability ($3100 – $2900). Thus, for a net outflow of only $2500 ($47,300 – $44,800), Samantha gets to invest $3600. That's a 30 percent return ($3600 – $2500 = $1100/$3600) on her "investment." Whoa! What a good deal!

	Not Participating in 401(k) Plan	Participating in 401(k) Plan
Income	$60,000	$60,000
Contribution to plan	– 0 –	3,600
Taxable income	60,000	56,400
Federal income tax	9,600	8,700
State income tax	3,100	2,900
Take-home pay	$47,300	$44,800

portfolio of stocks, bonds, and mutual funds that earns 8 percent annually. We use 35 years because that is the low end of the typical person's working life. Those who work, and save, longer can accumulate additional funds. Calculations are from Appendix A-4.

You Accumulate $334,300 by Making Annual After-Tax Investments That Are Not Tax Sheltered

The sum of $3000 in after-tax money is invested in a personal taxable account every year for 35 years. Because the 8 percent return is subject to annual income taxes, the return rate is effectively reduced to 6 percent [8 percent × (1 – 0.25)]. A $3000 annual investment for 35 years that earns 6 percent annually will grow to $334,300. The person has invested $105,000.

You Accumulate $516,950 by Making Annual After-Tax Investments That Are Tax Sheltered

The sum of $3000 in after-tax money is invested in a tax-sheltered account every year for 35 years. Because no income taxes are assessed on the interest, dividends, and capital gains while they accumulate, the return rate is 8 percent. A $3000 annual investment for 35 years that earns 8 percent annually will grow to $516,950. The person has invested $105,000. Examples of this type of investment program are the Roth 401(k) and Roth IRA plans (discussed later).

You Accumulate $516,950 by Making Annual Pretax Investments That Are Tax Sheltered

The $3000 in pretax money is invested in a tax-sheltered account every year for 35 years. Pretax contributions to retirement accounts reduce the current year's income tax liability, so the investor saves $750 ($3000 × 0.25) in income taxes. Instead of the $750 going to the government, those dollars are used to reduce the amount the person had to invest. A $3000 annual investment for 35 years that earns 8 percent annually will grow to $516,950. Of the $105,000 invested, the person put in only $78,750 because $26,250 was money that would have otherwise gone to the IRS. Examples of this type of investment program are the 401(k) and IRA plans (discussed later).

You Accumulate $646,188 by Making Annual Investments That Tax-Shelter Growth Plus Invest the Money That Would Have Gone to the IRS in Taxes

The $3000 in pretax money is invested in a tax-sheltered account every year for 35 years. Pretax contributions to qualified accounts reduce the current year's income tax liability, so the investor saves $750 ($3000 × 0.25) in income taxes. This time, however, the investor uses that $750 to help fund a larger contribution—$3750 instead of $3000. A $3750 annual investment for 35 years ($131,250 invested, although only $105,000 was the investor's money and $26,250 was money that would have otherwise gone to the IRS) that earns 8 percent annually will grow to $646,188.

DID YOU KNOW?

Tax Consequences in Retirement Planning

Tax-deferred retirement plans, like 401(k) plans and traditional IRAs, provide these benefits:

- *Your contributions are tax deductible and are not subject to federal, state, and local income taxes.*

- *No income taxes are due on any earnings on the assets until withdrawn.*

- *Withdrawals are subject to income taxes at your marginal tax rate, which in retirement may be lower than your tax rate today.*

- *Other retirement income, such as from Social Security, pensions, employment, interest, dividends, and capital gains, is subject to income taxes.*

- *When you die, any beneficiary may choose to roll your 401(k) assets into his or her IRA tax free.*

---

tax-free withdrawals
Removal of assets from a retirement account with no taxes assessed.

Third Benefit: Your Withdrawals Might Be Tax Free

A **tax-free withdrawal** is a removal of assets from an account with no taxes assessed. IRS regulations permit tax-free withdrawals from certain after-tax retirement accounts, such as the Roth IRA, which is discussed later. **Tax-free** means that withdrawals are never taxed.

 Concept Check 17.3

1. Distinguish between after-tax money put into investments and pretax money.

2. Give your impression of the logic of the "net outflow" numbers of participating in a 401(k) plan.

3. Explain what is meant by tax-sheltered investment growth on money invested through qualified retirement accounts.

 LEARNING OBJECTIVE   4

Distinguish among the types of employer-sponsored tax-sheltered retirement plans.

employer-sponsored retirement plan
An IRS-approved retirement plan offered by an employer (also called qualified plans).

Employee Retirement Income Security Act (ERISA)
Regulates employer-sponsored plans by calling for proper plan reporting and disclosure to participants in defined-contribution, defined-benefit, and cash-balance plans.

REACH YOUR GOAL THROUGH EMPLOYER-SPONSORED RETIREMENT PLANS

From the earlier discussion, you can see the fantastic benefits of saving for retirement via a tax-sheltered plan. Such plans are offered by many employers. Approximately one-third of all workers at small firms participate in an employer-sponsored retirement plan; at medium-size to large firms, about three-quarters participate. Unfortunately, one-half of all workers age 18 to 30 fail to save for retirement through their employer's retirement plans and, as a result, miss out on the many benefits of these plans. Don't let that be you. If you have a plan at work, use it. If not, set up and contribute to a personally established plan, as discussed later in this chapter.

Employer-Sponsored Retirement Plans Are Government Regulated

Employers usually offer retirement plans to their employees because the promise of a secure retirement represents an effective way to recruit and retain valuable workers. An **employer-sponsored retirement plan** is an IRS-approved plan offered by an employer. These are called **qualified plans**, meaning that they qualify for special tax treatment. The **Employee Retirement Income Security Act (ERISA)** does not require companies to offer retirement plans, but it does regulate those plans that are provided. ERISA calls for proper plan reporting and disclosure to participants. Participating in a plan, such as a 401(k) plan, can serve as the cornerstone of your retirement planning.

DID YOU KNOW?

About the Retirement Plan Contribution Tax Credit for Low-Income and Moderate-Income Savers

Young workers just starting out and low- to moderate-income workers often feel that they cannot afford to save for retirement. Congress has provided an added incentive to assist these workers. Singles with adjusted gross incomes of less than $27,750 and joint filers earning less than $55,500 can claim a nonrefundable retirement plan contribution credit (also known as a saver's tax credit). This credit ranges from 10 to 50 percent of every dollar they contribute to an IRA or employer-sponsored retirement plan up to $2000.

Assets held in tax-sheltered retirement accounts, even employer contributions, are always owned by the person who opened the account. Ownership means that you determine how the funds are to be invested and withdrawn. An added benefit of employer-sponsored plans is portability. **Portability** means that upon termination of employment, an employee can transfer the retirement funds from the employer's account to another tax-sheltered account without taxes or penalty.

ERISA also governs rules concerning eligibility, waiting periods, and vesting within employer-sponsored plans. To be eligible for any retirement benefits, an employee must first participate in the employer-sponsored retirement plan. Under ERISA, employers are allowed to require a waiting period of up to one year before allowing new employees to participate in the company's retirement plan.

Vesting ensures that a retirement plan participant has the right to take full possession of all employer contributions and earnings if the employee is dismissed, resigns, or retires. If an employee has not worked long enough for the employer to be vested before leaving his or her job, the employer's contributions are forfeited back to the employer's plan. The employee has no rights to any of those funds. Once vested, the worker has a legal right to the entire amount of money in his or her account in an employer's plan. Note that no matter when you leave an employer, you always have a vested right to the money that you personally contributed to that retirement account. Some employers permit immediate vesting, whereby the employee owns the money just as soon as the employer deposits funds into the retirement account.

Employees, under the ERISA law, must be vested no later than specified by one of the following options:

- **Cliff vesting**. The employee is fully vested within three years of employment.

- **Graduated vesting**. Employees must be at least 20 percent vested after two years of service and gain an additional 20 percent of vesting for each subsequent year until, at the end of year six, the account is fully vested.

Most Common Today Are Defined-Contribution Plans

A **defined-contribution retirement plan** voluntarily offered by an employer is designed to provide a retiring employee a lump sum at retirement. It is distinguished by its "contributions"—that is, the total amount of money put into each participating employee's individual account. The eventual retirement benefit in such an employer-sponsored plan consists solely of assets (including investment earnings) that have accumulated in the various individual accounts. In a **noncontributory plan**, money to fund the retirement plan is contributed only by the employer. In a **contributory plan**, money to fund the plan is provided by both the employer and the participant or solely by the employee. Most plans are contributory. This is the most popular retirement plan offered by employers today.

portability
Upon termination of employment, employees with portable benefits can keep their savings in tax-sheltered accounts, transferring retirement funds from employer's account directly to another account without penalty.

FINANCIAL POWER POINT

Beneficiary Designation Form

When you open a retirement account, you must sign a **beneficiary designation form**. This document contractually determines who will inherit the funds in that retirement account in case you die before the funds are distributed. This designation generally overrides any provisions in a will, and it keeps those assets out of one's estate, as discussed in Chapter 18.

vesting
Ensures that a retirement plan participant has the right to take full possession of all employer contributions and earnings if the employee is dismissed, resigns, or retires.

graduated vesting
Schedule under which employees must be at least 20 percent vested after two years of service and gain an additional 20 percent of vesting for each subsequent year until, at the end of year six, the account is fully vested.

defined-contribution retirement plan

A retirement plan designed to provide a lump-sum at retirement; it is distinguished by its "contributions"— the total amount of money put into each participating employee's individual account.

contributory plan

The most common type of employee-sponsored defined-contribution retirement plan; accepts employee as well as employer contributions.

matching contribution

Employer benefit that offers a full or partial matching contribution to a participating employee's account in proportion to each dollar of contributions made by the participant.

Many employers choose to make a **matching contribution** that may fully or partially match (up to a certain limit) the employee's elective deferral contribution to his or her employer-sponsored retirement account. The matching contribution may be up to a certain dollar amount or a certain percentage of compensation. For example, the match might be $1.00 for every $1.00 the employee contributes up the first 3 percent of pay. More common is $0.50 per $1.00 up to the first 6 percent of pay. When your employer makes a contribution to your account every time you do, you in effect obtain an "instant return" on your retirement savings. Saving $4000 a year with a $0.50 employer match immediately puts $2000 more into your retirement account. This concept is illustrated in Table 17-3. During times of low profitability, employers sometimes reduce or eliminate their matching contributions to retirement plans.

When you elect to participate and contribute to such a retirement plan, you take a portion of your salary and postpone receiving it. That money goes into your account. Because it goes there before you receive it, those funds are not subject to income taxes. Defined-contribution retirement plans are also known as **salary-reduction plans** because the contributed income is not included in an employee's salary. The tax-free contributions are designated as such on the employee's W-2 form. For tax purposes, a defined-contribution plan can be viewed as an interest-free loan from the government, via the income taxes saved, to help finance one's retirement.

Each employee's contributions are deposited with a **trustee** (usually a financial institution, bank, or trust company that has fiduciary responsibility for holding certain assets), which invests the money in various securities, including mutual funds, and sometimes the stock of the employer. Each employee's funds are managed in a separate account.

Employers who offer a defined-contribution account may choose to establish an **automatic enrollment plan** for employees. Employees are registered, and the employer withholds up to 3 percent of the employee's salary and puts that amount into each worker's account in an automatically diversified portfolio. Over time, the employer may choose to automatically increase the withholding to 6 percent, or the company maximum. Employees have the right to opt out of this kind of "automatic" plan, although taking such action defeats a valuable way to save for retirement and is usually a very bad idea.

Defined-contribution retirement plans are described as **self-directed** because the employee controls where the assets in his or her account are invested. The individual selects where to invest, how much risk to take, how much to invest, and how often contributions are made to the account.

Over time, the balance amassed in such an account consists of the contributions plus any investment income and gains, minus expenses and losses. The contributions devoted to the account are specified ("defined"). The future amount in the account at retirement will not be known until the individual decides to begin making withdrawals. This uncertainty occurs because the sum available to the retiree depends on the success of the investments made. At retirement, the retiree thus has a lump sum to manage and spend during the rest of his or her lifetime.

FINANCIAL POWER POINT

How Much Should You Save?

Only about half of twenty-somethings say they have a retirement plan, such as an IRA or 401(k). People who start saving and investing for retirement during their 20s should aim to reserve 12 to 15 percent of their pretax income every year, *including* employer contributions, for this purpose. Those who have delayed planning for retirement until their late 30s or 40s should begin investing 20 to 25 percent annually in an effort to catch up, and they also may have to be more risk aggressive in their investment choices. Saving too little will likely mean that you will work until you are 70 or 75 years old.

DID YOU KNOW?

The Power of Compounding

The benefits of (1) starting early, (2) saving an adequate amount yearly, and (3) taking on reasonable investment risk are all magnified by the power of compound interest and make a retirement nest egg in excess of $2 million entirely possible for those in their 20s.

Names of Defined-Contribution Plans

Several types of employer-sponsored defined-contribution plans exist. These include the 401(k), 403(b), and 457 plans (named after sections of the IRS tax code) and the SIMPLE IRA and SIMPLE 401(k). Each plan is restricted to a specific group of workers. You may contribute to these plans only if your employer offers them.

The **401(k) plan** is the best-known defined-contribution plan. It is designed for employees of private corporations. (You can rate the quality of your employer's 401(k) plan at www.brightscope.com.) Eligible employees of nonprofit organizations (colleges, hospitals, religious organizations, and some other not-for-profit institutions) may contribute to a **403(b) plan** that has the same contribution limits. Employees of state and local governments and non–church controlled tax-exempt organizations may contribute to **457 plans**. Only employees (not employers) make contributions into 457 plans. An employer offering 401(k), 403(b), and 457 plans may also offer Roth versions of these plans calling for after-tax (rather than tax-deferred) contributions but with provisions for tax-free withdrawals during retirement. When the employing organization has 100 or fewer employees, it may set up a **Savings Incentive Match Plan for Employees IRA (SIMPLE IRA)**. Employers with 25 or fewer employees can offer a **Salary Reduction Simplified Employee Pension Plan (SARSEP)** plan similar to a 401(k) plan. Regulations vary somewhat for each type of plan.

Limits on Contributions

There are limits on the maximum amount of income per year that an employee may contribute to an employer-sponsored plan. The maximum contribution limit to 401(k), 403(b), and 457 plans is $16,500; the maximum is $11,500 for SIMPLE IRA plans. These figures rise yearly with inflation.

Catch-Up Provision

A **catch-up provision** permits workers age 50 or older to contribute an additional $5500 to most employer-sponsored plans. Millions of people who are getting a late start on saving—including women who have gone back to work after raising children—can put more money away for retirement.

Defined-Benefit Plans Are Yesterday's Standard

The second type of employer-sponsored retirement plan, a **defined-benefit retirement plan**, pays lifetime monthly payments to retirees based on a predetermined formula. Defined-benefit plans are commonly called pensions. A **pension** is a sum of money paid regularly as a retirement benefit. Pensions are paid to retirees, and sometimes their survivors, by the Social Security Administration, various government agencies, and some

self-directed
In defined-contribution plans, employees control the assets in their account—how often to make contributions to the account, how much to contribute, how much risk to take, and how to invest.

401(k) plan
Defined-contribution plan designed for employees of private corporations.

What if You Inherit a 401(k)?

If you inherit a 401(k) or other qualified company retirement plan from someone other than your husband or wife, you may transfer the balance directly to an inherited IRA.

defined-benefit retirement plan
Employer-sponsored retirement plan that pays lifetime monthly annuity payments to retirees based on a predetermined formula.

How Much You Give Up Without Matching Employer Contributions

Table 17-3

You might consider working only for employers who offer matching contributions to your retirement account. For example, the matching 100 percent employer contributions shown below increase the retirement account balance after 30 years from $317,193 to $475,578 with a 2 percent match and to $634,386 with a 4 percent match. By increasing the employee's contribution from 4 percent ($70,000 × 0.04 = $2800) to 6 percent ($70,000 × 0.06 = $4200) to obtain the full 100 percent employer match on the first 6 percent of salary, the sum rises to almost $1 million after 30 years earning an 8 percent annual return. You should make contributions to your account at least up to the amount where you obtain the largest matching contribution from your employer. After all, the matching contributions are "free money."

Salary $70,000	Employee Contribution	100% Match of 2% of Salary	100% Match of 4% of Salary	100% Match of 6% of Salary
Employee contributions	$2,800	$2,800	$2,800	$4,200
Employer contributions	$0	$1,400	$2,800	$4,200
Total annual contributions	$2,800	$4,200	$5,600	$8,400
Account balance after 30 years earning 8%	$317,193	$475,578	$634,386	$951,579

employers. Defined-benefit plans were the standard a generation ago, but today they are offered by less than one-fifth of employers, primarily because 401(k) retirement plans are less costly to provide employees.

Benefits in defined-benefit plans are based on the years of service at the employer, average pay in the last few working years, and a percentage. For example, an employee might have a defined annual retirement benefit of 2 percent multiplied by the number of years of service and multiplied by the average annual income during the last five years of employment. In this example, a worker with 20 years of service and an average income of $48,000 over the last five years of work would have an annual benefit of $19,200 (20 × 0.02 × $48,000), or $1600 per month. In another example, an employee with 30 years of service might qualify for 60 percent of the average income over the last five years of work. With a $48,000 average salary over those five years, this worker might receive $28,800 annually, or $2400 per month.

Since the employer contributes all the money, it assumes all the investment risks associated with creating sufficient funds to pay future benefits. Some employers offer both defined-benefit and defined-contribution plans to their employees. Vesting requirements and participant rights are the same for all retirement plans offered by an employer.

Normal or Early Retirement? The earlier you retire, the smaller your monthly retirement pension from a defined-benefit plan will be because you will likely receive income for more years as a retired person. To illustrate, assume you are eligible for a full retirement pension of $28,800 per year at age 65. Your benefit may be reduced 5 percent per year if you retire at age 58 or reduced 3 percent per year if you retire at age 62. Smaller monthly pension payments are paid to the early retiree in a defined-benefit plan so that he or she will receive, in theory, the same present value amount of benefits as the person who retires later.

The financial advantage of taking early retirement depends in part on the person's life expectancy and the rate at which benefits are reduced. People who expect to live for a shorter period than the average expectancy may achieve a better financial position by retiring early. Most employees are allowed to work for as long as they choose, but companies generally do not increase benefits for employees who postpone retirement beyond age 65.

Disability and Survivors Benefits Survivors and disability benefits also represent concerns for workers who have spouses or children or are financially responsible for caring for others. A person's full retirement pension forms the basis for any benefits paid to survivors and, when part of a retirement plan, for disability benefits as well. **Disability benefits** may or may not be paid to employees who become disabled prior to retirement. People receiving either survivors or disability benefits are entitled to an amount that is substantially less than the full retirement amount. For example, if you were entitled to a retirement benefit of $2000 per month, your disability benefit might be only $1100 per month.

If a survivor is entitled to benefits, that pension amount must be paid over two people's lives instead of a single person's life; consequently, the monthly payment is different. Using the benefit described in the preceding example, if your surviving spouse is five years older than you, he or she might be entitled to $1300 per month. In contrast, if your spouse is five years younger, he or she might be entitled to only $900 per month.

A qualified **joint and survivor benefit** (or **survivor's benefit**) is an annuity whose payments continue to the surviving spouse after the participant's death, often equal to at least 50 percent of the participant's benefit. This requirement can be waived if desired, but only after marriage—not in a prenuptial agreement. Federal law dictates that a spouse or ex-spouse who qualifies for benefits under the plan of a spouse or former spouse must agree in writing to a waiver of the spousal benefit. This **spousal consent requirement** protects the interests of surviving spouses. If the spouse does waive his or her survivor benefits, the worker's retirement benefit will increase. Upon the worker's death, the spouse will not receive any survivor benefits when a waiver has been signed. Unless a spouse has his or her own retirement benefits, it is usually wise to keep the spousal benefit.

disability benefits
Substantially reduced benefits paid to employees who become disabled prior to retirement.

joint and survivor benefit/ survivor's benefit
Annuity whose payments continue to a surviving spouse after the participant's death; often equals at least 50 percent of participant's benefit.

spousal consent requirement
Federal law that protects the surviving rights of a spouse or ex-spouse to retirement or pension benefits unless the person signs a waiver of those rights.

Cash-Balance Plan—A Hybrid Employer-Sponsored Retirement Plan

Some employers have established or amended their existing retirement plans to create a third type of employer-sponsored retirement plan, a hybrid of the defined-contribution and defined-benefit plans. A **cash-balance plan** is a defined-benefit plan that gives each participant an interest-earning account credited with a percentage of pay on a monthly basis. It is distinguished by the "balance of money" in an employee's account at any point in time. The employer contributes 100 percent of the funds, and the employees contribute nothing. The employer contributes a straight percentage of perhaps 5 percent of the employee's salary every payday to his or her specific cash-balance account. Interest on cash-balance accounts is credited at a rate (perhaps 5 percent) guaranteed by the employer, and the employer assumes all the investment risk. As a result, the amount in the account grows at a regular rate. Employees can look ahead 5 or 25 years and calculate how much money will be in their account.

Many large employers are shifting to cash-balance retirement plans in part because they are much less costly to administer. Cash-balance plans are controversial because when substituted for a defined-benefit plan, they typically give older workers smaller benefits. Recognizing this concern, many cash-balance plans now provide a higher contribution, sometimes as large as 10 percent, for those employees age 55 and older. Younger workers who are more inclined to move from job to job may appreciate a benefit that can move with them, rather than a defined-benefit plan that offers a substantial payout only after decades of job loyalty.

Additional Employer-Sponsored Retirement Plans

Some employers offer supplemental savings plans to employees.

ESOP An **employee stock-ownership plan (ESOP)** is a benefit plan through which the employer makes tax-deductible gifts of company stock into a trust, which are then allocated into accounts for individual employees. When employees leave the company, they get their shares of stock and can sell them. In effect, the retirement fund consists of stock in the company. If the company prospers over time, the employees will own some valuable stock; if the company does poorly or goes bankrupt, the stock may be worthless. (Note that an ESOP is not an employee stock option, examined in Chapter 14, page 421, because an ESO is a gift, like a bonus, from an employer to an employee that allows employees to benefit from the appreciation of their employer's stock without putting any money down.)

To be properly diversified, experts recommend that employees have no more than 10 percent of their retirement assets invested in their employer's company stock. The Pension Protection Act provides that companies cannot require that you buy company stock to qualify for a match. If your contributions continue to be matched with stock, you are able to trade out of those shares after three years. If you already own company shares, you can sell a third at a time, over three years.

Profit-Sharing Plan A **profit-sharing plan** is an employer-sponsored plan that shares some of the profits with employees in the form of end-of-year cash or common stock contributions to employees' 401(k) accounts. The level of contributions made to the plan may reflect each person's performance as well as the level of profits achieved by the employer. Contributions might be fixed (perhaps at 10 percent of profits) or be discretionary. They can vary from year to year. Some companies offer a voluntary profit-sharing plan through which employees can regularly purchase shares of stock in the company at discounted prices.

cash-balance plan
Defined-benefit plan funded solely by an employer that gives each participant an interest-earning account credited with a percentage of pay on a monthly basis.

DID YOU KNOW?

Retirement Plan Insurance

ERISA established the Pension Benefit Guaranty Corporation (PBGC; www.pbgc.gov). The nation's 29,000 employer-sponsored defined-benefit pension plans pay insurance premiums to the PBGC, which guarantees a certain minimum amount of benefits of up to $4500 a month to 44 million eligible workers should those plans become financially unable to pay their obligations. The PBGC has taken over about 3800 plans. PBGC insurance never insures defined-contribution plans, but it does insure some cash-balance plans.

employee stock-ownership plan (ESOP)
Benefit plan in which employers make tax-deductible gifts of company stock into trusts, which are then allocated into employee accounts.

DID YOU KNOW?

Which Retirement Plan Is Most Generous?

Only the defined-benefit retirement pension program brings a guaranteed monthly pension benefit, possible reduced early retirement benefits, survivor annuities, and disability benefits. Cash-balance and 401(k) plans do not. Participants in the latter plans will need to tap into their retirement accounts to pay for disability and survivor needs, if they become necessary.

profit-sharing plan
Employer-sponsored plan that allocates some of the employer profits to employees in the form of end-of-year cash or common stock contributions to employees' 401(k) accounts.

 Concept Check 17.4

1. Summarize the main differences between defined-contribution and defined-benefit pension plans.

2. Explain why defined-contribution retirement plans are called self-directed.

3. Offer your impressions of working for an employer that offers a sizable matching contribution compared with one that does not.

4. Distinguish between an employee stock-ownership plan (ESOP) and a profit-sharing plan.

REACH YOUR GOAL THROUGH PERSONALLY ESTABLISHED RETIREMENT ACCOUNTS

LEARNING OBJECTIVE **5**

Explain the various types of personally established tax-sheltered retirement accounts.

If you do not have access to an employer plan, you should set up your own plan. IRS regulations allow you to take advantage of personally established, self-directed tax-sheltered retirement accounts such as an individual retirement account (IRA). Even if you do have a plan at work, you can benefit from contributing to one or more personally established plans. These plans include IRAs, Roth IRA accounts, Keogh plans, and SEP-IRAs. If you are not eligible for a 401(k) at work, consider starting a Roth or traditional IRA. Even if you are in a 401(k), once you have earned the full company match, it is wise to save extra money for retirement, future education expenses, or a home in a Roth IRA account.

individual retirement account (IRA)
Personal retirement account to which a person can make annual contributions that provide tax-deferred growth and then decide how to invest the funds within the IRA.

Individual Retirement Accounts (IRAs)

An **individual retirement account (IRA)** is a personal retirement account into which a person can make one or more annual contributions. These accounts are created and funded solely at the discretion of the individual who sets them up. An IRA is much like any other account opened at a bank, credit union, brokerage firm, or mutual fund company. An IRA is not an investment but rather an account in which to hold investments, like stocks and mutual funds. You can invest IRA money almost any way you desire, including collectibles like art, gems, stamps, antiques, rugs, metals, guns, and certain coins and metals. You may change investments whenever you please.

 DID YOU KNOW?

You Can Open a Personally Established Retirement Account Almost Anywhere

Individual retirement accounts (IRAs) offer flexibility on where you can invest. You may open an account at a bank, credit union, savings and loan association, or mutual fund company. Individuals often invest in stock mutual funds, particularly index funds. You can change investments whenever desired. You may choose to contribute once to a tax-sheltered retirement account and then never do so again, or you can contribute regularly for many years.

You should consider investing in an IRA to augment your retirement savings. IRAs are similar to 401(k) plans in that you do not pay taxes each year on capital gains, dividends, and other distributions from securities held within the account. The total maximum annual contribution you may make to any IRA (traditional or Roth) is $5000 (which is indexed to inflation). This overall maximum applies to workers with incomes up to $107,000 ($169,000 if married filing jointly) with reduced maximums for those with incomes up to $122,000 ($179,000 if married filing jointly) at which point the maximum contribution is $0. An additional catch-up contribution of $1000 to an IRA may be made by people age 50 and older. You may not borrow from an IRA.

To fund the account, you may make a new contribution or transfer a lump-sum distribution received from another employer plan or another IRA account to your IRA account. Taxpayers can even opt on their tax return to allocate part or all of their refund for direct deposit into an IRA account.

Traditional IRA Accounts Shelter Investment Growth A **traditional (or regular) IRA** offers tax-deferred growth. Your contributions may be tax deductible, which means that you can use all or part of your contributions to reduce your taxable income. Qualifying depends on how much your earnings are (restrictions exist to prevent some high-income earners from getting the deduction) and whether you and your spouse are eligible to participate in an employer-sponsored retirement plan. To see whether you qualify for a tax-deductible IRA, use the following guidelines:

traditional (regular) IRA
Account that offers tax-deferred growth; the initial contribution may be tax deductible for the year that the IRA was funded.

1. If you have no retirement plan at work, you can invest in a traditional IRA and deduct the entire amount from your taxes.
2. If you are married and you are not an active participant in an employer retirement plan but your spouse is an active participant, you may deduct all of your contribution to a traditional IRA.
3. If you have a retirement plan at work, you may fully or partially deduct your IRA contributions only if your adjusted gross income qualifies. The deductibility of your contribution is phased out depending on your adjusted gross income (AGI). For single taxpayers, the deductibility begins to phase out at $56,000 (and becomes $0 at $66,000), and for married taxpayers, the deductibility phases out beginning at $90,000 (and becomes $0 at $110,000).
4. If your spouse does not work outside the home, that person may contribute to a **spousal IRA**. Each partner may invest up to the limit and deduct the full amount if the combined compensation of both spouses is at least equal to the contributed amount.

spousal IRA
Account set up for spouse who does not work for wages; offers tax-deferred growth and tax deductibility.

Distributions from traditional IRAs may be fully or partially taxable. If the account is funded solely by tax-deductible contributions, any distributions are fully taxable when received. If you also made nondeductible contributions, logically some amount should not be taxed at withdrawal as it has already been taxed earlier. You should maintain adequate records of all IRA contributions—even for 40 years or more—to avoid paying too much in taxes. That means saving all annual reports of account activities. The IRS requires that withdrawals from traditional IRAs begin no later than age 70½.

DID YOU KNOW?

Sean's Success Story

Sean is now 52 years old. He has held four jobs, and two of his employers offered no retirement plan. When working at those jobs, he made monthly deposits into a Roth IRA account with low-fee mutual fund investments. He participated fully in the plans offered by the other two employers. Total annual contributions to retirement savings usually totaled about 12 percent, including the matches from his employers who offered retirement plans. When Sean changed employers, he always transferred the vested amounts in his retirement accounts to a rollover IRA account, which now has a value of $412,000. Sean

has been with his current employer for ten years, and his 401(k) account balance is $175,000. He has been careful to diversify his retirement investments. He started out almost entirely in stock funds, especially index funds. During the last two years, Sean started to move some of his money into lower risk options by focusing on high-rated bond funds. His current allocation is about 60 percent equities, 30 percent bonds, and 10 percent in a money market fund. His target percentages at a planned retirement at age 65 are 45 percent equities, 40 percent bonds, and 15 percent money market. Sean is looking forward to retirement in about 12 years with a nest egg of about $2 million.

Nondeductible Roth IRA Accounts Still Provide Tax-Free Growth A **Roth IRA** is a nondeductible, after-tax IRA that offers significant tax and retirement planning advantages. [Similar Roth 401(k)s and 403(b)s exist.] Contributions to Roth IRAs are not tax deductible, but funds in the account grow tax free. Withdrawals are tax free if taken at age 59½ or later (or if you are disabled) from an account held at least five years. Tax-free withdrawals may be made for qualifying first-time home-buyer expenses or to pay for educational expenses. Once you remove money from a Roth IRA, it is a withdrawal (not a loan), and you cannot put it back. There is no mandatory withdrawal schedule for Roth IRAs, and money in the account can pass to an heir free of estate taxes.

Roth IRA
IRA funded with after-tax money (and thus it is not tax deductible) that grows on a tax-deferred basis; withdrawals are not subject to taxation.

DID YOU KNOW?

How to Decide Between a Regular and Roth IRA

Mutual fund websites provide worksheets to help you look at the tax implications of deciding whether investing through a traditional IRA or a Roth IRA is better for you. Websites you can use to decide can be found at T. Rowe Price at (http://individual.troweprice.com/public/Retail/Retirement/IRA) and Fidelity Investments (http://personal.fidelity.com/products/retirement/iraeval/popup.shtml). The calculations will be based on your current age, current marginal tax rate, expected annual yield, years to retirement, years in retirement, and marginal income tax rate during the distribution years.

It is also possible to convert a traditional IRA to a Roth IRA. To do so, you must pay income taxes on the withdrawn amount based on your current marginal tax rate and then invest the proceeds into a Roth IRA. You can pay the additional income taxes with some of the proceeds taken out of the traditional IRA or with other money you have available. If you are under age 59½, you also must pay a 10 percent penalty.

Many websites are available to help you decide if a Roth conversion is right for you, including Vanguard (https://personal.vanguard.com/us/insights/taxcenter/planning/is-a-roth-conversion-right) and Fidelity (https://calcsuite.fidelity.com/rothconveval/app/launchPage.htm).

Keoghs and SEP-IRA Accounts Are for Self-Employed Individuals

Keogh
Tax-deferred retirement account designed for self-employed and small-business owners.

A **Keogh** (pronounced "Key-oh") is a tax-deferred retirement account designed for self-employed and small-business owners. Depending on the type of Keogh established (profit-sharing or money-purchase), an individual can save as much as 25 percent of self-employment earned income, with most plan contributions capped at $49,000 per participant. If the income comes from self-employment, contributions can still be made after age 70½. Money in Keoghs may be invested in real estate, and a Keogh can be converted to an SEP-IRA.

A **simplified employee pension–individual retirement account (SEP-IRA)** is a retirement savings account for a sole proprietor's self-employment income and owners of small businesses looking to save only in profitable years. A SEP-IRA is easier to set up and maintain than a Keogh. The maximum contribution limit to a SEP-IRA is the same as for a Keogh. People with income from a sideline business can contribute substantial amounts to a SEP-IRA account. There also is a one-person 401(k) plan, which allows larger contributions than a Keogh or SEP-IRA plan.

 Concept Check 17.5

1. What factors would lead someone to choose to save for retirement through a personally established retirement account?

2. List two differences between a traditional IRA and a Roth IRA.

3. Who would use a Keogh rather than an SEP-IRA to save for retirement?

REACH YOUR GOAL THROUGH WISE INVESTMENT CHOICES AND USE MONTE CARLO SIMULATIONS

 LEARNING OBJECTIVE **6**

Make wise investment choices when deciding on how to invest for retirement.

Two broad strategies are available when investing for retirement. Active investors can choose to manage their retirement portfolio, following a do-it-yourself approach. Passive or "hands-off" investors can put their retirement assets in an index fund or target-date retirement fund (both discussed in Chapter 15) or hire a professional to make the decisions. Professional advice for investing retirement assets is available, and advisers often use Monte Carlo simulations to help guide their recommendations.

Where to Invest Your Retirement Money

When you open any kind of defined-contribution retirement plan, you may invest in a number of alternatives. Options within employer-based plans are usually mutual funds and employer stock. With mutual funds, you will likely have, at a minimum, a stock fund, a growth stock fund, an index fund, a bond fund, and a money market fund from which to choose. You may have dozens of funds in which to invest. You will want to focus the investment returns and fees assessed by the various investment options available to you through your employer's plan. In addition, you will likely be able to invest in your own company's stock and perhaps in an annuity (discussed later). Self-established accounts such as IRAs have an even broader range of choices including individual company stocks and precious metals. So, where should you put your money?

In Chapter 13, we described several long-term investment strategies employed by wise investors (pages 395–400). The most notable of these for retirement investing is the buy and hold philosophy funded by a dollar-cost averaging approach with broad diversification using an asset allocation strategy. Retirement investors should never be jumping in and out of investments. Because retirement investing is usually accomplished on a regular basis through payroll withholding for an employer-based plan or regular savings in a personally established retirement plan, investors are using dollar-cost averaging. Diversification through asset allocation requires more planning.

One important principle in investing for retirement is to recognize that you can accept more risk in your investments the further away you are from retirement. Investing too conservatively almost guarantees low returns and not enough funds at retirement.

Here are some examples of accepting more risk. A young, risk-tolerant, long-term 401(k) or IRA investor with an aggressive investment philosophy might have a portfolio with 100 percent in a growth stock fund. A more moderate approach might have a stock fund/bond fund/money market fund portfolio allocated at 60/30/10 percent, respectively. As a young investor, you do not need to be conservative with your retirement money because you will have the time to ride out the ups and downs of the stock market. You can keep the same proportions of your asset allocation until your broad investment goals change—possibly not for another 25 or 30 years as you approach retirement.

You should allocate no more than 10 percent to your company's stock because of the need to diversify your portfolio. Similarly, until near retirement, you should not have more than 10 percent going into a money market fund because its returns are too low to build the financial nest egg you will need. So that leaves various stock and bond funds for your choices. The material on long-term investment strategies on pages 398–400 in Chapter 13 should be your guide for investing for retirement.

If you are just starting out in a 401(k) plan or have no other retirement assets, you might consider investing in a low-fee **target-date retirement fund** (see Chapter 15). These funds are the ultimate in disciplined, hands-off investing. To start, you pick a date that matches the year you plan to retire, perhaps in 2050. The fund will place your money in a diversified portfolio that automatically shifts the asset mix away from equities and toward more conservative fixed-income investments as you approach the year of your retirement.

Employees who participate in their employer-sponsored retirement plan may have access to services to automatically rebalance their retirement assets. Instead of being a do-it-yourself investor, a worker can sign up for the services of a **limited managed account**. Once you have signed a contract with a vendor approved by your employer, you and your advisor decide on your preferred asset allocation. Then the mutual fund company sells and buys your mutual fund assets, usually quarterly, on your behalf to adjust your portfolio back to your specified asset allocation percentages. Recommendations may or may not consider all of one's retirement assets, including those of a spouse or significant other, not just money in a 401(k) account. The service may be paid or subsidized by the employer. Annual fees are usually no more than one-half of 1 percent of the assets.

DID YOU KNOW?

Why You Should Avoid "High-Cost" Mutual Funds

Investing for retirement in low-cost or ultra-low-cost funds, such as an index fund or exchange-traded fund, is the single most effective strategy to fatten your retirement nest egg. The following calculations are based on research from T. Rowe Price and *Money*. Assume you are 30 years old, earn $40,000, and invest 6 percent of your salary with a $0.50 match on $1.00. Your salary increases 3 percent annually, and your investments earn 8 percent a year. Low mutual fund expenses dramatically increase your retirement nest egg.

Cost of Mutual Fund Expenses	Retirement Nest Egg at Age 65
High expenses (1.5%)	$664,000
Moderate expenses (1.0%)	$732,000
Low expenses (0.5%)	$819,000
Ultra-low expenses (0.25%)	$852,000

Valuable Retirement Investment Advice Is Based on Monte Carlo Simulations

Employer-based financial advice must follow the requirements of the Pension Protection Act, including keeping employees informed about any possible conflicts of interest. The advice must be based on computer simulations of projected investment performance. Monte Carlo simulations are an evolution of the long-term investment strategy of asset allocation and modern portfolio theory, as discussed in Chapter 13.

Monte Carlo simulations, named for the famous casino site, can be used to model the performance of hundreds or even thousands of individual mutual funds and stocks through thousands of fluctuating securities markets. The simulations allow you to estimate the probability of reaching your financial goals. This sophisticated application of asset allocation identifies the investor's acceptable level of risk tolerance and then finds an optimal portfolio of assets that will have the highest expected returns for that level of risk.

The mathematical simulations are based on long-term historical risk and return characteristics for various mixes of stock, bond, and short-term investment asset classes. Each simulation estimates how much you need to save if your investments performed better or worse than expected, and it gives the odds that your assets will last throughout the retirement time period after you choose a given set of investments and establish a withdrawal amount. Note that these calculations are probabilities, not certainties.

By using Monte Carlo simulations, investors can get a more realistic view of how much their current investments may yield in retirement. Investors may learn that they are playing it too safe by investing too conservatively, and this may prevent them from reaching their goals. By evaluating the trade-offs among various combinations of retirement plan contribution levels, diverse investment mixes, overall portfolio risk, projected retirement age, and retirement income goals, Monte Carlo simulations let you understand how certain changes in these factors will affect the chance that you will have enough money in retirement. Some investors may have to learn to be comfortable with increased risk, while others may have to save more or work longer. See Figure 17-2 for illustrative Monte Carlo calculations.

Software programs can be used to assist investors in creating an efficient portfolio using Monte Carlo simulations. Products are available from Financial Engines, Morningstar, Vanguard, and Financial Soundings. Many employers offer free or low-cost access to modern portfolio theory software as an employee benefit (such as less than $15 annually through Financial Soundings [www.financialsoundings.com]). Services might include retirement forecasts, annual report on progress toward retirement, portfolio monitoring, e-newsletters, and information on finances and investing. To try out interactive Monte Carlo simulations, see www.moneychimp.com/articles/risk/riskintro.htm.

Monte Carlo simulations
Mathematical calculations that can be used to find an optimal portfolio of mutual funds and stocks that will have the highest expected returns for a certain level of risk.

FINANCIAL POWER POINT

Remember...Buy Term and Invest the Rest

Insurance companies love to promote cash-value life insurance as a way to save for retirement. They call life insurance an investment. It is a highly overpriced way to save for retirement. If you need life insurance, buy term life insurance, not cash-value life insurance. Then use the savings from not buying cash value insurance to invest in mutual funds through tax-sheltered retirement accounts.

Monte Carlo Simulation from Financial Engines

Figure 17-2

(The analysis and recommendations pictured are hypothetical and are provided for illustrative purposes only. This illustration should not be relied on for investment advice.)

You're on track!

The Forecast for your new strategy looks good! Click the **Next** button to receive your Advice Action Kit.

Your decisions

	Current	New
Your contribution	$3,400/year	$6,100/year
Employer contribution	$1,300/year	$1,300/year
Your investments	Current	Advice
Your risk level	Mod. conserv.(0.82)	Mod. aggr.(1.25)
Retirement age	65	67
Desired income	$59,000	$59,000
Minimum income	$42,000	$42,000

Your outlook at age 65

	Current strategy	New strategy
Retirement Forecast Chance your investments and benefits will provide $59,000 per year. More...	 FORECAST 8%	 FORECAST 78%
Retirement income Estimated annual income you may have at age 65. More...		
■ Upside - excellent performance*	$63,200	$189,000
■ Median - average performance	$42,600	$82,100
▪ Downside - poor performance*	$31,400	$43,500
Possible 1-year loss Amount you could lose in the next 12 months. More...	9.1% or more	14.1% or more
	Assumptions	Assumptions

*Note: There is a 5% chance you'll have less than the downside amount and a 5% chance you'll have more than the upside amount. Amounts shown are in pre-tax dollars and have been adjusted for inflation.

Your personalized investment advice is based on your decisions. How we created your investment advice.

Investment advice

	Current strategy	New strategy
401(k) Account		
Redwood Money Market	5%	0%
Platinum Growth	17%	10%
Cypress Balanced Fund	11%	0%
Maple Bond Market	13%	13%
Sequoia Small Cap	25%	0%
Granite S&P 500 Index	29%	30%
Silver Growth and Income	0%	23%
Chestnut Idx:500 Idx	0%	24%

Source: Copyright © Financial Engines. Used with permission.

When you take the appropriate retirement planning action steps, including a moderate amount of risk when investing, you will be able to relax with the confidence that you are making wise decisions about your investment assets and the knowledge that your money will grow and will be there to fund your lifestyle during the last third of your life.

Concept Check 17.6

1. Do you visualize yourself as a "do-it-yourself" or as a "hands-off" type of investor of retirement funds? Explain why.

2. Summarize the importance of low-cost mutual fund fees to long-term investing success.

3. Offer some impressions of Monte Carlo simulations as a tool to use in retirement planning.

LEARNING OBJECTIVE **7**

Describe techniques for making your retirement money last.

AVOID WITHDRAWAL PENALTIES AND OUTLIVING YOUR RETIREMENT MONEY

Once you have accumulated a substantial retirement nest egg, you can congratulate yourself. For many years, you sacrificed some of your spending and invested instead. However, retirement planning does not end when retirement saving ends. You will also need to plan your retirement spending so you—and perhaps a significant other—can live during retirement without running out of money. To do so, you must avoid withdrawing your money early, carefully manage your retirement assets, plan appropriate account withdrawals once you do retire, consider purchasing an annuity with a portion of your retirement funds at retirement, and/or work part-time during your earliest retirement years.

Withdrawing Tax-Sheltered Retirement Money Early

For many people, the money accumulated in a 401(k) or IRA retirement account represents most—if not all—of their retirement savings. Withdrawing money early from a retirement account or borrowing some diverts the funds from their intended purpose, and the money is no longer there to grow tax-deferred. When other financial needs present themselves, there is often a desire to tap into the funds for nonretirement purposes. Such uses were not the intent of Congress when it set up the tax-favored status of the accounts. And, more importantly, making early withdrawals means that you either must retire later or retire at a lower level of living. You want to avoid both.

Some Penalty-Free Withdrawals Do Exist   Although your employer may have rules for its retirement plan that restrict withdrawals, the IRS imposes no penalty for early withdrawals in three situations:

1. **Expenses for medical, college, and home buying.** You can make penalty-free withdrawals from an IRA account (but not an employer-sponsored plan) if you pay for medical expenses in excess of 7.5 percent of your adjusted gross income, you pay medical insurance premiums after being on unemployment for at least 12 weeks, you are disabled, you pay for qualified higher-education expenses, or the distribution of less than $10,000 is used for qualifying first-time home-buyer expenses. You must pay income taxes on the amount withdrawn.

2. **Account loan.** You may borrow up to half of your accumulated assets in an employer-sponsored account, not to exceed 50 percent of the balance, or $50,000, whichever is less. The borrower pays interest on the loan, which is then credited to the person's account. Loans must be repaid with after-tax money. If the employee changes employers, he or she must repay the unpaid balance of the loan within 30 days. Otherwise, the loan is reclassified as a withdrawal, which may result in additional taxes and penalties. You may not borrow from IRA accounts.

3. **Early retirement.** You may avoid a penalty if you retire early (but not earlier than 59.5 years) or are totally or permanently disabled and you are willing to receive annual distributions according to an IRS-approved annuity method for a time period of no less than five years. You must pay taxes on the withdrawn amounts.

The IRS Has a 20 Percent Withholding Rule to Ensure Prepayment of Income Taxes

The IRS's **20 percent withholding rule** applies whenever a participant takes direct possession of the funds grown from pretax deposits into a retirement account. The rule applies whether the withdrawal occurs early or during retirement. This amount is forwarded to the IRS to prepay some of the income taxes that will be owed on the withdrawn funds. You can avoid the 20 percent withholding rule by transferring the money into a **rollover IRA**, which is simply an account set up to receive such funds. Another way to avoid the withholding rule is to make a **trustee-to-trustee rollover**. Here the funds go directly from the previous employer's trustee to the trustee of the new account, avoiding any payment to the employee.

For example, a $300,000 lump-sum distribution made directly to a former employee would result in that person receiving $240,000 and the employer withholding $60,000 for the IRS. Government regulations further require that the employee put the entire $300,000 into an account at another employer or a rollover IRA within 60 days—even though only $240,000 was actually received by the employee. The person must supply the difference ($60,000 in this instance) on his or her own. Substantial penalties are assessed for noncompliance. The 20 percent amount that was withheld may be retrieved the following tax year by filing an income tax return to claim a refund. Because of such penalties, smart people avoid taking such distributions. The IRS wants taxpayers to transfer retirement funds in such a way that the previously untaxed money remains accountable and, eventually, taxable.

trustee-to-trustee rollover
Retirement funds go directly from the previous employer's trustee to the trustee of the new account, with no direct payment to the employee occurring, thereby deferring taxation and the early withdrawal penalty.

DID YOU KNOW?

Turn Bad Habits into Good Ones

Do You Do This?	*Do This Instead!*
Put off saving for retirement	Save early and often
Avoid risk when saving for retirement	Accept risk knowing that you have time to ride out the highs and lows of the stock market
Invest solely in your employer's stock	Diversify your investments and limit company stock to no more than 10 percent of your portfolio
Rely only on your employer's plan when saving for retirement	Contribute to a Roth IRA to supplement your employer-sponsored plans if necessary to reach your calculated retirement savings goal
Withdraw or borrow money from your retirement accounts when money is desired for other reasons	Keep your hands off your retirement money

Beware of the Negative Impacts of Early Withdrawals

When money is directly withdrawn from a tax-sheltered retirement account before the rules permit—perhaps to buy a car, take a vacation, remodel a home, or pay off a credit card debt—three bad things happen:

1. **More taxes are due to the government.** Early withdrawals—typically defined as a premature distribution before age 59½—are taxed as ordinary income. Assume William Wacky, a 35-year-old with $25,000 in a tax-sheltered retirement account, withdraws $8000 out of the account. If he pays combined federal and state income taxes at the 30 percent rate, his $8000 withdrawal must be included as part of his taxable income. That will cost him an extra $2400 ($8000 × 0.30) in income taxes.

2. **Penalties are assessed.** The IRS assesses a 10 percent **early withdrawal penalty** on such withdrawals. Because William withdrew $8000, he must also pay a penalty tax of $800 ($8000 × 0.10).

early withdrawal penalty
A ten percent penalty over and above the taxes owed when money is withdrawn early from a qualified retirement account.

Planning an active retirement can include working part time at something you enjoy.

3. The investment does not grow. Withdrawing money means that the investment can no longer accumulate. The lost time for compounding will substantially shrink your retirement nest egg. William's withdrawal of $8000 out of the account that could have grown at 8 percent over the next 30 years costs him the forgone return of a whopping $80,502 (from Appendix A-1).

Summing up this example, William's early withdrawal of $8000 nets him only $4800 after taxes and penalties ($8000 − $2400 − $800), and he gave up a future value of more than $80,000 in his retirement account. More than 60 percent of workers age 18 to 34 take all the money out of their employer's tax-sheltered retirement account when they change jobs. Early withdrawals are unwise!

DID YOU KNOW?

How to Manage Your Retirement Money After Leaving Your Employer

When changing employers or retiring, you may have four choices:

1. *Leave it.* You may be able to leave the money invested in your account at your former employer until you wish to begin taking withdrawals.

2. *Transfer it.* You may be able to transfer the money to a retirement account at a new employer.

3. *Transfer it.* You can transfer the money to a rollover IRA.

4. *Take it.* You can take the money in cash and pay income taxes and penalties.

Options 2, 3, and 4 result in a **lump-sum distribution** because all the funds are removed from a retirement account at one time. Such a transfer must be executed correctly according to the IRS's rollover regulations or the taxpayer will be subject to a substantial tax bill and perhaps a need to borrow money to pay the IRS. A **rollover** is the action of moving assets from one tax-sheltered account to another tax-sheltered account or to an IRA within 60 days of a distribution. This procedure preserves the benefits of having funds in a tax-sheltered account.

Figure Out How Many Years Your Money Will Last Once You Retire

As you near retirement, you will want to ask "How long will my retirement nest egg last?" The answer to this question will depend on three factors: (1) the amount of money you have accumulated, (2) the real (after inflation) rate of return you will earn on the funds, and (3) the amount of money to be withdrawn from the account each year.

Appendix A-4 provides factors that can be divided into the money in a retirement fund to determine the amount available for spending each year. Consider the example of Kevin and Kelly Neu, 63-year-old retirees from Prescott, Arizona, who want their $500,000 retirement nest egg to last 20 years. They assume that the nest egg will earn a 6 percent annual return in the future and assume an annual inflation rate of 3 percent. The present value factor in the table in the "20 years" column and the "3 percent (6 percent investment return minus 3 percent inflation)" row in Appendix A-4 is 14.8775. Dividing

$500,000 by 14.8775 reveals that Kevin and Kelly could withdraw $33,608, or $2800 per month ($33,608 ÷ 12 months), for 20 years before the fund was depleted. Because they adjusted their rate of return for inflation, the Neus can safely increase their income by three percent each year to safeguard the spending power of their retirement income. But what if they live for 30 more years? The factor for 30 years is 19.6004, and the answer is $25,510, or $2126 per month; almost $700 less initially.

One of the mistakes that new retirees make is withdrawing money too fast. In the previous example, the Neus would be withdrawing at a 6.7 percent ($33,608/$500,000) annual rate if they planned on their nest egg lasting 20 years. Choosing a slightly lower rate of withdrawal can significantly increase their years of retirement income. By withdrawing $25,510, or about 5 percent per year, they extend their withdrawals for another ten years.

People beginning retirement should be cautious and withdraw at an even lower rate, perhaps 4 percent, because that rate is not likely to deplete their funds too rapidly. Then they can be more confident that their money will last the desired number of years. Table 17-4 indicates the likelihood that retirement money will last given certain withdrawal rates. As you can see, the Neus' initial withdrawal of 6.7 percent significantly reduces the likelihood that their money will last.

Should You Use an Annuity to "Guarantee" a Portion of Your Retirement Income?

The fear of running out of money in retirement looms large for people approaching retirement and during retirement. How can you be sure that declines in the stock market and/or high inflation will not cause you to have to significantly decrease your level of living as you age? Rather than continuing to manage their own investments and withdrawals in an effort to make the money last, some people use a portion of their retirement nest egg (such as one-third or one-half) to buy an annuity. An **annuity** is a contract made with an insurance company that provides for a series of payments to be received at stated intervals (usually monthly) for life or a specified time period. For retirees who buy an annuity, this means that an insurance company will receive a portion of their retirement nest egg and, in return, promise to send monthly payments according to an agreed-upon schedule, usually for the life of the person covered by the annuity (the **annuitant**).

Payments Start Right Away When You Buy an Immediate Annuity

Retirees typically buy an **immediate annuity** at or soon after retirement. The annuity income payments will then begin at the end of the first month after purchase. People who buy an immediate annuity typically do so with a lump sum of money rolled over from an IRA, from an employer's defined-contribution retirement account, from the cash-value or death benefit of a life insurance policy, or from other savings and investments.

annuity
Contract made with an insurance company that provides for a series of payments to be received at stated intervals (usually monthly) for a fixed or variable time period.

immediate annuity
Annuity, often funded by a lump sum from the death benefit of a life insurance policy or lump sum from a defined-contribution plan, that begins payments one month after purchase.

Table 17-4

How Long Will the Retirement Money Last?

The higher your withdrawal rate, the more likely it is that your portfolio will not last until you die. The basis for the following calculations is research by T. Rowe Price, Vanguard, and other online retirement planning websites. Here are the rates of withdrawals and the likelihood that a diversified portfolio earning a long-term historical rate of return will last through retirement, assuming 3 percent annual increases in withdrawals for inflation.

Withdrawal Rate Amount	Years in Retirement		
	20	30	40
3%	99%	99%	93%
4%	99%	86%	68%
5%	93%	61%	41%
6%	74%	35%	18%

deferred annuity
Annuity plan in which annuitants pay premiums during their working lives, then take income payments at some future date, such as retirement.

Payments Begin at a Later Date with Deferred Annuities Another type of annuity is a **deferred annuity**. Here the person pays premiums over a long period of time. Then he or she can elect to stop paying premiums and begin taking income payments immediately or at some future date, such as at retirement. Deferred annuities are often one of the choices you might have within your employer's retirement plan. They provide that part of your 401(k) contribution buys a dollar amount of annuitized retirement income. You can also buy deferred annuities through your IRA or other self-administered plan. When you purchase a deferred annuity, you name a beneficiary should you die before beginning withdrawals, and thus, a deferred annuity also provides a death benefit similar to a life insurance contract. Note that this death benefit provision ends once the annuitant begins receiving payments under a straight annuity as described later.

FINANCIAL POWER POINT

When Should You Buy an Annuity?

There are many reasons for not using an annuity while saving for retirement. Annuities, if desired, can readily be purchased when you retire, so wait until then to make that decision. Further, some 401(k) plans have retirement income or guaranteed income options available through a mutual fund or insurance company that mimic annuities with more flexibility.

You Have Several Income Options Once Your Annuity Payments Begin Annuities offer several options for receiving the annuity benefits. In the following examples of hypothetical income payments, assume that a 70-year-old retiree has purchased an annuity for $100,000. A **straight annuity** might provide a lifetime income of perhaps $790 monthly for the rest of the life of the annuitant only. An **installment-certain annuity** might provide a payment of $680 monthly for the rest of the life of the annuitant with a guarantee that if the person dies before receiving a specific number of payments, his or her beneficiary will receive a certain number of payments for a particular time period (such as ten years in this example). A **joint-and-survivor annuity** might provide $640 monthly for as long as one of the two people—usually a husband and wife—is alive.

All Annuities Carry Sales Commissions and Fees All annuities charge a variety of fees that reduce the amount of income paid out. Annual expense ratios that range as low as 0.25 percent to 0.75 percent or higher are common, as are first-year sales commissions exceeding 10 percent. The trade-off is between the guaranteed payouts from an annuity that often carry high costs and the potential high risks of managing one's own retirement investments, such as making poor investment choices. Those considering buying an annuity perhaps might begin with the AAA-rated, low-fee industry leader TIAA-CREF.

joint-and-survivor annuity
Provides monthly payments for as long as one of the two people—usually a husband and wife—is alive.

Variable Annuities Carry More Investment Risk Annuities can have a fixed or variable rate of return. With a **fixed annuity**, the insurance company guarantees a specified rate of return on your invested funds. The rate is relatively low, perhaps 4 percent, because of the lower risk. A more common type of annuity sold by insurance salespeople is called a **variable annuity**. This is an annuity whose value rises and falls like mutual funds. One type of variable annuity is the **equity-indexed annuity (EIA)**, which is a complex financial instrument that has characteristics of both fixed and variable annuities. An EIA's return varies more than a fixed annuity, but not as much as a variable annuity. So EIAs give you more risk (but more potential return) than a fixed annuity but less risk (and less potential return) than a variable annuity. EIAs offer a minimum guaranteed interest rate combined with an interest rate linked to a market index.

variable annuity
Annuity whose value rises and falls like mutual funds and pays a limited death benefit via an insurance contract. Not as efficient as a mutual fund; costs are high for little return.

Variable annuities are sold very aggressively because sellers earn the highest commissions and the insurance company charges the highest annual fees. An investor may have to wait 15 to 20 years before a variable annuity becomes as efficient as a direct investment in a mutual fund. When buying a variable annuity, make sure that you fully understand the fees, commissions, and other rules of the contract.

Should You Buy a Deferred Annuity as Your Retirement Plan? Many people are attracted to annuities since they provide a predictable source of income that can keep them from outliving their money. A deferred annuity is an after-tax, tax-deferred vehicle, meaning that your investment returns are tax sheltered until withdrawn as annuity payments. Nonetheless, people should absolutely, positively not consider investing in a deferred annuity until *all* other tax-sheltered vehicles to save and invest for retirement have been maximized. This means that people saving for retirement first contribute the legally permitted maximum amounts to 401(k), traditional IRA, and Roth IRA accounts, perhaps totaling $20,000 each year. The tax-sheltered benefits of these retirement accounts are far better than those of a deferred annuity. Further, annuities are replete with numerous restrictions, administrative charges, commissions, purchase fees, withdrawal charges, and penalties. Deferred annuities are subject to the same early withdrawal penalties and withholding rules as other forms of tax-deferred retirement savings accounts.

Stay Engaged by Working Part Time

Preparing for your life in retirement goes beyond the financial arena. The happiest retirees are physically and mentally active and engaged in a variety of social networks. For a variety of reasons, including reducing the worry of outliving one's retirement income, some people choose to work part time for a while during their early retirement years instead of retiring completely. Reasons include wanting the extra income, enjoying being with coworkers, and obtaining employer-provided health care benefits. Predictions are that many retirees will work part time if for no other reason than to continue to feel active and be a contributing member of society.

DO IT NOW!

You know more about personal finance after reading this chapter, so get started right now by:

1. *Calculating your annual Social Security benefit assuming you work for 35 or more years earning an average salary of perhaps $35,000 or $50,000.*

2. *Calculating your retirement savings goal at both age 60 and 67 based on your projected income following graduation, perhaps $30,000 or $40,000.*

3. *Deciding tentatively whether you would choose to make most of your investing for retirement through employer-sponsored plans or personally established retirement accounts.*

 Concept Check 17.7

1. List three negative impacts of withdrawing money early from a tax-sheltered retirement account.

2. Use Appendix A-4 to calculate how much could be withdrawn each year from a $900,000 retirement nest egg earning 5 percent if you wanted the nest egg to last 20 years. How much less could be withdrawn so that the nest egg lasts 25 years?

3. Offer some positive and negative observations on the wisdom of buying an annuity with all or some of your retirement nest egg money when you retire.

4. Explain the negative aspects of buying a deferred annuity as part of your retirement planning outside of your employer's retirement plans.

WHAT DO YOU RECOMMEND NOW?

Now that you have read the chapter on retirement and estate planning, what do you recommend to Maryanne and Bob Johnson in the case at the beginning of the chapter regarding:

1. The major steps in the process to determine the amount of Maryanne and Bob's retirement savings goal?

2. How Bob's net income could be invested in a personal tax-sheltered retirement account?

3. The kinds of investment accounts into which they might put additional money over the next 23 years if they determined they needed $1 million to meet their retirement savings goal?

4. The investment strategies that Maryanne and Bob might follow for accumulating their retirement funds?

BIG PICTURE SUMMARY OF LEARNING OBJECTIVES

LO1. Estimate your Social Security retirement income benefit.

The Social Security program is funded through FICA taxes on employees and employers, and the amounts withheld are put into trust fund accounts from which benefits are paid to current program recipients. Congress is expected to take action to maintain the solvency of the Social Security program. You must be fully insured under the Social Security program before retirement benefits can be paid.

LO2. Calculate the amount you must save for retirement in today's dollars.

Your retirement nest egg is the total amount of accumulated savings and investments needed to support your desired retirement. This is calculated by projecting your annual retirement expenses and income and determining the amount of annual savings you need to set aside in today's dollars to achieve your retirement goal.

LO3. Understand why you should save for retirement within tax-sheltered retirement accounts.

Saving in tax-sheltered retirement accounts has important tax advantages. Your contributions may be tax deductible and earnings may be tax deferred; thus, you can accumulate more money for retirement.

LO4. Distinguish among the types of employer-sponsored tax-sheltered retirement plans.

The three major types of employer-sponsored retirement plans are defined-contribution, defined-benefit, and cash-balance. Some employers make matching contributions to their employees' accounts. To receive benefits, an employee must be vested in an employer-sponsored retirement plan.

LO5. Explain the various types of personally established tax-sheltered retirement accounts.

IRS regulations allow you to take advantage of personally established tax-sheltered retirement plans, including the traditional individual retirement account, or IRA, for which contributions are tax deductible and withdrawals are taxed. After-tax contributions may be made to Roth IRAs in which earnings accumulate tax free and withdrawals are not taxed. Keogh plans and SEP-IRA plans are available for the self-employed and small business owners.

LO6. Make wise investment choices when deciding on how to invest for retirement.

Employers often provide financial advice for retirement assets, and the advice must be based in part on Monte Carlo simulations. These calculations allow you to estimate the probability of reaching your financial goals.

LO7. Describe techniques for making your retirement money last.

You can save on taxes and make sure your retirement money is maximized by not withdrawing it prior to retirement. Then, your choices at retirement are to carefully manage your retirement account withdrawals, consider purchasing an annuity with a portion of your retirement funds, and/or work part-time during your early retirement years. There are tables and techniques to calculate how long your money will last.

LET'S TALK ABOUT IT

1. **Retirement Investing Today.** What are your thoughts on this comment? "Younger workers today face some serious challenges in deciding where to invest their retirement funds."

2. **Why Calculate?** Do you know anyone who has estimated his or her retirement savings goal in today's dollars? Offer two reasons why many people do not perform those calculations. Offer two reasons why it would be smart for people to determine a financial target.

3. **Roth or Traditional IRA.** If you go to work for an employer that does not sponsor a retirement plan, which kind of personal retirement account would you establish? A traditional IRA or a Roth IRA? Give two reasons to support your response. How much money do you think could accumulate in the account before retirement?

4. **Help People Plan.** What kinds of people do you think are likely to not plan ahead and save for retirement in a tax-sheltered account? What might be done to help those people prepare for retirement?

5. **Retirement Planning Mistakes.** Of all the mistakes that people make when planning for retirement, which one might be likely to negatively affect your retirement planning? Give two reasons why.

6. **How to Invest.** If you had $10,000 in your employer's 401(k) plan retirement account, explain how you would invest these funds. Tell why.

DO THE MATH

1. **Tax-Sheltered Returns.** Timothy Clum, of Commerce, Texas, is in the 25 percent tax bracket and is considering the tax consequences of investing $2000 at the end of each year for 30 years, assuming that the investment earns 8 percent annually.

   (a) How much will the account total if the growth in the investment remains sheltered from taxes?

   (b) How much will the account total if the investments are not sheltered from taxes? (Hint: Use Appendix A-3 or the *Garman/Forgue* companion website.)

2. **Withdrawal Amount.** Over the years, Kyle and Erica Paget, of Elon, North Carolina, have accumulated $200,000 and $220,000, respectively, in their employer-sponsored retirement plans. If the amounts in their two accounts earn a 6 percent rate of return over Kyle and Erica's anticipated 20 years of retirement, how large an amount could be withdrawn from the two accounts each month? Use the *Garman/Forgue* companion website or Appendix A-4 to make your calculations.

   What if Kyle is an aggressive investor *and* lucky? Assume that his $200,000 retirement nest egg will earn 8 percent. How large an amount could be withdrawn from his fund each month over the next 20 years? Use the *Garman/Forgue* companion website or Appendix A-4 to make your calculations.

3. **Savings Amount Needed.** Christine and Nathan Riley, of Newport, Rhode Island, desire an annual retirement income of $40,000. They expect to live for 30 years past retirement. Assuming that the couple could earn a 3 percent after-tax and after-inflation rate of return on their investments, what amount of accumulated savings and investments would they need? Use Appendix A-4 or the *Garman/Forgue* companion website to solve for the answer.

4. **Annual Earnings.** Alicia and Juan Selenas, of Union, New Jersey, hope to sell their large home for $280,000 and retire to a smaller residence valued at $150,000.

   After they sell the property, they plan to invest the $130,000 in equity ($280,000 – $150,000, omitting selling expenses) and earn a 4 percent after-tax return. Approximately how much annual income will be earned? Use Appendix A-4 or the *Garman/Forgue* companion website to solve for the answer.

5. **Twins Invest.** Kathryn Ake, of Omaha, Nebraska, plans to invest $3000 in a mutual fund for the next 25 years to accumulate savings for retirement. Her twin sister, Kristin, plans to invest the same amount for the same length of time in the same mutual fund. Instead of investing with after-tax money, Kristin will invest through an employer-sponsored retirement plan. If both mutual fund accounts provide an 8 percent rate of return, how much more will Kristin have in her retirement account after 40 years? How much will Kristin have if she also invests the amount saved in income taxes? Assume both women pay income taxes at a 25 percent rate. Use Appendix A-3 or the *Garman/Forgue* companion website to solve for the answer.

6. **Total Sum Accumulated.** Jenna Cowley, of Dallas, Texas, is currently putting 9 percent per year into her tax-sheltered employer-sponsored retirement plan at work. Jenna's employer matches $0.50 for each $1 that each employee contributes to his or her retirement account, and Jenna deposits up to 6 percent of her salary. Jenna's annual salary is $70,000. How much will Jenna accumulate after 28 years if her annual investments plus the employer's contributions grow at a 7 percent rate of return? How can Jenna protect herself from inflation in this plan? Use Appendix A-3 or the *Garman/Forgue* companion website to solve for the answer.

7. **More Aggressive Investing.** Cliff Wong, of Fort Wayne, Indiana, wants to invest $4000 annually for his retirement 30 years from now. He has a conservative investment philosophy and expects to earn a return of 3 percent in a tax-sheltered account. If he took a more aggressive investment approach and earned a return of 5 percent, how much more would Cliff accumulate? Use Appendix A-3 or the *Garman/Forgue* companion website to solve for the answer.

FINANCIAL PLANNING CASES

CASE 1

The Johnsons Consider Retirement Planning
Harry Johnson's father, William, was recently forced into early retirement at age 63 because of poor health. In addition to the psychological drawbacks of the unanticipated retirement, William's financial situation is poor because he had not planned adequately for retirement. His situation has inspired

Harry and Belinda to take a look at their own retirement planning. Together they now make about $100,000 per year and would like to have a similar level of living when they retire. Harry and Belinda are both 27 years old and recently received their annual Social Security Benefits Statements indicating that they could expect about $28,000 per year in today's dollars as retirement benefits at age 67. Although their retirement is a long way off, they know that the sooner they put a plan in place, the larger their retirement nest egg will be.

(a) Belinda believes that the couple could maintain their current level of living if their retirement income represented 75 percent of their current annual income after adjusting for inflation. Assuming a 4 percent inflation rate, what would Harry and Belinda's annual income need to be over and above their Social Security benefits when they retire at age 67? (Hint: Use Appendix A-1 or visit the *Garman/Forgue* companion website.)

(b) Both Harry and Belinda are covered by defined-contribution retirement plans at work. Harry's employer will contribute $1170 per year, and Belinda's employer will contribute $1140 per year in addition to the $4620 total that Harry and Belinda can contribute. Assuming a 7 percent rate of return, what would their retirement nest egg total 40 years from now? (Hint: Use Appendix A-3 or visit the *Garman/Forgue* companion website.)

(c) For how many years would the retirement nest egg provide the amount of income indicated in Question (a)? Assume a 4 percent return after taxes and inflation. (Hint: Use Appendix A-4 or visit the *Garman/Forgue* companion website.)

(d) One of Harry's dreams is to retire at age 55. What would the answers to Questions (a), (b), and (c) be if he and Belinda were to retire at that age?

(e) How would early retirement at age 55 affect the couple's Social Security benefits?

(f) What would you advise Harry and Belinda to do to meet their income needs for retirement?

CASE 2

Victor and Maria's Retirement Plans

Victor, now age 61, and Maria, age 59, are retiring at the end of the year. Since his retail management employer changed from a defined-benefit retirement plan to a defined-contribution plan ten years ago, Victor has been contributing the maximum amount of his salary to several different mutual funds offered through the plan, although his employer never matched any of his contributions. Victor's tax-sheltered account, which now has a balance of $144,000, has been growing at a rate of 9 percent through the years. Under the previous defined-benefit plan, Victor is entitled to a single-life pension of $360 per month or a joint and survivor option paying $240 per month. The value of Victor's investment of $20,000 in Pharmacia stock eight years ago has now grown to $56,000.

Maria's earlier career as a dental hygienist provided no retirement program, although she did save $10,000 through her credit union, which was later used to purchase zero-coupon bonds now worth $28,000. Maria's second career as a pharmaceutical representative for Pharmacia allowed her to contribute about $37,000 to her retirement account over the past nine years. Pharmacia matched a portion of her contributions, and that account is now worth $130,000; its growth rate has ranged from 6 to 10 percent annually. When Maria's mother died last year, Maria inherited her home, which is rented for $900 per month; the house has a market value of $170,000. The Hernandezes' personal residence is worth $180,000. They pay combined federal and state income taxes at a 30 percent rate.

(a) Sum up the present values of the Hernandezes' assets, excluding their personal residence, and identify which assets derive from tax-sheltered accounts.

(b) Assume that the Hernandezes sold their stocks, bonds, and rental property, realizing a gain of $238,000 after income taxes and commissions. If that sum earned a 7 percent rate of return over the Hernandezes' anticipated 20 years of retirement, how large an amount could be withdrawn each month? How large an amount could be withdrawn each month if they needed the money over 30 years? How large an amount could be withdrawn each month if the proceeds earned 6 percent for 20 years? For 30 years?

(c) Victor's $144,000 and Maria's $130,000 in retirement funds have been sheltered from income taxes for many years. Summarize the advantages the couple realized by leaving the money in the tax-sheltered accounts. Offer them a rationale to keep the money in the accounts as long as possible before making withdrawals.

CASE 3

Julia Price Thinks About Retirement

Julia is now in her early 50s. She has had two jobs in her career so far and participated fully in the defined-contribution plans offered by both employers. When she left her first position, she rolled her retirement account over to the account at her new employer, and it is currently worth about $380,000. Now she is about to change jobs again. But this time, she is taking a job with the Consumer Financial Protection Agency in Washington, DC. She will also be taking about four months off from working before starting that government job. The federal government retirement program is a defined-benefit plan. That means she cannot transfer her private sector plan to the government plan and therefore must decide whether to leave the funds within her current employer's plan or open a traditional IRA account into which to roll over the funds tax-and penalty-free. Another alternative available to her is to withdraw the $240,000 from her current account, pay income taxes on it this year (probably at a federal marginal tax rate of 36 percent), and invest the proceeds (about $100,000) in a new Roth IRA account. Offer your opinions about her thinking.

CASE 4

Deciding How to Invest Retirement Money

Emily Borden, from Georgetown, Delaware, recently graduated from college and started her first full-time job with a midsize company. Emily's employer offers a 401(k) defined-contribution, tax-sheltered retirement account in which she and her employer can place funds. She must select one or more options from among these seven investment choices: (1) her company's stock, (2) a low-risk bond mutual fund, (3) a growth stock fund, (4) an aggressive growth stock fund, (5) a stock index fund, (6) a money market fund, or (7) an annuity. Into which option(s) would you suggest she invest, and indicate what percentage of the overall 100 percent of deposited funds she should put into that option. Explain the reasons for your choices.

CASE 5

Calculation of Annual Savings Needed to Meet a Retirement Goal

Jessica Amberlin, age 40, single, and from Victorville, California, is trying to estimate the amount she needs to save annually to meet her retirement needs. Jessica currently earns $30,000 per year. She expects to need 80 percent of her current salary to live on at retirement. Jessica anticipates that she will receive $800 per month in Social Security benefits. Using

the Run the Numbers worksheet on page 518, answer the following questions.

(a) What annual income would Jessica need for retirement?

(b) What would her annual expected Social Security benefit be?

(c) Jessica expects to receive $500 per month from her defined-benefit pension at work. What is her annual benefit?

(d) How much annual retirement income will she need from her retirement funds?

(e) How much will Jessica need to save by retirement in today's dollars if she plans to retire at age 65 and live to age 90?

(f) Jessica currently has $5000 in a traditional IRA. Assuming a growth rate of 8 percent, what will be the value of her IRA when she retires?

(g) How much additional money will she still need to save for retirement?

(h) What is the amount she needs to save each year to reach this goal?

CASE 6

Early and Normal Retirement Benefits

Patrick Dietrick of Murfreesboro, Tennessee, age 37, is single and is finally making belated plans for his retirement from employment in state government. Based on his family's medical history, he thinks he should base his plan on assuming he will live to age 85. He wants to maintain his current lifestyle without scrimping and needs to save more for his retirement to take advantage of compounding. Currently, Patrick earns $44,000 per year, with an adjusted gross income of $43,000 and an after-tax income of $33,000. He anticipates receiving $10,000 from Social Security annually and $14,000 per year from his employer's defined-benefit pension upon retirement at age 67. If he retires at age 62, his pension benefits will be lowered to approximately $11,000. To date, Patrick has about $10,000 in investments.

(a) Using the Run the Numbers worksheet on page 518, calculate the additional amount of annual savings that Patrick needs to set aside to reach his goal of retiring at age 62 with 80 percent of his current income.

(b) What amount is needed if he waits until his full benefit retirement age of 67? Use the same worksheet to solve for the answer.

(c) Why do you think the dollar amounts that Patrick will need to save are so drastically different for retiring at age 62 and at age 67?

(d) If Patrick had another $4000 to invest for retirement every year, would you recommend he invest those funds into a traditional IRA or a Roth IRA? Why or why not?

BE YOUR OWN PERSONAL FINANCIAL MANAGER

1. **Income Needed in Retirement Adjusted for Inflation.** Based on your expected income in your field after you graduate, make an estimate of the dollar amount you would need to make today to live comfortably as a retiree. Then assume that inflation will average 3 percent per year until you are age 67. Use Appendix A-1 to calculate the dollar amount you would need that year to live at the level of living you estimate as being comfortable today.

2. **Calculate Your Retirement Nest Egg.** Use the Run the Numbers worksheet and material on pages 518–519 or Worksheet 65: My Estimated Retirement Savings Goal in Today's Dollars from "My Personal Financial Planner" to estimate the amount you must save each year to reach your retirement goal. If you have not yet begun working in your career field, use an estimate of the typical starting salary for the income on line 1 of the worksheet. (Visit the Career Guide to Industries at www.bls.gov/oco/cg.)

MY PERSONAL FINANCIAL PLANNER

3. **How Long Will Your Retirement Money Last?** If you currently have begun a retirement savings nest egg and/or are currently setting aside funds into an account each year, use Appendix A-1 (for the nest egg) and Appendix A-2 (for the annual deposits) to estimate your full nest egg at an age that you would like to retire. Then use the material on page 537 and Worksheet 66: How Long Will My Retirement Money Last? from "My Personal Financial Planner" to estimate how long that money will last based on the result you obtained for item 1 above.

MY PERSONAL FINANCIAL PLANNER

4. **Questions to Ask About an Employer's Retirement Plan.** Are you currently employed and eligible to participate in an employer-sponsored retirement plan? Use the material on pages 522–527 and Worksheet 67: Questions to Ask About Your Employer's Retirement Plan from "My Personal Financial Planner" to assess the plan and make decisions about your enrollment in the plan.

MY PERSONAL FINANCIAL PLANNER

ON THE 'NET

Go to the Web pages indicated to complete these exercises.

1. **Calculate Your Benefits.** Visit the website for the Social Security Administration. There you will find a quick benefits calculator at www.ssa.gov/planners/calculators.htm that can be used to estimate your Social Security benefit in today's dollars. Use an income figure that approximates what you expect to earn in the first full year after graduating from college. When the calculator provides your answer, click on "break-even age" to see when you would be better off if you had waited until age 67 to begin taking benefits rather than age 62.

2. **Investigate 401(k) Fees.** Visit the website for the U.S. Department of Labor. There you will find an article on 401(k) fees and the effects they can have on retirement savings at www.dol.gov/ebsa/publications/undrstndgrtrmnt.html. Develop a list of six questions that employees with a 401(k) plan might ask their employers about the fees charged under their plans.

3. **Fixing Social Security.** Visit the website of the American Association of Retired Persons (AARP), where you will find AARP's views on how to fix the Social Security system at www.aarp.org/work/social-security/info-08-2009/keeping_Social_Security_strong.html. How would the suggestions affect your retirement planning? Which of the suggestions would you support? Which would you oppose?

ACTION INVOLVEMENT PROJECTS

1. **Views Concerning Social Security.** Talk to five fellow students who are not taking your personal finance class. Ask them to explain their feelings about the degree to which Social Security will meet their income needs during retirement. Then ask them how they plan to meet their retirement income needs beyond what Social Security might provide. Make a table that summarizes your findings. Then compare their views and plans with what you have learned from reading this chapter.

2. **What Is It Like to Be Retired?** Survey three individuals or couples who have been retired for more than one year. Ask them how financially well-prepared they felt before they retired. Then ask them to assess the

financial realities of retirement at the current point in time. Include a discussion of how their investment mix (mutual funds, stocks, bonds, annuities) may or may not have changed since they have retired. Write a summary of their responses and how their experiences may affect your thinking about being retired.

3. **Feelings About Approaching Retirement.** Survey three individuals or couples who are about 10 to 15 years away from retirement. Ask them to explain what steps they have taken to prepare for retirement and how prepared they feel. Also ask them to describe what they will do in the next decade to get ready for retirement. In addition, ask them about the types of investments (mutual funds, stocks, bonds) that they are using to save for retirement. Write a summary of their responses and how their experiences affected your own thinking about getting ready for retirement.

4. **Retirement Savings Behavior Early in One's Career.** Survey three individuals or couples who are less than ten years into their professional careers. Ask them if they have started saving for retirement and, if not, why not. Also ask them about the types of investments (mutual funds, stocks, bonds) that they are using or would use to save for retirement. Write a summary of their responses and how their efforts, or lack thereof, affected your thinking about saving for retirement.

5. **Comparing Boomers with Millennials.** Research reveals that about three-fourths of the Baby Boom Generation report they are inadequately prepared for retirement. Survey five individuals under age 30. Ask them if they feel that their generation will be more or less prepared for retirement than Baby Boomers and why. Write a summary of their responses and how their views might impact your thinking about your own retirement planning.

Visit the Garman/Forgue companion website at **www.cengagebrain.com**.

YOU MUST BE KIDDING, RIGHT?

Michael and Jessica are unmarried, have two children, and live in Fort Collins, Colorado. In addition, Michael has a 7-year-old child from his previous 10-year marriage to Ashley. Unfortunately, one day, a big bus hit and killed Michael. The assets in his IRA account amount to $200,000. Who is likely to get the $200,000 now that Michael has died?

A. First wife, Ashley

B. Current significant other, Jessica

C. Children of first or second wife

D. Michael's mother

The answer is D, Michael's mother. Why? If Michael was like many unmarried guys starting a career who designate their mothers as the beneficiary in their IRA, his mom will get all the money if he neglected to change the beneficiary and designate someone else, like Ashley, on his account. If instead of living together, Jessica and Michael had been married, her spousal right probably would legally override his mother's. While first wife Ashley has no rights to the retirement funds, she and her child may be eligible to receive Social Security survivor's benefits. As you can see, estate tasks, such as designating beneficiaries, are not just for old people!

LEARNING OBJECTIVES

After reading this chapter, you should be able to:

❶ Identify the ways that your estate can be transferred through contracts and a will.

❷ Determine how trusts can be used to transfer assets and reduce estate taxes.

❸ Summarize the benefits of preparing advance directive documents.

❹ List the questions and documents needed to simplify the settlement and transfer of your estate.

❺ Explain the potential impact of estate and inheritance taxes.

Orlando Molina, age 34, the ballet master at a professional ballet company, recently remarried after being single for several years. He shares custody of his son with his first wife. Orlando married into a ready-made family: Giselle, his new wife, who was divorced from her husband two years ago, has two children, Jamie and Jon. Like many married couples, Orlando and Giselle, who is a modern dance choreographer, have a variety of financial assets. These include bank accounts, money market accounts, mutual fund accounts, 401(k) plans, Roth IRAs, and whole life insurance policies. With home prices now low compared to their previous highs, the Molinas hope to buy a larger home in the near future. Soon after they returned from their honeymoon, Orlando's father, who is only 56 years of age, had a serious stroke. Despite undergoing physical therapy, he is now in a nursing home and likely will reside there for the remainder of his life. The financial and emotional impacts of the elder Mr. Molina's illness have forced Orlando and Giselle to talk about some delicate financial circumstances in their own family.

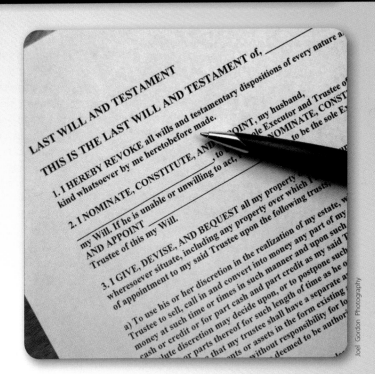

Joel Gordon Photography

What do you recommend to Orlando and Giselle on the subject of estate planning regarding:

1. Beneficiary designations for their financial assets?

2. Joint ownership of their home, vehicles, and other property?

3. Making a will?

4. Establishing guardianship for the children?

5. Using advance directive documents to avoid a situation like that confronting Orlando's father?

6. Establishing trusts for their children?

YOUR NEXT 5 YEARS

In the next five years, you can start achieving financial success by doing the following related to estate planning:

1. *Review the beneficiary and ownership designations in your life insurance policies, retirement plans, bank accounts, vehicles, and other assets to make certain they will transfer the property according to your wishes.*

2. *Write your will and a letter of last instructions.*

3. *Prepare advance directive documents so others can make the right decisions for you if you become incapacitated.*

4. *Discuss with your spouse or significant other your family's financial and estate plans once each year.*

5. *Inform one or two close family members and friends of the location of your financial records, advance directives, and will.*

Identify the ways that your estate can be transferred through contracts and a will.

estate
Your worldly possessions and financial assets less any debts you owe.

estate planning
The definite arrangements you make during your lifetime that are consistent with your wishes for the administration and distribution of your estate when you die.

probate
Court-supervised process that allows creditors to present claims against an estate and ensures the transfer of a decedent's assets to the rightful beneficiaries according to a properly executed and valid will or, when no will exists, to the people, agencies, or organizations required by state law.

Your **estate** consists of your worldly possessions and financial assets less any debts you owe. When you die, all of your creditors must be notified of your death and can collect what they are owed from your estate. The remainder will be distributed to your heirs. Creditors have absolutely no legal right to collect from your surviving relatives unless the relative was also a party to the debt or a cosigner. Experts recommend that when debt collectors make sympathetic calls to husbands, wives, children and other family members to urge them ever-so-gently to pay what the loved one owed, family members should simply hang up.

If you follow the guidance in this book, you will spend wisely, save and invest, protect your assets and income with insurance, donate, and build a retirement nest egg to eventually spend down. Now—not 10 or 20 years from today—is the time to think about the final financial planning task of transferring your estate to others. **Estate planning** comprises the specific arrangements you make during your lifetime for the administration and distribution of your estate when you die. Estate planning takes into consideration the needs of your survivors, making sure the greatest amount of the estate passes to the intended beneficiaries. It involves both financial and legal considerations, and a primary goal is to minimize both taxes and legal expenses. Protecting and transferring your estate can be an emotional process. It is both smart and practical to take the fundamental steps while you are young and then update them as your life progresses.

HOW YOUR ESTATE IS TRANSFERRED

You probably will work hard over the course of your life to build a substantial estate, but you already have an estate now. Should you die, your surviving family members will not conduct the distribution of your assets. The distributions are either set up by you before your death or through **probate** by which a special **probate court** allows creditors to present claims against an estate and ensures the transfer of a decedent's assets to the rightful beneficiaries. The probate court will make the distributions according to a properly executed and valid will or, when no will exists, to the people or organizations as required by state law.

Your Assets Should Be Set Up Right Now as Nonprobate Property

Figure 18-1 illustrates the different ways that your property can be distributed after your death. Importantly, **nonprobate property** is not transferred by the probate court. Nonprobate property includes assets transferred to survivors by contract such as by naming a beneficiary for your retirement plan or by owning assets with another person through joint tenancy with right of survivorship. Trusts (discussed in the next section) can also be used to transfer assets outside of probate court. One of the primary benefits of setting up assets as nonprobate property is time. Nonprobate property transfers immediately upon your death, whereas probate can take between 4 and 18 months, or longer if there is no will. Avoiding probate court may also save money since your estate pays the cost of the probate process based on the value of the assets it must distribute. Avoiding probate also maintains your privacy because a public record is maintained of the probate process.

Most Nonprobate Property Is Transferred by Contract

People of average economic means should be able to transfer by contract most or all of the remaining part of their estate outside of probate. Transferring your estate by contract is an easy, do-it-yourself project. You just have to take a few minutes of time to fill out the appropriate forms.

1. Transfers by Beneficiary Designation
When you open up investment accounts, you are given a form to complete in order to name your beneficiaries. Changes

How to Distribute Your Estate

Figure 18-1

YOUR ENTIRE ESTATE	
Your nonprobate property is transferred at your death before your estate goes through probate court. These transfers can be implemented:	Your probate property is transferred by the probate court in accordance with:
By contracts you set up before death, such as: ■ Beneficiary designations in life insurance and retirement plans ■ Assets owned by joint ownership with rights of survivorship ■ Payable-on-death clauses in bank accounts **By setting up trusts that designate who will receive the property at your death** ■ Living trusts established while you are still alive ■ Testamentary trusts designed to take effect at your death	Your wishes as outlined in your will **OR** If you have no will, the intestate succession laws in your state

are made in the same way; you complete a new beneficiary designation form. Examples of accounts like this are IRAs, 401(k) plans, Keogh plans, pension plans, bank and credit union accounts, stock brokerage accounts, mutual funds, annuities, and life and disability income insurance policies. A **beneficiary** is a person or organization designated to receive a benefit. A **beneficiary designation** is a legal form signed by the owner of an asset providing that the property goes to a certain person or organization in the event of the owner's death. The form also contains a place to designate a **contingent (or secondary) beneficiary** in case the first-named beneficiary has died after the form was filled out. If no one has been named as beneficiary for a particular asset or if that person and a named contingent beneficiary have died, the property will go to one's estate and to probate court for distribution. The lesson here: Be certain to name contingent beneficiaries as well as beneficiaries in contracts.

2. Transfers by Property Ownership Designation

Joint tenancy with right of survivorship (also called **joint tenancy**; see page 155) is the most common form of joint ownership of assets, especially for husbands and wives. In this case, each person owns the whole of the asset, such as a bank account or home, and can dispose of it without the approval of the other owners. Assets owned in this way include bank accounts, stocks, bonds, real estate, mutual funds, government bonds, and other assets. Upon the death of one owner, the surviving owners receive the property by operation of law rather than through the provisions of a will. Simply stated, the surviving owner(s) owned the entire asset before the death and own all of it after death. The lesson here: If you want an asset to immediately transfer to a particular person upon your death, own it as joint tenants with right of survivorship.

3. Transfers by Payable-on-Death Designation

It is often impractical, undesirable, or inappropriate to own certain types of property using joint tenancy. For example, two elderly unmarried siblings might want each other to have access to funds in individual savings accounts earmarked to pay for their funerals but not have those accounts be available to the other sibling during life. They could, of course, designate each other as heirs in their wills. However, the funds would then remain tied up until the probate process is complete. To solve this dilemma, each could name the other to receive the funds upon their death using a **payable-on-death designation** for the account. With a payable-on-death bank account, the beneficiary has no rights to the funds until you pass on. Until that time, you are free to use

nonprobate property
Does not go through probate; includes assets transferred to survivors by contract (such as beneficiaries listed on retirement accounts and bank accounts held with another person).

primary beneficiary
The person first in line in a will, trust, retirement plan, or life insurance policy to receive named benefits when the person setting up the account dies.

contingent (or secondary) beneficiary
The beneficiary in case the first-named beneficiary has died; also called the secondary beneficiary.

joint tenancy with right of survivorship/joint tenancy
Most common form of joint ownership, especially for husbands and wives, in which each person owns the whole of the asset, such as a bank account or home, and can dispose of it without the approval of the other owner(s).

FINANCIAL POWER POINT

Estate Planning on the Web

Some excellent basic resources for estate planning are on the Web:

- American Bar Association (www .abanet.org/rppt/public/home.html)
- Cornell Law School (http://topics.law .cornell.edu/wex/Estate_Planning)
- National Association of Estate Planners & Councils (www.naepc.org/ default-public.web)
- Nolo (www.nolo.com/legal -encyclopedia/wills-trusts-estates/)

Preparing a will ensures appropriate distribution of your assets upon your death.

payable-on-death designation
Status granted to individuals who are not joint tenants and who might need to access accounts without going through probate; the deceased signs the designation before death, and the designee simply presents a death certificate to access the accounts.

probate property
All assets other than nonprobate property.

will
Written document in which a person tells how his or her remaining assets should be given away after death; without a will, the property will be distributed according to state probate law.

lump-sum distribution
When money in a deceased person's retirement account is handed over to the beneficiary at once, rather than monthly payments, and the amount taken is taxable.

the money kept in the bank account, to change the beneficiary, or to close the account. The named party simply needs to present the death certificate to the bank and show proper identification, and access to the account will be granted. The only real drawback to a payable-on-death designation is that you cannot name contingent beneficiaries on an account. An alternative could be to set up multiple accounts with payable-on-death designations for different loved ones. The lesson here: Use a payable-on-death designation on assets that you solely control that you also desire to immediately transfer to a particular person upon your death.

The Rest of Your Estate Can Be Transferred via Your Will

Your **probate property** is simply all assets other than nonprobate property. Your probate property consists of what you owned individually and totally in your name, as well as the value of assets jointly owned through tenancy in common. In the latter case, your heirs will receive your share, but not the co-owner's share. A will is the smartest way to transfer your nonprobate assets upon your death. You definitely need a will unless all of your property is nonprobate property or will be transferred by contract. A will is not estate planning. It is written after all the other aspects of estate planning are completed.

Transfers with a Will Go to Your Desired Heirs A **will** is a written document in which a person, the **testator**, tells how his or her remaining assets should be given away after death. In your will,

---

DID YOU KNOW?

How Retirement Assets Transfer to Heirs

As a condition of opening almost any type of retirement account, such as an IRA or 401(k), you are required to complete the form identifying your named beneficiaries in case you die. The primary beneficiaries are those first in line to receive named benefits, and the contingent beneficiaries are those who will only receive benefits if the primary beneficiary has died. The beneficiaries of retirement account assets can include a spouse, child, parent, sibling, or anyone else, or an estate. You can name more than one beneficiary to share in the proceeds by simply specifying the percentage each beneficiary will receive. The shares do not have to be equal. Retirement plan administrators are required by the Employee Retirement Income Security Act (ERISA) to pay benefits in the plan to the beneficiaries identified in the plan documents.

Named beneficiaries of a qualified retirement plan are able to access the money even while the rest of the estate is in probate. Beneficiaries usually have three choices: (1) take the money in a lump-sum distribution, (2) transfer the funds to another tax-deferred account, or (3) disclaim ownership, in part or in full, so that the assets will pass to any remaining beneficiaries. If, for example, you choose to take a **lump-sum distribution** (where all the money is handed over to the beneficiary at once, rather than in monthly payments, and the amount taken is taxable), you will not have to pay the standard early withdrawal penalty tax. Receiving the lump sum, however, may create an immediate federal and state income tax burden and potentially push you into a higher tax bracket.

Beneficiaries may avoid paying income taxes in the current year by choosing to roll over the retirement assets into another tax-deferred account. This can be done via a direct trustee-to-trustee transfer only. If one attempts to personally execute a regular rollover, he/she might end up in possession of the funds, and this will be viewed by the IRS as a distribution and the total amount will be subject to income taxes in the current year.

No one can keep amounts in a retirement account indefinitely. Generally, one must begin receiving distributions by April 1 of the year following the year in which he or she reaches age 70½. Inherited retirement funds usually may be received over time in one of two ways: (1) over a **five-year payment schedule**, or (2) over a **life expectancy payment schedule**. The latter means that the beneficiary receives the savings over his or her life expectancy. In that instance, the **Uniform Lifetime Table**, which is updated annually by the Internal Revenue Service, must be used to calculate the annual **required minimum distribution** every year (www.irs.gov/pub/irs-pdf/p590.pdf). The rules of the deceased original account holder's plan typically stipulate that beneficiaries take the assets within 60 days. Employers do not want to be in the business of administering an account years into the future for former employees. Inherited assets in most retirement plans generally may be easily transferred to other accounts and invested in mutual funds, stocks, bonds, and/or annuities.

Protections for Surviving Spouses

Federal law dictates that a surviving spouse will become the automatic beneficiary of 401(k) retirement plan assets unless he or she signs a timely, written waiver giving up that legal right. This is the case even if you named your beneficiary when you were single. If you had named someone, such as your mother, and later got married, your spouse will trump the rights of the person you named.

This is not the case with IRA assets because, in general, the named beneficiary will get ownership no matter what other documents are signed. There are exceptions, however, because if the person who died lived in a state with community property laws,* the surviving spouse may have rights related to the IRA regardless of whether he or she is named as the primary beneficiary.

When the Surviving Spouse Is the Beneficiary

A spouse named as beneficiary can receive a lump-sum distribution, pay ordinary income taxes, and keep what's left; however, he or she has considerable flexibility for delaying distributions that may be subject to income taxes. On IRA accounts, you as a surviving spouse have two choices: (1) do a spousal rollover by transferring the money from the account of the deceased into your own traditional IRA, or (2) continue to own the account as a beneficiary by designating yourself as the account owner rather than the beneficiary. If you are a surviving spouse of 401(k) assets, you may choose to treat the assets as your own and make withdrawals according to the rules of the employer.

When a Nonspouse Is the Beneficiary

A nonspouse beneficiary of 401(k) or IRA money also can choose to receive a lump-sum distribution. However, the nonspouse beneficiary may not transfer the assets into an existing IRA to avoid paying income taxes. Instead the beneficiary can choose to roll the assets into a newly set up **inherited IRA** in the name of the original account holder for the beneficiary's benefit, and the beneficiary has total control of the account. The beneficiary can leave the money in the inherited IRA to continue to grow tax free, withdrawing only the minimum amounts required by the IRS in subsequent years.

The Lesson Here: Keep Beneficiary Designations Up to Date

Too often, people initially sign the papers to leave their retirement savings to their parents or siblings and never update the forms. Keep your beneficiary designations up to date when major life events occur, such as divorce, remarriage, or the birth of a child. If an employee dies before changing the beneficiary on a 401(k) account, an ex-spouse might inherit all of the retirement plan assets, even if state law generally views his or her children as the proper heirs. Divorce does not terminate an ex-spouse's status as the named beneficiary of a retirement plan or a life insurance policy even if the divorce decree says something to the contrary. The beneficiary designation itself must be changed.

five-year payment schedule
One way a beneficiary may receive distributions from an inherited retirement account whereby all the money must be distributed within five years of the end of the year in which the deceased original account holder died.

life expectancy payment schedule
One way a beneficiary may receive distributions from an inherited retirement account whereby all the money must be distributed in installments over his or her life expectancy.

Uniform Lifetime Table
The life expectancy table required by the Internal Revenue Service to be utilized every year by persons who are required to make annual distributions from their retirement accounts.

required minimum distribution
The amount that qualified retirement account owners must begin distributing from their retirement accounts by April 1 following the year they reach age 70 ½. Required minimum distribution amounts must then be recalculated and distributed each subsequent year.

inherited IRA
A new IRA account set up by a nonspouse beneficiary of money inherited from a deceased person's qualified retirement account, which must be in the name of the original account holder but is for the benefit of the beneficiary who has total control of the account.

* Arizona, California, Idaho, Louisiana, Nevada, New Mexico, Puerto Rico, Texas, Washington, and Wisconsin.

DID YOU KNOW?

Last Will and Testament of Harry Johnson

1 Introduction

Being of sound mind and memory, I Harry Johnson, do hereby publish this as my Last Will and Testament. I am married to Belinda Johnson, and my mother is Melinda Johnson.

2 Payment of Debts and Expenses

I hereby direct my Executor to pay my medical expenses, funeral expenses, debts, and the costs of settling my estate.

3 Distribution of Assets

I give my wife one-half of my possessions and all my personal effects. I give my mother one-quarter of my possessions. I give to Common Cause, a nonprofit organization, one-quarter of my possessions. If my wife, Belinda Johnson, predeceases me, I give her share to my mother, Melinda Johnson.

4 Simultaneous Death of Beneficiary

If any beneficiary of this Will, including any beneficiary of any trust established by this Will, other than my wife, shall die within 60 days of my death or prior to the distribution of my estate, I hereby declare that I shall be deemed to have survived such person.

5 Appointment of Executor and Guardian

I appoint my father-in-law, Martin Anderson, to be the Executor of this will and my estate, and provide if this executor is unable or unwilling to serve then I appoint the Trust Department of the Bank of America as alternate Executor. My Executor shall be authorized to carry out all provisions of this Will and pay my just debts, obligations, and funeral expenses.

6 Power of the Executor

The executor of this will has the power to receive payments, buy or sell assets, and pay debts and taxes owed on behalf of my estate.

7 Payment of Taxes

I direct my executor to pay all taxes imposed by governments.

8 Execution

In witness therefore, I hereby set my hand to this last Will and Testament, which consists of one page, this 31st day of January 2012.

_____   _____
Signature   Date

9 Witness Clause

The above-named person signed in our presence and in our opinion is mentally competent.

_____   _____   _____
Witness 1   Address   Date

_____   _____   _____
Witness 2   Address   Date

---

executor/personal representative
Person responsible for carrying out the provisions of a will and managing the assets until the estate is passed on to heirs.

you name an **executor** (or **personal representative**). The executor identifies assets, collects any money due, pays off debts, obtains life insurance proceeds, liquidates assets, files for Social Security burial benefits, prepares final income tax and estate tax returns, and with the court's permission distributes the balance of any remaining money and property to the beneficiaries. Relatives and friends are not necessarily the best choice to perform the executor's duties, and many people name an accountant or attorney to play this role since the work is time consuming and challenging for novices and may require the hiring of experts. The person should ideally live in the state where the will is to be probated. A legal background is not necessary, but honesty and maturity are key attributes of a good executor. The executor's fee for carrying out these complicated tasks is about 3 percent of the estate, or they can charge an hourly fee.

A simple will that is prepared by an attorney can cost $125 to $400. Minor changes in a will may be made with a **codicil** instead of revoking the existing will and writing a completely new one, as you would when making major changes.

codicil
Legal instrument with which one can make minor changes to a will.

A Valid Will Is Not Likely to Be Challenged

If you die with a valid will, the probate court will transfer or distribute your property according to your wishes. A person who inherits or is entitled by law or by the terms of a will to inherit some asset is called an **heir**. A will that is properly drafted, signed, and witnessed is unlikely to be successfully challenged by someone who is dissatisfied with the intended distribution of assets, thus reducing the likelihood of family disputes. If you have a complicated estate, you should seek the assistance of an attorney who specializes in estate planning.

heir
Person who inherits or is entitled by law or by the terms of a will to inherit some asset.

FINANCIAL POWER POINT

Prepare Your Will Online

People usually know exactly what they want to do with their property, so they can use software and online programs to prepare an uncomplicated will. Examples include BuildaWill.com, LegacyWriter, LegalZoom, Kiplinger's Quicken Will-Maker, and WillPower.

You Need to Appoint a Guardian in Your Will if You Have Minor Children If you have minor children, you should appoint a legal **guardian** for each child in your will. This person is responsible for caring for and raising any child under the age of 18 and for managing the child's estate. The guardian should be someone who shares your values and views on child rearing. Nationally syndicated financial columnist Michelle Singletary suggests that you might avoid as potential guardians those who are too old, too ill, or too tired from raising their own children, and those who don't really know the children. Consider naming an alternate candidate in case your first choice cannot take on this responsibility. If you have not taken steps to name a legal guardian, the court will appoint one.

guardian
Person responsible for caring for and raising any child under the age of 18 and for managing the child's estate.

Letter of Last Instructions Provides Guidance to Those Left Behind Many people prepare a **letter of last instructions** along with their will that may contain preferences regarding funeral and burial instructions, organ donation wishes, material to be included in the obituary, contact information for relatives and friends, and other information useful to the survivors, such as the location of important documents. Family members and others are not legally bound by details in a letter of last instructions, but such a letter relieves them of the stress of making sometimes emotional decisions. A letter of last instructions may specify that certain pieces of jewelry or art not specified in your will that have more sentimental than monetary value are to go to specific people. If the will contains different instructions on these matters, the will prevails.

Your original will and letter of last instructions should be kept in a safe place, such as a lockable filing cabinet or home safe or at an attorney's office. Copies may be given to certain family members or friends.

DID YOU KNOW?

Checklist for Topics to Include in Your Will

- Decide what property to include.
- Decide who will inherit which assets.
- Identify an executor.
- Choose a guardian for your children.
- Select someone to manage children's inherited assets.
- Sign your will in front of witnesses.
- Store your original will in an attorney's office or safe deposit box.

Without a Will, Your State Law Determines the Distribution of Your Property

If you do not care about what happens to your property, children, and favorite pieces of jewelry, the state will make those decisions. When a person dies without a valid will, the deceased is assumed to have died **intestate**. Dying intestate can cost much more in taxes and cause legal, bureaucratic, and emotional struggles for survivors. In such a case, the probate court first ensures that the debts, income taxes, and expenses of the deceased are paid. Then, the probate court will divide all property and transfer assets to the legal heirs according to state law. If no surviving relatives exist, the estate will go to the state by **right of escheat**. One's friends and charities will get nothing.

The manner in which the assets are divided varies enormously from state to state. For example, one state might make the following distributions of a $120,000 estate: If a person with no surviving kin except a spouse dies without a will, the spouse receives the entire estate of $120,000. If the deceased had children with that spouse, the spouse takes $60,000, and the balance is divided equally between the spouse and their children. If the couple was not married, the children would get 100 percent. If the deceased also had children from another marriage, one-half of the estate goes to the spouse, and the balance is divided among all of his or her children. If a spouse and a parent survive the decedent, the spouse receives $60,000 and one-half of the balance, with the remainder passing to the parent.

letter of last instructions
Nonlegal instrument that may contain preferences regarding funeral and burial, material to be included in the obituary, and other information useful to the survivors, such as the location of important documents.

intestate
When a person dies without a legal will.

FINANCIAL POWER POINT

Estate Planning for Unmarried Couples

Many couples live together without being married, and without careful estate planning, the surviving partner is likely to get nothing. Most state intestate laws do not recognize the rights of an unmarried partner. Disputes between the surviving partner and the family of the deceased often occur even when there is a will, so the couple should arrange to transfer assets to each other as nonprobate property using the advantages of beneficiary and payable-on-death designations, joint ownership with right of survivorship, and trusts.

As you can see, state laws contain a number of complex provisions that govern what constitutes a legal heir and how much (if any) of an estate an heir may be entitled to receive. What may appear least fair in the intestate distributions just described is that, if the decedent has no children, his or her spouse may be required to share the assets with a distant relative. Sadly, more than two-thirds of all adults including parents with dependent children do not have wills.

Spouses Have Legal Rights to Each Other's Estates

The **partnership theory of marriage rights** is an assumption in the law that presumes that wedded couples share their fortunes equally. Thus, property acquired during the marriage and titled in the name of only one partner (other than property acquired by gift or inheritance) becomes the property of both spouses. A decedent who disinherits a surviving spouse or who leaves that person with less than a fair share of the estate is judged to have reneged on the partnership. A surviving spouse disinherited in this manner has some claim in probate court to a portion of the decedent's estate if he or she chooses to elect that option. All states give a surviving spouse the right to claim one-fourth to one-half of the other spouse's estate, no matter what a will provides. The remaining portion may pass to other heirs.

Furthermore, in states with **community property laws**, the law assumes that the surviving spouse owns half of everything that both partners earned during the marriage, no matter how much was actually contributed by either partner and even if only one spouse held legal title to the property. States with community property laws provide the same spousal rights for marriages that end in divorce.

 Concept Check 18.1

1. What is probate, and why should people try to avoid probate court?

2. Distinguish between probate and nonprobate property.

3. Give three examples of how people transfer some estates by contract.

4. Give an example of what could happen to one's estate when one dies without a will.

5. Summarize how spouses have legal rights to each other's estates.

 LEARNING OBJECTIVE ❷

Determine how trusts can be used to transfer assets and reduce estate taxes.

trust
Legal arrangement between you as the creator of the trust and the trustee, the person designated to faithfully and wisely manage any assets in the trust to your benefit and to the benefit of your heirs.

grantor
Creator of a trust—the person who makes a grant of assets to establish a trust. Also called the settler, donor, *or* trustor.

trustee
Person charged with carrying out the trust for the benefit of the grantor(s) and heirs.

USE OF TRUSTS TO TRANSFER ASSETS AND REDUCE ESTATE TAXES

Properly drawn trusts can save you and your family time, trouble, and money. These laudable objectives can be achieved only with the assistance of an experienced attorney who specializes in carefully drafting, planning, and executing strategies and techniques in estate planning.

By creating one or more trusts, portions of an estate can be transferred in a contractual manner to others in a way that avoids probate and may reduce or eliminate the federal estate tax. A **trust** is a legal arrangement between you as the **grantor** or creator of the trust and the **trustee**, the person designated to control and manage any assets in the trust. The agreement requires the trustee to faithfully and wisely manage and administer the assets to the benefit of the grantor and others. Trusts can be established to take effect during the grantor's life as well as upon his or her death.

Who Should Consider Setting Up a Trust?

People who should consider setting up a trust include those who have complex estates, hold relatively few liquid assets, desire privacy for their heirs, fear a battle over the provisions of a will, or live in a state with high probate costs or cumbersome probate procedures. Trusts may be created to safeguard the inheritances of survivors, reduce estate taxes, fund a child's education, provide the down payment on someone's home, provide financial assistance for minor children, manage property for young children or disabled elders, and provide income for future generations.

Trust Terminology

Some of the terms associated with trusts are as follows:

- **Grantor:** The person who makes a grant of assets to establish a trust. Also called the **settler, donor, or trustor**.
- **Trustee:** The person or corporation to whom the property is entrusted to manage for the use and benefit of the beneficiary or beneficiaries.
- **Corpus:** The assets put into a trust. Also called the **trust estate or fund**.
- **Beneficiary:** The person for whose benefit a trust is created. Also called the **donee**.
- **Remainder beneficiaries:** The parties named in the trust who are to receive the corpus upon termination of the trust agreement.

Living Trusts Are Established While Grantor Is Alive

There are two types of trusts: (1) **living trusts** that take effect while the grantor is alive and (2) testamentary trusts (see next section) that go into effect upon death.

Revocable Living Trusts A **revocable living trust** is used to protect and manage a person's assets. The person creating the trust maintains the right to change its terms or cancel the trust at any time, for any reason, during his or her lifetime. Thus, living trusts often establish the grantor as the trustee. A revocable living trust can provide for the orderly management and distribution of assets if the grantor becomes incapacitated or incompetent. A new trustee can easily be named. A revocable living trust operates much like a will and proves difficult to contest. Its assets stay in the estate of the grantor at his or her death.

Use an Irrevocable Charitable Remainder Trust to Boost Your Current Income Effective use of an **irrevocable charitable remainder trust (CRT)** is popular for people who want to leave a portion of their estate to charity because it can boost one's income during the grantor's lifetime. You set up the trust and irrevocably give it assets. The trust then pays you income from the assets in the trust for a set period,

living trust
A trust that takes effect while the grantor is still alive.

revocable living trust
Grantor maintains the right to change the trust's terms or cancel it at any time, for any reason, during his or her lifetime.

usually for life, and possibly your spouse's life as well. The charity eventually receives the corpus of the CRT when you (and your spouse, if so arranged) die. For example, Amy Louisanta, a widow from Jefferson City, Tennessee, increased the after-tax income on her $60,000 investment portfolio from $1800 to $4800 per year by creating a CRT, thus giving the assets to the National Wildlife Federation. According to her attorney, Matthew Paul, the CRT then reinvested the proceeds, thus earning a higher return for the organization and providing more to Amy.

A CRT works well for people who show wealth on paper because of appreciated assets. The projected future value of the gift can be discounted to a present value. This amount can then be written off as a charitable contribution on Amy's current income tax return, saving her even more money. It is wise to give to a CRT because the donor can avoid capital gains taxes while still realizing the full benefit of the asset's current value.

irrevocable living trust

Arrangement in which the grantor permanently gives up ownership and the right to control of the property, to change the beneficiaries, and to change the trustees.

Irrevocable Living Trusts

An **irrevocable living trust** is an arrangement in which the grantor relinquishes ownership and control of property. Usually this involves a gift of the property to the trust. It cannot be changed or undone by the grantor during his or her lifetime. The grantor gives up three key rights under an irrevocable living trust: (1) control of the property, (2) change of the beneficiaries, and (3) change of the trustees. Because irrevocable trusts are generally considered separate tax entities, the trust pays any income taxes due. The assets in the trust bypass probate; however, transfers to a trust made within three years of death may be brought back into the decedent's estate.

FINANCIAL POWER POINT

Trusts for Special Needs Children and Adults

Some states have passed laws that allow parents to set aside money in a trust specifically for the benefit of a disabled child or adult while letting him or her retain all public benefits, like Medicaid or welfare. This kind of trust is called a **special needs trust**. This type of trust is used in situations where the grantee likely will never be able to handle his or her own affairs. It provides lifelong access to supplemental and emergency funds to cover expenses that public assistance does not. The trustee makes all the decisions to pay for access to assure suitable health, safety, and welfare. Without special arrangements, income from a trust will count against a child with special needs who is receiving public aid.

Testamentary Trusts Go into Effect Only upon the Death of the Grantor

testamentary trust

Becomes effective upon death of the grantor according to the terms of the grantor's will or a revocable living trust. Such trusts can provide money or asset management after the grantor's death for the heirs' benefit.

The second broad category of trusts used in connection with estate planning comprises **testamentary trusts**. A testamentary trust becomes effective upon the death of the grantor according to the terms of the grantor's will or a revocable living trust. Such trusts can be designed to provide money or asset management after the grantor's death, to provide income for a surviving spouse and children, and to give assets to grandchildren or great-grandchildren while providing income from the assets to the surviving spouse and children, among other things.

✔ Concept Check 18.2

1. List some reasons why people establish trusts.

2. Distinguish between a grantor and a trustee.

3. Summarize the difference between living and testamentary trusts.

4. Explain what is so important about the difference between revocable and irrevocable trusts.

CREATE ADVANCE DIRECTIVE DOCUMENTS IN CASE YOU BECOME INCAPACITATED

The U.S. Constitution and state laws provide that adults have the legal right to accept or refuse medical care, including life-sustaining treatments. Thus you have the right to request or consent to treatment, to refuse treatment before it has started, and to have treatment stopped once it has begun.

Your wishes, however, may not be carried out unless you have written them down in advance because accidents and many illnesses, such as Alzheimer's disease, strokes, and cancer, may result in a period of mental incompetence and physical disability before death. Eighty-five percent of Americans die in hospitals, rehabilitation facilities, and nursing homes where they may not be capable of making good decisions.

Advance directives refers to treatment preferences and the designation of a surrogate decision maker in the event that a person should become unable to make decisions on her or his own behalf as a result of coma, dementia, brain death, or other serious medical condition. These documents may be used to retain your dignity and save your loved ones the burden of making some very challenging and difficult decisions. In essence, you sign legal documents stating exactly what you want to happen if you become incapacitated. Four out of five adults have no advance directive documents.

There are three types of advance directives: (1) health care proxy, (2) living will, and (3) durable power of attorney for legal and financial matters. Thinking about advance directives makes one contemplate one's value system and definition of quality of life. Once you have created advance directive documents, give copies to members of your family and other responsible people in your life, and your wishes in these matters may then be controlled as you desire.

A Health Care Proxy Designates a Person to Make Health Care Decisions

A **health care proxy** is a legal document in which individuals designate another person to make health care decisions on their behalf if they are rendered incapable of making their wishes known. The authorized person executes such decisions or tries to make sure that health care professionals follow the maker's intentions. The person who is authorized is called a proxy or agent.

The proxy has broad authority over a person's care and has access to all of his or her medical records. The person designated as the health care proxy has, in essence, the same rights to request or refuse treatment that the individual would have if capable of making and communicating decisions. Filling out a health care proxy form does not deprive the maker of the right to make decisions about medical treatment as long as he or she is able to do so. If the individual regains the ability to make his or her own health-related decisions, the proxy may no longer make them. A health care proxy does not override directives in a living will.

A Living Will Specifies End-of-Life Medical Treatments

If you have no one you can appoint to make medical decisions for you or do not want to appoint someone, you can choose to give specific written instructions about treatment in advance. A **living will** allows you to document in advance your specific wishes concerning medical treatments in an emergency or during end-of-life health care. The document sets forth one's wishes in case of terminal illness or persistent unconsciousness where the individual is no longer capable of participating in his or her health care decisions. A living will may relieve family members of making a painful decision to allow a person's life to end as well as prevent the involvement of a court in such decision making.

Depending on state law, a living will may also designate one person to have decision-making priority over any other individuals who could, by law, make health care decisions. A living will is sometimes called an **advance medical directive** because similar

LEARNING OBJECTIVE

Summarize the benefits of preparing advance directive documents.

advance directives
Forms that allow one to specify his or her treatment preferences and the designation of a surrogate decision maker in the event that a person should become unable to make decisions on her or his own behalf as a result of coma, dementia, brain death, or other serious medical condition.

health care proxy/durable power of attorney for health care
A legal document in which individuals designate another person to make health care decisions on their behalf if they are rendered incapable of making their wishes known and executing such decisions; the proxy tries to make sure that health care professionals follow the maker's intentions.

living will (advance medical directive)
A legal documents that allows you to record in advance your specific wishes concerning medical treatments in an emergency or during end-of-life health care, in case of terminal illness or persistent unconsciousness where you are no longer capable of participating in your health care decisions.

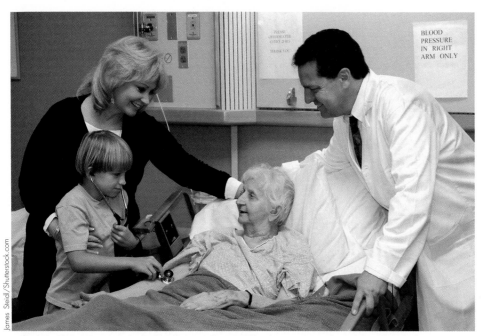

Advance directives can help family members make appropriate decisions when a loved one is incapacitated.

legal provisions are often contained within a single document. Living wills in some states contain provisions for a health care proxy and/or a living will.

General Phrasing for a Living Will A living will can be general or very specific. The most common general statement in a living will is an end-of-life preference stating: "If I should have an incurable or irreversible condition that will result either in death within a relatively short period of time or a state of permanent unconsciousness from which, to a reasonable degree of medical certainty, there can be no recovery, it is my desire that my life not be prolonged by the administration of life-sustaining procedures. If I am unable to participate in my health care decisions, I direct my attending physician to withhold or withdraw life-sustaining procedures that merely prolong the dying process and are not necessary to my comfort or freedom from pain."

Specific Phrasing for Life Sustaining Procedures in a Living Will Your general instructions about refusing treatment, even if written down, may not be effective. To avoid varying interpretations by physicians or well-meaning relatives, a living will must speak to specific circumstances; therefore, your instructions should clearly cover the exact treatment decisions that must be made.

The maker should declare his or her intention whether or not to withhold each of a list of life-sustaining procedures under circumstances of terminal illness or persistent unconsciousness, including analgesia (pain relief), antibiotics, kidney dialysis, chemotherapy, artificially supplied food (nutrition) or hydration (fluids), surgery, the use of life-support equipment including ventilators, and a "do not resuscitate order" for both heart and lung resuscitation efforts in case of cardiac or respiratory arrest. Whether one wants to donate organs may also be specified. Living wills need to conform precisely to the statutes in the state in which the person lives. Federal law requires hospitals to inform patients of their rights to make such decisions about medical care.

DID YOU KNOW?

Turn Bad Habits into Good Ones

Do You Do This?	*Do This Instead!*
Are not sure of your beneficiary designations	Check employer records and investment accounts
Own home only in your name	Change to joint ownership with significant other
Put off writing your will	Go online and create a will
Have no named guardian for your child	Discuss and name guardian in new will
Have no advance directive documents	Go online and fill out online forms
Don't know where key documents are stored	Store documents and give location to others
Have lots of assets but no trust agreement	See an estate planning attorney

A Durable Power of Attorney Appoints Someone to Handle Legal and Personal Finances

People over age 50, as well as young adults, are smart to create a **durable power of attorney** in advance of the onset of any incapacitating medical condition. This is a document in which you appoint someone, called an attorney-in-fact, to handle your legal or business matters and sign his or her name to documents. It allows an individual to make bank transactions, collect Social Security payments, apply for disability, and pay bills while an individual is medically incapacitated. It stays in effect as long as the person lives, unless he or she explicitly revokes it.

This document should detail the specific aspects of your affairs that it covers and should even mention specific institutions (banks or brokerage firms, for example) and account numbers. A durable power of attorney gives the designated person virtually absolute power to manage your financial affairs, so choose a trusted individual who knows your wishes. A **limited (or special) power of attorney** is narrower in scope and could be restricted to one specified act or a certain time period, such as signing the maker's name at the closing of the sale of a home or managing the maker's investment accounts.

Select someone you can thoroughly trust to give power of attorney and let him or her know what your wishes are. Experts suggest that it is wise to avoid giving power of attorney to caregivers. Share the information about your power-of-attorney arrangements with other family members because that puts them in a position to watch out for potential misconduct. Understand, too, that you may revoke your power of attorney and/or give it to another person as long as you are mentally capable to do so.

durable power of attorney
A legal document in which you appoint someone, called an attorney-in-fact, to handle your legal or business matters and sign his or her name to documents. It allows an individual to make bank transactions, collect Social Security payments, apply for disability, and pay bills while an individual is medically incapacitated. It stays in effect as long as the person lives, unless he or she explicitly revokes it.

limited (or special) power of attorney
A legal document, narrower in scope than a durable power of attorney, that can be restricted to one specified act or a certain time period, such as signing the maker's name at the closing of the sale of a home or managing the maker's investment accounts.

 Concept Check 18.3

1. Offer three reasons why people should create advance directive documents.

2. What does a health care proxy achieve, and how does it differ from a living will?

3. What does a living will commonly provide, and why should it be written very specifically rather than generally?

4. What does a durable power of attorney provide?

FINANCIAL POWER POINT

Advanced Directives for Unmarried Couples

While state laws are evolving on the rights of unmarried couples, a loved one can be protected and have some legal power. To do so, name each other as your durable power of attorney for finances and health care proxy.

CHECKLIST TO SETTLE AND TRANSFER YOUR ESTATE

Creating a master checklist to your financial world by providing answers to estate planning questions and detailing the locations of related documents will simplify the settlement and transfer of your estate.

1. *Current will.* Location? Contact information for attorney? For financial adviser? For insurance agent?

2. *Powers of attorney.* Living will? Health care proxy? Durable power of attorney?

3. *Letter of last instructions.* Document locations? Who has copies?

4. *Funeral and burial arrangements.* Written instructions? Who has copies?

5. *Trusts.* Location? Attorney contact information?

6. *Official documents.* Birth? Prenuptial agreements? Marriage? Divorce? Guardianship? Military?

7. *Social Security numbers.* Yours? Spouse? Children?

8. *Computer passwords.* Passwords for computer?

9. *Safe-deposit box.* Location? Key? Written record of contents?

LEARNING OBJECTIVE **4**

List the questions and documents needed to simplify the settlement and transfer of your estate.

10. *Employer.* Employee benefits? Contact information for supervisors and human resources department?
11. *Life insurance.* Policies? Employer group policy? Primary beneficiaries? Contingent beneficiaries? Agent(s)? Details on collecting benefits?
12. *Pension.* Potential benefits? Veteran's benefits?
13. *Retirement accounts.* IRA? 401(k)? Keogh? Annuities? Employer pension plans? Passwords?
14. *Social Security and Veterans Administration.* Current or potential benefits? Discharge papers? Records?
15. *Health insurance.* Coverage details? Employer policy?
16. *Disability income and long-term care insurance.* Policies?
17. *Financial statements.* Balance sheet, including artwork and family heirlooms? Cash-flow statement? Value of estate?
18. *Budget.* Details? Old records?
19. *Liabilities.* Credit cards? Vehicle loans/leases? Personal loans? Mortgages? Passwords?
20. *Cash management.* Bank information? Checking? Savings? Money market? Passwords? Certificates of deposit?
21. *Housing.* Deeds? Titles? Rental properties? Title insurance? Timeshares? Homeowner's policies?
22. *Automobiles/recreational vehicles.* Titles? Insurance policies?
23. *Investment assets.* Brokerage accounts? Mutual fund statements? Stocks? Bonds? Other assets? Written investment objectives? Passwords?
24. *Business interests.* Agreements? Ownership interest in a family-owned business? Legal counsel?
25. *Tax returns.* Last year's return? Previous returns? Current year's information? Gift and estate tax?

DID YOU KNOW?

Your Worst Financial Blunders in Estate Planning

Based on others' financial woes, you will make mistakes in personal finance when you:

1. Do not have a valid will.

2. Do not have signed advance directive documents.

3. Forget to update forms you have signed that contractually award assets, like life insurance and retirement and checking accounts, to ex-spouses, parents, or siblings.

 Concept Check 18.4

1. List five estate planning documents that should be easily found by your survivors.

2. List five different types of assets about which your survivors will need detailed information in order to claim them after your death.

ESTATE AND INHERITANCE TAXES

LEARNING OBJECTIVE 5

Explain the potential impact of estate and inheritance taxes.

federal estate tax
Assessed against a deceased person's estate before property (real estate, stocks and bonds, business interests, and so on) is transferred to heirs or assigned according to terms of a will or state intestacy laws.

The **federal estate tax** is assessed against the estate of a deceased person before property (real estate, stocks and bonds, business interests, and so on) is transferred to heirs or assigned according to terms of a will or state intestacy laws. It is a tax on the deceased's estate, not on the beneficiary who is to receive the property.

Only about 3500 of the nation's wealthiest estates are required to pay estate taxes. The tax law exempts the first $5 million of an individual's estate. This is called the **basic exclusion amount.** The tax rate on estates valued above these amounts is 35 percent. The law offers "portability" of the exemption between married couples because it allows them to add any unused portion of the $5 million estate tax exemption of the first spouse to die to the surviving spouse's estate tax exemption. Thus married couples may pass $10 million on to their heirs free from estate taxes with no planning whatsoever.

The estate tax law also has become unified with federal gift and generation-skipping transfer taxes with $5 million exemptions. The estate tax exemption and rate will be in effect through the end of 2012; however, if Congress does not pass a new law in 2013, everything goes back to the 2001 rules, so the estate tax exemption will be $1 million, with a 55% rate.

DID YOU KNOW?

Directing Life Insurance Benefits to Your "Estate" Is a Mistake

Life insurance proceeds are payable directly to the named beneficiary(ies) in the policy, and they transfer tax free. However, if the proceeds of life insurance are payable to the estate of the deceased—which is exactly the wrong thing to do—they are included in the estate for federal estate tax purposes.

Further, if the deceased, while alive, retained any ownership interest, such as the right to change beneficiaries or to borrow against any cash value of the policy, the proceeds are still included in the estate for estate tax purposes. To solve this problem, prior to death, assign ownership of a life insurance policy to someone else, such as the beneficiary.

ADVICE FROM A PRO

Ten Things Every Spouse Must Know

The following checklist contains items spouses should know about financial, estate, tax, and investment planning. After all, it is never what we know that will get us in trouble, but rather what we don't know.

1. *Understand your current financial situation—assets and liabilities, net worth, and family income and expenses.*

2. *Have a plan for all emergencies. Know exactly what financial resources would be needed if your spouse were to become disabled or unemployed. Make certain your auto, homeowner's, and medical insurance coverage are adequate for your situation. Have sufficient cash on hand to pay your deductibles.*

3. *Carry sufficient life insurance on yourself and your spouse. Determine whether sufficient resources are available to raise your family and provide for your children's education if you or your spouse were to die. Know what benefits your spouse's employer offers and what benefits have been selected. Know who are the beneficiaries at your spouse's death and if both you and your spouse were to die. Consider naming a trust as beneficiary instead of naming minor-age children as beneficiaries.*

4. *Verify that your estate documents (wills, trusts, guardianships, durable powers of attorney, and so on) reflect your current wishes for your family.*

5. *Understand your income taxes and pursue aggressive, but legal, strategies for reducing your tax liabilities. Don't sign a return you don't understand.*

6. *Create a written investment plan and follow it. Understand the rate of return that you must realize on your investments to achieve your goal. Monitor your results quarterly.*

7. *Know how to invest—when to buy and sell—so that you can consistently obtain a rate of return that will allow your family to achieve and maintain financial independence. Do not expect someone else to care more about your money than you do.*

8. *Have a plan for funding your children's education, home ownership, and your retirement. Complete sample FAFSA (Free Application for Federal Student Aid) forms when your child enters high school so you will understand what the government believes your family should be able to contribute for your child's college education.*

9. *Thoroughly understand your employer- and government-provided benefits. If they are not sufficient to achieve your goals, make a career change. There is no sense in riding a dead horse.*

10. *Communicate with your children and other members of your family to teach them about financial, estate, tax, and investment planning. Remember, the most expensive form of education is to learn through your own bad experiences.*

Lorraine R Decker
Decker & Associates Inc., www.DeckerUSA.com

Source: Decker, Lorraine R., CLU, ChFC, MSFS, President, Decker & Associates Inc., "Ten Things Every Spouse Must Know About Finance, Estate Tax, and Investment Planning." Copyright © 2009 by Decker & Associates Inc. Reprinted with permission.

Seventeen states and the District of Columbia also have a **state estate tax**, and most are coupled with the federal estate tax. So, when the federal estate tax is zero, those taxes are also zero.

Eight states* impose an **inheritance tax** assessed by the decedent's state of residence on beneficiaries who receive inherited property. This tax is based on how much the

inheritance tax
A tax imposed by eight states (i.e., Connecticut, Indiana, Iowa, Kentucky, Maryland, Nebraska, New Jersey, and Pennsylvania) that is assessed on the decedent's beneficiaries who receive inherited property.

* Connecticut, Indiana, Iowa, Kentucky, Maryland, Nebraska, New Jersey, and Pennsylvania.

DO IT NOW!

You know more about personal finance after reading this chapter, so get started right now by:

1. *Taking an inventory of your inheritable assets and deciding to whom you would like them to go in the event of your death.*

2. *Determining how all of your bank and investment accounts are owned and changing the ownership form as appropriate to individual or joint with someone else of your choosing.*

3. *Preparing a will.*

beneficiaries get and their right to receive it, and the rates range from 1 to 20 percent. In those states, transfers to spouses, children, and other close relatives may be either exempt or subject to a lower state inheritance tax rate. The beneficiaries are responsible for paying inheritance taxes, although typically, the estate pays the taxes before distributing any remaining assets to the heirs.

✔ Concept Check 18.5

1. What is the amount of an estate that is exempt from federal estate taxes?

2. Comment on the likely impact of estate taxes and inheritance taxes at the state level on most people.

Joel Gordon Photography

WHAT DO YOU RECOMMEND NOW?

Now that you have read the chapter on estate planning, what do you recommend to Orlando and Giselle Molina in the case at the beginning of the chapter regarding:

1. Beneficiary designations for their financial assets?

2. Joint ownership of their home, vehicles, and other property?

3. Making a will?

4. Establishing guardianship for the children?

5. Using advance directive documents to avoid a situation like that confronting Orlando's father?

6. Establishing trusts for their children?

BIG PICTURE SUMMARY OF LEARNING OBJECTIVES

LO1.   Identify the ways that your estate can be transferred through contracts and a will.

After inventorying everything you own and owe, you may find that you can readily transfer most or all of your estate with a will and via contracts. Nonprobate property, which does not go through the court process of probate, includes assets transferred to survivors by contract (such as naming a beneficiary for your retirement plan or with bank accounts owned with another person through joint tenancy with right of survivorship).

LO2.   Determine how trusts can be used to transfer assets and reduce estate taxes.

By creating one or more trusts, portions of an estate can be transferred in a contractual manner to others in a way that avoids probate and may reduce or eliminate the federal estate tax. A trust is a legal arrangement between you as the grantor or creator of the trust and the trustee, the person designated to control and manage any assets in the trust. Revocable and irrevocable trusts are used in estate planning as well as testamentary trusts.

LO3. **Summarize the benefits of preparing advance directive documents.**

Making advance directives can save your loved ones the burden of making some challenging decisions in case you become incapacitated. These documents include durable power of attorney, limited power of attorney, living will, and health care directive.

LO4. **List the questions and documents needed to simplify the settlement and transfer of your estate.**

Creating a master list of "CliffsNotes" to your financial world by providing answers to estate planning questions and listing the locations of related documents will simplify the settlement and transfer of your estate.

LO5. **Explain the potential impact of estate and inheritance taxes.**

The federal estate tax affects about 3500 estates. Some states have state estate and inheritance taxes.

LET'S TALK ABOUT IT

1. **Wills for College Students.** Do college students really need a will at this point in their lives? Why or why not? What probably would happen to the typical college student's assets if he or she died without a will?

2. **Choosing an Executor.** What are some criteria that you would use to select the executor for your estate or the guardian for your children if you and your spouse or significant other died at the same time?

3. **Writing a Living Will.** If you were thinking about signing a living will, what are some specific provisions that you might put into the document?

4. **Writing a Letter of Last Instructions.** Identify topics that you would cover in your letter of last instructions.

5. **Creating Trusts for Grandchildren.** Do you think it is appropriate for parents and grandparents to put conditions in a trust set up for their children or grandchildren that relate to the behavior of their heirs?

DO THE MATH

1. **Estimating the Size of an Estate.** Christopher Marcos, of Franklin Springs, Georgia, died in 2012 without a valid will. His probate estate for federal estate tax purposes was $12 million. Christopher's wife, Amanda, and three children were his only survivors. Answer the following questions, assuming that Christopher's state of residence followed the typical guidelines of division (one-half for the spouse with the children equally splitting the remainder):

   (a) What will be the dollar amount of the division of assets for the wife and children?

   (b) If Amanda has personal assets (beyond her inheritance from Christopher) that have a fair market value of $400,000, if she died soon after him in 2012, how much would her estate total?

   (c) If Amanda died without a will in 2012, what would be the dollar amount of the division of assets, assuming that she has no other children?

   (d) Assuming Amanda's estate paid $50,000 for her funeral expenses, $90,000 for probate costs, and $500,000 to pay off remaining debts and mortgages, what would be Amanda's taxable estate in 2012 before subtracting the exempt amount and how much in estate taxes will have to be paid?

   (e) How much in estate taxes would have to be paid if she died in 2013 instead of 2012, assuming Congress does not change the law?

2. **Estimating Estate Taxes.** Laura Kim of Hayward, California, lives with her elderly grandmother, Haejeong. Her grandmother owns two profitable auto parts stores that are worth millions. They are wondering how these estate taxes might affect Haejeong. Laura hopes that her grandmother, who is in excellent health, lives at least another 20 years. If she doesn't, the federal estate tax will apply. If Haejeong's probate estate is valued at $7.5 million, calculate the following:

   (a) The amount of the estate subject to the federal estate tax and the amount of that tax if she dies in 2012.

   (b) The amount of the federal estate tax if she dies in 2013 and Congress does not change the law.

FINANCIAL PLANNING CASES

CASE 1

Belinda Johnson Helps Her Uncle Plan His Estate

Belinda Johnson has been approached by her uncle, Ryan Lawrence, who seeks advice about planning his estate. She has been handling some of Ryan's investments, and he trusts her judgment on financial matters. Ryan has a net worth of $7,000,000. At age 54, he is concerned about preparing his finances so that as much as possible of his estate will go to his heirs according to his wishes. Ryan has no will but has written down some of his ideas. He has no wife or children but wants to be able to provide for his mother, four nephews, Belinda, and a disabled sister.

(a) What is the first action Ryan should take in planning his estate?

(b) Why might an irrevocable living trust be a good idea for Ryan in providing for his mother and sister?

(c) What other types of trusts might Ryan use in his estate planning?

CASE 2

Victor and Maria Update Their Estate Plans

Since retiring earlier this year, Victor and Maria have found that their assets amount to approximately $800,000, made up of the following: Victor's half-interest in their home ($90,000), his tax-sheltered pension plan ($144,000), his stock ($56,000), his personal property ($50,000), Maria's half-interest in their home ($90,000), the inherited home from her mother ($120,000), her tax-sheltered pension plan ($112,000), the present value (obtained from Victor's employer) of the survivors benefits under her husband's defined-benefit pension plan ($60,000), personal property ($50,000), and her zero-coupon bonds ($28,000).

(a) Offer the Hernandezes advice about how each might establish a durable power of attorney for finances.

(b) Should both Victor and Maria have living wills? Why or why not?

(c) Victor purchased his $100,000 term life insurance policy through his employer, and he has been paying on his privately purchased $50,000 whole life insurance policy for many years (which now has a cash value of $30,000). Maria is listed as the primary beneficiary on both policies. Assuming that Victor owns both

policies, what advice can you offer regarding ownership of the two policies?

(d) After adding up the value of the estate, what is the likelihood of Victor's estate having to pay federal inheritance taxes?

(e) Offer Victor and Maria some suggestions on how to ease the transfer of assets to their adult children and grandchildren.

CASE 3

Julia Price Is Frightened into Estate Planning

Mary Leakey, who was Julia's best friend at the engineering firm where she works, recently died from breast cancer at age 58. Like Julia, Mary never married. Later, Julia was surprised to receive letters informing her that she was designated as the primary beneficiary of Mary's retirement plan assets and that she was left some assets noted in Mary's will. Mary's generosity got Julia motivated to do all her estate planning as soon as possible, as you never know when a big bus will run you down and end your life. Since Julia has a substantial amount of assets from her own saving and investing in addition to what Mary passed on to her, she made appointments with her human resources department, her stock broker, and an estate planning attorney. Julia knows she needs to check her beneficiary designations, write a new will, fill out advance directive forms, make a letter of last instructions, and perhaps establish a trust for her brother Louis and his two children, Lucy and Tanszania. Offer your opinion about her thinking.

CASE 4

A Couple Considers the Ramifications of Dying Intestate

Melissa Merryweather of Sioux Falls, South Dakota, is a 34-year-old police detective earning $58,000 per year. She and her husband, Joshua, have two children in elementary school. They own a modestly furnished home and two late-model cars. Melissa also owns a snowmobile. Both spouses have 401(k) retirement accounts through their employers, and their employers also provide them with $50,000 group term life policies. Melissa also has a $50,000 term life policy of her own. The couple has about $5000 in their joint checking account. Neither has a will.

(a) List four negative things that could happen if either Melissa or Joshua were to die without a will.

(b) What would be the most important negative consequence of not having a will if both Melissa and Joshua were to die together in an accident?

(c) Which assets could be jointly owned so that they will automatically transfer to the other spouse if either Melissa or Joshua dies?

(d) What qualities should Melissa and Joshua look for when naming the executors of their wills?

(e) Once they have completed and signed their wills, where should the Merryweathers keep the original documents and any copies?

CASE 5

A Lottery Winner Practices Estate Planning

Your good friend, Brandon, has just announced that he has the sole winning ticket in the $7 million lottery drawing of last week. Brandon is 60 years old, divorced, and lives in St. Clairsville, Ohio. He has two adult children (Nicole and Heather) and four grandchildren. Recognizing that you are not an attorney, and knowing that your friend needs personal finance advice, offer some estate planning suggestions regarding the following points:

(a) Assume that Brandon's taxable estate now amounts to $7,200,000, and after the $5 million exemption, his remaining estate will be taxed at 35 percent. If he died in 2012, how much would he owe? Give him that figure and offer him one single piece of advice.

(b) Name two types of trusts that Brandon might consider to reduce his eventual estate taxes and summarize what those trusts might help him accomplish.

(c) Offer Brandon some suggestions for things he might want to put into his letter of last instructions.

BE YOUR OWN PERSONAL FINANCIAL MANAGER

1. **Your Beneficiary Designations.** Assume you have a full-time job with benefits, including a 401(k) retirement plan that now contains thousands of dollars in mutual fund shares. Write down who you want to be the primary beneficiaries of those assets, and if there is more than one beneficiary, write down what percentage each is to receive. Also make note of the names of your contingent beneficiaries.

2. **Will, Letter of Last Instructions, and Advance Directive Documents.** Complete Worksheet 68: My Will, Letter of Last Instructions, and Advance

MY PERSONAL
FINANCIAL
PLANNER

Directive Documents in "My Personal Financial Planner" by recording on the list of six documents the date you prepared each and the names of those who know about their location or have a copy.

3. **Beneficiary Designations.** Complete Worksheet 69: My Assets to Be Transferred by Beneficiary Designations in "My Personal Financial Planner" by recording your intended beneficiaries for the dozen or more types of assets you either own now or would expect to own in a few years.

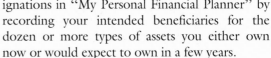

MY PERSONAL
FINANCIAL
PLANNER

ON THE 'NET

Go to the Web pages indicated to complete these exercises.

1. **Health Care Proxy.** Visit the website for the New York State Department of Health (www.health.state.ny.us/professionals/patients/health_care_proxy) and read the information on who will speak for you, clarify values and beliefs, choose a spokesperson, and discuss your wishes. Then click on "Appointing Your Health Care Agent." Print the form and complete it by writing in necessary information. Get some witnesses, sign the form, and make copies for those you think should know. This health care proxy is valid in New York and may or may not be valid in your state, although it does clearly state your desires.

2. **Living Will.** Visit the website for Hospice of the Valley (www.hov.org/health_care_decisions.aspx) and click on "Free Living Will and Health Care (Medical) Power of Attorney" (English or Spanish). Print the form and complete it by checking the appropriate boxes and writing in necessary information. Get some witnesses, sign the form, and make copies for those you think should know.

3. **Charitable Remainder Trusts.** View an example of a charitable remainder trust and read the logic behind the donors making such a gift (www.futurefocus.net/crutexample.htm). What are your thoughts about the value to both the donor and the recipient?

4. **Cost of a Will.** Go online and search Google or Bing for "will preparation software" to discover the cost of preparing a will. Find three companies that charge a fee to permit you to input information for them to prepare your last will and testament. Write a report of your findings.

ACTION INVOLVEMENT PROJECTS

1. **Written Record of Your Personal Information.** Make a written record of your personal information that would be helpful for your heirs. Be sure to include employer's human resource department contact information, Social Security number, bank and investment account names and numbers, credit accounts, vehicle title(s), property owned, life insurance, and location of safe-deposit box. Prepare a written list.

2. **Letter of Last Instructions.** Inventory what you own, including items of sentimental value, and write a letter of last instructions telling heirs who gets what items. Sign and date the form. It is not necessary to have it witnessed, but you can if you wish.

3. **Guardianship Criteria.** Assume you have children and wish to identify a guardian for them in the event you die before they are adults. Make a list of criteria you and a significant other might consider when making such a decision.

4. **Charitable Contributions.** Assume you have $1 million and have a terminal disease. Make a list of charitable organizations to which you want to give money before you pass.

Visit the Garman/Forgue companion website at **www.cengagebrain.com**

APPENDIXES

APPENDIX A

PRESENT AND FUTURE VALUE TABLES

Many problems in personal finance involve decisions about money values at varying points in time. These values can be directly and fairly compared only when they are adjusted to a common point in time. Chapter 1 introduced the basic time value concepts. This appendix offers more details about the time value of money. In addition, it provides tables listing the future and present value of $1 with which to make calculations.

Four assumptions must be made to eliminate unnecessary complications:

1. Each planning period is one year long.
2. Only annual interest rates are considered.
3. Interest rates are the same during each of the annual periods.
4. Interest is compounded and continues earning a return in subsequent periods.

Tables of present and future values can be constructed to make these adjustments. **Future values** are derived from the principles of compounding the dollar values ahead in time. **Present values** are derived by discounting (which is the inverse of compounding) the dollar values and transferring them to an earlier point in time.

It is usually unnecessary to precisely identify whether the interest is paid/received at the *beginning* of a period or at the end of a period, or to know whether interest compounds daily or quarterly instead of annually. (These calculations require even more tables.) The following present and future value tables assume that money is accumulated, received, paid, compounded, or whatever at the *end* of a period. The tables can be used to compute the mathematics of personal finance with high certainty and to confirm (or reject as inaccurate) what people tell you about financial matters.

The most significant task is to find the correct table. Accordingly, each table is clearly described here, and illustrations of its use appear on the facing page where possible. In addition, the appropriate mathematical equation is shown and can be easily solved using a calculator.

Illustrations Using Appendix A-1: Future Value of a Single Amount ($1)

To use Appendix A-1 on page A-4, locate the future value factor for the time period and the interest rate.

1. You invest $500 at a 15 percent rate of return for 12 years. How much will you have at the end of that 12-year period?

   The future value factor is 5.350; hence, the solution is $500 × 5.350, or $2675.

2. Property values in your neighborhood are increasing at a rate of 5 percent per year. If your home is presently worth $90,000, what will its worth be in 7 years?

   The future value factor is 1.407; hence, the solution is $90,000 × 1.407, or $126,630.

3. You need to amass $40,000 in the next 10 years to make a balloon payment on your home mortgage. You have $17,000 available to invest. What annual interest rate must be earned to realize the $40,000?

   $40,000 ÷ $17,000 = 2.353. Read down the periods (*n*) column to 10 years and across to 2.367 (close enough), which is found under the 9 percent column. Hence, the $17,000 invested at 9 percent for 10 years will grow to a future value of slightly more than $40,000.

4. An apartment building is currently valued at $160,000, and it has been appreciating at 8 percent per year. If this rate continues, in how many years will it be worth $300,000?

    $300,000 ÷ $160,000 = 1.875. Read down the 8 percent column until you reach 1.851 (close enough to 1.875). This number corresponds to a period of 8 years. Hence, the $160,000 property appreciating at 8 percent annually will grow to a future value of $300,000 in slightly more than 8 years.

5. You have the choice of receiving a down payment from someone who wants to purchase your rental property as $15,000 today or as a personal note for $25,000 payable in 6 years. If you could expect to earn 8 percent on such funds, which is the better choice?

    The future value factor is 1.587; hence, the future value of $15,000 at 8 percent is $15,000 × 1.587, or $23,805. Thus, it would be better to take the note for $25,000.

6. How much will an automobile now priced at $20,000 cost in 4 years, assuming an annual inflation rate of 5 percent?

    Read down the 5 percent column and across the row for 4 years to locate the future value factor of 1.216. Hence, the solution is $20,000 × 1.216, or $24,320.

7. How large a lump-sum investment do you need now to have $20,000 available in 5 years, assuming a 10 percent annual rate of return?

    The $20,000 future value is divided by 1.611 (10 percent at 5 years), resulting in a current lump-sum investment of $12,415.

8. You have $5000 now and need $10,000 in 9 years. What rate of return is needed to reach that goal?

    Divide the future value of $10,000 by the present value of the lump sum of $5000 to obtain a future value factor of 2.0. In the row for 9 years, locate the future value factor of 1.999 (very close to 2.0). Read up the column to find that an 8 percent return on investment is needed.

9. How many years will it take your lump-sum investment of $10,000 to grow to $16,000, given an annual rate of return of 7 percent?

    Divide the future value of $16,000 by the present value of the $10,000 lump sum to compute a future value factor of 1.6; look down the 7 percent column to find 1.606 (close enough). Read across the row to find that an investment period of 7 years is needed.

An alternative approach is to use a calculator to determine the future value, *FV*, of a sum of money invested today, assuming that the amount remains in the investment for a specified number of time periods (usually years) and that it earns a certain rate of return each period. The equation is

$$FV = PV(1.0 + i)^n \quad \textbf{(A.1)}$$

where

$$FV = Future Value$$
$$PV = Present\ Value \text{ of the investment}$$
$$i = Interest \text{ rate per period}$$
$$n = Number \text{ of periods the } PV \text{ is invested}$$

Future Value of a Single Amount ($1 at the End of n Periods)
(Used to Compute the Compounded Future Value of a Known Lump Sum)

n	1%	2%	3%	4%	5%	6%	7%	8%	9%	10%	11%	12%	13%	14%	15%	16%	17%	18%	19%	20%
1	1.0100	1.0200	1.0300	1.0400	1.0500	1.0600	1.0700	1.0800	1.0900	1.1000	1.1100	1.1200	1.1300	1.1400	1.1500	1.1600	1.1700	1.1800	1.1900	1.2000
2	1.0201	1.0404	1.0609	1.0816	1.1025	1.1236	1.1449	1.1664	1.1881	1.2100	1.2321	1.2544	1.2769	1.2996	1.3225	1.3456	1.3689	1.3924	1.4161	1.4400
3	1.0303	1.0612	1.0927	1.1249	1.1576	1.1910	1.2250	1.2597	1.2950	1.3310	1.3676	1.4049	1.4429	1.4815	1.5209	1.5609	1.6016	1.6430	1.6852	1.7280
4	1.0406	1.0824	1.1255	1.1699	1.2155	1.2625	1.3108	1.3605	1.4116	1.4641	1.5181	1.5735	1.6305	1.6890	1.7490	1.8106	1.8739	1.9388	2.0053	2.0736
5	1.0510	1.1041	1.1593	1.2167	1.2763	1.3382	1.4026	1.4693	1.5386	1.6105	1.6851	1.7623	1.8424	1.9254	2.0114	2.1003	2.1924	2.2878	2.3864	2.4883
6	1.0615	1.1262	1.1941	1.2653	1.3401	1.4185	1.5007	1.5869	1.6771	1.7716	1.8704	1.9738	2.0820	2.1950	2.3131	2.4364	2.5652	2.6996	2.8398	2.9860
7	1.0721	1.1487	1.2299	1.3159	1.4071	1.5036	1.6058	1.7138	1.8280	1.9487	2.0762	2.2107	2.3526	2.5023	2.6600	2.8262	3.0012	3.1855	3.3793	3.5832
8	1.0829	1.1717	1.2668	1.3686	1.4775	1.5938	1.7182	1.8509	1.9926	2.1436	2.3045	2.4760	2.6584	2.8526	3.0590	3.2784	3.5115	3.7589	4.0214	4.2998
9	1.0937	1.1951	1.3048	1.4233	1.5513	1.6895	1.8385	1.9990	2.1719	2.3579	2.5580	2.7731	3.0040	3.2519	3.5179	3.8030	4.1084	4.4355	4.7854	5.1598
10	1.1046	1.2190	1.3439	1.4802	1.6289	1.7908	1.9672	2.1589	2.3674	2.5937	2.8394	3.1058	3.3946	3.7072	4.0456	4.4114	4.8068	5.2338	5.6947	6.1917
11	1.1157	1.2434	1.3842	1.5395	1.7103	1.8983	2.1049	2.3316	2.5804	2.8531	3.1518	3.4785	3.8359	4.2262	4.6524	5.1173	5.6240	6.1759	6.7767	7.4301
12	1.1268	1.2682	1.4258	1.6010	1.7959	2.0122	2.2522	2.5182	2.8127	3.1384	3.4985	3.8960	4.3345	4.8179	5.3503	5.9360	6.5801	7.2876	8.0642	8.9161
13	1.1381	1.2936	1.4685	1.6651	1.8856	2.1329	2.4098	2.7196	3.0658	3.4523	3.8833	4.3635	4.8980	5.4924	6.1528	6.8858	7.6987	8.5994	9.5964	10.6993
14	1.1495	1.3195	1.5126	1.7317	1.9799	2.2609	2.5785	2.9372	3.3417	3.7975	4.3104	4.8871	5.5348	6.2613	7.0757	7.9875	9.0075	10.1472	11.4198	12.8392
15	1.1610	1.3459	1.5580	1.8009	2.0789	2.3966	2.7590	3.1722	3.6425	4.1772	4.7846	5.4736	6.2543	7.1379	8.1371	9.2655	10.5387	11.9737	13.5895	15.4070
16	1.1726	1.3728	1.6047	1.8730	2.1829	2.5404	2.9522	3.4259	3.9703	4.5950	5.3109	6.1304	7.0673	8.1372	9.3576	10.7480	12.3303	14.1290	16.1715	18.4884
17	1.1843	1.4002	1.6528	1.9479	2.2920	2.6928	3.1588	3.7000	4.3276	5.0545	5.8951	6.8660	7.9861	9.2765	10.7613	12.4677	14.4265	16.6722	19.2441	22.1861
18	1.1961	1.4282	1.7024	2.0258	2.4066	2.8543	3.3799	3.9960	4.7171	5.5599	6.5436	7.6900	9.0243	10.5752	12.3755	14.4625	16.8790	19.6733	22.9005	26.6233
19	1.2081	1.4568	1.7535	2.1068	2.5270	3.0256	3.6165	4.3157	5.1417	6.1159	7.2633	8.6128	10.1974	12.0557	14.2318	16.7765	19.7484	23.2144	27.2516	31.9480
20	1.2202	1.4859	1.8061	2.1911	2.6533	3.2071	3.8697	4.6610	5.6044	6.7275	8.0623	9.6463	11.5231	13.7435	16.3665	19.4608	23.1056	27.3930	32.4294	38.3376
21	1.2324	1.5157	1.8603	2.2788	2.7860	3.3996	4.1406	5.0338	6.1088	7.4002	8.9492	10.8038	13.0211	15.6676	18.8215	22.5745	27.0336	32.3238	38.5910	46.0051
22	1.2447	1.5460	1.9161	2.3699	2.9253	3.6035	4.4304	5.4365	6.6586	8.1403	9.9336	12.1003	14.7138	17.8610	21.6447	26.1864	31.6293	38.1421	45.9233	55.2061
23	1.2572	1.5769	1.9736	2.4647	3.0715	3.8197	4.7405	5.8715	7.2579	8.9543	11.0263	13.5523	16.6266	20.3616	24.8915	30.3762	37.0062	45.0076	54.6487	66.2474
24	1.2697	1.6084	2.0328	2.5633	3.2251	4.0489	5.0724	6.3412	7.9111	9.8497	12.2392	15.1786	18.7881	23.2122	28.6252	35.2364	43.2973	53.1090	65.0320	79.4968
25	1.2824	1.6406	2.0938	2.6658	3.3864	4.2919	5.4274	6.8485	8.6231	10.8347	13.5855	17.0001	21.2305	26.4619	32.9190	40.8742	50.6578	62.6686	77.3881	95.3962
26	1.2953	1.6734	2.1566	2.7725	3.5557	4.5494	5.8074	7.3964	9.3992	11.9182	15.0799	19.0401	23.9905	30.1666	37.8568	47.4141	59.2697	73.9490	92.0918	114.4755
27	1.3082	1.7069	2.2213	2.8834	3.7335	4.8223	6.2139	7.9881	10.2451	13.1100	16.7386	21.3249	27.1093	34.3899	43.5353	55.0004	69.3455	87.2598	109.5893	137.3706
28	1.3213	1.7410	2.2879	2.9987	3.9201	5.1117	6.6488	8.6271	11.1671	14.4210	18.5799	23.8839	30.6335	39.2045	50.0656	63.8004	81.1342	102.9666	130.4112	164.8447
29	1.3345	1.7758	2.3566	3.1187	4.1161	5.4184	7.1143	9.3173	12.1722	15.8631	20.6237	26.7499	34.6158	44.6931	57.5755	74.0085	94.9271	121.5005	155.1893	197.8136
30	1.3478	1.8114	2.4273	3.2434	4.3219	5.7435	7.6123	10.0627	13.2677	17.4494	22.8923	29.9599	39.1159	50.9502	66.2118	85.8499	111.0647	143.3706	184.6753	237.3763
40	1.4889	2.2080	3.2620	4.8010	7.0400	10.2857	14.9745	21.7245	31.4094	45.2593	65.0009	93.0510	132.7816	188.8835	267.8635	378.7212	533.8687	750.3783	1051.668	1469.772
50	1.6446	2.6916	4.3839	7.1067	11.4674	18.4202	29.4570	46.9016	74.3575	117.3909	184.5648	289.0022	450.7359	700.2330	1083.657	1670.704	2566.215	3927.357	5988.914	9100.438

Illustrations Using Appendix A-2: Present Value of a Single Amount ($1)

To use this table, locate the present value factor for the time period and the interest rate.

1. You want to begin a college fund for your newborn child; you hope to accumulate $30,000 by 18 years from now. If a current investment opportunity yields 7 percent, how much must you invest in a lump sum to realize the $30,000 when needed?

    The present value factor is 0.296; hence, the solution is $30,000 × 0.296, or $8880.

2. You hope to retire in 25 years and want to deposit a single lump sum that will grow to $250,000 at that time. If you can now invest at 8 percent, how much must you invest to realize the $250,000 when needed?

    The present value factor is 0.146; hence, the solution is $250,000 × 0.146, or $36,500. The present value of $250,000 received 25 years from now is $36,500 if the interest rate is 8 percent.

3. You have the choice of receiving a down payment from someone who wants to purchase your rental property as $15,000 today or as a personal note for $25,000 payable in 6 years. If you could expect to earn 8 percent on such funds, which is the better choice?

    The present value factor is 0.630; hence, the solution is $25,000 × 0.630, or $15,750. Thus, the present value of $25,000 received in 6 years is greater than $15,000 received now, and the personal note is the better choice.

4. You own a $1000 bond paying 8 percent annually until its maturity in 5 years. You need to sell the bond now, even though the market rate of interest on similar bonds has increased to 10 percent. What discounted market price for the bond will allow the new buyer to earn a yield of 10 percent?

    First, compute the present value of the future interest payments of $80 per year for 5 years at 10 percent (using Appendix A-4): $80 × 3.791, or $303.28. Second, compute the present value of the future principal repayment of $1000 after 5 years at 10 percent: $1000 × 0.621, or $621.00. Hence, the market price is the sum of the two present values ($303.28 + $621.00), or $924.28.

An alternative approach is to use a calculator to determine the present value, PV, of a single payment received some time in the future. The equation, which is a rearrangement of the future value Equation (A.1), is

$$PV = \frac{FV}{(1.0 + i)^n} \quad \textbf{(A.2)}$$

where

$$PV = Present\ Value\ of\ the\ investment$$
$$FV = Future\ Value$$
$$i = Interest\ rate\ per\ period$$
$$n = Number\ of\ periods\ the\ PV\ is\ invested$$

Appendix A-2

Present Value of a Single Amount ($1)
(Used to Compute the Discounted Present Value of Some Known Future Single Lump Sum)

n	1%	2%	3%	4%	5%	6%	7%	8%	9%	10%	11%	12%	13%	14%	15%	16%	17%	18%	19%	20%
1	0.9901	0.9804	0.9709	0.9615	0.9524	0.9434	0.9346	0.9259	0.9174	0.9091	0.9009	0.8929	0.8850	0.8772	0.8696	0.8621	0.8547	0.8475	0.8403	0.8333
2	0.9803	0.9612	0.9426	0.9246	0.9070	0.8900	0.8734	0.8573	0.8417	0.8264	0.8116	0.7972	0.7831	0.7695	0.7561	0.7432	0.7305	0.7182	0.7062	0.6944
3	0.9706	0.9423	0.9151	0.8890	0.8638	0.8396	0.8163	0.7938	0.7722	0.7513	0.7312	0.7118	0.6931	0.6750	0.6575	0.6407	0.6244	0.6086	0.5934	0.5787
4	0.9610	0.9238	0.8885	0.8548	0.8227	0.7921	0.7629	0.7350	0.7084	0.6830	0.6587	0.6355	0.6133	0.5921	0.5718	0.5523	0.5337	0.5158	0.4987	0.4823
5	0.9515	0.9057	0.8626	0.8219	0.7835	0.7473	0.7130	0.6806	0.6499	0.6209	0.5935	0.5674	0.5428	0.5194	0.4972	0.4761	0.4561	0.4371	0.4190	0.4019
6	0.9420	0.8880	0.8375	0.7903	0.7462	0.7050	0.6663	0.6302	0.5963	0.5645	0.5346	0.5066	0.4803	0.4556	0.4323	0.4104	0.3898	0.3704	0.3521	0.3349
7	0.9327	0.8706	0.8131	0.7599	0.7107	0.6651	0.6227	0.5835	0.5470	0.5132	0.4817	0.4523	0.4251	0.3996	0.3759	0.3538	0.3332	0.3139	0.2959	0.2791
8	0.9235	0.8535	0.7894	0.7307	0.6768	0.6274	0.5820	0.5403	0.5019	0.4665	0.4339	0.4039	0.3762	0.3506	0.3269	0.3050	0.2848	0.2660	0.2487	0.2326
9	0.9143	0.8368	0.7664	0.7026	0.6446	0.5919	0.5439	0.5002	0.4604	0.4241	0.3909	0.3606	0.3329	0.3075	0.2843	0.2630	0.2434	0.2255	0.2090	0.1938
10	0.9053	0.8203	0.7441	0.6756	0.6139	0.5584	0.5083	0.4632	0.4224	0.3855	0.3522	0.3220	0.2946	0.2697	0.2472	0.2267	0.2080	0.1911	0.1756	0.1615
11	0.8963	0.8043	0.7224	0.6496	0.5847	0.5268	0.4751	0.4289	0.3875	0.3505	0.3173	0.2875	0.2607	0.2366	0.2149	0.1954	0.1778	0.1619	0.1476	0.1346
12	0.8874	0.7885	0.7014	0.6246	0.5568	0.4970	0.4440	0.3971	0.3555	0.3186	0.2858	0.2567	0.2307	0.2076	0.1869	0.1685	0.1520	0.1372	0.1240	0.1122
13	0.8787	0.7730	0.6810	0.6006	0.5303	0.4688	0.4150	0.3677	0.3262	0.2897	0.2575	0.2292	0.2042	0.1821	0.1625	0.1452	0.1299	0.1163	0.1042	0.0935
14	0.8700	0.7579	0.6611	0.5775	0.5051	0.4423	0.3878	0.3405	0.2992	0.2633	0.2320	0.2046	0.1807	0.1597	0.1413	0.1252	0.1110	0.0985	0.0876	0.0779
15	0.8613	0.7430	0.6419	0.5553	0.4810	0.4173	0.3624	0.3152	0.2745	0.2394	0.2090	0.1827	0.1599	0.1401	0.1229	0.1079	0.0949	0.0835	0.0736	0.0649
16	0.8528	0.7284	0.6232	0.5339	0.4581	0.3936	0.3387	0.2919	0.2519	0.2176	0.1883	0.1631	0.1415	0.1229	0.1069	0.0930	0.0811	0.0708	0.0618	0.0541
17	0.8444	0.7142	0.6050	0.5134	0.4363	0.3714	0.3166	0.2703	0.2311	0.1978	0.1696	0.1456	0.1252	0.1078	0.0929	0.0802	0.0693	0.0600	0.0520	0.0451
18	0.8360	0.7002	0.5874	0.4936	0.4155	0.3503	0.2959	0.2502	0.2120	0.1799	0.1528	0.1300	0.1108	0.0946	0.0808	0.0691	0.0592	0.0508	0.0437	0.0376
19	0.8277	0.6864	0.5703	0.4746	0.3957	0.3305	0.2765	0.2317	0.1945	0.1635	0.1377	0.1161	0.0981	0.0829	0.0703	0.0596	0.0506	0.0431	0.0367	0.0313
20	0.8195	0.6730	0.5537	0.4564	0.3769	0.3118	0.2584	0.2145	0.1784	0.1486	0.1240	0.1037	0.0868	0.0728	0.0611	0.0514	0.0433	0.0365	0.0308	0.0261
21	0.8114	0.6598	0.5375	0.4388	0.3589	0.2942	0.2415	0.1987	0.1637	0.1351	0.1117	0.0926	0.0768	0.0638	0.0531	0.0443	0.0370	0.0309	0.0259	0.0217
22	0.8034	0.6468	0.5219	0.4220	0.3418	0.2775	0.2257	0.1839	0.1502	0.1228	0.1007	0.0826	0.0680	0.0560	0.0462	0.0382	0.0316	0.0262	0.0218	0.0181
23	0.7954	0.6342	0.5067	0.4057	0.3256	0.2618	0.2109	0.1703	0.1378	0.1117	0.0907	0.0738	0.0601	0.0491	0.0402	0.0329	0.0270	0.0222	0.0183	0.0151
24	0.7876	0.6217	0.4919	0.3901	0.3101	0.2470	0.1971	0.1577	0.1264	0.1015	0.0817	0.0659	0.0532	0.0431	0.0349	0.0284	0.0231	0.0188	0.0154	0.0126
25	0.7798	0.6095	0.4776	0.3751	0.2953	0.2330	0.1842	0.1460	0.1160	0.0923	0.0736	0.0588	0.0471	0.0378	0.0304	0.0245	0.0197	0.0160	0.0129	0.0105
26	0.7720	0.5976	0.4637	0.3607	0.2812	0.2198	0.1722	0.1352	0.1064	0.0839	0.0663	0.0525	0.0417	0.0331	0.0264	0.0211	0.0169	0.0135	0.0109	0.0087
27	0.7644	0.5859	0.4502	0.3468	0.2678	0.2074	0.1609	0.1252	0.0976	0.0763	0.0597	0.0469	0.0369	0.0291	0.0230	0.0182	0.0144	0.0115	0.0091	0.0073
28	0.7568	0.5744	0.4371	0.3335	0.2551	0.1956	0.1504	0.1159	0.0895	0.0693	0.0538	0.0419	0.0326	0.0255	0.0200	0.0157	0.0123	0.0097	0.0077	0.0061
29	0.7493	0.5631	0.4243	0.3207	0.2429	0.1846	0.1406	0.1073	0.0822	0.0630	0.0485	0.0374	0.0289	0.0224	0.0174	0.0135	0.0105	0.0082	0.0064	0.0051
30	0.7419	0.5521	0.4120	0.3083	0.2314	0.1741	0.1314	0.0994	0.0754	0.0573	0.0437	0.0334	0.0256	0.0196	0.0151	0.0116	0.0090	0.0070	0.0054	0.0042
40	0.6717	0.4529	0.3066	0.2083	0.1420	0.0972	0.0668	0.0460	0.0318	0.0221	0.0154	0.0107	0.0075	0.0053	0.0037	0.0026	0.0019	0.0013	0.0010	0.0007
50	0.6080	0.3715	0.2281	0.1407	0.0872	0.0543	0.0339	0.0213	0.0134	0.0085	0.0054	0.0035	0.0022	0.0014	0.0009	0.0006	0.0004	0.0003	0.0002	0.0001

Illustrations Using Appendix A-3: Future Value of a Series of Equal Amounts (an Annuity of $1 per Period)

To use this table, locate the future value factor for the time period and the interest rate.

1. You plan to retire after 16 years. To provide for that retirement, you initiate a savings program of $7000 per year in an investment yielding 8 percent. What will the value of the retirement fund be at the beginning of the seventeenth year?

    Your last payment into the fund will occur at the end of the sixteenth year, so scan down the periods (n) column for period 16, and then move across until you reach the column for 8 percent. The future value factor is 30.32. Hence, the solution is $7000 × 30.32, or $212,240.

2. What will be the value of an investment if you put $2000 into a retirement plan yielding 7 percent annually for 25 years?

    The future value factor is 63.250. Hence, the solution is $2000 × 63.250, or $126,500.

3. You are trying to decide between putting $3000 or $4000 annually for the next 20 years into an investment yielding 7 percent for retirement purposes. What is the difference in the value of investing the extra $1000 for 20 years?

    The future value factor is 41.0. Hence, the solution is $1000 × 41.0, or $41,000.

4. You will receive an annuity payment of $1200 at the end of each year for 6 years. What will be the total value of this stream of income invested at 7 percent by the time you receive the last payment?

    The appropriate future value factor for 6 years at 7 percent is 7.153. Hence, the solution is $1200 × 7.153, or $8584.

5. How many years of investing $1200 annually at 9 percent will it take to reach a goal of $11,000?

    Divide the future value of $11,000 by the lump sum of $1200 to find a future value factor of 9.17. Look down the 9 percent column to find 9.200 (close enough). Read across the row to find that an investment period of 7 years is needed.

6. If you plan to invest $1200 annually for 9 years, what rate of return is needed to reach a goal of $15,000?

    Divide the future value goal of $15,000 by $1200 to derive the future value factor 12.5. Look across the row for 9 years to locate the future value factor of 12.49 (close enough). Read up the column to find that you need an 8 percent return.

An alternative approach is to use a calculator to determine the total future value, *FV*, of a stream of equal payments (an annuity). The equation is

$$FV = \frac{[(1.0 + i)^n - 1.0] \times A}{i} \quad \text{(A.3)}$$

where

$FV = $ *Future Value* of the investment

$i = $ *Interest* rate per period

$n = $ *Number* of periods the *PV* is invested

$A = $ *Amount* of the annuity

Appendix A-3

Future Value of a Series of Equal Amounts (an Annuity of $1 Paid at the End of Each Period)
(Used to Compute the Compounded Future Value of a Stream of Income Payments)

n	1%	2%	3%	4%	5%	6%	7%	8%	9%	10%	11%	12%	13%	14%	15%	16%	17%	18%	19%	20%
1	1.0000	1.0000	1.0000	1.0000	1.0000	1.0000	1.0000	1.0000	1.0000	1.0000	1.0000	1.0000	1.0000	1.0000	1.0000	1.0000	1.0000	1.0000	1.0000	1.0000
2	2.0100	2.0200	2.0300	2.0400	2.0500	2.0600	2.0700	2.0800	2.0900	2.1000	2.1100	2.1200	2.1300	2.1400	2.1500	2.1600	2.1700	2.1800	2.1900	2.2000
3	3.0301	3.0604	3.0909	3.1216	3.1525	3.1836	3.2149	3.2464	3.2781	3.3100	3.3421	3.3744	3.4069	3.4396	3.4725	3.5056	3.5389	3.5724	3.6061	3.6400
4	4.0604	4.1216	4.1836	4.2465	4.3101	4.3746	4.4399	4.5061	4.5731	4.6410	4.7097	4.7793	4.8498	4.9211	4.9934	5.0665	5.1405	5.2154	5.2913	5.3680
5	5.1010	5.2040	5.3091	5.4163	5.5256	5.6371	5.7507	5.8666	5.9847	6.1051	6.2278	6.3528	6.4803	6.6101	6.7424	6.8771	7.0144	7.1542	7.2966	7.4416
6	6.1520	6.3081	6.4684	6.6330	6.8019	6.9753	7.1533	7.3359	7.5233	7.7156	7.9129	8.1152	8.3227	8.5355	8.7537	8.9775	9.2068	9.4420	9.6830	9.9299
7	7.2135	7.4343	7.6625	7.8983	8.1420	8.3938	8.6540	8.9228	9.2004	9.4872	9.7833	10.0890	10.4047	10.7305	11.0668	11.4139	11.7720	12.1415	12.5227	12.9159
8	8.2857	8.5830	8.8923	9.2142	9.5491	9.8975	10.2598	10.6366	11.0285	11.4359	11.8594	12.2997	12.7573	13.2328	13.7268	14.2401	14.7733	15.3270	15.9020	16.4991
9	9.3685	9.7546	10.1591	10.5828	11.0266	11.4913	11.9780	12.4876	13.0210	13.5795	14.1640	14.7757	15.4157	16.0853	16.7858	17.5185	18.2847	19.0859	19.9234	20.7989
10	10.4622	10.9497	11.4639	12.0061	12.5779	13.1808	13.8164	14.4866	15.1929	15.9374	16.7220	17.5487	18.4197	19.3373	20.3037	21.3215	22.3931	23.5213	24.7089	25.9587
11	11.5668	12.1687	12.8078	13.4864	14.2068	14.9716	15.7836	16.6455	17.5603	18.5312	19.5614	20.6546	21.8143	23.0445	24.3493	25.7329	27.1999	28.7551	30.4035	32.1504
12	12.6825	13.4121	14.1920	15.0258	15.9171	16.8699	17.8885	18.9771	20.1407	21.3843	22.7132	24.1331	25.6502	27.2707	29.0017	30.8502	32.8239	34.9311	37.1802	39.5805
13	13.8093	14.6803	15.6178	16.6268	17.7130	18.8821	20.1406	21.4953	22.9534	24.5227	26.2116	28.0291	29.9847	32.0887	34.3519	36.7862	39.4040	42.2187	45.2445	48.4966
14	14.9474	15.9739	17.0863	18.2919	19.5986	21.0151	22.5505	24.2149	26.0192	27.9750	30.0949	32.3926	34.8827	37.5811	40.5047	43.6720	47.1027	50.8180	54.8409	59.1959
15	16.0969	17.2934	18.5989	20.0236	21.5786	23.2760	25.1290	27.1521	29.3609	31.7725	34.4054	37.2797	40.4175	43.8424	47.5804	51.6595	56.1101	60.9653	66.2607	72.0351
16	17.2579	18.6393	20.1569	21.8245	23.6575	25.6725	27.8881	30.3243	33.0034	35.9497	39.1899	42.7533	46.6717	50.9804	55.7175	60.9250	66.6488	72.9390	79.8502	87.4421
17	18.4304	20.0121	21.7616	23.6975	25.8404	28.2129	30.8402	33.7502	36.9737	40.5447	44.5008	48.8837	53.7391	59.1176	65.0751	71.6730	78.9791	87.0680	96.0217	105.9306
18	19.6147	21.4123	23.4144	25.6454	28.1324	30.9057	33.9990	37.4502	41.3013	45.5992	50.3959	55.7497	61.7251	68.3941	75.8364	84.1407	93.4056	103.7403	115.2659	128.1167
19	20.8109	22.8406	25.1169	27.6712	30.5390	33.7600	37.3790	41.4463	46.0185	51.1591	56.9395	63.4397	70.7494	78.9692	88.2118	98.6032	110.2846	123.4135	138.1664	154.7400
20	22.0190	24.2974	26.8704	29.7781	33.0660	36.7856	40.9955	45.7620	51.1601	57.2750	64.2028	72.0524	80.9468	91.0249	102.4436	115.3797	130.0329	146.6280	165.4180	186.6880
21	23.2392	25.7833	28.6765	31.9692	35.7193	39.9927	44.8652	50.4229	56.7645	64.0025	72.2651	81.6987	92.4699	104.7684	118.8101	134.8405	153.1385	174.0210	197.8474	225.0256
22	24.4716	27.2990	30.5368	34.2480	38.5052	43.3923	49.0057	55.4568	62.8733	71.4027	81.2143	92.5026	105.4910	120.4360	137.6316	157.4150	180.1721	206.3448	236.4384	271.0307
23	25.7163	28.8450	32.4529	36.6179	41.4305	46.9958	53.4361	60.8933	69.5319	79.5430	91.1479	104.6029	120.2048	138.2970	159.2764	183.6014	211.8013	244.4868	282.3618	326.2368
24	26.9735	30.4219	34.4265	39.0826	44.5020	50.8156	58.1767	66.7648	76.7898	88.4973	102.1741	118.1552	136.8315	158.6586	184.1678	213.9776	248.8075	289.4945	337.0105	392.4842
25	28.2432	32.0303	36.4593	41.6459	47.7271	54.8645	63.2490	73.1059	84.7009	98.3471	114.4133	133.3339	155.6196	181.8708	212.7930	249.2140	292.1048	342.6035	402.0424	471.9811
26	29.5256	33.6709	38.5530	44.3117	51.1135	59.1564	68.6765	79.9544	93.3240	109.1818	127.9988	150.3339	176.8501	208.3327	245.7120	290.0883	342.7626	405.2721	479.4305	567.3773
27	30.8209	35.3443	40.7096	47.0842	54.6691	63.7058	74.4838	87.3508	102.7231	121.0999	143.0786	169.3740	200.8406	238.4993	283.5688	337.5024	402.0323	479.2211	571.5223	681.8527
28	32.1291	37.0512	42.9309	49.9676	58.4026	68.5281	80.6977	95.3388	112.9682	134.2099	159.8173	190.6989	227.9499	272.8892	327.1041	392.5027	471.3778	566.4808	681.1116	819.2233
29	33.4504	38.7922	45.2188	52.9663	62.3227	73.6398	87.3465	103.9659	124.1354	148.6309	178.3972	214.5827	258.5834	312.0937	377.1697	456.3032	552.5120	669.4474	811.5228	984.0679
30	34.7849	40.5681	47.5754	56.0849	66.4389	79.0582	94.4608	113.2832	136.3075	164.4940	199.0209	241.3327	293.1992	356.7868	434.7451	530.3117	647.4390	790.9479	966.7121	1181.882
40	48.8864	60.4020	75.4013	95.0255	120.7998	154.7620	199.6351	259.0565	337.8824	442.5925	581.8260	767.0914	1013.704	1342.025	1779.090	2360.757	3134.522	4163.212	5529.829	7343.856
50	64.4632	84.5794	112.7969	152.6671	209.3480	290.3359	406.5289	573.7701	815.0834	1163.908	1668.771	2400.018	3459.507	4994.522	7217.714	10435.65	15089.50	21813.09	31515.33	45497.17

Illustrations Using Appendix A-4: Present Value of Series of Equal Amounts (an Annuity of $1 per Period)

To use this table, locate the present value factor for the time period and the interest rate.

1. You are entering into a contract that will provide you with an income of $1000 at the end of the year for the next 10 years. If the annual interest rate is 7 percent, what is the present value of that stream of payments?

The present value factor is 7.024; hence, the solution is $1000 × 7.024, or $7024.

2. You expect to have $250,000 available in a retirement plan when you retire. If the amount invested yields 8 percent and you hope to live an additional 20 years, how much can you withdraw each year so that the fund will just be liquidated after 20 years?

The present value factor for 20 years at 8 percent is 9.818. Hence, the solution is $250,000 ÷ 9.818, or $25,463.

3. You have received an inheritance of $60,000 that you invested so that it earns 9 percent. If you withdraw $8000 annually to supplement your income, in how many years will the fund run out?

Solving for *n*, $60,000 ÷ $8000 = 7.5. Scan down the 9 percent column until you find a present value factor close to 7.5, which is 7.487. The row indicates 13 years; thus, the fund will be depleted in approximately 13 years with $8000 annual withdrawals.

4. A seller offers to finance the sale of a building to you as an investment. The mortgage loan of $280,000 will be for 20 years and requires an annual mortgage payment of $24,000. Should you finance the purchase through the seller or borrow the funds from a financial institution at a current rate of 10 percent?

$280,000 ÷ $24,000 = 11.667. Scan down the periods (*n*) column to 20 years and then read across to locate the figure closest to 11.667, which is 11.470. The column indicates 6 percent; thus, seller financing offers a lower interest rate.

5. You have the opportunity to purchase an office building for $750,000 with an expected life of 20 years. Looking over the financial details, you see that the before-tax net rental income is $90,000. If you want a return of at least 15 percent, how much should you pay for the building?

The present value factor for 20 years at 15 percent is 6.259, and $90,000 × 6.259 = $563,310. Thus, the price is too high for you to earn a return of 15 percent.

An alternative approach is to use a calculator to determine the present value, *PV*, of a stream of payments. The equation is

$$PV = \frac{[1.0 - 1.0/(1.0 + i)^n] \times A}{i} \quad \textbf{(A.4)}$$

where

PV = *Present Value* of the investment

i = *Interest* rate per period

n = *Number* of periods the *PV* is invested

A = *Amount* of the annuity

Appendix A-4

Present Value of a Series of Equal Amounts (an Annuity of $1 Received at the End of Each Period)
(Used to Compute the Discounted Present Value of a Stream of Income Payments)

n	1%	2%	3%	4%	5%	6%	7%	8%	9%	10%	11%	12%	13%	14%	15%	16%	17%	18%	19%	20%
1	0.9901	0.9804	0.9709	0.9615	0.9524	0.9434	0.9346	0.9259	0.9174	0.9091	0.9009	0.8929	0.8850	0.8772	0.8696	0.8621	0.8547	0.8475	0.8403	0.8333
2	1.9704	1.9416	1.9135	1.8861	1.8594	1.8334	1.8080	1.7833	1.7591	1.7355	1.7125	1.6901	1.6681	1.6467	1.6257	1.6052	1.5852	1.5656	1.5465	1.5278
3	2.9410	2.8839	2.8286	2.7751	2.7232	2.6730	2.6243	2.5771	2.5313	2.4869	2.4437	2.4018	2.3612	2.3216	2.2832	2.2459	2.2096	2.1743	2.1399	2.1065
4	3.9020	3.8077	3.7171	3.6299	3.5460	3.4651	3.3872	3.3121	3.2397	3.1699	3.1024	3.0373	2.9745	2.9137	2.8550	2.7982	2.7432	2.6901	2.6386	2.5887
5	4.8534	4.7135	4.5797	4.4518	4.3295	4.2124	4.1002	3.9927	3.8897	3.7908	3.6959	3.6048	3.5172	3.4331	3.3522	3.2743	3.1993	3.1272	3.0576	2.9906
6	5.7955	5.6014	5.4172	5.2421	5.0757	4.9173	4.7665	4.6229	4.4859	4.3553	4.2305	4.1114	3.9975	3.8887	3.7845	3.6847	3.5892	3.4976	3.4098	3.3255
7	6.7282	6.4720	6.2303	6.0021	5.7864	5.5824	5.3893	5.2064	5.0330	4.8684	4.7122	4.5638	4.4226	4.2883	4.1604	4.0386	3.9224	3.8115	3.7057	3.6046
8	7.6517	7.3255	7.0197	6.7327	6.4632	6.2098	5.9713	5.7466	5.5348	5.3349	5.1461	4.9676	4.7988	4.6389	4.4873	4.3436	4.2072	4.0776	3.9544	3.8372
9	8.5660	8.1622	7.7861	7.4353	7.1078	6.8017	6.5152	6.2469	5.9952	5.7590	5.5370	5.3282	5.1317	4.9464	4.7716	4.6065	4.4506	4.3030	4.1633	4.0310
10	9.4713	8.9826	8.5302	8.1109	7.7217	7.3601	7.0236	6.7101	6.4177	6.1446	5.8892	5.6502	5.4262	5.2161	5.0188	4.8332	4.6586	4.4941	4.3389	4.1925
11	10.3676	9.7868	9.2526	8.7605	8.3064	7.8869	7.4987	7.1390	6.8052	6.4951	6.2065	5.9377	5.6869	5.4527	5.2337	5.0286	4.8364	4.6560	4.4865	4.3271
12	11.2551	10.5753	9.9540	9.3851	8.8633	8.3838	7.9427	7.5361	7.1607	6.8137	6.4924	6.1944	5.9176	5.6603	5.4206	5.1971	4.9884	4.7932	4.6105	4.4392
13	12.1337	11.3484	10.6350	9.9856	9.3936	8.8527	8.3577	7.9038	7.4869	7.1034	6.7499	6.4235	6.1218	5.8424	5.5831	5.3423	5.1183	4.9095	4.7147	4.5327
14	13.0037	12.1062	11.2961	10.5631	9.8986	9.2950	8.7455	8.2442	7.7862	7.3667	6.9819	6.6282	6.3025	6.0021	5.7245	5.4675	5.2293	5.0081	4.8023	4.6106
15	13.8651	12.8493	11.9379	11.1184	10.3797	9.7122	9.1079	8.5595	8.0607	7.6061	7.1909	6.8109	6.4624	6.1422	5.8474	5.5755	5.3242	5.0916	4.8759	4.6755
16	14.7179	13.5777	12.5611	11.6523	10.8378	10.1059	9.4466	8.8514	8.3126	7.8237	7.3792	6.9740	6.6039	6.2651	5.9542	5.6685	5.4053	5.1624	4.9377	4.7296
17	15.5623	14.2919	13.1661	12.1657	11.2741	10.4773	9.7632	9.1216	8.5436	8.0216	7.5488	7.1196	6.7291	6.3729	6.0472	5.7487	5.4746	5.2223	4.9897	4.7746
18	16.3983	14.9920	13.7535	12.6593	11.6896	10.8276	10.0591	9.3719	8.7556	8.2014	7.7016	7.2497	6.8399	6.4674	6.1280	5.8178	5.5339	5.2732	5.0333	4.8122
19	17.2260	15.6785	14.3238	13.1339	12.0853	11.1581	10.3356	9.6036	8.9501	8.3649	7.8393	7.3658	6.9380	6.5504	6.1982	5.8775	5.5845	5.3162	5.0700	4.8435
20	18.0456	16.3514	14.8775	13.5903	12.4622	11.4699	10.5940	9.8181	9.1285	8.5136	7.9633	7.4694	7.0248	6.6231	6.2593	5.9288	5.6278	5.3527	5.1009	4.8696
21	18.8570	17.0112	15.4150	14.0292	12.8212	11.7641	10.8355	10.0168	9.2922	8.6487	8.0751	7.5620	7.1016	6.6870	6.3125	5.9731	5.6648	5.3837	5.1268	4.8913
22	19.6604	17.6580	15.9369	14.4511	13.1630	12.0416	11.0612	10.2007	9.4424	8.7715	8.1757	7.6446	7.1695	6.7429	6.3587	6.0113	5.6964	5.4099	5.1486	4.9094
23	20.4558	18.2922	16.4436	14.8568	13.4886	12.3034	11.2722	10.3711	9.5802	8.8832	8.2664	7.7184	7.2297	6.7921	6.3988	6.0442	5.7234	5.4321	5.1668	4.9245
24	21.2434	18.9139	16.9355	15.2470	13.7986	12.5504	11.4693	10.5288	9.7066	8.9847	8.3481	7.7843	7.2829	6.8351	6.4338	6.0726	5.7465	5.4509	5.1822	4.9371
25	22.0232	19.5235	17.4131	15.6221	14.0939	12.7834	11.6536	10.6748	9.8226	9.0770	8.4217	7.8431	7.3300	6.8729	6.4641	6.0971	5.7662	5.4669	5.1951	4.9476
26	22.7952	20.1210	17.8768	15.9828	14.3752	13.0032	11.8258	10.8100	9.9290	9.1609	8.4881	7.8957	7.3717	6.9061	6.4906	6.1182	5.7831	5.4804	5.2060	4.9563
27	23.5596	20.7069	18.3270	16.3296	14.6430	13.2105	11.9867	10.9352	10.0266	9.2372	8.5478	7.9426	7.4086	6.9352	6.5135	6.1364	5.7975	5.4919	5.2151	4.9636
28	24.3164	21.2813	18.7641	16.6631	14.8981	13.4062	12.1371	11.0511	10.1161	9.3066	8.6016	7.9844	7.4412	6.9607	6.5335	6.1520	5.8099	5.5016	5.2228	4.9697
29	25.0658	21.8444	19.1885	16.9837	15.1411	13.5907	12.2777	11.1584	10.1983	9.3696	8.6501	8.0218	7.4701	6.9830	6.5509	6.1656	5.8204	5.5098	5.2292	4.9747
30	25.8077	22.3965	19.6004	17.2920	15.3725	13.7648	12.4090	11.2578	10.2737	9.4269	8.6938	8.0552	7.4957	7.0027	6.5660	6.1772	5.8294	5.5168	5.2347	4.9789
40	32.8347	27.3555	23.1148	19.7928	17.1591	15.0463	13.3317	11.9246	10.7574	9.7791	8.9511	8.2438	7.6344	7.1050	6.6418	6.2335	5.8713	5.5482	5.2582	4.9966
50	39.1961	31.4236	25.7298	21.4822	18.2559	15.7619	13.8007	12.2335	10.9617	9.9148	9.0417	8.3045	7.6752	7.1327	6.6605	6.2463	5.8801	5.5541	5.2623	4.9995

ESTIMATING SOCIAL SECURITY BENEFITS

The Social Security Administration (SSA) provides basic benefits for your retirement, for a period of disability, or for your survivors. To qualify, you must have earned the number of credits required for each benefit program. Once you qualify, the level of benefits received is based on your income in years past that was subject to the Federal Insurance Contributions Act (FICA) taxes, commonly known as Social Security taxes. Benefits increase each year based on a cost of living adjustment (COLA) announced by the SSA each October for the following year. Due to low inflation, there were no COLA adjustments for 2010 and 2011. The discussion and Appendix B-1 provide the authors' estimates of Social Security benefits for 2012 for various income levels using calculators found at www.ssa.gov/planners/calculators.htm. The amounts are for a 30-year-old worker but would not differ significantly for workers ten years older or younger.

Social Security Retirement Benefits

To qualify for Social Security retirement benefits, any worker born after 1928 must have earned 40 credits of coverage. As noted in the text, it is possible to receive a maximum of four credits per year. In 2011, a worker would earn one credit for each $1120 of income subject to Social Security taxes (this figure is adjusted upward each year for inflation). Dependent children, spouses caring for dependent children, and retired spouses at age 62 (including former spouses if the marriage lasted at least ten years) may also collect benefits based on the eligibility of the retired worker.

You can use Appendix B-1 to estimate a person's Social Security retirement benefits in today's dollars, assuming the retiree worked steadily, received average pay raises, and retired at the full-benefit retirement age. If more than one person would receive a benefit under the retiree's account (retiree and spouse, for example), the amount of the second person's benefit would be one-half of the retiree's benefit, giving a couple a total benefit 50 percent higher than the individual figure listed in Appendix B-1.

Social Security Disability Benefits

Social Security will pay disability benefits to an insured worker, dependent children up to age 18 (or 19 if the child is still in high school), a spouse caring for a dependent child who is younger than age 16 or disabled, and a spouse (even if divorced, but not remarried, provided that the marriage lasted ten years) age 62 or older. The benefit amount depends on two factors. The first factor is the eligibility of the disabled worker. To qualify for disability benefits, workers need at least 40 credits of coverage under Social Security, with at least 20 of the credits attained in the previous ten years (depending on year of birth). A worker younger than age 31 must have attained at least six credits or one more than one-half of the total credits possible after age 21, whichever is greater. (For example, a 26-year-old worker would have five years, or 20 credits, possible and would need ten credits of coverage.) The second factor affecting benefit levels is the predisability income of the covered individual that was subject to the FICA tax.

You can use Appendix B-1 to estimate an individual's Social Security disability benefits, assuming the disabled person worked steadily and received average pay raises. To obtain figures more specific than those given in Appendix B-1, contact the Social Security Administration to obtain your Social Security Statement as described in Chapter 17 or log on to www.ssa.gov/mystatement/ or www.ssa.gov/planners/calculators.htm.

Social Security Survivors Benefits

Social Security will pay benefits to surviving children younger than age 18 (or 19 if the child is still in high school), to a surviving spouse (even if divorced from the deceased, but not remarried) caring for surviving children who are younger than age 16, and to a surviving spouse (even if divorced, if the marriage lasted at least ten years) age 60 or older. Two factors are important in such cases. The first factor is the eligibility of the covered worker. The deceased worker who has accrued at least 40 credits of coverage is considered to be "fully insured." Workers who have earned at least as many credits of coverage as years since turning age 21 will be fully insured as well. Other individuals may be considered "currently insured" if they have earned six credits of coverage out of the previous 13 possible calendar credits. The survivors of currently insured workers receive limited types of benefits compared with those available to fully insured workers. The second factor is the covered worker's level of earnings, as indicated in Appendix B-1.

You can use Appendix B-1 to estimate monthly survivors benefits from Social Security in today's dollars for eligible surviving family members. The table assumes that the deceased worker worked steadily and received average pay raises.

Appendix B-1   Estimates* of Social Security Benefits for the Three Major Social Security Programs

	Present Annual Earnings					
	$30,000	**$40,000**	**$50,000**	**$60,000**	**$75,000**	**$100,000**
Monthly Retirement Benefits at Age 67 in Today's Dollars						
Per month	$ 1,276	$ 1,543	$ 1,816	$ 1,943	$ 2,195	$ 2,516
Per year	$15,312	$18,156	$21,792	$23,316	$26,340	$ 30,192
As a percentage of income	51%	46%	44%	39%	35%	30%
Monthly Retirement Benefits at Age 67 in Future Dollars						
Per month	$ 4,772	$ 5,743	$ 6,743	$ 7,623	$ 8,327	$ 9,501
Per year	$57,264	$68,916	$80,916	$91,476	$99,924	$114,012
Monthly Disability Benefits if You Became Disabled in 2012						
Individual benefit per month	$ 1,150	$ 1,387	$ 1,623	$ 1,858	$ 2,058	$ 2,334
Individual benefit per year	$13,800	$16,644	$19,476	$22,296	$24,696	$ 28,008
As a percentage of income	46%	42%	39%	37%	33%	28%
Maximum family benefit per month	$ 1,955	$ 2,358	$ 2,759	$ 3,159	$ 3,499	$ 3,968
Maximum family benefit per year	$23,460	$28,296	$33,108	$37,908	$41,988	$ 47,616
Monthly Survivor's Benefits if You Died in 2012						
Individual benefit per month†	$ 889	$ 1,074	$ 1,259	$ 1,443	$ 1,573	$ 1,790
Individual benefit per year	$10,668	$12,888	$15,108	$17,316	$18,876	$ 21,480
As a percentage of income	36%	32%	30%	29%	25%	21%
Maximum family benefit per month	$ 1,974	$ 2,676	$ 3,005	$ 3,368	$ 3,671	$ 4,179
Maximum family benefit per year	$23,688	$32,112	$36,060	$40,416	$44,052	$ 50,148

* Authors' estimates in 2012 for a 30-year-old worker using Social Security Administration website calculators.
†A surviving spouse age 65 or older would receive a retirement benefit approximately one-third higher than these figures.

10-K report A firm's financial statements and activity details for any publicly traded company appear in this mandatory report sent to the SEC annually.

12b-1 fees/distribution fees Annual fees that some "no-load" fund companies deduct from a fund's assets to compensate salespeople and pay other expenses.

401(k) plan Defined-contribution plan designed for employees of private corporations.

403(b) plan Defined-contribution plan designed for eligible employees of not-for-profit institutions, such as colleges, hospitals, and religious organizations.

529 plan Provides a tax-free way to save for college in a state-run investment plan whereby the deposits into the fund are not deductible but the earnings at withdrawal are tax-free if used for qualified educational expenses.

above-the-line deductions Adjustments subtracted from gross income whether taxpayer itemizes deductions or not.

acceleration clause Part of a credit contract stating that after a specific number of payments are unpaid (often just one), the loan is considered in default and all remaining installments are due and payable upon demand of the creditor.

account reconciliation Comparing your records with your bank's records, checking the accuracy of both and identifying and correcting any errors.

accrual-basis budgeting A method of budgeting that recognizes earnings and expenditures when money is earned and expenditures are incurred, regardless of when money is actually received or paid.

active investor An investor who wishes to manage her own account by carefully studying the economy, market trends, and investment alternatives; regularly monitoring these factors; and buying and selling three to four times a year to rebalance her or his portfolio.

activities of daily living (ADLs) Insurance companies use the inability to perform a certain number of such activities as a criterion for deciding when the insured becomes eligible for long-term care benefits.

actual cash value (of personal property) Represents the purchase price of the property less depreciation.

add-on interest method Interest is calculated by applying an interest rate to the amount borrowed times the number of years to arrive at the total interest to be charged.

adjustable-rate mortgage (ARM)/variable-rate mortgage Mortgage in which the borrower's interest rate fluctuates according to some index of interest rates based on the rising or falling cost of credit in the economy—thus transferring interest rate risk to the borrower.

adjusted capitalized cost (adjusted cap cost) Subtracting the capitalized cost reductions from the gross capitalized cost.

adjusted gross income (AGI) Gross income less any exclusions and adjustments.

adjustments to income Allowable subtractions from gross income.

adoption tax credit A nonrefundable tax credit of up to $12,150 available for the qualifying costs of an adoption.

advance medical directive Statement of medical preferences, including designation of surrogate decision maker if patients become unable to make medical decisions for themselves in case of coma, dementia, or brain death.

adverse selection A situation involving certain types of perils such as earthquakes and floods where only those people with high probabilities of loss will want to buy the coverage, thereby violating the law of large numbers.

after-tax dollars Money on which employee has already paid taxes.

after-tax money Funds put into regular investment accounts; subject to income taxes.

after-tax profit Money left over after a firm has paid expenses, bondholder interest, and taxes.

after-tax yield The percentage yield on a taxable investment after subtracting the effect of federal income taxes that will need to be paid on the investment.

aggressive growth funds Funds that invest in speculative stocks with volatile price swings, seeking the greatest long-term capital appreciation possible. Also known as maximum capital gains funds and capital appreciation funds.

aggressive investment philosophy (risk seeker) Investors with this philosophy primarily seek capital gains, often with a short time horizon.

all-risk (open-perils) policies Cover losses caused by all perils other than those that the policy specifically excludes.

alpha statistic Quantifies the difference between an investment's expected return and its actual recent performance (outperforming or underperforming) given its risk; positive values indicate better-than-market performance.

alternative dispute resolution programs Industry- or government-sponsored programs that provide an avenue to resolve disputes outside the formal court system.

alternative minimum tax (AMT) A special higher tax rate of 26 or 28 percent that must be paid rather than the regular tax called for in the standard marginal tax brackets for certain high-income taxpayers that is triggered for people with excessive deductions.

American Opportunity Tax Credit A partially refundable tax credit of up to $2500 a year that to help defray college expenses for the first four years of postsecondary education.

amortization Loan repayment method in which part of the payment goes to pay interest and part goes to repay principal. Extra payments toward principal shorten the life of the loan and decrease total amount of interest paid.

amortization schedule List that shows all the monthly payments, the portions that will go toward interest and principal, and the debt remaining after each payment is made throughout the life of the loan.

annual fees Charges levied against cardholders for the privilege of having an open account but that are not included in the advertised APR.

annual fund operating expenses Normal operating costs of the business that are deducted from fund assets before shareholders receive earnings.

annual percentage rate (APR) Expresses the cost of credit on a yearly basis as a percentage rate.

annual percentage yield (APY) Return on total interest received on a $100 deposit for 365-day period, given the institution's simple annual interest rate and compounding frequency.

annual report Legally required yearly report about financial performance, activities, and prospects sent to major stockholders and made available to the general public.

annuitant Person covered by an annuity who is to receive the benefits.

annuity Contract made with an insurance company that provides for a series of payments to be received at stated intervals (usually monthly) for a fixed or variable time period.

any-occupation policy Provides full benefits only if the insured cannot perform any occupation.

appraisal fee Fee charged for a professionally prepared estimate of the fair market value of the property by an objective party.

approximate compound yield (ACY) A measure of the annualized compound growth of any long-term investment stated as a percentage.

aptitudes The natural abilities and talents that individuals possess.

as is Way for the seller to get around legal requirements for warranties; the buyer takes all risk of nonperformance or other problems despite any salesperson's verbal assurances.

ask price Declared lowest price that anyone is willing to accept to sell a security.

asset Property owned by a taxpayer for personal use or as an investment that has monetary value.

asset allocation Form of diversification in which investor decides on the proportions of an investment portfolio that will be devoted to various categories of assets.

asset allocation funds Investments in a mix of assets (usually stocks, bonds, and cash equivalents and sometimes international assets, gold, and real estate); they buy and sell regularly to reduce risk while trying to outperform the market.

asset management account (AMA, central asset accounts, or all-in-one account) Multiple-purpose, coordinated package that gathers most monetary asset management vehicles into a unified account and reports activity on a single monthly statement to the client.

assets Everything you own that has monetary value.

asset-to-debt ratio Compares total assets with total liabilities.

assumable mortgage Buyer pays the seller a down payment generally equal to the seller's equity in the home and takes responsibility for the mortgage loan payments for the remaining term of the seller's existing mortgage loan.

ATM transaction fee Payments levied each time an automated teller machine (ATM) is used.

automatic enrollment plan Plan in which the employer withholds up to 6 percent of an employee's salary and places it into a defined-contribution retirement plan.

automatic funds transfer agreement Agreement whereby the amount necessary to cover a bad check is transferred from your savings account to your checking account.

automatic premium loan Provision allows any premium not paid by the end of the grace period to be paid automatically with a policy loan if sufficient cash value or dividends have accumulated.

automatic reinvestment Investor's option to choose to automatically reinvest any interest, dividends, and capital gains payments to purchase additional fund shares.

automobile bodily injury liability Occurs when a driver or car owner is held legally responsible for bodily injury losses that other people, including pedestrians, suffer.

automobile insurance Combines the liability and property insurance coverages that most car owners and drivers need into a single-package policy.

automobile medical payments insurance Insurance that covers bodily injury losses suffered by the driver of the insured vehicle and any passengers, regardless of who is at fault.

automobile property damage liability Occurs when a driver or car owner is held legally responsible for damage to others' property.

average-balance account Checking account for which service fees are assessed if the account's average daily balance drops below a certain level during a specified time.

average daily balance Sum of the outstanding balances owed each day during the billing period divided by the number of days in the period.

average share cost Actual cost basis of the investment used for income tax purposes, calculated by dividing the total amount invested by the total shares purchased.

average share price Calculated by dividing the share price total by the number of investment periods.

average tax rate Proportion of total income paid in income taxes.

back-end ratio Compares the total of all monthly PITI expenditures plus auto loans and other debts with gross monthly income.

balanced funds Funds that keep a set mix of stocks and bonds, often 60 percent stocks and 40 percent bonds, in order to earn a well-balanced return of income and long-term capital gains.

balance sheet (or net worth statement) Snapshot of assets, liabilities, and net worth on a particular date.

balance transfer Full or partial payment on the balance of one credit card using a cash advance from another.

balloon automobile loan A loan that has a low monthly payment similar in amount to that required if the vehicle had been leased and with a large final payment similar in amount to the residual value under a lease.

bank credit card account Open-ended credit account with a financial institution that allows the holder to make purchases almost anywhere.

bankruptcy Constitutionally guaranteed right that permits people (and businesses) to ask a court to find them officially unable to meet their debts.

basic exclusion amount The amount of a taxable estate exempt from estate taxes.

basic (homeowner's insurance) form (HO-1) Named-perils policy that covers 11 property-damage–causing perils and provides three areas of liability-related protection: personal liability, property damage liability, and medical payments.

basic liquidity ratio Number of months you could meet expenses using only monetary assets if all income were to cease.

basic retirement benefit/primary insurance amount Amount of Social Security benefits a worker would receive at his or her full-benefit retirement age, which is 67 for those born after 1960.

bear market Market in which securities prices have declined in value by 20 percent or more from previous highs, often over the course of several weeks or months.

below-average costs Average costs of an investment if more shares are purchased when the price is down and fewer shares when the price is high.

beneficiary A person or organization designated to receive a benefit from a life insurance policy or estate or investment/savings account.

beneficiary designation form A form signed when opening a retirement account that contractually determines who will inherit the funds in that retirement account in case you die before the funds are distributed.

beneficiary designation Allowance of fund holder to name one or more beneficiaries so that the proceeds bypass probate proceedings if the original shareholder dies.

benefit amount Long-term care plans are generally written to provide a specific dollar benefit per day of care.

benefit period The maximum period between the onset of a disability and the date that disability benefits begin.

best buy Product or service that, in the buyer's opinion, represents acceptable quality at a fair or low price for that quality level.

beta value/beta coefficient A measure of stock volatility; that is, how much the stock price varies relative to the rest of the market.

bid price Declared highest price anyone wants to pay for a security.

billing/closing/statement date The last day for which any transactions are reported on the credit statement.

biweekly mortgage A form of growing-equity mortgage (GEM) that calls for payments of half of the normal payment to be made every two weeks; the borrower thus makes 26 payments a year and reduces the principal amount by one full payment each year; this reduces the mortgage term to about 20 years on a 30-year mortgage.

blue-chip stocks Stocks that have been around for a long time, have a well-regarded reputation, dominate its industry, and are known for being solid, relatively safe investments.

board of directors A group of individuals at a corporation that sets policy and names the principal officers of the company.

bond A debt instrument issued by an organization that promises repayment at a specific time and the right to receive regular interest payments during the life of the bond; from investor's standpoint, a loan that the investor makes to a government or a corporation.

bond funds Fixed-income funds that aim to earn current income higher than a money market fund without incurring undue risk by investing in a portfolio of bonds and other low-risk investments that pay high dividends and offer capital appreciation.

bond rating An impartial outsider's opinion of the quality—or creditworthiness—of the issuing organization.

book-entry form Bond certificates aren't issued; rather, account is set up in name of the issuing organization or the brokerage firm that sold the bond, and interest is paid into this account when due.

book value per share Reflects the book value of a company divided by the number of shares of common stock outstanding.

book value/shareholder's equity Net worth of a company, determined by subtracting total liabilities from assets.

breakeven price The point at which the cost of a options contract is negated by a profit (or the cost is reduced by hedging a loss).

broker/dealer A brokerage firm representing a buyer that communicates with another brokerage firm that has the desired securities, thus in effect "making a market" for one or more securities.

broker's commission Largest selling cost in selling a home; these commissions often amount to 6 percent of the selling price of the home.

budget Paper or electronic document used to record both planned and actual income and expenditures over a period of time.

budget controls Techniques to maintain control over personal spending so that planned amounts are not exceeded.

budget estimates Projected dollar amounts to receive or spend in a budgeting period.

budget exceptions When budget estimates differ from actual expenditures.

budget variance Difference between amount budgeted and actual amount spent or received.

bull market Market in which securities prices have risen 20 percent or more over time.

bunching deductions A technique to save on income taxes by prepaying tax deductible expenses in a year in advance so as to increase one's itemizations higher than the standard deduction threshold and taking the standard deduction in the following year.

business cycle/economic cycle Business cycles can be depicted as a wavelike pattern of rising and falling economic activity; the phases of the business cycle include expansion, peak, contraction (which may turn into recession), and trough.

business-cycle risk The risk that economic growth or the lack thereof will impact the profits of a particular business.

business failure risk (also called financial risk) The possibility that a business will fail, perhaps go bankrupt, and result in a massive or total loss of one's invested funds.

buy and hold/buy to hold Investment strategy in which investors buy a widely diversified mix of stocks and/or mutual funds, reinvest the dividends by buying more stocks and mutual funds, and hold onto those investments almost indefinitely.

buyer's order Written offer that names a specific vehicle and all charges; only sign such offers after the salesperson and sales manager have signed *first*.

buying long Buying a security (especially on margin) with the hope that the stock price will rise.

call option Stipulation in an indenture that allows issuer to repurchase the bond at par value or by paying a premium, often one year's worth of interest. Bonds are thus callable.

capital gain Net income received from sale of an asset above its purchase price.

capital gains distributions Distributions representing the net gains (capital gains minus capital losses) that a fund realizes when it sells securities that were held in the fund's portfolio.

capital improvements Costs incurred in making value-enhancing changes (beyond maintenance and repair) in real property.

capital loss The net loss of income that results when the sale of an asset brings less income than the costs of purchasing and selling an asset.

card registration service Firm that will notify all companies with which you have debit and credit cards if your cards are lost or stolen.

career The lifework chosen by a person to use personal talent, education, and training.

career fairs University-, community- and employer-sponsored events for job seekers to meet with many employers quickly to screen potential employers.

career goal Identifying what you want to do for a living, whether a specific job or field of employment.

career plan A plan that identifies employment that interests you; fits your abilities, skills, work style, and lifestyle; and provides strategic guidance to help you reach your career goal.

cash Cash equivalents such as Treasury securities.

cash account A brokerage account that requires an initial deposit (perhaps as little as $1000) and specifies that full settlement is due to the brokerage firm within three business days after a buy or sell order has been given.

cash advance A cash advance is the use of a credit card to obtain cash rather than to make a purchase.

cash advance (or convenience) checks A check-equivalent way to take a cash advance on a credit card.

cash-balance plan Defined-benefit plan funded solely by an employer that gives each participant an interest-earning account credited with a percentage of pay on a monthly basis.

cash basis Only transactions involving actual cash received or cash spent are recorded.

cash dividends Distributions made in cash to holders of common and preferred stock typically paid 4 times a year.

cash flow Amount of rental income you have left after paying all operating expenses.

cash-flow calendar Budget estimates for monthly income and expenses.

cash-flow statement (or income and expense statement) Summary of all income and expense transactions over a specific time period.

cash surrender value Represents the cash value of a policy minus any surrender charges.

cash-value life insurance Pays benefits at death and includes a savings/investment element that can provide a reduced level of benefits to the policyholder prior to the death of the insured person.

catch-up provision Permits workers age 50 or older to contribute an additional $5500 to most employer-sponsored plans ($1000 limit on IRA accounts).

certificate of deposit (CD) An interest-earning savings instrument purchased for a fixed period of time.

certificate of insurance Document or booklet that outlines group health insurance benefits.

certified check Personal check on which your financial institution imprints the word *certified*, signifying that the account has sufficient funds to cover its payment.

Chapter 7 of the Bankruptcy Act (straight bankruptcy) Provides for the liquidation of assets with proceeds applied to paying off excusable debts to the degree possible.

Chapter 13 of the Bankruptcy Act (wage earner or regular income plan) Designed for individuals with regular incomes who might be able to pay off some or all of their debts given certain court protections.

chargeback The amount of the transaction is charged back to the business where the transaction originated in the case of a dispute or challenge by the cardholder.

checking accounts At depository institutions, allow depositors to write checks against their deposited funds, which transfer deposited funds to other people and organizations.

child and dependent care credit A nonrefundable tax credit that may be claimed by workers who pay employment-related expenses for care of a child or other dependent if that care gives them the freedom to work, seek work, or attend school full time.

child tax credit A refundable tax credit of $1000 or more that may be taken by low and moderate income families for each qualifying child younger than age 17 claimed as a dependent.

chronological format Résumé that provides your information in reverse order, with the most recent first.

city indexes Comparing wages and cost of living for various employment locations.

claims adjuster Person designated by the insurance company to assess whether the loss is covered and to determine the dollar amount that the company will pay.

cliff vesting A time schedule under which an employee is fully vested in an employer-sponsored retirement plan within three years of employment.

closed-end lease/walkaway lease Agreement in which the lessee pays no charge if the end-of-lease market value of the vehicle is lower than the originally projected residual value.

closed-end mutual funds Funds that issue a limited and fixed number of shares at inception and do not buy them back; after purchase, fund shares trade at market prices.

closing costs Include fees and charges other than the down payment and may vary from 2 to 5 percent of the mortgage loan amount.

COBRA rights The Consolidated Omnibus Budget Reconciliation Act of 1985 allows a former employee to remain a member of a group health plan for as long as 18 months if the employee worked for an employer with more than 20 workers.

codicil Legal instrument with which one can make minor changes to a will.

coinsurance Method by which the insured and the insurer share proportionately in the payment for a loss.

coinsurance clause Requires the insured to pay a proportion of any loss suffered.

collectibles Cultural artifacts that have value because of their beauty, age, scarcity, or popularity, such as antiques, stamps, rare coins, art, baseball cards, and so on.

college savings plan One of the two types of qualified tuition programs that is set up for a designated beneficiary.

collision insurance Reimburses insureds for losses to their vehicles resulting from a collision with another car or object or from a rollover.

commissions Fees or percentages of the selling price paid to salespeople, agents, and companies for their services in buying or selling an investment.

common stock Most basic form of ownership of a corporation.

comparison shopping Process of comparing products or services to find the best buy.

compound interest When interest on an investment itself earns interest.

comprehensive automobile insurance Protects against property damage losses to an insured vehicle caused by perils other than collision and rollover.

comprehensive health insurance Insurance that provides protection against financial losses resulting from hospital, surgical, and medical expenditures.

condominium Form of ownership with the owners holding legal title to their own housing unit among many with common grounds and facilities owned by the developer or homeowners association.

conservative investment philosophy (risk aversion) Investors with this philosophy accept very little risk and are generally rewarded with relatively low rates of return for seeking the twin goals of a moderate amount of current income and preservation of capital.

consumer-driven health care An approach to health care protection in which the consumer elects a health care plan with a high deductible and high overall policy limits.

consumer finance company/small loan company Firm that specializes in making relatively small secured or unsecured loans that require monthly installment payments.

consumer price index (CPI) A broad measure of changes in the prices of all goods and services purchased for consumption by urban households.

consumer statement Your version of a credit issue that shows up on your credit report when the credit bureau refuses to drop a disputed claim.

contents replacement-cost protection Option sometimes available in homeowner's insurance policies (including the renter's form) that pays the full replacement cost of any personal property.

contingency clauses Specify that certain conditions must be satisfied before a contract is binding.

contingent (or secondary) beneficiary The beneficiary in case the first-named beneficiary has died; also called the secondary beneficiary.

contingent deferred sales charge A sales commission that is imposed only when shares are sold; often charges are on a sliding scale, with the fee dropping 1 percentage point per year that the investor stays in the fund.

contributory plan The most common type of employee-sponsored defined-contribution retirement plan; accepts employee as well as employer contributions.

conventional mortgage A fixed-rate, fixed-term, fixed-payment mortgage loan.

convertible preferred stock Can be exchanged at the option of the stockholder for a specified number of shares of common stock.

convertible term insurance Offers policyholders option of exchanging a term policy for a cash-value policy without evidence of insurability.

cooperative (co-op) Form of ownership in which the owner holds a share of the corporation that owns and manages a group of housing units as well as common grounds and facilities.

coordination-of-benefits clause Prevents an individual from collecting insurance benefits that exceed the loss suffered by noting the order in which plans will pay if the insured individual is covered by multiple plans.

copayment A variation of a deductible, requires you to pay a specific dollar amount each time you use your benefits for a specific covered expense item.

corporate bonds Interest-bearing certificates of long-term debt issued by a corporation.

corporate earnings The profits a company makes during a specific time period indicate to many analysts whether to buy or sell a stock.

corporation A state-chartered legal entity that can conduct business operations in its own name.

countercyclical (or defensive) stock A stock that exhibits price changes contrary to movements in the business cycle.

coupon rate/coupon/coupon yield/stated interest rate Interest rate printed on the certificate when the bond is issued.

cover letter A letter of introduction sent to a prospective employer to get an interview.

Coverage C—uninsured and underinsured motorist insurance Coverage that an insured can purchase as part of automobile insurance that covers the insured in an accident with an uninsured or underinsured driver at fault.

Coverdell education savings account (or education savings account) An IRS approved way to pay the future education costs for a child younger than age 18 whereby the earnings accumulate tax free and withdrawals for qualified expenses are tax free.

covered option Option for a security that the writer owns and thus the writer can settle any call options contract with relatively little risk.

covering a position When an investor using a margin account buys back securities sold short or sells securities bought long.

credit An arrangement in which goods, services, or money is received in exchange for a promise to repay at a future date.

credit agreement Contract that stipulates repayment terms for credit cards.

credit application Form or interview that provides information about your ability and willingness to repay debts.

credit bureau Firm that collects and keeps records of many borrowers' credit histories.

credit card blocking Hotels or other service providers use a credit card number to secure reservations and charge the anticipated cost of services.

credit cards Cards that allow repeated use of credit as long as the consumer makes regular monthly payments.

credit counseling agency (CCA) Agency that can arrange payment schedules with unsecured creditors for overly indebted consumers and can provide individuals with credit counseling.

credit history Continuing record of a person's credit usage and repayment of debts.

credit limit Maximum outstanding debt that a lender will allow on an open-ended credit account.

credit receipt Written evidence of any items returned that notes the specific amount and date of the transaction.

credit repair company (credit clinic) Firm that offers to help improve or fix a person's credit history for a (usually hefty) fee.

credit report Information compiled by a credit bureau from merchants, utility companies, banks, court records, and creditors about your payment history.

credit reporting service Allows you to access your credit report as often as daily and obtain your credit score for an annual fee.

credit score (risk score) Statistical measure used to rate applicants based on various factors deemed relevant to creditworthiness and the likelihood of repayment.

credit statement The monthly bill on a credit card account showing the charges and payments made, minimum payment required, and due date among other information; also called a *periodic statement.*

credit union (CU) Member-owned, not-for-profit insured financial institutions that provide checking, savings, and loan services to members.

crude annual rate of return A rough measure of the yield on amounts invested that assumes that equal portions of the gain are earned each year.

cumulative preferred stock Preferred stock for which dividends must be paid, including any skipped dividends, before dividends go to common stockholders.

current income Money received while you own an investment; usually received regularly as interest, rent, or dividends.

currently insured status Requires workers to earn six credits in the most recent three years; provides for some survivors or disability benefits but no retirement benefits.

current rate Rate of return the insurance company has recently paid to policyholders.

current yield Equals the bond's fixed annual interest payment divided by its bond price.

cyclical stock The stock of a company whose profits are greatly influenced by changes in the economic business cycle.

day trading Occurs when an investor buys and sells stocks quickly throughout a day with the hope that prices will move enough to cover transaction costs and earn some profits.

dealer holdback/dealer rebate Dealer incentive in which the manufacturer allows dealers to hold back a percentage of invoice price, thereby providing the dealer with additional profit on the vehicle.

death benefit Amount that will be paid to the beneficiary when the insured dies.

debt Any obligation to repay an amount borrowed.

debt collection agency Firm that specializes in collecting debts that the original lender could not collect.

debt-consolidation loan A loan taken out to pay off several smaller debts.

debt limit Overall maximum you believe you should owe based on your ability to meet repayment obligations.

debt management plan (DMP) Arrangement whereby consumer provides one monthly payment (usually somewhat smaller than the total of previous credit payments) that is distributed to all creditors.

debt payments-to-disposable income method Percentage of disposable personal income available for regular debt repayments aside from set obligations.

debt payments-to-disposable income ratio Divides monthly disposable personal income into monthly debt repayments.

debts Lending investments that typically offer both a fixed maturity and a fixed income.

debt service-to-income ratio Compares dollars spent on gross annual debt.

debt-to-equity ratio Ratio of your consumer debt to your assets.

declining-balance method Interest calculation method in which interest is assessed during each billing period (usually each month) based on the outstanding balance of the installment loan that billing period.

deductible clause Requires that the policyholder pays an initial portion of any loss.

deductibles Clauses in health care plans that require you to pay an initial portion of health expenses annually before receiving reimbursement.

deed Written document used to convey real estate ownership.

deeded timesharing The buyer obtains a legal title or deed to limited time periods of use of real estate and becomes a secured creditor.

default rate Percentage of bonds that do not repay the principal at maturity and sometimes cease interest payments in the interim.

default risk/credit risk Uncertainty associated with not receiving the promised periodic interest payments and the principal amount when it becomes due at maturity.

deferred annuity Annuity plan in which annuitants pay premiums during their working lives, then take income payments at some future date, such as retirement.

deficiency amount The difference between the amount owed on a mortgage loan and what the lender collects at a short sale of the property.

deficiency balance Occurs when money raised by sale of repossessed collateral doesn't cover the amount owed on the debt plus any repossession expenses.

deficit (or net loss) When expenses exceed income such as reported on a cash flow statement.

defined-benefit retirement plan Employer-sponsored retirement plan that pays lifetime monthly annuity payments to retirees based on a predetermined formula.

defined-contribution retirement plan IRS-approved retirement plan sponsored by employers that allows employees to make pretax contributions that lower their tax liability.

dental expense insurance Insurance that provides reimbursement for dental care expenses.

depository institutions Organizations licensed to take deposits and make loans.

depreciation Decline in value of an asset over time due to normal wear and tear and obsolescence.

derivative/derivative security A financial instrument that people trade in order to more easily manage the underlying asset upon which these instruments are based, which can be used to reduce risk or take on additional risk.

direct ownership Results when an investor holds the actual legal title to property.

direct sellers Companies that market insurance policies through salaried employees, mail-order promotions, newspapers, the Internet, and even vending machines.

disability benefits Substantially reduced benefits paid to employees who become disabled prior to retirement.

disability income insurance Insurance that covers a portion of the income lost when you cannot work because of illness or injury.

discharged debts Debts (or portions thereof) that are excused as a result of a bankruptcy.

discount brokers Charge commissions to execute trades that are often 30 to 80 percent less than the fees charged by full-service brokers, but also offer fewer services.

discounted cash-flow method Effective way to estimate the value or asking price of a real estate investment based on after-tax cash flow and the return on the invested dollars discounted over time to reflect a discounted yield.

discount method of calculating interest Interest is calculated based on a discount rate multiplied by the amount borrowed and by the number of years to repay. Interest is then subtracted from the amount of the loan and the difference is given to the borrower. In this method, interest is paid up front before any part of the payment is applied to the principal.

discount yield Difference between the original purchase price of a T-bill and what the Treasury pays you at maturity—the gain, or "par," is interest.

discretionary income The money left over once the necessities of living are covered, such as paying for housing, food, and other necessities; the money that is "controllable" and often makes up the bulk of money available to pay for one's variable expenses.

disposable income Amount of income remaining after taxes and withholding for such purposes as insurance and union dues.

diversification Process of reducing risk by spreading investment money among several investment opportunities.

dividend A portion of a company's earnings that the firm pays out to its shareholders.

dividend payout ratio Dividends per share divided by earnings per share (EPS); helps judge the likelihood of future dividends.

dividends per share Translates the total cash dividends paid out by a company to common stockholders into a per-share figure.

dividend yield Cash dividend to an investor expressed as a percentage of the current market price of a security.

dollar-cost averaging/cost averaging Systematic program of investing equal sums of money at regular intervals regardless of the price of the investment.

Dow Jones Industrial Average (DJIA) The most widely reported of all stock market indexes that tracks prices of only 30 actively traded blue-chip stocks, including well-known companies such as American Express and AT&T.

down payment Portion of the purchase price that is not borrowed.

due-on-sale clause Requires that the mortgage loan be fully paid off if the home is sold. It can impose a burden on the seller because it prohibits a buyer from assuming the mortgage loan.

dunning letters Notices that make insistent demands for repayment.

durable power of attorney for finances Document that appoints someone, called an attorney-in-fact, to handle your legal or business matters and sign your name to documents if illness prevents you from doing so yourself.

earned income credit (EIC) A refundable tax credit that may be claimed by workers with a qualifying child and in certain cases by childless workers.

earnest money Funds given to the seller as a deposit to hold the property until a purchase contract can be negotiated.

earnings per share (EPS) A firm's profit divided by the number of outstanding shares.

earnings yield Inverse of the P/E ratio; helps investors more clearly see investment expectations.

earthquake insurance Can be purchased only from a private insurance company either as a separate policy or as an endorsement to an existing homeowner's or renter's insurance policy.

economic growth A condition of increasing production (business spending) and consumption (consumer spending) in the economy and hence increasing national income.

effective marginal tax rate The total marginal rate reflects all taxes on a person's income, including federal, state, and local income taxes as well as Social Security and Medicare taxes.

electronic funds transfers (EFTs) Funds shifted electronically (rather than by check or cash) among various accounts or to and from other people and businesses.

employee benefit Compensation for employment that does not take the form of wages, salaries, commissions, or other cash payments.

Employee Retirement Income Security Act (ERISA) Regulates employer-sponsored plans by calling for proper plan reporting and disclosure to participants in defined-contribution, defined-benefit, and cash-balance plans.

employee stock option A contractual option to purchase a stock without putting any money down that is sometimes given to employees who might benefit from a hoped for increase in the employer's stock price.

employee stock-ownership plan (ESOP) Benefit plan in which employers make tax-deductible gifts of company stock into trusts, which are then allocated into employee accounts.

employer-sponsored retirement plan An IRS-approved retirement plan offered by an employer (also called **qualified** plans).

employment agency Firm that locates employment for certain types of employees.

envelope system Placing exact amounts into envelopes for each budgetary purpose.

equities Stocks and/or stock mutual funds.

escrow account Special reserve account at a financial institution in which funds are held until they are paid to a third party—in this case, for home insurance and for property taxes.

estate Your worldly possessions and financial assets less any debts you owe.

estate planning The definite arrangements you make during your lifetime that are consistent with your wishes for the administration and distribution of your estate when you die.

estimated taxes People who are self-employed or receive substantial income from an employer that is not required to practice payroll withholding (such as lawyers and owners of rental property) are required by the IRS to estimate their tax liability and pay their taxes in advance in quarterly installments.

estimate of the required rate of return on an investment A calculation that multiplies the beta value of an investment by the estimated market risk and adds the risk-free T-bill rate that suggests to investors the return required to put their money at risk.

excess mileage charge Fees assessed at the end of a lease if the vehicle was driven more miles than originally specified in the lease contract.

exchange fees Small amount charged to move money among funds within a mutual fund family.

exchange privilege Allowance for mutual fund shareholders to easily swap shares on a dollar-for-dollar basis for shares in another mutual fund within a mutual fund family. Also called switching, conversion, or transfer privilege.

exchange-traded fund (ETF) Basket of passively managed securities structured like an index fund; owns all or a representative set of securities that duplicate the performance of a market segment or index.

exclusion amount The value of assets that may be transferred to heirs without incurring an estate tax—currently $3.5 million.

exclusions Income not subject to federal taxation.

executor/personal representative Person responsible for carrying out the provisions of a will and managing the assets until the estate is passed on to heirs.

exemption (or personal exemption) Legally permitted amount deducted from AGI based on the number of people that the taxpayer's income supports.

expansion phase A stage in the economic cycle when production is at high capacity, unemployment is low, retail sales are high, and prices and interest rates are low or falling.

expense ratio Expense per dollar of assets under management.

expenses Total expenditures made in a specified time such as reported on a cash-flow statement.

expiration date An exact date, typically three, six, or nine months in the future from the date of purchase of an options contract after which the investor may not exercise the option to buy or sell shares of stock specified in the contract.

extended warranty/service contract/maintenance agreement/buyer protection plan Agreement between the seller and buyer of a product to repair or replace covered product components for some specified time period; purchased separately from the product itself.

face amount Dollar value of protection as listed in the policy and used to calculate the premium.

Fair Credit Billing Act (FCBA) Helps people who wish to dispute billing errors on revolving credit accounts.

Fair Credit Reporting Act (FCRA) Requires that credit reports contain accurate, relevant, and recent information and that only bona fide users be permitted to review a file for approved purposes.

Fair Debt Collection Practices Act (FDCPA) Prohibits third-party debt collection agencies from using abusive, deceptive, or unfair practices to collect past-due debts.

fair market value Amount a willing buyer would pay to a willing seller for a charitable item.

federal deposit insurance Insures deposits, both principal amounts and accrued interest, up to $100,000 per account for most accounts.

federal estate tax Assessed against a deceased person's estate before property (real estate, stocks and bonds, business interests, and so on) is transferred to heirs or assigned according to terms of a will or state intestacy laws.

federal funds rate The rate that banks charge one another for overnight loans; set by the Federal Reserve Board.

Federal Housing Administration (FHA) An arm of the U.S. Department of Housing and Urban Development (HUD) that insures loans that meet its standards to encourage home ownership.

Federal Insurance Contributions Act (FICA) Act that authorizes Social Security and Medicare tax withdrawals from employee paychecks; amounts withheld go into Social Security trust fund accounts, which pay benefits to current retirees.

filing status Description of a taxpayer's marital status on last day of tax year.

final expenses One-time expenses occurring just prior to or after a death.

finance charge Total dollar amount paid to use credit.

financial goals Specific objectives addressed by planning and managing finances.

financial literacy Knowledge of facts, concepts, principles, and technological tools that are fundamental to being smart about money.

financial planner An investment professional who evaluates the personal finances of an individual or family and recommends strategies to set and achieve long-term financial goals.

financial planning Managing income and wealth continuously through life to meet financial goals.

financial ratios Calculations designed to simplify evaluation of financial strength and progress.

financial records Documents that evidence financial transactions.

financial responsibility Means that you are accountable for your future financial well-being and that you strive to make wise personal financial decisions.

financial risk Possibility that an investment will fail to pay a return to the investor.

financial services industry Companies that provide monetary asset management and other services.

financial statements Snapshots that describe an individual or family's current financial condition.

financial strategies Preestablished action plans implemented in specific situations.

fixed expenses Expenses that recur at fixed intervals.

fixed income Specific rate of return that a borrower agrees to pay the investor for use of the principal (initial investment).

fixed maturity Specific date on which a borrower agrees to repay the principal to the investor.

fixed yield Interest income payment remains the same regardless of the bond's price.

flexible benefit plan An employer-sponsored plan that gives the employee a choice of selecting either cash or one or more qualifying nontaxable benefits; also known as a cafeteria plan.

flexible spending account (FSA) An employer-sponsored account that allows employee-paid expenses for medical or dependent care to be paid with an employee's pretax dollars rather than after-tax income.

flexible spending account (FSA) (or expense reimbursement account) An IRS approved plan for employers that allows an employee to fund qualified medical expenses on a pretax basis through salary reduction to pay for out-of-pocket unreimbursed expenses for health and dependent care that are not covered by insurance.

flexible spending arrangements Employer arrangements that allow employees to place a portion of their salary into an account that is used to pay some of their health care expenditures, including employee-paid health plan premiums.

floater policies Provide all-risk protection for accident and theft losses to movable property regardless of where the loss occurs.

floor broker Brokerage firm's contact person at an exchange.

foreclosure Process in which the lender sues the borrower to prove default and asks the court to order the sale of the property to pay the debt.

front-end load A sales charge paid when an individual buys an investment, reducing the amount available to purchase fund shares.

front-end ratio Compares the total annual PITI expenditures for housing with the loan applicant's gross annual income to assess the borrower's ability to pay the mortgage.

FSBO For sale by owner; commonly pronounced "fizbo"; home sold directly by the homeowner to save on sales commission paid to a real estate broker.

full warranty Warranty that meets three stringent promises: the product must be fixed at no cost to the buyer within a reasonable time, the owner will not have to undertake an unreasonable task to return the product for repair, and a defective product will be replaced with a new one or the buyer's money will be returned if the product cannot be fixed.

full-benefit retirement age Age at which a retiree is entitled to full Social Security benefits; 67 for those born in 1960 or later.

fully insured Social Security status Requires 40 credits and provides workers and their families with benefits under the retirement, survivors, and disability programs; once status is earned, it cannot be taken away even if the eligible worker never works again.

functional format Résumé that emphasizes career-related experiences.

fundamental analysis School of thought in market analysis that assumes each stock has an intrinsic (or true) value based on its expected stream of future earnings.

fund investment advisers Money managers, securities analysts, and traders of a mutual fund that have access to the best research; they select, buy, sell, and monitor the performance of the securities purchased; thus, they oversee the portfolio.

fund screener/fund-screening tool Permits investors to screen all of the mutual funds in the market to gauge performance.

futures contract Type of exchange-traded standardized forward contract that specifies the size of the contract, quality of product to be delivered, and delivery date.

future value The valuation of an asset projected to the end of a particular time period in the future.

garnishment Court-sanctioned procedure by which a portion of debtors' wages are set aside by their employers to pay debts.

general (full-service) brokerage firms Offer a full range of services to customers, including investment advice and research.

generic products Goods that carry store brand names or a general commodity name rather than an advertised brand, such as Del Monte.

gold bullion A refined and stamped weight of precious metal.

gold bullion coins Various world mints issue these coins, which contain 1 troy ounce (31.15 grams) of pure gold.

good-faith estimate Lender's list of all the costs associated with the loan, including the annual percentage rate (APR), application and processing fees, closing costs, and any other charges that must be paid when the deal is legally consummated.

government securities money market funds Funds that appeal to investor concerns about safety by investing solely in U.S. Treasury bills and other short-term securities backed by the U.S. government.

grace period Period (in days) for which deposits or withdrawals can be made without any penalty.

graduated-payment mortgage Mortgage in which the borrower pays smaller-than-normal payments in the early years but payments gradually increase to larger-than-normal payments in later years.

graduated vesting Schedule under which employees must be at least 20 percent vested after two years of service and gain an additional 20 percent of vesting for each subsequent year until, at the end of year six, the account is fully vested.

grantor Creator of a trust—the person who makes a grant of assets to establish a trust. Also called the *settler, donor,* or *trustor*.

gross capitalized cost (gross cap cost) Includes vehicle price plus cost of any extra features such as insurance or maintenance agreements.

gross domestic product (GDP) The nation's broadest measure of economic health; it reports how much economic activity (all goods and services) has occurred within the U.S. borders during a given period.

gross income All income in the form of money, goods, services, and/or property.

group health plan Sold collectively to an entire group of people rather than to individuals, such as the group health care policies offered by employers.

growth and income funds Funds that invest in companies that have a high likelihood of both dividend income and price appreciation; less risk-oriented than aggressive growth funds or growth funds.

growth funds Funds that seek long-term capital appreciation by investing in common stocks of companies with higher-than-average revenue and earnings growth, often the larger and well-established firms.

growth stock The stock of a company that offers the promise of much higher profits tomorrow and has a consistent record of relatively rapid growth in earnings in all economic conditions.

guaranteed insurability (guaranteed purchase option) Permits the cash-value policyholder to buy additional stated amounts of cash-value life insurance at stated times in the future without evidence of insurability.

guaranteed insurance contracts (GIC) An investment offered by an insurance company that guarantees the owner a fixed or floating interest rate for a predetermined period of time and the return of principal.

guaranteed minimum rate of return Minimum rate that, by contract, the insurance company is legally obligated to pay.

guaranteed portability Provision that allows an individual to convert group coverage to individual coverage within 180 days before COBRA ends.

guaranteed renewable policies Policies that must be continued in force as long as the policyholder pays the required premium.

guaranteed renewable term insurance Protects you against the possibility of becoming uninsurable.

guardian Person responsible for caring for and raising any child under the age of 18 and for managing the child's estate.

hazard Any condition that increases the probability that a peril will occur.

health care plan Generic name for any program that pays or provides reimbursement for direct health care expenditures.

health care proxy/durable power of attorney for health care Legal document that appoints another person to make health care decisions if the writer of the proxy is rendered incapable of making his or her wishes known.

health maintenance organizations (HMOs) Health insurance plans that provide a broad range of health care services for a set monthly fee on a prepaid basis.

health reimbursement account (HRA) Funds that employers set aside to reimburse employees for qualified health expenses.

health savings accounts (HSAs) Special savings account intended for people who have a high-deductible health care plan (with annual deductibles of at least $1000 for individuals and $2000 for families).

hedge funds Freewheeling risky investment pools for the extremely wealthy that are global companies beyond the regulations of the U.S. Securities and Exchange Commission (SEC) that use unconventional investment strategies.

heir Person who inherits or is entitled by law or by the terms of a will to inherit some asset.

high-balling Sales tactic in which a dealer offers a trade-in allowance that is much higher than the vehicle is worth.

high-deductible health care plan Can either be traditional health insurance or an HMO that follows the consumer-driven health care philosophy by charging relatively high deductibles.

high-risk investments Alternative investments that have the potential for significant fluctuations in return over short time periods, perhaps only days or weeks, such as collectibles, precious metals and stones, and options and futures contracts.

high-risk/speculative investments Present potential for significant fluctuations in return, sometimes over short time periods.

home inspection Conducted to ensure that the home is physically sound and that all operating systems are in proper order.

homeowner's equity Dollar value of the home in excess of the amount owed on it.

homeowner's general liability protection Applies when you are legally liable for another person's losses, other than those that arise out of use of vehicles or your professional duties.

homeowner's insurance Combines liability and property insurance coverages that homeowners and renters typically need into single-package policies.

I bonds Nonmarketable savings bonds backed by the U.S. government that pay an earnings rate that combines two rates: a fixed interest rate set when the investor buys the bond and a semiannual variable interest rate tied to inflation that protects the investor's purchasing power.

immediate annuity Annuity, often funded by a lump sum from the death benefit of a life insurance policy or lump sum from a defined-contribution plan, that begins payments one month after purchase.

income Total income received such as reported on a cash-flow statement.

income stock A stock that may not grow too quickly, but year after year pays a cash dividend higher than that offered by most companies.

incontestability clause Places a time limit on the right of the insurance company to deny a claim.

indenture Written, legal agreement between bondholders and debtor that describes terms of the debt by setting forth the maturity date, interest rate, and other details.

indexed A procedure used by the Social Security Administration to adjust the earnings during one's working years to reflect increases in average wages for all workers over time; used in the process of calculating SSA benefits.

index fund Mutual fund that seeks to achieve the same return as a particular market index by buying and holding all or a representative selection of securities in it.

indexing Yearly adjustments to tax brackets that reduce inflation's effects on tax brackets.

index of leading economic indicators (LEI) A composite index reported monthly by the Conference Board that suggests the future direction of the U.S. economy.

individual account Has one owner who is solely responsible for the account and its activity.

individual retirement account (IRA) Investment account that reduces current year income, and the funds in the account accumulate tax free.

inflation A steady and sustained rise in general price levels across economic sectors; measured by the changing cost over time of a "market basket" of goods and services that a typical household might purchase.

inflation risk (also called purchasing power risk) The danger that money saved or invested will not grow as fast as inflation and therefore not be worth as much in the future as it is today.

inheritance tax A tax imposed by eight states (i.e., Connecticut, Indiana, Iowa, Kentucky, Maryland, Nebraska, New Jersey, and Pennsylvania) that is assessed on the decedent's beneficiaries who receive inherited property.

initial public offerings (IPOs) New issues of stock issued by a public corporation.

insolvent A situation where a person's liabilities exceed their assets resulting in a negative net worth.

installment-certain annuity Provides monthly payments for the rest of the life of the annuitant with a guarantee that if the person dies before receiving a specific number of payments, the beneficiary will receive a certain number of payments for a particular time period.

installment credit (closed-end credit) Credit arrangement in which the borrower must repay the amount owed plus interest in a specific number of equal payments.

insurance Mechanism for transferring and reducing pure risk through which a large number of individuals share in the financial losses suffered by members of the group as a whole.

insurance agent Representative of an insurance company who is authorized to sell, modify, service, and terminate insurance contracts.

insurance claim Formal request to the insurance company for reimbursement for a covered loss.

insurance dividends Surplus earnings of the insurance company when the difference between the total premium charged exceeds the cost to the company of providing insurance.

insurance policy Contract between the person buying insurance (the insured) and the insurance company (the insurer).

insured Individual whose life is insured.

interest Charge for borrowing money; investors in bonds earn interest.

interest-adjusted net payment index (IANPI) If a policy will remain in force until death, this method allows you to effectively measure the cost of cash-value insurance. The lower the IANPI, the lower the cost of the policy.

interest-earning checking account Any account on which you can write checks that pays interest.

interest inventories Scaled surveys that assess career interests and activities.

interest-only mortgage Mortgage in which the borrower pays only the interest on the mortgage in monthly payments for a fixed term, then either refinances the principal, pays off the principal, or starts paying the higher monthly payment with the principal payments added in.

interest rate risk Risk that interest rates will rise and bond prices will fall, thereby lowering the prices on older bond issues.

intermediate-term goals Financial targets that can be achieved within one to five years.

intestate When a person dies without a legal will.

introductory rate A temporarily low initial interest rate to entice borrowers to apply for a credit card.

investing Putting saved money to work so that it makes you even more money.

investment (capital) assets Tangible and intangible items acquired for their monetary benefits.

investment assets-to-total assets ratio Compares investment asset value with total assets.

investment banking firms Financial organizations that serve as intermediaries between public companies issuing new stocks and bonds and the investing public.

investment-grade bonds Offer investors a reasonable certainty of regularly receiving periodic income (interest) and retrieving the amount originally invested (principal).

investment philosophy Investor's general tolerance for risk in investments, whether it is conservative, moderate, or aggressive, given the investor's financial goals.

investment plan An explanation of your investment philosophy and your logic on investing to reach specific goals.

investment risk The possibility that the yield on an investment will deviate from its expected return.

investments Assets purchased with the goal of providing additional income from the asset itself.

invoice price/seller's cost Reflects the price the dealer has been billed from the manufacturer.

irrevocable living trust Arrangement in which the grantor permanently gives up ownership and the right to control of the property, to change the beneficiaries, and to change the trustees.

IRS tax table Used to figure income tax returns for incomes up to $100,000.

itemized deductions Tax-deductible expenses.

item limits Specify the maximum reimbursement for a particular health care expense.

job interview Formal meeting between employer and potential employee to discuss job qualifications and suitability.

joint and survivor benefit/survivor's benefit Annuity whose payments continue to a surviving spouse after the participant's death; often equals at least 50 percent of participant's benefit.

joint-and-survivor annuity Provides monthly payments for as long as one of the two people—usually a husband and wife—is alive.

joint tenancy with right of survivorship Type of account ownership whereby each person owns the whole of the asset and can dispose of it without the approval of the other(s).

Keogh Tax-deferred retirement account designed for self-employed and small-business owners.

kiddie tax A tax on a portion of the unearned income of those 24 and younger typically earned on money placed in a savings or investment account by a parent in an effort to avoid capital-gains taxes.

land contract/contract for deed Brings greater risk for the buyer because all terms in the contract (including payment of the debt) must be satisfied before transfer of title will occur.

large-cap stocks Those public corporations that are capitalized by issuing $3 billion to $4 billion (or more) of stocks; most are considered blue-chip companies.

large-loss principal A basic rule of risk management that encourages us to insure the risks that we cannot afford and retain the risks that we can reasonably afford.

law of large numbers As the number of members in a group increases, predictions about the group's behavior become increasingly accurate.

layering term insurance policies Purchasing level-premium term policies so that coverage grows when you need it most and then can be decreased as your needs change.

LEAP (Long-term Equity AnticiPation Security) An option with a much longer term than traditional stock or index options.

lease In this context, a contract specifying both tenant and landlord legal responsibilities.

leasing Renting a product while ownership title remains with the lease grantor.

lemon laws State laws that provide guidelines for arbitrators to use to order a dealer's buyback of a "lemon" as defined under the law—commonly if a car that has been in the shop four or more times to fix the same problem.

lesser-known growth stocks Growth stocks that are not as popular with investors as more well known growth stocks; examples include regional businesses with strong earnings or companies that may be the third or fourth leading firm in an industry.

letter of last instructions Nonlegal instrument that may contain preferences regarding funeral and burial, material to be included in the obituary, and other information useful to the survivors.

level-premium term insurance Term policy with long term under which premiums remain constant. Also called guaranteed level-premium term insurance.

leverage Using borrowed funds to invest with the goal of earning a rate of return in excess of the after-tax costs of borrowing.

liabilities What you owe.

liability insurance Protection from financial losses suffered when you are held liable for others' losses.

lien A legal right to seize and dispose of (usually sell) property to obtain payment of a claim. Once the loan is paid, the lien is removed.

life insurance An insurance contract that promises to pay a dollar benefit to a beneficiary upon the death of the insured person.

lifestyle trade-offs Weighing the demands of particular jobs with your social and cultural preferences.

lifetime/aggregate limit Places an overall maximum on the total amount of reimbursement available under a policy.

lifetime learning credit A nonrefundable tax credit that may be claimed every year for tuition and related expenses paid for all years of postsecondary education undertaken to acquire or improve job skills.

limited liability The responsibility for business losses to stockholders is limited to the amount invested in the shares of stock owned. Stockholders vote to elect the company's.

limited managed account Services sometimes provided by a vender to employees in the employer-sponsored retirement plan that automatically rebalance (buy and sell) the retirement assets of employees according to their preferred asset allocations.

limited-pay whole life insurance Whole life insurance that allows premium payments to cease before the insured reaches the age of 100.

limited warranty Any warranty that offers less than the three conditions for full warranty.

limit order Instructs the stockbroker to buy or sell a stock at a specific price.

liquidity Speed and ease with which an asset can be converted to cash.

listing agreement Agreement that brokers require homeowners to sign that permits the broker to list the property exclusively or with a multiple-listing service.

living trust A trust that takes effect while the grantor is still alive.

load funds Mutual funds that always charge a "load" or sales charge upon purchase; the load is the commission used to compensate brokers.

loan Consumer credit that is repaid in equal amounts over a set period of time.

loan commitment/loan preapproval Lender's promise to grant a loan.

loan preapproval Oral commitment from a bank or credit union agreeing to furnish credit for a purchase; lets buyers know how much they can borrow and at what interest rate.

loan-to-value ratio Measures the amount of leverage in a real estate investment project by dividing the total amount of debt by the market price of the investment.

long-term care insurance Provides reimbursement for costs associated with intermediate-term and custodial care in a nursing facility or at home.

long-term disability income insurance plan Replaces a portion of one's income for an extended period of time of five years or more.

long-term gain/or loss A profit or loss on the sale of an asset that has been held for more than a year.

long-term goals Financial targets to achieve more than five years in the future.

long-term liability Debt that comes due in more than one year.

loss control Designing specific mechanisms to reduce loss frequency and loss severity.

low-balling A sales tactic where the seller quote and artificially low price to obtain a verbal agreement from a buyer and then attempts to raise the negotiated price when it comes time to finalize the written contract.

low-load funds Funds carrying sales charges of perhaps 1 to 3 percent; sold by brokers, via mail, and sometimes through mutual fund retailers located in shopping centers.

managed care plans Any health care plan that controls the conditions under which health care can be obtained.

managed funds Funds that employ professional managers who constantly evaluate and choose securities to buy or sell, using a specific investment approach.

management Those who run a corporation's day-to-day operations, such as the president and the chief financial officer.

manufacturer's suggested retail price (MSRP)/sticker price Suggested initial asking price.

margin account Account at a brokerage firm that requires a substantial deposit of cash or securities and permits the purchase of other securities using credit granted by the brokerage firm.

marginal cost The additional (marginal) cost of one more incremental unit of some item.

marginal tax bracket (MTB)/marginal tax rate One of six income-range segments at which income is taxed at increasing rates. Also known as **marginal tax rate**.

marginal tax rate The tax rates that apply to income in each tax bracket range. Also known as **marginal tax bracket**.

marginal utility The extra satisfaction derived from gaining one more incremental unit of a product or service.

margin buying Using a margin account to buy securities; allows the investor to apply leverage that magnifies returns—or losses.

margin call If a stock price declines to the point that the investor's equity is less than the required percentage, a representative of the brokerage firm makes a phone call and tells the investor to either put up more money or securities or face having the position bought on margin (liquidated).

margin rate Set by the Fed, percentage of the value (or equity) in an investment that is not borrowed—recently 25 to 50 percent.

marital deduction Allows an estate to pass on an unlimited amount of assets to a surviving spouse free of estate taxes.

marketability risk The risk that when you have to sell a certain asset quickly, it may not sell at or near the market price.

market efficiency The speed at which new information is reflected in investment prices suggesting that security prices are reflective of their true value at all times because publicly available information has driven market prices to the correct level.

market interest rates Current long- and short-term interest rates paid on various types of corporate and government debts that carry similar levels of risk.

market making A broker/dealer both buys and sells securities by maintaining an inventory of specific securities to sell to other brokerage firms and stands ready to buy reasonable quantities of the same securities at market prices.

market order Instructs the stockbroker to execute an order at the prevailing market price—that is, the current selling price of the stock.

market price The current price of a share of stock that a buyer is willing to pay a willing seller.

market risk/systematic risk/undiversifiable risk Risk that the value of an investment may drop due to influences and events that affect all similar investments.

market timers Long-term investors who pull out of stocks or bonds in anticipation of a market decline or hold back from investing until the market "settles down"—that is, when they expect prices to climb.

market timing Investing, perhaps speculatively, in an effort to "time" the markets by buying or selling on the anticipated direction of the overall market, hope to capture most of the upside of rising stock prices while avoiding most of the downside.

market volatility The likelihood of large price swings in securities due to a company's success (or lack of it) and various market conditions.

market-volatility risk All investments are subject to occasional sharp changes in price as a result of events affecting a particular company or the overall market for similar investments.

matching contribution Employer benefit that offers a full or partial matching contribution to a participating employee's account in proportion to each dollar of contributions made by the participant.

maturity date Date upon which the principal is returned to the bondholder.

maximum taxable yearly earnings (MTYE) The maximum amount To which the FICA tax is applied.

Medicaid A government health care program for low-income people funded jointly by the federal and state governments.

medicare The federal government's health care program for the elderly.

microcap stocks Stocks of public corporations with less than $100 million in capitalization, and perhaps as little as $10 million.

midcap stocks Stocks of public corporations that are quite substantial in terms of capitalization—perhaps $750 million to $3 billion in size—but not among the very largest firms.

minimum-balance account Checking account that requires customers to keep a certain minimum amount for a specified time period to avoid fees.

minimum-balance requirement A requirement of free checking accounts specifying that some minimum balance amount must be maintained to avoid a service charge.

minimum payment Payment that must be made to a credit account each month to cover interest and a portion of the amount owed.

minimum payment amount Lowest allowable monthly payment required by the lender.

moderate investment philosophy (risk indifference) Investors with this philosophy accept some risk as they seek capital gains through slow and steady growth in investment value along with current income.

modern portfolio theory (MPT) Goal is to identify the investor's acceptable level of risk tolerance and then find an optimal portfolio of assets that will have the highest expected returns for that level of risk.

monetary asset (cash) management How you handle your monetary assets.

monetary assets Cash and low-risk, near-cash items that can quickly be converted into cash.

money market account Interest-earning accounts that pay relatively high interest rates and offer limited check-writing privileges.

money market deposit account (MMDA) Government-insured money market account with minimum-balance requirements and tiered interest rates.

money market mutual fund (MMMF) Money market account in a mutual fund rather than at a depository institution.

Monte Carlo analysis Technique that performs a large number of trial runs of a particular portfolio mix of investments, called simulations, to find an optimal allocation for a particular investor's goals and risk tolerance.

Monte Carlo simulations Mathematical calculations that can be used to find an optimal portfolio of mutual funds and stocks that will have the highest expected returns for a certain level of risk.

mortgage broker Individual or company that acts as an intermediary between borrowers and lenders.

mortgage insurance Insures the difference between the amount of down payment required by an 80 percent LTV ratio and the actual, lower down payment.

mortgage interest tax credit A nonrefundable income tax credit of up to $2000 for persons who borrow money to buy a home under certain state and local government programs.

mortgage life insurance A life insurance policy specifically focused on paying the remaining balance on a mortgage loan.

mortgage loan Loan to purchase real estate in which the property itself serves as collateral.

municipal bonds (munis) Long-term debt issued by state and local governments and their agencies to finance public improvement projects; usually tax-free interest to buyer.

mutual fund Investment company that pools funds by selling shares to investors and makes diversified investments to achieve financial goals of income or growth, or both.

mutual fund ask (or offer) price Price at which an investor can purchase a mutual fund's shares; current NAV per share plus sales charges.

mutual fund bid price Shareholders receive this amount per share when they redeem their shares, which is the same dollar amount as the NAV.

mutual fund dividend Income paid to investors out of profits earned by the mutual fund from its investments.

mutual fund family Investment management company that offers a number of different funds to the investing public, each with its own investment objectives or philosophies of investing.

naked option Speculative option that the writer does not own, thus exposing the writer to unlimited risk (if selling a call) or substantial risk (if selling a put).

named-perils policies Cover only losses caused by perils that the policy specifically mentions.

NASDAQ National Association of Securities Dealers Automated Quotations system, which provides instantaneous information on securities offered by more than 3200 domestic and foreign companies.

National Flood Insurance Program A federal government program that makes flood insurance available in counties where flooding is common.

need Item thought to be necessary.

needs-based approach A superior method of calculating the amount of insurance needed that considers all of the factors that might potentially affect the level of need.

negative amortization Occurs when monthly payments are actually smaller than necessary to pay interest on the loan, which will result in a rising principal loan balance.

negative option plans You are automatically signed up for a purchase or subscription plan and your membership renews automatically unless you notify them that you want it to end.

negotiating/haggling Process of discussing actual terms of agreement with a seller, usually on higher-priced items.

net asset value (NAV) Per-share value of a mutual fund.

net surplus Amount remaining after all budget classification deficits are subtracted from those with surpluses.

net worth What's left when you subtract liabilities from assets.

new-vehicle buying service No-fee organization that arranges discount purchases for new-car buyers who are referred to nearby participating automobile dealers that have agreed to charge specific discount prices.

no-load funds Funds that allow investors to purchase shares directly at the net asset value (NAV) without the addition of sales charges.

nominal income Also called money income; income that has not been adjusted for inflation and decreasing purchasing power.

noncontributory plan An employer-sponsored defined-contribution retirement plan in which only the employer makes contributions.

nondeeded timesharing A timeshare property sold without a deed that gives the buyer a legal right-to-use purchase of a limited, preplanned timesharing period of use of a property; in effect a long-term lease that expires in 20 to 25 years.

nonforfeiture values Amounts stipulated in a life insurance policy that protect the cash value, if any, in the event that the policyholder chooses not to pay or fails to pay required premiums.

nonprobate property Does not go through probate; includes assets transferred to survivors by contract (such as beneficiaries listed on retirement accounts and bank accounts held with another person).

nonrefundable tax credit A tax credit that can reduce one's tax liability to below zero, with the excess being refunded to the taxpayer.

nonsalary benefits Forms of remuneration provided by employers to employees that result in the employee not having to pay out-of-pocket money for certain expenses; also known as employee benefits.

odd lot An amount of a security that is less than the normal unit of trading for that particular security; for stocks, any transaction less than 100 shares is usually considered to be an odd lot.

online brokers Such brokers, also called Internet or electronic brokers, have reduced the cost of executing a trade to perhaps $20 or even $10 because their primary business is online trading.

open-ended (revolving) credit Arrangement in which credit is extended in advance of any transaction so that borrowers do not need to reapply each time they need to use credit.

open-end mutual funds Investment that issues redeemable shares that investors purchase directly from the fund (or through a broker for the fund).

opportunity cost Most valuable alternative that must be sacrificed to satisfy a want or need.

option Contract to buy or sell a financial asset at a specified point in the future at a specified price.

option ARMs Adjustable-rate loans with low initial rates that give the borrower the option of paying the standard payment, an interest-only payment, and even worse, a less than interest payment resulting in negative amortization.

option holder Person who buys and then owns an option contract.

option premium Price of an option contract.

option writer Agrees to sell an option contract that promises either to buy or to sell a specified asset for a fixed striking price.

ordinary income dividend distributions Distributions that occur when the fund pays out dividend income and interest (monthly, quarterly, or annually) it has received from securities held in the fund.

organized exchanges Actual physical location for a market, at which some securities prices are set by open outcry.

overindebted When one's excessive personal debts make repayment difficult and cause financial distress.

over-the-counter (OTC) marketplace Electronic marketplace for securities transactions.

owner/policyholder Retains all rights and privileges granted by the policy, including the right to amend the policy and the right to designate who receives the proceeds.

paid-up Point at which the owner of a whole life policy can stop paying premiums.

participating policies Life insurance policies that pay dividends.

par value/face value Some multiple of $1000 that is printed on a bond when issued and repaid at maturity.

passive investor An investor who does not actively engage in trading securities or monitoring his or her investments; seeks to match the market return via mutual funds or other managed investments in the longer term.

payable-on-death designation Status granted to individuals who are not joint tenants and who might need to access accounts without going through probate—the deceased signs the designation before death and the designee simply presents a death certificate to access the accounts.

payroll withholding The IRS requirement that an employer withhold a certain amount from an employee's income as a prepayment of that individual's tax liability for the year. It is sent to the government where it is credited to the taxpayer's account.

pay yourself first Treating savings as the first expenditure after—or even before—getting paid rather than simply the money left over at the end of the month.

penny stock A speculative stock that sells for less than $1 per share typically issued by new companies with erratic sales, few profits, and only some hope of success; sometimes sold over the telephone by high-pressure salespeople to unsophisticated investors.

pension Sum of money paid regularly as a retirement benefit.

peril Any event that can cause a financial loss.

periodic rate The APR for a charge account divided by the number of billing cycles per year (usually 12).

periodic statements Monthly reports that show all electronic transfers to and from accounts, fees charged, and opening and closing balances.

personal finance The study of personal and family resources considered important in achieving financial success; it involves how people spend, save, protect, and invest their financial resources.

personal injury protection (PIP) Medical payments coverage for the driver and any passengers for bodily injury losses as well as possibly lost wages and rehabilitation expenses common in no-fault accident states.

personal line of credit Form of open-ended credit in which the lender allows the borrower access to a prearranged revolving line of credit.

PITI Elements of a monthly real estate payment consisting of principal, interest, real estate taxes, and homeowner's insurance.

plan See qualified tuition plan.

planned buying Thinking through all the details of a purchase from the initial desire to buy to your satisfaction after the purchase.

point/interest point Fee equal to 1 percent of the total mortgage loan amount.

policy limits Specify the maximum dollar amounts that will be paid under the policy.

portability Upon termination of employment, employees with portable benefits can keep their savings in tax-sheltered accounts, transferring retirement funds from employer's account directly to another account without penalty.

portfolio Collection of investments assembled to meet your investment goals.

portfolio diversification Practice of selecting a collection of different asset classes of investments (such as stocks, bonds, mutual funds, real estate, and cash) that are chosen not only for their potential returns but also for their dissimilar risk–return characteristics.

portfolio tracking Automatically updates the value of your portfolio after you enter the symbols of the stocks you own and the number of shares held.

potential rate of return A calculation of the approximate compound yield of an investment that sums up projected income and price appreciation, and the resulting figure may then be compared with returns on other investments.

predatory lending Dishonest or deceptive practices by lenders taking advantage of a borrower's lack of understanding of credit matters.

preemptive right Right of common stockholders to purchase additional shares before a firm offers new shares to the public.

pre-existing conditions Medical conditions or symptoms that the plan participant knew about or had been diagnosed within a certain time period before the plan effective date.

preferred employer Identifying employers that would suit you best.

preferred provider organization (PPO) Group of health care providers (doctors, hospitals, and other health care providers) who contract with a health insurance company to provide services at a discount.

preferred stock Type of fixed-income ownership security in a corporation that pays fixed dividends.

premium Comparatively small, predictable fee with which individuals or companies can replace an uncertain—and possibly large—financial loss.

premium conversion plans With premium conversion, the employee's share of the premiums is paid with pretax dollars; those amounts are not included when the employer reports the employee's income to the IRS.

premium-only plan (POP) An IRS approved plan offered by some employers that allows employees to withhold a portion of their pretax salary to pay their premium contributions for employer-provided health benefits.

premium quote service Offers computer-generated comparisons among 20 to 80 different companies.

prepaid educational service plan Type of qualified tuition program that allows purchase of a child's future college education at today's prices, locking in tuition prices. Also known as prepaid tuition plan.

prepayment penalty Special charge assessed to the borrower for paying off a loan early.

present value The current value of an asset (or stream of assets) that will be received in the future; also known as discounted value.

preservation of capital A concept suggesting that an investor does not want to lose any of the money invested thus they are risk averse.

preshopping research Gathering information before actually beginning to interact with sellers.

pretax dollars Money income that has not been taxed by the government.

pretax income The amount of income withheld from a worker's salary before taxes are calculated.

pretax money Investing before income taxes are calculated, thus gaining an immediate elimination of part of your income tax liability for the current year.

price/earnings (P/E) ratio (or multiple) The current market price of a stock divided by earnings per share (EPS) over the past four quarters; used as the primary means of valuing a stock.

price/sales ratio (P/S ratio) Tells the number of dollars it takes to buy a dollar's worth of a company's annual revenues; calculated by dividing company's total market capitalization by its sales for the past four quarters.

price-to-book ratio (P/B ratio) Current stock price divided by the per-share net value of a firm's plant, equipment, and other assets (book value).

price-to-rent ratio This ratio shows the average home price divided by annual rent in a community. Higher numbers, such as those above the national average of 15, mean that home values are high relative to the cost of renting.

principal Face amount of a bond, or price originally paid for a bond.

principle of indemnity Insurance will pay *no more* than the actual financial loss suffered.

privately-held corporation One that issues stock purchased by a relatively small number of people and is not traded on a public stock exchange.

private mortgage insurance (PMI) Mortgage insurance obtained from a private company.

probate Court-supervised process that allows creditors to present claims against an estate and ensures the transfer of a decedent's assets to the rightful beneficiaries according to a properly executed and valid will or, when no will exists, to the people, agencies, or organizations required by state law.

probate property All assets other than nonprobate property.

professional abilities Job-related activities that you can perform physically, mentally, artistically, mechanically, and financially.

professional interests Long-standing topics and activities that engage your attention.

professional liability insurance/malpractice insurance Protects individuals and organizations that provide professional services when they are held liable for their clients' losses.

professional networking Making and using contacts with individuals, groups, and other firms to exchange career information.

profile prospectus/fund profile Publication that describes the mutual fund, its investment objectives, and how it tries to achieve its objectives in lay terms rather than the legal language used in a regular prospectus.

profit Money left over after a firm pays all expenses and interest to bondholders.

profit-sharing plan Employer-sponsored plan that allocates some of the employer profits to employees in the form of end-of-year cash or common stock contributions to employees' 401(k) accounts.

progressive income tax Tax rate increases as taxable income increases.

projected P/E ratio Because investors need to look to the future rather than the past, this measure divides price by projected earnings over the coming four quarters. Also known as forward price/earnings ratio.

promissory note (note) Contract that stipulates repayment terms for a loan.

property insurance Protection from financial losses resulting from the damage to or destruction of your property or possessions.

prospectus Highly legalistic information presented by a firm to the SEC and to the public with any new issue of stock.

public corporation One that issues stock purchased by the general public and traded on stock markets such as the New York Stock Exchange.

purchase contract/sales contract Formal legal document that outlines the actual agreement that results from the real estate negotiations.

purchase offer/offer to purchase Written offer to purchase real estate.

purchasing power Measure of the goods and services that one's income will buy.

pure risk A situation that exists when there is no potential for gain.

put option Gives option holder the right to sell the optioned asset to the option writer at the striking price at any time before the option expires.

qualified plans Plans that the IRS has approved to encourage saving for retirement.

qualified tuition (Section 529) program Provides tax-sheltering when saving for a child's education.

qualified tuition program IRS approved plans whereby individuals may save and invest after-tax money for college and the withdrawals are free if made for qualified education expenses.

random/unsystematic risk Risk associated with owning only one investment of a particular type (such as stock in one company) that, by chance, may do very poorly in the future due to uncontrollable or random factors that do not affect the rest of the market.

rate of return/yield Total return on an investment expressed as a percentage of its price.

real estate Property consisting of land, all structures permanently attached to that land, and accompanying rights and privileges, such as crops and mineral rights.

real estate (or housing) bubble Rapid and unsustainable increases in home prices followed by sharp declines in values.

real estate broker Person licensed by a state to provide advice and assistance, for a fee, to buyer or sellers of real estate.

real estate investment trust (REIT) Special kind of closed-end mutual fund that invests in a portfolio of assets, such as properties, like office buildings and shopping centers, or mortgages.

real estate transfer taxes Community-assessed taxes paid by the seller and also sometimes by the buyer based on the purchase price of the home or the equity the seller has in the home.

real income Income measured in constant prices relative to some base time period. It reflects the actual buying power of the money you have as measured in constant dollars.

real rate of return Return on an investment after subtracting the effects of inflation and income taxes.

rebate A partial refund of a purchase price offered as an inducement to buy.

recession A recurring period of decline in total output, income, employment, and trade, usually lasting from six months to a year and marked by widespread contractions in many sectors of the economy.

record date Date that an issuer establishes to determine who is eligible to receive a dividend or distribution.

record keeping Recording sources and amounts of dollars earned and spent.

redeems When an investor sells shares.

redemption charge/exit fee Similar to a deferred load but often much lower; used to reduce excessive trading of fund shares.

redress Process of righting a wrong.

refundable tax credit A tax credit that can reduce one's income tax liability to below zero and the excess is refunded to taxpayer.

registered bond Bondholder's name is recorded so that checks or electronic funds transfers for payment of interest and principal can be safely forwarded when due.

reinvestment risk (or duration risk) The risk that the return on a future investment will not be the same as the return earned by the original investment in part because of falling interest rates.

release Insurance document affirming that the dollar amount of the loss settlement is accepted as full and complete reimbursement.

rent Cost charged for using an apartment or other housing space.

rental yield A computation of how much income the investor might pocket from rent each year (before mortgage payments) as a percentage of the purchase price; divide the annual rent by 2 and then divide by the purchase price.

renter's contents broad form (HO-4) Named-perils policy that protects the insured from losses to the contents of a rented dwelling rather than to the dwelling itself.

repairs Usually tax-deductible expenses necessary to maintain property value.

replacement-cost requirement Stipulates that a home *must* be insured for 80 percent of its replacement value (some companies require 100 percent) in order for any loss to be fully covered.

repossession/foreclosure Legal proceeding by which the lender seizes an asset.

residual claim Common stockholders have a right to share in the income and assets of a corporation after higher-priority claims are satisfied.

residual clause Feature of own-occupation policies that allows for some reduced level of disability income benefits when a partial—rather than full—disability strikes.

residual value Projected value of a leased asset at the end of the lease time period.

résumé Summary record of your education, training, experience, and other qualifications.

retail credit cards Allow customers to make purchases on credit at any of the outlets of a particular retailer.

retained earnings Money left over after firm has paid expenses, bondholder interest, taxes, preferred stockholder dividends, and common stockholder dividends.

retirement The time in life when the major sources of income change from earned income (such as salary or wages) to employer-based retirement benefits, private savings and investments, income from Social Security, and perhaps parttime employment.

retirement plan contribution credit/saver's tax credit Program to encourage low-income individuals to save for retirement, this tax credit ranges from 10 to 50 percent of every dollar they contribute to an IRA or employer-sponsored retirement plan up to $2000.

retirement savings contribution credit A nonrefundable tax credit (also known as a **saver credit**) of up to $1000 available for some low and moderate income taxpayers.

retirement savings goal/retirement nest egg Total amount of accumulated savings and investments needed to support a desired retirement lifestyle.

reverse mortgage/home-equity conversion loan Allows a home owner older than age 61 to continue living in the home and to borrow against the equity in a home that is fully paid for and to receive the proceeds in a series of monthly payments, often over a period of 5 to 15 years or for life.

revocable living trust Grantor maintains the right to change the trust's terms or cancel it at any time, for any reason, during his or her lifetime.

revolving savings fund Variable budgeting tool that places funds in savings to cover emergency or higher-than-usual expenses.

risk Uncertainty about the outcome of a situation or event.

risk management Process of identifying and evaluating purely risky situations to determine and implement appropriate management.

risk premium The difference between a riskier investment's expected return and the totally safe return on the T-bill; this premium is the compensation needed to encourage risk-averse investors to invest in equities rather than keeping money in safer investments, like T-bills.

risk reduction Includes mechanisms, such as insurance, that reduce the overall uncertainty about the magnitude of loss.

risk retention Accepting that some risks simply arise in the course of one's life and consciously retaining that risk.

risk tolerance An investor's ability and willingness to weather changes in security prices, that is, to weather market risk.

Roth IRA An individual retirement account of investments made with after-tax money; the interest on such accounts is allowed to grow tax free, and withdrawals are also tax free.

round lots Standard units of trading of 100 shares of stock and $1000 or $5000 par value for bonds.

rule of 72 A formula for figuring the number of years it takes to double the principal using compound interest; simply divide the interest rate that the money will earn *into* the number 72.

rule of 78s method/sum of the digits method for calculating prepayment penalties A common method of calculating the prepayment penalty on a loan which uses the add-on method for calculating the interest.

sales finance company Seller-related lender whose primary business is financing sales for its parent company.

savings Income not spent on current consumption.

savings account Account that provides an accessible source of emergency cash and a temporary holding place for extra funds that will earn some interest.

S-CHIP program A government program similar to Medicaid that covers children whose parents are middle income and lower and do not have access to a private health care plan.

secured bond Pledges specific assets as collateral in indenture or has the principal and interest guaranteed by another corporation or government agency.

secured loan Loan that is backed by collateral or a cosigner.

securities Assets suitable for investment, including stocks, bonds, and mutual funds.

securities exchange/stock market Market where agents of buyers and sellers can find each other easily by providing an orderly, open plan to trade securities.

securities market index Measures the average value of a number of securities chosen as a sample to reflect the behavior of a more general market.

securities markets Places where stocks and bonds are traded (or in the case of electronic trading, the way in which securities are traded).

security freeze With a freeze you tell the credit bureaus not to release your financial records to anyone without your consent.

security's street name Securities certificates kept in the brokerage firm's name instead of the name of the individual investor.

self-directed In defined-contribution plans, employees control the assets in their account—how often to make contributions to the account, how much to contribute, how much risk to take, and how to invest.

seller financing/owner financing When a seller self-finances a buyer's loan by accepting a promissory note from a buyer, who makes monthly mortgage payments.

selling short Investors selling securities they do not own (borrowing them from a broker) and later buying the same number of shares of the security at a lower price (returning them to the broker).

serial bonds Bonds that are retired serially; that is, each bond is numbered consecutively and matures according to a prenumbered schedule at stated intervals.

Series EE savings bonds Nonmarketable, interest-bearing bonds issued by the federal government that are issued at a sharp [MLC5] discount from face value and pay no annual interest, and that may be redeemed at full value upon maturity.

settlement options Choices from which the policyholder can choose in how the death benefit payment will be structured.

shareholder fees Fees charged directly to investors for specific transactions, such as purchases, redemptions, or exchanges.

short sale A circumstance in housing when a home is being foreclosed and a lender agrees to accept less than the full mortgage amount and often forgive whatever debt is left unpaid.

short-term (current) liability Obligation paid off within one year.

short-term disability income insurance plan Replaces a portion of one's income for a short period of time; perhaps up to two years.

short-term gain/loss A profit or loss on the sale of an asset that has been held for one year or less.

short-term health insurance Health care plans that can be paid for monthly for a term of 6-months or a year and may be renewable.

simplified employee pension–individual retirement account (SEP-IRA) A retirement savings account for sole proprietor's self-employment income and owners of small businesses looking to save only in profitable years.

single-family dwelling Housing unit that is detached from other units.

sinking fund Bond feature through which money is set aside with a trustee each year for repayment of the principal portion of the debt at maturity.

skilled nursing care Intended for people who need intensive care, that is, 24-hour-a-day supervision and treatment by a registered nurse under the direction of a doctor.

skills format Résumé that emphasizes your aptitudes and qualities.

small-cap stocks Stocks of a company that has a capitalization of $300 million to $2 billion.

small-claims court State courts in which civil matters are often resolved without attorney assistance.

socially conscious funds Funds that invest in companies that meet some predefined standard of moral and ethical behavior.

Social Security credits Accumulated quarterly credits to qualify for Social Security benefits obtained by paying FICA taxes.

Social Security Disability Income Insurance Under this government program, eligible workers can collect some income for up to one year if their disabilities are total, meaning that they cannot work at any job.

Social Security rider Provides an extra dollar amount of protection if a person fails to qualify for Social Security disability benefits (70 percent of all applicants are rejected).

Social Security statement A document that the Social Security Administration periodically sends to all workers, which includes earnings history, Social Security taxes paid, and an estimated benefit amount.

Social Security survivor's benefits Government program benefits paid to a surviving spouse and children.

special (homeowner's insurance) form (HO-3) Provides open-perils protection (except for the commonly excluded perils of war, earthquake, and flood) for four types of property losses.

specialist Person on the floor of an exchange who handles trades of a particular stock in an effort to maintain a fair and orderly market.

speculative-grade bonds Long-term, high-risk, high-interest-rate corporate (or municipal) IOUs issued by companies (or municipalities) with poor or no credit ratings. Also called junk bonds or high-yield bonds.

speculative risk Involves the potential for either gain or loss; equity investments might do either.

speculative stock A company that has a potential for substantial earnings at some time in the future although those earnings may never be realized.

speculator An investor who buys in the hope that someone else will pay more for an asset in the not-too-distant future.

spousal consent requirement Federal law that protects the surviving rights of a spouse or ex-spouse to retirement or pension benefits unless the person signs a waiver of those rights.

spousal IRA Account set up for spouse who does not work for wages; offers tax-deferred growth and tax deductibility.

spread Represents difference between the bid price at which a broker/dealer will buy shares and the higher ask price at which the broker/dealer will sell shares.

springing power of attorney "Springs" into effect when a specified event occurs, usually mental incapacitation or disability.

standard deduction Fixed amount that all taxpayers may subtract from their adjusted gross income if they do not itemize their deductions.

standard deviation A measure of a security's or mutual fund's volatility; also known as *beta*.

standardized expense table SEC-required information that describes and illustrates mutual fund charges in an identical manner so that investors can accurately compare the effects of all of a fund's fees and other expenses relative to other funds.

standard of living Material well-being and peace of mind that individuals or groups earnestly desire and seek to attain, to maintain if attained, to preserve if threatened, and to regain if lost.

start-up capital Funds initially invested in a business enterprise.

stated commission The sales charge as a percentage of the amount invested.

stockbroker/account executive Professional who is licensed to buy and sell securities on behalf of the brokerage firm's clients.

stock dividend A non-cash dividend declared by a public corporation in the form of shares of common stock given to current shareholders.

stockholder/shareholder Each person who owns a share of a company's stock holds a proportionate interest in firm ownership (a very small slice) and, therefore, in the assets and income of the corporation.

stock option Security that gives the holder the right to buy or sell a specific number of shares (normally 100) of a certain stock at a specified (striking) price before a specified expiration date.

stocks Shares of ownership in the assets and earnings of a business corporation.

stock-screening tools Enable you to quickly sift through vast databases of hundreds of companies to find those that best suit your investment objectives.

stock split When the shares of a stock owned by existing shareholders are divided into a larger number of shares.

stop order Instructs a stockbroker to sell your shares of stock at the market price if a stock declines to or goes below a specified price.

stop-payment order Notifying your bank not to honor a check when it's presented for payment.

straight annuity Provides lifetime payments for the life of the annuitant only.

striking price A specific price before a specified date in an options contract when the holder has the right, but not the obligation, to buy or sell a specific number of shares of a certain stock at a specified price.

subleasing An arrangement in which the original tenant leases the property to another tenant.

subordinate budget Detailed listing of planned expenses within a single budgeting classification.

subprime lending This market focuses on lending to people who normally would not qualify for credit due to low credit scores. The interest rates are commensurately higher.

subrogation rights Allow an insurer to take action against a negligent third party (and that party's insurance company) to obtain reimbursement for payments made to an insured.

surplus (or net gain or net income) When total income exceeds total expenses such as reported on a cash-flow statement.

sweat equity property Property that needs repairs but that has good underlying value; an investor buys the property at a favorable price and fixes it up to rent or sell at a profit.

take-home pay/disposable income Pay received after employer withholdings for taxes, insurance, and union dues.

tangible (use) assets Personal property used to maintain your everyday lifestyle.

target-date retirement funds/life-cycle funds Asset allocation funds that offer investors premixed portfolios of stocks, bonds, and cash that investors of a certain age and risk tolerance might prefer.

taxable income Income upon which income taxes are levied.

tax avoidance Reducing tax liability through legal techniques.

tax balance due Money you must pay to the IRS if withholding and quarterly payments are insufficient to cover tax liability.

tax credit Dollar-for-dollar decrease in tax liability; also known as credit.

tax deferred The individual does not have to pay current income taxes on the earnings (interest, dividends, and capital gains) reinvested in a retirement account.

tax-deferred compounding Tax-free growth of tax-deferred investments.

taxes Compulsory government-imposed charges levied on citizens and their property.

tax evasion Deliberately and willfully hiding income from the IRS, falsely claiming deductions, or otherwise cheating the government out of taxes owed; it is illegal.

tax-exempt income Income that is totally and permanently free of taxes.

tax-exempt money market funds Funds that limit their investments to tax-exempt municipal securities with maturities of 60 days or less.

tax free Withdrawals from retirement accounts that IRS regulations deem are never taxed, such as money taken out of Roth IRA accounts.

tax-free exchange Arises when a real estate investor trades equity in one property for equity in a similar property and no other forms of property or money change hands.

tax losses Paper losses that may not represent actual losses created when deductions generated from an investment exceed income from the investment.

tax planning Seeking legal ways to reduce, eliminate, or defer income taxes.

tax rate schedules Equations to figure taxes for returns with incomes above $100,000.

tax refund Amount the IRS sends back to the taxpayer if withholding and estimated payments exceed the tax liability.

tax-sheltered income Income exempt from income taxes in the current year but that will be subject to taxation in a later tax year.

tax-sheltered investments Investments that yield returns that are tax advantaged.

tax-sheltered retirement accounts Retirement account for which all earnings from the invested funds are not subject to income taxes.

tax-sheltered retirement plan Employer-sponsored, defined-contribution retirement plans including 401(k) plans and similar 403(b) and 457 plans.

T-bill One form of Treasury securities is the short-term Treasury bill, or T-bill, which is a government IOU of one year of less.

teaser rate Low interest rate that lenders sometimes use to lure buyers; these rates will be low for the first year or so and then will rise to more realistic rates.

technical analysis Method of evaluating securities that uses statistics generated by market activity, such as past prices and volume, over time to determine when to buy or sell a stock.

tech stocks Stock in the technology sector that offer technology-based products and services, biotechnology, Internet services, network services, wireless communications, and more.

term life insurance "Pure protection" against early death; pays benefits only if the insured dies within the time period (term) that the policy covers.

testamentary trust Becomes effective upon death of the grantor according to the terms of the grantor's will or a revocable living trust. Such trusts can provide money or asset management after the grantor's death for the heirs' benefit.

tiered interest Common type of NOW account that pays lower interest on smaller deposits and higher interest on larger balances.

time deposits Savings accounts that financial institutions expect to remain on deposit for an extended period.

time risk The more time your money is invested, the more it is at risk, thus the sooner your invested money is supposed to be returned to you—the time horizon of an investment—the less the likelihood that something could go wrong.

timesharing The joint ownership or lease of vacation property through which the principals occupy the property individually for set periods of time.

time value of money (TVM) A method by which one can compare cash flows across time, either as what a future cash flow is worth today (present value) or what an investment made today will be worth in the future (future value).

title Legal right of ownership interest to real property.

title insurance Protects the lender's interest if the title search is later found faulty.

total income Compensation from all sources.

total return Income an investment generates from current income and capital gains.

trade-off Giving up one thing for another.

traditional (regular) IRA Account that offers tax-deferred growth; the initial contribution may be tax deductible for the year that the IRA was funded.

trailing commission Compensation paid to salespeople for months or years in the future.

trailing P/E ratio Calculated using recently reported earnings, usually from the previous four quarters.

transaction fee Charge levied against cardholders per use of the card and are not included in the APR advertised.

transportation reimbursement plan An IRS approved plan offered by some employers that allows employees the opportunity to withhold a portion of their pretax salary to pay for work-related transportation expenses because it reduces the individual's income tax liability.

travel and entertainment (T&E) cards Bank credit cards that allow holders to make purchases at numerous businesses but that require the holder to repay the entire balance charged within 30 days.

treasury bills Known as T-bills, U.S. government securities with maturities of one year or less.

Treasury Inflation-Protected Securities (TIPS) Marketable Treasury bonds whose value increases with inflation. These inflation-indexed $1000 bonds are the only investment that guarantees that the investor's return will outpace inflation.

treasury note/treasury bond Fixed-principal, fixed-interest-rate government security issued for an intermediate term or long term. Notes mature in ten years or less; bonds mature in more than ten years.

treasury securities Known as Treasuries, securities issued by the U.S. government, including bills, notes, and bonds.

trust Legal arrangement between you as the creator of the trust and the trustee, the person designated to faithfully and wisely manage any assets in the trust to your benefit and to the benefit of your heirs.

trustee Person charged with carrying out the trust for the benefit of the grantor(s) and heirs.

Truth in Lending Act (TIL) Requires lenders to disclose to credit applicants both the interest rate expressed as an annual percentage rate (APR) and the finance charge.

U.S. government savings bonds Nonmarketable, interest-bearing bonds issued by the U.S. Treasury.

umbrella (excess) liability insurance Catastrophic liability policy that covers liability losses in excess of those covered by any underlying homeowner's, automobile, or professional liability policy.

unearned income Investment returns in the form of rents, dividends, capital gains, interest, or royalties.

uniform settlement statement Lists all of the costs and fees to be paid at the closing.

unit investment trust (UIT) Closed-end investment company that makes a one-time public offering of only a specific, fixed number of units; once the UIT closes, it becomes an unmanaged fund that is somewhat illiquid.

universal life insurance Provides the pure protection of term insurance and the cash-value buildup of whole life insurance, along with face amount variability, rate of cash-value accumulation, premiums, and rate of return.

unmanaged fund Fund with very low management fees since managers do not evaluate or select individual securities; ETFs and index funds are examples.

unsecured bond/debenture Does not name collateral as security for debt; backed only by the good faith and reputation of the issuing agency.

unsecured loan/signature loan Loan granted based solely on borrower's good creditworthiness.

use-it-or-lose-it rule An IRS regulation requiring that unspent dollars in a flexible spending account at the end of a calendar year be forfeited, unless the employer allows a 2½ month grace period for spending the funds.

value funds Funds specializing in stocks that are fundamentally sound whose prices appear to be low (low P/E ratios) based on the logic that such stocks are currently out of favor and undervalued by the market.

value investing Seeing to invest, in stocks for example, when they are underpriced and sell them when they rise.

value investor One who believes that the market isn't always efficient and that it is possible to find companies trading for less than they are worth, thus they try to buy stocks when they are quoted below their fair value and sell them when they rise above that level.

value stock A stock that tends to trade at a low price relative to its company fundamentals (dividends, earnings, sales, and so on) and thus is considered undervalued by a value investor.

values The principles, standards, or qualities that you consider desirable.

variable annuity Annuity whose value rises and falls like mutual funds and pays a limited death benefit via an insurance contract. Not as efficient as a mutual fund; costs are high for little return.

variable expenses Expenses over which you have substantial control.

variable interest rate cards Have rates that change monthly or annually according to general changes in the economy as a whole.

variable-rate (adjustable-rate) loans Loans for which the interest rate varies with the monthly payment going up or down, allowing the loan to be paid off by the original end date.

variable-universal life insurance Form of universal life insurance that gives the policyholder some choice in the investments made with the cash value accumulated by the policy. Also called flexible-premium variable life insurance.

variable value Because interest rates change, bonds may trade at a premium (more than face value) or at a discount (less than par) so that the yield equals the current yield for bonds with similar maturities and risk levels.

vesting Ensures that a retirement plan participant has the right to take full possession of all employer contributions and earnings if the employee is dismissed, resigns, or retires.

volatility A mutual fund's (or any security's) tendency to rise or fall in price over time.

voting rights Proportionate authority to express an opinion or choice in matters affecting the company.

waiting period The time period between the onset of a disability and the date that disability benefits begin.

waiver of premium Sets certain conditions under which an insurance policy would be kept in full force by the company without the payment of premiums.

want Item not necessary but desired.

warranty Sellers' assurances that goods are as promised and that certain steps will be taken to rectify problems if they arise.

well-known growth stocks Stocks of companies that are leaders in their fields, that dominate their markets, and that have several consecutive years of above-industry-average earnings.

whole life insurance Form of cash-value life insurance that provides lifetime life insurance protection and expects the insured to pay premiums for life. Also called straight life insurance.

will Written document in which a person tells how his or her remaining assets should be given away after death; without a will, the property will be distributed according to state probate law.

withdrawal A removal of assets from an account.

withdrawal options/systematic withdrawal plans Arrangements with a mutual fund company for shareholders who want to receive income on a regular basis from their mutual fund investments.

work-style personality Your own ways of working with and responding to job requirements, surroundings, and associates.

yield to maturity (YTM) Total annual effective rate of return earned by a bondholder on a bond if the security is held to maturity—takes into consideration both the price at which the bond sold and the coupon interest rate to arrive at effective rate of return.

zero-coupon bonds (zeros or deep discount bonds) Municipal, corporate, and Treasury bonds that are issued at a sharp discount from face value and pay no annual interest but are redeemed at full face value upon maturity.

zero-sum game Situation in which the wealth of all investors remains the same; the trading simply redistributes the wealth among those traders. Each profit must be offset by an equivalent loss; therefore, the average rate of return for all investors in futures is zero.

INDEX

Note: **Boldface** type indicates key terms defined in text.